Lecture Notes in Computer Science 3851

Commenced Publication in 1973
Founding and Former Series Editors:
Gerhard Goos, Juris Hartmanis, and Jan van Leeuwen

P.J. Narayanan Shree K. Nayar
Heung-Yeung Shum (Eds.)

Computer Vision – ACCV 2006

7th Asian Conference on Computer Vision
Hyderabad, India, January 13-16, 2006
Proceedings, Part I

Springer

Volume Editors

P.J. Narayanan
Centre for Visual Information Technology
International Institute of Information Technology
Gachibowli, Hyderabad 500032, India
E-mail: pjn@iiit.ac.in

Shree K. Nayar
Columbia University, Department of Computer Science
530 West 120th Street, New York, NY 10027, USA
E-mail: nayar@cs.columbia.edu

Heung-Yeung Shum
Microsoft Research Asia
49 Zhichun Road, Beijing 100080, China
E-mail: hshum@microsoft.com

Library of Congress Control Number: 2005938106

CR Subject Classification (1998): I.4, I.5, I.2.10, I.2.6, I.3.5, F.2.2

ISSN 0302-9743
ISBN-10 3-540-31219-6 Springer Berlin Heidelberg New York
ISBN-13 978-3-540-31219-2 Springer Berlin Heidelberg New York

Springer is a part of Springer Science+Business Media

springer.com

Printed in Germany

Typesetting: Camera-ready by author, data conversion by Scientific Publishing Services, Chennai, India
Printed on acid-free paper SPIN: 11612032 06/3142 5 4 3 2 1 0

Preface

Welcome to the 7th Asian Conference on Computer Vision. It gives us great pleasure to bring forth its proceedings. ACCV has been making its rounds through the Asian landscape and came to India this year. We are proud of the technical program we have put together and we hope you enjoy it.

Interest in computer vision is increasing and ACCV 2006 attracted about 500 submission. The evaluation team consisted of 27 experts serving as Area Chairs and about 270 reviewers in all. The whole process was conducted electronically in a double-blind manner, a first for ACCV. Each paper was assigned to an Area Chair who found three competent reviewers for it. We were able to contain the maximum load on the reviewers to nine and the average load to less than six. The review form had space for qualitative and quantitative evaluation of the paper on nine aspects. The submitted reviews underwent an elaborate process. First, they were seen by the Area Chair, who resolved divergences of opinion among reviewers, if any. The Area Chair then wrote qualitative comments and a quantitative score along with his/her initial recommendation on the paper. These were looked at by Program Co-chairs and compiled into a probables list. The Area Chairs and Program Co-chairs met in Beijing during ICCV to discuss this list and arrived at the final list of 64 oral papers and 128 posters. Naturally, many deserving papers could not be accommodated.

Katsushi Ikeuchi has been unflinching in his support of ACCV as a whole and ACCV 2006 in particular. His help was critical at many stages. We must thank the Area Chairs and the reviewers for their time and effort towards the conference. From IIIT Hyderabad, C V Jawahar and Anoop M. Namboodiri contributed in many ways with the program. The enthusiastic team of students from the Centre for Visual Information Technology (CVIT) was behind it fully. Karteek Alahari, Kiran Babu Varanasi, Sumeet Gupta, Sukesh Kumar, and Satyanarayana made all the logistics of the CFP, paper submission, review process, and preparation of the proceedings really possible. The International Institute of Information Technology was fully behind the conference as a team and deserves our deep gratitude. Finally – but most importantly – we wish to thank the authors who showed great enthusiasm for ACCV.

ACCV has been gaining in stature as a platform to showcase the best of computer vision research over the years. We hope the 2006 edition has brought it forward at least a little. Computer vision continues to be an exciting area and conferences like these provide the much needed light to many who will embark on a journey down its path.

P J Narayanan
Shree Nayar
Harry Shum
(Program Chairs)

Conference Committees

General Chairs
Narendra Ahuja
University of Illinois & IIIT Hyderabad
Takeo Kanade
Carnegie Mellon University
Tieniu Tan
Chinese Academy of Sciences

Program Chairs
P.J. Narayanan
IIIT, Hyderabad
Shree Nayar
Columbia University
Harry Shum
Microsoft Research Asia

Organizing Chairs
C.V. Jawahar
IIIT, Hyderabad
Santanu Chaudhury
IIT, Delhi

Advisory Committee
Masahiko Yachida, *Osaka University*
Eam Khwang Teoh, *Nanyang Technological University*
Roland Chin, *Hong Kong University of Science and Technology*
Wen-Hsiang Tsai, *Chiao Tang University*
David Suter, *Monash University*
Sang-Uk Lee, *Seoul National University*
Katsushi Ikeuchi, *Tokyo University*
B. L. Deekshatulu, *University of Hyderabad*
D. Dutta Majumdar, *Indian Statistical Institute*
B. N. Chatterjee, *Indian Institute of Technology, Kharagpur*

Area Chairs

Yaron Caspi	*Hebrew University*
Tat Jen Cham	*Nanyang Technological University*
Bhabatosh Chanda	*Indian Statistical Institute*
Subhasis Chaudhuri	*Indian Institute of Technology, Mumbai*
Yi-ping Hung	*National Taiwan University*
Prem Kalra	*Indian Institute of Technology, Delhi*
Chandra Kambhamettu	*University of Delaware*
Mohan Kankanahalli	*National University of Singapore*
In So Kweon	*Korean Advanced Institute of Science and Technology*
Sang Wook Lee	*Sogang University*
Ravikanth Malladi	*GE John Welch Technology Centre*
Hiroshi Murase	*Nagoya University*
Tomas Pajdla	*Czech Technical University*
Long Quan	*Hong Kong University of Science and Technology*
A.N. Rajagopalan	*Indian Institute of Technology, Madras*
Mubarak Shah	*University of Central Florida*
Takeshi Shakunaga	*Okayama University*
David Suter	*Monash University*
Tanveer Syeda-Mahmood	*IBM Almaden Research Center*
Chi-Keung Tang	*Hong Kong University of Science and Technology*
Xiaoou Tang	*Microsoft Research Asia*
Rin-ichiro Taniguchi	*Kyushu University*
Baba Vemuri	*University of Florida*
Yaser Yacoob	*University of Maryland*
Naokazu Yokoya	*Nara Institute of Science and Technology*
Changshui Zhang	*Tsinghua University*
Zhengyou Zhang	*Microsoft Research, Redmond*

Reviewers

Neeharika Adabala
Manoj Aggarwal
Amir Akbarzadeh
Yusuf Akgul
Kenichi Arakawa
Greg Arnold
Naoki Asada
Mark Ashdown
Tarkan Aydin
Noboru Babaguchi
Simon Baker
Hynek Bakstein
Alok Bandekar
Subhashis Banerjee
Musodiq Bello
Kiran Bhat
Rahul Bhotika
Prabir Kumar Biswas
Michael Brown
Sema Candemir
Lekha Chaisorn
Kap Luk Chan
Michael Chan
Sharat Chandran
Peng Chang
Parag Chaudhuri
Datong Chen
Chu-Song Chen
Xilin Chen
Yong-Sheng Chen
James Cheong
Tat-Jun Chin
Ondrej Chum
Antonio Criminisi
Shengyang Dai
Kristin Dana
James Davis
Amadou Diallo
Gianfranco Doretto
Lingyu Duan
Sumantra Dutta Roy
Ryan Eckbo
Alexei Efros
Hazim Kemal Ekenel
Sabu Emmanuel
Chris Engels
Mark Everingham
Zhimin Fan
Jan-Michael Frahm
Kazuhiro Fukui
Hui Gao
Theo Gevers
Christopher Geyer
Joshua Gluckman
Dmitry Goldgof
Girish Gopalakrishnan
Ralph Gross
Yanlin Guo
Keiji Gyohten
Mei Han
Wang Hanzi
Manabu Hashimoto
Jean-Yves Hervé
Shinsaku Hiura
Jeffrey Ho
Ki-Sang Hong
Anthony Hoogs
Osamu Hori
Kazuhiro Hotta
Changbo Hu
Gang Hua
Rui Huang
Szu-Hao Huang
Daniel Huber
Sei Ikeda
Ali Iskurt
C.V. Jawahar
Jiaya Jia
Seon Joo Kim
Ioannis Kakadiaris
Atul Kanaujia
Masayuki Kanbara
Moon Gi Kang
Sing Bing Kang
Mark Keck
Zia Khan
Ron Kimmel
Koichi Kise
Dan Kong
Ravi Kothari
Ryo Kurazume
Uday Kurkure
James Kwok
Shang-Hong Lai
Arvind Lakshmikumar
Shihong LAO
Kyoung Mu Lee
Wee Kheng Leow
Maylor Leung
Thomas Leung
Dahua Li
Liyuan Li
Min Li
Lin Liang
Chia-Te Liao

Jenn-Jier James Lien
Joo-Hwee Lim
Stephen Lin
Che-Bin Liu
Zhiheng Liu
Qingshan Liu
Tyng-Luh Liu
Xiaoming Liu
Zicheng Liu
Yogish Mallya
Jose Marroquin
Daniel Martinec
Bogdan Matei
Yasuyuki Matsushita
Scott McClosskey
Paulo Mendonca
Shabbir Merchant
Branislav Micusik
Karol Mikula
James Miller
Anurag Mittal
Daisuke Miyazaki
Kooksang Moon
Yasuhiro Mukaigawa
Dipti Prasad Mukherjee
Jayanta Mukhopadhyay
Kartik Chandra Muktinutalapati
Rakesh Mullick
Christopher Nafis
Anoop Namboodiri
Srinivasa Narasimhan
Ko Nishino
David Nister
Naoko Nitta
Takahiro Okabe
Shinichiro Omachi
Sean O'Maley
Taragay Oskiper
Jiazhi Ou
Dirk Padfield
Kannappan Palaniappan
Vladimir Pavlovic
Shmuel Peleg
A.G. Amitha Perera
Michael Phelps
Carlos Phillips
Marc Pollefeys
Daniel Pooley
Arun Pujari
Kokku Raghu
Deepu Rajan
Subrata Rakshit
Srikumar Ramalingam
Ravi Ramamoorthi
Visvanathan Ramesh
Anand Rangarajan
Sohan Ranjan
Cen Rao
Christopher Rasmussen
Alex Rav-Acha
Sai Ravela
Jens Rittscher
James Ross
Amit Roy-Chowdhury
Hideo Saito
Subhajit Sanyal
Alessandro Sarti
Imari Sato
Tetsu Sato
Tomokazu Sato
Yoichi Sato
Peter Savadjiev
Konrad Schindler
Andrew Senior
Erdogan Sevilgen
Shiguang Shan
Ying Shan
Vinay Sharma
Zhang Sheng
Sheng-Wen Shih
Ikuko Shimizu Okatani
K.S. Shriram
Kaleem Siddiqi
Terence Sim
Sudipta Sinha
Jayanthi Sivaswamy
Thitiwan Srinark
S.H. Srinivasan
Christopher Stauffer
Jesse Stewart
Henrik Stewenius
Svetlana Stolpner
Peter Sturm
Akihiro Sugimoto
Rahul Sukthankar
Qibin Sun
Srikanth Suryanarayananan
Bharath Kumar SV
Rahul Swaminathan
Gokul Swamy
Kar-Han Tan
Ming Tang
Hai Tao

SriRam Thirthala
Ying-Li Tian
Prithi Tissainayagam
George Toderici
Shoji Tominaga
Wai Shun Dickson Tong
Philip Torr
Lorenzo Torresani
Emin Turanalp
Ambrish Tyagi
Seiichi Uchida
Norimichi Ukita
Anton van den Hengel
Rajashekar Venkatachalam
Svetha Venkatesh
Ulas Vural
Toshikazu Wada
Meng Wan
Huan Wang
Liang Wang
Shu-Fan Wang
Chieh-Chih (Bob) Wang
Zhizhou Wang
Tomas Werner
Frederick Wheeler
Kwan-Yee Kenneth Wong
Woontack Woo
Wen Wu
Yihong Wu
Ying Wu
Jing Xiao
Jiangjian Xiao
Wei Xu
Yasushi Yagi
Shuntaro Yamazaki
Kazumasa Yamazawa
Shuicheng Yan
Hua Yang
Ming Yang
Changjiang Yang
Jie Yang
Ming-Hsuan Yang
Ruigang Yang
Qingxiong Yang
Jieping Ye
Dit-Yan Yeung
Ting Yu
Xinguo Yu
Jingyi Yu
Ali Zandifar
Xiang Zhang
Hongming Zhang
Li Zhang
Tao Zhao
Wenyi Zhao
Jiang Yu Zheng
Wei Zhou
Yongwei Zhu
Andrew Zisserman
Larry Zitnick

Table of Contents

Poster Session 1

Face Recognition

Variational Methods

Tracking

Geometry and Calibration

Lighting and Focus

Poster Session 2

Table of Contents – Part II

Detection and Applications

Statistics and Kernels

Segmentation

Geometry and Statistics

Signal Processing

Poster Session 3

Video Processing

On Using Silhouettes for Camera Calibration

Edmond Boyer

MOVI - Gravir - INRIA Rhône-Alpes, Montbonnot, France
Edmond.Boyer@inrialpes.fr

Abstract. This paper addresses the problem of camera calibration using object silhouettes in image sequences. It is known that silhouettes encode information on camera parameters by the fact that their associated viewing cones should present a common intersection in space. In this paper, we investigate how to evaluate calibration parameters given a set of silhouettes, and how to optimize such parameters with silhouette cues only. The objective is to provide on-line tools for silhouette based modeling applications in multiple camera environments. Our contributions with respect to existing works in this field is first to establish the exact constraint that camera parameters should satisfy with respect to silhouettes and second to derive from this constraint new practical criteria to evaluate and to optimize camera parameters. Results on both synthetic and real data illustrate the interest of the proposed framework.

1 Introduction

Camera calibration is a necessary preliminary step for most computer vision applications involving geometric measures. This includes 3D modeling, localization and navigation, am-ong other applications. Traditional solutions in computer vision are based on particular features that are extracted and matched, or identified, in images. This article studies solutions based on silhouettes which do not require any particular patterns nor matching or identification procedures. They represent therefore a convenient solution to evaluate and improve on-line a camera calibration, without the help of any specific patterns. The practical interest arises more specifically in multiple camera environments which are becoming common due, in part, to recent evolutions of camera acquisition materials. These environments require flexible solutions to estimate, and to frequently update, camera parameters, especially because often calibrations do not remain valid over time.

In a seminal work on motion from silhouettes, Rieger [1] used *fixed points* on silhouette boundaries to estimate the axis of rotation from 2 orthographic images. These fixed points correspond to epipolar tangencies, where epipolar planes are tangent to the observed objects' surface. Later on, these points were identified as *frontier points* in [2] since they go across the frontier of the visible region on a surface when the viewpoint is continuously changing. In the associated work, the constraint they give on camera motion was used to optimize essential matrices. In [3], this constraint was established as an extension of the traditional epipolar constraint, and thus was called the *generalized epipolar constraint*. Frontier points give constraints on camera motions, however they must first be localized on silhouette boundaries. This operation appears to be difficult:

P.J. Narayanan et al. (Eds.): ACCV 2006, LNCS 3851, pp. 1–10, 2006.

in [4] inflexions of the silhouette boundary are used to detect frontier points from which motion is derived, in [5] infinite 4D spaces are explored using random samples and in [6] contour signatures are used to find potential frontier points. All these approaches require frontier points to be identified on the silhouette contours prior to camera parameter estimation. However such frontier points can not be localized exactly without knowing epipoles. As a consequence, only approximated solutions are usually obtained by discrete sampling over a space of potential locations for frontier points or epipoles. We take a different strategy and bypass the frontier point localization by considering the problem globally over sets of silhouettes. The interest is to transform a computationally expensive discrete search into an exact, and much faster, optimization over a continuous space.

It is worth to mention also a particular class of shape-from-silhouette applications which use turntables and a single camera to compute 3D models. Such model acquisition systems have received noticeable attention from the vision community [7, 8, 9]. They are geometrically equivalent to a camera rotating in a plane around the scene. The specific constraints which result from this situation can be used to estimate all motion parameters. However, the associated solutions do not extend to general camera configurations as assumed in this paper.

Our approach is based first on the study of the constraint that both silhouettes and camera parameters must satisfy. We then derive two criteria: a quantitative smooth criterion in the form of a distance, and a qualitative discrete criterion, both being defined at any point inside a silhouette. This provides practical tools to qualitatively evaluate calibrations, and to quantitatively optimize their parameters. It appears to be particularly useful in multiple camera environments where calibrations often change, and for which fast on-line solutions are required.

This paper is organized as follows. Section 2 recalls background material. Section 3 precises constraints and respective properties of silhouettes, viewing cones and frontier points. Section 4 introduces the distance between viewing cones that is used as a geometric criterion. Section 5 introduces the qualitative criterion. Section 6 shows results on various data before concluding in section 7.

2 Definitions

Silhouette: Suppose that a scene, containing an arbitrary number objects, is observed by a set of pinhole cameras. Suppose also that projections of objects in the images are segmented and identified as foreground. $\mathcal{O}$ denotes then the set of observed objects and $\mathcal{I}_{\mathcal{O}}$ the corresponding binary foreground-background images. The foreground region of an image i consists of the union of objects' projections in that image and, hence, may be composed of several unconnected components with non-zero genus. Each connected component is called a *silhouette* and their union in image i is denoted $\mathcal{S}_i$.

Viewing Cone: Consider the set of viewing rays associated with image points belonging to a single silhouette in $\mathcal{S}_i$. The closure of this set defines a generalized cone in space, called *viewing cone*. The viewing cone's delimiting surface is tangent to the surface of the corresponding foreground object. In the same way that $\mathcal{S}_i$ is possibly

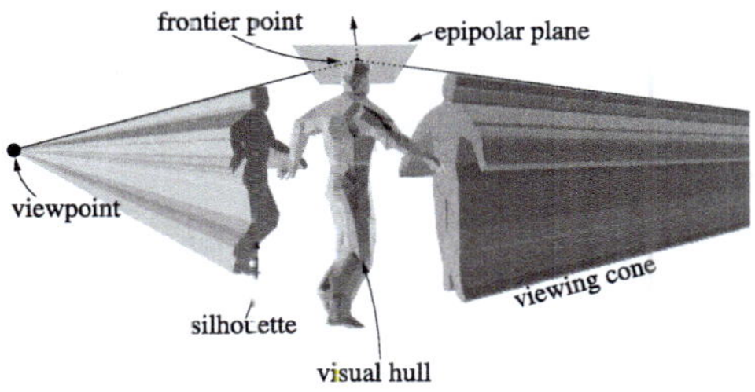

Fig. 1. A visual hull and 2 of its viewing cones

composed of unconnected components, the viewing cones of image i are possibly several distinct cones, one associated with each silhouette in $\mathcal{S}_i$. Their union is denoted $\mathcal{C}_i$. Note that individual objects are not distinguished here.

Visual Hull: The *visual hull* [10] is formally defined as the maximum surface consistent with all silhouettes in all images. Intuitively, it is the intersection of the viewing cones of all images (see figure 1). In practice, silhouettes are delimited by 2D polygonal curves, thus viewing cones are polyhedral cones and since a finite set of images are considered, visual hulls are polyhedrons. Assume that all objects are seen from all image viewpoints then:

$$\mathcal{VH}(\mathcal{I_O}) = \bigcap_{i \in \mathcal{I_O}} \mathcal{C}_i, \tag{1}$$

is the visual hull associated with the set $\mathcal{I_O}$of foreground images and their viewing cones $\mathcal{C}_{i \in \mathcal{I_O}}$. If all objects $\mathcal{O}$ do not project onto all images, then the reasoning that follows still applies to subset of objects and subsets of cameras which satisfy the common visibility constraint.

3 Geometric Consistency Constraint

In this section, the exact and optimal geometric consistency which applies with silhouettes is first established and its equivalence with more practical constraints is discussed.

3.1 Visual Hull Constraint

Calibration constraints are usually derived from geometric constraints reflecting geometric coherence. For instance, different image projections of the same feature should give rise to the same spatial location with true camera parameters. In the case of silhouettes, and under the assumption that no other image primitives are available, the only geometric coherence that applies comes from the fact that all viewing cones should correspond to the same objects with true camera parameters. Thus:

$$\mathcal{O} \subset \mathcal{VH}(\mathcal{I_O}),$$

and consequently by projecting in any image i:

$$S_i \subset P_i(\mathcal{VH}(\mathcal{I_O})), \; \forall i \in \mathcal{I_O},$$

where $P_i()$ is the oriented projection[1] in image i. Thus, viewing cones should all intersect, and viewing rays belonging to viewing cones should all contribute to this intersection. The above expression is equivalent to:

$$\bigcup_{i \in \mathcal{I_O}} [\mathcal{S}_i \; - \; P_i(\mathcal{VH}(\mathcal{I_O}))] = \emptyset, \tag{2}$$

which says that the visual hull projection onto any image i should entirely cover the corresponding silhouette $\mathcal{S}_i$ in that image. This is the constraint that viewing cones should satisfy with true camera parameters. It encodes all the geometric consistency constraints that apply with silhouettes and, as such, is optimal. However this expression in its current form does not yield a practical cost function for camera parameters since all configurations leading to an empty visual hull are equally considered, thus making convergence over cost functions very uncertain in many situations. To overcome this difficulty, viewing cones can be considered pairwise as explained in the following section.

3.2 Pairwise Cone Tangency

We can easily derive from the general expression (2) the pairwise tangency constraint. Substituting the visual hull definition (1) in (2):

$$(2) \Leftrightarrow \bigcup_{i \in \mathcal{I_O}} [\mathcal{S}_i \; - \; P_i(\bigcap_{j \in \mathcal{I_O}} \mathcal{C}_j)] = \emptyset.$$

Since projection is a linear operation preserving incidence relations:

$$(2) \Rightarrow \bigcup_{i \in \mathcal{I_O}} [\mathcal{S}_i \; - \; \bigcap_{j \in \mathcal{I_O}} P_i(\mathcal{C}_j)] = \emptyset.$$

Note that, in the above expression, the exact equivalence with (2) is lost since projecting viewing cone individually introduces depth ambiguities and, hence, does not ensure a common intersection of all cones as in (2). By distributive laws:

$$(2) \Rightarrow \bigcup_{(i,j) \in \mathcal{I_O} \times \mathcal{I_O}} [\mathcal{S}_i \; - \; P_i(\mathcal{C}_j)] = \emptyset. \tag{3}$$

Expression (3) states that all viewing cones of a single scene should be pairwise tangent. By pairwise tangent, it is meant that all viewing rays from one cone intersect the other cone, and reciprocally. This can be seen as the extension of the epipolar constraint to silhouettes (see figure 2). Note that this constraint is always satisfied by concentric viewing cones, for which no frontier points exist. Note also that if (3) and (2) are not strictly equivalent, they are equivalent in most general situations.

[1] i.e. a projection such that there is a one-to-one mapping between rays from the projection center and image points.

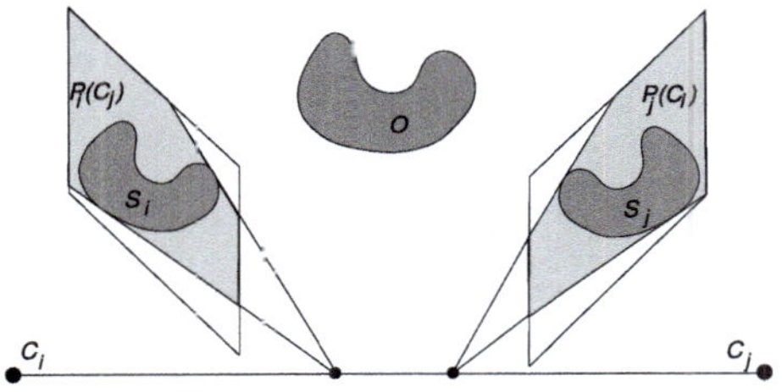

Fig. 2. Pairwise tangency constraint: silhouette S_i is a subset of the viewing cone projection $P_i(\mathcal{C}_j)$ in image i

3.3 Connection with Frontier Points

A number of approaches consider frontier points and the constraints they yield on camera configurations. Frontier points are particular points which are both on the objects' surface and the visual hull, which project onto silhouettes in 2 or more images, and where the epipolar plane is tangent to the surface (see figure 1). They satisfy therefore what is called the generalized epipolar constraint [3]. They allow thereby projective reconstruction when localized in images [5, 6]. The connection between the generalized epipolar constraint and the pairwise tangency constraint (3) is that the latter implies the former at particular frontier points. Intuitively, if two viewing cones are tangent then the generalized epipolar constraint is satisfied at extremal frontier points where viewing lines graze both viewing cones.

4 Quantitative Criterion

The pairwise tangency is a condition that viewing cones must satisfy to ensure that the same objects are inside all cones. In this section, we introduce a distance function that evaluates this condition.

4.1 Distances Between a Viewing Ray and a Viewing Cone

The distance function between a ray and a cone that we seek should preferably respect several conditions:

1. It should be expressed in a fixed metric with respect to the data, thus in the images since a 3D metric will change with camera parameters.
2. It should be a monotonic function of the respective locations of ray and cone.
3. It should be zero if the ray intersect the viewing cone. This intersection, while apparently easy to verify in the images, requires some care when epipolar geometry is used. Figure 3 depicts for instance a few situations where the epipolar line of a ray intersects the silhouette, though the ray does not intersect the viewing cone. These situations occur because no distinction is made between front and back of rays.
4. It should be finite in general so that situations in figure 3 can be differentiated.

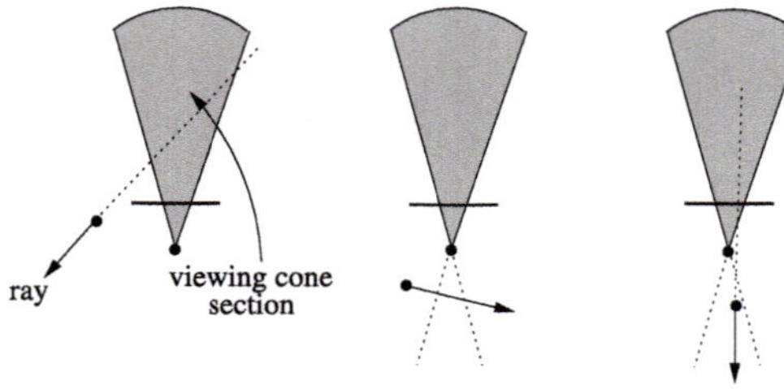

Fig. 3. A ray and the cross-section of the viewing cone in the corresponding epipolar plane. 3 of the situations where unoriented epipolar geometry will fail and detect intersections.

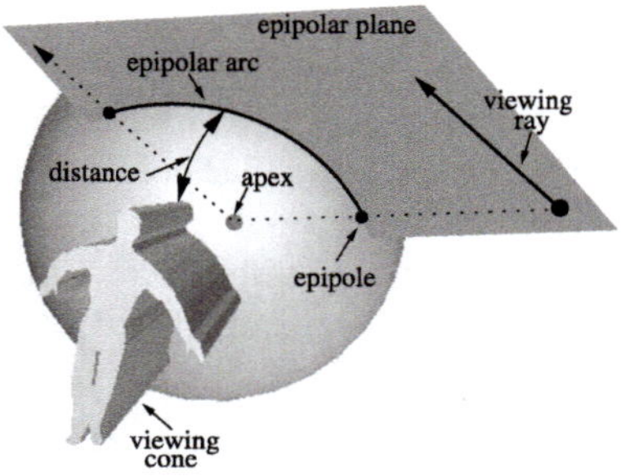

Fig. 4. The spherical image model: viewing rays project onto epipolars arcs on the sphere

In light of this, a fairly simple but efficient approach is to consider a spherical image model instead of a planar model (see figure 4), associated to an angular metric. The distance from a ray to a viewing cone is then the shortest path on the sphere from the viewing cone to the ray projection. This projection forms an epipolar circle-arc on the sphere delimited by the epipole and the intersection of the ray direction with the sphere. The ray projection is then always the shortest arc between these 2 points, which can coincide if the ray goes trough the viewing cone apex. Two different situations occur depending on the respective positions of the ray epipolar plane and the viewing cone:

1. The plane intersects the viewing cone apex only, as in figure 4. The point on the circle containing the epipolar arc and closest to the viewing cone must be determined. If such point is on the epipolar arc then the distance we seek is its distance to the viewing cone. Otherwise, it is the minimum of the distances between the arc boundary points and the viewing cone.
2. The plane goes through the viewing cone. The distance is zero in the case where the ray intersects the viewing cone section in the epipolar plane, and the shortest distance between the epipolar arc boundary points and the viewing cone section in the other case. This distance is easily computed using angles in the epipolar plane.

4.2 Distance Between 2 Viewing Cones

A distance function between a ray and a viewing cone has been defined in the previous section, this section discusses how to integrate it over a cone. The distance between

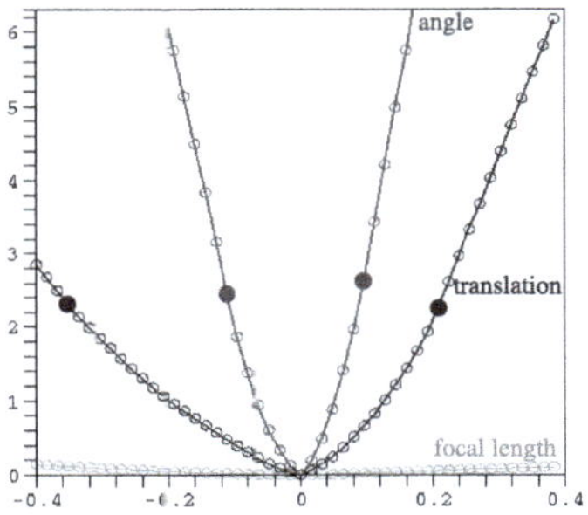

Fig. 5. The distance between 2 viewing cones as a function of: (green) one focal length which varies in the range $[f - 0.4f, f + 0.4f]$, with f the true value; (blue) one translation parameter to which is added from -0.4 to 0.4 of the camera-scene distance; (red) one Euler orientation angle which varies in the range $[\alpha - 0.4\pi, \alpha + 0.4\pi]$ with α the true value. The filled points denote the limit distances on curves above which the 2 cones do not intersect at all.

2 viewing cones is then simply defined by a double integration over the 2 concerned cones.

Recall that silhouettes and viewing cones are discrete in practice and thus defined by sets of contour points in the images and boundary rays in space. The simplest solution consists then in summing individual distances over boundary rays. Assume that r_i^k is the kth ray on the boundary of viewing cone C_i, and $d(r_i^k, C_j) = d_{ij}^k$ is the distance between r_i^k and C_j as defined in the previous section. Then the distance D_{ij} between C_i and C_j is:

$$D_{ij} = \sum_k d_{ij}^k + \sum_l d_{ji}^l = d_{ij} + d_{ji}. \quad (4)$$

Remark that $D_{ij} = D_{ji}$ but $d_{ij} \neq d_{ji}$. The above expression is easy to compute once the distance function is established. It can be applied to all boundary viewing rays, however mainly rays on the convex hulls of silhouettes are concerned by the pairwise tangency constraint, we thus consider only them to improve computational efficiency. Figure 5 illustrates the distance D_{ij} between 2 viewing cones of a synthetic body model as a function of various parameters of one cone's camera. This graph demonstrates the smooth behavior of the distance around the true parameter values, even when the cones do not intersect at all.

5 Silhouette Calibration Ratio

Following the quantitative criterion, we introduce a simple qualitative criterion which evaluates how silhouettes contribute to the visual hull for a given calibration.

Recall that any viewing ray, from any viewing cone, should be intersected by all other image viewing cones, along an interval common to all cones. Let ω_r be an interval along ray r intersected by viewing cones, and let us call $\mathcal{N}(\omega_r)$ the number of image contributing (image for which a viewing cone intersects ω_r) inside that interval. Then the sum over the rays r: $\sum_r \max_{\omega_r}(\mathcal{N}(\omega_r))$, should theoretically be equal to $m(n-1)$ if m rays and n images are considered. Now this criterion can be refined by considering each image contribution individually along a viewing ray. Let ω_r^i be an interval, along ray r, where image i contributes. Then the silhouette calibration ration C_r defined as:

$$C_r = \frac{1}{m(n-1)^2} \sum_r \sum_i \max_{\omega_r^i}(\mathcal{N}(\omega^i)), \tag{5}$$

should theoretically be equal to 1 since each image should have at least one contribution interval with $(n-1)$ image contributions. This qualitative criterion is very useful in practice because it reflects the combined quality of a set of silhouettes and of a set of camera parameters. Notice however that it can hardly be used for optimizations because of its discrete, and thus non-smooth, nature.

6 Experimental Results

The pairwise tangency presented in the previous section constraint camera parameters when a set of static silhouettes $\mathcal{I}_O$ is known. For calibration, different sets $\mathcal{I}_O$ should be considered. They can easily be obtained, from moving objects for instance, as in [5]. The distances between viewing cones are then minimized over the camera parameter space through a least square approach:

$$\hat{\theta}_{\mathcal{I}_O} = \min_{\theta} \sum_{(i,j) \in \mathcal{I}_O \times \mathcal{I}_O} D_{ij}^2, \tag{6}$$

where θ is the set of camera parameters to be optimized. $\hat{\theta}_{\mathcal{I}_O}$ is equivalent to a maximum likelihood estimate of the camera parameters under the assumption that viewing rays are statistically independent. The above quantitative sum can be minimized by standard non-linear methods such as Levenberg-Marquardt.

6.1 Synthetic Data

Synthetic sequences, composed of images with dimensions 300×300, were used to test the approach robustness. 7 cameras, with standard focal lengths, are viewing a running human body. All camera extrinsic parameters and one focal length per camera, assuming known or unit aspect ratios, are optimized. Different initial solutions are tested by adding various percentages of uniform noise to the exact camera parameters. For the focal lengths and the translation parameters, the noise amplitudes vary from 0% up to 40% of the exact parameter value; for the pose angle parameters, the noise amplitudes vary from 0% up to 40% of 2π. Figure 6 shows, on the left, the silhouette calibration ratios after optimization; and on the right, relative errors in the estimated camera parameters after optimization using 5 frames per cameras. These results first validate the silhouette calibration ratio as a global estimator for the quality of any calibration with respect to silhouette data. Second, they show that using only one frame per camera is intractable in most situations. However, they prove also that using several frames, calibration can be recovered with a good precision even far from the exact solution. Other

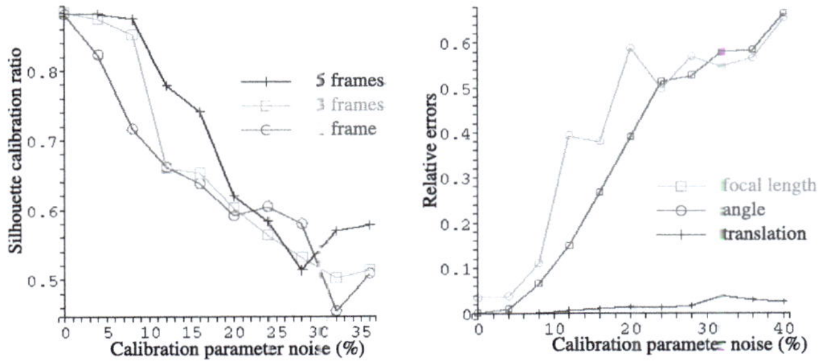

Fig. 6. Robustness to the initial calibration: right, the silhouette calibration ratio; left, the relative errors in the estimated camera parameters for the 5 frame case: errors relative to the true value for the focal length, errors relative to the distance camera-scene for the translation parameter and errors relative to π for the angle parameter

experiments, not presented due to lack of space, show that adding a reasonable amount of noise to silhouette vertices, typically a 1 pixel Gaussian Noise, only slightly changes these results.

6.2 Real Data

Our approach was also tested in a real environment with 6 firewire cameras viewing a moving person. A calibration obtained by optimizing an initial solution using known points is available and will be considered as the ground truth. In the following experi-

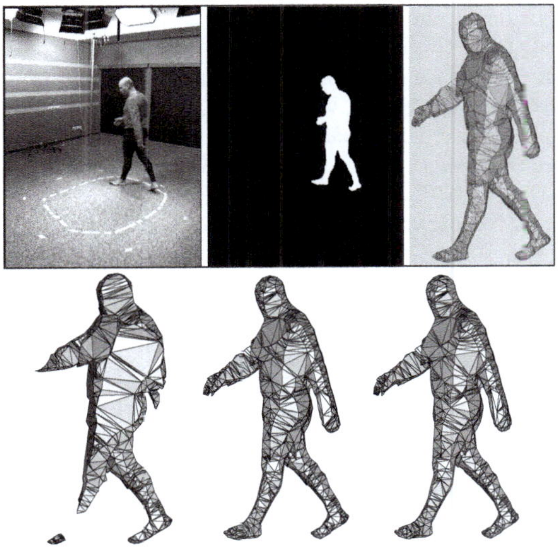

Fig. 7. Top, one of the original image, the corresponding silhouette and the visual hull model obtained with ground truth calibration. Bottom, 3 models which correspond to calibrations obtained with our method and using respectively 1, 3 and 5 frames per camera.

ments, we use the same initial solution for the calibration with viewing cones. As for the synthetic case, all camera extrinsic parameters and one focal length per camera are optimized. Figure 7 shows, on top, the input images and a visual hull model obtained using ground truth values for calibration. In the bottom, models obtained from the same silhouettes, but using our approach with respectively 1, 3 and 5 frames per camera. Apart from a scale difference, not shown and due to the fact that fixed dimensions were imposed for the ground truth solution, the 2 most-right models are very close to the ground truth one.

7 Conclusion

We have studied the problem of estimating camera parameters using silhouettes. It has been shown that, under little assumptions, all geometric constraints given by silhouettes are ensured by the pairwise tangency constraint. A second contribution of this paper is to provide a practical criterion based on the distance between 2 viewing cones. This criterion appears to be efficient in practice since it can handle a large variety of camera configurations, in particular when viewing cones are distant. It allows therefore multi-camera environments to be easily calibrated when an initial solution exists. The criterion can also be minimized using efficient and fast non-linear approach. The approach is therefore also aimed at real time estimation of camera motions with moving objects.

References

1. Rieger, J.: Three-Dimensional Motion from Fixed Points of a Deforming Profile Curve. Optics Letters **11** (1986) 123–125
2. Cipolla, R., strm, K., Giblin, P.: Motion from the Frontier of Curved Surfaces. In: Proceedings of 5th International Conference on Computer Vision, Boston (USA). (1995) 269–275
3. Åström, K., Cipolla, R., Giblin, P.: Generalised Epipolar Constraints. In: Proceedings of Fourth European Conference on Computer Vision, Cambridge, (England). (1996) 97–108 Lecture Notes in Computer Science, volume 1065.
4. Joshi, T., Ahuja, N., Ponce, J.: Structure and Motion Estimation from Dynamic Silhouettes under Perspective Projection. In: Proceedings of 5th International Conference on Computer Vision, Boston (USA). (1995) 290–295
5. Sinha, S., Pollefeys, M., McMillan, L.: Camera Network Calibration from Dynamic Silhouettes. In: Proceedings of IEEE Conference on Computer Vision and Pattern Recognition, Washington, (USA). (2004)
6. Furukawa, Y., Sethi, A., Ponce, J., Kriegman, D.J.: Structure from Motion for Smooth Textureless Objects. In: Proceedings of the 8th European Conference on Computer Vision, Prague, (Czech Republic). (2004)
7. Fitzgibbon, A., Cross, G., Zisserman, A.: Automatic 3d model construction for turn-table sequences. In: Proceedings of SMILE Workshop on Structure from Multiple Images in Large Scale Environments. Volume 1506 of Lecture Notes in Computer Science. (1998) 154–170
8. Mendoça, P., Wong, K.Y., Cipolla, R.: Epipolar Geometry from Profiles under Circular Motion. IEEE Transactions on PAMI **23** (2001) 604–616
9. Jiang, G., Quan, L., Tsui, H.: Circular Motion Geometry Using Minimal Data. IEEE Transactions on PAMI **26** (2004) 721–731
10. Laurentini, A.: The Visual Hull Concept for Silhouette-Based Image Understanding. IEEE Transactions on PAMI **16** (1994) 150–162

Towards a Guaranteed Solution to Plane-Based Self-calibration

Benoît Bocquillon, Pierre Gurdjos, and Alain Crouzil

Université Paul Sabatier, IRIT-TCI, 118, route de Narbonne,
31062 Toulouse, France
{bocquillon, gurdjos, crouzil}@irit.fr

Abstract. We investigate the problem of self-calibrating a camera, from multiple views of a planar scene. By self-calibrating, we refer to the problem of simultaneously estimate the camera intrinsic parameters and the Euclidean structure of one 3D plane. A solution is usually obtained by solving a non-linear system via local optimization, with the critical issue of parameter initialization especially the focal length. Arguing that these five parameters are inter-dependent, we propose an alternate problem formulation, with only three d.o.f., corresponding to three parameters to estimate. In the light of this, we are concerned with global optimization in order to get a guaranteed solution, with the shortest response time. Interval analysis provides an efficient numerical framework, that reveals to be highly performant, with regard to both estimation accuracy and time-consuming.

1 Introduction

The self-calibration of a camera consists in determining, either partially or completely, the metric properties of the camera and/or the scene, from a set of uncalibrated views. The principle of self-calibration is to use "absolute entities" as targets, geometrically constrained by some prior information about the internal or external parameters of the camera. Absolute targets are abstract entities, located at infinity, encoding the Euclidean structure (ES) of the considered d-dimensional space, with the characteristic property of being left invariant under similarities[1] in d-space [1, 2]. In 3-space, the target is the *absolute conic* (AC), which is a circle of imaginary radius on the plane at infinity π_∞. The AC has the well-known property that its image (IAC) is globally invariant under camera motion, providing the camera internal parameters are constant. This is the starting point of numerous 3D self-calibration methods (see [1, chapter 19] for a review). On the basis of a projective reconstruction of the scene, 3D self-calibration determines the ES of the 3D space in terms of the AC *and* the plane at infinity, in projective coordinates. This can be achieved either separately, or simultaneously. In the latter case, the AC is treated as a rank-3 envelope of 3D planes, known as absolute dual quadric in the literature. Assuming that the focal length is the only unknown, closed-forms and linear solutions can be obtained e.g., as in [3].

The problem up to discussion in this work is the 2D (or plane-based) self-calibration of a camera i.e., by observing a 3D plane π, with regard to general camera motion. In

[1] i.e., transformations preserving angles and changing distances in the same ratio.

P.J. Narayanan et al. (Eds.): ACCV 2006, LNCS 3851, pp. 11–20, 2006.

2-space, the self-calibration targets are the *circular points* (CP) that are two conjugate complex points of π on the line at infinity, meeting all the circles of π and the AC of π_∞. Since Triggs' work [4], it is known that 2D self-calibration is possible, using the constraint that the image of the CP (ICP) lie on the IAC, only involving inter-view homographies induced by π. Because no other (general) invariance of the ICP can be exhibited, very few 2D self-calibration methods have been reported [5, 6, 4], except for some specific camera motion [7, 8]. Furthermore, contrary to 3D self-calibration, even with a simplified model of the camera, no closed-form or linear solution exist. Such a problem, consisting in determining simultaneously the CP and the AC, is non-linear in essence. As stated in [4], the problem parameterization requires 4 d.o.f. for the ICP plus 5 d.o.f. for the AC. A solution can be obtained via local optimization, from at least 5 views, with the critical issue of parameter initialization, especially the focal length.

Our starting point is to reduce the number of parameters to estimate by using the fact that, since the CP lie on the AC, there is a redundancy in the problem parameterization. This inter-dependence of parameters in Triggs' statement is a modeling constraint that has no reason not to be exactly ensured. Actually, Triggs initially treated it as an equation, which does not really make sense as we will argue later. That said, our contribution is to propose a new minimal parameterization of the 2D self-calibration problem, by introducing as target a degenerate conic envelope, consisting of the point-pair at which the AC meets the line at infinity i.e., consisting of the CP. Thanks to our propositions (1) and (2), we show that we only require to estimate the affine structure of the plane along with the internal parameters. This leads to a formulation with seven unknowns/d.o.f. instead of the nine initially mentioned in [4]. Assuming that the constant focal length is the sole unknown, only three parameters have to be estimated. This paves the way for finding a guaranteed solution to the problem as this small number of unknowns is well adapted to the use of interval analysis [9]. Interval analysis has been widely used in global optimization problems [10] and afford the guarantee that the global minimum has been found. Interval analysis has been succesfully used to the 3D self-calibration problem [11]. It provides an efficient numerical framework, that reveals to be highly performant, with regard to both estimation accuracy and time-consuming.

This paper is structured as follows. First, starting with the basic 2D self-calibration equations of [4], we explain how to obtain a minimal parameterization of the problem from which we derive a cost function. Second, we review the main rules of interval analysis and the global minimization scheme used here. Eventually, we give the results obtained with synthetic and real data and conclusions are drawn.

2 Minimal Parameterization of 2D Self-calibration

2.1 Foreword and Notations

Our problem is that of recovering the Euclidean structure (ES) of some 3D plane π, called world plane, seen in multiple views, for some *uncalibrated* camera. What is only assumed to be *known* is the inter-view homographies induced by π.

Without any additional knowledge, this problem cannot be separated from that of calibrating the camera i.e., of recovering its intrinsic parameters. Stated together, these are then referred to as the plane-based self-calibration problem [4]. [5] describes an alternative to [4]. We will give in §2.2 the link between these two constraints.

We use some MATLAB-like notations: $1 : n$ denotes the range $1, \dots, n$. $\mathtt{M}_{(1:r,1:c)}$ denotes the $r \times c$ submatrix of M selected by the row range $1 : r$ and the column range $1 : c$. The notation $\mathtt{M}_{(:,1:c)}$, resp. $\mathtt{M}_{(1:r,:)}$, selects the first c (resp. r) columns, resp. rows, of M. We also define the canonical vectors:

$$\mathbf{e}_1 \equiv (1,0,0)^\top, \ \mathbf{e}_2 \equiv (0,1,0)^\top, \ \mathbf{e}_3 \equiv (0,0,1)^\top. \qquad (1)$$

The matrix $[\mathbf{x}]_\times$ refers to the skew-symmetric, order-3, matrix, such that $[\mathbf{x}]_\times \mathbf{y} = \mathbf{x} \times \mathbf{y}$, $\mathbf{y} \in \mathbb{R}^3$. In this paper, we will make a heavily use of the equality $[\mathtt{T}\mathbf{x}]_\times = \det(\mathtt{T})\mathtt{T}^{-\top} [\mathbf{x}]_\times \mathtt{T}^{-1}$. The notation i *always* refers to the imaginary number $\sqrt{-1}$.

In the following we assume some basic results on projective geometry. These can be found in standard textbooks e.g., in [1, 2]. We remind the reader some essential notions and establish some novel properties relevant to our work.

The *image of the absolute conic* (IAC) matrix satisfies $\omega = \mathbf{K}^{-\top}\mathbf{K}^{-1}$, where $\mathbf{K}$ is the calibration matrix [1, §5.1] that encodes the internal camera parameters, which is, in its more general form:

$$\mathbf{K} \equiv \begin{pmatrix} \alpha_u & \gamma & u_0 \\ 0 & \alpha_v & v_0 \\ 0 & 0 & 1 \end{pmatrix}, \qquad (2)$$

where α_u, α_v represent the focal length in terms of pixel dimensions in the u, v direction respectively, (u_0, v_0) are the principal point pixel coordinates and γ is the skew factor.

2.2 Plane-Based Self-calibration Equations

Let P denote the *unknown* (Euclidean) world-to-image homography, mapping entities of π to their projections on the image plane $\tilde{\pi}$, and let H_j be the *known* inter-view homography, induced by π, from the current view to some view number j.

The (Regular) Plane-Based Self-calibration Equations. Rigorously, the ES of π is given in terms of its *imaged circular points* (ICP) $P(\mathtt{I}_\pm)$, whereas the circular points (CP) $\mathtt{I}_\pm$ are, by definition [1, pp. 52-53], conjugate complex points at infinity in π, common to all of its circles. In any Euclidean representation, the CP have canonical coordinates $\mathbf{e}_\pm \equiv \mathbf{e}_1 \pm i\mathbf{e}_2 = (1, \pm i, 0)^\top$, which are invariant under any 2D similarity S of π i.e., $\mathbf{e}_\pm \sim \mathtt{S}\mathbf{e}_\pm$, where $\mathtt{S} \in \mathbb{R}^{3\times3}$ is the matrix of S. In image representation, the coordinates of the ICP $P(\mathtt{I}_\pm)$, denoted by $\mathbf{x}_\pm \equiv \mathbf{x}_1 \pm i\mathbf{x}_2$, satisfy $\mathbf{x}_\pm \sim \mathtt{PS}\mathbf{e}_\pm$, where $\mathtt{P} \in \mathbb{R}^{3\times3}$ is the matrix of P. Note that $\mathbf{x}_\pm$ only have four d.o.f., basically the eight d.o.f. of P minus the four d.o.f. of S.

The ICP are, by projective invariance, on the vanishing line, common to all imaged circles, including the image ω of the absolute conic [1, pp. 81-83] of the plane at infinity. The IAC ω is the locus of all ICP (i.e., of all 3D planes) which entails that $\mathbf{x}_\pm^\top \omega \mathbf{x}_\pm = 0$, or equivalently (see [1, p. 211] for more details):

$$\mathbf{x}_1^\top \omega \mathbf{x}_2 = 0 \quad \text{and} \quad \mathbf{x}_1^\top \omega \mathbf{x}_1 - \mathbf{x}_2^\top \omega \mathbf{x}_2 = 0. \qquad (3)$$

In view number j, the constraint is described by $\mathbf{x}_{\pm}^{\top}\mathtt{H}_j^{\top}\boldsymbol{\omega}_j\mathtt{H}_j\mathbf{x}_{\pm} = 0$, or:

$$\mathbf{x}_1^{\top}\mathtt{H}_j^{\top}\boldsymbol{\omega}_j\mathtt{H}_j\mathbf{x}_2 = 0 \quad \text{and} \quad \mathbf{x}_1^{\top}\mathtt{H}_j^{\top}\boldsymbol{\omega}_j\mathtt{H}_j\mathbf{x}_1 - \mathbf{x}_2^{\top}\mathtt{H}_j^{\top}\boldsymbol{\omega}_j\mathtt{H}_j\mathbf{x}_2 = 0, \tag{4}$$

where $\boldsymbol{\omega}_j$ is the matrix of the IAC in view number j and $\mathtt{H}_j$ is the matrix of H_j.

The Dual Plane-Based Self-calibration Equations. A (maybe) most intuitive parameterization of the ES can also be given in terms of any (Euclidean) world-to-image homography $P \circ S$, where S denotes an arbitrary 2D similarity. Indeed, by applying $(P \circ S)^{-1}$ to the image plane, we get an Euclidean reconstruction of π, $P \circ S$ being referred to as *rectifying homography.*

If we treat the ICP as a degenerate conic envelope i.e., as the assemblage of isotropic lines as tangents, we get a conic, referred to as the *image of the conic dual to circular points* (ICDCP) in [1, p.52], whose matrix is of the form:

$$\mathtt{C}^* \sim \mathbf{x}_-\mathbf{x}_+^{\top} + \mathbf{x}_+\mathbf{x}_-^{\top} \sim \mathtt{P}(\mathbf{e}_-\mathbf{e}_+^{\top} + \mathbf{e}_+\mathbf{e}_-^{\top})\mathtt{P}^{\top} \sim \mathtt{PS}(\mathbf{e}_-\mathbf{e}_+^{\top} + \mathbf{e}_+\mathbf{e}_-^{\top})\mathtt{S}^{\top}\mathtt{P}^{\top}, \tag{5}$$

where $\mathtt{S} \in \mathbb{R}^{3\times3}$ is the matrix of S. As $\mathbf{e}_-\mathbf{e}_+^{\top} + \mathbf{e}_+\mathbf{e}_-^{\top} \sim \mathrm{diag}(1,1,0)$, a rectifying homography can be obtained by the adequate factorization [1, pp.55-56] of $\mathtt{C}^*$ e.g., based on the singular value decomposition (SVD), with singular values $\sigma_1 \geq \sigma_2 > 0$ and $\sigma_3 = 0$:

$$\pm\mathtt{C}^* = \mathtt{U}\boldsymbol{\Sigma}\mathtt{U}^{\top} \equiv \mathtt{X}\,\mathrm{diag}(1,1,0)\mathtt{X}^{\top} = \begin{bmatrix}\mathbf{x}_1 \ \mathbf{x}_2\end{bmatrix}\begin{bmatrix}\mathbf{x}_1 \ \mathbf{x}_2\end{bmatrix}^{\top}. \tag{6}$$

Therefore, the ICP can be specified in the form of $\mathbf{x}_{\pm} = \mathtt{U}_{(:,1:2)}\sqrt{\boldsymbol{\Sigma}}_{(1:2,1:2)} \sim \mathtt{XS}\mathbf{e}_{\pm}$. Consequently, the constraints (4) can be put in the matrix form:

$$\begin{bmatrix}\mathbf{x}_1 \ \mathbf{x}_2\end{bmatrix}^{\top}\mathtt{H}_j^{\top}\boldsymbol{\omega}_j\mathtt{H}_j\begin{bmatrix}\mathbf{x}_1 \ \mathbf{x}_2\end{bmatrix} \sim \mathtt{I}_{2\times2}. \tag{7}$$

We now highlight an interesting decomposition of the ICDCP matrix $\mathtt{C}^*$. Basically, our aim is to put into equation the fact that the degenerate conic $\mathtt{C}^*$ consists of the two points at which the vanishing line $\mathbf{v}$ meets the IAC $\boldsymbol{\omega}$. Since the AC is a circle on the plane at infinity, these two points are the ICP.

Proposition 1. *The ICDCP matrix satisfies the following decomposition:*

$$\mathtt{C}^* \sim [\mathbf{v}]_{\times}\,\boldsymbol{\omega}\,[\mathbf{v}]_{\times}, \tag{8}$$

where $\boldsymbol{\omega}$ is the IAC matrix and $\mathbf{v}$ is the vanishing line vector.

Proof. Define $\Delta \equiv [\mathbf{v}]_{\times}\,\boldsymbol{\omega}\,[\mathbf{v}]_{\times}$. Clearly Δ is rank-2, so as a conic envelope, Δ consists of two distinct points $\mathbf{p}$, $\mathbf{q}$ i.e., $\Delta \sim \mathbf{p}\mathbf{q}^{\top} + \mathbf{q}\mathbf{p}^{\top}$. Let us show these are the ICP. On the one hand, we see that $\Delta\mathbf{v} = \mathbf{0}$ which implies that both $\mathbf{p}$, $\mathbf{q}$ are on the vanishing line $\mathbf{v}$. On the other hand, any line $\mathbf{w} \neq \mathbf{v}$, verifying $\mathbf{w}^{\top}\Delta\mathbf{w} = 0$, passes either through $\mathbf{p}$ or $\mathbf{q}$. Assume $\mathbf{w}$ contains $\mathbf{p}$: this entails that $\mathbf{v} \times \mathbf{w} \sim \mathbf{p}$ and so $\mathbf{p}^{\top}\boldsymbol{\omega}\mathbf{p} = 0$. As a result, since $\boldsymbol{\omega}$ is the locus of all ICP, $\mathbf{p}$ is one ICP of π and $\mathbf{q}$ its conjugate.

Minimal Parameterization. As explained above, the ICP can be specified from $\mathtt{C}^*$ in the form of $\mathbf{x}_1 \pm \mathbf{x}_2$, with $\begin{bmatrix}\mathbf{x}_1 & \mathbf{x}_2\end{bmatrix} \equiv \mathtt{U}_{(:,1:2)}\sqrt{\mathbf{\Sigma}_{(1:2,1:2)}}$ obtained from (6).

In this work, we will need a formal expression of $\mathbf{x}_1$ and $\mathbf{x}_2$.

Proposition 2. *Vectors $\mathbf{x}_1$, $\mathbf{x}_2$ satisfying (6), and so (7), can be written in the form of:*

$$\begin{bmatrix}\mathbf{x}_1 & \mathbf{x}_2\end{bmatrix} \sim \begin{bmatrix}[\mathbf{v}]_\times \mathbf{e}_k & \mu [\mathbf{v}]_\times \boldsymbol{\omega} [\mathbf{v}]_\times \mathbf{e}_k\end{bmatrix}, \quad k \in \{1, 2, 3\}, \tag{9}$$

where $\mu \equiv \alpha_u \alpha_v / \left\|\mathtt{K}^\top \mathbf{v}\right\|$ and $\mathbf{e}_k$ is a canonical vector, as defined in (1).

The proof requires to remind the reader that the vanishing line can be written as $\mathbf{v} = \mathtt{K}^{-\top}\mathbf{n}$, where $\mathbf{n}$ is the unit normal to π in the camera frame. Let us also define the 'calibrated' ICDCP $\bar{\mathtt{C}}^* \equiv \xi \mathtt{K}^{-1}\mathtt{C}^*\mathtt{K}^{-\top}$, where ξ is a scalar such that $\bar{\mathtt{C}}^* = [\mathbf{n}]_\times^\top [\mathbf{n}]_\times$.

Proof. The singular values of $\bar{\mathtt{C}}^*$ are $\{1, 1, 0\}$ so $\mathrm{ran}(\bar{\mathtt{C}}^*) = \mathrm{ran}([\mathbf{n}]_\times)$ and $\mathrm{null}(\bar{\mathtt{C}}^*) = \mathrm{null}([\mathbf{n}]_\times)$. Thanks to the SVD theorem [12], we know that the matrix $\mathtt{W} \in \mathbb{R}^{3\times 3}$, $\mathtt{W}\mathtt{W}^\top \sim \mathtt{I}_3$, such that $\bar{\mathtt{C}}^* \sim \mathtt{W}\,\mathrm{diag}(1, 1, 0)\mathtt{W}^\top$, has the properties that $\mathrm{ran}(\bar{\mathtt{C}}^*) = \mathrm{span}\{\mathbf{w}_1, \mathbf{w}_2\}$ and $\mathrm{null}(\bar{\mathtt{C}}^*) = \mathrm{span}\{\mathbf{w}_3\}$. As a result, we can compute:

$$\mathbf{w}_1 = [\mathbf{n}]_\times \mathbf{e}_k, \quad \mathbf{w}_2 = [\mathbf{n}]_\times^2 \mathbf{e}_k, \quad \mathbf{w}_3 = \mathbf{n}, \tag{10}$$

where $\mathbf{w}_2 = \mathbf{w}_3 \times \mathbf{w}_1 = [\mathbf{w}_3]_\times \mathbf{w}_1$. Substituting $\mathtt{K}^\top\mathbf{v}$ to $\mathbf{n}$ into (10), after some normalizations, we obtain (9).

The proposed form (9) offers an obvious advantage of minimal parameterization of the self-calibration problem. Substituting (9) into (4), there are now seven d.o.f. instead of the nine in [4].

Link with Malis' Constraint [5]. Introducing $\bar{\mathtt{H}}_j \equiv \mathtt{K}_j^{-1}\mathtt{H}_j\mathtt{K}_j$, the 'calibrated' ICDCP, in the view number j, is $\bar{\mathtt{C}}_j^* \equiv [\mathbf{n}_j]_\times^\top [\mathbf{n}_j]_\times \sim \bar{\mathtt{H}}_j [\mathbf{n}]_\times^\top [\mathbf{n}]_\times \bar{\mathtt{H}}_j^\top$, where $\mathbf{n}_j$ is the unit normal to π in the camera frame number j. Interestingly enough, since the singular values of $\bar{\mathtt{C}}_j^*$ are $\{1, 1, 0\}$, those of $\bar{\mathtt{H}}_j [\mathbf{n}]_\times^\top$ are also $\{1, 1, 0\}$, up to a scale factor. This latter property is the theoretical foundation of the self-calibration constraints of [5].

2.3 Formulation of the Problem

Assume that the IAC is constant in the views i.e., $\boldsymbol{\omega} \sim \boldsymbol{\omega}_j$. Given N views, *i.e.* $(N-1)$ inter-view homographies H_j, $2 \le j \le N$, the *self-calibration problem* of a camera is that of solving the system consisting of two equations (3) and $2(N-1)$ equations (4) for the p d.o.f. in the IAC matrix plus q in the ICP vectors. This is a non-linear, possibly constrained, problem which has, until now, been solved using iterative methods. It requires initial values which is a critical issue, already mentioned in [4].

Because of the proposed form (9) of ICP, compared to [4], our problem modeling only exhibits seven unknowns instead of nine. However, there is no magic: With the proposed form, the equation (3), related to the key view, is implicitly satisfied, while, in [4], it is considered as an equation to be satisfied. We ask the question: do we have to consider (3) as a constraint or as an equation? Since no input data i.e., no estimated homography is involved in (3), there is no logical reason for this equation not to be exactly satisfied. Actually, the nine parameters of [4] are not independent and must satisfy the additional constraint (3). More generally, with regard to the estimation of the homography, from key view to some view number j, using feature correspondences, there is no logical reason for assigning any error to the positions of the (arbitrary) features in the key view.

As one can expected, there are no more than two constraints for the plane-based self-calibration problem, but several ways of expressing them.

Simplified Camera Model. We investigate now the minimal parameterization of ICP under the assumption of a simplified camera model. Let the calibration matrix be $\mathtt{K} = \mathrm{diag}(\alpha, \alpha, 1)$, where α represents the focal length in pixels. Let $\mathbf{v} \equiv (\cos\phi, \sin\phi, -\rho)^\top$, where ρ is the orthogonal distance from the principal point to the vanishing line in pixels. This means that (9) can also be written in the form of (7), with:

$$\begin{bmatrix} \mathbf{x}_1 \; \mathbf{x}_2 \end{bmatrix} = \begin{bmatrix} -\sqrt{\alpha^2+\rho^2}\sin\phi & \rho\cos\phi \\ \sqrt{\alpha^2+\rho^2}\cos\phi & \rho\sin\phi \\ 0 & 1 \end{bmatrix}. \tag{11}$$

3 Global Optimization Using Interval Analysis

3.1 Interval Analysis

Interval analysis (IA) is born about forty years ago [13]. Several good introductions to IA are available in [10, 9].

An interval is denoted by $\mathbf{x} = [\underline{x}, \overline{x}]$, where $\underline{x}$ and $\overline{x}$ are the lower bound and the upper bound of $\mathbf{x}$ respectively. Interval vectors are called boxes. If $\mathbf{x}$ and $\mathbf{y}$ are two intervals, then the four elementary operations are defined by $\mathbf{x}$ op $\mathbf{y} = \{x \text{ op } y \mid x \in \mathbf{x} \text{ and } y \in \mathbf{y}\}$ for op $\in \{+, -, \times, \div\}$. By composing these operations, we can compute an extension of the range of a function over an interval. For instance, if $f(x) = x(x-1)$, then an extension of f over $[-1, 1]$ is $\mathbf{f}([-1, 1]) = [-1, 1]([-1, 1] - 1) = [-1, 1][-2, 0] = [-2, 2]$, which necessarily contains the exact range $[-1/4, 2]$ of f.

3.2 IA-Based Global Optimization

The idea of using IA for global optimization has been investigated by many authors [10, 14], to cite a few. In recent years, IA-based global optimization has exhibited many successes in various domains. It has also been successfully applied to 3D self-calibration [11]. The problem is the following: Find the global minimum $f^\star$ of a smooth function f, $f^\star = \min\{f(x) \mid x \in \mathbf{D}\}$, as well as the set of points for which it is obtained, $\mathbf{X}^\star = \{x \in \mathbf{D} \mid f(x) = f^\star\}$, where $\mathbf{D}$ is a box. IA-based global optimization usually uses IA along with a branch and bound algorithm. Let $\mathbf{X}$ be the box representing the search region and $\mathcal{L}$ a list of boxes to be processed. The basic scheme of the method can be stated as follows:

1. Initialize $\mathcal{L}$ by placing the initial search region $\mathbf{X}_0$ in it.
2. While $\mathcal{L} \neq \emptyset$ do:
   a Remove a box $\mathbf{X}$ from $\mathcal{L}$.
   b Process $\mathbf{X}$ (rejecting, reducing, critical point existence, ...).
   c Subdivise $\mathbf{X}$ and insert the boxes derived from $\mathbf{X}$ onto $\mathcal{L}$.

Many details, such as stopping criteria or tolerances have been omitted here. We refer the reader to [10] for a complete description of the method.

3.3 Implementation

We give here pratical details about our implementation. We use the simplified camera model described in §2.3. The cost function we minimize is the sum of the two squared residuals of the equations (4) in which we use the simplified form of the ICP (11):

$$f(\alpha, \rho, \phi) = \sum_{j=2}^{N} (\mathbf{x}_1^T H_j^T \omega H_j \mathbf{x}_1 - \mathbf{x}_2^T H_j^T \omega H_j \mathbf{x}_2)^2 + (\mathbf{x}_1^T H_j^T \omega H_j \mathbf{x}_2)^2.$$

We derived the symbolic expression of the residuals. At each function evaluation, the developped residuals are numerically evaluated. This choice seems to be a good compromise between the evaluation time and the quality of the function extension. We have implemented a C++ code based on the PROFIL/BIAS library[2].

4 Experimental Results

4.1 Synthetic Data

The experimental setup is the following: The world plane is a planar grid composed of 100 points, projected onto 720×576 images, adding a Gaussian noise with a standard deviation equal to σ pixels. In our simplified camera model, the principal point is fixed to the center of the image, aspect ratio is equal to 1 and skew is 0. The focal length α is set to 1024 pixels. The camera fixates the center of the plane from a varying distance of 1460 ± 570 pixels, from randomly generated orientations varying in $[10°, 70°]$ in the world plane X axis, by $\pm 30°$ in the Y axis and by $\pm 90°$ in the Z axis. The inter-view homographies are estimated using the normalized DLT method [1, chapter 4]. The homographies are then transformed such that the principal point coincides with the image frame origin and such that $\alpha \rightarrow \alpha/360$ and $\rho \rightarrow \rho/360$.

In order to assess the benefit of a global optimization method we have minimized the cost function using an iterative method: We have performed tests with 5 images and $\sigma = 1$ pixel. For each test, the unknowns have been randomly initialized such that $\alpha = \alpha^\star \pm 30\%$, $\rho = \rho^\star \pm 30\%$ and $\phi = \phi^\star \pm 30\%$, where $(\alpha^\star, \rho^\star, \phi^\star)$ was the real global minimum. The method converged to the global minimum (within a 20% tolerance) in 38% of cases. The global optimization method we used found the solution in 100% of cases. In our experiments, we have taken an initial interval corresponding to $[300, 3000] \times [100, 12000] \times [0, 360]$. The initial interval has no effect on the accuracy

[2] `http://www.ti3.tu-harburg.de/Software/PROFILEnglisch.html`

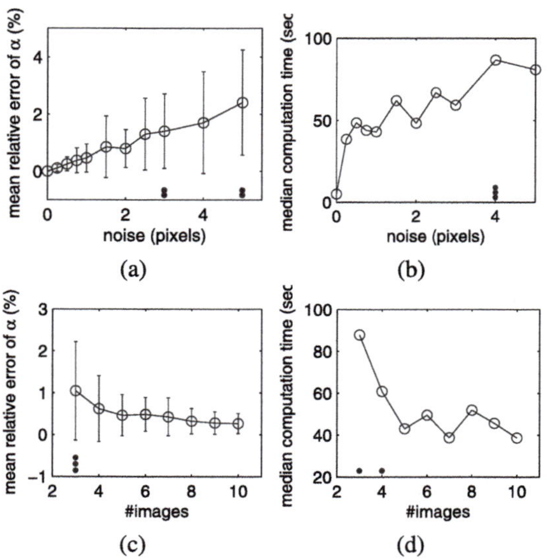

Fig. 1. Estimation error and computation time for varying noise level and varying image number. Each black point counts an excluded test (in (a) and (c)) or a failure (in (b) and (d)).

of the calculated minimum but only on the computation time. When a test cannot finish in a reasonable time, then we declare it as a *failure*. A few time-consuming tests will dramatically increase the mean computation time so we will present the median of computation time instead. Sometimes, the motion induced by the image sequence is closed to a degenerate configuration. In these cases, the global minimum is a bit far away from the real minimum. Therefore we exclude the tests such that the relative error is greater than 10% in the mean and standard deviation computations. The compuation times are given on a Pentium M 2GHz. Figure 1 gives some results about the estimation of α with respect to the noise level. Results for ρ and ϕ are very similar and are not presented here due to a lack of space. The accuracy remains quite good, even for σ=5 pixels. There are only a few excluded tests (there were 4 excluded tests over a total of 11000 tests). The estimation of α with respect to the image number is shown in the figure 1. The estimation error decreases when adding more images but the benefit is less relevant after 5-6 images. Figure 1 also shows the computation time with respect to noise and image number. In the first case, the presence of noise has a critical issue on the computation time whereas the noise level is less relevant. Indeed, the computation time does not dramatically increase with the noise level (the increasing looks linear). In the second case, the figure shows that after 5 images the computation time remains approximately the same: There are more terms to evaluate in the cost function whereas adding images makes the global minimum easier to enclose.

Since we have made hypotheses on τ, u_0 and v_0, we have assessed the tolerance of our method to a variation of these internal parameters. We first made the principal point varying randomly in a 50×50 pixels square. Second, we made τ varying in $[0.95, 1.05]$ (i.e. a variation of 5%). We used 5 images and $\sigma = 1$ pixel. The results are shown in table 4.1. Both varying principal point and varying τ have not critical consequences

Table 1. Estimation error and computation time for varying principal point and aspect ratio

Experiment	fixed (u_0, v_0), fixed τ	varying (u_0, v_0), fixed τ	fixed (u_0, v_0), varying τ
mean relative error of α (%)	0.5 ± 0.5	2.1 ± 1.8	2.7 ± 2.3
median computation time (sec)	43	92	83
number of failures	0	2	34

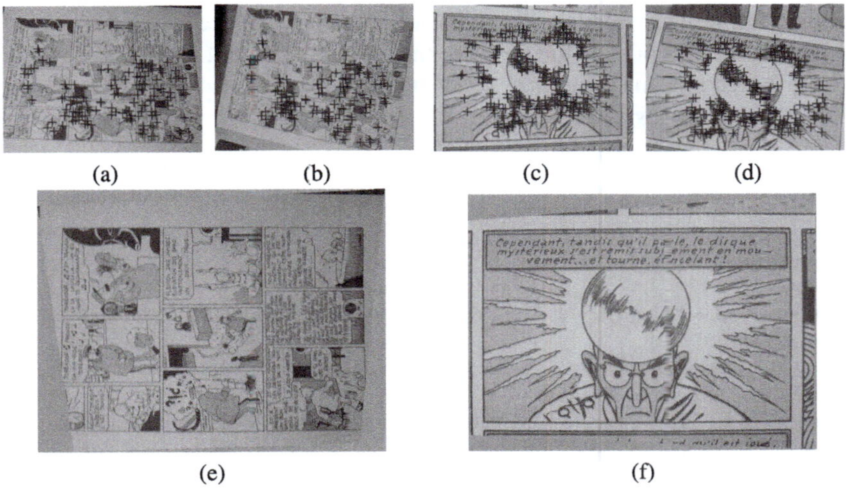

Fig. 2. Results for real images: (a) and (b) Key image and another image of the *tintin* sequence, along with the matched points. (e) The rectified image. (c), (d) and (f) Same results for *septimus*.

on the estimation of the parameters. However, we can see that varying τ has a critical impact on the number of failures. This is not a real limitation of the method since τ is usually very close to 1.

4.2 Real Data

We have tested the method on two sequences, *tintin* and *septimus*, composed of 7 and 4 640 × 480 images respectively. Homographies have been estimated by using the Kanatani optimal method [15], from automatically matched points. Then, we have applied a metric rectification of the key image. In the rectified image, the world plane should be parallel to the image plane and parallelism and angles should be recovered. Figure 2 shows two images of each sequence, including the matched points, and the rectified key image. We can see that the rectifications are quite good. The computation took 4 min 34 sec in the case of *tintin* and 8 min 14 sec in the case of *septimus*.

5 Conclusion

We proposed a minimal parameterization of the 2D self-calibration problem. Assuming the focal length is the only unknown, there are 3 parameters that can be estimated using a global minimization method, providing a guaranteed solution. A guaranteed solution to 3D self-calibration has been recently proposed by [11], for which closed-form solutions exist [3], contrary to 2D self-calibration. Although our constraint is more complex than Triggs' one, this not a real problem for the global optimization method we have used. Only the number of unknowns is relevant here. Our simplified camera model does not reveal some real limitation since we showed that the method is tolerant to consequent variations in the principal point position and since the hypothesis of a unit aspect ratio is quite realistic regarding recent digital cameras. The proposed method seems to work well provided the degeneracies of the problem are avoided. The study of such degeneracies is outside the scope of the current work, but reveals to be essential if we are aimed at using a minimal set of images [16]. We also aim at improving the performances of the algorithm we used.

Acknowledgement. The authors wish to acknowledge Frédéric Messine for fruitful discussions.

References

1. Hartley, R., Zisserman, A. In: Multiple View Geometry. Second ed. Cambridge University Press (2003)
2. Semple, J., Kneebone, G. In: Algebraic Projective Geometry. Oxford Classic Series, Clarendon Press (1952, reprinted, 1998)
3. Bougnoux, S.: From Projective to Euclidean Space under any Practical Situation, a Criticism of Self-Calibration. In: Proc. of the ICCV. Volume 1., Bombay, India (1998) 790–796
4. Triggs, B.: Autocalibration from Planar Scenes. In: Proc. of the ECCV. Volume 2., Freiburg, Germany (1998) 89–105
5. Malis, E., Cipolla, R.: Multi-view Constraints between Collineations: Application to Self-Calibration from Unknown Planar Structures. In: Proc. of the ECCV. Volume 2., Dublin, Ireland (2000) 610–624
6. Gurdjos, P., Sturm, P.: Methods and Geometry for Plane-Based Self-Calibration. In: Proc. of the CVPR. Volume 1., Madison, Wisconsin, USA (2003) 491–496
7. Jiang, G., Tsui, H., Quan, L.: Circular Motion Geometry Using Minimal Data. IEEE Trans. on PAMI **26** (2004) 721–731
8. Knight, J., Zisserman, A., Reid, I.: Linear Auto-Calibration for Ground Plane Motion. In: Proc. of the CVPR, Madison, Wisconsin, USA (2003) 503–510
9. Neumaier, A. In: Introduction to Numerical Analysis. Cambridge University Press (2001)
10. Hansen, E.R., Walster, G.W. In: Global Optimization Using Interval Analysis. Second ed. Marcel Dekker (2003)
11. Fusiello, A., Benedetti, A., Farenzena, M., Busti, A.: Globally Convergent Autocalibration Using Interval Analysis. IEEE Trans. on PAMI **26** (2004) 1633–1638
12. Golub, G., Loan, C.V. In: Matrix computations. Third ed. John Hopkins University Press (1996)
13. Moore, R.E. In: Interval Analysis. Prentice-Hall (1966)
14. Kearfott, R.B. In: Rigorous Global Search: Continous Problems. Kluwer Academic Publishers (1996)
15. Kanatani, K., Ohta, N.: Accuracy Bounds and Optimal Computation of Homography for Image Mosaicing Applications. In: Proc. of the ICCV. Volume 1., Kerkyra, Greece (1999) 73–78
16. Sturm, P., Maybank, S.J.: On plane-based camera calibration: A general algorithm, singularities, applications. In: Proc. of the CVPR. Volume 1., Fort Collins, Colorado, USA (1999) 432–437

Plane-Based Calibration and Auto-calibration of a Fish-Eye Camera

Hongdong Li and Richard Hartley

Research School of Information Sciences and Engineering,
The Australian National University,
Canberra Research Labs, National ICT Australia Ltd.

Abstract. We propose a systematic way for (auto)calibrating a fish-eye lens camera. By taking images of a planar scene with a fish-eye camera, our method automatically estimates the centre-of-distortion (COD), distortion parameters, and other conventional camera intrinsics. We fulfil this by a three-stage algorithm. Each stage accounts for one of the above three calibration tasks. Our main contributions reside in the second stages, in which we design a nine-point minimal solver for the purpose of distortion correction. Our method is applicable to both known planar scene and unknown planar scene. The later case corresponds to an auto-calibration version of the fish-eye camera calibration algorithm.

1 Introduction

Fish-eye camera (as well as other wide-angle and mirror-based omnidirectional camera), has a much larger field-of-view than most pinhole cameras. This has facilitated its wide and increasing applications in many computer vision tasks such as video surveillance, panoramic mosaic, vision reconstruction, augmented reality, etc.

Images captured by this type of cameras often contain large distortion. The distortion is often purposely designed to be so in order to enable the camera possessing a large field-of-view. We focus in this paper on **radial distortion**, as it is often the dominant type of lens distortion. Lens distortion effectively changes the geometric property of the camera, for example, the effective centre-of-projection are no longer unique. Conventional pinhole camera model no longer applies to such camera. Therefore, most classic vision algorithms, which were designed for *pinhole model*, can not be readily applied to fisheye camera. To better use these fisheye images, a procedure (algorithm) must be developed in order to handle such distortion. Besides, developing special procedure for calibrating fisheye camera, (i.e, to recover the Euclidean frame of the camera) are also crucial for many real world vision problems.

This paper aims at providing a systematic and automatic approach for fisheye camera (auto)calibration. Specifically, by *calibration* we mean a *procedure* that maps every image pixel into the direction of the corresponding incoming ray. To do so, we propose a three-stage procedure, first estimate the centre-of-distortion, then correct the radial distortion, and finally calibrate other conventional intrinsic parameters.

We use a planar scene for the calibration task. This is rather practical because planes abound in natural and man-made environments. This planar scene can be either known

P.J. Narayanan et al. (Eds.): ACCV 2006, LNCS 3851, pp. 21–30, 2006.

or unknown. For the later case, we in fact fulfil an **auto-calibration** algorithm for fish-eye image.

As will be explained later, our method has several unique advantages that make it distinct from existing algorithms: (1)In essence, it makes use of the *epipolar relationship*, however, it does not need to actually estimate any fundamental matrix. In other words, the method has successfully decoupled the estimation of lens distortion from the estimation of other camera parameters, thus gains more stability. (2) we propose a nine-point algorithm, which is basically high-degree nonlinear. However, we do not need to perform any iteration or minimization. Therefore, applying our method risks nothing in the convergence and local minima issues. (3) It successfully handles outliers or mismatches, by using a newly proposed `kernel-voting` technique, as oppose to the popularly adopted `RANSAC`. Experiments have demonstrated this technique very robust to outliers and noise. (4) Not like many previous distortion-correction methods, our method does not rely on a particular choice of radial distortion model.

2 Plane-Based COD Estimation

While it is common in the literature to assume the COD is known, usually at the principal point, we argue that this is not a safe assumption in general. The real COD can be displaced from the principal point. However, an accurate estimation of the COD is very crucial for a vision reconstruction algorithm. A small error in COD may lead to evident skewness in the final 3D reconstruction result [4].

Traditionally, the estimation of COD is obtained at the same time of performing a full-range camera calibration. For fish-eye camera, [8] suggests a method using the center of the circular (or elliptic) field-of-view as the COD. However, this method is valid only for situation where the whole field-of-view is seen in-full in the image plane. This is not always the case in reality, because the area of CCD imaging device is often not large enough to afford a full field-of-view.

With Known Planar Scene. Paper [10] first introduces a novel centre-of-distortion estimation algorithm. We employ this algorithm as the first stage of our calibration method. A brief description of the procedures of the COD algorithm is summarized below.

Consider a fish-eye camera observing a known planar calibration grid. Assume that the image have all square pixels. This assumption simplifies our derivation, and it can be relaxed easily. It is easy to verify that any two corresponding points in the image plane and in the calibration plane will remain **coplanar**. This is due to the fact that radial distortion only affects the radial component of image coordinates. *And this is nothing but a (generalized)* ***epipolar relationship***. Figure-1 illustrates the geometric configuration of the imaging process. We (bravely) write down this generalized *radial-epipolar relationship* as:

$$\mathbf{x}_d^T \mathrm{F}_\mathbf{r} \mathbf{x}_c = 0. \tag{1}$$

where the x_d, x_c are the coordinates of the distorted image point, and of the corresponding known planar calibration grid point, respectively. The matrix $\mathrm{F}_\mathbf{r}$ is called the *radial fundamental matrix*, which is a generalization of the conventional fundamental matrix [9].

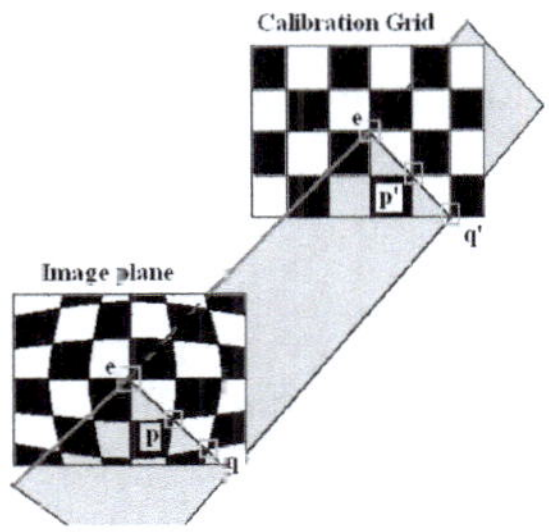

Fig. 1. The imaging process of a planar calibration grid by a camera with square pixels and radial distortion. The image point (e.g.,p) and its corresponding 3D scene point (e.g., p') are always coplanar, even under radial distortion. This coplanarity relationship is represented by a *radial-epipolar relationship*.

This matrix may be computed in the usual way (for example, by the eight point algorithm) from several point correspondences, and the COD extracted simply as the **left epipole**. More formal and mathematically rigorous derivations of the above algorithm can be found in [10].

With Unknown Planar Scene. The above idea of COD estimation can be easily extended to images of unknown planar scene, thus we obtain an auto-calibration algorithm for COD estimation. In this case, at least three views of an unknown planar scene will be needed. For example for three views, in a similar way a generalized three-view trilinear relationship—the so-called radial trifocal tensor—will be derived. This method resembles very much to *radial trifocal tensor* in [6] not only by their names, but also by their spirit. However, they made no attempt at estimating COD.

In order to *linearly* compute this radial trifocal tensor, at least 26 points across three views are needed. Simulations have given good results, which proves the feasibility of the theory and method. For simplicity, in the remaining parts of the paper, we simply assume that the COD $\mathbf{e}$ has already been estimated and subtracted from the point coordinates $\mathbf{x}_u$ and $\mathbf{x}_d$.

3 Plane-Based Distortion Estimation

Models for Radial Distortion. Polynomial Model (PM) [3]is the most popular distortion model. However it works best for lens with small distortions. For fish-eye lens, whose distortion is much larger, the PM model often requires too many terms than practical [3]. In this paper we adopt the Division Model (DM) [4] for describing the fisheye radial distortion:

$$\mathbf{x}_u - \mathbf{e} = (\mathbf{x}_d - \mathbf{e})/L(r_d, \mathbf{k}), \tag{2}$$

where $L(r_d, \mathbf{k}) = 1 + k_1 r_d^2 + k_2 r_d^4 + \cdots + k_p r_d^{2p}$, and $2p$ is the model order, $\mathbf{e}$ the centre-of-distortion (COD) and r_d the pixel radius to $\mathbf{e}$. The most remarkable advantage of this DM model is that it is able to express high distortion at much lower order. Often, one parameter suffices for many applications (see [4][7]). For demonstration purpose we adopt this DM model. However, in principle our method does not rely on any particular choice of distortion model, so long as it is algebraic. The reason will become clear later in this paper.

3.1 With Known Planar Scene

Consider a fisheye image of a known planar calibration grid, for example, as shown in figure-2. Let $\mathbf{x}_c$ denotes a point on the planar grid, and $\mathbf{x}_d$ the corresponding radially distorted image point. The ideal (i.e., un-distorted) version of the $\mathbf{x}_d$ is denoted by $\mathbf{x}_u$. Then $\mathbf{x}_c$ and $\mathbf{x}_u$ are related by a planar homography H. This homography will actually induce a *degenerate epipolar relationship*, namely,a fundamental matrix $\mathrm{F} = \mathrm{sH}$, where s is an arbitrary homogeneous 3-vector.

The epipolar relationship between corresponding pixels can be written as:

$$\mathbf{x}_u^{\mathbf{T}} \mathrm{F} \mathbf{x}_c = 0.$$

Assuming that image pixels are square (i.e.,zero-skew and unity aspect-ratio), we then plug an (algebraic) distortion model into it, thus get a generalized epipolar equation, which now explicitly depends on the distortion parameters $\mathbf{k}$. For example, using (2) we get $[\mathbf{x}_d^{\mathbf{T}}/L(r_d, \mathbf{k})]\mathrm{F}\mathbf{x}_c = 0$. Notice that the image coordinates being used are homogeneous, they therefore admit arbitrary changes in the scale without affecting the equality of the equation. We thus left-multiply a $L(r_d, \mathbf{k})$ to the left-hand side of the equation, and rearrange the result in a bilinear form using Kronecker product symbol $\otimes$, then get:

$$((x_d, y_d, L(r_d, \mathbf{k})) \otimes \mathbf{x}_c)\mathtt{vec}(\mathrm{F}^{\mathbf{T}}) = 0. \quad (3)$$

Now we do so for a group of nine points, whose coordinates denoted by matrices X' and X. We then stack the resulting nine bilinear equations together, and get a homogeneous equation system:

$$\mathrm{M}(\mathrm{X}', \mathrm{X}, \mathbf{k})\mathbf{f} = 0, \quad (4)$$

where the square matrix M is called *measurement matrix*, which depends explicitly on input distorted coordinates and the distortion parameter $\mathbf{k}$, and $\mathbf{f}$ the right null-vector. For simplicity, later we will drop the index of X and X' in M.

There are two important observations that justify this processing: firstly, we find that the $\mathbf{f}$ is no other but $\mathtt{vec}(\mathrm{F}^{\mathbf{T}})$. This is because the row-wise re-scaling of M does not affect its null-space at all; secondly, this row-wise re-scaling does not change its rank either. The above homogeneous equations will have non-trivial solution *if and only if* the matrix $\mathrm{M}(\mathbf{k})$ is singular.

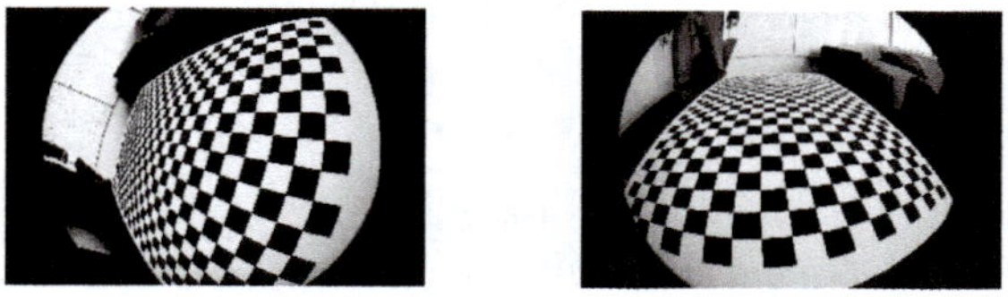

Fig. 2. One sample input image pair taken by a Canon-EOS camera with fish-eye lens

More precisely, since the plane-induced fundamental matrix is degenerate, it is thereby that a noise-free $\mathrm{M}(\mathbf{k})$ must be at most rank-six. This leads to: $rank(\mathrm{M}(\mathbf{k}))=6$.

In computation, we simply use the following procedures to enforce the above rank-condition. We keep only the 7×9 upper sub-matrix of the 9×9 measurement matrix, then arbitrarily choose seven columns from it and assemble a 7×7 sub-matrix $\mathrm{M}_7(\mathbf{k})$. Thus we use the following singularity condition to replace the above rank-six condition.

$$\det[\mathrm{M}_7(\mathbf{k})] = 0 \tag{5}$$

This condition, though not mathematically strict—since it is a necessary condition only—however, delivers good result in practice (partially also because of the kernel-voting scheme that we adopt).

Moreover, since the solution of Eq.-(4) **f** itself is a valid fundamental matrix, so it (after rearrangement) must be **singular** too. Hence obtain another equation:

$$\det(\mathtt{Mtx}[\mathtt{Ker}[\mathrm{M}(\mathbf{k})]]) = 0, \tag{6}$$

where the `Ker[]` is the null-space operator, and `Mtx[]` is the *matrix operator* which rearranges a vector into a matrix (i.e., the reverse operator of `vec[]`).

Equations (5) and (6) are the **basic equations** of our method. Note that the distortion parameters only depend on the above two equations, and there is no need to actually compute the value of the fundamental matrix F.

Now that having a group of nine correspondences, two nonlinear equations are established. If a distortion model involves two parameters only, then nine points are sufficient to compute them. When more parameters are required, in order to solve for them we can simply collect more groups of measurements. Now, we can even relax the square-pixel assumption, as the unknown aspect ratio can be regarded as a further parameter to be solved for. Moreover, the above method does not reply on any particular parametric form of the distortion model.

3.2 With Unknown Planar Scene

If the planar scene is unknown, then we are facing an *auto-calibration* problem. Now the rank-six condition is no longer hold. However, the singularity of the 9×9 measurement matrix is still valid. Then we can simply replace Eq.5 with the following one:

$$\det[\mathrm{M}(\mathbf{k})] = 0 \tag{7}$$

Except for this, there is few other thing needs to be changed. The only difference will be the degree of the resultant basic equations. For example, for unknown planar scene one now will get a sixth-degree and a eighteenth-degree basic equations for the one-parameter DM model. Nevertheless, the required solution technique and computational complexity remain very much the same. This constitutes another merit of our algorithm.

3.3 The Proposed Distortion Estimation Algorithm

In this section we demonstrate our algorithm on the DM model with a known plane. Remember the convention that the COD is assumed already estimated, and the image has been centered. The algorithm goes as follows.

The Nine Point Algorithm

1. Input two images; find feature point correspondences.
2. Normalize the image coordinates by an isotropic scaling so that the maximal radius is 1.0.
3. Collect a group of nine points, write down the pair of basic equations Eqns.(5) and (6).
4. Solve these two basic equations by, for example, the Sylvester resultant method or Groebner basis method.
5. Discard those non-real roots. Add the real root pairs into list $\mathcal{R}$.
6. Do the above three steps for other data groups, and add the resulting real root pairs into $\mathcal{R}$.
7. Choose the *best roots* from $\mathcal{R}$ by *kernel-voting* [11].
8. Substitute the best roots to the DM model to correct the images.

Kernel Voting. One could use RANSAC technique to find the best real root. But RANSAC is not particularly efficient in such context. First, unlike in the problem of estimating a line or a fundamental matrix where the inlier/outlier test can be performed fairly efficiently, for the distortion estimation problem there is no such simple way to do so; Second, because noise also affects the nine-point group, it significantly *distorts* the basic equations as well. In other words, the equation we just solved is not the *exact* equation that we intended to solve. In such case, there is little hope to obtain a genuine root from RANSAC.

We advocate the method of kernel-voting ([11]). The main operation of kernel-voting is to project every valid real root onto the real-line, then use a kernel density estimation technique to find the root distribution function. The peak position is thus considered to be the *best root*, as it is satisfied by the majority of the measurements. This scheme looks similar to the Randomized Hough Transforms [17]. However, the RHT works only in a discretized linear parameter space, while ours can easily deal with continuous nonlinear problem.

4 Estimate Other Intrinsincs

Once we successfully correct the radial distortion, what we obtained is an equivalent ideal pinhole camera. Then many conventional plane-based calibration and auto-calibration algorithms can be used here. For example the reader can simply use the methods reported in [3] [12] [19] [9], etc.

5 Results

This section gives some experimental results. We focus on the second stage: plane-based distortion estimation.

5.1 Distortion Estimation

Synthetic Images: With Known Planar Scene. We generated a 3D planar points scene, where the points are uniformly randomly distributed. Then perspectively projected them on two image planes at different viewpoints, and applied the radial distortion. We used one-parameter DM model with a single parameter k for better illustration. We added

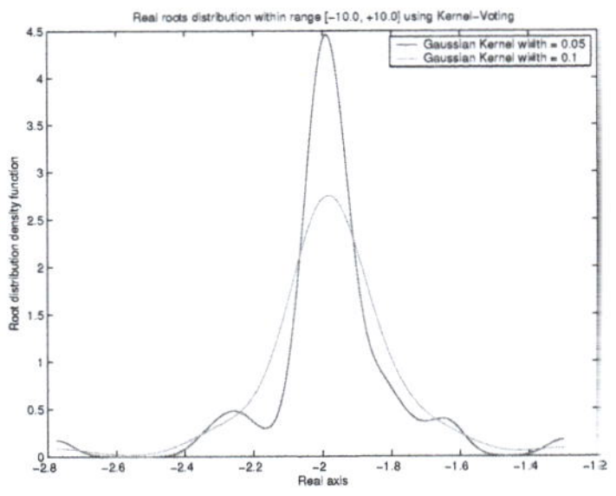

Fig. 3. Real-root voting result for synthetic known planar scene: 50 groups of data. STD Noise level at 0.1 pixels.

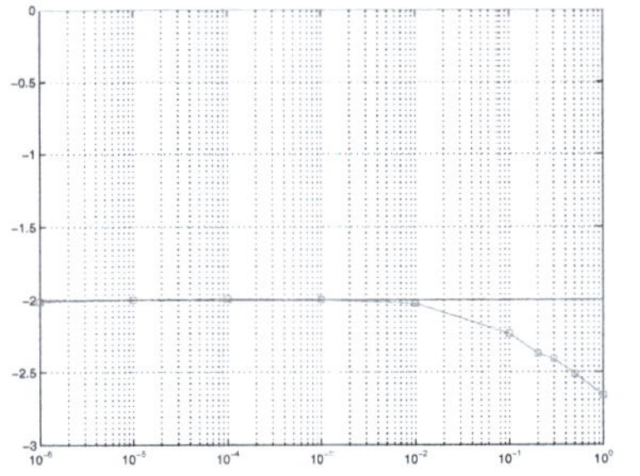

Fig. 4. k-Estimation vs noise-levels. Horizontal axis: std noise level in pixels; Vertical axis: estimated k values. The ground-truth $k = -2.00$.

noise to the image coordinates, then tested our method for different values of k. Randomly choosing nine-point data groups from 100 feature points, we then applied our nine-point algorithm to each group, and get a cubic polynomial equation corresponding to the first basic equation.

An example of real-root distribution is shown in figure-3. It is the average result of 200 random trials. The noise level was 0.1 pixels. From this figure we can easily find out the root value at the peak position to be $k = -2.014$, while the ground-truth value is $k = -2.000$. We tested the algorithm for different noise levels. Figure-4 shows the parameter estimation result versus noise. It is seen that the algorithm degrades smoothly and gracefully as the increasing of the noise. When the noise level is below 1.0 pixel,(obtaining which is not a difficult task for many corner detection methods,) the result is quite accurate. We have tested distortion-removal performance. Two synthetic images were first distorted by an inverse DM model, and add-into noise of 0.5 pixels (in std). Then fed the results into our algorithm to correct the distortion. After the correction, the maximal pixel deviation was reduced from 28.3 pixels to 3.7 pixels, while the average deviation is reduced from 4.3 pixels to below 0.5 pixels.

Synthetic Images: With Unknown Planar Scene. In this experiment we demonstrate that our algorithm works equally well for unknown planar scene. Essentially no change needs to be made to the algorithm. The only difference is that: now we have to solve a polynomial equation of **higher-degree**. For example for the one-parameter DM model, with known planar scene we get a cubic equation corresponding to the first basic equation. But now for an unknown plane, we get a degree-six equation. One example is given as:

$$Equ = -.2918e^{-17}k^6 - .9439e^{-15}k^5 - .7113e^{-14}k^4$$
$$-.1505e^{-13}k^3 + .1929e^{-14}k^2 + .3141e^{-13}k + .1771e^{-13}$$

Figure-5 gives the root distribution chart for the unknown-plane case. We test the reliability of our method against outliers (mismatches). In this experiment, we first rounded the image coordinates into integers, and arbitrarily added a small numbers of mismatches into the input data, then ran our algorithm again. We found that although the

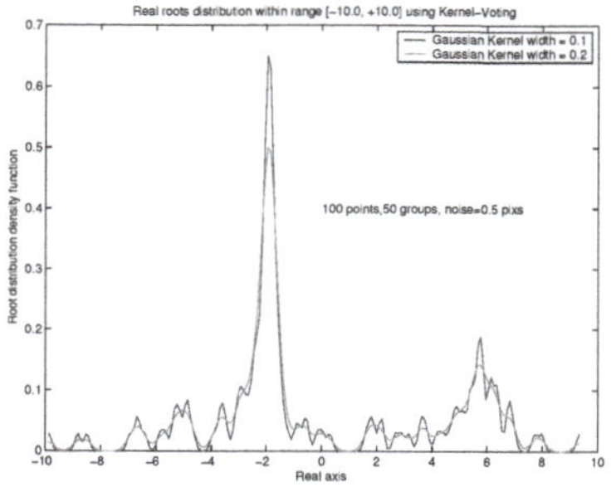

Fig. 5. Root distribution result for a synthetic unknown planar scene

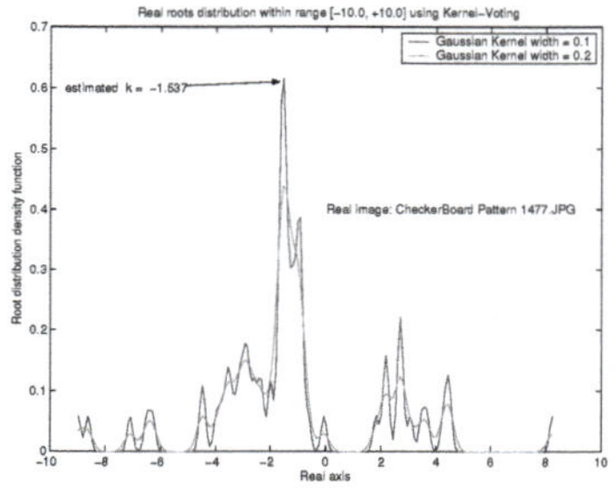

Fig. 6. Root distribution for the real images of figure-2

roots became more scattering, the peak position remained stable. Moreover, by increasing the sampling number of groups, the peak can always be made as sharp as that of the outlier-free case.

Test on Real Images: With Real Unknown Planar Scene. We tested our algorithm on a Canon-EOS digital camera equipped with a fisheye lens (image resolution 1536×1024). One obtained sample image pair is shown in figure-2. Note that in this experiment we assume that we are working with *unknown planar scene*. Image feature points were

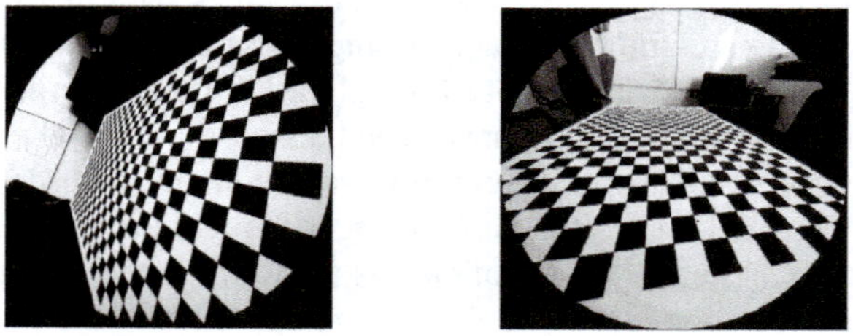

Fig. 7. Correction results for figure-2

Fig. 8. Left: white-board input image; Right: correction result

extracted by a corner detector. In fact we used in our experiments Lowe's SIFT code, since there are large distortions near the periphery of the image. After that, we manually identified the correspondences within the same planar region of the two images. After applying the nine-point algorithm, we obtained the following roots distribution result (See figure-6, from which we get the distortion parameter is $k = -1.537$. Using this value, the corrected images are shown in figure-7. Another example result of a planar white-board image is shown in figure-8.

6 Conclusions and Future Work

Our method allows the user to correct the fish-eye lens distortion simply from two images of a known or unknown planar scene. This facilitates many practical applications, such as panoramic image stitching, image-based location estimation (i.e, vision-based GPS), etc. The later is one of our current research focuses. To solve a system of inconsistent simultaneous equations, we suggest a kernel-voting technique. This technique gives much reliable and robust results with respect to noise and outliers. Moreover, it is easy to implement. With some necessary but minor modifications, our method is also useful for other types of distortion models, and other types of omnidirectional cameras, for examples, in [18] [23] [15], or the Ladybug^{R} camera [24].

In addition, as pointed out by one of the reviewers, the rank-six condition may suggest that less than nine points are already enough for solving the underlying problem. To verify this point will be one of our future work.

Acknowledgments. NICTA is funded through the Australian Governments Backing Australias Ability Initiative, in part through the Australian Research Council. Thank the anonymous reviewers for very valuable suggestions, especially on the analysis of the rank-6 condition.

References

1. T.Clarke,J.Fryer and W.Wang, The principal point for CCD cameras, Photogrammetric Record, 16(92):293-312,1998.
2. Z.Zhang, On the Epipolar Geometry Between Two Images with Lens Distortion, In proc. ICPR-96, 1996.
3. Z.Zhang, A Flexible New Technique for Camera Calibration, IEEE Trans. Pattern Analysis and Machine Intelligence. Vol.22, No.11. 1330C1334, November 2000.
4. A. Fitzgibbon, Simultaneous Linear Estimation of Multipleview Geometry and Lens Distortion, in IEEE-CVPR-2001, 2001.
5. Y.Xiong, Turkowski,K.,Creating image-based VR using a self-calibrating fisheye lens, In Proc CVPR-97, 1997.
6. S.Thirthala and M.Pollefeys, The radial trifocal tensor: A tool for calibrating the radial distortion of wide-angle cameras, In Proc CVPR-2005, June 2005.
7. D.Claus and A. Fitzgibbon, A rational function lens distortion model for general cameras. In Proc. CVPR-2005, June 2005.
8. B.Micusik and T.Pajdla, Estimation of omnidirectional camera model from epipolar geometry, in Proc. CVPR-2003, 2003.

9. R.Hartley,A.Zisserman, Multiview Geometry in Computer Vision,2nd Edition, Cambridge University Press, 2004.
10. R.Hartley, S.B.Kang, Parameter-free Radial distortion correction with centre of distortion estimation, In Proc. ICCV-2005, Oct, 2005.
11. Hongdong Li, R.Hartley, An easy non-iterative algorithm for radial lens distortion estimation, IEEE workshop on Omni-Vis-05, with ICCV-2005, 2005.
12. B.Triggs, Autocalibration from planar scenes, In Proc. ECCV-1998, 1998.
13. P. Gurdjos and P. Sturm,Methods and Geometry for Plane-Based Self-Calibration, In Proc IEEE-CVPR-03, 2003.
14. G.Stein, Lens distortion calibration using point correspondences, in Proc. CVPR-1997, 1997.
15. X. Ying, Z. Hu, Can We Consider Central Catadioptric Cameras and Fisheye Cameras within a Unified Imaging Model? In proc ECCV-2004,Prague, Czech, 2004.
16. J.Barreto and K. Daniilidis, Wide Area Multiple Camera Calibration and Estimation of Radial Distortion, Omnivis-2004, ECCV-2004 workshop, 2004.
17. Lei Xu, E.Oja, Randomized Hough Transform (RHT): Basic Mechanisms, Algorithms and Complexities", CVGIP:IU,Vol.57, No.2, March, 1993.
18. M.Grossberg and S.K.Nayar, A General Imaging Model and a Method for Finding its Parameters, in Proc ICCV-2001,Vancouver,Canada, July 2001.
19. M.Wilczkowiak and P.Sturm and E.Boyer,Using Geometric Constraints Through Parallelepipeds for Calibration and 3D Modelling, IEEE T-PAMI, 2005.
20. D. Liebowitz and A. Zisserman, Metric Rectification for Perspective Images of Planes, in Proc. IEEE-CVPR-1998, 1998.
21. F.Devernay and O.Faugeraus, Striaght lines have to be straight, MVA, 13(1), 14-24,2001.
22. S.B.Kang, Radial distortion snake,MVA, vol-12, 2000.
23. T.Svoboda, T.Pajdla,H.Hlavac. Epipolar geometry for panoramic cameras, ECCV-1998,1998.
24. Ladybug spherical camera, www.ptgrey.com/products/ladybug.

Stereo Matching Using Iterated Graph Cuts and Mean Shift Filtering

Ju Yong Chang, Kyoung Mu Lee, and Sang Uk Lee

School of Electrical Eng., ASRI,
Seoul National University, 151-600, Seoul, Korea
jangbon@diehard.snu.ac.kr, kyoungmu@snu.ac.kr, sanguk@sting.snu.ac.kr

Abstract. In this paper, we propose a new stereo matching algorithm using an iterated graph cuts and mean shift filtering technique. Our algorithm consists of following two steps. In the first step, given an estimated sparse RDM (Reliable Disparity Map), we obtain an updated dense disparity map through a new constrained energy minimization framework that can cope with occlusion. The graph cuts technique is employed for the solution of the proposed stereo model. In the second step, we re-estimate the RDM from the disparity map obtained in the first step. In order to obtain accurate reliable disparities, the crosschecking technique followed by the mean shift filtering in the color-disparity space is introduced. The proposed algorithm expands the RDM repeatedly through the above two steps until it converges. Experimental results on the standard data set demonstrate that the proposed algorithm achieves comparable performance to the state-of-the-arts, and gives good results especially in the areas such as the disparity discontinuous boundaries and occluded regions, where the conventional methods usually suffer.

1 Introduction

Stereo matching is one of the classical problems in computer vision and has many potential application areas including the robot navigation, 3D modelling, and image based rendering. In the stereo matching problem, we are given more than two images of the same scene. Then the goal of stereo matching is to compute the disparity map for the reference image. A disparity describes the difference in the positions of two corresponding pixels. Therefore, to get the disparity map, we have to solve the correspondence problem for each pixel. Generally, in binocular stereo, we assume that two input images are calibrated and rectified in advance, so that the epipolar line becomes horizontal. However despite those constraints, due to the ill-posed nature of the stereo matching problem, determination of accurate disparities is still a hard problem, especially in the occluded and textureless areas. To resolve this problem, many stereo matching algorithms have been proposed, and a detailed review of those algorithms can be found in [1].

In general, stereo algorithms can be classified into the local or global approaches. Local algorithms often use a finite-size window to increase the discrimination power of correspondence. Corresponding points can be found by

P.J. Narayanan et al. (Eds.): ACCV 2006, LNCS 3851, pp. 31–40, 2006.

comparing the intensity values of the local windows with various matching metrics like SSD, SAD, NCC, and Birchfield measure [2]. Local algorithms are very efficient, but they are sensitive to locally ambiguous regions (e.g., occlusion regions or regions with uniform texture) and disparity discontinuous boundaries.

Global algorithms use the smoothness constraint in order to resolve the ill-posed problem of stereo matching. By using this, the problem of textureless regions can be handled successfully. However, the discontinuous features of the disparity map usually cannot be recovered by the simple linear or quadratic smoothness constraint. Thus, the discontinuity preserving smoothness constraint such as Potts model has been employed for the stereo model, and the energy function including such a smoothness constraint is minimized through various minimization techniques. Among them, graph cuts [3, 4] and belief propagation [5] have attracted much attention due to their excellent performances. Nevertheless, since many global stereo algorithms still do not consider the occlusion problem explicitly, eventually reconstruction errors dominate in the occluded regions.

Recently, stereo matching algorithms using color segmentation has received a lot of attention [6, 7, 8, 9]. These algorithms are based on the assumption that there are no large disparity discontinuities inside homogeneous color segments. In general, we can get much sharper intensity boundaries by using color segmentation. Therefore color segmentation based stereo matching algorithms produce better performance on disparity boundaries. Tao et al. [6], Ernst et al. [7], and Hong and Chen [8] made an assumption that pixels inside each color segment produced by a color segmentation algorithm have the same disparity value. Under this assumption, the stereo matching problem can be formulated as an energy minimization problem in the segment domain instead of the pixel domain. Specifically, the energy function contains two parts; the data energy term and the smoothness term. The data energy measures the disagreement of corresponding segments given disparity value. The smoothness energy measures how smooth the disparities of neighboring segments are. In order to minimize both the data energy and the smoothness energy, Tao et al. [6] used a local greedy search algorithm, Ernst et al. [7] used the relaxation algorithm, and Hong and Chen [8] used the graph cuts technique. However these methods depend largely on the initial color segmentation result. Consequently, these methods usually get in trouble when there exist disparity boundaries inside the initial color segments.

In this paper, we present a new segmentation-based stereo matching algorithm using an iterated graph cuts and mean shift filtering technique. In contrast to most conventional segmentation based stereo matching methods that exploit only the color segmentation information or the disparity segmentation information independently, our proposed method considers the segmentation using both the color and disparity information simultaneously in the color-disparity space. Through the mean shift filtering [10] in the color-disparity space, the proposed method corrects the current disparity map coherently with the disparity distribution information as well as the color information. In order to reduce the effect of outliers and to obtain more reliable disparities, the disparity crosschecking (left-right checking) is performed before the mean-shift filtering. Thus, through the crosschecking and mean shift filtering, we obtain a RDM (Reliable Disparity Map) from the current disparity map, that is sparse but contains reliable disparities (of ground control points). Such a RDM is then used to guide more correct and dense disparity map through a constrained energy minimization framework that can handle the occlusion. The reliable disparity constrained energy minimization is solved via graph cuts, and it makes the proposed algorithm more robust to the occlusion problem.

The rest of the paper is organized as follows. First we present the constrained stereo matching method by the reliable disparities in Section 2. Then we explain how to compute the RDM through the crosschecking and mean shift filtering procedures in Section 3. And we describe the structure of the overall algorithm in Section 4. Experimental results on various data sets are shown in section 5, and finally, conclusions are drawn in Section 6.

2 Stereo Matching with the RDM

In this section, we present the first part of the proposed algorithm, that is, the stereo matching with the RDM. Firstly, we introduce the conventional energy-based stereo model. Then, we explain how to formulate and solve the constrained stereo model with a given RDM.

2.1 Energy-Based Stereo Matching Model

Let L and R be the sets of pixels in the left and right images, respectively. The goal of stereo matching is to determine a label f_p for each pixel p in the left image, which denotes a disparity value for that pixel. Then, the stereo matching can be modelled as the following energy minimization problem,

$$E(f) = E_{data}(f) + E_{smooth}(f). \tag{1}$$

The data term, $E_{data}(f)$, measures how consistent the disparity function f agrees with the input images, and can be written as

$$E_{data}(f) = \sum_{p \in L} D_p(f_p), \tag{2}$$

where $D_p(f_p)$ is a penalty function of the pixel p having the disparity f_p. This penalty function can be the usual SSD, SAD or normalized correlation. However, in this paper, we use the pixel dissimilarity measure proposed in [2], since it is known to be insensitive to the image sampling noise. The smoothness term, $E_{smooth}(f)$, encodes the smoothness assumption imposed by the algorithm, and can be written as

$$E_{smooth}(f) = \sum_{p,q \in N} V_{p,q} \cdot T(f_p \neq f_q), \tag{3}$$

where N is a neighborhood system for the pixels of the left image, $V_{p,q}$ is a function to control the level of smoothness, and $T(\cdot)$ is 1 if its argument is true and 0 otherwise. This is called the Potts energy model, and we adopt this smoothness model for its discontinuity preserving feature.

2.2 A New Modified Stereo Model

By employing the Potts energy model for the smoothness constraint, we can remedy the problems of disparity discontinuous boundaries as well as the textureless regions. However, the conventional energy-based stereo models still lack proper consideration of the occlusion problem. A simple example is shown in figure 1. The arrows indicate the true correspondences between pixels in two images. The true disparity value of white pixels is 0, and that of gray pixels is 1. According to the conventional stereo model, the data term for these true correspondences becomes $E_{data}(f) = D_p(0) + D_q(0) + D_r(1) + D_s(1)$. However, note that the pixel q is occluded by the pixel r, and true corresponding pixel does not exist in the right image. Thus, minimizing the penalty term of the occluded pixel q, D_q is meaningless, and produces false matching.

Therefore, in order to make the penalty term of each pixel in the left image contribute to the data term properly, we have to check the visibility of each pixel in the right image. For that purpose, we introduce a function Vis_p that indicates whether the occlusion is occurred or not for pixel p. When the pixel p is occluded, Vis_p is 0, otherwise, Vis_p is 1. Note that, in general, the occlusion of a pixel p depends not only f_p, the disparity at p, but also the disparities of the neighboring pixels that can occlude it. So, Vis_p should be a function of f_p and f. Now, the data term modified by the visibility function Vis_p can be written by

$$E'_{data}(f) = \sum_{p \in L} Vis_p(f_p, f) \cdot D_p(f_p). \tag{4}$$

Because of the dependency of the visibility function Vis_p on f, minimizing the total energy function $E(f)$ becomes a nontrivial problem. Actually, we can

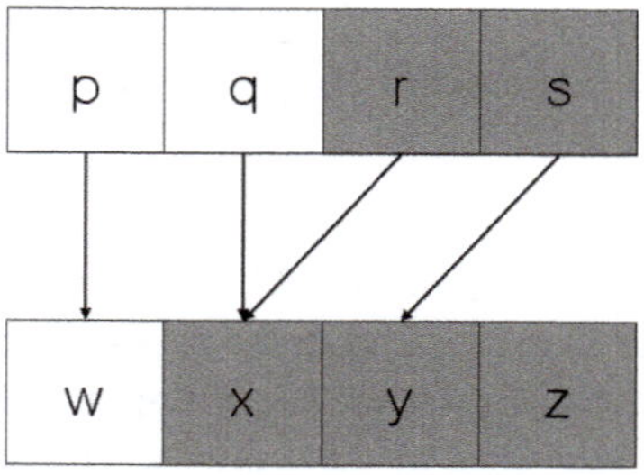

Fig. 1. An example of stereo matching with occlusion: $L = \{p, q, r, s\}$ and $R = \{w, x, y, z\}$. Arrows indicate the true correspondences between pixels in two images.

prove that the new energy function does not satisfy the regularity condition [11]. And, according to [11], the regularity condition is a necessary and sufficient condition for minimizing the energy function via graph cuts. Thus, the energy function involving the modified data term in (4) can not be solved by the graph cuts directly.

In order to minimize the modified energy function via graph cuts efficiently, we introduce a RDM, r in which each element r_p can have a label of reliable disparity value, or the UD label for the undetermined or invalid disparity. Thus, the RDM provides the information on each pixel whether its disparity has been already determined reliably or to be further estimated. By using a given RDM, we can modify (4) by

$$E''_{data}(f) = \sum_{p \in L} D'_p(f_p), \tag{5}$$

$$D'_p(f_p) = \begin{cases} Vis_p(f_p, r) \cdot D_p(f_p), & \text{if } r_p = UD; \\ 0, & \text{if } r_p \neq UD \text{ and } f_p = r_p; \\ \infty, & \text{if } r_p \neq UD \text{ and } f_p \neq r_p, \end{cases} \tag{6}$$

where $D'_p(f_p)$ is a modified data penalty term by the RDM constraint. For the pixels that have reliable disparities ($r_p \neq UD$), we do not change the current disparity values. While, for the pixels that need new disparity estimation ($r_p = UD$), by using the visibility function $Vis_p(f_p, r)$ constrained by the reliable disparities, we can eliminate the effect of the occluded pixels efficiently. Thus, by employing this new data term, we can resolve the occlusion problem effectively.

Now, the proposed energy function consists of the modified data term with given r in (5) and (6), and the traditional Potts energy model in (3) given by

$$E(f) = E''_{data}(f) + E_{smooth}(f). \tag{7}$$

Note that the modified data term is a summation of the new penalty terms that depend only on the disparity f_p of each pixel p, and has the same formation as the conventional data term in equation (2). Therefore the proposed energy function can be minimized via graph cuts. In this paper, we use the α-expansion algorithm [3].

3 Computing the RDM

In this section, we explain the second part of the proposed algorithm, that is, how to construct the RDM from the disparity map estimated in the first step. The RDM consists of pixels with reliable disparity values and pixels of which disparity values are invalid. For estimating whether given disparity values are reliable or not, we use the conventional crosschecking technique followed by clustering in the color-disparity space. Through the crosschecking of left and right disparity maps, only the disparity values that are consistent in both maps are survived as the reliable disparities, and the others are assigned by UD label that means undetermined disparity. Next, as in many other works [6, 7, 8, 9] that successfully applied the color segmentation information to stereo matching, we also use the color information to refine and correct the crosschecked disparity map. We adopt the mean shift algorithm [10] for this purpose.

3.1 Crosschecking Technique

Let f_p and $f'_{p'}$ be the disparity values of the corresponding pixels p and p' in the left and right images, respectively. Then, if $f_p = f'_{p'}$, we consider the disparity f_p at p as a reliable disparity value, otherwise an invalid one.

3.2 Mean Shift Algorithm

The mean shift algorithm is a nonparametric density estimation-based method for feature space analysis, proposed by Comaniciu and Meer [10]. It assumes that the feature space can be regarded as an empirical probability density function (p.d.f) of the represented parameter. Dense regions in the feature space correspond to local maxima of the p.d.f., that is, the modes of the unknown density. Once the location of a mode is determined, the cluster associated with it can be delineated based on the local structure of the feature space. Thus, the mode detection is an important part for the feature space analysis. In the mean shift algorithm, such a mode detection process is based on the mean shift procedure.

According to the work of Comaniciu and Meer [10], the mean shift procedure that is the successive iteration of the following two steps;

- computation of the mean shift vector $m_{h,G}(x)$,
- translation of the kernel $G(x)$ by $m_{h,G}(x)$,

is guaranteed to converge at a nearby point where the density estimator has zero gradient, that is, a mode. Here, $m_{h,G}(x)$ is the mean shift vector defined by

$$m_{h,G}(x) = \frac{\sum_{i=1}^{n} x_i g(\|\frac{x-x_i}{h}\|^2)}{\sum_{i=1}^{n} g(\|\frac{x-x_i}{h}\|^2)} - x, \tag{8}$$

where x_i, $i = 1, ..., n$, are data points, and the function $g(x)$ is the profile of the kernel. The set of all locations that converge to the same mode defines the basin of attraction of that mode. Thus, the delineation of the clusters is a natural outcome of the above mode detection process. After convergence, the basin of attraction of a mode, i.e., the data points visited by all the mean shift procedures converging to that mode, automatically delineates a cluster of arbitrary shape.

3.3 Mean Shift Filtering in Color-Disparity Space

Most conventional color segmentation based stereo matching algorithms use the segmentation information in the color space. However, the color segmentation algorithm cannot produce correct scene segmentation results, because it does not consider the disparity (or depth) information. Therefore, in this paper, we incorporate the disparity information with the color and spatial coordinates information through the mean shift algorithm. We compose the CSD (Color-Spatial coordinates-Disparity) space by adding the disparity component x^d to the conventional color-spatial coordinates space. We use the crosschecked disparity as the disparity component x_p^d at the pixel p. Then, the feature vector of each pixel p in the input image can be represented by $x_p = (x_p^c, x_p^s, x_p^d)$, a point in the 6-D CSD space. In this expression, x^c and x^s are the color and spatial coordinates part of the feature vector, respectively. We apply the mean shift procedure to such feature points in the CSD space repeatedly until it converges, and replace the disparity value of each pixel by that of the corresponding point of convergence. The mean shift filtering algorithm in the CSD space can be summarized as follows. Let x_p and z_p, $p = 1, ..., n$, be the input and filtered feature vector of a pixel p in the CSD domain, respectively. For each pixel,

1. Initialize $i = 1$ and $y_{p,1} = x_p$.
2. Compute $y_{p,i+1}$ according to $y_{p,i+1} = y_{p,i} + m_{h,G}(y_{p,i})$ until convergence. $m_{h,G}(y_{p,i})$ is the mean shift vector at the point $y_{p,i}$. Let $y_{p,c}$ be the converging point.
3. Assign $z_p = (x_p^c, x_p^s, y_{p,c}^d)$.

After convergence, we define a reliable disparity map r as $r_p = z_p^d$.

In order to perform the above mean shift clustering algorithm, we have to compute the mean shift vector $m_{h,G}(x)$. However, because of the characteristic of the disparity space different from the color and spatial coordinates space, we have to set a new definition of the mean shift vector.

Distance in Disparity Space. Let x be a point in the CSD space. Then, the mean shift vector at the point x can be computed by (8). In order to compute the mean shift vector, we have to compute the distance between the point x and the data points in the input image. We can compute the distance by the sum of the distances of each component normalized by the bandwidth in its domain. For the color and spatial component, we use the Euclidean distance. However, it is not appropriate for the disparity space, since we assume the piecewise constant constraint among local disparities by Potts model as in (3). Moreover, the UD label makes the Euclidean distance unusable. By the piecewise constant assumption, we enforce the same cost for the neighboring pixels with unequal disparities, regardless of the magnitude of the disparity difference. Thus, following this notion, let us define the distance in the disparity domain as follows:

$$\left\|\frac{x^d - x_i^d}{h_d}\right\| = \begin{cases} 0, \text{ if } x^d = x_i^d; \\ k, \text{ otherwise,} \end{cases} \tag{9}$$

where k is some constant.

Mean Shift Vector in Disparity Space. In the mean shift procedure, the position of the kernel is translated by the mean shift vector. The mean shift vector (8) implies the difference between the weighted means with the weighting kernel G. Therefore, by the mean shift procedure, the kernel is moved to the mean of data points that belong to the kernel G. However, for the disparity space, the arithmetic mean of disparity values is meaningless. Therefore, instead of the arithmetic mean, we define the mean value in the disparity domain as the most frequent disparity value (mode) among disparity values of points in the kernel:

$$m_{h,G}(x)^d = \arg\max_{j \in D} \sum_{x_i^d = j} g(\| \frac{x - x_i}{h} \|^2). \tag{10}$$

In this equation, D is the set of all possible disparity values.

4 Experimental Results

For the quantitative evaluation and comparison of different stereo algorithms, Scharstein and Szeliski [1] have proposed a test bed along with ground truths which is available at their website (http://www.middlebury.edu/stereo). We have evaluated the proposed algorithm on these test data sets. The evaluation metric is the percentage of bad pixels, of which disparity are different from the true values more than 1 pixel. This measure is calculated in three different parts of an input image including the entire image (all), untextured (untex), and discontinuity (disc) regions. And, only non-occluded pixels are considered in all three cases.

Our algorithm has four parameters; one parameter that controls the level of smoothness $V_{p,q}$ in the stereo matching part, and three parameters, h_c, h_s, and k for the mean shift filtering part. In this paper, following other researchers' works [1, 3], we employed the gradient-dependent smoothness cost for the smoothness control, given by

$$V_{p,q} = \begin{cases} 2\lambda, & \text{if } |I_p - I_q| \leq 5; \\ \lambda, & \text{otherwise,} \end{cases} \tag{11}$$

where I_p and I_q are intensity values of pixel p and q, respectively.

All the parameters were fixed for all the test sets, and the best results were obtained when $\lambda = 10$, $h_c = 6.5$, $h_s = 7$, and $k = 0.7$. The proposed algorithm has been implemented on a Pentium IV 3.0GHz PC. Typically, after few iterations, the RDM converged, and the final dense disparity map was computed within few minutes (e.g. Tsukuba data, 3 iterations, 95 seconds).

Figure 2 reports the detailed intermediate results on the Tsukuba data. We can see that through the crosschecking and mean shift filtering process, reliable disparities coherent with color information have been extracted from the given disparity map. And through the updating stereo matching process guided by those ground control points with reliable disparities, more undetermined pixels become fixed and the reliable disparity range expands.

Table 1 presents the overall performance of our algorithm, where it summarizes the quantitative evaluation results. The proposed algorithm performs quite well, and our overall rank is 4th out of about 30 algorithms. From the extracted disparity maps, we can observe that especially good performances have been

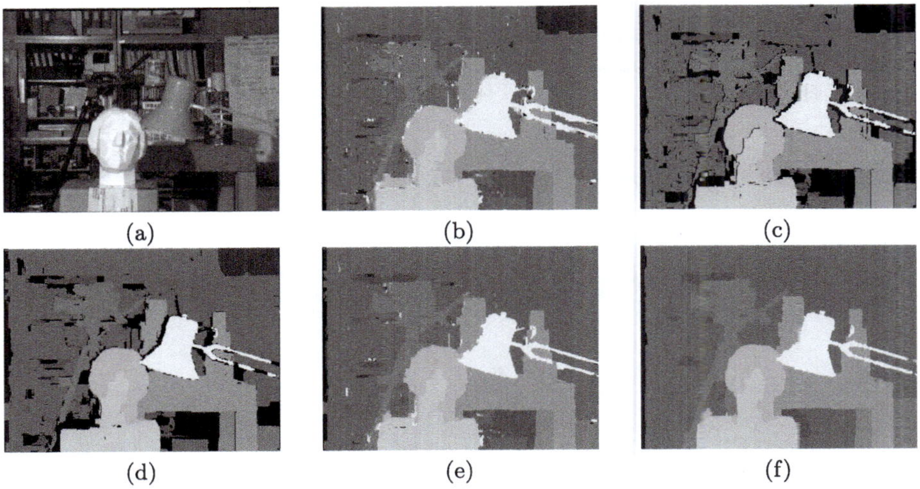

Fig. 2. Detailed results on the Tsukuba data. (a) Reference image. (b) disparity map in the first iteration, (c) RDM after crosschecking, (d) RDM after mean shift filtering, (e) disparity map in the second iteration, (f) final disparity map after convergence.

Table 1. Evaluation table of different stereo algorithms

Algorithms	Tsukuba			Sawtooth			Venus			Map	
	all	untex	disc	all	untex	disc	all	untex	disc	all	disc
Sym.BP+occl.	0.97	0.28	5.45	0.19	0.00	2.09	0.16	0.02	2.77	0.16	2.20
Segm.-based GC [8]	1.23	0.29	6.94	0.30	0.00	3.24	0.08	0.01	1.39	1.49	15.46
Graph+segm.	1.39	0.28	7.17	0.25	0.00	2.56	0.11	0.02	2.04	2.35	20.87
Our method	1.13	0.48	6.38	1.14	0.06	3.34	0.77	0.70	3.61	0.95	12.83
Segm.+glob.vis.	1.30	0.48	7.50	0.20	0.00	2.30	0.79	0.81	6.37	1.63	16.07
Layered	1.58	1.06	8.82	0.34	0.00	3.35	1.52	2.96	2.62	0.37	5.24
Belief prop. [5]	1.15	0.42	6.31	0.98	0.30	4.83	1.00	0.76	9.13	0.84	5.27
MultiCam GC	1.85	1.94	6.99	0.62	0.00	6.86	1.21	1.96	5.71	0.31	4.34
2-pass DP	1.53	0.66	8.25	0.61	0.02	5.25	0.94	0.95	5.72	0.70	9.32
GC+occl.	1.19	0.23	6.71	0.73	0.11	5.71	1.64	2.75	5.41	0.61	6.05

achieved in the areas such as disparity discontinuous boundaries and occluded regions, where the conventional stereo algorithms usually suffer.

5 Conclusion

In this paper, we presented a new stereo matching algorithm based on iterated constrained graph cuts with reliable disparities obtained by the mean shift filtering in the CSD space. Through the mean shift filtering in the CSD space, a RDM coherent with disparity information as well as color information is obtained. And computing the solution of a new constrained stereo energy model with given RDM enables the proposed algorithm to be more robust to the occlusion. Evaluation and comparison result shows that our algorithm is one of the state-of-the-arts.

Acknowledgements

This work has been supported in part by the ITRC (Information Technology Research Center) support program of Korean government and IIRC (Image Information Research Center) by Agency of Defense Development, Korea.

References

1. Scharstein, D., Szeliski, R.: A taxonomy and evaluation of dense two-frame stereo correspondence algorithms. IJCV **47** (2002) 7–42
2. Birchfield, S., Tomasi, C.: A pixel dissimilarity measure that is insensitive to image sampling. PAMI **20** (1998) 401–406
3. Boykov, Y., Veksler, O., Zabih, R.: Fast approximate energy minimization via graph cuts. PAMI **23** (2001) 1222–1239
4. Kolmogorov, V., Zabih, R.: Computing visual correspondence with occlusions using graph cuts. In: ICCV01. (2001) 508–515
5. Sun, J., Zheng, N.N., Shum, H.Y.: Stereo matching using belief propagation. PAMI **25** (2003) 787–800
6. Tao, H., Sawhney, H.: A global matching framework for stereo computation. In: ICCV01. (2001) I: 532–539
7. Ernst, F., Wilinski, P., Overveld, K.V.: Dense structure-from-motion: An approach based on segment matching. In: ECCV02. (2002) II: 217–231
8. Hong, L., Chen, G.: Segment-based stereo matching using graph cuts. In: CVPR04. (2004) I: 74–81
9. Wei, Y., Quan, L.: Region-based progressive stereo matching. In: CVPR04. (2004) I: 106–113
10. Comaniciu, D., Meer, P.: Mean shift: A robust approach toward feature space analysis. PAMI **24** (2002) 1–18
11. Kolmogorov, V., Zabih, R.: What energy functions can be minimized via graph cuts. PAMI **26** (2004) 147–159

Augmented Stereo Panoramas

Chien-Wei Chen[1], Li-Wei Chan[2], Yu-Pao Tsai[3,4], and Yi-Ping Hung[1,2,3]

[1] Dept. of Computer Science and Information Engineering, National Taiwan University, Taipei, Taiwan
[2] Graduate Institute of Networking and Multimedia, National Taiwan University, Taipei, Taiwan
[3] Institute of Information Science, Academia Sinica, Taipei, Taiwan
[4] Dept. of Computer and Information Science, National Chiao Tung University, Hsinchu, Taiwan

Abstract. Panoramas and object movies are popular image-based techniques for modeling and rendering 3D scenes and objects. In this paper, we present a method which allows the authors of virtual exhibition systems to produce an augmented stereo panorama by interactively integrating stereo object movies into a stereo panorama. When navigating in the augmented stereo panorama with a stereoscopic display, the user can directly browse the stereo object movies that he is interested in. With augmented stereo panoramas, the user can enjoy more persuasive interaction with better depth perception To our best knowledge, this paper is the first work to integrate stereoscopic image-based scenes with stereo object movies.

1 Introduction

Image-based modeling and rendering techniques have become popular approaches to yielding photorealistic rendering results. These techniques model the scenes/objects by a collection of images and generate novel images representing the scenes/objects appearance at arbitrary points. McMillan and Bishop [13] proposed an image-based rendering method to sample and render novel views using the 5D plenoptic function. The original 7D plenoptic function was presented by Adelson and Bergen1. The Light Filed [9] and the Lumigraph [5] are two methods which reduce the 5D plenoptic function into the 4D plenoptic function, but their large memory requirements make them impractical for real applications, especially for those requiring Internet transmission. The simplest way to model scenes is panorama, which is a 2D plenoptic function. The technique was first proposed by Chen [3], and allows the user to navigate the scene toward any viewing direction at a fixed view point.

An object movie (OM) is a set of images taken from different perspectives around a 3D object; when the images are played sequentially, the object seems to be rotated around itself. When captured, each image is associated with distinctive pan and tilt angles of the viewing direction, and thus some particular images can be chosen and shown on screen according to user interaction. This technique was first proposed in Apple QuickTime VR [8] which allows the users to interactively rotate the virtual artifacts. Recently, object movie is a popular image-based approach to model and

P.J. Narayanan et al. (Eds.): ACCV 2006, LNCS 3851, pp. 41 – 49, 2006.

render 3D objects, and has been widely applied to many areas, e.g., E-Commerce, digital Archive, Digital Museum [12], etc.

If we do not have 3D information of the 3D image-based objects and the panorama scenes, to integrate panoramas and object movies together is not a trivial problem. In [10], we proposed a pure image–based approach, which does not have to reconstruct the geometric models of the 3D objects, to augment a panorama with object movies in a visually 3D-consistent way.

Since the binocular vision provides the human depth perception of 3D objects in three-dimension, with stereo vision, the viewer can see where objects are in relation to them with much greater precision, especially when those objects are moving toward or away from them. To benefit from human binocular visions, we extend the work on augmented panorama to augmented stereo panorama.

The organization of this paper is as follows. First, the related works will describe in Section 2 followed by the methods to obtain stereo object movies and panoramas in Section 3 and 4, respectively. In Section 5, we describe the detail of our interactive method to augment stereo panoramas with stereo object movies. Some experimental results will be presented in Section 6. Finally, the conclusion will be given in Section 7.

2 Related Works

Our work involves creating stereo panoramas and object movies and integrating stereo object movies into stereo panoramas. To generate stereo panoramas, Huang and Hung [9] proposed a method to automatically generate a stereo panorama with two cameras. One of the cameras is rotating on the axis and the other is off-center rotating. This method generates two sets of panorama, one for the left view and the other for the right view.

In [14], Peleg and Herman proposed a new method to capture stereo panoramas by using only an off-center rotating camera. They assume the viewer's eyes are on a viewing circle. The projections of the left view and the right view are tangent to the viewing circle. One is clockwise and the other is counter-clockwise.

The method, named Parallel Ray Interpolation for Stereo Mosaicing (PRISM) proposed in [17], is to stitch mosaics seamlessly for aerial images. The authors generated stereo panorama from an aerial camera. The aerial camera, which undergoes a dominant translational motion, is mounted on an aerial plane. To calibrate the aerial camera, they estimate the extrinsic parameters of the camera by an aerial instrumentation system, such as GPS, INS and laser profiler. After estimating camera parameters, they rectified the captured images to eliminate rotational components.

Shum and He proposed concentric mosaic [15] to capture rays in the environment. Those rays are all tangent to several specific circles and form several cylindrical images with different radius. The concentric mosaic can render scenes at any view point toward any viewing direction inside the circle. Shum and Szeliski [7] further use the concentric mosaic to generate stereo. Because the depth of any vertical strip of captured rays is not identical, they apply depth correction for captured rays.

Based on augmented panorama, we developed a stereoscopic kiosk [12] for virtual museum, which consists of two display devices: one is a touch screen and the other is a stereoscopic display. In the kiosk system, artifacts are presented as object movies, and can be integrated with both image-based panoramas and geometry-based scenes for constructing virtual museum. Through the touch screen, the users can arbitrarily navigate in the virtual museum, select artifacts, and interactively view the detail information of the selected artifacts. Once an artifact on the touch screen is selected, the stereoscopic object movie of the selected artifact will be synchronously shown in the stereoscopic display. The kiosk system provides the user a better experience for browsing the 3D object through the stereoscopic display, however, the exhibition environment and the stereo OMs are displayed in separated devices. In this paper, we will integrate them together so that the user can navigate the virtual exhibition and browse the 3D objects using a stereoscopic display.

3 Stereo Object Movies

In this section, we discuss how to obtain stereo object movies (stereo OMs). A stereo OM consists of a pair of monocular OMs: one for left view (the left-OM) and the other for the right view (the right-OM). To acquire object movies (OMs), we use the motorized object rig, autoQTVR, developed by Texnai Inc. The motorized object rig is a computer-controlled 2-axis omniview shooting system, as shown in Fig. 1. By controlling the 2-axis, each captured image is associated with distinctive pan and tilt angles of the viewing direction. With the known pan and tilt angles, some particular images can be chosen and shown on screen according to user interactions.

For obtaining stereo OMs, we first acquire a monocular OM, e.g., for the left view, and then shift camera rightward to acquire the other monocular OM. Fig. 2 shows the 3D configurations when capturing a stereo OM. As it should be, we can use a stereo camera to acquire a pair of OMs simultaneously. Another method to obtain stereo OMs is to generate the right-OMs from the left-OMs using view morphing techniques.

In order to integrate a stereo OM into a new background, we have to remove the original background of the stereo OMs. In this work, we use the system proposed in [16] to remove the background of OMs. Using the system, we can perform background removal in less time with least human intervention.

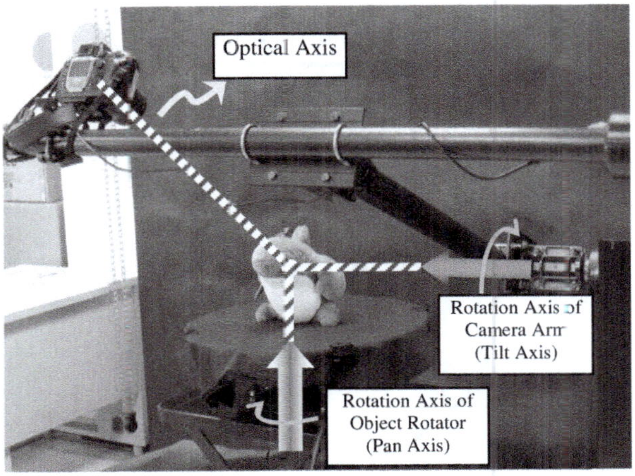

Fig. 1. The motorized object rig, autoQTVR, is used to acquire OMs

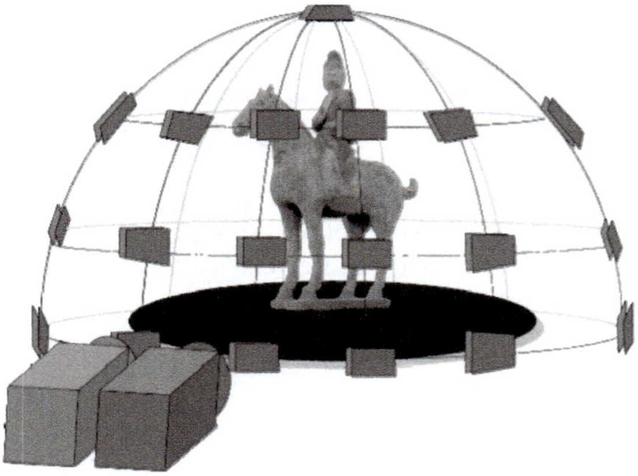

Fig. 2. The motorized object rig, autoQTVR, is used to acquire OMs

4 Stereo Panoramas

As mentioned in Section 2, there are many methods to obtain stereo panoramas. In this work, we adopt the method proposed in [14], because their method is easy to implement. Their method generates stereo panoramas by stitching vertical strips of a series images captured by a video camera. These image strips can approximate the desired circular projection on a cylindrical image surface. As shown in Fig. 3, the camera with an optical center O and an image plane is rotated about the rotation axis behind the camera. Strips at the left side of the image are seen from viewpoint V_r, and strips at right side of the image are seen from viewpoint V_l. The left strips are extracted for the right panorama and the right strips are for the left panorama. Therefore, the left panoramic image can be constructed from strips located at the right side of images and the right panoramic image can be constructed from strips located at the left side of images.

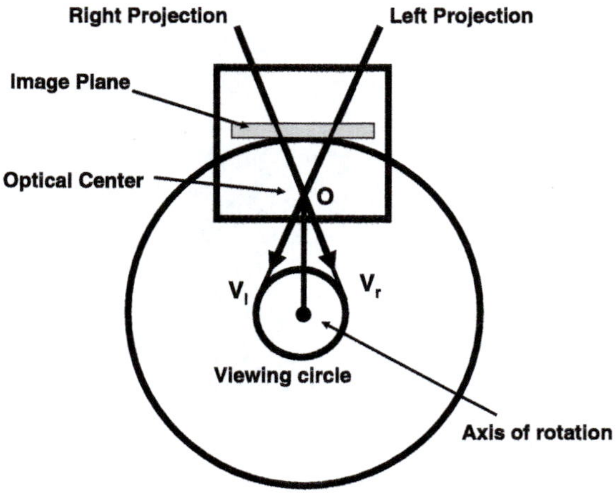

Fig. 3. A diagram of the method [14] to create a pair of stereo panoramic images

5 Augmented Stereo Panoramas

To integrate stereo OMs into a stereo panorama, we have to know where the objects will be inserted in. As mentioned in [10], to achieve the task for a monocular panorama, the user is only required to specify four vertices of a cuboid to define a 3D reference frame, named shadow reference frame (SRF), in a 2D dewarped view. This reference frame defines where the shadow of the object is supposed to be projected onto. Once the user has specified a SRF in the dewarped panoramic view, the geometric transformation between this SRF and the panorama reference frame (PRF) can be computed using this information [4]. By referring to the SRF, the user can insert stereo OMs into the stereo panorama in a visually 3D-consistent way. Each stereo OM is associated with a reference frame, named object reference frame (ORF), so the user can manipulate the stereo OM according to the orientation and location where the user desires. In this paper, we extend the method to augment a stereo panorama with stereo OMs. Our system provides two approaches for the users to quickly and accurately specify shadow reference frames in a stereo panorama. When rendering, the left panorama with left-OMs and right panorama with right-OMs are processed separately but in the same way.

5.1 Defining a Reference Frame

In this section, we will discuss two approaches allowing the user to specify where the stereo OMs will be inserted into a stereo panorama. One is a 2D approach, which the user can determine the SRFs in dewarped views of the stereo panorama. The other is a 3D approach, which allows the user to specify the SRFs in 3D space with stereoscopic display devices. The 3D approach is intuitive while the 2D approach does not require the stereoscopic devices.

(1) 2D approach
First, we let the user to define a SRF for the left panorama by specifying four vertices of a cuboid projected in the dewarped image, and the system can solve the geometric transformation between the SRF and the PRF. Furthermore, our system then automatically estimates the corresponding SRF in the right panorama by finding the corresponding vertices of the SRF. If the estimated result does not meet the user's expectations, the user can adjust the corresponding SRF in the right panorama. Here, our system provides a user interface to help the user performing the adjustments for more accuracy. First, we automatically find some corresponding features between both dewarped views of the stereo panorama using pyramidal KLT [2]. The extracted correspondences are shown on both dewarped images for the user to select good correspondences. After selecting correspondences (at least 8 correspondences), the fundamental matrix can be computed. Using the fundamental matrix, we can draw the epipolar line in the right dewarped image for a given point in the left dewarped image, as shown in Fig. 4. Therefore, the user can adjust the corresponding vertices of SRF in the right view with the help of epipolar lines.

(2) 3D approach
In this approach, the user is asked to wear a stereo glasses and directly manipulates a 3D SRF. By scaling, rotating and translating the 3D SRF, the user can determine the orientation and location of the SRF in 3D space.

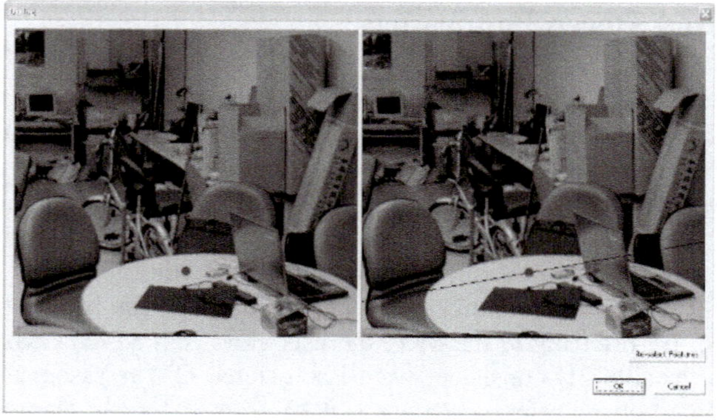

Fig. 4. An example of determining corresponding point with the help of the epipolar line

5.2 Rendering

An augmented stereo panorama consists of the left augmented panorama and the right augmented panorama. The left augmented panorama is composed by left OMs and the left panorama, and the right augmented panorama is composed by right OMs and the right panorama. We separately render the left augmented panorama and the right augmented panorama in the same viewing direction.

When rendering, we sequentially render the background layer, the shadow layer and the object layer. The background layer is composed by the de-warped view of the panorama. After the viewing direction of viewer is specified, we can dewarp the view according to the specified viewing direction and render it.

An OM with no 3D geometric model is impossible to generate a realistic shadow. To cope with this, we assume the shadow to be generated is produced by a set of parallel light sources. The lighting directions of the parallel sources can either be estimated from photographs containing the global illumination or manually specified by the user. We then can generate shadow of an OM by putting the correct shadow map at the correct position with respect to a user-specified SRF. As shown in Fig. 5, we generate a viewing image by composing the image of the OM correspond to the viewing direction n_L and its shadow, on the x-z plane of the SRF, produced by shadow map.

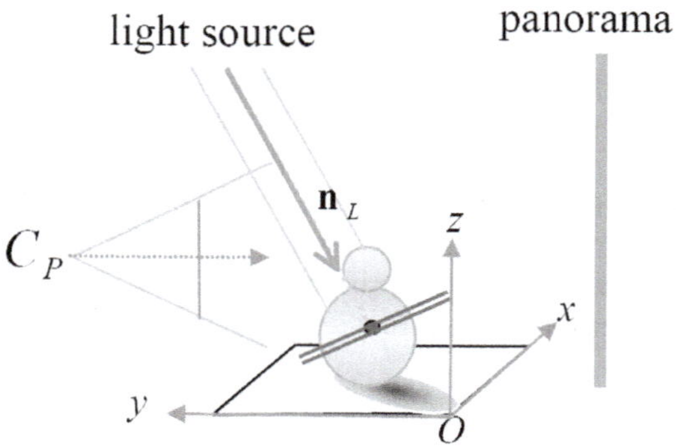

Fig. 5. Illustration of casting shadow for an object movie

To render object layer, we first compute the viewing direction from the center of PRF (C_p) to the center of the ORF, and select and render the image of the OM according to the viewing direction.

6 Experimental Results

Fig.6 shows the stitched results of a stereo panorama from photos taken in our laboratory. Fig. 7 shows the result of integrating a stereo OM into the stereo panorama. The shadow is properly rendered under the inserted object and the perceived depth of the OM is consistent with its nearby scene objects. Fig. 8 shows the consecutive views of rotating the stereo OM in the stereo panorama.

(a)

(b)

Fig. 6. Stitching result of a stereo panorama

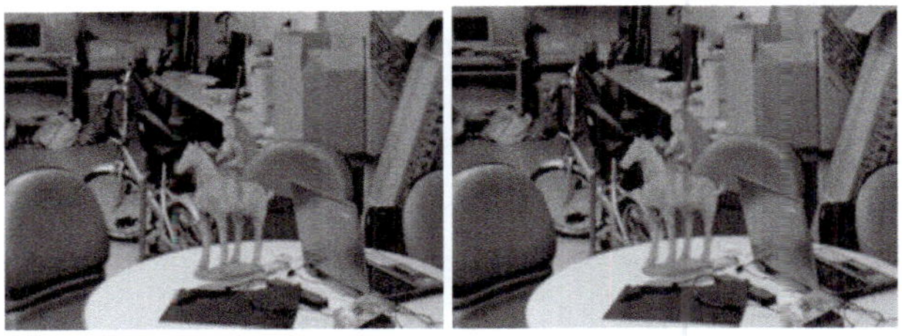

(a) (b)

Fig. 7. Result of the augmented panorama with a stereo OM. (a) shows the rendered left view, and (b) shows the right view.

7 Conclusion

In this paper, we extend our previous work on augmented panorama to augmented stereo panoramas. We develop an interactive system which allows the user to integrate stereo OMs into a stereo panorama, and interactively browse the augmented stereo

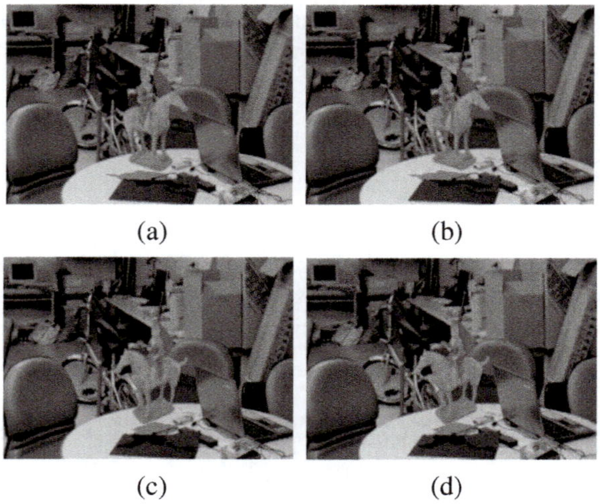

Fig. 8. Rotating the OM in the augmented stereo panorama. (a) and (c) are the left views. (b) and (d) are the right views.

panorama. In our system, we provide the users two approaches to determine the reference frames where the object will be inserted in a stereo panorama. After determining the reference frames, we render the left view and the right view separately. For each view, we first render the background layer, then the shadow layer and the object layer. When browsing the augmented panorama, the user can directly rotate and translate the stereo object movie that he is interested in. With augmented stereo panoramas, the user can enjoy more persuasive interaction with better depth perception.

Acknowledgements

This work is supported in part by National Science Council, Taiwan, under the grants of NSC- 93-2422-H-002-022 and NSC-94-2422-H002-019.

References

1. Adelson, E. H.andBergen. J. R.: The Plenoptic Function and the Elements of Early Vision. Computational Models of Visual Processing, Chapter 1, Edited by Michael Landy and J. Anthony Movshon. The MIT Press, Cambridge, Mass. (1991)
2. Bouguet, J.-Y.: Pyramidal Implementation of the Lucas Kanade Feature Tracker Description of the algorithm. Intel Corporation, Microprocessor Research Labs, OpenCV. Documents (1999)
3. Brown, M., and Lowe, D. G.: Recognising Panoramas. Proceeding of International Conference on Computer Vision, vol. 2, (2003) 1218-1225
4. Chen, C. S., Yu, C. K., Hung, Y. P.: New Calibration-free Approach for Augmented Reality Based on Parameterized Cuboid Structure. Proc. of International Conf. on Computer Vision, (1999) 30-37

5. Chen, S. E.: Quick Time VR: an image-based approach to virtual environment navigation. Proc. ACM conf. Computer Graphics, (1995) 29-38
6. Gortler, S. J., Grzeszczuk, R., Szeliski, R., and Cohen, M. F.: The Lumigraph. Proc. ACM conf. Computer Graphics, (1996) 43-54
7. H. Y. Shum and R. Szeliski, "Stereo Reconstruction from Multiperspective Panoramas," *Pattern Analysis and Machine Intelligence*, Vol. 26, pp. 45-62, Jan 2004.
8. http://www.apple.com/quicktime
9. Huang, H. C., and Hung, Y. P.: Panoramic Stereo Imaging System with Automatic Disparity Warping and Seaming. Graphical Models and Image Processing. vol. 60, no. 3, (1998) 196-208
10. Hung, Y. P., Chen, C. S., Tsai, Y. P. and Lin, S. W.: Augmenting panoramas with object movies by generating novel views with disparity-based view morphing. J. Visualization and Computer Animation, vol. 13, (2002) 237-247
11. Levoy, M., and Hanrahan, P.: Light Field Rendering. Proc. ACM conf. Computer Graphics, (1996) 31-42
12. Lo, W. Y., Tsai, Y. P., Chen, C. W., Hung, Y. P.: Stereoscopic Kiosk for Virtual Museum. Proc. International Computer Symposium (2004)
13. McMillan, L. and Bishop, G.: Plenoptic Modeling: An Image-Based Rendering System. Proc. ACM conf. Computer Graphics, (1995) 39-46
14. Peleg, S., and Ben-Ezra, M.:Stereo Panorama with a Single Camera. Proc. IEEE Conf. Computer Vision and Pattern Recognition,(1999) 395-401
15. Shum, H. Y., and He, L. W.:Rendering with Concentric Mosaics. Proc. ACM conf. Computer Graphics, (1999) 299-306
16. Tsai, Y. P., Hung, Y.P., Shih, Z. C., Su, J. J., and Tsai, S. R.: Background Removal System for Object Movies. Proc. of International Conf. on Pattern Recognition, Vol. 1, (2004) 608-611
17. Zhu, Z., Riseman, E. M., and Hanson, A. R.,: Parallel-Perspective Stereo Mosaics. Proc. of International Conf. on Computer Vision, vol. 1, (2001) 345-352

A Local Basis Representation for Estimating Human Pose from Cluttered Images

Ankur Agarwal and Bill Triggs

GRAVIR-INRIA-CNRS, 655 avenue de l'Europe, Montbonnot 38330, France
{Ankur.Agarwal, Bill.Triggs}@inrialpes.fr
http://lear.inrialpes.fr

Abstract. Recovering the pose of a person from single images is a challenging problem. This paper discusses a bottom-up approach that uses local image features to estimate human upper body pose from single images in cluttered backgrounds. The method takes the image window with a dense grid of local gradient orientation histograms, followed by non negative matrix factorization to learn a set of bases that correspond to local features on the human body, enabling selective encoding of human-like features in the presence of background clutter. Pose is then recovered by direct regression. This approach allows us to key on gradient patterns such as shoulder contours and bent elbows that are characteristic of humans and carry important pose information, unlike current regressive methods that either use weak limb detectors or require prior segmentation to work. The system is trained on a database of images with labelled poses. We show that it estimates pose with similar performance levels to current example-based methods, but unlike them it works in the presence of natural backgrounds, without any prior segmentation.

1 Introduction

The ability to identify objects or their parts in the presence of cluttered backgrounds is critical to the success of many computer vision algorithms, but finding descriptors that can distinguish objects of interest from the background is often very difficult. We address this problem in the context of understanding human body pose from general images. Images of people are seen everywhere. A system that was capable of reliably estimating the configuration of a person's limbs from images would have applications spanning from human computer interaction to activity recognition from images to annotating video content. In this paper, we focus on recognizing upper body gestures. Human arm gestures often convey a lot of information — *e.g.* during communication — and automated inference and interpretation of these could allow for critical understanding of a person's behaviour.

Current methods for human pose inference usually rely on background subtraction to isolate the subject. This limits their applicability to fixed environments. Model-based approaches use a manual/heuristic initialization of pose as a starting point to optimize over image likelihoods, or to track through subsequent frames in a video sequence. The application of such methods to 3D pose recovery requires camera parameter estimates and realistic human body models. We prefer to take a bottom-up approach to the problem, considering pose inference from general images in terms of two interdependent

P.J. Narayanan et al. (Eds.): ACCV 2006, LNCS 3851, pp. 50–59, 2006.

sub-problems: *(i)* identifying/localizing the human parts of interest in the image, and *(ii)* estimating 3D pose from them. We combine methods that are currently used mainly for object and pedestrian detection with recent advances in example-based pose estimation from human silhouettes or segmented images, implicitly using the knowledge contained in human body configurations to learn to localize body parts in the presence of cluttered backgrounds and to infer 3D pose.

Our approach to modeling human body parts is based on using SIFT-like histograms [5] computed on a uniform grid of overlapping patches on an image to encode the image content as an array of 128-d feature vectors. This scheme encodes local image content in terms of gradient patterns invariant to illumination changes, while still retaining spatial position information. It allows us to key on gradient patterns such as head/shoulder contours or bent elbows that are characteristic of humans and that contain important pose information, in contrast to limb based representations that either key on skin colour and face detection (*e.g.* [11]), or learn individual limb detectors and then apply kinematic tree based constraints [16,20].

As the human body is highly articulated, it is a complicated object to detect, particularly at the resolution of individual body parts. Although explicit kinematic tree based structures can be an effective tool in this regard, we avoid such assumptions, instead learning characteristic spatial configurations directly from images. Our patch based representation allows us to work on the scale of small body parts, and besides providing spatial information for each of these parts, enables us to mix and match part combinations for modeling generic appearance.

Previous work: There are currently only a few bottom up approaches to the estimation of human pose from images and video. Many of these methods use combinations of weak limb detectors to detect the presence of a person [16,9], but are not capable of deducing 3D poses accurately enough to infer actions and gestures. Similarly, in [15], loose 2D configurations of body parts are used to coarsely track people in video by filtering potential limb-like objects based on motion and color statistics.

Most methods for precise pose estimation adopt top-down approaches in the sense that they try to minimize projection errors of kinematic models, either using numerical optimization [21] or by generating large number of pose hypotheses [11]. With suitable initialization or sufficiently fine sampling such methods can produce accurate results, but the computational cost is high. Efficient matching methods such as [6] fall back to the assumption of having pre-segmented images. [20] discusses an interesting approach that combines weak responses from bottom-up limb detectors based on a statistical model of image likelihoods with a full articulated body model using belief propagation. However, this approach uses background subtraction and it also relies on multiple calibrated cameras.

A recent work that addresses upper body pose from single images in clutter is [11]. This is based on the use of heuristic image cues including a clothes model and skin color detection; and relies on generating and testing large numbers of pose hypotheses using a 3D body model. Here we adopt an example based approach inspired by [19] and [1]. Both of these approaches infer pose from edge feature representations of the input image using a model learned from a number of labeled training examples (image-pose pairs). However, both require clean backgrounds for their representations. Here

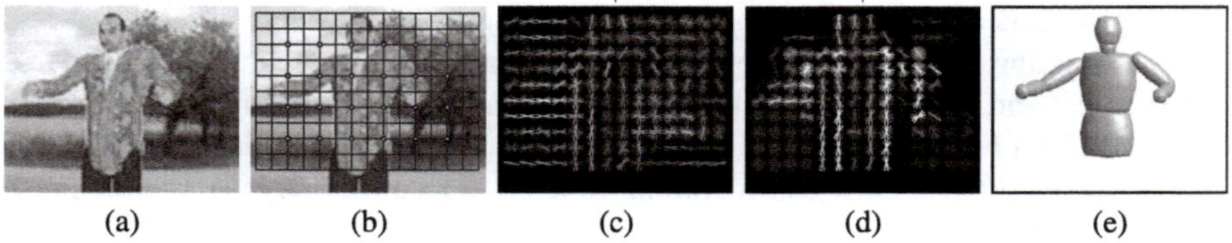

Fig. 1. An overview of our method of pose estimation from cluttered images. (a) original image, (b) a grid of fixed points where the descriptors are computed (each descriptor block covers an array of 4x4 cells, giving a 50% overlap with it's neighbouring blocks), (c) SIFT descriptors computed at these points, the intensity of each line representing the weight of the corresponding orientation bin in that cell, (d) Suppressing background using a sparse set of learned (NMF) bases encoding human-like parts, (e) final pose obtained by regression.

we develop a more general approach that works with cluttered backgrounds. Our image representation is based on local appearance descriptors extracted from a uniformly spaced grid of image patches. This notion, in the form of superpixels, or image sites, has previously been used in several different contexts, *e.g.* [4, 13, 17]. We also take inspiration from the image coding and object localization methods described in [22, 14].

2 Regression Based Approach

Example based methods often have problems when working in high dimensional spaces as it is difficult to create or incorporate enough examples to densely cover the space. This is particularly true for human pose estimation which must recover many articular degrees of freedom from a complex image signal. The sparsity of examples is usually tackled by smoothly interpolating between nearby examples. Learning a single smooth inference model in the form of a regressor was suggested in [1]. This has the advantage of directly recovering pose parameters from image observations, which obviates the need to attach explicit meanings or attributions to image features (*e.g.* labels designating the body parts seen). However it requires a robust and discriminative representation of the input image. Following [1], we take a regression based approach, extending it to deal with the presence of cluttered image background. Encoding pose by the 3D locations of 8 key upper body joint centres, we regress a 24-d output pose vector $\mathbf{y}$ on a set of image features $\mathbf{x}$:

$$\mathbf{y} = \mathbf{A}\,\phi(\mathbf{x}) + \epsilon \tag{1}$$

where $\phi(\mathbf{x})$ is a vector of basis functions, $\mathbf{A}$ is a matrix of weight vectors, and ϵ is a residual error vector. The matrix $\mathbf{A}$ is estimated by minimizing least squares error while applying a regularization term to control overfitting.

The method turns out to be relatively insensitive to the choice of regression methods. Here we work with a classical single-valued regressor as frontal upper body gestures have relatively few multimodality problems in comparison to the full body case, but the multimodal multi-valued regression method of [2] could also be used if necessary. Our main focus is on exploring suitable image representations and mechanisms for dealing with background clutter.

3 Image Features

Image information can be encoded in many different ways. Given the variability of clothing and the fact that we want to be able to use black and white images, we do not use colour information. Silhouette shape and body contours have proven effective in cases where segmentations are available, but with current segmentation algorithms they do not extend reliably to images with cluttered backgrounds [12]. Furthermore, more local, part-based representations are likely to be able to adapt better to the highly non-rigid structure of the human body. To allow the method to key on important body contours, we based our representation on local image gradients. For effective encoding, we use histograms of gradient orientations in small spatial cells. The relative coarseness of the spatial coding provides some robustness to small position variations, while still capturing the essential spatial position and limb orientation information. Note that owing to loose clothing, the *positions* of limb contours do not in any case have a very precise relation to the pose, whereas *orientation* of body edges is a much more reliable cue. Hence a SIFT-like representation is appropriate. We compute these histograms in the same way as SIFT descriptors [5], quantizing gradient orientations into discrete values in small spatial cells and normalizing these distributions over local blocks of cells to achieve insensitivity to illumination changes. To retain the information about image location that is indispensable for pose estimation, the descriptors are computed at fixed grid locations in the image window. Figure 1(c) shows the features extracted from a sample image. We denote the descriptor vectors at each of these L locations as $\mathbf{v}^l, l \in \{1 \ldots L\}$, and represent the complete image as a large vector $\mathbf{x}$, a concatenation of the individual descriptors: $\mathbf{x} \equiv (\mathbf{v}^{1\top}, \mathbf{v}^{2\top}, \ldots \mathbf{v}^{L\top})^\top$.

An alternate approach that failed to provide convincing results in our experiments is a *bag of features* style of representation. In the absence of reliable salient points on the human body, we computed SIFT descriptors at all edge points in the image and added spatial information by appending image coordinates to the descriptor vector. For effective pose estimation, though, it seems that coding location precisely is extremely important and extracting descriptors on a fixed grid of locations is preferable.

3.1 Similarity Based Encoding

Representations based on collections of local parts are commonly used in object recognition [18,3,7]. A common scheme is to identify a representative set of parts as a vocabulary for representing new images. In an analogous manner, the human body can be represented as a collection of limbs and other key body parts in particular configurations. To test this, we independently clustered patches at each image location to identify representative configurations of the body parts that are seen in these locations. Each image patch was then represented by *softly* vector quantizing the SIFT descriptor by voting into each of its corresponding k-means centers, *i.e.* as a sparse vector of similarity weights computed from each cluster center. Results from this and other representations are summarized in figure 4 and discussed in the experimental section.

3.2 Non-negative Matrix Factorization

Non-negative matrix factorization (NMF) is a recent method that can exploit latent structure in data to find part based representations [10,8]. NMF factorizes a non-

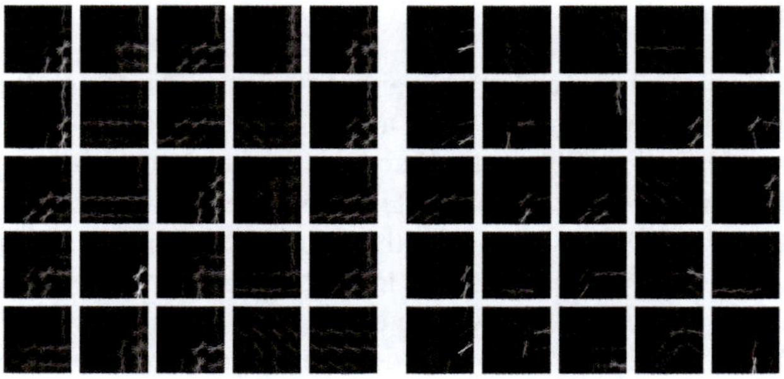

Fig. 2. Exemplars, or basis vectors, extracted from SIFT descriptors over 4000 image patches located close to the right shoulder. The corresponding block is shown in figure 3. *(left)* Representative examples selected by k-means. *(right)* Much sparser basis vectors obtained by non-negative matrix factorization. These capture important contours encoding a shoulder, unlike the denser examples given by k-means.

negative data matrix $\mathbf{V}$ as $\mathbf{V} \sim \mathbf{W}\mathbf{H}$, where $\mathbf{W}$ and $\mathbf{H}$ are both constrained to be non-negative. If the columns of $\mathbf{V}$ consist of feature vectors, $\mathbf{W}$ can be interpreted as a set of basis vectors, and $\mathbf{H}$ as corresponding coefficients needed to reconstruct the original data. Each entry of $\mathbf{V}$ is thus represented as $\mathbf{v}_i = \sum_j \mathbf{w}_j h_{ji}$. Unlike other linear decompositions such as PCA or ICA [23], this purely additive representation (there is no subtraction) tends to pull out local fragments that occur consistently in the data, giving a sparse set of basis vectors. The results of applying NMF to the 128-d descriptor space at a given patch location are shown in figure 2.

Besides capturing the local edges representative of human contours, the NMF bases allow us to compactly code each 128-d SIFT descriptor directly by its corresponding vector $\mathbf{h}$ of basis coefficients. This serves as a nonlinear image coding that retains good

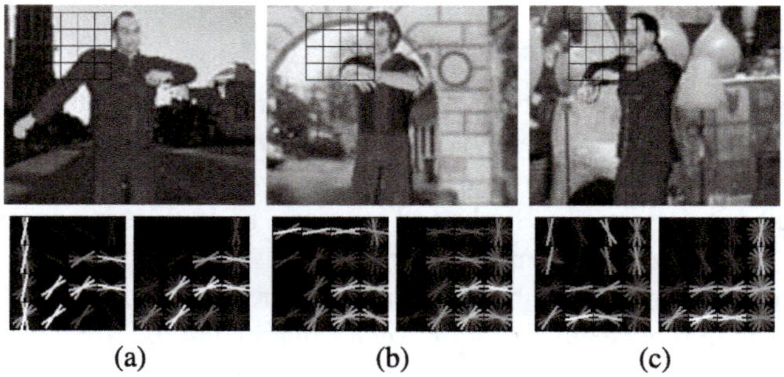

Fig. 3. To selectively encode foreground features and suppress unwanted background, we use NMF bases learned on clean images (with no clutter) to reconstruct the cluttered image patches. For each image, the original SIFT feature and its representation using the bases extracted using NMF are shown for the patch marked. Features corresponding to background edges such as those of the building on the left in (a) and the arch in (b) are clearly suppressed, while background clutter in (c) is downweighted.

locality for each patch: $\phi(\mathbf{x}) \equiv (\mathbf{h}^{1\top}, \mathbf{h}^{2\top}, \ldots \mathbf{h}^{L\top})^\top$ in (1). Having once estimated the basis $\mathbf{W}$ (for each image location) from a training set, we keep it fixed when we compute the coefficients for test images. In our case, we find that the performance tends to saturate at about 30-40 basis elements per grid patch.

Selectively removing clutter: An interesting advantage of using NMF to represent images is its ability to selectively encode only the foreground of regions of interest, hence effectively rejecting background. We find that by learning the bases $\mathbf{W}$ from a set of clean images (containing no background clutter), and using these only additively (with NMF) to reconstruct images with clutter, only the edge features corresponding to the foreground are reconstructed, while suppressing features in unexpected parts of the image. This happens because the bases are constructed from clean human images and hence forced to contain mass only in regions containing human-like features. Some examples illustrating this phenomenon are shown in figure 3.

4 Experimental Performance

We trained and evaluated the methods on two different databases of human pose examples. The first is a set of randomly generated human poses using a human model rendering package, POSER from Curious Labs. This is a subset of the data used in [19], kindly supplied to us by its authors. The second dataset contains motion capture data from human recordings of several sets of arm movements. It was obtained from http://mocap.cs.cmu.edu. Unfortunately neither set has significant background clutter, nor are we aware of any existing dataset that combines images of human poses with background clutter and motion capture data for training and ground truth. However, as all of this data was created under controlled conditions, we were able to artificially add random backgrounds to the images while retaining their 3D pose ground truth information for comparative testing with and without background clutter. So we have *clean* and *cluttered* versions of both image sets, albeit with somewhat artificial poses (for set 1) and backgrounds.

For descriptor computation, we quantized gradient orientations into 8 orientation bins (in $[0, \pi]$) in 4×4 spatial cells, as described in [5], using blocks 32 pixels across.

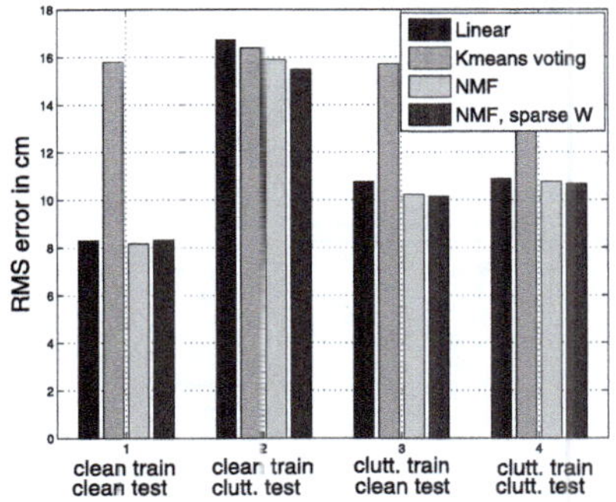

Fig. 4. A comparison of the performance of different feature encodings in regressing 3D pose, over different combinations of training and testing on clean and cluttered data. See text.

Our images are centered and resized to 118×95 pixels. The descriptor histograms are computed on a 4×6 grid of 24 uniformly spaced overlapping blocks on each image, giving rise to 3072-d image descriptor vectors $\mathbf{x}$.

Figure 4 shows the performance of different feature encodings over all combinations of training and testing on clean and cluttered images. The regularization parameter of the regressor was optimized using cross validation. These figures are reported for 4000 training and 1000 test points from the POSER dataset. The errors reported indicate, in centimeters, the RMS deviations for the 3D locations of shoulder, elbow, wrist, neck and pelvis joints. The best performance, as expected, is obtained by training and testing on clean, background-free images, irrespective of the descriptor encoding used. Training on clean images does not suffice for generalization to clutter. Using cluttered images for training provides reasonably good generalization to unseen backgrounds, but the resulting errors are larger by 2-3 cms on both clean and cluttered test sets than the best case. Surprisingly, a linear regressor on the vector $\mathbf{x}$ performs very well despite the clutter —

Fig. 5. Sample pose estimates from a test set of 1000 images in cluttered backgrounds. No knowledge of segmentation is used in the process.

an examination of the elements of the weight matrix **A** reveals this is due to automatic downweighting of descriptor elements that usually contain only background. On average, the k-means based representation performs the worst of all and the NMF-based representation gives the best performance. To study the space of encodings 'between' an extreme exemplar based k-means representation and the set of basis vectors obtained by NMF, we tested NMF with constraints on the sparsity level of the basis vectors and coefficients [8]. Varying the sparsity of the basis vectors **W** has very little effect on the performance, while varying the sparsity of the coefficients **H** gives results spanning the range of performances from k-means to unconstrained NMF. As the sparsity prior on **H** is increased to a maximum, NMF is forced to use only a few basis vectors for each training example, in the extreme case giving a solution very similar to k-means.

To see the effect of depth ambiguities on these results, we computed errors separately in the x and y coordinates corresponding to the image plane and z, corresponding to depth. We find that errors in depth estimation are a little higher than those in lateral displacement. *E.g.*, of the 10.88 cm of error obtained in the experiment on cluttered images, 9.65 cm comes from x and y, while 12.97 cm from errors in z. In the absence of clutter, we obtain errors of $\sim$8 cm. This is similar to the performance reported in [19] on this dataset (when transformed into the angle based error measure used in that paper), showing that regression based methods can match the performance of nearest-neighbourhood based ones, while avoiding having to store and search through exces-

Fig. 6. Pose reconstructions on real unseen images. The first 3 images are taken from a test sequence in our motion capture dataset which includes similar gestures made by another person, while the last 3 are example images obtained using Google. The results on the real images are not very precise if overlayed on the images, but they do capture the general appearance of the subject's gestures fairly well. They would probably improve considerably given more training data for common gestures.

sive amounts of training data. Examples of pose estimation on the cluttered test set are shown in figure 5.

For our second set of experiments, we use $\sim$1600 images from 9 video sequences of motion capture data. Performance on a test set of 300 images from a 10th sequence gives an error of 7.4 cm in the presence of clutter. We attribute this slightly improved performance to the similarity of the gestures performed in the test set to those in the training sequences, although we emphasize that in the test set they were performed by a different subject. Figure 6 shows sample reconstructions over test examples from the second database and from some natural images found with Google. We find that training on the second dataset also gives qualitatively better performance on a set of randomly selected real images. This suggests that it is important to include more 'natural', human-like poses in the training set, which are not covered by randomly sampling over the space of possible poses. We are currently collecting more training data to improve performance on typical human gestures.

5 Conclusion

We have presented a method that is capable of estimating 3D human upper body pose from a single image. To the best of our knowledge, this is the first totally bottom-up approach to this problem that works in the presence of background clutter. An image representation based on a set of local descriptors computed at known locations in the image allows us to model the appearance of different parts independently, before combining the information for pose regression. The regression based approach eliminates the need to store large numbers of training examples. We have also demonstrated a novel application of non-negative matrix factorization that allows us to discriminate features of interest from background. This is likely to prove useful in other applications including segmentation and recognition.

Future work: We currently work with centered images of people. The framework could be applied as it is on the output of a person detector to estimate pose or infer activity of multiple people in a scene. In fact, we are hoping to construct a unified person detector and pose estimator that uses a knowledge of human body configurations for complete detection. As regards immediate extensions, the method will be trained on a larger database of common gestures and extended to incorporate motion information for tracking full body motion in cluttered backgrounds.

References

[1] A. Agarwal and B. Triggs. 3D Human Pose from Silhouettes by Relevance Vector Regression. In *Int. Conf. Computer Vision & Pattern Recognition*, 2004.

[2] A. Agarwal and B. Triggs. Monocular Human Motion Capture with a Mixture of Regressors. In *IEEE Workshop on Vision for Human-Computer Interaction*, 2005.

[3] S. Agarwal, A. Awan, and D. Roth. Learning to detect objects in images via a sparse, part-based representation. *IEEE Transactions on Pattern Analysis and Machine Intelligence*, 26(11):1475–1490, 2004.

[4] N. Dalal and B. Triggs. Histograms of Oriented Gradients for Human Detection. In *Int. Conf. Computer Vision*, 2005.

[5] D.Lowe. Distinctive Image Features from Scale-invariant Keypoints. *International Journal of Computer Vision*, 60, 2:91–110, 2004.

[6] P. Felzenszwalb and D. Huttenlocher. Pictorial Structures for Object Recognition. *International Journal of Computer Vision*, 61 (1), 2005.

[7] R. Fergus, P. Perona, and A. Zisserman. Object Class Recognition by Unsupervised Scale-Invariant Learning. In *Int. Conf. Computer Vision & Pattern Recognition*, 2003.

[8] P. Hoyer. Non-negative Matrix Factorization with Sparseness Constraints. *J. Machine Learning Research*, 5:1457–1469, 2004.

[9] K.Mikolajczyk, C. Schmid, and A. Zisserman. Human Detection based on a Probabilistic Assembly of Robust Part Detectors. In *European Conference on Computer Vision*, volume I, pages 69–81, 2004.

[10] D. D. Lee and H. S. Seung. Learning the Parts of Objects by Non–negative Matrix Factorization. *Nature*, 401:788–791, 1999.

[11] M. Lee and I. Cohen. Human Upper Body Pose Estimation in Static Images. In *European Conference on Computer Vision*, 2004.

[12] J. Malik, S. Belongie, T. Leung, and J. Shi. Contour and texture analysis for image segmentation. *International Journal of Computer Vision*, 43(1):7–27, 2001.

[13] G. Mori, X. Ren, A. Efros, and J. Malik. Recovering Human Body Configurations: Combining Segmentation and Recognition. In *Int. Conf. Computer Vision & Pattern Recognition*, 2004.

[14] B. Olshausen and D. Field. Natural image statistics and efficient coding. *Network: Computation in Neural Systems*, 7(2):333–339, 1996.

[15] D. Ramanan and D. Forsyth. Finding and Tracking People from the Bottom Up. In *Int. Conf. Computer Vision & Pattern Recognition*, 2003.

[16] R. Ronfard, C. Schmid, and B. Triggs. Learning to Parse Pictures of People. In *European Conference on Computer Vision*, pages IV 700–714, Copenhagen, 2002.

[17] S. Kumar and M. Hebert. Discriminative Random Fields: A Discriminative Framework for Contextual Interaction in Classification. In *Int. Conf. Computer Vision*, 2003.

[18] E. Sali and S. Ullman. Combining Class-specific Fragments for Object Classification. In *British Machine Vision Conference*, 1999.

[19] G. Shakhnarovich, P. Viola, and T. Darrell. Fast Pose Estimation with Parameter Sensitive Hashing. In *Int. Conf. Computer Vision*, 2003.

[20] L. Sigal, M. Isard, B. Sigelman, and M. Black. Assembling Loose-limbed Models using Non-parametric Belief Propagation. In *NIPS*, 2003.

[21] C. Sminchisescu and Bill Triggs. Estimating articulated human motion with covariance scaled sampling. *International Journal of Robotics Research*, 22(6):371–391, June 2003. Special issue on Visual Analysis of Human Movement.

[22] J. Sullivan, A. Blake, M. Isaard, and J. MacCormick. Object Localization by Bayesian Correlation. In *Int. Conf. Computer Vision*, 1999.

[23] J. van Haateran and vander Schaaf A. Independent component filters of natural images compared with simlpe cells in preimary visual cortex. *Proc. R. Soc. Lond.*, B 265:359–366, 1998.

Alignment of 3D Models to Images Using Region-Based Mutual Information and Neighborhood Extended Gaussian Images

Hon-Keat Pong and Tat-Jen Cham

School of Computer Engineering,
Nanyang Technological University, Singapore
hkpong@pmail.ntu.edu.sg
astjcham@ntu.edu.sg

Abstract. Mutual information has been used for matching and registering 3D models to 2D images. However, in Viola's original framework [1], surface albedo variance is assumed to be minimal when measuring similarity between 3D models and 2D image data using mutual information. In reality, most objects have textured surfaces with different albedo values across their surfaces, and direct application of this method in such circumstances will fail. To solve this problem, we propose to include spatial information into the original formulation by using histogram-based features of local regions that are robust to local but significant albedo variation. Neighborhood Extended Gaussian Images (NEGI) are used as descriptors to represent local surface regions on the 3D model, while pixel intensity data are considered within corresponding region windows on the image. Experiments on aligning 3D car models in cluttered scenes using this new framework demonstrate substantial improvement as compared to the original pixel-wise mutual information approach.

1 Introduction

One of the difficult problems in computer vision is the registration of a 3D model to an image. 2D-3D alignment techniques are applied in the medical images domain to register 3D volumetric data with 2D images, with mutual information as one of the most popular similarity measures [2]. 3D geometric models are used for detecting faces and objects in 2D images by finding pose estimates through alignment.

Representations of object models have been studied extensively for varied detection techniques and application purposes. Some existing 2D-3D alignment-based detection methods use edges of the 3D geometric models as a matching cue, through finding invariant descriptors from 2D projection profiles or by defining shape signatures [3, 4, 5, 6]. Viola [1] and Maes *et al.* [7] proposed an alignment approach using a similarity measure derived from information theory [8]. An interesting application in [1] is that we can take surface normal samples (N) from a geometric model, collect the corresponding intensity values (I) in the image and then compute the mutual information (MI) between N and I. Object pose in the image is estimated by maximization of mutual information.

P.J. Narayanan et al. (Eds.): ACCV 2006, LNCS 3851, pp. 60–69, 2006.

As a similarity measure, mutual information does not assume a known functional relationship between the model and the image. Rather, it only assumes that a consistent relationship exists. The consistency principle states that similar model data will map to similar image data and it is observed that a correct alignment will generally lead to a consistent relationship (figure 3). This makes mutual information a more robust similarity measure for matching multi-modal data [2]. A likely situation for object detection is that functional relationships between 3D model and 2D image can be difficult to model or hard to establish due to complexities such as illumination changes and shadows, the 3D model being a weak descriptor (for instance, the available model is only a rough approximation of the object shape with low polygonal counts), or the rather unusual appearance of the object for its image being captured using a thermal camera. Mutual information has been shown to be a promising matching metric in such situation, but very little has been studied in the case of 2D-3D alignment beyond the initial framework in [1] and the medical image registration domain.

There is an important limitation to mutual information applied in alignment of 3D geometric models to image data: it fails on surfaces that have significant albedo variation. The reason for the failure is that, as mutual information takes into account only the relationship between single dimension points (i.e. a single model normal and intensity of a single pixel), the consistency principle breaks down when similar surface normals map to different intensity values (figure 2). In reality, many objects have textured surfaces with varying albedo values across their surfaces. To make mutual information more applicable to real world scenarios, it is important to handle the issue of varied albedo across object surface.

In this paper, a method to solve the aforementioned problem is presented. We propose to include spatial information into the original formulation by including a neighborhood set of points in a novel manner that makes it robust to albedo variation. To accommodate the extension to alignment of 3D models to 2D image data, we define the Neighborhood Extended Gaussian Images to represent shape within local surface regions on the model, and consider intensity data within region windows on the image. The method makes it more practical for 2D-3D alignment based on the mutual information for non-medical images.

The paper is organized as follows: section 2 contains review of related work. Section 3 presents discussion on the mutual information as a matching metric and an extension of its original formulation. Section 4 presents the Neighborhood Extended Gaussian Images. Section 5 presents our experimental results and finally Section 6 presents some conclusions and future research directions.

2 Previous Work

Instead of comparing images using singleton pixels, Russakoff *et al.* [9] extended mutual information to include spatial information by using more pixels in a neighborhood when computing the mutual information – this is applied to 2D medical image registration. The framework exploits the spatial relationship of pixels in a simple manner to provide greater regularization to the optimization problem, but does not deal with significant albedo variation. Our method not only extends the problem to 3D alignment, but is specifically designed to handle substantial (albeit local) albedo variation.

Campbell and Flynn provide a comprehensive survey of 3D object recognition techniques using 3D geometric models [3]. Two related works that use 3D vehicular models are that of Kollnig and Nagel [5] and Tan *et al.* [6]. Kollnig and Nagel made use of intensity discontinuities along projection contours to update object pose while Tan *et al.* estimated the model pose by matching 2D image and 3D model lines using the Hough Transform.

Recently, Suveg and Gosselman [4] aligned simple polyhedral block models to aerial views of buildings using mutual information as matching metric. Mutual information between gradient magnitude along model contour and image data is computed. Their framework is still subject to the consistency breakdown issue as no spatial information is included in the formulation.

In Viola's alignment approach [1], surface normals of the object are matched to intensity values by maximizing their mutual information with respect to a set of transformation parameters. Leventon and Grimson [10] extended the alignment framework to using multiple views of the object when single image does not provide enough information.

3 Mutual Information as Similarity Measure

Mutual information is a statistical measure assessing the dependency between two random variables, without requiring that functional forms of the random variables be known [8]. It can be thought of as a measure of how well one random variable explains the other, i.e. how much information about one random variable is contained in the other random variable. If random variable A explains random variable B well, their joint entropy is reduced. Defined in terms of entropies, the mutual information between two random variables A and B, $I(M, I)$ is

$$I(A, B) = H(A) + H(B) - H(A, B)$$

where $H(A)$ and $H(B)$ are marginal entropies derived from the probability distribution functions corresponding to A and B, i.e.

$$H(A) = -\sum_a p(a) \log p(a)$$

$$H(B) = -\sum_b p(b) \log p(b)$$

$H(A, B)$ is the joint entropy of the two random variables that is defined as

$$H(A, B) = -\sum_a \sum_b p(a, b) \log p(a, b)$$

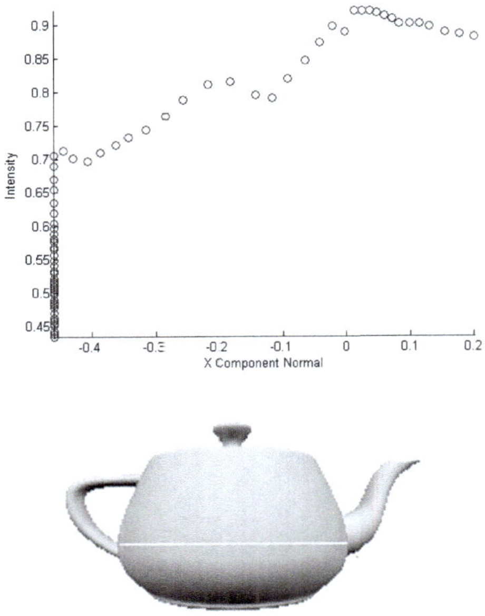

Fig. 1. Consistent relationship between model and image. The figure shows a scatter plot of the variation of intensity values on the white scan line of the teapot image versus variation of the corresponding x components of the surface normals for a correct alignment.

Mutual information is assumed to be maximal when the model is aligned correctly with the image for a set of transformation parameters (we consider six-parameter rigid transformation of the object model, i.e. 3 for rotations and 3 for translations).

For our 2D-3D alignment framework using polygonal models, mutual information is computed from the joint and marginal entropies of surface normals (using x and y components of the normals) and image intensities. However, the original formulation is only feasible for surfaces with minimal albedo variance. As mutual information does not contain information about spatial distributions of intensities and surface normals, ambiguity arises when the maximum mutual information doesn't occur at the correct object pose due to varying albedo on surface points. Longer-range interaction between point samples is ignored when they are considered independently in the mutual information formulation.

Russakoff *et al.* [9] extended the original formulation of mutual information (MI) to include spatial information by using higher dimensional points consisting of pixels in a neighborhood – the regional mutual information (RMI). For a sample point S, spatial information is brought into MI by grouping neighboring pixels within a chosen radius to form a higher dimensional vector. When applying Russakoff *et al.* 's formulation to our case, the normals in a neighborhood (here, a 4x4 window) are grouped into a higher dimensional vector N, and the corresponding pixels in the image form the vector I:

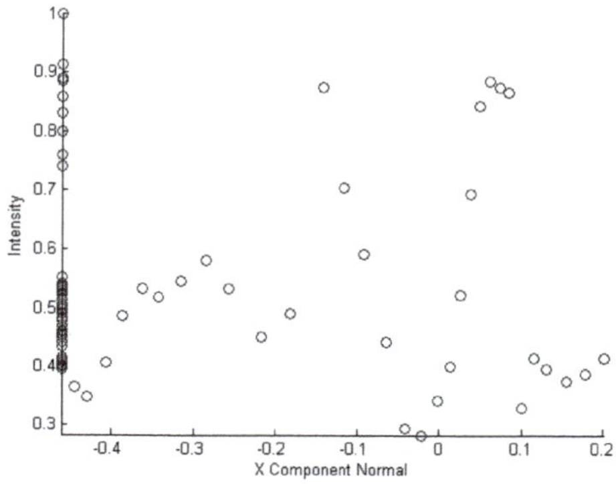

Fig. 2. Consistency breakdown: a scatter plot of the intensity values on the same scan line of the teapot image versus variation of the corresponding x components of the surface normals when the teapot is textured

$$N = \{x_1, x_2, x_3, x_4, y_1, y_2, y_3, y_4\}$$
$$I = \{i_1, i_2, i_3, i_4\}$$

where x_i and y_i are x and y components of the normals. i_i is intensity value for the corresponding image pixel.

To deal with the curse of dimensionality, the dimensions are assumed to be independent from each other to allow entropy calculation to be decoupled from one involving d-dimensional distribution to one involving d one-dimensional distributions. Shanon's entropy formulation for a set of points distributed in $\mathbb{R}^d$ with covariance matrix $\boldsymbol{\Sigma_d}$ is then used to calculate entropy of the high-dimensional points [11]:

$$H_g(\boldsymbol{\Sigma_d}) = \log((2\pi e)^{d/2}\det(\boldsymbol{\Sigma_d})^{\frac{1}{2}})$$

4 Region Mutual Information Using the Neighborhood Extended Gaussian Images

The straightforward concatenation of neighborhood pixel data into a high dimensional state vector does not automatically induce invariance to non-constant albedo. A different representation is therefore required.

In our framework, the assumption is that while albedo may be substantially different from one point on the object to the next and uncorrelated with the geometry of the object, the statistics of the albedo within a larger semi-local region on the object surface is much more strongly correlated to the geometry. This is based on the observation that, at least for the classes of objects that we are interested in, the portion of albedo variation that is *independent* of the object geometry is often only of higher spatial frequencies. These high-frequency variations are substantially reduced by considering histogram-based features of larger regions on the object and image. On the other hand, the portion of albedo variation that directly depends on the object geometry can be preserved and used in the computation of mutual information.

The Extended Gaussian Images (EGI) [12] is a 3D shape descriptor obtained by having each polygon vote on the bin corresponding to its normal direction, with a weight equal to the area of the polygon. It is a global representation of the model as normals on all polygons are mapped spherically to the histogram (figure 3).

The Neighborhood EGI (NEGI) describes local shape of surface regions by grouping neighborhood surface normals according to their spherical coordinates (i.e. latitude and longitude)$\{\theta, \phi\}$. When building the EGI, one has to tessellate

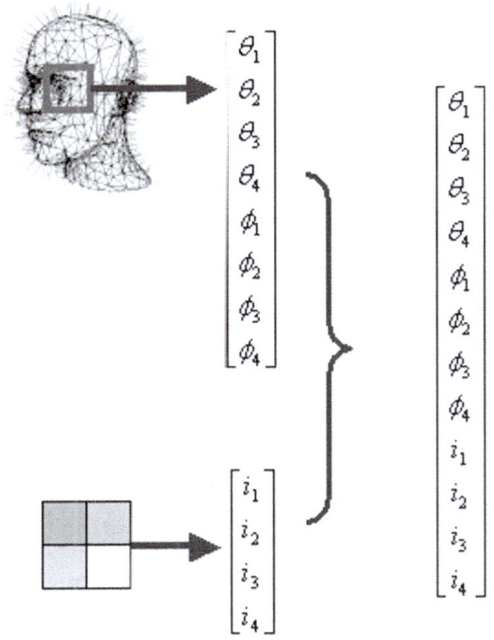

Fig. 3. High-dimensional point to include spatial information. The mannequin model is shown with normals on the triangles. For a 2D window on the projection screen of the 3D model, normals that fall within the window are collected. Spherical coordinates of each normal, N , are computed. Corresponding intensity values, I, in the image are collected. Both vectors then combined to form a high-dimensional point for estimation of joint entropy term in the mutual information formulation.

the Gaussian sphere into cells. These cells should have the same area and similar shape. As the NEGI represents local normals within a small region window, we can assume that the surface patch on the Gaussian sphere that corresponds to the region window is finely subdivided.

Normals are sampled from normal maps generated using OpenGL. All pixels on the object in the normal map have RGB corresponds to (x, y, z) of surface normals on surface points at the pixel locations. An example normal map is shown in figure 4. We note that instead of one normal for a polygon with area A on the geometric model, normals are *continuous* on the normal map. Therefore when only normals within a small 2D window on the normal map are considered, we can assume that the model has very high resolution and unit weight is associated with each normal sample.

Fig. 4. A sample normal map for a car model. We uniformly sample pixel locations on the normal map. RGB values of each pixel correspond to (x, y, z) components of surface normal at the pixel location.

As shown in figure 3, for a normal sample n on the normal map, neighboring normals within a 2D region window w (in this case, a 2 by 2 window) are collected to form a high-dimensional vector N:

$$N = \{\theta_1, \theta_2, \theta_3, \theta_4, \phi_1, \phi_2, \phi_3, \phi_4\}$$

and the corresponding image intensity values are collected to form the high-dimensional vector, I. N and I are then concatenated to form a high-dimensional point p:

$$p = \{\theta_1, \theta_2, \theta_3, \theta_4, \phi_1, \phi_2, \phi_3, \phi_4, i_1, i_2, i_3, i_4\}$$

4.1 Algorithm

The algorithm proceeds as follows:

- Given an object A and image B, render normal map of object A at current pose, generate sample locations on the normal map.
- For each sample location on the normal map, collect N and I. Concatenate N and I to form p.
- For n sample locations, we have n high-dimensional points, p_i, $P = [p_1, p_2, ..., p_n]$.
- Calculate covariance of the points [9], $C = (1/n)P_0 P_0^T$, where P_0 is zero-mean of P.
- Calculate joint entropy using $H_g(C)$ and marginal entropies using the method described in [9].

5 Experimental Results

5.1 Alignment Using the NEGI

In the first experiment, we looked at misalignment with respect to rotational offsets along the y-axis. Region mutual information is plotted with varying neighborhood sizes ($r = 2$, $r = 3$, $r = 4$, $r = 5$) (figure 5). As we consider region mutual information with larger neighborhoods, more spatial information is included and we get a stronger peak at the global optimum. This distinctiveness of the response at the ground truth point will help to reduce ambiguity, as shown in the following detection experiments.

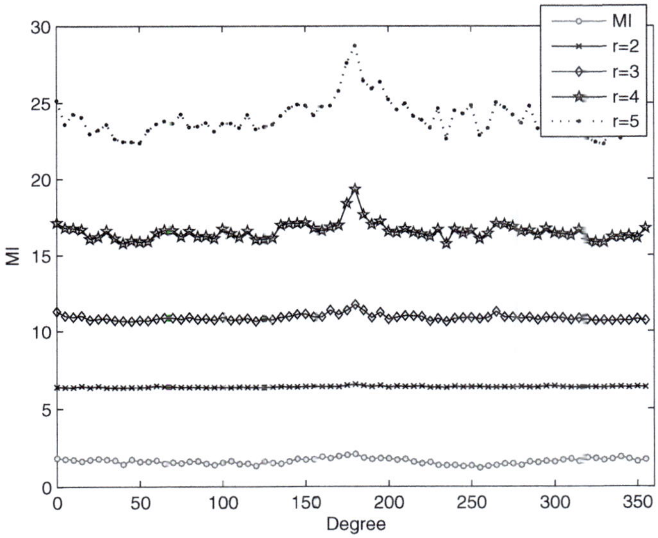

Fig. 5. Combined plots of RMI as a function of rotational misalignment in the y-axis with neighborhoods of varying sizes ($r = 2$, $r = 3$, $r = 4$, $r = 5$) to clearly show that a stronger peak is obtained at the global optimum when more spatial information is brought into the metric, thus reducing ambiguity when comparing model to image data. Original MI is also plotted in the graph.

5.2 Detection

For comparing detection performances, we did a naive search of the pose space. This allows us to obtain the global optimal pose parameters, without having to worry about the issues of local optimums and convergence failures. We manually aligned a detailed 3D car model to the test image (some of the test images are shown in figure 6). Ground truth poses for the model are recorded. When plotting the receiver operating characteristics (ROC) curves, these ground truth poses are the true positives. The average of the mutual information values at the

Fig. 6. Test images

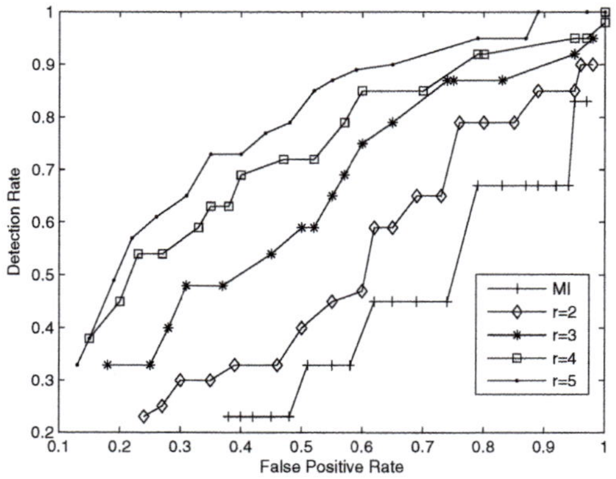

Fig. 7. ROC curves for RMI and MI

ground truth poses is used as detection threshold. ROC curves for original MI and RMI with varying neighborhood sizes are shown in figure 7. The plots show that when spatial information is included, there is gain in detection performance.

6 Conclusion

This paper presents a method to align 3D geometric model to image using mutual information (MI) as similarity measure. While MI has enjoyed a great deal of success in the medical image registration domain, its application to general object detection has been limited, one major reason being its failure in capturing longer-range information when comparing model to image data. To solve this issue, we propose to use a region-based method so that ambiguity due to albedo variance is reduced when spatial information is included. We defined the Neighborhood Extended Gaussian Images for the case of 3D model-2D image alignment. Experiments showed that the method works better than the original formulation. In the future, we plan to include regional edge information in the mutual information calculation, which we believe would make the metric more discriminative. Additionally, we have made some progress in designing an approach to allowing this framework to run much more quickly [13]. We would also like to validate the method more extensively with other data set.

References

1. Viola, P.: Alignment by Maximization of Mutual Information. PhD thesis, Massachusetts Institute of Technology (1995)
2. Pluim, J., Maintz, J., Viergiver, M.: Mutual information based registration of medical images: A survey. IEEE Transcations on Medical Imaging **22** (2003) 986–1004
3. Campbell, R., Flynn, P.: A survey of free-form object representation and recognition techniques. Computer Vision and Image Understanding **81** (2001) 166–210
4. Suveg, I., Gosselman, G.: Mutual information based evaluation of 3D building models. In: Proceedings of the International Conference on Pattern Recognition. Volume 3., Quebec City, Canada (2002) 188–197
5. Kollnig, H., Nagel, N.: 3D pose estimation by directly matching polyhedral models to gray value gradients. International Journal of Computer Vision **23** (1997) 283–302
6. Tan, T., Sullivan, G., Baker, K.: Model-based localization and recognition of road vehicles. International Journal of Computer Vision **27** (1998) 5–25
7. Maes, F., Collignon, A., Vandermeulen, D., Marchal, G., Suetens, P.: Multimodality image registration by maximization of mutual information. IEEE Transactions on Medical Imaging **16** (1997) 187–198
8. Cover, T., Thomas, J.: Elements of Information Theory. John Wiley (1991)
9. Russakoff, D., Tomasi, C., Rohlfing, T., Maurer, C.: Image similarity using mutual information of regions. In: Proceedings of the European Conference on Computer Vision, Prague, Czech Republic (2004) 596–607
10. Leventon, M., Wells III, W., Grimson, W.: Multiple view 2D-3D mutual information registration. In: DARPA Image Understanding Workshop. (1997) 625–630
11. Shannon, C.: A mathematical theory of communication. The Bell System Technical Journal **27** (1948) 379–423
12. Horn, B.: Extended gaussian images. Proceedings of the IEEE **72** (1984) 1656–1678
13. Pong, H., Cham, T.: Object detection using a cascade of 3D models. In: Proceedings of the Asian Conference on Computer Vision, Hyderabad, India (2006)

The Eigen-Transform and Applications

Alireza Tavakoli Targhi[1], Eric Hayman[1],
Jan-Olof Eklundh[1], and Mehrdad Shahshahani[2]

[1] Computational Vision and Active Perception Laboratory, School of Computer Science and Communication, Royal Institute of Technology (KTH), SE-100 44, Stockholm, Sweden
{att, hayman, joe}@nada.kth.se
[2] Institute for Studies in Theoretical Physics and Mathematics (IPM), Tehran, Iran
mehrdads@ipm.ir

Abstract. This paper introduces a novel texture descriptor, the *Eigen-transform.* The transform provides a measure of roughness by considering the eigenvalues of a matrix which is formed very simply by inserting the greyvalues of a square patch around a pixel directly into a matrix of the same size. The eigenvalue of largest magnitude turns out to give a smoothed version of the original image, but the eigenvalues of smaller magnitude encode high frequency information characteristic of natural textures. A major advantage of the Eigen-transform is that it does not fire on straight, or locally straight, brightness edges, instead it reacts almost entirely to the texture itself. This is in contrast to many other descriptors such as Gabor filters or the standard deviation of greyvalues of the patch. These properties make it remarkably well suited to practical applications. Our experiments focus on two main areas. The first is in bottom-up *visual attention* where textured objects pop out from the background using the Eigen-transform. The second is unsupervised *texture segmentation* with particular emphasis on real-world, cluttered indoor environments. We compare results with other state-of-the-art methods and find that the Eigen-transform is highly competitive, despite its simplicity and low dimensionality.

1 Introduction

Texture analysis has applications in several areas within computer vision such as image segmentation[15, 7], the classification of objects [19] or materials [9, 17, 10]. Many different descriptors for texture have been proposed such as filters, wavelets, co-occurrence matrices, energy measures from the Fourier transform, Markov random fields, local binary patterns, and texton histograms, to name but a few. In this paper we introduce a novel texture descriptor, the *Eigen-transform* which is derived in a manner very different to those descriptors reviewed above. The key idea is to investigate the eigenvalues of matrices formed directly from greyvalues of local patches. Eigenvalues play an important role in the analysis of many systems, for instance via linear ordinary differential equations, and can correspond to frequencies of vibration, critical values of stability parameters,

P.J. Narayanan et al. (Eds.): ACCV 2006, LNCS 3851, pp. 70–79, 2006.

energy levels of atoms and more. This inspired us to use eigenvalues to characterise image patches. More specifically, we consider a square patch around a pixel, insert the greyvalues of that patch into a matrix the same size as the original patch, and compute a descriptor as an average of some of those eigenvalues. It turns out that the eigenvalue with largest magnitudes essentially gives a smoothed version of the original image, but the *smaller* magnitudes eigenvalues encode high frequency variations characteristic of visual texture. This yields a texture descriptor with a number of properties which are desirable for bottom-up processing in real-world applications: (i) It captures small-scale structure in terms of roughness or smoothness of the image patch. (ii) It provides a compact representation which is easy to store and perform calculations on. (iii) Few parameters need tuning. The most significant parameter is a notion of scale provided by the size of the local image patch. (iv) Unlike most other texture descriptors, it does not generate spurious responses round brightness edges. (v) Last but not least, it is extremely easy to implement. Although the eigen-decomposition is commonly used in image processing and computer vision, to the best of our knowledge, and indeed somewhat to our surprise, it appears not to have been applied directly to the image patch in the manner proposed in the current paper. The quality of a texture-based algorithm should be defined as how well the final output agrees with human perception in tasks such as segmentation or classification. We demonstrate the effectiveness of the Eigen-transform in three applications: (i) *attention* for an autonomous robot; (ii) *texture segmentation* to locate textured areas in indoor scenes.

The rest of the paper is organised as follows. After reviewing some relevant literature in sec. 1.1, the Eigen-transform is presented in sec. 2. Applications are described in sec. 3 and conclusions are drawn in sec. 4.

1.1 Previous Work

The purpose of this section is to highlight differences between our work and previous papers which used the eigen-decomposition or SVD for related applications. Principal component analysis (PCA) performs eigen-decomposition of an $N \times N$ covariance matrix formed e.g. by considering N pixels as a single, large, vector. In recognition tasks it was used for objects [13] and faces [4] yielding a *global* rather than *local* representation since the entire object or face is captured. However, [5] used PCA to describe smaller image patches for texture segmentation. The singular value decomposition (SVD) has been applied to image compression and noise reduction [1]. The basic idea is to describe the original greyscale image as a matrix which is well approximated by its largest singular values and corresponding singular vectors, ignoring the contribution of the smaller singular values. Our work differs from the papers listed above in that (i) only the *smallest* eigenvalues are used; (ii) the eigenvectors (or singular vectors) are discarded completely; and (iii) unlike [13, 4, 5] we operate directly on local patches of greyscale images. In our own previous work [16] we studied the application of *singular values* within a similar framework to the current paper, while here we focus on *eigenvalues*.

2 Computing the Eigen-Transform

In this section we describe the computation of our texture descriptor based on the eigen-decomposition. We consider a $w \times w$ square neighbourhood centred at the pixel, and copy its greyvalues directly into a $w \times w$ real matrix, W. We proceed by computing the eigenvalues of W, taking their magnitude, and sorting them in decreasing order, $\{\|\lambda_1\|, \|\lambda_2\|, ..., \|\lambda_w\|\}$. We will not use the eigenvectors in this paper at all. At this stage we have a set of w numbers, the magnitude of the eigenvalues, describing each pixel in an image. What do these numbers tell us? This is best illustrated with an example. Fig. 1a shows an image of a table on which six different objects from a database [10] of materials are placed. Eigenvalues were computed from 32×32 patches. First consider the largest eigenvalue, $\|\lambda_1\|$, which is shown as an image in Fig. 1b where the intensities of the response image have been rescaled such that the highest response is white. It resembles a smoothed version of the original image, so the largest eigenvalue captures the DC component. This eigenvalue is therefore of no use for describing image texture. The smallest eigenvalue (Fig. 1d) corresponds to high frequencies, but is mainly noise. An intermediate eigenvalue (Fig. 1c) is somewhat similar to the smallest eigenvalue, but less noisy. It reveals some form of *roughness* of the texture: rougher regions like bread (labelled "3") appear light while smooth regions like cotton (labelled "5") appear dark in the eigenvalue response image, even though cotton was brighter than bread in the original image.

To reduce noise further we average over multiple eigenvalues, defining the *Eigen-transform*, Γ, at each pixel as

$$\Gamma(l, w) = \frac{1}{w - l + 1} \sum_{k=l}^{w} \|\lambda_k\| \quad , \quad 1 \leq l \leq w \ . \tag{1}$$

For a descriptor that reacts to texture as opposed to brightness, the largest few eigenvalues should be ignored; we typically choose l to be in the range $[2, w/3]$. An important aspect of this combination of eigenvalues is that it yields a more compact representation: w eigenvalues are reduced to a single number.

Fig. 1e shows the Eigen-transform for $l = 12$.

To further illustrate that the Eigen-transform responds to roughness, it was averaged over images of six different, natural materials. Fig. 2 shows the original images and the Eigen-transform values.

2.1 Interpretation of the Eigen-Transform

It is not trivial to explain exactly what properties are captured with the Eigen-transform, yet it is instructive to recall that the eigenvalues provide information about the dependence between rows and columns of the matrix W. In a patch of uniform brightness, all but the largest eigenvalue are zero. If any two rows or columns are identical, the matrix drops rank, that is the smallest eigenvalue becomes zero. If those two rows or columns are similar but not quite identical, the smallest eigenvalue will be close to, but not exactly equal to zero. Similarly,

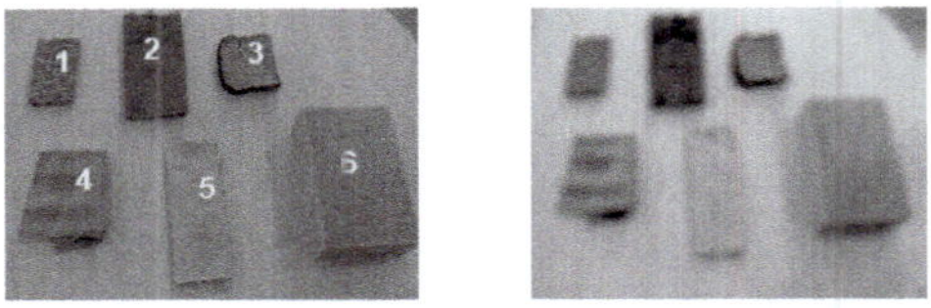

(a) Original image (b) Largest eigenvalue

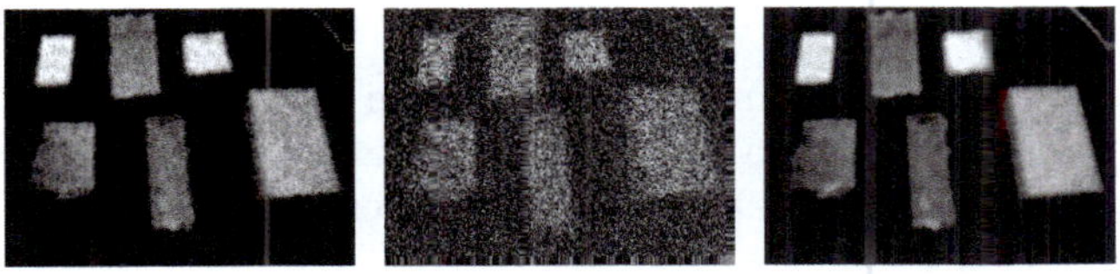

(c) 12th eigenvalue (d) Smallest eigenvalue (e) Averaging the 21 smallest eigenvalues

Fig. 1. A demonstration of what the eigenvalues of 32×32 image patches encode. (a) shows the original image with six materials placed on a table-top (1-cracker, 2-corduroy, 3-bread, 4-linen, 5-cotton, 6-sponge). (b) shows the largest eigenvalue which appears as a (brightened) smooth version of the original image. (c) and (d) show the 12th and 32nd eigenvalues respectively. (e) takes the mean of the 21 smallest eigenvalues, giving a less noisy response than in (c) and (d)

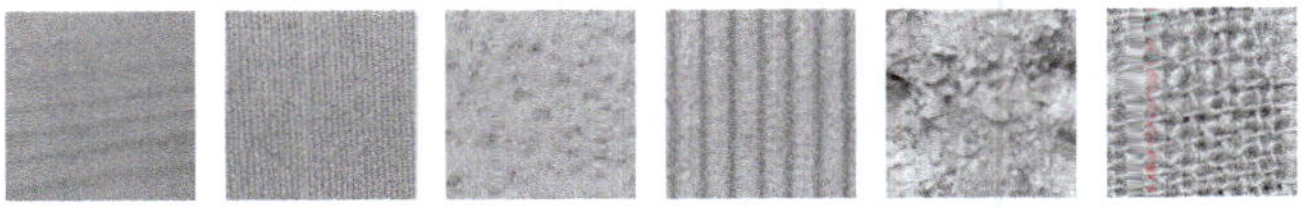

3.4 7.8 13.1 15.8 19.9 24.4

Fig. 2. The Eigen-transform $\Gamma(12, 32)$ on 6 materials from [10]. Higher scores are indicative of rough, coarse structure, while lower numbers correspond to smooth, fine materials.

n similar rows or columns yield $n-1$ small eigenvalues. Already at this stage we may therefore state that the Eigen-transform $\Gamma(l, w)$ of the $w \times w$ image patch W will be low if there is little variation in the rows or columns of W, implying that there is little 2D texture. It is also easy to think of patches that produce high values of the Eigen-transform. First, uncorrelated high-magnitude noise is clearly highly unlikely to produce linearly dependent rows or columns, and we may expect the same to apply to stochastic visual texture arising from natural materials. Second, a diagonal edge or bar produces independent rows and columns. We observe that a patch containing any number of horizontal or vertical brightness step edges will have zero Eigen-transform if $l > 1$. On the other hand another single channel approach like taking the standard deviation of greyvalues at each $w \times w$ patch, (see e.g. [20]) exhibits a strong response at illumination edges which tends to dominate over actual small-scale image structure.

2.2 The Minimum-Response Eigen-Transform

A simple solution to the problem of spurious responses at diagonal brightness edges is obtained by rotating the image patch at regular intervals between 0° and 90°, recomputing the Eigen-transform at each interval, and then storing only the *minimum* response over orientation θ,

$$\Gamma_{MR}(l, w, W) = \min_{\theta} \{\Gamma(l, w, \mathcal{R}_\theta(W)\} \ , \tag{2}$$

where $\mathcal{R}_\theta(W)$ represents the image patch rotated by θ. Note that it is sufficient to consider only a 90° interval since the eigenvalues of a matrix are invariant to rotations of the matrix by 90° . We found intervals of $\theta = 30°$ sufficient, implying that two rotated images need be created. The Minimum-Response Eigen-transform $\Gamma_{MR}(l, w)$ will be used by default in the remainder of this paper . It will be compared with the regular Eigen-transform in sec. 2.3.

2.3 The Effects of Illumination Change

A multiplicative scaling a of greyvalues within a patch, $W \to aW$, gives an Eigen-transform of $\Gamma(l, w, aW) = a\ \Gamma(l, w, W)$ from the property that $\lambda(aW) = a\ \lambda(W)$. Unfortunately, results are hard to predict for more complicated models involving for instance an additive term $W \to aW + b$.

We therefore settle for demonstrating robustness to lighting changes empirically. Fig. 3 shows the same image as Fig. 1 but with some squares of the original image artificially brightened or darkened in PhotoShop. In the Eigen-transform image (Fig. 3b) it is impossible to detect the presence of squares with edges of horizontal and vertical orientations, the Eigen-transform responds to the texture as opposed to the overall brightness. There are also a couple of diagonally oriented squares. Their edges give rise to a high response, as was predicted in Sec 2.1. However, using the Minimum Response Eigen-transform presented in Sec 2.2, it is possible to remove also these edges (Fig. 3c). It would, for instance, be easy to segment this transform image, despite the variations in illumination.

3 Applications

We now present results which use the eigen-transform in practical real-world applications. Our overall goal is a system for recognising objects or object categories, intended for use on autonomous, indoor assistive robots. Inspired by human visual processing, such a system may be split into three stages, (1) attention, (2) segmentation, and (3) recognition.

3.1 Attention and Object Detection

Attention [8, 18] concerns locating and ranking salient parts of the image, enabling subsequent processing to focus on a reduced amount of visual data. In our

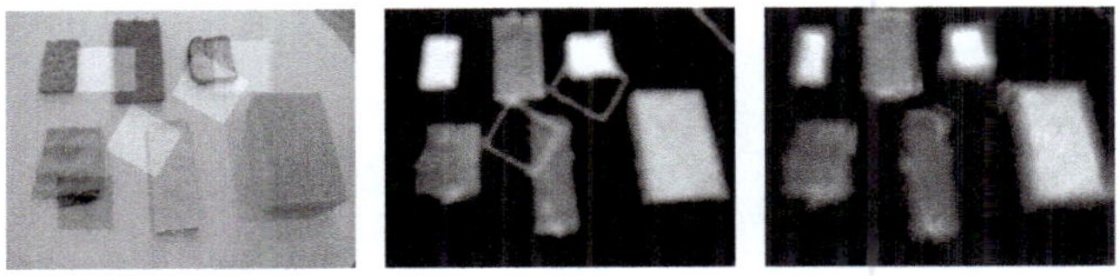

(a) Original image (b) Regular Eigen-transform $\Gamma(12, 32)$ (c) Minimum-Response Eigen-transform $\Gamma_{\mathrm{MR}}(12, 32)$

Fig. 3. The Eigen-transform is remarkably robust to illumination changes. (a) shows the same image as Fig. 1a, but four squares have been artificially brightened, and one darkened. The Eigen-transform in its original form (b) is robust to the horizontally-oriented squares and the internal regions of the diagonal squares, but responds to diagonal edges. The Minimum-Response Eigen-transform (c) is robust to edges of all orientations.

(a) Detected objects (b) $\Gamma_{\mathrm{MR}}(12, 32)$ (c) Segmentation

Fig. 4. An experiment using the Eigen-transform as a saliency map (b) for attention for a mobile robot. The objects on the table have saliency values of 57 and 50 whereas the next highest value (corresponding to the chair) is 20. Results using a very simple segmentation method by thresholding are also shown (c).

work the goal is to obtain a bottom-up texture cue capable of identifying the location and physical extent of objects. We demonstrate that the Eigen-transform may be used directly to form a saliency map well-suited to this purpose.

In a first experiment (Fig. 4), small, man-made textured objects on a table pop out from the striped tablecloth, and the wooden cupboards at the top of the image also have a much lower response. Our results compare very favourably with the method of [18] based on multiple cues. It appears that the Eigen-transform would provide an excellent texture feature for their system (they used edge filters).

We also show results from a more complex desktop scenario in Fig. 5. The scene was imaged from two very different positions, and a desk-lamp was turned off after the first image was taken. Various items are detected. The Minimum Response Eigen-transform was used. The same regions are detected as salient in both images, apart from the monitor where the screensaver blanked the screen after the first image. This degree of repeatability is not merely interesting for attention, it is also of potential use in wide-baseline matching, though we have not investigated this possibility further.

(a) Original image

(b) Objects detected in (a) via the Eigen-transform

(c) Same scene as (a), but with different pose and lighting

(d) Objects detected in (c) via the Eigen-transform

Fig. 5. Attention in complex, desktop scenes. Interesting objects are detected.

3.2 Texture Segmentation for Material Classification

Many objects are characterised not by their colour or shape, but by the material of which they are made, which in turn may be captured by the visual texture. Performing a segmentation based on texture can assist during subsequent classification of the materials.

Fig. 6a shows an image from a rather cluttered kitchen cupboard in which we placed a sponge, a slice of bread and a cracker, all of which are objects best represented by their visual texture as opposed to other cues. All three objects are evident in the Eigen-transform in Fig. 6b. Also note that the brightness edges caused by the shelves and frame of the cupboard are invisible in the transform, thus the descriptor is truly responding to texture and not to brightness edges. This transform image may then be input to a segmentation algorithm for greyscale images, the argument being that this transform image is easier to segment than the original greyscale or colour image. Fig. 6a shows good results achieved with publicly available code for JSEG [7, 6]. All three objects have been successfully segmented out from the background, and the number of other regions is remarkably low. Unlike some other methods from the literature, it was not necessary to supply the number of segments to the segmentation algorithm. This is a crucial requirement for fully unsupervised systems. As a proof of concept [1], this segmentation was used before computing a dense representa-

[1] As yet we have performed very few experiments on this, so by no means do we wish to give the impression that this is a solved problem.

(a) Original Image showing segmentation from the Eigen-transform in (b)

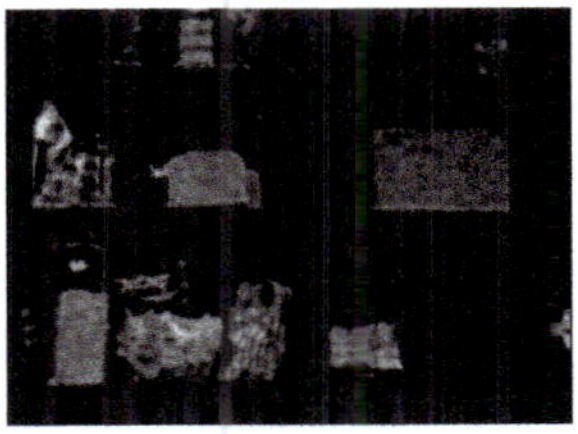

(b) The Eigen-transform $\Gamma_{\mathrm{MR}}(12, 32)$

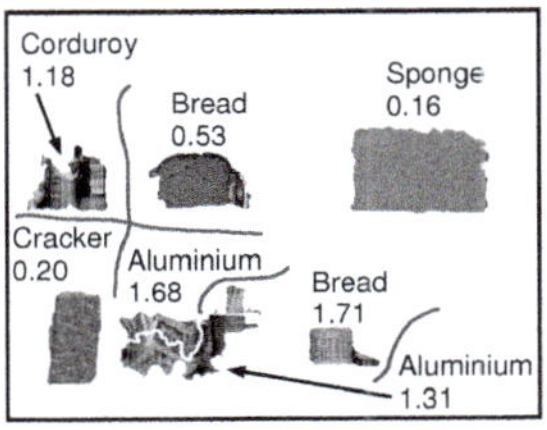

(c) Classification results. Nearest-Neighbour distances (×100) and the closest class.

(d) Segmentation from JSEG on RGB image gives a higher number of candidate regions.

Fig. 6. Segmenting materials out from a cluttered kitchen cupboard. JSEG was applied to the Eigen-transform (a-b). (c) The three materials for which models were trained are correctly identified with low distances to the training set, whereas "junk" regions have much higher distances and may therefore be removed by thresholding the distance.

tion of each region in an attempt to classify the materials. All three objects are taken from a ten-class database for material classification [10]. For each region we posed the question which of the ten materials it most closely resembled, and with what score. We used multi-scale histograms of LBP descriptors [17] and a Nearest-Neighbour classifier using the χ^2-distance between histograms as the similarity measure. Fig. 6c shows that all three materials were classified correctly. Note that all regions are forced to make a decision, but that the distances for the "junk" regions were considerably higher. Therefore it should be possible to set a threshold on this distance such that those segments would be labelled "unknown".

We also performed comparisons with other state-of-the-art texture segmentation algorithms. By applying JSEG [7, 6] directly to the RGB image (Fig. 6d), all three materials were successfully segmented out. Yet since JSEG combines both texture and colour information there are also many regions of constant colour as opposed to texture. Thus, if our task is to look for and recognise an object which we know, from training, is well characterised by its texture, we can save a lot of computation time in the recognition stage by using the segmentation from Fig. 6a rather than Fig. 6d since there are fewer regions to

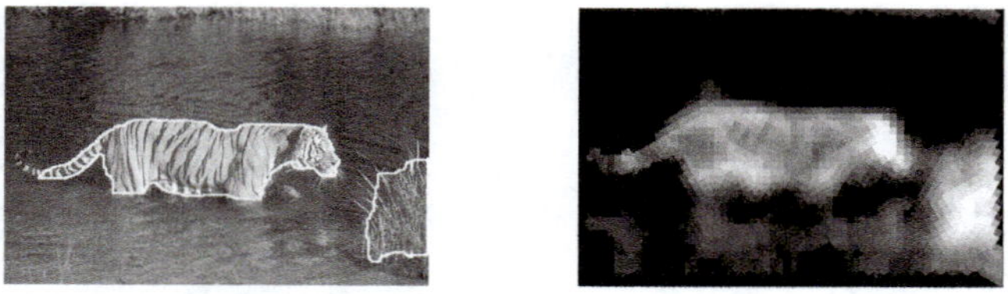

(a)Segmentation result (b) The eigen-transform $\Gamma_{\mathrm{MR}}(12, 32)$

Fig. 7. Using the Eigen-transform for segmentation of a sample image from the Berkeley database [12]

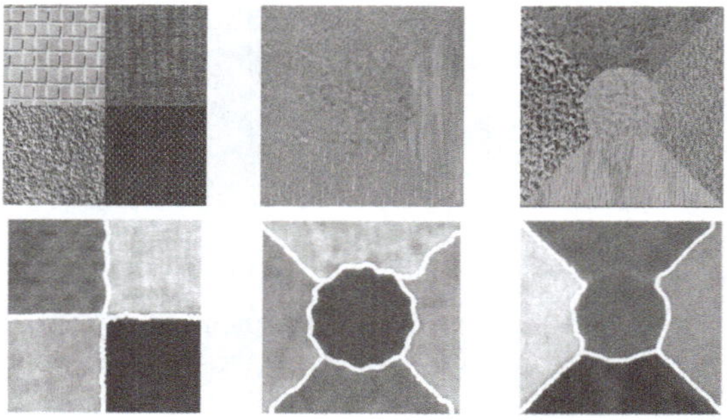

Fig. 8. Segmentation results for [2] and [14]. Mean-Shift is applied to the Eigen-transform. With only a single channel in the descriptor, it is obviously not possible to separate all textures, as in the rightmost example.

process. In experiments (not depicted due to space limitations) we also tested Normalised Cuts [21] using filter-bank texton histograms [11] as features. This yielded many superfluous regions. Similar results were obtained with Mean-Shift [3] on the RGB image. Other texture segmentation resuls are shown in Fig. 7 and Fig. 8.

4 Discussion

In this paper we presented a novel descriptor for texture, particularly well-suited to applications in autonomous indoor assistive robots. It is extremely easy to implement, reasonably fast to compute, and requires very little tuning of parameters. It responds to natural textures, but not to brightness edges, implying that spurious regions are not detected around those edges. As such it is very well suited for bottom-up attention or object detection, and it shows great promise for segmenting different materials out from the background with a view to subsequent classification. In our current work we are attempting to further interpret exactly what the eigenvalues represent, although this is by no means trivial. A promising framework is in the correlations of pixels with their neighbouring pixels, as modelled by 2D Markov random fields.

Acknowledgments

The support from the European Commission within the project MUSCLE (A. Tavakoli Targhi) and the Swedish Foundation for Strategic Research within the project VISCOS (E. Hayman) is gratefully acknowledged.

References

1. S. O. Aase, J. H. Husy and P. Waldemar. A critique of SVD-based image coding systems. In *Proc. ISCAS* pages 4:13–16, 1999.
2. P. Brodatz. *Textures*. Dover, 1966.
3. D. Comaniciu and P. Meer. Mean shift analysis and applications. In *Proc. ICCV*, pages 1197 – 1203, 1999.
4. T. Cootes, G. Edwards, and C. Taylor. Active appearance models. *PAMI*, 23(6):681–685, June 2001.
5. D. de Ridder, J. Kittler, O. Lemmers, and R. Duin. The adaptive subspace map for texture segmentation. In *Proc. ICPR*, 2000.
6. Y. Deng and B. Manjunath. JSEG. http://vision.ece.ucsb.edu/segmentation/jseg/software/, 1999.
7. Y. Deng and B. Manjunath. Unsupervised segmentation of color-texture regions in images and video. *PAMI*, 23(8):800–810, 2001.
8. L. Itti, C. Koch, and E. Niebur. A model of saliency-based visual attention for rapid scene analysis. *PAMI*, 20(11):1254–1259, 1998.
9. T. Leung and J. Malik. Representing and recognizing the visual appearance of materials using three-dimensional textons. *IJCV*, 43(1):29–44, June 2001.
10. P. Mallikarjuna, M. Fritz, A. Tavakoli Targhi, E. Hayman, B. Caputo and J.-O. Eklundh. The KTH-TIPS2 databases. www.nada.kth.se/cvap/databases/kth-tips
11. J. Malik, S. Belongie, T. Leung, and J. Shi. Contour and texture analysis for image segmentation. *IJCV*, 43(1):7–27, June 2001.
12. D. Martin, C. Fowlkes, D. Tal, and J. Malik. A database of human segmented natural images and its application to evaluating segmentation algorithms and measuring ecological statistics. In *Proc. ICCV*, volume 2, pages 416–423, July 2001
13. H. Murase and S. Nayar. Visual learning and recognition of 3D objects from appearance. *IJCV*, 14(1), 1995.
14. T. Ojala, T. Mäenpää, M. Pietikäinen, J. Viertola, J. Kyllonen, and S. Huovinen. Outex: New framework for empirical evaluation of texture analysis algorithms. In *Proc. ICPR*, pages I: 701–706, 2002.
15. T. Ojala and M. Pietikainen. Unsupervised texture segmentation using feature distributions. *Pattern Recognition*, 32(3):477–486, March 1999.
16. A. Tavakoli Targhi and A. Shademan. Clustering of Singular Value Decomposition of Image Data with Applications to Texture Classification. In *Proc. SPIE*, Vol. 5150, pp. 972-979, July 2003.
17. M. Pietikainen, T. Nurmela, T. Maenpaa, and M. Turtinen. View-based recognition of real-world textures. *Pattern Recognition*, 37(2):313–323, February 2004.
18. O. Ramström and H. Christensen. Object detection using background context. In *Proc. ICPR*, pages III: 45-48, 2004.
19. B. Schiele and J. Crowley. Recognition without correspondence using multidimensional receptive field histograms. *IJCV*, 36(1):31–50, January 2000.
20. E. Sharon, A. Brandt, and R. Basri. Segmentation and Boundary Detection Using Multiscale Intensity Measurements. In *Proc. CVPR*, pages I: 469–476, 2001.
21. J. Shi and J. Malik. Normalized cuts and image segmentation. *PAMI* 22(8), Aug 2000.

Edge-Model Based Representation of Laplacian Subbands*

Malay K. Nema and Subrata Rakshit

Centre for Artificail Intelligence and Robotics,
High Grounds, Bangalore, India 560001
{malay, subrata}@cair.res.in

Abstract. Multiresolution subbands have a characteristic structure composed of sparse positive and negetive linear patterns present in close spatial proximity. This implies that there must be efficient ways to represent these subband images as compared to general images. Pixel and block transform approaches based on regular spatial sampling are unale to take this structure into account. This work introduces a novel way of representing Laplacian subbands using (oriented) edge elements. The representation is based on selecting an appropriate set of 7×7 primitives that captures the type of structures present in Laplacians. Unlike contourlets, the primitive set does not constitute a basis but has the twin advantages of small set size and close correspondence between set elements and edge elements that can be interpolated using prior models. As the chosen primitive set is not a basis, the computed representation is formulated by matching given primitives to various image regions, as opposed to decomposing given regions in terms of a basis set. This representation can be used for edge sharpness preserving magnification required in super resolution. The representation can also be exploited for lossy compression and noise removal

Index terms: subband representation, primitive set, image magnification, scale-space interpolation, super-resolution.

1 Introduction

The ability to interpolate subbands across scales is relevant in the context of compression, super resolution and multiresolution theory. One approach has been to study the values of subband pixels across scales in order to predict pixel values for (assumed) higher resolution scales. The correlation across scales for zero (small) pixels is at the heart of the Zero Tree Wavelet [1] based coding schemes. Mallat and Zhong [2] have studied the variation of pixel values across subband scales to classify discontuities into three categories and predict pixel values in higher resolution scales. Freeman et. al. have used Markov Random Fields [3] to learn characteristics of Laplacians to synthesize high frequency details. Similar

* This work was funded by DRDO through Proj CAR-008. Authors wish to thank Director CAIR, ISYS-DO and colleagues in CVG for their support.

P.J. Narayanan et al. (Eds.): ACCV 2006, LNCS 3851, pp. 80–89, 2006.

learning based approaches form the basis of various learning based super resolution schemes [4] [5]. Greenspan and Anderson had formulated a scale-space interpolation scheme based on the idea of using existing high frequency components in images to introduce coherent higher frequencies that would enhance edges on magnification [6]. Inter-subband prediction also forms the basis of Symmetric Residue pyramids [7] that are a more sparse pyramid representation than the Laplacian pyramids [8]. In general, the correlation across subbands arise because strong step edges give rise to coherent harmonics at all scales. Knowing the components at one scale, it should be possible to predict the *coherent* high frequency harmonics. Alternately, one can postulate the sharpness of edges and introduce the required coherent harmonics at the (synthesized) higher level subbands to ensure that edges remain sharp after image magnification. Iterative super resolution schemes that need to create a putative high resolution image would benefit from such a technique. The present work is aimed at developing such a scheme for synthesis of Laplacian subbands having coherent high frequencies. As explained below, an ability to model subbands using suitable primitives is essential for this task.

In this work we represent Laplacians using a small set of fixed modelling elements, called the Primitive Set (PS). The endeavour is to have a fixed set of primitives that can suffice for all images, requiring no image specific learning. The scope of this paper is limited to showing that Laplacians can be satisfactorily modelled using a small set of functions that are suitable for later interpolation. The main challenges addressed here are the selection of model elements and the computation of a representation using a set that does not constitute a basis.

2 Representation of Laplacians with Primitive Set

The Burt Laplacian are composed of tightly coupled positive and negetive ridges, with the ridge width dependent on the filter order (W) for sharp edges. As shown in Figure 1, the Laplacians can be easily distinguished from randomly generated zero-mean images. It would appear that it should be easy to come up with an image model for Laplacians that explitly captures their characteristic linear structures. Unfortunately, any *arbitrary* $W \times W$ subimage is not guaranteed to be zero-mean or have both the positive and negetive linear patterns. As a result, when a PCA is done on a large sample set of $W \times W$ extracts from Laplacian subbands, the result looks similar to that for regular Gaussian images (in effect, one gets the DCT basis). When Laplacian images are represented as collection of individual pixel values (raw) or even as coefficients of a transform (Fourier transform, block DCT), it is not possible to manipulate these images in a manner consistent with their inherent structure. Consider the problem of having a Laplacian subband for a simple image (a solid square on a blank background) and trying to create the next level Laplacian. As shown in Figure 2, pixel based interpolation creates an uncharacteristically low frequency subband (Fig 2b) which will blur the edges in the resulting Gaussian. One would like to preserve the edge location but create a higher frequency subband like that shown in

Figure 2c. In effect, one would like to create linear structures of twice the length, corresponding to the ones present at the lower resolution, but without doubling the width of the structures. This paper formulates a model based representation of Laplacians that will allow one to synthesize magnified Laplacians with correct edge widths. This is in contrast to the work of Simoncelli [9] and Greenspan [10] that model edges present in images with oriented Laplacians. The work on image interpolation by Li and Orchard [11] is similar in intent to our work. The edges in images are interpolated anisotropically to preserve sharpness. However, they do not use multiscale intermediates and models. As a result, that approach cannot provide the flexibility to do prior-based interpolation, lossy compression, noise removal etc. that our model based representation allows.

We use the Laplacain pyramid as our multiresolution representation of choice, rather than the wavelets, as Laplacians are not critically subsampled. The edges representations in Laplacians are smooth and regular. In contrast, wavelet subbands - even when the three directional subbands are upsampled and combined - have irregular edges due to critical sampling. This effect is illustrated with an example in Figure 3. The Laplacian is made with a 5×5 filter and *daub6* wavelet H1, V1 and D1 subbands have been upsampled and combined to make it comparable to the non-directional Laplacian.

The approach used here is more akin to vector quantization than decomposition using basis functions. Vector quantization techniques do not require a basis set, but they also attempt to model extracts from an image sampled from a fixed grid. The proposed method therefore differs from standard VQ techniques in three ways: (i) it uses a fixed, small sized codebook, (ii) it uses a signal de-

a b c

Fig. 1. Laplacian images: (a), (c). Zero mean image: (b).

a b c

Fig. 2. Laplacian of square subband (L_0)

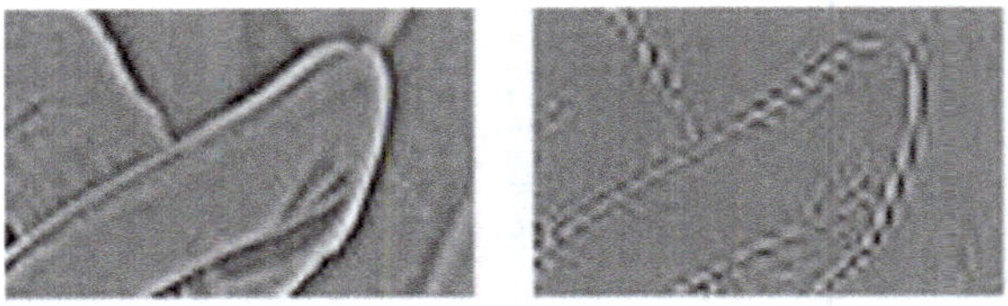

Fig. 3. Laplacian (left) and wavelet (right) edges

pendent sampling process to model what it can using the limited codebook and (iii) the reconstruction process uses a differect codebook in order to achieve the desired anisotropic interpolation between subbands at various levels. We select the model elements using our judgement to mirror the typical patterns found in Laplacians at the $W \times W$ scale. Then we move the model elements over the Laplacians to find $W \times W$ subimages that they can best model. The criteria for selecting members of the Primitive Set and the algorithm for computing the representation are described in detail in this section.

2.1 Selection of Primitive Set Elements

In order to generate the Primitive Set (PS) for Laplacians created with a 5-tap filter, we consider the various basic edges that may be defined at in a 7×7 window. In terms of ease of interpolation, straight edges would be the simplest: one can define model elements of twice the length along the same orientation to create a longer edge. In a 7×7 window, one can create edges with eight distinct orientations - at 0, 22.5, 45, 67.5, 90, 112.5, 135 and 157.5 degs. The PS with these 8 elements is designated as PS8. In order to capture sharp curves and isolated spots, additional elements would be needed to enhance the modelling ability. The four quadrants of a disk edge (radius = 4) were used to define four additional elements. For modelling spots, two more elements were defined using edges defined by a single pixel spot and a 3×3 blob. This enhanced primitive set, PS14, will need slightly more complex rules for interpolation than PS8 in order to deal with the curves and spots. However, the ability to deal with sharp curves was considered essential for modelling Laplacians of natural scenes. Images were created with the above type of sharp edges and their resulting Laplacian patterns were extracted to form PS14. These patterns are shown in Figure 4a.

It was found that though the representation based on PS14 was visually satisfactory, thick edges were not modelled accurately. The top most Laplacian subband, L_0, captures frequencies ranging from the highest frequencies to the midfrequency region. Primitives based only on abrupt edges were inadequate to model the smoother edges. To capture these, another set of 14 primitives were introduced based on slightly smoothed edges as shown in Figure 4b. This combined set of 14 sharp and 14 smoother patterns constitute the primitive set PS28 (Fig 4). The interpolation set corresponding to PS28 is constructed by synthetically creating the corresponding Gaussian images at twice the scale, computing their Laplacians and extracting 15×15 subimages. This set constitutes the

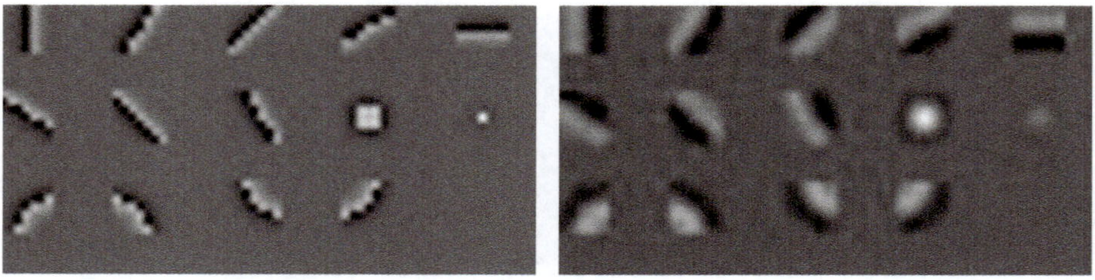

(a) PS14 elements based on sharp edges (b) 14 elements based on smoother edges

Fig. 4. The PS28 primitive set elements. The 7×7 elements, scaled for display.

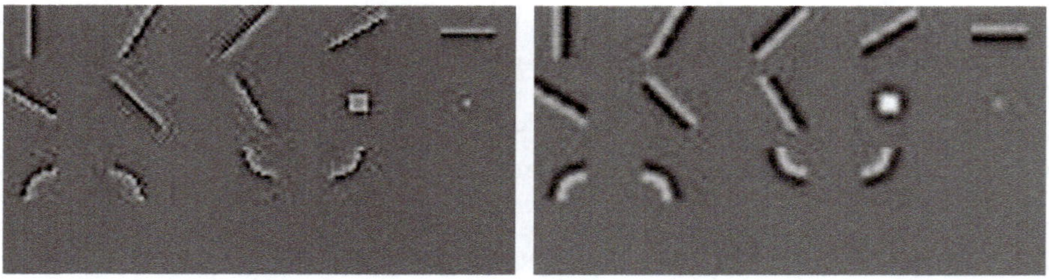

(a) Interpolation elements for sharp edges (b) Interpolation elements for smoother edges

Fig. 5. The IPS28 set elements. 15×15 images, scaled for disply.

Interpolation Primitive Set, IPS28. As can be seen from Figure 5, these elements are similar to those of PS28, except in the length to width ratios of the edge patterns.

2.2 Computing the Representation

The PS28 elements are defined as 7×7 images. At that image size there will be 49 degrees of freedom, requiring a basis set to have 49 elements. PS28 clearly does not have the ability to serve as a basis set (even if one were to perform an orthogonalisation procedure). As mentioned earlier, the problem simplifies if one moves away from the task of representing arbitrary 7×7 blocks to selecting 7×7 blocks that can be represented using the PS. The expectation is that the structure in Laplacians will enable such a method to create a reasonably good approximation. The method needs to be iterative as a given pixel or area could be covered by many possible 7×7 windows. One would like to first model those areas where the residual error will be small compared to the signal that is modelled. Subsequently, one could model both the initial residual errors and the unmodelled regions of the previous iterations. Hence we iterate the modelling process in a way that picks the Laplacian edges in the following order.

1. High amplitude edges that have a good fit to an element of the PS
2. Lower amplitude edges that have a good fit to an element of the PS

3. High amplitude edges that do not have a good fit to an element of the PS
4. Lower amplitude edges that do not have a good fit to an element of the PS

The quantification for the above enumerated criteria is done on the basis of energy and modeling error. For each 7×7 block extracted from the laplacian image, the following are computed. The energy of the extract determines the amount of signal present. Laplacians, like all subbands, are zero-mean and sparse. The energy is concentrated in only a few areas. Only blocks having energy above a threshold are considered for modelling. The threshold is initially set high and reduced with each iteration till it reaches a lower cut off. This cut off determines the termination of the iterative process, as errors below this threshold will not be further modelled. For blocks where the energy crosses the current threshold,the block is considered for modelling by elements of the primitive set (PS14 or PS28). Denoting the PS elements as $\boldsymbol{p_i}$ and the block to be modelled as $\boldsymbol{x}$, we need to find the model element and associated scalar α that minimises

$$J(\alpha, i) = ||(\mathbf{x} - \alpha.\mathbf{p_i})|| \tag{1}$$

For a given $\mathbf{p_i}$, the best α is given by

$$\alpha_{opt} = \frac{\mathbf{p_i}.\mathbf{x}}{||\mathbf{p_i}||} \tag{2}$$

A search over the elements gives the best fit. However, one cannot straight away commit to this modelling decision as it is possible that a neighboring (overlapping) extract may produce a $\boldsymbol{x}$ that is more ammenable for modelling. Thus a relaxation process is required to ensure that the best possible fits are committed first. This requires another iterative procedure, runing outside the iteration for energy, that ensures that better fits are explored and committed first. The quality of fit, γ, is defined as the ratio of the energy of the residual to the original when approximated by a $\boldsymbol{p_i}$ using the optimum α as given above.

$$\gamma = \frac{||\boldsymbol{x} - \alpha.\boldsymbol{p_i}||}{||\boldsymbol{x}||} \tag{3}$$

In performing the modelling, quantization effects arising due to integer arithmetic become significant. The edge signatures for low amplitude edges differ from that due to high amplitude edges. As we did not want to expand PS28 to include separate elements for low amplitudes, we introduced dynamic scaling of the model elements, prior to the computation of α. As the α computed above is determined both by the quality of fit (dot product between the vectors) and the relative norms of the two vectors, it cannot be used to determine the right scale factor. This factor, β, is computed based on the ratio of peak-to-peak amplitudes between the $\boldsymbol{x}$ and the $\boldsymbol{p_i}$. The scaled model element, $\beta.\boldsymbol{p_i}$ computed with integer precision, is then used in the computation of α and γ.

2.3 Modelling Algorithm

The parameters for modelling a given Laplacian using a primitive set can be computated as follows.

1. Set the modelling error threshold, Th_m, to 0 (or a very low value)
2. Set the energy threshold Th_e to a high value (say 20,000)
3. Extract 7×7 subimages, $\boldsymbol{x}$, from the Laplacian using single pixel shifts.
4. Check if the energy of this block, $(E(\boldsymbol{x}))$, is above Th_e. If $E(\boldsymbol{x}) < Th_e$, proceed to the next $\boldsymbol{x}$
5. Find the best model element from the PS by computing β, α and γ for each $\boldsymbol{p_i}$. Let the minimum γ be γ^* for element $\boldsymbol{p_{i^*}}$
6. If $\gamma^* < Th_m$, then commit $\alpha(\beta.\boldsymbol{p_{i^*}}$ as the representation for $\boldsymbol{x}$. Update $\boldsymbol{x}$ to $\boldsymbol{x} - \alpha(\beta.\boldsymbol{p_{i^*}}$ in the Laplacian.
7. On completing a pass through the Laplacian, decrement Th_e and start another pass over Laplacian
8. When Th_e reaches the lower cut off, increment Th_m, reset Th_e and iterate Step 3 - 7
9. When Th_m reaches the upper cut off, exit

The bounds on Th_e and Th_m depend on the application. If one wants to get as complete a representation as possible, the Th_e must be allowed to decrement to very small values. If the intent is to capture only strong edges and ignore the rest (*e.g.*, for a noise removal application), then Th_e must be given a fairly high lower cut off (500). If we wish to restrict the size of our PS, the Th_m must be allowed to increase to a higher cut off to get good modelling.On the other hand, if we wish to get compact representation, we should use a large PS with a lower upper cut off on Th_m (say 0.5).

3 Results

The ability of the modelling algorithm to compute the correct model parameters is established by testing it with a synthetic Laplacian composed of PS elements themselves. A Laplacian was created having the the PS28 elements with their original amplitudes and after scaling them by 0.1. The results for modelling this test Laplacian with PS14 and PS28, with and without the β logic, is shown in Table 1. It can be seen that PS28 with β is clearly the best strategy for generating accurate and compact models. Without β, some small amplitude structures are omitted in the model, leading to compact models but higher errors.

The PS28 set along with β logic was used to model the first Laplacian band (L_0) of the four natural images shown in Figure 6. These images have strong

Table 1. Effect of primitive set (PS) size and scaling (β) on accuracy and model size. The image consisted of 56 (scaled) primitive elements. The model size indicates the number of primitive set elements needed on average to model each scaled element in the test image.

	PS14	PS14+β	PS28	PS28+β
Err %	2.5	2.28	0.353	0.257
Size	1.57	2.86	0.98	1.82

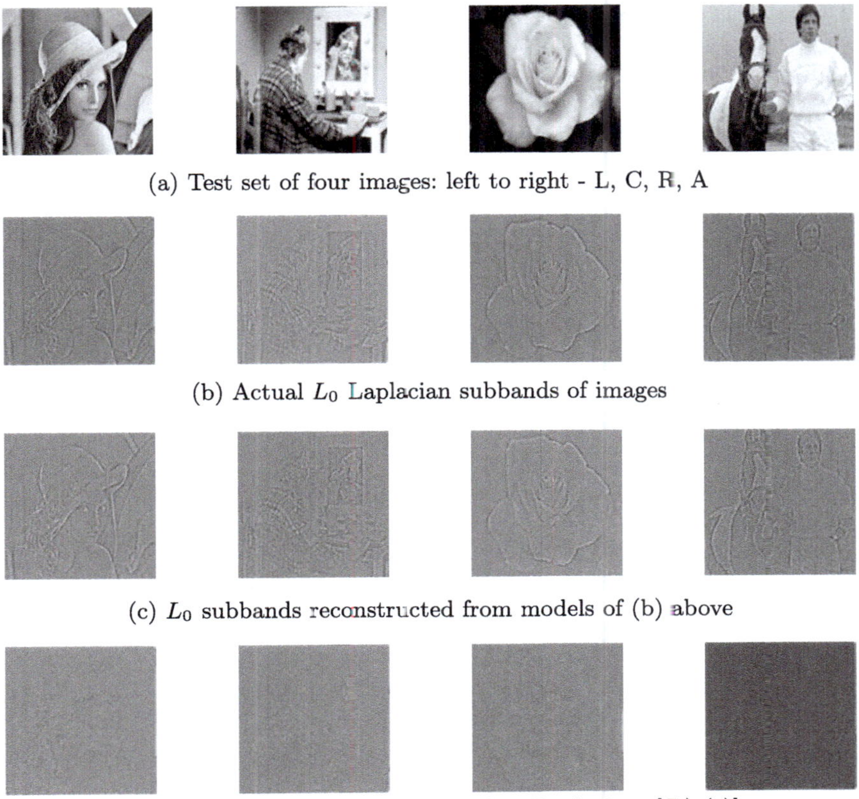

(a) Test set of four images: left to right - L, C, R, A

(b) Actual L_0 Laplacian subbands of images

(c) L_0 subbands reconstructed from models of (b) above

(d) Reconstruction errors for the four Laplacians [(b)-(c)]

Fig. 6. Modelling accuracy of Laplacians for natural images

Table 2. Modeling accuracy and model sizes for laplacians of four test images. The error energy is given as a % of the true laplacian subbands. The model size indicates the number of model elements used to represent the laplacians. The images are shown in Figure 6.

	L	C	R	A
Err %	39.8	32.9	31.0	31.5
Size	2083	3440	1306	3012

edges and curvilinear structures of varying degrees of sharpness. The original Laplacians, the model based reconstructed Laplacaians and the residual errors are also shown in Figure 6. The model sizes generated and the residual error energies are shown in Table 2. It is seen that the dominant edges are well modeled while the residuals are mainly the texture/small edges.

The model generated for Lena was also used to generate a magnified version using IPS28. This result is shown in Figure 7, where frequency extrapolation [6] and bilinear interpolation is also shown for comparison. The model based magnification is able to retain the sharpness of major edges by introducing correct coherent harmonics at the required places. The edges are slightly overemphasized by [6], which leads to ringing.

(a) Frequency (b) Spatial (c) Model

Fig. 7. Comparison of frequency extrapolation [6], spatial interpolation and model based magnification

When given a noisy image, the model ignores the unstructured edges due to noise. Thus the model based reconstruction can be used for noise removal without blurring the sharp edges. This is shown in Figure 8. The Lena image was corrupted by white noise. A one level pyramid was constructed $(G1, L_0)$, the L_0 was replaced by its model based reconstruction and the pyramid reconstructed. For comparison, the low pass and median filtered versions are also shown in Figure 8.

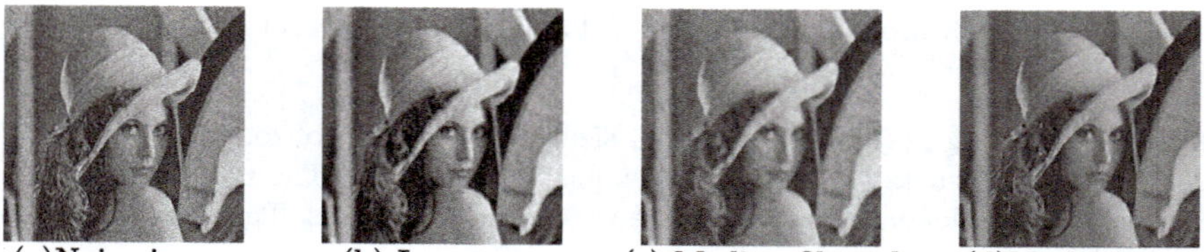

(a)Noisy image (b) Low pass (c) Median filtered (d)Model based

Fig. 8. Noise removal ability using L_0 modeling based approach

4 Conclusion and Future Work

The structure of Laplacians is exploited to generate a model of Laplacians. The algorithm for creating such a representation is developed and the ability to model Laplacians is demonstrated. Preliminary results of applications of this representation for magnification and noise filtering is shown. The problem of creating the optimum Primitive Set and exploring further applications of this representation are directions of future work.

References

1. Shapiro J.M., Staelin D.H.: Embedded image coding using zerotrees of wavelet coefficints. Signal Processing IEEE Transactions on Volume 41, Issue 12, (Dec. 1993) pp.3445 - 3462
2. Mallat S., Zhong S.: Characterization of signals from multiscale edges. Pattern Analysis and Machine Intelligence, IEEE Transactions on Volume 14, Issue 7, (July 1992) pp.710 - 732
3. William T. Freeman, Egon C. Pasztor, Owen T Carmichael: Learning Low-Level Vision IJCV (2000).
4. Jiji C.V. and S. Chaudhuri: Single Frame Image Super-Resolution Through Contourlet Learning. EURASIP Journal of Applied Signal Processing, Accepted
5. Baker S., Kanade T.: Limits on super-resolution and how to break them. IEEE Transactions on Pattern Analysis and Machine Intelligence vol. 24, issue 9, (Sept. 2002) pp.1167 - 1183
6. H Greenspan, CH Anderson, S Akber: Image enhancement by nonlinear extrapolation in frequency space. IEEE Transactions on Image Processing vol. 9, issue 6, pp. 1035-1048
7. Subrata Rakshit, M.K. Nema: Symmetric Residue Pyramids - An extension to Burt laplacian pyramids. IEEE - ICASSP, (2003).
8. P. Burt and E. Adelson The Laplacian Pyramid as a Compact Image Code. IEEE Transaction on Communication, COM-31 pp. 532-540,(1983).
9. Simoncelli E.P., Freeman W.T.: The steerable pyramid: a flexible architecture for multi-scale derivative computation. Image Processing, (1995). Proceedings., International Conference on Volume 3, 23-26 Oct. 1995 Page(s):444 - 447 vol.3
10. Greenspan H., Belongie S., Goodman R., Perona P., Rakshit S., Anderson C.H.: Overcomplete steerable pyramid filters and rotation invariance. Computer Vision and Pattern Recognition. IEEE Computer Society Conference on, 21-23 (June 1994) pp.222 - 228
11. Xin Li, Orchard M.T.: New edge-directed interpolation. Image Processing, IEEE Transactions on Volume 10, Issue 10, (Oct. 2001) pp.1521 - 1527

Fusion of Texture Variation and On-Line Color Sampling for Moving Object Detection Under Varying Chromatic Illumination

Chunfeng Shen, Xueyin Lin, and Yuanchun Shi

Key Lab of Pervasive Computing(MOE),
Dept. of Computer Science & Technology, Tsinghua University,
100084 Beijing, P.R. China
Spring98@mails.tsinghua.edu.cn
Lxy-dcs@mail.tsinghua.edu.cn, Shiyc@tsinghua.edu.cn

Abstract. In this paper, a novel approach to non-rigid moving object detection under varying chromatic illumination is proposed. Different from most algorithms that utilize color information, the assumption of smooth or global change of illumination is no longer needed. Our method is based on the observation that the color appearance of objects may alter as the change of light intensity and color, but their texture structures remain almost the same. Therefore, texture based invariant characteristic to varying illumination is extracted and modeled, which can be used to guide for obtaining color appearance model at each frame. By this philosophy, firstly texture variation, which is not sensitive to illumination, is extracted by comparing the current image with background image. Secondly, the instantaneous color model is created by a special sampling algorithm according to the texture variation and previous consecutive detection results. By fusing texture variation and on-line color sampling, an energy function is founded and minimized to obtain the target contour. Experiments show that this approach has a great capability in detecting non-rigid objects under global or local varying illumination even when the hue and saturation of the lighting change abruptly or locally.

1 Introduction

Moving object detection is one of the primary problems in computer vision, but most detection algorithms based on background subtraction strategy are suffering from illumination variation. However, the varying chromatic illumination is ubiquitous. In this paper, we focus on extracting the moving object contour under chromatic illumination, where light intensity or color may change abruptly or locally. The detection results represented as contours instead of rectangle or ellipse can benefit further analysis, e.g., pose estimation or action analysis.

In the literature, many methods have been proposed to deal with color illumination variation. For example, model based approach has been presented using features insensitive to chromatic illumination variation, such as edges or textures [1]. The limitation is high level knowledge dependence, since

P.J. Narayanan et al. (Eds.): ACCV 2006, LNCS 3851, pp. 90–99, 2006.

edge and texture cue alone is not strong enough to extract target from the scene.

Color constancy strategy has also been suggested to reduce the influence of varying illumination, where color is usually represented by two components of the YUV, HSV[2], rgb color space or by linear combinations of the RGB components[3]. But this method performs poorly if the light chromatic changes.

The third class of methods adopts estimation and prediction strategy to evolve color distributions. Some researchers proposed using parameter-based prediction and update, that is, generate a stochastic model of color distribution, and evolve model parameters over time [4]. Others proposed using non-parameter prediction and update based on statistic techniques[5]. Both of these methods are suitable for coping with smooth temporal illumination change only.

In [6], the input frames are decomposed into reflectance and illumination images, so detection algorithm can be performed on the reflectance images. This scheme utilizes the illumination eigenspace to capture the illumination variation due to environmental factors. But it needs to store a lot of illumination images captured under different illumination conditions in advance.

Recently, some papers have tried to integrate above methods together [7], which based on a new LDA color space that maximizes the foreground/background class separability. Then multiple hypotheses about the next state of the color distribution using CONDENSATION are derived and the best hypothesis is adopted to generate the best object segmentation by introducing a dynamic color model. But it has to keep a certain number of particles in order to cover the color distribution, so the computation is expensive.

Other papers also try to pursue accurate moving object contour[8][9], or integrate multiple cues[10], but them still suffer from light changes. In this paper a novel method is proposed for moving object detection indoor captured by a fixed camera under varying chromatic illumination. It means that the chroma and intensity of the illumination can vary abruptly within the whole image or partial of it, so temporal consistent color model is abandoned. Instead, based on the features insensitive to illumination variation, an on-line local color model is built by virtue of a special sampling strategy. Specially, a novel dynamic texture coefficient (DTC) is defined to measure the texture consistency of each pixel as insensitive feature between current frame and background image. Then the probability of each pixel belonging to the target or background color model is assigned. Finally, an energy function fusing DTC and on-line color model is introduced, leading to the solution via level set framework.

The main contributions in this paper include: 1) Propose a novel feature insensitive to varying chromatic illumination; 2) Develop an on-line color sampling scheme to deal with abrupt light changes; 3) Fuse texture variation and online color modeling via the level set framework; 4) No shape information about the moving objects is necessary, so it is especially suitable for the situation that the prior of shape information is hard to be obtained.

2 Dynamic Texture Coefficient

It is well known that illumination variation can make captured images look quite different. So features insensitive to illumination variation should be developed for distinguishing the target from the background reliably. It is observed that texture structure is very insensitive to illumination variation. For example, if the local texture structure of the current image is similar to that of the background image, it probably indicates that the corresponding background region still can be seen by the camera and not occluded by moving objects. Otherwise moving object is supposed to entry. Based on this observation a dynamic texture coefficient (DTC) is defined formally to describe the texture variation between the corresponding region of the current frame and the background image.

Texture variation is calculated block-wisely by using window with size $N \times N$ between the current frame and background image, denoted as block B and block C respectively as shown in Fig. 1. The intensity value in block B and C are represented by two N^2 dimensional vectors $V_b(x, y)$ and $V_c(x, y)$ corresponding to block B and C respectively with (x, y) the coordinates of the block centers.

Here normalized correlation is used to compute the local texture variation as

$$\frac{|\overline{V_c}^T \cdot \overline{V_b}|}{||\overline{V_c}|| \cdot ||\overline{V_b}||}$$

where $\overline{V_c} = V_c - mean\,(V_c)$, $\overline{V_b} = V_b - mean\,(V_b)$, $||\cdot||$ is vector norm, and $mean$ is the mean of vector elements. The reason of using such kind of description is based on the observation that if block B is a textured Lambert surface (no strong specular reflection) and not occluded by moving objects, then the correlation value will close to one. However, whenever it is occluded by a moving object, $V_c(x, y)$ will quite different from $V_b(x, y)$. As a result, it can be used to extract contours of the moving objects effectively.

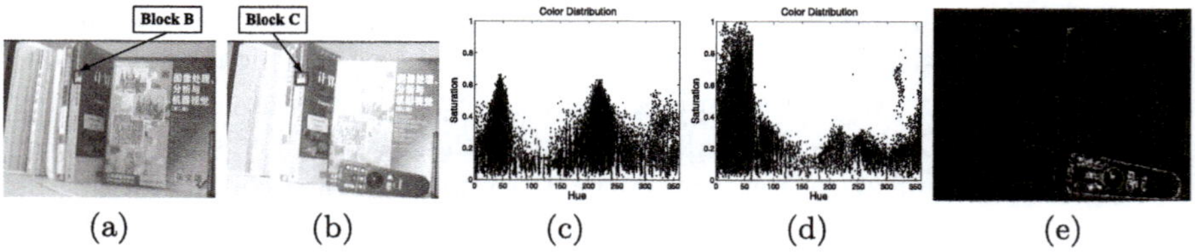

Fig. 1. Block extraction and color distribution. (a)(b): Two blocks extracted from background and current images in the same position for matching. (c)(d): Color distribution in HS space of background and current image. (e): Dynamic texture result.

In practice, however, four different kinds of situations should be concerned. For example, if both blocks are textured we can use the correlation value to judge whether the texture changes or not. If both blocks are uniform, then there is probably no target contour exists in this local area. If block B is uniform while block C is textured, we can make a strong judgment that there exist moving objects. The situation that block B is textured while block C is uniform should be considered carefully, as it may not necessarily relative to target occlusion but to strong illumination for camera saturation as well indicated some regions in Fig. 1 (a) and (b).

From above analysis, the DTC used to indicate moving objects as insensitive feature to varying illumination can be defined as

$$DTC(V_c, V_b) = \begin{cases} 1 - \frac{|V_c^T \cdot V_b|}{\|V_c\| \|V_b\|}, & \text{if } var(V_c) \geq T \ \& \ var(V_b) \geq T \\ 0, & \text{if } var(V_c) < T \\ 1, & \text{if } var(V_c) \geq T \ \& \ var(V_b) < T \end{cases} \quad (1)$$

where var means the variance of pattern vector, and T is the threshold discriminating whether textured or not. It is obvious that the DTC close to 1 means a moving object edge around.

For camera dither or image noise, we do not use calculated DTC value from each pixel directly, but choose the minimum DTC value in the neighborhood of each pixel instead. Then the following equation is added for modification:

$$DTC(x, y) = \min_{(x',y') \in N(x,y)} DTC\left(V_c(x', y'), V_b(x', y')\right) \quad (2)$$

where $N(x, y)$ is pixel (x, y) and its 4-neighborhood.

Fig. 1(e) illustrates the DTC result for image pair shown in Fig. 1(a) and (b), where bright region presents high confidence of non-matching degree. It is obvious that this result is very useful to extract moving object edges despite of dramatic illumination variations.

Some methods of moving object edge extraction have been proposed using edge magnitude. For instance, Jabri[11] proposed edge subtraction method by integrating edge magnitude and direction. But edge magnitude is unstable to illumination, because the surface reflectance on each side of an edge is not equal.

Fig. 2 illustrates the comparison between Jabri's and our algorithm. When the intensity varies drastically between Fig. 2(a) and (b), the performance of his algorithm is very poor, as many static edges of background are misclassified as moving edges, while our method can get good performance as shown in Fig. 2(d).

It is obvious that moving object edge (MOE) can be obtained by thresholding the DTC value. Since the DTC is region-based, actual MOE can be refined from the current image by applying Nonmaximum Suppression procedure.

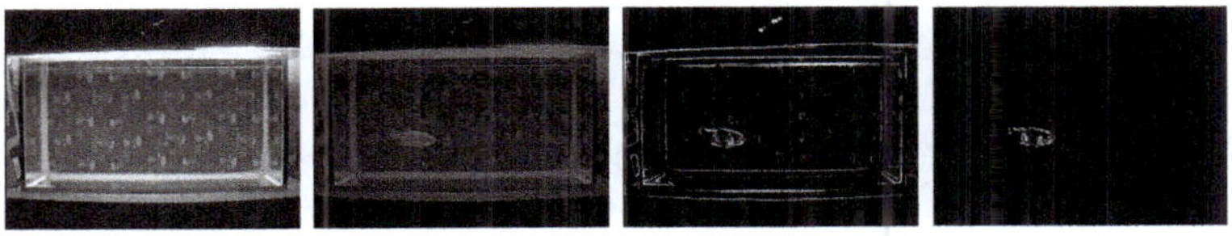

(a) (b) (c) (d)

Fig. 2. The comparison of algorithm performance between Jabri's and our algorithm. (a) Background image. (b) Current image. (c) Jabri's result. (d) Our DTC result.

3 On-Line Color Sampling

DTC distribution is usually fragmented when background texture structure is similar to moving object contour. So local color models of the background and foreground are established around the contours of the moving objects as a supplement used for extracting the nearby target area from background. The color models are calculated from the samples selected from both sides of the target contours. Since we use DTC for detecting the target contours, the samples are selected around the edges with high DTC values. The problem is, however, that such kind of edges may be inside the target area not on the boundary of the objects. As a result they should be excluded from the sample set. So we use predicted contour in combination, and restrict the samples around the MOE near the predicted contours. The on-line sampling sketch map is illustrated in Fig. 3(a), where blue curve is the predicted contour based on previous detection results and yellow short line is sampling route located in the gradient direction of pixel on moving object edges. The hollow red circle is background sampling pixels, while the solid red circle is the extracted foreground sampling pixels.

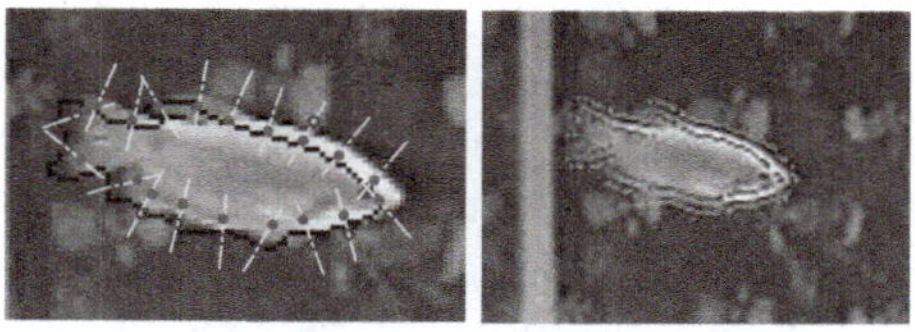

(a) (b)

Fig. 3. On-line color sampling. (a) Sketch map of on-line color sampling. (b) Distribution of two kinds of sampling pixels.

The key point of creating color model is to distinguish which sampling pixel is inside the target area and which is not. Then a special judgment scheme based on predicted target region and MOE, as shown in Fig. 4, has been developed.

First, a pixel on the MOE is selected as the base point. Then two pixels along its normal line with fixed distance from the base point but on different sides are sampled for color modeling, shown as red solid and hollow circles. There are two situations shown as Case one and Case two, as shown in Fig. 4. In Case one, MOE is located outside of predicted target region, and in Case two it is inside of that. Actually the role of the predicted target region plays is indicating which side of the MOE is inside of the target and which is outside. In case one the sampling point nearer to the predicted region is assigned as the sampling point of the target. In case two, however, the point far away from the predicted border is the target sample. The sampling result is shown in Fig. 3(b) where red points represent sampling target pixels and green points represent sampling.

Considering spatial information, the following color models are created. For concision, we define (x, y) as X, and (x', y') as X'. Let $I(X)$ be the RGB vector for a pixel at X, and $F(X)$, $B(X)$ be the foreground and background sampling

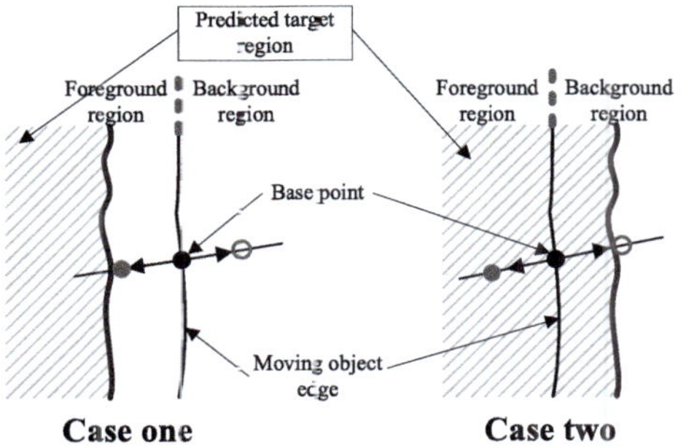

Fig. 4. The judgment scheme. Case one: moving object edge locating outside of the predicted target region. Case two: MOE locating inside of the predicted target region.

pixel sets in the neighborhood of X respectively. Using these sampling pixels, the foreground and background probability density functions, $P_f(X)$ and $P_b(X)$, can be estimated using the Gaussian function N as

$$P_{l_i}(X) = \frac{1}{\sum\limits_{X' \in S_i(X)} \alpha_{X'}} \sum_{X' \in S_i(X)} \alpha_{X'} N(I(X) - I(X'), \Sigma) \tag{3}$$

where $l = \{f, b\}$, $S = \{F, B\}$, $i = 1, 2$, and weighted coefficient $\alpha_{X'} = ((x - x')^2 + (y - y')^2)^{-1/2}$ controls the influence of sampling point such that the further from the current pixel to the sampling pixel, the weaker influence will be. Σ is the covariance matrix of RGB color.

4 Construction of Energy Function

Let $\{C(p) : [0,1] \to \mathbb{R}^2\}$ be a closed curve in a Euclidean plane $\mathbb{R}^2$. Our goal is to find the curve $C^*(p)$ which divides the whole image area into targets and background regions. Here, two items of energy functions about DTC and color probability are introduced, and we define energy function of color model as

$$E_{color} = -\int_{\omega} P_f(X)dX - \int_{\omega^-} P_b(X)dX \tag{4}$$

where ω means the inner region of curve $C(p)$, and ω^- means the outer region. Minimizing (4) means including pixels with similar color to foreground and excluding pixels with similar color to background.

On the other hand, since big DTC value presents high confidence of moving object existence, the Geodesic active contour model [12] is introduced to model DTC information and aims at attracting the curve to high DTC value region by minimizing the following energy function:

$$E_{DTC} = \oint_C \underbrace{g(|\nabla DTC(C(p))|)}_{Boundary\ attraction} \underbrace{|\dot{C}(p)|}_{Regularity} dp \tag{5}$$

where $\dot{C}(p)$ is the partial derivative of curve with respect to p, and $g(.)$ is a monotonically deceasing function such that $g(r) \to 0$ as $r \to \infty$, and $g(0) = 1$.

To combine color probability and dynamic texture, the goal for object detection is converted to find the curve $C^*(p)$ minimizing following energy function:

$$\begin{aligned} C^*(p) &= \min_C E(C(p)) \\ E(C(p)) &= \alpha E_{color} + \beta E_{DTC} \end{aligned} \tag{6}$$

where α and β are weighted coefficients which modulate the influence of color model and DTC model.

5 Contour Evolution Via Level Set

For (6), a time variable t is added and using gradient descent process:

$$\frac{\partial C}{\partial t} = -\frac{\delta E(C)}{\delta C} = -\left(\alpha \frac{\delta E_{color}}{\delta C} + \beta \frac{\delta E_{DTC}}{\delta C}\right) \tag{7}$$

Applying Euler-Lagrange equation and gradient descent process:

$$\frac{\delta E_{DTC}}{\delta C} = \left[g(\nabla DTC(C))k - \nabla g(\nabla DTC(C)) \cdot \vec{N}\right] \vec{N} \tag{8}$$

Let $\{\phi(x,y) : \mathbb{R}^2 \to \mathbb{R}\}$ be an implicit representation of $C(p)$, such that C is zero level set of $\phi : C = \{(x,y) : \phi(x,y) = 0\}$. Similar to the deduction in [13], a steady state solution of (8) can be given by:

$$\phi_{t,DTC} = g(\nabla DTC)k|\nabla \phi| + \nabla g(\nabla DTC) \cdot \nabla \phi \tag{9}$$

The normal $\vec{N}$, as well as the curvature value k, can be estimated directly from the level set function ϕ. Using step function $H(\phi) = \begin{cases} 1, \text{ if } \phi \geq 0 \\ 0, \text{ if } \phi < 0 \end{cases}$ and delta function $\delta(.)$, the first item of (7) about color energy is

$$\phi_{t,color} = -\alpha \frac{\delta E_{color}}{\delta C} = \alpha \left[P_f(X) - P_b(X)\right] \delta(H(\phi)) \tag{10}$$

Then level set function ϕ deduced from (6) is given as

$$\phi_t = \alpha \left[P_f(X) - P_b(X)\right] \delta(H(\phi)) + \beta \left[g(\nabla DTC)k|\nabla \phi| + \nabla g(\nabla DTC) \cdot \nabla \phi\right] \tag{11}$$

Eq.(11) indicates that the flow can be divided into three components. One is the force deduced from the color model which may raise the three dimensional surface ϕ if the region color is more like foreground, and descend it otherwise. The second part is a contractive item in proportion to the curvature. And the third part attracts the curve to the dynamic textures. By harmonizing these three forces via level set, the curve of moving objects can be extracted.

6 Experiments

This section shows the performance of proposed method with different illumination covering typical illumination, especially for sudden and local variation. The varying of chromatic illumination in these videos can not be dealt with correctly by previous methods, such as color prediction [14].

6.1 Human Body Detection

This video sequence is taken in a classroom equipped with a projector. A human body stands in front of a board full of pictures. The projector casts a beam of chromatic light onto the board and human body at the same time. The color light from the projector changes frequently from frame to frame, and the body also turns around continuously.

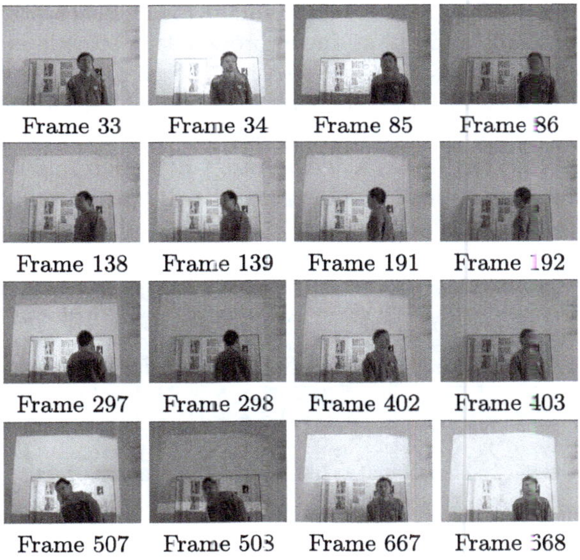

Fig. 5. Human body detection under abrupt local varying chromatic illumination in smart classroom

In Fig. 5, 8 pairs of consecutive frames with drastically different illumination condition are shown with the extracted contours of the person. These results indicate that our approach can get good performance despite of local abrupt light variation and target appearance alteration with time.

6.2 Fish Detection

Fig. 6 shows the experiment result of a fish sequence under synthesized chromatic sudden varying illumination to test the algorithm robustness. Each selected pair

Fig. 6. Fish detection under chromatic sudden varying illumination

of consecutive frames is under drastic different illumination conditions. Despite of the significant chromatic difference, it can still get good performance.

The video sequence is processed with a Pentium4 2.4 GHz processor, and the system can process averagely 15 fps with frame size 384 x 288. For comparison, the algorithm proposed by Stauffer [14] is adopt, where each pixel is modeled as a mixture of Gaussians and an on-line approximation scheme is used to update the model. Here we use three Gaussians to model each pixel and YUV color space to reduce the influence of light intensity, and update rate for model update is set as 0.2. The experiment results are shown in Fig. 7 where the upper row is original image and the low row is the result of foreground detection. It can be seen obviously that update algorithm can hardly produce good performance while illumination changes abruptly.

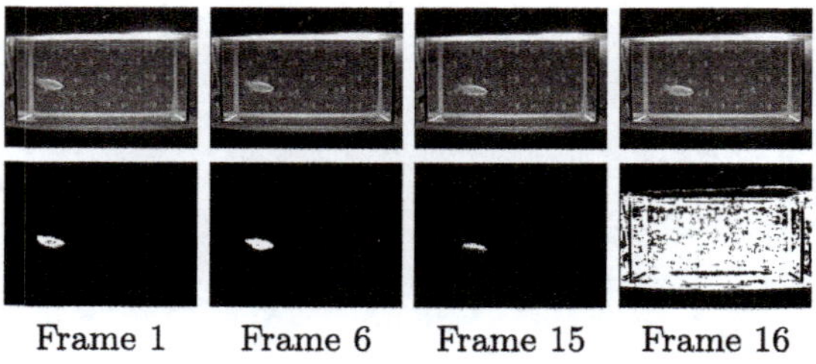

Fig. 7. Foreground detection using mixture Gaussian model and on-line update scheme. Upper row: original images; lower row: foreground detection results.

7 Conclusion

In this paper, we propose a new robust approach for moving object detection, which integrates the color and texture variation information within an energy function and carries out the tracking procedure in the framework of level set. The main contribution of this paper is that a feature, dynamic texture coefficient, insensitive to illumination variation is defined to extract moving object edge, and an on-line color model via sampling is created. Therefore texture variation information and on-line color model can be integrated to trace the target contour in level set framework under illumination variation environment.

We intend to explore several avenues in future work. First, a new scheme should be proposed for invariant feature derivation under chromatic illumination without textureless light assumption. We also plan to adopt target model for high level supervising to improve the robustness.

Acknowledgement. This research is supported partially by the National Grand Fundamental Research 973 Program of China (No. 2002CB312101) and the National Natural Science Foundation of China (No. 60433030).

References

1. Cascia, M., Sclaroff, S., Athitsos, V.: Fast, reliable head tracking under varying illumination: an approach based on registration of texture-mapped 3d models. IEEE Trans. PAMI **22** (2000) 322–336
2. Lee, Y., You, B., Lee, S.: A real-time color based object tracking robust to irregular illumination variations. In: Proc. IEEE Int. Conf. Robotics and Automation. Volume 2. (2001) 1659–1664
3. Korhonen, M., Heikkila, J., Silvcn, O.: Intensity independent color models and visual tracking. In: Proc. IEEE ICPR. Volume 3. (2000) 600–604
4. Wren, C.R., Azarbayejani, A., Darrell, T., Pentland, A.P.: Pfinder: real-time tracking of the human body. IEEE Trans. PAMI **19** (1997) 780–785
5. Sigal, L., Sclaroff, S., Athitsos, V.: Skin color-based video segmentation under time-varying illumination. IEEE Trans. PAMI **26** (2004) 862–877
6. Matsushita, Y., Nishino, K., Ikeuchi, K., M.Sakauchi: Illumination normalization with time-dependent intrinsic images for video surveillance. IEEE Trans. PAMI **26** (2004) 1336–1347
7. Moreno-Noguer, F., Sanfeliu, A., Samaras, D.: Fusion of a multiple hypotheses color model and deformable contours for figure ground segmentation in dynamic environments. In: Proc. IEEE Workshop on CVPR. (2004) 13
8. Ruzon, M., Tomasi, C. Alpha estimation in natural images. In: Proc. IEEE CVPR. Volume 1. (2000) 18–25
9. Paragios, N., Deriche, R.: Geodesic active contours and level sets for the detection and tracking of moving objects. IEEE Trans. PAMI **22** (2000) 266–280
10. Khan, S., Shah, M.: Object based segmentation of video using color, motion and spatial information. In: Proc. IEEE CVPR. Volume 2. (2001) 746–751
11. Jabri, S., Duric, Z., Wechsler, H., Rosenfeld, A.: Detection and location of people in video images using adaptive fusion of color and edge information. In: Proc. IEEE ICPR. Volume 4. (2000) 627–630
12. Caselles, V., Kimmel, R., Sapiro, G.: Geodesic active contour. In: Proc. IEEE ICCV. (1995) 694–699
13. Goldenberg, R., Kimmel, R., Rivlin, E., Rudzsky, M.: Fast geodesic active contours. IEEE Trans. Image Processing **10** (2001) 1467–1475
14. Stauffer, C., Grimson, W.: Adaptive background mixture models for real-time tracking. In: Proc. IEEE CVPR. Volume 2. (1999) 246–252

Combining Microscopic and Macroscopic Information for Rotation and Histogram Equalization Invariant Texture Classification

S. Liao, W.K. Law, and Albert C.S. Chung

Lo Kwee-Seong Medical Image Analysis Laboratory,
Department of Computer Science,
The Hong Kong University of Science and Technology,
Clear Water Bay, Kowloon, Hong Kong
{liaoshu, maxlawwk, achung}@ust.hk

Abstract. This paper presents a new, simple approach for rotation and histogram equalization invariant texture classification. The proposed approach is based on both microscopic and macroscopic information which can effectively capture fundamental intensity properties of image textures. The combined information is proven to be a very powerful texture feature. We extract the information at the microscopic level by using the frequency histogram of all pattern labels. At the macroscopic level, we extract the information by employing the circular Gabor filters at different center frequencies and computing the Tsallis entropy of the filter outputs. The proposed approach is robust in terms of histogram equalization since the feature is, by definition, invariant against flattening of pixel intensities. The good performance of this approach is proven by the promising experimental results obtained. We also evaluate our method based on six widely used image features. It is experimentally shown that our features exceed the performance obtained using other image features.

1 Introduction

Texture analysis plays an important role in computer vision and image processing. Translation, rotation, and histogram equalization invariant texture analysis methods have been of particular interest. Some researchers have considered to extract rotation-invariant features for image textures. Greenspan *et al.* [1] applied a set of oriented pyramid filters to an image texture and obtained a set of filtered energies. Porter and Canagarajah [2] removed the HH wavelet channels and combined the LH and HL wavelet channels to obtain rotation-invariant wavelet features. Haley and Manjunath [3] used Gabor filters to extract rotation-invariant features. Kashyap and Khotanzad [4] constructed an isotropic circular Gaussian Markov random field (GMRF). To capture directional information in the possibly non-isotropic textures, Deng and Clausi [5] extended the ICGMRF model [4] into anisotropic circular GMRF model. Utilizing similar circular neighborhoods, Arof and Deravi obtained rotation invariant features with 1D DFT transformation [6]. Also, Ojala *et al.* [7] proposed rotation invariant features

P.J. Narayanan et al. (Eds.): ACCV 2006, LNCS 3851, pp. 100–109, 2006.

by observing statistical distributions of uniform local binary patterns (LBP). Huang, Li and Wang extended the conventional LBP method to calculate the derivative-based local binary patterns in the application of face alignment [8].

In this paper, we propose a new approach to histogram equalization and rotation invariant texture classification by capturing and combining both **microscopic information**: characteristics of local details in the textures, and **macroscopic information**: blob-like texture pattern in the image. The main contributions of this work are as follows. First, along the same line of Ojala *et al.* [7], instead of just observing the "uniform LBP", we propose to use frequency histogram of all pattern labels. At the microscopic level, it is found that this can better represent the dominant patterns in the texture images than the conventional LBP method [7]. Second, we use the Gabor filters to extract macroscopic information [10], and represent the extracted macroscopic information by computing the Tsallis entropy from the histogram of the image filtered using the circular Gabor filters because of the fact that the histogram can be transformed into a vector of generalized image entropies [9]. Finally, we found that the microscopic and macroscopic features can complement with each other effectively. This can lead to higher classification accuracy when the resolution of the image is low, e.g. 16×16, or the textures in the images are difficult to be classified. In this paper, we employ the support vector machines for performing classification, and the grid search to find the best setting of parameters which can produce the highest classification accuracy for each feature.

The performance of the proposed approach is demonstrated with three experiments on three databases: Brodatz [11], Meastex [12] and CUReT textures [13]. Excellent experimental results demonstrate that our method is able to produce, from any random rotation angle, a representation that allows for discriminating a large number of textures at other random angles. The features are computationally attractive as they can be extracted in just a few operations.

2 Microscopic Information

At the microscopic level, we show how to derive features based on the modified version of local binary patterns (LBP) using frequency histogram of all pattern labels in the images. It will be experimentally shown that, using frequency histogram of all pattern labels, our new features outperform the conventional LBP and other five widely used image features (see Section 4 for details). Our features are simple, and robust to image histogram equalization and rotation.

An advantage of using frequency histogram of all pattern labels over using the histogram of "uniform LBP" in the conventional LBP method [7] is that, for some kinds of textures, the dominant patterns are not mainly the "uniform LBP", especially for the textures whose edges and shapes are not regular. For example, Table 1 lists the proportions of the "uniform LBP" in some sample images obtained from the Meastex database. As listed in the table, even with different values of radius R, the majority of textural information cannot be effectively represented by merely considering the histogram of "uniform LBP".

Table 1. Proportions (%) of "uniform LBP" for some samples in the Meastex database. It shows that, for some kinds of textures, the dominant patterns are not mainly the "uniform LBP".

Textures	P=8,R=1	P=16,R=2	P=24,R=3
Concrete0002	52.30	38.54	24.85
Concrete0003	63.72	45.05	31.95
Concrete0006	50.15	34.94	26.70
Concrete0007	40.64	26.07	13.58
Misc0000	58.61	42.50	30.84
Misc0001	46.40	32.78	20.80
Rock0015	56.80	41.83	27.32
Rock0016	64.42	50.52	24.10
Rock0017	44.93	31.70	16.33
Rock0018	51.68	36.85	22.78

It shows that the "uniform LBP" are not the dominant patterns in these sample images. Moreover, the approach of "uniform LBP" is not very robust against random rotation as the interpolation of pixel intensities of the rotated images can change the original "uniform" patterns into "non-uniform". Instead, the frequency histogram of all pattern labels can be more robust to random rotation as, no matter how much the images are rotated, the new patterns appear after the interpolation will also be considered in the frequency histogram of all pattern labels.

Based on the work of Ojala et. al [7], we first give the definition of pattern labels, and then describe how frequency histogram of all pattern labels is used for feature selection. Let V be a vector representing the neighboring intensity values (anti-clockwise direction) at each image pixel (x, y), $V(x, y) = (t_0, t_1, \ldots, t_{m-1})^T$, where (x, y) denote image pixel coordinates, and t_1, t_2, ... , t_{m-1} represent the intensity values of m equally spaced pixels around the pixel at (x, y). In order to maintain rotation invariance, a circular neighborhood system is used. Therefore, t_1, t_2, ... , t_{m-1} form a circularly symmetric neighbor set on a circle of radius R. Fig. 1 illustrates the circularly symmetric neighbor sets for different values of m and R. The intensity values of the neighboring pixels are estimated using the bilinear interpolation. Let t_0 be the intensity value of a neighboring pixel, which is $(R, 0)$, to the right of the center pixel t_c, $(0, 0)$, and t_1, t_2, ... , t_{m-1} denote the intensity values in the order of anti-clockwise from t_0. To achieve histogram equalization invariance, the intensity value t_c at the center pixel is subtracted from the intensity values of the neighbor sets t_1, t_2, ... , t_{m-1}. A vector is defined to represent the trend of each pixel to its neighbors in the image, $Trend(x, y) = (u(t_0 - t_c), u(t_1 - t_c), \ldots, u(t_{m-1} - t_c))^T$, where $u(x)$ is a step function, $u(x) = 1$ when $x \geq 0$; else, $u(x) = 0$. The vector $Trend$ at each pixel is a highly discriminative microscopic texture feature. It is robust to histogram equalization because the sign of difference between two pixels will not be changed after performing histogram equalization. Then, a binary weighted factor $2^i, i = 0, 1, ..., m-1$ is assigned to

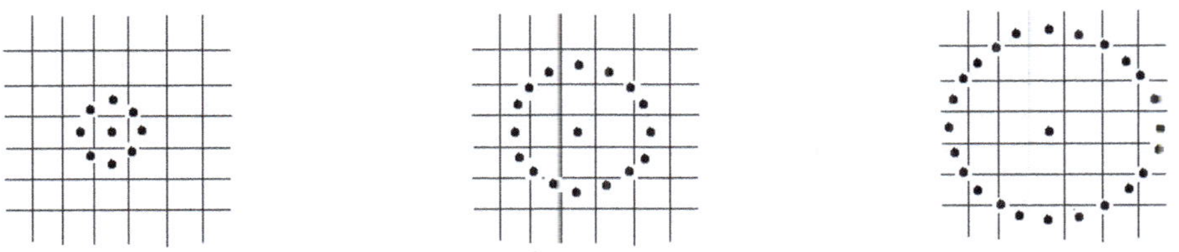

Fig. 1. Circularly symmetric neighbor sets for different values of m and R

each element in vector *Trend* in order to label each pattern, which is given as,

$$Mic(m, R) = \sum_{i=0}^{m-1} u(t_i - t_c)2^i. \quad (1)$$

This feature is an effective representation of the information at the microscopic level because its value denotes a unique label number which describes the pattern characteristics centered at a particular pixel.

Suppose that the image is rotated by an arbitrary angle, the intensity values of t_i will correspondingly move along the perimeter of the circle centered at t_c. Therefore, rotating the image with a particular angle naturally results in a different $Mic(m, R)$ value. To remove the rotation effect and achieve rotation invariance, we need to group two pattern structures together if one can be obtained by performing rotation with the other. To assign a unique identifier to each rotation invariant group, the feature is now re-defined as,

$$Mic^s(m, R) = \min(Cir(Mic(m, R), n)), \quad (2)$$

where $n = 0, 1, ..., m-1$, $Cir(x, n)$ performs a circular anti-clockwise bit-wise shift on the m-bit number by n times. Unlike the conventional LBP, we consider all the pattern combinations and group them into the same rotation invariance group. Therefore, no matter how much the image is rotated (randomly rotated), we can still map each pattern in the rotated image into one group, while for the approach of local binary patterns some kinds of rotation angles will lead to rotation variant effects due to interpolation of pixels intensities of rotated images.

In the real world applications, rotation angles are not always integers or regular angles. As such, any texture classification approach should be robust to random rotation. For the approach of "uniform LBP", some patterns that are uniform will be changed to non-uniform due to the interpolation of random rotated images. To solve this problem, we propose to consider all pattern labels and use the frequency histogram to find a minimum set of pattern labels that represent 80% of the pattern labels in an image because they should correctly represent the dominant pattern labels given the image. This is more robust to random rotation because no matter how much the image is rotated, the dominant texture pattern information will be captured by the frequency histogram of the dominant pattern labels. According to our experimental results, it appears that the first 20 pattern labels are generally sufficient to reach or exceed 80% of the pattern labels in the image, and can effectively reflect the characteristics of the dominant textures in the image.

3 Macroscopic Information

Although the microscopic information can effectively represent the small, local pattern distribution in the image, it is still not sufficient to represent all the information or characteristics of the whole image. It becomes obvious especially when the resolution of the image is relatively high. To overcome the shortage of the microscopic information, we need to derive the macroscopic information in the image so that the microscopic and macroscopic information can complement well with each other. We use the circularly symmetric Gabor filters to extract macroscopic features of the image. The magnitude of the filtered image measures existence of blob-like structures in textures, which describes whether the textural pattern forms clusters. Apart from the traditional approach that averages pixel magnitude of each filtered image, we compute the Tsallis entropy [14] from the filter outputs. The reason is that the average pixel magnitude can be affected by histogram equalization and suffered by the lost of individual general information because of taking the average value. The Tsallis entropy of the filter outputs can be expressed as a linear function of the histogram and is more robust to histogram equalization.

Gabor filters are often used in texture analysis to provide features for texture classification and segmentation [15], [16]. It functions over the whole image. Therefore, the features extracted from the filtered image are the macroscopic features. It is also resistant to histogram equalization as it takes the overall intensity distribution into consideration.

The traditional Gabor filter varies along one direction alone, thus making it highly orientation specific. As a result, the filter is not suitable for achieving rotation invariance. To achieve rotation invariance, we need to have circularly symmetric Gabor filter, which is given by $h(x,y) = g(x,y)e^{-2\pi jF\sqrt{x^2+y^2}}$ where F is the required center frequency. To extract macroscopic texture-based features from an image using the circularly symmetric filters, we use four circularly symmetric Gabor filters, with different center frequencies (measured in cycles/image) $F_1 = 2.0$, $F_2 = 3.17$, $F_3 = 5.04$ and $F_4 = 8.0$ so that they are spaced in geometric progression across the Fourier domain to achieve optimum coverage. These four filters overlap slightly and the Fourier domain is almost evenly covered. Finally, four filter responses to the input image can be obtained. We denote the histograms of four filter responses as H^1, H^2, H^3, H^4, respectively. The features at macroscopic level are then extracted from the individual histograms by computing the corresponding Tsallis entropy [14] $S_q = \frac{1-\sum_{j=0}^{m-1} h_j^q}{q-1}$, where q is a continuous parameter, m denotes the maximum bin number for the histogram, h_j is the value of the corresponding histogram density, e.g. H^1, H^2, H^3 or H^4. The Tsallis entropies are powerful features to represent the macroscopic information extracted from the histogram [18]. For texture classification, the four Tsallis entropies extracted from H^1, H^2, H^3 and H^4 are used as the features at the macroscopic level.

4 Experimental Results

We have evaluated our method on three different databases with large sets of texture images: (1) 24 source textures captured from the Brodatz album [11]; (2) all textures (28 kinds of texture in total) in the Meastex database [12], which is very challenging as most of the textures are very similar to each other; and (3) 47 textures selected from the CUReT database [13]. We have also reduced the resolution of the images to study the effect of different image resolutions on classification accuracy. In the experiments, we performed histogram equalization and randomly rotated each image in order to test the robustness of our method. The robustness of our approach is compared with six commonly used image features, which are listed below.

1. **Daubechies wavelet packet features (DWPF)** [17] and [2]: The feature vector consisted of the L_2 norms of the images of the wavelet packet transform [17]. The wavelet transform was combined with spatial sub-sampling to give critical image sampling. The rotation-invariant version **DWPFRT** [2] was also implemented.
2. **Traditional Gabor filters (Gabor)** [3]: Eight Gabor filters were chosen, spaced at the frequencies, $F = 2.0, 3.17, 5.04$ and 8.0 and oriented at angles of 0 and 90 degrees to achieve optimal coverage in the Fourier domain. Average pixel magnitude of each filtered image was used as feature. The circularly symmetric version **CGabor** was also implemented.
3. **Gaussian Markov random field parameters (GMRF)** [19]: Each pixel was assumed to be a linear combination of the intensities of its neighboring pixels. We utilized the 4th order neighborhood system. The linear parameters were computed with the least square estimation.
4. **Anisotropic Circular Gaussian MRF parameters (ACGMRF)** [5]: An improved version of the Gaussian MRF mentioned above was implemented. It was rotation invariant with strong response to directional features. In total, 36 parameters were calculated using approximated least square estimation from a 3rd order symmetrical 24 orientation neighborhood system.
5. **Multiresolution Histograms (MH)** [18]: The generalized Tsallis entropy and Fisher information were computed over different resolutions. In this experiment, generalized Tsallis entropy and Fisher information were computed over three resolution levels and let the continuous parameter $q = 2$.
6. **Local binary patterns (LBP)** [7]: The occurrence histogram of the uniform local binary patterns were computed when $P = 8, 16, 24$ with $R = 1, 2, 3$ respectively. The final features were the features obtained after combining the three sets of features computed over $P = 8, R = 1$; $P = 16, R = 2$; $P = 24, R = 3$ together. It was claimed to have the best performance of local binary patterns in Ojala *et al.*'s experiment [7].

Also, the microscopic information is denoted as **Mic** and the macroscopic information is denoted as **Mac**, and the combination of them is denoted as **MicMac**. We used the support vector machine (SVM) as the classifier in our experiments. SVM can perform binary classification and regression. They perform classification using the structural risk minimization principle. In particular, the SVM creates a classifier with minimized VC dimension.

4.1 Experiments on Brodatz Database

The image data set includes 24 texture classes from the Brodatz album [11]. For each texture class, there are 25 128×128 source images, in which initially we divide each 128×128 source image into 4 disjoint 64×64 subimages. As such, we have 100 samples for each texture class (25 source images×4 divisions). We use the first 50 samples for the training of the classifier and the other 50 images are used for the testing of the classifier.

Training and classification are first performed on the textures at their original orientation and resolution, and without histogram equalization and rotation. It produces the results listed in the first column of Table 2. Testing on the original textures only verifies the basic capability of each feature, and does not test its histogram equalization and rotation invariance. The training and testing sets are then presented after performing histogram equalization but without rotation. It yields the second column of results listed in Table 2. Then, the original training and testing sets are presented by rotating each of them in a randomly generated angle between 0 and 360 degrees (angles were uniformly distributed). It should be noted that the randomly generated angle is not necessary an integer value (e.g. generating 23.24 degree is possible), but without performing histogram equalization. The classification results are presented in the third column of Table 2. The fourth column in Table 2 gives the results of performing both histogram equalization and random rotation for each training set and testing set.

Table 2. Performance of different features of 64×64, (32×32) and [16×16] image resolutions in the **Brodatz Database**. Results of our methods are listed in the last three rows. For each test (column), the highest classification accuracy is highlighted in bold.

Features	Classification accuracy %			
	Original Textures	Histogram Equalized Textures	Randomly Rotated Textures	Histogram Equalized & Random Rotated Textures
DWPF [17]	98.61(88.89)[80.56]	89.35(72.69)[55.56]	83.06(79.63)[59.72]	56.94(64.81)[41.20]
DWPFRT [2]	91.67(79.17)[68.06]	75.00(52.78)[43.06]	91.20(78.24)[64.81]	78.70(60.19)[38.43]
Gabor [3]	96.76(79.17)[56.02]	91.67(62.96)[38.43]	64.35(47.69)[45.37]	54.63(34.26)[29.17]
CGabor [3]	90.07(62.50)[48.61]	51.85(26.40)[32.90]	87.87(58.80)[50.46]	55.09(33.80)[29.63]
GMRFs [19]	96.70(53.40)[36.81]	84.33(44.20)[27.11]	44.30(24.74)[23.90]	40.40(22.43)[14.62]
ACGMRFs [5]	95.22(75.00)[33.19]	86.52(75.46)[42.13]	93.72(76.94)[31.48]	80.56(74.33)[37.96]
MH [18]	96.35(78.31)[53.68]	63.61(48.74)[25.12]	87.64(80.21)[56.27]	54.86(41.43)[24.76]
LBP [7]	98.37(92.85)[83.24]	97.44(90.07)[78.22]	92.13(86.37)[80.91]	91.67(84.81)[74.30]
Mic	98.61(93.96)[89.91]	97.69(93.33)[83.98]	94.44(89.16)[82.80]	91.82(85.46)[80.93]
Mac	87.84(63.00)[52.12]	60.73(29.25)[38.06]	85.65(62.17)[55.24]	63.47(39.02)[35.43]
MicMac	**99.54(94.91)[93.02]**	**99.54(95.37)[92.18]**	**99.54(97.69)[92.35]**	**99.07(94.32)[90.11]**

To observe the robustness of different approaches, we reduce the original image resolution from 64×64 to 32×32, and to 16×16. To achieve the resolution reduction, we first perform histogram equalization and random rotation on the original 64×64 images. Then, we take the 32×32 and 16×16 resolution images from the 64×64 images. Table 2, (see the numbers in brackets for 32×32 and squares for 16×16), correspondingly lists the results of histogram equalization and random rotation perform on the textures when all training and testing images are reduced to resolution of 32×32 and 16×16. It is observed that our method based on both microscopic and macroscopic information outperforms other six widely used image features.

4.2 Experiments on Meastex Database

In the Meastex database [12], images are divided into 28 kinds of textures, each image is of resolution of 512×512, and there are 69 source images. It is a very challenging database because, in 28 kinds of textures, some of the images, which are very similar to each other, are divided into two different kinds of textures. Since the Meastex database is very challenging, we do not reduce the resolution less than 64×64 pixels. To setup the experimental environment, we first divide each (512×512) source images into 64 disjoint (64×64) subimages. Half of the subimages of each texture class is used as the training sets, while the other half of the subimages of each texture class is used as the testing sets.

Table 3. Performance of different features of 64×64 image resolution in the **Meastex Database**. Results of our methods are listed in the last three rows. For each test (column), the highest classification accuracy is highlighted in bold.

Features	Classification accuracy %			
	Original Textures	Histogram Equalized Textures	Randomly Rotated Textures	Histogram Equalized & Random Rotated Textures
DWPF [17]	50.74	42.34	36.31	30.50
DWPFRT [2]	42.53	31.63	48.52	27.39
Gabor [3]	56.06	52.63	46.23	39.61
CGabor [3]	51.30	42.63	53.68	38.10
GMRFs [19]	56.78	32.10	37.52	24.68
ACGMRFs [5]	60.73	58.71	50.31	48.64
MH [18]	51.66	26.74	46.32	22.64
LBP [7]	58.32	54.75	57.80	55.94
Mic	61.06	58.34	57.73	60.18
Mac	42.10	38.52	33.50	31.08
MicMac	**81.57**	**81.57**	**81.06**	**80.48**

The experimental results are listed in Table 3, which shows that Meastex is a very challenging database because the classification accuracies are generally lower that the Brodatz database. For our approach, if we just consider the microscopic information (see bottom third row in Table 3), it just has a mediocre performance on the original textures (63.40%). On the other hand, if we just consider the macroscopic information (see bottom second row in Table 3), its performance is not good (42.44%) because the detailed information is lost. However, if we combine the microscopic and macroscopic information (see last row in Table 3), we can see that the performance is greatly improved (81.57%), which is better than other methods listed in the table. This is a promising performance in such challenging database. Also, even in the most difficult condition, after performing histogram equalization and random rotation, our approach can still maintain a good performance (81.07%), its robustness against histogram equalization and random rotation is strongly implied.

4.3 Experiments on CUReT Database

For the CUReT database [13], there are 47 textures and each texture source image is of 320×320 pixels. We first divide each source image into 25 disjoint (64×64) subimages. Then, we use the first 12 subimages as the training set, and the other 13 subimages are used as the testing set. We choose the CUReT database to evaluate the performance of our approach because it contains more nature images. It is also a very challenging database. The experimental results are listed in Table 4, in which our method gives promising performance when both microscopic and macroscopic information is used.

Table 4. Performance of different features of 64×64 image resolution in the **CUReT Database**. Results of our methods are listed in the last three rows. For each test (column), the highest classification accuracy is highlighted in bold.

Features	Classification accuracy %			
	Original Textures	Histogram Equalized Textures	Randomly Rotated Textures	Histogram Equalized & Random Rotated Textures
DWPF [17]	88.30	57.98	75.53	36.70
DWPFRT [2]	79.26	35.64	65.96	32.98
Gabor [3]	57.45	39.89	57.45	21.81
CGabor [3]	45.74	24.47	48.94	20.56
GMRFs [19]	75.85	53.60	41.52	38.63
ACGMRFs [5]	64.89	63.29	39.36	38.83
MH[18]	67.08	40.31	53.75	33.38
LBP [7]	69.15	67.55	65.43	65.85
Mic	81.38	77.12	76.60	77.05
Mac	68.80	60.47	71.31	63.37
MicMac	**95.21**	**96.28**	**94.15**	**92.02**

5 Conclusion

It is experimentally shown that our approach is capable of effectively capturing and combining both microscopic and macroscopic information in the texture images. Moreover, its excellent classification performance in Brodatz, Meastex and CUReT databases was demonstrated experimentally. It was also shown to be robust to image histogram equalization and random rotation. Our method was compared with six widely used image features. It was shown that our approach is the most robust one. To make our method invariant to other complex textures, the macroscopic part of the method, i.e., the filters used in the method, can be modified.

References

1. H. Greenspan, S. Belongie, R. Goodman, and P. Perona, "Rotation Invariant Texture Recognition Using a Steerable Pyramid," *Proc. 12th IAPR ICPR*, vol. 2, pp. 162-167, 1994.
2. R. Porter and N. Canagarajah, "Robust Rotation-Invariant Texture Classification: Wavelet, Gabor Filter and GMRF Based Schemes," *IEE Proc. Conf. VISP*, vol. 144, no. 3, pp. 180-188, 1997.
3. G.M. Haley and B.S. Manjunath, "Rotation-Invariant Texture Classification Using a Complete Space-Frequency Model," *IEEE Trans. Img. Proc.*, vol. 8, no. 2, pp. 255-269, 1999.
4. R.L. Kashyap and A. Khotanzad, "A Model-Based Method for Rotation Invariant Texture Classification," *IEEE Trans. PAMI*, vol. 8, no. 7, pp. 472-481, 1986.
5. H. Deng and D.A. Clausi, "Gaussian MRF Rotation-Invariant Features for Image Classification," *IEEE Trans. PAMI*, vol. 26, no. 7, 2004.
6. H. Arof and F. Deravi, "Circular Neighborhood and 1-D DFT Features for Texture Classification and Segmentation," *IEE Proc. Conf. VISP*, vol. 145, no. 3, pp. 167-172, 1998.
7. T. Ojala, M. Pietikainen, and T. Maenpaa, "Multiresolution Gray-Scale and Rotation Invariant Texture Classification with Local Binary Patterns," *IEEE Trans. PAMI*, vol. 24, no. 7, pp. 971-987, 2002.
8. X. Huang, S.Z.Li and Y. Wang, "Shape Localization Based on Statistical Method Using Extended Local Binary Pattern," *IEEE Proc. Conf. Image and Graphics*, pp. 184 - 187, 2004.
9. J. Sporring and J. Weickert, "Information Measures in Scale-Spaces," *IEEE Trans. Information Theory*, vol. 45, no. 3, pp. 1051-1058, 1999.
10. I. Fogel and D. Sagi, "Gabor Filters as Texture Discriminator," *Biological Cybernetics*, vol. 61, pp. 103-113, 1989.
11. P. Brodatz, "Textures: A Photographic Album for Artists and Designers," *New York: Dover Publications*, 1966.
12. "MeasTex Image Texture Database and Test Suite," *Centre for Sensor Signal and Information Processing, the University of Queensland.*
13. K. Dana, B. Ginneken, S. Nayar, and J. Koenderink, "Reflectance and Texture of Real-World Surfaces," *ACM Trans. Graphics*, vol. 18, no. 1, pp. 1-34, 1999.
14. C. Tsallis, "Nonextensive Statistics: Theoretical, Experimental and Computational Evidences and Connections," *Brazilian J. Physics*, vol. 29, no. 1, 1999.
15. A.C. Bovik, M. Clark, and W.S. Geisler, "Multichannel texture analysis using localised spatial filters," *IEEE Trans. PAMI*, pp. 55-73, 1990.
16. A. Teuner, O. Pichler, and B.J. Hosticka, "Unsupervised texture segmentation of images using tuned matched Gabor filters," *IEEE Trans. Img. Proc.*, pp. 863-870, 1995.
17. A. Laine and J. Fan, "Texture Classification by Wavelet Packet Signatures," *IEEE Trans. PAMI*, vol. 15, no. 11, 1993.
18. H. Efstathios, D. Michael, and S. Nayar, "Multiresolution Histograms and Their Use for Recognition," *IEEE Trans. PAMI*, vol. 26, no. 7, 2004.
19. R. Chellappa, and S. Chatterjee, "Classification of textures using Gaussian Markov random fields," *IEEE Trans. ASSP*, pp. 959 - 963, 1985.

Gaussian Decomposition for Robust Face Recognition

Fumihiko Sakaue and Takeshi Shakunaga

Department of Computer Science, Okayama University,
3-1-1, Tsushima-naka, Okayama-shi, Japan
{sakaue, shaku}@chino.it.okayama-u.ac.jp

Abstract. This paper discusses Gaussian decomposition of facial images for robust recognition. While it cannot sufficiently extract an effective component, it can decompose an image into two effective components, the filtered image and its residual. The Gaussian component represents rough information for a lighting condition and small individuality. The residual represents individuality and the other information including small noise. The two components complement each other and they are evaluated independently in the framework of eigenface method. The image decomposition can also collaborate with parallel partial projections for robust recognition.

1 Introduction

The appearance of a human face changes with the conditions under which the face images are taken, and it is difficult to control these conditions in a natural environment. Although eigenfaces[1, 2] can efficiently represent changes in lighting conditions when a sufficient set of images are provided for the registration, they cannot be appropriately constructed when too few images are available for the registration. In this case, we must extract a component that is insensitive to the lighting conditions for the robust face recognition.

In image processing, simple filters, for example a Gaussian filter and a difference of Gaussian (DoG) filter, are widely used for extracting intrinsic information from an input image. In the present study, we attempt to utilize these filters for facial image recognition. An input image is decomposed by the filters into a filtered image and its residual. We show a novel method for robust face recognition using both the filtered images and their residuals. The basic idea of image decomposition is proposed in our previous work[3]. Further development of Gaussian decomposition and sufficient experimental results are extensively discussed in this paper.

2 Definitions

2.1 Normalized Eigenspace

Basic definitions and the notation scheme are summarized here. Since the proposed method is based on eigenspace, this section deals mainly with the concept

P.J. Narayanan et al. (Eds.): ACCV 2006, LNCS 3851, pp. 110–119, 2006.

of eigenspace. All images are normalized as follows: Let an N-dimensional vector $\mathbf{X}$ denote an original image composed of N pixels, and let $\mathbf{1}$ denote an N-dimensional vector in which each element is 1. The normalized image $\mathbf{x}$ of an original image $\mathbf{X}$ is defined as $\mathbf{x} = \mathbf{X}/(\mathbf{1}^T\mathbf{X})$. After the normalization, $\mathbf{x}$ is normalized in the sense that $\mathbf{1}^T\mathbf{x} = 1$. An image space constructed by a set of normalized images is called the Normalized Image Space (NIS).

An eigenspace constructed by mean vector $\overline{\mathbf{x}}$ and m-principal eigenvectors Φ_m in NIS is described as $\langle\overline{\mathbf{x}}, \Phi_m\rangle$. In the concept of NIS, an image $\mathbf{x}$ is projected onto eigenspace $\langle\overline{\mathbf{x}}, \Phi_m\rangle$ by $\tilde{\mathbf{x}}^* = \tilde{\Phi}_m^+\mathbf{x}$, where $\tilde{\Phi}_m = [\Phi_m \ \overline{\mathbf{x}}]$ and $\tilde{\Phi}_m^+ = (\tilde{\Phi}_m^T\tilde{\Phi}_m)^{-1}\tilde{\Phi}_m^T$.

In order to measure a similarity between an input image $\mathbf{x}$ and the eigenspace $\langle\overline{\mathbf{x}}, \Phi_m\rangle$, we define a normalized correlation in terms of NIS. It can be defined by a cosine of angle when an image $\mathbf{1}/N$ is regarded as the origin of NIS. That is, a normalized correlation C_I between $\mathbf{x}$ and $\langle\overline{\mathbf{x}}, \Phi_m\rangle$ is defined as

$$C_I = C(\mathbf{x}, \tilde{\Phi}_m\tilde{\mathbf{x}}^*) \tag{1}$$

where

$$C(\mathbf{x}, \mathbf{y}) = \frac{(\mathbf{x} - \mathbf{1}/N)^T(\mathbf{y} - \mathbf{1}/N)}{(||(\mathbf{x} - \mathbf{1}/N)||||(\mathbf{y} - \mathbf{1}/N)||)^{1/2}}.$$

A given image $\mathbf{x}$ can be evaluated in terms of NIS without explicit normalization in this definition.

2.2 Partial Projection

Let us define an indicator matrix P, which is an $N \times N$ diagonal matrix, each diagonal term of which is 1 or 0, which indicates whether the pixel is effective (1) or ineffective (0) for the projection. Then, $\mathbf{x}$ is partially projected onto $\langle\overline{\mathbf{x}}, \Phi_m\rangle$ with indicator matrix P by

$$\tilde{\mathbf{x}}_P^* = (P\tilde{\Phi}_m)^+P\mathbf{x}, \tag{2}$$

where $\tilde{\Phi}_m = [\Phi_m \ \overline{\mathbf{x}}]$ and $(P\tilde{\Phi}_m)^+ = (\tilde{\Phi}_m^TP\tilde{\Phi}_m)^{-1}(P\tilde{\Phi}_m)^T$. A partial residual is defined as

$$\tilde{\mathbf{x}}_P^\sharp = P(\mathbf{x} - \tilde{\Phi}_m\tilde{\mathbf{x}}_P^*). \tag{3}$$

The last element of $\tilde{\mathbf{x}}_P^*$ is important and denoted by β_P. β_P is equivalent to a total of pixel values estimated by the partial projection. When the eigenspace cannot be constructed since only one image is available, we can regard the image as a 0-dimensional eigenspace. The normalized correlation C_I can be extended to span the partial projection. A partial correlation C_P between $\mathbf{x}$ and $\langle\overline{\mathbf{x}}, \Phi_m\rangle$ within a pixel set indicated by P is defined as

$$C_P = C(P\mathbf{x}, P\tilde{\Phi}_m\tilde{\mathbf{x}}_P^*). \tag{4}$$

When P is an identify matrix, Eq. (4) is equivalent to Eq. (1).

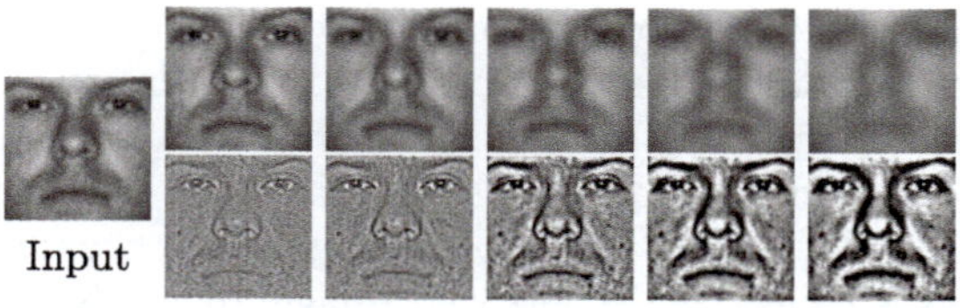

Fig. 1. Examples of the Gaussian decomposition: original images ($\mathbf{x}$)(left), Gaussian images ($\mathbf{x}_G^\$$)(upper row), and residuals ($\mathbf{x}_G^\sharp$)(lower row)

3 Gaussian Decompositions

3.1 Decomposition by Gaussian Filter

An image decomposition by a universal eigenspace, so called the canonical eigenface, is proposed by Shakunaga and Shigenari[4] when the eigenspace is constructed from a lot of facial images taken under various lighting conditions. The decomposition using the canonical eigenspace is useful when an appropriate learning set can be registered. However, when a face image is taken from a different camera under a different condition, the eigenspace may not properly decompose the image. In addition, when a test image contains a lot of noises, such as occlusions, the noises may affect the entire image by the projection onto the eigenspace. In order to refrain from these problems, we consider an alternative method without using the eigenspace for image decomposition.

Wang et al.[5] proposed a self quotient image (SQI) that extracts the insensitive component for illumination. In their method, the Gaussian filter is applied for getting the lighting information. The Gaussian filter is used in our method for image decomposition. The 2-d Gaussian function $G(u, v)$ is defined as

$$G(u,v) = (2\pi\sigma^2)^{-1} \exp\left(-\frac{u^2+v^2}{2\sigma^2}\right),$$

where σ is the standard deviation of the Gaussian function. Let G denote an $N \times N$ matrix that works as the Gaussian filter. Then, the decomposition of image $\mathbf{x}$ into a Gaussian image $\mathbf{x}_G^\$$ and its residual $\mathbf{x}_G^\sharp$ can be represented in

$$\mathbf{x}_G^\$ = G\mathbf{x} \tag{5}$$

and

$$\mathbf{x}_G^\sharp = \mathbf{x} - \mathbf{x}_G^\$. \tag{6}$$

An input image $\mathbf{x}$ is decomposed into the Gaussian image $\mathbf{x}_G^\$$ and the residual $\mathbf{x}_G^\sharp$. The two components complement each other. Figure 1 shows examples of the Gaussian decomposition. If the SQI should be made, each pixel value of the input image is divided by the corresponding pixel in the Gaussian image. In the proposed method, however, the Gaussian image is subtracted from the original image to calculate the residual.

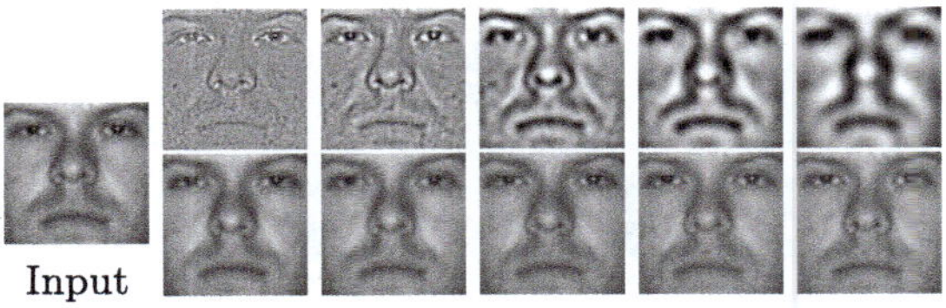

Fig. 2. Examples of the DoG decomposition: original images ($\mathbf{x}$) (left), DoG images ($\mathbf{x}_D^{\$}$)(upper row), and residuals ($\mathbf{x}_D^{\sharp}$) (lower row)

A face recognition algorithm is constructed in the ordinary way using the two components. In the registration stage, one eigenspace is constructed from a set of the filtered images and is denoted by $\langle \overline{\mathbf{x}}_G^{\$}, \Phi_{mG}^{\$} \rangle$. The other eigenspace is constructed from a set of the residuals and is denoted by $\langle \overline{\mathbf{x}}_G^{\sharp}, \Phi_{mG}^{\sharp} \rangle$. In the recognition stage, a filtered image $\mathbf{x}^{\$}$ and a residual $\mathbf{x}^{\sharp}$ are evaluated independently by

$$C^{\$} = C(\mathbf{x}_G^{\$}, \tilde{\Phi}_{mG}^{\$} \tilde{\Phi}_{mG}^{\$+} \mathbf{x}_G^{\$}) \tag{7}$$

and

$$C^{\sharp} = C(\mathbf{x}_G^{\sharp}, \tilde{\Phi}_{mG}^{\sharp} \tilde{\Phi}_{mG}^{\sharp+} \mathbf{x}_G^{\sharp}). \tag{8}$$

Finally, the image $\mathbf{x}$ is evaluated using the sum of $C^{\$}$ and $C^{\sharp}$.

3.2 Decomposition by Difference of Gaussian (DoG)

The Difference-of-Gaussian (DoG) filter is often used for edge detection[6]. Since edge features are effective for image recognition, the DoG filter provides a candidate feature for face recognition. The DoG $\mathbf{x}_D^{\$}$ of an image $\mathbf{x}$ is defined by $\mathbf{x}_D^{\$} = G_1\mathbf{x} - G_2\mathbf{x}$, where G_1 and G_2 are two Gaussian filters that have different standard deviations, σ_1 and σ_2, respectively. In this paper, σ_2 is equal to $1.6\sigma_1$. Here, the residual $\mathbf{x}_D^{\sharp}$ is defined as $\mathbf{x}_D^{\sharp} = \mathbf{x} - \mathbf{x}_D^{\$}$. These components are evaluated in face recognition in the same manner as discussed for the Gaussian decomposition. Figure 2 shows examples of the DoG decomposition. When σ_1 is small, the edge component is emphasized by the DoG filter and the residual $\mathbf{x}_D^{\sharp}$ is smoothed. On the other hand, when σ_1 becomes larger, the residual gets less smooth because the DoG image is excessively smoothed and the high-frequency component remains in the residual.

4 Face Recognition by Parallel Partial Projections

4.1 Parallel Partial Projections

When an input image contains local noises such as shadows or occlusions, the noises affect the recognition results. First, in the most commonly used method, although images for face recognition are normalized by some method, when the

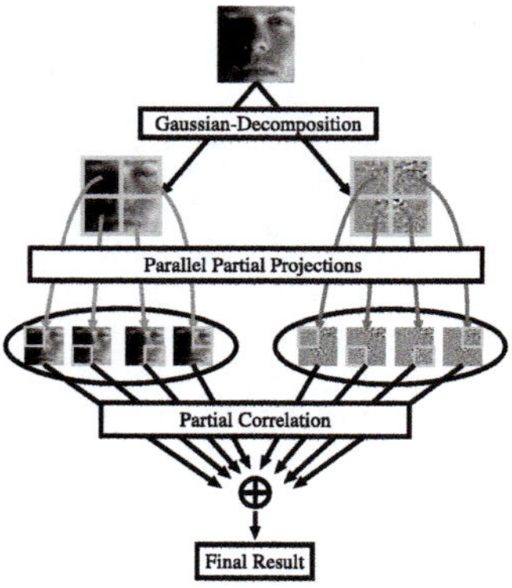

Fig. 3. Combination of Guassian and locational decompositions

image contains noises, the image cannot be properly normalized. Second, when we use an eigenspace, the effects of noises is spread to the entire image by the projection onto the eigenspace, affecting the face recognition results.

In order to avoid this problem, we use local information independently. In this section, we introduce a locational decomposition algorithm, which can use local information independently.

Parallel partial projection (PPP) onto eigenspaces is proposed for face recognition under various lighting conditions. This is one method for implementing the locational decomposition, and so local information is treated independently and the spread of noises is prevented. In this paper, this method is used as the locational decomposition of the image.

Let us describe the j-th partial projection $\tilde{\mathbf{x}}^*_{P_j}$ onto eigenspace $\langle \overline{\mathbf{x}}, \Phi_m \rangle$. Here, PPP is a set of partial projections $\{\tilde{\mathbf{x}}^*_{P_1}, \cdots, \tilde{\mathbf{x}}^*_{P_M}\}$, where M is the number of parts indicated by P_j. This can be represented by the backprojected image, which can be calculated as

$$\mathbf{x}^{\$'} = \sum_{j=1}^{M} P_j \tilde{\Phi}_m \tilde{\mathbf{x}}^*_{P_j}.$$

4.2 Discriminant Functions

A Gaussian decomposition and PPP can be combined in a simple manner. In the combination method, an input image is decomposed by the Gaussian decomposition, and the two decomposed components are evaluated in a framework of the PPP. Figure 3 shows the concept of the combination.

At first, an input image $\mathbf{x}$ is decomposed by Eqs. (5) and (6). The decomposition dose not affect parallel partial projections because the method decomposes an input image without any noise expansion.

The decomposed images are evaluated by a framework of PPP. In the combination method, the partial correlation should be defined for each component.

SS1	SS2	SS3	SS4	SS5
$\theta \leq 12°$	$\theta \leq 25°$	$\theta \leq 50°$	$\theta \leq 77°$	$\theta > 77°$

Fig. 4. Example images in subsets 1-5 (SS1-5), where θ is the angle between the light source direction and the camera axis

When an eigenspace constructed from a set of $\mathbf{x}_G^{\$}$ is denoted by $\langle \overline{\mathbf{x}}_G^{\$}, \Phi_{mG}^{\$} \rangle$, a partial correlation $C_{P_j}^{\$}$ between $\mathbf{x}_G^{\$}$ and $\langle \overline{\mathbf{x}}_G^{\$}, \Phi_{mG}^{\$} \rangle$ within a pixel set indicated by P_j is calculated by

$$C_{P_j}^{\$} = C(P_j \mathbf{x}_G^{\$}, P_j(\tilde{\Phi}_{mG}^{\$}(P_j \tilde{\Phi}_{mG}^{\$})^{+} \mathbf{x}_G^{\$})). \tag{9}$$

In the similar way, a partial correlation $C_{P_j}^{\sharp}$ between a residual $\mathbf{x}_G^{\sharp}$ and an eigenspace $\langle \overline{\mathbf{x}}_G^{\sharp} \Phi_{mG}^{\sharp} \rangle$ is calculated by

$$C_{P_j}^{\sharp} = C(P_j \mathbf{x}_G^{\sharp}, P_j(\tilde{\Phi}_{mG}^{\sharp}(P_j \tilde{\Phi}_{mG}^{\sharp})^{+} \mathbf{x}_G^{\sharp})). \tag{10}$$

where $\langle \overline{\mathbf{x}}_G^{\sharp} \Phi_{mG}^{\sharp}{}' \rangle$ is constructed from a set of the residuals defined in Eq. (6). Then, a total correlation $C_G{}'$ is defined as

$$C_G{}' = w \sum_{j=1}^{M} C_{P_j}^{\$} + (1 - w) \sum_{j=1}^{M} C_{P_j}^{\sharp}, \tag{11}$$

where w is a weight for the Gaussian components.

While the parallel partial projections provides robustness against local noises, effective information for face recognition does not increase in the whole image. The parallel partial projections still requires a sufficient number of registered images for each person since the conventional eigenface method requires a lot of images for the stable recognition. On the other hand, the Gaussian decomposition often provides stable results even when only a few images are registered. However, it is sometimes seriously affected by local noises. In the combination method, however, the parallel partial projections prevents local noises spreading to the whole image when the Gaussian decomposition provides a sufficient information for face recognition. Therefore, the combination method works better than the single method.

5 Experimental Results

5.1 Results for Yale Face Database B

Data Specifications: We performed discrimination experiments on 640 frontal face images of 10 people, which were taken from the Yale Face Database B [7].

Table 1. Discrimination rates(%) for Yale Face Database B when only one image is registered. NN indicates the Nearest Neighbor method, PPP indicates Parallel Partial Projections, Gaussian and DoG indicate Gaussian and DoG decompositions, and PPP-Gaussian and PPP-DoG are combination methods.

Method	NN	PPP	Gaussian	DoG	PPP-Gaussian	PPP-DoG
Subset 2	99.2	100	100	100	100	100
Subset 3	74.6	99.2	99.2	98.3	100	100
Subset 4	30.4	78.3	90.6	71.7	100	98.6
Subset 5	12.2	78.3	57.7	32.3	100	100

Table 2. Discrimination rates(%) for Yale Face Database B when seven images are registered: EF indicates the eigenface method and the other methods are as listed in Table 1

Method	EF	PPP	Gaussian	DoG	PPP-Gaussian	PPP-DoG
Subset 2	100	100	100	100	100	100
Subset 3	100	100	100	100	100	100
Subset 4	93.5	100	98.6	99.3	100	100
Subset 5	56.1	100	74.1	72.0	100	100

The database includes 65 frontal face images of each person. Sixty-four of the images were taken under different lighting conditions. Each image was converted to a 64×64 pixel image such that the eyes of all of the images are in the same coordinates.Discrimination experiments were performed using the segmented data set. Figure 4 shows examples of the five subsets (SS1-5).

Discrimination results: Table 1 shows the discrimination rates for the dataset when only one image is registered. In the methods which use the PPP, images were divided into sixty-four squares. In the Gaussian and DoG decompositions, σ and σ_1 are fixed to 0.5 and 1.0, respectively. Table 2 shows discrimination rates when seven images are registered. In the experiments, PPP and the combination methods give the complete discrimination because a sufficient number are registered. Gaussian and DoG decomposition methods give slightly worse results than PPP because they cannot sufficiently suppress the noises.

Table 3 shows results when the σ and σ_1 for Gaussian and DoG filters change. In the Gaussian decomposition, the best discrimination rate is given when $\sigma = 0.5$ and the best discrimination rate for DoG decomposition is given when $\sigma_1 = 1.0$. Almost all the rates become worse for a larger value of σ or σ_1. The results suggest that effective features for facial image recognition are contained in the high-frequency components. Table 4 shows results when the number of image parts changes. When the number is too big, the discrimination rate becomes worse because each part could not provide sufficient information for recognition because it is too small. In the experiments, the best result is provided when the number of parts is 4×4 and 8×8.

Tables 5 and 6 show results when images classified into SS4 are registered. In these experiments, images for registration are randomly selected from SS4.

Table 3. Comparison of the σ (or σ_1) for Gaussian (DoG) filter when only one image is registered from SubSet 1. Subset 4 and Subset 5 are used as test sets in the experiment.

	Test Class	σ (σ_1)					
		0.5	1.0	1.5	2.0	2.5	3.0
Gaussian	SS4	90.6	89.9	86.2	81.2	74.6	71.7
	SS5	57.7	55.6	45.5	37.0	27.0	22.2
DoG	SS4	26.8	71.7	58.7	37.7	31.9	23.2
	SS5	16.4	32.3	19.6	13.2	14.3	16.9
PPP-Gaussian	SS4	100	100	99.3	97.8	97.1	94.2
	SS5	100	100	100	100	100	100
PPP-DoG	SS4	75.4	98.6	79.0	43.5	35.5	34.1
	SS5	82.5	100	98.4	85.7	71.4	49.7

Table 4. Comparison of the number of segments for each algorithm when 7 images are registered from SubSet 1. Subset 4 and Subset 5 are used as test sets in the experiment.

# parts	Test Class	PPP	PPP-Gaussian	PPP-DoG
1 × 1	SS4	93.5	98.6	99.3
	SS5	56.1	74.1	72.0
2 × 2	SS4	96.4	99.3	100
	SS5	94.7	97.4	94.2
4 × 4	SS4	100	100	100
	SS5	100	100	99.5
8 × 8	SS4	100	100	100
	SS5	100	100	100
16 × 16	SS4	98.6	100	89.9
	SS5	96.3	99.5	87.3

Table 5. Discrimination rates(%) when one image from SS4 is registered

Method	NN	PPP	Gaussian	DoG	PPP-Gaussian	PPP-DoG
Subset 1	16.7	41.3	33.9	69.8	97.4	97.1
Subset 2	18.4	41.2	31.8	65.9	98.5	96.7
Subset 3	22.0	37.3	38.7	63.3	94.0	90.6
Subset 5	21.4	37.0	36.8	47.6	96.5	94.3

Table 6. Discrimination rates(%) when 7 images from SS4 are registered

Method	EF	PPP	Gaussian	DoG	PPP-Gaussian	PPP-DoG
Subset 1	86.7	99.5	100	100	100	100
Subset 2	91.3	99.9	99.9	100	100	100
Subset 3	95.5	97.8	99.4	97.4	100	100
Subset 5	7.09	98.1	87.0	88.2	100	100

Table 7. Discrimination rates(%) using other methods. Illumination cone (IC1), illumination cone with cast shadow (IC2), photometric alignment using RANSAC (PA), segmented linear subspace method (SLS) and proposed methods using 1 or 7 images.

Method	IC1[8]	IC2[8]	PA[9]	SLS[10]	PPP-Gaussian(1)	PPP-Gaussian(7)	PPP-DoG(1)	PPP-DoG(7)
Subset 2	100	100	100	100	100	100	100	100
Subset 3	100	100	100	100	100	100	100	100
Subset 4	91.4	100	100	100	100	100	92.8	100
Subset 5	-	-	81.5	-	100	100	100	100

This process was repeated twenty times and registered images for each person were varied. Most results in these experiments are worse than those shown in Tables 1 and 2 because images in SS4 include more shadows than SS1. However, results of the combination methods still keep high discrimination rates in these experiments. Table 7 shows results reported in literatures[8, 9, 10]. It shows all the algorithms provide good results when a sufficient number of images are registered. However, it should be noted that our method can provide almost same results even when only few images are registered.

In conclusions, the combination methods work better than the single decomposition methods. In addition, the combination methods have the advantages of both Gaussian decomposition and parallel partial projections and work well even when only one image is registered and the test images include a significant amount of shadows.

5.2 Results for the AR Database

The AR database[11] contains images of 135 people taken under various conditions for each person. For this experiment, we used database images taken under seven different conditions. The example images are as shown in Fig 5. In this

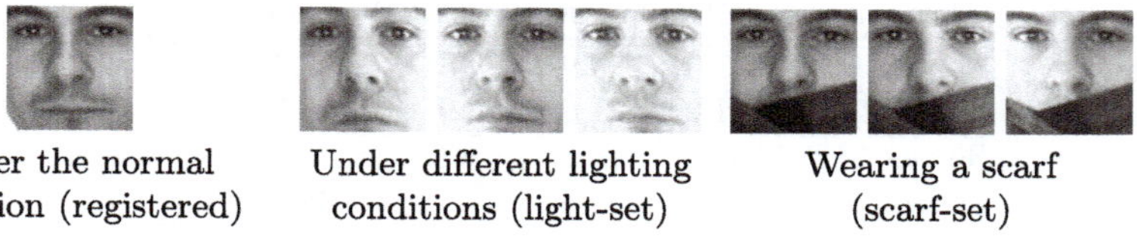

Fig. 5. Examples of segmented images in the AR Database. The top row shows registered images taken under normal conditions. The middle and bottom rows show test images taken under conditions that differed from those of the registered image.

Table 8. Discrimination rates(%) for the AR Database

Method	NN	PPP	Gaussian	DoG	PPP-Gaussian	PPP-DoG
light	40.5	70.1	76.8	81.0	94.1	93.1
scarf	3.7	45.3	55.1	64.4	86.2	84.4

experiment, only one image was registered and the other images were used as the test set from which test images were selected.

Table 8 shows the discrimination rates obtained in the experiments. The Gaussian decomposition and DoG decomposition gave better results than PPP because PPP cannot work when only one image is registered. The combination methods worked better than the other methods for both of the individual sets. The results of this experiment indicate that the combination methods work well when only one image is registered and the test images include a large occlusion.

6 Conclusions

The combination of the Gaussian/DoG decomposition and the parallel partial projections has the advantages of the both methods. While the use of only one of the method cannot handle complex problems, the combination of the decompositions can easily overcome such problems. works even when only one image is registered and test images include a lot of noises.

This work has been supported by Grant-In-Aid for Science Research under Grant No.15300062 from the Ministry of Education, Science, Sports, and Culture, Japanese Government. It has also been supported by National Institute of Information and Communications Technology.

References

1. Turk, M., Pentland, A.: Eigenfaces for recognition. Journal of Cognitive Neuroscience **3** (1991) 71–86
2. Moghaddam, B., Pentland, A.: Probabilistic visual learning for object representation. IEEE Trans. Pattern Analysis and Machine Intelligence **19** (1997) 696–710
3. Sakaue, F., Shakunaga, T.: Combination of projectional and locational decompositions for robust face recognition. In: Proc. IEEE International Workshop on Analysis and Modeling of Faces and Gestures. (2005) 407–421
4. Shakunaga, T., Shigenari, K.: Decomposed eigenface for face recognition under various lighting conditions. In: Proc. CVPR2001. Volume 1. (2001) 864–871
5. Wang, H., Li, S., Wang, Y.: Face recognition under varying lighting conditions using self quotient image. In: Proc. IEEE FG2004. (2004) 819–824
6. Marr, D., Hildreth, E.C.: Theory of edge detection. In: Proc. Royal Society, London B. Volume 207. (1980) 187–217
7. Georghiades, A., Belhumeur, P., Kriegman, D.: From few to many: Generative models for recognition under variable pose and illuminations. In: Proc. FG2000. (2000) 277–284
8. Georghiades, A., Belhumeur, P., Kriegman, D.: From few to many: illumination cone models for face recognition under variable lighting and pose. IEEE Trans. Pattern Analysis and Machine Intelligence **23** (2001) 643–660
9. Okabe, T., Sato, Y.: Object recognition based on photometric alignment using ransac. In: Proc. CVPR2003. Volume 1. (2003) 221–228
10. Batur, A., Hayes III, M.: Linear subspaces for illumination robust face recognition. In: Proc. ICCV2001. Volume II. (2001) 296–301
11. Martinez, A., Benavente, R.: The AR face database. Technical Report #24, CVC (1998)

Occlusion Invariant Face Recognition Using Selective LNMF Basis Images

Hyun Jun Oh[1], Kyoung Mu Lee[2], Sang Uk Lee[2], and Chung-Hyuk Yim[3]

[1] SK Telecom, Korea
purete5@nate.com
[2] School of Electrical Eng. and Computer Science,
Seoul National University, Korea
kyoungmu@snu.ac.kr, sanguk@sting.snu.ac.kr
[3] School of Mechanical Design and Automation Engineering,
Seoul National University of Technology, Korea
chyim@snut.ac.kr

Abstract. In this paper, we propose a novel occlusion invariant face recognition algorithm based on Selective Local Nonnegative Matrix Factorization (S-LNMF) technique. The proposed algorithm is composed of two phases; the occlusion detection phase and the selective LNMF-based recognition phase. We use local approach to effectively detect partial occlusion in the input face image. A face image is first divided into a finite number of disjointed local patches, and then each patch is represented by PCA (Principal Component Analysis), obtained by corresponding occlusion-free patches of training images. And 1-NN threshold classifier was used for occlusion detection for each patch in the corresponding PCA space. In the recognition phase, by employing the LNMF-based face representation, we exclusively use the LNMF bases of occlusion-free image patches for face recognition. Euclidean nearest neighbor rule is applied for the matching. Experimental results demonstrate that the proposed local patch-based occlusion detection technique and S-LNMF-based recognition algorithm works well and the performance is superior to other conventional approaches.

1 Introduction

One of the most important goals of computer vision is to achieve visual recognition ability comparable to that of human [11],[12],[13]. And among many recognition subjects, the face recognition problem has been researched intensively during last few decades, due to its great potential in the various practical applications such as HCI Human Computer Interface), intelligent robot, surveillance, and so on. And, if the face recognition is diverged further, obvious problem of occlusion by other objects or apparels such as sunglasses or scarves becomes eminent. Thus a robust algorithm for occluded faces is required for real applications. So far, several approaches dealing with occlusion have been proposed in the literature. A. Leonardis and H. Bischof [1],[2] proposed a robust PCA approach that could estimate the coefficients of eigenimages from partially degraded images. This approach presented successful reconstruction of partially occluded images, however the performance was usually

P.J. Narayanan et al. (Eds.): ACCV 2006, LNCS 3851, pp. 120 – 129, 2006.

depended on training set. S. Z. Li et al. proposed a novel method, called local non-negative matrix factorization (LNMF) [3], for learning spatially localized, parts-based subspace representation of visual patterns. In addition to the non-negativity constraint in the standard NMF, the prescribed objective function imposed localization constraints, [4]. Experimental results compared LNMF with the NMF and PCA methods for occluded face recognition, where the advantages of LNMF were demonstrated. A. M. Martinez [5] described a probabilistic approach that is able to compensate for imprecisely localized, partially occluded, and expression-variant faces when only single training sample per class was available to the system.

In this paper, we present a novel face recognition algorithm robust to occlusion using S-LNMF technique. The proposed algorithm is based on a local approach where face images are divided into a finite number of disjointed local patches. But, unlike previous approaches, we perform occlusion detection explicitly. The occluded regions in the face images are detected by 1-NN classifier. Afterwards, the recognition process is performed over selected LNMF bases of occlusion-free patches. We evaluate our algorithm on the occlusion subset of the AR database [6], and demonstrate that the proposed algorithm has superior performance than previous face recognition schemes.

2 Occlusion Detection

The proposed face recognition algorithm is based on selected LNMF subspace matching. Note that since each LNMF basis image exhibits high localization characteristics in spatial domain, local occlusion affects only the coefficients of the corresponding bases, so that the error becomes local and not global. So, by using the LNMF bases for occlusion-free regions exclusively, we can achieve robust matching for occlusion. However, in order to select relevant local bases, we need to determine the occluded regions in a face image in advance. In this section we propose an occlusion detection algorithm based on one class classifier in PCA space.

2.1 Local Subdivision of a Face Image

Partial occlusions in face images usually occurs when subjects wear adornments like sunglass or scarf, or when faces are covered by other objects such as hands, cup and so on. In order to detect the locally occluded regions in a face image, we first divide the image into a finite number of local disjoint patches as in Fig. 1, and then examine each patch individually [5].

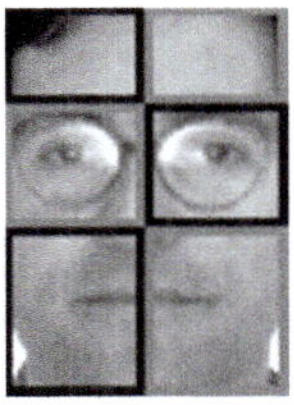

Fig. 1. Local subdivision of a face

2.2 Local Occlusion Detection in PCA

Occlusion detection of a given face image is accomplished for each local patch independently by employing pattern classification framework. Note that each local patch is still high dimensional data that are computationally infeasible. So we deal with each patch image in a low dimensional subspace after dimension reduction using PCA (Principal Component Analysis) [10],[14],[15],[16],[17].

6 PCA subspaces corresponding to 6 local patches of occlusion-free faces are trained by normal face images. When a test face image is given, it is divided into 6 local patches as shown in Fig. 1, and then each patch, $k=1,2,\ldots 6$, are projected onto the corresponding eigenspace, producing the PCA coefficients. So, the occlusion detection for each patch is accomplished by comparing the coefficient vectors of occlusion-free images with that of the test image in the corresponding eigenspace.

2.3 Supervised l-Nearest Neighbor Threshold Classfiers

To distinguish normal data from occluded ones in eigenspace, we need a proper classifier. Occlusion detection problem can be seen as a type of one class classification problem [7],[8]. That is, the goal of one class classification is to accurately describe one class of objects, disregarding a wide range of other objects that are not of interest.

In general, the performances of conventional classifiers such as k-NN and 1-NN classifier are highly dependent on the number of training samples. However, sufficient training samples are not always provided. To improve the classification performance when the number of training data is limited, we introduce a supervised 1-NN threshold classifier that employs absolute distance between samples contrast to the relative distance of k-NN classifier and 1-NN distance classifier. With a reasonable threshold value, making hyperspheres of target class data can reduce the classifier's dependency upon the number of training data. Fig. 2 (a) shows the concept of the proposed classifier. The radius of hypersphere is represented as the circles and outlier class data are illustrated as X. When an unknown input test data is entered, the nearest neighbor among training data is found. If the nearest neighbor is an outlier class data, the test data is labeled as outlier class data. If the nearest neighbor is a target class data, distance between the input data and the nearest one is measured.

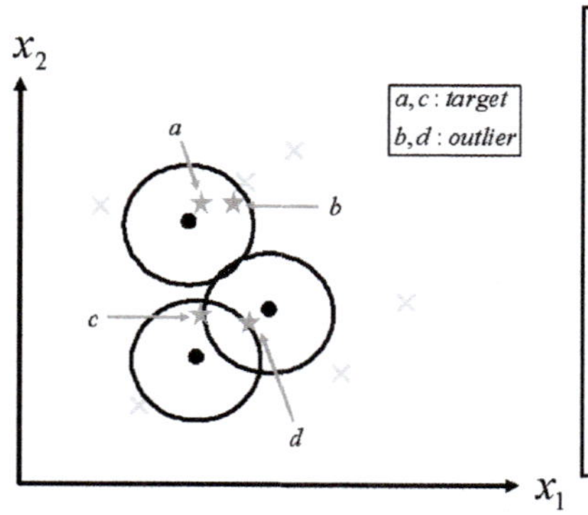

(a)

```
/* Supervised 1-NN threshold classifier */

Find the nearest neighbor of a test data.
If the nearest neighbor is an outlier,
   test data is assigned to the outlier class .
Else
   if distance < threshold,
      test data is assigned to the target class.
   else
      test data is assigned to the outlier class.
```

(b)

Fig. 2. Supervised 1-NN threshold classifier

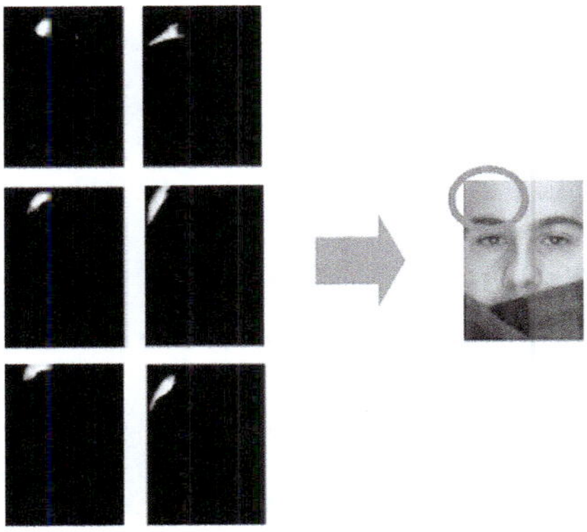

Fig. 3. Example of LNMF bases

If the distance is smaller than a threshold value, which is the hypersphere radius, the test data is labeled as target class data, or else outlier class data. The algorithm is summarized as in Fig.3 (b). According to this algorithm, data a and c are classified correctly as the target class since the nearest neighbor is the target class data and they are within the hypersphere. And although data b is located in the hypersphere, it is correctly classified as an outlier since its nearest neighbor is the outlier.

3 Face Recognition Using Selective LNMF Basis Images

After detecting occluded regions by the methods mentioned in the previous section, LNMF based matching technique is applied for recognition. Since the occluded regions are already identified, LNMF bases corresponding to only occlusion-free regions are to be integrated.

3.1 LNMF Basis Selection

Unlike PCA which exhibits holistic features of an image, LNMF can learn spatially localized, parts-based subspace representation [3]. Moreover, the significance between LNMF bases is non-hierarchic. Since the maximum number of LNMF bases that can be learned is infinite, we can initiate the number of bases. Note that LNMF bases are spatially localized; some are corresponding to occluded regions and the others are corresponding to occlusion-free regions. If we choose to indiscriminately use all the bases for face recognition, the bases corresponding to occluded regions will degrade the recognition performance. Therefore it is natural to employ the bases corresponding to the occlusion-free regions selectively. In Fig. 3, 6 images on left show an example of LNMF basis images corresponding to the occlusion-free upper left region of a face. These bases are nearly independent to the lower occluded part by scarf, and thus can be used to reconstruct the local region correctly. Similarly, other bases, not located at the occluded region can contribute to the recognition.

In order to detect bases for occluded region, let us define a measure for occluded energy per each basis as follows.

$$E^{i}_{Occlusion} = \frac{\sum_{x,y \in W} I_i^2(x,y)}{\sum_{x=1}^{C}\sum_{y=1}^{R} I_i^2(x,y)}, \quad i = 1,2,\ldots,N, \tag{1}$$

where $C \times R$ is the image size, $I_i(x,y)$ is the value of the i_{th} LNMF basis at x column and y row, W is the detected occluded region, and N is the number of bases.

3.2 Face Recognition in LNMF Subspace

Face recognition is performed in the LNMF subspace spanned by occlusion-free bases. Since LNMF bases set is not orthonormal like PCA bases set, in order to calculate the LNMF coefficients of an input image, we use pseudo inverse of the selected occlusion-free LNMF bases matrix. Let $\mathbf{B} = [\mathbf{b}_1\ \mathbf{b}_2\ \cdots \mathbf{b}_N]$ be the original LNMF bases set. For a given test face $\mathbf{y}$, we can determine the occlusion-free basis set associated with it, and denote it as $\mathbf{W} = [\mathbf{w}_1\ \mathbf{w}_2\ \cdots \mathbf{w}_M]\ (\mathbf{W} \subset \mathbf{B}, M \le N)$. Then the selected coefficient vector $\mathbf{h}$ of $\mathbf{y}$ can be obtained by

$$\mathbf{h} = \mathbf{W}^{+}\mathbf{y}, \tag{2}$$

where $\mathbf{W}^{+}$ is the pseudo inverse of $\mathbf{W}$. Similarly, each training face image $\mathbf{x}_i\ (i = 1,2,\cdots,K)$, where K is the total number of training faces, is projected into the same selected occlusion-free LNMF subspace with coefficient vector $\mathbf{g}_i\ (i = 1,2,\cdots,K)$.

$$\mathbf{g}_i = \mathbf{W}^{+}\mathbf{x}_i, \quad i = 1,2,\cdots,K. \tag{3}$$

Then, the recognition is performed by finding the closest training face in the feature space as follows.

$$\arg\min_i \| \mathbf{g}_i - \mathbf{h} \|, \quad i = 1,2,\cdots,K. \tag{4}$$

Since only selected basis images are used in the proposed algorithm, unlike original face recognition technique using LNMF [3], the number of basis images used for recognition changes according to the result of the occlusion detection.

4 Experimental Results

4.1 The AR-Face Database

We used the AR face database for our test [6]. For illustration, normal and partially occluded images by sunglass and scarf are shown in Fig. 4 (b) and (c). Localization and normalization for each face images are performed by aligning eye positions, removing background and warping, so that each face became a 64 x 88 array of 256 grayscale values. We performed experiments with 56 men and 44 women selected at random. We use normal (occlusion free), sunglass, and scarf images totaling 300 images. Among them, 100 normal images are used for LNMF bases learning. For the supervised classifiers for occlusion detection, 50 sunglass images and 50 scarf images are used as outlier class data in the training phase. The rest 50 sunglass and 50 scarf images are used for the test of face recognition.

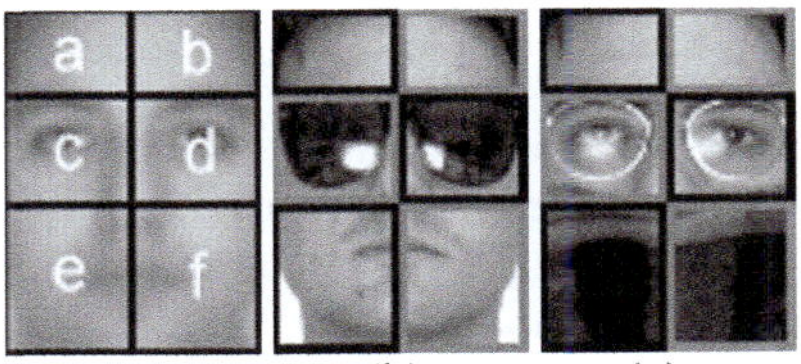

(a) (b) (c)

Fig. 4. Example of partially occluded faces

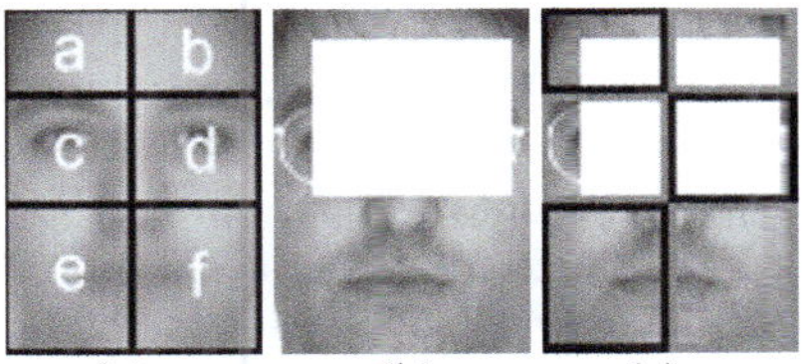

(a) (b) (c)

Fig. 5. Synthetic occlusion patterns

4.2 Occlusion Detection Results

4.2.1 The Performance Comparisons of the Classifiers

We quantitatively evaluated the performances of the occlusion detection schemes. Occluded regions are detected in the eigenspace, the feature space trained by PCA. Each training normal face image is divided into 6 disjoint patches as shown in Fig. 4 (a), and the corresponding 6 eigenspaces are learned. Fig. 4 (b) and (c) show examples of test occluded faces, in which patches (**c**, **d**) and (**e**, **f**) are occluded, respectively. Considering LNMF bases selection after occlusion detection, discarding the normal data labeled as the occluded data may reduce the information that can be used for recognition to some extent. However, using the occluded data labeled as the normal data in the recognition phase lowers the performance seriously since it delivers disturbed information. Thus, as a measurement compared with the performances of the classifiers, we evaluated the false alarm rate when the detection rate is 100% (false rejection rate is 0%).

The detection results on test images are shown in Table 1. In case of k-NN classifier the performance when $k = 3$ is worse than when $k = 1$. This shows that the finding numerous nearest neighbors lowers the detection performance. The supervised 1-NN threshold classifier and the k-NN with $k = 1$ gave the best results in this test. Now, these two classifiers were tested on test images with synthetic occlusion pattern that were quite different from the trained outlier patterns as shown in Fig. 5 (b) and (c). We have examined the occluded patches a, b, c, and d. Since no false alarm can occur in this test, detection rates were calculated and summarized in the Table 2. Note that the supervised 1-NN threshold classifier still gave robust performance, while the k-NN classifier didn't work at all under this circumstance. Based on the above results, we chose the supervised 1-NN threshold classifier as the occlusion detector for our face recognition system.

Table 1. The performance comparison of the classifiers on real occlusion

Classifier	Detection Rate / False Alarm Rate (%)				Average FAR (%)
	c	**d**	**e**	**f**	
k-NN (k=3)	100/0	100/0	100/4	100/2	1.5
k-NN (k=1)	100/0	100/0	100/0	100/0	0
Supervised 1-NN threshold	100/0	100/0	100/0	100/0	0

4.2.2 Subdivision of Face Image

Proposed partial occlusion detection and face recognition algorithm are developed based on local patches of a face image. Thus, different division methods may result in different performances on both occlusion detection and recognition. In this section, we examine the optimal subdivision method of face images in an empirical sense. Fig. 6 shows 12 possible subdivision layouts that we have considered in this experiment. The supervised 1-NN threshold classifier was used for the comparison of the occlusion detection performances. And the false alarm rate with 100% detection rate for each subdivision method was calculated for the performance evaluation. Table 3 shows the results of the test. From these results, we concluded that the method 6-1 is optimal.

Table 2. The performance comparison of classifiers on synthetic occlusion

Classifier	Detection Rate / False Alarm Rate (%)				Average DR (%)
	a	**b**	**c**	**d**	
k-NN (*k*=1)	0/-	0/-	0/-	0/-	0
Supervised 1-NN threshold	100/-	100/-	100/-	100/-	100

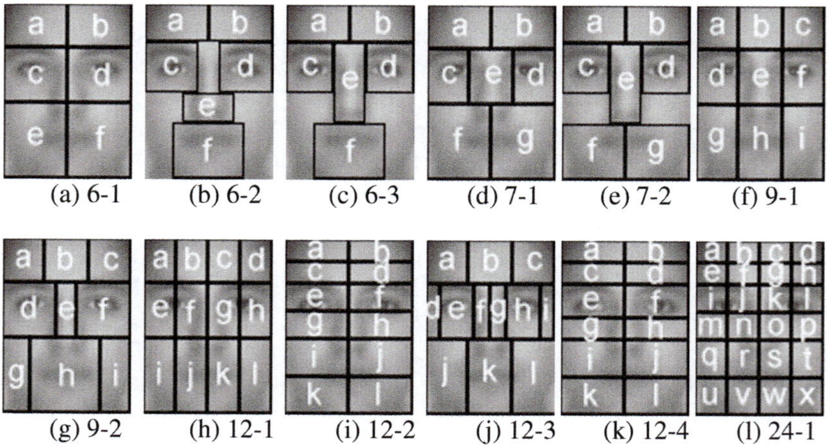

(a) 6-1 (b) 6-2 (c) 6-3 (d) 7-1 (e) 7-2 (f) 9-1

(g) 9-2 (h) 12-1 (i) 12-2 (j) 12-3 (k) 12-4 (l) 24-1

Fig. 6. Subdivision methods

Table 3. Detection performance of subdivision method

Method	**6-1**	**6-2**	**6-3**	**7-1**	**7-2**	**9-1**
Average FAR (%)	0	32.5	15.5	1.2	0.4	14.3
Method	**9-2**	**12-1**	**12-2**	**12-3**	**12-4**	**24-1**
Average FAR (%)	9.7	3.8	7.0	16.7	7.0	16.3

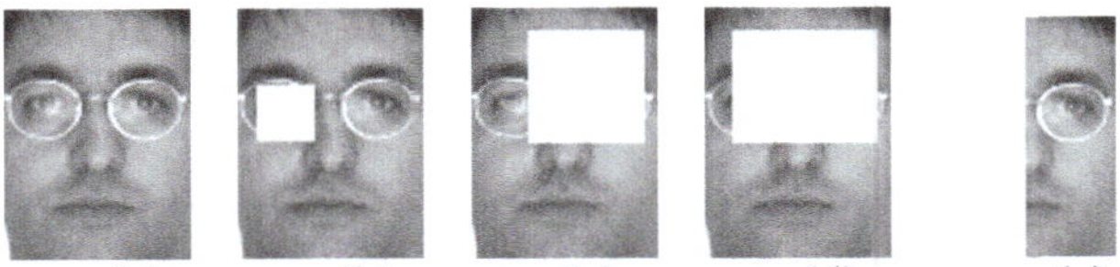

(a) (b) (c) (d) (e)

Fig. 7. Examples of Synthetically occluded test images

4.3 Face Recognition Results

4.3.1 LNMF Bases

We have trained 100 occlusion-free training face images in the AR database. The bases for occluded regions are detected by the equation (1) with a threshold of 0.1, which means that any basis, whose energy in an occluded region is greater than 10% of the total energy, will not be used for matching.

4.3.2 Experiments on Synthetic Occlusions

First, we tested our S-LNMF based recognition algorithm on synthetically occluded images as shown in Figs. 8 (b)-(e). Occlusion-free images as in Fig. 7 (a) were used for the training. Some conventional algorithms including PCA [10], LNMF [3] and R-PCA [1],[2] were also tested for the comparative performance evaluation. The recognition rate, defined as the percentage of correctly recognized faces, is used as the performance measure. Table 4 show the recognition results. The recognition rate of the proposed algorithm was obtained when the number of bases was 100. Experimental results show that the proposed algorithm achieved the highest recognition rate. Although R-PCA gave slightly better results than PCA and LNMF, the performance decreased drastically as the size of the occluded region became larger.

4.3.3 Experiments on Real Occlusions

We have tested our algorithm on real face images occluded by sunglass and scarf in AR database. All 135 people (76 men and 59 women) in the AR face database were used. Among these, all 135 normal face images and 70 occluded face images (35 sunglass images and 35 scarf images of 20 men and 15 women) were used for the training the target class and the outlier class, respectively. The remaining 100 sunglass images and 100 scarf images were used for probes and all the normal frontal faces were used for the gallery.

Table 4. Recognition rate (%) on synthetic occlusions

	(a)	(b)	(c)	(d)	(e)
PCA	100	100	24	8	6
LNMF	100	96	28	10	4
R-PCA	100	100	46	24	6
S-LNMF	**100**	**100**	**100**	**100**	**100**

Table 5. Recognition rate (%) on real occlusions

Algorithm	**smile**	**scream**	**sunglass**	**scarf**
PCA	94	44	40	14
LNMF	95	44	46	14
R-PCA	94	80	50	16
AMM	96	56	80	82
S-LNMF	**95**	**44**	**90**	**92**

Note that if there is no occlusion in a test face, then the algorithm becomes the very original LNMF-based recognition scheme, in which whole LNMF bases are integrated for matching, and the recognition performance of our algorithm will be the same as the original LNMF's [3]. Thus, in this paper, we investigate the performance of our algorithm on the occluded face images exclusively. Unlike the syntactic occlusion test where the occlusion-free parts of the gallery and the corresponding test images are exactly the same, in this case, those parts may differ since they are taken in different conditions. We found empirically that the optimal number of bases could be chosen from 200 to 400. The performances of PCA, LNMF, R-PCA and AMM (Martinez's algorithm [5]) were also evaluated and compared to that of the proposed algorithm, and the results are summarized in Table 5. The recognition rate of the proposed algorithm was obtained when the number of bases was 200.

From these results, we can conclude that our algorithm is more robust than other algorithms including AMM. AMM gave relatively better results than PCA, LNMF and R-PCA for both sunglass and scarf tests. This is because it also uses local approach. However, since the matching is done in probabilistic framework with the sum of the Mahalanobis distances between all the corresponding local parts, the effect of the occluded parts are not removed completely and still affects final matching.

5 Conclusion

In this paper we have dealt with the occlusion problem, which has been researched relatively less than illumination and pose problems in face recognition. We have proposed a new robust face recognition algorithm called S-LNMF to the partial occlusion, based on selective LNMF bases matching. Local occluded area in faces are first detected by a supervised 1-NN threshold classifier in PCA space, and then matching is performed in the LNMF subspaces with the selected occlusion-free bases. Experimental results demonstrated that the proposed algorithm could reliably recognize partially occluded faces with higher recognition rate than the existing methods.

Acknowledgement

This work has been supported in part by the ITRC and the Center for Intelligent Robotics, 21C Frontier program of Korean government.

References

1. A. Leonardis and H. Bischof, "Dealing with occlusions in the eigenspace approach," *Proc. IEEE Conf. Computer Vision and Pattern Recognition*, pp. 453-458 ,1996.
2. A. Leonardis and H. Bischof, "Robust recognition using eigenimages," *Computer Vision and Image Understanding*, vol. 78, pp. 99-118, 2000.
3. S. Z. Li, X. W. Hou, H. J. Zhang, and Q. S. Cheng, "Learning spatially localized, part-based representation," *Proc. IEEE Conf. Computer Vision and Pattern Recognition*, pp. 207-212, 2001.
4. D. D. Lee and H. S. Seung, "Learning the parts of objects by non-negative matrix factorization," *Nature*, vol. 401, pp. 788-791, 1999.
5. A. M. Martinez, "Recognizing imprecisely localized, partially occluded, and expression variant faces from a single sample per class," *IEEE Trans. Pattern Analysis and Machine Intelligence*, vol. 24, no. 6, pp. 748-763, 2002.
6. A. M. Marttinez and R. Benavente, "The AR Face Database," *CVC Technical Report*, no. 24, June 1998.
7. Tax, D., *One-Class Classification*, PhD thesis, Delft University of Technology, 2001.
8. D. De Ritter, D. Tax, R. P. W. Duin, "An experimental comparison of one-class classification methods," *Proc. Fourth Annual Conference of the Advanced School for Computing and Imaging*, ASCI, Delft, June 1998.
9. R. O. Duda, P. E. Hart, D. G. Stork. *Pattern Classification*, John Wiley & Sons Inc., 2001.
10. M. Turk and A. Pentland, "Face Recognition Using Eigenfaces," *Proc. IEEE Conf. Computer Vision and Pattern Recognition*, pp. 586-591, 1991.
11. A. Jain, *Fundamentals of Digital Image Processing*, Prentice-Hall Inc., 1982.
12. E. Trucco, and A. Verri, *Introductory Techniques for 3-D Computer Vision*, Prentice-Hall Inc., 1998.
13. L. G. Shapiro, and G. C. Stockman, *Computer Vision*, Prentice-Hall Inc., 2001.
14. L. Sirovich and M. Kirby, "Low-Dimensional Procedure for the Characterization of Human faces," *J. Optical soc. Am. A*, vol. 4, pp. 519-524. 1987.
15. M. Kirby and L. Sirovich, "Application of Karhunen-Love Procedure for the Characterization of Human Faces, *IEEE Trans. Pattern Analysis and Machine Intelligence*, vol. 12, no. 1, pp. 103-108, 1990.
16. M. Turk and A. Pentland, "Eigenfaces for recognition," *Journal of Cognitive Neuroscience*, vol. 3, pp. 71-86, 1991.
17. B. Moghaddam and A. Pentland, "Probabilistic Visual Learning for Object Recognition," *IEEE Trans. Pattern Analysis and Machine Intelligence,* vol. 19, no. 7, pp. 696-710, 1997

Two-Dimensional Fisher Discriminant Analysis and Its Application to Face Recognition

Zhizheng Liang[1], Pengfei Shi[2], and David Zhang[3]

[1] Shenzhen Graduate School, Harbin Institute of Technology, ShenZhen, China
zzliang76@yahoo.com.cn
[2] Department of automation, Shanghai, China
pfshi@sjtu.edu.cn
[3] Department of computing, Hongkong, China
csdzhang@comp.polyu.edu.hk

Abstract. Image matrices are often transformed into vectors prior to feature extraction, which results in the curse of dimensionality when the dimensions of matrices are huge. In order to effectively deal with this problem, a new technique for two-dimensional(2D) Fisher discriminant analysis is developed in this paper. In the proposed algorithm, the Fisher criterion function is directly constructed in terms of image matrices. Then we utilize the Fisher criterion and statistical correlation between features to construct an objective function. We theoretically analyze that the proposed algorithm is equivalent to uncorrelated two-dimensional discriminant analysis in some condition. To verify the effectiveness of the proposed algorithm, experiments on ORL face database are made. Experimental results show that the performance of the proposed algorithm is superior to those of some previous methods in feature extraction. Moreover, extraction of image features using the proposed algorithm needs less time than that of classical linear discriminant analysis.

1 Introduction

Linear subspace analysis is a popular technique for feature extraction, which has been successfully applied in many fields such as face recognition and character recognition. Among them, principal component analysis (PCA) and linear discriminant analysis (LDA) are two of the most commonly used methods for feature extraction, which can effectively reduce the number of features. The idea of PCA is to generate a set of orthogonal vectors by maximizing the variance overall the samples, while linear discriminant analysis seeks to find the direction which maximizes between-class scatter and minimizes the within-class scatter. Based on linear discriminant analysis, Foley and Sammon [1] proposed optimal discriminant vectors for two-class problems. Duchene and Leclercq [2] further presented a set of discriminant vectors to solve multi-class problems. Although Foley-Sammon optimal discriminant vectors(FOSDV) are orthogonal and perform well in some cases, the features which are obtained by optimal orthogonal discriminant vectors are statistically correlated. To avoid this problem, Jin et

P.J. Narayanan et al. (Eds.): ACCV 2006, LNCS 3851, pp. 130–139, 2006.

al.[3, 4] proposed a new set of uncorrelated discriminant vectors(UDV) which is proved to be more powerful than that of optimal orthogonal discriminant vectors in some cases. Then Jing et al.[5]further stated improvements on uncorrelated optimal discriminant vectors. Subsequently, Xu et al.[6]further researched the relationship of the Fisher criterion value between FOSDV and UDV. Recently, Xu et al [7] developed a new model for Fisher discriminant analysis, which applies the maximal Fisher criterion and the minimal statistical correlation between features. Since the methods mentioned above are based on vectors rather than matrices, these methods face the computational difficulty when the dimension of data is too huge. To overcome this problem, Liu et al.[8] firstly proposed a novel linear projection method, which performs linear discriminant analysis in terms of image matrices. However, feature vectors using Liu's method could be statistically correlated. In order to effectively deal with this problem, Yang et al.[9] proposed a set of 2D projection vectors which satisfy conjugate orthogonal constraints. Most importantly, feature vectors obtained by Yang's method are statically uncorrelated. Then Yang et al. [10, 11] proposed a two-dimensional principal component analysis for image presentation, whose idea is that 2D image matrices are used to directly construct the image covariance matrix. In short, one of advantages of linear subspace methods based on image matrices is their computational efficiency in feature extraction.

In this paper, we propose a new and effective method for 2D linear discriminant analysis, which applies the Fisher criterion and statistical correlation between extracted features. We also demonstrate that the Fisher criterion value obtained by the proposed algorithm corresponding to each vector is not smaller than that of corresponding uncorrelated image discriminant analysis(UIDA). Most importantly, we find a relationship between the proposed algorithm and UIDA. Experimental results on ORL face database show that neither the Fisher criterion nor statistical correlation is an absolute criterion for measuring the discriminatory power of discriminant vectors. Moreover, the recognition rate of the proposed method is higher than that of classical linear discriminant analysis.

The rest of paper is organized as follows. In Section 2, we briefly discuss two-dimensional linear discriminant analysis. Then we propose a novel method for two-dimensional linear discriminant analysis in Section 3, which applies the Fisher criterion and statistical correlation between extracted features. Experimental results and discussion are given in Section 4. Conclusions are made in Section 5.

2 Two-Dimensional Linear Discriminant Analysis

Without loss of generality, let the image A be an $m \times n$ matrix. Then the image A is projected onto an n-dimensional vector X. That is, the following transformation is adopted:

$$Y = AX. \tag{1}$$

It is obvious that the projection vector Y is an m-dimensional vector. In this case, the image A is transformed into an m-dimensional vector Y and each image corresponds to a vector. Let L be the number of classes and $n_j (j = 1, \cdots, L)$denote the number of samples in the jth class. Let A_{ij} denote the ith image in the jth class. Then we project the image onto X and obtain the following form:

$$Y_{ij} = A_{ij}X, i = 1,\ 2, \cdots, n_j, j = 1,\ 2, \cdots, L. \tag{2}$$

Let $m_j = \frac{1}{n_j}\sum_{i=1}^{n_j} Y_{ij}$and $P_j = n_j/M$, where M is the total number of training samples, m_j denotes the mean projection vector of class j and P_j is a prior probability of class j.Then the between-class scatter matrix S_b , within-class matrix S_w, and total population scatter matrix S_t are defined as

$$S_b = \sum\nolimits_{j=1}^{L} P_j[m_j - E(Y)][m_j - E(Y)]^T, \tag{3}$$

$$S_w = \sum\nolimits_{j=1}^{L} P_j E[(Y - m_j)(Y - m_j)^T\,|_j\,], \tag{4}$$

$$S_t = E\{[Y - E(Y)][Y - E(Y)]^T\} = S_b + S_w, \tag{5}$$

where $E(\ )$ denote the expectation value of vectors or matrices. In order to construct the criterion function for class separability, we need to transform the above matrices to numbers. The criteria should be larger when the between-class scatter is larger or the within-class scatter is smaller. To this end, the following function is constructed from Eqs. (3) and (5), which is a generalization of classical linear discriminant analysis.

$$J = \frac{tr(S_b)}{tr(S_t)}, \tag{6}$$

where tr() denote the trace of matrices. According to Eq.(3), we obtain the following equation:

$$tr(S_b) = \sum\nolimits_{j=1}^{L} P_j[m_j - E(Y)]^T[m_j - E(Y)]. \tag{7}$$

Substituting Eq.(2) into Eq. (7), we obtain

$$\begin{aligned} tr(S_b) &= \sum\nolimits_{j=1}^{L} P_j[A_jX - E(A)X]^T[A_jX - E(A)X] \\ &= X^T\sum\nolimits_{j=1}^{L} P_j[A_j - E(A)]^T[A_j - E(A)]X, \end{aligned} \tag{8}$$

where A_j is the average image matrix of class j. Define the matrix below

$$S_{b1} = \sum\nolimits_{j=1}^{L} P_j[A_j - E(A)]^T[A_j - E(A)]. \tag{9}$$

The matrix S_{b1} is called image between-class scatter matrix. It is obvious that S_{b1} is an $n \times n$ matrix. In a similar way, we can define the following two matrixes:

$$S_{w1} = \sum\nolimits_{j=1}^{L} P_j E[(A - A_j)^T(A - A_j)\,|_j\,], \tag{10}$$

$$S_{t1} = E\{[A - E(A)]^T [A - E(A)]\}. \tag{11}$$

The matrix S_{w1} is called image within-class scatter matrix and the matrix S_{t1} is called image total population scatter matrix. Accordingly, it is easy to verify that S_{w1} and S_{t1} are $n \times n$ matrices. In such a case, we transform Eq.(6) into the following form:

$$J(X) = \frac{X^T S_{b1} X}{X^T S_{t1} X}. \tag{12}$$

In general, the problem of Eq.(12) can be solved by the following generalized eigenvalue problem:

$$S_{b1} X = \lambda S_{t1} X. \tag{13}$$

In general, the matrix S_{t1} is nonsingular for two-dimensional linear discriminant analysis. As discussed in [9], the eigenvector corresponding to maximum eigenvalue of Eq.(13) is taken as the first uncorrelated discriminant vector. According to Jing's theory, the $(r+1)$th uncorrelated discriminant vector X_{r+1} is the eigenvector corresponding to maximum eigenvalue of the following eigenequation:

$$PS_{b1} X = \lambda S_{t1} X, \tag{14}$$

where $P = I - S_{t1} D^T (D S_{t1} D^T)^{-1} D$, $D = (X_1 \ X_2 \cdots X_r)^T$, and $I = diag(1, 1, \cdots, 1)$.

3 An Effective Method for 2D Linear Discriminant Analysis

In this section, we propose an effective method for two-dimensional linear discriminant analysis, which applies the Fisher criterion and statistical correlation between extracted features. Assume that optimal 2D projection vectors $X_1, \cdots, X_r$ are used for feature extraction. Let $Y_k = AX_k (k = 1, \cdots, r)$. Thus, the image space is transformed into the feature space. Let Y_i and Y_j be any two features. Then the covariance between them is defined as

$$cov(Y_i, Y_j) = E[(Y_i - EY_i)^T (Y_j - EY_j)] = X_i^T S_{t1} X_j. \tag{15}$$

Accordingly, the correlation coefficient between Y_i and Y_j is defined as

$$\rho(Y_i, Y_j) = \frac{cov(Y_i, Y_j)}{\sqrt{cov(Y_i, Y_i)}\sqrt{cov(Y_j, Y_j)}} = \frac{X_i^T S_{t1} X_j}{\sqrt{(X_i^T S_{t1} X_i)}\sqrt{(X_j^T S_{t1} X_j)}}. \tag{16}$$

For the sake of discussion, let $\rho(Y_i, Y_j) = f(X_i, X_j)$. In a similar way, we select the vector corresponding to maximum value of Eq.(12) as the first discriminant vector. Then the following optimization model is used to obtain the $(r+1)$th discriminant vector, denoted as

$$\max J(X), \tag{17}$$

$$\min f_1^2(X, X_1),$$

$$\vdots$$

$$\min f_r^2(X, X_r),$$

where $f_i(X, X_i) = \frac{X_i^T S_{t1} X}{\sqrt{X_i^T S_{t1} X_i}\sqrt{X^T S_{t1} X}}$, $i = 1, \cdots, r$.

It is obvious that the correlation between X and $X_i(i = 1, \cdots, r)$,namely Y and $Y_i(i = 1, \cdots, r)$, is the lowest when $f_i^2(X, X_r)(i = 1, \cdots, r)$are zero. This new model shows that the feature vector extracted by the $(r+1)$th discriminant vector has the lowest correlation with those extracted by previous r discriminant vectors.

In order to deal with the above model, the model is further transformed into the following equation:

$$G(X) = s_0 J(X) - \sum\nolimits_{i=1}^{r} s_i f_i^2(X, X_i), \tag{18}$$

where $s_i \geq 0(i = 0, \cdots, r)$ are weighting factors and $\sum_{i=0}^{r} s_i = 1$. From Eq.(18), we can see that the smaller $f_i^2(X, X_r)$ is and the bigger $J(X)$ is, the bigger $G(X)$ is. Therefore, it is necessary to obtain the $(r+1)$th discriminant vector corresponding to the maximal value of $G(X)$. Substituting Eqs. (12) and (16) into Eq.(18), we obtain

$$G(X) = s_0 \frac{X^T S_{b1} X}{X^T S_{t1} X} - \sum\nolimits_{i=1}^{r} s_i \frac{(X_i^T S_{t1} X)^2 / (X_i^T S_{t1} X_i)}{X^T S_{t1} X}. \tag{19}$$

From Eq. (19), it is straightforward to verify that for any nonzero constant μ, $G(\mu X) = G(X)$. In such a case, we add the constraint to $G(X)$ and the corresponding model is denoted as

$$\max G(X), \tag{20}$$

$$X^T S_{t1} X = 1.$$

In order to further deal with Eq. (20), we construct the following Lagrange function in terms of the Lagrange multiplier λ, denoted by

$$L(X) = G(X) - \lambda(X^T S_{t1} X - 1). \tag{21}$$

Setting the partial derivative of $L(X)$ with respect to X equal to zero, we obtain

$$2s_0 S_{b1} X - 2\lambda S_{t1} X - 2\sum\nolimits_{i=1}^{r} s_i S_{t1} X_i (X_i^T S_{t1} X)/(X_i^T S_{t1} X_i) = 0. \tag{22}$$

Then we obtain the following equation:

$$(s_0 S_{b1} - \sum\nolimits_{i=1}^{r} s_i S_{t1}(X_i X_i^T) S_{t1}/(X_i^T S_{t1} X_i))X = \lambda S_{t1} X, \tag{23}$$

From the above discussion, we obtain the following theorem.

Theorem 1. *The* $(r+1)th$ *discriminant vector is the vector corresponding to maximum eigenvalue of the following generalized eigenequation:*

$$PX = \lambda S_{t1} X, \tag{24}$$

where
$P = s_0 S_{b1} - \sum_{i=1}^{r} s_i S_{t1}(X_i X_i^T) S_{t1} / (X_i^T S_{t1} X_i)$, $\sum_{i=0}^{r} s_i = 1$, $s_i \geq 0 (i = 0, \cdots, r)$. Compared with Eq. (14), we can see that it is not necessary to use the matrix inverse in Eq. (24). Moreover, we can directly apply previous results to compute P in Eq. (24). Therefore, performing the proposed method costs less computational time than performing uncorrelated discriminant analysis. Applying Eq. (24), we can obtain optimal discriminant vectors $\{X_1, \cdots, X_r\}$. Then corresponding Fisher criterion values can be obtained by Eq.(12). As pointed out in [6], the Fisher criterion value of Liu's method corresponding to each discriminant vectors is not smaller than that of the corresponding uncorrelated discriminant vector. We ask: does there exist a relationship of Fisher criterion values between the proposed method and UIDA. To answer this question, we firstly give some related knowledge on generalized eigenvalue problems. Assume that $X_1, \cdots, X_n$ are linear independent eigenvectors of $S_{t1}^{-1} S_{b1}$corresponding to the eigenvalues $\lambda_1 \geq \cdots \geq \lambda_n$.

Let $W_1 = span\{X_{r+1}, \cdots, X_n\}$and $W_2 = span\{X_1, \cdots, X_r\}$. Then we obtain

$$\lambda_{r+1} = \max\{J(X) \,|0 \neq X \in W_1\}, \tag{25}$$

$$\lambda_r = \min\{J(X) \,|0 \neq X \in W_2\}. \tag{26}$$

According to the above theories, we can obtain the following proposition.

Proposition 1. *Let* $J_y(X_i)(i = 1, \cdots, n)$ *be Fisher criterion values obtained by uncorrelated image discriminant analysis and* $J_l(X_i)(i = 1, \cdots, n)$ *be Fisher criterion values obtained by the proposed method. Then we obtain*

$$J_l(X_i) \geq J_y(X_i)(i = 1, \cdots, n). \tag{27}$$

Proof. According to the theories of generalized eigenvalue problems, it is sure that $J_y(X_i) = \lambda_i (i = 1, \cdots, n)$,where X_i is obtained using uncorrelated image discriminant analysis. However, the discriminant vectors $\{X_1, \cdots, X_n\}$ obtained by the proposed method may not be a basis of R^n. Assume that the rth discriminant vector X_{r1} is obtained using the proposed method. If $X_{r1} \in W_2$, $J_l(X_{r1}) \geq \lambda_r = J_y(X_r)$; if $X_{r1} \in W_1, J_l(X_{r1}) \leq \lambda_{r+1} \leq \lambda_r = J_y(X_r)$. Therefore, the proposition holds.

Proposition 1 states that Fisher criterion values of the proposed algorithm must not be smaller than those of corresponding uncorrelated discriminant vectors.

Since we apply the Fisher criterion and the statistical correlation to construct the evaluation function, we guess there exists some relationship between the proposed method and uncorrelated discriminant analysis. To this end, we further analyze the proof of uncorrelated discriminant analysis which can be found in [3]. In deducing Eq.(14), the following equation is applied:

$$2S_{b1}X - 2\lambda S_{t1}X - \sum\nolimits_{i=1}^{r} S_{t1} X_i \mu_i = 0, \tag{28}$$

where $\mu_i = 2X_i^T S_{b1} X / (X_i^T S_{t1} X_i)$.

Substituting μ_i into Eq.(28), we obtain

$$S_{b1}X - \sum_{i=1}^{r} S_{t1} X_i X_i^T S_{b1} X / (X_i^T S_{t1} X_i) = \lambda S_{t1} X. \quad (29)$$

In what follows, we further discuss the relationship between Eq.(29) and Eq.(24). Let

$$c_i = S_{t1} X_i X_i^T S_{b1} / (S_{t1} X_i X_i^T S_{t1}).$$

Then we transform Eq.(29) into the following form:

$$(S_{b1} - \sum_{i=1}^{r} c_i S_{t1} X_i X_i^T S_{t1} / (X_i^T S_{t1} X_i))X = \lambda S_{t1} X. \quad (30)$$

Let $s_0 = \frac{1}{1+\sum_i^r c_i}$ and$s_i = \frac{c_i}{1+\sum_i^r c_i} (i = 1, \cdots, r)$. In such a case, it is obvious that $\sum_{j=0}^{r} s_j = 1$, which satisfies the constraint in Eq. (24). Therefore, Eq.(24)is a generalization of Eq.(14). In other words, if we choose suitable parameters in Eq.(24), the solutions to Eq.(24) is equivalent to the solutions to Eq.(14). As a result, we build a bridge between the proposed algorithm and UIDA. That is, the relationship between Eq.(24)and Eq.(14) is revealed. From the above discussion, we also find an efficient method for computing the matrix P in Eq.(14), which does not need to use the matrix inverse.

4 Experimental Results and Discussion

In order to verify and test the effectiveness of the proposed method, experiments are made on face images which are obtained from Olivetti Research Lab (ORL, http://www.cam-or.co.uk/facedatabase.html). This set of data consists of 40 distinct persons, with each containing 10 different images with variation in pose, illumination, facial expression and facial details. All the images are taken against a dark homogeneous background with the subjects in an upright, frontal position (with tolerance for some side movement). The original face images are sized 112×92 pixels with a 256-level gray scale. Each face image is downsampled to 28×23 pixels to reduce the computational complexity. In all experiments, we apply the first five images of each subject for training and others are for testing. Namely, 200 samples are used for training and 200 samples are used for testing.

The first set of experiments is used for showing the effectiveness of the number of features. The parameters in the proposed algorithm are set as follows: $s_i = 1/(r+1)(i = 0, \cdots, r)$. At the same time, the proposed method is compared with uncorrelated image discriminant analysis(UIDA) and Liu's method (LM). In addition, the nearest-neighbor classifier is adopted for classification due to the simplicity. Table 1 shows the classification performance of several methods when the number of feature vectors varies from 1 to 6. From Table 1, we can surprisedly see that the results of the proposed method are the same as those of UIDA. We also note that the classification performance of the proposed algorithm is superior to that of Liu's method.

Table 1. Recognition rates(%) of several methods when the number of features varies

The number of features	Methods (recognition rates(%))		
	UIDA	LM	Ours
1	83.5	83.5	83.5
2	89.0	84.5	89.0
3	88.5	86.5	88.5
4	88.5	85.5	88.5
5	89.0	85.5	89.0
6	89.0	85.0	89.0

In the second set of experiments, similarly, the nearest-neighbor classifier is used for classification and the parameters are set as follows: $s_i = 1/(r+1)(i = 0, \cdots, r)$. In such a case, the execution time for feature extraction and classification of several methods are compared, which is shown in Table 2. As can be seen from Table 2, the methods based on image matrices including UIDA, LM and the proposed method need less time than Eigenfaces [13]or Fisherface [12]. There is no remarkable difference in time for UIDA, LM and the proposed method. Since both Eigenfaces and Fisherfaces need to convert image matrices into vectors in the process of recognition, the classification time of these two methods are more than that of 2D linear discriminant analysis. Moreover, 2D linear discriminant analysis is superior to classical linear discriminant analysis in terms of the computational efficiency for feature extraction.

In the third set of experiments, similar experimental conditions are set. Based on this, the classification performance of the proposed algorithm is compared with other methods including Fisherfaces[12], Eigenfaces[13], ICA[14], uncorrelated image discriminant analysis(UIDA), Liu's method and direct recognition method(DRM). The detailed experimental results are listed in Table 3. From Table 3, we can see that the proposed method is better than other methods except for uncorrelated image discriminant analysis in recognition rates. To our surprise, the results of the proposed algorithm are the same as those of uncorrelated image discriminant analysis.

In the fourth set of experiments, we discuss the Fisher criterion values of several methods such as Liu's method and uncorrelated image discriminant analysis. Firstly, we set the parameters as follows: $s_i = 1/(r+1)(i = 0, \cdots, r)$. In addition, we also discuss another case, namely $s_0 = 0.0001$ and $s_i = 1/r(i = 1, \cdots, r)$. In such a case, we think that the Fisher criterion plays an insignificant role and the

Table 2. The execution time for feature extraction and classification of five methods

Methods	Eigenfaces	Fisherfaces	UIDA	LM	Ours
Dimension	1×200	1×39	32×2	32×3	32×2
The time for extraction(s)	27.85	97.14	4.23	7.18	4.03
Classification time(s)	59.51	34.46	4.01	5.81	3.96
The total time(s)	87.36	131.60	8.24	12.99	7.99

Table 3. Recognition rates (%) of several methods

Method	Dimension	Recognition rates
Eigenfaces	1×200	88.0
Fisherfaces	1×39	86.0
LM	32×3	86.5
UIDA	32×2	89.0
ICA	1×40	84.2
DRM	32×28	83.5
ours	32×2	89.0

Table 4. Fisher criterion values of several methods

$J(X_i)$	X_1	X_2	X_3	X_4	X_5	X_6
UIDA	0.8667	0.8315	0.6562	0.5804	0.5012	0.4725
LM	0.8667	0.8399	0.7479	0.6757	0.6498	0.5746
Ours(1)	0.8667	0.8315	0.6562	0.5804	0.5012	0.4725
Ours(2)	0.8667	0.8315	0.6563	0.5806	0.5014	0.4727

statistical correlation between feature vectors plays an important role in feature extraction, denoted by ours(2). From Table 4, it is obvious that the Fisher criterion value of UIDA corresponding to each feature vector is the smallest in all methods. From Table 3, we know the classification performance of the proposed algorithm is superior to that of Liu's method. This means the Fisher criterion value is not an absolute criterion for measuring the discriminatory power of discriminant vectors. We also find that the classification performance is not superior to that of uncorrelated image discriminant analysis in the sencond case, which also shows that statistical correlation is not an absolute criterion for measuring the discriminatory power of discriminant vectors. Therefore, in order to obtain powerful discriminant vectors, it is necessary to combine Fisher criterion values and statistical correlations among feature vectors.

5 Conclusions

In this paper, a novel method for two-dimensional linear discriminant analysis is developed for image feature extraction. The proposed algorithm directly utilizes image matrices to construct the Fisher criterion function, which doesn't need to convert image matrices into high-dimensional vectors such as classical PCA or LDA. Then discriminant vectors are obtained by maximizing Fisher criterion functions and minimizing statistical correlation between extracted features. Since the size of image matrices is much smaller that of vectors, the execution time of the proposed algorithm for feature extraction is much less than that of traditional linear discriminant analysis. Moreover, we demonstrate that the Fisher criterion values of the proposed algorithm are smaller than the Fisher criterion values of uncorrelated discriminant vectors. In addition, the feature vectors obtained by the proposed algorithm are the same as those obtained by uncorrelated discriminant vectors in some condition. Experimental results on ORL face database show the proposed method outperfoms some previous methods in feature extraction. At the same time, experiments also show that Fisher criterion values and statistical correlation must be simultaneously considered to obtain effective discriminant vectors. Finally, it should be pointed out that the proposed method requires more coefficients for feature extraction than LDA. In other words, the 2DLDA method needs more storage space than the classical LDA method, which is one of disadvantages of 2D linear discriminant analysis.

References

1. D.H.Foley, J.W. Sammon, Jr., "An optimal set of discriminant vector," IEEE Trans. Computer, 3, pp.281-289, 1975.
2. J.Duchene, S.Leclercq, "An optimal transformation for discriminant and principal component analysis,"IEEE trans. on PAMI, 6, pp. 978-983, 1988.
3. Z. Jin, J.Y Yang, Z. S. Hu, Z. Luo, "Face recognition based on the uncorrelated discriminant transformation," Pattern Recognition, Vol. 34, No.7, pp.1405-1416, 2001.
4. Z.Jin, J.Y. Yang, Z.Tang, Z.Hu, "A theorem on the uncorrelated optimal discriminant vectors," Pattern Recognition, Vol.34, No.10, pp. 2041-2047, 2001.
5. X.Y.Jing, D. Zhang , Z.Jin, "Improvements on the uncorrelated optimal discriminant vectors," Pattern Recognition, Vol.36, No. 8, pp.1921-1923, 2003
6. Y. Xu, J.Y.Yang, Z.Jin, "Theory analysis on FSLDA and ULDA," Pattern Recognition, Vol.36, No.12, pp.3031-3033,2003.
7. Y. Xu, J.Y.Yang, Z.Jin, "A novel method for Fisher discriminant analysis", Pattern Recognition, Vol. 37, No.2, pp.381-384, 2004.
8. K.Liu, Y.Q.Cheng, J.Y.Yang, "Algebraic feature extraction for image recognition based on an optimal discriminant criterion," Pattern Recognition, Vol.26, No. 6, pp.903-911,1993.
9. J.Yang, J.Y.Yang, A.F.Frangi, and D.Zhang, "Uncorrelated projection discriminant analysis and its application to face image feature extraction," Inter. J. of Pattern Recognition and Artificial Intelligence, Vol.17, No.8, pp.1325-1347, 2003.
10. J.Yang, J.Y.Yang, "From image vector to matrix: a straightforward image projection technique -IMPCA vs.PCA," Pattern Recognition, Vol. 35, No. 9, pp.1997-1999, 2002.
11. J. Yang, D.Zhang, A.F.Frangi, J.Y. Yang, "Two-dimensional PCA: a new approach to appearance-based face representation and recognition," IEEE Trans. on PAMI, Vol.26, No.1, pp.131-137, 2004.
12. P.N.Belhumeur, J.P.Hespandha, and D.J. Kriegman, "Eigenfaces vs Fisherfaces recognition using class specific linear projection," IEEE trans. on Pattern Recognition and Machine Intelligence, Vol.19, No.7, pp.711-720, July, 1997.
13. M. Turk and A. Pentland, "Eigenfaces for recognition", J. Cogn. Neruosci., Vol.3, No.1, pp.71-86, 1991.
14. P.C.Yuen and J.H.Lai, "Face representation using independent component analysis," Pattern Recognition, Vol.35, No.6, pp.1247-1257, June 2002.

Combining Geometric and Gabor Features for Face Recognition

P.S. Hiremath and Ajit Danti

Dept. of P.G. Studies & Research in Computer Science,
Gulbarga University, Gulbarga-585 106, Karnataka, India
hiremathps@yahoo.co.in, ajitdanti@yahoo.com

Abstract. In automated face recognition, a human face can be described by several features, but very few of them are used in combination to improve discrimination ability. This paper demonstrates how different feature sets can be used to enhance discrimination for the purpose of face recognition. We have used geometrical features and Gabor features in combination for face recognition. The geometrical features include distances, areas, fuzzy membership values and evaluation values of the facial features namely eyes, eyebrows, nose and mouth. The Geometric-Gabor features are extracted by applying the Gabor filters on the highly energized facial feature points on the face. These features are more robust to image variations caused by the imprecision of facial feature localization. An Extended-Geometric feature vector is constructed by combining both the feature sets and is found to achieve satisfactory results for face recognition using a simple matching function. The matching performance is analyzed for both the feature sets as well as for an Extended-Geometric feature vector. Experimental results demonstrate that no feature set alone is sufficient for recognition but the Extended-Geometric feature vector yields an improved recognition rate and speed at reduced computational cost and yet it is more discriminating and easy to discern from others.

1 Introduction

Face is one of the important biometric identifier used for human recognition. A number of other biometric identifiers namely finger print, hand geometry, iris, keystroke, signature and voice have been in use in various applications. Each biometric has its strengths and weaknesses and the choice depends upon the application [10]. The face recognition involves the computation of similarity between face images belonging to the determination of the identity of the face. The accurate recognition of face images is essential for the security based applications. A number of approaches for face recognition for real time applications have been proposed in the literature [16]. Many researchers have addressed face recognition based on geometrical features and template matching [1]. There are several well known face recognition methods such as Eigenfaces [14], Fisherfaces [2], [11], Laplacianfaces [7]. The wavelet based Gabor functions provide a favorable trade off between spatial resolution and frequency resolution [5]. Gabor wavelets provide superior representation capability for face recognition [17], [13], [12]. An information fusion based algorithm for retrieval and

P.J. Narayanan et al. (Eds.): ACCV 2006, LNCS 3851, pp. 140 – 149, 2006.

verification of person identity is presented in [6]. In face recognition, different facial local features have different contributions in personal identification. The use of geometrical features will always have the credit of reducing huge space that is normally required in face image representation, which in turn increases the recognition speed considerably [16]. With this as the motivation, in the proposed approach, the geometric features are extracted by exploiting the geometrical knowledge of the human face which includes distances, areas, fuzzy membership values, and evaluation values of the eyes, eyebrows, nose and mouth. These local features are optimized and are experimentally shown to be invariant to pose, scale and facial expressions [8]. The Geometric-Gabor features are extracted from the Gabor responses by applying the Gabor filters at the highly energized points on the face. The matching performance is analyzed for Geometric feature set and Geometric-Gabor feature set as well as for an Extended-Geometric feature vector using a matching function.

2 Feature Extraction

In the human ability of recognizing a face, the local features such as eyes, eyebrows, nose and mouth dominate the face image analysis. In the present study, these features are used for the recognition, and the efficacy of the approach is demonstrated.

2.1 Geometric Feature Extraction

The locations of the facial features are obtained from our face detector [9] based on the fuzzy face model as shown in the Fig. 1 using the face detection algorithm as follows.

Input: Preprocessed image
Output: Most probable face is detected
Step 1: Input image is binarized and feature blocks are labeled.
Step 2: Select any pair of feature blocks to be probable eye candidates in given image.
Step 3: Compute the slope angle θ_{HRL} of the line joining the two feature blocks and if it is between $\pm 45^\circ$, then compute the evaluation value E_{Eye} using the equation:

$$E_{Eye} = exp\left[-1.2\left((l_1 - l_2)^2 + (l_1 - l_2 - 1)^2 + (\theta_1 - \theta_{HRL})^2 + (\theta_2 - \theta_{HRL})^2\right)\right] \tag{1}$$

where l_1 *and* l_2 denote the semi major axis; and θ_1 *and* θ_2 denote the orientations of the two blocks. If E_{Eye} is greater than the empirical threshold value 0.7, then these feature blocks are accepted as the *potential eye candidates*. Further, with respect to these candidates, construct the fuzzy face model as shown in the Fig. 1 Otherwise, reject this pair of blocks and go to step 2.
Step 4: For searching left eyebrow, choose any feature block K located in the support region of the left eyebrow and determine its horizontal and vertical distances h_K *and* v_K , respectively from *Vertical Reference Line* (VRL) and *Horizontal Reference Line* (HRL). Then compute evaluation value E_K using the equation:

$$E_K = \frac{1}{2}\left(exp\left[-1.2\left(\frac{v_K - V_{Leb}}{D/2} \right)^2 \right] + exp\left[-1.2\left(\frac{h_K - H_{Leb}}{D/2} \right)^2 \right] \right) \tag{2}$$

where, H_{Leb} and V_{Leb} denote the estimated horizontal and vertical distances of the left eyebrows respectively and are normalized by the distance between eyes *D*. The estimated distances are determined experimentally based on the observation of several face images of the databases.

Step 5: Determine fuzzy evaluation value E_{Leb} of the left eyebrow and its membership value μ_{Leb} by computing the membership values μ_K of E_K for every feature block *K* in the support region of the left eyebrow using the *min-max* fuzzy composition rule given by the equations:

$$\mu_K = min(\mu_{h_K}, \mu_{v_K}), \text{ for each } K, \quad \mu_{Leb} = \max_K \{\mu_K\} \tag{3}$$

where μ_{h_K}, μ_{v_K} denote the trapezoidal fuzzy membership values for horizontal and vertical distance of the Kth block. For example, μ_{v_K} is given by equation:

$$\mu_{v_K} = \begin{cases} 0, & if\ v_K \le min\ v_{Leb} \\ \dfrac{(v_K - min\ v_{Leb})}{(\alpha - min\ v_{Leb})}, & if\ (min\ v_{Leb} \le v_K \le \alpha) \\ 1, & if\ (\alpha \le v_K \le \beta) \\ \dfrac{(max\ v_{Leb} - v_K)}{(max\ v_{Leb} - \beta}), & if\ (\beta \le v_K \le max\ v_{Leb}) \\ 0, & if\ (v_K \ge max\ v_{Leb}) \end{cases} \tag{4}$$

where $\alpha = \bar{v}_{Leb} - 0.5\sigma_{v_{Leb}}$ and $\beta = \bar{v}_{Leb} + 0.5\sigma_{v_{Leb}}$; and $min\, v_{Leb}$, $max\, v_{Leb}$, $\bar{v}_{Leb}$ and $\sigma_{v_{Leb}}$ are the empirically determined minimum, maximum, mean and standard deviation of the vertical distances of the centroid of the left eyebrow feature, respectively. These distances are normalized by the distance between eyes *D*.

Step 6: Perform steps, similar to step 4 & 5, for searching right eyebrow, nose and mouth and determine their fuzzy evaluation values E_{Reb}, E_{Nose} *and* E_{Mouth} and corresponding membership values μ_{Reb}, μ_{Nose} *and* μ_{Mouth} respectively.

Step 7: Compute overall fuzzy evaluation *E* of the fuzzy face with respect to the eye pair candidate chosen in the step 2 and its membership value μ_E using the fuzzy composition rule given by the equations:

$$E = 0.4E_{Eye} + 0.3E_{Mouth} + 0.2E_{Nose} + 0.05E_{Leb} + 0.05E_{Reb} \tag{5}$$

$$\mu_E = min\{\mu_{Mouth}, \mu_{Nose}, \mu_{Leb}, \mu_{Reb}\} \tag{6}$$

Step 8: Repeat the steps 2 to7 for every eye pair candidate to obtain the evaluation value *E* and its corresponding membership value μ_E for each potential fuzzy face.

Step 9: Perform the defuzzification process as following: For the set Ω of $\{E, \mu_E\}$ values computed in Step 8, find the maximum membership value $\mu_{E\,max}$ given by:

$$\mu_{E\,max} = \max_{E \in \Omega}\{\mu_E\} \tag{7}$$

Then the E value corresponding to $\mu_{E\,max}$ is the defuzzified evaluation value E_D of the face. If there is more than one E value corresponding to $\mu_{E\,max}$, the maximum among those values is the defuzzified evaluation value E_D of the face.

Step 10: The potential eyes, mouth, nose, and eyebrows corresponding to the overall evaluation value E_D constitute the most probable face in the given image provided E_D is greater than the empirical threshold value 0.7. Otherwise, the input image contains no face. Further, the detected facial features are projected on to the *Diagonal Reference Line* (DRL). For example, left eyebrow is projected on to DRL as shown in Fig. 2. The distances of all the facial features along the DRL are used to compute the distance ratios as follows.

$$R_{Leb2Reb} = \frac{MP_{Leb}}{MP_{Reb}} \quad \text{and} \quad R_{m2n} = \frac{MP_{Mouth}}{MP_{Nose}} \tag{8}$$

The triangular area A_{en} formed by eyes and nose; and, the triangular area A_{em} formed by eyes and mouth are used to compute the ratio of triangular area A_{Eyes}. Similarly, the triangular area A_{ebn} formed by eyebrows and nose; and, the triangular area A_{ebm} formed by eyebrows and mouth are used to compute the ratio of triangular area $A_{Eyebrows}$ using the equation:

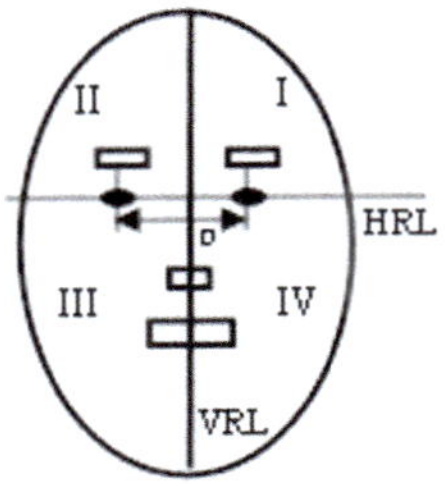

Fig. 1. Fuzzy face model with support regions for facial features shown in boxes

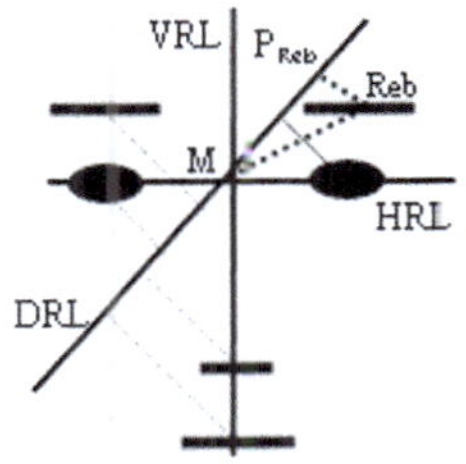

Fig. 2. Projection of Facial Features on to DRL

$$A_{Eyes} = \frac{A_{en}}{A_{em}} \quad \text{and} \quad A_{Eyebrows} = \frac{A_{ebn}}{A_{ebm}} \tag{9}$$

Finally, the geometrical feature set contains the fourteen geometrical features i.e.

$$GF = \begin{pmatrix} \mu_{Leb}, \mu_{Reb}, \mu_{Nose}, \mu_{Mouth}, E, E_{Eye}, E_{Leb}, E_{Reb}, \\ E_{Nose}, E_{Mouth}, R_{Reb2Leb}, R_{Mouth2Nose}, A_{Eyes}, A_{Eyebrows} \end{pmatrix} \tag{10}$$

Further, the locations of the facial features of the detected face namely eyes, eyebrows, nose, and mouth are considered as highly energized points on the face, which are used to determine the Geometric-Gabor features using Gabor responses as described below.

2.2 Geometric-Gabor Feature Extraction

The local information around the locations of the facial features is obtained by the Gabor filter responses at the highly energized points on the face. A Gabor filter is a complex sinusoid modulated by a 2D Gaussian function and it can be designed to be highly selective in frequency. The limited localization in space and frequency yields a certain amount of robustness against translation, distortion, rotation and scaling. The Gabor functions are generalized by Daugman [4] to the following 2D form in order to model the receptive fields of the orientation selective simple cells. The Gabor responses describe a small patch of gray values in an image *I(x)* around a given pixel $x=(x,y)^T$. It is based on a wavelet transformation, given by the equation:

$$R_i(x) = \int I(x')\psi_i(x-x')dx' \qquad (11)$$

which is a convolution of image with a family of Gabor kernels.

$$\psi_i(x) = \frac{\|k_i\|^2}{\sigma^2} e^{-\frac{\|k_i\|^2 \|x^2\|}{2\sigma^2}} \left[e^{jk_i x} - e^{-\frac{\sigma^2}{2}} \right] \cdot \text{ where } k_i = \begin{pmatrix} k_{ix} \\ k_{iy} \end{pmatrix} = \begin{pmatrix} k_v \cos\theta_\mu \\ k_v \sin\theta_\mu \end{pmatrix} \qquad (12)$$

Each ψ_i is a plane wave characterized by the vector k_i enveloped by a Gaussian function, where σ is the standard deviation of this Gaussian. The center frequency of ith filter is given by the characteristic wave vector k_i having a scale and orientation given by (k_v, θ_μ). The first term in the Gabor kernel determines the oscillatory part of the kernel and the second term compensates for the DC value of the kernel. Subtracting the DC response, Gabor filter becomes insensitive to the overall level of illumination. The decomposition of an image into these states is called the wavelet transform of the image given by the equation 11. Convolving the input image with complex Gabor filters with 5 spatial frequencies $(v = 0,...4)$ and 8 orientations $(\mu = 0,...7)$ will capture the whole frequency spectrum, both amplitude and phase, as shown in the Fig.3.

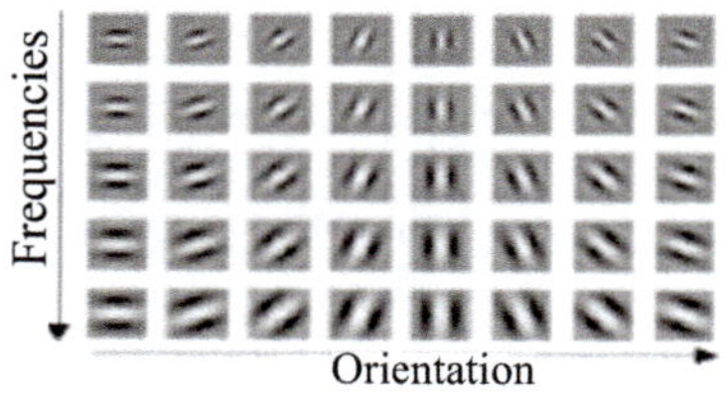

Fig. 3. Gabor filters (5 frequencies and 8 orientations)

Several techniques found in the literature for Gabor filter based face recognition consist of obtaining the response at grid points representing the entire facial topology using elastic graph matching for face coding [15], [3], which generate the high dimensional Gabor feature vector. In the proposed approach, however, instead of using the graph nodes on entire face, we have utilized only the locations of the facial features extracted by our face detector [9] as the highly energized face points and Gabor filter responses are obtained at these points only. This approach leads to reduced computational complexity and improved performance on account of the low dimensionality of the extended feature vector, which is demonstrated in experimental results. A feature point is located at (x_0, y_0) if

$$R_i(x_0, y_0) = \max_{(x,y)\in W_0} (R_i(x,y)) > \frac{1}{N_1 N_2} \sum_{x=1}^{N_1} \sum_{y=1}^{N_2} R_i(x,y) \tag{13}$$

where $i=1,\ldots,40$, R_i is the response of the image to the ith Gabor filter. The size of the face image is $N_1 \, X \, N_2$ and the center of the window, W_0, is at (x_0, y_0). The window size W must be small enough to capture the important features and large enough to avoid redundancy. In our experiments, 9x9 window size is used to capture the Gabor responses around the face points. For the given face image, we get 240 Gabor responses (40 filters applied to 6 energy points) as a Geometric-Gabor feature set. These feature vectors are used for the recognition of a face by applying the matching function as below.

3 Face Matching

The traditional PCA technique [14] considers each face image as a feature vector in a high dimensional space by concatenating the rows of the image and using the intensity of each pixel as a single feature. Hence, each image can be represented as an n-dimensional random vector x. The dimensionality n may be very large, of the order of several thousands, which accounts for more computational cost. In this paper, a face image is represented by Geometric feature set and also by Geometric-Gabor feature set. Further, these two feature sets are integrated into an Extended-Geometric feature vector, which is considerably very small compared to that of the feature vector used in [14]. The matching function is evaluated for all the feature sets of the training face images in order to assess the match between the images of the same person (or subject) and the images from different individuals. The match value d is determined by comparing a host face with the other face images using the negative exponential function given by:

$$d = \frac{1}{N} \sum_{i=1}^{N} exp(-|x_i - y_i|), \text{ where } 0<d<1 \tag{14}$$

where x_i and y_i are the feature elements of the face images X and Y, respectively, N is the total number of elements of the feature. The results of the matching performance for the database faces considering the Geometric feature set and for the Geometric-

Gabor feature set are shown in the Fig. 5(a) and 5(b) respectively. The match value for an Extended-Geometric feature vector is determined by the average of the match values of Geometric and Geometric-Gabor feature sets. The matching performance of extended vector is presented in the Fig. 5(c) in which the horizontal axis represents the face number and the vertical axis represents the match between faces for that feature set. The value of the match is within the range [0,1] and it can be given probability interpretation. The match is 1, when the host face is having highest match with that of the target face and the match is zero, when the host face is having lowest match with that of the target face. The performance of the features are analyzed by searching for target faces that match with the given host face. The targets are different images of the same person as the host. The analysis is based on the individual assessment of the two feature sets as well as the performance when both the feature sets are integrated into the extended feature vector.

4 Experimental Results

For experimentation, we have used ORL and MIT face databases, which are the publicly available benchmark databases, to evaluate our proposed method. The ORL database consists of 400 images, in which there are 40 subjects (persons) and each having 10 variations i.e. varying expressions, poses, lighting conditions under homogeneous background. The MIT database consists of 432 images, in which there are 16 subjects and each having 27 variations i.e. different head tilts, scales and lighting conditions under moderate background.

The experimentation is done with 40 face images, which consist of 10 subjects and each of 4 variations. To illustrate the analysis of experimental results, Fig. 4 depicts face no 21 as host face and face nos. 22, 23 and 24 as its target faces, i.e. these face images pertain to the same subject (person). Results of the match between the face 21 and the other 39 faces are shown in the Figs. 5(a), (b) and (c) for the Geometric feature set, the Geometric-Gabor feature set and the Extended-Geometric feature vector, respectively. In the Fig. 5(a), we observe that some of the non-target faces also yield a comparable match value as that of target faces leading to recognition errors, e.g. non-target face nos. 3, 26 and 27 have match values close to that of target faces no. 23. Further, many of the non-target faces have match values greater than 0.5 leading to the poor discrimination ability of the geometric feature set. Similar observations can be made in the Fig. 5(b), but the discrimination ability of Geometric-Gabor feature set is found to be better than the geometric feature set. Only few non-target faces have match values greater than 0.4 and close to the target faces. However, still improved match results are found in case of the integrated feature vector combining geometric as well as Geometric-Gabor features and are depicted in Fig. 5(c). All the non-target faces have their match values much less than 0.4 and are well discriminated from the target faces leading to enhanced recognition rate. The possibility of a good match of the non-target faces on individual feature sets have been reduced and such faces are well discriminated by combining both the feature sets as shown in the Fig. 5(c). Similar discrimination results are reported when comparing the effectiveness of template matching to geometric features [1]. In matching, the geometric features remain reasonably constant for a certain extent of variations in face orientation, expressions and tolerate side-to-side rotation better than up-down movement, which are attributed to the normalization by the distance between eyes. However for the geometric features, match fails for upside down faces and extreme illumination conditions, due to the fact that, the proposed fuzzy face model is constrained by the face orientation within the range $\pm 45^\circ$ and minimum face area of 500 pixels, otherwise the facial features are miss-detected. These factors are greatly affecting the matching performance of the Geometric feature set. The Geometric-Gabor feature set performed well on all the faces due to the fact that, Gabor features capture most of the information around the local features, which yields a certain amount of robustness against lighting variations, translation, distortion, rotation and scaling. Further, robustness of Gabor features is also because of capturing the responses only at highly energized fiducial points of the face, rather than the entire image. The Gabor filters are insensitive to the overall level of illumination, but fails for the images under extreme illumination conditions (too darkness). Hence, the match on the Extended-Geometric feature vector exhibits a balanced performance. Face movement not only affects feature translation and rotation but also causes variation in illumination by changing the position of shadows especially in case of up-down, and side-to-side face movements. Hence the proposed approach is tolerant not just to face movement but also to a certain extent of variations in illumination. The proposed method is compared with the well known algorithms for face recognition such as eigenface [14] and elastic graph matching [15] with respect to the recognition performance and the results are presented in the Table 1. The eigenface method did reasonably better on MIT database with 97% recognition and also has acceptable performance on ORL database with 80% recognition. Eigenface technique uses minimum Euclidian distance classifier, which is optimal in performance only if the lighting variation between training and testing images is around zero-mean. Otherwise, minimum distance classifier deviates significantly from the optimal performance, which is resulting in the deterioration of performance. Elastic matching method also performed well on the MIT database with 97% recognition and 80% recognition on ORL database. This method utilizes Gabor features covering entire face and it has some disadvantages due to their matching complexity, manual localization of training graphs and overall execution time. The proposed method performed reasonably well on MIT database with 89% recognition, which is comparable to the other two methods and significantly better performance on ORL database with 91% recognition in comparison to other two methods.

The comparison reveals that the Extended-Geometric feature vector is more discriminating and easy to discern from others and has a credit of low dimensional

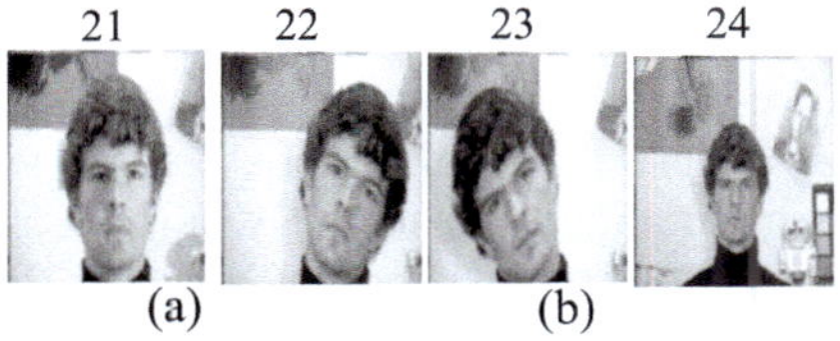

Fig. 4. Sample faces in MIT database images a) Host face b) Target faces

vector when compared to the high dimensional vectors used in [14] and [15]. The reduced dimension increases the recognition speed and reduces the computation cost considerably.

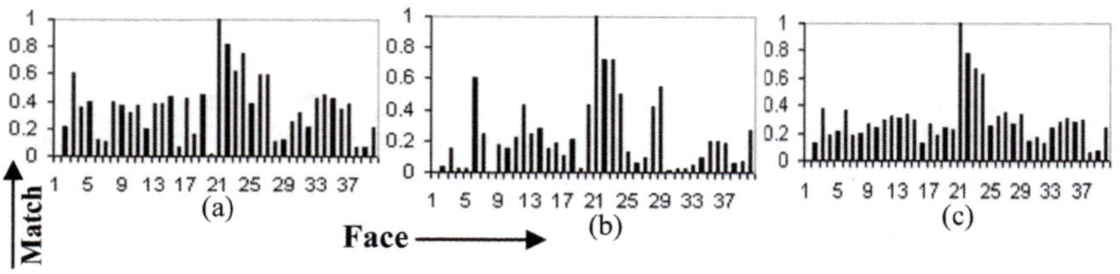

Fig. 5. Match between host face and training faces on feature sets a) Geometric b) Geometric-Gabor c) Extended-Geometric

Table 1. Recognition Performance

Method	Face Databases	
	MIT	ORL
Eigenface [14]	97%	80 %
Elastic graph Matching [15]	97%	80 %
Proposed Method	89 %	91 %

5 Conclusion

In this paper, human face is described by the Geometric feature set and Geometric-Gabor feature set. Further these two sets are combined into an Extended-Geometric feature vector. The discrimination ability of these feature sets are analyzed by comparing the face images using the matching function. The proposed method is compared with other well known methods. The Geometric features are extracted from the geometrical configuration of the facial features namely eyes, eyebrows, nose and mouth. These features are normalized by the distance between eyes and they are reasonably constant for a certain extent of face orientation, expressions and tolerate side-to-side rotation better than up-down movement. However, the geometric features are sensitive to the upside down faces and extreme illumination conditions, due to the constraints of the proposed fuzzy face model. Otherwise the facial features are miss-detected. These factors are greatly affecting the matching performance of the Geometric feature set. The Geometric-Gabor features are extracted by applying the Gabor filters only on the highly energized facial points namely eyes, eyebrows, nose and mouth. These features capture most of the information around the local features, which yield a certain amount of robustness against lighting variations, translation, distortion, rotation and scaling. Considering the Gabor responses only at the highly energized fiducial points of the face, instead of entire image will reduces the dimension of the feature vector to a minimum. The Gabor filters are insensitive to the overall level of illumination, but fail for the images under extreme illumination conditions. Hence, the match on the Extended-Geometric feature vector exhibits a balanced performance, and the proposed approach is tolerant not just to face movement but also to a certain extent of variations in illumination. Experimental results reveal that Extended-Geometric feature vector has a credit of low dimensionality when compared to the high dimensional vectors used in [14], [15]. The reduced dimension increases the recognition speed and reduces the computational cost considerably. The analysis of the matching performance shows that though the Extended-Geometric feature vector is low in dimension, yet it is more discriminating and easy to discern from others, when compared to only Geometric feature set or only Geometric-Gabor feature set. These results are expected to be useful in the design of efficient face recognition system.

References

1. Brunelli, R., Poggio T.: Face recognition: Features versus Templates. IEEE Trans. on PAMI, Vol. 15(10) (1993) 1042-1052
2. Belhumeur, P.N., Hespanha, J.P., Kriegman, D.J.: Eigenfaces vs. Fisherfaces: Recognition using class specific Linear Projection. IEEE Trans. on PAMI, vol. 19(7), (1997) 711-720
3. Duc, B., Fisher, S., and Bigün, J.: Face Authentication with Gabor Information on Deformable Graphs. IEEE Transactions on Image Proc., Vol. 8(4), (1999) 504-515
4. Daugman, J.D.: Two dimensional spectral analysis of cortical receptive field profiles. Vision Research, Vol. 20 (1980) 847-856
5. Gabor, D.: Theory of Communications. Jr. of Institute of Elect. Eng., Vol. 93 (1946) 429-557
6. Gutkowski, P.: Algorithm for retrieval and verification of person identity using bimodal biometrics. Jr. of Information fusion, Vol. 5(1) (2004) 65-71
7. He, X., Yan, S., Hu, Y., Niyogi, P., and Zhang, H-J.: Face Recognition Using Laplacianfaces. IEEE transactions on PAMI, Vol. 27(3) (March 2005) 328-340
8. Hiremath P.S., and Ajit Danti: Optimized Geometrical Feature Vector for Face Recognition. Proceedings of the International Conference on Human Machine Interface, Indian Institute of Science, Bangalore, (Dec. 2004) 309-320
9. Hiremath P.S., and Ajit Danti: Detection of multiple faces in an image using skin color information and Lines-of-Separability face model. Intl. Jr. of Pattern Recognition and Artificial Intelligence (Accepted on May 2005)
10. Jain, A.K., Ross, A., and Prabhakar, S.: An Introduction to Biometric Recognition. IEEE Trans on circuits and systems for video technology, Vol. 14(1) (Jan 2004) 4-20
11. Kim, T-K., and Kittler, J.: Locally Linear Discriminant Analysis for Multimodally Distributed Classes for Face Recognition with a Single Model Image. IEEE transactions on PAMI, Vol. 27(3) (March 2005) 318-327
12. Olugbenga, A., Yang, Y-H.: Face Recognition approach based on rank correlation of Gabor-Filtered images. Pattern Recognition, Vol. 35 (2002) 1275-1289
13. Shan, S., Gao, W., Chang, Y., Cao, B., Yang, P.: Review the strength of Gabor features for face recognition from the angle of its robustness miss-alignment. Proc. of the 17th Intl. Conference on Pattern recognition (ICPR 04) (2004)
14. Turk, M., Pentland, A.: Eigenfaces for recognition. Journal of Cognitive Neuroscience, Vol. 3(1) (1991) 71-86
15. Wiskott, L., Fellous, J.M., Krüger N., and Christoph von der Malsburg: Face Recognition by Elastic Graph Matching. In Intelligent Biometric Techniques in fingerprint and Face Recognition, CRC Press, Chapter 11 (1999) 355-396
16. Zhao, W., Chellappa, R., Rosenfeld, A. and Phillips, P.J.: Face recognition: A Literature survey. Tech. Reports of Comp. Vision Lab. of Univ. of Maryland (2000)
17. Zhang, H., Zhang, B., Huang, W., Tian, Q.: Gabor wavelet associate memory for face recognition. IEEE Trans. on Neural Network Vol. 16(1) (2005) 275-278

Complex Activity Representation and Recognition by Extended Stochastic Grammar

Zhang Zhang, Kaiqi Huang, and Tieniu Tan

National Laboratory of Pattern Recognition, Institute of Automation,
Chinese Academy of Sciences, Beijing 100080, China
{zzhang, kqhuang, tnt}@nlpr.ia.ac.cn

Abstract. Stochastic grammar has been used in many video analysis and event recognition applications as an efficient model to represent large-scale video activity. However, in previous works, due to the limitation on representing parallel temporal relations, traditional stochastic grammar cannot be used to model complex multi-agent activity including parallel temporal relations between sub-activities (such as "during" relation). In this paper, we extend the traditional grammar by introducing Temporal Relation Events (TRE) to solve the problem. The corresponding grammar parser appending complex temporal inference is also proposed. A system that can recognize two hands' cooperative action in a "telephone calling" activity is built to demonstrate the effectiveness of our methods. In the experiment, a simple method to model the explicit state duration probability distribution in HMM detector is also proposed for accurate primitive events detection.

1 Introduction

Activity recognition in video is a key problem in many computer vision applications, such as video indexing and retrieval, intelligent surveillance, human computer interaction and intelligent robot. In most previous works, the bottom-up method based on statistical learning is widely used. Some statistical tools were used to model the state transition process in the feature space. HMM and DBN are the typical statistical models. In early work [5], HMM was used to recognize the sign language. In [6], the authors exploited Coupled Hidden Markov Models to model more complicated interaction activity. In [7], the authors developed a Dynamically Multi-Linked Hidden Markov Model (DML-HMM) to interpret group activities involving multiple objects captured in an airport scene.

These statistical methods can model the activity automatically, but most works focus on the short-term activities, and the basic premise of the approach is that the observed feature sequence can be considered Markovian. However, the pure bottom-up method may fail due to the need of a large training data and the huge computation complexity of the model structure, when we consider a large temporal scale activity.

Fortunately a complex large-scale activity often can be considered as a combination of several simple sub-activities that have explicit semantic meanings. So, as

P.J. Narayanan et al. (Eds.): ACCV 2006, LNCS 3851, pp. 150 – 159, 2006.

proposed in [3], the activity recognition task can be split into two steps: first bottom-up statistical method can be used to detect simple sub-activities. Then the prior structure knowledge is used to construct a composite activity model.

In some examples, the prior structure knowledge has been combined into activity model successfully. In [9], the authors made up several concept hierarchies of actions to describe activities in an image sequence. In [10], the authors extended CASE that was used for language understanding previously to represent complex temporal relations between sub-events. In [11], the author propose an event ontology for representing complex spatio-temporal events, then a new model called as Event Recognition Language (ERL) was defined to represent the events of interest.

Stochastic grammar is also used to embed the prior structure knowledge. In [3], the authors gave a set of special solutions for handling uncertain input and errors in primitive detection. And some composite activities in gesture and surveillance applications were used to demonstrate the effectiveness of grammar parsing. In [1], the rules of Blackjack card game were specified by stochastic context-free grammar (SCFG), which was a multi-tasked activity including two player's interaction. In [2], the Towers of Hanoi task was analyzed by stochastic grammar, and the experiments demonstrated the high-level parser could give feedback to influence low level tracking result. In these studies, grammar method has shown some advantages for activity representation: (1) Event structures can be simply embedded in grammar productions. The representation is concise and easy understanding; (2) Many efficient parsing algorithms have been studied in speech recognition and natural language processing, which can be used for reference in computer vision; (3) Previous works have given good solutions to some problems appearing in computer vision application, such as the uncertainty input and various detection errors.

However, traditional stochastic grammar is only suited for the specification of temporally well-ordered activities. But different agents may play different roles simultaneously in many interaction activities. Traditional stochastic grammar may fail to encode these parallel relations in the interaction activities.

In order to solve the above problem, we extend traditional stochastic grammar by introducing Temporal Relation Event (TRE) and designing the corresponding parsing algorithm. Experiments have demonstrated the effectiveness of our methods. The main contributions of this paper are as follows:

(1) Extend traditional stochastic grammar to represent complex temporal relations and an event ontology is used to instruct the foundation of activity grammar.
(2) Modify the parsing algorithm to adapt for the extended grammar, and the new parser is compatible with traditional parsing.
(3) For primitive event detection, a simple alternative method is used to model the explicit state duration probability distribution in the HMM detector. The detector can identify the time interval of primitive events accurately.

The remainder of this paper is arranged as follows. In Section 2, the extended stochastic grammar is defined and the corresponding parsing algorithm is proposed. Section 3 introduces our experiment system architecture and the techniques to detect primitive events. Experimental results and some analysis are shown in Section 4.

2 Extended Stochastic Grammar Representation and Parsing

2.1 Grammar Representation

A hierarchical event ontology similar to that in [11] is introduced to instruct grammar's foundation. The events can be classified into three categories: primitive event, single-agent event and multi-agent event. Primitive event is the simplest event that is regarded as terminal in the grammar. Single-agent event is a combination of several primitive events with temporal sequencing. Multi-agent event is composed of single-agent events, and the composition operator may be complex temporal relation.

Different from previous works, single-agent event and multi-agent event are represented by different strategies. Traditional production is used to define single-agent event. For multi-agent event, we introduce seven temporal relation events (TRE) to handle the complex temporal relations. TREs include: "*before*", "*overlap*", "*during*", "*finish*", "*meet*", "*equal*", "*start*". The meanings can refer to Allen's interval logic relations [4]. A TRE connects two common events that belong to different agents or different agent groups involved in an interaction activity. For example, a production:

$$S \rightarrow A \quad during \quad B \quad [p] \tag{1}$$

That means if an agent completes event A, another agent completes event B, and the interval of event A is *during* the interval of event B, event S occurs. P is the conditional probability of the production being chosen.

By introducing TREs, a multi-agent event can be represented conveniently. But TREs are not actual primitive events. They are generated in the parsing process. So the parsing algorithm must be changed.

2.2 Grammar Parsing

Our parsing algorithm is derived from the Earley-Stolcke algorithm [12] and its subsequent application to computer vision by Ivanov and Bobick [3]. Some parsing details, such as uncertainty handling may be found in their works. In the following, we mainly explain our modification on the original parsing algorithm.

2.2.1 Parameters

Three parameters *agent, start* and *end* are augmented to characterize primitive event and parsing state. So a parsing state can be represented as follows:

$$i : X_j \rightarrow Y \cdot during \ Z \ [\alpha, \gamma, agent, start, end] \tag{2}$$

where *agent* indicates the executor of a primitive event or parsing state. [*start, end*] denotes the time interval of a primitive event or parsing state. α is called as forward probability, γ is called as inner probability, the dot is the marker of the current position in the input string. For simplicity, α γ's computation can refer to [3].

2.2.2 Parsing algorithm

The Earley-Stolcke algorithm [12] analyzes a symbol string iteratively through three steps: *scanning*, *completion* and *prediction*. We prefer to embed the modification in such framework to assure the compatibility with the traditional parsing.

Scanning:
According to the *agent* of the current scanned primitive event, new scanned states are generated for the current state set as follows:

$$\begin{cases} a\left[agent_a, start_a, end_a\right] \\ i-1: X_k \rightarrow \lambda \cdot a\mu\left[agent_s, start, end\right] \end{cases} if\ agent_a = agent_s$$
$$\Rightarrow \begin{cases} i: X_k \rightarrow \lambda a \cdot \mu\left[agent_a, start_a, end_a\right] & if\ \lambda = \varepsilon \\ i: X_k \rightarrow \lambda a \cdot \mu\left[agent_a, start, end_a\right] & otherwise \end{cases} \quad (3)$$

If the current scanned symbol is a TRE, the new scanned states should also be added into the *k*th state set, which is prepared for the backtracking in *completion* step.

If no state is matched successfully with the *agent* constraint, there may be a new agent appearing in the scene. Do scanning process again in those states whose *agent* is zero. Here *agent* is zero means the state has not been specified by any agents.

$$\begin{cases} a\left[agent_a, start_a, end_a\right] & if\ agent_a\ is\ a\ new\ agent \\ i-1: X_k \rightarrow \lambda \cdot a\mu\left[0,0,0\right] & appearing\ in\ the\ scene \end{cases}$$
$$\Rightarrow i: X_k \rightarrow \lambda a \cdot \mu\left[agent_a, start_a, end_a\right] \quad (4)$$

Besides the above operations, another function in scanning is to judge whether a TRE should be generated in the next *completion* step. A sign *flag* will be evaluated as *true*, if and only if the following conditions are satisfied:

a) In the last predicted state set, there is a predicted state that denotes the next scanned event should be a TRE. We define the primitive event on the right part of the TRE as the *post-event*, the left one as the *pre-event*;

b) The current scanned primitive event's *agent* is different from the state that satisfies condition a.

Completion:
If the current scanned symbol is a TRE, there will be no *completion* step, because there is no completed state in the current state set.

Otherwise, the completion process is implemented appending the *agent* constraint:

$$\begin{cases} i: Y_j \rightarrow v \cdot \left[agent_f, start_f, end_f\right] \\ j: X_k \rightarrow \lambda \cdot Y\mu\left[agent_m, start_m, end_m\right] \end{cases} if\ agent_f = agent_m$$
$$\Rightarrow i: X_k \rightarrow \lambda Y \cdot \mu\left[agent_m, start_m, end_f\right] \quad (5)$$

Then, if the sign *flag* is *true*, a TRE can be generated according to the following steps:

First, in the current state set, some states whose production head is identical with the *post-event* are selected out for the next temporal inference.

Then for each state selected in the last step, if the marker has been at the rightmost position of the production, which means *post-event* has been completed, two values are computed to measure the temporal relation between *pre-event*'s interval and *post-event*'s interval.

$$\eta_1 = \left(post.start - pre.start\right) / \left(pre.end - pre.start\right) \quad (6)$$

$$\eta_2 = (post.end - pre.end)/(pre.end - pre.start) \tag{7}$$

where the *post-start* means *post-event*'s start point, *post.end* means the end point; *post-start* means *pre-event*'s start point, *post.end* means the end point.

Finally, a TRE is generated according to Table 1. The threshold is selected empirically. If the *post-event* has not been completed, the end time must be later than the *pre-event*'s end time, which can be equal to $\eta_2 > 0.1$ So TRE also can be generated according to Table 1. The TRE's *agent* is to be specified by a group agent: one is the *pre-event*'s *agent*; another is the *post-event*'s *agent*.

Table 1. TRE generation

Conditions	TRE
$\eta_2 > 0.1 \wedge \eta_1 > 1.1$	*before*
$\eta_2 > 0.1 \wedge 0.9 < \eta_1 \le 1.1$	*meet*
$\eta_2 > 0.1 \wedge 0.1 < \eta_1 \le 0.9$	*overlap*
$\eta_2 > 0.1 \wedge -0.1 < \eta_1 \le 0.1$	*start*
$\eta_2 > 0.1 \wedge \eta_1 \le -0.1$	*during*
$\eta_2 \le 0.1 \wedge \eta_1 > 0.1$	*i-finish*
$\eta_2 \le 0.1 \wedge \eta_1 \le -0.1$	*finish*
$\eta_2 \le 0.1 \wedge -0.1 < \eta_1 \le 0.1$	*equal*

In the next iteration, the TREs become the scanned events. The event that triggered the generation of TRE should be handled again after the scanning of TRE.

Prediction:

If the current scanned primitive event is a TRE, the prediction step only rewrites all the predicted states in the last state set into the current state set. Otherwise, common prediction is processed.

If the predicted production includes a TRE, the *post-event* of the TRE should also be predicted:

$$\begin{cases} i: X_k \rightarrow \lambda \cdot Z\mu\,[agent, start, end] \\ \quad Y \rightarrow v\omega N \qquad\qquad if\ \ \omega\ \ is\ \ a\ \ TRE \\ \quad M \rightarrow \psi \end{cases}$$

$$\Rightarrow \begin{cases} i: Y_i \rightarrow \cdot v\omega N\,[agent, 0, 0] \\ \quad i: M_i \rightarrow \cdot\psi\,[0,0,0] \end{cases} \tag{8}$$

where $R_L(Z \Rightarrow {}_L Y)$ and $R_L(N \Rightarrow {}_L M)$ are both nonzero. Here, the R_L is the left corner relation matrix [12].

Finally, all predicted states in the last state set whose *agent* is different from the current scanned primitive event should be rewritten in the current state set, which are prepared for handling other agent's event in the next parsing iteration.

3 System Architecture and Primitive Event Detection

3.1 System Architecture

The system architecture is shown in Figure 1. First, the video signal is fed into the object detection and tracking module (red part of Figure 1) that includes the whole low level processing. In this module, we can robustly obtain the moving object's position, direction and other low level features. Then each moving object's feature sequence (such as trajectory, etc) is fed into the primitive event detection module (green part of Figure 1). In here, we train a HMM for each primitive event and a backward-looking algorithm is implemented to detect whether a primitive event has occurred. Once a primitive event has been detected, it is sent to the grammar parser module (blue part of Figure 1) where the event is analyzed with context information. Finally, higher semantic interpretation is inputted.

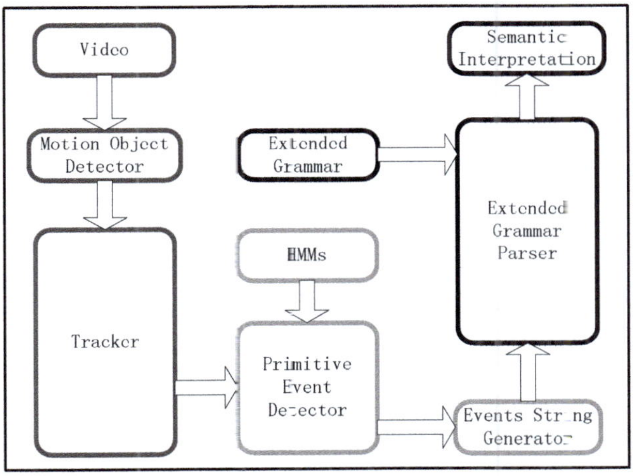

Fig. 1. System architecture

In our experiment, a tracking system was constructed, which used mean-shift tracker to get the robust multiple objects' trajectories and other low-level features. The details on the tracking method may be found in [8].

3.2 Primitive Event Detection

As shown in [3], we also choose HMM as the primitive events' detector. However traditional HMM has the limitation on modeling the state duration [13], which often leads to inaccurate detection results. In our experiment, the detected errors between the detected results and the ground truths can reach nearly 30 frames if we only use pure HMM as the primitive event detector. Such errors are unacceptable for the temporal inference in grammar parsing. For this problem, we use a simple histogram method to measure the state duration density. Different with directly measuring from the training sequences used in the segmental k-means procedure [13], we count each

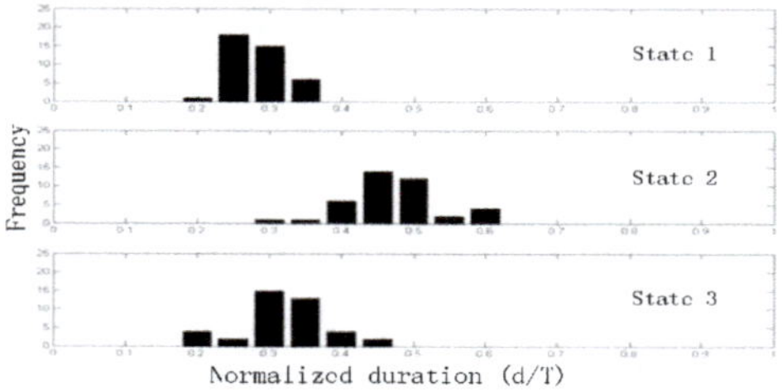

Fig. 2. Normalized duration Histograms for the 3-state HMM of a primitive event in our experiment

state's duration in Viterbi path to acquire each state's duration histogram. A histograms for a 3-state HMM of a primitive event in our experiment is shown in Figure 2.

For primitive event detection, first the Viterbi path and the corresponding probability is computed for an observed sequence. Then as proposed in [13], a post-processor is added to the Viterbi probability according to the explicit state duration histogram:

$$\log \tilde{p}(q, O \mid \lambda) = \log p(q, O \mid \lambda) + \sum_{j=1}^{N} \log p_j(d_j) \tag{9}$$

where d_j is the duration of state j along the Viterbi path, $p(q,O \mid \lambda)$ is the Viterbi probability and $p_j(d_j)$ is the duration probability of state j.

4 Experimental Results and Analysis

Here, "telephone calling" activity is introduced to demonstrate the effectiveness of our methods. In our study, a telephone calling activity can be decomposed into two hands' cooperative actions. The left hand and right hand are regarded as two agents. It is our experiment's target to recognize the temporal relation between "pick up phone" and "dial telephone number". The temporal relations between the two sub-events can be described as variant types: *before, during* and *overlap.*

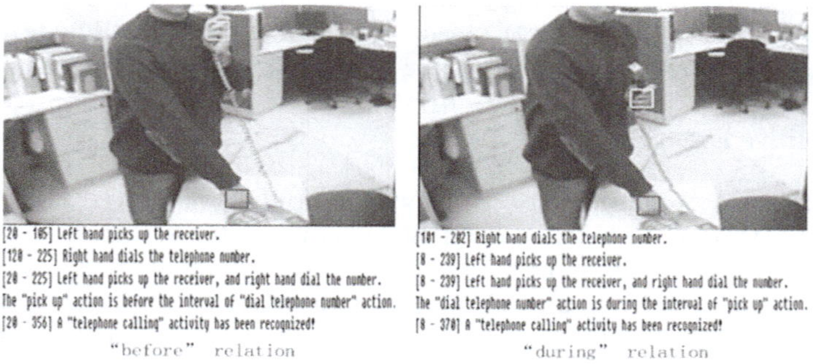

Fig. 3. Two types of "telephone calling" activities

Productions	Description
S → X b N [1.0]	Tele call → call to somebody *before* put down telephone
X → U b I [0.5]	Call to somebody → pick up phone *before* dial number
X → U o I [0.1]	Call to somebody → pick up phone *overlap* dial number
X → I g U [0.4]	Call to somebody → dial number *during* pick up phone
U → r p h t [0.5]	Pick up phone
U → r e [0.5]	Pick up phone
N → d w [1.0]	Put down phone
I → r a w [1.0]	Dial telephone number

Terminals	Description
r	One hand moves from body to phone
p	One hand moves from phone to bosom
h	One hand hangs around bosom
t	One hand moves from bosom to ear
e	One hand moves from phone to ear
d	One hand moves from ear to phone
w	One hand moves from phone to body
a	One hand linger over phone

Terminals	Description
b	"Before" relation
o	"Overlap" relation
g	"During" relation

Fig. 4. "Telephone calling" activity grammar

Two types of "telephone calling" activities are presented in Figure 3. The left picture shows the "pick up" action is *before* the "dial telephone number" action. The right one shows the "dial telephone number" action is *during* the "pick up" action. According to prior knowledge, we obtain the activity grammar, as shown in Figure 4.

We have recorded 12 consecutive "telephone calling" activities. Using our tracking system, 48 trajectories are acquired by specifying different initial tracking position. Among these 48 trajectories, 40 consecutive trajectories are used to train HMMs and explicit state duration model. Other trajectories are used to test. For each primitive event, we train 3-states HMM with a Gaussian Mixture output probability.

To compare primitive event detection accuracy between pure HMM and HMM with explicit state duration model, the results are evaluated by labeling each frame. For each frame a values is evaluated that specify whether a particular primitive event is active or inactive. By comparing these labels with ground truth, we can compute the overall-correct ratio as [*correct_positive*+ *correct_negative*]/[*all_frames*]. The statistical results are available in the left part of Table 2. As shown in this table, the detector with explicit duration model is more accurate than the pure HMM detector.

The middle part of Table 2 shows the results on primitive event detection. The right part is TREs recognition results through grammar parsing. We can find that the temporal relations are all recognized successfully, and all the true primitive events are recognized, but there are many insertion errors in primitive event detection. Two reasons may lead to the problem: (1) due to the influence of viewing angle, the trajectories of some primitive events are very similar in the image coordinate. So a trajectory segment may be received by two HMMs simultaneously. For example, the trajectory of action "w" is very similar to the trajectory of action "p" in our experiments. (2) Some primitive events are just a part of other primitive events in the trajectory space. For example, the trajectory the action "t" is just a part of the action "e". But these errors can be corrected completely through grammar parsing, as shown in the last column of middle part of Table 2.

Table 2. Recognition results. The left and middle parts are the results for primitive events detection. The right part denotes the recognition result of TREs. The symbols' meaning can be referred to Figure 4.

Primitive events	HMM	ED-HMM
r	95.4%	97.4%
p	90.4%	93.6%
h	88.8%	90.6%
t	94.7%	96.8%
e	81.3%	96.8%
d	92.5%	99.5%
w	94.9%	96.4%
a	96.1%	96.3%
Average	91.7%	95.9%

Primitive events	Ground truth	Actual test	Error rate	Recovery rate
r	16	24	33%	100%
p	4	4	0%	-
h	4	4	0%	-
t	4	8	50%	100%
e	4	4	0%	-
d	8	8	0%	-
w	16	24	33%	100%
a	4	4	0%	-

Temporal relation	Ground truth	Actual test	Error rate
b	11	11	0%
o	1	1	0%
g	4	4	0%

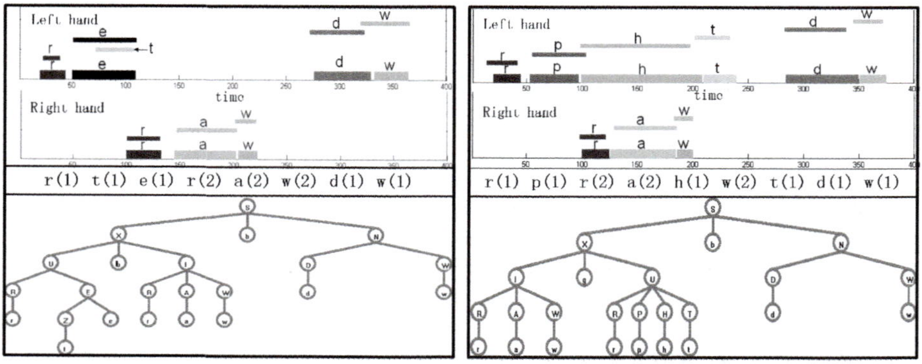

Fig. 5. Illustration of the "telephone calling" activity recognition process

Two activity recognition processes are shown in Figure 5. In the left part, the primitive events detection results are shown at the top, including left hand and right hand's actions. Compared with the ground truth (the thick line), the detection result is accurate enough for the temporal inference. The symbol string in the middle part is the primitive events string, the number in the bracket represent the primitive events' *agent* ("1" represents left hand, "2" two represents right hand). The events are ordered by their end times. At the bottom, the parsing tree is shown. The symbol "Z" and other capital letters of terminals ("R", etc) are all derived by the *skip* rule that is used for correcting insertion errors [3]. As we can see, the whole activity is recognized successfully, the "U" action (pick up) is *before* the "I" action (dial telephone number), and the insertion error "t" is corrected. The right part of Figure 5 shows another type of "telephone calling" activity, the temporal relation "*during*" between the "I" action (dial telephone number) and the "U" action (pick up) is also recognized successfully.

5 Conclusion

In this paper, we have extended the traditional stochastic grammar and designed the corresponding parsing algorithm to recognize complex activities involving parallel temporal relations. We have applied the extended stochastic grammar parser in an activity recognition system. For accurate primitive event detection, a simple method has been proposed to model the explicit state duration probability distribution in the HMM detector. Experimental results have demonstrated the validity of our method. An advantage of the two phases strategy is also shown: higher grammar parsing can correct the errors in lower primitive event detection that may be difficult to be identified only using image features due to some reasons (viewing angle, etc).

In this work, the grammar is defined manually. In the future work, the association rules between primitive events may be learned using some data mining techniques. The quantitative description of the temporal relations is also our future work.

Acknowledgment

This work is supported by research grants from the National Basic Research Program of China (No. 2004CB318100), the National Natural Science Foundation of China (No. 60335010) and the International Cooperation Program of Ministry of Science and Technology of China (Grant No. 2004DFA06900).

References

1. D.Moore, I.Essa, "Recognizing multitasked activities using stochastic context-free grammar", *CVPR WM vs. CV 2001*,Kauai, Hawaii, Dec 2001
2. D.Minnen, I.Essa, T.Starner, "Expectation Grammars: Leveraging High-Level Expectations for Activity Recognition", *Proc. CVPR2003*, vol.2.pp.626-632 Madison, WI, June 2003
3. Y.A.Ivanov, A.F.Bobick, "Recognition of visual activities and interactions by stochastic parsing", *IEEE TRANS.PAMI*, vol 22.no8, pp.852-872, Aug 2000
4. J.F. Allen, F. Ferguson, "Actions and events in interval temporal logic" *J. Logic and Computation* Volume 4, Number 5, pp. 531-579, Otc 1994
5. T.Starner, A.Pentland, "Real-Time American Sign Language Recognition From Video Using Hidden Markov Models" *Perceptual Computing Section Technical Report* No. 375, MIT Media Lab, Perceptual Computing Group, 1996.
6. N.M.Oliver, B.Rosario, A.P.Pentland, "A Bayesian Computer Vision System for Modeling Human Interactions" *IEEE TRANS.PAMI*, vol.22.no8, pp.831-843, Aug 2000
7. S. Gong, T. Xiang, "Recognition of group activities using dynamic probabilistic networks" *Proc. ICCV2003*, vol.2, pp. 742-749, Nice, France, Oct 2003
8. D. Comaniciu, V. Ramesh, P. Meer, "Real-time tracking of non-rigid objects using mean shift" *Proc. CVPR2000*, vol.2, pp.142-149, 2000
9. A.Kojima, T.Tamura, "Natural Language Description of Human Activities from Video Images Based on Concept Hierarchy of Actions ", *IJCV*, vol 50, num.2 PP.171-184, Nov 2002
10. A.Hakeem, Y.Sheikh, M.Shah "$CASE_E$: A Hierarchical Event Representation for the analysis of Videos" *Proc. AAAI2004*, pp.263-268, San Jose 2004
11. R.Nevatia, T.Zhao, S.Hongeng, "Hierarchical Language based Representation of Events in Video Streams" *Proc. CVPR03 Workshop on Event Mining*, Madison, Wisconsin 2003
12. A. Stolcke, "An efficient probabilistic context-free parsing algorithm that computes prefix probabilities", *Computational Linguistics*, v.21 no.2, pp.165-201, June 1995
13. L.R. Rabiner, "A tutorial on Hidden Markov Models and selected applications in speech recognition" *Proceedings of the IEEE*, Vol.77, No.2, pp.257–286, Feb 1989

Recognize Multi-people Interaction Activity by PCA-HMMs

Ying Wang, Xinwen Hou, and Tieniu Tan

National Laboratory of Pattern Recognition,
Institute of Automation, Chinese Academy of Sciences,
100080 Beijing, P.R. China
{wangying, xwhou, tnt}@nlpr.ia.ac.cn

Abstract. In this paper, we propose a new approach to multi-people activity recognition in outdoor scenes. The proposed method is based on Hidden Markov Models with parameters of reduced dimensionality. Most existing work is based on HMMs and DBNs, and focuses on the interactions between two objects. However, longer feature vectors of HMMs usually lead to covariance matrix singularity in parameter learning and activity recognition. Moreover, arbitrary structure of DBNs can introduce large computational complexity. Compared with former works, the proposed method named PCA-HMMs reduces the dimensionality of the model parameters while retains most of the original variability, and thus avoids overflowing and weakens the constraints on observations in conventional HMMs. The experimental results proved that the modified HMMs are effective solutions for multi-people interactive activity recognition.

1 Introduction

The visual analysis of human movements has long been one of the most compelling computer vision problems. In recent years, there have been more and more research efforts in providing machines with the ability to recognize human activities and analyze events. Although some successful algorithms from individual activity recognition have been developed, there is still much work to do for multi-people interaction analysis. In this paper, we propose an approach to multi-people activity recognition using modified HMMs.

HMMs are the most widely used solutions to model behaviors of dynamic systems because of their double stochastic processes, a marriage of low-level features and high-level semantic interpretation. Moreover, efficient algorithms for parameter estimation and recognition are available.

Since Yamoto et al. used HMMs to model simple tennis swings in 1992 [1], some extensions of HMMs have been employed to solve different problems. Galata et al. applied variable-length Markov models to recognize highly structured aerobics behavior [2]. The key idea of this approach is to use cross-entropy measure in optimizing memory length in order to capture different tempo-scale behaviors. However, complex activities and human interactions have not been

P.J. Narayanan et al. (Eds.): ACCV 2006, LNCS 3851, pp. 160–169, 2006.

modeled effectively because of the requirement of one-hidden node. Then CHMM (Coupled Hidden Markov model) is introduced by Brand et al. to recognize interactions with different state structures [3]. Conditional probability matrices of the coupled hidden states are used to model causal relationship between different action processes. Bui et al. constructs AHMM (Abstract Hidden Markov model) to describe behaviors in different scenarios over a long period of time [4]. Unfortunately, these extensions of HMMs have complex structures which need as complex algorithms for learning, and inference with large training samples. The learning algorithm of parameters is so intractable that it is difficult for generalization. In the case of multi-people activity recognition, much information is needed to represent the low-level features. Moreover, the dimension of the feature vector increases in proportion to the number of people and thus is often very long. Meanwhile, longer feature vectors usually cause more errors in the processes of parameter distribution estimation.

As the general form of HMMs, DBNs with arbitrary structure provide a detailed interpretation of events according to the state transition between different hidden nodes[5, 6]. DBNs take advantage of multi-node structure to decrease the dimensionality of low-level feature vector, however, the online recognition efficiency is much lower than the Baum-Welch algorithm of HMMs[7].

The proposed method uses the classic Baum-Welch algorithm in parameter learning. After PCA is applied, the recognition procedure is modified in state level with the conventional HMM. We call this model PCA-HMMs. The advantage of dimensionality reduction is to improve the recognition speed and fuse the observation data. Our experimental results have demonstrated its effectiveness.

The organization of this paper is as follows: Section 2 briefly introduces our method. Three different models are compared in this section. Section 3 analyzes the experimental results. Section 4 concludes the paper and discusses future work.

2 Activity Recognition

2.1 System Platform and Hardware Components

All videos in the experiment are real-life activities in a cluttered environment. They are obtained by surveillance platform which consists of multiple sensors distributed around the campus. There are tricolor CCD cameras with active pan, tilt and zoom control which can monitor a scene of interest effectively. Moreover, sixteen signal lines connecting to the fixed area supply adequate data.

2.2 Tracking and Low-Level Feature Extraction

Object tracking is the first step in human activity analysis. When tracking objects in the case of group merging and splitting, it is difficult to extract visual features of the occluded objects. However, the complete dynamic information, namely the low-level feature is important to activity recognition. Our system successfully uses a tracking algorithm to handle multi-target problems in complex

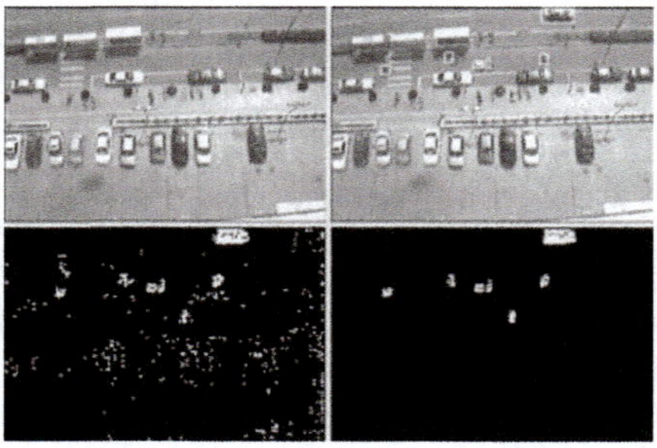

Fig. 1. The tracking results of our platform

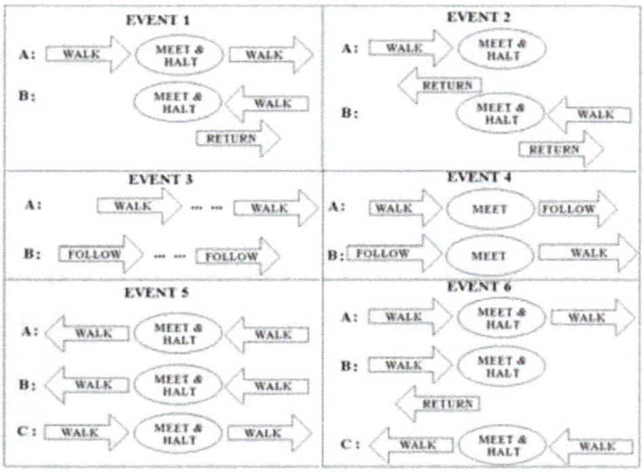

Fig. 2. Event description chart

and dynamic scenes. Detailed discussions about the algorithm can be found in [8]. Figure 1 shows the tracking results of our system. The figure on the top-left corner is the video sequence without any processing. The results of motion detection is shown on the top right of Figure 1. The experiment results before erosion and dilation are illustrated on the bottom left corner. This system yields robust, real-time outdoor tracking results even in the case of lighting changes, repetitive motions, or long-term scene changes[9]. Note that tracking is not the focus of this paper, we just use the low-level results to obtain required observation data of our graphical models.

For each object, its velocity, acceleration and distance between different objects forms a feature vector. It should be noted that the distance feature includes the distance to their respective initial positions and the relative distance to another interactive object. The relative distance is introduced in order to normalize the different start point. Since the relationship of these features is nonlinear, it is reasonable to reduce the dimensionality of the feature vector by PCA.

2.3 Event Models Via Different Graphical Models: DBNs, HMMs and PCA-HMMs

It is important for behavior understanding to model the reference behavior sequences from continuous time sequences. Then DBNs, HMMs and PCA-HMMs are presented to model activities not only for two-object interactions but also for three-object activities such as "meeting", " chasing" and "forming a new group in different directions".The details of each activity can be described as below:

Event 1: Two objects approach each other, and halt for a while when they meet, then one returns while the other goes in his original direction.

Event 2: Two objects approach in the same way in opposite directions, meet and halt, then they all return.

Event 3: One object walks ahead, another object follows him.

Event 4: One object walks, another object follows him, then overruns him.

Event 5: Three objects in two groups, A and B in group 1, C in group 2. The two groups approach in opposite directions, when they meet, they stop for a moment, and then they keep going in their original direction respectively.

Event 6: The activity relationships among three objects are similar to the beginning of Event 5. After meeting, B turns back and forms a new group with C, whereas A and C keep going in their respective original direction.

These events can be described clearly by Figure 2.

All the low-level features (distances, velocities and accelerations) for each event are shown clearly by Figure 3. All features for the same object are in the same color, and the same feature of different objects are represent by the same type of lines. Namely the lines in blue and red represent the features of A and B respectively, the lines linked by diamond, circle and x-mark denote the distance to each object's start point, velocity and acceleration respectively. In the case of three-objects activities, the relative distance between different objects are denoted by the line in black, magenta and yellow respectively. Since Event 1 is divided into three phases, each hidden node has three states representing its motion status. The distances, velocity and acceleration represent the motion features, and the relationship between these features is independent, so they can be extracted as the low-level features.

According to the prior knowledge of the specific events, the DBN's topology of the state-to-state and state-to-observation connection is illustrated in Figure 4. The number of states of each hidden node is different according to corresponding interaction.

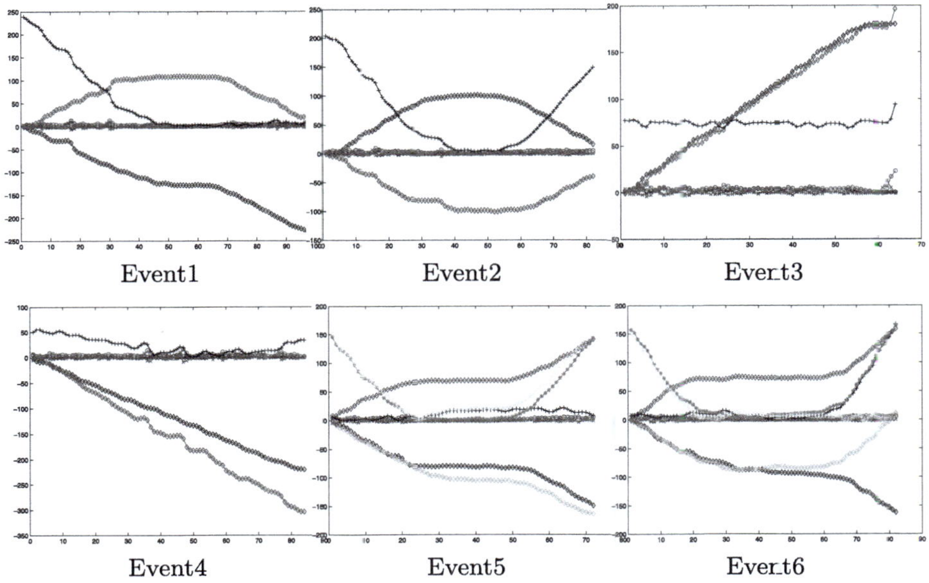

Fig. 3. The feature vectors for the six events

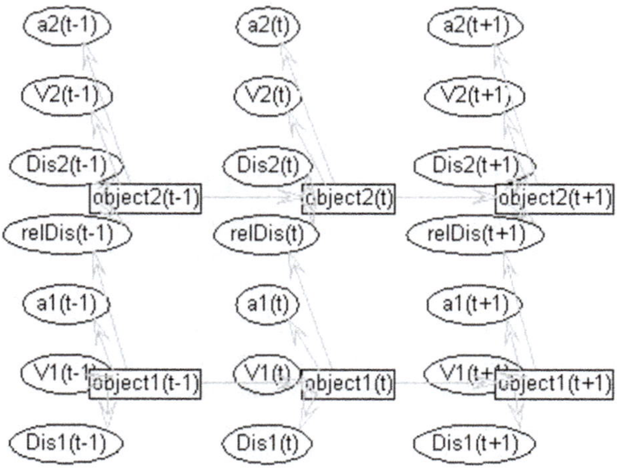

Fig. 4. The network structure of two-object activities where $\text{Dis}_{(i)}(t)$, $V_i(t)$ and $a_i(t)$, (i=1,2) represent the distance, velocity and acceleration respectively, relDis(t) is the relative distance between them. Object1 and object2 are hidden nodes representing different objects in each time slice.

It should be noted that the structure of HMMs and PCA-HMMs is conventionally ergodic. Considering the structure of HMM with one hidden node and one observation node, more objects result in longer feature vectors, decreasing the length of feature vectors without reducing the key components of the variables is needed for multi-object activity recognition, and hence comes our PCA-HMMs model.

2.4 Parameter Learning Via DBNs, HMMs and PCA-HMMs

Since the structure has been defined according to human understanding in our case, the learning task of DBNs is to estimate the conditional probability distribution associated with the network[10]. Meanwhile, [11] gives more details about HMMs learning. There are many ways to represent this distribution, which depends in part on whether nodes are discrete or continuous. Since the feature data coming from sequences are continuous, the output distribution is a mixture of M multivariate Gaussians to represent each state of these graphical models.

2.5 Recognition by DBNs, HMMs and PCA-HMMs

In the case of DBNs, there are many inference algorithms. To split the difference between speed and complexity, we use the conventional junction tree algorithm in the computation of pairs of neighboring slices [10].

In the recognition of HMMs, the Baum-Welch algorithm is efficient to calculate the probability of the observation sequence given the model parameters [7]. For convenience, we use the following symbols as the parameters of HMM [11].

The initial state distribution matrix $\pi = \{\pi_i\}$, where

$$\pi_i = P[q_i = S_i], \qquad 1 \le i \le N \tag{1}$$

N is the number of states in the model, S_i is the ith state.

The state transition probability distribution matrix $A = \{a_{ij}\}$, where

$$a_{ij} = P[q_{t+1} = S_j | q_t = S_i], \quad 1 \le i, j \le N \tag{2}$$

In this paper, considering the continuity of the trajectory data, the conditional probability distribution is presumed to be a mixture of M multivariate Gaussians for each state, then the observation symbol probability distribution matrix $B = \{b_j(o_t)\}$, where

$$b_j(o_t) = \sum_{l=1}^{M} c_{jl}\mathcal{N}(o_t|\mu_{jl}, \Sigma_{jl}) = \sum_{l=1}^{M} c_{jl} b_{jl}(o_t) \tag{3}$$

c_{jl} is the mixture coefficient for the lth mixture in state j and $\mathcal{N}$ denotes Gaussian distribution with mean vector μ_{jl} and covariance matrix Σ_{jl} for the lth mixture component in state j. Our approach distinguishes itself from the standard HMM work in that it uses the parameters with reduced dimensions by PCA in recognition, then, the dimensionality of the observation data is reduced based on the level of state. The main steps of the recognition in our method are as following:

1. Get the parameter $\pi_i, a_{ij}, \mu_{il}, \Sigma_{il}$ by the standard Baum-welch algorithm.
2. Get μ_i, Σ_i using the following equation

$$\mu_i = \sum_{l=1}^{M} c_{il}\mu_{il}, \qquad \Sigma_i = \sum_{l=1}^{M} c_{il}[\Sigma_{il} + (\mu_{il} - \mu_i)(\mu_i - \mu_i)^T] \tag{4}$$

3. Here PCA is used to reduce the dimensionality of the parameters but retain most of the original variability in the parameters. So we compute the principal components matrix Pc_i of the covariance matrix Σ_i, then the percentage of the total variance in the observations decides the dimensions to be reduced. So instead of working with all the original parameters, we use only some principal components Pc_i^* with largest variance to reduce the dimensionality of the mean vector, covariance matrix and observation data.

$$\mu_{il}^{'} = \mu_{il}Pc_i^*, \qquad \Sigma_{il}^{'} = Pc_i^T \Sigma_{il} Pc_i^*, \qquad o_t^{'} = o_t Pc_i^* \tag{5}$$

4. Calculate the probability of the observation sequence using the reduced dimension parameters of each competing model, and the model, which best matches the observations, is chosen as the recognition result.

$$b_j(o_t^{'}) = \sum_{l=1}^{M} c_{jl}\mathcal{N}(o_t^{'}|\mu_{jl}^{'}, \Sigma_{jl}^{'}) \tag{6}$$

Referring to the Baum-Welch procedure in the recognition[7, 11], we define

$$\alpha_i(t) = P(O_1 = o_1, ..., O_t = o_t, Q_t = S_i|\pi, A, B) \tag{7}$$

which is the probability of the partial observation sequence $o_1, ..., o_t$ and state S_i at time t, given the model parameters π, A, B.

$$\beta_i(t) = P(O_{t+1} = o_{t+1}, ..., O_T = o_T|Q_t = i, \pi, A, B) \tag{8}$$

which is the probability of the partial observation sequence $o_{t+1}, ..., o_T$, given the state S_i at time t and the model parameters π, A, B. where T is the length of the observation sequence. An efficient forward iterative computation is:

$$\alpha_i^{'}(1) = \pi_i b_i^{'}(o_1^{'}), \quad \alpha_j^{'}(t+1) = [\sum_{i+1}^{N} \alpha_i^{'}(t) a_{ij}] b_j^{'}(o_{t+1}^{'}),$$

$$P^{'}(O|\pi, A, B^{'}) = \sum_{i=1}^{N} \alpha_i^{'}(T) \tag{9}$$

Similarly the backward iterative computation is:

$$\beta_i^{'}(T) = 1, \quad \beta_i^{'}(t) = \sum_{j=1}^{N} a_{ij} b_j^{'}(o_{t+1}^{'}) \beta_j^{'}(t+1), \quad P^{'}(O|\pi, A, B^{'}) = \beta_i^{'}(1) \pi_i b_i^{'}(o_1^{'}) \tag{10}$$

However, from this iterative equations we should compute $b_j^{'}(o_{t+1}^{'})$ with the reduced dimension observation input, which is obtained from the third formula of equation (5). Moreover, we only use PCA in the recognition but not in parameter learning so that we can keep the characteristics of each activity and fuse the main features of the observation data.

3 Recognition Result Analysis

In our experiments, all images are 320×320 pixels in the video sequence from a stationary camera. Parameter learning was done offline with 20 to 60 training sequences for each event, depending on the complexity of the events. All trajectory data are obtained by the object tracking system described in Section

Table 1. The number of the states and training data for different events

DBN	States	Training data
Event1	3	40
Event2	3	40
Event3	2	25
Event4	3	22
Event5	3	60
Event6	3	50

2.1 and 2.2. Two or three states are used for each hidden node in DBN model according to the real trajectory data. Table 1 shows the the number of the states and training data for different events.

To compare the recognition performance of the three previously mentioned models we convert the DBN with discrete hidden nodes to an equivalent HMM. Compared with DBNs, HMMs compress all of the observation nodes and hidden nodes into one observation node and one state node, therefore the feature vector is 7-dimension because DBN has 7 observation nodes in the case of two-objects. Since DBN has 15 observation nodes in the case of three-objects, the feature vector of HMM is 15-dimension. Assume a DBN has n hidden nodes and each node has M states, then the equivalent HMM should have M^n states. Then we can get the states for each HMM according to Table 1. Moreover, the search space in training process for HMM is much larger, much more data are required for HMM to converge to true distribution during the training. However, if we use the same data to train, obviously, the number of iterations would increase during the parameter learning.

Figure 5 shows that the log likelihood of each event approaches the final convergence point quickly in the case of DBNs. The number of iterations for each event is shown in the brackets of Figure 5.

Figure 6 shows that the learning curve of four events approaches in the case of HMMs. The number of iterations for each event is shown in the brackets. Since state converting between DBN and HMM has the exponential relationship M^n, the number of the states for each HMM become so large that the convergence of the traditional HMMs is difficult. Unfortunately in the learning stage of Event 4 and Event 5, the final convergence is not achieved because of the longer feature vector and less training data. However, we have to use more data to train than that of DBNs.

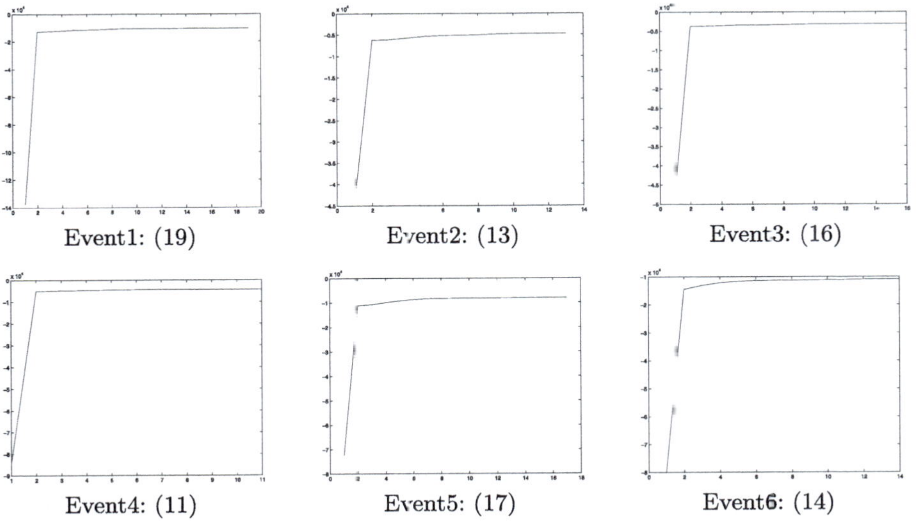

Fig. 5. The number of the states and training data for different events

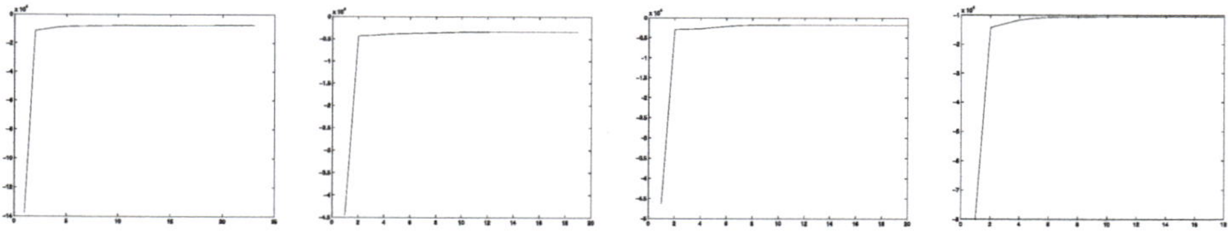

Event1: (23) Event2: (19) Event3: (20) Event6: (18)

Fig. 6. The learning curve of HMM: the vector of log-likelihood scores at each iteration of different events

Table 2. The percentage of variance in the observations of each eigenvector (in the case of two objects)

Event1	Event2	Event3	Event4
97.1154	98.2802	99.1350	99.3682
1.4095	1.6560	0.5125	0.5340
1.1937	0.0398	0.2518	0.0630
0.2241	0.0141	0.0903	0.0277
0.0409	0.0051	0.0063	0.0052
0.0147	0.0044	0.0036	0.0017
0.0016	0.0005	0.0005	0.0003

Table 3. Activity recognition rates in the six trained Events

Event	DBNs	HMMs	PCA-HMMs
Event1	86%	78.7%	95%
Event2	84.5%	80%	93%
Event3	91%	77%	100%
Event4	92%	91.6%	100%
Event5	95%	56%	96.7%
Event6	92%	60.4%	90%

Once all of parameters of each event are obtained, we reduce the dimensionality of mean vector and covariance matrix by PCA, then the percentage of the total variance in the observations are explained by each eigenvector in Table 2.

We find that almost all of the first two components of Pc_i for each covariance matrix account for 99% of the original variability. So instead of working with all the original parameters, we use only first two principal components.

In the stage of recognition, the values of log likelihood are applied to classify the activities. The experimental results of activity recognition rates are shown in Table 3.

For the three models, these recognition rates are all similar in the case of two-object activity whereas the results are so different in the case of three-objects. The recognition result of HMMs is not satisfactory because with the increasing of the objects, the number of states are larger and feature vectors are longer. When we reduce the dimensionality of the model parameters but retain most of the original variability using PCA, obviously, the recognition results for Event 5 and Event 6 are much better.

4 Summary and Conclusions

The model PCA-HMM was developed because the Baum-Welch theory allows a well-founded set of statistical estimation and PCA reduces dimensionality without sacrificing accuracy. During the learning process, we use the standard Baum-Welch algorithm to obtain the parameters. Then a new HMM is designed to reduce the dimensionality of the model parameters while retain most of the original variability using PCA and alleviate the constraints on observations in conventional HMMs. The advantage of this modified HMM is that it can reduce the dimensionality of the feature space and thus avoid overflowing. The promising experimental results demonstrate that the PCA-HMMs based approach to activity recognition is effective.

Acknowledgment

This work is supported by National Natural Science Foundation of China (Grant No. 60335010), International Cooperation Program of Ministry of Science and Technology of China (Grant No. 2004DFA06900) and National Basic Research Program of China (Grant No. 2004CB318100).

References

1. Yamato. J, Ohya. J, Ishii. K, "Recognizing human action in time-sequential images using hidden Markov model", *IEEE CVPR*, pp. 379-385, 1992.
2. Galata. A, Johnson. N, etc., " Learing Variable-length Markov Models of Behavior", *Computer Vision and Image Understanding*, Vol. 81, No. 3, pp. 398-413, 2001.
3. M. Brand, N.Oliver, A. Pentland, "Coupled Hidden Markov Models for Complex Action Recognition", *CVPR*, pp.994-998, 1997.
4. Bui, H., Venkatesh, S., West, G, "Policy Recognition in the Abstract Hidden Markov Model",*Journal of Artificial Intelligence Research*, vol. 17, pp. 451-499, 2002.
5. Ying Luo, Tzong-Der Wu, Jenq-Neng Hwang. "Object-based analysis and interpretation of human motion in sports video sequences by dynamic Bayesian networks", *Computer Vision and Image Understanding*, Vol. 92, pp.196-216,2003.
6. Nuria Oliver, Barbara Rosario, Alex Pentland."A Bayesian Computer Vision System for Modeling Human Interactions". *IEEE Trans. Pattern Anal. Mach. Intell.*, Vol. 22(8), pp.831-843, 2000.
7. Jeff A. Blimes, "A Gentle Tutorial Of The EM Algorithm And Its Application To Parameter Estimation For Gaussian Mixture And Hidden Markov Models", *International Computer Science Institute,* 1998.
8. Ismail Haritaoglu, David Harwood, Larry S. Davis, "W4: Real-Time Surveillance of People and Their Activities", *IEEE Transactions on Pattern Analysis and Mchine Intelligence*, Vol. 22, No. 8, August 2000.
9. Tao Yang, Stan Z. Li, Quan Pan, Jing Li: "Real-Time Multiple Objects Tracking with Occlusion Handling in Dynamic Scenes." *CVPR (1)*, 970-975, 2005.
10. K. Murphy, "Dynamic Bayesian Networks: Representation, Inference and Learning", *Ph.D. dissertation, UC Berkeley* , 2002.
11. LLawrence Rabiner. "A tutorial on hidden markov models and selective applications in speech recognition",*Proceedings of The IEEE,* Vol. 77, NO. 2, 1989.

Object Recognition Through the Principal Component Analysis of Spatial Relationship Amongst Lines

B.H. Shekar, D.S. Guru, and P. Nagabhushan

Department of Studies in Computer Science, University of Mysore,
Manasagangothri, Mysore 570 006, Karnataka, India
bhshekar@yahoo.com, guruds@lycos.com
pnagabhushan@hotmail.com

Abstract. This paper introduces a novel scheme which works on symbolizing every line in an object image for object recognition. Symbolizing is accomplished in terms of angles of intersection with regard to a line under consideration. Spatial relationship existing among the symbolized lines is represented using the notion of Triangular Spatial Relationship (TSR). A set of quadruples which preserves the TSR is subjected to principal component analysis to obtain the principal component vectors. These vectors are then stored in the knowledgebase for the purpose of recognition. Experimental results demonstrate that the proposed approach is efficient, invariant to linear transformations and capable of learning. To substantiate the success of the proposed model, a comparative study is performed with Murase and Nayar approach.

Keywords: Line drawing interpretation; Spatial relationship; Principal component analysis; Object recognition.

1 Introduction

Appearance-based object recognition models have been receiving much attention by researchers because of their efficiency and ease of implementation. Moreover, the combined effects of shape, reflectance properties, pose, and the illumination conditions will be learnt during learning phase and hence robust recognition is possible [8]. Murase and Nayar [10] devised an efficient approach that has *parametric eigenspace* representation for object recognition. The approach has been improved by many researchers [8, 9, 11, 13, 14]. In [10], for each object of interest, a set of images containing object in different poses and lighting conditions are obtained during training. Each object is represented as a manifold by projecting all the views of an object onto a subset of eigenvectors. During recognition, the image of a test object is projected to the subspace and the object is recognized based on the manifold it lies on. *Object eigenspace* is used to identify the pose parameters. Using a subset of the Columbia Object Image Library (COIL-100), they show that the 3D objects can be recognized accurately from their appearances in real-time. Although the approach is robust and efficient, as noticed by many rsearchers

P.J. Narayanan et al. (Eds.): ACCV 2006, LNCS 3851, pp. 170 – 179, 2006.

[8, 9, 11, 13, 14], the method in its standard form cannot handle problems such as occlusion, and of varying background. Pentland suggested the use of modular eigenspaces [14] to overcome the problem of occlusion. Ohba and Ikeuchi [13] proposed the eigen-window method in order to recognize partially occluded objects. But, due to local windows, these methods lack the global aspect and usually require further processing [8]. To eliminate the effects of varying background, Murase and Nayar [11] introduced a search window, which is the AND area of the object regions of all the images in the training image set. To alleviate the problem of occlusion and segmentation of an object from background, Leonardis et al. [9] proposed a robust and an efficient approach which is based on multiple eigenspaces. A novel self-organizing frame-work has been used in their work to construct multiple, low-dimensional eigenspace from a set of training images. Thus, the eigenspace approach has since been used in different vision tasks. However, in all these appearance-based approaches, all the images need to have the same dimension during training as well as in recognition and hence normalization is required which may result in loss of significant information. Moreover, these eigenspace approaches are not so robust to image transformations. Training a system on a data set which has linear transformation effects is time consuming and inclusion of a new object requires retraining of the system.

On the other hand, it could be seen in literature that there are several other models which work on geometrical properties of objects. Geometrical criteria such as line drawings invaraince is used by Bergevin and Levine [1] in their PARVO system. For the success of PARVO system, line drawings must satisfy a certain number of assumptions. Tsai [15] identified line invariants under various transformations for the recognition of 2D objects. Geometric hashing technique [7] was used in their system to speed-up the process of recognition. The system is capable of indentifying partially visible objects. However, complex trigonometric calculations involved in their approach to compute invariants and the performance of the system is shown against the model database only. ORASSYLL [6] - developed by Kruger and Peters is a robust object recognition system where objects are represented as a spatially organized set of local line segments. The symbolic representation used in ORASSYLL system has a parameterized description. Comparative analysis is presented in their work with PCA based models [10] too. However, the problem of representing 3D objects has not been addressed in their work. Cootes et al. [3] introduced an object recognition system based on line segments. A sort of similarity exists between ORASSYLL and Cootes approach.

In view of these, we propose a novel scheme for recognizing 3D objects invariant to image transformation. The proposed model being simple to implement, has efficient computing performance in terms of feature extraction and recognition. Since the feature extration of one object is independent of other objects, the proposed system possesses learnability. Representation of spatial relationship existing among the symbolized data through triangular spatial relationship further strengthen the claim that the method is invariant to image transformations.

The rest of the paper is organized as follows. Proposed methodology is presented in section 2. Experimental results are given in section 3. A comparative study is given in section 4. Discussions and conclusions are presented in section 5.

2 Proposed Methodology

The proposed model has three stages viz., line extraction from edge image, transformation of line image to symbolic image, and feature extraction and representation.

Quite often, object recognition systems were designed based on the nature of distribution of generic components or parts rather than the physical image itself. In such cases, components themselves are assumed to be the local features of the object and hence it is necessary to study the spatial topology existing among the components. In view of this, we decompose a gray image into a number of components. In our work, a gray image is considered as the physical image and each line segment in the line image is treated as a component and represented symbolically. Such a symbolically encoded image is called a symbolic image.

2.1 Transformation of Line Image to Symbolic Image

The line image obtained due to eigen transformation process [4] is used to obtain a symbolic image. For each line segment found in the line image, its angle of intersection with other line segments is computed. The computed angles are sorted in ascending order. The first k angles are called as *k-smallest angles* and the last k angles are called as *k-largest angles*. The ratio of the sum of *k-largest angles* to the sum of *k-smallest angles* is defined to be the label for a line segment under consideration. This process is repeated for all the line segments present in the line image. The resulting image is the desired image consisting only symbols (real values) instead of lines. This symbolic image is used for feature extraction purpose.

More formally, let m be the number of lines present in the line image. For each line, say l_i, $\alpha_1 \le \alpha_2 \le \ldots \le \alpha_k$ be the *k-largest angles* and $\beta_1 \le \beta_2 \le \ldots \beta_k$ be the *k-smallest angles*. The label of l_i is the ratio of sum of $\alpha_1, \alpha_2, \ldots, \alpha_k$ to the sum of $\beta_1, \beta_2, \ldots, \beta_k$.

$$i.e., \qquad label\ (l_i) = \frac{\sum_{j=1}^{k} \alpha_j}{\sum_{j=1}^{k} \beta_j} \tag{1}$$

The line image thus transformed is called as a symbolic image.

2.2 Feature Extraction and Representation

Spatial topology existing among the components of symbolic image is preserved with the help of Triangular Spatial Relationship [5]. A brief review of TSR is given below followed by feature extraction and representation.

2.2.1 Triangular Spatial Relationship

A TSR is defined by connecting three non-collinear components in a symbolic image. Let X, Y and Z are any three non-collinear components and L_x, L_y and L_z be their respective labels. Connecting the centroids of these components mutually forms a triangle as shown in Fig. 1. Let M_1, M_2 and M_3 be the mid points of the sides of the triangle and θ_1, θ_2, and θ_3 be the respective subtended smaller angles, as shown in Fig. 1. The TSR among the components X, Y, and Z is represented by a set of quadruples $\{(L_x, L_y, L_z, \theta_3), (L_x, L_z, L_y, \theta_2), (L_y, L_x, L_z, \theta_3), (L_y, L_z, L_x, \theta_1), (L_z, L_x, L_y, \theta_2), (L_z, L_y, L_x, \theta_1)\}$. Since there are six quadruples for every three non-collinear components, the representation is unwieldy and hence the following conventions were adopted to choose one out of six quadruples.

If $(L_{i1}, L_{i2}, L_{i3}, \theta)$ is the quadruple to be chosen, then the labels L_{i1}, L_{i2}, and L_{i3} must satisfy any one of the following conditions.

- The labels L_{i1}, L_{i2}, and L_{i3} are distinct and $L_{i1}>L_{i2}>L_{i3}$
- $L_{i1}=L_{i2}$ and $L_{i3} < L_{i1}$
- $L_{i1} > L_{i2}$ and $L_{i2} = L_{i3}$ and DIST(Comp(L_{i1}), Comp(L_{i2})) $\geq$ DIST(Comp(L_{i2}), Comp(L_{i3}))
- $L_{i1}=L_{i2}=L_{i3}$ and DIST(Comp(L_{i1}), Comp(L_{i2})) $\geq$ M where M = max(DIST(Comp(L_{i1}), Comp(L_{i3})), DIST(Comp(L_{i2}), Comp(L_{i3})).

Here, DIST(X, Y) is a function which computes the Euclidean distance between the mid-points of the components X and Y. max(a, b) denotes the maximum among *a* and *b*, and Comp(L) indicates the component, the label of which is L.

The TSR among any three non-collinear components in a symbolic image is invariant to translation and rotation since the distance between any two components is invariant to translation and rotation, and invariant to scale since the angle θ in the quadruple $(L_{i1}, L_{i2}, L_{i3}, \theta)$ remains same. Proof for linear transformation invariance can be found in [5].

2.2.2 TSR Model for Object Recognition

The triangular spatial relationship existing among every possible combination of three non-collinear components are computed and represented by a set S of quadruples. If there are *m* number of lines, then we have *m* number of components and hence the set S has ${}^{m}C_3 - N_c$ numbers of quadruples, where N_c is the number of triplets of collinear components (parallel line segments). The set S can itself be stored in the symbolic image database for the matching process at the time of recognition. However, it could be unwieldy as the size of S in general is $O({}^{m}C_3 - N_c)$. Thus, in order to minimize the storage requirement, we find the first principal component vector (PCV), D, the vector on which the variance of the corresponding projected points is maximally preserved after projecting the quadruples of S onto D, assuming that the set S is a set of four dimensional samples, each of which is represented as a point in 4-dimensional space. The first PCVs computed for each symbolic image are stored in the knowledgebase called symbolic image database (SID) for recognition purpose. Hence, the algorithm for object representation is as follows.

2.2.3 Algorithm: Object Representation (TRAINING)

Input: Set of Objects, say $\mathbf{O} = \{O_1, O_2, ..., O_m\}$
Output: Symbolic Image Database: SID

Procedure:

For each object, say O_i

For each view, say $v_{ij} \in O_i$

1. Extract the lines from the edge image of v_{ij}
2. Transform the line image to symbolic image.
3. Compute the set of quadruples, S using TSR.
4. Compute the variance-covariance matrix, CV of S
5. Find the eigenvectors of CV.
6. Choose the eigenvector, D associated with a largest eigenvalue of CV and store it as the representative of view v_{ij} in SID

Algorithm Object Representation *ends.*

Subsequently, the algorithm for recognition of an object is as follows:

Algorithm: Object Recognition

Input: Test object image, OI

Symbolic Image Database, SID

Output: Object class label of OI

Procedure:

1. Extract the lines from edge image of OI.
2. Transform the line image to symbolic image.
3. Compute the set of quadruples, Q.
4. Compute the variance-covariance matrix CV_Q of Q.
5. Find the eigenvectors of CV_Q.
6. Choose the eigenvector, E_j associated with the largest eigenvalue of CV_Q.
7. Use nearest neighbor classifier to find the nearest vector E_k in SID to E_j and return the corresponding Object class label.

Algorithm Object Recognition *Ends.*

In general and in most of the cases, it is found that the object class label returned on classification of test view using Euclidean distance measure is unique. If two different object views are almost similar, then there is a possibility of obtaining two different object class labels. In such cases, second principal component vector is used to resolve the problem of ambiguous classification. It is possible to go up to 4 principal component vectors to resolve the ambiguity. However, if the object view classification is still unresolved, then the test view is treated as ambiguous view and

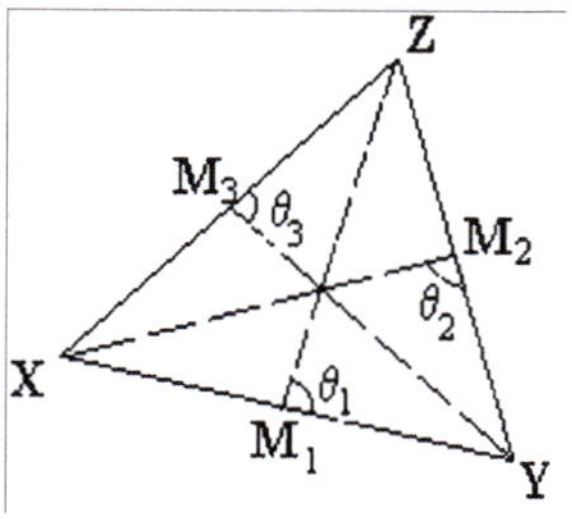

Fig. 1. Triangular Spatial Relationship

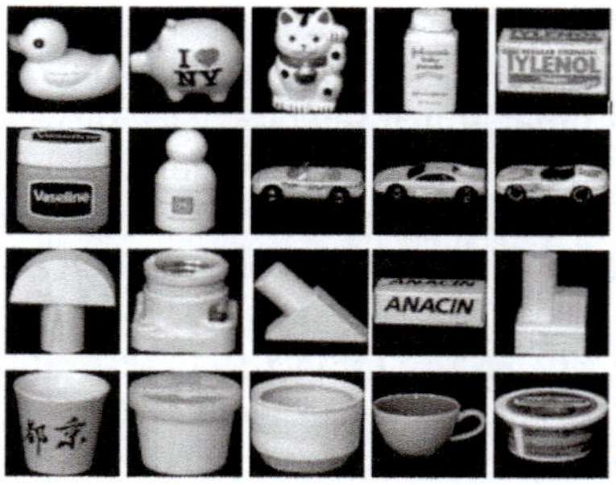

Fig. 2. COIL-20 database

could be resolved with the help of having an additional test view. This issue has not been addressed here since it is another major work under *'active object recognition'* theory.

A binary search technique could be employed to search for the computed PCVs of a given object image in the symbolic image database provided the PCVs are stored in a sorted order in SID, and hence the proposed algorithm requires ***O****(log n)* search time in the worst case. Here *n* represents the number of object views considered for training.

3 Experimental Results

In this section, we present several experiments conducted to demonstrate the performance of the proposed method. To corroborate the efficacy of the proposed model for 3-D object recognition, we performed all experiments on the standard set of images, COIL-20 [12] which is used by many researchers as a benchmark dataset. Fig. 2 shows the images of the 20 objects taken in frontal view, i.e., zero pose angle of COIL-20 database. Each object is represented in the database by 72 views obtained by rotation of the object through 360° in 5° steps (1440 views in total). To validate our claim of transformation invariance, each object view is rotated randomly in in-plane (rotation of an image perpendicular to the image plane) to generate 3 additional views and hence the total size of the database is 5760 views in total.

Table 1. Object recognition performance of the Proposed Method

Number of *k*-smallest and *k*-largest angles used for labeling	Computing time for recognition (5760 views) (in secs.)	% of Recognition with 1440 views knowledgebase	% of Recognition with 720 views knowledgebase
2	9490.14	63.453	50.819
3	9498.25	64.346	58.912
4	9396.53	62.753	51.597
5	9518.48	65.745	56.736
6	9399.00	64.677	57.684
7	9478.43	68.887	58.277
8	9978.11	64.227	60.694

An experiment has been conducted by considering the original 1440 views as training samples and the recognition rate is obtained with all 5760 views as testing samples. Similarly, we have conducted experimentation by considering the alternate views as training samples (720 views) and the recognition rate is obtained with 5760 views as testing samples. The percentage of recognition for different values of *k*, the parameter used to specify the number of smallest and largest angles considered for labeling purpose, and the computing performance is reported in Table-1. Recognition performance of the proposed methodology with varying number of *k* smallest/largest angles and training views is given in Fig. 3.

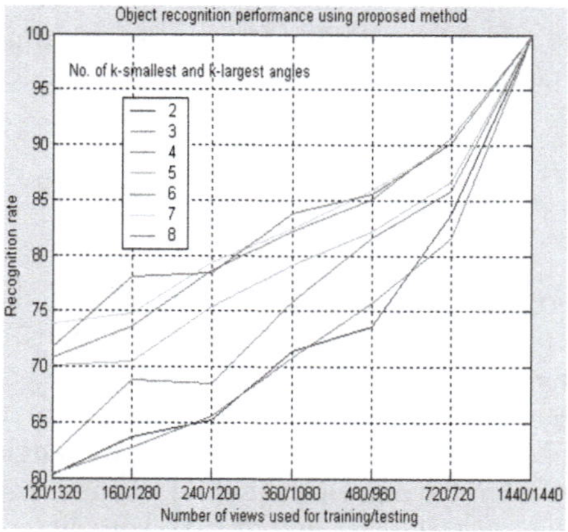

Fig. 3. Performance of the proposed method with varying number of training samples

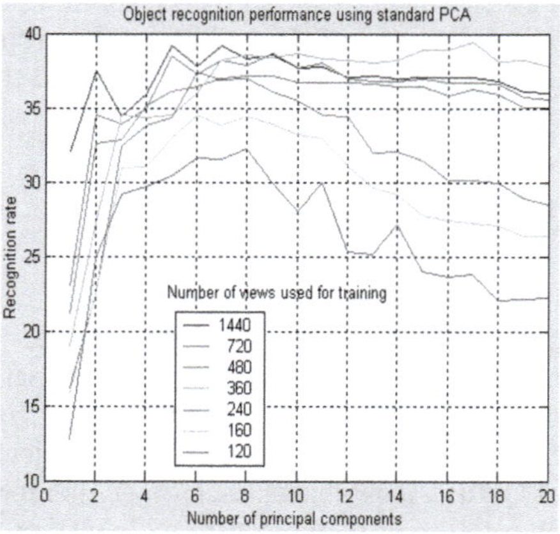

Fig. 4. Performance of the Standard-PCA with varying number of training samples

4 Comparative Study

We have conducted a series of experiments to compare the performance of the proposed method with the traditional PCA based approach [10] under the conditions where the number of training views varied. We performed seven tests with varying number of training views. More specifically, we have considered the original 1440 views of 20 objects as training views and the testing is performed with all views (5760 views). In the next case, we have chosen alternate views from the original 1440 views collection and testing is performed with all views. Similarly, we have conducted experiments considering 480, 360, 240, 160 and 120 views as training views of the COIL-20 database choosing 24, 18, 12, 8 and 6 views respectively from each object and the recognition performance is obtained considering the all views as test views. A nearest neighbor classifier was employed for recognition purpose. Recognition time taken by the proposed methodology and PCA based approach for different training samples are given in Table-2. Recognition accuracy is also given in Table-2. Here, it should be noticed that the traditional PCA consumes less recognition time when compared to our method and it is apparent when the number of training samples decreases. However, recognition rate is very high in the case of proposed methodology at the cost of computing time. Recognition performance of traditional PCA with varying number of principal components along with varying number of training views is given in Fig. 4.

Table 2. Recognition performance and computing time of Standard PCA and Proposed methodology

Number of training views	Number of testing views	Computing time for recognition (in secs.)		Percentage of Recognition	
		Standard PCA	Proposed method (*k*=8)	Standard PCA (20-D)	Proposed method (*k*=8)
1440	5760	766.532	9974.11	36 04	64.227
720	5760	609.955	9932.50	35 59	60.694
480	5760	605.334	9810.49	35 07	55.069
360	5760	528.462	9896.33	37 78	52.153
240	5760	522.906	9822.42	28 44	58.681
160	5760	510.953	9761.44	26 39	53.681
120	5760	489.765	9656.81	22 22	50.833

5 Discussions and Conclusions

Recognition of an object plays a vital role in machine vision applications. Devising an efficient object recognition system is a challenging issue. This paper proposes an efficient and linear transformation invariant object recognition system. The performance of the proposed system is based on low-level image processing.

Well-known appearance based model proposed by Murase and Nayar [10] works very well for noisy as well as unstructured environment and has traditionally been improved by many researchers. However, it is possible that the objects can be placed with at most one degree of freedom (i.e., it does not taken into account in-plane images). Besides, it suffers from illumination problem too. In the case of the proposed method, at the lowest level, we have used canny edge detector [2] and since canny edge detector tolerates noise to some extent, we have a claim that the proposed system is capable of withstanding noise. Moreover, we have used a linear transformation invariant scheme for transforming the line image to symbolic image and hence the proposed system provides two-degrees of freedom (i.e., in-plane images are considered during testing). In the case of Murase and Nayar approach, it is required to have the same size for both the training views as well as test view, which is not required in our approach. However, the proposed method has some limitations. The performance of the system is heavily dependent on low-level image processing such as lines/edges extraction unlike traditional PCA which works directly on intensity values without any intermediate processing. Moreover, labeling of lines depends on all the lines presence in an image. The proposed approach uses only first PCVs for the purpose of recognition. In order to improve the recognition rate, we can have second PCVs and so on. No doubt, incorporation of the second, third, etc., PCVs improve the recognition rate to some extent which can be realized from Fig. 5 and it is at the cost of increased recognition time and more memory. But, when compared to Murase and Nayar approach where it is required to have a minimum of 20-dimensional feature vector to have good recognition accuracy, we have used p-dimensional (p is at most 16) feature vector for the purpose of recognition. Moreover, it should be noticed that the incorporation of another object to the trained knowledgebase requires to re-train the system with the new object set introduced in the case of PCA based approaches which is not required in our method.

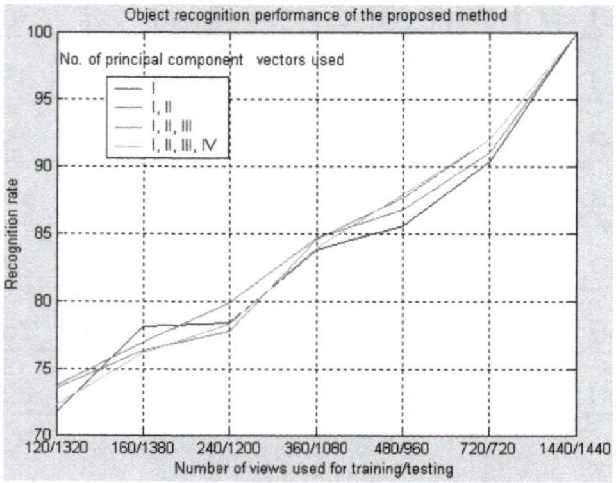

Fig. 5. Recognition performance of the proposed method with varying number of principal component vectors

In summary, we have proposed a simple and an efficient method for 3-D object recognition. The proposed method has three stages namely lines extraction from edge images, transformation of line image to symbolic image and feature extraction by employing PCA on a set of quadruples which are used to represent spatial relationship existing among the components. The proposed method is invariant to linear transformation and consumes less time not only for training, even for recognition too. The proposed method is capable of learning also when an unknown object is given as test object for recognition.

We believe that the system presented here will be a good basis for further improvement. Adaptation of local window technique to design a robust mapper to transform line image to symbolic image, efficient indexing data structure to represent spatial relationship among the components will certainly improve the recognition accuracy which is our future research.

References

1. Bergevin, R., and Levine, M., Generic Object Recognition: Building and matching coarse descriptions from line drawings, IEEE Transactions on Pattern Analysis and Machine Intelligence, vol. 15(1), pp. 19-36, 1993.
2. Canny, J.F. A Computational Approach to Edge Detection, IEEE Transactions on Pattern Analysis and Machine Intelligence, vol. 8(6), pp. 679-698, 1986.

3. Cootes, T.F., Taylor, C.J., Cooper, D.H., and Graham, J. Active shape models- their training and application, Computer Vision and Image Understanding, vol. 61(1), pp. 38-59, 1995.
4. Guru, D.S., Shekar, B.H., and Nagabhushan, P. A simple and robust line detection algorithm based on small eigenvalue analysis, Pattern Recognition Letters, vol. 25(1), pp. 1-13, 2004.
5. Guru, D.S., and Nagabhushan, P. Triangular spatial relationship: A new approach for spatial knowledge representation, Pattern Recognition Letters, vol. 22(9), pp. 999-1005, 2001.
6. Kruger, N., and Peters G. ORASSYLL: Object recognition with autonomously learned and sparse symbolic representations based on metrically organized local line detectors, Computer Vision and Image Understanding, vol. 77(1), pp. 48-77, 2000.
7. Lamdan, Y., and Wolfson, H. Geometric Hashing: A general and efficient model based recognition scheme, Second International Conference on Computer Vision, 1988.
8. Leonardis, A., and Bischof, H. Robust recognition using Eigenimages, Computer Vision and Image Understanding, vol. 78(1), pp. 99-118, 2000.
9. Leonardis, A., Bischof, H., and Jasna, M. Multiple Eigenspaces, Pattern Recognition, vol. 35(11), pp. 2613-2627, 2002.
10. Murase, H. and Nayar, S. K. Visual learning and recognition of 3-d objects from appearance, International Journal of Computer Vision, vol. 14(5), pp. 1-24, 1995.
11. Murase, H., and Nayar, S.K., Detection of 3D objects in cluttered scenes using hierarchical eigenspace, Pattern Recognition Letters, vol. 18(4), pp. 375-384, 1997.
12. Nene, S.A., Nayar, S.K., and Murase, H. Columbia Object Image Library (COIL-20), Technical Report CUCS-005-96, Columbia University, New York, 1996.
13. Ohba, K, and Ikeuchi, K. Detectability, Uniqueness, and Reliability of eigen windows for stable verification of partially occluded objects, IEEE Transactions on Pattern Analysis and Machine Intelligence, vol. 19(9), pp. 1043-1048, 1997.
14. Pentland, A., Moghddam, B., and Straner, T. View-based and Modular Eigenspaces for Face Recognition, Technical Report 245, MIT Media Laboratory, 1994.
15. Tsai, F.C.D. Geometric hashing with line features, Pattern Recognition, vol. 27(3), pp. 377-389, 1994.

Shift-Invariant Image Denoising Using Mixture of Laplace Distributions in Wavelet-Domain

B.S. Raghavendra and P. Subbanna Bhat

Department of Electronics and Communication Engineering,
National Institute of Technology Karnataka, Surathkal-575 025, India
r.bobbi@gmail.com, psb@nitk.ac.in

Abstract. In this paper, we propose a new method for denoising of images based on the distribution of the wavelet transform. We model the discrete wavelet coefficients as mixture of Laplace distributions. Redundant, shift invariant wavelet transform is made use of in order to avoid aliasing error that occurs with critically sampled filter bank. A simple Expectation Maximization algorithm is used for estimating parameters of the mixture model of the noisy image data. The noise is considered as zero-mean additive white Gaussian. Using the mixture probability model, the noise-free wavelet coefficients are estimated using a maximum a posteriori estimator. The denoising method is applied for general category of images and results are compared with that of wavelet-domain hidden Markov tree method. The experimental results show that the proposed method gives enhanced image estimation results in the PSNR sense and better visual quality over a wide range of noise variance.

1 Introduction

Wavelets have emerged as a new mathematical tool for statistical image processing. Many image processing tasks are efficiently carried out in the wavelet-domain. Wavelets provide a compact and decorrelated image representation. The wavelet transform uses a set of basis functions, which are shifted and dilated versions of a band pass wavelet function and shifted versions of low pass scaling function. The basis functions of wavelets are localized both in time and frequency. The wavelet coefficients are computed using filter banks, where the analysis and synthesis filters form a quadrature mirror filters. For images, separable transform is constructed by applying filter bank to each column and then to each row of the result. The multiresolution nature of wavelets gives both local and global view of an image. For an image the wavelet coefficients are naturally arranged in the form of quad trees. The children coefficients in the quad trees analyze the image at one scale finer than the parent does.

The wavelet transform can be redundant. The redundancy allows enriching the set of basis functions so that the representation is more efficient in capturing information contained in an image. Many applications such as edge detection and denoising can greatly benefit from redundant representations. In noise filtering, the study the signal is required in the domain where statistics of the clean signal and the noise are modeled effectively via appropriate transforms such as the wavelet transform.

P.J. Narayanan et al. (Eds.): ACCV 2006, LNCS 3851, pp. 180 – 188, 2006.

The simplest method for wavelet-based image denoising is a thresholding rule. More advanced image denoising approaches begin with a probability model for the wavelet coefficients and then obtain an estimator via Bayesian estimation techniques, such as the MAP or MMSE estimator [1]. In this direction, wavelet-domain Hidden Markov Tree (HMT) models have demonstrated superior performance in image denoising [2]. Wavelet-domain thresholding is used to get an optimal performance in [3]. Authors in [4] have proposed bivariate shrinkage function for denoising of images by modeling non-Gaussian nature of the wavelet statistics. They have used a bivariate probability distribution function for modeling the discrete wavelet coefficients.

The key point in signal denoising is to choose appropriate probability distribution functions (pdf) that represent the wavelet coefficients and estimation of parameters of that distribution from noisy data. In this paper, we propose a nonlinear image denoising algorithm based on mixtures of Laplacian distributions for modeling the discrete wavelet coefficients.

2 Background

Multiscale image expansions implemented with filter banks offers possibility of decomposition that is shift-invariant. In image denoising applications via thresholding in the wavelet-domain, the lack of shift-invariance causes pseudo-Gibbs phenomena around singularities. To solve this problem, it is recommended to use decomposition with less shift sensitivity than the standard maximally decimated wavelet decomposition [5]. Generally, cycle spinning algorithm is employed to improve the denoising performance of a non-shift-invariant design. It is equivalent to a shift-invariant denoising if all the possible shifts of the input image are used and it is computationally more expensive.

The wavelet coefficients of natural images are generally having heavy tailed distributions and approximately uncorrelated. There exists a strong dependence on adjacent coefficients in scale and space. This suggests that multivariate Gaussian model is not accurate for wavelet-domain modeling of natural images, even though it is easy to work with such models. In wavelet-based image denoising, non-Gaussian probability models may provide superior performance in achieving high quality results.

3 Formulation of Problem

In this section, mathematical formulation of image denoising problem is explained. An image corrupted with zero-mean additive white Gaussian noise is considered. In the orthogonal wavelet domain, the problem can be formulated as $y = w + n$, where y is the noisy wavelet coefficient, w is the noise free wavelet coefficient and n is the noise. For wavelet-based denoising using distributions, it is useful to know the distribution of the clean and noisy wavelet coefficients. Let $p_w(w)$ be the probability distribution function (pdf) of w and $p_n(n)$ be the pdf of n. In [6] pdf of wavelet coefficients is modeled as a generalized Gaussian with $p_w(w) = K(s,p)\exp\left(-\left|\frac{w}{s}\right|^p\right)$, where, s, p are the parameters of the model and $K(s,p)$ is the normalization factor.

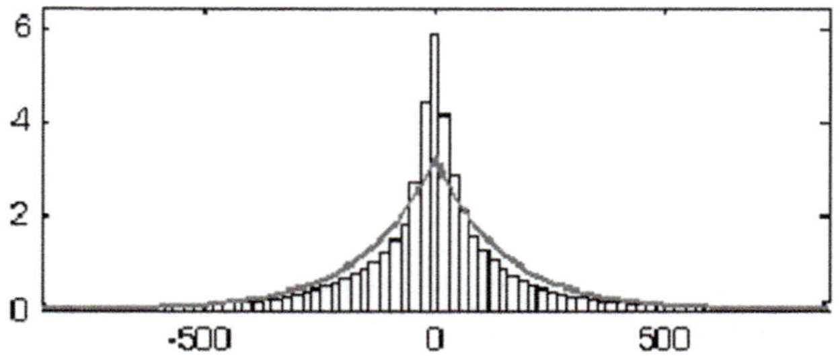

Fig. 1. Histogram of a subband of wavelet coefficients of Lena image. Solid line plot is the corresponding Laplacian distribution fit for the wavelet coefficients of the subband.

Figure 1 shows bar graph of histogram of a subband of wavelet coefficients for a noise-free Lena image. The distributions are characterized by a sharp peak at zero amplitude and extended tails on either side of the peak. The histograms of different subbands in different scales show that the marginal distributions of natural images in the wavelet-domain are highly non-Gaussian. Suppose consider that, the noise-free wavelet coefficients are modeled using Laplace distributions. The solid line plot in the Figure 1 shows the Laplace distribution fit for the data. The pdf of wavelet coefficients and noise are $p_w(w)=\frac{1}{\sqrt{2}\sigma_w}\exp\left(-\frac{\sqrt{2}}{\sigma_w}|w|\right)$, $p_n(n)=\frac{1}{\sqrt{2\pi}\sigma_n}\exp\left(-\frac{n^2}{2\sigma_n^2}\right)$ respectively, where σ_n^2 is the variance of the noise and σ_w^2 is the variance of wavelet coefficients. When the w and n are independent, the pdf of y is the convolution of the pdfs of w and n. Since the noise-free wavelet coefficient is Laplacian distributed and the noise is Gaussian distributed, the pdf of their sum is given by the formula [7].

$$p_y(y)=\frac{1}{2\sqrt{2}\sigma_w}\exp\left(-\frac{y^2}{2\sigma_n^2}\right)\times\left[erfcx\left(\frac{\sigma_n}{\sigma_w}-\frac{y}{\sqrt{2}\sigma_n}\right)+erfcx\left(\frac{\sigma_n}{\sigma_w}+\frac{y}{\sqrt{2}\sigma_n}\right)\right],$$

where $erfcx(x)=\exp(x^2)erfc(x)$, $erfc(x)=1-erf(x)$, $erf(x)=\frac{2}{\sqrt{\pi}}\int_0^x e^{-t^2}dt$. A maximum a posteriori (MAP) estimator is used to estimate w from the noisy observation y. The MAP estimator can be written as; $\hat{w}(y)=\arg\max_w p_{w|y}(w|y)$. Upon simplification, the MAP estimator of w uses a threshold $T=\frac{\sqrt{2}\sigma_n^2}{\sigma}$, where $\sigma=\sqrt{(\sigma_y^2-\sigma_n^2)}$. The estimate of wavelet coefficients is $\hat{w}(y)=sign(y)(|y|-T)_+$, where $(x)_+=\begin{cases}x & x\geq 0\\ 0 & otherwise\end{cases}$. We call this rule as *Tresh* and $\hat{w}(y)=Tresh(y,T)$. It is equivalent to soft-thresholding rule.

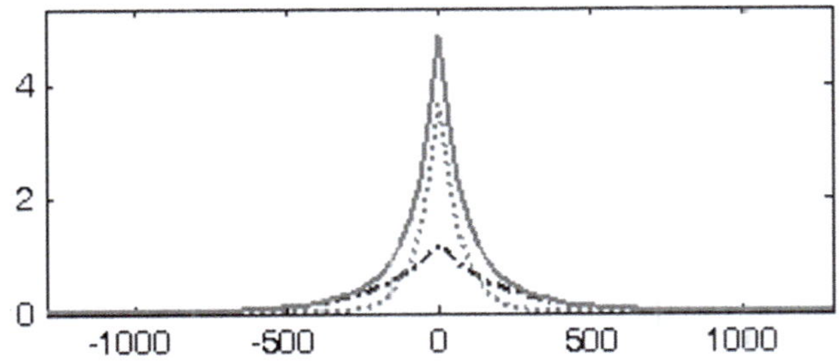

Fig. 2. Mixture of two Laplace distributions

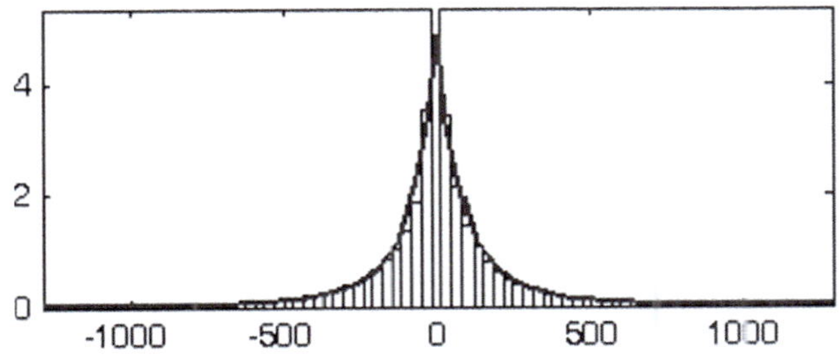

Fig. 3. Histogram of a subband of wavelet coefficients and solid line plot is modeling of wavelet coefficients with a mixture of two Laplace distributions

The plots in the Figure 1 show that the Laplace distribution does not follow the histogram very closely. To tackle this problem, we have used a mixture of two Laplace distributions. The estimation of the mixture model is performed using Expectation Maximization (EM) algorithm. The plots in the Figure 2 show that the mixture of two Laplace distributions. From the Figure 3, it is clear that, the mixture of two Laplace distributions matches the wavelet histogram quite well.

4 Mixture Model of Wavelets

A mixture model for a random variable has a pdf that is the sum of two simpler pdfs. The model can be written as; $p(x) = ap_1(x) + (1-a)p_2(x)$, where $p_1(x)$ and $p_2(x)$ are two pdfs and $p(x)$ is the combination of the two. Using a mixture of two Laplace pdfs to model the distribution of wavelet coefficients, the expression can be written as; $p(w) = a\frac{1}{\sqrt{2}\sigma_1}\exp\left(-\frac{\sqrt{2}}{\sigma_1}|w|\right) + (1-a)\frac{1}{\sqrt{2}\sigma_2}\exp\left(-\frac{\sqrt{2}}{\sigma_2}|w|\right)$. It is necessary to estimate three parameters, σ_1, σ_2 and a from the data. For the mixture model, an iterative EM algorithm is used to estimate the parameters.

4.1 EM Algorithm

The Expectation Maximization algorithm is an iterative numerical algorithm, each iteration of which consists of an E-step and an M-step. We use a simple EM algorithm as described in this section. For the mixture model $p(x) = ap_1(x) + bp_2(x)$ where $a + b = 1$, the observed data be x_n for $n = 1,...,N$.

Introduce auxiliary variables $r_1(n)$ and $r_2(n)$ that represent for each data point, how likely that the data point was generated by one or the other of the two components $p_1(x)$ and $p_2(x)$. The $r_1(n)$ represents how responsible $p_1(x)$ is for generating the data point x_n, while the $r_2(n)$ represents how responsible $p_2(x)$ is for generating the data point x_n. To start with, we have to initialize the variables a, b, σ_1 and σ_2. The initial values for a and b should satisfy $a + b = 1$. Sequences of E-M-steps are used until the parameters satisfy some convergence condition.

The E-step calculates the responsibility factors as;

$$r_1(n) = \frac{ap_1(x_n)}{ap_1(x_n) + bp_2(x_n)} \text{ and } r_2(n) = \frac{bp_2(x_n)}{ap_1(x_n) + bp_2(x_n)}.$$

These responsibility factors are between 0 and 1 and $r_1(n) + r_2(n) = 1$. The M-step updates the parameters a, b, σ_1 and σ_2. The mixture parameters a and b are computed as; $a = \frac{1}{N}\sum_{n=1}^{N} r_1(n)$ and $b = \frac{1}{N}\sum_{n=1}^{N} r_2(n)$. We estimate σ_1^2 as a weighted sum of the data point, where the weight for x_n is the responsibility of $p_1(x)$ for the data point x_n. The σ_1^2 and σ_2^2 are calculated as;

$$\sigma_1^2 = \frac{\left(\sum_{n=1}^{N} r_1(n) x_n^2\right)}{\left(\sum_{n=1}^{N} r_1(n)\right)} \text{ and } \sigma_2^2 = \frac{\left(\sum_{n=1}^{N} r_2(n) x_n^2\right)}{\left(\sum_{n=1}^{N} r_2(n)\right)} \text{ respectively.}$$

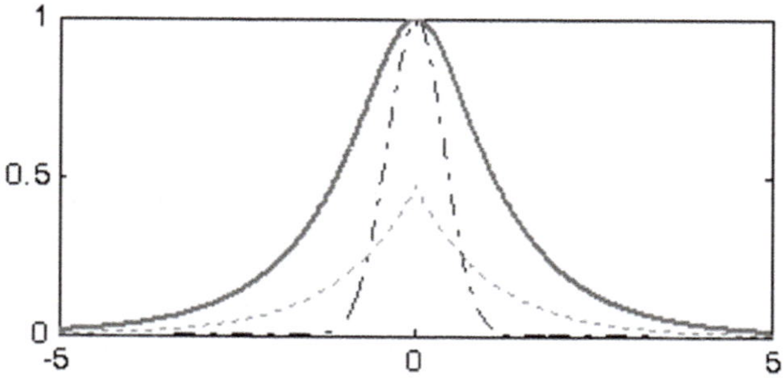

Fig. 4. Sum of Laplacian and Gaussian pdfs. The dotted plot is Laplacian pdf, the dash-dot plot is Gaussian pdf and solid plot is the sum of the two.

5 Image Denoising

The wavelet coefficient w is modeled as having the pdf $p_w(w) = ap_1(w) + bp_2(w)$ where $a+b=1$, and n is modeled as having the pdf $p_n(n)$, then the pdf of y is of the form $p_y(y) = ap_1(y) * p_n(y) + bp_2(y) * p_n(y)$, where * denotes convolution operation. Given the noisy data y, and assuming the noise standard deviation σ_n is known, we can estimate the model parameters a, σ_1 and σ_2 using the EM algorithm. The EM algorithm is modified to model y as a mixture of two Laplacian-Gaussian components. Figure 4 shows a sum of Laplacian and Gaussian pdfs.

Let $\hat{w}$ be the estimate of w. The estimate can be written as; $\hat{w} = p_a(y)\hat{w}_1(y) + p_b(y)\hat{w}_2(y)$, where $p_a(y)$ is the probability that w was generated by p_1 and where similarly $p_b(y)$ is the probability that w was generated by p_2. The $\hat{w}_1(y)$ is an estimate of w based on the assumption that n was generated by p_1 and that similarly $\hat{w}_2(y)$ is an estimate of w based on the assumption that w was generated by p_2.

We determine $p_a(y)$ and $p_b(y)$ respectively as;

$p_a(y) = \dfrac{a\ g_1(y)}{a\ g_1(y) + b\ g_2(y)}$, $p_b(y) = \dfrac{b\ g_2(y)}{a\ g_1(y) + b\ g_2(y)}$, where $g_1(y)$ is the pdf of y under the assumption that w was generated by p_1 and similarly where $g_2(y)$ is the pdf of y under the assumption that w was generated by p_2. Because y is the sum of w and independent Gaussian noise n, the pdf of y is the convolution of the pdf of w and the Gaussian pdf. This leads to the relations

$$g_1(y) = Laplace(y, \sigma_1) * Gaussian(y, \sigma_n)$$

$$g_1(y) = \frac{1}{\sqrt{2}\sigma_1} \exp\left(-\frac{\sqrt{2}}{\sigma_1}|y|\right) * \frac{1}{\sqrt{2\pi}\sigma_n} \exp\left(-\frac{y^2}{2\sigma_n^2}\right)$$

$$g_2(y) = Laplace(y, \sigma_2) * Gaussian(y, \sigma_n)$$

$$g_2(y) = \frac{1}{\sqrt{2}\sigma_2} \exp\left(-\frac{\sqrt{2}}{\sigma_2}|y|\right) * \frac{1}{\sqrt{2\pi}\sigma_n} \exp\left(-\frac{y^2}{2\sigma_n^2}\right).$$

Since p_1 and p_2 are Laplace pdfs with parameters σ_1 and σ_2 respectively, the threshold function *Tresh* can be used to get $\hat{w}_1(y)$ and $\hat{w}_2(y)$. The estimate of w can be written as follows $\hat{w}(y) = p_a(y)\ Thresh(y, T) + p_b(y)\ Thresh(y, T)$. Thus a nonlinear mixture shrinkage rule is derived from the mixture model. We call this method of denoising as Laplace Mixture Distribution Model (LMDM).

The nonlinearity shrinks the value of y to estimate w. Some of the shrinkage functions are given in the Figure 5. From the plots it is clear that, the nonlinear function does not shrink large values of y as much as the threshold function *Tresh* does.

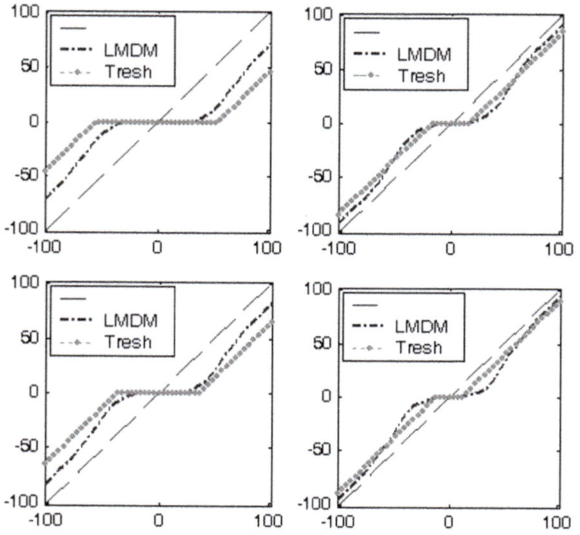

Fig. 5. Shrinkage functions for different subbands of the wavelet transform

6 Experimental Results

To evaluate the proposed algorithm, we performed several experiments by applying the algorithm on a variety of test images, all of size 512 x 512. The images are made corrupt by a zero-mean Gaussian noise with different standard deviations. We used Daubechies-4 wavelet to decompose images into five levels. The noise power in the transformed domain is calculated using the median estimate of the finest scale wavelet coefficients y_f as; $\sigma_n^2 = \dfrac{median(|y_f|)}{0.6745}$.

PSNR measure is used to compare the performance of the denoising results. Table 1 shows the denoising results for different noise powers. The denoising results of soft threshold rule *Tresh* and that of wavelet-domain HMT methods are also tabulated. The peak signal to noise ration (PSNR) is calculated as; $PSNR = 10\log 10\left(\dfrac{255^2}{MSE}\right)$, $MSE = \dfrac{1}{N^2}\sum_{i=1}^{N}\sum_{j=1}^{N}\left(X_{ij} - Y_{ij}\right)^2$, where the MSE is the mean squared error and X and Y are original and denoised images of size N x N respectively. In terms of PSNR, the Laplace Mixture Distribution Model (LMDM) gives the highest value of the other methods compared. Figure 6 shows the denoised results of a segment of Lena image. It is clear that the denoising scheme is capable of retaining edges and fine details. The algorithm removed most of the noise preserving high frequency details. The visual quality of the image is also improved.

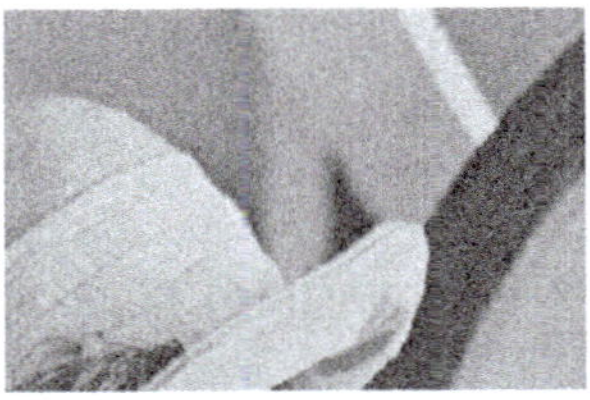 

(a) (b)

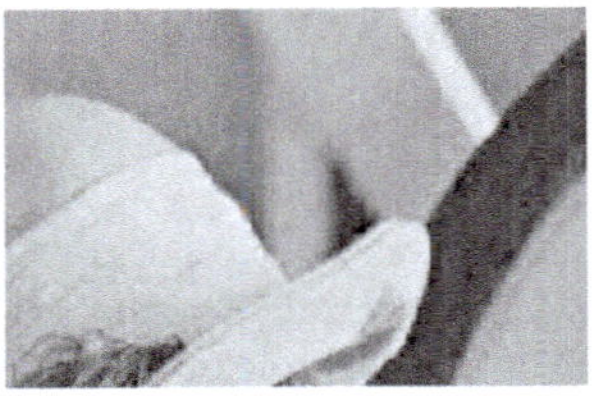 

(c) (d)

Fig. 6. Image denoising results. (a) Noisy image (b) Denoised image using HMT, PSNR=31.09dB (c) Denoised image using *Tresh*, PSNR=31.85dB (d) Denoised image using LMDM, PSNR=32.37dB.

Table 1. Denoising results for various noise powers

"Lena"	PSNR(dB)			
σ_n	Noisy	HMT	*Tresh*	LMDM
10	28.12	33.79	34.46	34.86
15	24.60	31.74	32.49	32.97
20	22.10	30.31	31.44	31.62
25	20.16	29.28	30.15	30.60
30	18.58	28.50	29.35	29.76
"Barbara"	PSNR(dB)			
σ_n	Noisy	HMT	*Tresh*	LMDM
10	28.12	31.34	31.94	32.34
15	24.60	28.98	29.59	29.83
20	22.10	27.47	27.76	28.06
25	20.16	26.38	26.42	26.72
30	18.58	25.47	25.35	25.69
"Boats"	PSNR(dB)			
σ_n	Noisy	HMT	*Tresh*	LMDM
10	28.15	32.17	32.97	33.13
15	24.63	30.23	30.88	31.13
20	22.13	28.82	29.35	29.70
25	20.19	27.72	28.18	28.59
30	18.61	26.91	27.29	27.61

7 Conclusion

Modeling is at the core of image denoising problem. In this paper, we have proposed a new method for denoising images based on MAP estimator by modeling wavelet coefficients as a mixture of Laplace distributions. A simple EM algorithm is used for estimating the parameters of the model. The proposed denoising method produces superior PSNR performance and better visual quality. The denoising results are comparable to that of the wavelet-domain HMT method.

References

1. M. S. Crouse, R. D. Nowak and R. G. Baraniuk.:Wavelet-based statistical signal processing using hidden Markov models. IEEE Trans. on Signal Proc., vol. 46, no. 4, (1998) 886-902.
2. J. Romberg, H. Choi, and R. Baraniuk.: Bayesian tree structured image modeling using wavelet-domain hidden Markov models. Proc. SPIE Technical Conference on Mathematical Modeling, Bayesian Estimation, and Inverse Problems, (1999) 31-44.
3. D. L. Donoho.: Denoising by soft-thresholding. IEEE Trans. Information Theory, vol. 41, no. 3, (1995) 613-627.
4. L. Sendur and I. W. Selesnick.: Bivariate shrinkage with local variance estimation. IEEE Signal Proc. Letters, vol. 9, no.12, (2002) 438-441.
5. M. Lang, H. Guo, J. E. Odegard and C. S. Burrus.: Noise reduction using an undecimated discrete wavelet transform. IEEE Signal Proc. Letters, vol. 3, no.1, (1996) 10-12.
6. E. P. Simoncelli.: Bayesian denoising of visual images in the wavelet domain. Lecture Notes in Statistics, Springer-Verlag, (1999).
7. M. Hansen and B. Yu.: Wavelet-thresholding via MDL for natural images. IEEE Trans. Information Theory, vol. 46, no. 5, (2000).

Blind Watermarking Via Pixel Modification with Regular Rule

Yulin Wang and Jinxu Guo

School of Information Engineering, Wuhan University of Technology,
122 Luoshi Road, Hongshan District, Wuchang,
Wuhan 430070, China
halfmooncity2@yahoo.com.cn
guojx@mail.whut.edu.cn

Abstract. Watermarking techniques that need no original information during watermark detection, the so-called blind watermark, are more desirable than informed ones for practical usage and convenience in watermark extraction. In this paper, a rule-based multi-bit watermarking technique is presented. Regular pixel patterns are used as base patterns in the watermark bit modulation, and each bit is embedded in one spreading pattern of 8x8 block, which is the combination with base patterns. Space division multiple access is applied to obtain high data-hiding capacity. The main advantage of the scheme is its simplicity, blindness and high capacity. Selected experimental results are reported.

1 Introduction

Digital watermarking is the communication of information by embedding it into multimedia data, called "host data," without introducing perceptual changes and receiving it later. The data with embedded watermark are denoted as "container". The embedded information can be used for copyright protection or covert message.

Most of the existing watermarking schemes are always based on some assumptions for watermark detection and extraction. Some schemes require the previous knowledge of watermark location, strength or some threshold. For example, to ensure the robustness and invisibility of a watermark, the optimum embedding location are generally different for different images. For a large image database, it could be a disadvantage if requiring watermark location and strength information for detection and extraction, since a large amount of information are needed to be stored. In the Internet distribution, the owner can always distribute the multimedia data by assigning different watermarks to different users in order to prevent illegal redistribution of data by a legal user. In such scenario, the watermark detection/extraction algorithms requiring the information of watermark location and strength, or the original watermark should fail, since the users do not know exactly which watermark is embedded in this copy of the watermarked image.

Thus a new blind watermarking scheme which overcomes the problems discussed above is proposed in this paper. One of the advantages of the proposed watermarking is that it has a general framework for covert message delivery, since extraction algorithm does not require any information on watermark locations and strengths.

P.J. Narayanan et al. (Eds.): ACCV 2006, LNCS 3851, pp. 189 – 195, 2006.

Secondly, due to its high payload, some readable signature or logo can be used as watermark. By using such a watermark, it is more robust semantically against attacks, because the signature or image pattern can always preserve a certain degree of structural information, which are meaningful and recognizable, can be more easy to be verified by human eyes rather than some objective similarity measurements.

The proposed algorithm operated in spatial domain, and watermark extraction is performed without resorting to the original image. Though at the expense of a slight loss of robustness, the proposed technique represents a major improvement to methods relying on the comparison between the watermarked and original images [1,2,3,4,5].

The detailed embedding scheme is introduced in section 2, including the information embedding and extraction. Selected experimental results are presented in section 3. The paper closes with concluding remarks in section 4.

2 Proposed Scheme

In most applications, the original host signal is not available to the watermark detector. Therefore, many watermarking schemes suffer considerably from the host-signal interference. The technique we present in this paper does not reply on the correlation detection, but on extracted patterns. For each pixel 8x8 block, regular-shape patterns are selected as Reference Patterns (RP), so the detection error due to attacks can be partially remedied by median filter and edge-detection image processing method. Though we can use the 64 separated pixels, which are mutually orthogonal in location, to make the distance as far as possible, it can not be remedied by filter for its shape is not a close set. Furthermore, we can select some regular-shape RPs which are invariant in shape after rotation. As for the shape, they can cover different area with any shape. The farther the distance among RPs is, the better for detection to distinguish. This is the part of the task, which we call it as top layer of watermark embedding. On the bottom layer, each pattern is constructed with the change of individual pixel. How can we change individual pixel?

In mathematics as we know, if g(i,j) which is an integer belongs to [0,255], for example, and if

$$\hat{g}(i,j) = \begin{cases} g(i,j), & if \quad p = k \\ g(i,j) + L*(k-p), & if \ p \neq k \ and \ |k-p| < \frac{K}{2} \\ g(i,j) - L*(K-|k-p|), & if \ p \neq k \ and \ (k > p) \ and \ |k-p| > \frac{K}{2} \\ g(i,j) + L*(K-|k-p|), & if \ p \neq k \ and \ (k < p) \ and \ |k-p| > \frac{K}{2} \end{cases} \quad (1)$$

Then $[\hat{g}(i,j) \div L] \bmod K = k$ always holds for all the above conditions.

In equation (1), $\hat{g}(i,j)$ represents the modified valued of g(i, j), and

K ------- the total different number of element k
L ------- the modification step, which is integer number

k ------- the possible element, which is integer number
p ------- [g(i,j) ÷L] mod K
[ ] ------ the truncation to an integer value, and mod is the modular operation.

The above formula means no matter how much the original value g(i,j) is modified, we can extract the same result from its counterpart ĝ(i,j). In this paper, we will use this formula to slightly modify the host image. The detailed technique is introduced in the following sub-section.

2.1 Watermark Embedding

We select 6 base block patterns of the size 8x8, which can be used to construct 26 different patterns, representing 64 self-defined ASCII codes if we embed text message in the image. The selected 6 base patterns RP1, RP2, …, RP6 are non-overlaid each other, or so-called orthogonal, which are shown in figure 1.

1	1	1	1	1	1	1	1
0	0	0	0	0	0	0	0
0	0	0	0	0	0	0	0
0	0	0	0	0	0	0	0
0	0	0	0	0	0	0	0
0	0	0	0	0	0	0	0
x	x	x	x	x	x	x	x
x	x	x	x	x	x	x	x

(a) RP_6

0	0	0	0	0	0	0	0
1	1	1	1	1	1	1	1
0	0	0	0	0	0	0	0
0	0	0	0	0	0	0	0
0	0	0	0	0	0	0	0
0	0	0	0	0	0	0	0
x	x	x	x	x	x	x	x
x	x	x	x	x	x	x	x

(b) RP_5

0	0	0	0	0	0	0	0
0	0	0	0	0	0	0	0
1	1	1	1	1	1	1	1
0	0	0	0	0	0	0	0
0	0	0	0	0	0	0	0
0	0	0	0	0	0	0	0
x	x	x	x	x	x	x	x
x	x	x	x	x	x	x	x

(c) RP_4

0	0	0	0	0	0	0	0
0	0	0	0	0	0	0	0
0	0	0	0	0	0	0	0
1	1	1	1	1	1	1	1
0	0	0	0	0	0	0	0
0	0	0	0	0	0	0	0
x	x	x	x	x	x	x	x
x	x	x	x	x	x	x	x

(d) RP_3

0	0	0	0	0	0	0	0
0	0	0	0	0	0	0	0
0	0	0	0	0	0	0	0
0	0	0	0	0	0	0	0
1	1	1	1	1	1	1	1
0	0	0	0	0	0	0	0
x	x	x	x	x	x	x	x
x	x	x	x	x	x	x	x

(e) RP_2

0	0	0	0	0	0	0	0
0	0	0	0	0	0	0	0
0	0	0	0	0	0	0	0
0	0	0	0	0	0	0	0
0	0	0	0	0	0	0	0
1	1	1	1	1	1	1	1
x	x	x	x	x	x	x	x
x	x	x	x	x	x	x	x

(f) RP_1

Fig. 1. Six base reference patterns (RPs) which are mutually orthogonal

Correspondingly, we divide one image into 8x8 blocks. In every block, by the combination of the 6 base reference patterns with each representing one bit watermark information, we can embed 6 bits in one 8x8 block. By using self-defined ASCII codebook which consists of 26 letters and digitals, we can embed text message in the host image. For example, if we want to embed a letter 'c' in one selected block, then we first look up the self-defined codebook to get the ASCII code of 'c', e.g. '001010', the map this bit-string into the combination of the 6 base reference patterns as shown in figure2. Sign '-' represents bit '0' and '+' represents bit '1'. Following the steps in the figure, we generate a modulation matrix, which consists of only 0s and 1s, as shown on the right of the figure 2.

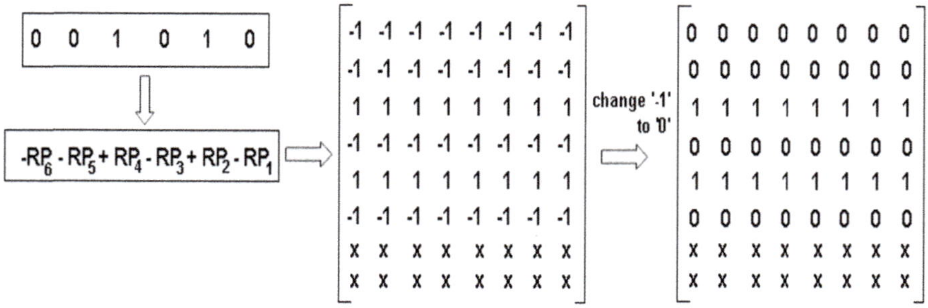

Fig. 2. The generation of modulation matrix with the Reference Patterns

Now we turn to the bottom layer. First of all, we convert the pixel value of the host image to the range of integer number [0, 255] if necessary. If we denote each element in the above modulation matrix in figure 2 as k, then k = {0,1}. If we denote the total statuses of k as K, then K=2. Then we can use the formula (1) to modify the luminance value of individual pixel in one image by assigning the meanings of the symbols as follows:

K ------- the total different number of k
L ------- watermark modulation depth
k ------- the logic value of the modification

The value of L affects the watermark imperceptibility. In our experiment, we select different values of L for comparison. The bigger the value of L, the higher the energy of the watermark, but at the same time the artifact will appear.

Inserting the k in the above modulation matrix, as well as L and K into formula (1), we modify the original pixel value g(i,j) in the pixel block, and get modified value $\hat{g}$(i,j). After all related pixels in the host image are modified, we get the watermarked image $\hat{g}$ of the original image g. Here we use g to denote image, and use g(i,j) to denote individual pixel at location (i,j), and similar notation is applied to $\hat{g}$ and $\hat{g}$(i,j).

2.2 Extraction of Watermark Bit

The watermark bit extraction from the watermarked image $\hat{g}$ is nearly the reverse process of the watermark bit embedding. We briefly describe it as follows:

- Getting one 8x8 pattern matrix WM', consisting of 1s and 0s, by the calculation of [$\hat{g}$(i,j) ÷L] mod K within one 8x8 block;
- Changing the 0s in WM' matrix to –1s;
- Obtaining the corresponding combination of the 6 base reference patterns by checking the new matrix row by row;
- Extracting the 6 watermark bits in the block;
- Repeating the above procedures until the all the watermark bits in the related blocks are extracted.

Since the watermark embedding is changing g(i,j) to $\hat{g}$(i,j) by k based on formula (1), and the watermark extraction is recovering k from $\hat{g}$(i,j). We needn't remember the value of change of individual pixel, since [ĝ(i,j) ÷L] mod K=k always holds. But if the watermarked image ĝ is attacked, some of the extract bits will be incorrect. If the watermark to be embedded is a binary logo as done in our experiment, the incorrectly extract bits are displayed as noise in the extracted logo.

3 Experimental Results

In figure 3, we embed the logo of Queen Mary in the image Lena with L=6. Figure 3(a) and 3(b) are the original image and the watermarked image respectively, but we can hardly identify their difference. After the watermarked image is compressed by JPEG with quality factor=60 (QF), the extracted logo as shown in 3(d), though noisy, can still be identified.

In figure 4, we repeat the same experiment with L=6, 26 and 36, respectively. The host image used is peppers. Since only part area of the image is needed to embed the small logo, we only demonstrate the enlarged watermarked area of the image for the clarity of comparison, as shown in figure 4(d), 4(f) and 4(h) for L=6, 26 and 36 respectively. You can find that the bigger the value of L, the artifact will appear due

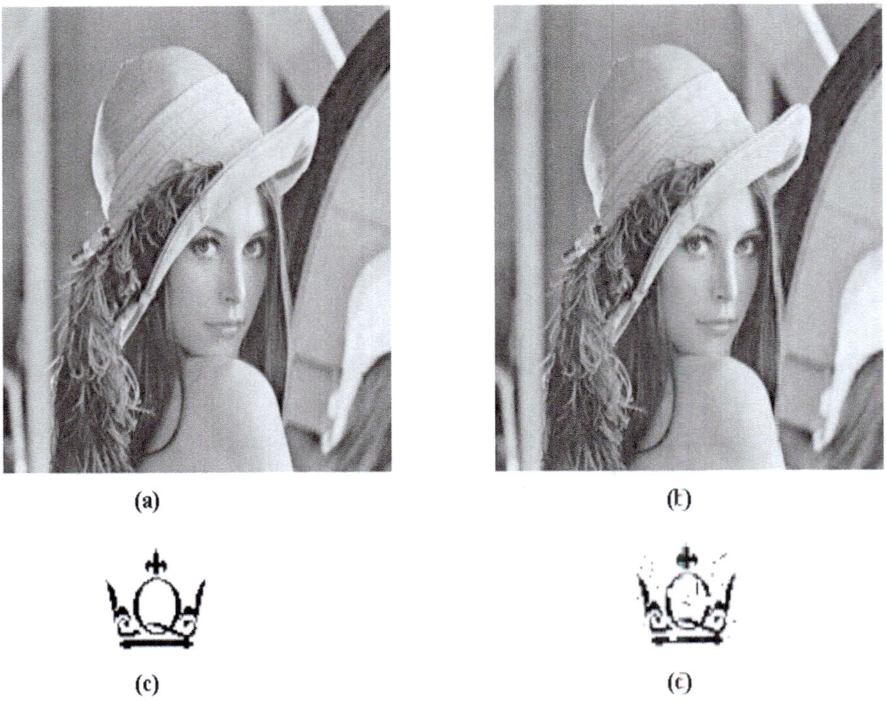

Fig. 3. Comparison between the original and watermarked image (L=6, PSNR= 43.4dB) (a) Original host image Lena (512x512); (b)Watermarked Lena, and compressed by JPEG with QF=60; (c) Queen Mary Logo embedded (50x45); (d) Extracted logo from b)

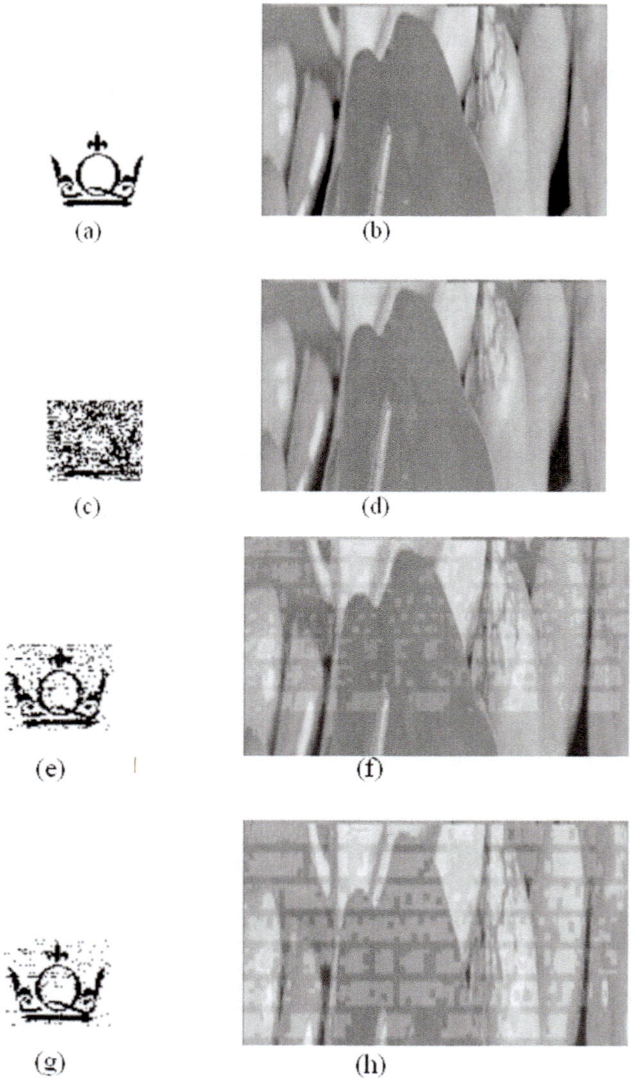

Fig. 4. Comparison with different L values, under the same attack, compressed by JPEG with QF=40). (a) Original Logo; (b) Original host image (part area of the image peppers); (c) Extracted Logo from (d); (d) Watermarked area of the image with L=6; (e) Extracted Logo from (f); (f) Watermarked area of the image with L=26; (g) Extracted Logo from (h); (h) Watermarked area of the image with L=36

to watermark embedding. Under the same attack ---- compressing by JPEG with quality factor=40 (QF), the Logo are extracted as shown in figure 4(c), 4(e) and 4(g) respectively. Obviously the bigger the value of L, the higher the energy of the watermark, and then the percentage of the incorrectly extracted bits is less.

4 Conclusion

In this paper, a novel technique based on regular-shape data patterns is presented. The energy of each watermark bit is spread into one of the possible patterns. If these basic reference patterns are the cyclically shifted versions each other, the modulation for watermarking is actually is phase-modulation. The great advantage of the scheme is its high payload, blindness and simplicity both in watermark embedding and extraction. Though it's slightly weak to numerical attacks, but has potential robustness against geometrical attack, such as rotation, re-sizing or ratio-changing if embedding concentric circular arcs globally in the whole image, and assisting with error correcting code (ECC), majority-voting rule and/or median filter.

High-payload data hiding is very useful in covert communication application, in which the main concerns are capacity and imperceptibility and blind extraction. This is also target of the proposed scheme in the paper.

References

1. I.J.Cox, J. Kilian, T.Leighton and T. Shamoon,"Secure spread spectrum watermarking for images, audio and video", Proc. IEEE Int. Conf. on Image Processing,Lausanne, Switzerland, 16-19 Sep 1996, vol. 3 pp. 243 –246.
2. F.M. Boland, W.J.Dowling and J.J.K.O Ruanaidh, "Phase watermarking of digital images", Proc. IEEE Int. Conf. Image Processing, Lausanne, Switzerland, 16-19 Sep 1996, vol. 3 pp. 239 –242..
3. C.Podilchuk and W.Zeng, "Perceptual watermarking of still images", Proc. The First IEEE Signal Processing Society Workshop on Multimedia Signal Processing, June 1997, Princeton, New Jersey.
4. M.D. Swanson, B. Zhu and A.H. Tewfik, "Transparent Robust Image Watermaking", Proc. IEEE Int. Conf. on Image Processing, Lausanne, Switzerland, 16-19 Sep 1996, vol. 3 pp. 211–214.
5. P. Wolfgang and E.J Delp, "A Watermark for Digital Images", Proc. IEEE Int. Conf. on Image Processing, Lausanne, Switzerland, 16-19 Sep 1996, vol. 3 pp. 219 –222.
6. J. Fridrich and M. Goljan, "Comparing robustness of water-marking techniques," in 11th Int. Symp. Electronic Imaging, vol. 3657. San Jose, CA: IS&T and SPIE, 1999.
7. M. Kutter, "Watermarking resisting to translation, rotation, and scaling," in Proc. SPIE Multimedia Systems and Applications, vol. 3528, Boston, MA, Nov. 1998, pp. 423–431
8. N. F. Johnson and S. Jajodia, "Steganalysis of images created using current steganography software," in Information Hiding:2nd Int. Workshop (Lecture Notes in Computer Science), vol.1525, D. Aucsmith, Ed. Berlin, Germany: Springer-Verlag,1998, pp. 273–289
9. S. Craver, B.-L. Yeo, and M. Yeung, "Technical trials and legal tribulations," Commun. ACM, vol. 41, no. 7, pp. 44–54, July 1998
10. N. A. Dodgson, "Quadratic interpolation for image resampling," IEEE Trans. Image Processing, vol. 6, pp. 1322–1326, Sept.1997
11. G. W. Braudaway, "Results of attacks on a claimed robust digital image watermark," in Optical Security and Counterfeit Deterrence Techniques II, vol. 3314, R. L. van Renesse, Ed. San Jose, CA: IS&T and SPIE, 1998

Surface Interpolation by Adaptive Neuro-fuzzy Inference System Based Local Ordinary Kriging

Coşkun Özkan

Erciyes University, Institute of Science, Computer Engineering Dept., and Engineering Faculty, Geodesy-Photogrammetry Eng., Dept., 38039, Kayseri, Turkey
cozkan@erciyes.edu.tr

Abstract. A new approach to the Ordinary Kriging interpolation method based on the combination of local interpolation and variogram modelling with Adaptive Neuro-Fuzzy Inference System (ANFIS) is proposed for surface interpolation. In this method, the experimental variogram is modelled by ANFIS and this model is used to interpolate the unknown values of specific points in a new local manner. In this local way, all the unknown points are grouped based on each reference point. As the study data, two types of data sets coming from mathematical functions and a 3D scanning system are used. The tests show that the proposed method produces better performances for all data sets in comparison to the well known and highly approved interpolation methods; Ordinary Kriging, Triangle Based Cubic and Radial Basis Function-Multiquadric. Moreover, by the proposed method the computational complexity impressively decreases compared to the global Ordinary Kriging.

1 Introduction

The surface interpolation is a process of constructing a multi-dimensional continuous function. This function defines a surface that passes the known scattered points. The dimensions of independent variables of a function are generally two or three. The surface interpolation process is needed in various fields including surveying, cartography, geology, medical imaging, some industrial designs and 3D visualization. The general approach in the surface interpolation is computing the unknown nodes of the underlying grid surface through interpolation function determined by known scattered data points. The interpolation of the single-valued data where underlying function has the form $f : R^2 \rightarrow R$ or $f : R^3 \rightarrow R$ is generally needed [1].

The interpolation methods can be generally classified into these categories; i- triangulation based methods, ii- inverse distance weighted methods, iii- radial basis function methods, iv- natural neighbor methods, and v- stochastic process methods based on the mathematical derivation. Based on the used reference points, global and local methods are also used. In the global methods, each interpolated value is affected by all of the data whereas in the local methods the interpolated value is only affected by the values at nearby points from the

P.J. Narayanan et al. (Eds.): ACCV 2006, LNCS 3851, pp. 196–205, 2006.

scattered point set. Because of the huge computational efforts, global methods are practically limited to small data. An addition or deletion of a data point, or a correction in any of the coordinates of a data point will change the interpolated values throughout the entire domain of definition. Opposed to global methods, local methods are capable of treating much larger data and they are less sensitive to data modifications. However, they may become quite complex, if a smooth result is required [1].

As a global method, Kriging interpolation algorithm belongs to the stochastic process category that generates spatial fields over the geographical region of interest. Kriging has been developed in the field of mining [3], and is one of the efficient tools of geostatistics. It has found many applications in other fields such as surveying, hydrogeology, environmental monitoring, meteorology, soil science and agriculture and ecology [4] and [7].

As a soft-computing technique, ANFIS model combines the learning capability of neural networks with the expressiveness and the capabilities for reasoning within uncertainty of the fuzzy logic. ANFIS is effectively used in different medical, engineering and computer vision applications [2], [13], [16], [18], [22].

The motivating factor of preparing this study is that ANFIS and Kriging have great potentials for surface data interpolation since Kriging can represent the spatial roughness mathematically enough and can be easily integrated with an effective soft-computing algorithm like ANFIS. The aim of this study is to develop a new surface interpolation method by integrating ANFIS and Kriging algorithms in a local manner. In this method, ANFIS is used to model the experimental variogram which is used to construct the spatial separation in Kriging. After the global variogram is modelled by ANFIS, the unknown spatial areas are interpolated in a different local method through Ordinary Kriging interpolation algorithm. The reference points within a specific range of a specific reference point are used to interpolate the unknown points closest to this reference point. Consequently, the combination of ANFIS and Kriging in a local manner impressively increases the interpolation performance while the processing time decreases.

2 Ordinary Kriging

In basic, an Ordinary Kriging estimate of an unobserved location is an optimized linear combination of the data at the observed locations. Ordinary Kriging is known as the best linear unbiased estimator. It is linear because its estimates are based on weighted linear combinations of available data. It is unbiased since it tries to have the mean error to be zero. It is the best because the error variance is minimized:

$$Var[\widehat{Z}_p - Z_p] = \min \tag{1}$$

Where;

$\widehat{Z}_p$: interpolated value of point p

Z_p: true value of point p

In the ordinary kriging, any drift function predefined over interpolation surface is not employed. So, the regional random variables are assumed as constant. Ordinary Kriging is an exact interpolator at the point of the data, i.e. the estimated value is equal to the data value. The general interpolation equation;

$$\hat{Z}_p = \sum_{i=1}^{n} W_i Z_i \tag{2}$$

Where;

Z_i: reference points used in the interpolation

W_i: weight values corresponding to each Z_i

n; number of reference points

The weighting model of Kriging supplies that the closer point more effective to the interpolation as in inverse distance weighted methods. The Kriging weights are completely a function of variograms of data set. A variogram function is as follow:

$$\gamma(h_m) = \frac{1}{2N(h)} \sum (Z(x_i, y_i) - Z(x_j, y_j))^2 \tag{3}$$

$$h_{ij} = \sqrt{(x_i - x_j)^2 + (y_i - y_j)^2} \tag{4}$$

Where;

γ(h): semi-variance value at distance h

h_{ij}: horizontal distance between i and j reference points

h_m: mean of h_{ij} distances

N(h): number of pairs with distance h

(x_i,y_i): planimetric coordinates of reference point i

Z(x_i,y_i): interpolated target value of reference point i

Semi-variogram values are computed at specific ranges. In order to compute an unknown value of a specific point, it is needed to determine the variogram values of the distances from this point to the reference points. So, it is needed a theoretical variogram model to determine the unknown variograms of these distances. The theoretical models are determined through the experimental values. The most common models used for theoretical variogram are linear, exponential and spherical models [6]. The exponential model is given in Equation 5;

$$\gamma(h) = C_0 + C(1 - e^{\frac{-h}{H}}) \tag{5}$$

where;

C_0: nugget effect, quantifies the sampling and assaying errors

C: vertical scale for the structured component of the variogram

H: the horizontal range of the variogram

After the theoretical variogram model has been constructed, the solution of the system based on ordinary kriging is done according to this set of equations:

$$\begin{array}{llllll} W_1\gamma_{11} & + W_2\gamma_{12} & + \cdots & + W_n\gamma_{1n} & + \lambda & = \gamma_{1P} \\ \vdots & & & \vdots & & \\ W_1\gamma_{n1} & + W_2\gamma_{n2} & + \cdots & + W_n\gamma_{nn} & + \lambda & = \gamma_{nP} \\ W_1 & + W_2 & + \cdots & + W_n & + 0 & = 1 \end{array} \quad (6)$$

Then, the weight values (W_i; i=1, 2,...,n) computed from Equation 2 are used in Equation 6. The difference between ordinary kriging and simple kriging is the constraint about weights of adding up to one to ensure the solution is unbiased. The balance between the number of equations and unknowns is supplied by using the Lagrange coefficient λ. The detailed mathematical and statistical equations of the solution for kriging and variogram can be found in [10].

3 Adaptive Neuro-fuzzy Inference System (ANFIS)

In the last decades, soft-computing techniques (artificial neural networks, fuzzy systems, genetic algorithms, etc.) have been successfully applied in the area of image processing [2] and computational geometry [17], [20]. The soft-computing techniques are preferred for different applications because of their ability to approximate complex nonlinear functions effectively [19]. A key advantage of the fuzzy system is its usage in representation of data information. Usually, a fuzzy system represents information in the form of logic rules, which effectively mimic the decision making of human brain. Neuro-fuzzy systems are hybrids of fuzzy systems and neural networks [11]. The goal of neuro-fuzzy systems is to combine the learning capability of a neural network with the intuitive representation of knowledge found in a fuzzy system.

ANFIS based on Sugeno type fuzzy inference system (FIS) uses a hybrid learning algorithm to identify the membership function parameters of single-output. The membership functions used in ANFIS can be Simple Gaussian, Generalized Bell Curve, 2-Sided Gaussian, Triangular, Trapezoidal, Sigmoid Curve and S-Shape Curve. The simple Gaussian membership function is defined as follows;

$$f(X;\alpha,\beta) = e^{\frac{-(X-\alpha)^2}{2\beta^2}} \quad (7)$$

In Equation 7, f(X;α,β) returns a matrix which is the Gaussian membership function evaluated at X. The parameters α and β determine the shape and position of this membership function. The optimal values of these parameters are computed by training ANFIS structures with enough epochs.

In ANFIS, the membership function parameters are tuned (adjusted) using either a backpropagation algorithm alone, or in combination with a least squares type of method using a given set of input/output data [12].

Some of the advantages of ANFIS are very fast convergence due to hybrid learning and the ability to construct reasonably good input membership functions. The most important advantage is that ANFIS provides more choices over membership functions [5]. The detailed information about neuro-fuzzy systems can be found in [14], [19].

4 The Proposed Method

The main novelty of the proposed method is using ANFIS to model the experimental variogram in stead of conventional parametric models in Ordinary Kriging. By this way, the modelling power of soft-computing techniques over nonlinear complex systems is introduced into an effective interpolation method and thus a new more effective hybrid method could be obtained. Moreover, the interpolation strategy has also been changed. In the classical way, Ordinary Kriging, as a global method, uses all the reference points to interpolate the unknown values of the specific points. Thus, all reference points are used recurrently at each interpolation point. This drives a computational complexity into the system. In the proposed method, each reference point is considered as a cluster center, and the unknown points of the closest Euclidean distances are assigned to this reference point. Then, by using the proposed method, the unknown values of the interpolation points are computed with respect to the reference points staying in a user defined circle centered at the reference point to which the unknown points are the closest. It is seen from application that this method decreases the computational complexity in an impressive manner whereas it increases the performance. The graphical representation of this local approach is given in Figure 1. The general steps of the proposed method in this study can be summarized as follows:

Construct the global experimental variogram model.

Construct the ANFIS object which models this experimental variogram.

Adjust the parameters of membership functions of ANFIS by training.

Cluster the unknown points assuming the reference points as cluster centers in one step.

Define the radius of interpolation circle and determine the reference points staying within this circle centered at each station reference point.

Interpolate the unknown points nearest to the target reference point by using the in-range reference points in the manner of Ordinary Kriging.

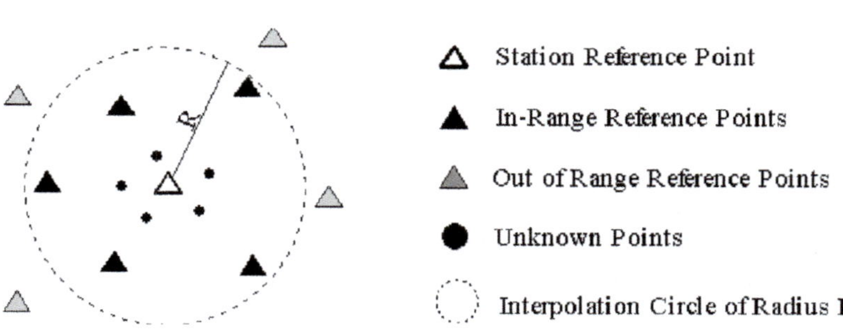

Fig. 1. Illustration of the local approach of the proposed interpolation method

In order to evaluate the performances of the interpolation processes, the root mean squared error function, (RMSE), is employed (Equation 8).

$$RMSE = \sqrt{\frac{1}{n}\sum_{i=1}^{n}(Z_i - \hat{Z}_i)^2} \tag{8}$$

Where $\hat{Z}_i$ is true values of test points, Z_i is interpolated values of test points and n is the number of test points

5 Study Data

Three study data sets are used in the application. The first of them is a mathematical surface defined with the Equation 9 as in [15], [21].

$$\begin{aligned} z = {} & 0.75e^{\frac{-(9x-2)^2+(9y-2)^2}{4}} + e^{\frac{(9x+1)^2}{49} - \frac{(9y+1)}{10}} + \\ & 0.50e^{\frac{-(9x-7)^2+(9y-3)^2}{4}} - 0.20e^{-(9x-4)^2-(9y-7)^2} + \\ & e^{-0.04\sqrt{(80x-40)^2+(90y-45)^2}} \cos(0.15\sqrt{(80x-40)^2+(90y-45)^2})) \end{aligned} \tag{9}$$

Where (x,y) is the pair of planimetric grid coordinates and z is the function values corresponding to each (x,y) pair. The planimetric grid coordinates of this surface is ranged from 0 to 1 The other two data sets are real 3D scanned models of a human face [9] and a rabbit model [8]. These two models are quantitatively diversified to enable the comparisons of interpolation methods in a gridding manner with a reasonable computation time.

The reference data points are selected uniform randomly from inside the known x, y, and z values [21], [23]. The numbers of reference points are 500 for mathematical surface, 6500 for rabbit model and 3000 for human face. After the reference points are extracted from the main population, the remaining points are employed as the test data sets. Consequently, the training and test data sets are (500-9500), (6500-58773) and (3000-20208). The mesh display of the mathematical surface and 3D point clouds of scanned data are displayed in Figure 2.

6 Application

In the application of the proposed method, firstly the experimental variogram model is generated from the reference points isotrophically, i.e. all possible distances in all possible directions. Then ANFIS objects are created to model these experimental variograms. Despite having relatively heavy computational cost, the simple Gaussian membership function is found as the most optimal membership function for all study data sets. The numbers of membership functions are determined experimentally. Optimization method used in the training is the default hybrid method, which combines least squares estimation with Backpropagation. The required parameters of ANFIS, i.e. training error goal, initial step

Fig. 2. Study data sets: Mathematical surface, 3D scanning results of Human face and Rabbit Model

size, step size decrease rate, step size increase rate, are used as default values, 0, 0.01, 0.9, and 1.1 respectively. And output membership function of system is considered as linear type. The optimal epoch number for each interpolation is determined analyzing the step-size parameter of ANFIS training. This parameter changes proportionally depending on the error value. All the tests show that the peak points of the step-sizes gathered from the training of ANFIS are critical points stand for the optimal size of the training epoch.

After the training of ANFIS, clustering process is done. By this clustering, each unknown point is assigned to the neighborhood of a reference point. The unknown points having the neighborhood of the same reference point are interpolated through the same in-range reference points within the circle centered at the center reference point. Here, another critical parameter is the radius of the interpolation circle. This parameter is experimentally determined, too. This parameter affects both the performance and the computation time. Moreover, the number of reference points in each local area is not allowed being less than 10 reference points. This threshold of 10 is also determined empirically. When the number of reference data points is less than 10, it is seen that the performance

Table 1. The optimal values of the parameters used in the proposed method

Data	**MF**	**Number-of-MF**	**Epoch**	**Radius**
Mathematical Surface	Simple Gaussian	5	4000	15
Face	Simple Gaussian	9	110	12
Rabbit	Simple Gaussian	5	190	15

dramatically decreases. The optimal values of the required parameters for the proposed interpolation method are listed in Table 1.

Finally, to determine the effectiveness of the proposed method, all the study data sets are interpolated by Ordinary Kriging, Radial Basis Function-Multiquadric and Triangle-Based Cubic methods. In Ordinary Kriging, an exponential model is used to model the experimental variogram. The RMSE performance results for all of the interpolation methods are given in Table 2.

Table 2. The RMSE performance results: Proposed Method (PM), Ordinary Kriging (OK), Triangle Based Cubic (TBC) and Radial Basis Function-Multiquadric (RBF-M) interpolation methods

Study Data	**Method**	**RMSE(10^{-3})**
Mathematical Surface	P.M.	1.812
	O.K.	9.554
	T.B.C.	16.504
	RBF-M.	6.158
Face	P.M.	1211.057
	O.K.	1234.686
	T.B.C.	1282.049
	RBF-M.	1299.000
Rabbit	P.M.	9.244
	O.K.	11.567
	T.B.C.	11.344
	RBF-M.	12.353

7 Results and Conclusions

In this study, a new surface interpolation method based on local ordinary Kriging with ANFIS variogram modelling is proposed. This proposed method is tested through three data sets; a mathematical surface and two 3D scanned models by comparing with the well known and highly approved interpolation methods; Ordinary Kriging, Triangle Based Cubic and Radial Basis Function-Multiquadric. It is seen from this comparison that the proposed method gives the best performances for all the data sets.

In the application, simple Gaussian membership function is found as the optimal one. It is seen that the optimal epoch number which is the most difficult parameter to determine than other parameters can be directly determined according to the step-size values of ANFIS training. The optimal length of the radius of the interpolation circle is both surface and number of reference data points dependent.

As a general conclusion, the proposed method is reasonably increased the performance of the surface interpolation compared to not only the Ordinary Kriging but also the other two well known methods; Triangle Based Cubic and RBF-Multiquadric. So, the results obviously point out that the fusion of geostatistical and soft computing methods is effective for surface interpolation and must be examined more detailed in future studies.

References

1. Amidror, I.: Scattered Data Interpolation Methods for Electronic Imaging Systems: A Survey, Journal of Electronic Imaging, **11** (2), (2002), 157–176.
2. Beşdok, E., Çiviciolu, P., Alçı, M.: Using an Adaptive Neuro-Fuzzy Inference System-Based Interpolant for Impulsive Noise Suppression from Highly Distorted Images, Fuzzy Sets and Systems, **150**, (2005), 525–543.
3. Cressie, N.: The Origins of Kriging, Mathematical Geology, **22**, (1990), 239–252.
4. Dunlap, L.E., Spinazola, J.M.: Interpolating Water-Table Altitudes in West- Central Kansas using Kriging Techniques, United States Geological Survey Water-Supply, Paper 2238, United States Government Printing Office, Washington, 1984.
5. Garzon, M.H., Prashant, A., Drumwright, E., Kozma, R.: Neurofuzzy Recognition and Generation of Facial Features in Talking Heads, IEEE International Conference on Fuzzy Systems, World Congress on Computational Intelligence, Honolulu-Hawaii, (2002), 926–931.
6. Golden Software Surfer, *User's Guide: Contouring and 3D Surface Mapping for Scientist and Engineers*, Colorado, USA, 1997.
7. Goodchild, M., Parks, B., Steyaert, L.: Environmental Modeling with GIS, Oxford University Press, (1993), 438–453.
8. http://www.cyberware.com/samples/
9. http://www.cs.wright.edu/~agoshtas/sample_range_data.html
10. Isaaks, E.H., Srivastava, R.M.: An Introduction to Applied Geostatistics, Oxford University Press, Oxford, (1989).
11. Jang, J.S.R., Sun, C.T., Mizutani, E.: Neuro-Fuzzy and Soft Computing: A Computational Approach to Learning and Machine Intelligence, Upper Saddle River, NJ, Prentice-Hall Inc., (1997).
12. MathWorks, Fuzzy Toolbox User's Guide, New York, USA, (2002).
13. Nedeljkovic, I.: Image Classification Based on Fuzzy Logic, XX. ISPRS Congress, Istanbul-Turkey, (2004), 83–87.
14. Pal, K., Mitra, S.: Multilayer Perceptron, Fuzzy Sets, and Classification, IEEE Transactions on Neural Networks, **3** (5), (1992), 683–697.
15. Renka, R.J., Brown, R.: Algorithm 792: Accuracy Tests of ACM Algorithms for Interpolation of Scattered Data in the Plane, ACM Transactions on Mathematical Software, 25, (1999), 78–94.
16. Russo, R.: Hybrid Neuro-fuzzy Filter for Impulse Noise Removal, Pattern Recognition, **32**(11), (1999), 1843-1855.
17. Sarzeaud, O., Stephan, Y.: Data Interpolation Using Kohonen Networks, IEEE In Proceedings of International Joint Conference on Neural Networks, **6**, (2000), 197–202.

18. Sharaf, R., Tarbouchi, M., El-Shafie, A., Noureldin, A.: Real-Time Implementation of INS/GPS Data Fusion Utilizing Adaptive Neuro-Fuzzy Inference, ION 2005 National Technical Meeting (The Institute of Navigation), San Diego, California, 2005.
19. Takagi, H., Sugeno, M.: Fuzzy Identification of Systems and Its Applications to Modeling and Control, IEEE Trans. SMC, **15** (1), (1985), 116–132.
20. Wong, K.W., Gedeon, T.D., Wong, P.M.: Spatial Interpolation Using Conservative Fuzzy Reasoning, 9th IFSA World Congress, Vancouver, (2001), 2825-2829.
21. Yanalak, M.: Effect of Gridding Method on Digital Terrain Model Profile Data Based on Scattered Data, Journal of Computing in Civil Engineering, ASCE, **17** (1), (2003), 58–67.
22. Zhuo, W., Dingxuan, Z.: An Adaptive Neuro-Fuzzy Inference System for Engineering-Vehicle Shift Decisions, International Journal of Heavy Vehicle Systems, **9**, (2002), 354–365.
23. Zimmerman, D., Pavlik, C., Ruggles, A., Armstrong, M.P.: An Experimental Comparison of Ordinary and Universal Kriging and Inverse Distance Weighting, Mathematical Geology, **31** (4), (1999), 375–390.

PCA-Based Recognition for Efficient Inpainting

Thommen Korah and Christopher Rasmussen

Dept. Computer and Information Sciences,
University of Delaware,
Newark, DE 19711
{korah, cer}@cis.udel.edu

Abstract. We present a technique for efficiently constructing a "clean" texture map of a partially occluded building facade from a series of images taken by a moving camera. After a robust registration procedure, building regions blocked by trees, signs, people, and other foreground objects are automatically inferred via the median absolute deviation of colors from different source images mapping to the same mosaic pixels. In previous work we extended an existing non-parametric inpainting algorithm for filling such holes to incorporate spatiotemporal appearance and motion cues in order to correctly replace the outlier pixels of the texture map. In contrast to other inpainting techniques that perform an exhaustive search over the image, in this work we introduce a principal components-based method that learns to recognize patches that locally adhere to the properties of the building being mapped, resulting in a significant performance boost with results of indistinguishable quality. Results are demonstrated on sequences where previous stitching and inpainting algorithms fail.

1 Introduction

As part of a vision-based architectural modeling project, we want to capture the visual appearance of buildings via robot-based "scanning." Assuming a polyhedral model of a building's structure [1, 2], a major subgoal of the task is to obtain a high-fidelity texture map of each planar section of its facade. Creating such a *mosaic* from a sequence of overlapping images via homography estimation has been thoroughly studied [3, 4, 5]. However, a complicating factor that motivated our work in [6] is the possible presence of other, unknown objects in the scene between the camera and building plane—e.g., trees, people, signs, poles, and other clutter of urban environments. These create "holes" in the mosaic by occluding parts of the building wall from particular views.

Image/video inpainting [7, 8, 9, 10], a method for image restoration or object removal, offers a principled way to fill such holes from contextual information surrounding them either spatially or temporally. In [6] we introduced two novel methods: (1) a technique for automatically identifying occluded regions (i.e., the areas to be filled) in building facade sequences, in contrast to existing inpainting algorithms that rely on manual segmentation; and (2) a novel spatiotemporal

P.J. Narayanan et al. (Eds.): ACCV 2006, LNCS 3851, pp. 206–215, 2006.

Fig. 1. Raw frames from Wolf Hall sequence (top row) and Hulliken sequence (bottom row) with frame numbers

inpainting algorithm that combines spatial information from pixels in a partially-completed mosaic with temporal cues provided by images in the *timeline*, or sequence of images captured. Like other non-parametric texture synthesis methods [8, 11], our algorithm required an exhaustive search to identify the most likely candidate pixels for replacement—over both the temporal and spatial domains. Though the visual results were satisfactory, for long sequences they could be very expensive to obtain, requiring on the order of hours to complete the inpainting procedure.

The key motivation of this work is to improve our earlier algorithm by framing the search problem in inpainting as one of learning and recognizing object classes, which is much more efficient than traditional Sum-of-Squared Distances (SSD)-based searching. In a similar vein to this work, eigenface methods for face identification [12] represent the whole image as a vector of weights in a linear subspace, and some recent techniques in image retrieval [13, 14] model the appearance of object classes with a constellation of discriminative features. Here we use Principal Component Analysis (PCA) to learn a lower dimensional representation of image patches that facilitates easy recognition of the most appropriate patch. Applied to building sequences, we exploit motion cues from the timeline to restrict the number of candidate pixels that will be filled. The problem then becomes one of "building-patch recognition", akin to the face recognition methods in [12]. The most likely building pixels can then be efficiently retrieved from these candidates using the PCA-based representation.

In the rest of the paper, we first explain our PCA-based inpainting technique that searches over a much lower dimensional feature space compared to other exemplar based methods. We then extend our synthesis from the spatial domain to include temporal information also and apply it to a vision-based application that aims to recover texture maps of occluded building façades. We compare these results to a previous technique and show equally good results at vastly improved efficiency.

2 Inpainting by PCA-Based Recognition

In this section we present an algorithm for filling holes in images that is built upon the work in Criminisi, Pérez, and Toyama [8], a patch-based copying method combining ideas from non-parametric texture synthesis and diffusion-based inpainting. We will refer to their method as *CPT inpainting* and briefly recapitulate the algorithm.

An empty target region Ω's pixels are filled from its border $d\Omega$ inward by copying square image patches from a source region Φ to target patches $\Psi_{\mathbf{p}}$ centered on $\mathbf{p} = (x, y) \in d\Omega$. Given the next target patch $\Psi_{\hat{\mathbf{p}}}$, an *exemplar* patch $\Psi_{\hat{\mathbf{q}}}$ is selected from Φ and pixels are copied to the unfilled portion of the target patch $\Psi_{\hat{\mathbf{p}}} \cap \Omega$ from the corresponding part of $\Psi_{\hat{\mathbf{q}}}$. Letting the entire image region be denoted by $\mathcal{I}$, $\Psi_{\hat{\mathbf{q}}}$ is chosen as the source patch with the minimum distance d (commonly the SSD) between it and the already-filled part of the target patch $\Psi_{\hat{\mathbf{p}}} \cap (\mathcal{I} - \Omega)$ (normalized for area). As inpainting proceeds Ω shrinks while Φ remains constant, leaving a band of filled pixels $\Omega_0 - \Omega_t$ at step t.

In the mold of [15, 8], a priority function $P(\mathbf{p}) = C(\mathbf{p})D(\mathbf{p})$ sets the order in which patches along $d\Omega$ are filled. $C(\mathbf{p})$ is a *confidence* term that measures the amount of reliable information around $\mathbf{p}$ with the formula

$$\sum_{\mathbf{q} \in \Psi_{\mathbf{p}} \cap (\mathcal{I} - \Omega)} \frac{C(\mathbf{q})}{|\Psi_{\mathbf{p}}|}$$

Initially, $C(\mathbf{p}) = 0 \; \forall \mathbf{p} \in \Omega_0$ and $C(\mathbf{p}) = 1 \; \forall \mathbf{p} \in \mathcal{I} - \Omega_0$. When pixels in $\Psi_{\hat{\mathbf{p}}} \cap \Omega$ are filled in, their confidence values are updated from 0 to $C(\hat{\mathbf{p}})$, having the effect of preferring higher confidence sections of $d\Omega$ to grow before low confidence regions. $D(\mathbf{p})$ is a *data* term proportional to the dot product of the tangent vector to $d\Omega$ at $\mathbf{p}$ and the gradient vector $\nabla_{\mathbf{p}}$ with the maximum magnitude in $\Psi_{\mathbf{p}} \cap (\mathcal{I} - \Omega)$. This encourages the extension of linear structures by boosting the priorities of patches with a strong edge "flowing into" them.

Most exemplar-based methods [11, 15] use the SSD as the distance function $d(\cdot, \cdot)$ between two image patches. In addition to the lack of perceptual uniformity in RGB space, for large search regions (as typically occurs with panoramas or videos), this could be very inefficient. For an 11×11 color image patch, the SSD to find the closest matching feature in Φ would require matching pairs of 363-element vectors over Φ. This can be potentially unmanageable. We therefore choose to encode image patches from Φ as a set of compact feature vectors in a lower dimensional eigenspace that allows much more efficient matching.

2.1 Computing the Patch Eigenspace

Given several image patches from Φ, we wish to capture almost all the variability across those patches with as few dimensions as possible. PCA has been a very popular dimensionality reduction technique widely used in recognition. It generates a set of orthonormal basis vectors, that maximize the scatter of all training samples. In spite of various limitations (gaussian distribution, orthogonal linear combinations), we have found it to be simple and adequate for the task at hand. Moreover, PCA is considered to be the most optimal with respect to the reconstruction error. Given an image to be inpainted and the source region Φ, we extract $n \times n$ patches from Φ that will be used to guide the inpainting. For regular inpainting, we extracted patches at every pixel, but this can be a more

Fig. 2. Given a set of image patches, classify them as belonging to bulding or foreground. Note the analogy with face recognition/detection schemes.

coarse sampling as we show in the timeline mosaicing application. Typical patch sizes that we've used are $n = 9$ and $n = 11$. We then create a vector out of these patches by concatenating all 3 color channels.

PCA is then applied to the set of $3n^2$-element vectors to build the eigenspace of patches that capture the statistics of these image patches. A similar method was also used in PCA-SIFT [16] to encode SIFT features for image retrieval applications. After PCA, each $n \times n$ patch is expressed as a vector of coordinates along the first k principal components. The value of k is chosen based on the decreasing magnitude of eigenvalues as well as empirical evaluation of the quality of reconstruction. Given a new high-dimensional patch, it is projected into feature space, where euclidean distance between points can be used to measure similarity.

3 PCA-Based Timeline Inpainting for Mosaicing

In this section we present an efficient algorithm for filling holes in sequence-based mosaics using the PCA-based recognition scheme. The goal of the application is to construct high-fidelity texture maps of building facades from an image sequence, even though parts of the building might be occluded by foreground objects such as trees or signs in a majority or even all of the views. Assuming that the building plane accounts for the majority of pixels in the sequence, with robust methods we can estimate the dominant motion of the building and stabilize it against the camera motion. If the foreground objects are small or fleeting, a temporal median filter can effectively recover the background from the stabilized sequence. Here we describe how our recognition-based inpainting method can efficiently recover the background even when these assumptions do not hold.

3.1 Pre-processing

Image registration is carried out to warp each frame in the sequence to a mosaic-aligned frame $\mathbf{W}_t$. Every location $\mathbf{p} = (x, y)$ in the mosaic reference frame has a set of pixels from the warped images $\{\mathbf{W}_t(\mathbf{p})\}$ associated with it which we call its *timeline* $\mathcal{T}(\mathbf{p})$. The size of each timeline $|\mathcal{T}(\mathbf{p})|$ may vary from 0 to N depending whether the pixel at $\mathbf{p}$ was imaged or not in each frame. Intuitively, since all pixels on the building facade exhibit the dominant motion, they should appear stationary in the mosaic whereas foreground objects such as trees and signs move due to parallax. This variability is measured using the median absolute deviation (MAD), and a high MAD at $\mathbf{p}$ indicates an outlier pixel in the median mosaic $\mathbf{M}_{med}(\mathbf{p})$ that needs to be inpainted.

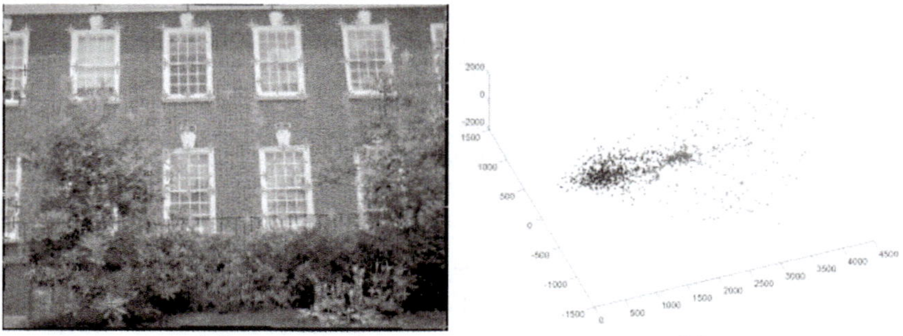

(a) (b)

Fig. 3. (a) KLT features labeled as RANSAC inliers (green) and outliers (red) can be used to extract training examples. (b) Plot of first 3 principal components in feature space for the training set.

Given that each $\mathcal{T}(\mathbf{p})$ contains an unknown mixture of background and foreground object pixels, our goal is to correctly pick or estimate each background pixel $\mathbf{M}(\mathbf{p})$ where $|\mathcal{T}(\mathbf{p})| > 0$, forming a building mosaic $\mathbf{M}$. Our inpainting framework from the previous section fits in well with the solution of this problem. The temporal information available from the timeline has already limited the possible number of candidate pixels that can be copied into the mosaic. The appearance matching problem has now become one of "recognizing" the appropriate background from a set of patches consisting of building and foreground objects (Fig. 2).

As explained in the previous section, we use PCA to project a set of labeled training image patches into a lower dimensional feature subspace. The positive examples of building patches are automatically extracted from Φ by uniformly sampling from 11×11 grids. The negative patches belonging to trees, grass and so on could either be marked manually in a semi-supervised learning fashion or automatically inferred from the RANSAC outliers in the image registration step (Fig 3a). Since the labeling of negative training examples is performed only once and offline, it doen not affect the run time. The original patches used to construct the eigenspace can be discarded after this step.

3.2 Timeline Inpainting by Recognition

Let the MAD outlier pixels be the target region Ω and the rest of the median mosaic $\mathbf{M}_{med}$ be the source region Φ. Our problem differs from pure spatial inpainting in that the timeline $\mathcal{T}$ for each $\mathbf{p} \in \Omega$, provided it contains at least one background pixel, should constrain the filling process. Thus, our major goals are to determine which, if any, pixels in $\mathcal{T}(\mathbf{p})$ are from the building background, and to integrate this information into the inpainting process. Letting $\mathcal{T}(\Psi_{\mathbf{p}}) = \{\Psi_{\mathbf{p}}^1, \ldots, \Psi_{\mathbf{p}}^{|\mathcal{T}(\mathbf{p})|}\}$ be the timeline of patches centered on $\mathbf{p}$, we create a *timeline mosaic* $\mathbf{M}_{time}$ by modifying CPT inpainting in three major ways:

1. In the first of two stages, each patch-wise pixel copy to Ω comes *from one timeline patch* $\Psi^*_{\hat{\mathbf{p}}} \in \mathcal{T}(\Psi_{\hat{\mathbf{p}}})$ maximally likely to have come from the building
2. During stage one, the updated confidences $C(\mathbf{p})$ of newly-filled pixels are set to the motion-based *background likelihoods* $p^*_{motion}(\mathbf{p})$ of the pixels in $\Psi^*_{\hat{\mathbf{p}}}$
3. If the mean background likelihood $\bar{p}_{motion}(\Psi^t_{\hat{\mathbf{p}}})$ for every patch in $\mathcal{T}(\Psi_{\hat{\mathbf{p}}})$ is below a threshold τ_{motion}, $\Psi_{\hat{\mathbf{p}}}$ is *not filled* at that time. Stage two begins when all remaining areas of Ω meet this definition, and consists simply of CPT inpainting

Each of these three modifications is explained below:

Timeline patch selection. Consider a patch $\Psi_{\hat{\mathbf{p}}}$ in the mosaic $\mathbf{M}_{time}$ that is the next to be inpainted. Pixels in its unfilled part $\Psi_{\hat{\mathbf{p}}} \cap \Omega$ will come from the corresponding part of one timeline patch $\Psi^*_{\hat{\mathbf{p}}} \cap \Omega$. We copy pixels from the timeline rather than Φ to maximize correctness, improve feature alignment, and allow for the retention of unique features not present in Φ. To pick a $\Psi^*_{\hat{\mathbf{p}}}$ that is most likely to contain building pixels rather than foreground pixels, we rely upon two cues: (1) *Appearance-based similarity* to other features in the presumed "all-building" region Φ; and (2) *Minimal motion energy* (indicating no occlusion in that frame).

Most buildings have repeated patterns such as windows, doors, columns, bricks, etc., so building (as opposed to foreground) timeline patches in Ω are likely to have a similar appearance to features in Φ. However, appearance matching alone is a less reliable indicator of "buildingness" in homogeneous areas, and can be improved by incorporating the likelihood that motion occurred in that patch in a particular timeline frame. By combining the unfilled portions of each timeline patch with the filled part from the mosaic to create a timeline of *composite patches* $\mathcal{T}(\tilde{\Psi}_{\hat{\mathbf{p}}}) = \{(\Psi^t_{\hat{\mathbf{p}}} \cap \Omega) \cup (\Psi_{\hat{\mathbf{p}}} \cap (\mathcal{I} - \Omega))\}$, we jointly measure patch t's building similarity and motion energy with the formula

$$B(\tilde{\Psi}^t_{\hat{\mathbf{p}}}) = p_{app}(\tilde{\Psi}^t_{\hat{\mathbf{p}}})\bar{p}_{motion}(\Psi^t_{\hat{\mathbf{p}}}),$$

where the probabilities measure the likelihood of a patch belonging to the background building based on appearance and motion cues respectively. Pixels are then copied from $\Psi^*_{\hat{\mathbf{p}}}$ determined by $* = \text{argmax}_t\, B(\tilde{\Psi}^t_{\hat{\mathbf{p}}})$.

The evaluation of p_{app} can be expressed in a probabilistic framework using the N-Nearest Neighbor rule. Given a test patch $\Psi_{\mathbf{y}}$, we can classify it as belonging to class $\hat{\nu}$ that has the maximum posterior probability:

$$\hat{\nu} = \text{argmax}_{\nu \in V} P(\nu|\Psi_{\mathbf{y}}).$$

V is the set of classes and in our case would be building and foreground. A straightforward method of computing the likelihood for each class is based on a voting scheme that returns the fraction of N-neighbors belonging to that class, but this is sub-optimal if the number of training image patches from each class is not guaranteed to be approximately the same. To evaluate the appearance properties, we first project the patch $\Psi_{\mathbf{y}}$ into the k-dimensional eigenspace. Let

$(<\mathbf{x}_1, V(\mathbf{x}_1)> \ldots <\mathbf{x}_N, V(\mathbf{x}_N)>)$ be the N nearest neighbors and their associated labels from the training examples. Then we return a distance weighted likelihood

$$p_{app}(\Psi_{\mathbf{y}}) = \frac{\sum_{i=1}^{N} w_i(\Psi_{\mathbf{y}}, \mathbf{x}_i)\delta(Building, V(\mathbf{x}_i))}{\sum_{i=1}^{N} w_i(\Psi_{\mathbf{y}}, \mathbf{x}_i)}$$

where $w(\cdot,\cdot)$ is the reciprocal of the euclidean distance between the two patches and $\delta(a,b) = 1$ if $a = b$ and 0 otherwise. Compared to [6], computing distances in a 25-dimensional eigenspace that captures almost all the variance across the patches is much more efficient than performing the SSD over the whole timeline for 11×11 patches.

The intersection of a pair of successive, thresholded difference images was suggested in [17] as a method for identifying foreground pixels. By converting the warped images to grayscale and scaling their intensity values to $[0,1]$ to get $\{\mathbf{W}'_t\}$, we can adapt this approach to define a motion energy or *foreground image* at time t as $\mathbf{F}_t = (|\mathbf{W}'_t - \mathbf{W}'_{t-1}|) \otimes (|\mathbf{W}'_{t+1} - \mathbf{W}'_t|)$ where $|\cdot|$ is the absolute value and $\otimes$ is the pixelwise product.[1] Letting μ be the mean foreground image value over all t, we define the *background likelihood* for pixel $\mathbf{p}$ in warped image t as $p^t_{motion}(\mathbf{p}) = e^{-\mathbf{F}_t(\mathbf{p})/\mu}$, and $\bar{p}_{motion}(\Psi^t_{\hat{\mathbf{p}}})$ as the mean pixelwise background likelihood over all pixels in $\Psi^t_{\hat{\mathbf{p}}} \cap \Omega$.

Confidence term. The background likelihoods $p^*_{motion}(\Psi_{\hat{\mathbf{p}}} \cap \Omega)$ are copied as the confidence values of the newly filled-in pixels in $\Psi_{\hat{\mathbf{p}}} \cap \Omega$. This tends to limit the propagation of bad choices in subsequent iterations—i.e., patches bordering areas of higher motion energy are bypassed for low motion energy areas first. The decaying confidence scheme of CPT inpainting does not apply in our case because timeline patch pixels in the interior of Ω are no less reliable than those near its edges.

Stopping criterion. With no patch in $\mathcal{T}(\Psi_{\hat{\mathbf{p}}})$ from the background, there are no temporal constraints on what pixels to fill it with. Because unique features in Ω may not be similar to any patches in Φ, we detect all-foreground timelines solely on the basis of excessive motion energy. Specifically, if for every patch in $\mathcal{T}(\Psi_{\hat{\mathbf{p}}})$ the mean background likelihood $\bar{p}_{motion}(\Psi^t_{\hat{\mathbf{p}}}) < \tau_{motion}$, $\Psi_{\hat{\mathbf{p}}}$ is not filled. Subsequent inpainting in adjacent areas may allow some skipped pixels to be filled later, but stage one halts when this condition is true at every remaining $\mathbf{p} \in \Omega$. The holes that are left are generally much smaller than Ω_0, with more building structure revealed, and thus stage two can consist of pure CPT inpainting with much better results than if it had been run in place of stage one.

4 Results

We show the result of our facade construction algorithm on image sequences that would not work well with current stitching or inpainting algorithms. The Wolf

[1] This of course excludes the timeline's first and last images.

Hall sequence consists of 17 subsampled images from an 801 frame sequence, and captured at 30 fps from a camera moving parallel to a building facade. Examples of these are shown in the top row of Fig. 1. Several objects at different depths occlude parts of the building including trees, bushes, and a large sign. The sequence was taken in early fall and some of the leaves closely match the color of the brick, making the case for highly discriminative encoding - even in a low dimensional space. We have found our technique to be robust to these effects. The Hullihen Hall sequence is a short sequence of 6 images taken by a camera, meant to illustrate the efficacy of our technique in recovering even unanimously occluded building regions. The first and last frames, shown in the bottom row of Fig. 1, emphasize how some parts of the facade behind the bushes are never seen throughout the sequence.

Fig. 4 shows the result of our recognition-based inpainting algorithm that looks into the timeline of image sequences. The initial set of positive training patches to construct the eigenspace was selected from Φ. The negative examples of trees and leaves were extracted from a manually marked section in a single frame. RANSAC outliers could also be used for automatic segmentation of negative examples. In both mosaics, the ground plane outside the region of the facade was excluded from timeline inpainting.

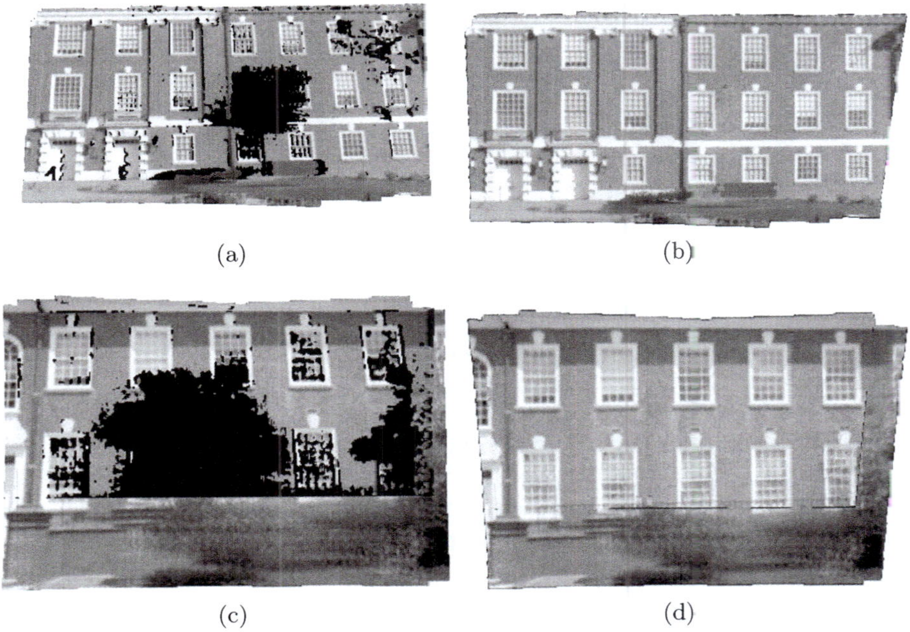

Fig. 4. (a) Median mosaic outliers for Wolf Hall sequence to be inpainted; (b) Result of PCA-based timeline inpainting followed by CPT inpainting after affine rectification (c) Median mosaic outliers for Hullihen Hall sequence (d) Result of inpainting and rectification as in (b)

(a) (b)

Fig. 5. Comparison of solutions in a problem area around the central window of the Wolf Hall Sequence. (a) Result of timeline inpainting using SSD measure; (b) Result of timeline inpainting using the PCA-based recognition scheme. Results are comparably good, but the runtime for (b) was many times faster.

Fig. 5 compares the result of our technique to [6]. Compared to [6] that used optimized SSD code in C as the distance function, our recognition-based approach was as much as 30 times faster even with unoptimized Matlab code. There are a couple of factors that have contributed to this improvement. Firstly, the reduced number of dimensions from 363-element vectors to $k = 25$ dimensions in the PCA eigenspace, while still retaining the distinctiveness of the patch improves the search procedure. Secondly, by our use of temporal information, we have at most $|\mathcal{T}(\mathbf{p})|$ patches that can be copied to the mosaic at $\mathbf{p}$. Since these frames are all aligned in the mosaic frame, it is theoretically enough to give a binary classification of $\{Builiding, Foreground\}$. However, by using $N = 10$ nearest neighbors, we are able to give a probabilistic likelihood without having to do the fine-grained appearance matching over every pixel as is done with the SSD function.

5 Conclusion

We have presented an approach to inpainting for sequences using a PCA-based recognition as opposed to exhaustive searching. We claim that representing image patches in a lower dimensional search space can vastly improve the efficiency of the search, especially in spatio-temporal analysis. We demonstrate the effectiveness of our technique in removing occlusions of building facades in image sequences using a combination of temporal and spatial inpainting.

There are several aspects of the problem that is the current focus of research. An important unaddressed image processing issue is the photometric artifacts that can be introduced due to shadows or different lighting conditions through a long sequence. Much work has been done in the face recognition community to make PCA robust to illumination. We would like to examine the adaptability of those techniques to smaller patches. We could also potentially have more speedup with better searching to find the N-nearest neighbors in the PCA eigenspace. Methods such as k-means or approximate nearest neighbor can be used to index into the feature vectors. We are also examining low-level texture-based segmentation for recovery of the building planes that will be fed to the inpainting.

References

1. Teller, S., Antone, M., Bodnar, Z., Bosse, M., Coorg, S., Jethwa, M., Master, N.: Calibrated, registered images of an extended urban area. Int. J. Computer Vision (2003)
2. van den Heuvel, F.: Automation in Architectural Photogrammetry; Line-Photogrammetry for the Reconstruction from Single and Multiple Images. PhD thesis, Delft University of Technology, Delft, The Netherlands (2003)
3. Davis, J.: Mosaics of scenes with moving objects. In: Proc. IEEE Conf. Computer Vision and Pattern Recognition. (1998)
4. Hansen, M., Anandan, P., Dana, K., van der Wal, G., Burt, P.: Real-time scene stabilization and mosaic construction. In: DARPA Image Understanding Workshop. (1994)
5. Szeliski, R.: Video mosaics for virtual environments. IEEE Computer Graphics and Applications **16** (1996) 22–30
6. Rasmussen, C., Korah, T.: Spatiotemporal inpainting for recovering texture maps of partially occluded building facades. In: IEEE Int. Conf. on Image Processing. (2005)
7. Bertalmio, M., Sapiro, G., Caselles, V., Ballester, C.: Image inpainting. In: SIGGRAPH. (2000) 417–424
8. Criminisi, A., Pérez, P., Toyama, K.: Region filling and object removal by exemplar-based image inpainting. IEEE Trans. Image Processing **13** (2004)
9. Jia, J., Wu, T., Tai, Y., Tang, C.: Video repairing: Inference of foreground and background under severe occlusion. In: Proc. IEEE Conf. Computer Vision and Pattern Recognition. (2004)
10. Wexler, Y., Shechtman, E., Irani, M.: Space-time video completion. In: Proc. IEEE Conf. Computer Vision and Pattern Recognition. (2003)
11. Efros, A., Freeman, W.: Image quilting for texture synthesis and transfer. In: SIGGRAPH. (2001)
12. Turk, M., Pentland, A.: Face recognition using eigenfaces. In: Proc. IEEE Conf. Computer Vision and Pattern Recognition. (1991)
13. Deselaers, T., Keysers, D., Ney, H.: Discriminative training for object recognition using image patches. In: Proc. IEEE Conf. Computer Vision and Pattern Recognition. (2005)
14. Fergus, R., Perona, P., Zisserman, A.: Object class recognition by unsupervised scale-invariant learning. In: Proc. IEEE Conf. Computer Vision and Pattern Recognition. (2003)
15. Bornard, R., Lecan, E., Laborelli, L., Chenot, J.H.: Missing data correction in still images and image sequences. In: ACM Multimedia. (2002)
16. Ke, Y., Suthanker, R.: A more distinctive representation for local image descriptors. In: Proc. IEEE Conf. Computer Vision and Pattern Recognition. (2004)
17. Toyama, K., Krumm, J., Brumitt, B., Meyers:, B.: Principles and practice of background maintenance. In: Proc. Int. Conf. Computer Vision. (1999)

Texture Image Segmentation: An Interactive Framework Based on Adaptive Features and Transductive Learning

Shiming Xiang, Feiping Nie, and Changshui Zhang

State Key Laboratory of Intelligent Technology and Systems,
Department of Automation, Tsinghua University, Beijing 100084, China
{xsm, nfp03, zcs}@mail.tsinghau.edu.cn

Abstract. Texture segmentation is a long standing problem in computer vision. In this paper, we propose an interactive framework for texture segmentation. Our framework has two advantages. One is that the user can define the textures to be segmented by labelling a small part of points belonging to them. The other is that the user can further improve the segmentation quality through a few interactive manipulations if necessary.

The filters used to extract the features are learned directly from the texture image to be segmented by the topographic independent component analysis. Transductive learning based on spectral graph partition is then used to infer the labels of the unlabelled points. Experiments on many texture images demonstrate that our approach can achieve good results.

1 Introduction

Automatic texture segmentation [1, 2] is a tough problem as witnessed in the past decades. It is challenging since it is under-constrained for the following reasons:

The first is the intrinsic ambiguities in texture perception. We can distinguish a texture when we see it. However, it is difficult to give an accurate definition [1] which can be applied to a vast amount of vision patterns in generical images. Texture is a scale-related regional process, which may be understood in different ways by different people for different purposes.

The second is the scale selection. Texture features for segmentation are all computed over local windows, whose size should be selected properly to contain the wide range of basic patterns. It is difficult to determine automatically an adaptive size without any prior information.

The third is the uncertainty in quantity. In real applications, an image region may be explained as a texture or a combination of several vision objects. It is important to know the number of the textures in an image for later statistical pattern analysis.

Motivated to the above observations, this paper addresses the problem of texture segmentation in a user controllable environment. The goal is to achieve good performance at the cost of modest human-computer interaction.

The interactive framework needs the user to define his/her own textures by labelling some points belonging to them, supply the total number of the textures

P.J. Narayanan et al. (Eds.): ACCV 2006, LNCS 3851, pp. 216–225, 2006.

in the texture image and the size of the local window for feature extraction. So the segmentation is controlled by the user.

Through human-computer interaction, the class IDs (labels) of labelled points are all known. Then the task is to infer the labels of the unlabelled points based on those labelled ones. This is a typical learning problem.

We use transductive learning via spectral graph partition [3] to solve the learning problem. Different from inductive learning and semi-supervised learning [4, 5], transductive learning only aims to infer the labels of the points in a given data set. Statistical learning results suggest that better results can be achieved [6]. In addition, a small part of labelled points are often enough to design an effective transductive learner (transducer). This means that the user is only required to label relatively few points.

To extract the adaptive texture features, we use the topographic independent component analysis (TICA) [7] to learn the filters directly from the texture image to be segmented.

2 Related Work

Interactive image segmentation. The recent years have seen a surge of interest in interactive image segmentation[8, 9, 10]. By indicating certain pixels that absolutely belong to the parts of the objects, the background or the foreground, hard constraints are imposed to the segmentation system to alleviate the problems inherent to fully automatic segmentation. Another advantage is that the user can make final decision whether the current result is good or not.

There exists a lot of work on this topic (refer to [8, 9, 10] for more literatures). Most of the approaches are based on color and gray information. To our knowledge, currently little work is developed on interactive texture segmentation.

Transductive learning. The setting of transductive learning is introduced in [6]. A transducer is constructed on a set of fixed data points, which contains two subsets [11]: a training set of labelled points and a working set, i.e. test set, of unlabelled points. The general transduction task is to infer the labels of the points in the working set. But in the traditional inductive setting, a classification function is learned first and only later tested on a test set chosen after the learning has been completed [11]. Algorithms for designing a transducer can be found in [3, 11, 12, 13] and so on.

Texture segmentation. Texture segmentation includes two main steps: feature extraction and pattern classification.

Literatures on feature extraction are rich [2, 14]. Among the majority of existing methods, filter based methods have won an emerging consensus [15]. Almost all existing filters are designed under some mathematical framework, for example, the optimized Gabor filter bank [16]. Differing from the traditional approaches [15], Zeng et al. [17] apply the classical independent component analysis (ICA) [18] to natural scene images to learn the filters, and have achieved good results. In applications, filters adaptive to the texture image to be segmented are desired.

Classification can be performed in an unsupervised or supervised way. Generally, most unsupervised clustering algorithms are designed on some prior knowledge. Naturally, the prior knowledge can be supplied by an interactive way.

3 Interactive Texture Segmentation Framework

3.1 Basic Formulation

Suppose the texture image to be segmented is converted to an array of feature vectors, $\mathbf{X} = (\mathbf{x}_1, \mathbf{x}_2, \cdots, \mathbf{x}_n)$. Each data point, $\mathbf{x}_i (\in R^N)$, corresponds to a pixel P_i and has a desired label of texture class $y_i \in \{1, 2, \cdots, C\}$, here C is the total number of the textures that the user supplies. Let $\mathbf{X} = \mathbf{X}_T \cup \mathbf{X}_W$, where $\mathbf{X}_T$ is the training set and $\mathbf{X}_W$ is the working set. The labels of the points in $\mathbf{X}_T$ are given by the user when defining his/her textures. Now the task is to infer the labels of the points in $\mathbf{X}_W$. This is a typical transductive learning problem.

We use Joachims's spectral graph transducer (SGT) [3] to infer the labels. The SGT is a transductive version of the k-NN classifier, which is very suitable for our task since texture can often be modelled as a Markov random field.

The SGT is initially designed for two-class classification problems. For multi-class problems ($C > 2$) [6], the labelled data should be divided into two subsets to construct a basic SGT. This may result in that they are unbalanced in quantity. But this factor is considered into the global optimization when using spectral methods to design a SGT. A key advantage of the algorithm is that it does not need additional heuristics to avoid unbalanced splits.

However, the SGT needs to perform singular value decomposition (SVD) of Laplacian matrix whose size is equal to the number of the data points in $\mathbf{X}$. Performing SVD may need a huge amount of computing resource for large matrices. Alternatively, to avoid labelling each pixel, we can label a representative subset of all pixels. The points in this subset can be chosen uniformly from the image by the user with proper resolution.

Actually, it is reasonable only to consider a representative subset for texture image segmentation. This results from the fact that texture is a region process. Every pixel in a window patch[1] of a texture should be labelled as the same class. We can use the center point as their representative. Thus, the total data points to be considered can be reduced to a large degree. This skill is similar to the technique applied in [19] to image segmentation.

However, this treatment will not produce pixel-level accuracy in the edge regions between textures. The user can choose to increase the resolution by reducing the size of the window patch to alleviate this problem.

3.2 Overview of the Framework

The interactive texture segmentation framework consists of five main modules: initialization, feature extraction, transductive learning, filtering and user evaluation.

[1] Note that it is not the "local window" used to extract the features.

Initialization. First, the user is required to provide four integers x_0, y_0, x_s and y_s to construct a representative subset $P = \{(x_0, y_0), (x_0 + x_s, y_0), \cdots, (x_0, y_0 + y_s), (x_0 + x_s, y_0 + y_s), \cdots\}$. Here, x_s and y_s control the resolution of representatives.

Second, the user is required to supply the total number of textures C and the size of the local window (w_l, h_l).

The third step is to define the textures. For user's convenience, the user can only need to mark a rectangle region R. A subset is uniformly selected from $R \cap P$ with two controlling parameters of row step s_r and column step s_c. For example, s_r/s_c=2 means that the points in every two rows/columns will be selected. The user can also label single important points to define a texture. Alternatively, the user can also choose to provide a data file of labelled information. In this way, the user is only required to supply the array with zeros for unlabelled pixels and positive integers for labelled ones.

Feature extraction. We use TICA to learn the filters to extract the features (Subsection 4.1).

Transductive learning. Based on the features of the points, single SGT is used to solve two-class classification problem, while a group of transducers is designed for multi-class problems (Subsection 4.2). The output of transductive learning is an array of point labels.

Filtering. To smooth the labels, median filter is performed on the label array according to the space relationship of data points.

User evaluation. The user can further improve the segmentation results until s/he is satisfied. This provides a mechanism for the user to correct the errors.

Usually, there are two kinds of errors. One is due to the reason that some basic vision patterns miss to be labelled. A part of image regions may be labelled as error textures. Another error often appears in the edge regions of different textures. When a patch in an edge region between textures is separated from the image setting, the ambiguity in pattern classification increases. Supplying more labelled points in the edge regions is desired.

4 Algorithm

4.1 Texture Feature Extraction

Recent researches suggest that ICA process of nature scene images can result in edge detection [20]. Zeng et al. use the classic ICA to learn the filters from images of four nature scenes [17]. Differing from their work, we use the TICA to learn the filters directly from the texture image to be segmented. The reason is that the TICA is more suitable for image decomposition [7], compared with classic ICA.

According to image decomposition, each image patch $\mathbf{x}$, treated as a vector here, can be formulated as a linear combination of a set of image bases, i.e. $\mathbf{x} = \mathbf{A} \cdot \mathbf{s}$. Equivalently, we have $\mathbf{s} = \mathbf{W} \cdot \mathbf{x}$. Each column of $\mathbf{A}$ is a mixing basis

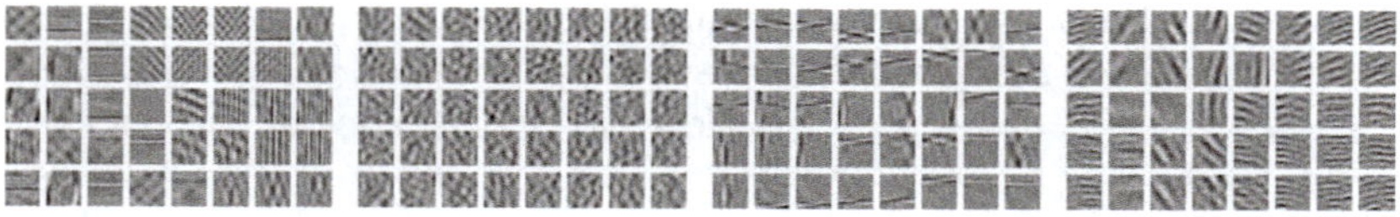

Fig. 1. Four groups of filters learned by the TICA. Here, $w_p = h_p = 16$, $N_{tica} = 6000$. The dimensionality after PCA is reduced to 64 and N_f is equal to 40.

and each row of $\mathbf{W}$ is an unmixing basis. Note that the computation of $\mathbf{W} \cdot \mathbf{x}$ is similar to the convolution operation in signal processing and each row of $\mathbf{W}$ can be viewed as a filter. The steps of feature extraction are as follows:

(1) Given the size of image patch (w_p, h_p), we randomly choose N_{tica} patches and convert each one (gray data) to a vector respectively to get samples $\{\mathbf{x}\}$. Then principal component analysis (PCA) is performed to reduce the redundancy and construct the eigen-space. After whitening the eigenspace transformed data, the TICA is used to learn the matrix $\mathbf{W}$.

By reconverting each row of $\mathbf{W}$ to a patch form, we get a group of filters denoted by $F = (f_1, f_2, \cdots, f_{N_f})$, where N_f is the total number of the filters learned by the TICA. Figure 1 shows four groups of filters, which correspond orderly to the source images in Figure 2. We can see that these filers are similar, to some degree, to the vision patterns that the texture contains. Thus, they are adaptive to the image data.

(2) convolute the texture image with F. For each pixel $p(x, y)$, a response vector is obtained, i.e. $\mathbf{R}_{p(x,y)} = (R^1_{p(x,y)}, R^2_{p(x,y)}, \cdots, R^{N_f}_{p(x,y)})^T$.

(3) construct filter channels by pixel-to-filter mapping [24]. Each filter channel I_i corresponds to a filter, which is a subset of pixels where the given filter gets maximal response [17]. It can be calculated from $\mathbf{R}_{p(x,y)}$:

$$I_i = \{(x, y) | i = \arg\max_j \{R^j_{p(x,y)}, (x, y) \in I\}$$

Obviously, $\{I_1, \cdots, I_{N_f}\}$ is an equivalent partition of I, namely, $I = \cup I_i$ and $I_i \cap I_j = \emptyset$, $\forall i \neq j$.

(4) For each $p(x, y)$, calculate a locally windowed filter histogram from all filter channels [17, 24]:

$$\mathbf{H}_{p(x,y)} = (|H^1_{p(x,y)}|, |H^2_{p(x,y)}|, \cdots, |H^{N_f}_{p(x,y)}|)^T$$

here $H^i_{p(x,y)} = \{(s, t) | (s, t) \in I_i \cap N_{p(x,y)}\}$, $N_{p(x,y)}$ is the local window of $p(x, y)$ and $| \cdot |$ is the cardinality of a set. The size of the local window, (w_l, h_l), is given by the user.

(5) Choose a N_d−dimensional sub-vector $\mathbf{F}_{p(x,y)}$ from $\mathbf{H}_{p(x,y)}$ by discarding its components with small values.

(6) Let $M = \max_{(x,y) \in I, 1 \leq j \leq N_d} \{F^j_{p(x,y)}\}$. After normalizing $\mathbf{F}_{p(x,y)}$ with M, we obtain the texture feature.

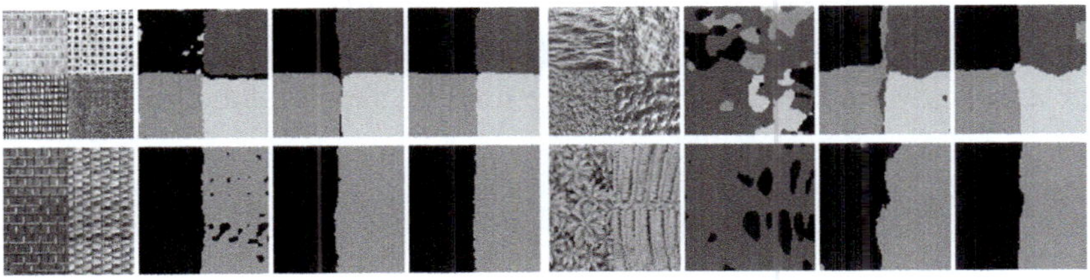

Fig. 2. Comparable experimental results by k-means cluster. In each of the four panels, from the first to the fourth column are the source image [21, 22], the results by the Gabor filter bank [16], by the filters learned from the 13 natural images [23] by TICA, and by the filters learned from the image to be segmented. The upper and lower bounder of interesting frequencies of Gabor filter bank are taken as 0.4 and 0.05, while the scale number and orientation number are 4 and 6. For TICA, $N_f = 40$ and $N_d = 20$.

Gabor filter bank [16] is often used to extract texture features. However, it may not be effective for the textures with irregular and non-periodic vision patterns [17]. Some comparable results are reported in Figure 2.

4.2 Transductive Learning by Spectral Graph Partition

Joachims's approach to transductive learning is a tranductive version of the kNN rule. Without a greedy search, the global optimization problem can also be solved effectively by spectral methods [3].

Two-class problem. The main steps of constructing a SGT are as follows:

(1) Construct the similarity-weight kNN graph:

$$A'_{ij} = \begin{cases} \frac{sim(\mathbf{x}_i,\mathbf{x}_j)}{\sum_{\mathbf{x}_k \in knn(\mathbf{x}_i)} sim(\mathbf{x}_i,\mathbf{x}_k)} & \text{if } \mathbf{x}_j \in knn(\mathbf{x}_i) \\ 0 & \text{otherwise} \end{cases}$$

where $\mathbf{x}_i$, $\mathbf{x}_j$ and $\mathbf{x}_k$ are texture features, and $sim(\mathbf{x}_i, \mathbf{x}_j)$ is the similarity between $\mathbf{x}_i$ and $\mathbf{x}_j$, calculated as $sim(\mathbf{x}_i, \mathbf{x}_j) = (\mathbf{x}_i \cdot \mathbf{x}_j)/(\|\mathbf{x}_i\| \ \|\mathbf{x}_j\|)$.

(2) Compute weighted matrix $\mathbf{A} = \mathbf{A}' + \mathbf{A}'^T$, diagonal degree matrix B, $B_{ii} = \sum_j A_{ij}$, and Laplacian matrix $\mathbf{L} = \mathbf{B}^{-0.5} \cdot (\mathbf{B} - \mathbf{A}) \cdot \mathbf{B}^{-0.5}$.

(3) Compute the smallest 2 to $d+1$ eigenvalues and the corresponding eigenvectors of $\mathbf{L}$.

(4) Construct a SGT. According to the labels, we first divide the training set into two subsets, i.e. positive training subset and negative training subset. Then, We compute the indicative vectors [3] for these two subsets and the working set, and evaluate the ratio of positive/nagetive points. Given the selected eigenvectors and a parameter c that trades off training error versus cut value, a SGT is finally constructed [3].

Multi-class problem. We use a method similar to *one-versus-rest* strategy [6] to deal with the multi-class problem. Given a combination of the class labels, we first partition the training set into positive and negative training subsets.

A SGT is then constructed. According to different combinations of class labels, we can get a group of transducers. Majority voting principle is applied to the outputs of these transducers to infer the final labels of unlabelled points.

5 Results

5.1 Textures in Benchmarks

To demonstrate the effectiveness of our approach, we apply the SGT and our texture features to many texture images constructed from two benchmarks, the Brodatz and MIT VisTex texture libraries [21, 22], which are mostly used in texture research. Some results are shown in Figure 3.

The upper row in Figure 3 shows the source texture images. The segmentation results are demonstrated in the lower row. To construct a representative subset, we input 16, 16, (10,10) for r_s, c_s and (x_0,y_0), respectively. Then the data points used to define each texture are labelled by a window, as illustrated respectively in the upper row in Figure 4. In Figure 3(a), 3(b), 3(c), 3(d), the numbers of the labelled points for each texture are 8, 20, 8, and 12, respectively. The size of local window (w_l, h_l) is 41×41.

(a) (b) (c) (d)

Fig. 3. Artificial texture images and the segmentation results. Only gray data are used.

When designing a SGT, we take $k = 10$, $c = 5000.0$ and $d = 200$. For feature extraction, we take N_d=15. All the other parameters related to PCA and TICA are the same as those used in the experiments demonstrated in Figure 2.

These parameters for transductive learning and feature extraction are fixed for all experiments. For four experiments reported in Figure 3, we achieve 100%, 98.05%, 97.27% and 94.14% correct rate, respectively.

5.2 Natural Texture Images

Figure 4 shows some results by applying our approach to real natural texture images. In Figure 4(a), we use two windows to label 12 data points, taking s_r=2 and s_c=1. We can see, from the result demonstrated in Figure 4(b), that only a few data points are incorrectly classified. To improve the performance, we add three labelled data points as shown in Figure 4(c) with yellow circles[2]. Then the transducer is reconstructed according to the new labelled information. New result is shown in Figure 4(d).

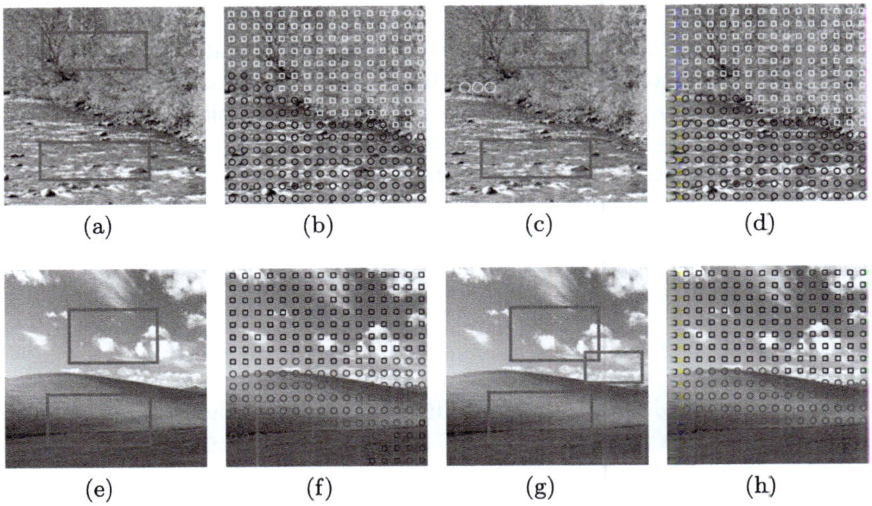

Fig. 4. Natural texture images and the segmentation results. Only gray data are used.

Figure 4(e) shows another texture image. 16 data points are labelled for the two textures respectively, taking $s_r = 1$ and s_c=2. The segmentation result is shown in Figure 4(f). The error rate is about 12%. One reason is that the blue-sky and white cloud texture is very complex. Besides the windowed vision patterns in Figure 4(e), the cloud patterns located in the second window as demonstrated in Figure 4(f) are also fundamental. Another reason is that the meadow patterns labelled in Figure 4(e) are not enough to represent the patterns located in the shadow region. To get better result, we add two labelled subsets of data points as shown in Figure 4(g). The result is illustrated in Figure 4(h). We can see that almost all data points are correctly labelled.

The sizes of local window used to extract the texture features for Figure 4(a) and Figure 4(e) are 41 × 41 and 51×51, respectively. All the other parameters are the same as those used in the experiments in Subsection 5.1.

---

[2] This is equivalent to performing heuristic post-processing.

6 Conclusion

In conclusion, a new framework for texture image segmentation has been proposed and demonstrated, which can obtain good segmentation quality with a few interactive operations. This framework allows the user to define his/her own textures by supplying several labelled data points and make final decision by evaluating the results. In this interactive setting, texture image segmentation is formulated as one of designing transductive learners.

In addition, the TICA is used to learn the filters directly from the image to be segmented. These filters are adaptive to the image data. Comparable experimental results shows that the features extracted by these filter are more separable for classification.

The limit of our framework is that currently it is only suited for texture images. However, most natural images include not only texture objects but also other non-texture objects, such as objects with uniform color distribution, lines, shapes, etc.. In the future, the main work is to integrate different perception objects together into an interactive framework.

Another limit of our work is that we can not obtain pixel-level accuracy. In the future, we would like to introduce hierarchical technique into our segmentation framework.

Acknowledgements

This study is carried out as a part of "R&D promotion scheme funding international joint research" promoted by NICT (National Institute of Information and Communications Technology) of Japan

We would like to thank the reviewers for their valuable suggestions, and thank Doctor Yangqiu Song and Shiliang Sun for valuable discussions.

References

1. Tuceryan, M., Jain, A. K.: Texture analysis. In Chen, C. H., Pau, L. F., Wang, P.S.P., eds: The handbook of pattern recognition and computer vision. 2nd edn. Singapore: World Scientific Publishing Company (1998) 207–248
2. Reed, T. R., du Buf, J. H. M.: A review of recent texture segmentation and feature extraction techniques. Computer Vision, Graphics, and Image Processing: Image Understanding, **57** (1993) 359–372
3. Joachims, T.: Transductive learning via spectral graph partitioning. In: Proc. of Int. Conf. on Machine Learning (ICML), Washington DC, USA (2003) 87–93
4. Vapnik, V. N.: The Nature of Statistical Learning Theory. Springer-Verlag, New York, 2nd edn, (2000)
5. Zhu, X. J.: Semi-Supervised Learning with Graphs. PhD thesis, Carnegie Mellon University (2005)
6. Vapnik, V. N.: Statistical Learning Theory. John Wiley, New York (1998)
7. Hyvarinen, A., Hoyer, P. O., Inki, M.: Topographic independent component analysis. Neural Computation, **13** (2001) 1525–1558

8. Boykov, Y., Jolly, M. P.: Interactive graph cuts for optimal boundary and region segmentation of objects in n-d images. In: Proc. of IEEE Int. Conf. on Computer Vision (ICCV), Vancouver, Canada (2001) 105–112
9. Rother, C., Kolmogorov, V., Blake, A.: Grabcut - interactive foreground extraction using iterated graph cuts, In: Proc. of ACM SIGGRAPH, Los Angeles, USA (2004) 309–314
10. Sun, J., Jia, J. Y., Tang, C. K., Shum, H. Y.: Poisson matting. In: Proc. of ACM SIGGRAPH, Los Angeles, USA (2004) 315–321
11. De Bie, T., Cristianini, N.: Convex methods for transduction, In: Advances in Neural Information Processing Systems. Vancouver, Canada (2003) 73–80
12. Blum, A., Mitchell, T.: Combining labeled and unlabeled data with co-training. In: Proc. of Conf. on Computational Learning Theory, Amsterdam, Holand (1998) 92–100
13. Joachims, T.: Transductive inference for text classification using support vector machines. In: ICML, Bled, Slovenia (1999) 200–209
14. Zhang, J. G., Tan, T. N.: Brief review of invariant texture analysis methods. Pattern Recognition, **35** (2002) 735–747
15. Randen, T., Husoy, J. H.: Filtering for texture classification: A comparative study. IEEE Trans. On Pattern Analysis and Machine Intelligence, **21** (1999) 291–310
16. Manjunath, B. S., Ma, W. Y.: Texture features for browsing and retrieval of image data. IEEE Trans. On Pattern Analysis and Machine Intelligence, **18** (1996) 837–842
17. Zeng, X. Y., Chen, Y. W., Nakao, Z., Lu, H. Q.: Texture segmentation based on pattern maps obtained by independent component analysis. In: Proc. of Int. Conf. On Neural Information Processing, Shanghai, China (2001) 1189–1193
18. Hyvarinen, A.: Survey on independent component analysis. Neural Computing Surveys, **2** (1999) 94–128
19. Yu, S. X., Shi, J. B.: Segmentation given partial grouping constraints. IEEE Trans. On Pattern Analysis and Machine Intelligence, **26** (2004) 173–183
20. Bell, A. J., Sejnowski, T. J.: The independent components of natural scenes are edge filters. Vision Research, **37** (1997) 3327–3338
21. Brodatz, P.: Textures: A Photographics Album for Artists and Designers. Dovery, New York (1966)
22. MIT Vision and Modeling Group: Texture image library. Http://www.media.mit.edu/vismod/, (1998)
23. Natural Image Collection for ICA Experiments: Texture image library. http://www.cis.hut.fi/projects/ica/data/images/ (2001)
24. Malik, J., Belongie, S., Shi, J. B., Leung, T.: Textons, contours and regions: Cue integration in image segmentation. In: ICCV, Corfu, Greece (1999) 918–925

Image Segmentation That Merges Together Boundary and Region Information

Wei Wang and Ronald Chung

Department of Automation and Computer Aided Engineering,
Chinese University of Hong Kong, HongKong
{wangwei, rchung}@acae.cuhk.edu.hk

Abstract. Segmentation is a classical yet important problem in vision. Most of the previous works are either region-based or boundary-based. The two approaches own complementary merits - while the region-based one always produces closed boundaries, the boundary-based one involves primarily local operations and avoids the complexity of deciding how homogeneous a region and how inhomogeneous neighboring regions should be. In this paper, we propose a new solution mechanism that makes use of both cues. We use the boundary processing and a particular field model to come up with a number of coarse, initial closed boundaries about the image first. Such coarse boundaries will then, through an adaptation of the Four Color Theorem, serve as the initialization to a level-set method-based minimization that acts on the intensity distribution of the image, and allows the final crispy segmentation result to emerge. Compared with the existing solutions, our method requires no initialization from the user, and the automatically extracted closed contours do provide guidance to derive more optimal and smoother segmentation result. Experimental results with some benchmarking image-sets show that the proposed solution could deliver accurate segmentation boundary.

1 Introduction

To segment an image into a number of regions so that each region corresponds to a surface or an object in the imaged scene is trivial to humans but remains a challenge to machine vision [1]. Previous works could be classified to either boundary-based or region-based. The boundary-based methods first detect places where there are sharp jumps of intensity, and aim at bridging such fragments of boundaries to form closed boundaries. In contrast, the region-based methods aim at dividing the image into a number of regions that have intensity distributions almost homogeneous within regions but inhomogeneous across neighboring regions.

The edge detection algorithms such as those based on Roberts operator, Sobel operator, Laplacian operator etc. [1] generally cannot provide closed contours; they work on the local intensity gradients merely to detect edge elements. The double-thresholding Canny edge detector [2] can outline longer chains of edge elements but gaps still remain at places where intensity contrast is weak. The

P.J. Narayanan et al. (Eds.): ACCV 2006, LNCS 3851, pp. 226–235, 2006.

saliency-enhancing operators proposed by Guy and Medioni [3] are capable of highlighting features which are considered perceptually relevant; in other words, they can provide gap-filling function in places where gradient information is almost absent, so as to construct closed contours. However, such segmentation decisions, which do not get involved more global information like intensity homogeneity in a region, sometimes do not correspond to meaningful features.

In contrast, the parametric active-contour such as snake method starts with a closed contour and seeks to refine its shape in accordance with the intensity gradients that the contour could perceive from the image data over the contour element positions where it holds. The active contour is guided by internal forces (to maintain the continuity or even smoothness of the contour at all time) as well as external forces (the intensity gradients in the image data over the contour element positions where the contour holds at any given time) [4]. However, good initialization of the contour is required, or else the contour will be easily trapped in some local minimum.

Level set algorithms provide more freedom on the indication of the initial contours in the active-contour methods. According to Chan and Vese [5], the initial curve can be almost anywhere in the image and good segmentation result could still be attained. In their formulation, the dynamics of the active contours' deformation does not depend on the intensity gradients in the image data, but is instead related to certain intensity partitioning threshold that distinguishes what intensity should be inside the final boundary and what should be outside it, and the threshold is determined from the initial contours. In another work of theirs [6], they adopted multiple seed initialization in which the initial contours such as circles are evenly and systematically distributed in the image. The results have been much improved over those of the previous methods. However, the dynamics of the active contours is dependent on a particular intensity partitioning threshold, which means the contours could still be arrested at local minima. In other words, the initialization of the contours still contribute substantially to the final result.

In our approach, the boundary information and the region homogeneity properties for the desired result are combined together to provide a more accurate segmentation yet requiring minimal input from the user. First, an algorithm is implemented on the image data to detect the edgel data in the form of linear elements; both the orientation, edge strength, and inter-segment relationship of the detected line segments are to be used in a later stage. Here, line segments instead of edge elements are used for two purposes: to enhance the globality of the processed features, and to reduce the computational complexities. Then, a field model is constructed from the end-points (not all points) of the segments, that indicates the probability distribution of the subjective contours' location. After that, we truncate the field with a threshold to form a binary image which include the image positions that are of high values in the probability distribution. Medial axes are then extracted from such image positions, and only closed contours are retained to provide initial contours to the subsequent processes. We then use an algorithm adapted from the Four Color Theorem to label the regions separated by those closed contours. Finally, a level set algorithm is implemented on the labeled regions to give the final segmentation result.

Compared with the previous methods, our approach combines information from both boundaries and regions so as to enhance the quality of the solution. The approach is without requiring the user to input initial contours. Experiments on some real images show promising performance.

2 Previous Methods

2.1 Tensor Voting Method

In this method, each image position collects voting information including orientation and strength contributed by all other line segments in the image. Then, based on the collected voting data, a measure on the agreement is performed to give the salient feature on each image position [3]. An example is illustrated in Fig. 1: (a) is the original image; (b) shows the field model adopted in this case – a ball field in which the strength's distribution is evenly spread out in all directions and decays from the point in the center of the field with increase of distance; (d) shows the extracted curves basing on the field shown in (c). The same original image is processed with a stick field as shown in (f), in which the field strength decays with the increase of distance to the center point and the increase of angle deviated from the direction of center point. Obviously, in this case, the voting segments need to own orientation information along with the intensity information. The images in Fig. 1 are derived from a matlab toolbox

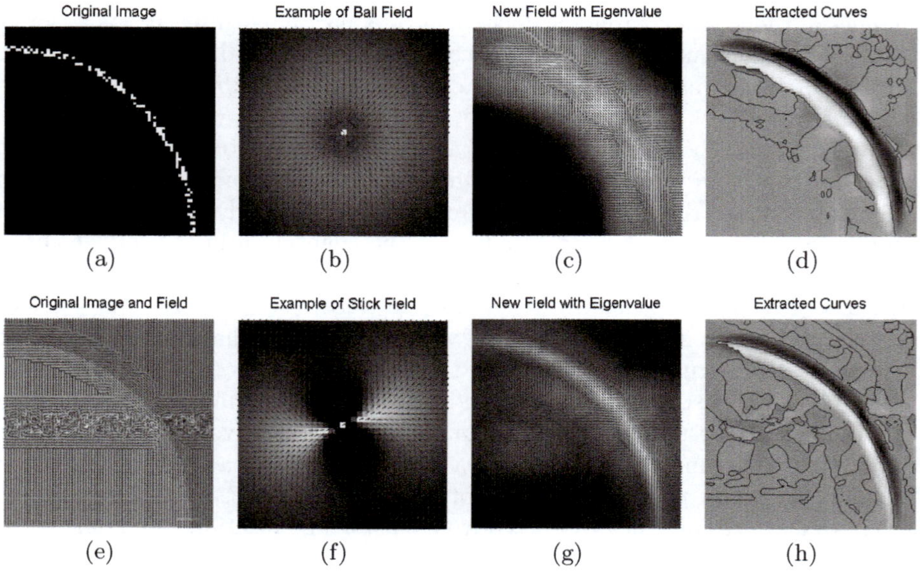

Fig. 1. Tensor voting result

that is based upon the work of Medioni [3]. We can find that the extracted curves are quite noisy and the stick field provides a thinner curve containing original point elements.

2.2 Level Set Method

Originally proposed by Osher and Sethian for capturing moving fronts, the level set method has been developed to be a numerical tool for image segmentation [7]. In the framework proposed by Chan and Vese [5], [6], Mumford-Shah functional is expressed in the level set formulation and compute the associated Euler-Lagrange equations to evolve contours and derive the segmentation. The model can detect contours with or without gradient, and closed contours can be promised. Although it is said that the initial curve for the model can be anywhere in the image, the fact that the stopping term of the Mumford-Shah functional is related to the evolution of PDE deduced from the associated Euler-Lagrange equation indicates that the location of initial curves will influence the final segmentation.

3 Discription of Our Approach

Our approach consists of two substantial parts: in the first part, closed contours are outlined from the detected separated edge elements by some edge detection algorithm, in which regions in the closed contours correspond to features with higher possibility to be objects; in the second part, image regions separated by above closed contours are labeled under Four Color Theorem with four labels, and then level set method is adopted to provide more homogeneous segmentation on the labeled regions. Steps of the procedure are listed in the following diagram.

In the first step of Fig. 2, a linear edge element detection algorithm is performed to extract line segments in one image and record the segment features including orientation, average intensity value, length and the inter-segment relationship to each other. An example is shown in Fig. 3 (a) and (b) corresponding to the original image and the extracted line segments separately.

Since the often separated and opened line segments can not be served as the initial segmentation contours, a field model similar as that mention in [8] is adapted to outline a saliency map to indicate the possibility distribution of subjective contours in the image. As the schematic diagram shown in Fig. 4, we consider the induced field contribution on a nearby position C around end point A of a line segment AB with length c and orientation θ_1, in which position C locates at a distance r to end point A with an orientation angle θ_2.

In our algorithm, in order to reduce the calculation consumption, the field contributed by an line segment is restricted in a fan shaped region from the corresponding end of the line segment with an angle spanned from -θ_0 to θ_0 relative to the line segment direction, which means, for example in the case of Fig. 4, once $|\theta_2 - \theta_1|$ is bigger than θ_0 there will be no field contributed by line segment AB. Currently in our algorithm, we set θ_0 as $\pi/4$ since normally the accepted smooth contours will not own a direction change over this range.

$$\sigma = K \frac{\cos^3\left(\frac{\pi|\theta_1 - \theta_2|}{2\theta_0}\right)}{\gamma^{(c_0/c)}} \tag{1}$$

In equation 1, the field calculation equation: σ is the strength of field element with orientation angle θ_2; K is a constant; c_0 is a length effect parameter to control the field descent rate as well as the computation consumption, which is set as one fifth of the length of the image here. The field element strength decays with the increase of distance from the image position such as point C to the end point of the considered line segment such as AB, and also decays with the increase of the deviation to the line segment direction. Of course positions on line segments possess highest strength values relative to the field generated by them, and the values are proportional to the strength values of line segments.

After field calculation, one position will own several field elements with different directions and strength values. To derive the saliency map on image positions, the principle direction and strength of the field on each site is required which is realized with Singluar Value Decomposition (SVD) in our work.

On the saliency map, we eliminate the sites with weak strength values under a threshold and derive a binary image as the instance shown in Fig. 3 (c). In this step, the threshold can be adjusted to detect strong or weak contours in the image. As the fourth and fifth steps shown in Fig. 2, central lines are extracted

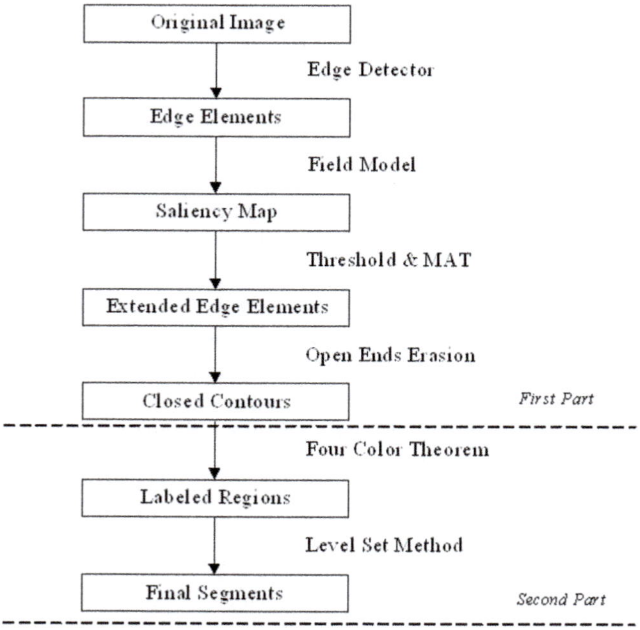

Fig. 2. Image processing steps of our approach

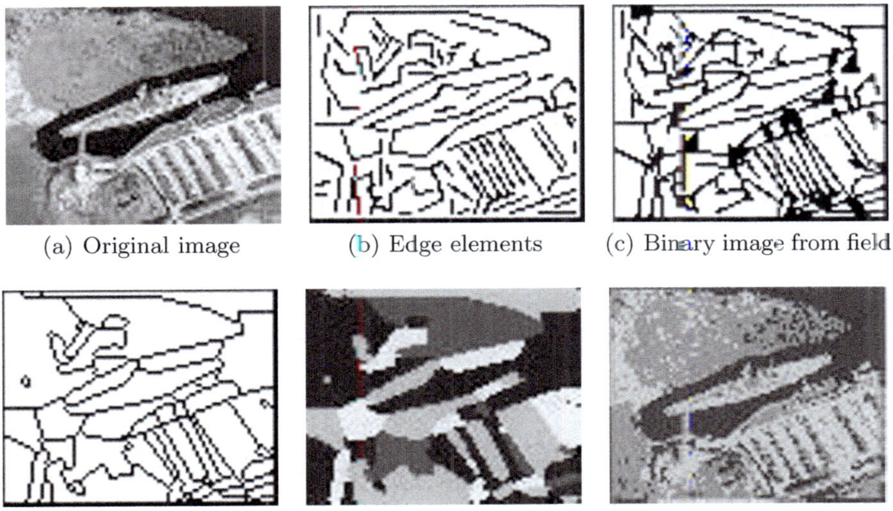

(a) Original image (b) Edge elements (c) Binary image from field

(d) Closed contours (e) Labeled segments (f) Final segments

Fig. 3. Image results from main step

from the regions occupied by the points with higher strength values through medial axis transformation (MAT) and only closed contours are retained in the following step as the example shown in Fig. 3(d).

The derived closed contours divide the image into pieces adjacent to each other. If the boundary of each piece is represented by a level set function, then N pieces will require N level set functions which increase a large amount of calculation expense as illustrated in [9]. Here, we adapt the method mentioned in [6] that based on Four Color Theorem, then merely two level set functions are sufficient to detect and represent distinct segments. Two C^1 level set functions ϕ_1, ϕ_2 are defined on the image, and $\phi_1 = 0, \phi_2 = 0$ are used to represent the closed contours, then according to Four Color Theorem all separated pieces can be labeled by $(\phi_1(x) > 0, \phi_2(x) > 0)$ or $(\phi_1(x) > 0, \phi_2(x) < 0)$ or $(\phi_1(x) < 0, \phi_2(x) > 0)$ or $(\phi_1(x) < 0, \phi_2(x) < 0)$ and any adjacent pieces can own different labels. Using the notation $\mathbf{\Phi} = (\phi_1, \phi_2)$ to represent the two level set functions

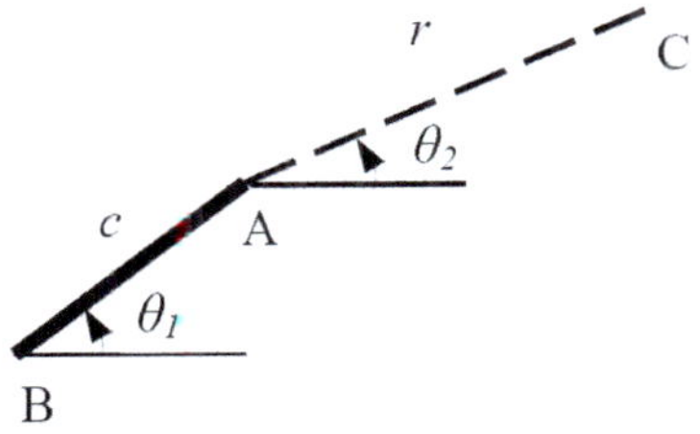

Fig. 4. Field element calculation model

in which $\mathbf{\Phi} = 0$ represents the contours, we introduce an energy in level set formulation, based on the Mumford-Shah functional [6]:

$$\begin{aligned} F(u, \mathbf{\Phi}) = & \int_{\Omega} |u^{++} - u_0|^2 H(\phi_1)H(\phi_2)dx \\ & + \mu \int_{\Omega} |\nabla u^{++}|^2 H(\phi_1)H(\phi_2)dx \\ & + \int_{\Omega} |u^{+-} - u_0|^2 H(\phi_1)(1 - H(\phi_2))dx \\ & + \mu \int_{\Omega} |\nabla u^{+-}|^2 H(\phi_1)(1 - H(\phi_2))dx \\ & + \int_{\Omega} |u^{-+} - u_0|^2 (1 - H(\phi_1))H(\phi_2)dx \\ & + \mu \int_{\Omega} |\nabla u^{-+}|^2 (1 - H(\phi_1))H(\phi_2)dx \\ & + \int_{\Omega} |u^{--} - u_0|^2 (1 - H(\phi_1))(1 - H(\phi_2))dx \\ & + \mu \int_{\Omega} |\nabla u^{--}|^2 (1 - H(\phi_1))(1 - H(\phi_2))dx \\ & + \nu \int_{\Omega} |\nabla H(\phi_1)| + \nu \int_{\Omega} |\nabla H(\phi_2)| \end{aligned} \tag{2}$$

Herein u is a C^1 function defined on the image to represent the resumed image in a smooth way, u^{++}, u^{+-}, u^{-+}, u^{--} are u in $\phi_1(x) > 0$ and $\phi_2(x) > 0$, $\phi_1(x) > 0$ and $\phi_2(x) < 0$, $\phi_1(x) < 0$ and $\phi_2(x) > 0$, $\phi_1(x) < 0$ and $\phi_2(x) < 0$ respectively. In order to express the equation uniformly, each integration is defined on the whole image region Ω, so, u^{++}, u^{+-}, u^{-+} and u^{--} are all zeros outside of their defined regions. The Heaviside function $H(\phi)$ is defined as one if $\phi \geq 0$ and zero if $\phi < 0$. The last two items in Eqn. 2 is served as boundary smooth constraints to prevent the zero level set contour to be too long; $\mu > 0$, $\nu > 0$ are variable parameters to weight the region smooth constraints and the boundary smooth constraints. A minimizer of the above energy will be an "optimal" piecewise-smooth approximation of the initial image u_0.

Examples of the labeled initial segments and the final segmentation result are shown in Fig. 3 (e) and (f) respectively in which segments are expressed with different grey levels.

4 Experimental Results

We compare the results derived from our method with those gotten from other methods including JSEG method [10] and active contours algorithm based on level set method [5], [6]. The active contour algorithm will run in two initialization modes, i.e., with two seeds and with multiple seeds for segmentation and the results are shown in the third and fourth row of Fig. 6.

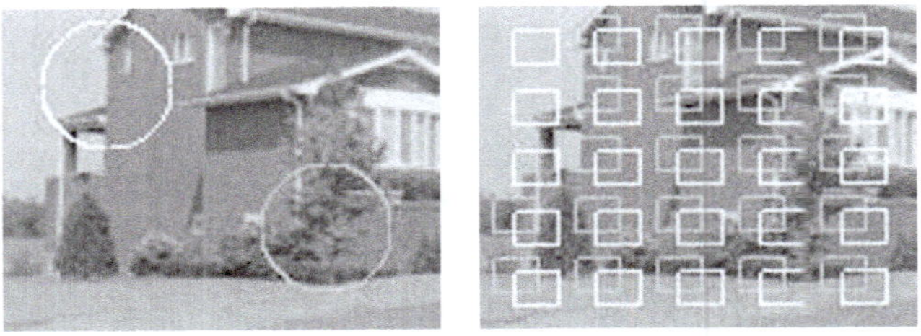

(a) (b)

Fig. 5. Initial segmentation seeds

Compared with the results derived from JSEG method as shown in the second row, the segmentation by our method exhibit smoother boundaries as shown in the last row of Fig. 6 especially in (m) and (n). The Fig. 6 (c) shows more separated and small segments than (f) however it can be found that the boundaries are still more smoother than those in (f). Since the JSEG method develops region growing and merging under the influence of the J values distributed in the image, the region's evolution does not involve a constraint on boundary smoothness as in our method. And in the comparison with the above mentioned active contour algorithm, our method can derive more suitable segmentation and operate more effectively. Fig. 6 (g) - (i) exhibit the segmentation results from initial seed segments indicated by two circles as shown in Fig. 5 (a); Fig. 6 (j) - (l) exhibit results from multiple seed initial segments as that shown in Fig. 5 (b). These kinds of initialization will induce under-segmentation result as shown in (g) and (i) or over-segmentation as shown in (j) and (l) separately. On another simple image (b), results derived from these methods are similar.

Our approach can automatically provide initial segments in the first part as shown in Fig. 2. In the field generation and binary image generation steps, the length effect parameter and the cutting threshold on saliency map can be adaptive to the image size and the field strength.

5 Conclusion and Future Work

In this work, an image segmentation method which combines the boundary and region information is presented. The segmentation consists of first closed-contour extraction based on edge detection result, and subsequently region homogeneity processing based on level set method. Compared with the existing solutions, our method requires no initialization from the user on the approximate boundary locations, and the automatically extracted closed contours which served as initial segmentation boundaries result in more optimal and smoother segmentation.

The current scheme however has the processes of closed-contour initialization and region-based optimization separated. Future work will be about how they could be integrated more closely together for more thorough communication between the two modules.

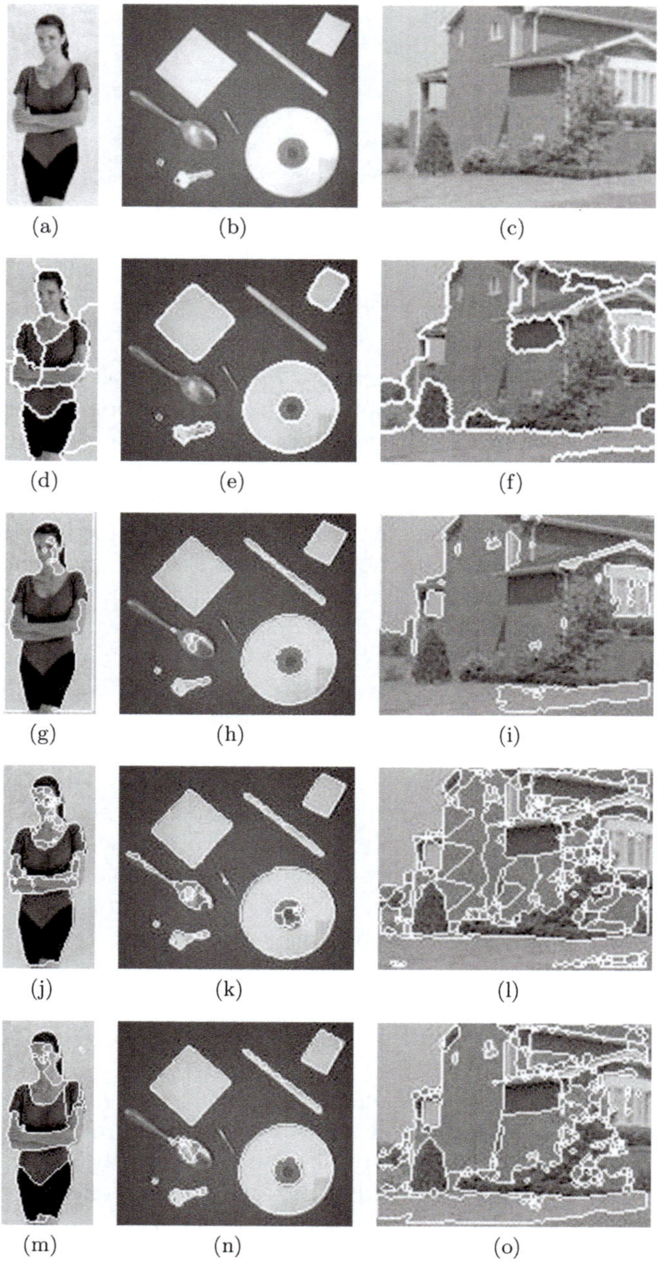

Fig. 6. Comparison result : (a)-(c) original images with size by pixel 58 $\times$ 131, 128 $\times$ 112 and 128 $\times$ 96 respectively; (d)-(f) results derived from JSEG method; (g)-(i) results derived from active contour method with two initial seed segments; (j)-(l) results derived from active contour method with multiple initial seed segments; (m)-(o) results derived from our method

References

1. Jain, R., Kasturi, R., Schunck, B.G., eds.: Machine Vision. McGraw-Hill Companies, Inc. (1995)
2. Canny, J.F.: A computational approach to edge detection. IEEE Trans. Pattern Analysis and Machine Intelligence **8(6)** (1986) 679 – 688
3. Guy, G., Medioni, G.: Perceptual grouping using global saliency-enhancing operators. In: Pattern Recognition, Conference A: Computer Vision and Applications, Proceedings , 11th IAPR International Conference on. Volume 1. (1992) 99 – 103
4. Kass, M., Witkin, A., Terzopoulos, D.: Snakes: Active contour models. International Journal of Computer Vision (1988) 321 – 331
5. Chan, T.F., Vese, L.A.: Active contours without edges. IEEE Transactions on Image Processing **10** (2001)
6. Chan, T.F., Vese, L.A.: A level set algorithm for minimizing the mumfor-shah functional in image processing. In: Variational and Level Set Methods in Computer Vision, Proceedings. IEEE Workshop on. (2001) 161 – 168
7. Tsai, Y.H., Osher, S.: Level set methods in image science. In: International Conference on Image Processing. (2003) 14 – 17
8. Wang, W., Chung, R.: Image segmentation via brittle fracture mechanism. In: IEEE International Conference on Image Processing. (2004) 909 – 912
9. Zhao, H.K., Chan, T., Merriman, B., Osher, S.: A variational level set approach to multiphase motion. Journal of Computational Physics **127** (1996) 179 – 195
10. Deng, Y., Manjunath, B., Shin, H.: Color image sementation. In: IEEE Computer Society Conference on Computer Vision and Pattern Recognition. (1999) 23 – 25

Extraction of Main Urban Roads from High Resolution Satellite Images by Machine Learning

Yanqing Wang[1,2], Yuan Tian[2], Xianqing Tai[2], and Lixia Shu[1]

[1] National Laboratory of Pattern Recognition, Institute of Automation, Chinese Academy of Sciences, Beijing, 100080, P.R. China
{yqwang, lxshu}@nlpr.ia.ac.cn
[2] Integrated Information System Research Center, 100080, P.R. China
{yuan.tian, xianqing.tai}@ia.ac.cn

Abstract. This paper focuses on automatic road extraction in urban areas from high resolution satellite images. We propose a new approach based on machine learning. First, many features reflecting road characteristics are extracted, which consist of the ratio of bright regions, the direction consistency of edges and local binary patterns. Then these features are input into a learning container, and AdaBoost is adopted to train classifiers and select most effective features. Finally, roads are detected with a sliding window by using the learning results and validated by combining the road connectivity. Experimental results on real Quickbird images demonstrate the effectiveness and robustness of the proposed method.

Keywords: AdaBoost, Local Binary Pattern, Machine Learning, Road Extraction.

1 Introduction

Road extraction in urban areas has been an important task for generating geographic information systems (GIS). Especially in recent years, the rapid development of urban areas makes it urgent to provide up-to-date road maps. The timely road information is very useful for the decision-makers in urban planning, traffic management and car navigation fields, etc.

Nowadays, we are experiencing an explosion in the amount of satellite image data, which provides us abundant data and also brings challenges to the road extraction task at the same time. The conventional road extraction methods by manual are time consuming and tedious, and cannot meet the increasing requirement for such tremendous data. Therefore, it has drawn considerable attention of many researchers on how to develop automatic road extraction systems. And much work has been done for this task. However, automatic extraction of urban roads from high resolution remote sensing imagery is still a challenging problem in digital photogrammetry and computer vision. The main reason is that the diverse road surfaces and the complex surrounding environments such as trees, vehicles and shadows induced by high buildings make the urban roads take on different textures and gray levels in images.

P.J. Narayanan et al. (Eds.): ACCV 2006, LNCS 3851, pp. 236–245, 2006.

1.1 Related Work

In the past decades, a large number of papers have been published for automatic road extraction. However, most of them focus on extracting roads in rural or open areas. By contrast, the efforts made for urban road extraction are relatively few [1], [2], [3], [4], [5], [6]. These methods can be roughly divided into two categories: heuristic-based methods and Bayesian-based methods.

Heuristic-based approaches usually model roads in a semantic way and group the extracted road components with the "hypothesis and test" paradigm. Hinz et al [1] used road substructures such as markings and lanes to extract road segments and further linked them into a global road network. In their later work [2] road details from multiple sources were integrated and then roads were found by iteratively grouping. The approach presented by Price [3] modelled the road network as a regular grid. He assumed that the roads crossed at the specific angles and the road width was approximately constant. After three initial seed points on the grid were given by manual, the grid propagation, verification and refinement process was performed based on edge and contextual information. McKeown et al described a multi-level cooperative methods for road tracking by assuming that there existed some specific patterns or textures for road surface [4]. They used a texture-correlation-based tracker and an edge linker to obtain the road candidates.

By contrast, Bayesian approaches generally build stochastic process models for road data and find roads by probability methods. For example, Barzohar and Cooper [5] established a geometric-stochastic model for road image generation and used maximum a posteriori probability to estimate road boundaries.

As can be seen from these methods, road details such as markings and structural information of road surface, are valuable cues for urban road detection from high resolution images. Furthermore, it is advisable to combine the local and global properties to extract road network. However, the two types of methods described above are limited because of the difficulties for building comprehensive road models covering all possible situations. As is known, the diversity of roads, the complexity of surrounding environments, the variation of illumination, the appearance of cars and trees and different view angles of sensors, make it very difficult to built a general road model.

1.2 Overview of the Proposed Method

In order to deal with the difficulties for building comprehensive road models and to make full use of the characteristics of urban roads, we propose an automatic approach based on machine learning. It can be divided into three steps. First, a series of features reflecting road characteristics are extracted. They include the ratio of bright lines on the road surface, the directional consistency of road markings and local binary patterns (LBP). These features are then input into a learning container, and AdaBoost is adopted to train classifiers and select distinct features. Finally, on the basis of the learning results roads are detected with a sliding window and further validated by combing the road connectivity.

The road extraction process is performed based on the essential features of urban roads which can be achieved by learning from a great amount of training examples with diverse appearances.

The remainder of this paper is organized as follows. Section 2 and Section 3 describe the features and the machine learning process based on AdaBoost, respectively. The experimental results and discussions are given in Section 4. Finally, Section 5 concludes the paper.

2 Features

There are many valuable indications about urban roads in high resolution images, for example, road markings are bright and parallel lines; road markings cover only a part of road surfaces; there exist some patterns or textures for urban roads.

Obviously, these assumptions are reasonable because the majority of main urban roads satisfy these conditions, especially those in built-up areas. To make the best use of these characteristics, it is important to extract features that are robust to illumination variations, building shadows and disturbances by cars or trees.

Here, three kinds of features are extracted, namely, the coverage ratio, the direction consistency of road markings and LBP-based features for road textures. There are mainly three reasons for choosing LBP as the road texture descriptor. First, the adopted LBP-based features are invariant to orientations and the monotonic transform of gray levels. Secondly, it can perform multi-resolution analysis by combining different neighborhoods for LBP. Furthermore, LBP is theoretically simple and easy to implement.

2.1 Coverage Ratio of Bright Lines

This feature is used to describe the distribution of road markings. First, the image is segmented to obtain bright lines. This can be accomplished by ridge detection based on the methods presented by Steger [12]. If bright regions are denoted as foreground with 1, and dark regions as background with 0, then the coverage ratio of the bright lines can be computed by the formula:

$$ratio = \frac{\sum_{i=1}^{M}\sum_{j=1}^{N} I(i,j)}{M \times N}$$

where

$$I(i,j) = \begin{cases} 1, \text{foreground;} \\ 0, \text{background.} \end{cases}$$

Here, M and N are the number of rows and columns of the image, respectively.

As is known, road markings cover only a part of road surface, therefore, the ratio feature can be used as one of the indicators for urban roads.

2.2 Direction Consistency

Most of road markings are parallel, so the direction consistency feature is considered to make use of their direction information. First, we obtain edges with Canny edge detector, and then Hough transform is carried out to further get their direction information. The results are shown in Figs. 1 and 2. The first two rows in these figures are roads and their edge features, and the last two ones are non-roads and their results. It can be seen that the directions of road markings are obviously consistent. Fig. 2 (b) is obtained by accumulating the votes of straight lines at different directions. The horizontal axis denotes the angles ranging from 0 to 179, and the vertical axis is the number of occurring times. Furthermore, the standard deviation can be computed directly from this figure. In Fig. 2, one can see that when the directions of edges are similar, the accumulation values converge on a small range of direction angles; otherwise,

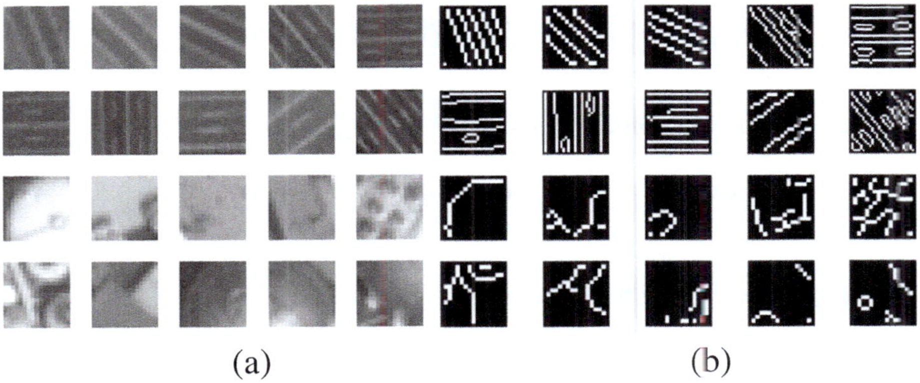

Fig. 1. (a) Original sub-images. (b) Detected edges.

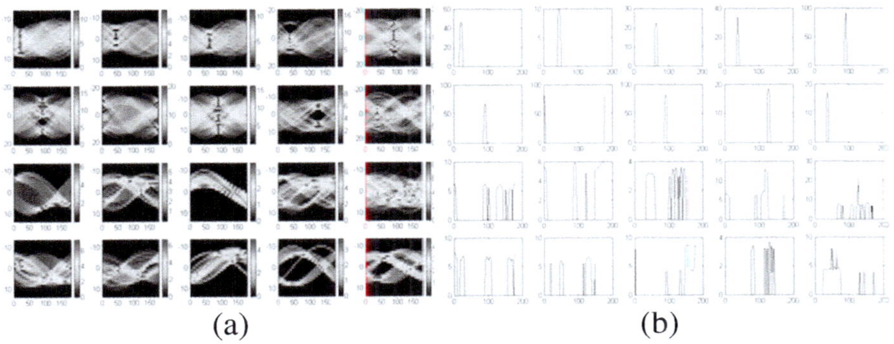

Fig. 2. (a) Hough transform. (b) Accumulation of the threshold result according to different directions.

they are spread on different angles. It shows that the direction consistency is a good feature for urban road extraction.

2.3 Features Based on LBP

Local Binary Pattern (LBP) [7], [8] is a descriptor for local texture. The original LBP operator labels each pixel in an image by comparing the gray values in a circularly symmetric neighborhood with that of the center pixel and then transforming the binary pattern into an integer. An example for LBP formation is shown in Fig. 3. The operator is denoted as $LBP_{P,R}$ for a neighborhood of P pixels that are symmetrically located on a circle of radius R. It can produce 2^P different binary patterns by the P pixels in the neighbor set. LBP is insensitive to the monotonic intensity transformation, because it is only dependent on the relative order of the gray levels. From its formation process, one can see that

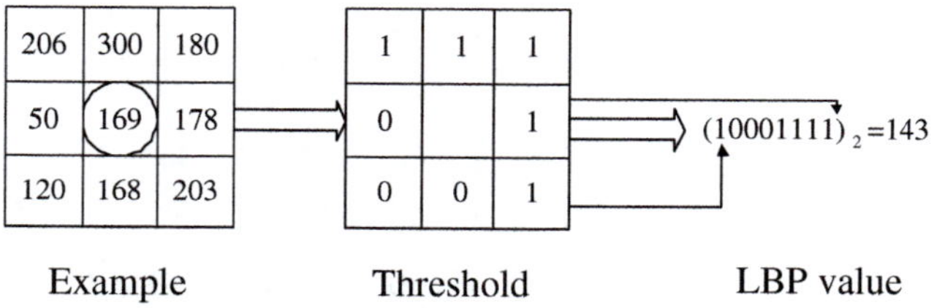

Fig. 3. An example for $LBP_{8,1}$ formation

$LBP_{P,R}$ is sensitive to image rotation, and cannot provide good discrimination for small size images because of the divergence of pattern occurrences. Therefore, as a variant of $LBP_{P,R}$, $LBP_{P,R}^{riu2}$, is introduced in [7]. This improved operator is rotation invariant and deals with the frequently occurring patterns and the less occurring ones in a different way. The procedure for $LBP_{P,R}^{riu2}$ is detailed as follows:

$$LBP_{P,R}^{riu2} = \begin{cases} \sum_{p=0}^{P-1} s(p), & \text{if } U(LBP_{P,R}) \leq 2; \\ \text{P+1}, & \text{otherwise.} \end{cases}$$

where

$$U(LBP_{P,R}) = |s(p-1) - s(0)| + \sum_{p=1}^{P-1} |s(p) - s(p-1)|,$$

and s(x)= 0 or 1.

$LBP_{P,R}^{riu2}$ has only P+2 different output values, less than 2^P ones, which makes it more convergent for texture discrimination.

Choosing different P and R, we can get operators of different spatial resolutions. Consequently, multi-resolution analysis can be realized by combining multiple operators with different (P, R) pairs.

Here, by simultaneously using $LBP_{8,1}^{riu2}$, $LBP_{16,2}^{riu2}$ and $LBP_{24,3}^{riu2}$ to extract road texture features, we are able to get 54 (10+18+26)-bin histogram of LBP-based features. Together with the two features described above, i.e., the coverage ratio of bright lines and the direction consistency, 56 features are obtained for the learning process.

3 Learning Based on AdaBoost

Given the road and non-road samples and their features, the current important task is to choose a suitable learning algorithm. Consideration of the redundancy of the 56-dimensional features, AdaBoost, which can serve as both a classifier trainer and a feature selector, is used in this study.

AdaBoost is an adaptive learning algorithm that aims to build a strong classifier by linearly combining a set of weak learners [10], [11]. It works by updating the weights of training samples dynamically according to the training error. Freund and Schapire have proved that the training error of the strong classifier decreases exponentially with the number of iterations. Furthermore, AdaBoost achieves a good generalization performance because it manages to maximize the margin between positive and negative examples.

In order to select important features, the weak learner of AdaBoost can be constrained to rely on a single feature. Consequently, AdaBoost obtains a strong classifier and effective features simultaneously during its learning process.

Motivated by the work of Viola et. al [11] we introduce the pyramid idea into the learning process to improve the system efficiency. Similar to a pyramid running from the top to bottom, at the first layer of the learning process a simple classifier with less features is trained to obtain a high detection rate, while propagating to the next layers more accurate and complex classifiers with more features are built to remove those false positives. The sub-images rejected by earlier classifiers will not be evaluated by subsequent classifiers. So the highly distinguishable but complex classifiers are only required to examine those potential regions, which can reduce the system spending effectively. As for the number of pyramid layers and the number of features, they are determined by considering the detection rate and false positive rate. The learning algorithm for each layer of the pyramid AdaBoost can be summarized as follows:

- Given training examples (x_i, y_i), $i = 1, 2, ..., n$, where x_i is a 56-D feature vector, and y_i= 0, 1 for road (positive) and non-road (negative) samples respectively.
- Initialize weights $w_{1,i} = \frac{1}{2m}, \frac{1}{2l}$ for y_i=0, 1 respectively, where m and l are the number of positive and negative samples respectively.
- t=0; While (FAR and AR are not satisfied):
  1. Update t: $t := t + 1$;
  2. Normalize the weights:

$$w_{t,i} := \frac{w_{t,i}}{\sum_{j=1}^{n} w_{t,j}}.$$

3. Train a classifier h_j for each feature j, the error related to w_t is $\epsilon_j = \Sigma_i w_i |(h_j(x_i) - y_i)|$.
   Choose the classifier $h_t = h_{argmin_j \epsilon_j}$.
4. $\beta_t = \frac{\epsilon_t}{1-\epsilon_t}$, $\alpha_t = log\frac{1}{\beta_t}$, $e_i = |(h_t(x_i) - y_i)|$.
5. Update the weights:

$$w_{t+1,i} = w_{t,i}\beta_t^{1-e_i}.$$

- Obtain the number of weak classifiers: T= t.
- Output the strong classifier of this layer:

$$h(x) = \begin{cases} 1, \sum_{t=1}^{T} \alpha_t h_t(x) \geq \frac{1}{2}\sum_{t=1}^{T} \alpha_t; \\ 0, \text{otherwise.} \end{cases}$$

From the above, it can be seen that for a certain layer features and weak classifiers will be continuously added until both the FAR and AR requirements are met. Then these weak classifiers are combined to get a strong classifier for this layer. The number of layers can also be obtained when FAR and AR both reach the expected value. Once the learning process is completed, all of the classifiers for different layers and the selected features obtained by AdaBoost are regarded as a paradigm. For a given image, urban roads are then detected according to this paradigm.

4 Experiments

In order to demonstrate the performance of the proposed method, Quickbird imagery, whose resolution is 0.61 m/pixel, is used in this study.

4.1 Training Data

We collected 833 positive samples from Quickbird images manually. These sub-images consisted of various road directions and appearances, and their sizes were also different, ranging from 14×14 to 30×30 pixels. In order to enlarge the training data set, we rotated the road samples by $2°$, $4°$, $6°$, $8°, 10°$, respectively. Therefore, we obtained 4998 road samples in all for training. Some of the road examples are shown in Fig. 4(a). The negative samples came from 320 gray-level images which were manually examined and found no roads in them. Here, 5000 negative sub-images are used for the learning process, which are obtained randomly from these gray-level images.

4.2 Experimental Results

The features extracted from the training set are input into the pyramid AdaBoost procedure for learning. Three learning curves are obtained in this process, as shown in Fig. 4(b). The horizontal axis in Fig. 4(b) denotes the learning layers, and the vertical axis denotes false accept rate (FAR), accept rate (AR) and correct classification rate (CCR), respectively. The curves reflect the fluctuating trends of these indices according to different layers. As can be seen, FAR and AR

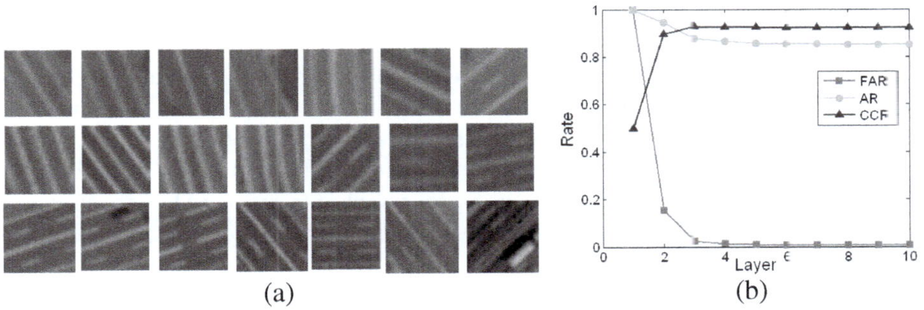

Fig. 4. (a)Road examples and (b)FAR, AR and CCR curves

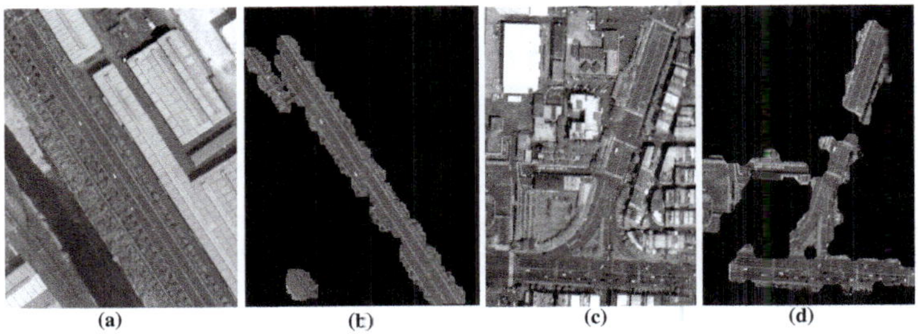

Fig. 5. Experiment 1: (a) original image1 and (b) road extraction result of image1. Experiment 2: (c) original image2 and (d) road extraction result of image2.

curves decrease with layers while CCR increases with layers, and the three curves almost keep unchanged after four layers. Therefore, it is sufficient to choose the first four layers for our AdaBoost. The corresponding number of selected features is 1, 1, 4, 6, respectively. As is expected, the coverage ratio and the direction consistency features are selected successfully.

When given an image, urban roads are to be detected with a sliding window. First, feature extraction is performed for the window of interest according to the learning results, which is followed by the multi-layer classification. Only when

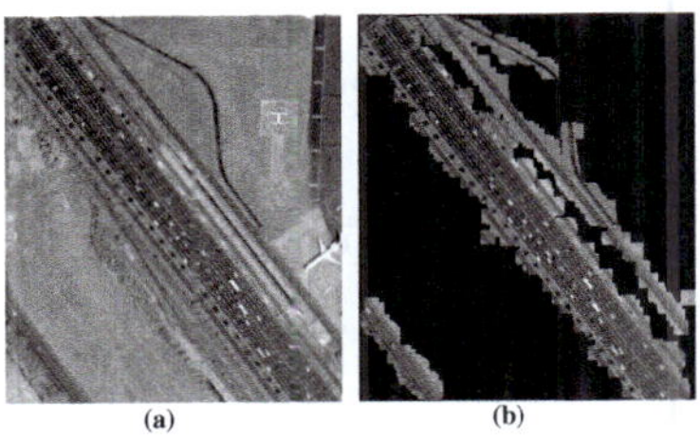

Fig. 6. Experiment 3: (a) original image3 and (b) road extraction result of image3

the window is considered as a road candidate by the earlier classifiers will it be examined by the next classifiers. Road candidates can be found by altering the size of the sliding window. Decisions are made by the majority-vote method for these different windows, and the largest window of the voting for ones are kept. Finally, the global connectivity of roads is integrated to obtain the final results.

Figs. 5, and 6 are three examples of our road extraction results on real Quickbird Pan imagery. Most of the roads are detected correctly though there are many disturbances, such as, buildings, trees and cars in the image.

4.3 Analysis and Discussions

In Fig. 5(a), there are buildings, trees and a few cars around or on the roads. Roads and buildings have a high similarity in intensity and local edges. Moreover, cars on roads have a negative effect on detection results. However, our method works very well on this image, as shown in Fig. 5(b), the majority of main urban roads has been extracted correctly. Other experiments with more complex surrounding environments and dense traffic flow in Figs. 5(c)(d)and 6 also give fairly good results. All of them demonstrate the effectiveness and robustness of the proposed method.

The qualitative evaluation results are shown in Table 1. Here, we select two evaluation measures provided by [13], namely, completeness and correctness. The reference road maps are obtained by manual, and the evaluation is based on the length of extraction results and reference roads. One can see that both the completeness and correctness are fairly good. The correctness for Experiment 1 and 3 are 100% and both of their completeness exceed 92%. Even for the complex environments in Experiment 2, the completeness and correctness are 89.3% and 84.6%, respectively.

One reason for the robustness of the proposed method is likely because that the vehicles on roads are aligned with the road direction and also appear as bright lines, which resemble road markings. Therefore, vehicles, road markings and road surfaces can be considered as an organic element. The robustness also benefits from the fusion of many features, namely, the coverage ratio of bright lines, the direction consistency and $LBPs$. Integrating these features is favorable to distinguish urban roads from buildings. Although the results are encouraging, there are some places to be improved further. For example, the road boundary is not very precise. Our future work will focus on integrating the road boundary detection into the current system. Additionally, some efforts are needed to promote the proposed method in an operational road detection system.

Table 1. External evaluation of the extraction results

Quality measures	Experiment 1	Experiment 2	Experiment 3
Completeness	92. 6%	89. 3%	94.9%
Correctness	100%	84. 6%	100%

5 Conclusion

In this paper, we present a new approach for main road extraction in urban areas from high resolution satellite images. This method is distinguished from previous work by two highlights. One is that a large number of robust features reflecting the structural and texture properties of urban roads are extracted. The other is to adopt the AdaBoost-based learning algorithm. AdaBoost can not only train the classifiers but select most effective features as well. The experimental results on real Quickbird imagery demonstrate that it is an effective way to detect urban roads by learning from many intrinsic road features.

References

1. S. Hinz, A. Baumgartner, C. Steger, H. Mayer, W. Eckstein, H. Ebner and B. Radig, "Road Extraction in Rural and Urban Areas," *Semantic Modeling for the Acquistion of Topographic Information from Images and Maps*, pp. 7-27, 1999.
2. S. Hinz, "Automatic Road Extraction in Urban Scenes and Beyond," *ISPRS*, Vol. 35, pp. 349-354, July 2004.
3. K. Price, "Road Grid Extraction and Verification," *International Archives of Photogrammetry and Remote Sensing*, Vol. 32, Part 3-2W5, pp. 101-106, 1999.
4. D. M. McKeown and J. L. Denlinger, "Cooperative Methods for Road Tracking in Aerial Imagery," *CVPR*, pp. 662-672, 1988.
5. Meir Barzohar and David B. Cooper, "Automatic Finding of Main Roads in Aerial Images by Using Geometric-Stochastic Models and Estimation," *IEEE Trans. PAMI*, Vol. 18, No. 7, pp. 707-721, July 1996.
6. Geman, D., B.Jedynak, "An active testing model for tracking roads in satellite images," *IEEE Trans. PAMI*, Vol.18, No.1, pp.1-14, January 1996.
7. T. Ojala, M. Pietikainen and T. Maenpaa, "Multiresolution Gray-Scale and Rotation Invariant Texture Classification with Local Binary Patterns", *IEEE Trans. Pattern Anal. Mach. Intell.*, Vol. 24, No. 7, pp. 971-987, July 2002.
8. A. Hadid, M. Pietikainen and T. Ahonen, "A Discriminative Feature Space for Detecting and Recognizing Faces," *CVPR*, Vol. 2, No. 2, pp. 797-804, 2004.
9. Xiangyun Hu and C.Vincent Tao, "Automatic Main Road Extraction from High Resolution Satellite Imagery," *ISPRS*, XXXIV, August 2002.
10. Y. Freund and R. E. Schapire, "A Decision-Theoretic Generalization of on-Line Learning and an Application to Boosting," *European Conference on Computational Learning Theory*, Springer-Verlag, pp. 23-37, March 1995.
11. P. Viola and M. Jones, "Rapid object detection using a boosted cascade of simple features," *CVPR*, Vol. 1, pp. 511-518, 2001.
12. C. Steger, "An unbiased detector of curvilinear structures," *IEEE Trans. PAMI*, Vol. 20, No. 2, pp. 113-125, 1998.
13. C. Wiedemann, "Automatic Evaluation of Road Networks," *ISPRS Archives*, Vol. XXXIV, Part 3/W8, Munich, pp. 17-19, September 2003.

Texture Classification Using a Novel, Soft-Set Theory Based Classification Algorithm

Milind M. Mushrif[1], S. Sengupta[2], and A.K. Ray[2]

[1] Department of Electronics and Communication Engineering,
Yeshwantrao Chavan College of Engineering, Wanadongri, Hingna Road,
Nagpur 44 11 10, Maharashtra, India
milindmushrif@yahoo.com

[2] Department of Electronics and Electrical Communication Engineering,
Indian Institute of Technology, Kharagpur 72 13 02, West Bengal, India
ssg@ece.iitkgp.ernet.in, ajoy_ray2004@yahoo.com

Abstract. In this paper, we have presented a new algorithm for classification of the natural textures. The proposed classification algorithm is based on the notions of soft set theory. The soft-set theory was proposed by D. Molodtsov which deals with the uncertainties. The choice of convenient parameterization strategies such as real numbers, functions, and mappings makes soft-set theory very convenient and practicable for decision making applications. This has motivated us to use soft set theory for classification of the textures. The proposed algorithm has very low computational complexity when compared with Bayes classification technique and also yields very good classification accuracy. For feature extraction, the textures are decomposed using standard dyadic wavelets. The feature vector is obtained by calculating averaged L_1-norm energy of each decomposed channel. The database consists of 25 texture classes selected from Bordatz texture Album. Experimental results show the superiority of the proposed approach compared with some existing methods. ...

1 Introduction

Textures provide important characteristics for the analysis of many machine vision and image processing problems such as image classification, segmentation, synthesis and retrieval. Even though we recognize a texture when we see it, no formal and complete definition of texture exists. Different people have defined textures in different ways, depending upon the particular application in which the textures are used or their perceptual motivation [1], [2]. One of the major applications of texture processing is classification, which involves a decision as to which texture category does a sample image belong to, using apriori knowledge of the classes and classical pattern classification techniques.

For accurate classification, it is essential that proper features that differentiate among textures for classification are extracted from the image. According to Tuceryan and Jain [1], different categories of features used for texture identification are statistical, geometrical, model-based, and signal processing features.

P.J. Narayanan et al. (Eds.): ACCV 2006, LNCS 3851, pp. 246–254, 2006.

In recent times, signal processing features obtained using wavelet transform, have been widely used for texture classification. Unser [3] used wavelet based features for texture analysis and segmentation. Ganesan [4] used wavelet statistical and wavelet co-occurrence features for texture classification. Chang and Kuo [5] used wavelet packets for texture classification. Y. Chitre [6] employed M-band wavelets for texture discrimination. The spatial/frequency information of texture provided by wavelets is very useful for applications such as texture classification, segmentation and retrieval.

We have presented herein, a novel method for classification of textures using an algorithm based on soft-set theory. The concept of soft-set theory was proposed by D. Molodotsov [7] to deal with the uncertainties which are free from the inadequacy in the parameterization tool of fuzzy set theory. In the soft set theory, the initial description of the object has an approximate nature. We can use any convenient parameterization strategies, such as real numbers, functions, mappings, words and so on. The problem of setting the membership function does not arise in soft set theory, which makes soft set theory very convenient and practicable. Maji et al. [8] have used soft sets in a decision making problem. We have experimentally found that our classification method has low computational complexity as compared to Bayes classification whereas the classification accuracy is much higher than that of the minimum distance classifier based on Euclidean distance and slightly higher than that of the Bayes method.

The organization of the paper is as follows. Section 2 briefly overviews 2-dimensional discrete wavelet transform. Section 3, presents the notions of soft-set theory and relevant definitions used in the proposed work. Section 4 is about the algorithm used for classification. Section 5 gives experimental results and section 6 concludes the paper.

2 Discrete Wavelet Transform

The 2-dimensional discrete wavelet transform can be obtained by applying 1-dimensional discrete wavelet transform over image rows and columns separately and then down sampling. In one level, the transform decomposes an image into four sub-bands with an overall scale factor of 4 and provides one low resolution subimage LL_1 and three wavelet coefficient sub-band images labeled LH_1, HL_1, HH_1 respectively. To obtain the next coarse level of wavelet coefficients, the low resolution sub-band image is further decomposed and down sampled to obtain low resolution sub-band image LL_2 and wavelet coefficients LH_2, HL_2, and HH_2 respectively. This process continues until some final scale is reached. The sub-band decomposition used for obtaining the textures features is shown in Fig. 1. Every sub-band image contains the information of a specific scale and orientation. The magnitudes of wavelet coefficients in a particular channel are greater for images with a strong textural content at the frequency and orientation represented by that channel. Therefore, the texture of an image can be represented by a feature vector that contains the average coefficient magnitude, known as averaged L_1-norm energy function. We have used L_1-norm energy sig-

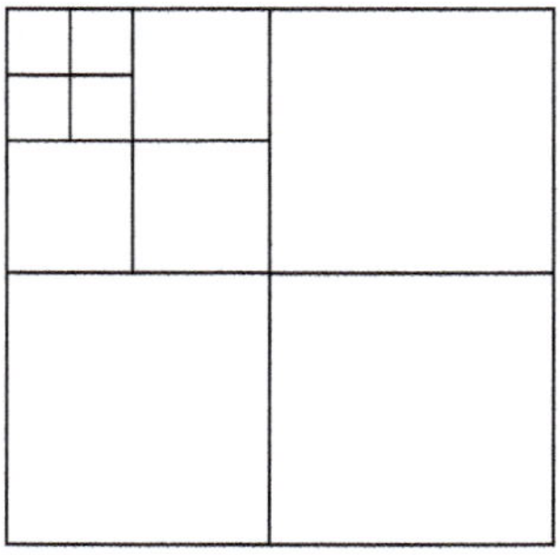

Fig. 1. The wavelet decomposition structure

nature for extraction of texture features as it reflects the distribution of energy along the frequency axis over scale and orientation and has been proven to be a very powerful for texture characterization. The L_1-norm of the image is given by,

$$E = \frac{1}{M^2} \sum_{m=1}^{M} \sum_{n=1}^{M} |x(m,n)| \tag{1}$$

where the image x is of dimension MxM. For k-level decomposition of the image, the size of the feature vector is *(3*k+1)*. In the proposed work we have used *3*-level decomposition, so the feature vector is of length 10.

3 Soft-Set Theory

In this section, we present the notions of soft sets, fuzzy soft sets and some useful related definitions introduced by Molodtsov in [7].

3.1 Definition of Soft Set

Let U be an initial universe set and let E be a set of parameters.

Definition 1. *A pair (F, E) is called a soft set over U if and only if F is a mapping of E into the set of all subsets of the set U: i.e.* $F : E \rightarrow P(U)$, *where P(U) is the power set of U.*

In other words, the soft set is a parameterized family of subsets of the set *U*. Every set *F(*ϵ*)*, for $\epsilon \in E$, from this family may be considered as the set of ϵ-elements of the soft set *(F, E)*, or as the set of ϵ-approximate elements of the soft set.

For example, we may consider a soft set, characterized by *(F, E)* over *U*, where *U* represents a set of textures and *E* represents a set of texture features and *F* is the mapping of all the above features onto the set *U*. Thus, a texture database of a number of textures may easily be mapped onto a soft set.

Table 1. Representation of Soft-Set

U	e_1	e_2	e_3
x_1	0.5	0.5	1.0
x_2	0.9	0.1	0.2
x_3	0.4	0.6	0.8
x_4	0.7	0.3	0.6
x_5	0.2	0.8	0.4
x_6	0.8	0.2	0.4

Let us consider U as a universe set of such objects (say textures) given by $U = \{x_1, x_2, x_3, x_4, x_5, x_6\}$ and E as a set of parameters (say texture features) given by $E = \{e_1, e_2, e_3\}$.
Suppose that,

$$F(e_1) = \{\frac{x_1}{0.5}, \frac{x_2}{0.9}, \frac{x_3}{0.4}, \frac{x_4}{0.7}, \frac{x_5}{0.2}, \frac{x_6}{0.8}\}$$

$$F(e_2) = \{\frac{x_1}{0.5}, \frac{x_2}{0.1}, \frac{x_3}{0.6}, \frac{x_4}{0.3}, \frac{x_5}{0.8}, \frac{x_6}{0.2}\}$$

$$F(e_3) = \{\frac{x_1}{1.0}, \frac{x_2}{0.2}, \frac{x_3}{0.8}, \frac{x_4}{0.6}, \frac{x_5}{0.4}, \frac{x_6}{0.4}\}$$

then we can represent a soft-set in the form of a table as shown in Table 1., in which the entries h_{ij} corresponds to the texture x_i and the texture feature e_j, where h_{ij} is the value of x_i in $F(e_j)$.

3.2 Comparison Table of a Soft Set (F, E)

It is a square table in which number the of rows and number of columns is equal, the rows and the columns both are labeled by object names $x_1, x_2, ..x_n$ of the universe, and the entry g_{ij} is the number of parameters for which the value of x_i exceeds or equals to the value of x_j for $i, j = 1, 2, ..., n$.

Clearly, $0 \leq g_{ij} \leq d$ and $g_{ij} = d, \forall i, j$ where d is the number of parameters in E. Therefore, g_{ij} is a numerical measure that indicates the dominance object x_i over an object x_j in g_{ij} number of parameters out of d parameters.

3.3 Row Sum, Column Sum and Score of an Object x_i

Row sum of an object x_i is denoted by r_i and is calculated by using the formula,

$$r_i = \sum_{j=1}^{n} g_{ij} \tag{2}$$

Column sum of an object x_j is denoted by t_j and is calculated by using the formula,

$$t_i = \sum_{i=1}^{n} g_{ij} \tag{3}$$

Clearly, r_i indicates the total number of parameters in which x_i dominates all the members of U and t_j indicates the total number of parameters in which x_j is dominated by all the members of U.

Difference between r_i and t_i is called a score of an object and is given by the formula,

$$S_i = r_i - t_i, i = 1, 2, ..., n \tag{4}$$

The score S is a vector containing n elements and the x_i is the most favorable object in the database where the index i corresponds to the largest element in S.

4 Classification Algorithm

Soft set theory has rich potential for applications in many areas. In [7] Molodtsov presented applications of soft set theory in areas like study of smoothness of functions, game theory, operations research etc., whereas Maji [8] presented its application in decision making theory. Taking a motivation from this, we have applied soft set theory for classification of natural textures.

In this section, we discuss the algorithm used for classification of textures.

4.1 Classification Algorithm

Training phase

1. Given N samples obtained from the texture w, decompose each sample with wavelet transform.
2. Compute the L_1- norm of each channel of the wavelet decomposition using equation (1) and obtain a feature vector $E_{wi}, i = 1, 2, ..., N$.
3. Calculate the cluster center vector E_w using equation (5) given below,

$$E_w = \frac{1}{N} \sum_{i=1}^{N} E_{wi} \tag{5}$$

4. Repeat the process for all W classes.
5. Obtain a soft-set *(F, E)* which is basically a W x D table of cluster centers in which an element of the table is $g_{wd}, w = 1, 2, ..., W$ and $d = 1, 2, ..., D$ and a row g_w is a cluster center vector for class w having D features.

Classification phase

1. Decompose an unknown texture with the wavelet transform.
2. Compute the L_1- norm of each channel of the wavelet decomposition using equation (1) and obtain a feature vector *Ef*.

3. Obtain a soft set *(F, A)* in which an element p_{wd}, $w = 1, 2, ..., W$ and $d = 1, 2, ...D$ is calculated using equation (6)

$$p_{wd} = 1 - \frac{|g_{wd} - Ef_d|}{\underbrace{max}_{w}(g_{wd})} \tag{6}$$

4. Compute a comparison table of soft-set *(F, A)* as explained in section 3.2
5. Computer the score vector S using equations (2), (3), and (4).
6. Assign the unknown texture to class w if

$$w = arg\left[max_{w=1}^{W}(S)\right] \tag{7}$$

5 Experimental Results

Effectiveness of the proposed method for texture classification has been thoroughly tested using a database of 25 natural texture images from Brodatz's texture album [9]. The textures are shown in Fig. 2. The database is created by dividing each image of size 256 x 256 pixels with 256 gray levels into 49 64 x 64 texture regions with an overlap of 32 pixels. Out of these 49 images, 14 randomly selected images are used for training the classifier and remaining 35 images are used for testing. Thus, there are 49 x 25 = 1225 images in the image database, 14 x 25 = 350 images are used as training samples and remaining 35 x 25 = 875 samples are used for testing.

For designing a classifier, 14 randomly selected textures of each class are decomposed using a standard *2*-dimensional discrete wavelet transform up to level 3, thus, giving 10 sub-band images. The 10 element feature vector is then obtained by calculating averaged L_1-norm energy for each sub-band using equation (1). Thus we get 14 feature vectors for each class. The cluster centre vector is then obtained by using equation (5). These steps are repeated for all 25 classes and finally we obtain a table of cluster centers of size 25 x 10.

In the testing phase, remaining 35 textures from each class are used as test samples. The *3*-level wavelet decomposition is performed and a *10*-element feature vector is obtained. A soft-set theory based classification algorithm, as discussed in previous section, is then used to classify the sample.

We conducted 4 experiments using 4 different wavelet decomposition filters namely 4th order Daubechis (db4), Daubechis *16*-tap filter, 4th order Symlets (sym4) and Haar wavelets. The decomposition filters are given in the Table 2.

In order to compare effectiveness of the proposed classification method, the classification is also obtained using the Bayes classier that uses Mahalanobis distance function and the minimum distance classifier based on Euclidean distance function. The results of these experiments are summarized in Table 3 and Table 4.

The experiments are performed on a Pentium IV, 2.4 GHz computer using MATLAB version 7.0. From Table 3, we observe that when the minimum distance classifier based on Euclidean distance is used, the classification accuracy

Fig. 2. Twenty five classes of textures from Brodatz album. Row 1: D1, D6, D9, D11, D15. Row 2: D16, D21, D26, D32, D34. Row 3: D38, D49, D53, D55, D56. Row 4: D57, D65, D77, D78, D82. Row 5: D83, D84, D95, D104, D105.

in the range of 51.49% to 83.54% is achieved for different wavelet decomposition filters. The accuracy is only 51.49% when 4th order Daubechis filter is used, whereas, it is 83.54% when Haar wavelet is used. A better accuracy, in the range of 88.8% to 96.46%, is obtained when Bayes classifier is used. The classification accuracy is the lowest, i.e. 88.8% in case of Daubechis *16*-tap filter and the highest in case a 4th order Daubechis filter is employed for decomposition. However, the best results are obtained when soft-set based classification algorithm is used. Classification accuracy is 97.49% for the 4th order Daubechis filter and best accuracy of 98.51% is achieved in case of 4th order Symlet.

The computation time for classification of all the 875 test samples is also calculated. From Table 4, we observe that the computation time in soft-set based classification method is nearly the same as that in case of minimum distance classifier using Euclidean distance. But, when compared with Bayes classifier, the soft-set method is almost 7 times as fast as the Bayes classifier. Thus, we

Table 2. Different wavelet decomposition filters used in the experiment

4th order Daubechis	-0.0106	0.0329	0.0308	-0.1870	-0.0280	0.6309	0.7148
	0.2304						
Daubechis 16-tap	0.0544	0.3129	0.6756	0.5854	-0.0158	-0.2840	0.0005
	0.1287	0.0544	0.3129	0.6756	0.5854	-0.0158	-0.2840
	0.0005	0.1287					
4th order Symlet	-0.0758	-0.0296	0.4976	0.8037	0.2979	-0.0992	-0.0126
	0.0322						
Haar	0.7071	0.7071					

Table 3. Classification accuracy for minimum distance classifier using Euclidean distance, Bayes classifier and Soft-set based classifier and different wavelet bases

Wavelet basis	**Minimum distance classifier using Euclidean distance**	**Bayes classifier**	**Soft-set based classifier**
4th order Daubechis	51.43%	96.46%	97.49%
Daubechis 16-tap	76.57%	88.80%	98.06%
4th order Symlet	68.00%	94.97%	98.51%
Haar	83.54%	94.97%	98.40%

Table 4. Classification time for minimum distance classifier using Euclidean distance, Bayes classifier and Soft-set based classifier and different wavelet bases

Wavelet basis	**Minimum distance classifier using Euclidean distance**	**Bayes classifier**	**Soft-set based classifier**
4th order Daubechis	0.19 sec	1.49 sec	0.17 sec
Daubechis 16-tap	0.19 sec	1.72 sec	0.24 sec
4th order Symlet	0.20 sec	1.58 sec	0.19 sec
Haar	0.20 sec	1.52 sec	0.19 sec

have shown that the soft-set theory based classification algorithm yields best results in terms of classification accuracy and the computation time.

6 Conclusions

We have presented a novel method for classification of natural textures using the notions of soft set theory. Feature vectors of the length 10 of energy features extracted from *3*-level decomposition of textures from 25 different texture classes were used for training and testing. It is experimentally demonstrated that this method yields very high accuracy when compared with conventional classification methods such as Bayes classifier and a minimum distance classifier based on Euclidean distance. We have also proved that the computation time for classification is much less in case of soft set method in comparison with Bayes classification method.

References

1. Chen, C.H., Pau, L.F., Eds: The Handbook of Pattern Recognition and Computer Vision. World Scientific (1998)
2. Fan, G., Xia, X.G.: Wavelet-based texture analysis and synthesis using hidden morkov models. IEEE Transactions on Circuits and Systems-I Fundamental Theory and Applications **50** (2003) 106–120
3. Unser, M.: Texture classification and segmentation using wavelet frames, ieee transactions on image processing. IEEE Transactions on Image Processing **4** (1995) 1549–1560
4. Arivazhagan, S., Ganesan, L.: Texture classification using wavelet transform. Pattern Recognition Letters **24** (2003) 1513–1521
5. T. Chang, T., Kuo, C.: Texture analysis and classification with tree structured wavelet transform. IEEE Transactions on Image Processing **2** (1993) 42–44
6. Chitre, Y., Dhawan, A.P.: M-band wavelet discrimination of natural textures. Pattern Recognition **32** (1999) 773–789
7. Molodtsov, D.: Soft set theory - first results. Computers and mathematics with applications **37** (1999) 19–31
8. Maji, P.K., Roy, A.R., Biswas, R.: An application of soft sets in a decision making problem. Computers and mathematics with applications **44** (2002) 1077–1083
9. Brodatz, P.: Texture: A Photographic Album for Artists and Designers, New York: Dover (1966)

Learning Multi-category Classification in Bayesian Framework

Atul Kanaujia and Dimitris Metaxas

CBIM, Rutgers University
{kanaujia, dnm}@cs.rutgers.edu

Abstract. We propose an algorithm for Sparse Bayesian Classification for multi-class problems using Automatic Relevance Determination(ARD). Unlike other approaches which treat multiclass problem as multiple independent binary classification problem, we propose a method to learn the multiclass predictor directly. The usual approach of "one against rest" and "pairwise coupling" are not only computationally demanding during training stage but also generates dense classifiers which have greater tendency to overfit and have higher classification cost. In this paper we discuss the algorithmic implementation of Multiclass Classification model and compare it with other multi-class classifiers. We also empirically evaluate the classifier on viewpoint learning problem using features extracted from human silhouettes. Our experiments show that our algorithm generates sparser classifiers, with performance comparable to state-of-the-art multi-class classifier.

1 Motivation and Related Work

Classification is a task of inferring a set of known or unknown classes based on some similarity measure, to explain an observed set of data points. Many supervised algorithms exist for classification ranging from simplest Nearest Neighbor, pairwise linear classifiers to complex RBF Networks, MLP, Tangent Distance Classifier(TDC) and Optimal Margin classifiers. However most of the classification algorithms are designed for binary classification problems. The multiclass classification can be decomposed into several independent binary classification problems. Classical approach for this decomposition had been *one against rest* and *pairwise coupling* proposed by Hastie et. al.[1]. Dietterich [2] suggested a more general approach to multi-category classification using a coding matrix that associates each row of l columns to a class label $y \epsilon Y$ where Y is set of lables and l are set of hypothesis. A binary classifier is run on each column and the prediction is made based on which row of the coding matrix is closest to l hypothesis. This approach is called *error correcting output codes.* Allwein et al.[3] discusses a unifying approach for reducing multiclass to binary problems for margin classifiers. Other extensions to multi-class problems have been applied by Breiman et al. [5] using decision tree learning and by Schapire and Freund, [16] as an extension for AdaBoost classification. These approaches although powerful

P.J. Narayanan et al. (Eds.): ACCV 2006, LNCS 3851, pp. 255–264, 2006.

and accurate, however, fail to capture relationship between different classes. The generated classifier is denser and has more tendency to overfit the training data.

A number of attempts have been made to directly approach the multi-class classification problem for optimal margin classifiers(SVM). These approaches extends the quadratic optimization for two classes to muliple classes by adding constraints for each class. The number of constraints grows exponentially with the number of classes. Bredensteiner et al.[6] and Weston [18] were among the first works on reducing multi-class learning problem to single large optimization problem.

There have been many works recently that attempt to solve this optimization in lesser time by breaking them into subproblems [4]. Tsochantaridis et al.[7] generalized the large margin method proposed by Weston et al.[18], to learning of structured response. Their algorithm is tunable to specific loss function and uses working set of active constraints that ensures sufficiently accurate solution.

However max-margin classifiers do not provide probabilistic measure for the predictions. Margin classifiers, although sparse, needs post-processing to get rid of unnecessary support vectors [17]. The smootheness parameters of margin classifiers have to be set by cross-validation.

Bayesian methods [10] do not possess above drawbacks. Sparse bayesian learning automatically embodies Occam's razor that penalizes complex models thereby smoothing the model. In this paper we propose an algorithm for learning sparse multi-category classifier in Bayesian framework as proposed by Mackay[10]. The algorithm uses multinomial distributions for multiple variables with one-of-all encoding for each class. The multiple outputs of the model is learnt as a kernel basis function with softmax as the canonical link function. The parameters are learnt using Automatic Relevance Determination(ARD). ARD is a model selection mechanism that ensures sparsity and smoothness.

To the best of our knowledge, this has not been attempted in past and our work provides complete algorithm to learn multiple class posterior probabilities directly in bayesian framework. Our work has three contributions: (1) We propose sparse bayesian classifiers for multi-class problems; (2) We empirically compare performance of our classifier with other algorithms for handling multi-class problems; (3) We use multi-class classifiers to infer viewing angle from features extracted from Human silhouettes. Section 2 gives a brief overview of the bayesian framework. In Section 3 we discuss the formulation of classification problem and our algorithm in detail. Section 4 discusses the experimental results. Theoretical proofs for convergence has been omitted from current discussion.

2 Bayesian Learning Framework

Bayesian learning intrinsically embodies regularization and model selection using Occam's razor[10] [8]. Bayesian learning is a three stage process. In the first stage the model is fit to the observed data by maximizing posterior distribution over the model parameters θ.

$$P(\theta|D,\alpha,\beta,M) = \frac{P(D|\theta,\beta,M)P(\theta|\alpha,M)}{P(D|M)} \tag{1}$$

The normalizing constant is called the evidence of the model M and is not required for fitting a given model M to the data set D. The first term on right hand side(likelihood) is the loss function and second term(prior distribution) is the smoothing factor. α and β are the scale parameters of these distributions. Taking the distributions as gaussians with appropriate normalization factor:

$$P(D|\theta, \beta, M) = \frac{e^{-\beta L_\theta(D)}}{(2\pi/\beta)^{N/2}} \tag{2}$$

$$P(\theta|\alpha, M) = \frac{e^{-\alpha P(\theta)}}{\int e^{-\alpha P(\theta)} d\theta} \tag{3}$$

where L_θ is the loss function to be minimized and $P(\theta)$ is the penality term for penalizing complex models with larger $|\theta|$ (smoothing). The posterior obtained is a joint function of scale parameters α, β for the loss function and smoothing prior respectively. Given α and β, most probable θ_{MP} can be obtained by maximizing the posterior distribution (1). For maximum margin classifiers these parameters corresponds to error/margin tradeoff parameter 'C' and insensitivity parameter ϵ [7] that have to be learnt using cross-validation. This is wasteful both for the data and computation.

Second stage of bayesian learning involves model selection by estimating the most probable scale parameters α_{MP} and β_{MP} by maximizing the posterior distribution:

$$P(\alpha, \beta|D, M) \propto P(D|\alpha, \beta, M)P(\alpha|M)P(\beta|M) \tag{4}$$

For a given prior distributions of α and β, maximizing (4) is equivalent to maximizing the evidence $P(D|\alpha, \beta, M)$. This evidence maximization procedure is called *Type II Maximum Likelihood* maximization and yields the equations for computing most probable α_{MP} and β_{MP}.

The posterior of parameters θ is approximated as

$$P(\theta|D, \alpha, \beta, M) \approx P(\theta|D, \alpha_{MP}, \beta_{MP}, M) \tag{5}$$

(5) and (1) can be used to estimate most probable $\theta = \theta_{\mathbf{MP}}$ (mode of the posterior distribution(1)) by substituting values for α_{MP} and β_{MP}. The update equations for θ_{MP}, α_{MP} and β_{MP} can be used iteratively to estimate the model with maximum evidence.

The third stage of Bayesian Framework allows us to quatitatively rank different basis functions and the prior distributions of the scale parameters α and β. Different priors corresponds to different hypothesis about the unknown data generation process and can be compared by evaluating evidence. [10] [19] [20] proposed Gamma distribution for the prior for scale parameters α and β. Using gamma priors causes posterior distribution of scale parameters to concentrate at large values for inputs which contribute little towards the data interpolant to be predicted. The θ parameters corresponding to these low relevance inputs can be pruned. The parameter set θ so obtained is much sparser compared to those obtained by Maximum Margin approches. This formulation is a form of *Automatic Relevance Determination* and has been applied in different optimization methods in the past.

3 Sparse Bayesian Multi-category Classification

Bayesian learning framework can be used to learn multi-class classifier which are much sparser and have low classification cost. For K classes and N observed data pairs (y_i, x_i) we use the conventional classification framework to learn the class posterior distribution as kernel basis function with canonical link function as $\sigma_j\{\mathbf{f}\} = e^{-f_j(x)}/\sum_i^K e^{-f_i(x)}$ where $f_i(x) = \sum_m^N \theta_{m,i}\Phi_m(x)$, is the kernel basis functions at N training points. The likelihood can be expressed as:

$$P(\mathbf{D}|\boldsymbol{\Theta},\mathbf{M}) = \prod_{k=1}^{K}\prod_{n=1}^{N} \sigma_k\left\{\mathbf{f}(\mathbf{x_n})\right\}^{y_{nk}} \tag{6}$$

In the classification formulation, β parameter has no significance as the likelihood (6) has no noise variance.

$\boldsymbol{\Theta} = \{\theta_1, \theta_2, \cdots, \theta_\mathbf{K}\}$ are the weight parameters for each class and $\mathbf{A} = \{\alpha_1, \alpha_2, \cdots, \alpha_\mathbf{K}\}$ are the scale parameters for the weight priors. We assume independent weight priors for each class,

$$P(\boldsymbol{\Theta}|\mathbf{A}) = \prod_{k=1}^{K} P(\theta_\mathbf{k}|\alpha_\mathbf{k}) \tag{7}$$

In the following subsections, we discuss our algorithm for estimating model parameters $\boldsymbol{\Theta}$ and $\mathbf{A}$ in bayesian framework.

3.1 Approximating Posterior Distribution for $\boldsymbol{\Theta}$

The posterior distribution can be conveniently formulated as log:

$$\log\{P(\boldsymbol{\Theta}|\mathbf{D},\mathbf{A})\} = \sum_{k=1}^{K}\sum_{n=1}^{N} c_{nk}\log\{\sigma_k\{\mathbf{f}(\mathbf{x_n})\}\} - (\sum_{k=1}^{K} \theta_\mathbf{k}\alpha_\mathbf{k}\theta_\mathbf{k}^\mathbf{T}) \tag{8}$$

The $\alpha_\mathbf{k} = diag(\alpha_{k1}, \alpha_{k2}, \cdots, \alpha_{kN})$ are the individual prior scale parameters for each class k and N training data points. The Posterior distribution has complex non-gaussian form and cannot be estimated in usual way using (1). We use Laplace's approximation [14] to estimate the posterior distribution as a gaussian distribution

$$P(\boldsymbol{\Theta}|\mathbf{D},\mathbf{A}) \simeq P(\boldsymbol{\Theta}_\mathbf{MP}|\mathbf{D},\mathbf{A}) * \exp\left\{-\tfrac{1}{2}(\boldsymbol{\Theta}-\boldsymbol{\Theta}_\mathbf{MP})\mathbf{C}^{-1}(\boldsymbol{\Theta}-\boldsymbol{\Theta}_\mathbf{MP})^\mathbf{T}\right\} \tag{9}$$

Laplace's approximation assumes that the posterior distribution of $\boldsymbol{\Theta}$ has a strong peak at most probable parameters $\boldsymbol{\Theta}_\mathbf{MP}$. Training the multi-class classifier essentially becomes learning the most probable model parameters $\boldsymbol{\Theta}_\mathbf{MP}$, as the modes of approximate posterior distribution (9).

Assuming block diagonal covariance matrix $\mathbf{C} = \mathbf{diag}\{\mathbf{C_1}, \mathbf{C_2}, \cdots, \mathbf{C_K}\}$ for K classes we can factorize (9) as:

$$P(\mathbf{\Theta}|\mathbf{D},\mathbf{A}) \simeq \left\{\prod_{k=1}^{K} P(\theta_{\mathbf{k},\mathbf{MP}}|\mathbf{D},\alpha_{\mathbf{k}})\right\} \exp\left\{\sum_{k=1}^{K} -\frac{1}{2}(\theta_{\mathbf{k}} - \theta_{\mathbf{k},\mathbf{MP}})\mathbf{C}_{\mathbf{k}}^{-1}(\theta_{\mathbf{k}} - \theta_{\mathbf{k},\mathbf{MP}})^{\mathbf{T}}\right\} \tag{10}$$

$\mathbf{\Theta}_{\mathbf{MP}}$ can be obtained by finding $\theta_{\mathbf{k},\mathbf{MP}}$ for each class k independently, using gradient based optimization methods. The covariance matrices $\mathbf{C}_{\mathbf{k}}$ are evaluated as hessian of log-posterior of class k[14].

3.2 Estimating Most Probable Parameters $\theta_{\mathbf{k},\mathbf{MP}}$

For each class k we estimate $\theta_{\mathbf{k},\mathbf{MP}}$ as modes of the posterior distribution of $\theta_{\mathbf{k}}$. We use iterative Newton's method to estimate $\theta_{\mathbf{k},\mathbf{MP}}$ that maximizes posterior (8). The gradient updates for the weights are:

$$\theta_{\mathbf{k}}^{\mathbf{t+1}} = \theta_{\mathbf{k}}^{\mathbf{t}} - \frac{\partial \log\{P(\mathbf{\Theta}|\mathbf{D},\mathbf{A})\}}{\partial\theta_{\mathbf{k}}}\left[\frac{\partial^2 \log\{P(\mathbf{\Theta}|\mathbf{D},\mathbf{A})\}}{\partial\theta_{\mathbf{k}}^{\mathbf{2}}}\right]^{-1} \tag{11}$$

The gradient and hessian can be evaluated as:

$$\nabla_{\theta_{\mathbf{k}}}(\mathbf{log}\{\mathbf{P}(\mathbf{\Theta}|\mathbf{D},\mathbf{A})\}) = -\sum_{n=1}^{N} \Phi_k(x_n)(c_{nk} - \sigma_k\{f(x_n)\}) - \theta_{\mathbf{k}}\alpha_{\mathbf{k}} \tag{12}$$

$$\nabla_{\theta_{\mathbf{k}}}\nabla_{\theta_{\mathbf{k}}}(\mathbf{log}\{\mathbf{P}(\mathbf{\Theta}|\mathbf{D},\mathbf{A})\}) = -((\mathbf{\Phi}_{\mathbf{k}}^{\mathbf{T}}\mathbf{B}_{\mathbf{k}}\mathbf{\Phi}_{\mathbf{k}}) + \alpha_{\mathbf{k}}) \tag{13}$$

where $\mathbf{B}_{\mathbf{k}} = diag(\beta_{k1}, \beta_{k2}, \cdots, \beta_{kN})$, $\mathbf{\Phi}_{\mathbf{k}}$ is the kernel basis function and $\beta_{kn} = \sigma_k\{f(x_n)\}[1 - \sigma_k\{f(x_n)\}]$. The hessian computed in (13) is used as covariance inverse $\mathbf{C}_{\mathbf{k}}^{-1}$ of the approximated posterior (10) for class k. The exact Newton's updates are expensive due to computation of hessian(13). We use quasi-newton method, limited memory BFGS [21], for approximating hessian at each iteration using M vectors $\theta_{\mathbf{k}}$ obtained from previous iterations.

3.3 Estimating Most Probable Regularization Scale Parameters $\alpha_{k,MP}$

The regularization scale parameter $\alpha_{k,MP}$ for each class k is obtained by maximizing the marginal evidence with respect to α_k. The marginal evidence is obtained by marginalising evidence over the parameter $\theta_{\mathbf{k}}$ for class k. For quadratic regularizing term $P(\theta_k)(3)$, we can approximate the marginal evidence as (10) [14]. For some initial value of $\alpha_{\mathbf{k},\mathbf{i}}$ and $\theta_{\mathbf{k}}$, the $\alpha_{k,MP}$ is obtained as an update equation:

$$\alpha_{\mathbf{k},\mathbf{MP}} = \frac{1 - \alpha_{\mathbf{k},\mathbf{i}}\mathbf{Trace}\{\mathbf{C}_{\mathbf{k}}^{-1}\}}{\theta_{\mathbf{k}}^{\mathbf{2}}} \tag{14}$$

$\alpha_{\mathbf{k},\mathbf{MP}}$ are computed for all the classes by substituting $\theta_{k,MP}$ (as obtained in Section 3.2) in (14). The updated $\alpha_{\mathbf{k}}$ values are used to re-estimate classifier parameters $\theta_{\mathbf{k}}$ for each class. The iterative procedure is run till $\alpha_{\mathbf{k}}$ for all the classes

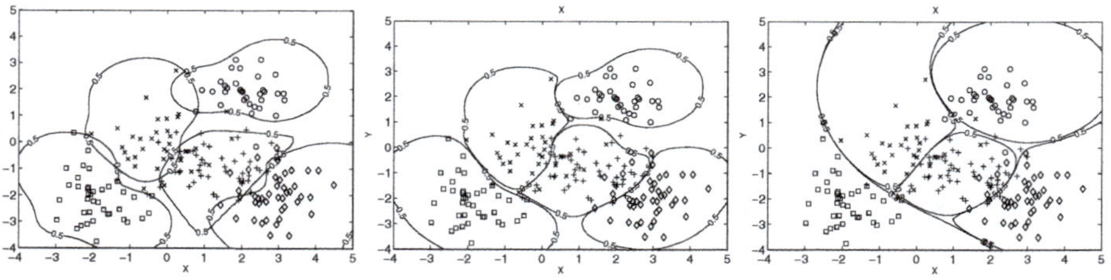

Fig. 1. (Left) Classification results for 5 class synthetic dataset, using "one against rest" classifier constructed using 5 RVM classifiers [8]. The contours are 0.5 probability points. The boundaries are not separated well and data points lying near boundaries are ambiguously classified. **(Middle)** Sparse Bayesian Multiclass Classifier for 5 clases. The boundaries are well demarcated as the normalization constraint is maintained throughtout optimization procedure. **(Right)** Bayesian Multiclass Classifier obtained from smoother radial bases functions obtained by varying the scale parameter.

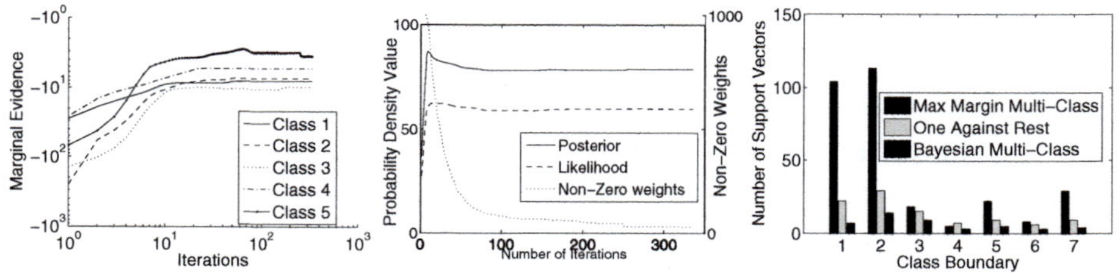

Fig. 2. (Left) Marginal Evidence for scale parameters of each class $\alpha_{\mathbf{k}}$ on log-scale for the artificial data in fig. 1. Notice that the marginal evidence increases with iterations for every class simultaneously. **(Middle)** *Left scale* Corresponding change of Posterior and Likelhood values with iterations. *Right Scale* Corresponding non-zero weights(model complexity) with no. of iterations. Note here that most of the change occurs in first 50 iterations only. This can be used make training faster. **(Right)** Number of support vectors for 3 multi-class classifier obtained for the Synth. dataset in Fig. 3.

do not change more than prespecified threshold. At every iteration step, $\alpha_{\mathbf{k}}$ values more than some maximum threshold can be pruned and the corresponding $\theta_{\mathbf{k}}$ values are made zero.

The critical assumption of this algorithm is the block diagonal covariance matrix in (10) which enables us to treat posterior distribution of $\theta_{\mathbf{k}}$ for each class independently. The $\theta_{\mathbf{k}}$ updates for all the classes at every iteration ensures simultaneous increase of marginal evidence at each iteration as shown in Fig. 2(Left).

4 Experiments

We conducted experiments to empirically evaluate and compare performance of the proposed classifier with other approaches for multi-class classification. The more classical approach is to combine several binary classifiers in probablistic framework to obtain multi-class classification. Classifiers obtained in this way are usually dense(due to modelling many class boundaries), have high classification cost or do not model class boundaries correctly.

The two generic approaches are, "One-against-Rest" and "Pairwise Coupling" [12],[1]. For comparison we use RVM classifier,[8] to learn "One-against-Rest" (1-REST) with logistic link function. We use RVM in "Pairwise Coupling" (PAIR) framework as proposed in [12]. We also compare the results with max margin classifier [7](MM) and generalized linear model (GLM) learnt using Iterative Reweighted Least Square (IRLS). Fig. 1 compares the classification boundaries obtained using 1-ALL classifier and Bayesian Multiclass Classifier. on 5-class synthetic dataset generated by sampling GMM. In all the experiments we used gaussian RBF kernel. For the comparisons, the global parameters of the classifiers were appropriately tuned to give best results.

4.1 Benchmark Comparison Results

We performed experiments on classification benchmarks from UCI Machine Learning database. Fig. 2(Right) compares bayesian multi-class classifier with max margin multi-class classifier [7] and 1-REST classifier in terms of complexity. The histogram represents the number of support vectors(non-zero parameters in the semi-parametric class boundary interpolant) in the multi-class classifier. The number of support vectors for bayesian classifier is much lower compared to other 2 classifiers.

Fig. 3(**left**) compares prediction rates of Bayesian multiclass classifiers(SBC) with other classifiers. The training datasets used were of varying size and ranged from 150 to 2000. The table shows consistent good performance of SBC compared

Pred.(%)	MM	SBC	1-REST	PAIR	GLM
Synth. (300/7)	62	65.5	62.7	68.6	53.8
Dermat. (292/6)	90	96	95.3	94.6	96
Glass (160/7)	85.6	72.2	66.7	68.5	66.7
OPT (1912/10)	89.1	93.3	93.4	93.2	87.2
PEN Dig. (1500/10)	89.5	94.4	94.2	88.8	85
MFeature (2000/10)	89.6	91.8	92	88.3	82.1

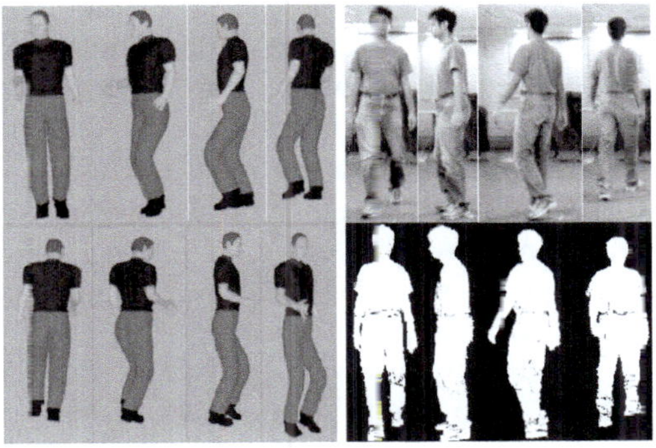

Fig. 3. (left) Comparison of prediction rates for different multi-class classifiers. The value in the brackets shows (training dataset size/Classes). All the recognition rates are in (%). Notice that SBC consistently performs good **(center)** Row-wise ordered, 8 classes of viewpoints at rotation angles of $0^o, 45^o, 90^o, 135^o, 180^o, 225^o, 270^o$ and 315° around Z-axis, **(right)** Class 1,Class 3, Class 4 and Class 5 Real motion sequences.

to other classifiers. Max Margin classifier performs good for some datasets but worse for others. Prediction rate of SBC is always slightly more than 1-REST due to inaccurate boundary modeling in 1-REST.

We also compare the classification time of different classifiers for OPT Digits recognition dataset. Classification of 2000 points for bayesian multi-class classifier was 6 times faster than pairwise classifier and 100 times faster than max-margin classifier. This is due to very sparse model obtained for SBC with typically less than $1\% - 2\%$ of number of training points. The "One-against-Rest" classifier was denser as the number of support vectors were more compared to SBC. The pairwise classifier obtained from multiple RVM classifiers, although were sparser, required computing posterior classification probabilities from $\frac{K(K-1)}{2}$ classifiers. This takes time which increase with the number of classes quadratically. MM classification time largely depended on the constraints' working set size, which was tuned to maximize the prediction rate.

4.2 Estimating Viewpoint from Human Silhouettes

We use Bayesian multi-class classifier to learn viewing angle from the human silhouettes. Estimating viewpoint directly has direct application in the context of human body tracking and 3D pose reconstruction. Several human motions are difficult to track from a viewpoint but are easier to track from other. Knowledge of viewpoint can be used to dynamically modify the tracker parameters and adjust to current viewing conditions.

We formulate the problem in classification framework by defining 8 classes based on viewing angles around vertical Z axis(at regular rotation angles of 45°). The framework can be extended to consider rotation around X and Y axes. However these variations are not relevant in the context of tracking human motion which seldom involves rotation around X and Y axes.

We train the SBC on 2D images rendered using MAYA. The motion capture data for generic motion[13] is imported to MAYA model constructed using standard human specification for joints and segments. The silhouettes extracted from the rendered images(Fig. 3(Right)) are used to generate shape context histogram[15](12 angular bins, 5 radial bins). The overall dimension is reduced to 60 by clustering to few bases means.

We train our classifier on 4 different activities' images rendered from 8 or 4 different viewpoints. We tested the classifier on both artificial and real motion sequences. For artificial test sequence, we rendered images from similar but unseen sequences at angles $\pm 15^o$ of the 8 class viewing angles. Table 1 gives the details of each sequence and the confusion matrix obtained from predictions using bayesian multi-class classifier.

We also tested on a real sequence captured from 8 different viewpoints. Fig. 3(**right**) shows 4 of these viewpoints. The viewing angle of the motion capture was changed by performing the motion at different angles with respect to camera plane. For extracting silhouettes from real images, we use non-parametric background subtraction and assumed stationary background with single foreground object.

Notice that training silhouettes are quite different from the testing silhouettes and also contained variations due to multiple subjects. The class boundaries are also not very well defined as the shape contexts[15] are invariant to small rotations. We used the artificial walking sequence in Table 1 for training. The test sequences contained varying number of frames for 8 classes of viewpoints. Table 1(**e**) shows the classification rate of real data set for 8 classes of viewpoint using sparse multi-class classifier. The classification rate is not encouraging due to forward backward ambiguities and the invariability of the shape context to small rotations.

Table 1. Confusion Matrix for the artificial test. Notice the bright tridiagonal band due to inaccuracy in classifying bordering points of adjoining classes. Also class 1 and class 5 have larger inaccuracies due to forward backward ambiguities. **(a)** Walking - 1000 training, 125 samples for each class. Recognition rate - *70%* **(b)** Running - 1000 training points, 125 samples for each class. Recognition rate - *73.67%* **(c)** Jumping - 1000 training points, 125 samples for each class, Recognition rate - *61.25%* **(d)** Bending - 4 Classes at viewing angles 0°, 90°, 180° and 270°, 1000 training samples, 250 samples for each class, recognition rate - *92.5%*, Notice the bright cell in row 1,column 3 due to misclassification of forward facing pose as backward facing pose. **(e)**Recognition Rates for Classes on Real Walking sequence. Notice the very low recognition rates for class 1 (person facing the camera) due to forward-backward ambiguities Overall recognition rate was **51.3%**.

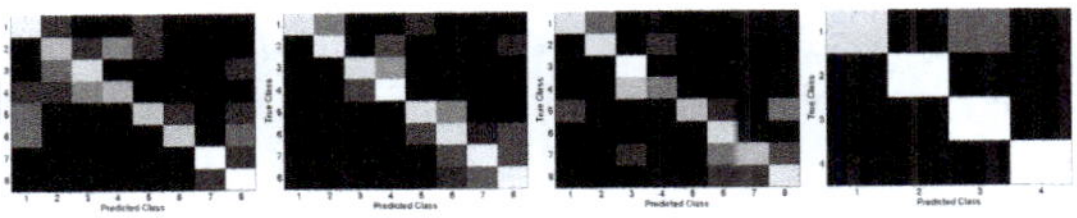

(a) (b) (c) (d)

Class	1	2	3	4	5	6	7	8
Pred. Rate(%)	30	45	53	43	59	55	47	4[illegible]

(e)

Nevertheless, the proposed bayesian classifier, in general gives consistently good performance compared to other approaches for multi-class classification and can be used effectively for other machine learning problems. Although the training time for the classifier is more, the classification time is extremely low compared to other multi-class classifers.

5 Conclusions and Future Work

In this paper we propose an extension for bayesian classification [10] to multi-class problems which gives improvement both in classification accuracy and time. The improvement occurs essentially due to sparse non-linear modeling of the class boundaries and maintaining the normalization constraint during the optimization procedure. The future work would involve making the training algorithm faster. The training time for bayesian multi-class classifier is comparable to max margin classifier and GLM but more than "pairwise coupling" and "One-against-Rest" implementation.

References

1. T. Hastie, R. Tibshirani, "Classification by pairwise coupling" *The Annals of Statistics, 1998*
2. T. G. Dietterich, G. Bakiri, "Solving multiclass learning problems via error-correcting output codes" *Journal of Artificial Intelligence Research, 1995*
3. E. L. Allwein, R. E. Schapire and Y. Singer, "Reducing multiclass to binary: A unifying approach for margin classifiers" *ICML, 2000*
4. B. E. Boser, I. M. Guyon, V. N. Vapnik, "A training algorithm for optimal margin classifiers" *Computational Learning Theory, 1992*
5. Leo Breinman, Jerome H. Friedman, Richard A. Olshen, and Charles J. Stone, "Classification and Regression Trees" *Wadsworth and Brooks,1984*
6. E. J. Bredensteiner and K. P. Bennet, "Multicategory classification using Support Vector Machines" *Computational Optimization and Applications,1999*
7. I. Tsochantaridis, T. Hofmann, T. Joachims, and Y. Altun, "Support Vector Learning for Interdependent and Structured Output Spaces," *ICML, 2004.*
8. M. E. Tipping, "Sparse Bayesian Learning and the Relevance Vector Machine" *JMLR, 2001.*
9. Ian T. Nabney, "Efficient Training of RBF Networks for Classification" *International Journal of Neural Systems, 2004*
10. D. J.C. Mackay, "Bayesian Interpolation" *Neural Computation, 1991*
11. K. Crammer, Y. Singer "On Algorithmic Implementation of Multiclass Kernel-bases Vector Machines, *JMLR, 2001*
12. T. Hamamura, H. Mizutani, B. Irie, "A Multiclass classification method based on multiple pairwise classifiers" *ICDAR, 2003*
13. "CMU Human Motion Capture Database" *http://mocap.cs.cmu.edu*
14. D. J. C. MacKay. "Choice of basis for Laplace approximation", *Machine Learning, 1998*
15. S. Belongie, J. Malik, and J. Puzicha. "Shape Matching and Object Recognition Using Shape Contexts", *PAMI 2002*
16. Y. Freund, R. E. Schapire. "A decision-theoretic generalization of on-line learning and an application to boosting." *Journal of Computer and System Sciences, August 1997*
17. C. Burges. "A tutorial on support vector machines for pattern recognition." *KDD, 1998*
18. J. Weston, C. Watkins "Support vector machines for multi-class pattern recognition" *European Symposium on ANN, April 1999*
19. R.M. Neal, "Bayesian Learning for Neural Networks", *Springer,1996*
20. J. O. Berger, "Statistical decision theory and Bayesian analysis", *Springer, 1985*
21. J. Nocedal, "Updating quasi-Newton matrices with limited storage" *Mathematics of Computation, 1980*

Estimation of Structural Information Content in Images*

Subrata Rakshit and Anima Mishra

Center for Artificial Intelligence and Robotics,
Bangalore, India
{subrata, anima}@cair.res.in

Abstract. We address the problem of formulating a measure of image information content that is consistent with human perception of information present in a given image. When presented with an image, humans can assess the amount of interesting structural details present as well as the quality of an image in terms of sharpness and noise level. This assessment can be performed independent of any reference image or prior knowledge of ground truth. The challeng is to formulate measures that are sensitive to structurally significant intensity variations in images but which can also reject noise and clutter in a way similar to humans. It is shown that conventional measures known in literature for evaluating single images (no ground truth) fail to reject noisy images. The limitations of the published methods based on statistics, edges and entropy lead us to define a new technique based on an extension of Shannon's entropy measure and multiresolution representations. This implicitly postulates a model of perceived structures that is able to reject noise while giving high scores for sharp, clean natural images.

Index terms: Perceptual quality, information, entropy, multiresolution, image model.

1 Introduction

Humans are capable of evaluating images independent of context for their content richness, level of detail and over-all quality. This (subjective) evaluation does correlate well across individuals. This is what we refer to as the structural information content in images: a sense of content quantity and quality independent of object recognition. If this can be formulated as a computable function, then one can have an automated (numerical) evaluation of images that can be used to assess various other image processing algorithms.

The difference between image information and image quality needs to be emphasized. Measures of quality compare images with identical contents for their appearance. A measure of information must evaluate the different amount of structural details present (edges, textures, shading) as well as their degradation due to any noise that may be present. There exist many published methods for

* This work was funded by DRDO through Proj CAR-008. Authors wish to thank Director CAIR, ISYS-DO and colleagues in CVG for their support.

P.J. Narayanan et al. (Eds.): ACCV 2006, LNCS 3851, pp. 265–275, 2006.

evaluating image quality and changes in images as listed in [1]. In situations where there exists a desired or target image, the use of error and correlation based measures are possible [2]. In practise, one often has only a noisy image that needs to be denoised. Images generated synthetically using image fusion also have no ground truth. For such cases, it is necessary to have a method of evaluating an image without recourse to comparison with a 'true' image. For the rest of this paper, we only consider measures of quality and content that can be applied to *single* images.

This paper is organized as follows. Some existing methods are examined first and their limitations are shown. One of these methods, computation of Shannon entropy, is extended to define a second order measure. In combination with multiresolution representations, it is used to define a new family of measures. Finally, results are presented for caliberation of images, evaluation of image enhancement approaches and quantitative evaluation of perceptual significance of noise patterns.

2 Single Image Measures

The challenge in defining single image measures is to able to codify the ability of the HVS to assess structural information. The two image version of the problem, where one wants to asses the relative change, has been studied in [2]. It is far harder to estimate information for single images (no ground truth) and indirect methods are often invoked. For example, Narayanan *et. al.* in [3] have used the performance of a classifier on given image sets to infer information content. These measures are problem specific and say as much about the application domain as about the image. For single image information content, one must be able to model the prior knowledge of the world used by the HVS as well: there is a sense of what is to be expected and, consequently, the unexpected. This brings into question the model order that one should use. A first order model would declare any change as unxpected, a second order would declare any change in the expectation of change as unexpected etc. The first order is obviously inappropriate as it would make noise very interesting. In this work we develop a measure based on a second order approach.

2.1 Desired Properties

The evaluation of the information estimate itself can only be made in terms of its qualitative behaviour in certain situations. The list below serves to set these conditions and limit the scope of our proposed measures.

1. It should only depend on pixel values of that image.[No reference, context or IU]
2. Blank (constant) images should get a score of 0.[No structures present]
3. White noise should also score (close to) 0.[No structure seen by HVS]
4. Textures should score higher than noise.[Some structure seen by HVS]
5. Images with plenty of well defined objects should score highest.

6. The measure should be sensitive to the spatial distribution of pixel values. Scrambling an image should *not* leave the measure unchanged.[Undesirable invariance]
7. The evaluated score should be attributable to contributions from each pixel, *i.e.*, it should be localizable.

The first condition defines the scope to context independent single image measures. The second and third can be considered as boundary conditions on image variance. The next three (4,5,6) are an attempt to capture characteristics of human evaluation of an image. The localization property (7) is desirable for any image measure in terms of utility. Knowing which parts of an image are contributing to its measure of information can facilitate further processing such as image fusion [4].

2.2 Existing Measures

Among the existing choices for characterizing single images, one may consider three basic approaches:

- Statistical measures: These include range, variance, energy and correlation. The 'Universal Image Quality Index' of Wang [5] as extended for single images by Piella [4] is an example.
- Entropy: Shannon entropy of intensity histogram, expressed as bits/pix. Variations such as mutual information and other definitions of entropy for defining image quality use two images as in [1], [6].
- Image Processing primitives: Measures based on detection of various edges and textures. Though we have not seen such measures defined explicitly, the present art would certainly allow for such measures to be defined for specific situations.

Each of these measures have some merit and can be used in certain situations. The principal drawback is that all these measures keep increasing the score as intensity variations keep increasing, even when such variations begin to constitute clutter and noise. For humans, a sense of 'background' is essential to the appreciation of a 'foreground' object[1] In addition, the statistical and entropy based measures are *invariant to the spatial distribution of pixels in images.* The scores from these measures remain unchanged even when the picture is scrambled by interchanging various pixels within an image. Last, but not least, one would like to have a measure that does not get influenced by just a minority of pixels as is the case for dynamic range and, to a lesser extent, for variance and energy.

In this work, we formulate a measure based on an extension of Shannon entropy that is specifically designed to discount noise. Multiresolution representation is used to induce sensitivity to spatial distribution of pixels. The issue of localization is explicitly addressed to enable location specific processing using the measures developed.

[1] In audio, the removal of silence periods renders speech incoherent.

2.3 A New Measure of Image Information

In his seminal paper, C.E. Shannon focussed his attention on the problem of communicating the value of a (random) variable across a communication channel. That approach, based on probability and entropy, has since blossomed into Information Theory. It should be noted that the 'information' refered to in Information Theory relates to the amount of information required to be conveyed *about* a variable. It does not indicate the information being conveyed *by* the variable. As a perfectly random variable is the hardest to communicate, the entropy of such a variable is maximum (for a given number of discrete states). As a signal from a measurement process, however, such an output would be unequivocally termed 'noise'. The formulation of a measure of information conveyed *by* a variable necessiates a modification to Shannon's measure of entropy.

2.4 Second Order Entropy

We begin by considering the definition for the entropy of a discrete variable. If the variable x can assume values $x_i, i = 1..N$ with probabilities $p_i, i = 1..N$, the entropy of x, denoted by $H(x)$ is defined as

$$H(x) = \sum_i -p_i \cdot \log p_i \qquad (1)$$

This definition of entropy is maximized when each state becomes equally probable. The drawback is that the equiprobable distribution that maximizes this measure does not correspond to our human perception of 'structure' or 'information' in a signal.

To address the above drawback in $H(X)$, we propose to extend the classical definition of entropy as given by Eqn 1. The basic idea is this: just as $H(x)$ goes to 0 when the variable is present in only one state, one would like the new measure to go to zero when $p_i = const$ for all i. This can be done by computing $H(p_i)$, which can be seen as a second order entropy (SOE) of the original variable x, denoted as $H_2(x)$. Irrespective of the dynamic range of x, the dynamic range of p_i is 0...1 and there will be exactly N samples (N = number of states of x). This, in practise, limits the quantization that one can perform for p_i. Assuming that one has quantized the [0..1] interval into M segments and computed the probability distribution of p_i as $q_j, j = 1..M$, then

$$H_2(x) = \sum_j -q_j \cdot \log q_j = H(p(x)) \qquad (2)$$

There exists a degree of freedom in going from p_i to its probability distribution q_j, so long as noise rejection is the sole criterion. One could have used any monotonic function of p_i, $f(p_i)$, to compute the distribution q_i. This choice of a monotonic function determines the type of input distribution, $p(x)$, that will maximize $H_2(x)$. If f is the identity function, $p(x) = x$ maximizes $H_2(x)$. This $p(x)$ forces some values to be much more likely than others, in effect forcing a background-foreground distribution. The choice of $f(p) = -\log p_i$ maximizes $H_2(x)$ for $p(x) = e^x$. This forces an even sharper separation of probabilities between the more probable (background) values and the rare (foreground) values. The exploration of higher orders and various nonlinear functions is beyond the scope of this work. They do constitute two ways in which the framework can be tuned towards specific models of the HVS.

2.5 Localization of Entropy

As stated in Sec 2.1, one desirable property is localization. The property of entropy is inherently a global one belonging to the distribution as a whole. However, it is possible to come up with an 'entropy map' for an image that is consistent with Eqn 1. Note that Eqn 1 involves a sum over the index i of terms of type $p_i \cdot -\log p_i$. For images, i would range over possible pixel values and p_i would be equal to N_i/N_{tot} where N_i is the number of pixels with intensity i and N_{tot} is the total number of pixels in the image. Thus the summation can be changed to a summation over all pixels, with each pixel contributing $(-\log p_i)/N_{tot}$ to $H(x)$, where the pixel intensity is i and p_i is the corresponding probability. Then the entropy $H(x)$ for an image can be seen as a summation of specific contributions from individual pixels. As the denominator is constant for all pixels, it can be disregarded as a scaling constant. Thus for each image, one can define an entropy map where each pixel of value i is replaced by $\alpha \cdot (-\log p_i)$ with α being a fixed scaling term meant to ensure that the computed values are in some desired dynamic range.

Having achieved the localization of $H(x)$, one can iterate the process to achieve both computation and localization of $H_2(x)$. Given an image, one computes its entropy map as mentioned above. By a suitable choice of α, this can also be made into an image within an identical dynamic range. The entropy of this image gives $H_2(x)$ for the original image and the entropy map of this derived image gives the second order entropy map for the original image. Note that this iterative method is simplest for the choice of $-\log p$ for the monotonic function.

2.6 Inducing Spatial Dependency Using Multiresolution

Both forms of entropy discussed so far depend only on the intensity histograms of images. The spatial arrangement of the pixels is not taken into account in the evaluation of these measures. Entropy characterizes a random variable based on a collection of samples, where ordering is irrelevant. For a signal, where sampled values are generated by sampling a physical dimension such as time or space, the ordering cannot be ignored. Thus direct evaluation of entropy on sampled values fails to take cognizance of an essential aspect of signals. The ordering can be made relevant by considering deviations of a sampled value from its local average and computing the entropy of these derived values. The multiresolution representations of signals like wavelets and Laplacian pyramids capture such deviations. The bandpass subbands measure deviations from local means at various scales. The Laplacian pyramid [7] is easier to use in this context as it does not decompose each level into oriented components. The results in this paper are quoted for Laplacian pyramid decompositions. However, wavelet decompositions can also be used. Evaluating SOE ($H_2(.)$) for images by evaluating the SOE of its multiresolution subbands gives a measure that takes cognizance of the spatial ordering of pixels with respect to each other.

The use of multiresolution for image information does more than just take into account the spatial ordering of pixel values. Evaluation of H_2 for each subband enables us to tailor the measure to HVS models. The use of multi-scale representations has been advocated for image quality assessment by Wang, Simoncelli and Bovik [8] as it enables one to model the scale-space dependency of the contrast sensitivity function (CSF) of the HVS. One could also build in a bias towards sharp edges (as those produced by occlusion) by requiring consistency across scales for the entropy maps of each subband. Last, but not least, one can use the Shannon entropy of the first subband (L_0 for Laplacians) to normalize the over all measure for input contrast and sensor dynamic range. These issues are brought out next during the formulation of the proposed measures of image information.

2.7 Algorithm for Estimating Information

The composite method for computing image information involving $H_2(x)$ and pyramid (multiresolution) for an image $\mathcal{I}$ is as follows:

1. Given $\mathcal{I}$, compute multiresolution subbands $M(\mathcal{I}) = L_0, L_1, L_2, ..., L_{n-1}, G_n$
2. For each subband, compute the corresponding $H_2(L_k)$
3. Compute $H_2(M(\mathcal{I}))$ as a function $\mathbf{F}$ of the subband SOE's
$$H_2(M(\mathcal{I})) = \mathbf{F}(\mathbf{H_2}(\mathbf{L_0}), \mathbf{H_2}(\mathbf{L1}), ...\mathbf{H_2}(\mathbf{G_n})) \quad (3)$$
4. Normalize the measure using entropy of L_0
$$H_2^*(M(\mathcal{I})) = H_2(M(\mathcal{I}))/(H(L_0))^\gamma \quad (4)$$
5. Consider the subband entropy maps as a pyramid and reconstruct it, consistent with $\mathbf{F}$, to generate the entropy map of $\mathcal{I}$.

The $H_2(M(\mathcal{I}))$ computed above is the multiscale second order entropy (MSOE) of the image $\mathcal{I}$. The $H_2^*(M(\mathcal{I}))$ is the normalized multiscale second order entropy (NMSOE). The NMSOE is useful when comparing images acquired with sensors having different dynamic ranges or ignoring the effect of contrast.

The choice of the combination function $\mathbf{F}$ in Eqn 3 plays an important role in selecting models of the HVS. The simple summation would give equal weightage to all scales while a weighted summation would prefer some scales over others. It could also be based on a projection operation that would favour consistency of edges across scales. We report results based on the following implementations of $\mathbf{F}$. Let $\mathbf{u_1(i,j)}$ and $\mathbf{u_2(i,j)}$ be the entropy maps of two neighboring subbands interpolated to the resolution of the larger of the two. They can be combined to define the resultant entropy map $\mathbf{u_r(i,j)}$ as

$$\mathbf{u_r(i,j)} = \{\mathbf{u_1(i,j)} + \mathbf{u_2(i,j)}\}/2 \qquad (5)$$

for the simple averaging case. For the consistency across scales model, we use

$$\mathbf{u_r(i,j)} = \frac{\mathbf{u_1.u_2}}{\|\mathbf{u_1}\|.\|\mathbf{u_2}\|}.\{\mathbf{u_1(i,j)} + \mathbf{u_2(i,j)}\}/2. \qquad (6)$$

Such a model would favour occlusion induced sharp edges while ignoring shading and textures. The choice of γ in Eqn 4 decides the importance of contrast in $\mathcal{I}$. It also determines the trade-off between discounting distributed high frequencies as sensor noise or attributing them to texture. The proposed framework for defining measures of image information is thus versatile enough to incorporate various HVS models and application specific priors.

3 Results

The results reported here are based on the Laplacian pyramid as the multiresolution representation. Four different choices of models were used. For brevity of notation we define them as
(i) HA : **F** is an averaging and $\gamma = 0$,[Weak noise rejection, no edge model]
(ii) HA^* : **F** is an averaging and $\gamma = 0.5$,[Stronger noise rejection]
(iii) HP : **F** is a projection and $\gamma = 0$, [Edge model favoring sharp edges]
(iv) HP^* : **F** is a projection and $\gamma = 0.5$.[Sharp edges, strong noise rejection]
where the projection operation is implemented as previously defined.

3.1 Ranking of Assorted Images

The ability of the proposed measures to quantify human perception of image content and quality is tested by a ranking task. A set of eight images, as shown in Figure 1, is to be ranked. The images range from a simple square ($\mathcal{T}$), white noise ($\mathcal{N}$), textures ($\mathcal{P}, \mathcal{S}$), natural images ($\mathcal{L}, \mathcal{B}, \mathcal{M}$) and a black/white diagram ($\mathcal{D}$). Besides the four MSOE based measures defined above, we also report results based on variance (V), the standard entropy (H), energy in output of Sobel operator (SB) and Canny edges (CE). Each measure assigns a numerical score to each image and the images are sorted in decreasing order to produce the ranking indiced by that measure. The result is shown in Table 1.

The key ability to reject noise is demonstrated by the proposed methods. The Canny edge detector was implemented with an adaptive method of selecting the threshold. Thus is was the only non-MSOE method capable of ignoring noise. It is also seen that large values of γ penalise textures and the use of projections favour images with well defined edges. To get more insight into the scoring process, we need to look at the relative scores given to the images. As each measure uses a different dynamic range, we facilitate comparison by normalising the scores for

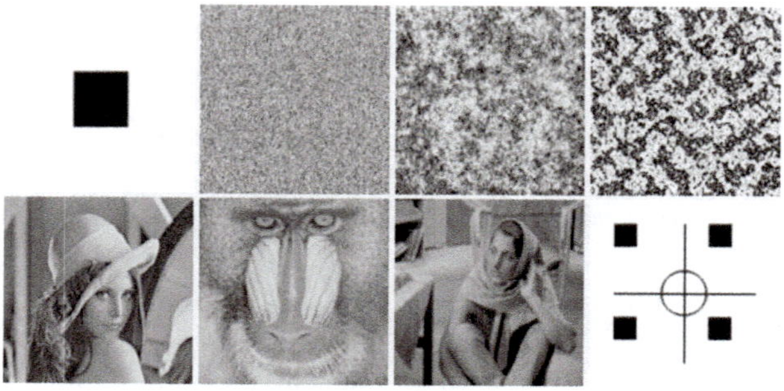

Fig. 1. Set of four images used for ranking test. Top row, left to right: $\mathcal{T}, \mathcal{N}, \mathcal{P}, \mathcal{S}$. Bottom row, left to right: $\mathcal{L}, \mathcal{M}, \mathcal{B}, \mathcal{D}$.

Table 1. Ranking of the eight images in decreasing order of information content by four proposed measures and four prior methods. Discounting noise and textures $(\mathcal{N}, \mathcal{P}, \mathcal{S})$ and differentiating between the binary images $(\mathcal{D}, \mathcal{T})$ are the key challenges.

V	$\mathcal{S}$	$\mathcal{P}$	$\mathcal{N}$	$\mathcal{D}$	$\mathcal{T}$	$\mathcal{L}$	$\mathcal{B}$	$\mathcal{M}$
H	$\mathcal{N}$	$\mathcal{L}$	$\mathcal{P}$	$\mathcal{M}$	$\mathcal{B}$	$\mathcal{S}$	$\mathcal{D}$	$\mathcal{T}$
SB	$\mathcal{S}$	$\mathcal{N}$	$\mathcal{P}$	$\mathcal{D}$	$\mathcal{M}$	$\mathcal{L}$	$\mathcal{B}$	$\mathcal{T}$
CE	$\mathcal{M}$	$\mathcal{B}$	$\mathcal{L}$	$\mathcal{S}$	$\mathcal{P}$	$\mathcal{N}$	$\mathcal{D}$	$\mathcal{T}$
HA	$\mathcal{B}$	$\mathcal{M}$	$\mathcal{L}$	$\mathcal{S}$	$\mathcal{P}$	$\mathcal{N}$	$\mathcal{D}$	$\mathcal{T}$
HA^*	$\mathcal{D}$	$\mathcal{L}$	$\mathcal{B}$	$\mathcal{M}$	$\mathcal{T}$	$\mathcal{S}$	$\mathcal{P}$	$\mathcal{N}$
HP	$\mathcal{L}$	$\mathcal{D}$	$\mathcal{B}$	$\mathcal{M}$	$\mathcal{T}$	$\mathcal{S}$	$\mathcal{P}$	$\mathcal{N}$
HP^*	$\mathcal{D}$	$\mathcal{L}$	$\mathcal{B}$	$\mathcal{M}$	$\mathcal{T}$	$\mathcal{S}$	$\mathcal{P}$	$\mathcal{N}$

each method by the maximum score assigned by it to any of the eight images. These normalised scores are shown in Table 2.

The ability of the proposed metrhods to localize the measured information is shown in Figure 2. The information maps for images $\mathcal{S}, \mathcal{L}, \mathcal{B}$ are shown for the method HP. Note that the sparse sharp edges of $\mathcal{L}$ score high, but the excessive

Table 2. Relative numerical scores assigned to the eight images by five selected methods. The scores for each measure are normalised by the maximum assigned by it to any of the eight images.

	H	CE	HA	HA^*	HP
$\mathcal{N}$	1.00	0.24	0.91	0.59	0.04
$\mathcal{P}$	0.92	0.38	0.95	0.62	0.09
$\mathcal{S}$	0.70	0.39	0.97	0.62	0.21
$\mathcal{T}$	0.05	0.04	0.36	0.66	0.22
$\mathcal{D}$	0.05	0.15	0.68	1.00	0.74
$\mathcal{L}$	0.94	0.57	0.98	0.79	1.00
$\mathcal{B}$	0.89	0.80	1.00	0.78	0.65
$\mathcal{M}$	0.91	1.00	0.99	0.75	0.44

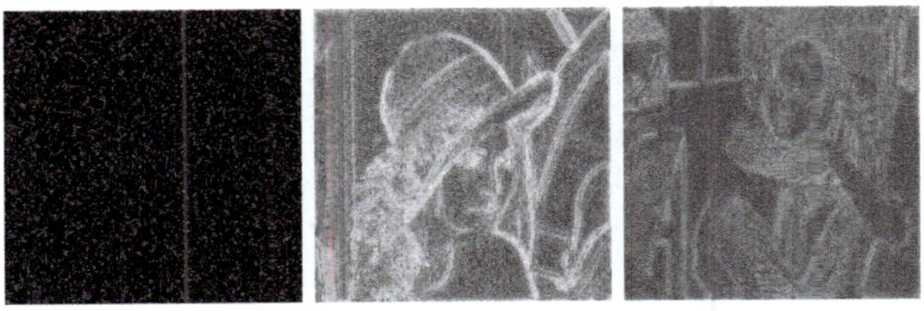

Fig. 2. The information maps of $\mathcal{S}, \mathcal{L}, \mathcal{B}$ for HP. The brighter regions indicate regions of the image that contributed more to the overall score for that image The image model underlying HP emphasizes sparse sharp edges.

amount of edges present in $\mathcal{S}$ lead to them being discounted. This ability to evaluate discontuities in the overall context of their abundance in an image is a key feature of MSOE measures.

3.2 Ranking of Enhancements

Noise removal for image enhancement does not have a unique solution. Various techniques are employed based on the nature of noise. When faced with a variety of images coming from unknown or uncaliberated sources, an ability to numerically evaluate each enhancement method is essential for automating the noise removal process. In such situations, one never has the noise free ground truth. Thus the reference image based structural information techniques and the

Fig. 3. The scores assigned by HA^* and HP^* are shown for each processed image. The left column shows two noisy images. The middle column shows the output of LPF while the right column shows the output of median filtering. The scores can be used to pick the better method/output for each case, without reference to the original image.

RMS based SNR methods cannot be applied. The proposed MSOE based measures can be used in such situations as shown in Figure 3. There are two noisy images (Fig 3 left column), one with white noise and the other with salt and pepper noise. Two noise removal techniques are employed - low pass filtering (Fig 3 center column) and median filtering (Fig 3 right column). The relative scores assigned by HA^*, HP^* both indicate that the LPF has done better for white noise and median filter has done better for salt and pepper noise. Thus the measures can be used to adaptively select best enhancement methods without ground truths and human judgement.

3.3 Noise Pattern Evaluation

Another class of problems often encountered is one where the noise in a noisy image can be accurately isolated because of the avalibility of a perfect reference image. A key problem then is in evaluating the significance of the error or noise. SNR based on RMSE does not correlate well with human perception of interference or degradation. Since the proposed measures provide a model for what is perceived by the HVS, it can be used to predict the visual impact of any noise pattern. In Figure 4 we consider four bipolar noise patterns that have identical energy (RMSE wrt 0). They however get different scores as per HA. The visual effect of the noise patterns can be appreciated when they are added to an image (Figure 4 bottom row). The ranking induced by HA seems to match human percetion of visually disruptive interference, while the ground truth based SNR would have scored all the four noisy images as of equal quality.

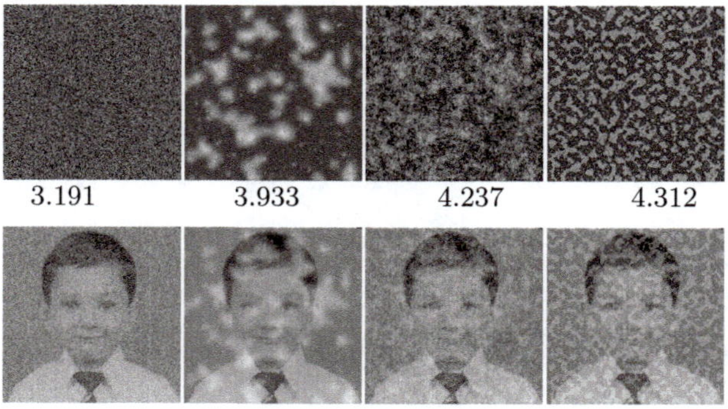

Fig. 4. The scores assigned by HA to the four noise patterns are used to rank them in increasing order of expected disruption (top row). The effect of these patterns on an image is shown (bottom row). As the noise patterns have identical energy, the noisy images have identical SNR.

4 Conclusion and Future Work

The present work proposes a framework based on multiresolution and second order entropy to define measures that can model the ability of the HVS to assess the presence of information in images. It has been shown that Shannon's measure of entropy does not model our ability to reject clutter. A second order extension has been formulated that is better able to model the HVS by requiring a certain amount of sparseness. The multiresolution representation is necessary to capture spatial relationships that are relevant for images. The framework allows for a series of measures to be defined. Results have been presented for ranking diverse images, adaptive selection of enhancement methods, noise rejection and noise evaluation. Future work will try to optimise the measures for specific HVS models and exploit the information maps for image fusion, lossy compression and steganography.

References

1. A. J. Ahumada(Jr.), Computational Image Quality Metrics. http://vision.arc.nasa.gov/personnel/al/papers/93sidaja/93sid.htm
2. Z Wang, A.C. Bovik, H.R Shiek and E. Simoncelli, Image Quality Assessment: From Error Visibility to Structural Similarity IEEE Trans in Img Proc, vol 13, no 4, 600-612, 2004.
3. R. M. Narayan, T. S. Sankaravadivelu and S. E. Reichenbach, Dependency of Image Information Content on Grey-Scale Resolution Geocarto International, vol 15, no 4, 15-27, 2000.
4. G. Piella and H. Hejimans, A New Quality Metric for Image Fusion Proc of International Conference on Image Processin, Barcelona, 2003.
5. Z. Wang and A.C. Bovik, A Universal Image Quality Index IEEE Signal Processing Letters, vol 9, no 3, 81-84, Mar 2002.
6. M. Jagersand, Saliency Maps and Attention Selection in Scale and Spatial Coordinates: An Information Theoretic Approach Proc of 5th International Conf on Computer Vision, 195-202, 1995.
7. P. Burt and E. Adelson, The Laplacian Pyramid as a Compact Image Code IEEE Transaction on Comm, COM-31 pp. 532-540, 1983.
8. Z. Wang, E.P. Simoncelli and A.C. Bovik, Multi-scale Structural Similarity for Image Quality Assessment IEEE Asilomar Conf on Signals, Systems and Computers, Invited Paper, Nov, 2003.

Automatic Moving Object Segmentation with Accurate Boundaries

Jia Wang, Haifeng Wang, Qingshan Liu, and Hanqing Lu

National Laboratory of Pattern Recognition, Institute of Automation,
Chinese Academy of Sciences, Beijing 100080, China
{wangjia, hfwang, qsliu, luhq}@nlpr.ia.ac.cn

Abstract. This paper presents a layer-model based method to segment moving objects from image sequence with accurate boundaries. The segmentation framework involves three stages: Motion seed detection, Motion layer expansion and Motion boundary refinement. In the first stage, motion seeds, which determine the amount and initial position of motion layers, are detected by corner matching between consecutive frames, and classified by global motion analysis. In the second stage, the detected motion seeds are expanded into motion layers. To preserve the spatial continuity, an energy function is defined to evaluate the spatial smoothness and accuracy of the layers. Then, Graph Cuts technique is used to solve the energy minimization problem and extract motion layers. In the last stage, the extracted layers are combined with edge information to find accurate boundaries of moving objects. The proposed method is tested on several image sequences and the experimental results illustrate its promising performance.

1 Introduction

Moving object segmentation is very important for many video processing applications, such as video representation, analysis, compression and synthesis. In the past, a number of algorithms have been proposed, each of which has its particular features and applications.

Arch and Kaup [1] proposed a segmentation technique using a statistical approach. They model the difference of pixels in background as a gaussian distribution and change detection mask (CDM) is yielded by finding the frame difference. Since this technique relies on the intensity information, there are always hollows within the detected motion regions when there is no plenty of textures. This shortcoming is partly overcome by Mech and Wollborn in [2] using morphological closing operation.

Meier and Ngan proposed an automatic segmentation technique for moving objects using a binary image model [3]. The binary model is derived from an edge image and is updated every frame to keep the changes in location and shape. The detection of a moving object is based on the binary model matching between two consecutive frames using Hausdoff distance. The advantage of this technique lies in its capable of tracking an object that stops moving for a certain

P.J. Narayanan et al. (Eds.): ACCV 2006, LNCS 3851, pp. 276–285, 2006.

period of time. However, the segmentation results depend on the success of the initial segmentation at the first frame.

In [4], Nicolescu and Medioni have employed a tensor voting procedure to obtain piecewise smooth motion region. They used two successive frames as input. For every pixel in the first frame, a normalized cross- correlation procedure is used to produce candidate matches for the second image. Then, 4-D tensor voting is performed to find the best match motion vector. After that, another 2-D tensor voting is used to obtain the motion boundary. While in some cases this method gives fairly nice results, its accuracy is influenced by the initial computation of candidate matches. Furthermore, it has the same problem as [1] that the spatial continuity of motion regions also depends on the abundance of textures.

In this paper, a new algorithm is proposed for automatic moving object segmentation, which can solve the above problems. The segmentation scheme consists of three steps: *Motion seed detection*, *Motion layer expansion* and *Motion boundary refinement*. In the first stage, motion seeds, which determine the amount and initial position of motion layers, are detected by corner matching between consecutive frames, and classified by global motion analysis. In the second stage, the detected motion seeds are expanded into motion layers. During the expansion process, an energy function is defined to evaluate the spatial smoothness and accuracy of the motion layers, by means of what the layer can keep its spatial continuity even when there is no plenty of textures. Then, Graph Cuts technique is used to settle the energy minimization problem and expand the motion layers. In the last stage, the extracted layers are combined with edge information to find the accurate boundaries of moving objects.

2 Motion Seed Detection

Layered models [5][6][7][8] provide a natural way to detect motion areas with different velocities. Computationally, the problem is addressed by first estimating motion vectors for all the pixels, then pixels are grouped into different layers based on their motion cues. Thus, to extract motion layers, it is necessary to first find out how many motions are there in the video and where they are. In this paper, such motions are regarded as seeds for the further extracted motion layers.

In this section, we extract the motion seeds by tracking corners between consecutive frames.

First, Harris detector is performed to detect corners in the current frame. The detected corners are tracked back to the previous frame to find their correspondences. Based on the coordinate difference between corresponding corners, the motion vectors between them are achieved. Then, the extracted corners together with their motion vectors are regarded as *motion seeds*.

Since the extracted motion seeds are disordered, to distinguish those belonging to moving objects, global motion analysis is used to cluster them into *global motion seeds* and *local motion seeds*based on their motion vectors, where global motion seeds have motion vectors consistent with global motion caused by the motion of camera, and local motion seeds have motion vectors corresponding to local motions caused by the moving objects.

For global motion analysis, a 3-parameter model is proposed to describe global motion, which can be expressed as

$$\begin{bmatrix} v_x \\ v_y \end{bmatrix} = a_1 \begin{bmatrix} x \\ y \end{bmatrix} + \begin{bmatrix} a_2 \\ a_3 \end{bmatrix} \tag{1}$$

In the above model, (x, y) is a pixel's coordinates with respect to the center of the image, and (v_x, v_y) is the motion vector of the pixel. The three parameters are

$$a_1 = z_{xy},\ a_2 = f_1(p_x, z_{xy}),\ a_3 = f_2(p_y, z_{xy}) \tag{2}$$

where z_{xy} is the zoom factor of the moving camera and (p_x, p_y) is the pan vector.

Based on the 3-parameter model, all the candidate *motion seeds* are compared with the global motion to find out whether they belong to the global motion or not. Such process is performed as follows:

STEP 1. The 3 parameters in formula (1) are estimated based on potential *global motion seeds.* (Note that for the first iteration, all the seeds are regarded as potential *global motion seeds.*)

Suppose there are N potential *global motion seeds.* Let (v_x^k, v_y^k) be the motion vector of a seed $k(k = 0, 1, \cdots, N-1)$, whose coordinate is (s_x^k, s_y^k) with respect to the center of the frame. The parameters (a_1, a_2, a_3) are estimated using the following criteria:

$$(a_1, a_2, a_3) = \arg\min \sum_{k=0}^{N-1} [(v_x^k - a_1 s_x^k - a_2)^2 + (v_y^k - a_1 s_y^k - a_3)^2] \tag{3}$$

Differentiating (3) with respect to the parameters and setting the derivatives to zero, the following solution can be achieved as:

$$a_1 = \frac{N\Psi_1 - \Psi_2}{N\Psi_3 - \Psi_4} \tag{4}$$

$$a_2 = \Psi_3 \sum v_x^k - \Psi_1 \sum s_x^k + \frac{\Psi_5}{N} \sum s_y^k \tag{5}$$

$$a_3 = \Psi_3 \sum v_y^k - \Psi_1 \sum s_y^k - \frac{\Psi_5}{N} \sum s_x^k \tag{6}$$

where
$\Psi_1 = \sum v_x^k s_x^k + \sum v_y^k s_y^k, \Psi_2 = \sum v_x^k \sum s_x^k + \sum v_y^k \sum s_y^k,$
$\Psi_3 = \sum (s_x^k)^2 + \sum (s_y^k)^2, \Psi_4 = (\sum s_x^k)^2 + (\sum s_y^k)^2,$
$\Psi_5 = \sum v_y^k \sum s_x^k + \sum v_x^k \sum s_y^k.$

STEP 2. Based on the estimated parameters (a_1, a_2, a_3) by **STEP 1**, each potential *global motion seed* k is checked by

$$\Delta_k = (v_x^k - a_1 s_x^k - a_2)^2 + (v_y^k - a_1 s_y^k - a_3)^2 \tag{7}$$

If Δ_k lies within a predefined threshold, seed k will be maintained as a potential *global motion seed.* Otherwise, it will be regarded as a *local motion seed.*

STEP 3. Return to **STEP 1** and re-estimate (a_1, a_2, a_3) based on the remaining potential *global motion seeds.*

The detected *motion seeds* will be used as the initial state of motion layer expansion in the following section, where the local motion seeds will be expanded into motion layers corresponding to moving objects and global motion seeds to layers corresponding to background. Fig. 1 shows an example of detected motion seeds on *Hall-monitor.*

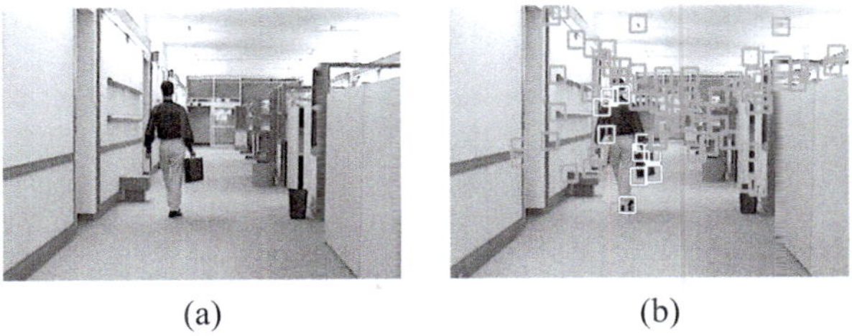

Fig. 1. Motion seed detection: the white squares illustrate the detected *global motion seeds*, and the black squares are the *local motion seeds*

3 Motion Layer Expansion

In this section, Graph cuts technique [9][10] is used to expand the motion layers from the detected motion seeds. Based on Graph cuts theory, motion layer expansion is regarded as an image-labelling process, where the labels correspond to motion vectors. During the labelling process, pixels belonging to different motion layers will have different labels.

3.1 Energy Function Definition

According to [8], many layer models have a weakness that each pixel is assigned to a layer independently of its neighbor pixels. As the result, the extracted layers always don't manifest the constraint that most physical objects are spatially coherent. In this paper, this spatial coherency constraint is formulated into an energy minimization problem, and then settled by graph cuts technique.

For the image-labelling process, the assigned labels should be consistent with the image data and be piecewise smooth, viz. they should remain unchanged or vary smoothly on the surface of an object, but change dramatically at object boundaries. Such problem can be described as: Finding a labelling f that assigns each pixel $p \in P$ a label $f_p \in L$, where f is both piecewise smooth and consistent with the observed data.In this paper, the above problem is formulated into an energy minimization problem with the energy function

$$E(f) = E_{data}(f) + E_{smooth}(f) \tag{8}$$

Here E_{smooth} evaluates the extent of how f is piecewise smooth, while E_{data} evaluates the disagreement between f and the observed data. The form of E_{data} is typically

$$\begin{aligned} E_{data}(f) &= \textstyle\sum_{p \in P} D_p(f_p) \\ D_p(f_p) &= |I_{current}(p) - I_{previous}(q)| \end{aligned} \tag{9}$$

where $I_{current}(p)$ is the intensity of p in the current frame. And q is the corresponding pixel of p in the next frame. The E_{smooth} is defined as

$$\begin{aligned} E_{smooth}(f) &= \textstyle\sum_{\{p,q\} \in P} V_{p,q}(f_p, f_q) \\ V_{p,q}(f_p, f_q) &= \begin{cases} 0 & if\ f_p = f_q \\ const & if\ f_p \neq f_q \end{cases} \end{aligned} \tag{10}$$

where N is the set of interacting pairs of pixels. *const* is the energy evaluating the smoothness of adjacent labels.

3.2 Motion Layer Expansion

Graph cuts technique [9] is used to minimize the energy defined in (8). The construction of the graph is the same as that used in [10]. This section illustrates how to achieve motion layers from *motion seeds* using such method.

First, some of the graph nodes are labelled initially according to the different type of the *motion seeds*. All nodes corresponding to the *global motion seeds* will be assigned a uniform label l_0. Nodes corresponding to *local motion seeds* will be labelled independently: For to a *local motion seeds* k, with coordinates (s_x^k, s_y^k) and motion vector (v_x^k, v_y^k), its graph node will be assigned an special label l_k. Based on the labelled graph, the nodes assigned l_0 will be regarded as belonging to background, and nodes assigned other labels will be regarded as belonging to moving objects, whose motion is described by (v_x^k, v_y^k). Then, the process of motion layer expansion from *motion seeds* can be summarized as:

STEP 1. Start with initial labelling f, where only the nodes corresponding to *motion seeds* are labelled;
STEP 2. Compute the $E(f)$ of (8);
STEP 3. Set $success := 0$;
STEP 4. For each label $l \in L$:
4.1. Find $\hat{f} = \arg\min E(f^c)$ using Graph cuts technique;
4.2. If $E(\hat{f}) < E(f)$, set $f := \hat{f}$ and $success := 1$;
STEP 5. If $success = 1$ goto **STEP 2**; else, goto **STEP 6**;
STEP 6. Output the final f.

In the final f, each node in the graph is assigned a label corresponding to its motion, based on what motion layers are naturally extracted. Pixels who were assigned label l_0 are segmented as background. Then, the rest pixels with other labels can be regarded as the moving objects. The motion layers extracted for Fig. 1 are shown in Fig. 2. it can be seen that the spatial continuity of layers is well preserved by graph cuts technique. According to Fig. 2, it is clear that

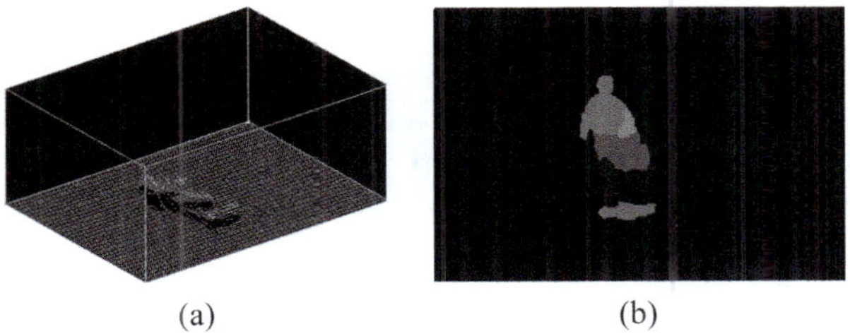

Fig. 2. Motion layers: (a) shows the extracted motion layers in 3-D space, where the horizontal dimensions correspond to (x, y) coordinates in image plane and vertical dimension v correspond to $v = (v_x^2 + v_y^2)^{1/2}$. The extracted layers can also be described by velocity map as shown in (b), where a higher velocity v has a higher intensity.

4 Motion Boundary Refinement

When the motion layers are extracted, the objects can be roughly identified by their motion, but the extracted motion layers may still be inaccurate along the motion boundaries. This section will combine edge information to refine the motion boundaries.

In this paper, morphological watershed transform [11] is used to detect intensity edges, which can produce an image partition with regions enclosed by one-pixel-wide contours. To deal with the over-segmentation problem of watershed segmentation, a region merging method presented in [12] is used to post-process the image.

Suppose the current image is partitioned into n regions $\Re = \{R_1, R_2, \cdots, R_n\}$, and every region R_i is enclosed by a one-pixel-wide edge $\overline{E_i}$. Based on the segmented edge map, following information are calculated: $||R_i||$, area of region R_i; $||\overline{E_i}||$, length of edge $\overline{E_i}$. On the other hand, velocity map provides us an initial Object Mask (OM), regions not labeled by l_0, with rough boundaries. Fig. 3(a) shows the initial OM by white regions. Then, considering the edge map together with the initial OM, object segmentation is regarded as a region classification process, in which all the regions will be classified into two groups: *object regions* and *background regions*. The classification is based on

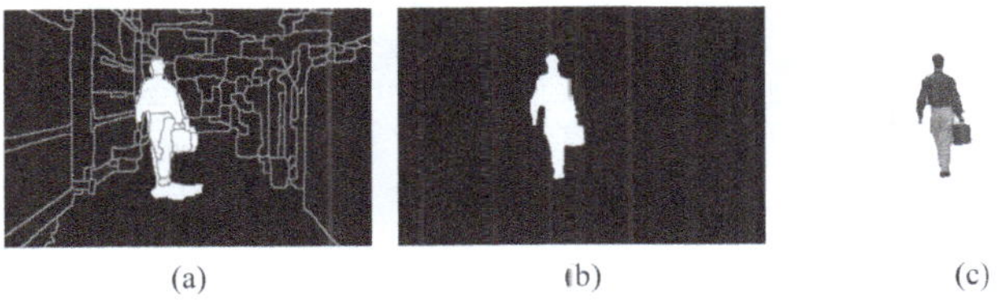

Fig. 3. Moving object extraction: (a) shows the initial OM and the edge map; (b) is the refined OM; the extracted object is shown in (c)

the motion analysis from both the regions and the edges. Two criteria are defined: $RP_i = ||R_i^*||/||R_i||$, where$R_i^* = \{p|p \in OM, p \in R_i\}$; $EP_i = ||\overline{E_i^*}||/||\overline{E_i}||$, where$\overline{E_i^*} = \{p|p \in OM, p \in \overline{E_i}\}$. Considering the possible inaccuracy of initial OM at boundaries, regions are classified as:

A region R_i is determined to be a object region, if, and only if, $RP_i > threshold_R$ & $EP_i > threshold_E$.

In our experiments, the thresholds are simply selected as $threshold_R = threshold_E = 0.7$. Based on the above criterion, all the regions in the image are analyzed and classified. Finally, the refined OM with accurate boundaries is used to extract the moving object. Fig. 3 shows an example of moving object extraction. From the segmentation result in Fig. 3(c), we can see the boundaries are very close to the real edge of moving object.

5 Experiments

The proposed method is tested on a number of video sequences. In this section, experimental results on *Mom-daughter* and *Table-tennis* are presented.

To further evaluate the performance of the proposed method we manually extract the objects in the video sequences as the ground truth or actual objects, and we evaluate the results obtained by the proposed method with the ground truth as follows:

$$SA = \frac{P_e}{P_a} \tag{11}$$

where SA is the spatial accuracy of extracted object. p_e is the number of error pixels belonging to the grey regions in Fig. 6(b). p_a is the total number of actual object pixels belonging to the grey region in Fig. 6(a).

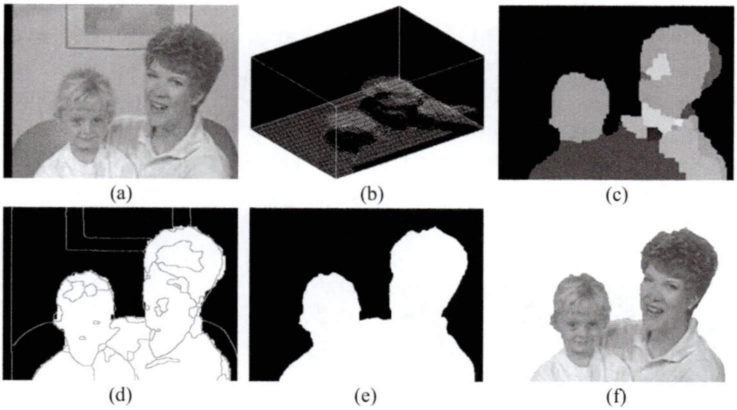

Fig. 4. Experiment on *Mom-daughter*: (a) is the original image; (b) gives the extracted motion layers (because the motion of a human body is non-rigid, the motion layers are fluctuant correspondingly, which can also be seen in velocity map (c)); By combining the edge information in (d) with the initial OM, the final results are shown in (e) and (f)

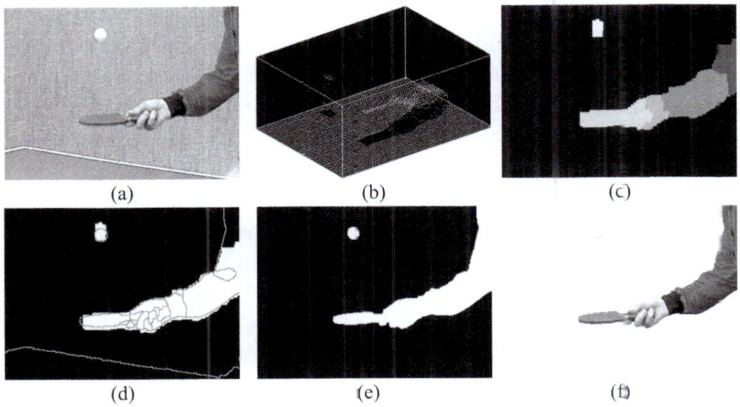

Fig. 5. Experiment on *Table-tennis*

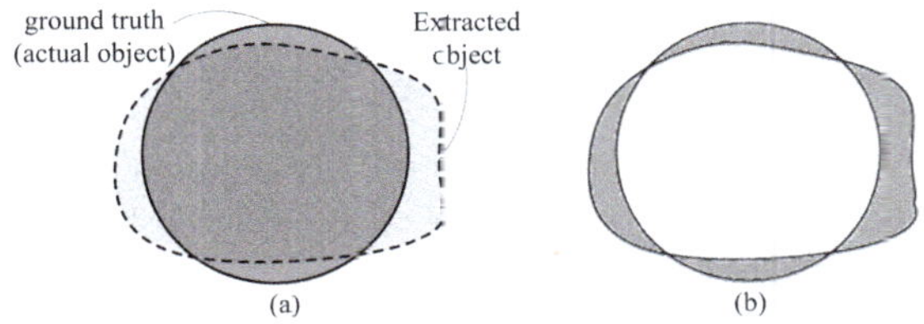

Fig. 6. Spatial accuracy definition

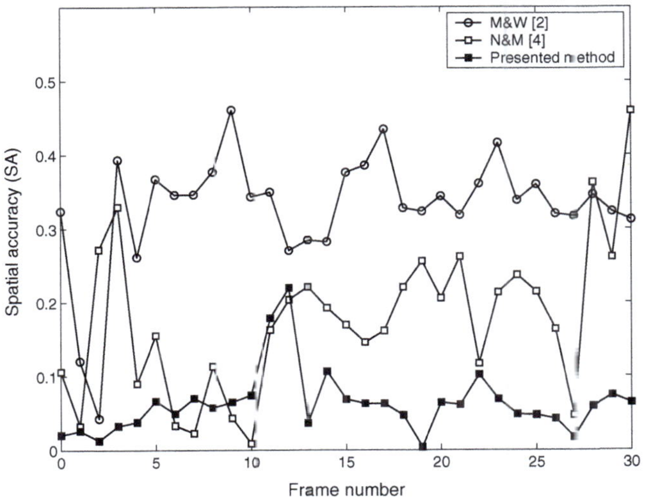

Fig. 7. Evaluation results

Using such objective performance evaluation criteria, we compare the proposed method with the techniques in [2] and [4]. Fig. 7 shows the evaluation results using Table-tennis sequence. From Fig. 7, we can see that, in many cases, the presented method can produce more accurate segmentation results than the other two. This partly comes from that graph cuts technique can preserve spatial coherency in motion layers, even when there is no manifest texture information. Besides, watershed segmentation together with WCA region merging algorithm also provide satisfying edge information for the extraction of moving objects.

One remaining problem for the proposed method is that only the motion cue between two frames is used to extract motion layer, which is not enough to extract meaningful objects in many cases. We will intend to embed tracking technique into the segmentation system in our future work. Another problem lies in the stage of motion boundary refinement, where the accuracy of object boundaries depends on the edge information too much. If edge map fails to describe the actual boundary information precisely, the extracted object will lose its accuracy.

6 Conclusion

This paper presented an approach to automatically segment moving objects from image sequences with accurate boundaries. The contribution of the presented method can be summarized as follows: Motion seed detection, which finds out how many motions are there in the video and where they are, provides a reasonable initial state for Motion layer expansion. Then during the expansion process, energy function and graph cuts technique preserve the spatial coherency of motion layers. Such layers, combined with edge information, produce the segmented moving objects with accurate boundaries. Several experimental results are shown in the paper, which illustrate the promising performance of the proposed method.

Acknowledgements

This research is sponsored by France Telecom R&D, and the National Natural Science Foundation of China (Grant No. 60135020, 60475010 and 60121302).

References

1. Arch, T., Kaup, A.: Statistical model-based change detection in moving video. Signal Processing **31** (1993) 165–180
2. Mech, R., Wollborn, M.: A noise robust method for 2d shape estimation of moving objects in video sequences considering a moving camera. Signal Processing **66** (1998) 203–217
3. Meier, T., Ngan, K.: Automatic segmentation of movings for video object plane generation. IEEE Trans. on Circuits & Systems for Video Technology **8** (2003) 525–538

4. Nicolescu, M., Medioni, G.: Motion segmentation with accurate boundaries-a tensor voting approach. Proceedings of the IEEE Computer Society Conference on Computer Vision and Pattern Recognition **1** (2003) 382–389
5. Wang, J., Adelson, E.: Layered representation for motion analysis. Proceedings of the IEEE Computer Society Conference on Computer Vision and Pattern Recognition (1993)
6. Darrell, T., Pentland, A.: Cooperative robust estimation using layers of support. IEEE Trans. on Pattern Analysis and Machine Intelligence **17** (1995) 474–487
7. Ayer, S., Sawhney, H.: Layered representation of motion video using robust maximum-likelihood estimation of mixture models and mdl encoding. 5th International Conference on Computer Vision (1995)
8. Jepson, A., Fleet, D., Black, M.: A layered motion representation with occlusion and compact spatial support. 7th European Conference on Computer Vision **1** (2002) 692–706
9. Boykov, Y., Kolmogorov, V.: An experimental comparison of min-cut/max-flow algorithms for energy minimization in vision. IEEE Trans. on Pattern Analysis and Machine Intelligence **26** (2004) 1124–1137
10. Wang, J., Lu, H., Liu, Q.: Moving object segmentation using graph cuts. IEEE Int'l Conf. on Signal Processing **1** (2004) 777–780
11. Vincent, L., Soille, P.: Watersheds in digital spaces: An efficient algorithm based on immersion simulations. IEEE Trans. on Pattern Analysis and Machine Intelligence **13** (1991) 583–598
12. Wang, J., Lu, H., Liu, Q.: A fast region merging algorithm for watershed segmentation. IEEE Int'l Conf. on Signal Processing **1** (2004) 781–784

A Bottom Up Algebraic Approach to Motion Segmentation

Dheeraj Singaraju and René Vidal

Center for Imaging Science, Johns Hopkins University,
301 Clark Hall, 3400 N. Charles St., Baltimore, MD, 21218, USA
{dheeraj, rvidal}@cis.jhu.edu
http://www.vision.jhu.edu

Abstract. We present a bottom up algebraic approach for segmenting multiple 2D motion models directly from the partial derivatives of an image sequence. Our method fits a polynomial called the multibody brightness constancy constraint (MBCC) to a window around each pixel of the scene and obtains a local motion model from the derivatives of the MBCC. These local models are then clustered to obtain the parameters of the motion models for the entire scene. Motion segmentation is obtained by assigning to each pixel the dominant motion model in a window around it. Our approach requires no initialization, can handle multiple motions in a window (thus dealing with the aperture problem) and automatically incorporates spatial regularization. Therefore, it naturally combines the advantages of both local and global approaches to motion segmentation. Experiments on real data compare our method with previous local and global approaches.

1 Introduction

Motion segmentation is a fundamental problem in many applications in computer vision, such as traffic surveillance, recognition of human gaits, etc. This has motivated the recent development of various local and global approaches to motion segmentation.

Local methods such as Wang and Adelson [1] divide the image in small patches and estimate an affine motion model for each patch. The parameters of the affine models are then clustered using the K-means algorithm and the regions of support of each motion model are computed by comparing the optical flow at each pixel with that generated by the "clustered" affine motion models. The drawback of such local approaches is that they are based on a local computation of 2-D motion, which is subject to the aperture problem and to the estimation of a single model across motion boundaries.

Global methods deal with such problems by fitting a mixture of motion models to the entire scene. [2] fits a mixture of parametric models by minimizing a Mumford-Shah-like cost functional. [3, 4, 5, 6, 7, 8] fit a mixture of probabilistic models iteratively using the Expectation Maximization algorithm (EM). The drawback of such iterative approaches is that they are very sensitive to correct initialization and are computationally expensive.

To overcome these difficulties, more recent work [9, 10, 11, 12] proposes to solve the problem by globally fitting a polynomial to all the image measurements and then factorizing this polynomial to obtain the parameters of each 2-D motion model. These algebraic approaches do not require initialization, can deal with multiple motion models across motion boundaries and do not suffer from the aperture problem. However,

P.J. Narayanan et al. (Eds.): ACCV 2006, LNCS 3851, pp. 286–296, 2006.

these algebraic techniques are sensitive to outliers in the data and fail to incorporate spatial regularization, hence one needs to resort to some ad-hoc smoothing scheme for improving the segmentation results.

1.1 Paper Contributions

In this paper, we present a bottom up approach to direct motion segmentation, that integrates the advantages of the algebraic method of [12], and the non-algebraic method of [1], and at the same time reduces the effect of their individual drawbacks.

Our approach proceeds as follows. We first consider a window around each pixel of the scene and fit a polynomial called the multibody brightness constancy constraint (MBCC) [12] to the image measurements of that window. By exploiting the properties of the MBCC, we can find the parameters of the multiple motion models describing the motion of that window. After choosing a dominant local motion model for each window in the scene, we cluster these models using K-means to obtain the parameters describing the motion of the entire scene [1]. Given such global models, we segment the scene by allotting to every pixel the dominant global motion model in a window around it.

This new approach to motion segmentation offers various important advantages.

1. With respect to local methods, our approach can handle more than one motion model per window, hence it is less subject to the aperture problem or to the estimation of a single motion model across motion boundaries.
2. With respect to global iterative methods, our approach has the advantage of not requiring initialization.
3. With respect to global algebraic methods, our approach implicitly incorporates spatial regularization by assigning to a pixel the dominant motion model in a window around it. This also allows our method to deal with a moderate level of outliers.

2 Problem Statement

Consider a motion sequence taken by a moving camera observing an *unknown* number of independently and rigidly moving objects. Assume that each one of the surfaces in the scene is Lambertian, so that the optical flow $\boldsymbol{u}(\boldsymbol{x}) = [\mathrm{u}, \mathrm{v}, 1]^\top \in \mathbb{P}^2$ of pixel $\boldsymbol{x} = [x, y, 1]^\top \in \mathbb{P}^2$ is related to the spatial-temporal image derivatives at pixel $\boldsymbol{x}$, $\boldsymbol{y}(\boldsymbol{x}) = [I_x, I_y, I_t]^\top \in \mathbb{R}^3$, by the well-known *brightness constancy constraint* (BCC)

$$\boldsymbol{y}^\top \boldsymbol{u} = I_x \mathrm{u} + I_y \mathrm{v} + I_t = 0. \tag{1}$$

We assume that the optical flow in the scene is generated by n_t 2-D translational motion models $\{\boldsymbol{u}_i \in \mathbb{P}^2\}_{i=1}^{n_t}$ or by n_a 2-D affine motion models $\{A_i \in \mathbb{R}^{3\times 3}\}_{i=1}^{n_a}$

$$\boldsymbol{u} = \boldsymbol{u}_i \quad i = 1, \ldots n_t \qquad \text{or} \qquad \boldsymbol{u} = A_i \boldsymbol{x} = \begin{bmatrix} \boldsymbol{a}_{i1}^\top \\ \boldsymbol{a}_{i2}^\top \\ 0, 0, 1 \end{bmatrix} \boldsymbol{x} \quad i = 1, \ldots, n_a, \tag{2}$$

respectively. Under these models, the BCC (1) reduces to

$$\boldsymbol{y}^\top \boldsymbol{u}_i = 0 \qquad \text{and} \qquad \boldsymbol{y}^\top A_i \boldsymbol{x} = 0 \tag{3}$$

for the 2-D translational and 2-D affine motion models, respectively.

In this paper, we consider the following problem.

Problem 1 (Direct 2-D motion segmentation). Given the spatial-temporal derivatives $\{(I_{xj}, I_{yj}, I_{tj}))\}_{j=1}^N$ *of a motion sequence generated by a known number of* $n = n_t$ *translational or* $n = n_a$ *affine motion models, estimate the optical flow* $\boldsymbol{u}(\boldsymbol{x})$*, the motion model at each pixel* $\{\boldsymbol{x}_j\}_{j=1}^N$ *and the segmentation of the image measurements, without knowing which measurements correspond to which motion model.*

3 Global Algebraic Motion Segmentation from the Multibody Brightness Constancy Constraint

In this section, we review the global algebraic approach to direct motion segmentation introduced in [12], which is based on a generalization of the BCC to multiple motions.

Let $(\boldsymbol{x}, \boldsymbol{y})$ be an image measurement associated with any of the motion models. According to the BCC (1) there exists a 2-D motion model, say the kth model, whose optical flow $\boldsymbol{u}_k(\boldsymbol{x})$ satisfies $\boldsymbol{y}^\top \boldsymbol{u}_k(\boldsymbol{x}) = 0$. Therefore, the following *multibody brightness constancy constraint* (MBCC) must be satisfied by every pixel in the image

$$\text{MBCC}(\boldsymbol{x}, \boldsymbol{y}) = \prod_{i=1}^{n} (\boldsymbol{y}^\top \boldsymbol{u}_i(\boldsymbol{x})) = 0. \tag{4}$$

From equation (4) we can see that in the purely translational case, the MBCC is a homogeneous polynomial of degree n_t which can be written as a linear combination of the monomials $y_1^{l_1} y_2^{l_2} y_3^{l_3}$ with coefficients $\mathcal{U}_{l_1,l_2,l_3}$. By stacking all the monomials in a vector $\nu_{n_t}(\boldsymbol{y}) \in \mathbb{R}^{M_{n_t}}$ and the coefficients in a *multibody optical flow* vector $\mathcal{U} \in \mathbb{R}^{M_{n_t}}$, where $M_{n_t} = \frac{(n_t+1)(n_t+2)}{2}$, we can express the MBCC as

$$MBCC(\boldsymbol{x}, \boldsymbol{y}) = \nu_{n_t}(\boldsymbol{y})^\top \mathcal{U} = \prod_{i=1}^{n_t} (\boldsymbol{y}^\top \boldsymbol{u}_i). \tag{5}$$

The vector $\nu_{n_t}(\boldsymbol{y}) \in \mathbb{R}^{M_{n_t}}$ is known as the Veronese map of $\boldsymbol{y}$ of degree n_t.

Similarly, if the entire scene can be modeled by affine motion models only, the MBCC is a bi-homogeneous polynomial of degree n_a in $(\boldsymbol{x}, \boldsymbol{y})$. The coefficients of this polynomial can be stacked into a *multibody affine matrix* $\mathcal{A} \in \mathbb{R}^{M_{n_a} \times M_{n_a}}$, so that the MBCC can be written as

$$MBCC(\boldsymbol{x}, \boldsymbol{y}) = \nu_{n_a}(\boldsymbol{y})^\top \mathcal{A} \nu_{n_a}(\boldsymbol{x}) = \prod_{j=1}^{n_a} (\boldsymbol{y}^\top A_j \boldsymbol{x}). \tag{6}$$

3.1 Computing the Multibody Motion Model

As the MBCC holds at every image measurement $\{(\boldsymbol{x}_j, \boldsymbol{y}_j)\}_{j=1}^N$, we can compute the multibody motion model $\mathcal{M} = \mathcal{U}$ or $\mathcal{A}$ by solving the linear system

$$L_n \boldsymbol{m} = 0, \tag{7}$$

where $\boldsymbol{m}$ is the stack of the columns of $\mathcal{M}$. In the case of translational models, the jth row of $L_{n_t} \in \mathbb{R}^{N \times M_{n_t}}$ is given by $\nu_{n_t}(\boldsymbol{y}_j)^\top$. In the case of affine models, the jth row of $L_{n_a} \in \mathbb{R}^{N \times (M_{n_a}^2 - Z_{n_a})}$ is given by a subset of the entries of $(\nu_{n_a}(\boldsymbol{y}_j) \otimes \nu_{n_a}(\boldsymbol{x}_j))^\top$. The dimension of L_{n_a} is $N \times (M_{n_a}^2 - Z_{n_a})$ rather than $N \times M_{n_a}^2$, because Z_{n_a} elements of $\mathcal{A}$ are zero, as the $(3,1)$ and $(3,2)$ elements of every affine motion model $\{A_i\}_{i=1}^{n_a}$ are zero. The enforcement of this constraint leads to a more robust calculation of $\mathcal{A}$.

With noisy data the equation $\text{MBCC}(\boldsymbol{x}, \boldsymbol{y}) = 0$, becomes $\text{MBCC}(\boldsymbol{x}, \boldsymbol{y}) \approx 0$. Nevertheless, since the MBCC is linear in the multibody motion parameters $\mathcal{U}$ or $\mathcal{A}$, we can solve a linear inhomogeneous system by enforcing the last entry of $\boldsymbol{m}$ to be 1. It is easy to prove, that when $n_t = 1$ or $n_a = 1$, this method of solving the linear system, reduces to the standard local approaches of fitting a single motion model to a given window.

3.2 Motion Segmentation Using the MBCC

In this subsection, we demonstrate how one can calculate the parameters of the multiple motion models associated with the entire scene from its MBCC.

A very important and powerful property of the MBCC is that one can compute the optical flow $\boldsymbol{u}(\boldsymbol{x})$ at each pixel in closed form, without knowing which motion model is associated with each pixel. Since each pixel $\boldsymbol{x}$ is associated with one of the n motion models, there is a $k = 1, \ldots, n$ such that $\boldsymbol{y}^\top \boldsymbol{u}_k(\boldsymbol{x}) = 0$, so $\prod_{\ell \neq i}(\boldsymbol{y}^\top \boldsymbol{u}_\ell(\boldsymbol{x})) = 0$ for all $i \neq k$. Therefore, the optical flow at a pixel obeying model k can be obtained as

$$\frac{\partial \text{MBCC}(\boldsymbol{x}, \boldsymbol{y})}{\partial \boldsymbol{y}} = \sum_{i=1}^{n} \boldsymbol{u}_i(\boldsymbol{x}) \prod_{\ell \neq i} (\boldsymbol{y}^\top \boldsymbol{u}_\ell(\boldsymbol{x})) \sim \boldsymbol{u}_k(\boldsymbol{x}). \tag{8}$$

For 2-D translational motions, the motion model is the optical flow at each pixel. Hence, we can take the optical flow at all the pixels in the scene and obtain the n_t different values $\{\boldsymbol{u}_i\}_{i=1}^{n_t}$ using any clustering algorithm in $\mathbb{R}^2$. Alternatively, one can choose n_t pixels $\{\boldsymbol{x}_i\}_{i=1}^{n_t}$ with reliable optical flow and then obtain $\boldsymbol{u}_i = \boldsymbol{u}(\boldsymbol{x}_i)$. As shown in [12], under the assumption of zero-mean Gaussian noise in $\boldsymbol{y}$ with covariance $\Lambda \in \mathbb{R}^{3\times 3}$, one can choose a measurement $(\boldsymbol{x}_{n_t}, \boldsymbol{y}_{n_t})$ that minimizes

$$d_{n_t}^2(\boldsymbol{x}, \boldsymbol{y}) = \frac{|\text{MBCC}(\boldsymbol{x}, \boldsymbol{y})|^2}{\|\Lambda \frac{\partial \text{MBCC}(\boldsymbol{x}, \boldsymbol{y})}{\partial \boldsymbol{y}}\|^2}. \tag{9}$$

The remaining measurements $(\boldsymbol{x}_{i-1}, \boldsymbol{y}_{i-1})$ for $i = n_t, n_t - 1, \ldots, 2$ are chosen as the ones that minimize

$$d_{i-1}^2(\boldsymbol{x}, \boldsymbol{y}) = \frac{d_i^2(\boldsymbol{x}, \boldsymbol{y})}{\frac{|\boldsymbol{y}^\top \boldsymbol{u}_i|^2}{\|\Lambda \boldsymbol{u}_i\|^2}}. \tag{10}$$

Notice that in choosing the points there is no optimization involved. We just evaluate the distance functions d_i at each point and choose the one giving the minimum distance.

In the case of 2-D affine motion models, one can obtain the affine motion model associated with an image measurement $(\boldsymbol{x}, \boldsymbol{y})$ from the cross products of the derivatives of the MBCC. More specifically, note that if $(\boldsymbol{x}, \boldsymbol{y})$ comes from the ith motion model, i.e. if $\boldsymbol{y}^\top A_i \boldsymbol{x} = 0$, then

$$\frac{\partial \text{MBCC}(\boldsymbol{x}, \boldsymbol{y})}{\partial \boldsymbol{x}} \sim \boldsymbol{y}^\top A_i. \tag{11}$$

Thus, the partials of the MBCC with respect to $\boldsymbol{x}$ give linear combinations of the rows of the affine model at $\boldsymbol{x}$. Now, since the optical flow $\boldsymbol{u} = [\text{u}, \text{v}, 1]^\top$ at pixel $\boldsymbol{x}$ is known, we can evaluate the partials of the MBCC at $(\boldsymbol{x}, \boldsymbol{y}_1)$, with $\boldsymbol{y}_1 = [1, 0, -\text{u}]^\top$, and $(\boldsymbol{x}, \boldsymbol{y}_2)$, with $\boldsymbol{y}_2 = [0, 1, -\text{v}]^\top$, to obtain the following linear combination of the rows of A_i

$$\boldsymbol{g}_{i1} \sim \boldsymbol{a}_{i1} - \text{u}e_3 \quad \text{and} \quad \boldsymbol{g}_{i2} \sim \boldsymbol{a}_{i2} - \text{v}e_3, \tag{12}$$

where e_i is given by the ith column of the 3×3 identity matrix. Let $\boldsymbol{b}_{i1} = \boldsymbol{g}_{i1} \times e_3 \sim \boldsymbol{a}_{i1} \times e_3$ and $\boldsymbol{b}_{i2} = \boldsymbol{g}_{i2} \times e_3 \sim \boldsymbol{a}_{i2} \times e_3$. Although the pairs $(\boldsymbol{b}_{i1}, e_1)$ and $(\boldsymbol{b}_{i2}, e_2)$ are not actual image measurements, they satisfy $e_1^\top A_i \boldsymbol{b}_{i1} = \boldsymbol{a}_{i1}^\top \boldsymbol{b}_{i1} = 0$ and $e_2^\top A_i \boldsymbol{b}_{i2} = \boldsymbol{a}_{i2}^\top \boldsymbol{b}_{i2} = 0$. Therefore, we can immediately compute the rows of A_i up to scale factors λ_{i1} and λ_{i2} as

$$\tilde{\boldsymbol{a}}_{i1}^\top = \lambda_{i1}^{-1} \boldsymbol{a}_{i1}^\top = \left. \frac{\partial \text{MBCC}(\boldsymbol{x}, \boldsymbol{y})}{\partial \boldsymbol{x}} \right|_{(\boldsymbol{b}_{i1}, e_1)}, \tilde{\boldsymbol{a}}_{i2}^\top = \lambda_{i2}^{-1} \boldsymbol{a}_{i2}^\top = \left. \frac{\partial \text{MBCC}(\boldsymbol{x}, \boldsymbol{y})}{\partial \boldsymbol{x}} \right|_{(\boldsymbol{b}_{i2}, e_2)}. \tag{13}$$

Finally, from the optical flow equations $\boldsymbol{u} = A_i \boldsymbol{x}$ we have that $\text{u} = \lambda_{i1} \tilde{\boldsymbol{a}}_{i1}^\top \boldsymbol{x}$ and $\text{v} = \lambda_{i2} \tilde{\boldsymbol{a}}_{i2}^\top \boldsymbol{x}$, hence the unknown scales are automatically given by

$$\lambda_{i1} = \frac{\text{u}}{\tilde{\boldsymbol{a}}_{i1}^\top \boldsymbol{x}} \quad \text{and} \quad \lambda_{i2} = \frac{\text{v}}{\tilde{\boldsymbol{a}}_{i2}^\top \boldsymbol{x}}. \tag{14}$$

In order to obtain the n_a different affine matrices, we only need to apply the method to n_a pixels corresponding to each one of the n_a models. We can automatically choose the n_a pixels at which to perform the computation using the same methodology proposed for 2-D translational motions, i.e. by choosing points that minimize (9) and a modification of (10). For the 2-D affine models, (10) is modified as

$$d_{i-1}^2(\boldsymbol{x}, \boldsymbol{y}) = \frac{d_i^2(\boldsymbol{x}, \boldsymbol{y})}{\frac{|\boldsymbol{y}^\top A_i \boldsymbol{x}|^2}{\|\Lambda(A_i \boldsymbol{x})\|^2}}. \tag{15}$$

Once the n models have been computed, the scene is segmented using the following scheme: assign $(\boldsymbol{x}_j, \boldsymbol{y}_j)$ to group i if

$$i = \arg \min_{\ell=1,\ldots,n} \frac{|\boldsymbol{y}_j^\top \boldsymbol{u}_\ell|^2}{\|\Lambda \boldsymbol{u}_\ell\|^2} \quad \text{for the translational case,} \tag{16}$$

$$i = \arg \min_{\ell=1,\ldots,n} \frac{|\boldsymbol{y}_j^\top A_\ell \boldsymbol{x}_j|^2}{\|\Lambda(A_\ell \boldsymbol{x}_j)\|^2} \quad \text{for the affine case.} \tag{17}$$

4 A Bottom Up Approach to Direct 2-D Motion Segmentation

The local method of [1] considers a window around every pixel, fits a single motion model to each window, and then clusters the locally estimated motion models. As earlier pointed out, this method can suffer from the aperture problem and hence, one would be required to take a large window to avoid it. However, using a large window can lead to the estimation of a single motion model across motion boundaries. The global method of [12] helps in overcoming these two problems by globally fitting a MBCC to the entire scene. However, this purely algebraic method does not incorporate spatial regularization, because the segmentation is point-based rather than patch-based, as suggested by equations (16) and (17). This results in noisy segmentations, which need to be post-processed using ad-hoc techniques for spatial smoothing. In addition, the method does not deal with outliers in the image measurements.

In this section, we propose a bottom up approach to motion segmentation which integrates the local and algebraic approaches by exploiting their individual advantages. We propose to fit multiple motion models to a possibly large window around each pixel using the algebraic method, to then cluster these locally estimated models. The details of our approach are given in the following subsections.

4.1 Local Computation of Multiple Motion Models

We consider a window $\mathcal{W}(\boldsymbol{x})$ around a pixel $\boldsymbol{x}$ and fit a MBCC to the measurements in that window. In doing so, we use a variable number of models $n = 1, \ldots, n_{\max}$, where $n_{\max}$ is the maximum number of motion models in the scene. For every n, we use the method described in Section 3 to calculate n motion models $M_n^1 \ldots M_n^n$ for that window. As n varies, this gives a total of $\frac{n_{\max}(n_{\max}+1)}{2}$ motion models for every window. From these candidate local models, we choose the *dominant local motion model* for that window as the one that minimizes the sum of the squares of the brightness constancy constraint evaluated at every pixel in the window. That is, we assign to $\boldsymbol{x}_j$ the model

$$M(\boldsymbol{x}_j) = \min_{\substack{n=1\ldots n_{\max} \\ l=1\ldots n}} \{M_n^l : \sum_{\boldsymbol{x}_k \in \mathcal{W}(\boldsymbol{x}_j)} (\boldsymbol{y}_k^\top \boldsymbol{u}_n^l(\boldsymbol{x}_k))^2\}, \tag{18}$$

where $\boldsymbol{u}_n^l(\boldsymbol{x}_k)$ is the optical flow evaluated at $\boldsymbol{x}_k$ according to M_n^l, i.e. the lth motion model estimated assuming n motion models in the window. This is equivalent to assigning to a window the motion model that gives the least residual with respect to the BCC for that window. By applying this procedure to all pixels in the image, $\{\boldsymbol{x}_j\}_{j=1}^N$, we estimate a collection of N local motion models for the entire scene.

Note that, in comparison with the local approach of [1], our method can account for more than one motion model in a window. In addition, the structure of the MBCC lets us choose the size of the window as large as necessary without having to worry about the motion boundary problem. In fact [12] deals with the case where the window size is the size of the entire image and hence fits the motion models to the entire scene.

An additional feature of our method is that equation (18) can also be used to estimate the number of motion models in a window. However, an accurate estimation of the number of models is not critical, as long as $n_{\max}$ is larger than or equal to the true number of models in the window. This is because if the true number of motion models is over estimated, then the estimated MBCC in (4) has additional factors apart from the true factors. Once can show that these additional factors do not affect the calculations described in equations (8) - (15). We omit the details of the proof due to space limitations.

4.2 Clustering the Model Parameters

Ideally, pixels corresponding to the same motion should have the same motion parameters. However, due to noise and outliers, the locally estimated motion model parameters may not be the same for pixels corresponding to the same motion.

In order to obtain a set of reliable motion model parameters that define the motion of the entire scene, we apply the K-means algorithm in the space of model parameters. Note that if we were to apply [12] to the entire scene followed by the K-means algorithm, we would have had problems due to outliers. However, in our approach, even for windows centered at outliers, we choose the pixels with most reliable motion model parameters in the window, thus providing better estimates of the local motion model at a pixel than [12]. We also provide better estimates than [1] that evaluates just one motion model per pixel, because we can evaluate multiple motion models at motion boundaries. Though we finally consider only one motion model per pixel on motion boundaries also, we claim that this motion model is more accurate than the motion model given by [1], because we choose the best among multiple local models.

4.3 Segmentation of the Motion Models

Once the motion model parameters describing the motion of the entire scene are calculated, it remains to be decided as to how one should segment the scene. While [12] performs well to a great extent, it does not incorporate spatial regularization. As a result the segmentation has a lot of holes and one has to use some ad-hoc method for smoothing the results.

We would like to design a segmentation scheme which incorporates spatial regularization, because it is expected that points that are spatially near by will obey the same motion model. Hence, we consider a window $\mathcal{W}(\boldsymbol{x}_j)$ around every pixel $\{\boldsymbol{x}_j\}_{j=1}^N$ and assign to it the *dominant global motion model* for that window, that is, the global model that minimizes the residual with respect to the BCC for the entire window. In the case of translational models, this can be expressed mathematically as follows

$$\boldsymbol{u}(\boldsymbol{x}_j) = \min_{i=1\ldots n_t} \{\boldsymbol{u}_i : \sum_{\boldsymbol{x}_k \in \mathcal{W}(\boldsymbol{x}_j)} (\boldsymbol{y}_k^\top \boldsymbol{u}_i)^2\}. \tag{19}$$

In the case of affine motion models, the segmentation of the scene is obtained as follows

$$A(\boldsymbol{x}_j, \boldsymbol{y}_j) = \min_{i=1\ldots n_a} \{A_i : \sum_{\boldsymbol{x}_k \in \mathcal{W}(\boldsymbol{x}_j)} (\boldsymbol{y}_k^\top A_i \boldsymbol{x}_k)^2\}. \tag{20}$$

5 Results

In this section, we test our algorithm on real world data and compare its performance with that of the algorithms in [1] and [12]. For all methods, we model the scene as a mixture of 2-D translational motion models. For the method in [12], we post process the segmentation results by spatially smoothing them with a median filter in a window of size 10×10.

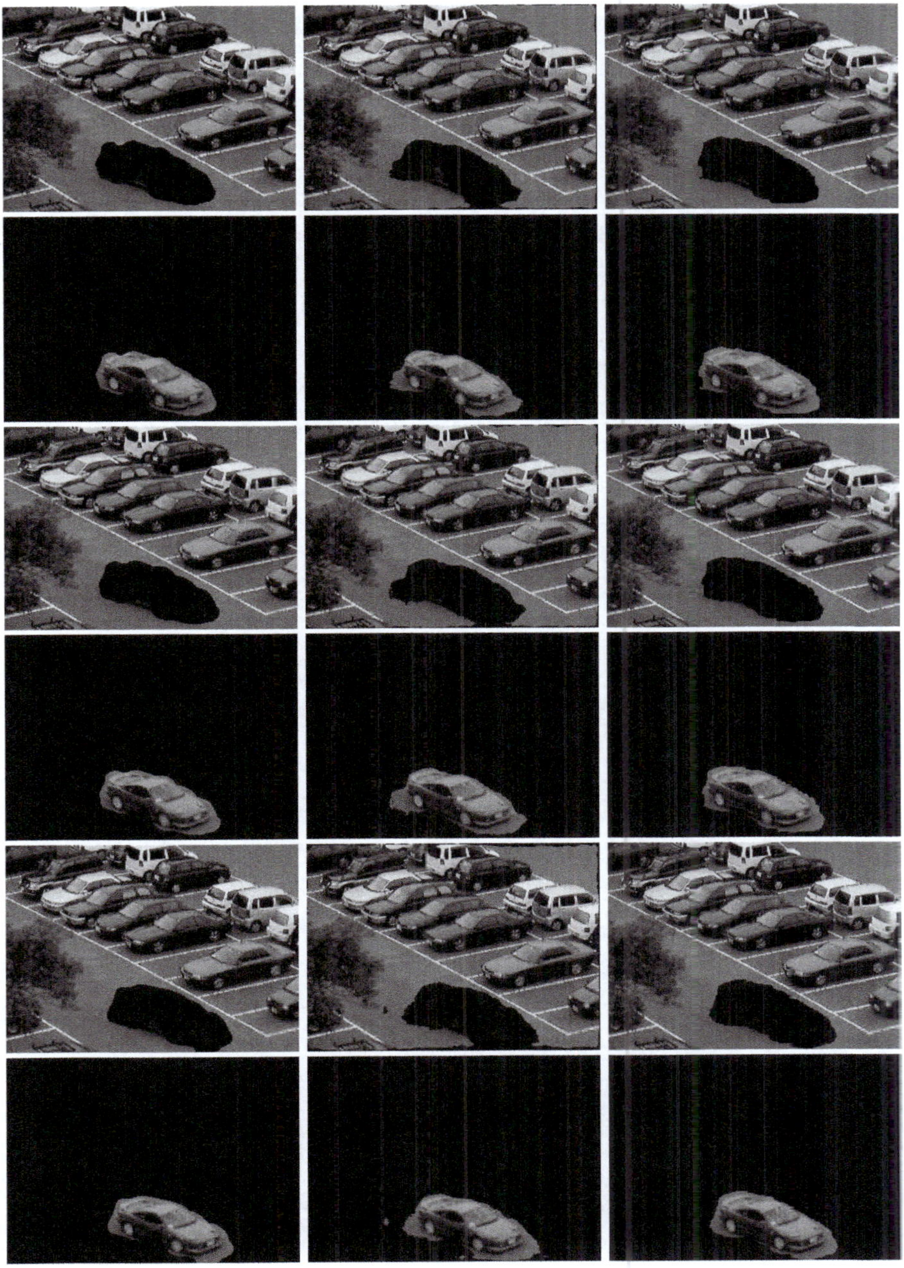

Method in [1] | Method in [12] | Our method

Fig. 1. Segmenting 3 frames from the car-parking lot sequence

Fig. 2. Segmenting 3 frames from the head-lab sequence

Figure 1 shows an example of segmentation of a 240×320 sequence of a car leaving a parking lot. The scene has 2 motions, the camera's downward motion and the car's right-downward motion. We use a window size of 10 × 10 to define the local neighborhoods for the method in [1] and for our method. The first and second columns of Figure 1 show the segmentation obtained using the methods in [1] and [12], respectively. The final column shows the results obtained using our method. In each image, the pixels that do not correspond to the group are colored black. Note that the best segmentation results are obtained using our approach. Although the improvement with respect to the method in [1] is not significant, the segmentation of the car is very good as compared to the method in [12] in the sense that very less amount of the parking lot is segmented along with the car.

Figure 2 shows an example of segmentation of a 240 × 320 sequence of a person's head rotating from right to left in front of a lab background. The scene has 2 motions, the camera's fronto-parallel motion and the head's motion. We use a window size of 20 × 20 to define the local neighborhoods for the method in [1] and for our method. The first and second columns of Figure 2 show the segmentation obtained using the methods in [1] and [12], respectively. The final column shows the results obtained using our method. In each image, pixels that do not correspond to the group are colored red. Notice that we cannot draw any conclusion for this sequence as to which algorithm performs better, because essentially all the methods misclassify the regions that have low texture. However, our method does perform better than [12] in terms of spatial regularization of the segmentation.

6 Conclusions and Future Work

We have presented a bottom up approach to 2-D motion segmentation that integrates the advantages of both local as well as global approaches to motion segmentation. An important advantage of our method over previous local approaches is that we can account for more than one motion model in every window. This helps us choose a big window without worrying about any aperture problem or motion boundary issues, and also reduces the need for iteratively refining the motion parameters across motion boundaries. An important advantage of our method over global algebraic approaches is that we incorporate spatial regularization into our segmentation scheme and hence we do not need to apply any ad-hoc smoothing to the segmentation results. Future work entails developing a robust algorithm for determining the number of motions in a window.

References

1. Wang, J., Adelson, E.: Layered representation for motion analysis. In: IEEE Conference on Computer Vision and Pattern Recognition. (1993) 361–366
2. Cremers, D., Soatto, S.: Motion competition: A variational framework for piecewise parametric motion segmentation. International Journal of Computer Vision **62** (2005) 249–265
3. Darrel, T., Pentland, A.: Robust estimation of a multi-layered motion representation. In: IEEE Workshop on Visual Motion. (1991) 173–178
4. Jepson, A., Black, M.: Mixture models for optical flow computation. In: IEEE Conference on Computer Vision and Pattern Recognition. (1993) 760–761

5. Ayer, S., Sawhney, H.: Layered representation of motion video using robust maximum-likelihood estimation of mixture models and MDL encoding. In: IEEE International Conference on Computer Vision. (1995) 777–785
6. Weiss, Y.: A unified mixture framework for motion segmentation: incoprporating spatial coherence and estimating the number of models. In: IEEE Conference on Computer Vision and Pattern Recognition. (1996) 321–326
7. Weiss, Y.: Smoothness in layers: Motion segmentation using nonparametric mixture estimation. In: IEEE Conference on Computer Vision and Pattern Recognition. (1997) 520–526
8. Torr, P., Szeliski, R., Anandan, P.: An integrated Bayesian approach to layer extraction from image sequences. IEEE Trans. on Pattern Analysis and Machine Intelligence **23** (2001) 297–303
9. Shizawa, M., Mase, K.: A unified computational theory for motion transparency and motion boundaries based on eigenenergy analysis. In: IEEE Conference on Computer Vision and Pattern Recognition. (1991) 289–295
10. Vidal, R., Sastry, S.: Segmentation of dynamic scenes from image intensities. In: IEEE Workshop on Motion and Video Computing. (2002) 44–49
11. Vidal, R., Ma, Y.: A unified algebraic approach to 2-D and 3-D motion segmentation. In: European Conference on Computer Vision. (2004) 1–15
12. Vidal, R., Singaraju, D.: A closed-form solution to direct motion segmentation. In: IEEE Conference on Computer Vision and Pattern Recognition. Volume II. (2005) 510–515

A Multiscale Co-linearity Statistic Based Approach to Robust Background Modeling

Prithwijit Guha[1], Dibyendu Palai[1], K.S. Venkatesh[1], and Amitabha Mukerjee[2]

[1] Department of Electrical Engineering,
Indian Institute of Technology, Kanpur,
Kanpur, 208016, Uttar Pradesh,
{pguha, palai, venkats}@iitk.ac.in
[2] Department of Computer Science & Engineering,
Indian Institute of Technology, Kanpur,
Kanpur, 208016, Uttar Pradesh,
amit@cse.iitk.ac.in

Abstract. Background subtraction is an essential task in several static camera based computer vision systems. Background modeling is often challenged by spatio-temporal changes occurring due to local motion and/or variations in illumination conditions. The background model is learned from an image sequence in a number of stages, viz. preprocessing, pixel/region feature extraction and statistical modeling of feature distribution. A number of algorithms, mainly focusing on feature extraction and statistical modeling have been proposed to handle the problems and comparatively little exploration has occurred at the preprocessing stage. Motivated by the fact that disturbances caused by local motions disappear at lower resolutions, we propose to represent the images at multiple scales in the preprocessing stage to learn a pyramid of background models at different resolutions. During operation, foreground pixels are detected first only at the lowest resolution, and only these pixels are further analyzed at higher resolutions to obtain a precise silhouette of the entire foreground blob. Such a scheme is also found to yield a significant reduction in computation. The second contribution in this paper involves the use of the co-linearity statistic (introduced by Mester et al. for the purpose of illumination independent change detection in consecutive frames) as a pixel neighborhood feature by assuming a linear model with a signal modulation factor and additive noise. The use of co-linearity statistic as a feature has shown significant performance improvement over intensity or combined intensity-gradient features. Experimental results and performance comparisons (ROC curves) for the proposed approach with other algorithms show significant improvements for several test sequences.

1 Introduction

Extracting foreground regions through background subtraction is a primary task in (quasi) static camera based computer vision systems spanning the application domains of automated video surveillance, activity analysis, smart rooms, human

P.J. Narayanan et al. (Eds.): ACCV 2006, LNCS 3851, pp. 297–306, 2006.

computer interfaces etc. The process of background subtraction is performed in two phases, viz. learning (background modeling) and classification (foreground extraction). In the learning phase, the background images are pre-processed and transformed to suitable color spaces (RGB, nRGB, HSI etc.) and are subjected to pixel (neighborhood) feature extraction. Finally statistical modeling is performed to approximate the distribution of extracted features. During operation (classification phase), each new image undergoes similar pre-processing, color space conversion and feature extraction operations and any foreground pixels present are detected by computing the belongingness of their extracted features to the learned statistical background model. Finally, at the post-processing stage, the occurrences of misclassified pixels are removed through morphological or spatial voting operations. Figure 1 shows a block diagram depicting the several stages of background subtraction.

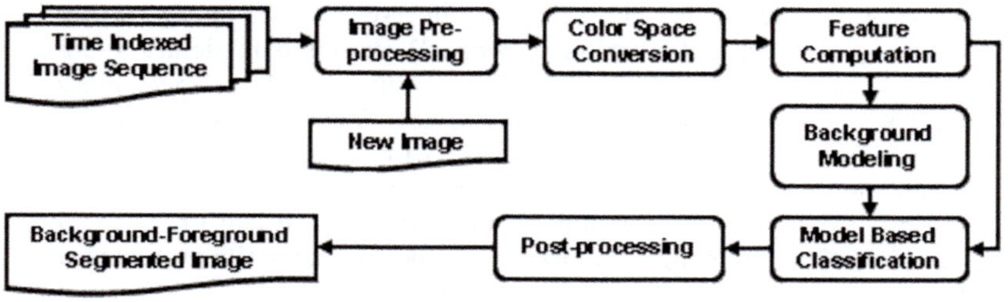

Fig. 1. Block diagram of the background subtraction procedure

The naive approach to background modeling assumes a temporal constancy of a pixel (or neighborhood) feature with very little variations caused by image noise leading to the modeling of feature distribution with a single Gaussian [1]. However, in most practical cases, spatio-temporal changes do occur due to disturbances caused by motion (swaying trees, sea waves etc) and/or variations in illumination conditions (cast shadows, changing ambient illumination over the day etc.). The computer vision community has proposed a number of algorithms to overcome the difficulties caused by such spatio-temporal changes. Koller et al. [2] have suggested Gaussian pre-filtering of the training sequences (with a filter bank) prior to further modeling, which is so far the only contribution in the pre-processing stage. A judicious selection of an operating color space also led to some success in handling illumination changes. Apart from using the naive RGB intensity values [3, 4], researchers have experimented with normalized RGB [5, 6, 7] and HSI [8] to deal with cast shadows and illumination fluctuations. Most of the works have adopted the pixel intensity value in a particular color space as a suitable feature [5, 9, 4, 7]. Performance improvements are witnessed while using the image gradients [3] or optical flow [6] features along with the pixel intensity values leading to an invariance toward illumination variations and motion disturbances. Contributions are also observed in the statistical modeling of the feature distributions. Grimson-Stauffer [4] have introduced the use of the mixture of Gaussians (MOG) to model the inherent multi-modality in the feature space caused by motion disturbances. This approach has shown significant improvement in dealing with persistent background motion. Elgammal et al. [9] have proposed a non-parametric approach based on Gaussian kernel functions. Apart from these, researchers have also proposed the applications of several other distribution generators like Markov random fields [5] or hidden Markov models [10].

The present work makes two distinct contributions. The first contribution in this paper is in the pre-processing stage, where an image pyramid is formed at multiple resolutions prior to background modeling. Such a representation gradually suppresses local motion disturbances in the background regions at lower resolutions. Thus, the background is learned at multiple scales and the combined model is used for the purpose of foreground extraction. During operation, the foreground pixels are first detected only at the lowest resolution and only the local neighborhood of the detected pixels are processed further at higher resolutions to acquire a more precise silhouette of the foreground region. This approach, on the one hand, takes care of small localized disturbances in the background and on the other hand, reduces the overall computations. The performances of the multiscale background models are studied against the corresponding single scale ones which shows significant improvements in the receiver operating characteristic (ROC, henceforth) curves irrespective of the feature chosen. Thus, using a multiscale representation for any existing background subtraction algorithm improves its performance as well as reduces computations. The second contribution deals with the use of the co-linearity statistic as an image feature, which assumes a linear model considering a signal modulation factor and an additive noise component in the observed signal. Mester et al. [11] have introduced the co-linearity statistic for the purpose of illumination invariant change detection in consecutive frames. In this paper we discuss the application of the co-linearity statistic in the domain of background subtraction. ROC curves are plotted comparing the performances of the co-linearity statistic with respect to the algorithms using intensity or intensity-gradient features and they reveal the significant superiority of this statistic as a feature for background subtraction.

This paper presents our work in the following manner. Section 2 discusses the proposed multiscale background model along with its advantages and performance evaluation. The application of co-linearity statistic in the domain of background subtraction is described in section 3. The experimental results and performance curves for the combined multiscale co-linearity statistic based background modeling algorithm are presented in section 4. Finally, we conclude in section 5 and discuss further extensions to the present contributions.

2 Multiscale Background Modeling

Spatio-temporal changes due to motion disturbances restricted to a local neighborhood are found to disappear at lower resolutions, when the lower resolutions are generated by averaging over contiguous, disjoint, blocks of pixels of size

$S_x \times S_y$ taken from the next higher resolution. Motivated by this observation, we propose to form an image pyramid by scaling down the original image at the pre-processing stage and learn background models at every scale of the pyramid. During the operating phase, foreground extraction in a new image is first performed at the lowest resolution. The detected foreground pixels and their immediate neighbors alone are zoomed in to the next higher resolution for further analysis. The zoomed-in foreground region thus formed is subjected to a morphological dilation with a 3×3 square structuring element so as to grow a single pixel boundary layer around it. The zoomed-in region along with the new grown boundary pixels are further subjected to background subtraction with the model learned at that resolution. Including the grown boundary layer pixels ensures a more precise detection of the foreground silhouette with a smooth contour. This process is repeated as we move further to higher resolutions. Figure 2 shows the improvements in the ROC curves as the depth of the image pyramid increases for a simple background subtraction algorithm with intensity feature distribution modeled as a single Gaussian.

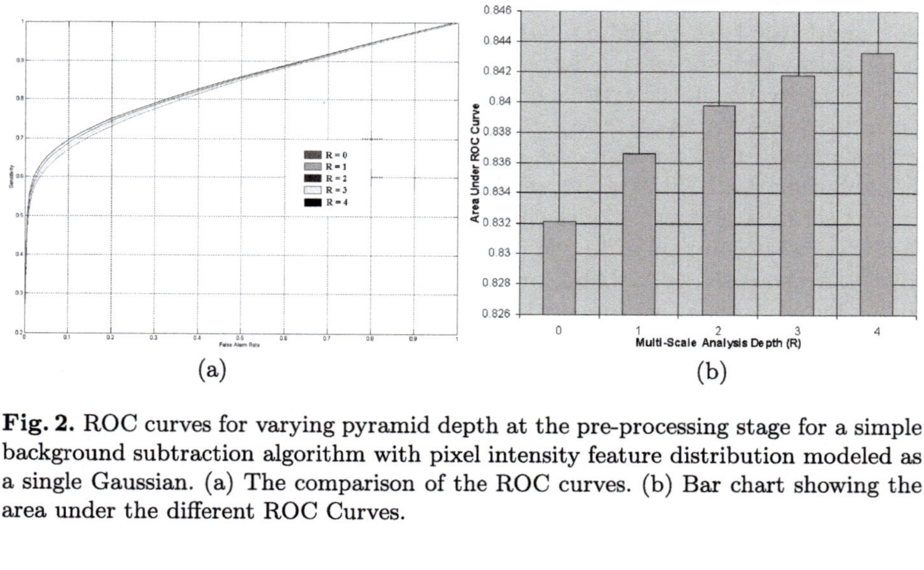

(a) (b)

Fig. 2. ROC curves for varying pyramid depth at the pre-processing stage for a simple background subtraction algorithm with pixel intensity feature distribution modeled as a single Gaussian. (a) The comparison of the ROC curves. (b) Bar chart showing the area under the different ROC Curves.

Consider an image with N_0 pixels from which we make an image pyramid of depth R by scaling down with factors S_x and S_y along the width and height respectively. Let the size of the image at the rth depth ($r = 0, \ldots, R$) of the pyramid be given by $N_r = \frac{N_0}{(S_x S_y)^r}$. Let the total number of pixels processed by a pyramidal background model of depth R for a particular background subtraction algorithm be C_R. Now, the same algorithm, without taking recourse to such a multiscale pre-processing stage will process $C_0 = N_0$ pixels. Let, P_r be the number of pixels processed at the rth depth. According to the proposed (multiscale modeling) scheme, background subtraction for a new image is first performed at the lowest resolution. Thus, at the Rth depth, we process $P_R = N_R$ pixels, of which, say, a fraction (equal to α) of pixels are declared as foreground. The detected foreground region(s) is (are) zoomed in to the next higher resolution to $\alpha N_R S_x S_y$ pixels. A morphological dilation with a 3×3 square structuring element is performed at this level to incorporate the pixels connected to the perimeter of the foreground region at the $(R-1)^{th}$ depth. Thus, the number of pixels processed at this depth is given by,

$$P_{R-1} = \alpha N_R S_x S_y + \beta \alpha N_R S_x S_y = \alpha(1+\beta) N_R S_x S_y \tag{1}$$

where β is the fractional gain in the number of foreground pixels owing to the process of dilation and hence is approximately equal to the perimeter to area ratio of the foreground region. If we consider the worst case, where all the pixels visited in the $(R-1)^{th}$ scale are selected as foreground candidates, then, following a similar procedure again, the number of pixels processed at the $(R-2)^{th}$ depth is given by $P_{R-2} = P_{R-1}(S_x S_y) + \frac{\beta}{S} P_{R-1}(S_x S_y)$.

We point out that as the detected foreground region inflates in higher resolutions, the perimeter to area ratio decreases by a factor of S, which is a function of S_x, S_y and the shape of the region. The effect of shape on the value of S is highest for a circular shape, and is the least for a highly elongated shape, whose perimeter to area ratio is largest. We can categorically state that S always exceeds unity even in the latter case, and is greatest for a circular shape. Using $S = 1$ as a loose lower bound on its value, a loose upper bound on P_{R-2} can be deduced as $(1+\beta)P_{R-1}(S_x S_y) = \alpha N_R [S_x S_y (1+\beta)]^2$. Thus, by induction we can write the loose upper bound on the number of pixels processed at $(R-r)^{th}$ depth as $P_{R-r} < \alpha N_R [S_x S_y (1+\beta)]^r$. Hence, the loose upper bound on the total number of pixels processed C_R for a pyramidal background model of depth R is given by,

$$\begin{aligned} C_R &= P_R + \sum_{r=1}^{R} P_{R-r} < N_R + \alpha N_R \sum_{r=1}^{R} [S_x S_y (1+\beta)]^r \\ &= \frac{N_0}{(S_x S_y)^R} \left[1 + \alpha(1+\beta) S_x S_y \frac{\{S_x S_y (1+\beta)\}^R - 1}{\{S_x S_y (1+\beta)\} - 1} \right] \end{aligned} \tag{2}$$

Define the quantity γ_R as the ratio of the number of pixels processed by a background subtraction algorithm with a pyramidal model to the one without it. Thus, from equation 2, we can deduce the loose upper bound on γ_R as,

$$\gamma_R = \frac{C_R}{C_0} < \frac{1}{(S_x S_y)^R} \left[1 + \alpha(1+\beta) S_x S_y \frac{\{S_x S_y (1+\beta)\}^R - 1}{\{S_x S_y (1+\beta)\} - 1} \right] \tag{3}$$

Evidently, we save on computations if $\gamma_R < 1.0$. Figure 3 shows the dependence of γ_R on α, β and R. In these simulation plots (and our experiments as well), we have chosen the scale factors to be $S_x = S_y = 2.0$.

It can be observed from figure 3(a) that the region of reduced computation in the (α, β) plane shrinks as R is increased. Also, from figure 3(b), it can be observed that choosing a value of $R = 3$ is good enough for all practical purposes.

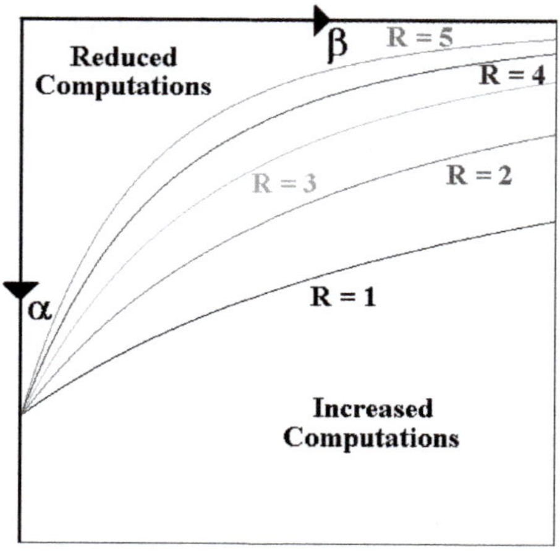

(a)

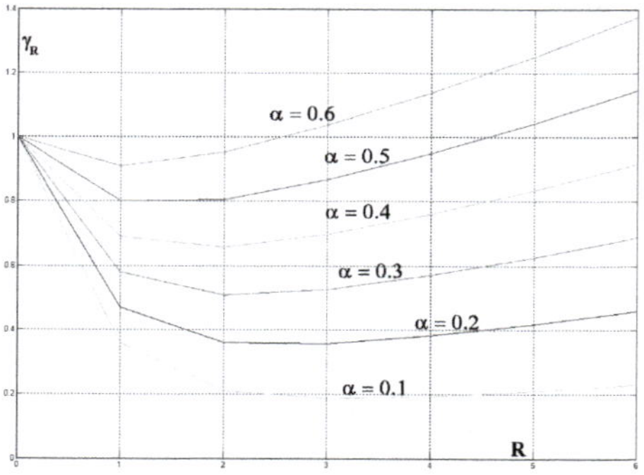

(b)

Fig. 3. Dependence of γ_R on α, β and R for scaling factors of $S_x = S_y = 2.0$. (a) Shrinking of *reduced computations* region in $(\alpha, \beta) \in [0, 1]$ plane as R varies from 1 to 5; (b) γ_R vs. R for different values of α and $\beta = 0.1$.

More so, we can see from figure 2 that the performance improvement in the ROC curves gradually saturates with increasing R. Hence, going for $R > 3$ does not yield significantly higher performance or reduced computations.

The pre-filtering technique proposed by Koller et al. [2] learns background models on the outputs of different filters. Thus for an image size of N_0 pixels and filter-bank size R, the memory requirement for the background model will be proportional to RN_0 pixels. However, in our case, if the background is learned over an image pyramid up to a depth of R, the total memory requirement will be proportional to $\sum_{r=0}^{R} \frac{N_0}{(S_x S_y)^r} = \frac{N_0\{(S_x S_y)^{R+1}-1\}}{(S_x S_y)^R (S_x S_y-1)}$. Further still, the number of pixels processed will also be increased by a factor of R to RN_0 for the pre-filtering approach, whereas the proposed algorithm will definitely reduce computations under most practical conditions. Hence, our method is superior to the one proposed by Koller et al. from both the view point of memory usage and computational cost.

3 The Co-linearity Statistic

Change detection in consecutive frames is often challenged by sudden illumination fluctuations. Recently, Mester et al. [11] have introduced the co-linearity statistic to handle the problems caused by illumination changes. The proposed approach assumes a linear model, where the observed data is represented as a sum of a modulated signal (modulation accounting for illumination change) and superimposed image noise. In this section, we discuss the use of co-linearity statistic as a pixel neighborhood feature for the purpose of background subtraction.

The background classification system initializes by computing the reference image $\overline{\Omega} = \frac{1}{T}\sum_{t=1}^{T} \Omega_t$ from the first T frames Ω_t $(t = 1, \ldots, T)$, which are assumed to be unintruded by any foreground object(s) (training conditions). Let the rectangular neighborhood regions of the $(x, y)^{th}$ pixel position in $\overline{\Omega}$ and Ω_t be $\omega(x, y)$ and $\omega_t(x, y)$ respectively. Let, $\overline{v}_{xy}$ and $\overline{v}_{xyt}$ be the respective column vectors obtained by stacking the rows of $\omega(x, y)$ and $\omega_t(x, y)$. Now, if no structural changes occur in the image within these rectangular windows, deviations from the reference vector can only happen due to multiplicative change in illumination (assumed to be uniform over the local neighborhood) and additive noise. However, neither the observed images nor the reference image $\overline{\Omega}$ provide us with the pure signal. Hence, both of them can be treated as an additive composition of the scalar modulation of the unknown pure signal unit vector $\overline{u}_{xy}$ and white noise.

$$\overline{v}_{xy} = \kappa_{xy}\overline{u}_{xy} + \overline{\xi}_{xy} \tag{4}$$

$$\overline{v}_{xyt} = \kappa_{xyt}\overline{u}_{xy} + \overline{\xi}_{xyt} \tag{5}$$

where κ_{xy}, κ_{xyt} and $\overline{\xi}_{xy}$, $\overline{\xi}_{xyt}$ are the modulation and white noise components for $\overline{v}_{xy}$ and $\overline{v}_{xyt}$ respectively. Let us define the quantity d_{xyt} as the norm squared sum of the white noise components $\overline{\xi}_{xy}$, $\overline{\xi}_{xyt}$ and is given by,

$$d_{xyt} \stackrel{def}{=} \|\overline{\xi}_{xy}\|^2 + \|\overline{\xi}_{xyt}\|^2 \tag{6}$$

The co-linearity statistic c_{xyt} is obtained by minimizing d_{xyt} with respect to $\overline{u}_{xy}$, and can be proved [11] to be the minimum eigen value $\lambda_{xyt}^{(min)}$ of the matrix $\mathbf{V}_{xyt}\mathbf{V}_{xyt}^T$, where $\mathbf{V}_{xyt} = (\overline{v}_{xy}\overline{v}_{xyt})^T$.

The background model at the $(x, y)^{th}$ pixel position is thus learned by computing the mean $\mu_c(x, y)$ and the standard deviation $\sigma_c(x, y)$ of the co-linearity statistic c_{xyt} from the T training frames. The Chebyshev inequality [12] ensures that $(1 - \frac{1}{k^2})$ fraction of the random variable sample values lie within $(\mu_c(x, y) \pm k\sigma_c(x, y))$ irrespective of the distribution. However, in our case, higher disparity from the model implies a higher value of the co-linearity statistic. Hence, we define the set of foreground pixels $\mathbf{F}_t$ for a new image Ω_t $(t > T)$ as,

$$\mathbf{F}_t = \{\Omega_t(x, y) : c_{xyt} \geq \mu_{xy} + k\sigma_{xy}\} \tag{7}$$

The processing time per pixel increases with larger pixel neighborhood size. When speed is preferred over spatial accuracy, the processing can be performed on a block raster instead of a pixel-wise classification. In all our experiments, however, a 3×3 neighborhood is chosen with pixel-wise classification. Figure 4 shows the comparison of the ROC curves of background subtraction algorithms using co-linearity statistic, intensity (single Gaussian and GMM) and combined intensity-gradient features. It is evident from the figure that the co-linearity statistic based feature extraction scheme provides significant improvement in performance as compared to the others.

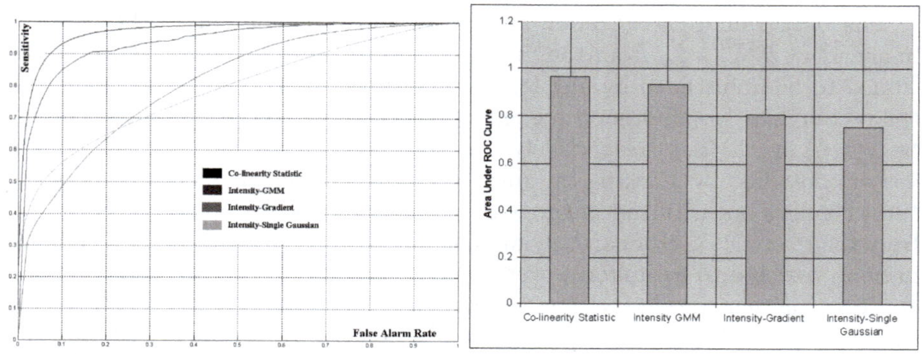

(a) (b)

Fig. 4. Performance analysis. (a) ROC curve of co-linearity statistic based approach compared to standard algorithms; (b) Bar chart showing the area under the ROC curves of (a).

4 Results

The experiments are performed on a number of test sequences comprising of both mild and violent motions in the background regions. In this section, we compare the performance of proposed multiscale co-linearity statistic based approach with the standard algorithms (intensity/intensity-gradient features with single (mixture of) Gaussian(s)) using pyramidal background models. In all these cases, a scaling factor of $S_x = S_y = 2.0$ is assumed with $R = 3$. Figure 5 shows the performance comparisons by the ROC curves of the corresponding algorithms.

The results of background subtraction using the proposed approach along with the comparisons with that of other algorithms are shown in figure 6. Sig-

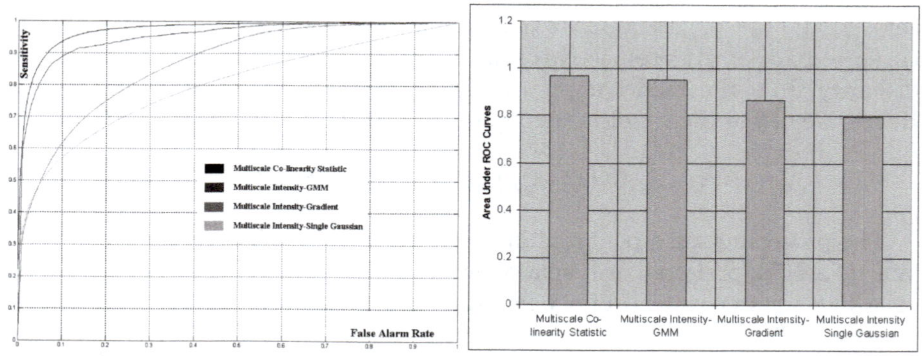

(a) (b)

Fig. 5. Performance analysis. (a) ROC curve of proposed multiscale co-linearity statistic compared to standard algorithms. (d) Bar chart showing the area under the ROC curves of (c).

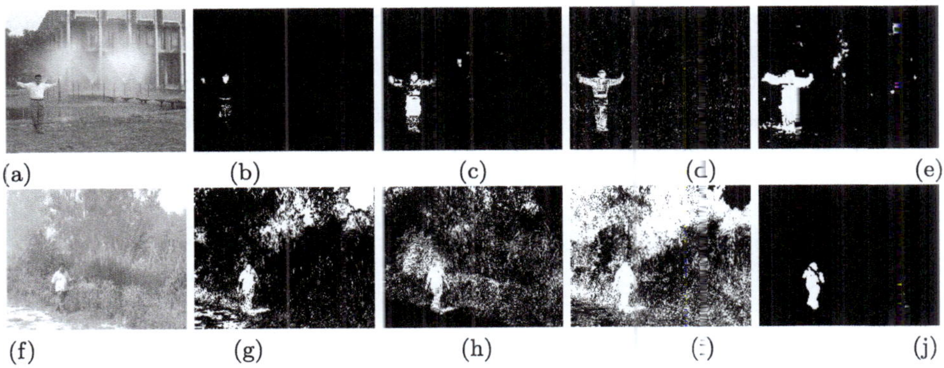

Fig. 6. Results of fountain sequence with mild background motion. (a) foreground image; results using (b) multiscale-intensity-single Gaussian; (c) multiscale-intensity GMM; (d) multiscale-intensity-gradient-GMM; (e) proposed multiscale and co-linearity statistic based approach. Results of forest sequence with violent background motion. (f) foreground image; results using (g) multiscale-intensity-single Gaussian; (h) multiscale-intensity GMM; (i) multiscale-intensity-gradient-GMM; (j) proposed multiscale-co-linearity statistic based approach.

nificant improvements are witnessed in both the sequences (forest sequence with violent background motion and the fountain sequence with mild disturbances) while employing the proposed approach. The current implementation (with un-optimized coding) of the proposed algorithm operates at $7.0Hz$ while executing on 320×240 images on a $2.8GHz$ Pentium-IV PC with $1GB$ RAM.

5 Conclusion

The process of background subtraction is composed of the several stages of image pre-processing, pixel/region feature extraction and statistical modeling of the same in the feature space. Afterwards, a post-processing stage is often involved for the purposes of shadow removal and suppression of classification noises by voting or morphological operations. This paper presents two significant contributions at the pre-processing and feature extraction stages. First, the multiscale approach to background modeling that improves the performance of any existing algorithm and reduces computations in most practical cases is discussed. Secondly, we introduce the use of a co-linearity statistic based feature extraction scheme that is shown to outperform intensity and combined intensity-gradient based approaches. The paper proposes the combination of the multiscale and the co-linearity statistic based approach which gives superior results compared to other algorithms. Experimental results have been presented while the comparison is performed by ROC curves and visual results are also outlined.

The current work assumes the availability of a few unintruded frames for the purpose of background model learning. Thus, a natural extension is the formulation of an automatic multi-scale co-linearity statistic based background model initialization algorithm. More so, we adopt another assumption regarding the structure of the background, primarily that it consists exclusively of objects located at infinite depth. Hence, a further improvement could involve the evolution of a multi-layered model. This would lead to a 2.5D modeling of the scene where the background model would segment the scene into a portion at infinity and yet include objects at finite distances.

References

1. Wren, C.R.Azarbayejani, A.Darrell, T.Pentland: Pfinder: real time tracking of human body. IEEE Transactions on Pattern Analysis and Machine Intelligence **19** (1997) 780–785
2. Koller, D., Weber, J., Malik, J.: Robust multiple car tracking with occlusion reasoning. Technical Report UCB/CSD-93-780, University of Californea, Berkley (1993)
3. Javed, O., Shafique, K., Shah, M.: A hierarchical approach to robust background subtraction using color and gradient information. In: Proceedings of the Workshop on Motion and Video Computing, IEEE Computer Society (2002) 22–27
4. C.Stauffer, W.E.L.Grimson: Adaptive background mixture models for real-time tracking. In: IEEE Computer Society Conference on Computer Vision and Pattern Recognition. Volume 2. (1999) 252
5. N.Paragios, V.Ramesh: A mrf based approach for real-time subway monitoring. In: CVPR 2001: Proceedings of the IEEE Computer Society Conference on Computer Vision and Pattern Recognition. Volume 1., IEEE Computer Society (2001) 1034–1040
6. Mittal, A., Paragios, N.: Motion-based background subtraction using adaptive kernel density estimation. In: CVPR 2004: Proceedings of the IEEE Computer Society Conference on Computer Vision and Pattern Recognition. Volume 2., IEEE Computer Society (2004) 302–309
7. Monnet, A., Mittal, A., Paragios, N., Ramesh, V.: Background modeling and subtraction of dynamic scenes. In: Proceedings of the Ninth IEEE International Conference on Computer Vision, IEEE Computer Society (2003) 1305–1312
8. S.J.McKenna, Y.Raja, S.Gong: Tracking color objects using adaptive mixture models. In: Image and Vision Computing. (1999) 225–231
9. Elgammal, A.M., Harwood, D., Davis, L.S.: Non-parametric model for background subtraction. In: Proceedings of the 6'th European Conference on Computer Vision-Part II, Springer-Verlag (2000) 751–767
10. Stenger, B., Ramesh, V., Paragios, N., Coetzee, F., Buhmann, J.: Topology free hidden markov models: Application to background modeling. In: Proceedings of Eighth IEEE International Conference on Computer Vision. Volume 1. (2001) 294–301
11. Mester, R., Aach, T., Dumbgen, L.: llumination-invariant change detection using a statistical colinearity criterion. In: Proceedings of the 23rd DAGM-Symposium on Pattern Recognition, Springer-Verlag (2001) 170–177
12. Bhat, B.: Modern Probability Theory. 2nd Edition, Halsted Press (John Wiley and Sons) (1981)

Motion Detection in Driving Environment Using U-V-Disparity

Jia Wang[1], Zhencheng Hu[2], Hanqing Lu[1], and Keiichi Uchimura[2]

[1] National Laboratory of Pattern Recognition, Institute of Automation, Chinese Academy of Sciences, Beijing 100080, China
{wangjia, luhq}@nlpr.ia.ac.cn
[2] Department of Computer Science, Kumamoto University, Kumamoto 860-8555, Japan
{hu, uchimura}@cs.kumamoto-u.ac.jp

Abstract. Motion detection in driving environment, which aims to detect REAL moving objects from continuously changing background, is vital for *Adaptive Cruise Control* (ACC) applications. This paper presents an efficient solution for such problem using a stereovision based method. First, a comprehensive analysis about 3D global motion is given based on "U-V-disparity" concept, in which a 5-parameter model is deduced to describe global motion within U-V-disparity domain and an iterative Least Square Estimation method is proposed to estimate the parameters. Then, in order to identify separate objects, geometric analysis segments the road scene into 3D object-surfaces based on U-V-disparity features of road surfaces, roadside structures and obstacles. Finally, the motions of the segmented object-surfaces are compared with the estimated global motion to find REAL moving surfaces, which correspond to the real moving objects. The proposed algorithm has been tested on real road sequences and experimental results verified its efficiency.

1 Introduction

Motion detection in driving environment, which aims to detect REAL moving objects from continuously changing background, is vital for *Adaptive Cruise Control* (ACC) applications.

Conventionally, optical flow forms the basis of vision-based motion analysis and obstacle detection [1][2][3], which detect moving objects by measuring the flow vectors difference between the objects and background. Yet most optical flow algorithms assume that the only motion between the camera and the environment is translation, which may not be true in most driving situations.

Recent researches have paid more attention to road scene analysis based on stereovision [4][5][6][7][8][9]. Stereo analysis is the process of measuring range to an object by comparing the object projection on two or more images [9]. Based on stereo information, obstacles can be segmented by distinguishing the features belonging to them from those belonging to road surface. However, most

P.J. Narayanan et al. (Eds.): ACCV 2006, LNCS 3851, pp. 307–316, 2006.

stereovision based method analyzes the road scene without considering the motion of cameras (*Global motion*), as well as the influence of such motion to the stereovision analysis.

In this paper, a comprehensive analysis about 3D global motion in stereovision is given based on "U-V-disparity" concept, in which a 5-parameter model is deduced to describe global motion within U-V-disparity domain and an iterative Least Square Estimation method is proposed to estimate the parameters. In order to identify separate objects, geometric analysis segments the road scene into 3D object-surfaces based on U-V-disparity features of road surfaces, roadside structures and obstacles. After that, the motions of the segmented object-surfaces are compared with the estimated global motion to find REAL moving surfaces, which correspond to the real moving objects.

2 Motion Detection Using U-V-Disparity

2.1 Stereovision

We have implemented a fast stereo module based on SSDA block matching algorithm. By careful management of cache memory and SSE technology on Pentium processor, our module can achieve real-time processing speed for dense disparity computation on a 320 by 240 image with the maximum disparity of 32 pixels. Fig. 1 shows a example of calculated disparity map.

Fig. 1. Disparity map: the right figure shows the disparity map of the left image, which following a pseudo color LUT (warmer color shows a bigger value of disparity, which means closer to the observer). The grey mask area indicate "don't care" region.

2.2 Global Motion Analysis Based on U-V-Disparity

Motion detection in driving environment always involves continuously changing background caused by the motion of observer or camera itself. Such problem is called global motion in the literature.

To analyze global motion within U-V-disparity domain, we approximately assume that the stereo rig mounted on the vehicle has two coplanar cameras with the same intrinsic parameters and their horizontal co-axis is parallel to the road surface (see Fig. 2), where the pitch angle to the ground plane is θ. By putting the origin of World Coordinate System WCS (X_w, Y_w, Z_w) to the centre

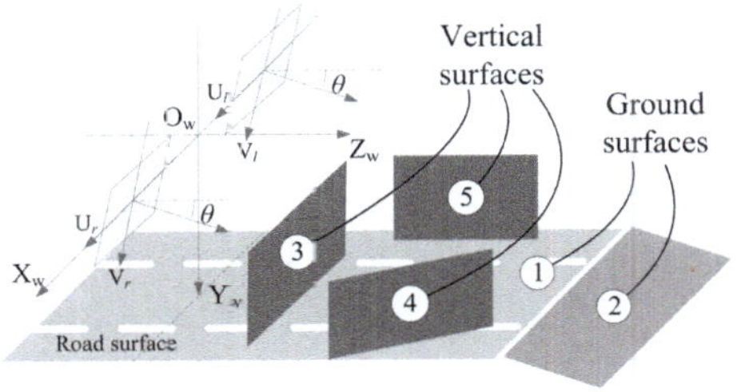

Fig. 2. Coordinate systems: The optical axis of the WCS is parallel to the ground plane and indicates the vehicle's direction of motion. The origin of camera coordinate system CCS (U, V) is put to the center of the image.

of the two stereo camera planes: O_w (as shown in Fig. 2), the transformation from WCS to CCS is achieved by:

$$\begin{cases} U_{l,r} = f\frac{X_w \pm b/2}{Y_w \sin\theta + Z_w \cos\theta} \\ V_{l,r} = f\frac{Y_w \cos\theta - Z_w \sin\theta}{Y_w \sin\theta + Z_w \cos\theta} \end{cases} \tag{1}$$

Then, disparity Δ can be deducted as:

$$\Delta = U_l - U_r = f\frac{b}{Y_w \sin\theta + Z_w \cos\theta} \tag{2}$$

Generally, global motion with respect to WCS can be described by

$$\begin{bmatrix} x \\ y \\ z \end{bmatrix} = \begin{bmatrix} r_{11} & r_{12} & r_{13} \\ r_{21} & r_{22} & r_{23} \\ r_{31} & r_{32} & r_{33} \end{bmatrix} \begin{bmatrix} x' \\ y' \\ z' \end{bmatrix} + \begin{bmatrix} t_1 \\ t_2 \\ t_3 \end{bmatrix} \tag{3}$$

which consists of translations along X, Y, Z axis and rotations about them. In the following, global motion will analyzed within U-V-disparity domain, using the basic relationship between WCS and U-V-disparity. Note that the pitch angle θ usually remains unchanged during the vehicles/cameras are moving, which means it doesn't influence the analysis. Only concerning about the left image, We can simplify formula (1) and (2) by making θ =0 as

$$X_w = U\frac{b}{\Delta} - \frac{b}{2}, Y_w = V\frac{b}{\Delta}, Z_w = f\frac{b}{\Delta} \tag{4}$$

Based on equation (3) and (4), different global motions are analyzed separately.

1) Translation along X axis

Using WCS, translation along X axis is described by

$$\begin{bmatrix} x \\ y \\ z \end{bmatrix} = \begin{bmatrix} x' \\ y' \\ z' \end{bmatrix} + \begin{bmatrix} t_1 \\ 0 \\ 0 \end{bmatrix} \tag{5}$$

Accordingly in U-V-disparity domain, such motion, combining (5) with (4), is described by

$$\begin{cases} u = u' + \Delta' \cdot t_1/b \\ v = v' \\ \Delta = \Delta' \end{cases} \tag{6}$$

2) Translation along Y axis
Similarly, translation along Y axis is described by

$$\begin{bmatrix} x \\ y \\ z \end{bmatrix} = \begin{bmatrix} x' \\ y' \\ z' \end{bmatrix} + \begin{bmatrix} 0 \\ t_2 \\ 0 \end{bmatrix} \Rightarrow \begin{cases} u = u' \\ v = v' + \Delta' \cdot t_2/b \\ \Delta = \Delta' \end{cases} \tag{7}$$

3) Translation along Z axis
Translation along Z axis is described by

$$\begin{bmatrix} x \\ y \\ z \end{bmatrix} = \begin{bmatrix} x' \\ y' \\ z' \end{bmatrix} + \begin{bmatrix} 0 \\ 0 \\ t_3 \end{bmatrix} \Rightarrow \begin{cases} u = u'/(1 + \Delta' \cdot t_3/fb) \\ v = v'/(1 + \Delta' \cdot t_3/fb) \\ \Delta = \Delta'/(1 + \Delta' \cdot t_3/fb) \end{cases} \tag{8}$$

4) Rotation about X axis
Using WCS, rotation about X axis can be described by

$$\begin{bmatrix} x \\ y \\ z \end{bmatrix} = \begin{bmatrix} 1 & 0 & 0 \\ 0 & \cos\alpha & \sin\alpha \\ 0 & -\sin\alpha & \cos\alpha \end{bmatrix} \begin{bmatrix} x' \\ y' \\ z' \end{bmatrix} \tag{9}$$

Mapping into U-V-disparity domain, there is:

$$\begin{cases} u = u'/(\cos\alpha - \sin\alpha \cdot v'/f) \\ v = (\cos\alpha \cdot v' + f \sin\alpha)/(\cos\alpha - \sin\alpha \cdot v'/f) \\ \Delta = \Delta'/(\cos\alpha - \sin\alpha \cdot v'/f) \end{cases} \tag{10}$$

If the rotation angle α is small, there is

$$\begin{cases} u \approx u' \\ v \approx v' + f \sin\alpha \\ \Delta \approx \Delta' \end{cases} \tag{11}$$

5) Rotation about Y axis
Similarly, rotation around Y axis is described by

$$\begin{cases} u = \frac{\cos\beta \cdot u' - f \sin\beta}{\cos\beta + \sin\beta \cdot (u' - \Delta'/2)/f} \overset{\beta \to 0}{\approx} u' - f \sin\beta \\ v = \frac{v'}{\cos\beta + \sin\beta \cdot (u' - \Delta'/2)/f} \overset{\beta \to 0}{\approx} v' \\ \Delta = \frac{\Delta'}{\cos\beta + \sin\beta \cdot (u' - \Delta'/2)/f} \overset{\beta \to 0}{\approx} \Delta' \end{cases} \tag{12}$$

6) Rotation about Z axis

Rotation around Z axis is described by

$$\begin{cases} u = (u' - \Delta'/2)\cos\gamma + v'\sin\gamma + \Delta'/2 \\ v = -(u' - \Delta'/2)\sin\gamma + v'\cos\gamma \\ \Delta = \Delta' \end{cases} \tag{13}$$

Based on the above analysis of separate motions, complex global motion within U-V-disparity domain can be modeled by the combination of them.

In order to find a simple expression of global motion, we only concern about the special cases when the cameras are firmly mounted on the vehicle and share the same motion with it. In this case, the most frequent and notable global motion is *translation along Z axis* (when the car is running forward/backward). Global motion will also include slight *translation along X axis* and *rotation about Y axis* when the car is wheeling. If the car is running on a slope, there will be slight *translation along Y axis* and *rotation about X axis. Rotation about Z axis* is the most infrequent motion and will not be considered in the estimation.

Therefore, we use such a simple combination of separate motions to model the complex global motion within U-V-disparity domain as

$$\begin{cases} u = \frac{1}{1+\Delta'\cdot T_Z}u' + \Delta'\cdot T_X + R_Y \\ v = \frac{1}{1+\Delta'\cdot T_Z}v' + \Delta'\cdot T_Y + R_X \\ \Delta = \frac{1}{1+\Delta'\cdot T_Z}\Delta' \end{cases} \tag{14}$$

There are 5 parameters in the model. T_X, T_Y and T_Z characterized the translation motions along X, Y and Z axis. R_X , R_Y correspond to the rotation about X, Y axis.

2.3 Object-Surface Segmentation

To extract moving objects, an initial segmentation of the road scene is necessary. In this paper, the U-V-disparity method in [9] is improved for the segmentation.

ROI Extraction. From Fig. 1, it can be seen that objects appear as surfaces in the 3D disparity map. In addition, moving objects generally appear as *Vertical surfaces* (defined by Fig. 2), and exist in the region between the *Ground surfaces* and sky. We name such regions as the *Regions of Interest*(ROI). In this paper, ROI is extracted by checking the Y coordinate in WCS, by means of which regions near (¿h_2) or far from (¡h_1) the ground are removed.

$$h_1 \le Y_w \le h_2 \Leftrightarrow \frac{h_1}{b} \le \frac{V}{\Delta} \le \frac{h_2}{b} \tag{15}$$

Fig. 3(c) illustrates the ROI extraction, where pixels not satisfying equation (15) are masked by the grey, and only *Vertical surfaces* within a certain range of altitude from the ground are remained for further analysis.

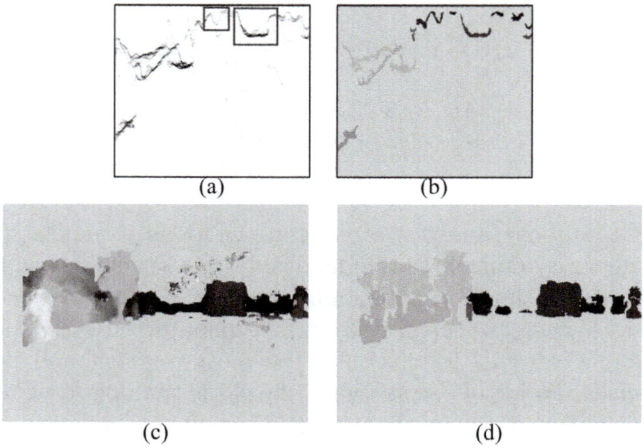

Fig. 3. ROI and object-surface segmentation: (a) U-disparity image; (b) Detected "U" curves; (c) ROI; (d) Object-surface segmentation

Object-Surface Segmentation. Following the U-V-disparity concept in [9], disparity map can be projected into U-disparity image and V-disparity image for analysis. Fig. 3(a) shows the U-disparity image of Fig. 1, in which regions with low intensity correspond to the projections of vertical surfaces. To segment the surfaces corresponding to different objects, their projections can be clustered separately by the spatial discontinuity and shape features within U-disparity image.

Since objects generally have higher disparities (closer to the observer) than the background, they always project as convex surfaces in 3D disparity maps. As the result, the convex surfaces will be projected as 2D convex curves (shapes similar to letter "U") in U-disparity iamge. An example is shown in Fig. 3(a), where the vehicles are projected as convex curves like "U" within the blue rectangles.

Based on the above analysis, we segment the surface-projections in U-disparity image as follows:

Step 1: Scanning U-Δ domain along Δ axis from Δ_{max} to 0. For each Δ, search U axis to find a *seed* pixel whose projection density is larger than a predefined threshold.

Step 2: The *seed* is expanded into a region based on the directions shown in Fig. 4. Such expanding process stops when all the candidate pixels' densities are smaller than a predefined threshold.

Step 3: Return to *Step1* to find a new *seed*.

Step 4: When the entire domain was scanned, several regions are clustered separately by the *seeds* and the expanding process. After a post-process of merging small regions to their adjacent large regions, the resultant regions in U-disparity map will be regarded as the separate projections of object-surfaces.

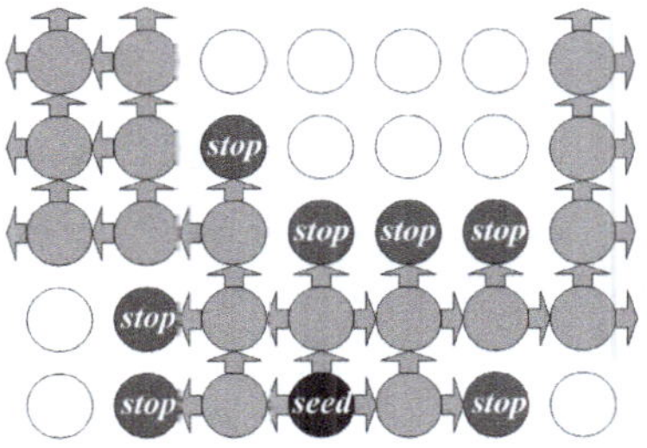

Fig. 4. Region expanding

The clustered regions are shown in Fig. 3(b). Each region is characterized by the disparity of *seed* following the pseudo color LUT. When such regions are mapped back into 3D disparity map, the segmentation result of object-surfaces is shown in Fig. 3(d).

2.4 Moving Object Detection

Iterative Least-square Estimation (ILSE) method is used to estimate the global motion parameters: First, corners are tracked through successive frames to find their correspondences. Suppose there are N corners, let (u_k, v_k, Δ_k) be the U-V-disparity coordinates for a corner k in the current frame. Its correspondence in the previous frame is (u'_k, v'_k, Δ'_k). Then, based on the N corner-pairs, ILSE method can compute the parameters as follows

$$T_Z = \frac{\sum \Delta' - \sum \Delta}{\sum \Delta \Delta'} \tag{16}$$

$$T_X = \frac{N \sum u\Delta' + \sum Zu' \sum \Delta' - N \sum Zu'\Delta' - \sum u \sum \Delta'}{N \sum (\Delta')^2 - (\sum \Delta')^2} \tag{17}$$

$$R_Y = \frac{(\sum u - \sum Zu') \sum (\Delta')^2 + (\sum Zu'\Delta' - \sum u\Delta') \sum \Delta'}{N \sum (\Delta')^2 - (\sum \Delta')^2} \tag{18}$$

$$T_Y = \frac{N \sum v\Delta' + \sum Zv' \sum \Delta' - N \sum Zv'\Delta' - \sum v \sum \Delta'}{N \sum (\Delta')^2 - (\sum \Delta')^2} \tag{19}$$

$$R_X = \frac{(\sum v - \sum Zv') \sum (\Delta')^2 + (\sum Zv'\Delta' - \sum v\Delta') \sum \Delta'}{N \sum (\Delta')^2 - (\sum \Delta')^2} \tag{20}$$

where

$$Z = 1/(1 + \Delta' T_Z) \tag{21}$$

Note that in the above equations, the subscript k is omitted for simplification purpose.

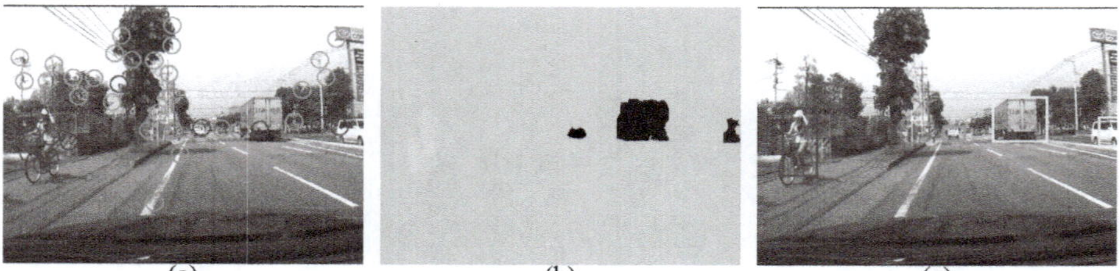

(a) (b) (c)

Fig. 5. Moving objects detection: (a) Detected corners and their 2D motion vectors, where corners matching the estimated global motion field are colored as green, and those who don't match are colored as red; (b) Detected moving objects; (c) The color of the rectangles indicates the distance between observer and detected objects, where *red*, *yellow* and *green* correspond to *close*, *middle* and *far*

To eliminate the influence of moving objects, the estimation procedure is performed iteratively. During each iteration, the estimated (T_Z, T_X, T_Y, R_X, R_Y) are used to construct a global motion field. Such field will be compared with the U-V-disparity of each corner-correspondence, and those who do not match with the current field will be discarded. Here "match" means that U-V-disparity lies within a threshold distance from the corresponding global motion field. After that, the remaining corners are used to re-estimate (T_Z, T_X, T_Y, R_X, R_Y) and enter a new iteration. Using such iterative scheme, those corners who don't follow global motion will be removed gradually, and after several iterations, the estimated parameters will converge to the final results.

Based on the segmented object-surfaces and estimated global motion parameters, moving objects (surfaces) are detected as follows: An object-surface, if

most of its including pixels follow the global motion in equation (14) with the estimated parameters, will be regarded as background. Otherwise, it will be regarded as having local motions and be extracted as real moving objects. Fig. 5 shows the detected moving objects of Fig. 1.

3 Experiments

The presented method has been tested on various road sequences. This section gives another two experimental results in Fig. 6 and Fig. 7. Segmentation result in Fig. 6 verifies that presented algorithm can properly handle slight rotations and translations to detect the real moving objects. In Fig. 7, the proposed algorithm makes use of equation (15) to successfully eliminate the bridge and extract the on-road objects.

Fig. 7. Experimental results on traffic image: a road scene including an over-pass bridge, which may be easily confused as obstacles and disturb the real objects detection

4 Conclusion

Detecting REAL moving objects from moving camera is a difficult task, especially for the applications in driving environment. This paper presents an efficient algorithm for motion detection in driving environment based on stereovision analysis. On the one hand, a 5-parameter model is deduced to describe 3D global motion in stereovision using "U-V-disparity" concept, based on what an iterative Least Square Estimation method is proposed to estimate the parameters. Then, the road scene is segmented into 3D object-surfaces corresponding to separate objects based on geometric features in U-V-disparity domain. Finally, the motions of the segmented object-surfaces are compared with the estimated global motion to find REAL moving object-surfaces, which correspond to the real moving objects. The proposed algorithm has been tested on real road sequences and experimental results verified its efficiency.

Acknowledgements

This research is sponsored by the National Natural Science Foundation of China (Grant No. 60135020, 60475010 and 60121302).

References

1. Nelson, R., Aloimonos, J.: Using flow field divergence for obstacle avoidance: towards qualitative vision. International Conference on Compute Vision (1988)
2. Enkelmann, W.: Obstacle detection by evaluation of optical flow fields form image sequence. Image and Vision Computing (1991)
3. Young, M., Hong, T., Yang, A.: Obstacle detection for a vehicle using optical flow. SAE Intelligent Vehicle (1992)
4. Luong, Q., Weber, J., Koller, D., Malik, J.: An integrated stereo-based approach to automatic vehicle guidance. International Conference on Computer Vision (1995)
5. Bertozzi, M., Broggi, A., Fascioli, A., Nichele, S.: Stereo vision based vehicle detection. IEEE Intelligent Vehicle Symposium (2000)
6. Talukder, A., Manduchi, R., Rankin, A., Matthies, L.: Fast and reliable obstacle detection and segmentation for cross-country navigation. IEEE Intelligent Vehicle Symposium (2002)
7. Labayrade, R., Aubert, D., Tarel, J.: Real time obstacle detection in stereovision on non flat road geometry through "v-disparity" representation. IEEE Intelligent Vehicle Symposium (2002)
8. Sole, A., Mano, O., Stein, G., Kumon, H., Tamatsu, Y., Shashua, A.: Solid or not solid: Vision for radar target validation. IEEE Intelligent Vehicle Symposium (2004)
9. Hu, Z., Uchimura, K.: U-v-disparity: An efficient algorithm for stereovision based scene analysis. IEEE Intelligent Vehicle Symposium (2005)

Visual Surveillance Using Less ROIs of Multiple Non-calibrated Cameras

Takashi Nishizaki, Yoshinari Kameda, and Yuichi Ohta

Graduate School of Systems and Information Engineering,
University of Tsukuba, 1-1-1 Tennoudai, Tsukuba, Ibaraki, 305-8573, Japan
{tanishi, kameda, ohta}@image.esys.tsukuba.ac.jp
http://www.image.esys.tsukuba.ac.jp

Abstract. With a large number of surveillance cameras, it is not an easy task to determine which camera should be monitored and which region of the camera images should be checked so that all the activities and/or events in a scene are examined. We present a new method to realize effective visual surveillance under an environment in which a number of non-calibrated fixed surveillance cameras are being operated. We also show two applications that are useful for surveillance tasks based on our proposed method. One is *"suggestion of associative blocks"*, and the other is *"dominant camera selection"*. Our approach exploits co-occurrence between two regions of interest (ROIs) over the surveillance cameras, and it needs neither calibration nor supervised training. We have conducted preliminary tests with forty cameras installed in a room and a corridor next to the room, and some promising results of the two applications are shown in this paper.

1 Introduction

Recently, there are increasing social demands to observe and detect usual and/or unusual events by exploiting cameras in various environments. Such a surveillance camera system is thought to be useful for security in public areas, road traffic monitoring, and so on. As surveillance cameras are being more and more installed and utilized in a scene for surveillance task, sometimes it becomes impractical and cumbersome to remember their locations and their visible areas. In addition, since surveillance cameras cannot always be set perpendicular to the ground/floor, images from surveillance cameras may not be comfortable to recognize instantly. Therefore, with a large number of surveillance cameras, it is not an easy task for people to recognize which camera should be monitored and which region of the camera images should be checked so that all the activities and/or events in a scene can be examined. This problem becomes prominent especially when a number of cameras are widely scattered because it is impractical to calibrate them consistently.

Fig. 1 shows snapshots of 36 cameras taken simultaneously. The cameras are installed in a room and a corridor adjacent to the room. It is apparently difficult to locate a person in the images. As the number of the surveillance cameras increases, maintaining the consistency of their geometric information (their locations and directions) is cumbersome. Therefore, there is a demand

P.J. Narayanan et al. (Eds.): ACCV 2006, LNCS 3851, pp. 317–327, 2006.

Fig. 1. An Example of Multi-view Videos (36 cameras)

to a sophisticated visual assistance method that can support visual surveillance tasks against a large number of cameras, which are not geometrically calibrated precisely.

We present a new method to realize effective visual surveillance under an environment in which a number of non-calibrated fixed surveillance cameras are being operated. We also show two applications that are useful for surveillance task based on our proposed method. One application of the method is "suggestion of associative blocks". If there is an event that an user should check and he/she has noticed it by checking one region on a surveillance camera on the system, the system can point out regions of different cameras that are helpful to examine the event. The other application is "dominant camera selection". Out of many surveillance cameras, our method can tell which cameras are worth watching in general case.

Our approach exploits co-occurrence between two regions of interest (ROIs) over the surveillance cameras, and it needs neither calibration nor supervised training. We divide camera images into small blocks. Each small block has foreground regions when it captures motions in a scene. Our system first eliminates redundant blocks that apparently do not contribute to event recognition. The elimination algorithm consists of two stages. In the first stage, the blocks that never detect motions are eliminated. Then, in the second stage, we exploit PCA to sweep out the blocks that do not contribute to describe events. We call the remaining blocks regions of interest (ROIs). The system then calculates co-occurrence of any pair of ROIs in which foreground regions related with an event are found simultaneously. Once the co-occurrence matrix is obtained, it can determine a set of ROIs that should be taken care of when an event in focus is found in a certain ROI. In other words, the ROIs are associative to the specified ROI. In addition, dominant camera selection can be conducted based on the co-occurrence matrix.

The rest of the paper is formed as follows. In section 2, recent reseaches related with our research are mentioned. Section 3 explains our surveillance system. Section4 describes the elimination algorithm of (small) blocks in surveillance camera images. In section 5, we show two applications, *"suggestion of associative blocks"* and *"dominant camera selection"*. The concluding remarks are shown in section 6.

2 Related Works

There are many visual surveillance systems for human tracking, traffic monitoring, and detection of unusual objects. In order to cover large area and/or to track objects in complex motion, surveillance systems uses multiple cameras. As shown in previous works, the multi-camera surveillance systems usually rely on manual camera calibration [1][2][3][4] or complex automated calibration method[5]. The surveillance systems with calibrated cameras can surely provide accurate geometry of objects in an environment. However, manual camera calibration is too cumbersome to cope with large-scale surveillance systems, and it is impractical to apply fragile automated calibration methods to such systems. Therefore, there are many demands for surveillance methods that only assume rough geometry information of cameras.

In order to track moving objects on surveillance videos, and to know where to see in videos for surveillance tasks, correspondences in videos captured by cameras are thought to be useful. Therefore, many methods that have correspondence models and estimate correspondences of locations or trajectories of moving objects have been proposed [6][7][8][9]. We also use the correspondences to calculate co-occurrence of objects observed in multiple cameras. Our proposed method is different on the point that it is a monitoring support method and can be applied to a large-scale camera system easily.

3 Surveillance System

In this section, we present a framework of our multi-camera surveillance system, and discuss image features to be used for estimating correspondence

3.1 Camera Network System

Fig. 2 shows a framework of our system and Fig. 1 shows an example of multi-view videos captured by the system. The system consists of multiple network-cameras(web-cameras) and multiple PCs for image processing. We employed the off-the-shelf web cameras because of the following advantages.

- Installation flexibility: One camera only requires one LAN cable (that also provides power to each camera) at its mounting point.
- Process scalability: We can change the number of cameras assigned to one PC easily.

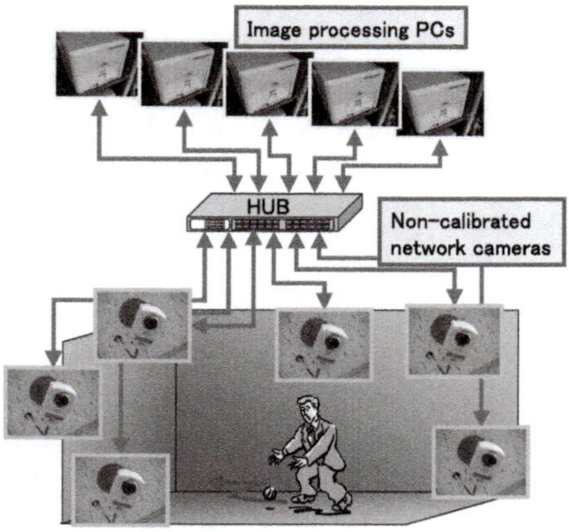

Fig. 2. A Framework of Our Surveillance System

On the other hand, they have following problems.

- It is difficult to synchronize videos.
- Frame rate of captured videos is unstable because it may be affected by network congestion.

To estimate co-occurrence matrix and apply it for the surveillance, we must take care of these factors. In our current implementation, however, synchronization of cameras does not matter because the cameras can output 10.0 to 30.0 fps and the motions in a scene are not so fast compared with the frame rate. Network congestion can also be avoided if network hubs are properly connected so as not to exceed the maximum bandwidth for each connection. Our system consists of 45 cameras and 22 PCs currently. We are planning to extend the system to 80 cameras.

3.2 Image Feature

We consider only basic image features so that our method can cover any kinds of events. Cameras capture images in RGB format and the system divides them into small rectangular blocks. An image is divided into R small blocks (currently, $R = 64$).

Fig. 3. Image Feature of One Captured Image. The left image is an input image and the right image is a display of its saved data.

In our research, the system extracts foreground regions by calculating background subtraction for input images. It calculates the mean intensity value of the foreground regions in each small block, and stores it in INT-type 32 bit data format. Fig. 3 shows an image of one saved data. The data is saved in compressed format. The data size depends on situations. For example, we captured a scene for about 290 hours by 4 cameras, and the compressed data size was about 1.3 GBytes.

4 ROI Selection

In this section, we present a method to select ROIs from the small blocks.

4.1 Data Structure

We define an event vector $\mathbf{x}(t)$ at time t $(1 \leq t \leq T)$, where T is a number of observed event vectors.

$$\mathbf{x}(t) = \{\ x_1(t),\ \cdots\ ,\ x_i(t),\ \cdots\ ,\ x_N(t)\ \} \tag{1}$$

The size(number of dimensions) of the vector is $N = C \times R$, where C is a number of cameras and R is a number of small blocks in an image Each event vector represents which camera and where in the captured image objects are observed. Each element $x_i(t)$ denotes a feature of an object detected in a region i at time t, and represents what object is observed there. We use the mean intensity values of the small blocks in an image as image features. Note that other features can also be applied in our method.

We call the small blocks that can contribute to event recognition "regions of interest (ROIs)". ROIs are obtained by eliminating redundant blocks among all the N blocks, and the elimination algorithm consists of two stages. In the first stage, the blocks that never detect foreground regions are eliminated. In the second stage, we exploit principal component analysis (PCA) to sweep out the blocks that do not contribute to describe events.

4.2 Block Elimination Based on Foreground Region Detection

First, a mean vector $\mathbf{M}$ is calculated for the input N dimensional event vector $\mathbf{x}(t)$ for $1 \leq t \leq T$ before the block elimination process starts. If M_i that is a mean of features observed in a small block i is zero, the block i is eliminated because it means the region i never detects any motions for all the T frames. Then, we get N' $(N' \leq N)$ dimensional vector $\mathbf{x}'(t)$ by eliminating the blocks that are useless to detect foreground regions.

4.3 Block Elimination by PCA

After the first stage, we apply principal component analysis (PCA) to $\mathbf{x}'$ by using the variance-covariance matrix $\mathbf{V}'$. PCA is a multivariate procedure that rotates the data in a multi-dimensional space so that variances projected onto the new axes have large variability. It is mainly used for dimensionality reduction. The resultant new rotated axes are called principal axes of $\mathbf{x}'$, and after applying the PCA, principal axes $z_k (1 \leq k \leq N')$ are given by linear combinations of the original variables as shown in the following equations.

$$\mathbf{z} = \mathbf{A}\,\mathbf{x}' \tag{2}$$

$$z_k = a_{1k}x'_1 + a_{2k}x'_2 + \cdots, a_{N'k}x'_{N'} \tag{3}$$

We select a set of variables $\{x'_j\}$ that have larger weight $\{a_{jk}\}$ for more significant principal axes $\{z_k\}$. The principal axes $\{z_k\}$ that have higher contribution ratio are thought to be useful both to recognize and to classify the original data. The followings are the detailed description of block elimination algorithm using PCA.

Step 1: Sorts the principal axes z_k by contribution ratios p_k. A contribution ratio p_k indicates how the principal component z_k represents data better, and it is represented by a variance λ_k of z_k.

$$p_k = \frac{\lambda_k}{\sum_{l=1}^{N'} \lambda_l} \tag{4}$$

Step 2: Calculates accumulated contribution ratio by

$$c_k = \sum_{l=1}^{k} p_l \tag{5}$$

and selects the principal components z_k whose accumulated contribution ratios are larger than a threshold c_{th}. Currently, c_{th} is set to 0.9. We denote the selected principal axes by $\{z'_k\}$.

Step 3: Given a principal axis z'_k, the method calculates the mean value $\bar{a}_k$ of $\{a_{jk}\}$ that are coefficients of $\{x'_j\}$. A score s_j of the variable x'_j obtains the contribution ratio p'_k of z'_k when the coefficient a_{kj} is larger than $\bar{a}_k$.

Step 4: Apply Step 3 to all the principal components $\{z'_k\}$. Calculate the mean value $\bar{s}$ of the scores $\{s_j\}$. Then, select the variables x'_j whose score s_j are higher than $\bar{s}$. Finally, block j corresponding to x'_j is regarded as a ROI.

4.4 Experimental Results of ROI Selection

Fig. 4 shows a layout of cameras in an experiment environment, and Fig. 5,6 show resultant ROIs. In the figures, the small blocks marked in a bright color are ROIs, where people walking around in a room were observed frequently. In the case of 12 cameras(Fig. 6), 525 blocks were selected from 768 blocks in the elimination process of the first stage, and 253 blocks were selected in the elimination process of the second stage. Some ROIs extracted in the case of 4 cameras(Fig. 5) were eliminated in the case of 12 cameras(Fig. 6) because they became less important than the other ROIs in the case of 12 cameras.

In the experiments, Calculation of ROI extraction was conducted on a PC of Pentium4 2.80 GHz, and its memory size is 1.0 GByte. We applied the ROI

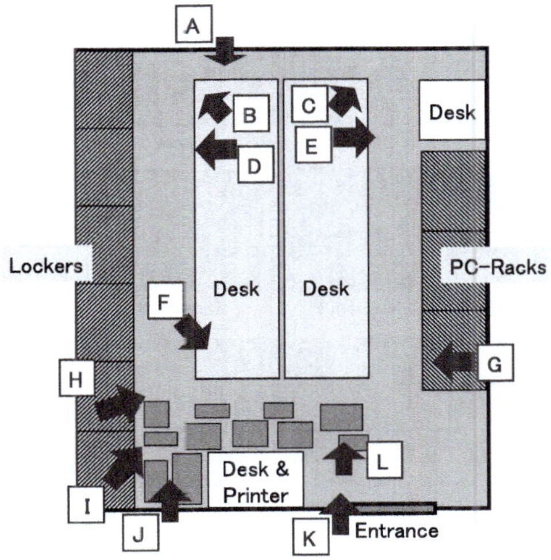

Fig. 4. Camera Layout. Alphabets indicate camera names and arrows show their directions.

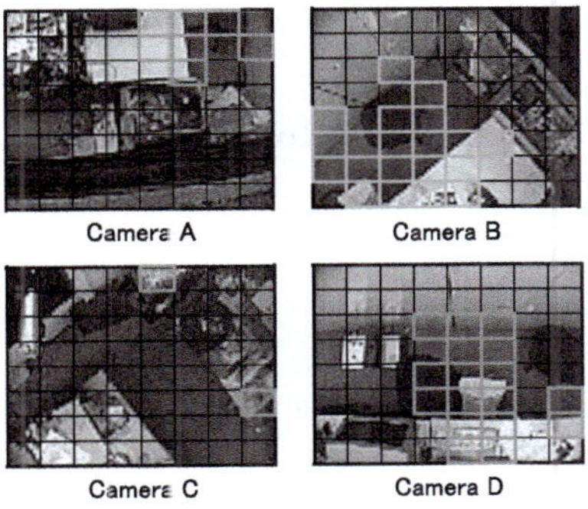

Fig. 5. Resultant ROIs (4 cameras)

extraction method to a scene of two hour length. In the case of 4 cameras, the calculation needed 181.70 seconds; 48.27 seconds to calculate a mean vector **M**, 133.30 seconds to calculate a variance-covariance matrix $\mathbf{V}'$, and 0 13 seconds to eliminate redundant blocks. In the case of 12 cameras, the calculation spent 1347.19 seconds; 147.7 seconds to calculate a mean vector, 1190.6 seconds to calculate a variance-covariance matrix, and 8.89 seconds to eliminate redundant blocks.

Currently, we are exploring an on-line clustering method for event vectors using extracted ROIs. We expect that the clustering method can be applied to a large-scale camera network because our redundancy elimination algorithm reduces the data size to be processed to a great extent.

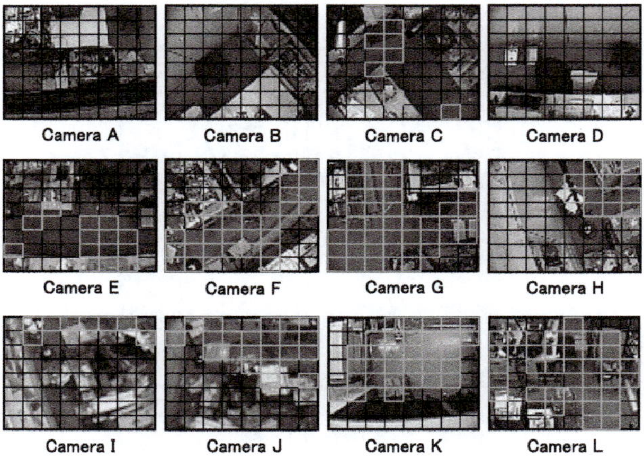

Fig. 6. Resultant ROIs (12 cameras)

5 Visual Surveillance Support Applications

Once the ROIs are calculated, the system can provide various support functions for visual surveillance. Two useful applications are introduced in this section.

5.1 Suggestion of Associative Blocks

One application of the method is suggestion of associative blocks. If there is an event that a user should examine and he/she notice it by having checked a certain region on one surveillance camera, the system can select associative ROIs that are helpful to examine the event.

To select the associative ROIs, we calculate the co-occurrence between two ROIs m, n. A feature value observed in a ROI m is shown as $y_m(t)$ $(1 \leq t \leq T)$, and a set of y_m is shown as a following vector.

$$\mathbf{y}_m = \{\ y_m(1),\ \cdots\ ,\ y_m(t),\ \cdots\ ,\ y_m(T)\ \} \tag{6}$$

We calculate a correlation value c_{mn} $(0 \leq c_{mn} \leq 1)$ by the following equations, and use it as a measure of the co-occurrence between two ROIs.

$$c_{1mn} = \frac{\mathbf{y}_m \cdot \mathbf{y}_n}{|\mathbf{y}_m||\mathbf{y}_n|} = \frac{\sum^T y_m(t) y_n(t)}{|\mathbf{y}_m||\mathbf{y}_n|} \tag{7}$$

$$c_{2mn} = \begin{cases} \frac{|\mathbf{y}_m|}{|\mathbf{y}_n|} & if\ |\mathbf{y}_m| < |\mathbf{y}_n| \\ \frac{|\mathbf{y}_n|}{|\mathbf{y}_m|} & \text{otherwise} \end{cases} \tag{8}$$

$$c_{mn} = c_{1mn}\ c_{2mn} \tag{9}$$

Fig. 7. Associative ROIs (1). The regions with bright frames have high co-occurrences with a white region.

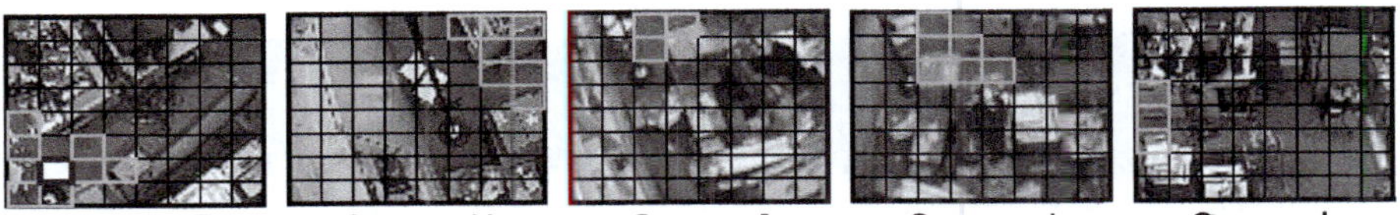

Fig. 8. Associative ROIs (2). The regions with bright frames have high co-occurrences with a white region.

We calculated the co-occurrence matrix of the 12 cameras shown in section 4.4. In Fig. 7 and Fig. 8, the regions with bright frames have high co-occurrences with the white region shown in Camera K and F respectively. The result means that if a user is interested in some motions in white block, the system suggests the user to check the brightly framed blocks too because it is likely to find something in them when some motions are found in the white block.

5.2 Dominant Camera Selection

The other application is dominant camera selection, which means the system can tell which cameras are worth watching in general case. It is useful as the number of cameras C becomes larger.

First, the system sorts all the pairs of any ROIs by their co-occurrences. Then, it selects the upper pairs that have higher co-occurrences, and increments the score u_c of the camera c $(1 \leq c \leq C)$ when the camera c has a block in the pairs. The system selects cameras whose scores are higher than the mean score $\bar{u}$. The selected cameras will be dominant for recognition purpose.

Fig. 9. Dominant Cameras (2 cameras were selected from 4 cameras)

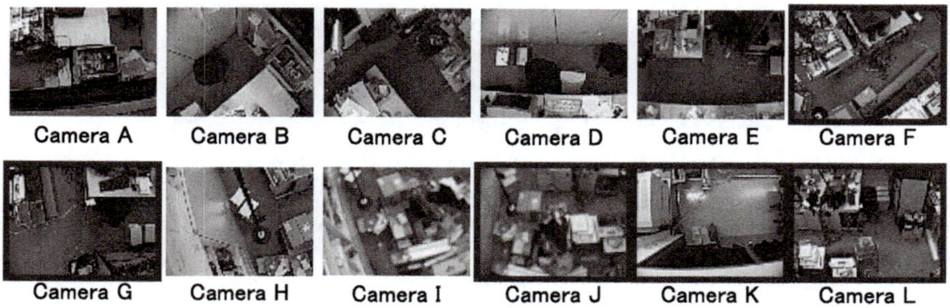

Fig. 10. Dominant Cameras (5 cameras were selected from 12 cameras)

Fig. 9 and Fig. 10 are the experimental results of the dominant camera selection. In the case where there are only 4 cameras (A, B, C, and D), the 2 cameras (B and D) are suggested to be checked for coming events (Fig. 9). On the other hand, if the system has 12 cameras, the system then suggests to check the 5 cameras (F, G, J, K, and L) (Fig. 10).

6 Conclusion

We presented a method to realize effective visual surveillance support under an environment in which a number of non-calibrated fixed surveillance cameras are being operated. Our method divides all camera images into small blocks and selects some blocks that can capture what kind of event is going on. We exploited PCA-based region selection algorithm, and succeeded in presenting useful data expression that can result in achieving two promising visual surveillance support applications; "suggestion of associative blocks" and "dominant camera selection".

As future works, we should examine the relevance of the ROI selection algorithm and the co-occurrence calculation method. In addition, we need to verify the proposed methods with large-scale camera network for very long time period.

References

1. M. D. Beynon, D. J. Van Hook, and M. Seibert abd A. Peacock, "Detecting abandoned packages in a multi-camera video surveillance system," in *IEEE Int. Conf. on Advanced Video and Signal Based Surveillance*, 2003, pp. 221–228.
2. T. Chang, S. Gong, and E. Ong, "Tracking multiple people under occlusion using multiple cameras," in *11th British Machine Vision Conference*, 2000.
3. N. T. Nguyen, S. Venkatesh, G. A. W. West, and H. H. Bui, "Hierarchical monitoring of people's behaviors in complex environments using multiple cameras," in *16 th Int. Conf. on Pattern Recognition*, 2002, pp. 13–16.
4. G. Wu, Y. Wu, L. Jiao, Y. Wang, and E. Y. Chang, "Multi-camera spatio-temporal fusion and biased sequence-data learning for security surveillance," in *11th ACM Int. Conf. on Multimedia*, 2003, pp. 528–538.

5. G. Stein, R. Romano, and L. Lee, "Monitoring activities from multiple video streams: Establishing a common coordinate frame," in *IEEE Transactions on Pattern Analysis and Machine Intelligence August 2000 (Vol. 22, No. 8)*, 2000, pp. 258–767.
6. O. Javed, K. Sha que, and M. Shah, 'Appearance modeling for tracking in multiple non-overlapping cameras," in *IEEE Int. Conf. on Computer Vision and Pattern Recognition*, 2005, vol.II, pp.26–33.
7. P. KaewTraKulPong and R. Bowden, "A real-time adaptive visual surveillance system for tracking low resolution colour targets in dynamically changing scenes," in *Image and Vision Computing, Volume 21, Number 10*, 2003, pp. 913–929.
8. V. Kettnaker and R. Zabih, "Bayesian multi-camera surveillance," in *IEEE Conf. on Computer Vision and Pattern Recognition*, 1999, vol.II, pp.253–259
9. C. Stauffer and K. Tieu, "Automated multi-camera planar tracking correspondence modeling," in *Computer Vision and Pattern Recognition*, 2003, pp. 259–266.

A Novel Robust Statistical Method for Background Initialization and Visual Surveillance

Hanzi Wang and David Suter

Department of Electrical and Computer Systems Engineering,
Monash University, Clayton 3800, Victoria, Australia
{Hanzi.wang, D.suter}@eng.monash.edu.au

Abstract. In many visual tracking and surveillance systems, it is important to initialize a background model using a training video sequence which may include foreground objects. In such a case, robust statistical methods are required to handle random occurrences of foreground objects (i.e., outliers), as well as general image noise. The robust statistical method *Median* has been employed for initializing the background model. However, the Median can tolerate up to only 50% outliers, which cannot satisfy the requirements of some complicated environments. In this paper, we propose a novel robust method for the background initialization. The proposed method can tolerate more than 50% of foreground pixels and noise. We give quantitative evaluations on a number of video sequences and compare our proposed method with five other methods. Experiments show that our method can achieve very promising results in background initialization: including applications in video segmentation, visual tracking and surveillance.

1 Introduction

Visual tracking and surveillance has gained a wide range of applications including monitoring freeways [1], recognizing human action [2, 3], motion segmentation [4], etc. Background subtraction, which detects changes from a background model, is a crucial step in these applications. To extract foreground objects, one usually needs to model the background scene using a short training video sequence.

There are a number of methods (for example, [2, 3, 5-8]) that have been proposed for modeling background scene in recent years. Simple methods represent background features by an average of either grey-level or color samples at each pixel over a training time. Pfinder [3] is one of the examples. It assumes that the values of the pixels, over a time window at a particular image location, are Gaussian distributed. Such kind of methods does not address scenes with dynamic backgrounds, or where foreground objects are present in the training stage. Some methods have been proposed to model dynamic background scenes,: for example, Mixture of Gaussians (MOG) [5, 8, 9]. In MOG, the background features are characterized by a mixture of several Gaussians. Each Gaussian represents a distribution per pixel. Thus, MOG can efficiently model dynamic background scenes. However, when the background involves a wide distribution in color/intensity, modeling the background with a mixture of a small number of Gaussian distributions is not efficient, when foreground objects are included in the training frames, MOG does not work well and it will misclassify [6].

P.J. Narayanan et al. (Eds.): ACCV 2006, LNCS 3851, pp. 328 – 337, 2006.

Among the above-mentioned methods, almost all of the methods require that the training sequence is *free of any foreground objects*. In practical cases, for example, in a busy road or in a public area, it is hard to control the environments. Such a requirement can not be always satisfied. We must initialize the background model in a way that is robust to the presence of foreground objects in the background training data. In contrast to background model representation and model maintenance, only a few studies of background model initialization have been made (e.g., [1, 4, 10, 11]).

For example, the authors of [11] proposed a Smoothness Detector (SD) Method. They assumed that a background value always has the longest stable value. They employed a moving window along time at each pixel to search for the stable intervals. However, we find one problem of the method is that when the data include multimodal distributions (i.e., some modes from foreground objects and some modes from background as shown in Fig. 2 and Fig. 3), and when the modes from foreground objects tend to be relatively stable, this method can not differentiate these modes from those from the background.

In order to decide the window length (L) and the intensity flicker of the window (T_f) for each pixel, the authors of [11] also proposed an Adaptive Smoothness Detector (ASD) method. Because the ASD method tries different L and T_f at each iteration until the solution is found, the computational cost of the ASD method is greatly increased.

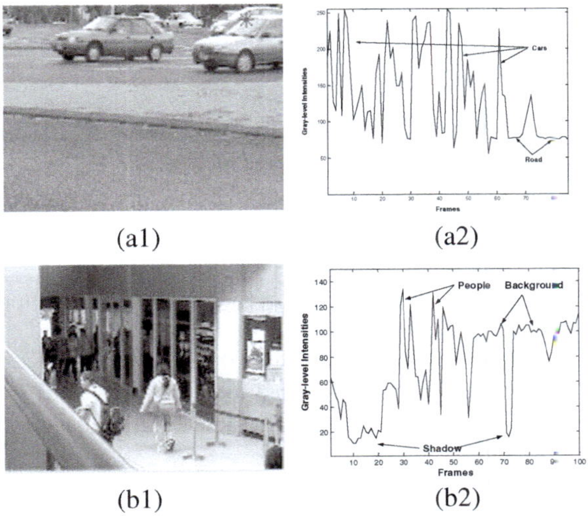

Fig. 1. Two examples that background is visible less than 50 percent of the training time: (a1) and (b1) show one frame of each training sequence; (a2) and (b2) show the intensity distributions over time at one pixel (marked by red star) of the sequence

Motivated by [11], a Local Image Flow (LIF) algorithm [10] was proposed. Two steps are used: in the first step, all stable sub-intervals in a training sequence are located for each pixel. In the second step, the method locates the sub-interval with the greatest average likelihood using local motion information, and produces background value by computing the mean value over the chosen sub-interval. Optical flow is computed for each consecutive pair of images and used to estimate the likelihood.

While this potentially adds valuable information, most optical flow computation methods themselves are computationally complex and very sensitive to noise.

In [1], the authors used the Median intensity value over observations at each pixel, to initialize the background for a traffic monitoring system. The underlying assumption is that the background at each pixel can be seen for more than 50 percent of time in the training sequence. However, the requirement that background appear more than 50% of time in a video sequence may not be always satisfied. Fig. 1 illustrates two such examples. In Fig. 1, we can see that the background value at the marked pixel (with red star) is visible less than 50 percent of the training time. The noise is either from the moving foreground objects or the shadows of the foreground objects.

A robust method which can tolerate more than 50% of noise is possible [12]. Examples include RANdom Sample Consensus (RANSAC) [13], Adaptive-Scale Sample Consensus (ASSC) [14], etc. To overcome the problems inherent in methods based on the Median, we propose a new robust method for background initialization. The major advantage of the proposed method is that it can tolerate over 50% of noise (including foreground pixels) in the data. The essential idea of the proposed method has been previously published in [15] which was restricted to only the background initialization problem. This paper also provides applications of the proposed method to video segmentation, visual tracking and surveillance.

This paper is organized as follows: in Sect. 2, we propose a new robust method for background initialization. In Sect. 3, experiments showing the advantages of, and applications of, our method are provided. We conclude in Sect. 4.

2 The Proposed Method for Background Initialization

2.1 Assumptions

In our method, we make some assumptions which are similar to those in [10, 11]:

1. The background at each pixel should be revealed at least for a short interval during the training period.
2. A background value tends to be relatively stable and constant.
3. A foreground object can remain stationary for a short interval in the training sequence. However, the interval should be no longer than the interval from the revealed static background.
4. The background scene remains relatively stable.

Stability is one characteristic of essentially stationary backgrounds. The foreground value at a pixel is assumed to have no less variance in grey-level intensity than a background value.

2.2 The Proposed Method

We employ a two-step framework:

(1) locate all non-overlapping stable subsequences of pixel values; (2) choose the most reliable subsequence (from which we use the mean value of either the grey-level intensities or the color intensities over that subsequence as the model background value).

In the first step, we use a sliding window with a minimum length L_w to locate all stable sub-intervals $\{l_k\}$ (similar to [10, 11]). For a test sequence of N frames, we have N observations at each pixel $\{x_i \mid i = 1,\dots,N\}$. Let $x_{l_k(t)}$ be a pixel value of the kth subsequence l_k at time t. The kth stable subsequence candidate should satisfy:

$$\forall (t-1,t) \in l_k,\ \begin{cases} \left| x_{l_k(t)} - x_{l_k(t-1)} \right| \le T_f \\ \left| x_{l_k(t)} - \overline{x}_{l_k(t-1)} \right| \le T_f \end{cases} \tag{1}$$

where $\overline{x}_{l_k(t-1)}$ is the mean value from the beginning of the subsequence l_k to time t-1.

If we cannot find any candidate subsequence with a minimum length L_w we use the longest stable candidate subsequence. We experimentally set L_w to 5 and T_f to 10, for all test sequences. Note: even after this step, the chosen subsequences can contain pixels from foreground, background, shadows, highlights, etc. (e.g., see Fig. 1 b).

The second step is a crucial step, because in this step, a reliable subsequence, which is most likely to arise from the background, will be chosen. Our definition of reliability is motivated by RANSAC [13]. We build in to our objective function the notions of consensus and of scale estimation. We consider both the number (n) of data points "agreeing" with a model (contained in the candidate interval), and the distribution of these data (e.g. standard variance S): n should be large, and S should be small. We define our objective function as finding the most stable interval from the non-overlapping sub-intervals $\{l_k\}$ by:

$$\widehat{l_k} = \arg\max_k (n_{l_k} / S_{l_k}) \tag{2}$$

where n_{l_k} and S_{l_k} are respectively the number of values (length) of, and the standard variance of, the observations in the kth subsequence l_k.

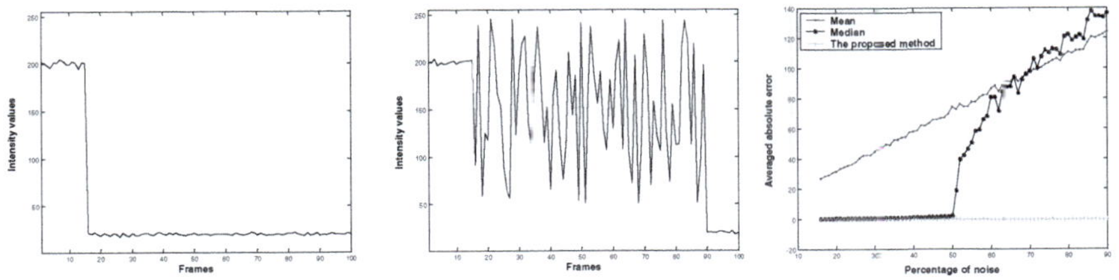

(a) (b) (c)

Fig. 2. Estimating background value from noisy data: (a) and (b) illustrate two cases of the distributions of the simulated data; (c) the results obtained by the three methods

To illustrate the robustness of the proposed method we generate synthetic data to simulate the observations over time at a pixel. One hundred data values (i.e., 100 frames) were generated. The first fifteen data values (i.e., a relatively stationary foreground object pixel) have intensity value of 200 and standard variance of 2. From the sixteenth to the i'th data, we simulate random noise (such as foreground objects in transit at that pixel) with intensity values ranging from 50 to 250. We simulate a background value in the sub-interval from the $(i+1)$'th data to the 100th data, with unit variance. We increase i value from 16 to 90 with step 1 each time. We repeat the experiment ten times and output the average value.

Fig. 2 (c) shows the results of finding backgrounds by three statistics: Mean, Median, and the proposed method. We see that the Mean is not robust to noise at all. The Median can only tolerate noise occupying less than 50 percent of the data. In contrast, the proposed method is much more robust.

However, we note that equation (2) might be erroneous when S_{l_k} is very small. This can happen when some pixels of a short subinterval have saturated colors. The saturated pixel values are clipped within the range from 0 to 255 and sequences containing these saturated pixels have a very small (or zero) standard variance [16]. For this case, the assumption (1) in Sect. 2.1 is violated. When we detect such a case happens, we use the following equation instead of equation (2):

$$\widehat{l}_k = \arg\max_k (n_{l_k}) \tag{3}$$

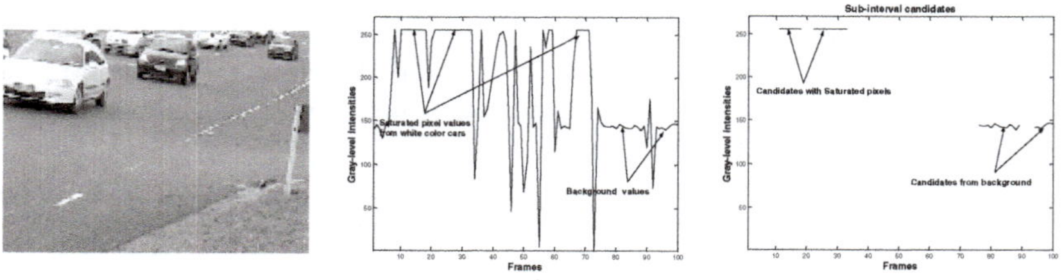

(a) (b) (c)

Fig. 3. One example showing that the intensities of the saturated pixels are clipped: (a) one frame of the test sequence. We investigate the grey-level intensity distribution of the observations at one pixel, which was marked with a red star. In (b), we can see that there are some saturated pixels corresponding to white colored cars. The sub-interval candidates obtained in the first step are shown in (c). The two candidates corresponding to saturated pixels have a standard variance of zero. In such case, we should use equation (3) instead of equation (2).

Fig.3 shows an example where the intensities of some saturated pixels are clipped.

3 Experiments

3.1 Background Model Construction Test

The test sequences are recorded by a Canon MV750i digital video camera. We stored the sequences at a resolution of 160x120, and a sample rate of five frames per second. We have deliberately chosen different background including both indoor and outdoor scenes (including within these scenes, foreground objects, shadows, highlights, and illumination changes to simulate true situations that a visual surveillance system may meet in practice).

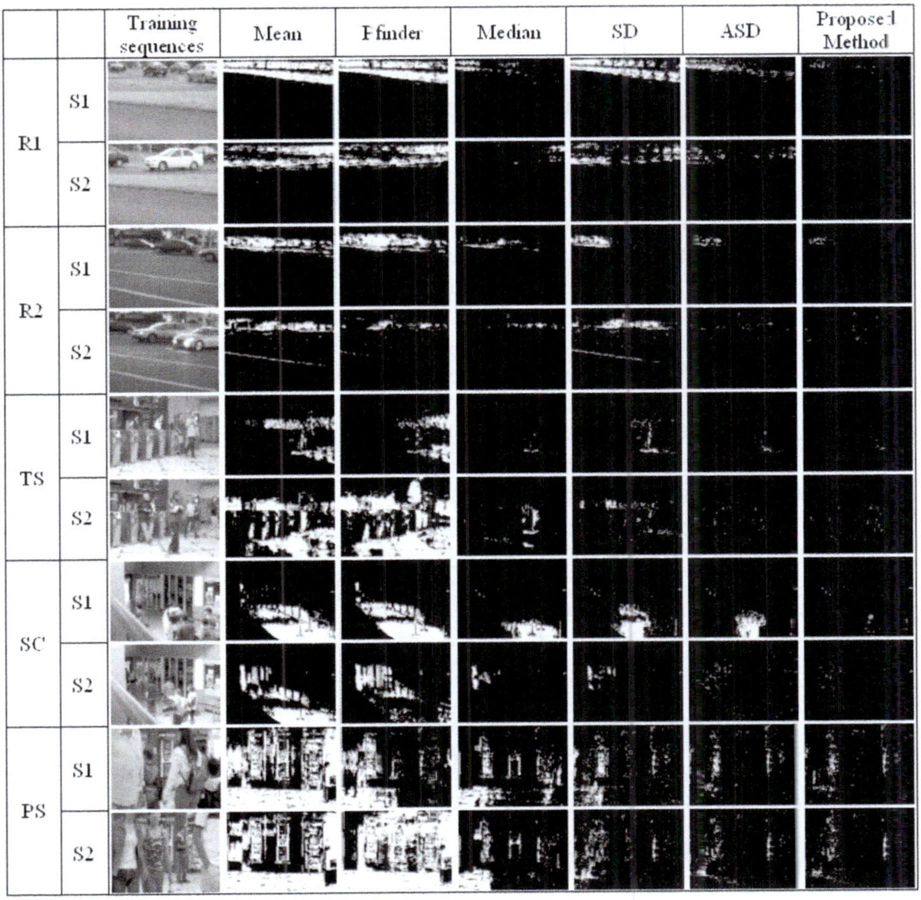

Fig. 4. Ten video sub-sequences of five test videos. The third column shows one frame of each training subsequence; the remaining columns show the difference between the background and the background estimate obtained by the competing methods. The results obtained by the proposed method are shown in the last column.

Road1 (R1): Heavy traffic in daytime (some shadows on the road).

Road2 (R2): Vehicles passed by a crossing road in the evening. Some parts of the road were highlighted when vehicles (with lights on) got close to those parts.

Train Station (TS): A gate of a train station. Many people exited or entered the station through that gate.

Sport Center (SC): In an indoor sport center, people walked through a corridor. Shadows of people were cast on the glass wall and the floor of the corridor. Also some illumination changes happened when people exited the back door and covered the light outside.

Pharmore Shop (PS): A pharmacy shop, which is located inside a big shopping center. People walked in front of the shop. The illumination of the background scene sometimes changed because of the reflected sunlight outside the shopping center.

We compare the proposed method with five other methods. All of the methods perform at pixel-level for background initialization (in contrast to methods that use region level analysis). To test each method, we choose two sub-sequences (S1 and S2) which include a number of frames ranging from 30 to 100 in each sub-sequence, from each test sequence. To evaluate the performance of each method, we employ three criteria, similar to those used in [10]: a) the Average gray-level Error (AE); b) the Number of Error pixels (NE); and c) the Number of Clustered error pixels (NC). We use the Mean value of Total error (MT) of the ten sub-sequences over each criterion as the overall measurement for each method.

We generate a Reference Frame (RF) for each test sequence by using the mean value of selected frames that are free of foreground objects. An error pixel is one whose grey-level value differs from the value of the reference pixel by a threshold 20. We define a clustered error pixel when the 4-connected neighbors of that error pixel consist of more than 4 error pixels.

Fig. 4 shows one frame of each test subsequences and the resulting error pixels (corresponding to the white color pixels), obtained by the five other methods and the proposed method. A quantitative comparison is given in Table 1. From these results, we can see that the Mean and the Pfinder methods are the most inaccurate in background initialization. The Mean takes all observations at each pixel in the test subsequence into account. The Pfinder, using a temporal smoothing technique, gives larger weight value to recent observations. When the observations contain pixels from other than background, these two methods break down.

Table 1. Experimental results by different methods on test sequences

		R1		R2		TS		SC		PS		MT
		S1	S2	S1	S2	S1	S2	S1	S2	S1	S2	
Mean	**AE**	**9.61**	**10.27**	**5.79**	**9.10**	**5.81**	**14.12**	**11.69**	**8.75**	**26.48**	**25.12**	**12.67**
	NE	2994	2369	1630	1320	1323	4992	3537	3102	10253	9799	4132
	NC	2965	2273	1571	1231	1211	4811	3436	3023	10031	9677	4023
Pfinder	AE	9.14	9.17	6.25	6.01	5.50	20.89	10.08	9.92	12.99	38.82	12.88
	NE	2790	2127	1917	411	1125	7805	3402	1822	3969	12690	3806
	NC	2752	2016	1866	312	1042	7605	3347	1699	3746	12573	3696
Median	AE	5.14	4.58	2.69	3.45	2.89	4.15	6.63	3.14	9.51	8.49	5.07
	NE	352	159	276	142	40	353	1349	271	2559	2092	759
	NC	282	127	239	114	28	296	1301	247	2347	1947	693
SD	AE	7.99	5.94	2.83	5.58	2.96	3.50	6.10	2.77	7.85	5.43	5.10
	NE	2097	976	515	872	226	399	1304	217	1400	921	893
	NC	2018	840	487	741	153	228	1195	181	961	603	741
ASD	AE	5.59	6.01	2.43	3.58	2.66	2.81	7.62	2.94	6.47	4.64	4.48
	NE	588	252	114	55	44	56	892	123	598	559	328
	NC	443	152	82	11	22	0	819	15	420	306	227
The proposed method	AE	4.33	4.32	2.05	3.00	2.54	2.77	2.81	2.46	6.27	4.36	3.49
	NE	70	10	57	37	21	63	76	51	541	484	141
	NC	23	0	23	4	7	5	28	15	296	238	64

Compared with the Mean and the Pfinder, the Median method achieves a much better result because of its robustness to noise (from foreground objects, shadows, etc.). However, when the test subsequence includes too many foreground objects, or if the background value is visible for less than 50 percent of the test subsequence (more noticeable, in the S1 of Sport Center sequence, and in the S1 and S2 of the Pharmore Shop sequence), the Median method fails to estimate the background.ï

SD obtained more accurate results than the Median in the SC and PS sequences, but less accurate results in the R1, R2, and TS sequences. ASD achieves better results than the SD method in all test sequences because it uses different window length L and T_f at each pixel location. However, the cost is about 30-50 times slower than SD in computational time.

Among the six methods, the proposed method achieves the most accurate results and it also is about three times faster than SD, and about 100 times faster than ASD.

3.2 Applications

The proposed method can be applied in a wide range of practical computer vision tasks such as video segmentation, vehicle surveillance, tracking, etc. Fig. 5 and Fig. 6 show the application to segmentation and tracking.

In Fig. 5, we use an image sequence from http://www.ecse.rpi.edu/~cvrl/humanbody/. The sequence shows an office with several people walking around. Almost every frame of the sequence includes people. The ground truth background image is not available. We use frames 310 to 359 as training images, which include two people walking around (Fig. 5 (a) and (b) show frame 310 and frame 359 of the image sequence). We initialize the background using the six methods. Because the MOG method is frequently used in many vision tasks, in this experiment, we also include MOG.

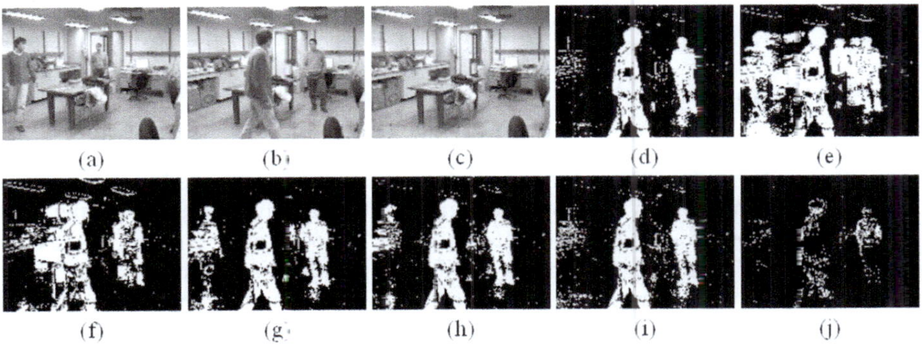

Fig. 5. (a) and (b) are frames 310 and 359. (c) The initialized background image by the proposed method; (d) The detected foreground pixels by the proposed method; (f) to (j) are respectively the foregrounds obtained by Mean, Pfinder, Median, SD, ASD, and MOG.

From Fig. 5, we can see that the proposed method outputs an accurate initialized background, and thus, it effectively extracts foreground objects (i.e., in this case, the two people). Because the Mean and Pfinder methods can not tolerate outliers at all, they totally broke down when the training frames include foreground objects. Although the Median method is robust to noise and outliers, it breaks down when data involves more than 50 percent. Thus, we can clearly see there is a ghost in the detected foreground. SD and ASD work better than the Mean, Pfinder, and Median. However, we can still see a ghost in the detected foreground in the result of SD. Although ASD produced a result close to that of the proposed method, the result of ASD is less accurate and the computational time is much higher. The result of MOG tends to give less false positive but more false negative pixels. This is because MOG blindly treats the pixels of the persons as background modes in the training stage.

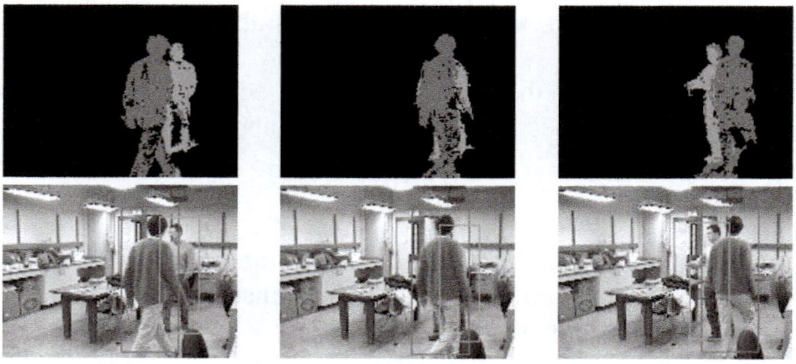

377 383 390

Fig. 6. Segmentation and tracking results (sample frames 377, 383 and 390)

In Fig. 6, we use the background initialized by the proposed method as the background model to segment/track people inside the office. The segmentation and tracking results (on frames 377, 383, 390) are shown in Fig. 6. We see the proposed method provides a good background initialization image for the tracking/segmentation system even when every frame in the training stage contains foreground objects.

4 Conclusion

In this paper, a new robust method is proposed for the task of background initialization. The proposed method is very robust to outliers and can be used in many places where foreground objects can not be avoided in the training stage. One of the main strength of the proposed method is that it is highly robust to noise and outliers in data. The method is a great improvement over the traditional Median method.

We have evaluated our method on various environments including outdoor and indoor, daytime and nighttime, different illumination conditions. Comparisons with several other methods on background initialization show that our method can achieve very promising results even when the background is revealed much less than half of time in the training sequences. Furthermore, we show the method can be successfully used in video segmentation, tracking and surveillance.

Acknowledgements

This work is supported by ARC grant DP0452416. This work was carried out within the Monash University Institute for Vision Systems Engineering.

References

1. Gloyer, B., et al. Video-based Freeway Monitoring System Using Recursive Vehicle Tracking. in Proc. of IS&T-SPIE Symposium on Electronic Imaging: Image and Video Processing. 1995. p. 173-180.
2. Haritaoglu, I., D. Harwood, and L.S. Davis, W4: Real-Time Surveillance of People and Their Activities. IEEE Trans. Pattern Analysis and Machine Intelligence, 2000. 22(8): p. 809-830.
3. Wren, C.R., et al., Pfinder: real-time tracking of the human body. IEEE Trans. Pattern Analysis and Machine Intelligence, 1997. 19(7): p. 780-785.
4. Cristani, M., M. Bicego, and V. Murino. Multi-level background initialization using Hidden Markov Models. in First ACM SIGMM international workshop on Video surveillance. 2003. p. 11 - 20.
5. Stauffer, C. and W.E.L. Grimson Adaptive Background Mixture Models for Real-time Tracking. in Proc. IEEE Int'l Conf. on Computer Vision and Pattern Recognition. 1999. p. 246-252.
6. Toyama, K., et al. Wallflower: Principles and Practice of Background Maintenance. in 7th International Conference on Computer Vision. 1999. p. 255-261.
7. Harville, M. A Framework for High-Level Feedback to Adaptive, Per-Pixel, Mixture-of-Gaussian Background Models. in 7th European Conference on Computer Vision. 2002. p. 543-560.
8. Friedman, N. and S. Russell. Image Segmentation in Video Sequences: A Probabilistic Approach. in Proc. Thirteenth Conf. on Uncertainty in Artificial Intelligence. 1997. p. 175-181.
9. Harville, M., G. Gordon, and J. Woodfill. Foreground Segmentation Using Adaptive Mixture Models in Color and Depth. in IEEE Workshop on Detection and Recognition of Events in Video. 2001. p. 3-11.
10. Gutchess, D., et al. A Background Model Initialization Algorithm for Video Surveillance. in IEEE Int'l Conference on Computer Vision. 2001. p. 733-740.
11. Long, W. and Y.H. Yang, Stationary Background Generation: An Alternative to the Difference of Two Images. Pattern Recognition, 1990. 23(12): p. 1351-1359.
12. Stewart, C.V., Robust Parameter Estimation in Computer Vision. SIAM Review, 1999. 41(3): p. 513-537.
13. Fischler, M.A. and R.C. Rolles, Random Sample Consensus: A Paradigm for Model Fitting with Applications to Image Analysis and Automated Cartography. Commun. ACM, 1981. 24(6): p. 381-395.
14. Wang, H. and D. Suter, Robust Adaptive-Scale Parametric Model Estimation for Computer Vision. IEEE Trans. Pattern Analysis and Machine Intelligence, 2004. 26(11): p. 1459-1474.
15. Wang, H. and D. Suter. Background Initialization with A New Robust Statistical Approach. IEEE International Workshop on Visual Surveillance and Performance Evaluation of Tracking and Surveillance. 2005. p. 153-159.
16. Horprasert, T., D. Harwood, and L.S. Davis. A Statistical Approach for Real-Time Robust Background Subtraction and Shadow Detection. in ICCV'99 Frame-Rate Workshop. 1999.

Exemplar-Based Human Contour Tracking

Shiming Xiang, Feiping Nie, and Changshui Zhang

State Key Laboratory of Intelligent Technology and Systems,
Department of Automation, Tsinghua University, Beijing 100084, China
{xsm, nfp03, zcs}@mail.tsinghau.edu.cn

Abstract. We propose an exemplar-based tracking framework for human contour tracking. The exemplars, i.e. the contour representatives, are used to construct a contour ensemble. The main task of contour ensemble is to generate contours to fill in the gaps in-between in the test sequences, and to supply the dynamics for updating the target contour by fast contour query. As a result, a normal dynamic Bayesian network is only used to infer the location and the size of the target contour. The effectiveness of the proposed method is tested by many human motion sequences.

1 Introduction

Vision based deformable contour tracking is a tough problem, due to non-rigidity of human body, complex dynamical system, occlusions and cluttered environments. Sequential Monte Carlo (SMC) estimation based on Dynamic Bayesian Network (DBN) is a popular approach for this problem [1, 2]. In SMC framework, tracking can be interpreted as a process of density propagation governed by the dynamic model and the observation model, which are both tightly associated with target state representation.

The state of the target contour consists of two parts: location and size and contour curve. Location and size can be stipulated by a geometrical transformation, while contour curve is related to geometrical representation.

However, representing the deformable contour may be a dilemma. The representations with high dimensionality can describe the local details. But the density function would be propagated in a high dimensional space. Accordingly, the tracker needs to employ more particles to keep a good adaptability. However, simple representations may lead the tracker to lose the target to be tracked, due to inaccurate measurements in cluttered environments. Crucially, compact and powerful representations are needed.

To avoid parameterizing the contour curves, exemplars of contours can be used to implicitly describe the target. Exemplars provide us with rich information [3, 4, 5]. But in real applications of contour tracking, there lacks of an explicit mechanism to generate in-between ones to fill in the gaps in the test sequences. To this end in this paper, a contour ensemble is constructed from the exemplars and in turn used to explain them and generate new contours.

Theoretically, the contour ensemble contains all the possible contours which are associated with a kind of human motion. To update the target contour, a

P.J. Narayanan et al. (Eds.): ACCV 2006, LNCS 3851, pp. 338–347, 2006.

neighbor search mechanism is introduced to find the appropriate candidates from this contour ensemble. This can be achieved for the contour at the next frame is definitely similar to those of the neighbors of the current one. As a result, we need not use the exemplars to learn the probabilistic metric mixture parameters and the dynamic model [5]. The SMC estimation is only used to estimate the location and size parameters.

The location and size and contour curve are separately treated and then integrated together to use the observation model. Therefore, we solve the dilemma of state representation.

2 Related Work

In SMC framework, one needs to deal with the following three aspects: contour representation, dynamic model and observation model. Typical contour representation includes parameterized shapes [1, 6, 7], exemplar-based models [5], and intrinsic representation in manifold space [8], and etc. All these representations are either suitable for the simple appearance models [1, 7] or need to learn complex probabilistic models [5, 8].

Linear dynamic model is usually used in real applications. To improve the adaptability, mixture models are developed via learning approaches [9]. Tracking can be implemented by switching among different models [10].

For observation model, the computation is tightly connected to image measurement [1, 11, 12]. In [13], joint probability data association filter is used to incorporate multiple cues. Shen et al. use color and edge feature to measure the observation data [14]. In addition, automatic switching model is proposed in [7].

Exemplar-based approach is used in [3, 4, 5, 15]. In [3], exemplars are used, non-probabilistically, to match the image features by distance transformation. Tomasi et al. propose a tracking paradigm where the tracker relies on the recognition of familiar exemplars [15]. On the contrary in [4] and [5], exemplars are considered into a probabilistic framework. Thus, it is necessary to perform exemplar-based learning. Furthermore, there lacks of a mechanism to deal with the in-between objects, which are not in the exemplar set, and may not be learned directly from the training data.

3 Contour Generation

3.1 Contour Ensemble

The methodology about ensemble is originated from statistical physics in 1930's, which is successfully applied to texture synthesis [16] during the past few years. Here we use the idea to describe contour ensemble.

Definition. Contour ensemble is a sextuple $\Gamma \triangleq < E, \tilde{E}, G, T, \varepsilon, D >$:

(1) E is a finite set of contours, which are chosen as representatives to specify some type of human motion;

(2) $\tilde{E}$ is an infinite set deduced from E, which contains all the possible meaningful contours similar to those in E. $E \subset \tilde{E}$;

(3) G is a generative operator. $\forall \mathbf{e}_1, \mathbf{e}_2 \in E$, $G(\mathbf{e}_1, \mathbf{e}_2) \in \tilde{E}$ produces a new contour. G is anti-symmetrical, i.e. $G(\mathbf{e}_1, \mathbf{e}_2) \neq G(\mathbf{e}_2, \mathbf{e}_1)$;

(4) T is a transformation. Given T, $\forall \mathbf{e} \in E$, $T(\mathbf{e}) \in \tilde{E}$;

(5) ε is a random vector. $\forall \mathbf{e} \in \tilde{E}$, $\mathbf{e} + \varepsilon \in \tilde{E}$;

(6) D is an operator of Euclidean distance measure in contour feature space.

Actually, contour ensemble Γ uses the finite to describe the infinite to model the continuous changes in real situations. Given $\mathbf{e}_1$, $\mathbf{e}_2 \in E$, we can generate new contours as follows:

$$\mathbf{e} = G(T(\mathbf{e}_1), T(\mathbf{e}_2)) + \varepsilon \tag{1}$$

3.2 Generate New Contour in Geometric Space

Given $\mathbf{e}_1$, $\mathbf{e}_2 \in E$, the task of G is to produce a new contour to fill in the gaps where a contour in a test sequence may not be equal to anyone in E.

Geometrically, in-between contours can be generated by interpolation based on the results of contour matching. Typically, Chui et al. introduce an accurate matching algorithm by minimizing bending energy [18]. Although a point-to-point mapping can not be directly obtained, we can achieve this by 1-NN mapping. For order preserving, we use linear regression to correct the possible cross matching pairs. The steps are summarized as follows:

(1) Use Chui's shape matching algorithm and 1-NN mapping to construct a point-to-point mapping between $\mathbf{e_1}$ and $\mathbf{e_2}$; (2) Use linear regression to make the mapping orderly; (3) Give a step ratio r, each point on new contour can be generated as follows:

$$P_N = P_S + r \cdot (P_D - P_S) \tag{2}$$

where $P_S \in \mathbf{e}_1$ and $P_D \in \mathbf{e}_2$. Figure 1(a) and 1(b) give an example.

However, Chui's approach is not rotation invariant since it is essentially based on Euclidean distance between contour points. This may produce wrong matching results. To achieve rotation invariance, we treat the unsigned distance maps [17] of $\mathbf{e}_1$ and $\mathbf{e}_2$ as normal images and registrate $\mathbf{e}_2$ to $\mathbf{e}_1$ by minimizing the sum of squared differences. After rotating $\mathbf{e}_2$ and matching it to $\mathbf{e}_1$, we can directly get the point-to-point correspondences (see Figure 1(c) and 1(d)).

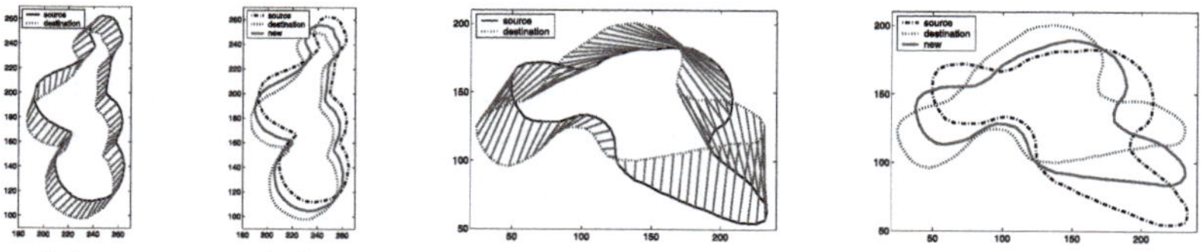

(a) (b) (c) (d)

Fig. 1. (a): Corresponds; (b): The generated contour according to the corresponds in (a), where the step ratio is 0.5; (c): Corresponds under rotation invariance; (d): The generated contour according to the corresponds in (c), where the step ratio is 0.5

Finally, we note that matching the contours in E can be done off-line among the neighbors. Matching those being non-neighbors is no meaningful in the context of contour tracking.

3.3 Contour Recognition

The elements in E should be preprocessed for contour recognition since in-between contours are generated from two neighbors. To this end, for each contour in E the indices of its neighbors are stored to build a lookup table. We use Hu moments as well as Euclidean distance measure (D opterator in Γ) to construct the feature space for fast query. Query can then be performed in a k-NN way.

3.4 Probabilistic Interpretation

E can be regarded as an optimal set of cluster centers, which can be learned from training contours, either supervised or semi-supervised or even manually defined by users. Taking the elements in E as clusters, the contours in $\tilde{E}$ can be globally modelled as some mixture model, for example, Gaussian mixture model. Human motion can then be interpreted as a process of model switching.

By dealing with each contour in E as a node, we can also construct a graphical model via k-NN method. The 2D contour sequence in a video sequence to be tracked can be viewed as an instance of a random walk on this graph. Being walking along the edge, new contours can be generated and used to fit the test data. In this way, the construction of the probabilistic model [5] is replaced by near-neighbor search, which is more effective in practical applications, as proven in texture synthesis [16].

4 Tracking Algorithm

4.1 Overview of Tracking Framework

Figure 2(a) illustrates our tracking framework. The sub-graph connected by solid-line arrows is a normal DNB structure, which is used to infer the location and size parameters by Monte Carlo sampling. The sub-graph connected by dashed-line arrows is introduced to provide the dynamics for contour update.

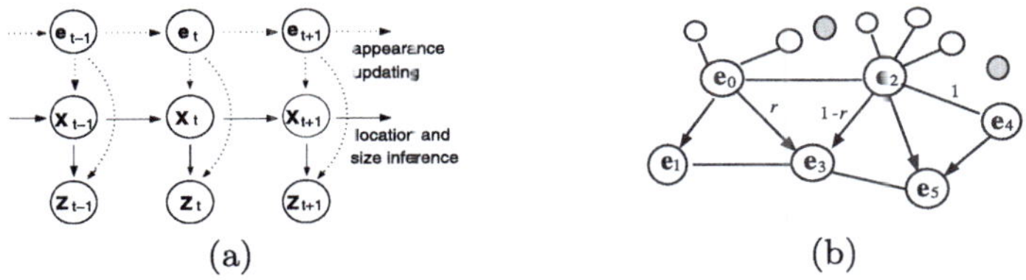

Fig. 2. (a): Exemplar-based contour tracking framework; (b): Contour generation

During tracking, each particle is associated with a contour, which is generated via operator G. Observation measurement will be finally performed on each particle and its associated contour.

4.2 Generating Contours Dynamically

In the tracking context, generating in-between contours should be implemented according to the following equation:

$$\mathbf{e} = G(\mathbf{e}_1, \mathbf{e}_2) + \varepsilon \tag{3}$$

Here $\mathbf{e}_1 (\in \tilde{E})$ is the currently estimated contour of a particle, and $\mathbf{e}_2 \in E$. However, if contour matching is done during tracking, the computation cost is expensive because there may be hundreds of thousands of particles. To fast produce a new contour, we record its parents from which $\mathbf{e}$ is generated. Since the parents are well matched in advance, generating new contour is a simple interpolation according to (2). Figure 2(b) shows the process.

Suppose $\mathbf{e}_3$ is generated by $\mathbf{e}_1$ and $\mathbf{e}_2$ at time t and its two parents are $\mathbf{e}_0$ and $\mathbf{e}_2$. To generate a new contour, we first search in E to obtain the neighbors of $\mathbf{e}_3$, and denote the set by $N(\mathbf{e}_3)$. Then, partition $N(\mathbf{e}_3)$ such that $N(\mathbf{e}_3) = N(\mathbf{e}_0) \cup N(\mathbf{e}_2) \cup N_0$. The elements in N_0, shown as shadow nodes in Figure 2(b), will not be accounted for any more. Take each one in $N(\mathbf{e}_0) \cup N(\mathbf{e}_2)$, for example $\mathbf{e}_4 \in N(\mathbf{e}_2)$, as a destination contour. Now, we define the distance between $\mathbf{e}_3$ and $\mathbf{e}_4$ as $2 - r$. Given a new step ratio $r_1 \in [0, 1]$, if $r_1 > (1 - r)/(2 - r)$, a new contour $\mathbf{e}_5$ is generated by $\mathbf{e}_2$ and $\mathbf{e}_4$. Thus, the parents of $\mathbf{e}_5$ are $\mathbf{e}_2$ and $\mathbf{e}_4$. Otherwise, $\mathbf{e}_5$ is generated from $\mathbf{e}_0$ and $\mathbf{e}_2$.

The step ratio r can be treated as a latent random variable. This will increase the complexity of probabilistic inference. We descretize it in experiments.

Note that generating contour according to ε requires to know parameters of the probabilistic mixture model and requires us to smooth the generated contours. Thus we omit this term in computation.

4.3 Tracking with Exemplars

We use the SMC framework to track the state w.r.t. location and size parameters, which are the centroid coordinate (x_c, y_c) of the associated contour and the scaling parameter s. Note that here we need not deal with the rotation angle as it is implicitly considered in contour generation (Subsection 3.2). Thus a state vector can be formulated as $\mathbf{x} = (x_c, y_c, s)^T$. The system dynamic equation we use is as follows:

$$\mathbf{x}_t = \mathbf{A}\mathbf{x}_{t-1} + \mathbf{B}\mathbf{N}_t \tag{4}$$

where $\mathbf{A}$ and $\mathbf{B}$ are matrices representing the deterministic and stochastic components of the dynamic model respectively and $\mathbf{N}_t$ is a Gaussian noise vector.

To calculate the likelihood value $p(\mathbf{z}_t|\mathbf{x}_t)$, we must combine $\mathbf{x}_t$ with the candidate contour $\{\mathbf{e}_k\}$. Namely, we should compute $p(\mathbf{z}_t|\mathbf{x}_t, \mathbf{e}_k)$, where $\mathbf{z}_t$ is treated as image feature. For deformable object tracking, color information is an appealing feature due to its robustness to spatial rotation, non-rigidity and partial occlusion [14]. But color does not contain any information about the spatial adjacency of pixels corresponding to the object. In contrast, edge feature can be used to describe the shape information. Thus, we use the following multi-cue likelihood model [14]:

$$p(\mathbf{z}_t|\mathbf{x}_t, \mathbf{e}_k) = [p_e(\mathbf{z}_t|\mathbf{e}_k(\mathbf{x}_t))]^{\alpha_e} \cdot [p_c(\mathbf{z}_t|\mathbf{e}_k(\mathbf{x}_t))]^{\alpha_c} \quad (5)$$

where $\mathbf{e}_k(\mathbf{x}_t)$ is the contour $\mathbf{e}_k$ scaled and translated according to $\mathbf{x}_t$, α_c and α_e are edge and color reliability factors. $p_e(\mathbf{z}_t|\mathbf{e}_k(\mathbf{x}_t))$ can be calculated as [1]:

$$p_e(\mathbf{z}_t|\mathbf{e}_k(\mathbf{x}_t)) \propto \prod_{i=1}^{M} [1 + \frac{1}{\sqrt{2\pi}\sigma q\lambda} \sum_{j=1}^{n_i} \exp(-\frac{v_i^j}{2\sigma^2})] \quad (6)$$

where λ is the mean of the Poisson distribution, σ is the standard deviation of the normal distribution, q is the non-detection probability, M is the number of measured lines in the clutter, n_i is the number of detected feature points along the ith measurement line, and $v_i^j = z_j - x_i$, here $x_i \in \mathbf{e}_k(\mathbf{x}_t)$. Finally, we scale $p_e(\mathbf{z}_t|\mathbf{e}_k(\mathbf{x}_t))$ to [0,1], and still denote the result by $p_e(\mathbf{z}_t|\mathbf{e}_k(\mathbf{x}_t))$.

To be robust to illumination changes, we consider the normalized HS histogram in HSV color space , $\mathbf{b}(\mathbf{e}_k(\mathbf{x}_t))$. Let $\mathbf{b}(\mathbf{e}_k(\mathbf{x}_t)) = (b^j(\mathbf{e}_k(\mathbf{x}_t)))_{j=1,\cdots,N}$, which is computed from the region of $\mathbf{e}_k(\mathbf{x}_t)$. Then we obtain [19]

$$p_c(\mathbf{z}_t|\mathbf{e}_k(\mathbf{x}_t)) = \frac{1}{\sqrt{2\pi}\sigma} \exp(-\frac{\rho(k,t)}{2\sigma^2}) \quad (7)$$

where $\rho(k,t) = 1 - \sum_{j=1}^{N} b^j(\mathbf{e}_k(\mathbf{x}_t)) \cdot b^j$, $(b^j)_{j=1,\cdots,N}$ is the HS histogram of a reference color model and σ is the variance calculated from $\{\rho(k,t)\}$.

Suppose the associated contour of $\mathbf{x}_{t-1}$ be $\mathbf{e}_{t-1}$. We first generate a set of candidate contours for $\mathbf{x}_t$ and denote it as $E_t(\mathbf{e}_{t-1})$. Then, each contour is scaled according to the predicted $\mathbf{x}_t$. Now we have:

$$\begin{aligned} p(\mathbf{z}_t|\mathbf{x}_t) &= \sum_{\mathbf{e}_k \in \tilde{E}} p(\mathbf{z}_t|\mathbf{x}_t, \mathbf{e}_k) P(\mathbf{e}_k) \approx \sum_{\mathbf{e}_k \in E_t(\mathbf{e}_{t-1})} p(\mathbf{z}_t|\mathbf{x}_t, \mathbf{e}_k) P(\mathbf{e}_k) \\ &\approx \frac{1}{N} \sum_{\mathbf{e}_k \in E_t(\mathbf{e}_{t-1})} p(\mathbf{z}_t|\mathbf{x}_t, \mathbf{e}_k) \end{aligned}$$

Here, we simply abandon the contributions of the contours in $\tilde{E}$ far from $\mathbf{e}_{t-1}$ according to k-NN criterion and assume that $\{P(\mathbf{e}_k)\}$ bear an uniform distribution. Finally, a contour for $\mathbf{x}_t$ can be obtained by maximum a posterior:

$$\mathbf{e}_t = \mathbf{e}_{k^*} = \arg\max_{\mathbf{e}_k} \{p(\mathbf{z}_t|\mathbf{x}_t, \mathbf{e}_k)\} \quad (8)$$

The steps of generating $\{\mathbf{x}_t^{(n)}, \mathbf{e}_t^{(n)}, w_t^{(n)}\}$ from $\{\mathbf{x}_{t-1}^{(n)}, \mathbf{e}_{t-1}^{(n)}, w_{t-1}^{(n)}\}$ based on SMC estimation are as follows:

Step1: Re-sampling. Generate $\{\mathbf{x'}_{t-1}^{(n)}\}$ from $\{\mathbf{x}_{t-1}^{(n)}\}$ according to the weights $\{w_{t-1}^{(n)}\}$, then copy the corresponding contour $\mathbf{e}_{t-1}^{(n)}$ to construct $\{\mathbf{x'}_{t-1}^{(n)}, \mathbf{e'}_{t-1}^{(n)}\}$

Step2: Prediction. For each $(\mathbf{x'}_{t-1}^{(n)}, \mathbf{e'}_{t-1}^{(n)})$

(1) Generate $\mathbf{x}_t^{(n)}$ from $\mathbf{x'}_t^{(n)}$ according to $p(\mathbf{x}_t|\mathbf{x}_{t-1})$.

(2) Query with $\mathbf{e'}_{t-1}^{(n)}$ in E and then generate a candidate set $E_t(\mathbf{e'}_{t-1}^{(n)})$

Step3: Correction. Select a contour for $x_t^{(n)}$ by (8). Accordingly, $w_t^{(n)}$ can be calculated based on $p(\mathbf{z}_t|\mathbf{x}_t)$. All the weights are normalized finally.

For initialization, we use the feature matching algorithm [20] to select the associated contours of particles from E.

5 Experimental Evaluation

The proposed tracking framework has been tested by several types of human motions. Here we report three experiments. The backgrounds in the first two experiments are static, while in the third it is non-static.

5.1 Tracking Squatting Action

The first experiment is to track a kind of squatting action. The seven elements in E are manually selected from the video to be analyzed and demonstrated in Figure 3(a).

To calculate $p(\mathbf{z}_t|\mathbf{x}_t)$, we take $k = 4$ when perform k-NN search for contour generation. When generating new contours, we descretize the step ratio r as 0, 1/8, 2/8, $\cdots$, 1.0. Thus we can produce at most 36 candidate contours for each particle to choose its associated contour by MAP. In (4), $\mathbf{A}$ and $\mathbf{B}$ are both

Fig. 3. (a) and (b): The exemplars used in the first and second experiments. The contours are filled for print.

Fig. 4. Some tracking results in the first experiment. The video includes 110 frames. The frame numbers of the bigger sub-images are 10, 16, 36, 56, 76, 96.

identical matrices. $\mathbf{N}_t = (x, y, s)^T$; $x \sim N(0, \sigma_x)$, $y \sim N(0, \sigma_y)$ and $s \sim N(1, \sigma_s)$. Here, $\sigma_x = 4$, $\sigma_y = 10$, $\sigma_s = 0.0$. Thus only x and y are inferred. The particle number is 600. In (5), $\alpha_e = 0.3$ and $\alpha_c = 0.7$. In (6), M=20, $n_i = 15$, $\sigma = 3$, $q = 0.6$, and $\lambda = 0.8$. The reason that we take larger λ and q is that the frame images are smoothed before edge detection. The reference color used in (7) is manually obtained from the clothing and facial skin. Figure 4 shows some results.

5.2 Tracking Human Body and Barbell

The second experiment is to track the whole contour shaped by a human body and a barbell in weight-lifting exercise. The sixteen elements in E are manually obtained from the video to be analyzed (Figure 3(b)).

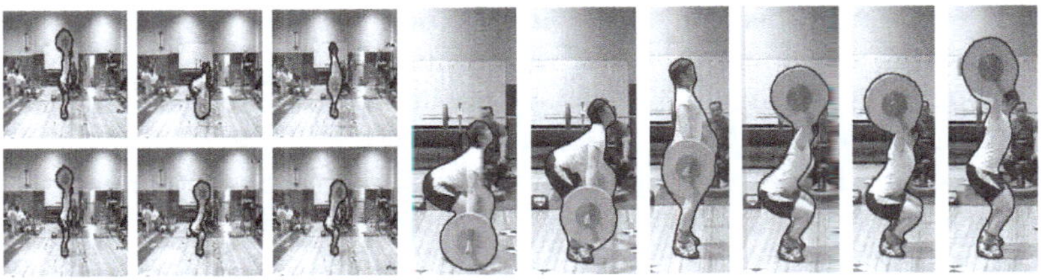

Fig. 5. Some tracking results in the second experiment. The video includes 98 frames. The frame numbers of the bigger sub-images are 10, 25, 40, 55, 70, 85.

Here, we take $k = 4$ when perform k-NN search. The step ratio r is descretized as 0, 1/6, 2/6, $\cdots$, 1.0. In (4), $\sigma_x = 4$, $\sigma_y = 12$ and $\sigma_s = 0.0$. The particle number is 600. All the other parameters are the same as those used in the first example. Figure 5 shows some results. We effectively treat the occlusions.

5.3 Tracking Human Body in Diving

The third experiment is to track human body in diving. The set E includes 96 different contours obtained by a hierarchical cluster [3] from 540 training contours, which are drawn by hand according to nine groups of standard training sequences. Due to space limited, we do not demonstrate them in a figure.

We take $k = 8$ for contour search. The step ratio r is descretized as 0, 0.25, 0.5, 0.75, 1.0. In (4), $\sigma_s = 0.05$, $\sigma_y = 2\sigma_x$ and $\sigma_x = 8$. The reasons that we take these values are: (1) the motion of the centriod of the body is roughly controlled by gravity and the motion in the horizontal direct is limited; (2) The motion of the camera leads the pictures translated. The particle number is 4000. The color reference model is built only based on the skin color of the divers since the clothing colors of the divers are different from each other. Figure 6 shows some extracted results of three dives.

The size of image frame in the first two experiments is 720×576, while the third is 352×288. The CPU of the PC computer is 2.4GHz and the RAM is

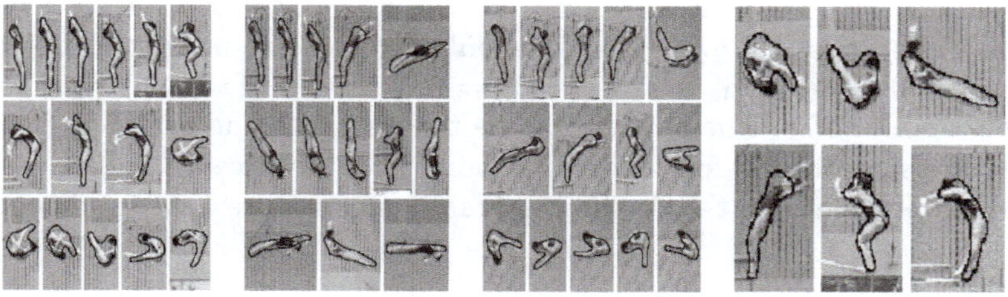

Fig. 6. (a), (b), (c) and (d): Some tracking results from three diving sequences. The number of frames in each video is about 60.

512M. The tracking speed in these three experiments is about 2-4 frames per second. Most time is spent on color computation in (7).

Note that, besides the factors of image quality, the tracking accuracy is tightly related to the exemplars. When the motion is slow, the change of the target contour is smooth. Thus a small quantity of exemplars may be enough to obtain good results. When the motion is fast, more exemplars are required. Simultaneously, when performing k-NN search, a larger k should be taken for fast motions such that the candidates of the target contour for the next time can be included into some neighboring subsets.

6 Conclusion

This paper proposes an exemplar-based human contour tracking approach. The examples are managed by a contour ensemble and not prepared to develop the probabilistic mixture model [5]. Distinctly, we use shape matching method to generate in-between contours to improve the tracker's adaptability. During tracking, the near-neighbor search mechanism provides the tracker with the dynamics for updating the target contours. Consequently, we can effectively use SMC estimation in a low dimensional state space, since the degree of freedom of state parameters is reduced to 3.

Although the work of this paper aims to track human contours, the proposed framework can be applied to other deformable contour tracking tasks. It is easy to use since one only needs to construct a set of contour exemplars.

Acknowledgements

This study is carried out as a part of "R&D promotion scheme funding international joint research" promoted by NICT (National Institute of Information and Communications Technology) of Japan.

We would like to thank Professor Xiaoping Chen, Doctor Guoyi Liu, Yu Deng and Rui Chen for their preparing the video data.

References

1. Isard, M., Blake, A.: Condensation conditional-density propagation for visual tracking. Jour. of Computer Vision, **29** (1998) 5–28
2. Doucet, A., De Freitas, N., Gordon, N.: Sequential Monte Carlo Methods in Practice, Springer-Verlag (2001)
3. Gavrila, D., Philomin, V.: Real-time object detection for smart vehicles. In: Proc. of IEEE Int. Conf. on Computer Vision (ICCV), Corfu, Greece (1999) 87–93
4. Frey, B. J., Jojic, N.: Learning graphical models of images, videos and their spatial transformations. In: Proc. of the Conf. on Uncertainty in Artificial Intelligence, Stanford, CA, USA (2000) 184–191
5. Toyama, K., Blake, A.: Probabilistic tracking with exemplars in a metric space. Jour. of Computer Vision, **48** (2002) 9–19
6. Cootes, T. F., Cooper, D., Taylor, C., et al.: Active shape models, their training and application. Computer Vision and Image Understanding **61** (1995) 38–59
7. Wu, Y., Hua, G., Yu, T.: Switching observation models for contour tracking in clutter. In: Proc. of IEEE Int. Conf. on Computer Vision and Pattern Recognition (CVPR), Madison Wisconsin (2003) 295–302
8. Wang, Q., Xu, G. Y., Ai, H. Z.: Learning object intrinsic structure for robust visual tracking. In: CVPR, Madison Wisconsin (2003) 227–233
9. Pavlovic, V., Sharma, R., Cham, T. J., Murphy, K. P.: A dynamic bayesian network approach to figure tracking using learned dynamic models. In: ICCV, Corfu, Greece (1999) 94–101
10. Isard, M., Blake, A.: A mixed-state condesation tracker with automatic model-switching. In: ICCV, Bombay, India (1998) 94–101
11. MacCormick, J. Blake, A.: A probabilistic contour discriminant for object localization. In: ICCV, Bombay, India (1998) 390–395
12. MacCormick, J., Blake, A.: A probabilistic exclusion principle for tracking multiple objects. In: ICCV, Corfu, Greece (1999) 572–578
13. Chen, Y.Q., Rui, Y., Huang, T.: Jpdaf based hmm or real-time contour tracking. In: CVPR, Cambridge, MA (2001) 543–550
14. Shen, C. H., van den Hengel, A., Dick, A.: Probabilistic multiple cue integration for particle filter based tracking, In: Proc. of Digital Image Computing: Techniques and Applications, Sydney, Australia (2003) 399–408
15. Tomasi, C., Petrov, S., Sastry, A.: 3d tracking = classification + interpolation. In: ICCV, Pairs, France (2003) 1441–1448
16. Efros, A., Leung, T.: Texture synthesis by non-parametric sampling. In: ICCV, Corfu, Greece (1999) 1033–1038
17. Sethian, A.: Level Set Methods: Evolving Interfaces in Geometry, Fluid Mechanics, Computer Vision and Materials Sciences. Cambridge University Press (1996)
18. Chui, H., Rangarajan, A.: A new algorithm for non-rigid point matching. In: CVPR, Hilton Head Island, SC (2000) 44–51
19. Comaniciu, D., Ramesh, V., Meer, P.: Kernel-based object tracking. IEEE Trans. On Pattern Analysis and Machine Intelligence (PAMI), **25** (2003) 564–577
20. Huttenlocher, D. P., Klanderman, G. A., Rucklidge, W. A.: Comparing images using the hausdorff distance. PAMI, **15** (1993) 850–863

Tracking Targets Via Particle Based Belief Propagation

Jianru Xue, Nanning Zheng, and Xiaopin Zhong

Institute of Artificial Intelligence and Robotics,
XI'AN Jiaotong University, 710049 Xi'an, China
{jrxue, nnzheng, xpzhong}@aiar.xjtu.edu.cn

Abstract. We first formulate multiple targets tracking problem in a dynamic Markov network(DMN)which is derived from a MRFs for joint target state and a binary process for occlusion of dual adjacent targets. We then propose to embed a novel Particle based Belief Propagation algorithm into Markov Chain Monte Carlo approach (MCMC) to obtain the maximum a posteriori (MAP) estimation in the DMN. In the message propagation,a stratified sampler incorporates information both from a learned bottom-up detector (e.g. SVM classifier) and a top-down dynamic behavior model. Experimental results show that the proposed method is able to track varying number of targets and handle their interactions.

1 Introduction

Multiple targets tracking (MTT) in video remains a challenging research problem because of difficult issues such as cluttered background, varying number, and interactions amongst targets. To adequately capture the uncertainty due to these issues, a probabilistic framework is required.

Sequential Bayesian estimation provides a promising framework for MTT, much work has been done on MTT in video within this framework [1, 2, 3, 4, 5, 6, 7, 11, 13]. These works broadly fall into two categories:centralized approaches and distributed approaches. The first solves MTT by extending the state-space to include components for all the targets of interest, e.g.[2, 3, 11]. It allows the reduction of the multi-target case to less difficult single-target case, and overcomes multi-modality in filtering distribution. A variable number of targets are accommodated by either dynamic changing the dimension of the joint state space, or by a corresponding set of indicator variables signifying whether an target is present or not.The second category, e.g[4, 7, 10], in contrast, abstains from concatenating targets and proposes single target tracking algorithm that tracks object individually but still simultaneously. They build multi-target trackers by multiple instantiations of single target tracking algorithms. Strategies with various levels of sophistication have been developed to interpret the output of each tracker.

Recently,Okuma et.al [6] propose a boosted particle filter based on the mixture particle filter[5] to track a varying number of hockey players. Both [6] and [5]

P.J. Narayanan et al. (Eds.): ACCV 2006, LNCS 3851, pp. 348–358, 2006.

are actually single particle filter tracking framework to address MTT with the help of mixture density model. Zhao et.al[13] propose a method of detection and tracking of multiple humans in the context of surveillance.These methods alleviate ambiguities due to varying number and interactions in MTT somewhat, how to handle these problems still remains an open problem.

In this paper, we formulate MTT in a dynamic Markov network. Two major contributions are made in this paper. First, we model targets' state and their interaction explicitly by using two MRFs and subsequently approximate it to an ad hoc DMN. Second, we embed a novel particle based belief propagation algorithm in the MCMC framework to obtain the MAP estimation in the DMN.

2 Problem Formation and Basic Model

At each time step t, Let m_t be the unknown number of targets to be tracked, the state of each target is parameterized as $x_{i,t} = (p_{i,t}, v_{i,t}, a_{i,t}, s_{i,t})$, $i = 1, ..., m$, where $p_{i,t}, v_{i,t}, a_{i,t}, s_{i,t}$ is its image location,2D velocity, appearance and scale, respectively. Denote the joint state by $\mathbf{X}_t = \{x_{1,t}, ..., x_{m,t}\}$, the image observation of $x_{i,t}$ by $y_{i,t}$, and the joint observation by $\mathbf{Y}_t$. Given image observation $\mathbf{Y}_t$ at time t and $\mathbf{Y}_{1:t}$ through t, MTT problem is to obtain the maximum a posterior probability of the joint state $P(\mathbf{X}_t|\mathbf{Y}_{1:t})$, e.g. the filtering distribution(1)

$$P(\mathbf{X}_t|\mathbf{Y}_{1:t}) \propto P(\mathbf{Y}_t|\mathbf{X}_t) \int P(\mathbf{X}_t|\mathbf{X}_{t-1})P(\mathbf{X}_{t-1}|\mathbf{Y}_{1:t-1})d\mathbf{X}_{t-1} \tag{1}$$

To estimate $P(x_{i,t}|\mathbf{Y}_{1:t})$, the joint dynamics $P(\mathbf{X}_t|\mathbf{X}_{t-1})$ and the joint likelihood $P(\mathbf{Y}_t|\mathbf{X}_t)$ need to be factorized, and then can $P(x_{i,t}|\mathbf{Y}_{1:t})$ be obtained by marginalizing $P(\mathbf{X}_t|\mathbf{Y}_{1:t})$.

It is generally assumed that targets are moving according to independent Markov dynamics. However, it is generally difficult to distinguish and segment these spatially adjacent targets from image observation, thus we can't simply factorized $P(\mathbf{Y}_t|\mathbf{X}_t)$, and $P(\mathbf{X}_t|\mathbf{Y}_{1:t})$ still couple through the observation when targets move close or present occlusion. To overcome this problem, we present in this section a novel distributed MTT model.

At each time step t, we model $\mathbf{X}$ by a MRFs with an auxiliary spatial binary process $\mathbf{O}$. Each node in MRFs represents a target and each node in $\mathbf{O}$ is located on the dual targets node to indicate their occlusion($O_{i,j} = 0$ for occlusion and $O_{i,j} = 1$ for no occlusion). Using Bayes' rule, the joint posterior probability over $\mathbf{X}$ and$\mathbf{O}$ given image observation $\mathbf{Y}$ is:

$$P(\mathbf{X},\mathbf{O}|\mathbf{Y}) = P(\mathbf{Y}|\mathbf{X},\mathbf{O})P(\mathbf{X},\mathbf{O})/P(\mathbf{Y}) \tag{2}$$

2.1 Prior Model

Assume $\mathbf{X}$ and $\mathbf{O}$ follow the Markov property, by specifying the first order neighborhood $\Gamma(i) = \{j|d(x_i, x_j) < \delta, x_j \in \mathbf{X}\}$ of target i , where $d(x_i, x_j)$ is the distance of targets i, j in the state space, δ is the threshold to determine the neighborhood, the prior can be expanded as:

$$P(\mathbf{X},\mathbf{O}) = \prod_{i} \prod_{j \in \Gamma(i)} \exp(-\varphi_c(x_i, x_j, O_{i,j})) \times \prod_{i} \exp(-\varphi_1(x_i)) \tag{3}$$

where $\varphi_c(x_i, x_j, O_{i,j})$ and $\varphi_1(x_i)$ are clique potential functions for single site x_i and neighboring sites x_i, x_j and $O_{i,j}$,respectively. $O_{i,j}$ is a binary variable between x_i and x_j. $\varphi_c(x_i, x_j, O_{i,j})$ and $\varphi_1(x_i)$ are user-customized functions to enforce the contextual constraints for enforcing spatial interaction and potential of single site, we define $\varphi_c(x_i, x_j, O_{i,j})$ as:

$$\varphi_c(x_i, x_j, O_{i,j}) = \varphi(x_i, x_j)(1 - O_{i,j}) + \gamma(O_{i,j}) \tag{4}$$

where $\varphi(x_i, x_j)$ penalizes sharing one common measurement with neighboring sites and $\gamma(O_{i,j})$ penalizes the occurrence of an occlusion between neighboring sites i and j. Typically, $\gamma(0) = 0$. Further, we define $\varphi_1(x_i)$ as the prior probability on the image size $A(x_i)$ of target i

$$\varphi_1(x_i) = (1 - exp(-\lambda_1 A(x_i))) \tag{5}$$

It penalizes very small target size since it is more likely to be noise. In the experiment in section 5, we set $\lambda_1 = 2.6$.

2.2 Observation Likelihood

Likelihood $P(\mathbf{Y}|\mathbf{X},\mathbf{O})$ describes how the underline state $\mathbf{X},\mathbf{O}$ of the system fits the observation $\mathbf{Y}$ and it is a very complicated distribution. Roughly speaking, image-based [3, 13]and target-based[4, 5, 6, 7, 10] are two widely used approaches in decomposing observation likelihood. One advantage of image based likelihood is that raw image contains almost all necessary information for targets detection and tracking. However, extracting target-like features needs complicated processing such as background modelling. For simplicity, we adopt target-based likelihood, it is often computed as a matching score of the target model with its estimated image projection in the image.

Since observation $\mathbf{Y}$ is the target-based ,given x_i,y_i can be decomposed from $\mathbf{Y}$. We addressed mutual occlusion of tracked targets by sampling the prior in the joint state space. We have modelled the occlusion explicitly in the prior, so we can build up a joint measurement, and directly assess its likelihood without incurring the combinational penalty associated with the JPDAF[1]. Assume the observation noise follows an independent identical distribution (i.i.d), we can define the target-based likelihood as

$$P(\mathbf{Y}|\mathbf{X},\mathbf{O}) \propto \prod L_i(x_i, y_i) \tag{6}$$

As to $L_i(x_i, y_i)$, we get the object size and appearance from the original image according to $p_{i,t}$ and $s_{i,t}$, and use color histogram to represent the target appearance. Similar to[16], we apply the Bhattacharyya similarity coefficient to define a distance on HSV histogram, and adopt the similar likelihood distribution.

Substitute(6), (3), (4),(5) into(1), we get

$$P(\mathbf{X},\mathbf{O}|\mathbf{Y}) \propto \prod_i \exp(-L_i(x_i,y_i))(1-\exp(-\lambda_1 A(x_i))) \times \prod_i \prod_{j\in\Gamma(i)} \exp(-\varphi(x_i,x_j)(1-O_{i,j})+\gamma(O_{i,j})) \tag{7}$$

3 Approximate Inference

3.1 Model Approximation

Maximization of the posterior (7) can be written as

$$\max_{\mathbf{X},\mathbf{O}} P\,(\mathbf{X},\mathbf{O}|\mathbf{Y}) = \max_{\mathbf{X}}\{\prod_i \exp(-(L_i(x_i,y_i))(1-\exp(-\lambda_1 A(x_i))) \times \max_{\mathbf{O}} \prod_i \prod_{j\in\Gamma(i)} \exp(-(\varphi(x_i,x_j)(1-O_{i,j})+\gamma(O_{i,j}))\} \tag{8}$$

Now we relax the binary process $O_{i,j}$ to analog process $O^{'}_{i,j}$ by allowing $0 \le O^{'}_{i,j} \le 1$. Since

$$\begin{aligned}&\max_{\mathbf{O}} \textstyle\prod_i \prod_{j\in\Gamma(i)} \exp(-(\varphi(x_i,x_j)(1-O_{i,j})+\gamma(O_{i,j})))\\ &= \exp(-\min_{\mathbf{O}'} \textstyle\sum_i (\varphi(x_i,x_j)(1-O^{'}_{i,j})+\gamma(O^{'}_{i,j})))\end{aligned} \tag{9}$$

the right hand side of (9) is just the objective function of a robust estimator according to [12], we can define the robust function as:

$$\psi_p(x_i,x_j) = \min_{O^{'}_{i,j}}(\varphi(x_i,x_j)(1-O^{'}_{i,j})+\gamma(O^{'}_{i,j})), \tag{10}$$

so we get the posterior probability over $\mathbf{X}$ defined by $\psi_p(x_i,x_j)$:

$$P(\mathbf{X}|\mathbf{Y}) \propto \prod_i \exp(-L_i(x_i,y_i))(1-exp(-\lambda_1 A(x_i))) \times \prod_i \prod_{j\in\Gamma(i)} \exp(-\psi_p(x_i,x_j)) \tag{11}$$

Thus far, we eliminate the analog processes and convert the task of modelling the prior terms $\{\varphi(x_i,x_j),\gamma(O_{i,j})\}$ explicitly into defining the robust function $\psi_p(x_i,x_j)$ which models occlusion implicitly. We derive $\psi_p(x_i,x_j)$ from the Total Variance (TV) model[15] with a potential function $\rho(z) = |z|$ because of its discontinuity preserving property:

$$\psi_p(x_i,x_j) = -\ln((1-e_p)\exp(-\frac{|A(x_i,x_j)|}{\sigma_p})-e_p) \tag{12}$$

where $A(x_i,x_j)$ depends on the number of overlapping pixels of two adjacent targets. It is maximal when two targets coincide and gradually falls off as targets move apart. Unlike Yu's upside-down Gaussian[7], our robust function has the property in maintaining discontinuity, this is very important in preventing particles of occluded targets from fast depletion because of temporal lacking of image evidence. By varying parameters e_p and σ_p , we can control the shape of the robust function and, therefore, the posterior probability. Also,the eliminated occlusion process can be recovered from through the robust function by identifying when the robust function reaches its upper bound.

3.2 Algorithm Approximation

Consider a Markov network $G = (V, E)$, where V denotes node set and E denotes edge set. Nodes $\{x_i, i \in V\}$ are hidden variables and nodes $\{y_i, i \in V\}$ are observed variables. By denoting $\mathbf{X} = \{x_i\}$ and $\mathbf{Y} = \{y_i\}$, the posterior $P(\mathbf{X}|\mathbf{Y})$ can be factorized as

$$P(\mathbf{X}|\mathbf{Y}) \propto \prod_i \rho_i(x_i, y_i) \prod_i \prod_{j \in \Gamma(i)} \rho_{i,j}(x_i, x_j) \tag{13}$$

where $\rho_{i,j}(x_i, x_j)$ is the compatibility function between nodes x_i and x_j , and $\rho_i(x_i, y_i)$ is the local evidence for node x_i . It can be observed that the form of our posterior (11) is the same form of (13), if we define

$$\rho_{i,j}(x_i, x_j) = \exp(-\psi_p(x_i, x_j)) \tag{14}$$

$$\rho_i(x_i, y_i) = \exp(-L_i(x_i, y_i))(1 - \exp(-\lambda_1 A(x_i))) \tag{15}$$

Thus inferring states of targets can be defined as estimating believes in the Markov network.

Loopy Belief propagation (LBP)[14] is an iterative inference algorithm that propagates messages in the network with loops. At iteration n of the BP algorithm, each node $i \in V$ calculates a message $m^n_{ij}(x_j)$ to be sent to each neighboring nodes $j \in \Gamma(i)$, $\Gamma(i) \equiv \{j|(i,j) \in E\}$ is the set of all nodes that are directly connected to i.

$$m^n_{ij}(x_j) = \kappa \int_{x_i} \rho_{i,j}(x_i, x_j)\rho_i(x_i, y_i) \prod_{u \in \Gamma(i) \backslash j} m^{n-1}_{ui}(x_i) dx_i \tag{16}$$

where κ is a normalization constant. At each iteration, each node can produce an approximation $\hat{p}^n(x_i|\mathbf{Y})$ to the marginal distributions $p(x_i|\mathbf{Y})$ by combining the incoming messages with the local observation potential.

$$\hat{p}^n(x_i|\mathbf{Y}) = \kappa_1 \rho_i(x_i, y_i) \prod_{j \in \Gamma(i)} m^n_{ji}(x_i) \tag{17}$$

where κ_1 is a normalization constant.

We use a MC approximation to the integral in (16). Each message is represented by a set of weighted particles, i.e., $m_{ji}(x_j) \sim \{s^{(n)}_j, w^{(i,n)}_j\}^N_{n=1}, i \in \Gamma(j)$, where $s^{(n)}_j$ and $w^{(i,n)}_j$ denote the sample and its weight of the message passing from x_i to x_j, respectively. The marginal posterior probability in each node is

Table 1. Algorithm 1-Stratified Sampling message updating and belief computing

Generate $\{s^{(n)}_{j,t,k+1}, w^{(i,n)}_{j,t,k+1}\}_{n=1}^{N}$ *and* $\{s^{(n)}_{j,t,k+1}, \pi^{(n)}_{j,t,k+1}\}_{n=1}^{N}$ *from* $\{s^{(n)}_{j,t,k}, w^{(i,n)}_{j,t,k}\}_{n=1}^{N}$, *and* $\{s^{(n)}_{j,t,k}, \pi^{(n)}_{j,t,k}\}_{n=1}^{N}$

1. *Stratified Sampling*
   (a) *For* $1 \leq n < \nu N$, *sample* $s^{(n)}_{j,t,k+1}$ *from a suitable proposal function* $H(x_{j,t})$,*set weight* $\tilde{w}^{(i,n)}_{j,t,k+1} = 1/H(s^{(n)}_{j,t,k+1})$
   (b) *For* $\nu N \leq n \leq N$,*sample* $s^{(n)}_{j,t,k+1}$ *from* $P(x_{j,t}|\mathbf{Y}_t)$, *set* $\xi^{(i,n)}_{j,k+1} = 1/\pi^{(n)}_{j,t,k}$
   (c) *For* $\nu N \leq n \leq N$
   $$\tilde{\xi}^{(i,n)}_{j,,t,k+1} = (1-v)\xi^{(i,n)}_{j,t,k+1}/(\sum\nolimits_{l=vN}^{N} \xi^{(i,l)}_{j,t,k+1})$$
   (d) *for* $\nu N \leq n \leq N$,$w^{(i,n)}_{j,t,k+1} = \tilde{u}^{(i,n)}_{j,t,k+1}$.
   (e) *for* $\nu N \leq n \leq N$,$\tilde{w}^{(i,n)}_{j,t,k+1} = u^{(i,n)}_{j,t,k+1} \times \tilde{\xi}^{(i,n)}_{j,t,k+1}$
2. *Importance correction: for* $1 \leq n \leq N$, $w^{(i,n)}_{j,t,k+1} = \tilde{w}^{(i,n)}_{j,t,k+1} \times m_{ij}(s^{(n)}_{j,t,k+1})$ *where* $m_{ij}(\cdot)$ *is defined in (20)*
3. *Normalize* $\{w^{(i,n)}_{j,t,k+1}, i \in \Gamma(j)\}$,*set* $\pi^{(n)}_{j,t,k+1}$ *according to (21) and normalize,then get* $\{s^{(n)}_{j,t,k+1}, w^{(i,n)}_{j,t,k+1}\}_{n=1}^{N}, \{s^{(n)}_{j,t,k+1}, \pi^{(n)}_{j,t,k+1}\}_{n=1}^{N}$.
4. $k \leftarrow k+1$,*iterate 1→4 until convergence.*

also represented by a set of weighted samples, i.e. $P(x_j|\mathbf{Y}) \sim \{s_j^{(n)}, \pi_j^{(n)}\}_{n=1}^{N}$. Then the message updating process is based on these set of weighted samples

Both PAMAPS [8] and NBP [9] approximate messages with Gaussian Mixture, and result in sampling from product of Gaussian Mixture. Different from using Gaussian Mixture model, we use importance sampling with a stratifier sampler to approximate messages, the proposal $H(x)$ is built based on the prior of target state. To make use of as much information as possible, we adopt a stratified sampler to sample $(1-v)N$ particles ($0 \leq v \leq 1$) from the current belief estimate, and vN particles from the proposal distribution for message. The resulting belief propagation is described in Table 1, where step 1(a)performs sampling from $H(x)$, and steps 1(b),1(c),1(d) and 1(e)perform sampling from belief node. Details of computing $m_{ij}(s^{(n)}_{j,t,k+1})$ and $\pi^{(n)}_{j,t,k+1}$ are given in section 4. Although we have not obtained the rigorous results on the convergence rate, we always observe the convergence in less than 5 iterations in our experiments.

4 Information Fusion

The joint state at time t and $t-1$ are described by two Markov network G_t and G_{t-1}, where $G_t = (V_t, E_t)$,V_t be the set of nodes of active targets, i.e. the targets appear in the view, and E_t be the possible occlusions. DMN shown in Fig.1 shows the evolution of G_t, it reflects the motion correlation among targets, due to the change of their spatial relation, occurrence of new targets and disappearance of tracked targets.

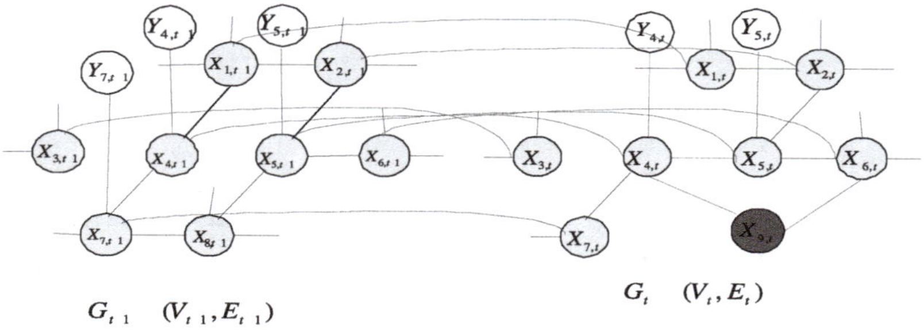

Fig. 1. DMN for MTT, the link between each paired hidden nodes indicates occurrence of occlusion. Graph G_{t-1} and G_t describe joint target state at two consecutive time instants. Link and node in red indicates new occlusions and the addition of new target, respectively.

By assuming independent dynamics,$P(\mathbf{X}_t|\mathbf{X}_{t-1})$ can be factorized as:

$$P(\mathbf{X}_t|\mathbf{X}_{t-1}) \propto \prod_{i \in V_t \cap V_{t-1}} P(x_{i,t}|x_{i,t-1}) \prod_{j \in V_t \setminus V_{t-1}} P_a(p_{j,t}) \prod_{k \in V_{t-1} \setminus V_t} P_d(p_{k,t}) \quad (18)$$

where $P(x_{i,t}|x_{i,t-1})$ represents target dynamics,$P_a(p_{i,t})$ and $P_d(p_{i,t})$ are probabilities for occurrence of new targets and disappearance of old targets, they are set empirically according to the distance of $(p_{i,t})$ to the boundaries of the image.

With G_t evolving, dimension of $\mathbf{X}_t$ is varying , corresponding to different number of targets. To inferring $P(x_{i,t}|\mathbf{Y}_{1:t})$, we embed algorithm 1 into a MCMC framework using a Metropolis sampler. The key to the efficiency of this sampler rests on the informed proposal. We build three proposal using (18)and a learned SVM detector[17] for existed tracks, a new initialized tracks and terminated tracks, respectively. At each sampling step, we switch G_t to $G_t^{'}$ by changing one target state, the acceptance probability for each transition is set to $min\{1, \frac{P(\mathbf{X}_t^{'})|\mathbf{Y}_{1:t}}{P(\mathbf{X}_t)|\mathbf{Y}_{1:t}}\}$.

The proposal for targets existed from time $t-1$ to t is $p(x_{i,t}|x_{i,t-1})$. For varying number case, proposals are based on a learned SVM detector,other detectors can also be adopted in the same way. One expects detector to be noisy in that they sometimes may fail, even these noisy information proves to be valuable in improving tracker's reliability[6]. Our proposals for adding new target and deleting old target have the similar form as follows:

$$P(\mathbf{X}_t|\mathbf{X}_{0:t-1}, \mathbf{Y}_{1:t}) = R(Q_s(\mathbf{Y}_t), P(\mathbf{X}_t|\mathbf{X}_{t-1})), \quad (19)$$

where Q_s is a Gaussian distribution center around the detected targets by the SVM detector. $R(\cdot)$ is a similarity function which compute the distance between a sample cluster in Q_s and that in $P(\mathbf{X}_t|\mathbf{X}_{t-1})$. The proposal for adding new target is $R_a(\cdot)$, which is a Gaussian mixture of the clusters in Q_s excluding those in $P(\mathbf{X}_t|\mathbf{X}_{t-1})$, the weight of each Gaussian component is in proportion to the distance of centroid of the cluster to the boundaries of the image. Similarly, the

Table 2. Algorithm 2-Particle based Belief Propagation

Generate $\{s_{j,t}^{(n)}, \pi_{j,t}^{(n)}\}_{n=1}^{N}$ *from* $\{s_{j,t-1}^{(n)}, \pi_{j,t-1}^{(n)}\}_{n=1}^{N}$
1. *Initialization:*
(a) *Re-sampling: for each* $j \in V, i \in \Gamma(j)$, *sample* $\{s_{j,t-1}^{(n)}\}_{n=1}^{N}$ *according to the weights* $\pi_{j,t-1}^{(n)}$ *to obtain* $\{s_{j,t-1}^{(n)}, 1/N\}_{n=1}^{N}$.
(b) *Prediction: for each* j, *for each sample in* $\{s_{j,t-1}^{(n)}, 1/N\}_{n=1}^{N}$, *sample* $\{s_{j,t}^{(n)}\}_{n=1}^{N}$ *from* $p(x_{j,t}\|x_{j,t-1})$.
(c) *Initialize Belief and message: for each* $j = 1, .., M$, *assign weight* $w_{j,t,k}^{(i,n)} = 1/N, \pi_{j,t,k}^{(n)} = p_j(y_{j,t,k}^{(n)}\|s_{j,t,k}^{(n)})$ *and normalize, where* $i \in \Gamma(j)$.
2. *Iterate L times: choose following(a),(b)and(c)randomly with probabilities 0.8,0.1 and 0.1 to obtain a new graph* G'
(a) *Randomly select a target* $j \in V$ *to move, obtain* G'
(b) *Sample from* $R_a(\cdot)$, *delete the corresponding node from* V *to obtain* G'
(c) *Sample from* $R_d(\cdot)$,*add the corresponding node into* V *to obtain* G'
3. *Do algorithm 1 on* G' *with proposal function* $p(x_{i,t}\|x_{i,t-1}), i \in G'$
4. *Inference result* $p(x_{j,t}\|\mathbf{Y}_t) \sim \{s_{j,t}^{(n)}, \pi_{j,t}^{(n)}\}_{n=1}^{M}$, *where* $s_{j,t}^{(n)} = s_{j,t,k+1}^{(n)}$ *and* $\pi_{j,t}^{i,n} = \pi_{j,t,k+1}^{(i,n)}$

proposal $R_d(\cdot)$for deleting an target is built from the clusters in $P(\mathbf{X}_t|\mathbf{X}_{t-1})$ excluding those in Q_s, the weight is set in the same way as that in adding a new target proposal.

The detailed steps of the sequential stratified sampler are presented in algorithm 2 in Table 2, and $m_{ij}(s_{j,t,k+1}^{(n)})$ and $\pi_{j,t,k+1}^{(n)}$ in algorithm 1 is computed as

$$m_{ij}(s_{j,t,k+1}^{(n)}) = \sum_{m=1}^{N} \{\pi_{i,t,k}^{(m)} \rho_i(y_{i,t,k}^{(m)}, s_{i,t,k}^{(m)}) \prod_{l \in \Gamma(i) \backslash j} w_{i,t,k}^{(l,m)}$$

$$\times [\sum_{r=1}^{N} p(s_{i,t,k}^{(m)}|s_{i,t-1}^{(r)})] \rho_{ij}(s_{i,t,k}^{(m)}, s_{j,t,k+1}^{(r)})\} \quad (20)$$

$$\pi_{j,t,k+1}^{(n)} = \rho_j(y_{j,t,k+1}^{(n)}, s_{j,t,k+1}^{(n)}) \prod_{u \in \Gamma(j)} w_{j,k+1}^{(u,n)} \times \sum_{r} p(s_{j,t,k+1}^{(n)}|s_{j,t-1}^{(r)}) \quad (21)$$

5 Experiments

We test our algorithm with two video sequences. The first is a synthetic example, in which we didn't use stratified sampler, parameters in our algorithm were set as $\nu = 1$. The second is a real video sequence of hockey game in which stratified sampler is used, the parameters are $\nu = 0.8$.

In the synthesized video, there are five identical and moving balls in a noisy background. Each ball presents an independent constant velocity motion and

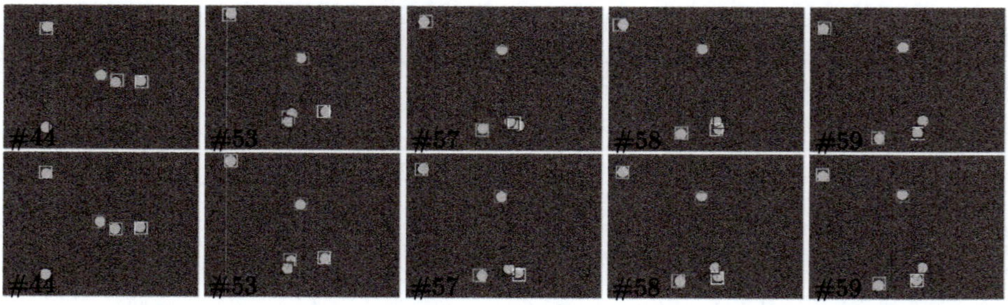

Fig. 2. Tracking balls by M.I.T and our algorithm. The result of MIT is Shown on the top with the result of our algorithm at the bottom.

is bounded by the image borders. The synthesized sequence challenges many existing methods due to the frequent presence of occlusion. We compare our results with those obtained by a multiple independent trackers(M.I.Tracker), which we implemented using color model[16]. Fig.2 shows some samples, the results of M.I.Tracker are on the top and ours at the bottom. we used 20 particles for each ball in both M.I.Tracker and our algorithm. The red lines in Fig.2 that link balls are the visual illustration of the structure of the Markov network. We find out that our approach can handle 98.6% of the 234 occlusions occurring in the 634 frames synthesized video, while M.I.Tracker can't produce satisfactory results.

Our algorithm has also been tested on a real video sequence of hockey game. We have trained a SVM classifier to detect hockey players, we got 34 SVs from a total of 1300 figures of hockey players finally. Fig.3 shows M.I.Tracker results on the top, and our algorithm tracking results on the bottom. As expected, our approach provides robust and stable results, while M.I.Tracker can't. Note that a fixed set of parameters $e_p = 0.05, \sigma_p = 1$ is used in both synthesized and real video. Obviously, this set of parameters is not the optimal for both video sequence, because their occlusion situation are quite different. Finally, we compare our algorithm with the latest multiple targets tracking algorithm, boosted particle filter[6]. Both the performance are almost the same, however, for

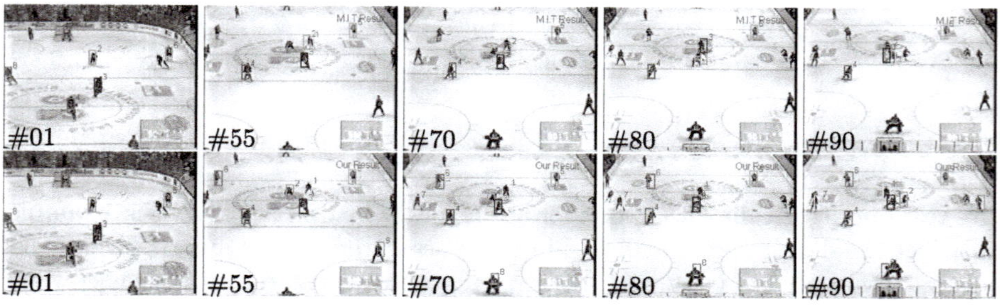

Fig. 3. Hockey players tracking result: the top is the result of M.I.T, and the bottom is the final result of our algorithm

each tracked player,boosted particle filter use multiple sub-region color model, while our algorithm uses a single region color model. It seems that in occlusion handling, boosted particle filter depends heavily on the discriminability of its likelihood function, while ours can handle occlusion mainly due to the better modelling of interactions among multiple targets.

6 Summary and Conclusions

This paper proposed to model multiple targets tracking problem in a dynamic Markov network which is derived from two MRFs:a MRFs for joint target state and a binary process for occlusion of dual adjacent targets. We then propose to embed a novel Particle based Belief Propagation algorithm into Markov Chain Monte Carlo approach (MCMC) to obtain the maximum a posteriori (MAP) estimation in the DMN. In the message propagation,a stratified sampler incorporates information both from a learned detector (e.g. SVM classifier) and dynamic behavior model. The proposed method is able to track varying number of targets and handle their interactions, and it was illustrated on a synthetic and a real world tracking problem.

References

1. Bar-Shalom, Y., Li, X.R.: Multitarget Multisensor Tracking: Principles and Techniques. YBS Publishing. (1995)
2. Hue, C., Le Cadre, J.P., Perez, P.: Tracking multiple objects with particle filtering. IEEE Transactions on Aerospace and Electronic Systems. Vol. 38, No. 3 (2002) 791–812
3. Isard, M., MacCormick, J.P.: Bramble: A Bayesian multiple-blob tracker. In Proceedings of International Conference on Computer Vision 2001. No. 2 (2001) 34–41
4. Tweed, D., Calway, A.: Tracking Objects using subordinated condensation. In Proceedings of the British Machine Vision Conference 2002. (2002) 283–292
5. Vermaak, J., Doucet, A., Perez, P.: Maintaining Multi-Modality through Mixture Tracking. In Proceedings of International Conference on Computer Vision 2003. (2003) 1110–1116
6. Okuma, K., Taleghani, A., Freitas, N., Little, J., Lowe, D.: A Boosted Particle filter: Multitarget detection and tracking. In Proceedings of European Conference on Computer Vision 2004, (2004) 28–39
7. Yu, T., Wu, Y.: Collaborative Tracking of Multiple Targets. In Proceedings of International Conference on Computer Vision and Pattern Recognition 2004. (2004) 834–841
8. Isard, M.: PAMPAS: Real-valued graphical models for computer vision. In Proceedings of International Conference on Computer Vision and Pattern Recognition 2003. (2003) 613–620
9. Sudderth, E., Ihler, A., Freeman, W., Willsky, A.: Nonparametric belief propagation. In Proceedings of International Conference on Computer Vision and Pattern Recognition 2003. (2003) 605–612
10. MacCormick, J.P., Blake, A.: A probabilistic exclusion principle for tracking multiple objects. In Proceedings of Internatioal Conference on Computer Vision 1999. (1999) 572–578

11. Tao, H., Sawhney, H.S., Kumar, R.: A sampling algorithm for tracking multiple objects. In Proceedings of the International Workshop on Vision Algorithms. (1999) 53–68
12. Black, M.J., Rangarajan, A.: On the unification of line processes, Outlier Rejection and Robust statistics with applications in Early vision. Internatioal Journal of Computer Vision. Vol. 19, No. 1 (1996) 57–91
13. Zhao, T., Nevatia, R.: Tracking Multiple Humans in Crowded Environment. In Proceedings of Internatioal Conference on Computer Vision and Pattern Recognition 2004. (2004) 406–413
14. Murphy, K., Weiss, Y., Jordan, M.: Loopy-belief propagation for approximate inference: An empirical study. In Proceedings of Fifteenth Conference on Uncertainty in Artificial Intelligence. (1999) 467–475
15. Osher, S., Rubin, L.I., Fatemi, E.: Nonlinear Total Variation based noise removal algorithms. Physica D. Vol. 60, No. 60 (1992) 259–268
16. Perez, P., Hue, C., Vermaak, J., Gangnet, M.: Color-based Probabilistic Tracking. In Proceedings of Europe Confernce on Computer Vision 2002. (2002) 661–675
17. Cristianini, N., Shawe-Taylor, J.: An Introduction to Support Vector Machines. Cambridge University Press. (2000)

Multiple-Person Tracking Using a Plan-View Map with Error Estimation

Kentaro Hayashi[1], Takahide Hirai[1], Kazuhiko Sumi[2], and Koichi Sasakawa[1]

[1] Advanced Technology R&D Center, Mitsubishi Electric Co.,
8-1-1, Tsukaguchi-Honmachi, Amagasaki, Hyogo 661-8661, Japan
{Hayashi.Kentaro, Hirai.Takahide, Sasakawa.Koichi}@wrc.melco.co.jp
[2] Graduate School of Informatics, Kyoto University,
36-1 Yoshida-Honmachi, Sakyo-ku, Kyoto 606-8501 Japan
sumi@vision.kuee.kyoto-u.ac.jp

Abstract. In this paper we describe a new method for detecting and tracking multiple persons with a stereo camera. The method is based on the idea of the plan-view map, i.e., the 2D histogram of projected 3D measurements from the camera. It estimates the statistical feature in an optimal window, e.g., a rectangular region, on the histogram, considering stereo measurement error, human breadth, and height. Then, it measures the actual statistical feature in the same window on the input histogram and compares estimated feature with measured one to detect and track persons. Experimental results show that our method can achieve higher performance than a normal plan-view map.

1 Introduction

Person tracking systems by vision are useful for many applications, including human-computer interaction, traffic counters, and surveillance systems. In this paper, we mainly consider surveillance systems.

In many surveillance systems, a camera may be installed in a limited space. Especially in a building, space is limited by its ceiling. Therefore, the camera should be located at a low height. In this situation, human silhouette is strongly effected by projection, and half-occlusion frequently occurs. 3D information, such as depth from a stereo camera, enables us to easily handle these issues.

However, a lot of past methods [1–5] assume that the camera position is low and faces a horizontal direction. These methods do not deal with long-term half-occlusion.

Beymer has proposed a person counting method using a stereo camera[6]. Although this method assumes that the stereo camera is above the path of a person and looking downward, it can deal with great changes in the viewing direction by a simple way using a plan-view map. The plan-view map is a 2D rectangular histogram that counts the number of 3D measurements in the vertical square pole on each bin(histogram component). Stereo measurements are distributed vertically on a standing person, so it can be assumed that the value of the bin under the person is higher than the others. Several papers[7, 8] have

P.J. Narayanan et al. (Eds.): ACCV 2006, LNCS 3851, pp. 359–368, 2006.

improved this basic idea. For instance, Harville[8] introduced a novel idea "plan-view height map" that applies object's height to the plan-view map. However, he did not clearly deal with the measurement error of a stereo camera.

Generally speaking, stereo measurement error grows as depth increases. Therefore, detection and tracking performance degenerates in areas far from the camera. This motivates us to take measurement error in account. In this paper we propose a new method, that analyzes the measurement error of depth from a stereo camera and reduces the effect of measurement error. This method is general enough to collaborate with another methods, such as Harville's plan-view height map.

First we derive the simplified formula of stereo measurement error and analyze the error of voting to 2D histogram, i.e., the plan-view map. Next we calculate an adaptive window at a position on the histogram using both the nature of the error and the breadth and the height of a person. The larger the window, the more reliable detection and tracking of people. However, too large window decreases the precision of the position. Therefore, we calculate the optimal window size. Lastly, we estimate the statistical feature, e.g., the average of values in the window and measure the same feature of the input histogram in the same window. We compare the estimated feature with the measured one to detect a person candidate at each position on the histogram. If these features are similar, the person exists at that position. Experimental results show that our method has higher performance than a normal plan-view map.

2 Problem Definition

2.1 Camera Configuration

Figure 1 shows the configuration of a stereo camera, its right image plane, a world coordinate system, persons, and a 2D histogram. The camera modules are

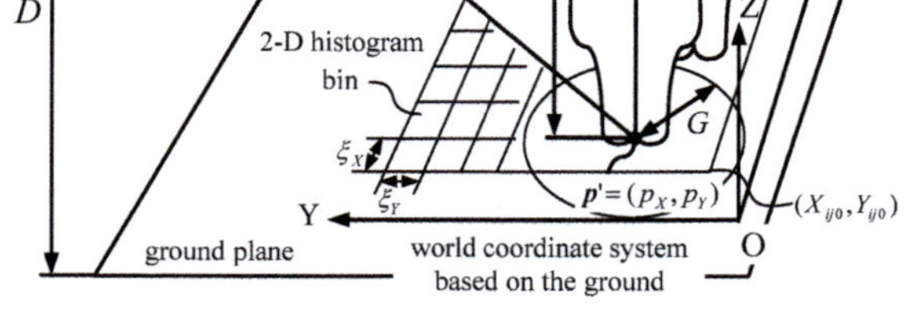

Fig. 1. Configuration of stereo camera, image plane, and world coordinate system

placed parallel at distance B, at height D from the ground, and those slanting angles are θ. These cameras have wide-angle lenses of horizontal angle α. We calculate a disparity d based on the image right image, whose coordinate system is represented by $u - v$. The width and height of the right image are a_u and a_v respectively. The stereo camera observes 3D point $\boldsymbol{p}$ on an object that exists in the world coordinate system $X - Y - Z$. For simplification, we set axis Y to be parallel to the axis u and fix the origin O to the ground plane. The 2D histogram is attached to the $X - Y$ plane, and its bins are arranged in a lattice shape parallel to the X and Y axes. The origin of the histogram is (X_{ij0}, Y_{ij0}). The size of the bin is $\xi_X \times \xi_Y$. H can be calculated from observations, or we can fix H to an average human height. We assume another person is outside of the circle whose center and radius are $\boldsymbol{p}$ and G, respectively. When G is large enough, e.g., 1m, we can ignore heavy occlusion. Our method outputs 2D positions of standing and/or walking persons from the input images.

2.2 Stereo Measurement Error Model

First, we correct the input images undistorted, smooth the images by Gaussian filter, calculate a dense disparity map by a block matching algorithm[9], and subtract the background depth map from the input depth map by a conventional background subtraction method such as [10]. We start from this depth map.

Rodriguez et.al.[11] analyzed stereo depth errors with respect to d. In this paper we first derive simpler formula so as to focus on the errors on the 2D histogram.

Suppose a 3D point $\boldsymbol{p}^c$, which is on the camera coordinate system, is observed at (u, v) on the right image plane and at $(u + d, v)$ on the left. $\boldsymbol{p}^c$ is presented as

$$\begin{aligned} \boldsymbol{p}^c &= [(u - u_0)B/d \;\; (v - v_0)B/d \;\; \zeta/d]^t \\ &= (1/d)\boldsymbol{p}^c_m \end{aligned} \tag{1}$$

$$\zeta = \frac{a_u B}{2\tan(\alpha/2)}, \tag{2}$$

where $\boldsymbol{x}^t$ means the transpose of $\boldsymbol{x}$. We can translate $\boldsymbol{p}^c$ into $\boldsymbol{p}$ on the world coordinate system using appropriate matrix $\mathbf{M}$ and vector $\boldsymbol{C}$ as

$$\boldsymbol{p} = \mathbf{M}\boldsymbol{p}^c + \boldsymbol{C}. \tag{3}$$

Let $\underline{d}$ be the true value of disparity at $\boldsymbol{p}^c$. We assume that d has a noise that has a Gaussian distribution, whose expectation and variation are 0 and σ_d^2 respectively, that is,

$$d = \underline{d} + \delta_d. \tag{4}$$

The expectation $\boldsymbol{\mu}_{p^c}$ of $\boldsymbol{p}^c$ at $d = \underline{d}$ is

$$\boldsymbol{\mu}_{p^c} = \boldsymbol{p}^c \mid_{d=\underline{d}} . \tag{5}$$

Applying 1-dimensional Taylor expansion to $\boldsymbol{p}^c$, we can obtain

$$\boldsymbol{p}^c \simeq \dot{\boldsymbol{p}}^c \mid_{d=\underline{d}} (d - \underline{d}) + \boldsymbol{p}^c \mid_{d=\underline{d}} . \tag{6}$$

$\dot{\boldsymbol{p}}^c$ is the differential of $\boldsymbol{p}^c$. Subtracting expectation $\boldsymbol{\mu}_{p^c}$ and substituting $d^* = (d - \underline{d})/\sigma_d$ into the right term, it is simplified as

$$\sigma_d \dot{\boldsymbol{p}}^c \mid_{d=\underline{d}} d^*. \tag{7}$$

Expectation of d^* is 0, and its variance is 1. Assuming that each component of $\dot{\boldsymbol{p}}^c$ is independent, the standard deviation $\boldsymbol{\sigma}_{p^c}$ of $\boldsymbol{p}^c$ is obtained from equations 1 and 7,

$$\boldsymbol{\sigma}_{p^c} = \frac{\sigma_d}{\underline{d}^2} \mathrm{diag}(\boldsymbol{p}^c_m), \tag{8}$$

where diag($\boldsymbol{p}$) is a matrix whose diagonals are the components of $\boldsymbol{p}$. Expectation $\boldsymbol{\mu}_p$ and standard deviation $\boldsymbol{\sigma}_p$ on the world coordinate system are obtained by applying equation 3,

$$\boldsymbol{\mu}_p = \mathbf{M}\boldsymbol{p}^c \mid_{d=\underline{d}} + \mathbf{C} \tag{9}$$

$$\boldsymbol{\sigma}_p = \frac{\sigma_d}{\underline{d}^2} \mathbf{M}\mathrm{diag}(\boldsymbol{p}^c_m)\mathbf{M}^t. \tag{10}$$

3 Detecting and Tracking Method

As described in section 1, a simple and effective way for detecting a standing/walking person is to use a 2D histogram. We improve the performance of this basic idea by considering measurement error.

3.1 Generating 2D Histogram

First we describe how to generate a 2D histogram. A 3D point $\boldsymbol{p} = [p_X \ p_Y \ p_Z]^t$ is projected on the bin at

$$(i, j) = (\lfloor (p_X - X_{ij0})/\xi_X \rfloor, \lfloor (p_Y - Y_{ij0})/\xi_Y \rfloor). \tag{11}$$

$\lfloor x \rfloor$ is a maximum integer less than x. The value of the bin at (i, j) is increased by the projection. After all 3D points are projected on appropriate bins, it is expected that the bin under a person has higher value than the others. We denote bin value at (i, j) by $h(i, j)$.

3.2 Analyzing 2D Histogram

A 3D point $\boldsymbol{p}$ includes measurement error, which increases along with the distance from the camera. Therefore, in general, the histogram generated by equation 11 has a broad and low peak underneath a person. Additional measurement error, such as extra depth attached to a person, decreases signal-noise ratio.

We propose a new method considering the measurement error that is processed as follows:

1. Calculate a window on the histogram from the variance of noises and human breadth. The window size varies along with distance from the camera.

2. Estimate statistical feature(s) in the window that can be an average, a variance, and/or, and so on. Since features are independent of the actual measurements, we can estimate all of them on the histogram in advance. In this paper we adopt an average as the feature.
3. Calculate the same feature in the same window on the measured histogram.
4. Compare estimated features with measured features at the same position. If they are similar, the probability of the person will be high at the position. We get this probability map by comparing features at each position of the histogram.
5. Detect and track peaks on the probability map.

The detailed algorithm is explained in the following subsections.

3.3 Calculating Optimal Window Size

We assume a rectangular window on the histogram. We calculate a minimum window that contains most of the measurement points on one person. For simplification, we consider the diagonals of $\boldsymbol{\sigma}_p$, $[\sigma_X \;\; \sigma_Y \;\; \sigma_Z]^t$. Let W denote the average human breadth, and $W_D (< W)$ denote the depth. Window size (w_w, h_w) is expressed as

$$w_w = F_q \sigma_X \tag{12}$$

$$F_q \sigma_Y + W_D \leq h_w \leq F_q \sigma_Y + W, \tag{13}$$

using a constant F_q. Figure 2 shows these relations.

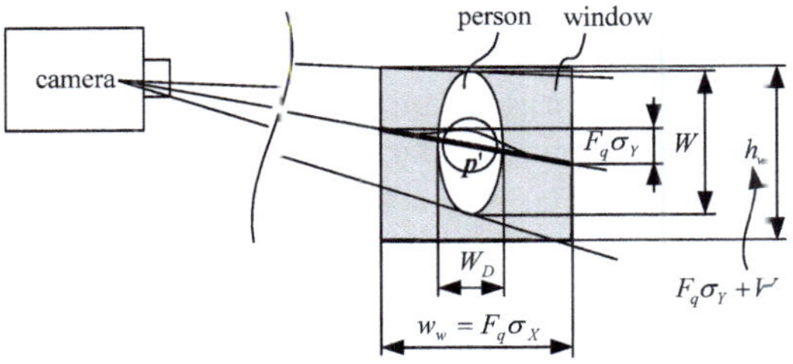

Fig. 2. Relation between standard deviation σ_X, σ_Y and window size

If most persons move along the lines with depth direction, h_w can be approximated as $h_w = W$.

3.4 Estimating Statistical Feature(s) in the Window

We describe how to calculate an average in the window. We use a simple human model, which is a plane vertical to the ground and its normal direction is facing to the camera. The model plane size is $W \times H$. Imagine that the plane is projected to the image, the distance from the bottom to the top of the plane is n pixels in the image coordinates, and bin width ξ_Y is m pixels. All $n \cdot m$ measurement points are projected into the same bin of the histogram if we ignore noises and measurement errors. Therefore, the true bin value $\underline{k}$ is $\underline{k} = n \cdot m$.

Let ρ_r be the probability of acquiring measurements on the human model plane and ν_k be the variance of the bin value caused by random noises on the image. $\underline{k}\rho_r + \nu_k$ measurement points are distributed in window width w_w because of the noise on the depth. Therefore, an average μ_k is

$$\mu_k = (\underline{k}\rho_r + \nu_k)/w_w. \tag{14}$$

ν_k can be calculated as follows. Let ρ_d be the occurrence probability of a uniform disparity in a pixel. Randomly generated disparity d' is projected to the bin if $\underline{d'} - \delta_d/2 < d' < \underline{d'} + \delta_d/2$ and its pixel is on the vertical line through the bin. Using the distance from the ground to the image boundary along the vertical line and maximal disparity d_{max},

$$\nu_k = h_{max} m \rho_d (\delta_d / d_{max}). \tag{15}$$

If ρ_d is small enough, ν_k is also small.

We can estimate other statistical features such as standard deviation. Since we are focusing on the effectiveness of our general framework, the simplest feature, i.e., the average, is sufficient for evaluating our method.

3.5 Measuring Statistical Feature(s) in the Window

An average $A_k(\boldsymbol{p})$ in the window on the input histogram is

$$A_k(\boldsymbol{p}) = \left(\sum_{(i,j)\in\mathcal{W}(\boldsymbol{p})} h(i,j)\right) / (w_w w_h). \tag{16}$$

Here $\mathcal{W}(\boldsymbol{p})$ is the window on the histogram corresponding to $\boldsymbol{p}$.

To calculate all averages on the histogram, we use a fast algorithm developed by Viola et.al.[12], i.e., the integral image. Let M^2 be the average area of a window, and N^2 the area of the histogram. A computational order of A_k by a brute-force method is $O(M^2N^2)$, which we can be reduced this into $O(N^2)$ using the integral image.

3.6 Detecting and Tracking Persons

From equations 14 and 16, we obtain μ_k and A_k at each point of the histogram. Although A_k will vary because of occlusion and other ignored noises, the high probability that a person is at the point may be expected when these are similar. Their similarity can be evaluated in a number of ways. For example,

$$h' = 1 - |A_k - \mu_k| / \mu_k. \tag{17}$$

If $A_k \leq \mu_k$, this can be simplified to $h' = A_k/\mu_k$.

We can detect the candidate of a person at a point when $h' \geq T_\mu$. After detection, we can track the peak near the previous peak by such filtering methods as Kalman filter, condensation method[13], or dynamic-programming[7]. We take map h' as a probability map and adopt a condensation method to track each peak on it.

4 Experiments

4.1 Simulating μ_k and A_k

The objective of the simulation is: (a) to check the correctness of the statistical feature estimates by comparing estimated features and simulated ones, and (b) to find appropriate thresholds that will work in actual situation.

We simulate μ_k and A_k as follows. (1) Locate a vertical plane whose size is $W \times H$ at position $\boldsymbol{p}$. (2) Scan all optical rays that go through both the image and the plane. (3) Calculate the disparity of each ray and add Gaussian noise to the disparity. (4) Count all 3D points calculated from the disparity map to the histogram. (5) Move $\boldsymbol{p}$ in the range of $-1500 \leq p_Y \leq 1500$ and $2000 \leq p_X \leq 5500$, and calculate μ_k and A_k at each position of $\boldsymbol{p}$.

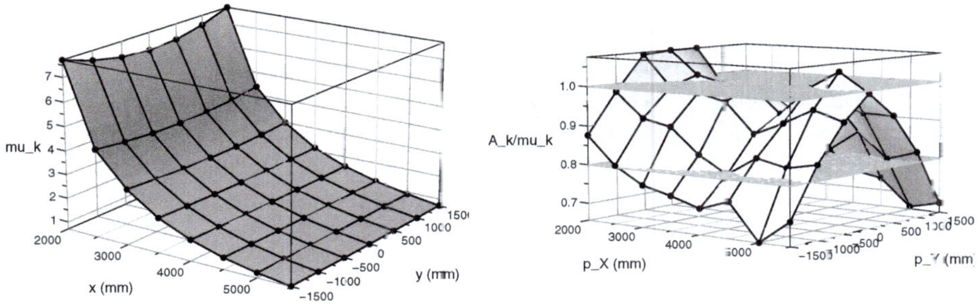

(a) Simulated μ_k at each point $\boldsymbol{p}$ (b) Simulated A_k/μ_k at each point $\boldsymbol{p}$

Fig. 3. Simulated results

Figure 3(a) shows μ_k at each point $\boldsymbol{p}$. μ_k decreases nonlinearly as the distance from the camera increases because window size increases and the number of measurement points decreases along with the distance. A_k behaves similar to μ_k. Most methods in the past approximated this behavior as linear. Therefore, it was difficult to maintain detection and tracking performance at all points.

We analyze the behavior of A_k more precisely. Figure 3(b) shows the A_k/μ_k ratio, i.e., A_k/μ_k. From this simulation, when p_Y is near 0, A_k/μ_k is close to 1. However, as $|p_Y|$ increases, A_k/μ_k also decreases. The reason for this phenomenon is that the window shape and the actual peak shape is different, especially when $|p_Y|$ is large. Nevertheless, we can detect persons at most positions, for instance, by setting $T_\mu = 0.8$.

4.2 Detecting and Tracking Actual Images

We consider Beymer's method as a baseline because his idea is so basic that everyone can comprehend it. Therefore, we compare the two methods. We developed a person tracking system using our method and also his method on a

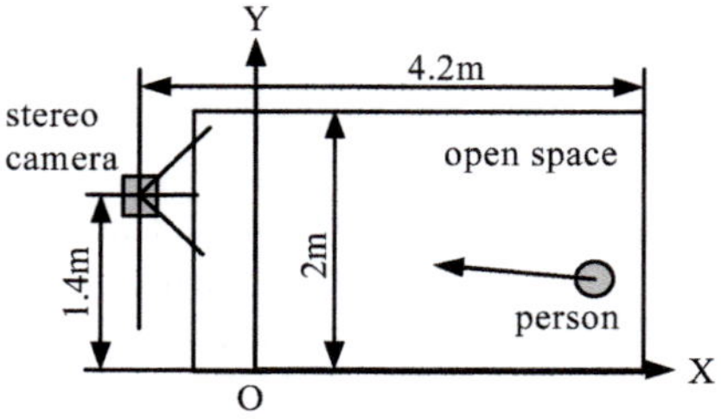

Fig. 4. Specifications of camera locations in our experimental setup

standard PC. Many performance evaluation methods have been proposed, in this paper we use Pingali's method[14], which investigates success and false alarm duration rates of total tracking.

Pingali defines one track from the appearance to the disappearance of the person in the field of view. A video sequence contains multiple tracks. Let A be the true number of tracks in a sequence, A' the number of true tracks that correspond to detected tracks, R' the number of detected tracks that correspond to true tracks, and R'' the number of detected tracks that do not correspond to the true tracks. $T(X)$ is the total duration of X tracks. Durational miss detection rate m_d and durational false alarm rate f_d are represented as

$$m_d = 1 - T(A')/T(A) \quad (18)$$

$$f_d = T(R'')/T(A). \quad (19)$$

$m_d = 0, f_d = 0$ denotes ideal tracking.

We located the stereo camera 2m high at a 40 degree slanting angle. The field of view angle was 109deg, and the base line length was 150mm. While multiple persons walked freely in the open space shown in figure 4, we captured video from the stereo camera about 73sec; the multiple persons were walking or running in the open space. The video contained 44 true tracks that were detected and tracked by a human operator, Beymer's method, and our method. We set parameters $\sigma_d = 0.1, F_q = 6$, which means $\pm 3\sigma$. We used the tracks picked by the operator as true tracks, and calculated m_d and f_d by comparing them with Beymer's tracks and our method's tracks.

Figure 5 shows the relationship between m_d and f_d calculated from the above experiment. Triangles(Beymer's method) were calculated using true tracks and his tracks of several different threshold values. Circles(proposed method) were calculated using true tracks and our proposed method's tracks of them. The solid line in the figure means the envelope of Beymer's, which is the boundary of its best performance. The dashed line denotes the same envelope of ours. One point dashed line stands for the equal error rate(EER). Obviously, our method shows higher performance than Beymer's. Table 1 shows the EERs of Beymer's and ours.

We show an example of the tracking process by our system in figure 6. The figure shows the moment when the system is tracking four persons. The top

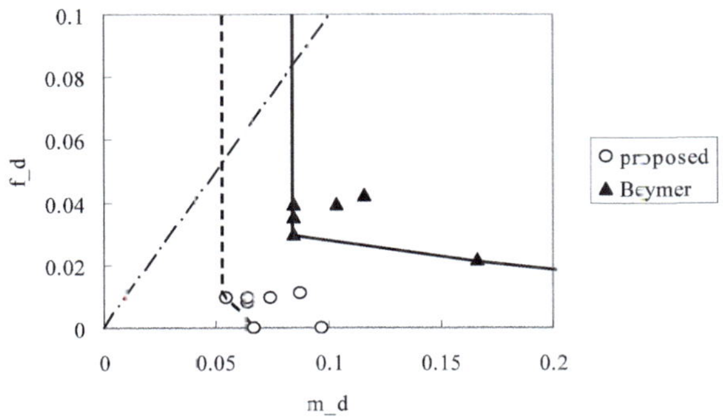

Fig. 5. Relation between miss detection(m_d) and false alarm detection(f_d)

Table 1. Equal error rate(EER) of Beymer's and our proposed methods

	Beymer	proposed
EER(%)	8.5	5.5

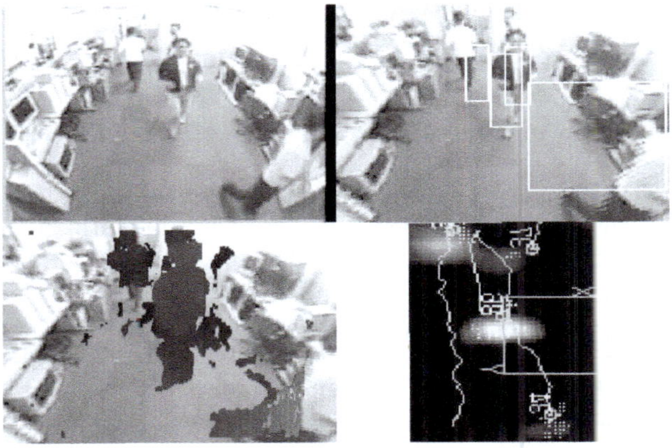

Fig. 6. Example of tracking results. Top left shows original image, bottom left shows disparities overlaid on the original, bottom right shows the map of h', tracking trajectories, and the world coordinate system, and top right shows rectangular person regions projected from tracking results.

left corner shows the original image, the bottom left shows disparities overlaid on the original, the bottom right shows the map of h', tracking trajectories, and the world coordinate system, and the top right shows rectangular person regions which are projected from the tracking results. Although the farthest person is heavily occluded by another person, the system can continue to track him because the occlusion duration is short.

5 Conclusions

We described a new method for detecting and tracking multiple persons with a stereo camera, that estimated statistical feature(s) in the optimal-sized window on the histogram, considering stereo measurement error and human breadth. Then the method measured the feature(s) in the same window on the input histogram and compared estimated feature with measured one. The experimental results showed that our method reduced both miss detection and false alarms more than the normal plan-view map.

References

1. Haritaoglu, I., Harwood, D., Davis, L.S.: W^4S: A real-time system for detecting and tracking people in $2\frac{1}{2}D$. In: European Conf. on Computer Vision. (1998) 877–892
2. Okada, R., Shirai, Y., Miura, J.: Object tracking based on optical flow and depth. In: IEEE/SICE/RSJ Intl. Conf. on Multisensor Fusion and Integration for Intelligent Systems. (1996)
3. Rehg, J.M., Loughlin, M., Waters, K.: Vision for a smart kiosk. In: Intl. Conf. on Computer Vision and Pattern Recognition. (1997) 690–696
4. Darrell, T., Gordon, G., Harville, M., Woodfill, J.: Integrated person tracking using stereo, color, and pattern detection. Intl. Journal of Computer Vision **37** (2000) 175–185
5. Beymer, D., Konolige, K.: Real-time tracking of multiple people using stereo. In: Intl. Conf. on Computer Vision. (1999)
6. Beymer, D.: Person counting using stereo. In: Intl. Workshop on Human Motion. (2000) 127–133
7. Darrell, T., Demirdjian, D., Checka, N., Felzenszwalb, P.: Plan-view trajectory estimation with dense stereo background models. In: Intl. Conf. on Computer Vision. (2001) 628–635
8. Harville, M.: Stereo person tracking with adaptive plan-view templates of height and occupancy statistics. Image Vision Computing **22** (2004) 127–142
9. Faugeras, O., Hots, B., Mathieu, H., Vieville, T., Zhang, Z., Fua, P., Theron, E., Moll, L., Berry, G., Vuillemin, J., Bertin, P., Proy, C.: Real time correlation-based stereo: Algorithm, implementations and applications. Technical Report N. 2013, INRIA (1993)
10. Stauffer, C., Grimson, W.E.L.: Learning patterns of activity using real-time tracking. IEEE Trans. on Pattern Analysis and Machine Intelligence **22** (2000) 747–757
11. Rodriguez, J.J., Aggarwal, J.: Stochastic analysis of stereo quantization error. IEEE Trans. on Pattern Analysis and Machine Intelligence **12** (1990) 467–470
12. Viola, P., Jones, M.J.: Robust real-time object detection. Technical Report CRL2001/01, COMPAQ Cambridge Research Laboratory (2001)
13. Isard, M., Blake, A.: Contour tracking by stochastic propagation of conditional density. In: European Conf. on Computer Vision. (1996) 343–355
14. Pingali, S., Segen, J.: Performance evaluation of people tracking systems. In: Works. on Application of Computer Vision. (1996)

Extrinsic Camera Parameter Estimation Based-on Feature Tracking and GPS Data

Yuji Yokochi*, Sei Ikeda, Tomokazu Sato, and Naokazu Yokoya

Nara Institute of Science and Technology, Graduate School of Information Science,
8916-5 Takayama-cho, Ikoma-shi, Nara, 630-0192 Japan
{sei-i, tomoka-s, yokoya}@is.naist.jp
http://yokoya.naist.jp/

Abstract. This paper describes a novel method for estimating extrinsic camera parameters using both feature points on an image sequence and sparse position data acquired by GPS. Our method is based on a structure-from-motion technique but is enhanced by using GPS data so as to minimize accumulative estimation errors. Moreover, the position data are also used to remove mis-tracked features. The proposed method allows us to estimate extrinsic parameters without accumulative errors even from an extremely long image sequence. The validity of the method is demonstrated through experiments of estimating extrinsic parameters for both synthetic and real outdoor scenes.

1 Introduction

Extrinsic camera parameter estimation from an image sequence is one of important problems in computer vision, and accurate extrinsic camera parameters are often required for a widely moving camera in an outdoor environment to realize outdoor 3D reconstruction and new view synthesis [1, 2]. In this field, accumulative errors in estimated camera parameters often cause un-desired effects for each application. This problem is unavoidable as long as we use only relative constraints among multiple frames [3, 4].

To avoid the accumulative error problem, some kinds of prior knowledge about surroundings and external position and posture sensors have been often used in the literatures [5–9]. As prior knowledge about surroundings, known 3D-positions [5, 6] (called feature landmarks) and wire frame of CAD models [7, 8] are used. The method using feature landmarks [5, 6] is based on the feature tracking approach. Extrinsic camera parameters and 3D positions of feature points are estimated by minimizing the re-projection error of feature landmarks and image feature points tracked in each frame. The method described in [7, 8] is based on matching silhouettes of CAD models with edges in input images. Such image based methods do not require any other sensors. However, the acquisition of these kinds of prior knowledge requires much human cost in a large scale outdoor environment. On the other hand, in the method using a sensor combination [9],

* Presently at Tochigi R&D Center, Honda R&D Co., Ltd.

P.J. Narayanan et al. (Eds.): ACCV 2006, LNCS 3851, pp. 369–378, 2006.

an RTK-GPS (Real Time Kinematic GPS), a magnetometer and a gyro sensor are sometimes integrated to obtain position and posture data without accumulative errors. However, it is difficult to reconstruct high frequency component in motion by only these sensors because the acquisition rate of position information from a general GPS receiver is 1Hz and is significantly lower than video rate. Moreover, highly accurate calibration and synchronization among sensors is needed but this problem has hardly been treated in the literature.

The most hopeful solution for the accumulative error problem is combination of camera and GPS [10, 11]. In this paper, we propose a method to estimate extrinsic parameters for a widely moving camera using both video sequence and GPS position data. To estimate accurate parameters, our method is based on structure-from-motion with extrinsic parameter optimization using the whole of GPS positions and video frames as an offline process; this is the main difference from the conventional methods described in [10, 11]. In the proposed method, tentative extrinsic parameters are estimated from GPS position data and are used to avoid mismatching in feature tracking. In the optimization process, a new error function defined by using GPS position data and re-projection error is minimized to determine some calibration parameters between camera and sensor. In our method, the following conditions are assumed. (i) Camera and GPS have been already synchronized. (ii) Position relation between camera and GPS receiver is always fixed. (iii) Distance between camera and GPS receiver is known, and direction of GPS receiver in camera coordinate system is unknown. In this paper, it is also assumed that cameras have been calibrated in advance and the intrinsic camera parameters (including lens distortion, focal length and aspect ratio) are known.

In the remainder of this paper, we firstly describe the proposed method that handle GPS position data for estimation of extrinsic parameters in Section 2. In Section 3, the validity of the proposed method is demonstrated through experiments of estimating extrinsic parameters for both synthetic and real outdoor scenes. Finally, we present conclusion and future work in Section 4.

2 Extrinsic Camera Parameter Estimation Using Features and GPS

The goal of this research is to obtain extrinsic camera parameters and a direction of GPS receiver from camera when multiple video frames and GPS positions are given. The main topic described in this section is how to integrate GPS position data to the structure-from-motion problem. In the proposed method, the general structure-from-motion algorithm is enhanced to treat GPS position information.

This method basically consists of feature tracking and optimization of camera parameters as shown in Figure 1. Tow process of (A) feature tracking and (B) initial parameter estimation are performed in order. At constant frame intervals, the local optimization process (C) is done to reduce accumulative errors. Finally, estimated parameters are refined using the tracked feature points and feature landmarks in the global optimization process (D). In the processes (C) and (D), a

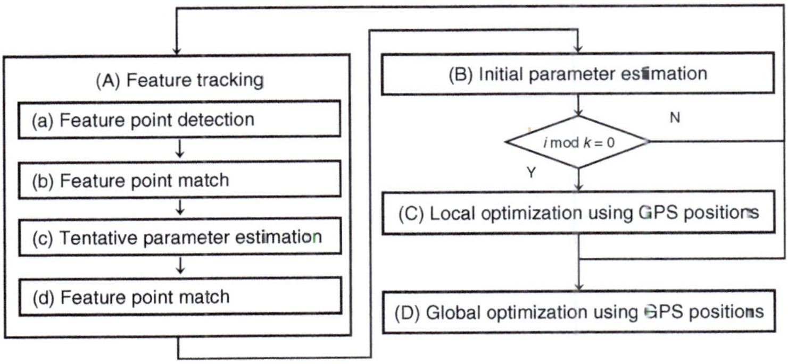

Fig. 1. Procedure of the proposed algorithm

common optimization is performed. The difference in both processes is the range of optimized frames. In the process (C), the range of optimization is limited in a part of the input image sequence because future data cannot be treated in sequential process. On the other hand, in the process (D), all the frames are simply optimized and updated.

In the following sections, we firstly define a new error function that treats both re-projection errors and GPS position errors. After that, each process is also detailed.

2.1 Formulation of Error Function with GPS Position

In this section, we define a new error function E which is combination of the error function concerning GPS and the re-projection error. The way of error minimization will be also mentioned. First, re-projection error is briefly explained as an error function of general structure-from-motion problem. Then, error function concerning GPS is also defined by modeling geometric relation between camera and GPS. Finally, we describe a new error function combining re-projection error and the error function concerning GPS.

Re-projection Error: Re-projection error is generally used for extrinsic camera parameter estimation based on feature tracking. The method minimizing the sum of squared re-projection error is called bundle adjustment. This error Φ_{ij} is defined as $|\mathbf{q}_{ij} - \hat{\mathbf{q}}_{ij}|$ for feature j in the i-th frame, where $\hat{\mathbf{q}}$ represents the 2D projected position of the feature's 3D position and $\mathbf{q}$ represents the detected position of the feature in the image.

Error of GPS: Generally, if GPS positions and estimated extrinsic parameters do not contain any errors, the following equation is satisfied in the i-th frame among the extrinsic camera parameters (position $\boldsymbol{t}_i$, posture $\boldsymbol{R}_i$), GPS position $\boldsymbol{g}_i$ and the position of GPS receiver $\boldsymbol{d}$ in the camera coordinate system.

$$\boldsymbol{R}_i\boldsymbol{g}_i + \boldsymbol{t}_i = \boldsymbol{d} \ (i \in \mathcal{F}), \tag{1}$$

where $\mathcal{F}$ denotes a set of frames in which GPS position is obtained. However, if GPS position $\boldsymbol{g}_i$ and extrinsic parameters $\boldsymbol{R}_i$ and $\boldsymbol{t}_i$ contain some errors, we must introduce an error vector $\boldsymbol{n}_i$.

$$\boldsymbol{R}_i \boldsymbol{g}_i + \boldsymbol{t}_i = \boldsymbol{d} + \boldsymbol{n}_i. \tag{2}$$

In this paper, we introduce an error function Ψ_i related to GPS receiver by using the length of the error vector $\boldsymbol{n}$: $\Psi_i = |\boldsymbol{n}_i|$. This function means the distance between the measured position of the GPS receiver and the predicted position of the receiver using the extrinsic parameters $\boldsymbol{R}_i$ and $\boldsymbol{t}_i$ and GPS position. Next, we describe a new error function E which is a combination of the error function Ψ_{ij} related to GPS receiver and the re-projection error Φ.

Error Function Concerning Feature and GPS: The new error function E is defined as follows:

$$E = \frac{\omega}{|\mathcal{F}|} \sum_{i \in \mathcal{F}} \Psi_i^2 + \frac{1}{\sum_i |\mathcal{S}_i|} \sum_i \mu_i \sum_{j \in \mathcal{S}_i} w_j \Phi_{ij}^2, \tag{3}$$

where ω means a weight for Ψ_i, and $\mathcal{S}_i$ denotes a set of feature points detected in the i-th frame. The coefficients μ_i and w_j mean the confidences for frame and feature, respectively. w_j represents the confidence coefficient of feature point j, which is computed as an inverse variance of re-projection error Φ_{ij}. The coefficient μ_i denotes the confidence of the i-th frame. Two terms in the right-hand side in Eq. (3) is normalized by $|\mathcal{F}|$ and $\sum_i |\mathcal{S}_i|$ each other so as to set ω as a constant value independent of the number of feature and GPS positioning points.

Note that it is difficult to obtain a global minimum solution because there are a large number of local minima in the error function E. In order to avoid this problem, we currently adopt a method to change the weight μ_i in the iteration of the optimization, which is experimentally derived from computer simulations. In this method, the weight is changed whenever optimization process is converged. We expect that local minima can be avoided because the global minimum does not move largely even if local minima move by changing the weight μ_i.

2.2 Implementation of Each Process

(A) Feature Tracking: The purpose of this process is to determine corresponding points between the current frame i and the previous frame $(i-1)$. The main strategy to avoid mismatching in this process is that feature points are detected at corners of edges by Harris operator [12] and detected feature points are tracked robustly with RANSAC approach. In the first process (a), natural feature points are automatically detected by using the Harris operator for limiting feature position candidates on the images. In the next process (b), every feature in the $(i-1)$-th frame is tentatively matched with the candidate feature points in the i-th frame by using a standard template matching. Then, in the third process (c) Tentative extrinsic parameters are then estimated by selecting correct matches using RANSAC approach [13]. In the final process (d), every feature is re-tracked within a limited searching area that can be computed by the tentative extrinsic parameters and 3D positions of the features.

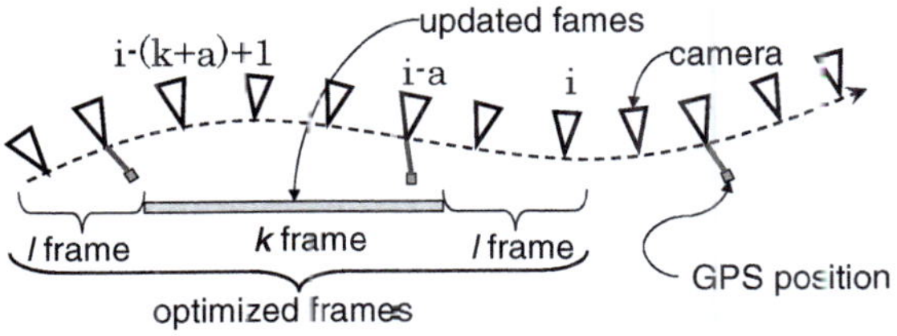

Fig. 2. Optimization frames in the process (C)

(B) Initial Parameter Estimation: This procedure computes 3D position of feature points and extrinsic parameters which minimize the sum of squared re-projection errors. In this process, extrinsic parameters of all the frames are refined to reduce the accumulated errors by the bundle adjustment using feature points. The error function E_{init} defined by Eq. (4) is minimized to optimize both extrinsic camera parameters of all the frames and 3D positions of all the feature points.

$$E_{init} = \sum_{h=1}^{i} \mu_h \sum_j w_j \Phi_{hj}^2. \tag{4}$$

(C) Local Optimization: In this process, the frames from the $(i-(k+2l)+1)$-th to the current frame are used to refine the camera parameters from $(i-(k+2l)+1)$ to $(i-l)$-th frame, as illustrated in Figure 2. This process is designed to use feature points and GPS positions obtained in the frames around the updated frames. To reduce computational cost, this process is performed every k frames. Note that the estimation result is insensitive to the value of l if it is large enough. The constant l is set as tens of frames to use a sufficient number of feature points reconstructed in the process (B). The constant k is set as several frames, which is empirically given so as not to accumulate errors in the initial extrinsic parameters estimated in the process (B).

(D) Global Optimization: The optimization in the process (C) dose not provide enough accuracy as the final output because it is performed for a part of whole of frames and GPS positions for feedback to feature tracking process (A). The purpose of this process is to refine extrinsic camera parameters by using whole of tracked features and GPS positions. The algorithm of this process is the same as the local optimization process (C) when l is set as zero and k is set as the total number of frames.

3 Experiment

In this section, we demonstrate experiments for both synthetic and real outdoor scenes. First, the experiment for synthetic data is carried out to evaluate the accuracy of extrinsic parameters estimated by the proposed method when the correspondences of feature points are given. The experiment for real data is then demonstrated to confirm the validity of the whole proposed method.

Note that some parameters used in the optimization process (C) and (D) are set as follows. The weight coefficient ω in the error function E defined by Eq. (3) was set as 10^{-9}. When a GPS position was obtained, the weight μ_i of the corresponding frame is always set as 1.0. When it was not obtained, 1.0 and 2.0 were alternately set as the weight μ_i whenever the optimization step was converged. In the local optimization process (C), we set the number of updated frames $k = 5$ and the number of optimized frames 49 ($l = 22$). The positions of the first and 15th frames were set as GPS positions. The postures of these frames were set as the true value for synthetic scene, and as the design value of the car system for real scene.

3.1 Synthetic Data

The purpose of this simulation is to evaluate extrinsic parameters estimated in the global optimization process (D). In addition, the validity of the proposed method is confirmed by comparison with the conventional method [6]. We gave a point set as a virtual environment that was used to generate 2D feature positions in synthetic input images. The virtual camera takes 990 images by moving in the virtual environment. The intrinsic parameters of the virtual camera are set the same as the real camera described in the next section. The position of GPS receiver in the camera coordinate system is set as (600,600,600)[mm]. We added errors to input data as follows. The GPS positions with Gaussian noise (σ =30 mm) are given every 15 frames. The feature points are projected to the virtual camera, and detected with Gaussian noise (σ =0.6 pixel) and quantization error. The initial extrinsic parameters $\boldsymbol{R}_i$ and $\boldsymbol{t}_i$ are generated by adding Gaussian noise (position: σ = 500 mm, posture: σ = 0.020 rad) to the ground truth. In the compared method, all the frames is set as key frames in which more than 15 feature landmarks appear. The landmarks are given as feature points whose confidence coefficient is set as large enough, and the 2D positions of the landmarks in each frame are given without any errors. In this simulation, 200 feature points are observed on average in each frame.

Position and posture errors in the simulation result for the synthetic data are shown in Figure 3. In the compared method, the position error is 39.8 mm, and the postures error is 0.0019 rad on average. In the proposed method, the position error is 32.9 mm, and the posture error is 0.0036 rad on average. We have also confirmed this extrinsic parameters obtained in this experiment are not converged to local minima in this simulation.

These results indicate that the proposed method enable us to obtain extrinsic parameters in the same order precision as the conventional method without any manual acquisitions of surrounding information. The difference of the accuracy between the proposed method and the compared one can be caused by the difference of behavior of the given absolute position information such as GPS positions and landmarks. Concretely, we consider that posture errors of the compared method becomes smaller than the proposed one because landmark position

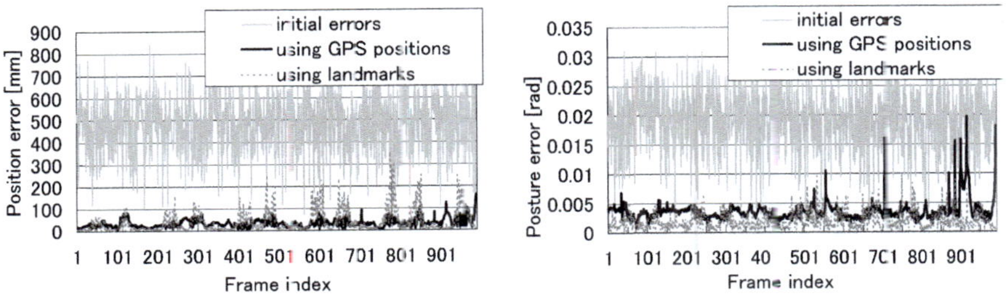

Fig. 3. Position and posture errors of estimated extrinsic parameters

information obtained from images is more sensitive to postures of camera than GPS position information.

3.2 Real Scene

The purpose of this experiment using real data is to confirm the validity of the proposed method which includes the feature tracking and the error models of feature point detection. In this section, first, we describe the condition of this experiment. After that, two kinds of experimental results are shown.

In the first experiment, we used a video camera (Sony DSR-PD-150, 720x480 pixel, 14.985fps, progressive scan) with a wide conversion lens (Sony DSR-PD-150) and a GPS receiver (Nikon LogPakII, accuracy ±3.0 cm) that were mounted on a car. We acquired 3600 frames and GPS positions while the car was moving 1.1km distance at 16.5km/h. The acquired frames and GPS positions were manually synchronized. Intrinsic parameters are estimated by Tsai's method [14]. The distance between camera and GPS receiver is 1020 mm which is manually measured.

First, to confirm the effect to the process (C), we compared the result of the sequential process of camera parameter estimation using the fully activated proposed method and the proposed method without the process (C). In both methods, the same extrinsic parameters of the first frame and the 15th frame are manually given.

The two comparison of the result of both methods are shown in Figure 4. In the method not using GPS position, the process has been terminated at the 1409th frame because tracked feature points decrease. On the other hand, 300 of feature points on average are tracked at all the frames in the method using GPS positions. This result indicates that the performance of the feature tracking is improved by using GPS positions.

Figure 8 shows the result of extrinsic parameters estimation after the global optimization process (D). In this figure, the camera path is smoothly recovered even at the frames where GPS positions are not obtained. The match move using the estimated extrinsic parameters is also demonstrated in Figure 6. The virtual objects were inserted to the input images. We have confirmed that estimated extrinsic parameters do not contain fatal errors because the virtual objects seem to be located at the same position in the real environment in most part of the input sequence (`http://yokoya.naist.jp/pub/movie/yokochi/match_move.mpg`).

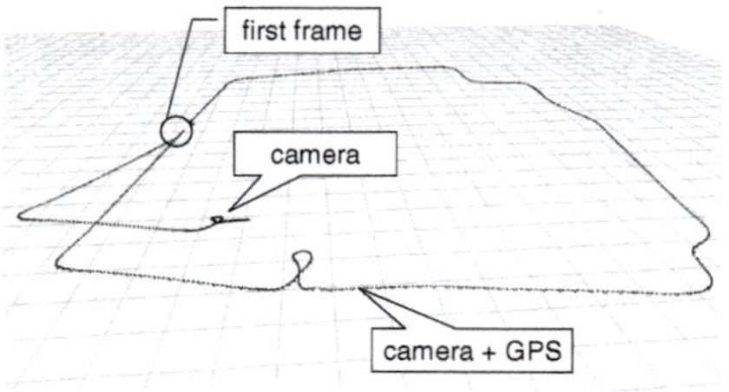

Fig. 4. Accumulative errors of extrinsic parameters

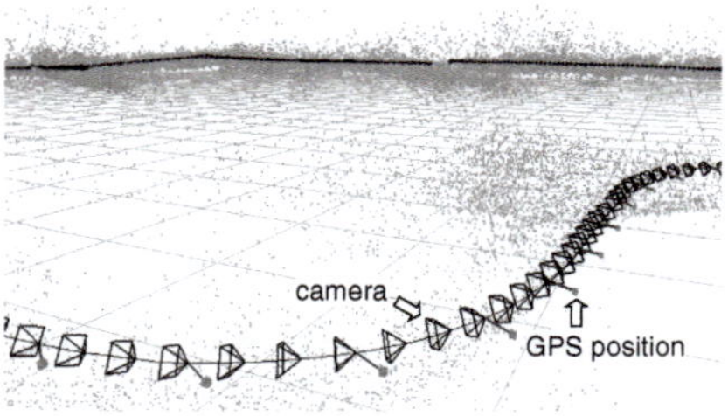

Fig. 5. Result of estimated extrinsic parameters

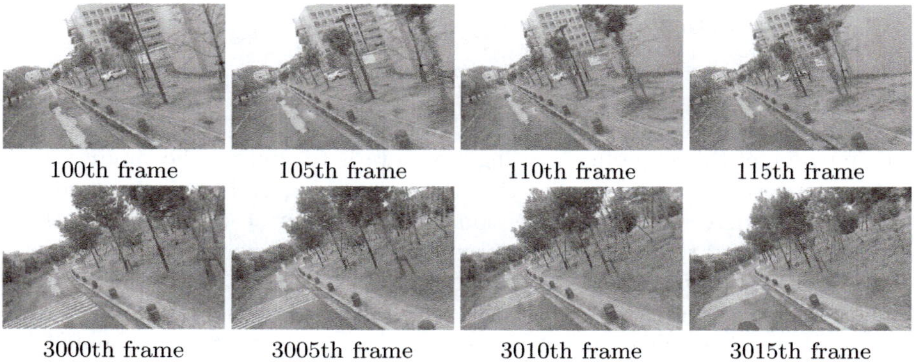

Fig. 6. Match move using estimated extrinsic parameters

Fig. 7. Examples of incorrect match move

However, the virtual objects are drifted from the 995th to the 1030th frames as shown in Figure 7. This position drift is due to the multi-path effect of GPS, which is the corruption of the direct GPS signal by one or more signals reflected

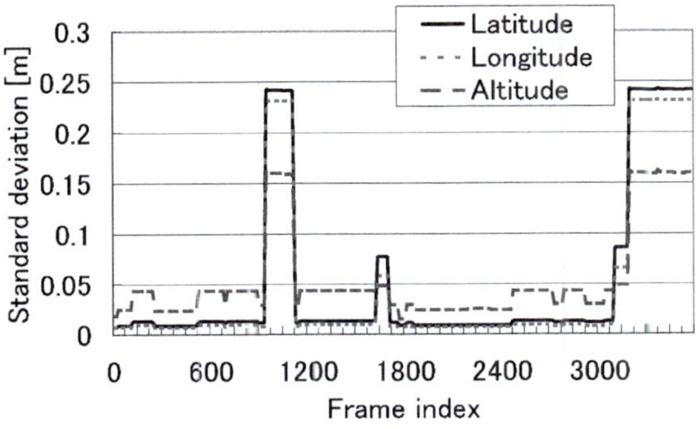

Fig. 8. Standard deviations in GPS data

from the local surroundings. The standard deviation as a degree of confidence of GPS positioning are also obtained from our RTK-GPS receiver. It increases from the 995th to the 1030th frames as shown in Figure 8. To detect the occurrence of the multipath effect, we will explore to design an estimation method using a degree of confidence of GPS positioning.

4 Conclusion

In this paper, we have proposed a method to estimate extrinsic camera parameters of a video sequence without accumulative errors by integrating feature tracking with GPS positions. In the proposed method, GPS position information is used for both feature tracking and optimization of extrinsic parameters.

We have confirmed that the proposed method allows us to obtain extrinsic parameters in the same order precision as the conventional shape-from-motion method using a large number of landmarks in every frame through experiments using both synthetic and real outdoor data. However, the multipath error of GPS is not acceptable for the proposed method. To detect the occurrence of the multipath effect, we will explore to design an estimation method using a degree of confidence of GPS positioning.

References

1. Feiner, S., MacIntyre, B., Höllerer, T., Webster, A.: A touring machine: Prototyping 3D mobile augmented reality systems for exploring the urban environment. In: Proc. 1st IEEE Int. Symp. on Wearable Computers. (1997) 208–217
2. D. Kotake, T. Endo, F. Pighin, A. Katayama, H. Tamura, M. Hirose: Cybercity Walker 2001 : Walking through and looking around a realistic cyberspace reconstructed from the physical world. In: Proc. 2nd IEEE and ACM Int. Symp. on Mixed Reality. (2001) 205–206
3. Fitzgibbon, A.W., Zisserman, A.: Automatic camera recovery for closed or open image sequences. In: Proc. 5th European Conf. on Computer Vision. Volume I. (1998) 311 – 326

4. Pollefeys, M., Koch, R., Vergauwen, M., Deknuydt, B., Gool, L.V.: Three-dimentional scene reconstruction from images. In: Proc. SPIE. Volume 3958. (2000) 215–226
5. Davison, A.J.: Real-time simultaneous localisation and mapping with a single camera. In: Proc. 9th IEEE Int. Conf. on Computer Vision. Volume 2. (2003) 1403–1410
6. Sato, T., Kanbara, M., Yokoya, N., Takemura, H.: Dense 3-D reconstruction of an outdoor scene by hundreds-baseline stereo using a hand-held video csamera. Int. Jour. of Computer Vision **47** (2002) 119–129
7. Comport, A.I., Marchand, É., Chaumette, F.: A real-time tracker for markerless augmented reality. In: Proc. 2nd ACM/IEEE Int. Symp. on Mixed and Augmented Reality. (2003) 36–45
8. Vacchetti, L., Lepetit, V., Fua, P.: Combining edge and texture information for real-time accurate 3D camera tracking. In: Proc. 3rd IEEE and ACM Int. Symp. on Mixed and Augmented Reality. (2004) 48–57
9. Güven, S., Feiner, S.: Authoring 3D hypermedia for wearable augmented and virtual reality. In: Proc. 7th IEEE Int. Symp. on Wearable Computers. (2003) 118–126
10. Nistér, D., Naroditsky, O., Bergen, J.: Visual odometry. In: Proc. IEEE Computer Society Conf. on Computer Vision and Pattern Recognition. Volume 2. (2004) 964–971
11. Hu, Z., Keiichi, U., LU, H., Lamosa, F.: Fusion of vision, 3D gyro and GPS for camera dynamic registration. In: Proc. 17th Int. Conf. on Pattern Recognition. (2004) 351–354
12. Harris, C., Stephens, M.: A combined corner and edge detector. In: Proc. Alvey Vision Conf. (1988) 147–151
13. Fischler, M.A., Bolles, R.C.: Random sample consensus: A pradigm for model fitting with applications to image analysis and automated cartography. Communications of the ACM **24** (1981) 381–395
14. Tsai, R.Y.: An efficient and accurate camera calibration technique for 3D machine vision. In: Proc. IEEE Conf. on Computer Vision and Pattern Recognition. (1986) 364–374

A Method for Calibrating a Motorized Object Rig

Pang-Hung Huang[1], Yu-Pao Tsai[2,3], Wan-Yen Lo[1], Sheng-Wen Shih[4], Chu-Song Chen[2], and Yi-Ping Hung[1,2,5]

[1] Department of Computer Science and Information Engineering, National Taiwan University, Taipei, Taiwan
[2] Institute of Information Science, Academia Sinica, Taipei, Taiwan
[3] Department of Computer and Information Science, National Chiao Tung University, Hsinchu, Taiwan
[4] Department of Computer Science and Information Engineering, National Chi Nan University, Nantou, Taiwan
[5] Graduate Institute of Networking and Multimedia, National Taiwan University, Taipei, Taiwan
hung@csie.ntu.edu.tw

Abstract. Object Movies (OMs) have been successfully used in many applications. However, the techniques for acquiring OMs still need to be improved if high-quality and efficient OMs are desired. In this paper, we present a method for calibrating a motorized object rig to facilitate the acquisition of OMs. We first apply the CPC kinematic model to formulate the 3D configuration of the device, and then propose a method to estimate the parameters of the CPC model of the device. Furthermore, a visual tool is provided for users to adjust the controllable axes of the rig according to the estimated results. After this calibration, more accurate camera parameters can be obtained and then be used for different purposes. In this work, we use the parameters to reconstruct, from an OM, the 3D model of the object, and then adjust the OM according to the center of the 3D model so that a high-quality OM can be obtained for rendering.

1 Introduction

Recently, image-based techniques for modeling and rendering high-quality and photo-realistic 3D objects have become a popular research topic. Having the advantage of being photo-realistic, object movie is especially suitable for delicate artifacts and thus has been widely applied to many areas, e.g., e-commerce, digital archive, digital museum, etc. This technique was first proposed in Apple QuickTime VR [4]. An object movie is a set of images taken from different perspectives around a 3D object; when the images are played sequentially, the object seems to be rotating around itself. Each image in an OM is associated with a pair of distinctive pan and tilt angles of the viewing direction, and thus a particular image can be chosen and shown on screen according to mouse motion of the user. In this way, users can interactively rotate the virtual artifacts arbitrarily and enjoy freely manipulating the object.

To acquire object movies (OMs), we use the motorized object rig, AutoQTVR, developed by Texnai Inc. The motorized object rig is a computer-controlled 2-axis omniview shooting system, as shown in Fig. 1. It has two rotary axes: the pan-direction

P.J. Narayanan et al. (Eds.): ACCV 2006, LNCS 3851, pp. 379–388, 2006.

object rotator and the tilt-direction camera arm rotator. For convenience, we will refer to the rotation axes of the both rotators by the tilt and the pan axes, respectively.

In order to acquire high quality OMs that rotate smoothly, one should manage to make the three axes intersect at a common point first. However, since the optical axis of the camera is invisible, aligning these three axes is inherently a difficult problem. To our knowledge, there is no simple and efficient method for solving this three-axis alignment problem. In this paper, we propose a method to calibrate the motorized object rig to make the three axes as close as possible. With our calibration method, accurate camera parameters can be easily estimated and consequently the quality of the acquired OMs can be remarkably improved.

To calibrate the motorized object rig, we first develop a method to estimate the three axes of it. We then provide a visual tool for users to adjust the motorized object rig according to the estimated results. After the adjustment, the three axes will intersect at a common point $\boldsymbol{C_S}$, as shown in Fig. 1. The details of the calibration process will be described in Section 2. The experimental results and conclusions will then be described in Section 3 and Section 4, respectively.

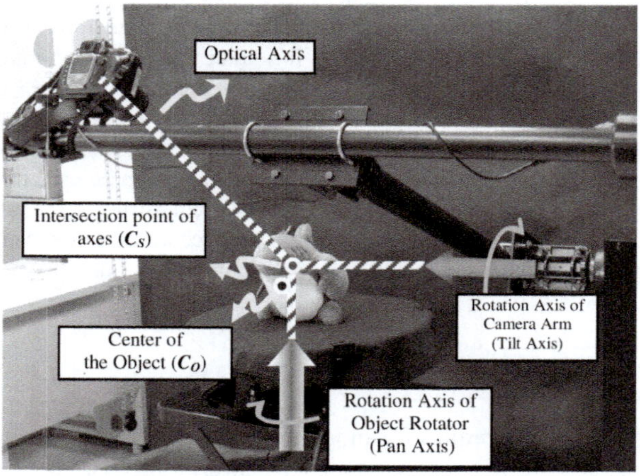

Fig. 1. Motorized object rig – AutoQTVR

2 Calibration of Motorized Object Rig

To calibrate the motorized object rig, we first use the camera mounted on the AutoQTVR to capture some feature points, whose 3D positions are known beforehand. The 2D and 3D positions of the feature points are used to estimate the intrinsic and extrinsic camera parameters. With the estimated extrinsic camera parameters, we can reconstruct the kinematic model of the rig. Then, we apply a simple and practical model, completely and parameter continuous (CPC) model [1][11], to formulate the relation among the three axes. Finally, we provide a visual tool showing the axes for users to adjust the motorized object rig. If the intersections of the rays are not close enough, the user can adjust the motorized object rig according to the estimated result, and then the axes will be estimated again. The whole process will be repeated until the intersections of the rays are close enough. After calibration, reliable extrinsic parameters of the camera will be available with the kinematic model.

2.1 Estimation of Camera Parameters

We adopt the method proposed by Zhang [10] to estimate the intrinsic camera parameters. The method performs camera calibration with at least two images of a known planar pattern captured at different orientations.

On the other hand, we adopt the method presented in [2] and [5] to estimate the extrinsic camera parameters, by first using the method proposed by Kato et al. [7] to obtain a set of initial extrinsic parameters, and then applying Iterative Closest Point (ICP) principle [2] to refine them.

2.2 CPC Model

A CPC model stands for the completely and parameter continuous kinematic model [11]. A complete model means the model provides enough parameters to express any variation of the actual robot structure, and parameter continuity implies no model singularity by adopting a singularity-free line representation [8].

This model was motivated by the special needs of robot calibration. It is assumed that the robot links are rigid. A CPC kinematic model for a revolution/prismatic joint can be represented as follows (we refer the reader to [11] for detail descriptions):

$$ {}^{i}T_{i+1} = Q_i V_i \tag{1}$$

where ${}^{i}T_{i+1}$ denotes the transformation matrix between any two consecutive joint frames, i.e., the *(i+1)-th* reference frame to the *i-th* reference frame. Q_i is the motion matrix defined as follows:

$$ Q_i = \begin{cases} Rot_z(sign \times q_i') & ;\text{for revolute joint} \\ Trans([0\ 0\ sign \times q_i']^t) & ;\text{for prismatic joint} \end{cases} \tag{2}$$

q_i' denotes joint value, which means the rotation angle for a revolution joint, or the amount of displacement for a prismatic joint, and V_i denotes the constant shape matrix. The shape matrix is a general transformation matrix given by

$$ V_i = [R \mid t] = R_i Rot_z(\beta_i) Trans(l_{i,x}, l_{i,y}, l_{i,z}) \tag{3}$$

where

$$ R_i = \begin{bmatrix} 1 - \frac{b_{i,x}^2}{1+b_{i,z}} & \frac{-b_{i,x}b_{i,y}}{1+b_{i,z}} & b_{i,x} & 0 \\ \frac{-b_{i,x}b_{i,y}}{1+b_{i,z}} & 1 - \frac{b_{i,y}^2}{1+b_{i,z}} & b_{i,y} & 0 \\ -b_{i,x} & -b_{i,y} & b_{i,z} & 0 \\ 0 & 0 & 0 & 1 \end{bmatrix} \tag{4}$$

and

$$Trans(l_{i,x}, l_{i,y}, l_{i,z}) = \begin{bmatrix} 1 & 0 & 0 & l_{i,x} \\ 0 & 1 & 0 & l_{i,y} \\ 0 & 0 & 1 & l_{i,z} \\ 0 & 0 & 0 & 1 \end{bmatrix} \quad (5)$$

The rotation matrix R_i is used to describe the relative orientation of the two consecutive joint axes, $Rot_z(\beta)$ is used to align the x- and the y-axes. Notice that the CPC convention requires that any two consecutive joint axes have a nonnegative inner product, i.e., $b_{i,z} \geq 0$. In general, this requirement can be achieved by changing the sign of one of the joint values of consecutive joints. This is because changing the sign of the joint value is equivalent to reversing the joint axis for both revolution and prismatic joints [9].

With the CPC kinematic model [11], the kinematic parameter identification problem can be decomposed into many kinematic parameter calibration sub-problems for each prismatic or revolute joint. Suppose we have a robot with n joints. The transformation matrix from world reference frame, w, to end-effector reference frame, n, can be expressed as follows:

$${}^{n}T_{w} = {}^{n}T_{n-1} \cdots {}^{0}T_{w} = Q_0 V_0 \cdots Q_n V_n \quad (6)$$

2.3 Kinematic Calibration Using the CPC Model

In this section, we will introduce how to apply the CPC model to estimate the transformation matrices among the coordinate systems defined on the motorized object rig. As shown in Fig. 2, we define three axes of three different reference frames on the rig. Let z_c, z_t, and z_p detnoe the z-axes of the camera coordinate system (CCS), the tilt-axis coordinate system (TCS), and the pan-axis coordinate system (PCS), respectively.

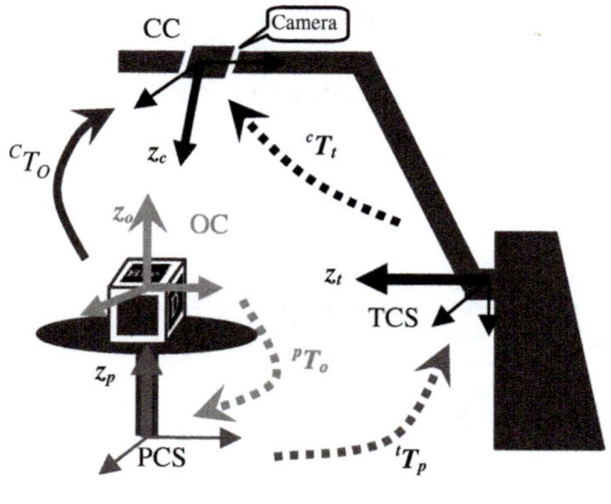

Fig. 2. The schema of motorized object rig

For convenience, let the camera be the "end-effector" of the motorized object rig. Thus, we can obtain the corresponding robot pose with the method described in Section 2.1. In general, the orientations of the x- and the y-axes of the coordinate systems need not to be specified in formulating the kinematics of the motorized object rig [9][11]. Therefore, the redundant parameter β_i can be set to zero, and the transformation matrix from object coordinate system (OCS) to camera coordinate system (CCS) can be simplified as follows:

$$ {}^{c}T_{o} = {}^{c}T_{t} \times {}^{t}T_{p} \times {}^{p}T_{o} = Q_0 \times V_0 \times Q_1 \times V_1 \times Q_2 \times V_2 \quad (7) $$

where ${}^{b}T_{a}$ denotes the transformation matrix from coordinate system a to coordinate system b.

Since the motorized object rig is composed of two revolution joints, the motion matrix Q_0 is a constant matrix which can be set to identity, whereas Q_1 and Q_2 are the rotation matrices about the z_t- and the z_p-axes, respectively. The equations of Q_0, Q_1 and Q_2 are given by

$$ \begin{aligned} Q_0 &= I_{4\times 4} \\ Q_1 &= Rot_z(\theta_t), \text{ where } \theta_t = sign_t \times q_t' \\ Q_2 &= Rot_z(\phi_p), \text{ where } \phi_p = sign_p \times q_p' \end{aligned} \quad (8) $$

where $sign_t$ and $sign_p$ are either +1 or -1, and q_t' and q_p' are the rotation angle about the tilt and the pan axes, respectively. Substituting (8) into (7), we have

$$ \begin{aligned} &{}^{c}T_{o} \\ &= R_0 \times Trans(l_0) \times Rot_z(\theta_t) \times R_1 \times Trans(l_1) \times Rot_z(\phi_p) \times R_2 \times Trans(l_2) \\ &= \begin{bmatrix} \left[{}^{c}r_o(\theta_t,\phi_p)\right]_{3\times 3} & \left[{}^{c}t_o(\theta_t,\phi_p)\right]_{3\times 1} \\ 0 & 1 \end{bmatrix} \end{aligned} \quad (9) $$

where ${}^{c}r_o$ and ${}^{c}t_o$ are the rotation matrix and the translation vector of the transformation matrix ${}^{c}T_o$. From (9), we have

$$ {}^{c}r_o(\theta_t,\phi_p) = R_0 \times Rot_z(\theta_t) \times R_1 \times Rot_z(\phi_p) \times R_2 \quad (10) $$

$$ {}^{c}t_o(\theta_t,\phi_p) = R_0 \times l_0 + R_0 \times Rot_z(\theta_t) \times R_1 \times l_1 + R_0 \times Rot_z(\theta_t) \times R_1 \times Rot_z(\phi_p) \times R_{22} \quad (11) $$

In the following subsections, we will show how to solve the parameters, R_0, l_0, R_1, l_1, R_2, l_2 in (10) and (11).

2.3.1 Rotation Parts

In order to simplify the calibration process, we calibrate one axis at a time. Therefore, when calibrating the tilt-axis, the pan-axis is held still, i.e., ψ_p can be regarded as a constant, and thus $R_1 \times Rot_z(\phi_p) \times R_2$ becomes a constant term denoted by X. By substituting X into (10), we have

$$ {}^{c}r_{o}(\theta_{t},\phi_{p}) = R_{0} \times Rot_{z}(\theta_{j}) \times X \quad (12)$$

Equation (12) can be rewritten in the following form

$$ X = Rot_{z}(-\theta_{j}) R_{0}^{-1} {}^{c}r_{o}(\theta_{i},\phi_{p}) \quad (13)$$

By maneuver the tilt axis to two different joint values, θ_i and θ_j, from (12) and (13), we have

$$ {}^{c}r_{o}(\theta_{i},\phi_{p}) \times {}^{c}r_{o}(\theta_{j},\phi_{p})^{-1} \times R_{0} = R_{0} \times Rot_{z}(\theta_{i}-\theta_{j}) \quad (14)$$

Multiplying $[0\ 0\ 1]^t$ on both sides of (14), we have

$$ \left[{}^{c}r_{o}(\theta_{i},\phi_{p}) \times \left({}^{c}r_{o}(\theta_{j},\phi_{p}) \right)^{-1} - I \right]_{3\times 3} \times \vec{b_{0}} = \varepsilon \approx \vec{0} $$

where ε denotes the error vector induced by the observation noise, and $\vec{b}_0$ can be estimated by minimizing $\|\varepsilon\|^2$. It is well known that $\vec{b}_0$ is the unit eigenvector of A^tA corresponding to the smallest eigenvalue λ. Note that the direction of $\vec{b}_0$ has to be determined such that its z-component is positive. By substituting the estimated $\vec{b}_0$ into (4), we have the orientation matrix R_0.

Once R_0 is available, (14) can be rewritten as follows

$$ \begin{aligned} {}^{c}r_{o}(\theta_{i},\phi_{p}) \times \left({}^{c}r_{o}(\theta_{j},\phi_{p}) \right)^{-1} \times R_{0} &= R_{0} \times Rot_{z}(\theta_{i}-\theta_{j}) \\ &= R_{0} \times Rot_{z}(sign_{t} \times \Delta q_{i}') \end{aligned} \quad (15)$$

The sign parameter $sign_t$ can be determined by minimizing the following function

$$ sign_{t} = \arg\left\{ \min_{sign_{t}=+1,-1} \sum_{j=1}^{M} \left\| R_{0} \times Rot_{z}(sign_{t} \times \Delta q_{i}') - {}^{c}r_{o}(\theta_{i},\phi_{p}) \times ({}^{c}r_{o}(\theta_{j},\phi_{p}))^{-1} \times R_{0} \right\|^{2} \right\} \quad (16)$$

Our next step is to solve the rotation matrix R_1 of ${}^{t}T_{p}$ also using (10). Now that R_0 is calibrated, the tilt axis can be moved when calibrating R_1. For convenience, let us define

$$ \left({}^{c}r_{o}(\theta_{t},\phi_{p}) \right)' = \left(R_{0} \times Rot_{z}(\theta_{t}) \right)^{-1} \times {}^{c}r_{o}(\theta_{t},\phi_{p}) \quad (17)$$

By maneuvering the pan axis to two joint angles, say ϕ_i and ϕ_j, from (10) and (17), we have

$$ \left({}^{c}r_{o}(\theta_{i},\phi_{i}) \right)' = R_{1} \times Rot_{z}(\phi_{i}) \times R_{2}, \left({}^{c}r_{o}(\theta_{j},\phi_{j}) \right)' = R_{1} \times Rot_{z}(\phi_{j}) \times R_{2} \quad (18)$$

$$ \left({}^{c}r_{o}(\theta_{i},\phi_{i}) \right)' \times \left(\left({}^{c}r_{o}(\theta_{j},\phi_{j}) \right)' \right)^{-1} \times R_{1} = R_{1} \times Rot_{z}(\phi_{i}-\phi_{j}) \quad (19)$$

Multiplying $[0\ 0\ 1]^t$ on both sides of (19), we have

$$\left[\left({}^c r_o(\theta_i,\phi_i)\right)' \times \left(\left({}^c r_o(\theta_j,\phi_j)\right)'\right)^{-1} - I\right]_{3\times 3} \times \vec{b_1} = \varepsilon \approx \vec{0}, \tag{20}$$

Again, by solving an eigenvalue problem, we obtain $\vec{b_1}$ which leads to the rotation matrix R_1. The sign parameter $sign_p$ for ψ_p, and also be determined by minimizing an objective function similar to (16).

The final orientation parameter R_2 can be computed with the following objective function derived from (10).

$$\min_{R_2} \sum_{i,j} \left\| {}^c r_o(\theta_i,\phi_j) - R_0 \times Rot_z(\theta_i) \times R_1 \times Rot_z(\phi_j) \times R_2 \right\|_F^2$$

subject to $R_2^t R_2 = I$ and $\det R_2 = 1$. This constrained optimization problem can be solved with a method similar to the one proposed in [2].

2.3.2 Translation Parts

By substituting the estimated rotation matrices into (11), we have the following linear equations for the translation parameters:

$${}^c t_o = M_{3x9} \begin{bmatrix} l_{0,x} & l_{0,y} & 0 & l_{1,x} & l_{1,y} & 0 & l_{2,x} & l_{2,y} & l_{2,z} \end{bmatrix}^t$$

where $M_{3\times 9} = \begin{bmatrix} R_0 & R_0 \times Rot_z(\theta_1) \times R_1 & R_0 \times Rot_z(\theta_1) \times R_1 \times Rot_z(\phi_2) \times R_2 \end{bmatrix}$. By moving the pan and the tilt joints to different positions, we have an over-determined system of the translation parameters which can be solved using the least square method.

2.3.3 Axes Adjustment

After solving the kinematic parameters of the motorized object rig, we can compute its forward kinematic model as (9). Given the tilt angle, θ_t, and the pan angle, ψ_p, we can use (9) to determine the pose of the camera. Also, the forward kinematic model can be used to find the representations of z_c, z_t and z_p axes, i.e., the orientation and position of these three axes. First, the transformation matrix from the reference frame of the tilt axis to the CCS can be determined as ${}^C T_t = V_0$. Thus, the unit direction vector of the tilt axis z_t, denoted by ori_{tilt}, can be derived as follows

$$ori_{tilt} = {}^c T_t \times [0 \quad 0 \quad 0 \quad 1]^t = V_0 \times [0 \quad 0 \quad 1 \quad 0]^t \tag{21}$$

The position of the tilt axis, denoted by pos_{tilt}, is given by

$$pos_{tilt} = {}^c T_t \times [0 \quad 0 \quad 0 \quad 1]^t = V_0 \times [0 \quad 0 \quad 0 \quad 1]^t \tag{22}$$

Similarly, the orientation and position of the pan axis z_p, denoted by ori_{pan} and pos_{pan}, can be found to be

$$ori_{pan} = V_0 \times Rot_z(\theta_t) \times V_1 \times [0 \quad 0 \quad 1 \quad 0]^t \tag{23}$$

$$pos_{pan} = V_0 \times Rot_z(\theta_t) \times V_1 \times [0 \quad 0 \quad 0 \quad 1]^t \tag{24}$$

By using equations (21)-(24), the positions and orientations of the three axes of z_c, z_t and z_p can be evaluated and then can be illustrated as shown in Fig. 4(a). The positions of these three axes can be adjusted to minimize the distance among them. According to our experiences, when the maximum distance among these three axes is smaller than a threshold value of 15 mm, the effect of the miss-alignment of these three axes is negligible.

3 Experimental Results

Fig. 3(a)-(b) shows the result before aligning the three axes of the rig where the estimates of the three axes are shown in Fig. 3(a), and the acquired OM of a toy shark is shown in Fig. 3(b). The estimation and adjustment process is repeated five times to align the three axes of the rig and the result is shown in Fig. 3(c)-(f). From the frontal view of Fig. 3(f), we show that the tilt axis can be effectively adjusted to be perpendicular to the pan axis and optical axis of camera with our method. Moreover, from the top view of Fig. 3(f), the intersections of the three axes are close enough. Some images of the OM of the toy shark are shown in Fig. 3(c). After the visual hull of the toy shark is constructed, shown in Fig. 3(e), the centralization process can be performed, and the resulted OM is shown in Fig. 3(d).

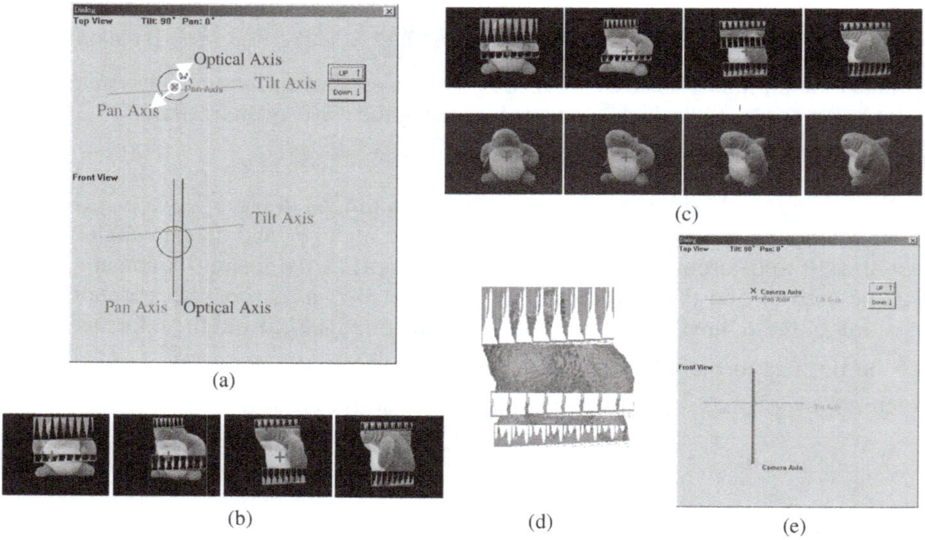

Fig. 3. The OM of the toy shark before/after the calibration. (a) shows the estimated relation among 3 axes, and (b) shows the OM of the toy shark. The cross markers indicate the center of images. (c) shows some images of the OM of the toy shark after calibration, while (d) shows that after centralization. (e) shows the Visual Hull of the toy shark, and (f) shows the estimated axes after calibration.

The process time (including capturing and computing) of the calibration process highly relies on the amounts of the photographs used. In order to find out the minimal number of photographs needed, we then did the following experiment: first, we reconstructed the 3D configurations of the rig, and generated the transformation matrix with different numbers of images (48, 24 and 12 images, respectively), where 48 images are taken from 4 different tilt angles (90, 60, 30, 0) and 12 different pan angles, 24 images are taken from 3 different tilt angles (90, 60, 30) and 8 different pan angles, and 12 images are taken in 3 different tilt angles (90, 60, 30) and 4 different pan angles. For each set with different number of images, we can obtain transformation matrices of 48 views based on the result of CPC estimation, and then can calculate the errors by comparing these matrices to those estimated using 48 images with the use of Frobenius Norm. According to the experiment results it can be shown that 12 images are enough to obtain high accurate camera parameters, and the process time is about only 7 minutes. For detail experimental details, please refer to [6].

4 Conclusion

In this paper, we presented a method for calibrating the motorized object rig, and introduced a visual tool for users to adjust the axes of the motorized object rig. After adjustment, the distances among all the three axes of the motorized object rig can be minimized, and more reliable camera parameters could be obtained after the calibration process. Furthermore, by utilizing the obtained camera parameters, we proposed a software method for automatically adjusting the acquired OM to improve its quality. This work should be useful for promoting future adoption of OMs.

Acknowledgements

This work is supported in part by National Science Council, Taiwan, under the grants of NSC- 93-2422-H-002-022 and NSC 93-2422-H-001-0004.

References

[1] M. Agrawal and L. S. Davis, "Complete Camera Calibration Using Spheres : A Dual-Space Approach," *IEEE International Conference on Computer Vision*, vol. 2, 2003.

[2] K. S. Arun, T. S. Huang and S. D. Blostein, "Least-Squares Fitting of Two 3-D Point Sets," *IEEE Transactions on Pattern Analysis and Machine Intelligence*, vol. 9, no. 5, pp. 698-700, 1987.

[3] C.-S. Chen and W.-Y. Chang, "On Pose Recovery for Generalized Visual Sensors," *IEEE Transactions on Pattern Analysis and Machine Intelligence*, vol. 26, no. 7, pp. 848-861, July 2004.

[4] S. E. Chen, "QuickTime VR – An Image-Based Approach to Virtual Environment Navigation," *Proceedings of the 22nd annual conference on Computer graphics and interactive techniques,* SIGGRAPH '95, pp. 29–38, 1995.

[5] C. R. Huang, C. S. Chen and P. C. Chung, "Tangible Photo-Realistic Virtual Museum," *IEEE Computer Graphics and Applications*, vol. 25, no.1, pp. 15-17, 2005.

[6] Pan-Hung Huang, Calibration of Motorized Object Rig and Its Applications, Master Thesis 2005
[7] H. Kato and M. Billinghurst, "Marker Tracking and HMD Calibration for a Video-based Augmented Reality Conferenciing", *Proceedings of the 2nd IEEE and ACM International Workshop on Augmented Reality,* IWAR, 1999.
[8] K. S. Roberts, "A New Representation for a Line", *Proceedings of Computer Vision and Pattern Recognition*, pp. 635-640, June 1988.
[9] S. W. Shih, Kinematic and Camera Calibration of Reconfigurable Binocular Vision Systems, Ph.D. thesis, National Taiwan University, 1995.
[10] Z. Zhang, "A Flexible New Technique for Camera Calibration," *IEEE Transactions on Pattern Analysis and Machine Intelligence*, vol. 22, no. 11, pp. 1330-1334, Nov 2000.
[11] H. Zhuang, Z. S. Roth and F. Hamano, "A Complete and Parametrically Continuous Kinematic Model for Robot Manipulators," *IEEE Transactions on Robotics and Automation*, vol. 8, no. 4, pp.451-463, Aug 1992.

Calibration of Rotating Line Camera for Spherical Imaging

Tomoyuki Hirota, Hajime Nagahara, and Masahiko Yachida

Osaka University, 1-3, Machikaneyama-cho, Toyonaka, Osaka, Japan
{t-hirota, nagahara, yachida}@yachi-lab.sys.es.osaka-u.ac.jp

Abstract. A number of applications in many fields, including virtual reality, digital archiving, etc., now require the capturing of large fields of view (FOV) and high-resolution images. Recently, rotating line cameras have been used for high-resolution and wide field of view panorama imaging. Some are equipped with a fish-eye lens and can observe a full spherical panorama image. We proposed a calibration method for rotating line cameras, using a spherical imaging model for the application of a full spherical panorama image. For the calibration, the proposed method uses 3D line segments that variously exist in man-made environments.

1 Introduction

There are a lot of requirements for taking a wide field of view (FOV) image in applications used in the fields of digital archiving, virtual reality, and the like. For example, Quicktime VR requires a wide FOV panoramic image to show free fields of view. Moreover, recently high-resolution images have also been required for wide FOV imaging in such applications. Many panoramic image sensors and imaging methods have been proposed previously [1], with the main two ways proposed for panorama imaging methods being those using catadioptric cameras and rotating cameras With the rotating-type camera it is easy to capture a panorama images with higher resolution and wider vertical FOV. Much research and many products have proposed high-resolution panorama cameras with high-resolution line cameras [2][3][4]. Some of them are equipped with fish-eye lens and can observe a full spherical panorama image. We also have constructed a prototype rotating line camera that can capture high-resolution full spherical panorama images (see the specifications in Table 1).

Generally speaking, it is first necessary to model the imaging of the camera and calibrate the parameters for rectifying image distortion or restoring the 3D geometry from an image. Tsai's method [5] has long been used for common camera calibration. However, this method cannot be applied in the case of a rotating line camera because it deals with only the perspective projection of common cameras. Moreover, such methods, which require a known calibration pattern, are difficult to apply to rotating cameras because a large calibration pattern must be prepared which covers the large FOV of the panorama camera. For this reason, some researchers have investigated calibration methods for rotating line cameras. Huang et al. [6] have proposed three calibration methods: point-based, image correspondence, and parallel-line-based for cylindrical

P.J. Narayanan et al. (Eds.): ACCV 2006, LNCS 3851, pp. 389–398, 2006.

panorama sensors. The point-based approach minimizes the difference between ideal projections and the actual projections of known 3D points, such as those of calibration objects or localized 3D scene points. A large set of 3D points is needed for accurate estimation. The image correspondence approach recovers epipolar geometry from a panoramic pair for estimating the camera parameters. The extrinsic parameters, namely that are camera rotation and translation, cannot be estimated in this approach. The parallel-line-based approach uses the related geometric properties such as the distances, lengths, and orthogonalities of a few straight lines for estimating the parameters. In this approach, it is difficult to set the environment for calibration because we need to know a lot of the geometric information of the 3D objects. Smadja et al. [7] have proposed a method for cylindrical sensor calibration using 3D line segments. This approach uses the lines that variously exist in the environment, and therefore the environment for calibration does not need to be set. However, this method assumes an image as a cylindrical projection, and therefore it cannot be applied to rotating line cameras that can capture a full spherical image. Against this problem, Pajdla et al. [8] proposed a spherical camera model, and estimated the camera parameters by using a known calibration chart.

In this paper, we propose a calibration method for rotating line cameras for spherical imaging. Our proposed method uses spherical projection for the application of full spherical images (360 × 180 degree FOV). A large known calibration chart for calibration is not needed because the method uses 3D line segments that variously exist in the man-made environment.

2 Spherical Imaging Model

2.1 Prototype Rotating Line Camera

We constructed a prototype rotating line camera system for spherical imaging. The prototype system consists of a color tri-linear CCD camera (NUCL7500D:

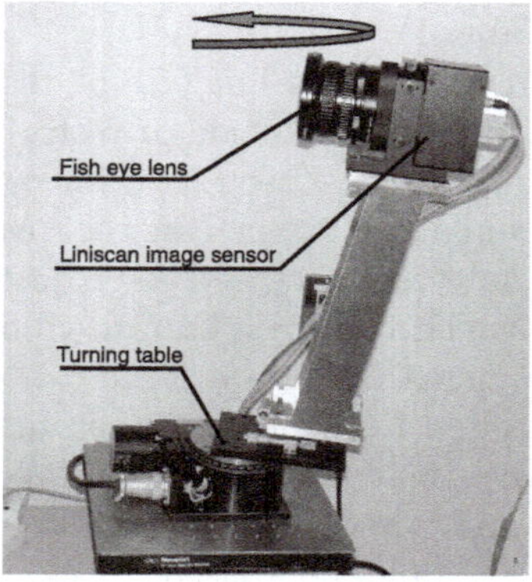

Fig. 1. Prototype rotating line camera

Fig. 2. Spherical image

Table 1. Specifications of the prototype system

Angular resolution (degree/pixel)	Image size (pixel)	Image aquisition time (sec)	Field of view (degree)
0.024×0.024	7500×15000	11.25	180×360

NED), a fish eye lens (smc PENTAX67 Fish-eye 35mm F4: PENTAX), and a rotating stage (KSA-120: SIGMA KOKI). The principal point of the lens is aligned at the rotation axis for taking the single viewpoint image. Figure 1 shows a photo of the prototype. Figure 2 shows an image captured by the prototype. The prototype can capture full spherical images with high-resolution. Table 1 shows the specifications of the prototype.

2.2 Imaging Model

A projection model of a common camera is assumed as a perspective projection. Figure 3 and Equation (1) indicate the relation of perspective projection, where y is the image coordinates, f is the focal length, and ϕ is the incidence angle. On the other hand, a projection of a camera with a fish-eye lens can be modeled as an equidistance projection. Image point y is proportional to the incidence angle ϕ on the equidistance projection, as shown in Figure 4 and Equation (2). The relation indicates that the line camera with the fish-eye lens captures one slice of a spherical image. Hence, the rotating line camera can capture a full spherical image by rotating around the principal point of the lens. We modeled the imaging of the camera as the projection, the lens distortion, and the line scanning models separately. Figure 5 shows the projection model of the rotating line camera.

$$v = f \tan \phi \tag{1}$$

$$v = f\phi \tag{2}$$

$O-X-Y-Z$ indicates the camera coordinates in Figure 5. The lens center O must be aligned with the center of the camera rotation in order to have a single viewpoint. The rotating speed is ω. Hence, the projection model can be modeled as a spherical projection centered on the origin O. The radius of the image sphere f is the focal length of the camera. An arbitrary point $\mathbf{P} = (X, Y, Z)^T$ in the

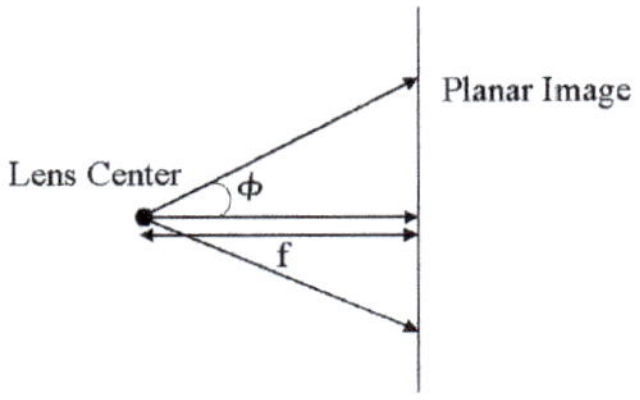

Fig. 3. Perspective projection

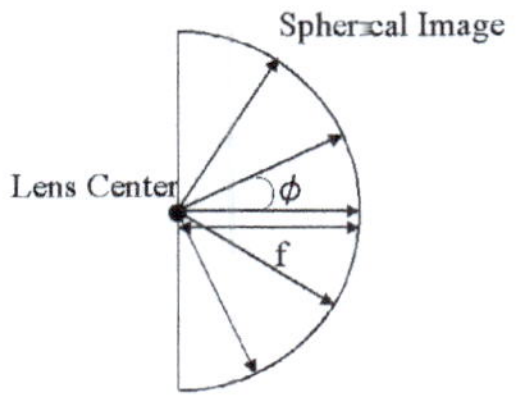

Fig. 4. Equidistance projection

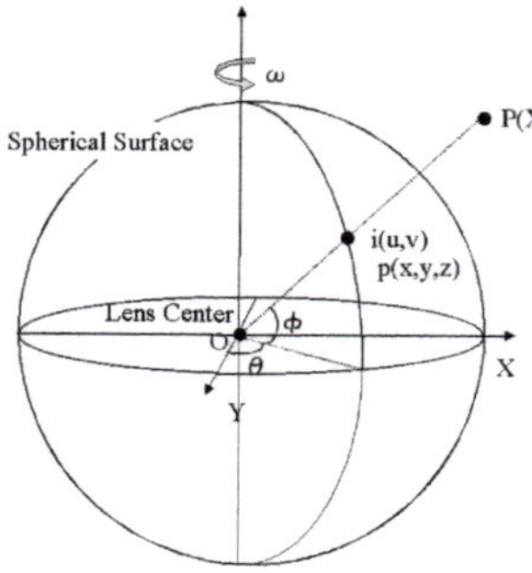

Fig. 5. Projection model

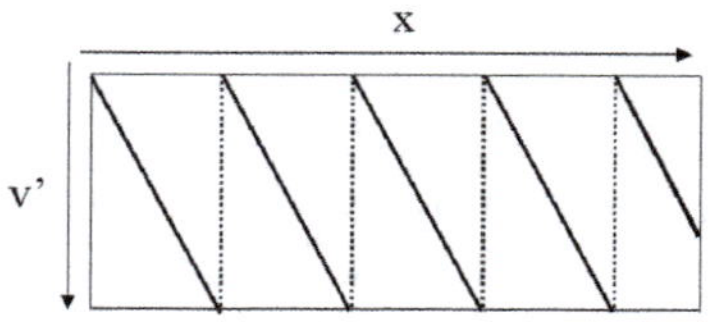

Fig. 6. Relationship between image coordinates and scanning

environment is projected on a point $\mathbf{p} = (x, y, z)^T$ on the image sphere, as given by:

$$\mathbf{p} = \begin{bmatrix} x \\ y \\ z \end{bmatrix} = \begin{bmatrix} f \sin\theta \cos\phi \\ f \cos\theta \cos\phi \\ f \sin\phi \end{bmatrix} = \begin{bmatrix} f \frac{X}{Z} \cos(\arctan(\frac{Z}{r})) \\ f \frac{Y}{Z} \cos(\arctan(\frac{Z}{r})) \\ f \arctan(\frac{Z}{r}) \end{bmatrix}, \tag{3}$$

where θ and ϕ are the longitude and latitude of the incident ray, respectively, and $r = \sqrt{X^2 + Y^2}$.

The image point $\mathbf{i} = (u, v)^T$, which is point $\mathbf{p}$ on the image coordinates, is directly expressed from (r, θ, Z) by the relation:

$$\mathbf{i} = \begin{bmatrix} u \\ v \end{bmatrix} = \begin{bmatrix} f_u \theta \\ v_0 - f_v \phi \end{bmatrix} = \begin{bmatrix} f_u \arctan(\frac{Y}{X}) \\ v_0 - f_v \arctan(\frac{Z}{r}) \end{bmatrix}, \tag{4}$$

where f_u and f_v are the focal lengths along the longitude and latitude, respectively. f_u is the scanning angular step calculated by the rotating speed ω and the scanning speed of the line image, and f_v is the focal length of the camera f. v_o is the principal point of the image (i.e., an equator of the acquired image).

The image point is practically dislocated by the lens distortion. The rotating line camera has only vertical lens distortion. Hence, we can model the lens distortion by a five-dimensional polynomial equation:

$$v' = v + k_1 v^3 + k_2 v^5, \tag{5}$$

where v' is the image coordinates included in the lens distortion and κ_1, κ_2 are coefficients of the lens distortion.

Finally, here we describe the scanning model. Figure 6 shows the relation of the image plane and scanning lines. Solid lines indicate scanning lines, and the image sphere is described as a Mercator projection in this figure. The line camera repeatedly scans L pixels corresponding to the line image by the cycle of S from the top to the bottom of the image. The scanning lines slant corresponding to the camera rotating speed ω, as shown in Figure 6. We can obtain the sequential one-dimensional image data by the speed of V [pixel/sec.]. The relationship between the acquired one-dimensional image and the point on the image sphere can be defined as:

$$u = f_u \omega T \tag{6}$$
$$v' = Vt \tag{7}$$
$$V = \frac{L}{S} \tag{8}$$
$$T = t + nS, \tag{9}$$

where T is the time from the start of scanning, t is the time of the scanning cycle, and n is the number of scanning. Equation (9) shows the relationship between T, t, and n.

3 Calibration

We propose a calibration method for rotating line cameras that can capture a full spherical image. The proposed method uses 3D line segments in the environment for calibration. Hence, the method does not need a known calibration chart. We estimate the rotation matrix $\mathbf{R}$ and translation vector $\mathbf{T}$ as extrinsic parameters and the focal length f_v, principal point of the image v_0, and the coefficients of lens distortion κ_1, κ_2 as intrinsic parameters. We describe the methods for estimating these intrinsic and extrinsic parameters in the following this sections.

3.1 Estimation of Intrinsic Parameters

Let us consider a point $\mathbf{P} = (X, Y, Z)^T$ lying on a 3D line segment in the environment, as shown in Figure 7. We define the line as a plane with the viewpoint O. The equation of the plane, called the view plane, is given by:

$$N_1 X + N_2 Y + N_3 Z = 0, \tag{10}$$

where $\mathbf{N} = (N1, N2, N3)^T$ is the normal vector of the view plane. Equation (10) can be expressed by:

$$\tfrac{Z}{r} = -\tfrac{N_1}{N_3}\tfrac{X}{r} - \tfrac{N_2}{N_3}\tfrac{Y}{r}. \tag{11}$$

Combining Equation (4), (11), $X/r = \cos\theta$, and $Y/r = \sin\theta$ leads to:

$$\mathrm{i} = \begin{bmatrix} u \\ v \end{bmatrix} = \begin{bmatrix} f_u \theta \\ v_0 - f_v \arctan(-\tfrac{N_1}{N_3}\cos(\tfrac{u}{f_u}) - \tfrac{N_2}{N_3}\sin(\tfrac{u}{f_u})) \end{bmatrix}. \tag{12}$$

Hence, the condition that an image point belongs to a line segment can be expressed by:

$$v = v_0 - f_v \arctan(A\cos(\frac{u}{f_u}) + B\sin(\frac{u}{f_u})), \tag{13}$$

where

$$A = -\tfrac{N_1}{N_3}, B = -\tfrac{N_2}{N_3}.$$

f_u is a known parameter because we assume that the camera rotating speed is controlled.

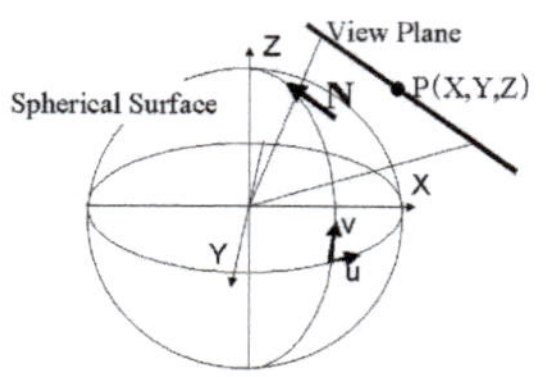

Fig. 7. Normal of a view plane

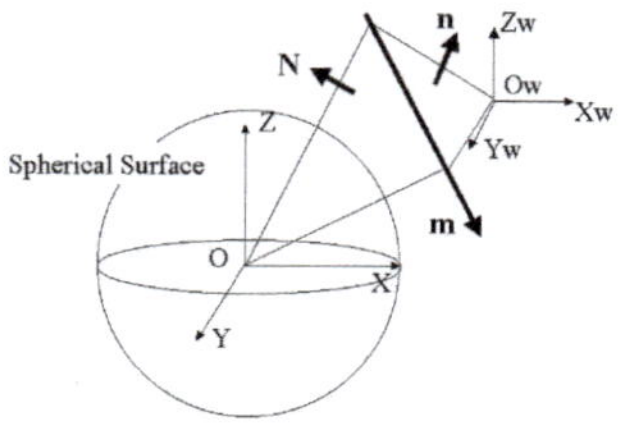

Fig. 8. Line vector and a normal of a view plane

Next, we explain the process for estimating the intrinsic parameters ($f_v, v_0, \kappa_1, \kappa_2$) and the normals of the view planes (A_k, B_k) through the line segments. We use the J points on each of the K line segments in the environments. Therefore, we use $J \times K$ points $\mathbf{i}_{j,k} = (u_{j,k}, v'_{j,k})^T$, $\{j = 0, 1, , J,\ k = 0, 1, , K\}$ to estimate the parameters. We calculate the parameters (v_0, f_v) and the coefficients of the lens distortion parameters (κ_1, κ_2) separately in order to estimate them stably. Equation (13) shows a relationship between the view plane and the intrinsic parameters (v_0, f_v). We estimate v_0, f_v, A_k, and B_k by using nonlinear estimation. First, we derive initial values of A_k and B_k. If v_0 and f_v are fixed as arbitrary initial values, Equation (13) can be regarded as a linear equation. Therefore, initial values of A_k and B_k are calculated by least square estimation from the image points $\mathbf{i}_{j,k}$ of each line. Next, we estimate the optimal values v_0, f_v, A_k, and B_k by using the Levenberg-Marquart Method [9] to minimize the function:

$$f(v_0, f_v, A_k, B_k) = \tan(\tfrac{v'_{j,k} - v_0}{f_v}) + A_n \cos(\tfrac{u_{j,k}}{f_u}) + B_n \sin(\tfrac{u_{j,k}}{f_u}), \qquad (14)$$

which is transformed from Equation (13).

Next, we estimate the lens distortion parameters κ_1 and κ_2 using the estimated parameters v_0, f_v, A_k, and B_k. κ_1 and κ_2 can be estimated by using nonlinear estimation to minimize the function:

$$\begin{aligned} g(\kappa_1, \kappa_2) &= v'_{n,i} - (v_{n,i} + \kappa_1 v^3_{n,i} + \kappa_2 v^5_{n,i}), \\ v_{n,i} &= v_0 - f_v \arctan(A_i \cos(\frac{u_{n,i}}{f_u}) + B_i \sin(\frac{u_{n,i}}{f_u})), \end{aligned} \qquad (15)$$

which is transformed from the lens distortion model of Equation (5).

Finally, we estimate v_0, f_v and κ_1, κ_2 iteratively to reduce the estimation error. The intrinsic parameters v_0, f_v, κ_1, and κ_2 can be estimated through these processes.

3.2 Estimation of Extrinsic Parameters

Here we describe a method for estimating the extrinsic parameters $\mathbf{R}$ and $\mathbf{T}$. We define a line vector $\mathbf{L_W}$ by Plucker coordinates [10]. Plucker coordinates constitute a simple representation of the 3D lines. Let us consider two arbitrary points $\mathbf{P} = (X_w, Y_W, Z_w)^T$ and $\mathbf{Q} = (X'_W, Y'_w, Z'_w)^T$ lying on the line segment in the world coordinates $O_W - X_W - Y_W - Z_W$. The line vector $\mathbf{L_W}$ is defined by:

$$\mathbf{L_W} = [\mathbf{P} - \mathbf{Q}, \mathbf{P} \times \mathbf{Q}]^T. \tag{16}$$

We express $\mathbf{L}_W = [\mathbf{m}, \mathbf{n}]^T$ here. $\mathbf{m}$ is clearly the line direction vector, whereas $\mathbf{n}$ corresponds to the normal vector of the plane formed by the line and the origin of the world coordinate system. Figure 8 shows the relation of $\mathbf{m}$ and $\mathbf{n}$. The world coordinate system $O_W - X_W - Y_W - Z_W$ can transform the camera coordinate system $O - X - Y - Z$ by using rotation vector $\mathbf{R}$ and translation vector $\mathbf{T}$. Therefore the line vector on the camera coordinates $\mathbf{L_C}$ can be expressed by:

$$\mathbf{L_C} = [\mathbf{Rm}, -\mathbf{R}(\mathbf{T} \times \mathbf{m} + \mathbf{n}).]^T \tag{17}$$

We also express $\mathbf{L_C} = [\mathbf{m}', \mathbf{n}']^T$ here, where $\mathbf{n}'$ is the normal vector $\mathbf{N}$ of the view. Therefore, the 3D line segment in the world coordinates $\mathbf{L_W}$ can be associated with $\mathbf{N}$:

$$\mathbf{N} = \begin{pmatrix} N_1 \\ N_2 \\ N_3 \end{pmatrix} = -\left[\mathbf{RT}_\times | \mathbf{R}\right] \begin{bmatrix} \mathbf{m} \\ \mathbf{n} \end{bmatrix}_{O_W}. \tag{18}$$

Combining Equations (13) and (18), the model for estimating the extrinsic parameters is given by:

$$N_3 \begin{pmatrix} A \\ B \\ 1 \end{pmatrix} = \left[\mathbf{RT}_\times | \mathbf{R}\right] \begin{bmatrix} \mathbf{m} \\ \mathbf{n} \end{bmatrix}_{O_W}. \tag{19}$$

We can estimate $\mathbf{R}$ and $\mathbf{T}$ from $\mathbf{L_W}$, $\mathbf{A}$, and $\mathbf{B}$ from Equation (19). We need more than three independent lines to estimate the parameters because there are 5 unknown parameters (Rotation 3 + Translation 3-Scaling 1) in $\left[\mathbf{RT}_\times|\mathbf{R}\right]$. However, if we estimate the parameters from only 3 lines, we have to solve the nonlinear equation as Equation (19). In this paper, we describe the linearized solution for a stable estimation. Equation (19) can be expressed by using the 18 parameters c_{11}-c_{36} as:

$$N_3 \begin{pmatrix} A \\ B \\ 1 \end{pmatrix} = \begin{bmatrix} c_{11} & c_{12} & c_{13} & c_{14} & c_{15} & c_{16} \\ c_{21} & c_{22} & c_{23} & c_{24} & c_{25} & c_{26} \\ c_{31} & c_{32} & c_{33} & c_{34} & c_{35} & c_{36} \end{bmatrix} \begin{bmatrix} \mathbf{m} \\ \mathbf{n} \end{bmatrix}_{O_W} \tag{20}$$

We can get two equations from Equation (20) as follows:

$$\begin{aligned} c_{11}m_1 + c_{12}m_2 + c_{13}m_3 + c_{14}n_1 + c_{15}n_2 + c_{16}n_3 - c_{31}m_1A \\ - c_{32}m_2A - c_{33}m_3A - c_{34}n_1A - c_{35}n_2A - c_{36}n_3A = 0, \end{aligned} \tag{21}$$

$$\begin{aligned} c_{21}m_1 + c_{22}m_2 + c_{23}m_3 + c_{24}n_1 + c_{25}n_2 + c_{26}n_3 - c_{31}m_1B \\ - c_{32}m_2B - c_{33}n_3B - c_{34}n_1B - c_{35}n_2B - c_{36}n_3B = 0, \end{aligned} \tag{22}$$

where

$$\mathbf{m} = [m_1, m_2, m_3]^T, \mathbf{n} = [n_1, n_2, n_3]^T.$$

If 9 or more lines of $\mathbf{Lw}_k$ are known and the corresponding A_k and B_k have been estimated as described in section 3.1, the matrix elements c_{11}-c_{36} can then be estimated to solve:

$$\begin{bmatrix} \mathbf{m_1^T}, \mathbf{n_1^T} & 0\ldots0 & A_1\mathbf{m_1^T}, A_1\mathbf{n_1^T} \\ 0\ldots0 & \mathbf{m_1^T}, \mathbf{n_1^T} & B_1\mathbf{m_1^T}, B_1\mathbf{n_1^T} \\ \vdots & \vdots & \vdots \\ \mathbf{m_K^T}, \mathbf{n_K^T} & 0\ldots0 & A_K\mathbf{m_K^T}, A_K\mathbf{n_K^T} \\ 0\ldots0 & \mathbf{m_K^T}, \mathbf{n_K^T} & B_K\mathbf{m_K^T}, B_K\mathbf{n_K^T} \end{bmatrix} \begin{bmatrix} c_{11} \\ \vdots \\ c_{36} \end{bmatrix} = \begin{bmatrix} 0 \\ \vdots \\ 0 \end{bmatrix} \tag{23}$$

where kth line vector is:

$$\mathbf{Lw}_k = [\mathbf{m}_k, \mathbf{n}_k]^T. \tag{24}$$

Equation (23) can be replaced by $\mathbf{Mc} = 0$. $\mathbf{c}$ can be solved as an eigenvector corresponding to an eigenvalue of $\mathbf{M^TM}$. The extrinsic parameters can be estimated from the matrix elements of $\mathbf{c}$ through these processes.

In this paper, we describe a method for estimating the extrinsic parameters by linear estimation, and this requires at least more than 9 known 3D line segments. If it is difficult to obtain at least 9 known lines of information, then a nonlinear estimation method can be used for calibration withby at least 4 known lines.

4 Experiment

4.1 Simulation

Simulations were carried out for evaluating the proposed calibration method. We simulated the sensor assumed as our prototype. Table 2 shows the setting parameters of the simulated camera, where ξ_x, ξ_y, and ξ_z are the elements of $\mathbf{R}$, and t_x, t_y, and t_z are the elements of $\mathbf{T}$. We estimated the intrinsic parameters v_0, f_v, κ_1, and κ_2 and the extrinsic parameters $\mathbf{R}$ and $\mathbf{T}$. f_u was given by the scan speed and the rotation speed as a known parameter. The prototype camera scans 15000 lines during a rotation of 360 degrees. Therefore f_u was given by $\frac{2\pi}{15000}$.

We used 10 random line segments in the environment, and 100 image points lying on each line were used, for a total of 1000 observation points for the simulation. We also added sampling noise to the image points as assumed at the resolution 0.024[degree/pixel] of the prototype camera.

Next it was necessary to set the initial values for estimating the intrinsic parameters. v_0 and f_v were given by adding the 0-200% errors of the true value. The orders of κ_1 and κ_2 are very small, and therefore the initial values of κ_1 and κ_2 were given by 0.

Table 3 shows the maximum errors of estimated intrinsic parameters. In total, 300 trials were carried out for deriving the result. The maximum errors of v_0 and f_v were small because the error values were 0.6367[pixel] and 0.4329[pixel/rad], respectively. The errors of κ_1 and κ_2 were $8.72e-12$ and $6.45e-18$, and the line vectors A_k and B_k were also small, even if the initial values of v_0 and f_v were added as 200% error. Hence, the method is stable for the estimation of the parameters independent of the initial values. The average geometric error

Table 2. The setting of camera parameters

v_0	3750 [pixel]
f_v	$7500/\pi$ [pixel/rad]
κ_1	2.3e-9
κ_2	-2.7e-16
ξ_x, ξ_y, ξ_z	40 [degree]
t_x, t_y, t_z	4 [m]

Table 3. Maximum errors of the estimated intrinsic parameters

v_0	0.6367 [pixel]
f_v	0.4329 [pixel/rad]
κ_1	8.72e-12
κ_2	6.45e-18

Table 4. Maximum errors of estimated extrinsic paremeters **R** and **T**

ξ_x	2.0e-8 [degree]
ξ_y	1.0e-8 [degree]
ξ_z	2.0e-8[degree]
t_x	2.2e-7[m]
t_y	4.5e-7[m]
t_z	3.4e-7[m]

Table 5. Initial values and the estimated values

	initial value	estimated value
v_0(pixel)	3750.0	3659.5
f_v(degree/pixel)	2384.0	2647.5
κ_1	0.0	3.6e-9
κ_2	0.0	-3.1e-16

of the points between the true image and the calibrated image was 0.73 [pixel] when the estimated intrinsic parameters were used for rectifying the simulated image distortion. Therefore we could confirm that all intrinsic parameters were sufficient to converge because the error was less than 1.0 [pixel].

Next we evaluated the estimation of the extrinsic parameters. We used the estimated intrinsic parameters, the estimated line parameters A_k and B_k k=1,2, . . . ,10, and the corresponding 10 known line vectors $\mathbf{L_w}_k$. Table 4 shows the maximum errors of the estimated parameters. Equation (19) shows that the estimated extrinsic parameters **R** and **T** were affected by the estimated errors of A_k and B_k. However, these errors were not large enough for practical use. Thus we could confirm that the proposed calibration method worked in the simulation experiments.

4.2 Experiment of the Proposed Calibration Method Using a Real Image

We applied the proposed calibration method to a real input image captured by the prototype system. We estimated the intrinsic parameters v_0, f_v, κ_1, and κ_2 in order to rectify the image distortion. Nine random lines and 30 points lying on each line were used, for a total of 270 points used for the calibration in this experiment. We manually took the points on the line segments by mouse pointing. Table 5 shows the initial values and estimated values of v_0, f_v, κ_1, and κ_2. The estimated parameters were converged even if the initial values were set on arbitrary values such as the simulation settings. Figures 9 and 10 show the raw input image and the rectified image using the estimated intrinsic parameters. These images represent the perspective projection image that shows the around zenith of the full spherical input image, and this is the most distorted part, so it is easy to identify the image distiortion. Figure 9 shows the barrel-like distortion, whereas the distortion has been rectified in Figure 10. From these results, we could confirm the effectiveness of the proposed calibration method.

Fig. 9. Raw input image

Fig. 10. Rectified image

5 Conclusion

Rotating line cameras have been used recently for virtual reality and digital archiving applications because it is easy to take high-resolution and wide field of view panorama images with such cameras. In this paper we proposed a calibration method for rotating line cameras for taking a full spherical panorama image. Though previous methods have used cylindrical imaging models, we used a spherical imaging model and applied it to a full spherical panorama image. For the calibration, the proposed method uses 3D line segments that variously exist in the man-made environment. We carried out both simulation and real experiments in order to evaluate the proposed calibration method. We confirmed that the calibration method worked in the experiments.

References

1. R. Benosman and S. B. Kang, " Panoramic Vision: Sensors, Theory, and Applications", *Springer*, 2001.
2. K. Scheibe, H. Korsitzky, R. Reulke, M. Scheele and M. Solbrig, "EYESCAN - A High Resolution Digital Panoramic Camera", *Proc. Int. Workshop on Robot Vision*, pp.77-83, 2001.
3. "Panoscan Mark III", http://www.panoscan.com.
4. "SPHERON VR", http://www.spheron.com.
5. R. Y.Tsai, "A Versatile Camera Calibration Technique For High-accuracy 3D Machine Vision Metrology Using Off-the-shelf TV Cameras And Lenses", *IEEE Journal Robotics and Automatioins*, vol. 3, no. 4, pp. 323-344, Aug, 1987.
6. F. Huang, S.K.Wei, R.Klette, "Comparative Studies of Line-based Panoramic Camera Calibration", *IEEE Int. Conf. Computer Vision and Pattern Recognition*, vol.7, pp. 16-22, June, 2003.
7. L. Smadja, R.Benosman, J. Devars, "Cylindrical Sensor Calibration using Lines", *Proc. Workshop Omnidirectional Vision and Camera Networks*, 2004.
8. H. Bakstein, T. Pajdla, gPanoramic Mosaicing with a 180Field of View Lensh, *Proc. Workshop Omnidirectional Vision and Camera Networks* , 2002.
9. P. E. Gill, W. Murray, M. H. Wrigth, "Practical Optimization", *Academic Press*, 1981.
10. K.Shoemake, "Plucker coordinate tutorial", *Ray-Tracing News*, vol. 11, Jul, 1998.

Viewpoint Determination of Image by Interpolation over Sparse Samples

Bodong Liang and Ronald Chung

Department of Automation and Computer-Aided Engineering,
The Chinese University of Hong Kong,
Shatin, N.T., Hong Kong, China
{bdliang, rchung}@acae.cuhk.edu.hk

Abstract. We address the problem of, given an image, determining the viewpoint from which the image was taken, and that is to be achieved without referencing to or estimating any explicit 3-D structure of the imaged scene. Used for reference are a small number of sample snapshots of the scene, each of which having the associated viewpoint supplied with it. By viewing image and its associated viewpoint as the input and output of a function, and the given snapshot-viewpoint pairs as samples of that function, we have a natural formulation of the problem as an interpolation or learning one. The interpolation formulation has at least two advantages: it allows imaging details like camera intrinsic parameters to be unknown, and the viewpoint specification to be not necessarily physical, i.e., the specification could consist of any set of values that adequately describe the viewpoint space and need not be measured in metric units. We describe an interpolation-based solution that guarantees that all given sample data are satisfied exactly with the least complexity in the interpolated function. Experimental results on benchmarking image dataset show that the solution is effective in arriving at good solution even with sparse input samples.

1 Introduction

Given an image of a scene, how can we tell from which viewpoint the image was taken? The problem, which we refer to as the viewpoint determination problem, is a central one in a variety of tasks including robot self-localization [1], robot navigation [2], human pose estimation, image-based rendering [3], and augmented reality [4].

We address the problem in the following light. There is no requirement of referencing to or estimating any explicit 3-D structure of the imaged scene. Used for reference are instead a number of sample snapshots of the scene, each of which having the associated viewpoint supplied with it.

The problem is related to the camera pose estimation problem formally defined in [5], [6]. Solutions proposed in the literature to camera pose estimation include [7], [4], in which closed-form solution was acquired under the assumption of calibrated cameras, and [8], [9], in which iterative methods were used to relax the requirement of prior calibration.

P.J. Narayanan et al. (Eds.): ACCV 2006, LNCS 3851, pp. 399–408, 2006.

Here we term our problem differently – viewpoint determination as opposed to camera pose estimation – because we allow the viewpoints to be specified in terms of any value set that is sufficient for the description, not necessarily in metric coordinates. For example, if the camera would only travel approximately along a line or curve, the user could just name the viewpoints of the sample images as 1, 2, 3 and so on in the order of their viewpoints along that line or curve. The viewpoints of all possible images would then be indexed linearly in accordance with their resemblance in the image space with those of the sample images; for instance, the image mid-way between sample image 1 and sample image 2 will then be of viewpoint 1.5. In a way, viewpoint determination is a relaxed form of camera pose estimation. It is particularly useful for tasks in which viewpoints are required to be indexed and ordered but not necessarily expressed in physical position coordinates.

By viewing image and the associated viewpoint (here by associated viewpoint we mean viewpoint expressed in terms of any convenient indexed terms, not necessarily in positional metric units) as the input and output of a function, and the supplied image-viewpoint pairs as samples of that function, we have a natural formulation of the problem: an interpolation or learning one. The formulation regards the mapping from an image to the associated viewpoint as a black box, and seeks to find a mapping surface that adequately describes it at least over the sample images. Compared to the closed-form solutions like [7], [4] and iteration solutions like [8], [9], the interpolation-based formulation has the advantage that it allows the explicit addressing of perspective projection and other complexities in the original mapping to be bypassed. It also allows imaging details like the focal length, pixel size, lens distortion etc. of the camera to be unknown.

The interpolation method we used is so-called *Example-Based Interpolation* (EBI) [10], which is a mechanism that learns or interpolates, from examples, a function that crosses all the input examples with minimal oscillations between the examples. It has promising results, even with very sparse examples given, in a number of applications including object detection and character recognition [11], computer animation and graphics [12], image synthesis [3], and others.

There has not been much previous work on camera pose or related problems that adopts the interpolation and learning approach. Beymer and Poggio's work [13] is the only one, but their approach need compute optical flow to establish dense correspondences over sample images. Since EBI scheme can ensure that the interpolated function always passes through all the examples exactly and smoothly, our EBI-based method can tackle the camera viewpoint transition as a continuous and smooth transition between the viewpoints of all sample images, even with sparse correspondences across sparse input sample images given.

2 Review of EBI

The interpolation problem could be stated as this: given S input-output pairs $\{(\mathbf{V}_s, f_{\mathbf{V}_s})\} : s = 1, 2, \cdots, S\}$ as examples of a function $f : \mathbb{R}^D \rightarrow \mathbb{R}$, construct the scalar function value $f_{\mathbf{V}} = f(\mathbf{V})$ for any arbitrary input $\mathbf{V}$ in $\mathbb{R}^D$ such that it satisfies $f_{\mathbf{V}_s} = f(\mathbf{V}_s)$ for all the S given examples. We shall refer to each $\mathbf{V}_s$ ($s \in \{1, 2, \cdots, S\}$) as the sth *example point*, and $f_{\mathbf{V}_s}$ the sth *example value*.

A natural inference of $f_{\mathbf{V}}$ for any $\mathbf{V}$ is a weighted sum of the example values:

$$f_{\mathbf{V}} = \left[f_{\mathbf{V}_1}, f_{\mathbf{V}_2}, \cdots, f_{\mathbf{V}_S}\right] \mathbf{W}_{\mathbf{V}} , \tag{1}$$

where *weight matrix* $\mathbf{W}_{\mathbf{V}} = [w_{1,\mathbf{V}}, w_{2,\mathbf{V}}, \cdots, w_{S,\mathbf{V}}]^{\mathrm{T}}$ represents, for computing $f_{\mathbf{V}}$ at any arbitrary input $\mathbf{V}$, the respective weights given to the S example values. The problem thus boils down to the design of the weight matrix $\mathbf{W}_{\mathbf{V}}$.

$\mathbf{W}_{\mathbf{V}}$, in which the sum of all S weights is equal to 1 for any particular $\mathbf{V}$, is a function of $\mathbf{V}$ since naturally it varies with $\mathbf{V}$ in this way: the contributions of the various example values $f_{\mathbf{V}_1}, f_{\mathbf{V}_2}, \cdots, f_{\mathbf{V}_S}$ are in accordance with the relative proximity of their examples points $\mathbf{V}_1, \mathbf{V}_2, \cdots, \mathbf{V}_S$ to $\mathbf{V}$. This implies:

$$\begin{bmatrix} 1 \\ \mathbf{V} \end{bmatrix} = \begin{bmatrix} 1 & 1 & \cdots & 1 \\ \mathbf{V}_1 & \mathbf{V}_2 & \cdots & \mathbf{V}_S \end{bmatrix} \mathbf{W}_{\mathbf{V}} . \tag{2}$$

To allow the interpolated function to satisfy the given input-output pairs exactly, if $\mathbf{V}$ happens to be one of the example points $\mathbf{V}_s$, where $s = 1, 2, \cdots, S$, the sth entry of $\mathbf{W}_{\mathbf{V}}$ is 1 while all the other entries are 0, i.e., for all s and $\mathbf{V}_\alpha$, where $s, \alpha \in \{1, 2, \cdots, S\}$,

$$w_{s,\mathbf{V}_\alpha} = \begin{cases} 1 & \text{if } s = \alpha \ , \\ 0 & \text{otherwise} \ . \end{cases} \tag{3}$$

With a minimum of only $(D-1)$ examples that do not lie in a same hyperplane in $\mathbb{R}^D$, a nonlinear design of $\mathbf{W}_{\mathbf{V}}$ [12], [14] could be determined by radial basis functions. This solution could ensure that the interpolated function $f_{\mathbf{V}}$ satisfies (2), (3) and passes through the input examples exactly and smoothly. We shall utilize this solution in this paper but do not list it here for lack of space.

3 EBI-Based Viewpoint Determination

3.1 Problem Statement and Overview to Approach

In its simplest form, the viewpoint determination problem could be stated as this: suppose we have S sample images $\mathbf{I}_{\mathbf{V}_s}$'s ($s = 1, 2, \cdots, S$) of a scene that are captured at S known viewpoints $\mathbf{V}_s$'s in a particular viewpoint space (which could be a subset of the 3-D space) under unknown imaging settings, for any given input image $\mathbf{I}_{\mathbf{V}}$ captured about the same scene in the viewpoint space, estimate the associated viewpoint $\mathbf{V}$.

To have a solvable problem, naturally we assume that the sample images cover all dimensions of the target viewpoint space, and the user shall index the viewpoint space with adequate number of dimensions and supply index values of the sample images in an orderly fashion, i.e., in accordance with their order in space along each of the above dimensions.

Our interpolation solution could be outlined as the following. From the given sample images we first extract distinct features and match such features across the samples. We keep only the set of features in each sample image that find correspondences in other samples, and we call such features the *seed features.* Suppose the total number of seed features in each sample image is C, and let us refer to such C seed features for each sample image $\mathbf{I}_{\mathbf{V}_s}$'s ($s = 1, 2, \cdots, S$) as $\mathbf{x}_{c,\mathbf{V}_s}$'s ($c = 1, 2, \cdots, C$), or together as:

$$\mathbf{X}_{\mathbf{V}_s} = \left[\mathbf{x}_{1,\mathbf{V}_s}{}^{\mathrm{T}}, \mathbf{x}_{2,\mathbf{V}_s}{}^{\mathrm{T}}, \cdots, \mathbf{x}_{C,\mathbf{V}_s}{}^{\mathrm{T}}\right]^{\mathrm{T}},$$

where $\mathbf{x}_{c,\mathbf{V}_s} = [u_{c,\mathbf{V}_s}, v_{c,\mathbf{V}_s}]^{\mathrm{T}}$ stands for the image position of the cth seed feature in the sth example (with viewpoint at $\mathbf{V}_s$).

Each sample image $\mathbf{I}_{\mathbf{V}_s}$ is therefore identified by the image positions of the seed feature set $\mathbf{X}_{\mathbf{V}_s}$ in it. The mapping function we interpolate from the sample data is therefore transformed from the original $\mathbf{I}_{\mathbf{V}_s} \rightarrow \mathbf{V}_s$ to $\mathbf{X}_{\mathbf{V}_s} \rightarrow \mathbf{V}_s$, i.e., one that maps a set of image positions (of the seed features in the image) to a viewpoint. We use EBI to interpolate that function from the pairings of feature positions versus viewpoint in the sample data.

For any input image $\mathbf{I}_{\mathbf{V}}$ whose viewpoint $\mathbf{V}$ is to be determined, we must also extract the same C seed features' image positions $\mathbf{x}_{c,\mathbf{V}}$'s ($c = 1, 2, \cdots, C$):

$$\mathbf{X}_{\mathbf{V}} = \left[\mathbf{x}_{1,\mathbf{V}}{}^{\mathrm{T}}, \mathbf{x}_{2,\mathbf{V}}{}^{\mathrm{T}}, \cdots, \mathbf{x}_{C,\mathbf{V}}{}^{\mathrm{T}}\right]^{\mathrm{T}}.$$

Thus the mapping function will map such features $\mathbf{X}_{\mathbf{V}}$ to the viewpoint $\mathbf{V}$ we desire. In the process we also make use of robust estimation to pick out the most consistent subset of $\mathbf{x}_{c,\mathbf{V}}$'s for determining viewpoint $\mathbf{V}$, thus allowing certain tolerance to positioning error on the seed feature set $\mathbf{x}_{c,\mathbf{V}}$'s.

3.2 Initial Correspondences Establishment

The interpolation process requires correspondence establishment – the determination of image locations in all sample images that are projected by the same 3-D feature of the imaged scene. The problem is a well studied one [15] and high quality toolkits are available. In our system, we use the IMAGE-MATCHING system developed by Zhang *et al.* [16] that exploits constraints like the epipolar constraint and other quasi-invariant properties of the features. However, other correspondence systems could serve the purpose just as well, since all needed is a small set of distinct features that find correspondences over the sample images.

3.3 Interpolation Process

With the above, for any given image $\mathbf{I}_{\mathbf{V}}$, we could proceed with the EBI scheme to estimate the viewpoint $\mathbf{V}$.

The determination of viewpoint $\mathbf{V}$ for image $\mathbf{I}_{\mathbf{V}}$ hinges at how seed feature $\mathbf{x}_{c,\mathbf{V}}$ is positioned relative to all $\mathbf{x}_{c,\mathbf{V}_s}$'s in the viewpoint space, for every seed feature. We could use solution of EBI in Sect. 2 to learn a $S \times 1$ weight matrix $\mathbf{W}_{\mathbf{V}}^{C}$ from $\mathbf{X}_{\mathbf{V}}$ and $\mathbf{X}_{\mathbf{V}_s}$'s such that

$$\begin{bmatrix} 1 \\ \mathbf{X}_{\mathbf{V}} \end{bmatrix} = \begin{bmatrix} 1 & 1 & \cdots & 1 \\ \mathbf{X}_{\mathbf{V}_1} & \mathbf{X}_{\mathbf{V}_2} & \cdots & \mathbf{X}_{\mathbf{V}_S} \end{bmatrix} \mathbf{W}_{\mathbf{V}}^{C} .$$

We then could use (1) in Sect. 2 to determine the viewpoint $\mathbf{V}$ as following:

$$\mathbf{V} = \left[\mathbf{V}_1, \mathbf{V}_2, \cdots, \mathbf{V}_S\right] \mathbf{W}_{\mathbf{V}}^{C} .$$

However, since each image position $\mathbf{x} = [u, v]^{\mathrm{T}}$ has two parameters and there are total C seed features, the dimension D of EBI we just applied is equal to $2C$, which is generally larger than the number of image samples, i.e., $D = 2C > S$, if we take it that the sample size could be sparse. We know there exist solutions for EBI in Sect. 2 only when $S \geq (D+1)$. Now that we generally have $S < (2C+1)$, we must choose less seed features than what we have on image $\mathbf{I}_{\mathbf{V}}$ to use as examples to the EBI mechanism.

We should first decide the size N of the needed subset of seed features. We determine N from the constraints that $S \geq (2N+1)$ and $S < [2(N+1)+1]$, then adopt robust estimation method (e.g. RANSAC [5], Least Median of Squares (LMedS) [17] etc.) to choose the most consistent N features of subset from the total C seed features for interpolating the viewpoint $\mathbf{V}$. That way we also allow certain tolerance to positioning error in the seed features of image $\mathbf{I}_{\mathbf{V}}$. In our implementation, we first choose the N-set from the C seed features and then apply the LMedS method to get the robust result.

Outliers Detection. More precisely, our first step is to detect the outliers from the whole C seed features. Using the Russian Roulette Wheel Selection or Monte Carlo method, we draw M (please refer to [17] and [16] for the process of determining M) random subsamples of the N features. For the mth drawing ($m = 1, 2, \cdots, M$), the N seed features are:

$$_{m}\mathbf{X}_{\mathbf{V}}^{N} = \left[\mathbf{x}_{P_1,\mathbf{V}}{}^{\mathrm{T}}, \mathbf{x}_{P_2,\mathbf{V}}{}^{\mathrm{T}}, \cdots, \mathbf{x}_{P_N,\mathbf{V}}{}^{\mathrm{T}}\right]^{\mathrm{T}} ,$$

$$_{m}\mathbf{X}_{\mathbf{V}_s}^{N} = \left[\mathbf{x}_{P_1,\mathbf{V}_s}{}^{\mathrm{T}}, \mathbf{x}_{P_2,\mathbf{V}_s}{}^{\mathrm{T}}, \cdots, \mathbf{x}_{P_N,\mathbf{V}_s}{}^{\mathrm{T}}\right]^{\mathrm{T}} ,$$

where $P_n \in \{1, 2, \cdots, C\}$, $n = 1, 2, \cdots, N$, and $P_i \neq P_j$ if $i \neq j$.

Then we could apply EBI to determine $_{m}\mathbf{W}_{\mathbf{V}}^{N}$ such that

$$\begin{bmatrix} 1 \\ _{m}\mathbf{X}_{\mathbf{V}}^{N} \end{bmatrix} = \begin{bmatrix} 1 & 1 & \cdots & 1 \\ _{m}\mathbf{X}_{\mathbf{V}_1}^{N} & _{m}\mathbf{X}_{\mathbf{V}_2}^{N} & \cdots & _{m}\mathbf{X}_{\mathbf{V}_S}^{N} \end{bmatrix} {}_{m}\mathbf{W}_{\mathbf{V}}^{N} . \quad (4)$$

For any cth seed feature ($c = 1, 2, \cdots, C$), we could predict, from its image positions $\mathbf{x}_{c,\mathbf{V}_s}$'s ($s = 1, 2, \cdots, S$) at the sample images, its image position $_{m}\mathbf{x}_{c,\mathbf{V}}^{N}$ at the unknown viewpoint $\mathbf{V}$ as below:

$$_{m}\mathbf{x}_{c,\mathbf{V}}^{N} = \left[\mathbf{x}_{c,\mathbf{V}_1}, \mathbf{x}_{c,\mathbf{V}_2}, \cdots, \mathbf{x}_{c,\mathbf{V}_S}\right] {}_{m}\mathbf{W}_{\mathbf{V}}^{N} . \quad (5)$$

Then the squared error for each feature ($c = 1, 2, \cdots, C$) is:

$$ {}_m\mathrm{SErr}^N_{c,\mathbf{V}} = \sqrt{\left({}_m\mathbf{x}^N_{c,\mathbf{V}} - \mathbf{x}_{c,\mathbf{V}}\right)^{\mathrm{T}} \left({}_m\mathbf{x}^N_{c,\mathbf{V}} - \mathbf{x}_{c,\mathbf{V}}\right)} \ . \tag{6} $$

So the median of squared error is:

$$ {}_m\mathrm{MedSErr}^N_{\mathbf{V}} = \mathrm{median}\left\{ {}_m\mathrm{SErr}^N_{1,\mathbf{V}},\ {}_m\mathrm{SErr}^N_{2,\mathbf{V}}, \cdots,\ {}_m\mathrm{SErr}^N_{C,\mathbf{V}} \right\} . $$

For each ${}_m\mathbf{W}^N_{\mathbf{V}}$, we can determine the median of squared error ${}_m\mathrm{MedSErr}^N_{\mathbf{V}}$ with respect to the whole C seed features. By adopting LMedS method [17], the outliers can be estimated and discarded at ${}_J\mathrm{MedSErr}^N_{\mathbf{V}}$ ($J \in \{1, 2, \cdots, M\}$) is minimum among all ${}_m\mathrm{MedSErr}^N_{\mathbf{V}}$'s ($m = 1, 2, \cdots, M$), i.e.:

$$ {}_J\mathrm{MedSErr}^N_{\mathbf{V}} = \min\left\{ {}_1\mathrm{MedSErr}^N_{\mathbf{V}},\ {}_2\mathrm{MedSErr}^N_{\mathbf{V}}, \cdots,\ {}_M\mathrm{MedSErr}^N_{\mathbf{V}} \right\} . $$

Suppose the number of seed features without outliers in each sample image is C^{R}, where $C^{\mathrm{R}} \leq C$.

Interpolation Without Outliers. The next step is to obtain the $S \times 1$ weight matrix from the C^{R} seed features without outliers. Same as above, we draw M subsamples of N seed features from the C^{R} seed features. For the mth ($m = 1, 2, \cdots, M$) drawing, the N seed features are:

$$ {}^{\mathrm{R}}_m\mathbf{X}^N_{\mathbf{V}} = \left[\mathbf{x}_{P_1,\mathbf{V}}{}^{\mathrm{T}}, \mathbf{x}_{P_2,\mathbf{V}}{}^{\mathrm{T}}, \cdots, \mathbf{x}_{P_N,\mathbf{V}}{}^{\mathrm{T}}\right]^{\mathrm{T}} , $$

$$ {}^{\mathrm{R}}_m\mathbf{X}^N_{\mathbf{V}_s} = \left[\mathbf{x}_{P_1,\mathbf{V}_s}{}^{\mathrm{T}}, \mathbf{x}_{P_2,\mathbf{V}_s}{}^{\mathrm{T}}, \cdots, \mathbf{x}_{P_N,\mathbf{V}_s}{}^{\mathrm{T}}\right]^{\mathrm{T}} , $$

where $P_n \in \{1, 2, \cdots, C^{\mathrm{R}}\}$, $n = 1, 2, \cdots, N$, and $P_i \neq P_j$ if $i \neq j$.

With ${}^{\mathrm{R}}_m\mathbf{X}^N_{\mathbf{V}}$ and ${}^{\mathrm{R}}_m\mathbf{X}^N_{\mathbf{V}_s}$'s ($s = 1, 2, \cdots, S$) defined above, we can get the weight matrix ${}^{\mathrm{R}}_m\mathbf{W}^N_{\mathbf{V}}$, the seed feature's image positions ${}^{\mathrm{R}}_m\mathbf{x}^N_{c,\mathbf{V}}$'s and the squared errors ${}^{\mathrm{R}}_m\mathrm{SErr}^N_{c,\mathbf{V}}$'s ($c = 1, 2, \cdots, C^{\mathrm{R}}$) from a same flow described in (4), (5) and (6) respectively.

Thus the mean of squared error for whole C^{R} seed features is:

$$ {}^{\mathrm{R}}_m\mathrm{MeanSErr}^N_{\mathbf{V}} = \frac{\sum_{c=1}^{C^{\mathrm{R}}} {}^{\mathrm{R}}_m\mathrm{SErr}^N_{c,\mathbf{V}}}{C^{\mathrm{R}}} \ . $$

For each ${}^{\mathrm{R}}_m\mathbf{W}^N_{\mathbf{V}}$, we can determine the mean of squared error ${}^{\mathrm{R}}_m\mathrm{MeanSErr}^N_{\mathbf{V}}$ with respect to the C^{R} seed features. Finally we retain the ${}^{\mathrm{R}}_J\mathbf{W}^N_{\mathbf{V}}$ for which ${}^{\mathrm{R}}_J\mathrm{MeanSErr}^N_{\mathbf{V}}$, where $J \in \{1, 2, \cdots, M\}$, is minimum among all ${}^{\mathrm{R}}_m\mathrm{MeanSErr}^N_{\mathbf{V}}$'s ($m = 1, 2, \cdots, M$), i.e.:

$$ {}^{\mathrm{R}}_J\mathrm{MeanSErr}^N_{\mathbf{V}} = \min\left\{ {}^{\mathrm{R}}_1\mathrm{MeanSErr}^N_{\mathbf{V}},\ {}^{\mathrm{R}}_2\mathrm{MeanSErr}^N_{\mathbf{V}}, \cdots,\ {}^{\mathrm{R}}_M\mathrm{MeanSErr}^N_{\mathbf{V}} \right\} . $$

With the ${}^{\mathrm{R}}_{J}\mathbf{W}^{N}_{\mathbf{V}}$ robustly estimated as above described, we then use (1) in Sect. 2 to determine the viewpoint $\mathbf{V}$ as below:

$$\mathbf{V} = [\mathbf{V}_1, \mathbf{V}_2, \cdots, \mathbf{V}_S]\ {}^{\mathrm{R}}_{J}\mathbf{W}^{N}_{\mathbf{V}} .$$

The above is the ultimate interpolation we desire: the function value $\mathbf{V}$ for any given image $\mathbf{I}_{\mathbf{V}}$.

4 Experimental Results

We present here experimental results on image data of the *Castle* scene, a widely used benchmarking image dataset available at Calibrated Imaging Laboratory (CIL) of CMU (`http://www-2.cs.cmu.edu/~cil/cil-ster.html`).

In the original dataset provided by CIL, there are a total of 11 calibrated images with 28 feature points matched across them. In this dataset, the camera's orientation is made fixed relative to the scene; there is only translation between the camera and the scene in the 3-D space. To test the performance of the proposed algorithm under a sparse input, we picked only 7 images (out of the original 11) as our image examples, whose viewpoints (indexed in topological order not in metric units) are located at 3-D positions of (2,0,0), (1,0,0), (–1,0,0), (0,1,0), (–1,1,0), (0,0,1), and (0,1,2) respectively. The images we used were of resolution 500 × 374 pixels.

Fig. 1(a) shows one of the 7 sample images. Fig. 1(b) shows another sample image on which we overlay the 28 feature points that were matched across all the sample images for initiation of the interpolation process. The sample images appear alike, but in fact the disparity of the corresponding image positions in the dataset could be as large as 85 pixels in the image space. Notice that in the whole process we did not make use of the image-set calibration information provided by CIL. The only two pieces of information we used are: (1) the associated viewpoints in the 3-D space of the 7 sample images; and (2) the 28 point correspondences across all the 7 sample images.

Fig. 1(c)–(d) are two original real images provided by CIL (but not among the sample images to the interpolation process) with associated viewpoints at (0,1,1) and (–2,0,0). For visual evaluation, two images shown in Fig. 1(e)–(f) are synthesized by applying the image synthesis method detailed in [3] at the viewpoints that are same as those in Fig. 1(c)–(d). We then apply the EBI-based viewpoint determination presented above to determine the viewpoints of images shown in Fig. 1(c) and Fig. 1(d); the results are (–0.0013, 0.9981, 0.9915) and (–2.0015, 0.0031, 0.2295) respectively. Putting these two viewpoints into the same synthesis module of [3], we could synthesize two new images, which are shown in Fig. 1(g)–(h). Each image in the two image-sets of Fig. 1(c)-(e)-(g) and Fig. 1(d)-(f)-(h) resembles others in the same set closely.

Remember that in viewpoint determination problem, only image positions in real (input) images of Fig. 1(c)–(d) are ground truth, the two viewpoints of (0,1,1) and (–2,0,0) for them are only for reference and need to be confirmed. The more accurate determined viewpoint is, the more close to zero difference between

(a) $\mathbf{V} = (2, 0, 0)$

(b) $\mathbf{V} = (-1, 0, 0)$

(c) $\mathbf{V} = (0, 1, 1)$

(d) $\mathbf{V} = (-2, 0, 0)$

(e) $\mathbf{V} = (0, 1, 1)$

(f) $\mathbf{V} = (-2, 0, 0)$

(g) $\mathbf{V} = (-0.0013, 0.9981, 0.9915)$

(h) $\mathbf{V} = (-2.0015, 0.0031, 0.2295)$

Fig. 1. Experiment on the *Castle* scene. (a) One of the 7 input image samples; (b) 28 feature points matched across the input image samples; (c)–(d) Two original images captured by real camera but not among the input image samples. The two viewpoints, provided by dataset for reference, are not ground truth and need to be confirmed; (e)–(f) Two synthesized images at the same viewpoints as those to be confirmed of the images in (c) and (d); (g)–(h) Two synthesized images at the viewpoints determined from the EBI-based viewpoint determination for the input images of (c) and (d).

Table 1. Image positions of the first 5 of the 28 corresponding points in the images shown in Fig. 1(c)–(h)

Point No.	Ground truth in Fig. 1(c)		Synthesized in Fig. 1(e)		Synthesized in Fig. 1(g)	
	u	v	u	v	u	v
1	78.87	106.43	78.82	106.48	78.87	106.44
2	56.49	138.09	56.44	138.13	56.49	138.09
3	96.21	137.35	96.17	137.39	96.21	137.35
4	40.52	150.38	40.47	150.42	40.52	150.38
5	109.34	149.62	109.29	149.66	109.33	149.62
Mean of squared error for total 28 points	0		0.07		0.01	

Point No.	Ground truth in Fig. 1(d)		Synthesized in Fig. 1(f)		Synthesized in Fig. 1(h)	
	u	v	u	v	u	v
1	128.97	82.78	129.29	82.74	128.96	82.66
2	107.40	113.94	107.79	113.88	107.41	113.87
3	146.36	113.18	146.63	113.12	146.33	113.10
4	92.08	125.94	92.52	125.87	92.10	125.89
5	159.56	125.16	159.82	125.09	159.54	125.10
Mean of squared error for total 28 points	0		0.30		0.08	

real image and synthesized image at the determined viewpoint should be. To evaluate the quality of the EBI-based viewpoint determination, we compare the image positions of the 28 feature points in Fig. 1(g)–(h) and Fig. 1(e)–(f) with those in Fig. 1(c)–(d). The comparison results, partially tabulated in Table 1, show that not only are all 28 points positioned in the image space by the EBI-based solution with error no more than one pixel, but that the image positions in Fig. 1(g)–(h) created at the estimated viewpoints are more closely located around the true positions in image space. Because the same image synthesis method is used for creating Fig. 1(g)–(h) and Fig. 1(e)–(f), we believe that Fig. 1(c) is more accurately located at determined (–0.0013, 0.9981, 0.9915) than at original (0,1,1) in 3-D space, and Fig. 1(d) at (–2.0015, 0.0031, 0.2295) than at (–2,0,0).

5 Conclusion and Future Work

We have described an interpolation mechanism that could determine the viewpoint of any given input image based upon some example data. It turns out the mechanism could, by using the positions of a number of image features to represent an image, interpolate from the example data the mapping from image to viewpoint and determine viewpoint robustly. Experimental results show that, even with few example images and sparse distinct features on the image data and no knowledge of the imaging parameters, the mechanism gives satisfactory solution.

Heavy occlusions, depth discontinuities, and other types of distortion in the example data could compromise the accuracy of the interpolation process. Future work will address such issues.

References

1. Abidi, M., Chandra, T.: A new efficient and direct solution for pose estimation using quadrangular targets: algorithm and evaluation. IEEE Trans. Pattern Anal. Machine Intell. **17(5)** (1995) 534–538
2. Chesi, G., Hashimoto, K.: Camera pose estimation from less than eight points in visual servoing. In: Proc. 2004 IEEE Int. Conf. on Robotics and Automation. (2004) 733–738
3. Liang, B., Chung, R.: Novel view synthesis via indexed function interpolation. In: Proc. 2004 IEEE/RSJ Int. Conf. on Intelligent Robots and Systems. (2004) 2319–2324
4. Simon, G., Berger, M.: Pose estimation for planar structures. IEEE Comput. Graph. Appl. **22(6)** (2002) 46–53
5. Fischler, M., Bolles, R.: Random sample consensus: a paradigm for model fitting with applications to image analysis and automated cartography. Communications of the ACM **24(6)** (1981) 381–395
6. Haralick, R., Joo, H., Lee, C., Zhuang, X., Kim, M.: Pose estimation from corresponding point data. IEEE Trans. Syst., Man, Cybern **19(6)** (1989) 1426–1446
7. Quan, L., Lan, Z.: Linear n-point camera pose determination. IEEE Trans. Pattern Anal. Machine Intell. **21(8)** (1999) 774–780
8. Hartley, R.: Estimation of relative camera positions for uncalibrated cameras. In: ECCV. (1992) 579–587
9. Kumar, R., Hanson, A.: Robust methods for estimating pose and a sensitivity analysis. CVIU **60** (1994) 313–342
10. Poggio, T., Girosi, F.: Networks for approximation and learning. Proc. IEEE **78(9)** (1990) 1481–1497
11. Papageorgiou, C., Poggio, T.: A trainable system for object detection. IJCV **38(1)** (2000) 15–33
12. Rose, C., Cohen, M., Bodenheimer, B.: Verbs and adverbs: multidimensional motion interpolation. IEEE Comput. Graph. Appl. **18(5)** (1998) 32–40
13. Beymer, D., Poggio, T.: Image representations for visual learning. Science **272** (1996) 1905–1909
14. Liang, B., Chung, R.: On desirable properties of example-based interpolation. In: Proc. 2003 IEEE Intelligent Automation Conf., Hong Kong, China. (2003) 81–86
15. Hartley, R., Zisserman, A.: Multiple View Geometry in Computer Vision. Cambridge University Press (2000)
16. Zhang, Z., Deriche, R., Faugeras, O., Luong, Q.: A robust technique for matching two uncalibrated images through the recovery of the unknown epipolar geometry. Artificial Intelligence **78** (1995) 87–119
17. Rousseeuw, P., Leroy, A.: Robust Regression and Outlier Detection. Wiley, New York (1987)

Inverse Volume Rendering Approach to 3D Reconstruction from Multiple Images

Shuntaro Yamazaki, Masaaki Mochimaru, and Takeo Kanade

Digital Human Research Center, AIST,
Water Front 3F, 2-41-6, Aomi, Koto-ku, Tokyo 135-0064, Japan
{shun-yamazaki, m-mochimaru, t.kanade}@aist.go.jp
http://www.dh.aist.go.jp

Abstract. This paper presents a method of image-based 3D modeling for intricately-shaped objects, such as a fur, tree leaves and human hair. We formulate the imaging process of these small geometric structures as volume rendering followed by image matting, and prove that the inverse problem can be solved by reducing the nonlinear equations to a large linear system. This estimation, which we call *inverse volume rendering*, can be performed efficiently through expectation maximization method, even when the linear system is under-constrained owing to data sparseness. We reconstruct object shape by a set of coarse voxels that can model the spatial occupancy inside each voxel. Experimental results show that intricately-shaped objects can successfully be modeled by our proposed method, and the original and other novel view-images of the objects can be synthesized by forward volume rendering.

1 Introduction

Reconstruction of 3D scene information from multiple view-images is a major research topic in computer vision. Most of the existing methods of scene reconstruction attempt to create a model of the object as a solid, using boundary representation. Many real objects, however, have extremely intricate shapes, such as human hair and fur, on the surface. It is therefore difficult to represent their geometry using boundary-based representation.

It is difficult to model intricately-shaped objects for two reasons. Firstly, the boundary-based shape representation is not suitable for such objects as human hair. Secondly, the resolution of optical sensors, such as Charge-Coupled Devices (CCD), is usually much lower than that of object geometry. Hence, it is inherently impossible to reconstruct complete geometry from given images.

Although it is difficult to capture and reconstruct intricate shape on the object surface, the captured image can preserve the appearance of these objects in sufficient quality. This fact implies that photorealistic view can be synthesized from a reconstructed model even if the resolution of the model is not as high as that of object shape.

In this paper, we propose a method of volumetric scene reconstruction using the voxels that model the spatial occupancy and color of the object. In practice, the spatial occupancy is stored in the voxel as α value (opacity), and the synthetic view images are generated through conventional volume rendering techniques.

P.J. Narayanan et al. (Eds.): ACCV 2006, LNCS 3851, pp. 409–418, 2006.

2 Related Work

2.1 Multi-view Reconstruction

The research on the method of 3D scene reconstruction from multiple view-images has a rich history. Here we briefly describe the related work.

One of the first attempts for image-based modeling of 3D scene in computer vision is two-view stereo reconstruction [1]. Okutomi et al. [2] extended the conventional two-view stereo reconstruction into the multiple-view problem and achieved convincing results. Kang et al. [3] discussed a method of multi-view stereo reconstruction from images with large occlusions. These methods are designed to reconstruct depth maps from particular viewpoints. Hence, they are not suitable for full 3D scene reconstruction from images obtained from multiple surrounding cameras.

Visual hull reconstruction [4] is another approach to 3D scene reconstruction from multiple view-images. The algorithm does not need to solve the correspondence problem. Instead, it simply calculates the convex hull of silhouettes in all view images. While the visual hull method works robustly when cameras surround the object, a concave object cannot be reconstructed using silhouettes alone. This problem was solved by Seitz et al. [5] in the voxel coloring method. The original voxel coloring has a limitation on the location of input view images, which is overcome in the space carving method proposed by Kutulakos et al. [6] The opacity hull [7] method proposed by Matusik et al. is another approach to this problem. They simply use a visual hull model as an rough geometric proxy, and map opacity images using view-dependent texture mapping. This method avoids the difficulty in geometric reconstruction, but requires a lot of input images to achieve photorealistic rendering.

Our proposed method is inspired by the space carving method, but has been extended so that it can deal with intricate shape within a framework of voxel modeling. Specifically, the geometrical structure within a voxel is represented as its spatial occupancy. Our method is similar to Roxels method [8] in that both can reconstruct spatial occupancy/opacity of voxels from images. The convergence of the Roxels method, however, is not proven, and the method cannot reconstruct the voxels in high resolution owing to the high computational cost.

2.2 Alpha Estimation

When a scene is captured by the digital optical sensors, such as CCD, what the device can record is not the light energy of a single light ray, but the averaged radiance incoming from a finite space in the scene. If a part of an object is observable from a single device cell, the recorded radiance is the combination of radiance coming from the corresponding foreground and background.

Alpha estimation is the process that decomposes an RGB color C_p of each image pixel into three components: foreground color F_p, background color B_p, and foreground opacity A_p. The relationship between the variables can be described by *matting equation*.

$$C_p = F_p + (1 - A_p)B_p. \tag{1}$$

The foreground opacity, or simply, opacity $A_p \in [0, 1]$ represents the contribution of the foreground object color to the pixel. When the background color in the images is controllable, we can separate these three components perfectly by capturing two images with different background colors and computing F_p and A_p which are common in the images [9]. The natural image matting methods [10, 11, 12] can solve this problem even when the background cannot be controlled and only one image is available.

3 Inverse Volume Rendering

3.1 Assumption and Preprocess

In this paper, the scene is assumed to be static and the surface reflection follows the Lambertian law. Under this assumption, the radiance emanating from the scene can be observed as a single color. Our proposed method deals with the scene composed of foreground object $\mathcal{O}$, which we are interested in, and background $\mathcal{B}$, which should be removed in the modeling process. The background component is removed beforehand by an appropriate method of alpha estimation described in Section 2.2.

The input to our modeling algorithm is a set of color images taken at N_{view} different viewpoints. The accuracy of reconstruction and robustness to noise and other factors not modeled in our assumption can be increased by using as many images as possible. About 30 images uniformly distributed on the upper hemisphere surrounding $\mathcal{O}$ could achieve good reconstruction in our experiments. Both intrinsic and extrinsic camera parameters are supposed to be known. The output from our algorithm is a set of voxels v_i which has both RGB color c_i and occupancy α_i.

3.2 Volume Rendering Equation

When the interest object $\mathcal{O}$ is captured and digitized into images by CCD, the intensity of pixel color C_p is in proportion to the sum of radiance emanating from the surfaces within a frustum spanning between the scene and the device cell. At each depth along viewing rays in the frustum, the transferred radiance is the sum of those emanating at the point ($\mathcal{S}_f$) and those coming from the behind ($\mathcal{S}_b$). Hence, the pixel colors in input images can be described by the following *volume rendering equation* [13].

$$C_p = \sum_{i \in \{\text{along a viewing ray}\}} c_i \alpha_i \prod_{j=0}^{i} (1 - \alpha_j), \tag{2}$$

c_i represents the radiance coming from light sources and reflected on the scene object at the depth i along viewing rays. $\alpha_i \in [0, 1]$ is the ratio by which the object located at i occludes others behind it. Thus, this ratio α can be regarded as equivalent to the spatial occupancy of the foreground object at the location. Supposing that c_i and α_i are view-independent, they can be parameterized by the location in 3D space. We voxelize the 3D space and assign c_i and α_i to each voxel.

3.3 Matting Equation

First the background components observed in input images are removed from each image pixel C_p, which is combination of radiance transferred from the foreground object and the background scene. This process is essential in order to associate each voxel's values c_i and α_i with pixel intensity C_p to create a 3D model of the object from the observed images.

Suppose that a voxel grid spreads infinitely in 3D space. Then, we can define the mapping between the voxel coordinate (x, y, z) and the 1D coordinate s along viewing rays. For each viewing ray that goes through the foreground object O, there is a position that separates O and background $\mathcal{B}$. Dividing the 1D ray coordinate into the *front* and *back* parts, equation (2) is rewritten in

$$C_p = F_p + (1 - A_p)B_p, \tag{3}$$

where

$$A_p = 1 - \prod_{k \in front} (1 - \alpha_k) \tag{4}$$

$$F_p = \sum_{i \in front} c_i \alpha_i \prod_{j=0}^{i} (1 - \alpha_j) \tag{5}$$

$$B_p = \sum_{i \in back} c_i \alpha_i \prod_{j \in back}^{i} (1 - \alpha_j). \tag{6}$$

Intuitively, A_p is the contribution of the spatial occupancy of voxels along a viewing ray to an image pixel, F_p is the contribution of accumulated colors of the voxels, and B_p is the background color.

Compared with equation (1), it turns out that equation (3) is equivalent to the matting equation. The values A_p and F_p can be estimated from C_p before modeling voxels, by one of several methods of alpha estimation introduced in Section 2.2. Once the foreground components A_p and F_p in input images is associated with the voxel values c_i and α_i, we can estimate voxel values using equation (4) and equation (5) as constraints. We refer to the estimation of 3D voxel values from 3D pixels values composed of foreground components as *inverse volume rendering*.

3.4 Derivation of Constraints

We reconstruct the color c_i and spatial occupancy α_i of voxels from the accumulated color F_p and occupancy A_p of image pixels in the following two-step procedure.

In the first step, we reconstruct only the voxel occupancy α_i using foreground opacity A_p. Taking the logarithm of equation (4) for each $A_p \neq 1$ and replacing opacity with transparency as $T_p = 1 - A_p$ and $t_i = 1 - \alpha_i$, we obtain the following equation.

$$\log(T_p) = \sum_i \log(t_i) \tag{7}$$

Since $\log(T_p)$ have already been estimated in preprocess, and therefore are regarded as constants, equation (7) comes down to a simple linear system in which $\log(t_i)$ are unknowns.

In the second step, we then reconstruct voxel color c_i from foreground color F_p. Now, the spatial occupancy α_i has been reconstructed in the first step. Thus, equation (4) can be reduced again into a linear system

$$F_p = \sum_{i \in front} \left[\alpha_i \prod_{j=0}^{i} (1 - \alpha_j)\right] c_i \tag{8}$$

where $[\ldots]$ and F_p are constants, and c_i are the unknowns that we want to estimate.

4 Implementation

4.1 Iterative Back-Projection Based on EM

Various methods of solving linear systems have been proposed. When the coefficient matrix of the linear system is full-rank, we can solve the system either by using a direct method such as the Gauss-Jordan elimination, or an iterative method such as the conjugate gradient method. If the system is either under- or over-constrained, the solution that maximizes the certain likelihood measure is estimated, for instance, by singular value decomposition.

Our linear system, however, cannot be solved directly by these conventional methods owing to the gigantic size of the system. The number of unknowns in equation (7) and equation (8) is equivalent to the number of voxels that increases in a cubic order. On the other hand, the number of equations in the linear system is roughly equal to the number of image pixels. Thus, the computational cost of our problem can be extremely high. It is also the case that the coefficient matrix cannot be stored in the limited working memory of a standard computer.

In order to overcome these difficulties, we propose an algorithm that can solve such a gigantic linear system within a framework of the EM (Expectation Maximization) method [14]. This algorithm starts with an initial estimation of the solution, and iteratively improves the solution through the maximization of an objective function. The algorithm can improve the solution monotonically, and can reach the global optimum.

The EM estimation is composed of two steps, namely, E-step and M-step. In the E-step, the expectation of certain probabilistic phenomena is calculated using the current estimation of parameters. In the M-step, the parameters are modified so that the expectation is maximized. Repeating E-step and M-step alternatively can maximize the expectation function even when some parameters cannot be measured directly.

The parameters that we want to estimate are the color c_i and occupancy α_i of voxels. The observed data that we have is F_p and A_p. In the E-step of the inverse volume rendering, we simply perform forward projection of voxel values. This is equivalent to the volume rendering according to equation (2). In the M-step of the inverse volume rendering, we improve either the color or the occupancy of voxels using back-projection for each viewing ray. The expectation can be calculated as a linear combination of unknowns. Hence, the function is concave and has a single global optimum.

Let the n-th estimations of unknowns in a linear system be $\{x_j^{(n)}\}$, the coefficients of the system be $\{r_{i,j}\}$, the constants of the system be $\{c_i\}$, then the $n+1$-th estimation of unknowns can be obtained by

$$x_j^{(n+1)} = \frac{x_j^{(n)}}{\sum_i r_{i,j}} \sum_i \frac{r_{i,j}c_i}{\sum_j r_{i,j}x_j^{(n)}} \tag{9}$$

where $\sum_j r_{i,j}x_j^{(n)}$ is the result of forward projection in the E-step, and the summation of projections with regard to $r_{i,j}c_i$ corresponds to the result of back projection. This relationship is illustrated in Fig. 1. It is worth noting that this EM estimation is a generic framework for solving linear systems.

The EM algorithm in our estimation can be accelerated by dividing the problem into several subsets. First, we divide the set of input images into several subsets. Then, the linear system is solved using one of the subsets. Once the algorithm has been converged, the linear system is solved using another subset using the previous solution as an initial estimation. This scheme is called OSEM (Ordered Subset EM) [15]. In our experiments, we made subsets by choosing four images such that the distances between their viewpoints are as large as possible.

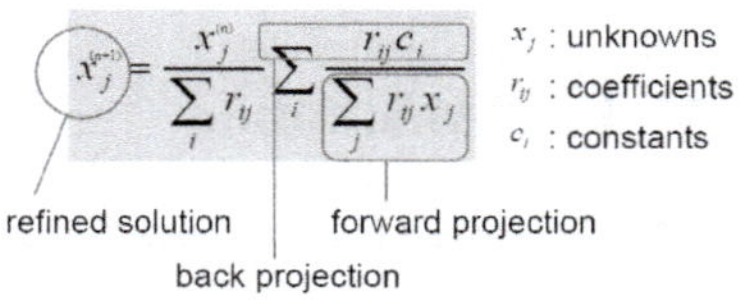

Fig. 1. Interpretation of the update law in EM

4.2 Shell Voxels

The voxels in which no foreground object exists ($\alpha_i = 0$) do not affect the estimation of other voxels along the viewing rays that pass through the empty voxel. Similarly, the voxels that are completely occupied by foreground object ($\alpha = 1$) neither affect the estimation of the voxels along the viewing rays. We can reduce computational cost by just omitting the computation for these rays.

After the alpha estimation for each input image has been completed, the voxels are classified into three types according to the opacities of corresponding image pixels.

1. background voxel: $A_p = 0$ in at least one image
2. internal voxel: $A_p = 1$ in all images
3. shell voxel: otherwise

The classification of voxels is performed as follows. Firstly, we classify as background the voxels whose projection is completely transparent (the corresponding pixels are all $A_p = 0$) at least in one of input images. Secondly, we construct the visual hull [4] of completely opaque pixels ($A_p = 1$), and classify the voxels enclosed by the hull as internal. The rest are shell voxels.

4.3 Optimization of Voxel Traversal

In each EM estimation, a set of coefficients in the left hand of equation (7) has to be prepared. This calculation requires the voxel traversal along arbitrary viewing rays and therefore is computationally expensive. Therefore, we precompute the set of voxels along every viewing ray beforehand, and store the result into LDI structures [16] for each input pixel. We can omit the LDI entry for the pixels where $A_p = 0$ and $A_p = 1$.

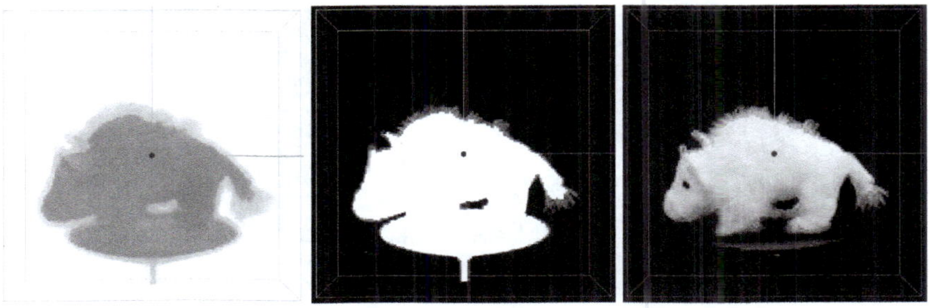

Fig. 2. Example of voxel reconstruction. (left) shell voxels in green and internal voxels in red, (center) reconstructed spatial occupancy, and (right) reconstructed color distribution.

5 Experimental Results

We have implemented the proposed method of inverse volume rendering and conducted some experiments on a standard PC with Pentium4 3.4GHz CPU and 2G byte main memory. Input images are captured from 36 viewpoints around the object that we want to model. The size of input images are 320×240, and the voxel resolution is set to 64^3 and 128^3.

5.1 Alpha Estimation

We adopted the multi-background scheme proposed by Smith et al.[9] for alpha estimation from input images. The background color of images is controlled by a liquid crystal projector. For each viewpoint, two images with different background color, C_{k1} and C_{k2} in RGB color space, were taken. Let the observed image color at the same pixel be C_{m1} and C_{m2} respectively, then the foreground opacity A_p of the pixel can be estimated by the following equation.

$$A_p = 1 - \frac{(C_{m1} - C_{m2}) \bullet (C_{k1} - C_{k2})}{(C_{k1} - C_{k2}) \bullet (C_{k1} - C_{k2})} \tag{10}$$

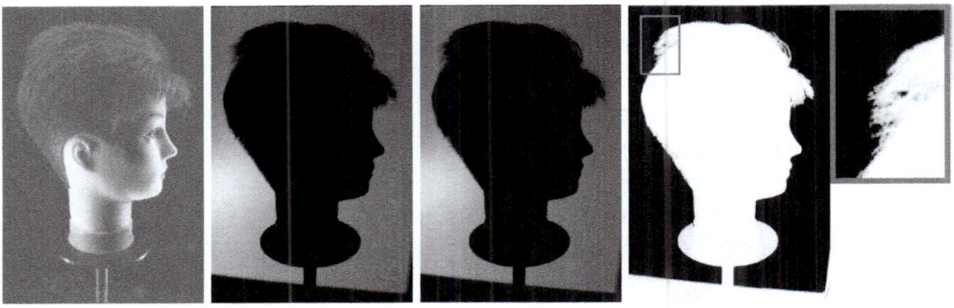

(a) object (b) green back (c) blue back (d) estimated α image

Fig. 3. Multi-background matting

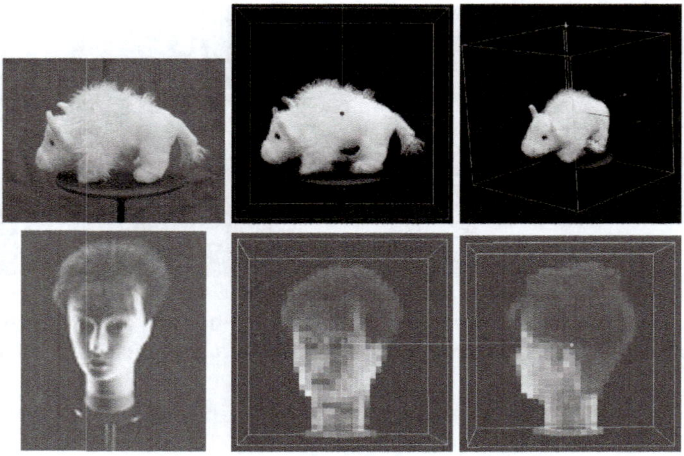

(a) input image (b) rendered voxel model

Fig. 4. Results of volume rendering

where an operator (•) represents dot-product of RGB vectors. The foreground color F_p of the pixel is calculated as follows.

$$F_p = (C_{m1} + C_{m2} - (1 - A_p)(C_{k1} + C_{k2}))/2 \tag{11}$$

An example of input images in alpha estimation and obtained alpha image is shown in Fig. 3.

5.2 Results of Volume Rendering

The reconstructed voxel model is rendered in Fig. 4. The voxels are rendered using the volume rendering equation (equation (2)) with the viewpoints not included in the input images.

5.3 Convergence

In Fig. 6, the convergence of our proposed method is illustrated. The upper and lower rows show the process of estimating α_i and c_i respectively. The resolution of reconstructed voxels is 128^3. The figure indicates that the visually sufficient result can be obtained in 10 iterations.

Fig. 5 is the plot of reprojection error in the EM estimation for the data shown in Fig. 6. The lines indicate the decreases in error for two different voxel resolutions. The error decreases rapidly within 5 iterations, and then gradually converges into the minimum value.

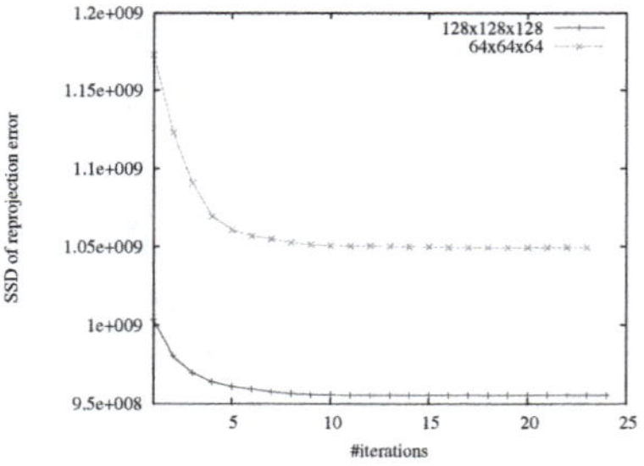

Fig. 5. Convergence

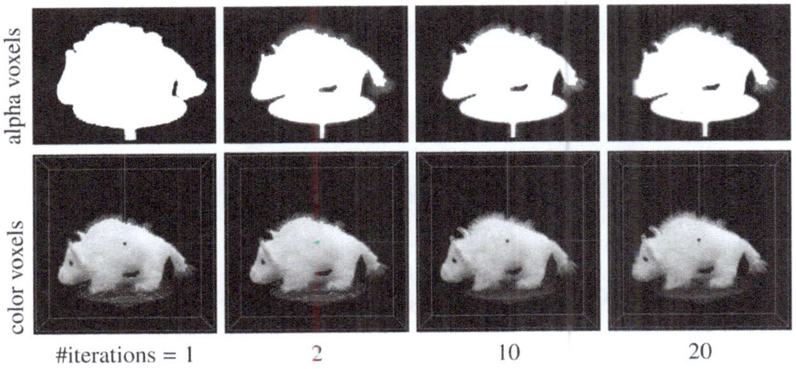

Fig. 6. Iterative optimization

5.4 Computational Cost

Table 1 shows the figures of memory usage and computational time. We have recorded these figures in the experiments using voxel resolutions of 64^3 and 128^3. Owing to the limitation of computer hardware, we could not conduct experiments with larger resolution. For example, reconstruction of a mannequin object with the resolution of 128^3 failed because of limited memory space on 32 bit computer.

Table 1. Performance

object	#shell vxl		memory(byte)		time(min)	
#voxels	64^3	128^3	64^3	128^3	64^3	128^3
cow	23379	185013	~256M	~2.1G	~30	~186
mannequin	32531	254123	~510M	—	~45	—

6 Discussion and Future Work

In this paper we proposed a novel method of voxel reconstruction that can deal with an object with intricate shapes such as a fur and hairs. We formulate our reconstruction process as the *inverse volume rendering* problem, and show how to solve it. We also present an effective implementation and conduct experiments on real objects to demonstrate the usefulness of the proposed method.

In Fig. 4, we see artifacts in the fur where the spatial occupancy seems higher than the real value. The reason for this is that computing $\log(1 - A_p)$ and $\log(1 - \alpha_i)$ become erroneous when α_i and A_p is close to 1, and therefore the small errors in alpha estimation for input image drastically affect the estimation of voxel occupancy.

We implemented some measures to reduce the computational costs in the inverse volume rendering. However, the cost is still high, and therefore we cannot reconstruct the object in a proper spatial resolution. We are planning to adopt adaptive voxel structures, such as octree and k-d tree, and to extend our algorithm so that it can be executed on parallel computers.

References

1. Marr, D.C., Poggio, T.: A computational theory of human stereo vision. Proceedings of the Royal Society of London **B 204** (1979) 301–328
2. Okutomi, M., Kanade, T.: A multiple-baseline stereo. IEEE Transactions on Pattern Analysis and Machine Intelligence **15** (1993) 353–363
3. Kang, S.B., Szeliski, R., Chai, J.: Handling occlusions in dense multi-view stereo. In: Proc. Computer Vision and Pattern Recognition 2001. (2001) I:103–110
4. Laurentini, A.: The visual hull concept for silhouette-based image understanding. IEEE Transactions on Pattern Analysis and Machine Intelligence **16** (1994) 150–162
5. Seitz, S.M., Dyer, C.M.: Photorealistic scene reconstrcution by voxel coloring. In: Proc. Computer Vision and Pattern Recognition '97. (1997) 1067–1073
6. Kutulakos, K.N., Seitz, S.M.: A theory of shape by space carving. In: Proc. International Conference on Computer Vision '99. (1999) 307–314
7. Matusik, W., Pfister, H., Ngan, A., Beardsley, P., Ziegler, R., McMillan, L.: Image-based 3D photography using opacity hulls. In: Proc. SIGGRAPH 2002. (2002) 427–437
8. Bonet, J.S.D., Viola, P.A.: Roxels: Responsibility weighted 3d volume reconstruction. In: Proc. International Conference on Computer Vision '99. (1999) 418–425
9. Smith, A.R., Blinn, J.F.: Blue screen matting. In: Proc. SIGGRAPH '96. (1996) 259–268
10. Ruzon, M.A., Tomasi, C.: Alpha estimation in natural images. In: Proc. Computer Vision and Pattern Recognition 2000. (2000) 24–31
11. Chuang, Y.Y., Curless, B., Salesin, D.H., Szeliski, R.: A bayesian approach to digital matting. In: Proc. Computer Vision and Pattern Recognition 2001. Volume 2. (2001) 264–271
12. Sun, J., Jia, J., Tang, C.K., Shum, H.Y.: Poisson matting. ACM Transactions on Graphics **23** (2004) 315–321
13. Lacroute, P., Levoy, M.: Fast volume rendering using a shear-warp factorization of the viewing transformation. In: Proc. SIGGRAPH '94. (1994) 451–458
14. Lange, K., Carson, R.: EM reconstruction algorithms for emission and transmission tomography. Journalof Computer Assisted Tomography (1984) 306–316
15. Hudson, H.M., Larkin, R.S.: Accelerated image reconstruction using ordered subsets of projection data. IEEE Transactions on Medical Imaging **13** (1994) 601–609
16. Shade, J., Gortler, S., wei He, L., Szeliski, R.: Layered depth images. In: Proc. SIGGRAPH '98. (1998) 231–242

Gaze Direction Estimation with a Single Camera Based on Four Reference Points and Three Calibration Images

Shinjiro Kawato, Akira Utsumi, and Shinji Abe

ATR Intelligent Robotics and Communication Laboratories,
Keihanna Science City, Kyoto 619-0288, Japan
{skawato, utsumi, sabe}@atr.jp

Abstract. We propose a method to estimate gaze direction in real time with a single camera based on four reference points and three calibration images. First, the position at which the eyeball center is projected is calculated as a linear combination of those of the reference points. Then, the gaze direction is estimated as a vector connecting the calculated eyeball center and the detected iris center. The algorithm is head pose free. We implemented the algorithm on a PC with a Xeon 2.2-GHz CPU, which works at a rate of 30 fps.

1 Introduction

Gaze estimation is one of the key technologies for human-computer interaction systems. A good review of recent advancements on this topic is presented in [1]. In this paper, we will propose a vision-based practical method for gaze estimation that uses a single camera.

Among various gaze tracking systems, intrusive methods, including head-mounted types, are in general more accurate than remote ones[1]. However, they are troublesome and impose a burden on users; therefore, non-intrusive methods are preferable.

Non-intrusive methods are classified into two categories: active and passive. Active methods use controlled lighting, usually infrared (IR) LEDs, for two different purposes. One is to detect pupils robustly. On-axis and off-axis lighting respectively produce bright-pupil and dark-pupil images[1], and the difference between the images enables robust pupil detection. The other is to make a glint or reflection of the LED on the cornea. The gaze can then be estimated based on the glint position and the center of the pupil.

The glint, however, is a very small spot, and thus an image of high resolution is required to detect it. This means the eye almost fills the screen. Consequently, not only does the focusing depth of field become very shallow, but also a slight movement of the head causes a large displacement in the image. This means the eye can easily fall out of the field of view, thus making it difficult to track. Some systems incorporate an extra wide-angle camera to track the eye and control the

P.J. Narayanan et al. (Eds.): ACCV 2006, LNCS 3851, pp. 419–428, 2006.

pan and tilt angle of the gaze camera [2][3], though this makes such systems very complicated.

One of the constraints present when using this type of system is that the distance between the user and the camera (and the LEDs) should be very short because of the limited LED power. Usually, users are supposed to be sitting in front of the system within one meter from it.

Among passive methods, systems featuring binocular stereo architectures have a similar constraint. A system described in [4] tracks not only irises but also other predefined feature points such as eye corners and mouth corners. Furthermore, the location of eyeball centers in 3D space are calculated from these feature points calibrated in advance. The gaze direction then is estimated as a line in 3D space connecting an eyeball center and the center of an iris. It works very well. However, in a binocular stereo system, a face should be within a region visible from both cameras. Therefore, the distance from the cameras to the user is very limited with respect to an appropriate image resolution and a base line. A similar system is reported in [5] that uses artificial marks as tracking features and a bright/dark pupil imaging technique.

Here, we propose a single-camera method that allows the use of long shot images after appropriate zooming-up if necessary.

As for single-camera methods, some neural network approaches have been proposed[6][7] that results in very fast calculation. However, it is pointed out that the trained neural network is too sensitive to changes in users, lighting conditions, and even changes within the user[8].

Another single-camera approach is the so-called "circle algorithm." If two circles on parallel planes are observed as ellipses, the normal direction of the support planes can be determined uniquely (two-circle algorithm)[9][10]. Therefore, if the irises are assumed to be circles and both of their images are extracted as ellipses, the gaze direction can be calculated. If we have only one iris image or one ellipse, there will be two possible solutions for the normal direction. Even in such a case, the true solution can also be selected using other cues (one-circle algorithm)[11].

The circle-algorithm approach is very attractive because no calibration is required beforehand. However, it is very difficult to develop a system with current video rate imaging techniques in terms of image resolution. Consider a case when an iris gazing at the camera is a circle in the image with a diameter of 100 pixels. When the eyeball turns ten degrees, the circle changes to an ellipse with the minor axis of 98.5 pixels (see $\cos 10° = 0.9848$) while the major axis remains at 100 pixels. It is quite difficult to detect such small changes stably and accurately.

On the other hand, iris displacement is much greater in the same situation. An eye model used in the simulation in [11] is such that the ratio of the radius of the eyeball to the radius of the iris is 2. According to this model, when the diameter of the iris is 100 pixels, the radius of the eyeball is also 100 pixels. Then, 10-degree rotation of the eyeball results in iris displacement of about 17 pixels (see $\sin 10° = 0.1736$), which seems to be easier to detect than a 1.5-pixel change.

In [8], iris displacement from the inner eye corner is measured to estimate the gaze direction. However, when the face rotates, while the gaze direction is fixed, the iris position relative to the eye corner changes. Therefore, the face direction should be fixed as it is in the calibration processes.

To overcome this problem a special reference point has been proposed in [12]. It is the middle point between the centers of the right and left eyeballs, called the virtual eyeball center. Cleverly, Miyake et al. put two marks on the face where the line connecting two eyeball centers intersects with the surface of the face, and assumed that the middle point of them in the image is the virtual eyeball center. They also detected both of the irises and calculated their middle point. This is called the virtual iris center. The line connecting the virtual eyeball center and the virtual iris center determines the gaze direction.

This idea makes the system head pose free, because the relative position of the virtual eyeball center and the virtual iris center does not change while the gaze is fixed, even when the face rotates. However, one of the marks placed on both sides of the face is likely to be occluded by the face itself when the face turns about twenty degrees or so. Consequently, the system cannot take full advantage of the head pose free algorithm.

Here, we propose another head pose free algorithm in which we use four marks instead of two. However, the constraint on the positions of them is far less restrictive than that used in [12]. Therefore, not only we can place them to be visible for a wide range of head poses, but also we have the scope to replace them with natural image feature points on faces in the future.

We calculate the position of the eyeball center by a linear combination of the positions of the four marks, detect the iris center, and estimate the gaze direction as a line connecting the calculated eyeball center and the detected iris center.

In the next section, we explain the principle of calculating of the fifth point position from the four reference points, and in Section 3, how the principle can be applied to gaze estimation. In Section 4, we briefly describe the image processing technique used in the experiment, and present some experimental results in Section 5. Section 6 concludes the paper.

2 Estimation of the Fifth Point Position

We express a point in 3D space as a vector $\boldsymbol{X}_i = (x_i, y_i, z_i)^T$. When we select four points $\boldsymbol{X}_0$, $\boldsymbol{X}_1$, $\boldsymbol{X}_2$, and $\boldsymbol{X}_3$ on a 3D object such that not all of them are on a plane, the vectors $(\boldsymbol{X}_1 - \boldsymbol{X}_0)$, $(\boldsymbol{X}_2 - \boldsymbol{X}_0)$, and $(\boldsymbol{X}_3 - \boldsymbol{X}_0)$ are linearly independent. Then, for any arbitrary point $\boldsymbol{X}_c$ on the object, there exist α, β, and γ such that

$$(\boldsymbol{X}_c - \boldsymbol{X}_0) = \alpha(\boldsymbol{X}_1 - \boldsymbol{X}_0) + \beta(\boldsymbol{X}_2 - \boldsymbol{X}_0) + \gamma(\boldsymbol{X}_3 - \boldsymbol{X}_0). \tag{1}$$

Because only relative vectors from $\boldsymbol{X}_0$ appear in Eq. (1), selecting the origin of the coordinate as well as its pose makes no difference. For convenience, hereafter, we assume the origin is at the center of gravity, and consider only the rotation of the object.

Our camera model here is the orthogonal projection model. It means that a point $(x, y, z)^T$ in 3D space is projected to $(x, y)^T$ on the image plane. It is known that the modeling error is small when the depth of the object is sufficiently small compared to the distance between the camera and the object.

From Eq. (1), for the image of the object in arbitrary pose,

$$\begin{pmatrix} x_c - x_0 \\ y_c - y_0 \end{pmatrix} = \alpha \begin{pmatrix} x_1 - x_0 \\ y_1 - y_0 \end{pmatrix} + \beta \begin{pmatrix} x_2 - x_0 \\ y_2 - y_0 \end{pmatrix} + \gamma \begin{pmatrix} x_3 - x_0 \\ y_3 - y_0 \end{pmatrix} \tag{2}$$

is always satisfied.

When a rotation, expressed by a rotation matrix $\boldsymbol{R}^k$, is applied to the object, a point$\boldsymbol{X}_i$ moves to $(x_i^k, y_i^k, z_i^k)^T = \boldsymbol{R}^k(x_i, y_i, z_i)^T$. Then, from Eq. (2), observed points on the image after rotations $\boldsymbol{R}^0$, $\boldsymbol{R}^1$, and $\boldsymbol{R}^2$ satisfy the following equation.

$$\begin{pmatrix} x_c^0 - x_0^0 \\ x_c^1 - x_0^1 \\ x_c^2 - x_0^2 \\ y_c^0 - y_0^0 \\ y_c^1 - y_0^1 \\ y_c^2 - y_0^2 \end{pmatrix} = \begin{pmatrix} x_1^0 - x_0^0 & x_2^0 - x_0^0 & x_3^0 - x_0^0 \\ x_1^1 - x_0^1 & x_2^1 - x_0^1 & x_3^1 - x_0^1 \\ x_1^2 - x_0^2 & x_2^2 - x_0^2 & x_3^2 - x_0^2 \\ y_1^0 - y_0^0 & y_2^0 - y_0^0 & y_3^0 - y_0^0 \\ y_1^1 - y_0^1 & y_2^1 - y_0^1 & y_3^1 - y_0^1 \\ y_1^2 - y_0^2 & y_2^2 - y_0^2 & y_3^2 - y_0^2 \end{pmatrix} \cdot \begin{pmatrix} \alpha \\ \beta \\ \gamma \end{pmatrix} \tag{3}$$

First, we solve Eq. (3) and obtain the values of α, β, and γ. Then, for an arbitrary rotation of the object even if the point $\boldsymbol{X}_c$ is not observed in the image, its projection point can be calculated from the coordinates $(x_0^k, y_0^k)^T$, $(x_1^k, y_1^k)^T$, $(x_2^k, y_2^k)^T$, and $(x_3^k, y_3^k)^T$ of observed points $\boldsymbol{X}_0$, $\boldsymbol{X}_1$, $\boldsymbol{X}_2$, and $\boldsymbol{X}_3$ using Eq. (2) as follows,:

$$\begin{pmatrix} x_c^k \\ y_c^k \end{pmatrix} = \alpha \begin{pmatrix} x_1^k - x_0^k \\ y_1^k - y_0^k \end{pmatrix} + \beta \begin{pmatrix} x_2^k - x_0^k \\ y_2^k - y_0^k \end{pmatrix} + \gamma \begin{pmatrix} x_3^k - x_0^k \\ y_3^k - y_0^k \end{pmatrix} + \begin{pmatrix} x_0^k \\ y_0^k \end{pmatrix}. \tag{4}$$

For Eq. (3) to be solvable, not all the axes of rotations $\boldsymbol{R}^0$, $\boldsymbol{R}^1$, and $\boldsymbol{R}^2$ should be parallel. Since Eq. (3) is over-constrained, we can solve it by the least-squares method.

3 Gaze Estimation

We assume the gaze direction is a vector from the eyeball center to the iris center. Since the iris is observable, we can calculate its center on the image; on the other hand, the eyeball center is not observable. Therefore, we calculate its position from the observable reference points $\boldsymbol{X}_0$, $\boldsymbol{X}_1$, $\boldsymbol{X}_2$, and $\boldsymbol{X}_3$ as a linear combination of them as mentioned in the previous section.

The gaze direction in the image plane is a vector from the calculated eyeball center to the detected iris center. The angle θ between the gaze direction and the normal of the image plane is calculated as follows, where r is the radius of the eyeball and d is the distance between the calculated eyeball center and the detected iris center in the image (Fig.1).

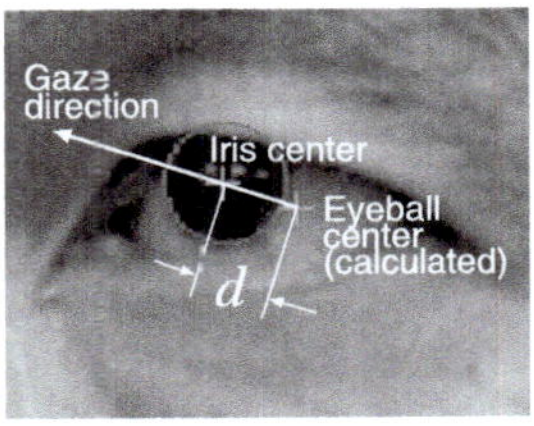

Fig. 1. Gaze direction model

$$\theta = \sin^{-1}(\frac{d}{r}) \tag{5}$$

As for the value of r, an anatomical model can be used like in [11], or we can acquire it from other calibration mean.

The eyeball center corresponds to $\boldsymbol{X}_c$ in the previous section. Although of course it is not observable, in order to calculate α, β, and γ, its projection point should be known in the face images with rotations of $\boldsymbol{R}^0$, $\boldsymbol{R}^1$, and $\boldsymbol{R}^2$. But how? Well, we consider a special case in which we can observe the eyeball center in the image.

In our gaze model, the gaze line is a line in 3D space connecting an eyeball center and the center of an iris. When we gaze at the camera lens, the three points of the center of the lens, the center of the iris, and the eyeball center align. Then, on the image, the center of the iris and the eyeball center are projected at the same point. In other words, in such a special case, the eyeball center is observed as the center of the iris.

In summary, the gaze estimation process is as follows.

(1) Place four reference marks around an eye as $\boldsymbol{X}_0$, $\boldsymbol{X}_1$, $\boldsymbol{X}_2$, and $\boldsymbol{X}_3$. They should not be on the same plane.
(2) Take three images, including the eye and four marks with different head poses while looking at the camera. (Calibration images)
(3) Extract the positions of $\boldsymbol{X}_0$, $\boldsymbol{X}_1$, $\boldsymbol{X}_2$, $\boldsymbol{X}_3$, and the center of the iris as $\boldsymbol{X}_c$. Now, we have Eq. (3).
(4) Solve Eq. (3) to acquire α, β, and γ.
(5) For an arbitrary gaze and head pose image, extract the positions of $\boldsymbol{X}_0$, $\boldsymbol{X}_1$, $\boldsymbol{X}_2$, $\boldsymbol{X}_3$, and the center of the iris.
(6) Calculate the projection point of the eyeball center using Eq. (4).
(7) The gaze direction is estimated as a line connecting the calculated eyeball center and the extracted iris center. The angle of the gaze line from the normal of the image plane is calculated by Eq. (5).

4 Experimental System

We developed a simple experimental system to examine the validity of our algorithm. For eye detection and tracking, we use a commercial software[13]. This software library returns locations of both eyes. However, this does not mean the

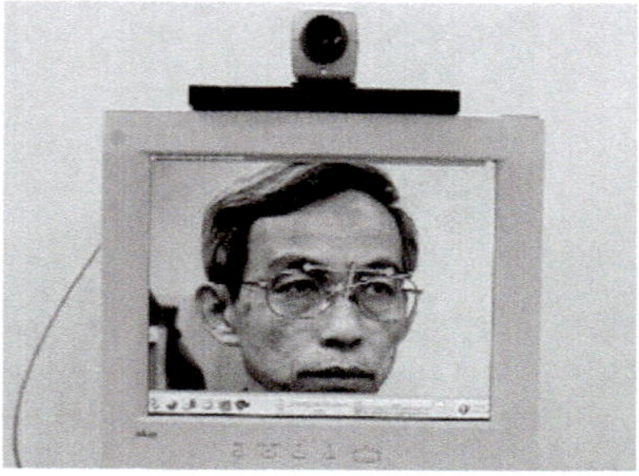

Fig. 2. Camera setup

iris locations, just dark regions. Therefore, we have to develop an iris detection process. This commercial software detects and tracks eyes under the condition that both are visible. Thus, we take the same approach as in [12], i.e. instead of using a single iris, we use the virtual iris center, which is the middle point of the centers of the right and left irises. Equation (4) then calculates the virtual eyeball center's location..

The camera is of IEEE 1394 interface with an image resolution of 640×480 pixels. The focal length of the lens is $f = 16mm$. The camera is placed on top of the display monitor, with the subject sitting about 90 cm from it. Figure 2 shows the camera setup and the relative face scale in the image.

Figure 3 shows a frame of reference marks. The one and only constraint on the alignment of marks is that not all of them can be on a same plane. The mark is designed for easy detection: it is a white disc 6 mm in diameter with a black circle 3 mm in diameter at the center. The size of the frame is about the distance between the eyes, and it is attachable to the nose part of the glasses so as not to distract the eyes. The mark in the upper-left of the figure is about 17 mm above the plane defined by the other three marks. Figure 4 shows a view of the marks attached to the face. When eye locations are extracted, the region where each mark can exist becomes predictable (see Fig. 4). Each mark is searched in such a region with a simple template matching technique.

The software library we used for eye detection and tracking returns position data where the average gray level of a certain square is lowest in the eye regions.

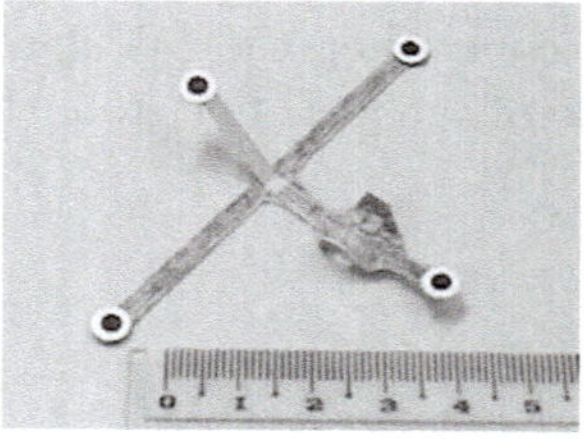

Fig. 3. A frame of reference marks

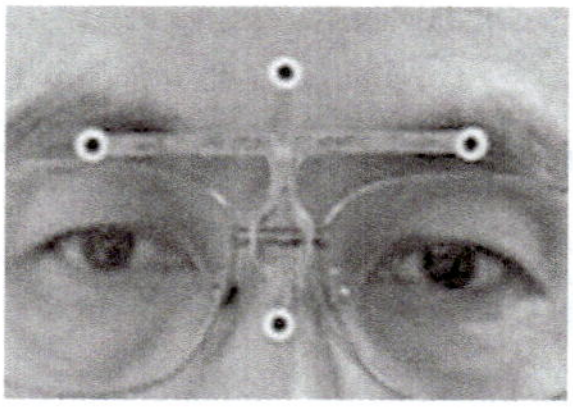

Fig. 4. Reference marks attached to the face

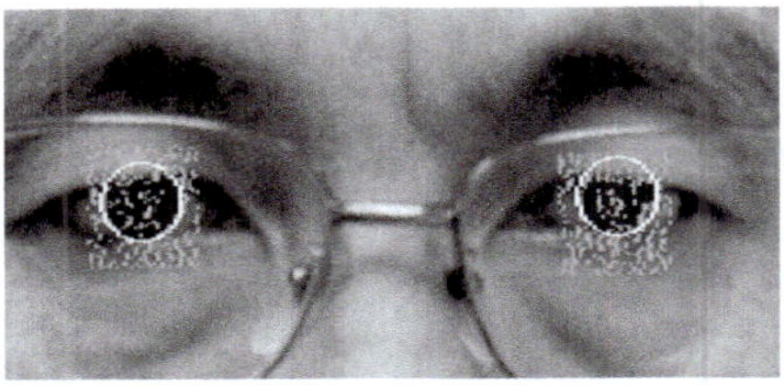

Fig. 5. Example of iris extraction

If the eyes are open, we can expect those positions to be on the irises. However, they are not the center of the irises. Therefore, the center of irises should be searched in a more precise manner.

In many previous works[9][12][10][11], the iris image is binarized, and regions not likely to be iris are eliminated by some means, and then an ellipse is fitted to the edges of the remaining region to extract the center of the iris. However, when binarizing an image, determining an appropriate threshold is almost always a difficult problem. We, therefore, take a different approach. We apply a Laplacian filter and extract zero-cross points as edges in a small region where an iris is likely to exist. We then apply a Hough transform technique for circles for those very many iris edge candidates in order to extract an iris as a circle.

Because the upper and lower parts of the iris are likely to be hidden by the eyelids, only vertical edges are extracted. Consequently, a one-dimensional (horizontal) Laplacian filter is applicable. We can expect that the center of the iris search region is on the iris. Thus, at a zero-cross point, the gradient direction is also taken into account so that the inside is the dark side. In applying the Hough transform for circles, voting to the upper part and lower part (over 60 degrees from the horizontal line) of a circle is suppressed, because that part of the iris is likely to be hidden by the eyelids.

Figure 5 shows an example of iris detection. The two circles are iris locations determined by the Hough transform, while the noisy dots are edge pixels extracted as Laplacian zero-crosses. There are many edges even in the iris region because of reflections of white papers, windows, light sources, etc.

5 Experiment

5.1 Calibration

For Eq. (3), we require three calibration images. The head poses in the calibration images should be different from each other, and the gaze should be directed to the camera. To satisfy these conditions with simple instructions, we showed a target mark at the center of the screen, and asked the subject: for each reference mark except the top one, (1) fit the mark on the target mark by adjusting the head pose; and (2) look at the camera; then (3) press the button. Image of the subject on the screen was flipped horizontally, so that the subject felt it was a mirror. This made it easier for the subject to feed back the image as a head pose

Fig. 6. A set of calibration images. (peripherally clipped)

adjustment, because people are familiar to their own mirror images. Figure 6 shows an example of a set of calibration images.

5.2 Head Pose Independency

Figure 7 shows gaze vectors in different head poses while the subject is gazing at the center of the monitor display. The monitor screen has a 5x5 grid, and the image in Fig. 7 is its 3x3 middle component. The two "+" marks are the calculated virtual eyeball center and the detected virtual iris center. The direction of the gaze vector is from the former to the latter, and its magnitude shown here is a summation of the results for the last 15 frames (0.5 seconds). Actual numbers of them in pixels are shown below each. Notice the origin of the coordinate is in the upper-left corner of the input image. Since the camera is set up on top of the monitor display, the estimated gaze direction is downward when the subject

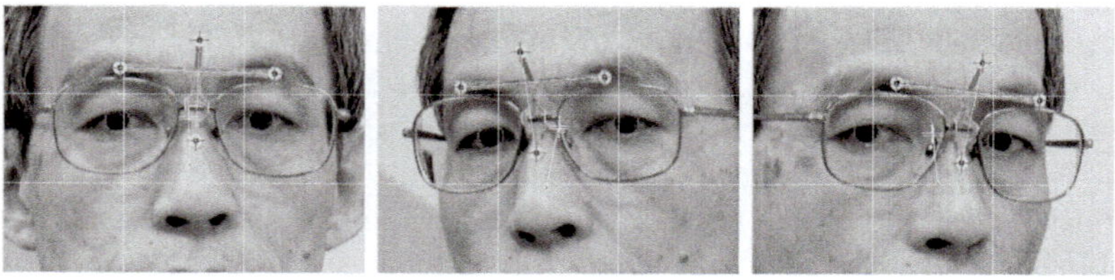

(a) (0, 51) (b) (-12, 66) (c) (5, 54)

Fig. 7. Estimated gaze directions with different head poses while looking at the center of the monitor

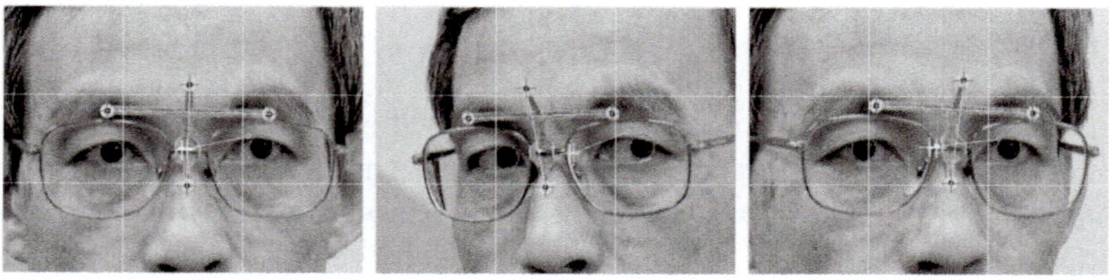

(a) (72, -15) (b) (62, -26) (c) (73, -9)

Fig. 8. Estimated gaze directions with different head poses while looking at the upper-right corner of the bezel is looking at the center of the monitor. The faces in Fig. 7(b) and (c) turn right and left so much that one of the marks used in [12] will be hidden. Nevertheless, the estimated gaze vectors in the three cases are very similar. Actually, figures of gaze directions show that the differences between each of them in both the x-direction and the y-direction are within ±15 pixels (±1 pixel when averaging frames).

Figure 8 shows the cases when the subject is looking at the upper right corner of the bezel. Even in these cases, the results show the head pose independency of our method; figures of gaze directions show that the differences between each of them in both x-direction and y-direction is within ±15 pixels.

5.3 Discussion

Although we cannot observe the location of the eyeball center, the results shown in Figs. 7 and 8 demonstrate that our algorithm to calculate its projected points from the four reference points as described in Section 2 works well.

The estimated gaze directions in Fig. 7(b) and (c) are slightly different. We noticed in experiments that there was a tendency in the drift of estimated gaze direction according to face orientation, and we think this comes from the camera modeling error. However, we employed the orthogonal projection model instead of the perspective model, which made our algorithm simple and robust.

The image resolution we used was rather coarse: the diameter of an iris was about 27 pixels, leading to the distance between the projected points of the eyeball center and the iris center being very short. Consequently, mainly due to fluctuations of the video signal, the estimated gaze direction fluctuates frame by frame. Therefore, in our experiment, we had to employ time averaging (0.5 seconds or 15 frames) to attain stable results. Consequently, the system contained a time delay, even though it processed 30 frames per second

6 Conclusions

We proposed a method to estimate the gaze direction using a single camera. The position of the eyeball center is calculated by a linear combination of four reference points. To determine the coefficients of the linear combination, we need three calibration images with different head poses. The gaze direction is estimated as a vector from the calculated eyeball center to the detected iris center. We demonstrated the validity of the algorithm in experiments. The algorithm is head pose independent; or in other words, head pose is determined with respect to four reference points. The system, implemented on a PC with Xeon 2.2-GHz processor, could process 30 frames per second. A demonstration video clip can be opened at the author's home page (http://www.mis.atr.jp/~skawato)

In the prototype system, locations of reference marks and irises are detected with pixel accuracy. However, because the eyeball center and the iris center are very close, one pixel error causes a relatively large direction error. Therefore, detecting their locations at sub-pixel accuracy remains as future work. In the future, we plan to apply natural feature points extracted on the face, instead of artificial reference marks, to calculate the location of the eyeball center.

This research was supported in part by the National Institute of Information and Communications Technology.

References

1. Morimoto, C.H., Mimica, M.R.M.: Eye gaze tracking techniques for interactive applications. Computer Vision and Image Understanding **98** (2005) 4–24
2. Ohno, T., Mukawa, N., Kawato, S.: Just blink your eyes: A head-free gaze tracking system. Proc. of CHI 2003 (2003) 950–951
3. Yoo, D.H., Chung, M.J.: A novel non-intrusive eye gaze estimation using corss-ratio under large head motion. Computer Vision and Image Understanding **98** (2005) 25–51
4. Matsumoto, Y., Zelinsky, A.: An algorithm for real-time stereo vision implementation of head pose and gaze direction measurement. Proc. IEEE 4th Int. Conf. on Automatic Face and Gesture Recognition (2000) 499–504
5. Tomono, A., Kishino, F., Kobayashi, Y.: Pupil exraction processing and gaze point detection system allowing head movement (in japanese). IEICE(D-II) **J76-D-II** (1993) 636–646
6. Baluja, S., Pomerleau, D.: Non-intrusive gaze tracking using artificial neural networks. Technical Report CMU-CS-94-102 (1994)
7. Schiele, B., Waibel, A.: Gaze tracking based on face-color. Proc. Int. Workshop on Automatic Face and Gesture Recognition (1995) 344–349
8. Zhu, J., Yang, J.: Subpixel eye gaze tracking. Proc. Int. Conf. on Automatic Face and Gesture Recognition (2002) 124–129
9. Wang, J.G., Sung, E.: Gaze determination via images of irises. Image and Vision Computing **19** (2001) 891–911
10. Wu, H., Chen, Q., Wada, T.: Conic-based algorithm for visual line estimation from image. Proc. Int. Conf. on Automatic Face and Gesture Recognition (2004) 260–265
11. Wang, J.G., Sung, E., Venkateswarlu, R.: Estimating the eye gaze from one eye. Computer Vision and Image Understanding **98** (2005) 83–103
12. Miyake, T., Haruta, S., Horihata, S.: Image based eye-gaze estimation irrespective of head direction. Proc. IEEE Int. Symposium on Industrial Electronics **1** (2002) 332–336
13. : http://www.red.atr.jp/product/08/pro_08.html. (2004)

3D Shape Recovery of Smooth Surfaces: Dropping the Fixed Viewpoint Assumption

Yael Moses[1] and Ilan Shimshoni[2]

[1] The Interdisciplinary Center, Herzliya, Israel
yael@idc.ac.il
[2] University of Haifa, Israel
ishimshoni@mis.haifa.ac.il

Abstract. We present a new method for recovering the 3D shape of a featureless smooth surface from three or more calibrated images. The main contribution of this paper is the ability to handle general images which are taken from unconstrained viewpoints and unconstrained illumination directions. To the best of our knowledge, no other method is currently capable of handling such images, since correspondence between such images is hard to compute. Our method combines geometric and photometric information in order to recover a dense correspondence between the images and successfully computes an accurate 3D shape of the surface. The method is based on a single pass and local computation and does not make use of global optimization over the whole surface. While we assume a Lambertian reflectance function, our method can be easily modified to handle more general reflectance models as long as it is possible to recover local normals from photometric information. Experimental results are presented for simulated and real images.

1 Introduction

We present a method for recovering the 3D shape of a smooth featureless surface. Our system accepts inputs consisting of three or more calibrated images of the surface, taken from different viewpoints (can be wide-baseline) and illuminated by different known distant point light sources. The surface is assumed to be Lambertian, and the perspective projection model is assumed. This is a challenging problem for which classical methods for shape recovery, both geometric or photometric, are inadequate, since correspondence between such images is hard to compute. Geometric methods, such as stereo or structure from motion, are based on the recovery of corresponding points in different images. Determining correspondence for images of the type considered in this paper is hard since the surface is assumed to be featureless and the grey-level values of corresponding points can vary considerably between images due to the change in light source direction. In photometric stereo [16, 9] the input images are taken with different lighting directions but from the same viewpoint. The fixed viewpoint assumption provides the correspondence for such methods, but since it does not hold in our case these methods cannot be directly used on our images.

P.J. Narayanan et al. (Eds.): ACCV 2006, LNCS 3851, pp. 429–438, 2006.

Our method computes an accurate 3D shape of the surface by combining geometric and photometric information to recover a dense correspondence between the set of input images. The general idea is to propagate correspondence over the surface and simultaneously recover the 3D shape of the surface. Given a set of corresponding points, we can compute the 3D location using geometric stereo triangulation. We can also compute the normal to the point using local photometric information (e.g., photometric stereo [16, 9]). The recovered 3D point and surface normal define the local shape of the surface, which is then used to propagate the correspondence in a more accurate manner than in SFS algorithms [4], and by relaxing the assumptions made by SFS (e.g., the albedo is not necessarily fixed). This process is repeated to recover the full 3D shape. In contrast to methods that are based on global optimization (e.g. [5, 11]), our method performs the shape recovery in a single pass, similar to [2, 7].

The combination of geometric and photometric information draws on the strengths of the geometric and photometric methods and overcomes their weaknesses. Unlike photometric stereo, we also deal with a perspective projection model, similar to the new SFS algorithms [10, 14]. We can overcome the weaknesses of SFS since the shape information in our method is based on three or more images compared with a single image in the SFS approach. As a result, we can relax the assumption of fixed albedo and obtain more accurate results. We overcome the weakness of photometric stereo, since we drop the fixed viewpoint assumption, and we use additional geometric information. Finally we overcome the weaknesses of geometric stereo since we can handle images of featureless smooth surface illuminated by different light sources, and obtain the support for the reconstructed 3D shape by photometric information.

The results of running our algorithm on synthetic and real data show that combining the photometric and geometric constraints is a powerful tool for handling general (unconstrained viewpoint and illumination) images of smooth surfaces. Our one-pass results can be used as a starting point for higher level iterative methods for shape recovery [11, 4]. Moreover, since the surface shape is over determined when both photometric and geometric information are used, we expect that in future work the camera and light parameters will also be obtainable directly from the images.

Recent studies address the problem of shape recovery of smooth surfaces under non-fixed viewpoint but under limited illumination variations. In [13, 8], the shape of a moving object is recovered. The consistency of the changes of the lighting and viewing conditions on the object is exploited to yield a modified stereo algorithm. In [17], an iterative scheme is introduced which is able to recover the 3D structure and the camera motion under the same settings. A work that uses a similar experimental setup as ours was presented in [15]. There however, the photometric constraints are used only to verify the 3D structure that was computed based on a space carving approach. This method requires many more images to determine the 3D shape. In [6], a setting of constant lighting and a moving camera is used. This is a less general setting than ours. In our previous work [12] we addressed the problem of recovering the shape of a smooth bilaterally symmetric surface from a single image by integrating geometric and photometric constraints. In that study the geometric and photometric constraints were integrated to compute correspondence between the two halves of the symmetric surface and hence to compute the 3D shape of the surface. To the best of our knowledge, our method is the only method that can recover the 3D shape of a smooth textureless object from a set of images that were taken under uncontrolled light source and viewpoint directions.

2 The Basic Approach

Consider n calibrated images of a featureless surface taken from different known camera positions under different lighting conditions which are also known. The number n must be sufficient for local normal recovery from photometric information when correspondence is known. Here we consider $n \geq 3$ images, perspective projection and a Lambertian surface. Photometric stereo is used to recover the local normal. When constant albedo is assumed two images suffice, otherwise at least three images are required.

In this section we show that a single set of corresponding points is sufficient for propagating the correspondence over the entire image and to compute the 3D shape. We first introduce some known notations of geometry and photometry image analysis which are used in existing geometric and photometric methods to recover the 3D structure.

Geometry: Let M_i, $1 \leq i \leq n$, be the known calibrated perspective projection matrices of the n images. Given a 3D surface point $P^{(0)}$, the projection of the point to the n images is given by:

$$p_i^{(0)} \cong M_i P^{(0)}, \qquad 1 \leq i \leq n.$$

The inverse problem is to recover $P^{(0)}$ given its projections to the images $p_1^{(0)}, p_2^{(0)}, \cdots, p_n^{(0)}$ using geometric stereo. In this case, each instance of Eq. 2 can be converted into two linear equations in the coordinates of $P^{(0)}$. Thus, when given two or more projections of a point its 3D position can be recovered [3].

Photometry: Let l_i, $1 \leq i \leq n$, be the known lighting vectors, where the direction of each l_i is pointing to the light source and its magnitude is the light source intensity. Denote by $\mathbf{L} = [l_1, \cdots, l_n]^T$ the matrix of all light vectors.

Let $P^{(0)}$ be a surface point whose normal and albedo are given by the vector $N^{(0)}$. The direction of $N^{(0)}$ is the normal direction at the point $P^{(0)}$ and its magnitude is the albedo at that point. Denote by $I_i^{(0)}$ the intensities at $p_i^{(0)}$ for $1 \leq i \leq n$. The vector $I^{(0)} = \left[I_1^{(0)}, \cdots, I_n^{(0)}\right]^T$ is the intensity vector of the corresponding points. Under the Lambertian model where $I_i^{(0)} = \ell_i N^{(0)}$ we obtain: $I^{(0)} = LN^{(0)}$. Thus, when L and $I^{(0)}$ are given, $N^{(0)}$ is recovered by

$$N^{(0)} = L^+ I^{(0)},$$

where L^+ is the pseudo inverse of L.

We next turn to propose our new method for combining photometry and geometry constraints.

Combining Photometry and Geometry: Given a corresponding set of points, $p_i^{(0)}$, $1 \leq i \leq n$, we can compute the surface point $P^{(0)}$ (by geometric stereo, based on Eq. 2) and its normal to the surface $N^{(0)}$ (by photometric stereo, Eq. 2). The task then is to compute a new point on the surface based on $P^{(0)}$ and $N^{(0)}$. Consider a small step, δ, on the first image to a neighboring point $p_1^{(1)} = p_1^{(0)} + \delta$. This point is the projection of the ray

$$P(\alpha) = (1-\alpha)O_1 + \alpha P_\delta, \tag{1}$$

where O_1 is the known center of projection of the first camera and $[P_\delta, 1] \cong M_1^+ p_1^{(1)}$ is a specific point on the ray. The value of α uniquely determines the location of the new point on the recovered surface.

As a first order approximation we require that $P(\alpha)$ lie on the tangent plane at $P^{(0)}$ which is given by the computed normal $N^{(0)}$. Thus, $P(\alpha)$ satisfies:

$$N^{(0)}(P(\alpha) - P^{(0)}) = 0.$$

This constraint together with Eq. 1 yields a unique value for α

$$\alpha = \frac{(P^{(0)} - O_1)^T N^{(0)}}{(P_\delta - O_1)^T N^{(0)}}. \tag{2}$$

Once $P^{(1)} = P(\alpha)$ has been estimated its projection to all the images $p_i^{(1)}, 1 \leq i \leq n$ is computed, yielding a new set of corresponding points. The surface normal to this point, $N^{(1)}$, can now be computed.

In the first order approximation, the surface was assumed to be locally planar. Clearly for highly curved regions, first order approximations might be insufficient. A more general second order estimate to the surface can also be considered. In this case, α can be determined by solving a quadratic equation, as is described in the full version of this paper.

Surface Propagation: Given a point in the first image for which the correspondence is known, it is possible to propagate the correspondence to any of its neighboring pixels. In order to reduce error accumulation, we propagate the correspondence such that the length of the path between the original pixel and the target pixel is minimal. This is done by propagating the correspondence in all directions from the given pixel. To this end we use a queue data structure in which the candidate propagation target pixels are kept, yielding a Breadth First Search (BFS) traversal of the image. This traversal circumvents regions for which the propagation cannot be computed (e.g., shadowed pixels).

3 Extensions

The basic approach can be extended to improve the quality of the reconstruction and reduce the negative impact of noise. In this section we present several extensions of the basic method.

Approximation based on multi-neighbors: When estimating the correspondence for a given target pixel, the 3D location and normal were already computed for at least one of its neighboring pixels. The basic approach uses this neighbor to compute the new point location. As a result, it is sensitive to errors since a single error can affect the rest of the reconstruction. To reduce the errors caused by noise and improve the reconstruction, we suggest using *multi-neighbor* propagation exploiting the information from all the neighbors of the target pixel that have already been computed. Thus, we compute the location of the new point as an average of the locations computed based on each of its neighbors. In addition, the neighbors can be used to choose a subset of good neighbors. As shown in the real experiments (Figure 4 Run A5 compared to Run B5), multi-neighbor propagation improves the reconstruction in problematic regions and reduces the effects of propagation errors.

Error correction based on local continuity: Local continuity of the object shape and albedo can be used to improve the reconstruction. A computed target point is evaluated based on local continuity which is defined by a *continuity score* function. Then the 3D location of the target point which minimizes this score is found.

Here we use the 3D location, the normal direction and the albedo of the already computed neighbors of a target point. The 3D location, the normal and the albedo of the target point are first computed using the basic method. The continuity score reflects their local continuity. Clearly, more complex measures of continuity can be applied under this framework. A threshold on this score can also be used to detect bad pixels. We then avoid computing their 3D position and refrain from using them for propagation. As shown in the real experiments (Figure 4 Run B5 compared to Run C5) error correction based on local continuity also improves the reconstruction in problematic regions and reduces the effects of propagation errors.

Using more than three images: Clearly, more images contain more information. Hence, by using more than three images we improve the reconstruction. Our basic propagation scheme uses three or more images in a straightforward manner. When more than three images are available, the least squares solution clearly reduces the sensitivity to image noise.

The additional images can also be used to detect and avoid bad pixels which exist in some of the images. A shadowed pixel or an occluded pixel can be avoided by ignoring its value when the normal is computed. This is done in the following way. For each set of intensities of corresponding points, we evaluate the consistency of these values with a single normal:

$$s^{(0)} = I^{(0)} - LL^{+}I^{(0)}.$$

This score is used to detect when a bad pixel exists and disregard it. Results in Section 4 (Figure 4 Run C5 compared to Run C3) show that more images improve the quality of the reconstruction.

4 Experimental Results

We have implemented our algorithm and tested it on simulated and real image sets. Simulated image sets enable us to compare the results with the ground truth. Running the algorithm on real image sets is more challenging because we have to supply the algorithm with projection matrices and lighting information which also have to be recovered from the images, and thus the algorithm has to be able to deal with these parameters which are inherently noisy. In addition the algorithm has to deal with image noise and the inaccuracies of the Lambertian model.

Simulated images: We generated three simulated images (see first row Fig. 1) of a bust of Mozart's head from 3D range data used also in [10]. The algorithm is given the parameters of the images (cameras and lightening) that were used to generate the images and an initial known 3D-point to start the propagation.

We present here a comparison between the ground truth 3D surface and three variants of our algorithm: the basic scheme (**Run A**), multi-neighbors approxi-

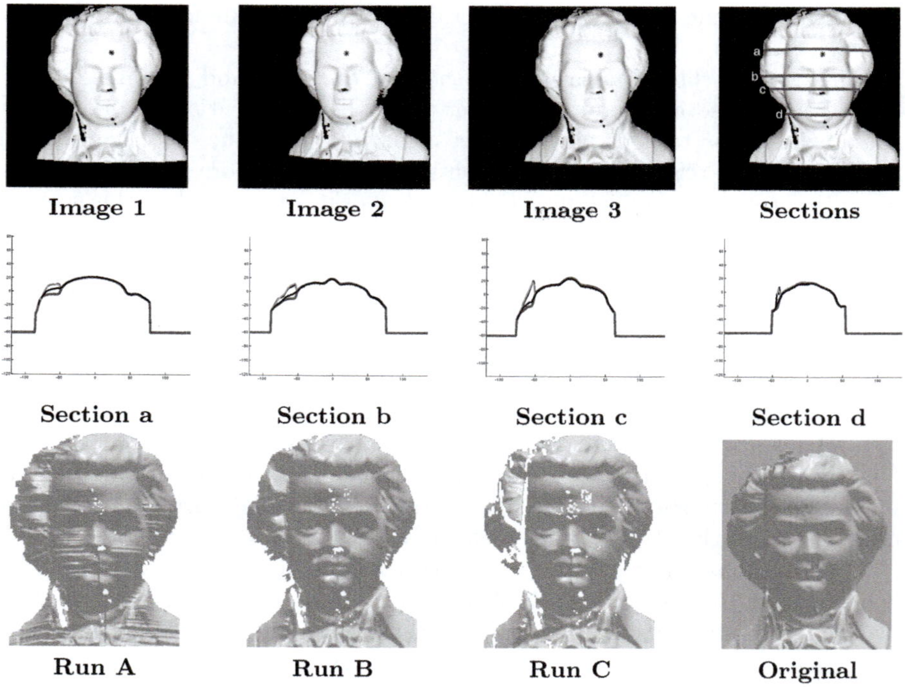

Fig. 1. Simulated images experiments. The first row consists of the three input images and an image with four cross sections. Comparison between the real and the recovered 3D shape from synthetic images are shown in the second row. Graphs (a-d) correspond to the depth values along the lines marked on the image termed Sections. The red, blue, green and black lines correspond to the ground truth and runs A, B and C respectively. The reconstructed surfaces of the three variants of the algorithm, Run A, Run B and Run C, and the original surface are shown on the third row.

mation (**Run B**), and multi-neighbors approximation and local continuity error correction (**Run C**). To evaluate the performance of the method the cross sections of the ground truth and the recovered 3D structures are compared (second row of Figure 1). The graphs, show that the reconstruction of the surfaces is very accurate in all the three runs for most of the face. The reconstruction starts to drift in dark image regions, which are less reliable. This is compensated for in Run C (Black graph), when multi-neighbors approximation and local continuity error correction are applied.

To visualize the performance of the three runs we present the reconstructed surfaces in the last row of Figure 1. The surface reconstructed by the basic scheme (Figure 1 Run A) is relatively good, however, using multi-neighbors (Run B) improves it. The reconstructed surface when both multi-neighbors and the local continuity error correction are applied (Run C) is very similar to the original one, except that some regions are not recovered at all. This is because the algorithm detects that there is not enough information for reliable recovery using local continuity. However, as can be seen from the graphs, the reconstruction is more accurate in this run.

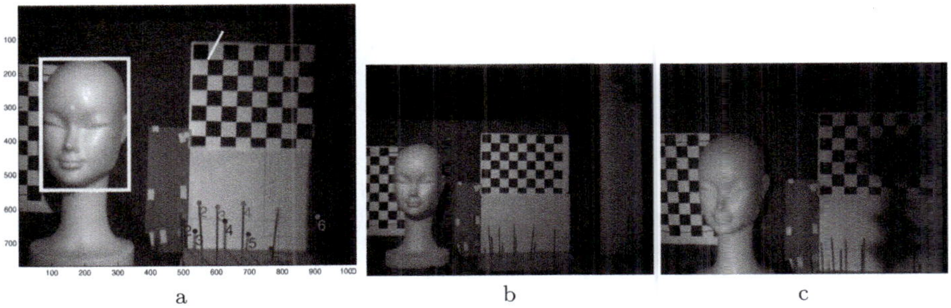

Fig. 2. (a) The real images experimental setup. A calibration paper in the background was used to calibrate the camera location, a subset of the nail shadows which are clearly visible were marked by hand to compute the light source direction. The projection of the head of the nails and their shadows are marked in blue and red respectively based on their computed 3D location. The yellow line is the projection of the light source position to the image plane. (b-c) Two additional original images used in the experiment.

Real images: We ran our algorithm on real images taken by a standard CCD camera calibrated by the geometric calibration toolbox [1]. An image of the setup is shown in Figure 2(a). The light source direction was estimated using a set of nails and their shadows whose 3D positions are estimated from the images. Vectors connecting nail tips to their shadows intersect at the light source position. The ambient light was determined to be the intensity value in the shadow of the mannequin and the light source intensity was chosen to be the maximal intensity value on the mannequin after reducing the ambient value.

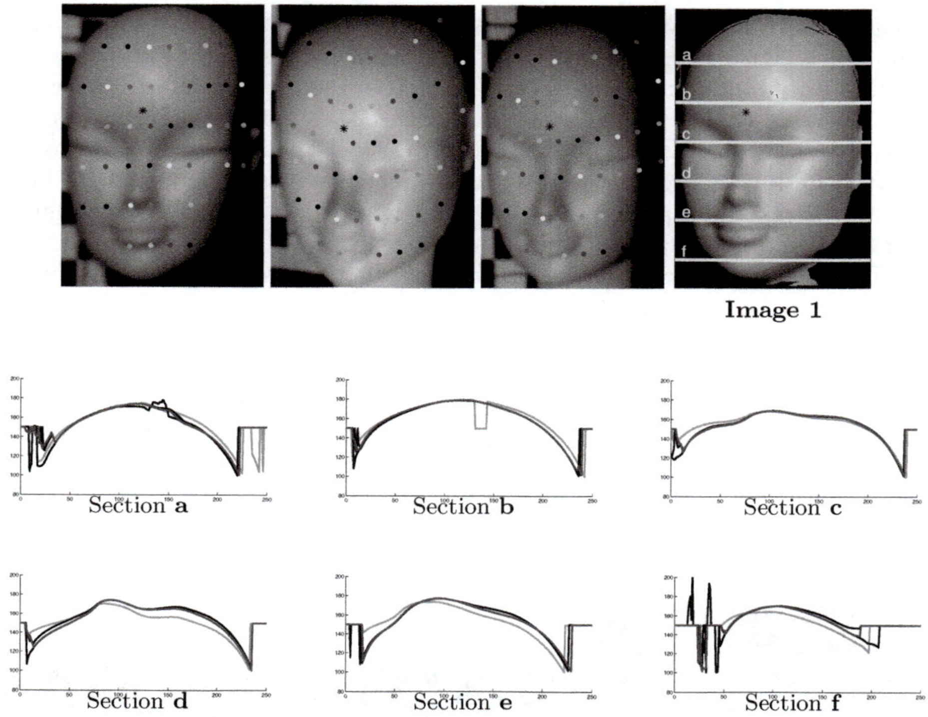

Fig. 3. Three of the five cropped images used in the experiment. Note that each of them was taken from a different viewpoint and with a different light source direction. The black star is the corresponding point given to the algorithm. A grid of automatically computed corresponding points in the images are marked such that corresponding points have the same color in the different images. Six cross sections of Image 1 are presented. The Red, Black, Blue Green lines represent results obtained for Runs **C5**, **B5**, **D5** and **A3**, respectively.

Two of the original images are shown in Figure 2(b-c) and three of the five cropped images that were used in the experiment are shown in the first row of Figure 3. The initial corresponding points, marked on the images in black, were chosen by hand and then fine tuned to minimize the cost function in Eq. 3. The basic scheme (**Run A**), its multi-neighbors approximation extension (**Run B**), and multi-neighbors approximation and local continuity error correction extension (**Run C**) were implemented in Matlab on three and five images. We denote by **Run A3, A5, B3, B5, C3, C5** the method used and the number of images used. In addition we denote by **Run D5** the basic scheme without multi-neighbors approximation but with error correction applied to five images.

To illustrate the quality of the results, we present the performance of the algorithm in the following figures: The correspondence of several image points as computed by the algorithm are shown in the first row of Figure 3. Figure 4 shows the reconstructed surfaces obtained by five variants of the algorithm: Runs **C5,**

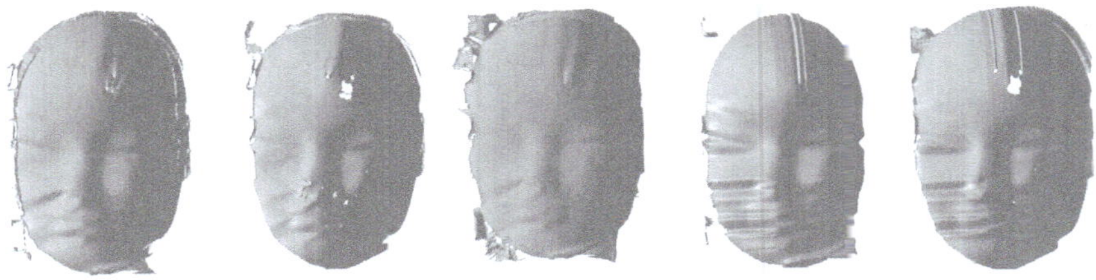

Fig. 4. 3D surfaces obtained by several variants of our method, as explained in the text. The best reconstruction is Surface C5, where both multi-neighbors and error-correction are applied.

C3, B5, A5, and **A3**. Finally, several cross sections of the surfaces recovered by the algorithms are displayed in the second and third rows of Figure 3.

The results show that the correspondence and the reconstruction is fairly good on most of the mannequin. This happens even in regions that are far from the starting point (marked by a black star). When only the basic scheme is performed, the results are noisy, but the rough shape of the mannequin is perceived. Using the multi-neighbor approximation improves the performance considerably (compare Surface A5 to B5), so does the error correction which is based on local continuity (compare Surface B5 to C5). Using more images improves the results (compare Surface C3 to C5 and Surface A3 to A5), however the improvement is not dramatic and it mainly helps in filling in the gaps. Using both extensions, averaging over the neighbors of the pixel and error correction yields the best results for three and five images (Surfaces C3 and C5).

5 Summary and Conclusions

In this paper we introduced a new shape reconstruction algorithm for smooth featureless surfaces under the perspective projection model. By enabling independent motion of the camera and the light source an accurate reconstruction algorithm is created. It builds on the strengths of photometric stereo, geometric stereo and shape from shading while avoiding their weaknesses.

The algorithm has been tested in realistic settings using an experimental setup that enables us to recover the input parameters to the algorithm from images. Even though these parameters were estimated from the images, the resulting recovered surfaces were quite accurate. These results can be improved by modifying the reflectance model to deal with specularities and non-distant light sources, which is relatively straightforward in our setup

Future research will focus on methods to use more than the minimal number of images to better detect and deal with bad pixels. Moreover, they can be used to detect the initial set of corresponding points used to start the algorithm and even to detect automatically the camera positions and light source directions from the images.

Acknowledgment. This research was supported by the Israel Science Foundation (grant No. 133/0-125). We would like to thank Avi Barliya, Gil Ben-Artzi, and Benjamin Neeman for working on the implementation of our method.

References

1. J. Y. Bouguet. Camera calibration toolbox for matlab. http://www.vision.caltech.edu/bouguetj/calib_doc.
2. P. Dupuis and J. Oliensis. Direct method for reconstructing shape from shading. In *Proc. IEEE Conf. Comp. Vision Patt. Recog.*, pages 453–458, 1992.
3. R.I. Hartley and P. Sturm. Triangulation. *Comp. Vis. Im. Understanding*, 68(2):146–157, November 1997.
4. B. K. P. Horn and M. Brooks. *Seeing shape from shading.* MIT Press, Cambridge, Mass., 1989.
5. K. Ikeuchi and B.K.P. Horn. Numerical shape from shading and occluding boundaries. *Artificial Intelligence*, 17:141–184, 1981.
6. H. Jin, D. Cremers, AJ. Yezzi, and S. Soatto. Shedding light on stereoscopic segmentation. In *Proc. Int. Conf. Comp. Vision*, 2004.
7. R. Kimmel and A. Bruckstein. Global shape from shading. *Comp. Vis. Im. Understanding*, 62(3):360–369, 1995.
8. A. Maki, M. Watanabe, and C. Wiles. Geotensity: Computing motion and lighting for 3D surface reconstruction. *Int. J. of Comp. Vision*, 48(2):75–90, 2002.
9. R. Onn and A.M. Bruckstein. Integrability disambiguates surface recovery in two-image photometric stereo. *Int. J. of Comp. Vision*, 5(1):105–113, August 1990.
10. E. Prados and O.D. Faugeras. Perspective shape from shading and viscosity solutions. In *Proc. Int. Conf. Comp. Vision*, pages 826–831, 2003.
11. D. Samaras and D. Metaxas. Incorporating illumination constraints in deformable models for shape from shading and light direction estimation. *IEEE Trans. Patt. Anal. Mach. Intell.*, 25(2):247–264, February 2003.
12. I. Shimshoni, Y. Moses, and M. Lindenbaum. Shape reconstruction of 3d bilaterally symmetric surfaces. *Int. J. of Comp. Vision*, 39(2):97—110, September 2000.
13. D. Simakov, D. Frolova, and R. Basri. Dense shape reconstruction of a moving object under arbitrary, unknown lighting. In *Proc. Int. Conf. Comp. Vision*, pages 1202–1207, 2003.
14. A. Tankus, N.A. Sochen, and Y. Yeshurun. A new perspective [on] shape-from-shading. In *Proc. Int. Conf. Comp. Vision*, pages 862–869, 2003.
15. M. Weber, A. Blake, and R. Cipolla. Towards a complete dense geometric and photometric reconstruction under varying pose and illumination. In *British Mach. Vis. Conf.*, pages 83–92, 2002.
16. R. J. Woodham. Photometric stereo: A reflectance map technique for determining surface orientation from image intensity. *In Proc. SPIE*, 155:136–143, 1978.
17. L. Zhang, B. Curless, A. Hertzmann, and S.M. Seitz. Shape and motion under varying illumination: unifying structure from motion, photometric stereo, and multi-view stereo. In *Proc. Int. Conf. Comp. Vision*, pages 618–625, 2003.

Stereo Matching by Interpolation

Bodong Liang and Ronald Chung

Department of Automation and Computer-Aided Engineering,
The Chinese University of Hong Kong,
Shatin, N.T., Hong Kong, China
{bdliang, rchung}@acae.cuhk.edu.hk

Abstract. Stereo vision is a long-studied problem in computer vision. Yet, few have approached it from the angle of interpolation. In this paper, we present an approach, *Interpolation-based Iterative Stereo Matching* (IISM), that regards stereo matching as a mapping that maps image position from one view to the corresponding position in the other view, and the mapping is to be learned or interpolated from some samples that could be just some initial correspondences over some distinct image features that are easy to match. Once the mapping is interpolated, it could be used to predict correspondences beyond the samples, and once such predicted correspondences are corrected and confirmed through local search around the predicted positions in the image data, they could be used together with the original samples as a new and larger sample for another round of interpolation. In other words, interpolation for the mapping is not one-time, but about a number of rounds of interpolation, correspondence prediction, prediction correction, sample set enlargement, and so on, each round producing a more accurate stereo correspondence mapping. IISM utilizes the *Example-Based Interpolation* (EBI) scheme, but in IISM the existing EBI is adapted to ensure the established correspondences satisfy exactly the epipolar constraint of the image pair, and to a certain extent preserve discontinuities in the stereo disparity space of the imaged scene. Experimental results on a number of real image datasets show that the proposed solution has promising performance even when the initial correspondence samples are sparse.

1 Introduction

Stereo matching is about pairing image positions across two images, that are projected by the same 3D features of the imaged scene. It is one of the most active research areas in computer vision. Many stereo algorithms have been published in the literature. Survey papers like [1], [2], [3], [4] reviewed the major techniques and methods proposed in the period from mid 1970's to early 1990's. Recently, Scharstein and Szeliski [5] provided a comprehensive discussion on stereo implementations, taxonomy, test data and results, as well as a test platform for the stereo algorithms.

Existing stereo algorithms can be classified into two classes: window-based algorithms and feature-based algorithms. In the window-based methods, disparity is computed by matching intensity windows cut out from each image about

P.J. Narayanan et al. (Eds.): ACCV 2006, LNCS 3851, pp. 439–448, 2006.

almost every image position. It has the advantage that a dense disparity map could be attained, but then it suffers from the problem that not all intensity windows are distinct enough to be matched with accuracy. In contrast, in the feature-based algorithms, each image is first converted into a sparse set of distinct features that are to be matched across the images, and the matching is often formulated as an optimization problem that makes use of the scene-smoothness assumption. The established correspondences are often more reliable since they are about distinct features, but then the dense disparity map is often available only with some post-processings.

Our approach belongs to the latter class. We match distinct features only, but then we formulate the matching problem not as an optimization problem but an interpolation one, allowing correspondence establishment and interpolation to be interplayed in alternative phases so as to result in having (1) correspondences over only the distinct features in the image data, and (2) a dense disparity map at the end. In the literature few have approached stereo vision in this direction, for example, the process in [6] was cast within a Bayesian inference framework.

The interpolation tool we adopt is the so-called *Example-Based Interpolation* (EBI) [7], [8], which is a mechanism that learns or interpolates, from examples, a function that passes all the input examples with minimal oscillations between the examples. It has promising results, even with very sparse given example, in a number of applications including object detection and recognition [9], computer animation and graphics [10], image processing [11], and others.

We refer to our approach as *Interpolation-based Iterative Stereo Matching* (IISM), in which we first extract initial correspondences over very distinct features that are easy to match across the input images. By applying EBI, we then treat stereo matching as a mapping that maps image position in one view to the corresponding position in another view, and interpolate the mapping from the existing examples of correspondences – the initial correspondences we extracted earlier. Here, the EBI mechanism is adapted so that the mapping result satisfies exactly the epipolar geometry that is estimated robustly from the given examples of correspondences. Once the mapping is interpolated, it could be used to predict more correspondences than the initial samples, and once such predicted correspondences are corrected and confirmed through local search around the predicted positions in the image data, they could be used together with the original samples as a new and larger sample for another round of interpolation. In other words, interpolation for the mapping of stereo matching is not one-time, but about a number of rounds of interpolation, correspondence prediction, prediction correction, sample set enlargement, and so on, each round producing a more accurate stereo correspondence mapping.

With IISM, even though correspondences are to be established over only distinct features in the image data so as to boost the correspondence accuracy, a dense disparity map could still be resulted at the end. Furthermore, correspondence establishment and interpolation are not separate but go hand-in-hand.

In essence, our approach views disparity map as a distribution of continuous and smooth transitions over the initially obtained sparse correspondences. It has the scene-smoothness assumption implicitly embedded in the formulation and would handle well those parts of the scene that are without occlusions. However, it wouldn't be adequate for the occlusion boundaries in the image scene.

In the interpolation formulation, the key to occlusion handling is that the disparity value at an image position is interpolated from not necessarily the disparities of its entire neighborhood. If the image position is about a point over a smooth surface in 3D, the disparities of the entire neighborhood of the image position will be used. However, if it is about a point over an occlusion boundary, only part of the neighborhood should be involved in the interpolation process.

Based upon the above analysis, we propose a way to adapt the EBI-based solution so that occlusions could be better handled. The idea is that the neighborhood of an image position that is involved in interpolation is automatically adjusted, which does not have to the entire neighborhood, so as to avoid over-smoothing.

2 Review of EBI

The interpolation problem could be stated as this: given S input-output pairs $\{(\mathbf{V}_s, f_{\mathbf{V}_s})\} : s = 1, 2, \cdots, S\}$ as examples of a function $f : \mathbb{R}^D \to \mathbb{R}$, construct the scalar function value $f_{\mathbf{V}} = f(\mathbf{V})$ for any arbitrary input $\mathbf{V}$ in $\mathbb{R}^D$ such that it satisfies $f_{\mathbf{V}_s} = f(\mathbf{V}_s)$ for all the S given examples. We shall refer to each $\mathbf{V}_s$ ($s \in \{1, 2, \cdots, S\}$) as the sth *example point*, and $f_{\mathbf{V}_s}$ the sth *example value*.

A natural inference of $f_{\mathbf{V}}$ for any $\mathbf{V}$ is a weighted sum of the example values:

$$f_{\mathbf{V}} = [f_{\mathbf{V}_1}, f_{\mathbf{V}_2}, \cdots, f_{\mathbf{V}_S}] \mathbf{W}_{\mathbf{V}} \ . \tag{1}$$

where $S \times 1$ *weight matrix* $\mathbf{W}_{\mathbf{V}} = [w_{1,\mathbf{V}}, w_{2,\mathbf{V}}, \cdots, w_{S,\mathbf{V}}]^{\mathrm{T}}$ represents, for computing $f_{\mathbf{V}}$ at any arbitrary input $\mathbf{V}$, the respective weights given to the S example values. The problem thus boils down to the design of the weight matrix $\mathbf{W}_{\mathbf{V}}$

$\mathbf{W}_{\mathbf{V}}$, in which the sum of all S weights is equal to 1 for any particular $\mathbf{V}$, is a function of $\mathbf{V}$ since naturally it varies with $\mathbf{V}$ in this way: the contributions of the various example values $f_{\mathbf{V}_1}, f_{\mathbf{V}_2}, \cdots, f_{\mathbf{V}_S}$ are in accordance with the relative proximity of their examples points $\mathbf{V}_1, \mathbf{V}_2, \cdots, \mathbf{V}_S$ to $\mathbf{V}$. This implies:

$$\begin{bmatrix} 1 \\ \mathbf{V} \end{bmatrix} = \begin{bmatrix} 1 & 1 & \cdots & 1 \\ \mathbf{V}_1 & \mathbf{V}_2 & \cdots & \mathbf{V}_S \end{bmatrix} \mathbf{W}_{\mathbf{V}} \ . \tag{2}$$

To allow the interpolated function to satisfy the given input-output pairs exactly, if $\mathbf{V}$ happens to be one of the example points $\mathbf{V}_s$, where $s = 1, 2, \cdots, S$, the sth entry of $\mathbf{W}_{\mathbf{V}}$ is 1 while all the other entries are 0, i.e., for all s and $\mathbf{V}_\alpha$, where $s, \alpha \in \{1, 2, \cdots, S\}$,

$$w_{s,\mathbf{V}_\alpha} = \begin{cases} 1 & \text{if } s = \alpha \ , \\ 0 & \text{otherwise} \ . \end{cases} \tag{3}$$

One nonlinear design of $\mathbf{W}_{\mathbf{V}}$ determined by radial basis functions (RBFs), as outlined in [10], [12], could ensure that the interpolated function $f_{\mathbf{V}}$ satisfies (2), (3) and passes through the input examples exactly and smoothly. We shall make use of this solution in this paper but do not list it here for lack of space.

3 Applying EBI to Stereo Matching Problem

Suppose in image pair of $\mathcal{I}$ and $\mathcal{I}'$, we have C initial corresponding points $(\mathbf{m}_1, \mathbf{m}_1{}')$, $(\mathbf{m}_2, \mathbf{m}_2{}')$, $\cdots$, $(\mathbf{m}_C, \mathbf{m}_C{}')$, where $\mathbf{m}_c = [u_c, v_c]^{\mathrm{T}}$ in image $\mathcal{I}$ and $\mathbf{m}_c{}' = [u_c{}', v_c{}']^{\mathrm{T}}$ in image $\mathcal{I}'$, $c = 1, 2, \cdots, C$. The 3×3 fundamental matrix $\mathbf{F}$ and epipoles, $\mathbf{e} = [u_{\mathbf{e}}, v_{\mathbf{e}}]^{\mathrm{T}}$ in image $\mathcal{I}$ and $\mathbf{e}' = [u_{\mathbf{e}}{}', v_{\mathbf{e}}{}']^{\mathrm{T}}$ in image $\mathcal{I}'$, are known. Given any point $\mathbf{m} = [u, v]^{\mathrm{T}}$ in image $\mathcal{I}$, then determine its corresponding point $\mathbf{m}' = [u', v']^{\mathrm{T}}$ in image $\mathcal{I}'$ such that $\mathbf{m}$ and $\mathbf{m}'$ satisfy the epipolar constraint.

We apply EBI scheme to the stereo matching problem here and treat the given image point $\mathbf{m}$ and its matching point $\mathbf{m}'$ as the input and output of a function, the given C corresponding points, $(\mathbf{m}_1, \mathbf{m}_1')$, $(\mathbf{m}_2, \mathbf{m}_2')$, $\cdots$, $(\mathbf{m}_C, \mathbf{m}_C')$, as examples of that function, and regard stereo matching as a problem of interpolating the function from the examples.

3.1 Applying EBI Without Epipolar Constraint

For any general feature whose image position in image $\mathcal{I}$ is $\mathbf{m}$, we are to predict its corresponding image position $\mathbf{m}'$ in image $\mathcal{I}'$. The prediction is derived from how $\mathbf{m}$ is positioned relative to all $\mathbf{m}_c$'s ($c = 1, 2, \cdots, C$) in image space. We could use the solution of EBI in Sect. 2 to learn a $C \times 1$ weight matrix $\mathbf{W}_{\mathbf{m}}$ from $\mathbf{m}$ and $\mathbf{m}_c$'s such that

$$\begin{bmatrix} 1 \\ \mathbf{m} \end{bmatrix} = \begin{bmatrix} 1 & 1 & \cdots & 1 \\ \mathbf{m}_1 & \mathbf{m}_2 & \cdots & \mathbf{m}_C \end{bmatrix} \mathbf{W}_{\mathbf{m}} \, .$$

With $\mathbf{W}_{\mathbf{m}}$, we could use (1) in Sect. 2 to determine the image position $\mathbf{m}'$ of the same feature in image $\mathcal{I}'$ as following:

$$\mathbf{m}' = \left[\mathbf{m}_1{}', \mathbf{m}_2{}', \cdots, \mathbf{m}_C{}'\right] \mathbf{W}_{\mathbf{m}} \, .$$

Note that the above method does not consider the epipolar constraint, so the results might not satisfy the epipolar geometry [13] listed in the following:

$$\left[\mathbf{m}'^{\mathrm{T}}, 1\right] \mathbf{F} \left[\mathbf{m}^{\mathrm{T}}, 1\right]^{\mathrm{T}} = 0 \, . \tag{4}$$

3.2 Bundling EBI with Epipolar Geometry

Since the fundamental matrix and epipoles are known, given any point in one image, its corresponding point in another image must locate on the epipolar line, the search problem decreases to one dimension. To incorporate the epipolar constraint, we show all image points in both images $\mathcal{I}$ and $\mathcal{I}'$ are represented by polar coordinate instead of Cartesian coordinate as illustrated in Fig. 1, i.e.,

$$\mathbf{m}_c = \left[u_c, v_c\right]^{\mathrm{T}} \equiv \left[\theta_c, r_c\right]^{\mathrm{T}} \quad \text{and} \quad \mathbf{m}_c{}' = \left[u_c{}', v_c{}'\right]^{\mathrm{T}} \equiv \left[\theta_c{}', r_c{}'\right]^{\mathrm{T}} ,$$

where $c = 1, 2, \cdots, C$. r_c ($r_c{}'$) is the Euclidean distance between $\mathbf{m}_c$ ($\mathbf{m}_c{}'$) and $\mathbf{e}$ ($\mathbf{e}'$), θ_c ($\theta_c{}'$) is the epipolar line given by the image point $\mathbf{m}_c{}'$ ($\mathbf{m}_c$) such that

$$\theta_c \equiv \mathbf{F}^{\mathrm{T}} \left[\mathbf{m}_c{}'^{\mathrm{T}}, 1\right]^{\mathrm{T}} \quad \text{and} \quad \theta_c{}' \equiv \mathbf{F} \left[\mathbf{m}_c{}^{\mathrm{T}}, 1\right]^{\mathrm{T}} .$$

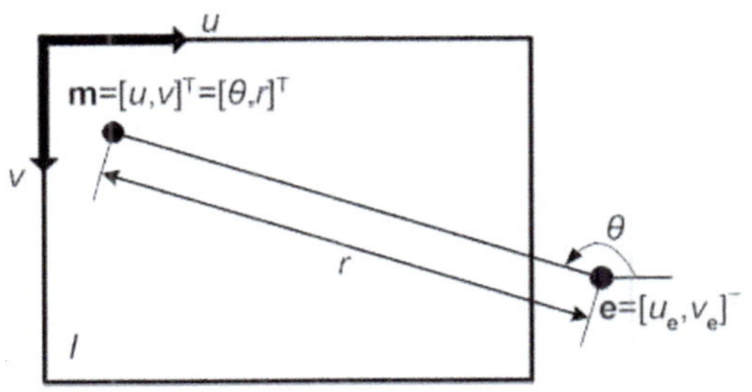

Fig. 1. Cartesian coordinate and polar coordinate for image point in image

For the matching problem, given any point $\mathbf{m} = [u, v]^{\mathrm{T}} \equiv [\theta, r]^{\mathrm{T}}$, we firstly calculate its corresponding point $\mathbf{m}'$'s polar coordinate and then determine its Cartesian coordinate, the detail steps are:

Step 1: According to epipolar geometry, $\mathbf{m}'$ must locate on the epipolar line

$$\theta' \equiv \mathbf{F}\left[\mathbf{m}^{\mathrm{T}}, 1\right]^{\mathrm{T}} .$$

Like above, using EBI to compute the $C \times 1$ weight matrix $\mathbf{W_m}$ such that

$$\begin{bmatrix} 1 \\ \theta \\ r \\ \theta' \end{bmatrix} = \begin{bmatrix} 1 & 1 & \cdots & 1 \\ \theta_1 & \theta_2 & \cdots & \theta_C \\ r_1 & r_2 & \cdots & r_C \\ \theta_1' & \theta_2' & \cdots & \theta_C' \end{bmatrix} \mathbf{W_m} .$$

$\mathbf{W_m}$ so determined must satisfy the epipolar geometry.

Step 2: In image $\mathcal{I}'$, computing the distance r' between $\mathbf{m}'$ and $\mathbf{e}'$:

$$r' = \left[r_1', r_2', \cdots, r_C'\right] \mathbf{W_m} .$$

Step 3: Determining the Cartesian location of $\mathbf{m}'$ in image $\mathcal{I}'$:

$$\mathbf{m}' = \left[\theta', r'\right]^{\mathrm{T}} \equiv \left[u', v'\right]^{\mathrm{T}} .$$

The above is the ultimate mapping we desire: for any arbitrary point $\mathbf{m}$ in image $\mathcal{I}$, map it to its matching point $\mathbf{m}'$ in image $\mathcal{I}'$, which satisfies the epipolar constraint defined in (4) exactly.

4 Matching from Sparse to Dense with IISM

In our approach referred to as *Interpolation-based Iterative Stereo Matching* (IISM), we firstly extract initial correspondences, estimate initial epipolar geometry robustly and then apply the EBI to have an interpolation to map the initial correspondences. Such EBI applied is improved to have each mapping satisfied exactly the epipolar constraint. Once the mapping is interpolated, it could be used to predict more correspondences than the initials, and once such predicted correspondences are corrected and confirmed through local search around the predicted positions in the image data, they could be used together with the original samples as a new and larger sample for another round of interpolation. In other words, the interpolation for the mapping of stereo matching is not one-time, but about a number of rounds of interpolation, correspondence prediction, prediction correction, sample set enlargement, and so on, each round producing a more accurate and dense stereo correspondence mapping than previous. The following are detail descriptions to the procedures of IISM:

Step 1: Extracting initial sparse correspondences at distinct features from the given stereo image pair. We utilize the software of IMAGE-MATCHING, developed by Zhang *et al.* [14], to create the initial corresponding points.

Step 2: Discarding the outliers. We could apply some robust estimation methods such as RANSAC [15] and Least Median of Squares (LMedS) [14], [16] to detect the outliers in the initial matches. Our purpose is to estimate the 3×3 fundamental matrix $\mathbf{F}$, which has only 7 degrees of freedom, so only 7 matches can give at least one solution of fundamental matrix. In our procedure, we firstly choose 7 point matches from the whole given correspondences with the techniques so-called Russian Roulette Wheel Selection or Monte Carlo method, and then apply the LMedS method to get the robust matches without outliers.

Step 3: Estimating the epipolar geometry from the matches determined by LMedS. With these matches, we firstly run the 8-point algorithm [17], [18] to obtain an initial estimation of fundamental matrix, and then use the non-linear method discussed in [16] to robustly estimate the epipolar geometry (including fundamental matrix and epipoles in two images).

Step 4: Matching from sparse to dense by applying EBI scheme. So far, we have the epipolar geometry and the correspondences, both are robustly estimated, in hand. As described in Sect. 3.2, for any general image position in one image, we can apply EBI to predict its corresponding point, under condition of satisfying the epipolar constraint, in another image. In this step, we can get dense matching and produce a dense disparity map between the images.

Step 5: Adjusting the dense matching with image local information. In dense matching established in Step 4, only geometric constraint, i.e., the epipolar geometry and geometric relation among the input image point and all given correspondences, has been used. The local information, such as texture, correlation, intensity ordering etc., is not yet utilized, thus many matches are possibly false. Here, we tune each pair of matches with normalized cross-correlation and then double-check the adjusted matches with epipolar constraint. Those adjusted matches not satisfying the epipolar geometry are discarded. Lastly, we get a new set of correspondences which satisfy not only the global constraint, but also the local information. They will be used as a new and larger sample for another round of interpolation.

Step 6: Running iteratively to get more promising results. Here our procedure goes back to Step 2 and run from there once again.

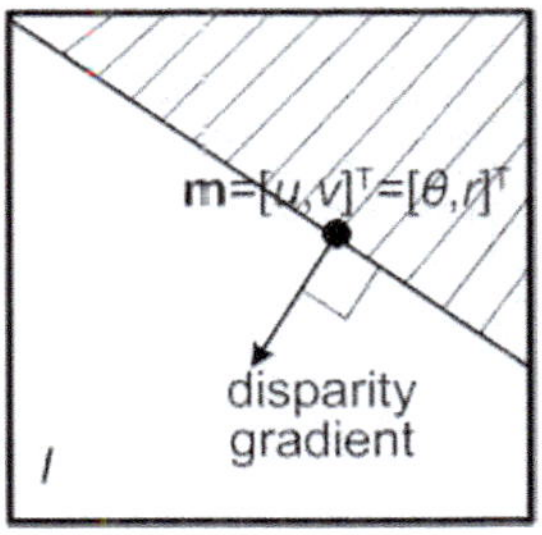

Fig. 2. For preserving the discontinuity of disparity, only those correspondences locating on shadow half-plane, anti-pointing to disparity gradient, are chosen as examples to apply the next iterative EBI

IISM can be considered as the combination of global method and local method. In fact we also incorporate the coarse-to-fine technique [19] in our approach to get more fast and accurate dense matching. In our real process, we use 3 different resolution levels and run 4 times of IISM in each level to get our experimental results.

5 Preserving Discontinuity

EBI is a powerful method for constructing function from examples with minimal oscillations between the example points. Thus at occlusion areas in image, the discontinuity of disparity is generally smoothed by interpolation process, we need develop the EBI to preserve the discontinuity.

Thanks to our iterative approach, we have last iterative result of disparity in hand. In general, the magnitude of disparity gradient has large value at occlusion areas. Along the tangent direction of disparity gradient with large magnitude value is the discontinuity boundary. If we only choose the example points on one side of the discontinuity boundary as final examples to apply EBI, the disparity discontinuity could be preserved.

While given one image point, the disparity gradient and its magnitude are calculated firstly. If the magnitude of disparity gradient on this point is larger than threshold value, this point could be located in occlusion areas. We pay more attentions to this situation and separate the image window to two half-planes along the disparity gradient's tangent direction, then we only choose those corresponding points on the half-plan of anti-pointing the direction of disparity gradient, the shadow area in Fig. 2, as the examples to apply IISM and find the matching point in next round.

6 Experimental Results

We have implemented the proposed algorithm. In this section we present two sets of experimental results on stereo image pairs of *Rocks* and *Map* to illustrate the performance of the EBI-based solution to stereo matching.

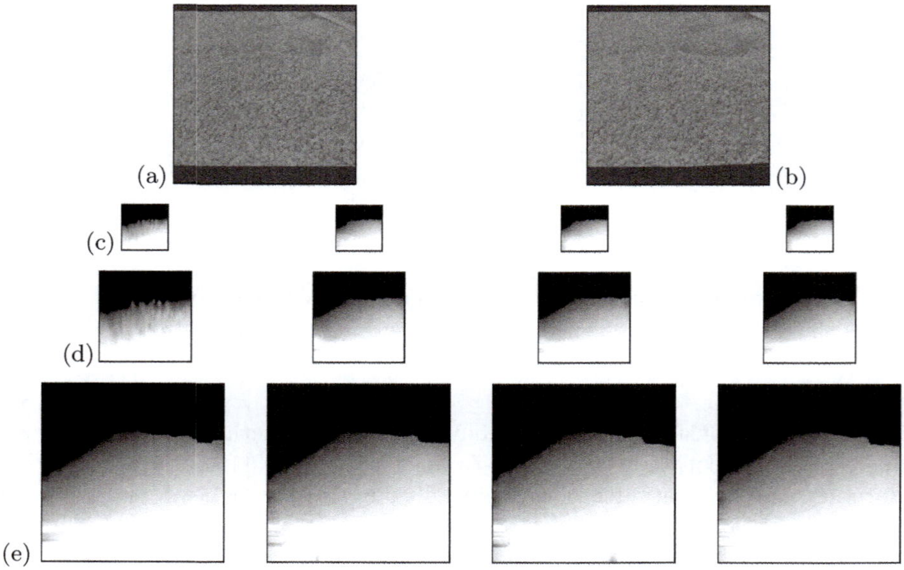

Fig. 3. Experiment on stereo image of *Rocks*. (a) left image. (b) right image; (c) disparity map produced by IISM in smallest resolution; (d) dense disparity map produced by IISM in smaller resolution; (e) dense disparity map produced by IISM in full resolution. The 4 disparity maps from left to right in (c)–(e) are 4 iterative results respectively.

Fig. 3(a)–(b) are the original left and right images of stereo image pair of *Rocks*, which are available at `http://vasc.ri.cmu.edu/idb/html/stereo/`. No considering the discontinuity smoothing problem, here we only use the IISM detailed in Sect. 4 and the algorithm of coarse-to-fine. In coarse-to-fine processing, we use 3 different resolution levels and run 4 iterations in each level. All produced dense disparity maps are shown in Fig. 3(c)–(e). The 4 disparity maps from left to right in Fig. 3(c) are 4 iterative results with 2nd subsampling resolution. Similarly, the 4 ones, from left to right, in Fig. 3(d) and 3(e) are 4 iterative results of dense disparity map with 1st subsampling and full resolution, respectively.

The stereo image pair of *Map*, shown in Fig. 4 (a)–(b), is a widely used benchmarking dataset available at `http://www.middlebury.edu/stereo/`. Fig. 4(c) is the disparity ground truth for the left image. In this experiment, we apply the IISM method plus preserving discontinuity method to produce the dense disparity map.

There are 2 objects in stereo image of *Map*, one is so-called front object and another back object. Seeing from viewpoint at left view of Fig. 4(a), some areas in back object just locating at right side of front object is occluded, but which can be seen from the right view of Fig. 4(b). On the other hand, some areas in back object just locating at left side of front object cannot be seen from right view. Since we are considering the disparity for left image, the dense matching

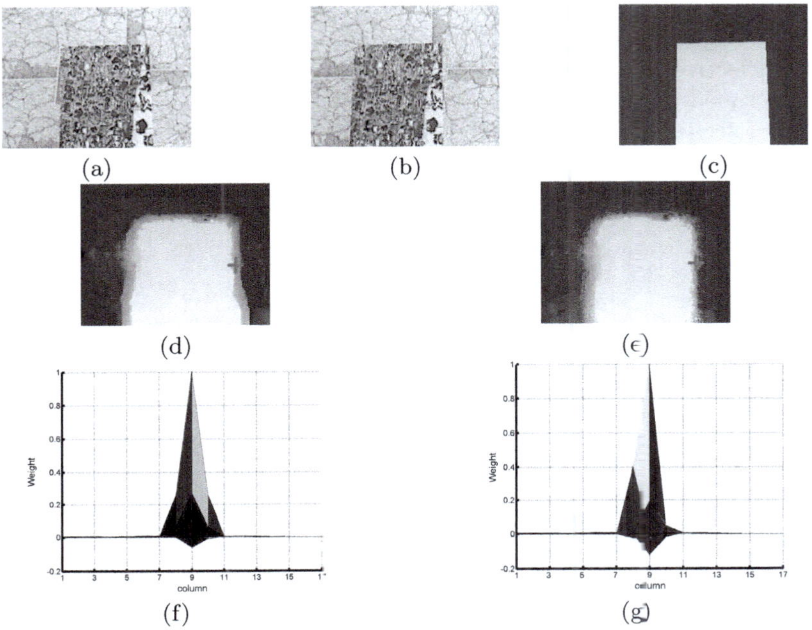

Fig. 4. Experiment on stereo image of *Map*. (a) left image; (b) right image; (c) disparity ground truth for left image; (d) dense disparity map produced by IISM; (e) dense disparity map produced by IISM with preserving discontinuity method; (f) while processing by IISM, side view of symmetrical radial basis function centered on the point marked with a plus in (d) and (e); (g) while processing by IISM with preserving discontinuity method, side view of radial basis function centered on the point marked with a plus in (d) and (e), the function is not symmetrical.

cannot be found correctly in the area where cannot be seen from right view, but can be constructed in the occlusion area in right side of front object so we can only improve the results at occlusion area in this case.

To applying the method discussed in Sect. 5, we adjust our RBFs in EBI algorithm and have the example points only in back object to affect the interpolation results in this discontinuity area. The RBFs are then not symmetrical (see Fig. 4(g)). The produced dense disparity map is shown in Fig. 4(e). Comparing it to the result (see Fig. 4(d)) without using the method of preserving discontinuity, we can see that the occlusion area shrinks very clearly.

7 Conclusion and Future Work

We have described a new interpolation mechanism IISM that could construct dense correspondences in stereo image from sparse initial correspondences. IISM utilizes the refinement technique of coarse-to-fine, iteratively applies the improved EBI algorithm, satisfies the robustly estimated epipolar geometry, preserves to a large extent the discontinuities in the imaged scene, and produces the dense disparity map for stereo image pair. Experimental results show that IISM is effective in producing, even from sparse correspondences, dense disparity. Experimental results also show that the approach could achieve reasonable results for scenes without heavy occlusions.

Future work includes how the approach could be further adapted to address discontinuities explicitly, so as to handle heavy occlusions in the scenes better.

References

1. Barnard, S., Fischler, M.: Computational stereo. ACM Comp. Surveys **14(4)** (1982) 553–572
2. Dhond, U., Aggarwal, J.: Structure from stereo-a review. IEEE Trans. Syst., Man, Cybern **19(6)** (1989) 1489–1510
3. Brown, L.: A survey of image registration techniques. ACM Comp. Surveys **24(4)** (1992) 325–376
4. Jones, G.: Constraint, optimization, and hierarchy: reviewing stereoscopic correspondence of complex features. CVIU **65(1)** (1997) 57–78
5. Scharstein, D., Szeliski, R.: A taxonomy and evaluation of dense two-frame stereo correspondence algorithms. IJCV **47(1/2/3)** (2002) 7–42
6. Zhang, Z., Shan, Y.: A progressive scheme for stereo matching. In: SMILE2000, LNCS2018. (2001) 68–85
7. Poggio, T., Girosi, F.: Networks for approximation and learning. Proc. IEEE **78(9)** (1990) 1481–1497
8. Powell, M.: A review of methods for multivariable interpolation at scattered data points. In Duff, I., Watson, G., eds.: The State of the Art in Numerical Analysis. (1997) 283–309
9. Papageorgiou, C., Poggio, T.: A trainable system for object detection. IJCV **38(1)** (2000) 15–33
10. Rose, C., Cohen, M., Bodenheimer, B.: Verbs and adverbs: multidimensional motion interpolation. IEEE Comput. Graph. Appl. **18(5)** (1998) 32–40
11. Ruprecht, D., Muller, H.: Image warping with scattered data interpolation. IEEE Comput. Graph. Appl. **15(2)** (1995) 37–43
12. Liang, B., Chung, R.: On desirable properties of example-based interpolation. In: Proc. 2003 IEEE Intelligent Automation Conf., Hong Kong, China. (2003) 81–86
13. Faugeras, O., Luong, Q.: The Geometry of Multiple Images. MIT press (2001)
14. Zhang, Z., Deriche, R., Faugeras, O., Luong, Q.: A robust technique for matching two uncalibrated images through the recovery of the unknown epipolar geometry. Artificial Intelligence **78** (1995) 87–119
15. Fischler, M., Bolles, R.: Random sample consensus: a paradigm for model fitting with applications to image analysis and automated cartography. Communications of the ACM **24(6)** (1981) 381–395
16. Zhang, Z.: Determining the epipolar geometry and its uncertainty: a review. IJCV **27(2)** (1998) 161–195
17. Longuet-Higgins, H.: A computer algorithm for reconstructing a scene from two projections. Nature **293(5828)** (1981) 133–135
18. Hartley, R.: In defence of the 8-point algorithm. In: ICCV. (1995) 1064–1070
19. Bergen, J., Anandan, P., Hanna, K., Hingorani, R.: Hierarchical model-based motion estimation. In: ECCV. (1992) 237–252

Novel View Synthesis Using Locally Adaptive Depth Regularization*

Hitesh Shah and Subhasis Chaudhuri

Department of Electrical Engineering,
Indian Institute of Technology, Bombay Powai, Mumbai 400 076, India
{hitesh, sc}@ee.iitb.ac.in

Abstract. In this paper we attempt to solve the problem of synthesizing a novel view corresponding to a virtual camera given the scene description in the form of images captured from other view points. We project each line of sight emerging from the virtual camera on each of the given views, align them geometrically and assign a color that is photo consistent as per the radiance model. This being ill-conditioned, a smooth variation of depth in the scene is utilized as the regularizing constraint. It leads to development of an algorithm which is computationally fast and generates visually realistic images with negligible artifacts even with a limited number of input views. The proposed approach puts no restriction on the view points from which the input images are captured.

1 Introduction

In past decade there has been a major research interest in developing methods that will allow three-dimensional graphical interaction with objects and scenes whose original specification began as images or photographs, unlike traditional polygonal models. Novel view synthesis describes this class of techniques. Such methods would lend themselves readily to applications like virtual reality, scientific visualization, computer games and special effects for films.

Present novel view synthesis techniques can be classified into three categories [1] according to their dependence on amount of geometric information used.

- **Rendering with explicit geometry:** Bill boards, view-dependent texture mapping [2], 3D warping, layered depth image, etc.
- **Rendering with implicit geometry:** View interpolation, view morphing [3], etc.
- **Rendering with no geometry:** Plenoptic modeling [4], light field [5], lumigraph [6], concentric mosaics [7], image mosaics [8], etc.

Most of the techniques in the last category are based on sampling and reconstruction of the plenoptic function [9]. Performance of these techniques, in general, is limited by the fact that they fail to exploit the inherent structure of the scene as they view it purely as a function reconstruction problem. On the

* Funded under the *Swarnajayanti Project* of DST.

P.J. Narayanan et al. (Eds.): ACCV 2006, LNCS 3851, pp. 449–459, 2006.

other hand rendering with explicit geometry requires extraction of the geometry of the scene which is still a challenging research problem. The use of scene geometry implicitly tries to combine the advantages of both of these techniques, albeit it invites additional problems like incompatibility with currently available graphics processing hardware making it computationally demanding.

Our approach can be put in the category of rendering with implicit geometry. The precursor to it are Irani *et al.*[10] and Fitzgibbon *et al.*[11]. Fitzgibbon *et al.* use local texture statistic to regularize the solution. This requires performing a combinatorial optimization for solving the labeling problem which makes their approach computationally expensive. We utilize the concept of smooth variation in depth in a small neighborhood of the scene to regularize the solution. Use of this locally adaptive depth regularization helps in limiting the search space which leads to reduction in the rendering time, making our approach very efficient compared to that of Fitzgibbon *et al.* Our approach generates comparable result with a fewer number of input images. It can be adapted for different radiance models allowing it to target a wide variety of scenes. Proposed approach does have some resemblance with that of ray tracing in computer graphics making it possible to utilize the current graphics processing hardware to improve the performance.

2 Problem Formulation and Assumptions

A set of n 2D images $I_1, ..., I_n$ are given along with the corresponding 3x4 projection matrix $P_1, ..., P_n$ [12]. The internal and external camera parameters which characterize the novel view to be rendered are provided by specifying the projection matrix P_{nv} for it. The minimum and the maximum depth, Z_{min} and Z_{max}, of the scene with respect to the image plane of the novel view are approximately known. Currently a scene with diffuse and opaque objects is addressed.

The input requirement of the projection matrix, maximum and minimum depth are not very restrictive. Recent advances in computer vision have made it possible to estimate various camera parameters from the images themselves [12]. Moreover, only rough estimates for Z_{min} and Z_{max} are needed as we use them primarily only to cut down the initial search space. As the rendering process progresses they are adaptively adjusted by the algorithm.

3 Proposed Approach

The motivation for the present approach lies in the fact that the color visible at a particular image point is the color of the first physical point in the scene which is on the line of sight emerging from the camera center through the image point. Figure 1(a) illustrates a typical scene, input views, a novel view and the line of sight. To decide on the color at the point $\mathbf{x}$ in the novel view we back project it to obtain line of sight in the scene. Projections of this line of sight on given input images are extracted, geometrically aligned and stacked such that the projections of a given point on the line of sight are all in the same column as shown in figure

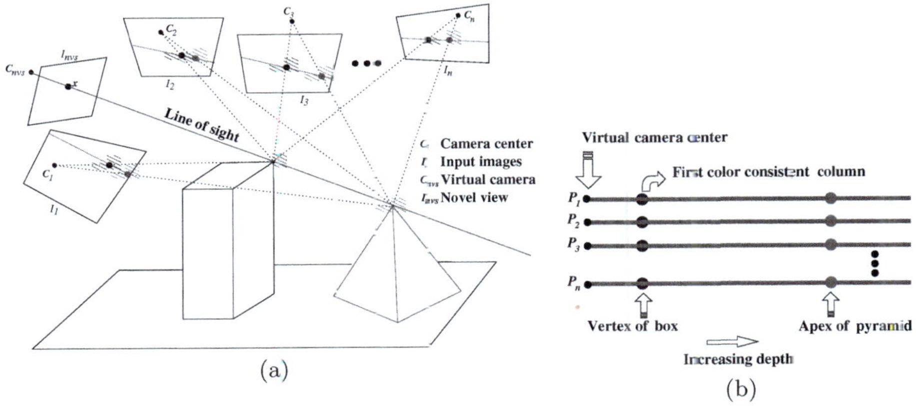

Fig. 1. Overview of the proposed approach. (a) Illustrative example of a scene. (b) P_i is geometrically aligned projection of the line of sight from image I_i.

1(b). Columns corresponding to the physical points, which are not obstructed in any of the input views, on the line of sight will satisfy the radiance model. The first such column that is encountered as we move away from the virtual camera center is used to calculate the new color using the radiance model.

Given an image I and its projection matrix P, a homogeneous 3D point $\mathbf{X}$ in the space can be projected on the image point $\mathbf{x}$, where $\mathbf{x} = P\mathbf{X}$. $I(\mathbf{x})$ denotes the pixel in the image to which the world point $\mathbf{X}$ projects.

$$I(\mathbf{x}) = I(\pi(P\mathbf{X})), \quad \pi(x, y, \omega) = (x/\omega, y/\omega). \tag{1}$$

Let I_{nv} denotes the novel image to be synthesized and P_{nv} is its projection matrix. To decide on the color of $I_{nv}(\mathbf{x})$ we need to determine the set of all points in the space that map to this point. This set will constitute a ray in the space passing through the camera center and the pixel location on the image plane. To obtain this ray we split up the projection matrix as $P_{nv} = [M|p_4]$, where M is a 3x3 matrix containing the first 3 columns of the P_{nv} and p_4 is the last column of it. Two end points of this ray, the camera center, are given by $-M^{-1}p_4$ and, the point of intersection of the back projected ray and the plane at infinity, by the point $((M^{-1}\mathbf{x})^T, 0)^T$. Hence the points along this ray are given by $\mathbf{X}(z)$, where z varies such that the points are confined from Z_{min} to Z_{max}.

$$\mathbf{X}(z) = z\begin{pmatrix} M^{-1}\mathbf{x} \\ 0 \end{pmatrix} + \begin{pmatrix} -M^{-1}p_4 \\ 1 \end{pmatrix}. \tag{2}$$

To decide on which color to select we need to find a point on this ray that satisfies the radiance model. For this we define photo consistency and its measure at a point.

Photo consistent point: A point P is photo consistent if the color set obtained by projecting the point on each of the available images is consistent with the radiance model for the surface on which P occurs.

Error measure for photo consistency at a point: It is an increasing, non-negative function which is representative of deviation of the point from being photo consistent for a given radiance model. A smaller value reflects a better match between the observed color set and the predicted color set using the radiance model.

Let $\mathbf{X}(z)$ be a point on the line of sight at a depth z as obtained by equation (2). The color of pixel in the ith image where this point projects is

$$C(i,z) = I_i(\pi(P_i\mathbf{X}(z))). \tag{3}$$

The set of colors of pixels on which the point $\mathbf{X}(z)$ projects is given as

$$C(:,z) = \{C(i,z)\}_{i=0}^{n}. \tag{4}$$

We calculate this set at a regular interval between Z_{min} and Z_{max}. Let $\mathbf{C}$ denote the collection of all such sets for a given point $\mathbf{x}$ in the I_{nv}

$$\mathbf{C} = \{C(i,z)|1 \leq i \leq n, Z_{min} < z < Z_{max}\}. \tag{5}$$

This collection $\mathbf{C}$ is now analyzed to locate the photo consistent point. For each depth z we take the color set and evaluate the error measure of photo consistency

$$Err[z] = PhotoConsistencyErr(C(:,z)). \tag{6}$$

The points where such an error measure is below a threshold Θ form a set $\mathbf{S}$ of feasible points that are likely to be the physical points on the line of sight.

$$\mathbf{S} = \{\mathbf{X}(z)|Err[z] \leq \Theta, Z_{min} < z < Z_{max}\}. \tag{7}$$

This set of points $\mathbf{S}$ will contain possibly a few points corresponding to the actual physical points on the line of sight and a few others on account of noise and occlusion in input images, and errors in the projection matrix. We need to select a point which is most likely to be the first physical point on the line of sight from the set $\mathbf{S}$.

Novel view synthesis is a poorly conditioned problem and to obtain a fairly good solution we need to regularize it. We use a smooth variation in depth as the regularizing constraint. A point, P_{phy}, from $\mathbf{S}$ which satisfies the above constraint is selected to calculate the color for the point in novel view. To prevent over smoothening due the above constraint, a check that the error measure at P_{phy} is in a small neighborhood of the error measure at the neighboring points is also done. Thus we have

$$P_{phy} = \mathbf{X}(z^*). \tag{8}$$

such that z^* satisfies following constraints.

$$(z_{nb} - \Delta z \leq z^* \leq z_{nb} + \Delta z) \& (Err[z_{nb}] - \Delta E \leq Err[z^*] \leq Err[z_{nb}] + \Delta E) \tag{9}$$

where z_{nb} is the depth value where the photo consistent point for neighbor of $\mathbf{x}$ was obtained and $Err[z_{nb}]$ is the measure of error in the photo consistency at this point. If there is no point in $\mathbf{S}$ that satisfy both the constraints then point which is nearest to the image plane from it is selected as P_{phy}.

After P_{phy} is calculated we need to decide on the color to be filled at the pixel. For this we use the color set $C(:, z^*)$ and the radiance model to predict the color that is visible along the direction of the line of sight. This color is assigned to the point $\mathbf{x}$ in the I_{nv}. The above procedure is repeated for each image location in I_{nv} to generate the entire image. But the search space in the depth is reduced by constraining the search to lie within the range $[z^* - \Delta z, z^* + \Delta z]$ where z^* is the depth at the previously rendered point and Δz is a suitably chosen measure of possible local variation in depth. In case equation (9) is not satisfied for the chosen range due to occlusion or disocclusion, the range is relaxed to $[Z_{min}, Z_{max}]$ to prevent any possible propagation of error, still maintaining the advantages of an adaptive search.

4 Implementation

The implementation of the algorithm is as given below.

INPUT:
Input Images I_i, where $i = 1, ..., n$.
Projection matrices P_i, where $i = 1, ..., n$.
Projection matrix of the novel view P_{nv}.
Minimum and maximum depths: Z_{max} and Z_{min}.
OUTPUT:
Image as seen from the novel view I_{nv}.
BEGIN:
$minz = Z_{min}$; $maxz = Z_{max}$; $numofstep = Fullstep$;
For all pixel $\mathbf{x}$ in the image I_{nv}
Calculate the set of points in space that project to P,
between $minz$ and $maxz$ as per $numofstep$
For all Point $\mathbf{X}(z)$ in the set
$C(i, z) = I_i(\pi(P_i\mathbf{X}(z)))$; Project point on each image
$C(:, z) = \{C(i, z)\}_{i=0}^{n}$; Calculate the set of color
Calculate the error in photo consistency
$Err[z] = PhotoConsistencyErr(C(:, z))$
End For
$minErr = minimum(Err[:])$
Set threshold
$\Theta = Fraction * minErr$
Calculate set of plausible points
$\mathbf{S} = \{\mathbf{X}(z) | Err[z] \leq \Theta, Z_{min} < z < Z_{max}\}$
Calculate z^* satisfying the constraint (9)
Estimate color for current pixel

$I_{nv}(\mathbf{x}) = filter(C(:, z^*))$
Readjust parameters $minz$ & $maxz$
$minz = z^* - \Delta z$
$maxz = z^* + \Delta z$
$numofstep = Reducestep$
End For

For the current implementation we have addressed a scene having diffuse and opaque objects. Hence a point on surface of any object will have the same color in each of the image, where it is visible. So we have used variance of the color set $C(:, z)$ as the error measure for photo consistency. The threshold Θ is obtained by scaling the minimum value of error measure by a fraction greater than unity. In our case we found the value of 1.6 for the $fraction$ to give good result.

Ideally, all colors in the set $C(:, z^*)$ should be same but due to noise and round off errors during quantization both in intensity domain and spatial domain while digitizing the images, this may not hold true. Function $filter(\,)$ is used to estimate the most likely color from the color set. We have tested mean filtering, mode filtering, median filtering for this. Visual quality of the result obtained using median filtering surpasses that of the others.

At each pixel location initially the search for the photo consistent point is restricted to the small length of the line of sight around which the neighboring pixels photo consistent point was found. This small length is divided into less number of steps *Reducestep*. Only when the search fails to find a plausible point in this small length then exhaustive search for such a point is carried out along the entire length of line of sight with more number of steps $Fullstep$. This strategy helps in reducing the computation as for most of the pixel the photo consistent point is obtained in the initial restricted search itself.

5 Experimental Results

The image sequence and the camera projection matrices used to test the algorithm were the same as used by [11] and were downloaded from *http://www.robots.ox.ac.uk/~awf/ibr*. They have been captured using a hand held camera and calibrated using a commercially available camera tracking software developed by 2d3 Ltd. The images were converted to 8-bit monochrome images for testing. A few of the images from the sequence are shown in figure 2.

For testing we select a sample of 8 images and render an image (serves as a ground truth) from it using other 7 images. The results of the test are shown in figure 3 and figure 4. Figure 3(a) shows the ground truth and figure 3(b) shows the corresponding rendered image using the proposed approach. Visually, the rendered image is a good reproduction of the ground truth. The difference between the ground truth and the rendered image is shown in the figure 3(c). The errors are quite insignificant and, as expected, are concentrated near the depth discontinuities. The white areas in figure 3(d) show where the search in the neighborhood of the previous pixel's location has sufficed to obtain the

Fig. 2. Examples of some of the input images taken from [11]

photo consistent point. It can be seen from the image that the exhaustive search is required only in a few cases (dark points) where there is a discontinuity in depth. Since most of the pixels need only a local search, the performance of the

(a) Ground truth

(b) Rendered image

(c) Difference image

(d) Locality of computation

Fig. 3. Results of an experimentation

(a) Ground truth (b) Rendered image (c) Ground truth (d) Rendered image

Fig. 4. Results of experiments for two other views

algorithm is improved. Figure 4 displays the ground truths and the rendered images for a couple of other views.

Figure 5(b) shows the error in photo consistency as a function of varying depth for three neighboring pixel in the rendered image shown in figure 5(a). Observe that error functions exhibit very similar behavior in all the three cases. The surface is almost smooth and equidistant from the camera center hence the minima in each case occur in the same neighborhood of depth. This supports our contention that depth can be used locally as the regularization parameter.

The piecewise smooth nature of the functions shown in figure 5(b) is attributed to the fact that the line of sight is over sampled by taking $Fullstep = 2000$. This brings to notice that for large, fixed number of sampling of the line of sight there will be a lot of redundant computation as many of the adjacent points on the line of sight will project onto the same pixels in each of the images. Such a redundancy will lead to a computationally expensive implementation. The maximum number of steps for any line of sight can be bounded by the maxi-

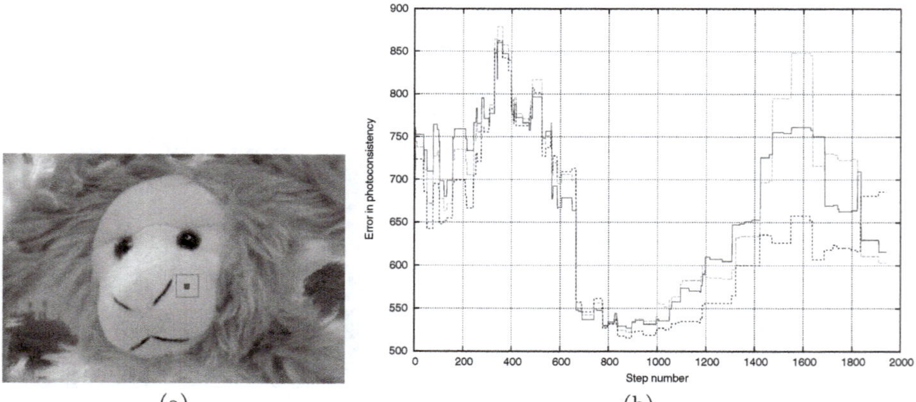

(a) (b)

Fig. 5. Illustration of the usefulness of local depth constraint. (a) Selection of three neighboring pixels. (b) Error in photo consistency of the points on the line of sight, of the pixels shown at the highlighted region in (a).

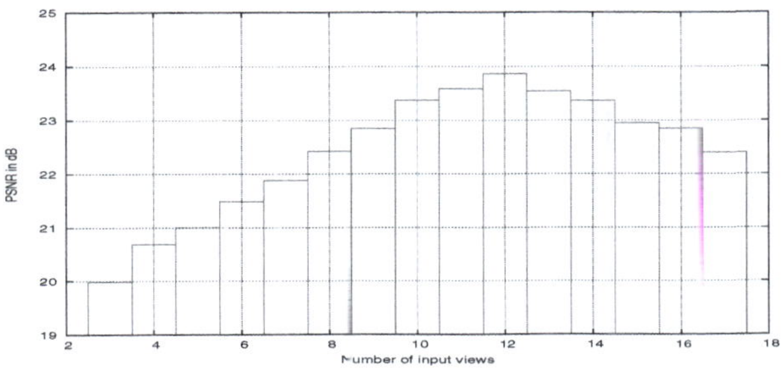

Fig. 6. PSNR as a function of number of input images while rendering

mum number of pixel along the diagonal in the input images, assuming same magnification in all input images. But this bound will be a very loose one for majority of line of sights as it accounts for the case in which the projection of line of sight will extend to the entire diagonal of one of the input images. This is very unlikely to occur. A better strategy would be to calculate the number of steps for each pixel by projecting the end points of the part of line of sight to be searched in each of the image. The optimal number of step will be given by the maximum number of pixels occurring on the line joining the two projected endpoints, among all input images. Such an adaptive approach to determine the number of steps leads to a computationally fast implementation.

The algorithm was implemented in C and tested on Fedora core 3 release 2.6.9 system having a Intel Pentium IV 3.00 GHz CPU and 256 MB RAM. Rendering of the image in figure 3(b) of the size 490 x 490 pixels was done with *Fullstep* = 75 and *Reducestep* = 10 in 10.132 sec.

Figure 6 shows the peak signal to noise ratio (PSNR) in the rendered image as a function of number of input images and figure 7 shows a few rendered images with different number of input images. Observe, performance of the algorithm degrades gracefully as the number of available images decreases. This is an important merit for practical systems. It can be ascertained visually from figure 7(b) that even with 7 images the algorithm performs well. The decrease in the PSNR as the number of images increases beyond 12 is because the new

(a) 4 input views (b) 7 input views (c) 12 input views (d) 17 input views

Fig. 7. Rendering results with varying number of input views

views added had relatively large deviations in camera directions and the distance between camera center with that of the novel view, thus increasing the occlusion.

In the presented approach when the input images are constrained to have an identical focal length and co-planar image planes, a scenario similar to that of light field [5] occurs. Conventional light field rendering assumes a constant depth for the entire scene. This leads to aliasing for the large depth of scene [13]. In the above approach constant depth assumption is not made for rendering. In fact the depth information is estimated implicitly and used for rendering thus counteracting the aliasing artifact. Lumigraph [6] performs depth correction of rays to reduce the effect of aliasing. For this it requires a rough geometric model of the object. In the present approach no such geometric model is needed.

6 Conclusion

We have proposed a computationally fast and accurate novel view synthesis technique. Our approach utilizes the constraint of smooth variation in depth for regularization. This also helps in limiting the search space, thus improving the performance. Such a locally adaptive search has the possibility of error propagation. But in our case, as exhaustive search was done initially and the photo consistency measure in the locality was also considered, such error propagation was not experienced in the results. Even though in this paper a Lambertian radiance model is considered for the objects in the scene during the development of the algorithm it is possible to extend our approach to other radiance model. We have applied our algorithm to the set of real-life images and the visual fidelity of the synthesized novel views is satisfactory.

References

1. Shum, H., Kang, S.B.: Review of image-based rendering techniques. Volume 4067., SPIE (2000) 2–13
2. Debevec, P.E., Taylor, C.J., Malik, J.: Modeling and rendering architecture from photographs: A hybrid geometry- and image-based approach. Computer Graphics **30** (1996) 11–20
3. Seitz, S.M., Dyer, C.R.: View morphing. In: SIGGRAPH '96: Proceedings of the 23rd annual conference on Computer graphics and interactive techniques, New York, NY, USA, ACM Press (1996) 21–30
4. McMillan, L., Bishop, G.: Plenoptic modeling: An image-based rendering system. Computer Graphics **29** (1995) 39–46
5. Levoy, M., Hanrahan, P.: Light field rendering. In: SIGGRAPH '96: Proceedings of the 23rd annual conference on Computer graphics and interactive techniques, New York, NY, USA, ACM Press (1996) 31–42
6. Gortler, S.J., Grzeszczuk, R., Szeliski, R., Cohen, M.F.: The lumigraph. Computer Graphics **30** (1996) 43–54
7. Shum, H.Y., He, L.W.: Rendering with concentric mosaics. Computer Graphics **33** (1999) 299–306
8. Chen, S.E.: QuickTime VR — an image-based approach to virtual environment navigation. Computer Graphics **29** (1995) 29–38

9. Adelson, E.H., Bergen, J.R.: The plenoptic function and the elements of early vision. M. Landy and J. A. Movshon, (eds) *Computational Models of Visual Processing* (1991)
10. Irani, M., Hassner, T., Anandan, P.: What does the scene look like from a scene point? In: ECCV '02, London, UK, Springer-Verlag (2002) 883–897
11. Fitzgibbon, A., Wexler, Y., Zisserman, A.: Image-based rendering using image-based priors. In: ICCV '03, Washington, DC, USA, IEEE Computer Society (2003) 1176
12. Hartley, R., Zisserman, A.: Multiple view geometry in computer vision Cambridge University Press, New York, NY, USA (2000)
13. Chai, J.X., Chan, S.C., Shum, H.Y., Tong, X.: Plenoptic sampling. In: SIGGRAPH '00: Proceedings of the 27th annual conference on Computer graphics and interactive techniques, New York, NY, USA, ACM Press (2000) 307–318

View Synthesis of Scenes with Multiple Independently Translating Objects from Uncalibrated Views

Geetika Sharma[1], Santanu Chaudhury[2], and J.B. Srivastava[1]

[1] Department of Mathematics
geetikas@gmail.com, jbsrivas@maths.iitd.ernet.in
[2] Department of Electrical Engineering, Indian Institute of Technology, Delhi Hauz Khas, New Delhi-110016, India
santanuc@ee.iitd.ernet.in

Abstract. We propose a technique for view synthesis of scenes with static objects as well as objects that translate independent of the camera motion. Assuming the availability of three vanishing points in general position in the given views, we set up an affine coordinate system in which the static and moving points are reconstructed and the translations of the dynamic objects are recovered. We then describe how to synthesize new views corresponding to a completely new camera specified in the affine space with new translations for the dynamic objects. As the extent of the synthesized scene is restricted by the availability of corresponding points, we use a voxel-based volumetric scene reconstruction scheme to obtain a scene model and synthesize views of the entire scene. We present experimental results to validate our technique.

1 Introduction

In this work we have addressed the problem of view synthesis of a scene containing multiple independently translating objects from views taken by arbitrary and uncalibrated cameras. This problem is different from the well researched structure from motion problem in that the camera *as well as* some objects in the scene are in motion. The motion of the objects is independent of that of the camera and we assume, in particular, that while the camera can undergo rotation as well as translation, the objects undergo translational motion only. Our technique does not require that the internal parameters of the camera remain fixed. We also describe a method to synthesize new views corresponding to a completely new camera with novel translations for the dynamic objects.

We require that there be some static objects in the scene which provide three vanishing points in general position. The vanishing points along with a static scene point are used to set up a world coordinate system. Assuming the correspondence of points on the static objects and the translating objects, we provide a technique for recovering the affine structure of static points as well as points on moving objects and their translations in this coordinate system. We also describe a technique to specify a new camera in the affine space different from

P.J. Narayanan et al. (Eds.): ACCV 2006, LNCS 3851, pp. 460–469, 2006.

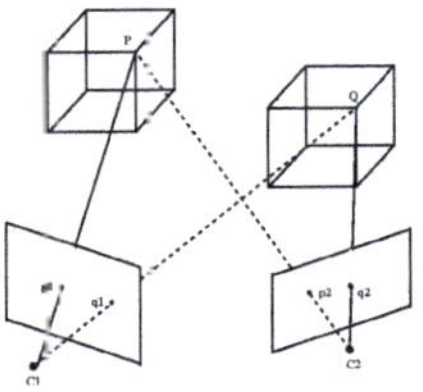

Fig. 1. The two instances of an object translating in time may be considered as two separate objects in a static scene

those of the given views and a method to synthesize new views of the scene with interactively chosen translations for the dynamic objects. Our technique also works with multiple views of the scene in which the motion of the dynamic objects need not be uniform.

As only points with known correspondence can be reconstructed, only the images of such points can be computed in the new views. While triangulation followed by texture mapping may be used to synthesize a large part of the scene, the given images contain more information about the scene which is left unexploited because of the lack of correspondences. To overcome this problem, we propose using a volumetric scene reconstruction algorithm to obtain a voxel-based model of the scene. Our approach is based upon the technique proposed in [1]. Although this technique requires calibrated cameras, we show that it can be used with an affine reconstruction without fully calibrating the camera. We also propose a new geometry-based photo-consistency computation technique.

For reconstructing dynamic objects we consider the two instances of a moving object in time as two different static objects in the scene. As shown in figure 1, the two objects have two projections in the given images - a true projection of the object in its actual position and a virtual projection of the object in its other position. Since all objects are now static, a single fundamental matrix suffices, contrary to the treatment in [2]. The epipolar constraints involving the true and the virtual projections act as additional constraints, linear in the structure and motion of the objects.

In [3] and [4] Homography Tensors are used for view synthesis of dynamic points. However, the motion of dynamic points is confined to the same planar straight line path across all given views, while our scheme can handle a change in the direction of translation in 3D space. In [5], the problem of reconstruction of a point moving on a straight line or conic-shaped path has been addressed. They assume the camera matrices to be known and require at least five views of points with straight line trajectories and nine views of points with conic-shaped trajectories. We do not assume knowledge of the camera matrices and can reconstruct the points even with two views. In [6], an analysis of the constraints imposed by moving objects on the calibration parameters of the camera is presented. While their aim is obtain a metric reconstruction, most of the constraints are nonlinear and require nonlinear optimization techniques to be solved. In [7], a method for reconstruction of scenes with multiple objects moving linearly with constant velocities. While knowledge of internal camera parameters is not required, the work focuses on varying focal lengths with all other internal parameters known. Although we work with an affine reconstruction, the motion need not be constant and linear. Work on view synthesis of static scenes includes [8] and [9].

The paper is organised as follows. In section 2 we describe the affine reconstruction, view-synthesis scheme and experimental results in section 3. The volumetric reconstruction technique is described in section 4. We conclude in section 5.

2 Synthesis from Two Views

We start with two views I_1 and I_2 of a scene containing some static objects and a single object in translational motion. The case for multiple translating objects will be discussed later. We assume that correspondences on the static and moving objects can be obtained from the two images.

2.1 Relating the Two Views

Without any loss of generality, we may choose one of the static scene points with known correspondence, $\mathbf{p_0^1}$ and $\mathbf{p_0^2}$, in I_1 and I_2, respectively, as the world origin. Let $\mathbf{v_1^1}, \mathbf{v_2^1}$ and $\mathbf{v_3^1}$ be three vanishing points in I_1 obtained by intersecting parallel lines in the static part of the world. Then, we may choose the directions of the world axes in the scene directions corresponding to $\mathbf{v_1^1}, \mathbf{v_2^1}$ and $\mathbf{v_3^1}$.

With this choice of coordinate system, the camera matrix for I_1 becomes $M_1 = [\alpha\mathbf{v_1^1}\ \beta\mathbf{v_2^1}\ \gamma\mathbf{v_3^1}\ \mathbf{p_0^1}]$, where α, β and γ are unknown scale factors. If $\mathbf{v_1^2}, \mathbf{v_2^2}$ and $\mathbf{v_3^2}$ are the corresponding vanishing points in I_2, the second camera matrix may be written as $M_2 = [\alpha'\mathbf{v_1^2}\ \beta'\mathbf{v_2^2}\ \gamma'\mathbf{v_3^2}\ \delta'\mathbf{p_0^2}]$. Next we derive a relation between the parameters α, α' and δ', β, β' and δ' and γ, γ' and δ'.

Let $\mathbf{X} = (X, 0, 0, 1)^T$ be a point on the world X axis. Let $\mathbf{x^1}$ and $\mathbf{x^2}$ be the images of $\mathbf{X}$ in the two images respectively. Then,

$$\begin{aligned} \lambda_1\mathbf{x^1} &= \alpha\mathbf{v_1^1}X + \mathbf{p_0^1} \\ \Rightarrow (\lambda_1\mathbf{x^1}) \times \mathbf{x^1} &= \alpha X(\mathbf{v_1^1} \times \mathbf{x^1}) + (\mathbf{p_0^1} \times \mathbf{x^1}) = 0 \\ \Rightarrow \alpha X &= -\frac{||\mathbf{p_0^1} \times \mathbf{x^1}||}{||\mathbf{v_1^1} \times \mathbf{x^1}||} \end{aligned} \tag{1}$$

Similarly, from the second view,

$$\frac{\alpha'}{\delta'}X = -\frac{||\mathbf{p_0^2} \times \mathbf{x^2}||}{||\mathbf{v_1^2} \times \mathbf{x^2}||} \tag{2}$$

Dividing (2) by (1), we get,

$$\frac{\alpha'}{\alpha\delta'} = \frac{||\mathbf{p_0^2} \times \mathbf{x^2}||\,||\mathbf{v_1^1} \times \mathbf{x^1}||}{||\mathbf{p_0^1} \times \mathbf{x^1}||\,||\mathbf{v_1^2} \times \mathbf{x^2}||} \quad \Rightarrow \alpha' = C_1\alpha\delta'$$

where $C_1 = \frac{||\mathbf{p_0^2} \times \mathbf{x^2}|| \, ||\mathbf{v_1^1} \times \mathbf{x^1}||}{||\mathbf{p_0^1} \times \mathbf{x^1}|| \, ||\mathbf{v_1^2} \times \mathbf{x^2}||}$. Similarly, choosing $\mathbf{Y} = (0, Y, 0, 1)^T$ on the world Y axis and $\mathbf{Z} = (0, 0, Z, 1)$ on the world Z axis, we get $\beta' = C_2 \beta \delta', \quad \gamma' = C_3 \gamma \delta'$ where, $C_2 = \frac{||\mathbf{p_0^2} \times \mathbf{y^2}|| \, ||\mathbf{v_2^1} \times \mathbf{y^1}||}{||\mathbf{p_0^1} \times \mathbf{y^1}|| \, ||\mathbf{v_2^2} \times \mathbf{y^2}||}$ and $C_3 = \frac{||\mathbf{p_0^2} \times \mathbf{z^2}|| \, ||\mathbf{v_3^1} \times \mathbf{z^1}||}{||\mathbf{p_0^1} \times \mathbf{z^1}|| \, ||\mathbf{v_3^2} \times \mathbf{z^2}||}$.

To be able to compute the constants C_i, $i = 1, 2, 3$, we need the correspondences of the points $\mathbf{X}$, $\mathbf{Y}$ and $\mathbf{Z}$. We describe here how to compute $\mathbf{x^1}$ and $\mathbf{x^2}$; correspondences $\mathbf{y^1}$, $\mathbf{y^2}$ and $\mathbf{z^1}$, $\mathbf{z^2}$ can be computed in a similar manner. The image of the world X axis in the first view is the line through $\mathbf{p_0^1}$, the image of the origin and $\mathbf{v_1^1}$, the vanishing point in the X direction. So, $\mathbf{x^1}$ may be chosen to be any point on this line. The corresponding point $\mathbf{x^2}$ will lie on the epipolar line, $\mathbf{l_x^2}$, of $\mathbf{x^1}$. $\mathbf{l_x^2}$ can be computed from the fundamental matrix, F_{12}, from the first to the second view. Also, $\mathbf{x^2}$ must lie on the image of the X axis in the second view, which is the line through $\mathbf{p_0^2}$ and $\mathbf{v_1^2}$. Thus, $\mathbf{x^2}$ is the intersection of $\mathbf{l_x^2}$ and the image of the X axis in the second view. So, the required correspondences can be computed and the constants C_i, $i = 1, 2, 3$ can be determined. The camera matrix M_2 may then be parametrised as $M_2 = \delta'[C_1 \alpha \mathbf{v_1^2} \; C_2 \beta \mathbf{v_2^2} \; C_3 \gamma \mathbf{v_3^2} \; \mathbf{p_0^2}]$.

2.2 Obtaining Structure

We now describe how to obtain the structure of the static and dynamic points in the scene and the translation of the dynamic points.

Let $\mathbf{P}$ be a point on the translating object. Assume that $\mathbf{P} = (X, Y, Z)^T$ when the first image is taken, and moves to $\mathbf{Q} = \mathbf{P} + \mathbf{t}$, $\mathbf{t} = (t_x, t_y, t_z)^T$ when the second image is taken. Let $\mathbf{p^1}$ be the image of $\mathbf{P}$ in the first view I_1 and $\mathbf{q^2}$ be the image of $\mathbf{Q}$ in the second view I_2. Then, projecting $\mathbf{P}$ to I_1 using M_1 and $\mathbf{Q}$ to I_2 using M_2, we get

$$\lambda^1 \mathbf{p^1} = \mathbf{v_1^1}(\alpha X) + \mathbf{v_2^1}(\beta Y) + \mathbf{v_3^1}(\gamma Z) + \mathbf{p_0^1} \tag{3}$$

$$\frac{\mu^2}{\delta'} \mathbf{q^2} = C_1 \mathbf{v_1^2}(\alpha X + \alpha t_x) + C_2 \mathbf{v_2^2}(\beta Y + \beta t_y) + C_3 \mathbf{v_3^2}(\gamma Z + \gamma t_z) + \mathbf{p_0^2} \tag{4}$$

where, λ^1 and μ^2 are scale factors required to have equality instead of projective equivalence in equations (3) and (4). Let $\mathbf{p^2}$ be the virtual image of the point $\mathbf{P}$ in I_2. Then,

$$\frac{\lambda^2}{\delta'} \mathbf{p^2} = C_1 \mathbf{v_1^2}(\alpha X) + C_2 \mathbf{v_2^2}(\beta Y) + C_3 \mathbf{v_3^2}(\gamma Z) + \mathbf{p_0^2}$$

Also, since $\mathbf{p^1}$ and $\mathbf{p^2}$ are corresponding points, $\mathbf{p^2}$ must lie on the epipolar line $\mathbf{l^2} = (l_x^2, l_y^2, l_z^2)$ of $\mathbf{p^1}$ in I_2. So, we must have $\mathbf{l^2}^T \mathbf{p^2} = 0$, which implies

$$\mathbf{l^2}^T \{C_1 \mathbf{v_1^2}(\alpha X) + C_2 \mathbf{v_2^2}(\beta Y) + C_3 \mathbf{v_3^2}(\gamma Z) + \delta \mathbf{p_0^2}\} = 0 \tag{5}$$

Similarly, if $\mathbf{q^1}$ is the virtual image of the point $\mathbf{Q}$ in I_1 and $\mathbf{l^1}$ is the epipolar line in I_1 corresponding to $\mathbf{q^2}$, then $\mathbf{l^1}^T \mathbf{q^1} = 0$ and

$$\mu^1 \mathbf{q^1} = \mathbf{v_1^1} \alpha (X + t_x) + \mathbf{v_2^1} \beta (Y + t_y) + \mathbf{v_3^1} \gamma (Z + t_z) + \mathbf{p_0^1}$$

$$\Rightarrow \mathbf{l^1}^T \{\mathbf{v_1^1} \alpha (X + t_x) + \mathbf{v_2^1} \beta (Y + t_y) + \mathbf{v_3^1} \gamma (Z + t_z) - \mathbf{p_0^1}\} = 0 \tag{6}$$

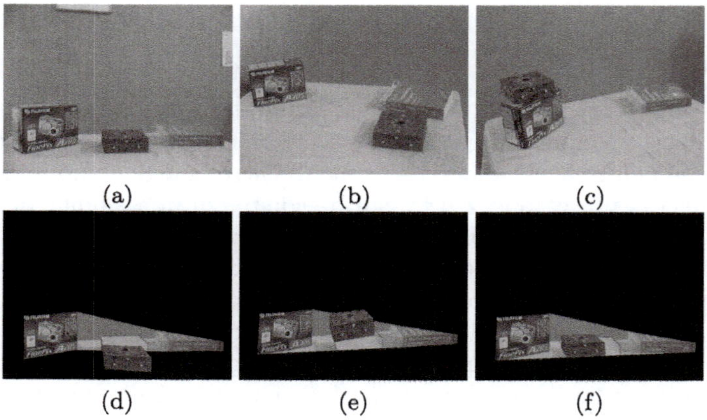

Fig. 2. (a), (b) and (c) are three input images of an indoor scene with a single translating object. (d)-(f) are the synthesized views.

Once $\mathbf{l^1}$ and $\mathbf{l^2}$ are obtained from the fundamental matrix between the two views, we get additional constraints on the structure. Equations (3), (4), (5) and (6) provide 8 linear equations in the unknowns αX, βY, γZ, λ^1, $\frac{\lambda^2}{\delta'}$, αt_x, βt_y and γt_z of which αt_x, βt_y and γt_z are the constant for all points on the moving object. Thus, given m points on the moving object, we have $8m$ equations and $5m + 3$ unknowns, forming an overdetermined linear system that can be solved using SVD.

If there are two or more translating objects in the scene, with known point correspondences, we can set up equations (3), (4), (5) and (6) for each additional object and solve for the structure and translation. Thus, our scheme can handle multiple dynamic objects with different translations. The structure of the static points can also be obtained from the equations derived. We only require equations (3) and (4) to solve for the unknown structure using SVD.

Our method can be extended to handle three or more input views. We only require that the correspondence of the three vanishing points in different directions be available in all the given views and that the origin be visible in all the views. The constants C_i relating the parameters α, β, γ of the first camera with those of other cameras may be computed as before. Structure and translation of points may be obtained by setting up equations (3), (4), (5) and (6), for all views that the point is visible in. Thus, our scheme recovers the structure of static points, the structure and translation of moving objects and the cameras of the given views in an affine coordinate system.

3 Synthesis with a New Camera

The reconstruction scheme described above can be used to synthesize views in which the camera undergoes rotation as well as translation. However, since the reconstruction is in an affine space, we cannot directly specify a rotation and

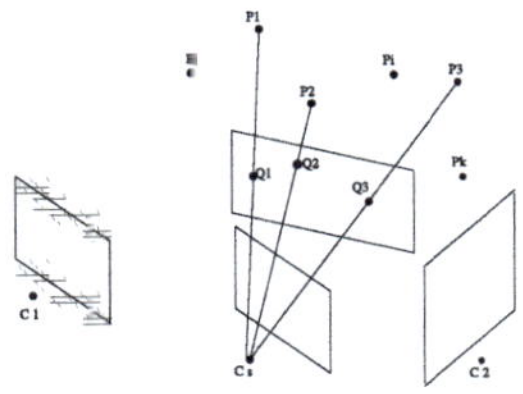

Fig. 3. Selecting a New Image Plane

translation for the virtual camera. We now describe a method for specifying a new image plane and centre of projection (COP) for the virtual camera.

We first describe how to specify the COP, $\mathbf{C_s}$, for the virtual view. It is well known that if the camera matrix is given by $M_s = [M\ \mathbf{p_0^s}]$, where, M is a 3×3 non-singular matrix and $\mathbf{p_0^s}$ is a 3×1 vector, then the COP is $\mathbf{C_s} = -M^{-1}\mathbf{p_0^s}$. Also, $\mathbf{p_0^s}$ is the image of the world origin in the virtual view. The virtual COP may be specified in two ways- either directly by choosing suitable coordinates for $\mathbf{C_s}$, or by choosing the image, $\mathbf{p_0^s}$, of the origin in the virtual view and computing $\mathbf{C_s}$ by the above formula. In our implementation, we have chosen the second method. The camera matrix for a view with this COP and image plane parallel to the image plane I_1 is then given by $M_{trans} = [\alpha\mathbf{v_1^1}\ \beta\mathbf{v_2^1}\ \gamma\mathbf{v_3^1}\ \mathbf{p_0^s}]$. If a view of the scene with only translational motion of the camera is required, we can use M_{trans} to obtain the projections of the reconstructed scene points. The new view is then triangulated using the projections of the reconstructed points and texture mapped from the given views.

If a view with a general motion of the camera is required, we need to specify a new image plane. We select three points in the first image with known correspondences to act as look at points for the new camera. The new image plane is chosen so that it intersects the rays from the new COP to the reconstructions of these points. Let the reconstructions of the chosen image points be $\mathbf{P_1}, \mathbf{P_2}$ and $\mathbf{P_3}$. We obtain the equations of the rays $\mathbf{C_sP_1}, \mathbf{C_sP_2}$ and $\mathbf{C_sP_3}$. As shown in Figure 3, we choose a point, $\mathbf{Q_i}$, $i = 1, 2, 3$, on each of the three chosen back projected rays and the new image plane is taken to be the plane passing through these points.

Next, we need to setup a coordinate system on the image plane to express the coordinates of the projections of the scene points. For this we make use of the camera matrix M_{trans}. We have

$$M_{trans} = [\alpha\mathbf{v_1^1}\ \beta\mathbf{v_2^1}\ \gamma\mathbf{v_3^1}\ \mathbf{p_0^s}] = \begin{bmatrix} \pi_{\mathbf{y}}{}^T \\ \pi_{\mathbf{x}}{}^T \\ \pi^T \end{bmatrix}$$

It is well known ([10]) that the the first row of a camera matrix represents a plane $\pi_{\mathbf{y}}$ through the COP and the y axis of the image plane, the second row represents a plane $\pi_{\mathbf{x}}$ through the COP and the x axis and the third row represents a plane π through the COP parallel to the image plane. We take the intersections of $\pi_{\mathbf{x}}$ and $\pi_{\mathbf{y}}$ with the new image plane. This gives two lines, $\mathbf{l_x}$ and

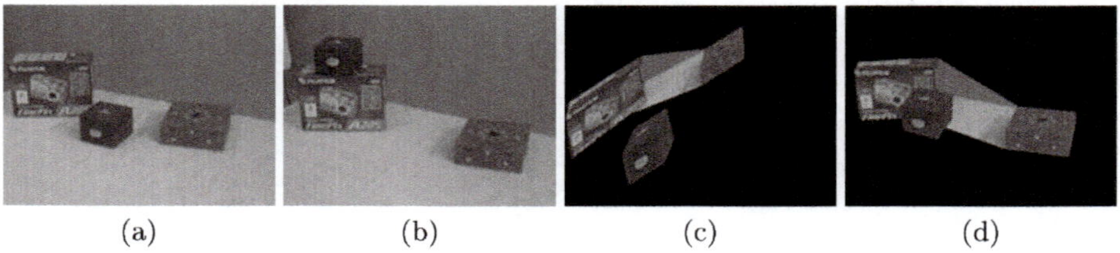

Fig. 4. (a) and (b) are input images of an indoor scene with a single translating object.(c)-(d) are synthesized views with a user chosen translation of the moving object.

$\mathbf{l_y}$, on the new image plane and although $\pi_\mathbf{x}$ and $\pi_\mathbf{y}$ are orthogonal, $\mathbf{l_x}$ and $\mathbf{l_y}$ need not be. However, we may choose one the lines, say $\mathbf{l_y}$, as the y axis and the point of intersection of $\mathbf{l_x}$ and $\mathbf{l_y}$ as the origin of the image coordinate system. The x axis is then a line passing through the origin and perpendicular to the y axis. Once the coordinate axes have been computed, we may obtain the camera matrix, M_{arb}, as follows. The first row of M_{arb} is the plane through $\mathbf{C_s}$ and the new y axis and the second row is the plane through the new x axis. The third row is a plane through $\mathbf{C_s}$ parallel to the image plane. Since the equation of the image plane is known, the equation of this plane can also be obtained. Thus, we can compute all the three rows of the camera matrix M_{arb}. The images of all scene points can be obtained by projecting them using M_{arb}. Next, a window is chosen on the image plane which defines the finite portion of the image plane to which the scene projects. The window is scaled to the desired image size using a transformation similar to the window to view-port transformation of the graphics pipeline. Finally, the new image is rendered by triangulation and texturing mapping from the given images. Although the choice of the points, $\mathbf{Q_1}, \mathbf{Q_2}$ and $\mathbf{Q_3}$, defining the image plane is arbitrary, in practice it is beneficial

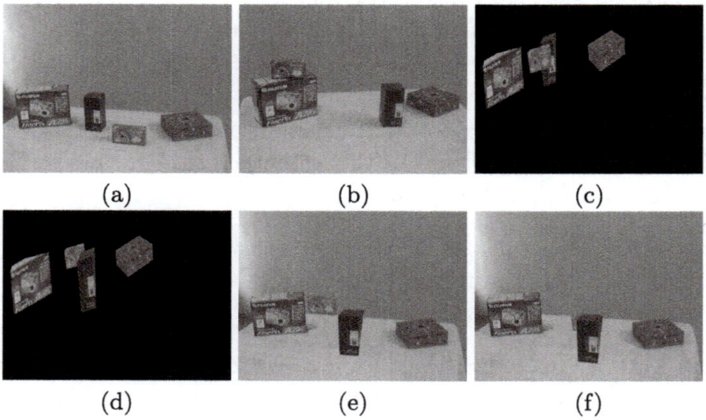

Fig. 5. (a) and (b) are input images of an indoor scene with two translating objects.(c) -(f) are synthesized views.

to restrict the set of possible image planes by imposing additional constraints like fixing the distance of $\mathbf{Q_i}$, $i = 1, 2, 3$ from the principle plane.

Figure 4 shows two views (a) and (b) of an indoor scene with a translating object with synthesized views (c)-(d). In (c), the dynamic object undergoes different translations, while in (d) the translation of the dynamic object is fixed and the camera changes. Three vanishing points in general position were made available by requiring that the scene contain man-made objects. In figure 5, we have taken two images (a) and (b) of a scene with two translating objects. (c)-(d) are synthesized views with different translations for the two objects and a new camera. Note that there is a scale distortion in the synthesized views because the reconstruction is up to the three unknown scale factors. Views (e)-(f) have the same camera as the first view, while the dynamic objects undergo user chosen translations. Figure 2 shows three images, (a)-(c), of a scene with a translating object. Note that in the three views the object does not move on the same straight-line path and translates in different directions. In (d) the translation of the object is interpolated between (a) and (b), while in (e) and (f) it is between (a) and (c).

4 Voxel-Based Scene Reconstruction

In this section we present the voxel-based scene reconstruction algorithm we have used to obtain a model of the scene. We have adapted the technique proposed in [1] to work with our affine reconstruction scheme as follows.

The reconstructed points are used to define a bounding volume containing the scene in the chosen affine coordinate system. A list of surface voxels is intialized and copied to another list of voxels to be checked for photo-consistency. Since the cameras are known in the affine space, each surface voxel can be projected into the given images and the set of pixels in its projection is determined. The set of pixels to which the voxel projects to in each image is used to decide the photo-consistency of the voxel. If the voxel is photo-consistent, it is retained otherwise it is carved out. Voxels that become visible as a result of a voxel being carved out are added to the list of voxels to be checked for photo-consistency. The algorithm terminates when this list becomes empty.

Since the scene may contain surfaces with considerable amount of texture as well as surfaces of uniform colour, the photo-consistency test should be able to make correct decisions in both cases. While [1] proposes a number of photo-consistency tests, most of them are based on statistical quantities like standard deviation and colour histograms. We propose a consistency test that computes a correspondence between the sets of pixels that a voxel projects to in the given images. The idea is to compute the homography between the images with respect to the front face of the voxel. This homography can be easily computed as the world coordinates of the four corners of the front face and their projections in the images are known. Once the homography is computed, for each pixel in the voxel's projection in the first image, we can find a corresponding pixel in the voxel's projection in the second image. We define the difference between the two

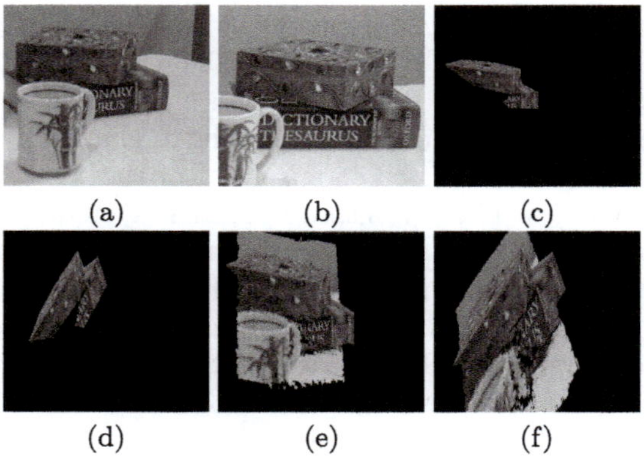

Fig. 6. (a) and (b) are input images of a static indoor scene. (e) and (f) are new views synthesized using the voxel model while (c) and (d) are views synthesized using corresponding points alone. (c) and (e) correspond to the same camera as do (d) and (f).

sets as the sum of the absolute differences in the intensities of corresponding pixels. If this quantity is below a certain threshold, the voxel is declared to be consistent and retained in the model, else it is carved out. Note that this consistency test can make correct decisions about both textured regions as well as regions of uniform colour.

Fig 6 shows two images (a) and (b) of an indoor scene with a considerable amount of texture and colour variations. (e) and (f) are synthesized views corresponding to new camera locations and orientations. (c) and (d) are views synthesized corresponding to the same cameras as (e) and (f), respectively, without using the voxel model. Since no correspondences were available on the mug and the background, they could not be synthesized in (c) and (d). Also, even if correspondences on the mug were available, its shape would not be sufficiently approximated by the triangles used for texture mapping. Fig 7 shows two images (a) and (b) of an indoor scene with relatively less textured objects and (c) and (d) are the synthesized views. In both cases, our algorithm is able to construct a model with sufficient amount of detail. The quality of the synthesized images can be further improved by texture mapping the areas which are covered by the triangulation of the corresponding points and using the model for the other parts. The quality of the model improves if the number of input images is increased.

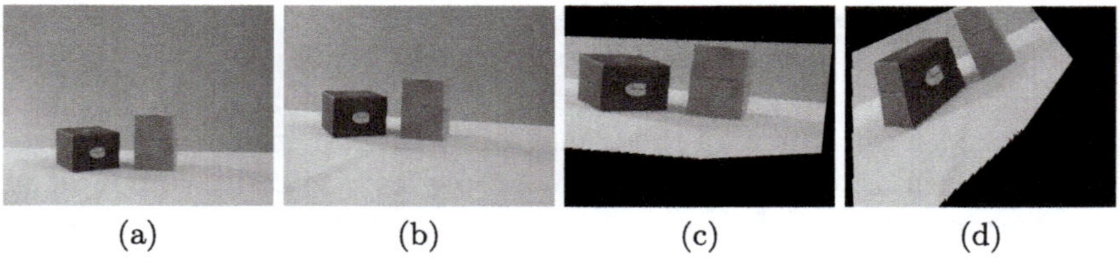

Fig. 7. (a) and (b) are input images of a static indoor scene. (c) and (d) are new views synthesized using the voxel model.

5 Conclusion

We have proposed a technique for view synthesis of scenes with independently translating objects using the correspondence of three vanishing points in general position. The static and moving objects are reconstructed in an affine coordinate system and the translations of the objects are also recovered. We also provide a technique to synthesize new views with a user chosen translation for the moving object and a completely new camera specified in the affine space. We have used a voxel-based volumetric reconstruction algorithm to obtain a model of the scene. This removes the dependence on corresponding points and allows for a larger portion of the scene to be synthesized in the new views. We have experimented the scheme on a number of scenes and while it produces good results in most cases, there was an affine distortion in some cases due to unknown scale factors.

References

1. Slabaugh, G.G., Culbertson, W.B., Malzbender, T., M. R. Stevens, R.W.S.: Methods for Volumetric Reconstruction of Visual Scenes. International Journal of Computer Vision **57** (2004) 179–199
2. Vidal, R., Ma, Y., Saotto, S., Sastry, S.: Two-View Multibody Structure from Motion. International Journal of Computer Vision (2002)
3. Shashua, A., Wolf, L.: Homography Tensors: On Algebraic Entities that Represent Three Views of Static or Moving Planar Points. In: Proc. European Conference on Computer Vision. (2000)
4. Wexler, Y., Shashua, A.: On the Synthesis of Dynamic Scenes from Reference Views. In: Proc. Computer Vision and Pattern Recognition. (2000)
5. Avidan, S., Shashua, A.: Trajectory Triangulation: 3D Reconstruction of Moving Points from a Monocular Image Sequence. IEEE Transactions on Pattern Analysis and Machine Intelligence **22** (2000)
6. Fitzgibbon, A., Zisserman, A.: Multibody Structure and Motion: 3-D Reconstruction of Independently Moving Objects. In: Proceedings of the European Conference on Computer Vision, Springer-Verlag (2000) 891–906
7. Han, M., Kanade, T.: Multiple Motion Scene Reconstruction with Uncalibrated Cameras. IEEE Transactions on Pattern Analysis and Machine Intelligence **25** (2003) 884–894
8. Seitz, S., Dyer, C.: View Morphing. In: Proc. SIGGRAPH. (1996) 21–30
9. Fitzgibbon, A., Wexler, Y., Zisserman, A.: Image-Based Rendering Using Image-Based Priors. In: IEEE International Conference on Computer Vision. Volume 2. (2003)
10. Hartley, R., Zisserman, A.: Multiple View Geometry. Cambridge University Press (2000)

Generating Free Viewpoint Images from Mutual Projection of Cameras

Koichi Kato and Jun Sato

Department of Computer Science and Engineering, Nagoya Institute of Technology, Nagoya 466-8555, Japan
kato@hilbert.elcom.nitech.ac.jp, junsato@nitech.ac.jp

Abstract. In augmented reality, accurate geometric adjustment of real scene and virtual 3D models is important. In this paper, we propose a new method for generating arbitrary views of 3D motion events accurately by using the mutual projections between user's cameras and cameras around the user. In particular, we show that the trifocal tensors computed from the mutual camera projections can be used efficiently for generating accurate user's views of 3D motion events from multiple camera images. We also show a method for identifying cameras projected in other cameras by using the invariance in multiple view geometry. The proposed method is implemented and tested in the real scene.

1 Introduction

In this paper, we propose a method for generating images viewed from arbitrary viewpoints very reliably in augmented reality systems. Recent progress in computer vision research enables us to generate realtime images viewed from arbitrary viewpoints. Kanade et al. showed that it is possible to reconstruct 3D objects from a large amount of cameras and show motion pictures viewed from arbitrary viewpoints [1]. It was also shown that by assuming the planarity of objects, we can efficiently generate arbitrary views of non-rigid objects in the scene[2].

Unfortunately these methods do not count the difficulty of adjusting generated virtual scenes with real scenes. For generating high quality images in augmented reality systems, it is very important to keep the consistency between the viewer's motions and image motions viewed from the viewer. Even if we can generate smooth and high quality images at given positions and orientations, the actual quality of images viewed from the viewer is bad, if the measurement of the positions and orientations of the viewer is bad. Thus, in augmented reality systems, we cannot separate the generation of arbitrary views from the computation of viewer's positions and orientations.

On the other hand, the research on multiple view geometry showed that multifocal tensors can be used efficiently for generating arbitrary views from multiple images without reconstructing the 3D structure of the scene [3, 4, 5]. Since the multiple view geometry is computed from images used for generating user's views, the adjustment of virtual models to the user's views is quite good if the

P.J. Narayanan et al. (Eds.): ACCV 2006, LNCS 3851, pp. 470–479, 2006.

computation of multifocal tensors is accurate. Unfortunately, the computation of multifocal tensors is unstable, if the configurations of 3D points and cameras are close to the so called critical configuration[5]. For example, if 3D points in the scene are close to coplanar, the multifocal tensors computed from these points are very sensitive to image noises. As a result, the augmented reality images generated from the multifocal tensors are also unstable under such cases. Since, in general, planes such as floors and walls are dominant in the augmented reality scene, this is a very big disadvantage of the method.

On the other hand, it has recently been shown that if the cameras are projected each other, we can extract strong constraints on the multifocal tensors from camera images, and thus we can compute multifocal tensors very accurately from less image correspondences[6]. Moreover, it is known that the multifocal tensors can be computed even if the 3D points are completely coplanar. In this paper, we apply the method for generating augmented reality images, and show that by using the mutual projections between user's cameras and the cameras surrounding the user, we can generate augmented reality images very reliably, even from planar scenes. Unfortunately, however, the use of mutual projections cause a problem, that is if we have many cameras in the scene, we have to identify which cameras are projected each other. In this paper, we also propose a method for identifying surrounding cameras projected to user's cameras by using the invariance in multiple view geometry.

2 Mutual Projection of Multiple Cameras

Let us consider M surrounding cameras, $\mathbf{C}_i$ $(i = 1, \cdots, M)$, around the field. The motion events occurred in the field are recorded in these M surrounding cameras as shown in Fig. 1 (a). After recording the motion events, the user goes into the field as shown in Fig. 1 (b). The user wears a HMD with a camera, $\mathbf{C}_U$. Then, our task is to show the replay of the 3D motion events to the user, so that the user can see the events at his viewpoints. For generating high quality views

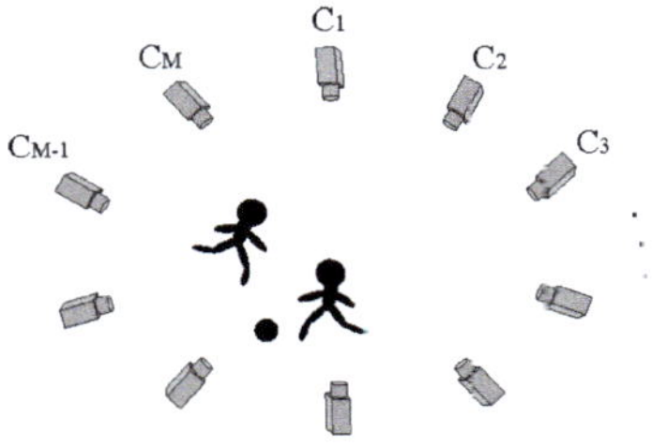

(a) recording motion events

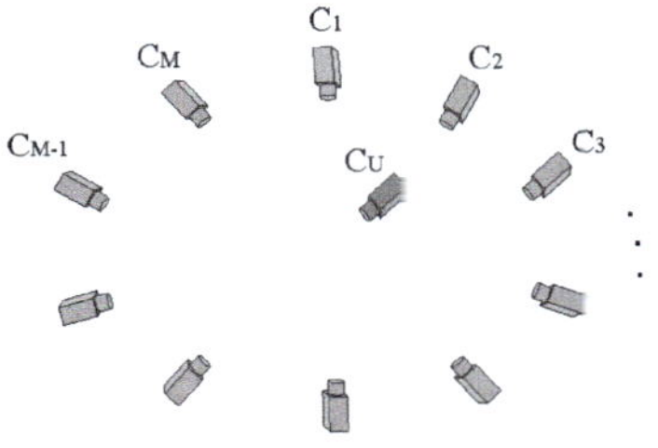

(b) replaying motion events

Fig. 1. Recording and Replaying the motion events. First, the motion events in the field are recorded in M surrounding cameras, $\mathbf{C}_i$ $(i = 1, \cdots, M)$ as shown in (a). After recording the motion events, the user's camera $\mathbf{C}_U$ goes into the field as shown in (b). Then, the image of $\mathbf{C}_U$ is generated from the images of $\mathbf{C}_i$ $(i = 1, \cdots, M)$.

(a) image of $\mathbf{C}_i$ (b) image of $\mathbf{C}_j$ (c) image of $\mathbf{C}_U$

Fig. 2. Mutual projections between a user's camera and two surrounding cameras. The projection of cameras in other camera images can be considered as epipoles.

of users from surrounding cameras, we propose a method for generating user's views by using the projection of cameras in other cameras.

Let us consider user's camera, $\mathbf{C}_U$, and M surrounding cameras, $\mathbf{C}_i$ $(i = 1, \cdots, M)$, around the user. We assume that the user's camera $\mathbf{C}_U$ is at around the center of the surrounding cameras $\mathbf{C}_i$, so that $\mathbf{C}_U$ is projected to $\mathbf{C}_i$ $(i = 1, \cdots, M)$. We also assume that at least 2 surrounding cameras are projected to the user's camera $\mathbf{C}_U$. If we have many surrounding cameras, such situations occur in general.

Let us consider a 3D point, $\mathbf{X}$, and let $\mathbf{X}$ be projected to $\mathbf{m}_U = [m_U^1, m_U^2, m_U^3]^\top$ in the user's camera, and $\mathbf{m}_i = [m_i^1, m_i^2, m_i^3]^\top$ and $\mathbf{m}_j = [m_j^1, m_j^2, m_j^3]^\top$ in the i th and j th surrounding cameras respectively $(i, j = 1, \cdots, M)$. Then, we have the following trilinear relationship on these image points:

$$m_U^a m_i^b m_j^c \epsilon_{bqu} \epsilon_{crv} \mathcal{T}_a^{qr} = 0_{uv} \tag{1}$$

where, $\mathcal{T}_a^{qr}$ denotes a trifocal tensor, and $\epsilon_{ijk}(i, j, k = 1, 2, 3)$ denotes a tensor whose value is 1 if $\{i, j, k\}$ is even permutation to $\{1, 2, 3\}$, and -1 if $\{i, j, k\}$ is odd permutation to $\{1, 2, 3\}$.

Let $\mathbf{t}$ be a vector which consists of the components of $\mathcal{T}_a^{qr}$, that is $\mathbf{t} = [\mathcal{T}_1^{11}, \cdots, \mathcal{T}_3^{33}]^\top$. If we have N corresponding points in three views, we have a system of linear equations on $\mathbf{t}$ from (1) as follows:

$$\mathbf{Mt} = \mathbf{0} \tag{2}$$

where, $\mathbf{M}$ is a $9N \times 27$ matrix and consists of the coordinates of corresponding points.

The linear method for computing the components of trifocal tensors is to find linear solutions, $\mathbf{t}$, in (2). If we have N corresponding points, we have $4N$ independent equations in (2), and thus minimum of 7 corresponding points provide us solutions $\mathbf{t}$.

Unfortunately, the linear solutions of (2) do not satisfy the geometric constraints of multiple views, since geometrically the DOF of the trifocal tensor is 18, while the rank of linear systems is 26 for unique solutions, $\mathbf{t}$, up to a scale. As a result, trifocal tensors computed from linear methods is sensitive to image noises, if the number of corresponding points is small or the configuration of 3D points and cameras is close to the critical configuration.

To cope with this problem, a method for computing multifocal tensors by using the mutual projection of multiple cameras has been proposed [6]. This method enables us to compute multifocal tensors which fully satisfy geometric constraints of multiple views, although it is a linear method. Since we apply the mutual projection method for generating arbitrary views, we quickly review the method.

Suppose a user's camera, $\mathbf{C}_U$, is projected to two surrounding cameras, $\mathbf{C}_i$ and $\mathbf{C}_j$. These projections can be considered as epipoles, $\mathbf{e}_{iU}$ and $\mathbf{e}_{jU}$ in the images of two surrounding cameras as shown in Fig. 2. If these surrounding cameras are projected to the user's camera, we also have two epipoles, $\mathbf{e}_{Ui}$ and $\mathbf{e}_{Uj}$, in a user's image. Then, we have the following relationships between trifocal tensors and epipoles [6]:

$$\mathbf{e}_{iU}^b \mathbf{e}_{jU}^c \epsilon_{bqu} \epsilon_{crv} \mathcal{T}_a^{qr} = \mathbf{0}_{uva} \tag{3}$$

$$\mathbf{e}_{Ui}^a \mathbf{e}_{ji}^c \epsilon_{crv} \mathcal{T}_a^{qr} = \mathbf{0}_v^q \tag{4}$$

$$\mathbf{e}_{Uj}^c \mathbf{e}_{ij}^b \epsilon_{bqu} \mathcal{T}_a^{qr} = \mathbf{0}_u^r \tag{5}$$

Similar relationships between multilinear tensors were also studied in [10]. Thus, if one camera is projected to other two cameras, we have 12 independent equations on $\mathcal{T}_a^{qr}$ from (3). If two cameras are projected to other cameras, (3) and (4) provide us 16 independent equations. If all three cameras are projected each other, (3), (4) and (5) provide us 20 independent equations on $\mathcal{T}_a^{qr}$. Since a set of corresponding points provides us 4 linear equations on $\mathcal{T}_a^{qr}$ from (1), the number of corresponding points required for computing $\mathcal{T}_a^{qr}$ is 5 for mutual projection of one camera, 4 for mutual projection of two cameras, and 2 for mutual projection of three cameras respectively [6].

If we have the mutual projection of L cameras in three cameras, $2L$ epipoles are available, and the remaining DOF in the three view geometry is $18 - 4L$. On the other hand, the mutual projections of one, two and three cameras provide us 12, 16 and 20 linearly independent equations. Thus the remaining DOF in the linear system (2) is 14, 10 and 6 respectively, and these numbers coincide with the remaining DOF in the three view geometry. Thus, if we have the mutual projection of one, two or three cameras, we can linearly compute trifocal tensors which fully satisfy the geometric constraints of three views.

3 Generating Users' Views from Mutual Projection of Cameras

By computing the trifocal tensors $\mathcal{T}_a^{qr}$ between the user's camera and 2 surrounding cameras from mutual projections in realtime, we can generate images in the user's camera, $\mathbf{m}_U$, from images in 2 surrounding cameras, $\mathbf{m}_1$ and $\mathbf{m}_2$, from the trilinear relationship (1).

The number of corresponding points required for computing $\mathcal{T}_a^{qr}$ is depend on the situations. If the surrounding cameras are not calibrated, we can only use the mutual projection of one camera, that is $\mathbf{e}_{1U}$ and $\mathbf{e}_{2U}$, and thus we need

5 corresponding points in three views for computing $\mathcal{T}_a^{qr}$ and generating new views. If the surrounding cameras are projectively calibrated, that is if we know the fundamental matrix, $\mathbf{F}_{ij}$, between ith and jth surrounding cameras, then we need just 2 corresponding points for computing $\mathcal{T}_a^{qr}$ and generating new views. This is because $\mathbf{e}_{ij}$ and $\mathbf{e}_{ji}$ are available from $\mathbf{F}_{ij}$, and $\mathbf{e}_{iU}$, $\mathbf{e}_{Ui}$, $\mathbf{e}_{jU}$ and $\mathbf{e}_{Uj}$ are given from the mutual projection of cameras, and as a result (3), (4) and (5) can be used for computing $\mathcal{T}_a^{qr}$.

As we will show in the experimental section, user's views generated by using the proposed method is very stable comparing with the views generated from the standard linear method [7].

4 Identifying Cameras from Invariance in Multiple View Geometry

Up to now, we showed an efficient method for generating user's views from surrounding cameras by using the mutual projection of multiple cameras. In this method, however, we have to identify which surrounding cameras are projected to the user's camera mutually. That is given two projections of cameras in a user's image, what is the serial number of these two cameras. Unless we have the identification of the projected surrounding cameras, we cannot use mutual projection of cameras for computing $\mathcal{T}_a^{qr}$ and for generating images. In this section, we describe a method for identifying surrounding cameras projected in user's cameras by using the invariance in multifocal tensors.

If the user's camera moves in the field, the trifocal tensor, $\mathcal{T}_a^{qr}$, between the user's camera and two surrounding cameras changes. However, since the surrounding cameras are stationary, the fundamental matrix, $\mathbf{F}$, between these two surrounding cameras does not change, even if the user's camera moves. Thus, if we extract a fundamental matrix between two surrounding cameras from the trifocal tensor, $\mathcal{T}_a^{qr}$, it is invariant. Thus, we can use the invariance of $\mathbf{F}$ for identifying cameras observed in the user's camera.

Suppose M surrounding cameras are calibrated projectively, that is $\mathbf{F}_{ij}$ $(i, j = 1, \cdots, M)$ are known. Since the surrounding cameras are stationary, we can calibrate these cameras projectively in advance by using the bundle adjustment based method [8]. Now, let us consider user's camera in the field, in which 2 surrounding cameras are projected. Then, we can compute trifocal tensor $\mathcal{T}_a^{qr}$ between the user's camera and 2 surrounding cameras. Then, by using the relationship between trifocal tensors and fundamental matrices [9], we can compute the fundamental matrix $\mathbf{F}$ between these 2 surrounding cameras. Since we know $\mathbf{F}_{ij}$ for any pair of surrounding cameras, the surrounding cameras projected in a user's camera can be identified by finding i and j which minimize the square distance between $\mathbf{F}$ and $\mathbf{F}_{ij}$ as follows:

$$\{i, j\} = \arg\min(\mathbf{f} - \mathbf{f}_{ij})^\top(\mathbf{f} - \mathbf{f}_{ij}) \tag{6}$$

where, $\mathbf{f}$ denotes a 9 vector which consists of the components of $\mathbf{F}$, and $\mathbf{f}_{ij}$ denotes that of $\mathbf{F}_{ij}$. Both $\mathbf{f}$ and $\mathbf{f}_{ij}$ are normalized so that they have a unit length.

Once the surrounding cameras observed in the user's camera are identified, we can compute trifocal tensors $\mathcal{T}_a^{qr}$ accurately from just 2 corresponding points, and can generate user's views from the surrounding cameras as described in section 3.

5 Experiments

5.1 Generating User's Views

We first show some experimental results on generating arbitrary user's views of 3D motion events from surrounding cameras. In this experiment, we used two surrounding cameras, $\mathbf{C}_1$ and $\mathbf{C}_2$, and a user's camera, $\mathbf{C}_U$ Fig. 3 (a) and (b) show images viewed from two surrounding cameras. The fundamental matrix between these two cameras is computed from many corresponding points in advance. Then, we put a ball which is bounding in the scene. The image motions of the bounding ball viewed from two surrounding cameras are recorded. We next

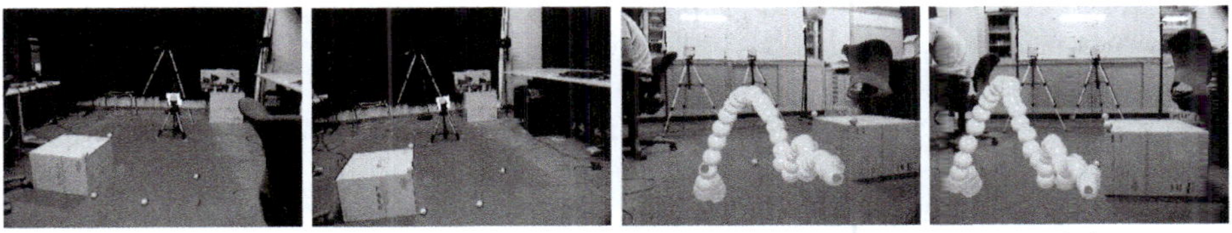

(a) (b) (c) (d)

Fig. 3. User's view of motion events generated from two surrounding cameras by using the mutual projection method. (a) and (b) show images viewed from two surrounding cameras, and (c) and (d) show user's images viewed at two different viewpoints. The blue points in these images show camera centers extracted and tracked by using color information. The two red points in each image show corresponding points used for computing trifocal tensors from the mutual projection method. The motion of a bounding ball is recorded to the surrounding cameras and is projected to the user's views as shown in (c) and (d).

(a) (b) (c) (d)

Fig. 4. User's view of motion events generated from two surrounding cameras by using the normalized linear method. The red points show 7 corresponding points used for computing trifocal tensors from the normalized linear method. See the caption of Fig. 3 for the explanation.

generated user's views of the bounding ball from the recorded images by using the proposed method. Fig. 3 (c) shows motions of the ball viewed from the user's camera, which are generated from the proposed method. The blue points in (a) and (b) show the user's camera projected in two surrounding cameras, and two blue points in (c) show two surrounding cameras projected in a user's camera. These points are extracted and tracked in realtime by using the color markers attached on the cameras, and are used as epipoles in three view geometry. Two red points in (a), (b) and (c) show corresponding points used for computing trifocal tensors and for generating arbitrary views. As shown in Fig. 3 (c), the bounding motions of a ball in the user's view generated by using the proposed method is very smooth and reasonable. Fig. 3 (d) shows the image motions of the same bounding motions viewed from a different viewpoint. As shown in these figures, we can generate very stable arbitrary views of the user by using the proposed method.

We next generated the user's views of the same bounding motions by using trifocal tensors computed from the normalized linear method [7]. Fig. 4 (a) and (b) show images of two surrounding cameras, and (c) and (d) show images of a user's camera at two different viewpoints. The red points in Fig. 4 (a), (b), (c) and (d) show 7 corresponding points used for computing trifocal tensors in the normalized linear method. 2 of these 7 points coincide with 2 points used in the proposed method for a fair comparison. As shown in (c) and (d), the image motions of a ball generated from the normalized linear method is not so stable. From these results, we can see that the proposed method can generate much more stable views of users from smaller number of corresponding points.

5.2 Accuracy and Stability Evaluation

We next evaluate the stability of the proposed method numerically by using synthetic images. Fig. 5 shows a synthetic scene of a tower used in our experiment. red point shows user's camera and green and blue points show two of M surrounding cameras. The synthetic images of these two surrounding cameras

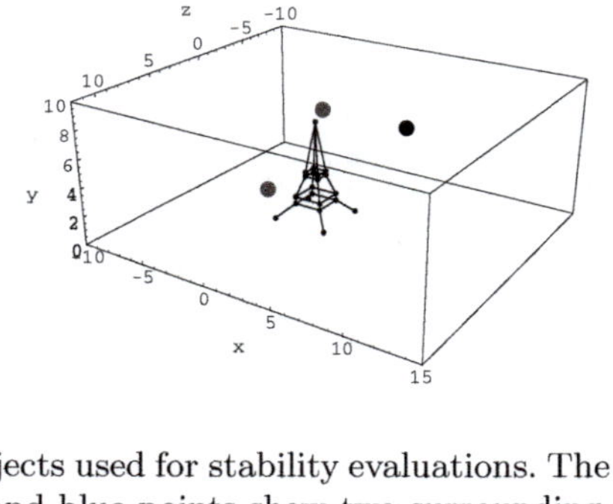

Fig. 5. Cameras and objects used for stability evaluations. The red point shows a user's camera, and the green and blue points show two surrounding cameras. The images of the tower are taken from the two surrounding cameras and are used for generating the image of user's camera.

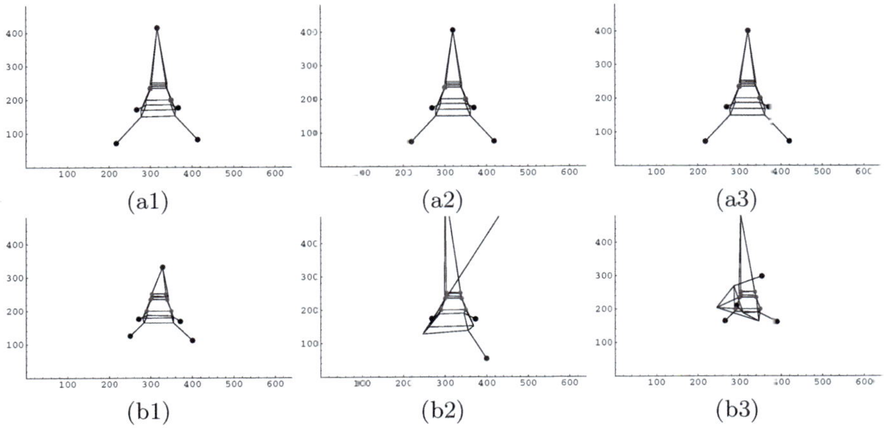

Fig. 6. Stability of user's images generated from two surrounding cameras. (a1), (a2) and (a3) show example images generated from the proposed method, and (b1), (b2) and (b3) show those from the normalized linear method. The red points show corresponding points used for computing trifocal tensors in each method.

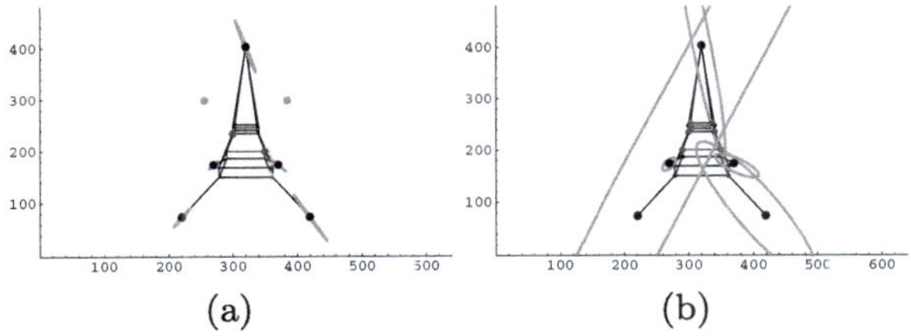

Fig. 7. Stability of user's images generated from two surrounding cameras. The green ellipses in (a) and (b) show the uncertainty bounds of image points generated from the proposed method and the normalized linear method respectively.

are used for generating user's images. We generated user's images 100 times by adding random Gaussian noises with the standard deviation of 1 pixel to all image features including epipoles given as the projection of cameras. Fig. 6 (a1), (a2) and (a3) show 3 example images generated from the proposed method, and (b1), (b2) and (b3) show example images generated by using the normalized linear method. The red points in these figures show corresponding points used for computing trifocal tensors between the user's camera and two surrounding cameras. Note, 2 corresponding points used for the proposed method are the subset of 7 corresponding points used for the normalized linear method. The green ellipses in Fig. 7 show the uncertainty bounds of generated points in user's images. Fig. 7 (a) shows the result from the proposed method and (b) shows that from the normalized linear method. As shown in Fig. 6 and Fig. 7, images generated from the proposed method is much more stable than those from the normalized linear method, although the proposed method is also a linear method.

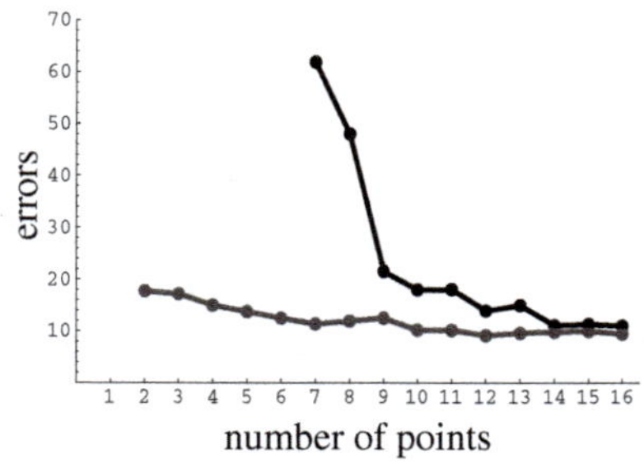

Fig. 8. The number of corresponding points and the errors of generated image points in the user's view

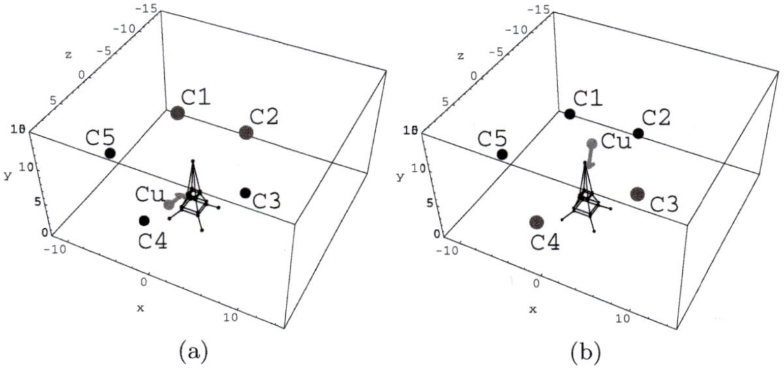

Fig. 9. Identification of cameras in user's images. (a) and (b) show two synthetic configurations of a user's camera and surrounding cameras. The green arrows show the directions of a user's camera, and the large red points show surrounding cameras identified as mutual projection cameras by using the proposed method.

We next show the relationship between the number of corresponding points and the errors of user's images generated from two surrounding cameras. The number of corresponding points is changed from 2 to 16, and the mean square errors of generated image points are computed in the proposed method and the normalized linear method. The red and blue lines in Fig. 8 show the mean square errors computed from the proposed method and the normalized linear method respectively. As shown in this figure, both methods provide us good accuracy if we have enough number of corresponding points. However, if the number of corresponding points is small, the proposed method provides us much better accuracy.

5.3 Identification of Cameras in Images

We next show the results on the identification of surrounding cameras which are visible from user's cameras. Fig. 9 (a) shows a 3D configuration of a user's camera, $\mathbf{C}_U$, and 5 surrounding cameras, $\mathbf{C}_i$ $(i = 1, \cdots, 5)$. The green arrow in the figure shows the direction of the user's camera. The synthetic images of these cameras are generated and used for identifying surrounding cameras observed in the user's camera. The Gaussian noises with the standard deviation of 1 pixel are added to all the image points including visible epipoles in each image. The fundamental matrix, **F** between two surrounding cameras observed in a user's image is computed from a trifocal tensor and used for identifying cameras observed in the user's image by using the proposed method. The red points in Fig. 9 (a) show two surrounding cameras identified as the mutual projection cameras observed in the user's camera. From the red points and the green arrow, we find that a correct pair of surrounding cameras is selected. Fig. 9 (b) shows another 3D configuration of cameras and identified surrounding cameras. As shown in these figures, correct pairs of surrounding cameras can be identified.

6 Conclusion

In this paper, we proposed a method for generating arbitrary user's views of 3D motion events from multiple camera images by using the mutual projection of these cameras. In particular, we showed that the trifocal tensors computed from the mutual camera projections can be used efficiently for generating accurate user's views of 3D motion events from multiple surrounding cameras. We also proposed a method for identifying surrounding cameras projected into user's cameras by using the invariance in multifocal tensors. The proposed method is implemented and tested for generating realtime motion images of 3D motion events viewed from arbitrary viewpoints.

References

1. T. Kanade, P.W. Rander, and P.J. Narayanan, "Virtualized reality: Constructing virtual worlds from real scenes," *IEEE Multimedia*, vol. 4, no. 1, 1997.
2. N. Inamoto and H. Saito, "Intermediate view generation of soccer scene from multiple views," in *Proc. International Conference on Pattern Recognition*, 2002.
3. S. Avidan and A. Shashua, "Novel view synthesis in tensor space," in *Proc. Conference on Computer Vision and Pattern Recognition*, pp. 1034–1040, 1997.
4. B. Boufama, "The use of homographies for view synthesis," in *Proc. International Conference on Pattern Recognition*, pp. 1563–1566, 2000.
5. R.I. Hartley and A. Zisserman, *Multiple View Geometry*, Cambridge University Press, 2000.
6. J. Sato, "Recovering multiple view geometry from mutual projection of multiple cameras," *International Journal of Computer Vision*, 2005 (to appear).
7. R.I. Hartley, "Minimizing algebraic error in geometric estimation problems," in *Proc. 6th International Conference on Computer Vision*, pp. 469–476, 1998.
8. B. Triggs, P. McLauchlan, R.I. Hartley, and A. Fitzgibbon, "Bundle adjustment – A modern synthesis," in *Vision Algorithms: Theory and Practice*, B. Triggs, A. Zisserman, and R. Szeliski, Eds., pp. 298–375. Springer Verlag, 2000.
9. A. Heyden, "A common framework for multiple view tensors," in *Proc. 5th European Conference on Computer Vision*, vol. 1, pp. 3–19, 1998.
10. B. Triggs, "The geometry of projective reconstruction I: Matching constraints and the joint image, *unpublished paper*, 1995.

Video Synthesis with High Spatio-Temporal Resolution Using Motion Compensation and Image Fusion in Wavelet Domain

Kiyotaka Watanabe[1], Yoshio Iwai[1], Hajime Nagahara[1], Masahiko Yachida[1], and Toshiya Suzuki[2]

[1] Osaka University, Graduate School of Engineering Science,
1–3 Machikaneyama-cho, Toyonaka,
Osaka 560–8531, Japan
{watanabe, iwai, nagahara, yachida}@yachi-lab.sys.es.osaka-u.ac.jp
[2] Eizoh Co., LTD, 2–1–10 Nanko-Kita,
Suminoe, Osaka 559–0034, Japan
suzuki@eizoh.co.jp

Abstract. This paper presents a novel algorithm for obtaining a high spatio-temporal resolution video from two video sequences. These sequences are high resolution with low frame rate and low resolution with high frame rate. To this end, we introduce a dual sensor camera that can capture these sequences with the same field of view simultaneously. The proposed method observes motion information through the video with high frame rate. Moreover, the method conducts both motion compensation for the high resolution sequence and image fusion in the wavelet domain. We confirmed that the proposed method improves the resolution and frame rate of the synthesized video.

1 Introduction

In recent years, charge coupled devices (CCD) and CMOS image sensors have been widely used to capture digital images. With the development of sensor manufacturing techniques, the spatial resolution of these sensors has been increased. As the resolution increases, however, the frame rate generally decreases because the sweep time is limited. Hence, high resolution is incompatible with high frame rate. There are some high resolution cameras available for special use, such as a digital cinema. However, these are very expensive and thus unsuitable for general purpose use.

Various methods have been proposed to obtain high resolution images from low resolution images by utilizing image processing techniques. One of the methods to enhance spatial resolution is known as super resolution, which have been actively studied for a long time. Conventional techniques of obtaining super resolution images from still images have been summarized in the literature [1], and several methods for obtaining a high resolution image from a video sequence have also been proposed [2, 3].

P.J. Narayanan et al. (Eds.): ACCV 2006, LNCS 3851, pp. 480–489, 2006.

Frame rate conversion algorithms have also been investigated in order to convert the frame rate of videos or to increase the number of video frames. Frame repetition and temporal linear interpolation are straightforward solutions for the conversion of the frame rate of video sequences, but they also produce jerkiness and blurring at moving object boundaries, respectively. It has been shown that frame rate conversion with motion compensation provides the best solution in temporal up-sampling applications [4, 5].

Conventinal techniques mentioned above enhance either spatial or temporal resolution. We adopt a novel stragety to synthesize a high spatio-temporal resolution video (i.e., high spatial resolution video with high frame rate). Our approach synthesizes the video from two video sequences. These sequences are high resolution with low frame rate and low resolution with high frame rate. To this end, we introduce a dual sensor camera [6, 7] that can capture two video sequences with the same field of view simultaneously. The dual sensor camera consists of conventional image sensors, allowing for inexpensive construction of the camera. Moreover, another advantage of this approach is that the amount of video data obtained from the dual sensor camera can be small.

Several works that are related to our approach have been conducted. Shechtman et al. have proposed a method [8, 9] for increasing the resolution both in time and in space. Matsunobu et al. have proposed a method to solve the same problem covered in this paper using image morphing [10]. In their methods, all processes are conducted in the image domain. However, it is difficult to extract and track the feature points in that approach, so there exist several cases where resolution enhancement of the video cannot be achieved. Another algorithm proposed by Watanabe et al. [11] conducts motion compensation for the high resolution images in the image domain, and fuses the spectrum of the compensated image with that of the temporally corresponding low resolution image in the DCT domain. That is, motion compensation and spectral fusion are done in distinct domains, so the algorithm can be complicated.

To solve these issues, this paper presents a novel method for synthesizing a high spatio-temporal resolution video using wavelet transform. The proposed method conducts both motion compensation and fusion of two video sequences in the wavelet domain, and thus can be uncomplicated. In our method, we use redundant discrete wavelet transform (RDWT) [12], which is an extension of traditional discrete wavelet transform (DWT). Shift-invariant property of RDWT

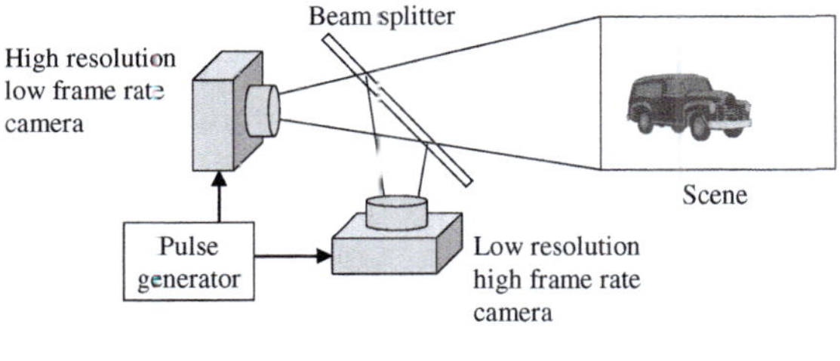

Fig. 1. Concept of dual sensor camera

allows motion compensation in the wavelet domain. In addition, our method conducts motion compensation for all pixels in the image, i.e., it doesn't contain difficult problems such as feature extraction and tracking.

The rest of the paper is organized as follows. We present the dual sensor camera in the following section. Next, we describe DWT and its property, and then introduce RDWT in Sect. 3. Section 4 demonstrates the proposed algorithm for synthesizing a high spatio-temporal resolution video. Section 5 shows some experimental results. Finally, we conclude this paper in Sect. 6.

2 Dual Sensor Camera

The concept of the dual sensor camera used in our method is shown in Fig. 1. The camera has a beam splitter and two CCD sensors. The beam splitter divides an incident ray into the two CCDs. The camera can capture two video sequences simultaneously, using two different CCDs which can capture high resolution video with low frame rate and low resolution video with high frame rate. Synchronized frames between low resolution and high resolution sequences can be obtained by means of the input of synchronization pulse. We call the synchronized frames "key frames" in this paper.

We define the resolution ratio between the high resolution and low resolution sensors as $2^{\alpha} : 1$ ($\alpha \in \mathbf{N}$) and the frame rate ratio as $1 : \rho$ ($\rho \in \mathbf{N}$). Moreover, we assume $\sigma = 2^{\alpha}$. Two video sequences satisfying $\alpha = 2$ (i.e., $\sigma = 4$) and $\rho = 7$ are obtained from the two video sequences captured through the dual sensor camera [6, 7].

3 Discrete Wavelet Transform

DWT is one of the frequency transforms. In contrast to some frequency transforms such as DFT, DCT, etc., DWT preserves the spatial information in the frequency domain. We employ this property for motion compensation and image fusion in order to conduct both operations in the wavelet domain.

It is known that the traditional DWT is shift-variant [13]. Hence, DWT coefficients of the image $I(x, y)$ is generally very different from that of one-pixel shifted image $I_s(x, y) = I(x - 1, y)$, so motion compensation of the wavelet coefficients causes large error.

Shift-variance of DWT arises from the downsampling operation in the DWT decomposition. To overcome this property, we introduce RDWT [12]. RDWT removes the downsampling operation from the traditional DWT to ensure shift-invariance at the cost of a redundant representation. Because of the shift-invariant property of RDWT, the shift in the image domain is just the same as in the wavelet domain. Therefore, motion compensation for each subband in the RDWT domain can be performed essentially in the same manner as in the image domain. The proposed method conducts both motion compensation and image fusion in the wavelet domain, and thus can be simplified.

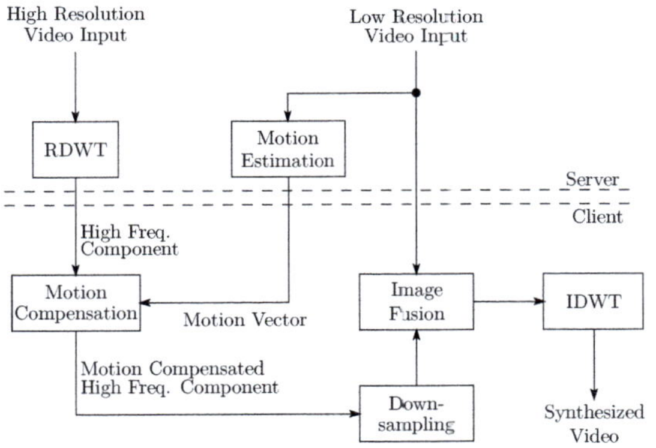

Fig. 2. Block diagram of proposed algorithm

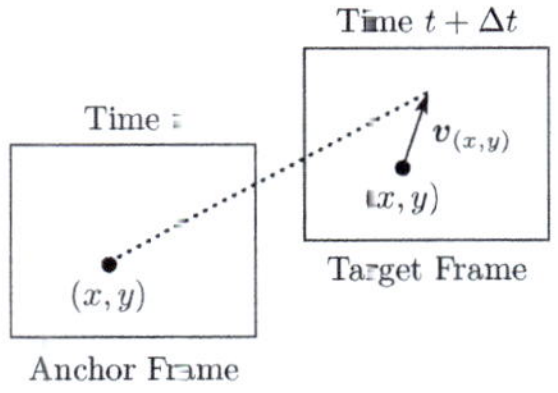

Fig. 3. Terminology of ME

Let $Lf^{(j)}$ and $Hf^{(j)}$ be the j-th level low-band and high-band DWT coefficients of f, respectively. Moreover, we denote $\widehat{L}f^{(j)}$ and $\widehat{H}f^{(j)}$ as the j-th level low-band and high-band RDWT coefficients of f, respectively, where $\widehat{}$ represents the RDWT coefficients.

DWT coefficients are correlated to RDWT coefficients as the following formulae;

$$Lf^{(j)} = \widehat{L}f^{(j)} \downarrow 2^j, \quad Hf^{(j)} = \widehat{H}f^{(j)} \downarrow 2^j. \tag{1}$$

where $\downarrow \alpha$ denotes downsampling by a factor of α. That is, if $y(n) = x(n) \downarrow \alpha$, then $y(n) = x(\alpha n)$. Therefore, RDWT reconstruction can be done as DWT reconstruction (inverse DWT) by using the formulae.

4 Video Synthesis in Wavelet Domain

Figure 2 shows the outline of the proposed algorithm that synthesizes high resolution images. The method estimates motion information in the low resolution video with high frame rate. Each frame of the high resolution video is decomposed by using RDWT. High frequency components of the RDWT coefficients are motion-compensated, based on the estimated motion information, and then downsampling is done for these components. Downsampled coeffficients are fused with low resolution video frames. Finally, by applying inverse DWT, we obtain a high resolution video with high frame rate.

In cases of streaming the video, RDWT and motion estimation are processed on the server side, while the other processes are processed on the client side.

4.1 Terminology of Motion Estimation

The computation of the motion information is referred to as motion estimation (ME). As shown in Fig. 3, if the motion from the frame at t to $t + \Delta t$ is estimated, then the frame at t and $t + \Delta t$ are called the "anchor frame" and "target frame" respectively. We distinctly call the estimation process "forward motion

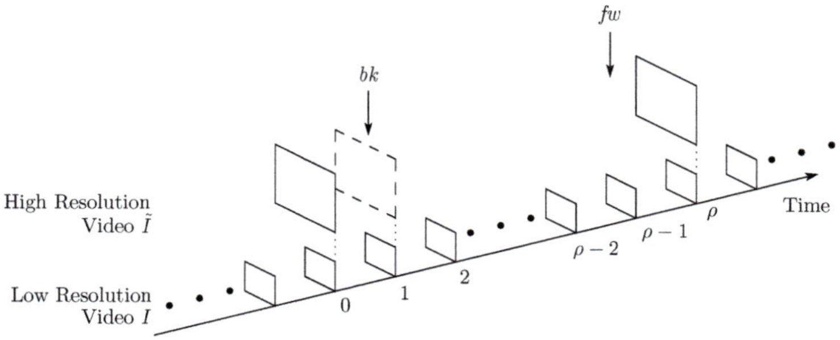

Fig. 4. Initial settings of proposed method

estimation" if $\Delta t > 0$ and "backward motion estimation" if $\Delta t < 0$. A motion vector is assigned for every pixel of the frame at t in this case.

4.2 Process for Synthesizing High Resolution Video

We assume, as shown in Fig. 4, that there exist two pairs of key frames, $(I_0, \tilde{I}_0)$ and $(I_\rho, \tilde{I}_\rho)$. We also suppose that the intermediate frames of these key frames, $I_1, I_2, \cdots, I_{\rho-1}$, are obtained. Under the assumptions mentioned above, the proposed algorithm synthesizes high resolution images $\tilde{I}_1, \cdots, \tilde{I}_{\rho-1}$ in accordance with the following process. The order of the synthesis of each frame is $\tilde{I}_1$, $\tilde{I}_{\rho-1}$, $\tilde{I}_2$, $\tilde{I}_{\rho-2}$, $\cdots$ in this instance.

Step 1. (Initial Settings) Set $bk = 1$ and $fw = \rho - 1$, as shown in Fig. 4.
Step 2. Set $s = bk$, $r = bk - 1$ and $c = fw + 1$.
Step 3. (RDWT Decomposition) Calculate the following high frequency components

$$\widehat{LH\tilde{I}_r}^{(j)},\ \widehat{HL\tilde{I}_r}^{(j)},\ \widehat{HH\tilde{I}_r}^{(j)} \quad (j = 1, 2, \cdots, \alpha) \tag{2}$$

by means of the RDWT decomposition for the high resolution image $\tilde{I}_r$, which has already been obtained. If the standard RDWT is used, then the low frequency component $\widehat{LH\tilde{I}_r}^{(\alpha)}$ can be obtained. However, $\widehat{LH\tilde{I}_r}^{(\alpha)}$ is not used in our method, so we do not need to calculate this.

Step 4. (Motion Estimation) Estimate the motion vector for each pixel of low resolution image I_s by the phase correlation method [14] where the anchor frame and target frame are the low resolution images I_s and I_r, respectively. The motion vector is measured to an accuracy of $1/\sigma$ pixel.

Step 5. (Motion Compensation) Estimate each subband of $\tilde{I}_s$ by conducting motion compensation for corresponding subbands of $\tilde{I}_r$. Motion compensation for each subband is conducted according to the following equations;

$$\widehat{LH\tilde{I}_s}^{(j)}(x_s, y_s) = \widehat{LH\tilde{I}_r}^{(j)}(x_r, y_r) \tag{3}$$

$$\widehat{HL\tilde{I}_s}^{(j)}(x_s, y_s) = \widehat{HL\tilde{I}_r}^{(j)}(x_r, y_r) \tag{4}$$

$$\widehat{HH\tilde{I}_s}^{(j)}(x_s, y_s) = \widehat{HH\tilde{I}_r}^{(j)}(x_r, y_r), \tag{5}$$

where

$$x_s = 2^\alpha x + \Delta_x,\ y_s = 2^\alpha y + \Delta_y$$
$$x_r = 2^\alpha(x + v^x_{(x,y)}) + \Delta_x,\ y_r = 2^\alpha(y + v^y_{(x,y)}) + \Delta_y,$$

for $0 \leq \Delta_x, \Delta_y \leq 2^\alpha - 1$.

The failure to estimate a motion vector may occur when there is no candidate of motion vector for which MSE is lower than certain threshold in phase correlation method. If there exist positions where the method fails to assign motion vectors, the motion estimation is conducted differently from the method mentioned above. In this case, I_s and I_c are used as the anchor frame and target frame respectively, and each subband of $\tilde{I}_s$ are estimated by conducting motion compensation for respective subbands of $\tilde{I}_c$.

If the method fails to assign motion vectors to the coordinate (x, y) with either procedure described above, zeros are substituted for each subband as shown below.

$$\widehat{LH\tilde{I}_s}^{(j)}(x'_s, y'_s) = 0,\ \widehat{HL\tilde{I}_s}^{(j)}(x'_s, y'_s) = 0,\ \widehat{HH\tilde{I}_s}^{(j)}(x'_s, y'_s) = 0$$
$$(j = 1, 2, \cdots, \alpha) \tag{6}$$

where

$$x'_s = 2^\alpha x' + \Delta_x,\ y'_s = 2^\alpha y' + \Delta_y,\ \text{for } 0 \leq \Delta_x, \Delta_y \leq 2^\alpha - 1. \tag{7}$$

Step 6. (Downsampling) Conduct downsampling operation for each subband of $\tilde{I}_s$ in accordance with (1), i.e., calculate the following DWT coeffients from RDWT coeffients.

$$LH\tilde{I}_s^{(j)},\ HL\tilde{I}_s^{(j)},\ HH\tilde{I}_s^{(j)}\ (j = 1, 2, \cdots, \alpha)$$

Step 7. (Image Fusion) Replace the low frequency component of $\tilde{I}_s$, $LL\tilde{I}_s^{(\alpha)}$, with temporally corresponding low resolution image I_s. That is, let $LL\tilde{I}_s^{(\alpha)} = I_s$.
Step 8. (IDWT) Conduct IDWT for each subband of $\tilde{I}_s$. As a result, we will obtain a high resolution image $\tilde{I}_s$.
Step 9. Add 1 to bk.
Step 10. If $bk = fw$, then terminate this algorithm. Otherwise proceed to Step 11.
Step 11. Set $s = fw$, $r = fw + 1$, and $c = fw + 1$, and then execute Steps 3 to 8.
Step 12. Subtract 1 from fw.
Step 13. Repeat from Step 2 to Step 12 until $bk = fw$.

5 Experiments

5.1 Simulation Experiments

We conducted simulation experiments to confirm that the proposed method synthesizes high resolution video. We used simulation input image sequences from

Table 1. Description of test sequences

Sequence Name	Spatial Resolution	Frame
Coast guard	352 × 288	1–295
Football	352 × 240	1–120
Foreman	352 × 288	1–295
Hall monitor	352 × 288	1–295

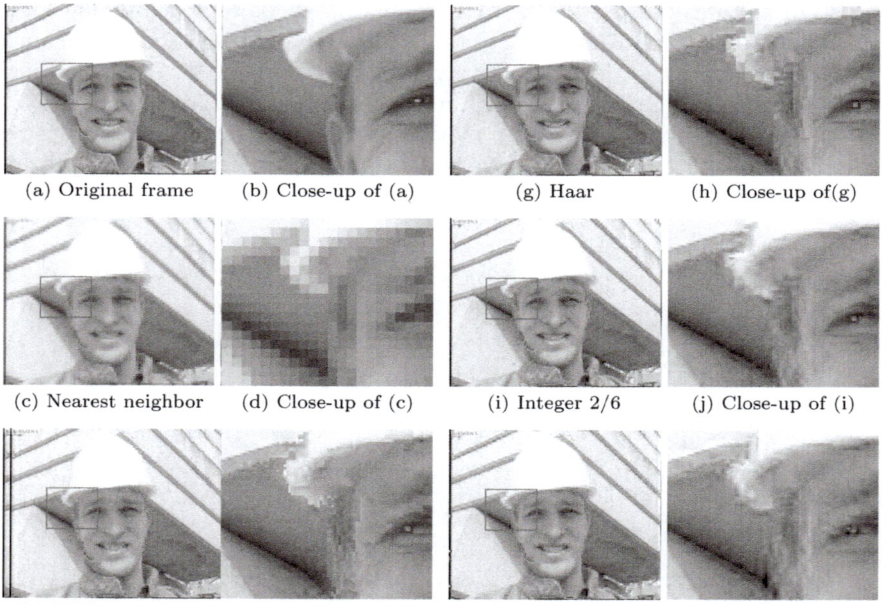

(a) Original frame (b) Close-up of (a) (g) Haar (h) Close-up of(g)
(c) Nearest neighbor (d) Close-up of (c) (i) Integer 2/6 (j) Close-up of (i)
(e) DCT fusion[11] (f) Close-up of (e) (k) Daubechies 4-tap (l) Close-up of (k)

Fig. 5. Test sequence "Foreman" 46th frame

the dual sensor camera. The simulated input images were made from MPEG test sequences as described below. The low resolution image sequence ($M/4 \times N/4$ [pixels], 30 [fps]) was obtained by a 25 % scaling down of the original MPEG sequence ($M \times N$ [pixels], 30 [fps]), i.e., $\sigma = 4$. The high resolution image sequence ($M \times N$ [pixels], 4.29 [fps]) was obtained by picking up every seven frames of the original sequence, i.e., $\rho = 7$. The proposed method synthesized $M \times N$ pixel video with 30 [fps] as the synthesized high resolution video with high frame rate. Table 1 shows the original MPEG sequences used in these experiments.

In these experiments, we used three wavelet functions for the image fusion; Haar wavelet, Daubechies 4-tap filter [15], and integer 2/6 wavelet [16]. We investigated the difference in the quality of the synthesized images between these functions.

Figure 5 shows the original frame (a)(b) and an upsampled low resolution frame using nearest neighbor method(c)(d). Figure 5 (e)(f) shows a synthesized

Table 2. PSNR results

Sequence Name	Haar Wavelet	Integer 2/6 Wavelet	Daubechies 4-tap filter	DCT spectral fusion[11]	Nearest Neighbor
Coast guard	23.59	23.65	22.47	23.38	21.28
Foreman	26.08	26.27	24.29	25.88	23.37
Football	20.06	20.52	19.78	20.15	19.38
Hall monitor	31.90	32.08	25.44	30.81	21.78

frame by means of DCT spectral fusion method [11]. In Fig. 5, (g)(h), (i)(j) and (k)(l) are synthesized frames using Haar wavelet, integer 2/6 wavelet and Daubechies 4-tap filter, respectively.

Blocking artifacts are produced in the synthesized image using Haar wavelet (Fig. 5(g)(h)), e.g., near the brim of the helmet. At these areas high frequency coefficients of RDWT are replaced with zero because the motion vector is not estimated. Haar wavelet is discontinuous, and thus the interpolation is conducted roughly at these areas. This nature causes blocking artifacts. On the other hand, these artifacts are reduced in the synthesized images using integer 2/6 wavelet and Daubechies 4-tap filter (see Fig. 5(i)-(l)). This results from the smoothness of these wavelet functions against Haar wavelet, so the smooth interpolation is carried out.

Table 2 shows the simulation results of each test sequence. We compared the peak signal to noise ratio (PSNR) between the synthesized and original images. The obtained results using integer 2/6 wavelet are better in PSNR than the results by means of up-sampling of the low resolution video (nearest neighbor) and DCT spectral fusion method for all the four test sequences. This result shows that the proposed method improved the resolution and frame rate.

PSNR results for the "Football" and "Foreman" sequences are relatively worse. These sequences contain large amount of dynamic region. Hence there are some regions where the motion information cannot be estimated, and thus the PSNR results decreased. On the other hand, static region and pure translation mainly dominate in the "Coastguard" and "Hall monitor" sequences. So the accurate motion estimation and compensation could be achieved and better PSNR results were obtained.

5.2 Synthesis from Real Video Sequences

By calibrating two video sequences captured through the prototype dual sensor camera [6, 7], two sequences were made;

- Size: 4000×2600 [pixels], Frame rate: 4.29 [fps]
- Size: 1000×650 [pixels], Frame rate: 30 [fps]

High resolution (4000×2600 [pixels]) video with high frame rate (30 [fps]) is synthesized from two video sequences mentioned above using our algorithm.

Figure 6(a) shows an example of the synthesized frames. Enlarged image of Fig. 6(a) is shown in Fig. 6(b). Figure 6(c) shows the low resolution image which

(a) (b) (c)

Fig. 6. Synthesized high resolution image from real images. (a) Synthesized frame, (b) Close-up of (a), and (c) Corresponding low resolution image.

temporally corresponds to Fig. 6(a)(b). We can observe sharper edges in Fig. 6(b), while the edges in Fig. 6(c) are blurred. This result shows that our method can also synthesize a high resolution video with high frame rate from the video sequences captured through the dual sensor camera.

6 Conclusion

In this paper we have proposed a novel algorithm for obtaining a high resolution video with high frame rate from two video sequences with different spatio-temporal resolution. The proposed algorithm synthesizes a high spatio-temporal resolution video using motion compensation and image fusion in the wavelet domain. We confirmed through the experiments that the proposed method improves the resolution and frame rate of video sequences.

Acknowledgments

A part of this research is supported by "Key Technology Research Promotion Program" of the National Institute of Information and Communication Technology.

References

1. Park, S.C., Kang, M.K., Kang, M.G.: Super-resolution image reconstruction: A technical overview. IEEE Signal Processing Mag. **20** (2003) 21–36
2. Shekarforoush, H., Chellappa, R.: Data-driven multi-channel super-resolution with application to video sequences. J. Opt. Soc. Am. A **16** (1999) 481–492

3. Tom, B.C., Katsaggelos, A.K.: Resolution enhancement of monochrome and color video using motion compensation. IEEE Trans. Image Processing **10** (2001) 278–287
4. Choi, B.T., Lee, S.H., Ko, S.J.: New frame rate up-conversion using bi-directional motion estimation. IEEE Trans. Consumer Electron. **46** (2000) 603–609
5. Ha, T., Lee, S., Kim, J.: Motion compensated frame interpolation by new block-based motion estimation algorithm. IEEE Trans. Consumer Electron. **50** (2004) 752–759
6. Hoshikawa, A., Shigemoto, T., Nagahara, H., Iwai, Y., Yachida, M., Tanaka, H.: Dual sensor camera system with different spatio-temporal resolution. In: Proc. SICE Annual Conf. (2005)
7. Nagahara, H., Hoshikawa, A., Shigemoto, T., Iwai, Y., Yachida, M., Tanaka, H.: Dual-sensor camera for acquiring image sequences with different spatio-temporal resolution. In: Proc. IEEE Int. Conf. Advanced Video and Signal based Surveillance. (2005)
8. Shechtman, E., Caspi, Y., Irani, M.: Increasing space-time resolution in video. In: Proc. European Conf. Computer Vision. (2002) 753–768
9. Shechtman, E., Caspi, Y., Irani, M.: Space-time super-resolution. IEEE Trans. Pattern Analysis and Machine Intelligence **27** (2005) 531–545
10. Matsunobu, T., Nagahara, H., Iwai, Y., Yachida, M., Tanaka, H.: Generation of high resolution video using morphing. In: Proc. SICE Annual Conf. (2005)
11. Watanabe, K., Iwai, Y., Nagahara, H., Yachida, M., Tanaka, H.: Video synthesis with high spatio-temporal resolution using motion compensation and spectral fusion. In: Proc. SICE Annual Conf. (2005)
12. Shensa, M.J.: The discrete wavelet transform: wedding the à trous and mallat algorithms. IEEE Trans. Signal Processing **40** (1992) 2464–2482
13. Park, H.W., Kim, H.S.: Motion estimation using low-band-shift method for wavelet-based moving-picture coding. IEEE Trans. Image Processing **9** (2000) 577–587
14. Girod, B.: Motion-compensating prediction with fractional-pel accuracy. IEEE Trans. Communications **41** (1993) 604–612
15. Daubechies, I.: Ten Lectures on Wavelets. Society for Industrial and Applied Mathematics (1992)
16. Zandi, A., Allen, J.D., Schwartz, E.L., Boliek, M.: CREW: Compression with reversible embedded wavelets. In: Proc. IEEE Data Compression Conf. (1995) 212–221

Estimating Illumination Parameters in Real Space with Application to Image Relighting

Feng Xie, Linmi Tao, Guangyou Xu, and Huijun Di

Key Laboratory of Pervasive Computing (Tsinghua University), Ministry of Education,
Department of Computer Science and Technology, Tsinghua University,
Beijing 100084, P.R. China
xiefeng97@mails.tsinghua.edu.cn
{linmi, xgy-dcs}@tsinghua.edu.cn
dhj98@mails.tsinghua.edu.cn

Abstract. A novel algorithm is presented in this paper for estimating the direction and strength of point light with the strength of ambient illumination. Existing approaches estimate these illumination parameters directly in the high dimensional image space, while we estimate the parameters in two steps: first to project the image to an orthogonal linear subspace based on spherical harmonic basis functions; then to calculate the parameters in the low dimensional subspace. The experimental results on CMU PIE database and Yale Database B showed the stability and effectiveness of this method. The resulting illumination information can help to synthesize more realistic relighting images and recognize object under variable illumination.

1 Introduction

Illumination condition is a fundamental problem in both computer vision and graphics. In computer vision, we frequently need to undo the effects of the reflection operator: to invert the interaction between the bidirectional reflectance distribution function (BRDF) and lighting. In computer graphics, the interaction between the incident illumination and the BRDF is a basic building block in most rendering algorithms. For instance, the estimation of lighting condition is important in face relighting and recognition, since synthesized realistic images can alleviate the small sample problem in face recognition applications.

Many algorithms [1-6] have been proposed to estimate the illumination parameters directly in the image space. Some of these algorithms [3-5] use a calibration sphere to estimate illumination condition which is impracticable under some circumstance. Y. Zhang [6] and W. Yang [1] introduce a novel algorithm to find the critical points from which the illumination parameters could be determined. But for complex surface such as human face, it's very hard to determine the critical points. D. Samaras [2] gives an iterative process to estimation of lighting direction and shape from shading but the computational cost is very heavy.

Recently Basri [7, 8] and Ramamoorthi [9, 10] independently apply the spherical harmonics techniques to explain the low dimensionality of differently illuminated images for convex Lambertian object. Ramamoorthi even derives analytically the principal components of this low dimensional image subspace. The incident illumina-

P.J. Narayanan et al. (Eds.): ACCV 2006, LNCS 3851, pp. 490–499, 2006.

tion is described as a set of coefficients in the frequency space. This method have already been widely applied to the areas of inverse rendering [11], image relighting [12], face recognition [13, 14], etc.

One of the limitations of this method is that the cast shadows are ignored. In the experiment results of [15], the cast shadows improve the face recognition result on the most extreme light directions. How to overcome this limitation is one of the motivations of our work. Another reason is that if we want to render a realistic image, usually we need the real light direction. Although the spherical harmonics coefficient of illumination could be easily estimated, how to recover the real light direction from these coefficients is still a problem.

In this paper we consider an illumination model consisting of one point light source and ambient illumination. We propose a novel algorithm for estimating the illumination parameters including the direction and strength of point light with the strength of ambient illumination. Images are projected into the analytical subspace derived in [10] according to a known 3D geometry, then the illumination parameters are estimated from these projected coefficients. Our primary experiments proved the stability and effectiveness of this method.

The rest of this paper is organized as follows. In section 2 we describe the illumination parameters estimation algorithm in detail. Experimental results on synthesized sphere images and real face images, and stability analysis of nonlinear least-square method are demonstrated in section 3. In section 4 we show our image relighting result and compared with the result of other image relighting algorithm. Finally, we conclude in section 5 with discussions and future work.

2 Estimation of Illumination Parameters

Consider a convex Lambertian object of known geometry with uniform albedo illuminated by distant isotropic light sources, the irradiance could be expressed as a linear combination of the spherical harmonic basis functions [9, 10]:

$$\begin{aligned} E(\vec{n}) &= \sum_{l=0}^{\infty}\sum_{m=-l}^{l} \hat{A}_l L_{l,m} Y_{l,m}(\vec{n}) \\ &\approx \sum_{l=0}^{2}\sum_{m=-l}^{l} \hat{A}_l L_{l,m} Y_{l,m}(\vec{n}), \end{aligned} \tag{1}$$

where $\vec{n}$ is the surface normal, $Y_{l,m}(\vec{n})$ is the spherical harmonics basis function, and $\hat{A}_l$ is a constant which vanishes for odd $l>1$ and decays rapidly. So we can obtain good approximation by limiting $l \le 2$. In fact, 99% of the energy of the Lambertian BRDF filter is constrained by $l \le 2$ [10].

In this paper we consider a simple illumination model consisting of one distant directional point light source and ambient illumination. As mentioned in [8,10], the point light source acts as a delta function, so its spherical harmonics coefficients $L_{l,m}=Y_{l,m}$. The ambient illumination only contributes to $L_{0,0}$ [16]. So the illumination coefficients could be expressed as:

$$L_{l,m} = \begin{cases} S_a + S_p Y_{0,0}(\alpha,\beta) & l = m = 0, \\ S_p Y_{l,m}(\alpha,\beta) & \text{otherwise,} \end{cases} \tag{2}$$

where (α, β) is the direction of point light, and S_a and S_p is the strength of ambient illumination and point light respectively. Altogether there are nine coefficients and four parameters, so it could be solved by nonlinear least-square method.

One problem is that, although the spherical harmonic basis functions are orthogonal in the sphere coordinates, they are not orthogonal in the image space. This property causes the algorithm unstable in some case. This problem can be solved by means of projecting the image to an orthogonal linear subspace. One approach is to use PCA [17] on large number of images under different lighting condition to estimate the subspace, but it requires a lot of training data. Alternatively, we choose the analytical subspace constructed in [10], which requires no training data.

We project the image to the subspace, get the coefficients γ:

$$\begin{aligned} \gamma_i &= E(\vec{n}) \cdot u_i \\ &= \left(\sum_{l,m} \hat{A}_l L_{l,m} Y_{l,m}(\vec{n}) \right) \cdot \left(\sum_{p,q} c_{p,q} Y_{p,q}(\vec{n}) \right) \\ &= \sum_{l,m} \left(\hat{A}_l Y_{l,m}(\vec{n}) \sum_{p,q} c_{p,q} Y_{p,q}(\vec{n}) \right) L_{l,m}, \end{aligned} \tag{3}$$

where

$$u_j = \sum_{l=0}^{\infty} \sum_{m=-l}^{l} c_{l,m} Y_{l,m}(\vec{n}) \tag{4}$$

is the eigenvectors of analytical PCA subspace in [10] and could be computed beforehand.

Defining

$$R_{l,m} = \hat{A}_l Y_{l,m}(\vec{n}) \sum_{p,q} c_{p,q} Y_{p,q}(\vec{n}), \tag{5}$$

where R is constant matrix, and plugging into (4), we obtain

$$\gamma_i = \sum_{l,m} R_{l,m} L_{l,m}. \tag{6}$$

Then we apply nonlinear least-square method to estimate the four unknown parameters α, β, S_a and S_p from the coefficients γ:

$$\arg \min_{\alpha,\beta,S_a,S_p} \left\| \gamma - R \cdot L \right\|. \tag{7}$$

Finding a global extreme of nonlinear problem is very difficult. We choose the popular Gauss-Newton method to solve this minimal problem, which might stay on local minima.

But the experimental results in section 3.3 show that if we choose enough coefficients, the energy surface guarantee the local minima is same as the global minima. (Note that we can use only a part of the PCA coefficients to solve this nonlinear minimal problem.) Actually the first five coefficients are enough for estimate these parameters stably.

3 Illumination Estimating Result

We experimented on both synthesized sphere images and real face images in CMU PIE database [18] and Yale Database B [15].

3.1 Synthesized Sphere Images Result

First, we randomly select the four illumination parameters and synthesize 600 sphere images under the different illumination, in which the incident directions are limited to the upper hemisphere and the light strength parameters are normalized to satisfy $S_a + S_p = 1$. Then we test our algorithm on these synthesized sphere images. Similar to the Yale Database B, we divide the images into 5 subsets (12°, 25°, 55°, 77°, 90°) according to the angle which the light source direction makes with the camera's axis. Fig. 1 shows five synthesized images and first five principal components computed analytically, in which the positive values of principal components are shown in green and the negative values are shown in red. The average estimation errors of illumination parameters on each subset are shown in Fig. 2 separatively.

From Fig. 2 we could see that the estimated light direction is accurate except on the extreme illumination direction. The average error of lighting direction on all images is not beyond 1 degree. For lighting strength the estimation error decreased when the angel light source direction makes with the camera's axis increase. Since the strength is normalized, the intensity level of 0.03 means about 7 grey levels in the image.

In the above experiment, we use only 9 harmonics (Order 2) to calculate the eigenvectors in (4). We use high order harmonics Order 8 instead of Order 2, to repeat the

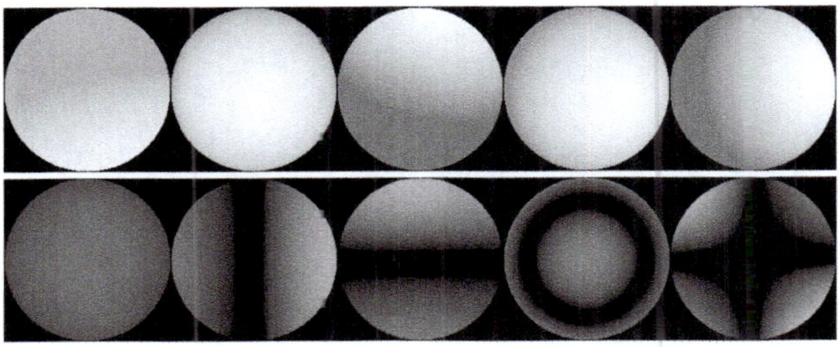

Fig. 1. (a) First row shows five synthesized sphere images; (b) second row shows first five principal components of sphere images

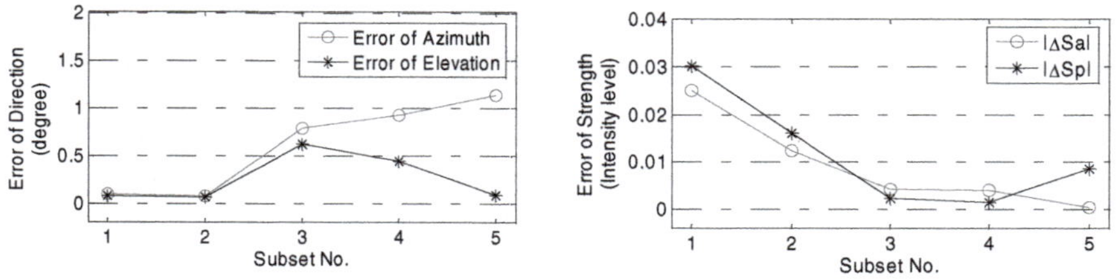

Fig. 2. The estimation errors of illumination parameters on synthesized sphere image set, using Order 2 harmonics

experiment. The result is more accurate, the average error of direction is within 0.01 degree and the average error of strength is within 0.001. For limited length of this paper, the figure of the result is omitted.

3.2 Real Images Database Result

Then we apply this method on real images in CMU PIE database [18] and Yale Database B [15]. One problem is that for real object the uniform albedo assumption is seldom satisfied. The work of [12] proves that when the albedo contains no first four order components (except the constant component), the approximation in (1) is still exact. For the albedo map of human face, [12] gives the conclusion that the coefficients of order 1,2,3,4 is very small, hence we could directly apply this algorithm on face images as [12, 14] did.

We applied a generic 3D face model (shown in Fig. 3(a)) to approximate the 3D shape of faces for the fact that human faces have similar shape. Given a 2D image, to create the correspondence between the vertices of the mesh and the 2D image, we first create the correspondence between the feature points on the mesh and the 2D image. The feature points on the 2D image are marked manually as shown in Fig. 3(b). Then the rest of the vertices on the mesh and the 2D image are aligned with image warping technique.

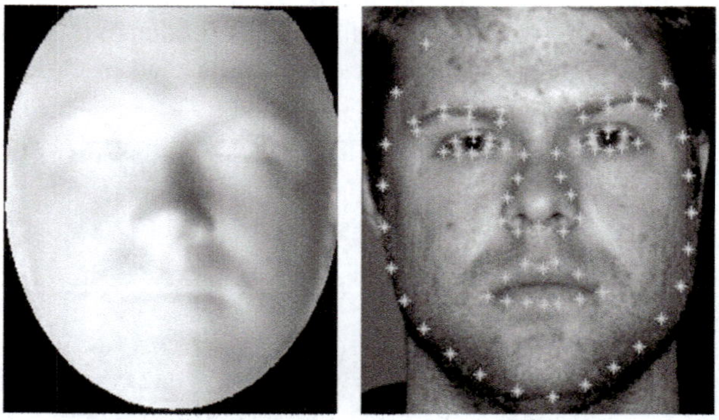

(a) (b)

Fig. 3. (a) generic 3D face model; (b) feature points

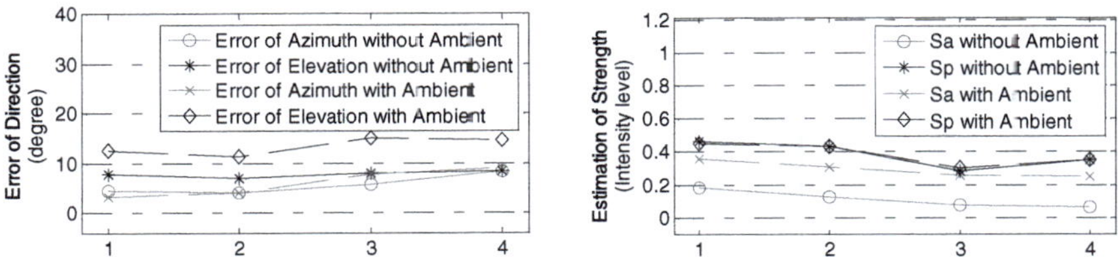

Fig. 4. The estimation result of illumination parameters on CMU-PIE database

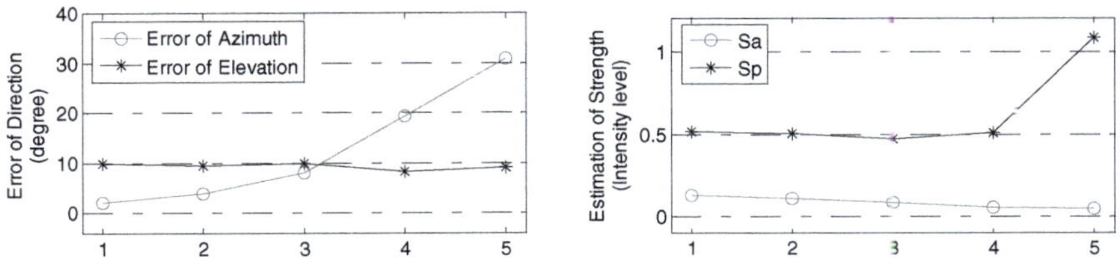

Fig. 5. The estimation result on Yale Database B

There are 68 persons in CMU PIE database. For frontal pose, each person has 22 images with different light point source plus ambient lights on and off. We apply our method on the selected 15 peoples images and the result is shown in Fig. 4. Similar to the Yale Database B, we divide the images into 4 subsets (12°, 25°, 55°, 77°) according to the angles the light source direction make with the camera's axis.

We could see that the estimated strength is stable whether the ambient lights on or off, but the estimated error of light direction increases when the ambient light is on. The reason of estimation error lies in three aspect: the face skin is not perfect Lambertian surface, the albedo is not constant, and the 3D shape is not accurate since we only use a generic face model. Considering these reasons, the estimated result is reasonably acceptable.

The Yale B database used above contains 5760 single light source images of 10 subjects, in which each was seen under 576 viewing conditions. Because our focus is illumination problem, only 640 images of frontal pose is considered and the result is shown in Fig. 5.

Fig.5 shows that the estimated strength is stable except on the most extreme light condition. With the extreme light condition the specular component of face skin become important in the image, but the model couldn't handle it. So the estimated S_a on subset 5 is quite bigger than normal value. The estimated error of direction also increases when the light direction is far from camera's axis.

3.3 Stability of Nonlinear Least-Square Method

In this section we discuss the stability of nonlinear least-square method since we choose the Gauss-Newton method to solve this minimal problem. If the iteration process stops on the undesired local minima, it will give the wrong result.

For simplicity, we restrict the minimal problem on two unknown parameters (α, β), and define the energy function:

$$F = \left\| \gamma - R \cdot L \right\| \tag{8}$$

Now we could compute the value of energy function on all possible values of (α, β). Choosing different number of coefficients derive different energy function. Fig. 6 shows four different energy function, using 2, 3, 5, 9 coefficients respectively (x-y plane is the domain of (α, β), while the z-axis is the value of energy function F).

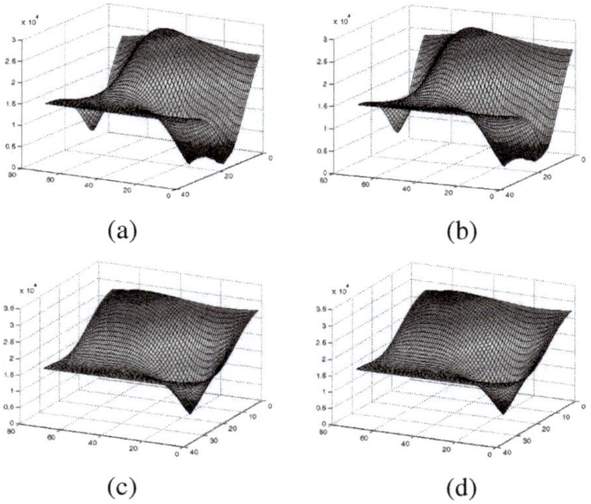

Fig. 6. Energy function over α, β plane. (a) use 2 coefficients; (b) use 3 coefficients; (c) use 5 coefficients; (d) use 9 coefficients.

From Fig. 6 we could see that when we use only 2 or 3 coefficients, the Gauss-Newton method might stay on the wrong local minima and give the wrong result, but if we use 5 or more coefficients, the Gauss-Newton method will always give the correct answer since the global minima is the only one local minima.

For four unknown parameters α, β, S_a and S_p, the experimental results yield similar result. So the first five coefficients are enough for estimate these parameters stably.

4 Image Relighting Result

Generating photo-realistic images under different lighting conditions is a challenging problem. Ratio image technique [12, 19, 20] has been used widely in this field.

But one problem of ratio image technique is that it could not handle the cast shadow. If there is no cast shadow in the original image, it won't generate cast shadow in the re-rendered image though cast shadow exists in the reference image and vice versa.

We could compute the cast shadow in the re-rendered images according the estimation of the light direction in the reference image. Then we apply this cast shadow mask on the re-rendered image derived by ratio image technique to generate more realistic images. Fig. 7 shows the image relighting result.

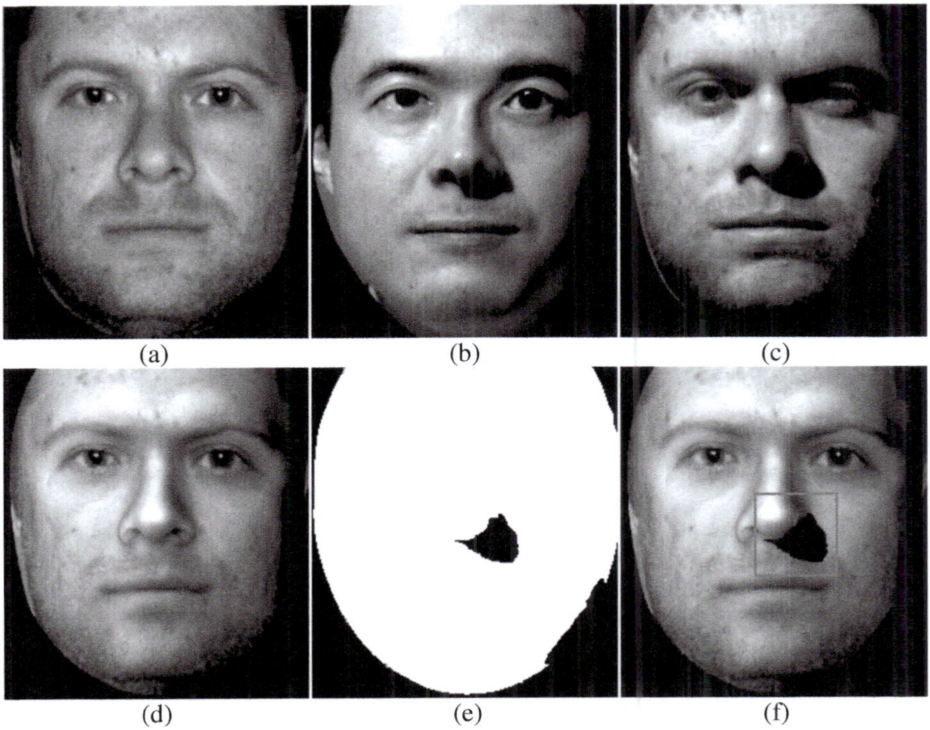

Fig. 7. Image relighting results. (a) original image; (b) reference image; (c) ground truth; (d) relighting image by ratio image technique; (e) generated cast shadow mask; (f) (c)*(e) yield the final relighting result.

From Fig. 7 we could see that there is no cast shadow in the original image, but it appears in the relighting images (f)(mainly the cast shadow of the nose). Since we only use a generic 3D model, the position of generated cast shadow is not very accurate. If we could get the accurate 3D model of the specified person, the result will be better but it needs more training images.

5 Conclusion and Future Works

This paper presents an algorithm for estimating the parameters of single point light source plus ambient light from spherical harmonics coefficients in frequency space by a known 3D geometry. This algorithm project the image to a low dimensional orthogonal linear subspace, then estimate the illumination parameters in this subspace via nonlinear optimization method. So the speed of this algorithm is very fast, the time cost for a 276*225 image is only 0.27s on AMD 2.2G CPU. The experimental results on synthesized images and real face databases show the effectiveness of the algorithm on first 3 subsets (<55°). When the light direction is far from camera's axis, there are some cast shadows in the image since human face is not totally convex which cause the estimation result deteriorate.

To solve this problem, we plan to iteratively calculate the cast shadow region on face model and remove it from the template according the result of the last step, henceforth estimate the new lighting direction parameters and update the cast shadow region.

The estimated lighting direction could be used to generating more realistic image than popular methods based on ratio image technique, since we could calculate the cast shadow regions by ray-casting techniques. Furthermore it could be used in face recognition application to improve the recognition rate as in [15].

Acknowledgement. This work is supported by the National Natural Science Foundation of China (No. 60433030).

References

1. Yang, W., Samaras, D.: Estimation of multiple directional light sources for synthesis of mixed reality images. Proc. 10th Pacific Conference on Computer Graphics and Applications (2002) 9-11
2. Samaras, D., Metaxas, D.: Coupled Lighting Direction and Shape Estimation from Single Images. Proc. of the International Conference on Computer Vision (1999) 868-874
3. Ortiz, A., Oliver, G.: Estimation of Directional and Ambient Illumination Parameters by means of a Calibration Object. Proceedings of the IAPR International Conference on Image Analysis and Recognition (2004)
4. Zhou, W., Kambhamettu, C.: A Unified Framework for Scene Illuminant Estimation. 15th British Machine Vision Conference (2004)
5. Bouganis, C.-S., Brookes, M.: Multiple light source detection. IEEE Trans. Pattern Analysis and Machine Intelligence, vol. 26 (2004) 509-514
6. Zhang, Y., Yang, Y.-H.: Multiple illuminant direction detection with application to image synthesis. IEEE Trans. Pattern Analysis and Machine Intelligence, vol. 23 (2001) 915-920
7. Basri, R., Jacobs, D.: Lambertian Reflectance and Linear Subspaces. Proc. Eighth IEEE Int'l Conf. Computer Vision (2001) 383-390
8. Basri, R., Jacobs, D.: Lambertian reflectance and linear subspaces. IEEE Trans. Pattern Analysis and Machine Intelligence, vol. 25 (2003) 218-233
9. Ramamoorthi, R., Hanrahan, P.: On the Relationship between Radiance and Irradiance: Determining the Illumination from Images of a Convex Lambertian Object. J. Optical Soc. Am. A, vol. 18 (2001) 2448-2459
10. Ramamoorthi, R.: Analytic pca construction for theoretical analysis of lighting variability in images of a lambertian object. IEEE Trans. Pattern Analysis and Machine Intelligence, vol. 24 (2002) 1322-1333
11. Ramamoorthi, R., Hanrahan, P.: A Signal-Processing Framework for Reflection. ACM Transactions on Graphics, vol. 23 (2004) 1004-1042
12. Wen, Z., Liu, Z., Huang, T.: Face Relighting with Radiance Environment Maps. Proc. Com-puter Vision and Pattern Recognition Conf. (2003) 158-165
13. Lee, K.C., Ho, J., Kriegman, D.J.: Nine Points of Light: Acquiring Subspaces for Face Recognition under Variable Lighting. Proc. Computer Vision and Pattern Recognition Conf. (2001) 519-526

14. Qing, L., Shan, S., Gao, W.: Face Recognition with Harmonic De-lighting. Proc. ACCV (2004)
15. Georghiades, A., Belhumeur, P.: From Few to many: Illumination cone models for face recognition under variable lighting and pose. IEEE Trans. Pattern Analysis and Machine In-telligence, vol. 23 (2001) 643-660
16. Sirovitch, L., Kirby, M.: Low-Dimensional Procedure for the Characterization of Human Faces. J. Optical Soc. Am. A, vol. 2 (1987) 519-524
17. Turk, M., Pentland, A.: Eigenfaces for Recognition. J. Cognitive Neuroscience, vol. 3 (1991) 71-96
18. Sim, T., Baker, S., Bsat, M.: The CMU Pose, Illumination, and Expression Database. IEEE Trans. Pattern Analysis and Machine Intelligence, vol. 25 (2003) 1615-1618
19. Riklin-Raviv, T., Shashua, A.: The quotient image: Class based re-rendering and recongnition with varying illuminations. Proceedings of CVPR 1999 (1999) 566-571
20. Liu, Z., Shan, Y., Zhang, Z.: Expressive expression mapping with ratio images. Proceedings of SIGGRAPH 2001 (2001) 271-276

An Efficient Real Time Low Bit Rate Video Codec

Shikha Tripathi[1], R. Vikas[2], and R.C. Jain[1]

[1] Electrical & Electronics Group,
Birla Institute of Technology & Science, Pilani, India
{shikha, rcjain}@bits-pilani.ac.in
[2] Electronics & Instrumrntation Group,
Birla Institute of Technology & Science, Pilani, India
vikas_84bf@rediffmail.com

Abstract. The implementation of a codec for real time applications such as video-conferencing at low bit rates is discussed. The discrete cosine transform has been used for compression, both in two spatial axes as well as in the time axis of the video sequence. A new method of frame by frame processing is proposed which reduces the real time delay associated with processing and transmission of successive video frames, with minimal memory and processing overhead. This implementation is inherently simple and also provides improved performance compared to other popular codecs

1 Introduction

The need for compression is constantly increasing due to the multimedia nature of mobile data. Video compression helps overcome this problem and is a necessary step for widespread introduction of applications of video based mobile phones like teleconferencing and video broadcasting. A satisfactory video compression technique must have the following characteristics:

- It should produce levels of compression comparable to MPEG based and other standards without objectionable artifacts.
- It should be able to compress as well as play back in real time with inexpensive hardware support.
- It should incorporate minimal delay, memory and computational complexity.
- It should not degrade much under network overload or on a slow platform
- It should be resilient to expected types of errors like packet loss during transmission.

The proposed scheme aims at satisfying almost all the above mentioned criteria. A simplified scheme of the compressor with various components is given Fig.1.

In the next section, the scheme, which implements the DCT in the third dimension or time axis, is discussed. In the sections that follow, the mathematical analysis of the proposed algorithm is explained, where a formula for error function has been derived and a method to minimize the cumulative error has been proposed. This is followed by a discussion of the actual results obtained. Other components are based on standard methods [1,3,5].

P.J. Narayanan et al. (Eds.): ACCV 2006, LNCS 3851, pp. 500 – 508, 2006.

Nth frame →2-D spatial DCT → FFT based time axis DCT with modified algorithm → Qunatizer → EntropyCoding → Compressed video frame.

Fig. 1. The Proposed Encoded Structure

2 The 3-D DCT and the Proposed Algorithm

The DCT is popular for its property of compact energy redistribution among fewer components in the transform domain compared to the original image. The formula for the three dimensional DCT (size 8X8X8) is :

$$F(u,v,w) = C(u)C(v)C(w)\sum_{x=0}^{7}\sum_{y=0}^{7}\sum_{z=0}^{7} f(x,y,z)[\cos(2x+1)u\pi/16]*[\cos(2y+1)v\pi/16][\cos(2z+1)w\pi/16] \quad (1)$$

where x,y,z are pixel indices in pixel space; f(x,y,z) is the value of a pixel in pixel space; u,v,w are pixel indices in DCT space; F(u,v,w)is a translated pixel value in DCT space; C(i)=1/√2 for i=0 and C(i)=1 for i>0.

Although standards like MPEG use different methods like motion compensation, to take advantage of correlation among successive frames, it has been found that such methods are computationally very complex and are therefore not well suited for transmission at low bit rates whenever computational simplicity is desired. Hence, of late, some research has been directed towards pure transform based techniques, which are simpler to implement, the 3-D DCT being one among them. Since an efficient real time fast algorithm for a "true" 3-D DCT has not been found yet, Eq(1) is implemented by running the one dimensional transform once in all three axes: namely the X-Y spatial axes and the temporal axis T. DCT is found to perform optimally for all the three axes if the number of elements is 8[2]. Detailed structure of this algorithm is given in [7]. However, research has also been conducted on adaptive block size based on the estimation of the amount of motion present in the sequence. [6]

In the conventional method using 3-D DCT [1], for every raw uncompressed video frame arriving at the coder, the DCT is first run in the X and Y directions for every 8X8 block in the frame. Then, the temporal DCT is run on each row in the time axis, for 8 such successive frames collected. For example, one of these temporal rows on which the time axis DCT acts is a set of pixels in positions (X=2,Y=3) in frames 1,2,3,4,5,6,7and 8, which means a pixel in the same spatial location is taken from 8 successive frames and the DCT is run on the row of 8 pixels thus formed along the temporal axis. This is repeated for all such possible rows along time axis. This is equivalent to splitting the whole video sequence of frames into 3 dimensional cubes of size 8X8X8 and running 3-D DCT on all such 3-D cubes formed. However, this conventional method presently used for 3-D DCT implementation [1] that has proved to be much simpler to implement compared to MPEG and motion based techniques, has the following drawbacks:

- The transform in time axis runs on 8 frames at a time, therefore each time it has to wait for 8 frames to accumulate before it can be run. This would lead to considerable time delay at the encoder as well as at the decoder.
- This algorithm requires storage of 8 frames at any instance of time, thus requiring considerable memory space.
- Accumulation of 8 frames and their simultaneous transmission after processing requires large bandwidth.

Our proposed algorithm, given below, eliminates these drawbacks and also maintains the simplicity in computation:

Step 1: We are required to wait only for the first frame to accumulate and initialize the sum buffer B_{sum} to 0.
Step 2: Then the intraframe 2-D DCT is run on all 8X8 blocks of the first frame and transmit the data (after quantization and entropy coding).
Step 3: This is repeated for the next 6 frames and the buffer B_{sum} is kept updated, by adding the pixel values of each new frame to B_{sum}. It is to be noted that only the buffer B_{sum} is stored (which is of the size of a single frame) and not the frames themselves, thus saving on memory space.
Step 4: The buffer B_{sum} is stored, which corresponds to the first 7 frames that have been coded. This frame consists of the sum of the values of those pixels that occupy the same spatial position in successive frames. Eg: Sum of pixels in position (1,1) in frames 0 to 6.
Step 5: From frame 7 onwards, for every new frame coming in, the intraframe 2-D DCT is performed on that frame. Then, the temporal axis DCT is run for a group of 2 frames: the most recent frame and the other stored frame (B_{sum}). This is run starting from the most recent frame moving towards the other stored frame (B_{sum}). After this, B_{sum} is updated based on the modified algorithm explained in the next section.

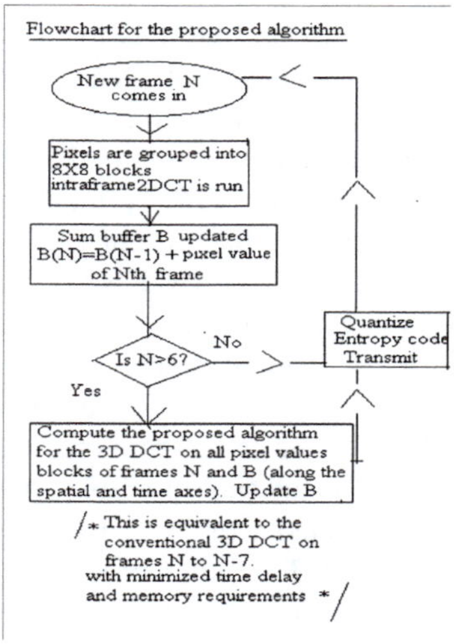

Fig. 2. Flowchart for the proposed algorithm

Step 6: Unlike the conventional 3-D DCT algorithm, which requires storing of 7 previous frames at any time, the proposed algorithm makes use of a single frame storage approach. This frame stored is the buffer B_{sum}.
Step 7: Thus for each new frame N (N>6) which comes in now, use the frame N and buffer B_{sum} to encode this frame N using the 3-D DCT (followed by the standard quantization and entropy coding). This requires a modification of the 3-D DCT, which is explained in the next section.

The flowchart for the proposed algorithm is given in Fig. 2.

3 Modification of the 3-D DCT

The 3-D DCT for each new frame N coming into the encoder (frame 8 onwards) can be expressed in terms of the 2-D intraframe DCT applied on the frame N as well as the temporal axis DCT applied on the Frame N along with 7 other previous frames.

An important difference from the conventional method is that the temporal DCT is applied here in the reverse direction to that of the order of frame arrival, i.e. for frames N to N-7, by considering the most recent frame (frame N) as the first frame (frame '0') for the temporal DCT. Since these previous frames are not stored, let only one "Sum" frame S be desired to be stored due to memory constraints, we adapt and modify the 3-D DCT to be applied on these 2 frames S and N only. Note that this frame S, which should contain the sum of pixels from frames N to N-7, is different from the actually stored buffer B mentioned earlier. The reason why this difference arises as well as the relation between S and B is derived later in this section. It will be shown that DCT frame '0' (frame N in this case, since we are running the DCT in the reverse direction, from frame N moving towards frames N-1, N-2 and so on up to frame N-7) can be thought of as the DC frame, conveying the information common to each of the image frames. The other DCT frames all convey AC information, which corresponds to motion in the original image sequence. frame '0' (frame N here) is 2-D-Discrete-Cosine-Transformed to produce one frame F(0), with 2-D-DCT coefficients. Next, let all 8 frames (i.e. frame N to frame N-7) be 3-D-Discrete-Cosine-Tansformed to produce a set of cubes (8X8X8 sized) of 8 frames with 3-D-DCT coefficients F(u,v,w). The coefficients F(0,v,u), which correspond to frame '0' (frame N in this case) can be calculated using Eq(1) by setting w=0 and rearranging w, y and x axes coefficients.

$$F(0,v,u) = C(u)C(v)C(w)\sum_{x=0}^{7}\sum_{y=0}^{7}\sum_{z=0}^{7} f(x,y,z)[\cos(2x+1)u\pi/16]*[\cos(2y+1)v\pi/16][1] \qquad (2)$$

The rearrangement is done as it enables the use of the proposed algorithm along the temporal axis. Then, letting original image sequence F(z,y,x) = F(0,y,x) + δ(z,y,x), the operations on F(0,y,x) and δ(z,y,x) can be considered separately [2,4]. Here, F(0,y,x) is frame '0' which when transformed, gives the 'DC' coefficient frame F(0,v,u) containing the average pixel values for the 8 frame sequence considered. δ(z,y,x) is the term proportional to the amount of motion present in the frame sequence. We are interested in the transform coefficient set of frame '0' (which is frame N in our frame sequence) F(0,y,x) which is F(0,v,u) and it is explored further below.

F(0,v,u), which is the 3-D DCT coefficient set for frame '0' (frame N) can be decomposed into two components: these components are: 1) a term proportional to F(0) which contains the 2-D DCT coefficients; and 2) a term proportional to the amount of motion present in the 8 image frames (frames N-1 to N-7), relative to the first frame.(frame N).Thus, this gives:
$F(0,v,u) = \sqrt{8} * F(0) + S_\delta(v,u)$; Where, the relative motion term,

$$S_\delta(v,u) = C(u)C(v)C(w)\sum_{x=0}^{7}\sum_{y=0}^{7}\sum_{z=0}^{7}\delta(x,y,z)[\cos(2x+1)u\pi/16]*[\cos(2y+1)v\pi/16]*[1] \tag{3}$$

Here, δ(x,y,z) is a pixel value relative to the corresponding pixel in the first frame (frame '0') of the 8 frame sequence, with the same spatial location (x,y). Thus, the values in Sδ (v,u) depends on δ(x,y,z) for a given X and Y coordinate. Thus, Sδ (v,u) is directly dependent on the relative values of pixels in frames 1 to 7 (N-1 to N-7) with respect to the pixels (with same spatial coordinates) in frame '0' (frame N). Thus for a particular spatial location (x=X,y=Y) and corresponding transform domain location (u=U,v=V),

$$S_\delta(v=V, u=U) = KD \tag{4}$$

where,

$D(x=X, y=Y) = \sum_{z=1}^{7} f(X,Y,z) - f(X,Y,0)$ and K is a proportionality constant.

D(X,Y) can be re-written as,

$$D(X,Y) = \sum_{z=1}^{7} f(X,Y,z) - [7 * f(X,Y,0)] \tag{5}$$

Thus, for each frame, we require the sum of the 7 previous frames. For the first frame coded in this manner (frame 7), the sum frame S(x=X,y=Y) for a particular spatial location (X,Y) is given by,

$$S_1(X,Y) = \sum_{z=0}^{6} f(X,Y,z) - [7 * f(X,Y,7)] \tag{6}$$

Note that frame '0' for this case is frame 7, which depends on pixel values of previous frame numbers 6, 5, 4, 3, 2, 1 and 0. Similarly, for the second frame encoded in this manner (frame 8),

$$S_2(X,Y) = \sum_{z=1}^{7} f(X,Y,z) - [7 * f(X,Y,8)] \tag{7}$$

Extending this idea to any frame N, let f(X,Y,z) be denoted by f(z) and $S_N(X,Y)$ by S_N. Then, from Eq(7), the desired frame sum S_2 requires the sum $f_1 + f_2 + f_3 + f_4 + f_5 + f_6 + f_7$. However, the sum buffer B_{sum}, which has been maintained in the encoder as stated earlier, actually has the value of buffer sum equal to $B_{sum} = f_0 + f_1 + f_2 + f_3 + f_4 + f_5 + f_6 + f_7$. It is clearly seen that the buffer B_{sum} contains an extra term f_0 (an unwanted contribution from frame 0) that should be removed. However, the problem is that we no longer have the values of pixels from frame 0. To overcome this problem and still minimize the effect of the pixels from frame 0 as desired (which is what would have happened had we been able to directly remove the extra term f_0 from B_{sum}), the following procedure is followed:

Subtract the mean M of pixel values f_0 to f_6 from the buffer B_{sum} and store it as B', instead of storing B_{sum}.

$$B' = B_{sum} - M \tag{8}$$

where $M = (f_0 + f_1 + f_2 + f_3 + f_4 + f_5 + f_5)/7$
This results in an error due to the approximation of desired frame sum S(X,Y) by the actually stored sum buffer value B', which is:
Error,
$E_2 = E_N = S(X,Y) - B' = (f_1 + f_2 + f_3 + f_4 + f_5 + f_6 + f_7) - [(f_0 + f_1 + f_2 + f_3 + f_4 + f_5 + f_6) - (f_0 + f_1 + f_2 + f_3 + f_4 + f_5 + f_6)/7] - f_7$. On simplification,

$$E_2 = (f_0 + f_1 + f_2 + f_3 + f_4 + f_5 + f_6)/7 - f_0 \tag{9}$$

Since for a slowly moving video, the changes in the pixel values are gradual, expected value of mean M is f_0, hence error E→0. thus this method is proved to be convergent, which has also been validated with experimental results. Therefore, the approach we follow is to find the Error for frame N, $E_N = S_N(X,Y) - B'$ and try to minimize it. For a frame N+6 (run N of this motion based approach after the first 7 frames have been intraframe coded), E_{N+6} can be minimized by considering another related value C, which is defined as the error due to the unwanted contribution of a frame L (L<N+6). As an example, $C_{N+6}(0)$, which is the error due to the unwanted contribution of first frame, frame 0 to the above described processing of frame N+6 expressed as a percentage of the pixel values in frame 0 is obtained by extending Eq(8) and Eq(9) for any value N, and is given by,

$$C_{N+6}(0) = [1/7 + 1/8 + \ldots\ldots + 1/(N+5) - 1] * 100 \tag{10}$$

Similarly, percent error due to contribution of pixels of frame 1 in the processing of frame N+6 is,

$$C_{N+6}(1) = [1/8 + 1/9 + \ldots\ldots + 1/(N+5) - 1] * 100 \tag{11}$$

and so on. We design the receiver structure in order to minimize this cumulative error. Extending Eq(10) and Eq(11) for any general frame value L (L<N+6), the total cumulative error sum due to C(0), C(1) etc. totally affecting a transmitted (and hence received frame) N+6, is given by a recursive relation,

$$Q_{N+6} = Q_{N+5} + \left[\sum_{i=0}^{N+4} f_i / (N+5) \right] - f_{N-2} \tag{12}$$

Thus, at the receiver, we need to have a Q buffer, which we keep on updating by adding Q_N whenever a new frame received is decoded. This buffer Q thus contains the cumulative error history which takes care of the (recursive) first term in the right hand side of Eq(12).This value can be subtracted from the received coefficient values to remove first error term. Also, similar to the transmitter, we also have a received frames sum buffer R, which is constantly updated by adding the scaled values (i.e. multiplied by N+5) of the pixels in the latest frames decoded. This removes the second error term in the right hand side of Eq(12). The last term is of concern since this requires the storage of a frame that has been decoded 8 frames before the present frame. This requires a buffer H of the most recent 8 frames at the receiver, which is updated constantly, which is the main memory requirement for the decoder, similar to the 3-D DCT decoder. If this is done, the third term in the right hand side of Eq(12) is also eliminated thus removing all error terms.

4 Results

The encoder and decoder were simulated using MATLAB 6.1. The simulation was carried out for the conventional 3-D DCT, the proposed codec, and also the intraframe 2-D DCT based codec. The original and encoded/decoded frames from a real time captured video are shown in Fig. 3. and Fig. 4. The calculation of the PSNR is in Table. 1.

Although not evident here, there is a fair degradation of quality in this case, unlike the next sequence "Seaplane" where the quality is not lost much. This is because the original "Seaplane" sequence is of medium quality.

Also, Table. 1 indicates that even before quantization and entropy coding, the bits per pixel value of 0.7 gives a PSNR of 15 to 24 dB that is acceptable for real time streaming. Further, in Table. 2, the comparison of the proposed method with the conventional 3-D DCT is given.

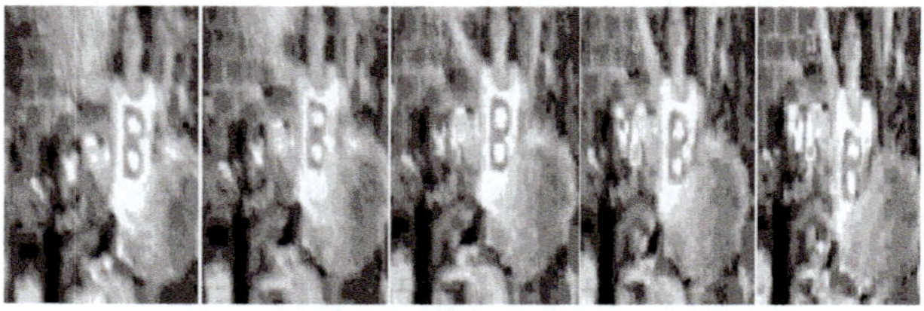

(a)

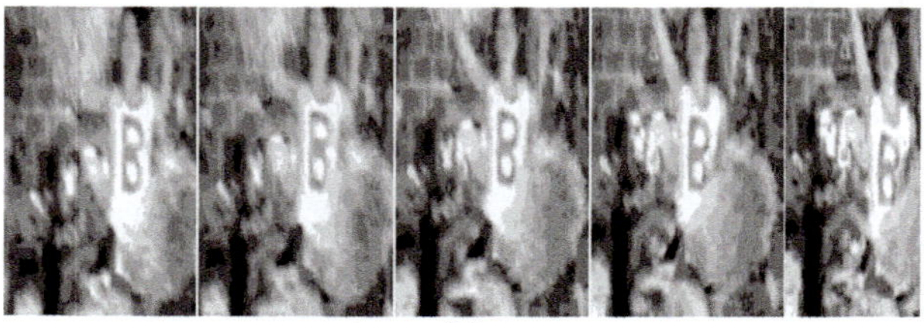

(b)

Fig. 3. (a) "Girl"-Original sequence (noisy in nature, typical of low quality streaming video)at 8 bits/pixel. (b) "Girl" sequence passed through the codec at 0.7 bits/pixel.

(a)

(b)

Fig. 4. (a) "Seaplane" at 8 bits/pixel (A medium quality video). (b) "Seaplane" after compression to 0.7 bits/pixel. The medium video quality is maintained even after compression in this case.

Table 1. Statistics of the 2 video sequences

Sequence	Bits per pixel (b.p.p)	PSNR(dB) (proposed method)	PSNR(dB) (conventional method)
1.Girl (noisy/streaming quality)	0.7	15.10	15.94
2.Seaplane (medium quality)	0.7	23.66	24.49

Table 2. Comparison between conventional 3-D DCT, simple intraframe 2-D DCT & proposed method for various test video sequences

Method of compression used	Time Delay in frame accumulation (in seconds)	Encoder Memory requirement (for a 340*240 sized video sequence) in kilobytes	Bits per pixel (b.p.p) (before quantization and entropy coding)
Conventional 3-D DCT	0.25	614.4	0.7
Proposed algorithm	0.03	153.6	0.7
Intraframe 2-D DCT only (for each frame)	0.03	76.8	1.875

For completeness, simple intraframe 2-D DCT has also been considered (which is similar to motion JPEG and does not take advantage of the temporal correlation among frames). It is clear from Table. 2 that the proposed algorithm retains the higher compression property of 3-D DCT. However, at the same time it does away with the time delay by reducing it to nearly (1/8)th of the delay in the 3-D DCT method. Additionally, the proposed method has the advantage of requiring lesser memory, which is (1/4)th that of 3-D DCT and is almost comparable to the minimal memory requirements of the basic 2-D DCT method.

5 Conclusion

The proposed algorithm has a performance, which is considerably superior to the conventional algorithm. In terms of time, the improvement is almost of an order of magnitude and requirement of memory is only about 25% of that required for the conventional method. These advantages are achieved while still retaining almost the same video quality as that obtained by the conventional 3-D DCT. As shown in the mathematical analysis in section-4, this method is convergent leading to zero error. However, there is scope for further improvement in finding the function, which minimizes the buffer H memory requirement at the decoder further over a large range of frame number N.

References

1. R. Westwater, B. Furht.: Real-Time Video Compression. Techniques and Algorithms. Kluwer Academic Publishers. Boston (1997)
2. M Servais, G Jager.: Video Compression using the 3 dimensional Discrete Cosine Transform. Proceedings of IEEE, COMSIG '97 (1997) 27-32.
3. Video Coding for Low Bit Rate Communication, H.263 Standard, ITU-T Recommendation H.263, February (1998)
4. B.P.Lathi.: Signal Processing and Linear Systems. Oxford University Press (1998)
5. P. Clarkson, H. Stark(Ed).: Signal Processing Applications for Audio, Images and Telecommunications. 2nd Edition. Academic Press (1995)
6. Furht, B., Gustafson, K., Huang, H., and Marques, O.: An adaptive three-dimensional DCT compression based on motion analysis. In Proceedings of the 2003 ACM Symposium on Applied Computing. ACM Press, New York. (2003) 765-768
7. Xiuqi Li and Borko Furht.: An Approach to Image Compression Using Three-Dimensional DCT. Proceedings of the Visual 2003 Conference. Miami, Florida. (2003)

Employing a Fish-Eye for Scene Tunnel Scanning

Jiang Yu Zheng[1] and Shigang Li[2]

[1] Dept. of Computer Science, Indiana University Purdue University Indianapolis,
723 W. Michigan St. Indianapolis, IN46202, USA
jzheng@cs.iupui.edu
http://www.cs.iupui.edu/~jzheng
[2] Dept. of Computer and Information Science, Iwate University,
4-3-5 Ueda, Morioka, Iwate 020-8551, Japan
li@cis.iwate-u.ac.jp
http://cv.lk.cis.iwate-u.ac.jp

Abstract. This work employs a fish-eye to scan cityscapes along a street and register scenes in a compact scene tunnel image. A fish-eye has complete field of view along a route. We mount the fish-eye camera on a vehicle and estimate its pose initially with respect to the vehicle by referring to 3D structure lines of such as roads and buildings on a street. Sampling curves are then allocated in the image frame for dynamic scanning route scenes as the vehicle moves forward. The accurate alignment of the curves ensures less distortion of shapes in the scene tunnel image. We also analyze the scanned results and evaluate alignments of the sampling curves to improve the scanning. The resulting scene tunnel is a continuous archive of the entire route in a city, which can be used for environment visualization and assessment, Internet based virtual navigation, city information indexing, etc.

1 Introduction

To register cityscapes for a visual map, the *route panorama* has been proposed to archive street scenes [1][2], which is a continuous image different from local panoramic views at static positions. A video camera moves along a smooth path and a long image of the path is generated with the slit scanning mechanism [3][4][5][6][10][17]. The slit scanning differs from most of the image patch stitching [12] or video mosaicing, since only a pixel line is collected at an instance when the camera undertakes translation. The slit scanning requires no inter-frame matching and morphing in creating the image so that it is suitable for transiting cameras viewing scenes even with complex occlusions, and real time route scene archiving. In order to capture both sides of a street, multiple cameras have been stacked to scan a *scene tunnel* that contains complete heights, three distinct aspects, and a long image length [6]. The compact data size and complete coverage of scenes benefit scene visualization, texture mapping on urban models, image transmission for navigation, virtual tour, etc.

In this paper, we explore the use of a fish-eye camera to achieve the scene tunnel acquisition. A fish-eye camera can capture half space scenes in an image, and thus is efficient to scan entire scene around the camera trajectory. It avoids many issues so far such as calibrating and synchronizing multiple cameras, integrating scenes at

P.J. Narayanan et al. (Eds.): ACCV 2006, LNCS 3851, pp. 509 – 518, 2006.

different heights and sides, and normalizing photometric properties in the connected images for generating the scene tunnel. In this paper, we explore the following issues.

(1) How to mount a fish-eye camera properly on a vehicle for route scenes?
(2) How to align sampling pixels (lines/curves) in the image frame to scan a scene tunnel so that the shapes of typical structures on the street can be preserved?
(3) How to calibrate the camera external parameter with respect to the street structure for localizing the sampling curves, if the camera is not set ideally on the vehicle?
(4) How the shapes are distorted due to an imprecise setting of a sampling curve, and how it can be improved?

Many works on the fish-eye camera calibration have been reported for 360 degree local panoramic view acquisition [7][8][9][13][14][15]. We will use these results for the calculation of the camera pose in an outdoor environment, in order to locate sampling curves and implement scene tunnel scanning for long distances.

In the following, we introduce the plane of scanning to acquire a scene tunnel, and the setting of a fish-eye camera in section 2. The selection of the sampling curves and their initial calibration in the image frame are discussed in section 3. The scanned results are analyzed and the refinement is given in section 4.

2 Acquiring Scene Tunnel Along a Camera Path

There is an expectation to project long route scenes to a single image, which can be simply retrieved with maps in GIS and many other applications. To capture complete views, a spherical retina is located on a vehicle *O-X'Y'Z'* moving along a smooth path on a horizontal roadway. The ideal vehicle motion has a translation $\boldsymbol{V}$ in the heading direction and a rotation R_y around the vertical axis, realized by a four-wheeled vehicle with a good suspension system.

2.1 Scene Tunnel Scanning Under Ideal Camera Setting

To capture non-redundant scenes for a compact representation, a *plane of scanning (PoS)* is set from the retina center to scan scenes along its trajectory [5]. As the vehicle moves forward, the temporal data on the *PoS* are projected towards the retina center and are imaged at a pixel curve $C(\theta)$ that is the intersection of the *PoS* and the retina surface. Here θ is azimuth angle of a line of sight in the *PoS* (correspond to latitude on the sphere). If we copy the temporal data from the sampling curve $C(\theta)$ and list them along the time axis, a scene tunnel $T(t, \theta)$ is obtained. The reason to select a 3D plane for scanning is that many structure lines such as building rims and road edges exist in urban environments. A plane can scan them instantaneously to obtain straight shapes in the resulting scene tunnel.

A *PoS* is desired to be set vertically in the 3D space when the vehicle is moving on a horizontal road; all architectures projected in the *scene tunnel* thus keep vertical for visualization and texture mapping [1][2]. The *scene tunnel* is the generalization of the *route panorama* that extends a pixel line to a sampling ring for the complete heights and sides [6]. To achieve this goal, multiple cameras are directed to different heights, which increases the system complexity.

Denote the angle between the vertical *PoS* and heading direction ***V*** by α. If a *PoS* is non-orthogonal to ***V*** (α≠π/2), the scanned scene tunnel includes not only building fronts but also partial side façades on the street. If three *PoS* (α<π/2, α=π/2, α>π/2) are set for fore-side, side, and rear-side scenes along a street, scene tunnels can cover all the visible route scenes.

Because the scene tunnel image is composed of consecutive 1D views, it has special object shape distortion under the parallel-central projection [1][2]. We focus on three types of lines in the analysis. In a street space, there are vertical lines, horizontal lines orthogonal to the roadway, and lines along the roadway on the street structures (Fig. 1). These lines, denoted as line sets ***L***, ***M***, and ***N***, are orthogonal to each other, and the remaining lines can be expressed as the linear combinations of them. The projections of ***L***, ***M***, and ***N*** sets in the image are denoted by ***l***, ***m***, and ***n***, respectively. Considering the camera motion along ***N***, *PoS* are set parallel to ***L*** and ***M*** for scanning architectures and ground.

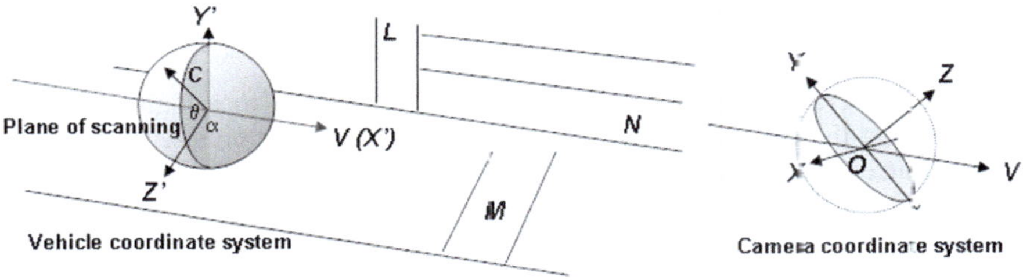

Fig. 1. Scanning a scene tunnel by a spherical retina along a path with typical structure lines

2.2 Scene Scanning with a Fish-Eye Camera

A fish-eye camera *O-XYZ* maps half-space scenes onto a circular image *I(x,y)*. According to the equidistance projection model of the fish-eye lens [8], point *P(X,Y,Z)* in the space is projected to *p(x,y)* in the image and is represented in a polar coordinates system $p(\varphi, \gamma)$ as

$$\rho = (x^2+y^2)^{1/2} \qquad \tan\varphi = y/x \qquad \gamma = \rho/f \tag{1}$$

where γ is the angle between the line of sight *OP* and the optical axis *OZ*, and *f* is the camera focal length. The line of sight can also be represented by a vector in the *O-XYZ* as

$$(X,Y,Z) = v(\varphi,\gamma) = (\sin\gamma\cos\varphi,\ \sin\gamma\sin\varphi,\ \cos\gamma) \tag{2}$$

We use a fish-eye lens (Olympus FCON-w2) in front of a video camera to capture image *I'(x',y')*. By calibrating the internal parameters of the lens [15] such as optical center $\boldsymbol{o}(x_0,y_0)$, focal length *f*, and radial distortion, the coordinates of a point in *I'(x',y')* can be converted to that in *I(x,y)* that obeys the equidistance model.

There are several ways to set the fish-eye camera for street scanning as depicted in Fig. 2. The camera can be mounted at front, side, top of the vehicle to face forward, side, up, or fore-up directions, respectively. The sampling curves allocated must scan optical flows in the fish-eye image, in order to generate the scene tunnel image.

(1) The forward setting obtains both building fronts and the ground. Two curves aligned with $\boldsymbol{l}$ and another curve on $\boldsymbol{m}$ can be set for scanning. The drawback is incapable of taking rear-side views. Moreover, angle α cannot be close to $\pi/2$. Otherwise, the image perimeter is sampled and the image quality is low. The same defect appears at the top. A large FOV is assigned to the ground that is not considered as important as the side scenes.
(2) The camera set at the vehicle top can scan fore-side, side and rear-side scene tunnels with three sampling curves. Scenes lower than the camera position are not included in the scene tunnel. It wastes a large FOV on sky area if most scenes along a street are low.
(3) Placing a fish-eye camera sideways covers entire side scenes and the camera is easy to mount. Three curves can be set for fore-side, side, and rear-side scene tunnels. However, two fish-eye cameras are needed for both-side scenes.
(4) Directing the camera forward-up to include full building heights and partial road surface. It is an ideal setting we employ for our street scanning.

For all the camera settings, the angular resolutions assigned to a high-rise are the same; directing the camera upward does not increase the building size in the image. The sampling curves are set according to the distinct *PoS* to scan $\boldsymbol{L}$ and $\boldsymbol{M}$ lines in *O-X'Y'Z'*. As the vehicle traverses a street, a video is taken and the 1D data on the sampling curves is copied to the scene tunnel at a fixed rate (30~60Hz).

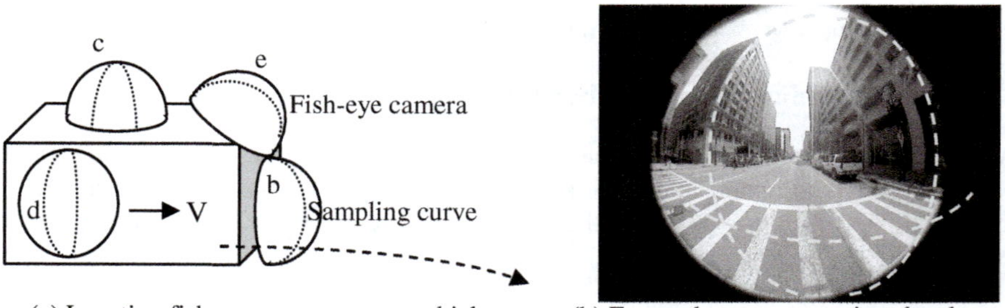

(a) Locating fish-eye cameras on a vehicle (b) Forward: curves scanning l_{left}, l_{right}, m

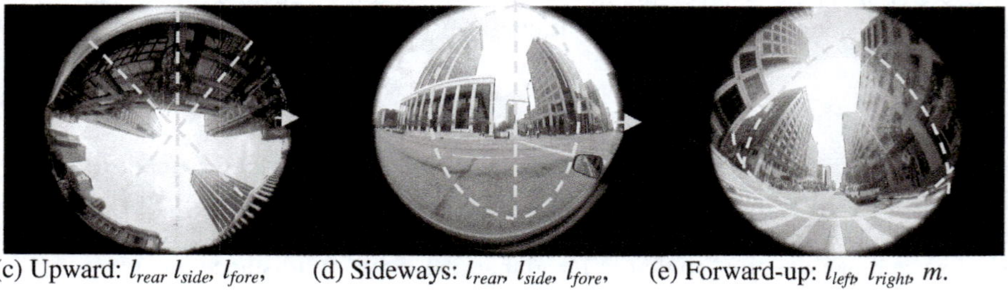

(c) Upward: l_{rear} l_{side}, l_{fore}, (d) Sideways: l_{rear}, l_{side}, l_{fore}, (e) Forward-up: l_{left}, l_{right}, m.

Fig. 2. Different settings of a fish-eye camera and their images with designed sampling curves

3 Calibration of Sampling Curves for Scene Scanning

After the fish-eye camera is mounted, there is no guarantee that the camera axis is exactly aligned with the **V** direction. We have to calibrate the orientation of the camera system *O-XYZ* with respect to the vehicle system *O-X'Y'Z'*. This ensures a correct allocation of sampling curves for the designed *PoS*. We park the vehicle on a straight road with high buildings around. The road surface is measured to be horizontal and the mounted camera takes a sample image with many straight lines. Different from the fish-eye lens calibration focusing on the internal parameters, we use parallel structure lines in the real scene to locate their vanishing points, which characterize the camera pose. Then the sampling curves are computed accordingly for vertical *PoS*. Although the located *PoS* may change instantly in the route scanning afterwards due to vehicle bumping on uneven roads, the major road sections will yield reasonably good results.

3.1 Calibrating Camera Pose Using Structure Lines in Sample Images

Let us examine the shapes of structure lines **L**, **M**, and **N** in the fish-eye images (Fig. 3). In general, the projection of a line in the fish-eye image is a curve. A line in the space determines its *plane of sight* Γ with *O*. The plane Γ intersects the spherical retina at a *great circle* *C*. A 3D line segment P_1P_2 determines the normal of Γ from $OP_1 \times OP_2$. Further, parallel lines in the space determine planes of sight Γ_j, $j=1,2,3,\ldots$. These planes intersect each other at a vector **Q** through **O**, which is parallel to the line set. Its projection to the spherical retina is the penetrating point at **q** as Fig. 3(c) depicted. A Γ_j is projected to a great circle C_j on the retina. Since **Q** is the intersection of all Γ_j, **q** is the crossing point of all C_j. Therefore, **q** is the *vanishing point* of the line set. Detecting the position of the vanishing point in the image tells the camera orientation with respect to the line set. Fig. 3 shows a forward and a slanted setting of a fish-eye camera and their images. We can find structure lines **L**, **M**, and **N** projected as curves **l**, **m**, and **n** in Fig. 4. These lines can be characterized by three pairs of vanishing points $\mathbf{q}_L$, $\mathbf{q}_M$, and $\mathbf{q}_N$, respectively. Some points are not in the image (on the other half of the spherical retina).

We first extract line segments on buildings in the sample image $I'(x',y')$ by edge detector and tracking algorithm, and convert the coordinates to that in the non-distorted image $I(x,y)$. Denoting the *i*th point on *j*th curve by $\mathbf{x}_{ij}=(x_{ij},y_{ij})$, $i, j=1,2,3\ldots$ in $I(x,y)$, we calculate the line of sight through $\mathbf{x}_{ij}$ is (X_{ij}, Y_{ij}, Z_{ij}) according to (2). Manually selecting an extracted line $\mathbf{l}_j$, all its points are filled into a total least squared error method for the normal $\mathbf{n}_j=(a_j, b_j, c_j)$ of Γ_j in the *O-XYZ*, where $a_j^2+b_j^2+c_j^2=1$. It minimizes

$$\Sigma_i[(X_{ij}, Y_{ij}, Z_{ij})\bullet(a_j, b_j, c_j)]^2 \rightarrow \min \tag{3}$$

Denote the coordinates of vanishing point by $\mathbf{Q}(X_L, Y_L, Z_L)$ in *O-XYZ*, it can be obtained through the second least squared error estimation from multiple normal $\mathbf{n}_j$, by

$$\Sigma_j[(X_L, Y_L, Z_L)\bullet(a_j, b_j, c_j)]^2 \rightarrow \min \tag{4}$$

By tracking edge points on **n** and **m** curves, we calculate the vanishing points $\mathbf{q}_N$ and $\mathbf{q}_M$ in the same way as for $\mathbf{q}_L$.

(a) (b) (c)

Fig. 3. Different fish-eye camera poses and their captured images. (a) An ideal forward setting of fish-eye camera. (b) An inclining camera setting by changing camera yaw, pitch and roll. (c) Vanishing point on spherical retina surface.

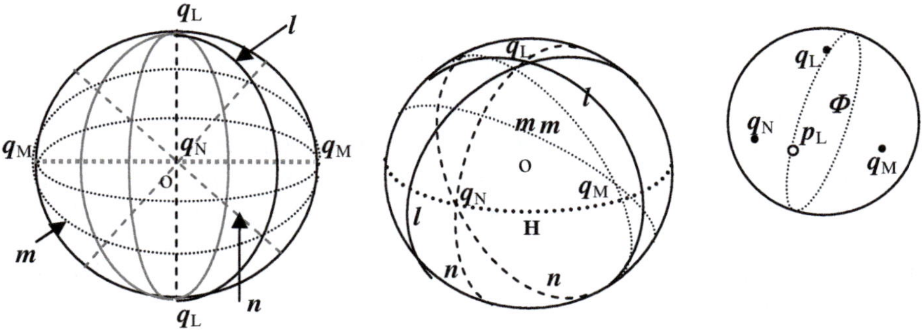

Fig. 4. Projected structure lines and the corresponding vanishing points in the fish-eye image. (a) Ideal camera setting in Fig. 3(a). (b) Projected curves *l*, *m*, *n* converge to their vanishing points in Fig. 3(b). (c) Vanishing point and pin point for setting PoS.

3.2 Initial Setting of Sampling Curves in Fish-Eye Image Frame

Because the fish-eye camera *O-XYZ* captures a half space, at least one quadrant of the *O-X'Y'Z'* system is covered. Among six vanishing points of three orthogonal line sets $\boldsymbol{L}$, $\boldsymbol{M}$, and $\boldsymbol{N}$ in *O-X'Y'Z'*, at least one set $\boldsymbol{q}_L$, $\boldsymbol{q}_M$, and $\boldsymbol{q}_N$ can be found within the fish-eye image. After detecting their positions from tracked curve sets $\boldsymbol{l}$, $\boldsymbol{m}$, and $\boldsymbol{n}$, we generate sampling curves for scene tunnel scanning.

For the calculated vanishing point $\boldsymbol{q}_L$, we select a pin point $\boldsymbol{p}_L$ in the image (Fig. 4(c)), considering the orientation of $PoS(\alpha)$. The lines of sight $\boldsymbol{v}(\boldsymbol{q}_L)$ and $\boldsymbol{v}(\boldsymbol{p}_L)$ through the two points can form a *PoS* parallel to line set $\boldsymbol{L}$, with the normal

$$\boldsymbol{n}_{\mathrm{L}} = \boldsymbol{v}(\boldsymbol{q}_L) \times \boldsymbol{v}(\boldsymbol{p}_L) \tag{5}$$

A line of sight $\boldsymbol{v}(\varphi, \gamma)$ on such a *PoS* must satisfy

$$\boldsymbol{n}_{\mathrm{L}} \bullet \boldsymbol{v}(\varphi, \gamma) = 0 \tag{6}$$

(a) Two sides only. (b) Stationary blurred. (c) Sampling curve inaccurate. (d) Refined tunnel

Fig. 5. Fish-eye camera scanned scene tunnels T(θ, t), $\theta \in [0,800]$ pixels along urban and suburban streets

Given $\varphi \in [0, 2\pi]$ with a fine interval, we can obtain corresponding γ for the sampling curve. It is further converted to (x,y) by using (2) and then to (x',y') in the fish-eye image frame. The distinct pixels on the curve are accumulated as a continuous C for sampling. Figure 5(a) displays a scene tunnel $T(t,\theta)$ copied from C_{Lleft} and C_{Lright} curves aligned with $\boldsymbol{l}$ lines in the image of 640×480 pixels.

For line set $\boldsymbol{M}$, the process to locate a curve for scanning the ground is similar. The resulting ground part thus has all the crossing pedestrians appearing straight in the scene tunnel from a linear vehicle path. Lines $\boldsymbol{N}$ appear straight and parallel to the t axis in the scene tunnel, and are disturbed if the vehicle deviates from a straight path.

4 Result Analysis and Refinement

4.1 Scene Tunnel Affected by Feature Distance

How important the alignment of sampling curves is and what happens if they are not precisely located? An immediate result one can imaging is that buildings are all slanted. However, some more serious defect is caused from an imperfect alignment. Fig. 6 shows a section of a scene tunnel where vertical lines at distance are more slanted than close ones. Because the *scene tunnel* at two sides contains scenes with different depth, a 2D skew transform is unable to rectify the image. This additional effect happens because the physical width of the sampling curve (one pixel) is not infinitely thin. The fish-eye video camera has a low-resolution image in over a half space. A pixel has a large angular coverage in the space. Through a pixel, the *Point Spread Function* (PSF) gets wide as the distance increases.

When the *PSF* moves across features at speed V (Fig. 7), a distant feature has longer response duration than a close feature because a wider *PSF* covers on it. This causes the distant edge blurred in the scene tunnel, which is named *stationary blur* in [11]. The degree of blur is more significant as the depth increases. Fig. 5(b) shows a scene tunnel from two side sampling curves. Stationary blur is obvious on the houses and trees because of their far distances from the roadsides. The close parts are sharp; it even has no motion blur on the vehicle shadow on the road surface. If the sampling line is non-parallel to the vertical edges as shown in Fig. 7, the responses at different heights are more sheared for a large *PSF* than a small *PSF*, even if the PSF regions are slanted in the same degree. This difference makes the edges incline differently.

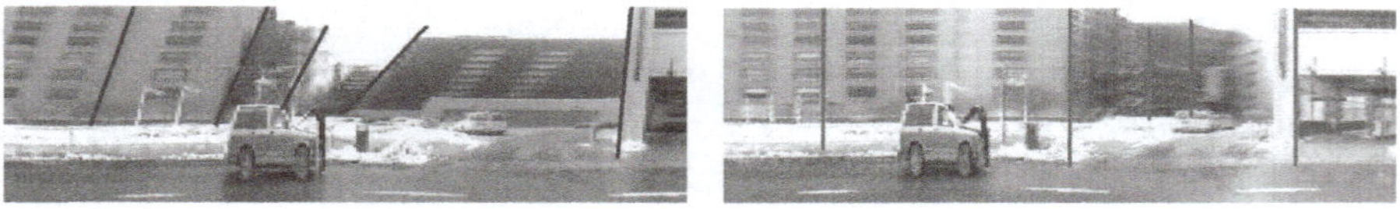

Fig. 6. Slanted vertical rims in the scene tunnel if the sampling line is not precisely aligned with the projection of a vertical line. (a) Declined edges due to imperfect alignment of the pixel line. (b) A precisely set sampling line generates a good shape of vertical lines.

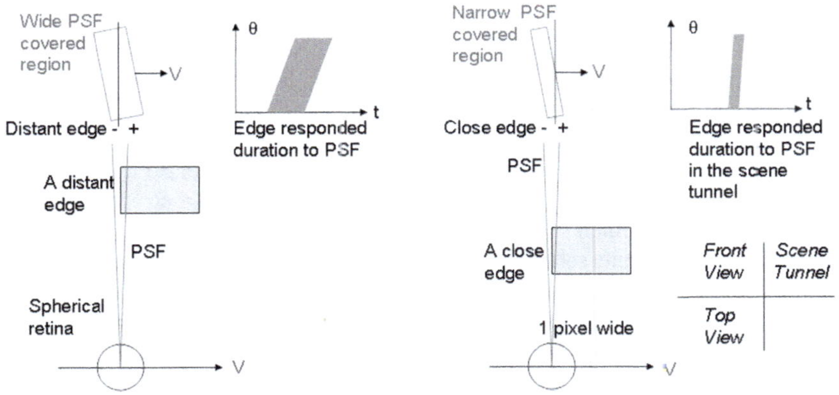

Fig. 7. Different sizes of the Point Spread Function of a sampling line at different distances, and the scanned edges in the scene tunnel. Edges at different depths have different slanting angles.

Based on above analysis, close features are less influenced from slanted sampling curves than distance features. If a street has close building fronts, the error caused from the calibration of the sampling lines is not significant. For distance features, we can observe large, coarse edges slanted in the background. If a sampling line is located imperfectly, a common slanting direction and bending can be observed in the resulting scene tunnel (Fig. 5(c)).

4.2 Scanning Refinement of Scene Tunnel

From a limited number of sample images in a long video sequence, it is difficult to obtain an accurate camera pose for scanning all the routes. Based on the scanned result of a scene tunnel, we can refine the position and shape of the sampling curves for the second scanning of the recorded video.

Because the setting of sampling curves has position error, we have to assess the calibration based on the scanned scene tunnel. On the time axis of the scene tunnel, we locate long periods without shaking, verified by consistent orientations (or slanting directions) of the projected building rims. From these periods, we pick up some time instances when a high building (or a high rim) is imaged. The video frames at such moments are loaded again for the refinement of the sampling curves. A curve segment is adjusted precisely on a projection of the long rim in the image. The recorded video is scanned again with the updated sampling curve. This refinement guarantees that most parts of a route are scanned in good shape (except the shaking road segments). If no structure line can be found in the entire scanned scene tunnel, no sample image will be retaken from the video sequence for further refinement. The deformed shapes in the remaining nature scenes are not critical to the visualization. Fig. 5(c) shows such an initial scanning with bended structure lines on the ground and slightly on buildings. Some shaking road segments are at the street crossings. Such defects are reduced after the refinement in Fig. 5(d).

5 Conclusion

This work explores the using of a fish-eye camera, localization and calibration of sampling curves for scanning scene tunnels from a moving vehicle. It avoids many system issues with multiple cameras in the scene scanning. We located multiple sampling curves on the projection of structure lines in order to generate the scene tunnel with preserved shapes. We calculated the camera pose from the structure lines, and scanned long scene tunnels successfully. We further analyzed the influences on shapes from an inaccurate setting of the sampling line. The future work will be the scene tunnel scanning with a high-definition TV camcorder, in order to obtain high-resolution scene tunnel with less stationary blurs. The scene tunnel is then a digest of street views for VR visualization, information indexing, and environment assessment.

References

1. Zheng, J.Y., Route Panorama, *IEEE Multimedia*, 10(3), 57-68, 2003.
2. Zheng, J. Y., Shi, M., Mapping cityscapes into cyberspace for visualization, J. Computer Animation and Virtual Worlds, 16(2), 97-107, 2005.
3. Zheng, J. Y., Tsuji, S., Panoramic Representation for route recognition by a mobile robot, *IJCV*, 9(1), 55-76, 1992.
4. Gupta, R., Hartley, R., Linear pushbroom cameras, IEEE PAMI, 19(9), 963-975, 1997.
5. Zheng, J. Y., Tsuji, S., Generating dynamic projection images for scene representation and recognition, Computer Vision and Image Understanding, 72(3), 237-256, 1998.
6. Zheng, J. Y., Zhou, Y., Shi, M., Scene tunnels for seamless virtual tour, 12th ACM Multimedia, 448-451, 2004.
7. Xiong, Y., Turkowski, K., Creating image-based VR using a self-calibrating fisheye lens, IEEE CVPR, 237-241, 1997.
8. Kannala, J., Brandt, S., A General Camera Calibration Method for fish-eye lens, ICPR2004, Vol. 1, 692-695, 2004.
9. Li, S., Nakano, M., Chiba, N., Acquisition of spherical image by fish-eye conversion lens, IEEE VR04 235-236, 2004.
10. Peleg, S., Rousso, B., Rav-Acha, A., Zomet, A., Mosaicing on adaptive manifolds, IEEE PAMI, 22(10), 1144-1154, 2000.
11. Shi, M., Zheng, J. Y., A slit scanning depth of route panorama based on stationary blur, IEEE CVPR05, Vol. 1, 1047-1054, 2005.
12. Zhu, Z., Hanson, A., Riseman, E. M., Generalized parallel-perspective Stereo Mosaics from Airborne Video. *IEEE PAMI* 26(2): 226-237, 2004
13. Bakstein, H., Bajdla, T., Panoramic mosaicing with 180 field of view lens, Omnidirectional vision workshop, 60-68, 2002.
14. Swaminathan, R., Nayar, S. K., Nonmetric calibration of wide-angle lenses and polycameras, IEEE PAMI 22(10), 2000.
15. Li, S., Estimating head orientation based on sky-ground representation, IEEE/RSJ Int. Conf. Intelligent Robots and Systems 05.
16. Uyttendaele, M. *et al.* Image-based interactive exploration of real-world environments. *IEEE Computer Graphics and Applications,* 24(3), 2004.
17. Li, S., Hayashi, A., Robot navigation in outdoor environments by using GPS information and panoramic views, IEEE/RSJ Conf. Intelligent Robots and Systems, 570-575, 1998.

Automatically Building 2*D* Statistical Shapes Using the Topology Preservation Model GNG

José García Rodríguez[1], Anastassia Angelopoulou[2], Alexandra Psarrou[2], and Kenneth Revett[2]

[1] Departamento de Tecnología Informática y Computación, Universidad de Alicante, Apdo. 99. 03080 Alicante, Spain
jgarcia@dtic.ua.es

[2] Harrow School of Computer Science, University of Westminster, Harrow HA1 3TP, United Kingdom
{agelopa, revettk, psarroa}@wmin.ac.uk

Abstract. Image segmentation is very important in computer based image interpretation and it involves the labeling of the image so that the labels correspond to real world objects. In this study, we utilise a novel approach to automatically segment out the ventricular system from a series of MR brain images and to recover the shape of hand outlines from a series of 2*D* training images. Automated landmark extraction is accomplished through the use of the self-organising model the growing neural gas (GNG) network which is able to learn and preserve the topological relations of a given set of input patterns without requiring *a priori* knowledge of the structure of the input space. The GNG based method is compared to other self-organising networks such as Kohonen and Neural Gas (NG) maps and results are given showing that the proposed method preserves accurate models.

1 Introduction

Modelling the shape of a class of non-rigid objects in two-dimensions requires the recovery of their structure from a set of images. A common modelling approach is the observation and analysis of a set of examples of the object or class of objects using standard statistical methods such as principal component analysis (PCA). This approach has turned out to be very effective in image segmentation and interpretation. The basic idea of statistical shape modelling is to establish new unseen legal instances of shapes taken from a given set of training examples, using as few parameters as possible. Shape training sets usually come from manually annotated boundaries. The difficulty arises over the need to automate the process. For example, in a clinical setting the first stage in the post-processing step of a T1-weighted MRI technique is to segment out the ventricles, which can be difficult in many cases if the patient is not properly aligned in the scanner. These post-processing step is laborious and must be very accurate if the purpose of the scan is to help determine the extent of disease progression. In very overburdened medical facilities, performing this task manually may not be

P.J. Narayanan et al. (Eds.): ACCV 2006, LNCS 3851, pp. 519–528, 2006.

feasible. An automated procedure may provide the means of yielding objective and consistent results across various institutions. It is imperative therefore that an accurate, rapid and automated algorithm be developed and deployed. That is the subject of the rest of this paper.

In literature, various attempts have been made to automate the process of landmark based image registration and correct correspondences among a set of shapes. Baumberg's *et al.* [1] method, which generates flexible shapes models by using equally spaced spline control points around the boundaries of walking pedestrians, is an example of arbitrary parameterisation. The process is automatic, but it is arbitrary since it uses properties of the specific shape being modelled (each shape has a principal axis) thus, not generally applicable. Davies *et al.* [2] method of automatically building statistical shape models by re-paremeterising each shape from the training set and optimising an information theoretic function to assess the quality of the model has received a lot of attention recently. The quality of the model is assessed by adopting a minimum description length (MDL) criterion to the training set. The MDL is obtained from information theoretic considerations and has been used quite extensively by a number of researchers due to its ability to locate dense correspondence between the boundaries [3, 2, 4]. This is a very promising method and the models that are produced are comparable to and often better than the manual built models. However, due to very large number of function evaluations and nonlinear optimisation the method is computationally expensive. Recently, Fatemizadeh *et al.* [5] have used modified growing neural gas to automatically correspond important landmark points from two related shapes by adding a third dimension to the data points and by treating the problem of correspondence as a cluster-seeking method by adjusting the centers of points from the two corresponding shapes. This is a promising method and has been tested to both synthetic and real data, but the method has not been tested on a large scale for stability and accuracy of building statistical shape models.

In this work, we introduce a new and computationally inexpensive method for the automatic selection of landmarks along the contours of $2D$ MRI slices of human brain and hand outlines. The incremental Neural Network, the growing neural gas (GNG) is used to automatically annotate the training set without using *a priori* knowledge of the structure of the input patterns. Unlike other methods, the incremental character of the model avoids the necessity to previously specify a reference shape. The method is used for the representation of $2D$ ventricles and hand shapes, which can be extended to $3D$. To evaluate the accuracy of the method we have tested it with other self-organising models such as Kohonen maps and Neural Gas (NG) maps and global distance error [6] have been applied to measure the quality of the adaptation of the network.

The remaining of the paper is organised as follows. Section 2 introduces the statistical shape models. Section 3 provides a detailed description of the topology learning algorithm GNG. A set of experimental results along with qualitative analysis is presented in Section 4, before we conclude in Section 5.

2 Statistical Shape Models

Statistical shape models are flexible models that have been used to capture the variability of a class of objects using a set of examples. The most well known statistical shape models are Cootes *et al.* [7] "Point Distribution Models" (PDMs) that models the shape of an object and its variation by using a set of n_p landmark points from a training set of S_i shapes. In this work, PDM represents the shape of an object as a set of n_p automatically extracted landmarks in a vector $\mathbf{x} = [x_{i0}, x_{i1}, ..., x_{in_{p-1}}, y_{i0}, y_{i1}, ..., y_{in_{p-1}}]^T$. In order to generate flexible shape models the S_i shapes are aligned (translated, rotated, scaled) and normalised (removing the centre-of-gravity and placing it at the origin) to a common set of axes. The modes of variations of the hand are captured by applying principal component analysis (PCA). Using PCA, valid shapes can be represented by allowing the landmark points to undergo displacements relative to the mean shape and in directions defined by the eigenvectors of the covariance matrix Σ. The K most significant eigenvectors are ordered according to the magnitudes of their corresponding eigenvalues to form the matrix of column vectors $\Phi = (\phi_1 \mid \phi_2 \mid \phi_3 \mid ..... \mid \phi_k)$ where $\lambda_1, \lambda_2, \lambda_3, ...\lambda_k$, is the order of the magnitude of the eigenvectors [8]. By retaining only the modes of variation with the highest variance plausible and compact shapes can be generated Any shape can be back-projected to the input space by a linear model of the form:

$$\mathbf{x} = \overline{\mathbf{x}} + \Phi\beta_i \tag{1}$$

where $\overline{\mathbf{x}}$ is the mean shape, Φ describes a set of orthogonal modes of shape variations, and β_i is a vector of weights for the ith shape. To ensure that the above weight changes describe reasonable variations we restrict the weight β_i to the range $-3\sqrt{\lambda} \leq \beta_i \leq 3\sqrt{\lambda}$. PCA works well as long as good correspondences exist. To obtain the correspondences and represent the contour of the hands and the ventricles the self-organising network GNG was used.

3 Topology Learning

One way of selecting points of interest along the contour of 2*D* shapes is to use a topographic mapping where a low dimensional map is fitted to the high dimensional manifold of the contour, whilst preserving the topographic structure of the data. A common way to achieve this is by using self-organising neural networks where input patterns are projected onto a network of neural units such that similar patterns are projected onto units adjacent in the network and vice versa. As a result of this mapping a representation of the input patterns is achieved that in postprocessing stages allows one to exploit the similarity relations of the input patterns. Such models have been successfully used in applications such as speech processing [9], robotics [10, 11] and image processing [12]. However, most common approaches are not able to provide good neighborhood and topology preservation if the logical structure of the input patten is not known *a priori*. In fact, the most common approaches specify in advance the number of neurons in the network and a graph that represents topological relationships between them, for example, a two-dimensional grid, and seek the best match to the given input pattern manifold. When this is not the case the networks fail to provide good topology preserving as for example in the case of Kohonen's algorithm.

The approach presented in this paper is based on self-organising networks trained using the Growing Neural Gas learning method [13]. This is an incremental training algorithm where the number of units in the network are determined by the unifying measure for neighborhood preservation [14], the topographic product. The links between the units in the network are established through competitive hebbian learning [15]. As a result the algorithm can be used in cases where the topological structure of the input pattern is not known *a priori* and yields topology preserving maps of feature manifold [16].

3.1 Growing Neural Gas

In this Section we describe the complete growing neural gas algorithm and ending condition as used in this work. The network is specified as:

- A set N of nodes (neurons). Each neuron $c \in N$ has its associated reference vector $w_c \in R^d$. The reference vectors can be regarded as positions in the input space of their corresponding neurons.
- A set of edges (connections) between pairs of neurons. These connections are not weighted and its purpose is to define the topological structure. An *edge aging scheme* is used to remove connections that are invalid due to the motion of the neuron during the adaptation process.

The GNG learning algorithm to approach the network to the input manifold is as follows:

1. Start with two neurons a and b at random positions w_a and w_b in R^d.
2. Generate at random an input pattern ξ according to the data distribution $P(\xi)$ of each input pattern. In our case since the input space is the contour, the input pattern is the (x, y) coordinate of the edges. Typically, for the training of the network we generated 1000 to 10000 input patterns depending on the complexity of the input space.
3. Find the nearest neuron (winner neuron) s_1 and the second nearest s_2 by:
$$s_1 = \arg\min_{c \in A} \| \xi - w_c \| \quad (2)$$
and
$$s_2 = \arg\min_{c \in A\{s_1\}} \| \xi - w_c \| \quad (3)$$
4. Increase the age of all the edges emanating from s_1:
$$age_{(s_1,i)} = age_{(s_1,i)} + 1 \ (\forall i \in N_{s1}) \quad (4)$$
5. Add the squared distance between the input signal and the winner neuron to a counter error of s_1 such as:
$$\Delta error(s_1) = \|w_{s_1} - \xi\|^2 \quad (5)$$

6. Move the winner neuron s_1 and its topological neighbours (neurons connected to s_1) towards ξ by a learning step ϵ_w and ϵ_n, respectively, of the total distance:
$$\Delta w_{s_1} = \epsilon_w(\xi - w_{s_1}) \tag{6}$$
$$\Delta w_{s_n} = \epsilon_w(\xi - w_{s_n}) \tag{7}$$
for all direct neighbours n of s_1.
7. If s_1 and s_2 are connected by an edge, set the age of this edge to 0.
$$age_{(s_1,s_2)} = 0 \tag{8}$$
If it does not exist, create it.
8. Remove the edges larger than a_{max}. If this results in isolated neurons (without emanating edges), remove them as well.
9. Every certain number λ of input patterns insert a new neuron as follows:
   - Determine the neuron q with the maximum accumulated error:
   $$q = \arg\max{}_{c \in A} E_c \tag{9}$$
   - Determine among the neighbours of q the neuron f with the maximum accumulated error:
   $$f = \arg\max{}_{c \in N_q} E_c \tag{10}$$
   - Insert a new neuron r between q and its further neighbour f:
   $$w_r = 0.5(w_q + w_f) \tag{11}$$
   - Insert new edges connecting the neuron r with neurons q and f, removing the old edge between q and f.
10. Decrease the error variables of neurons q and f multiplying them by a fraction α:
$$\Delta error_(q) = -\alpha E_q \tag{12}$$
$$\Delta error_(f) = -\alpha E_f \tag{13}$$
11. Initialize the error variable of r with the new value of the error variable of q and f.
$$E_r = \frac{(E_q + E_f)}{2} \tag{14}$$
12. Decrease all error variables by multiplying them with a constant γ.
13. If the stopping criterion is not yet achieved (in our case 144 neurons), go to step 2.

The parameters used in all simulations were: $\lambda = 1000$, $\varepsilon_w = 0.1$, $\varepsilon_n = 0.001$, $\alpha = 0.5$, $\gamma = 0.95$, $a_{max} = 250$. The testing involved two cases were the number of neurons were too few or too excessive for the training set of the images. In the former the topological map is lost, not enough neurons to represent the contour of the ventricles and the hands and in the later an overfit is performed.

4 Experiments

4.1 Hands

The hand database, was composed of images of four individuals who contributed with four images of their right hand and at different poses. We used 16 hand shapes which were extracted from the training set by thresholding. All images were of same size 395x500 pixels. In Figure 1 the modes are displayed by varying the first three shape parameters $\beta_i\{\pm 3\sigma\}$ over the training set. The first mode

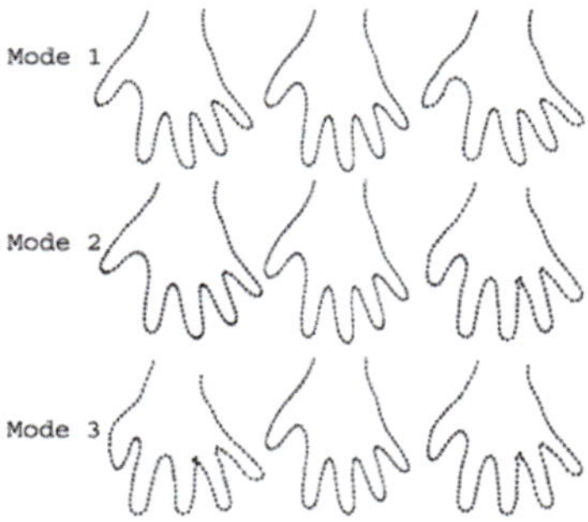

Fig. 1. The first three modes ($m = 1, 2, 3$) of variation of the automatically hand built model. Range of variation $-3\sqrt{\lambda} \leq \beta_i \leq 3\sqrt{\lambda}$.

β_1 varies the shape of the thumb and increases the distance between the middle and the index finger. The second mode β_2 varies the distance between the thumb and the index finger, and bends the middle finger. The third mode β_3 varies the shape of the middle finger and the thumb. In Figure 2 two shape variations from the automatically generated landmarks were superimposed to the training set and the in between shape instances are drawn which shows the flexing of middle finger and hand rotation. These modes effectively capture the variability of the training set and present only valid shape instances. Table 1 shows the

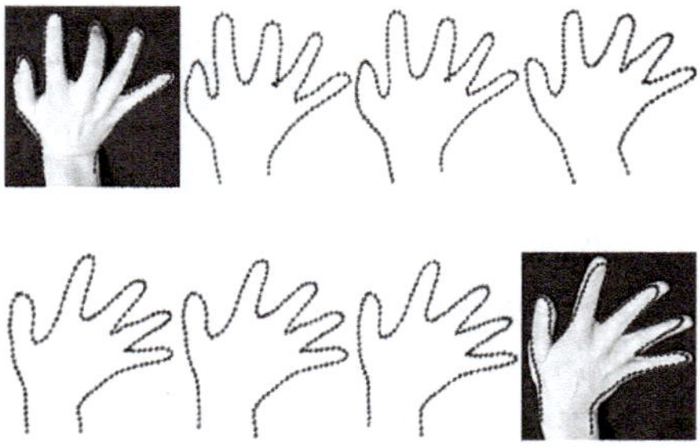

Fig. 2. Superimpose shape instances to the training set and taking the in between steps

Table 1. A quantitative comparison of various neurons adapted to the hand model with variances for the first six modes and the total variance

Mode	25 neurons	61 neurons	100 neurons	144 neurons	169 neurons
1	2.1819	4.2541	3.2693	1.5253	2.5625
2	1.2758	2.2512	1.4869	1.1518	0.9266
3	0.6706	0.5681	0.6154	0.9808	0.5734
4	0.4317	0.4645	0.4977	0.3968	0.3101
5	0.3099	0.2844	0.3532	0.3716	0.2491
6	0.2305	0.2489	0.1292	0.1980	0.1927
V_T	5.7486	8.6170	6.4108	5.1783	5.2470

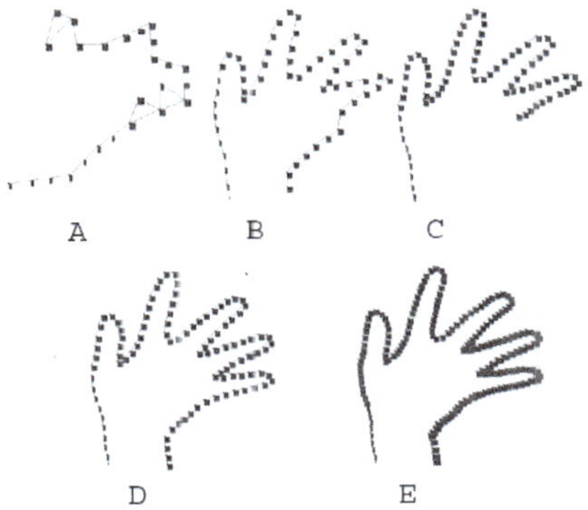

Fig. 3. Adaptation to an object with network of 25 (Image A), 61 (Image B), 100 (Image C), 144 (Image D), and 169 (Image E), neurons

total variance achieved by maps containing varying number of neurons (25, 61, 100, 144, 169) used for the automatic annotation (Figure 3). The map of 144 neurons is the most compact since it achieves the least variance. It is interesting to note that whilst there is significant difference between 25, 61 and 100 neurons the mapping with 169 is good and has no significant difference with the mapping of 144 neurons. The reason is that for the current size of the images the distance between the neurons is short enough so adding extra neurons does not give more accuracy in placement. The introduction of extra neurons slows down the adaptation process.

4.2 Ventricles

The data that we used in this study was obtained from the MNI BIC Centre for Imaging at McGill University, Canada. These images are 1 mm thick, 181x217 pixels per slice, 3% noise and 20% INU. These images are used as our gold standard for segmentation, as every voxel in the entire volume has been correctly labeled to a tissue class by the McGill Institute. The entire brain volume consisted of 181 slices, from which we extracted those that contained ventricles (slices 49-91). Since most typical clinical MRI volumes are on average 5 mm

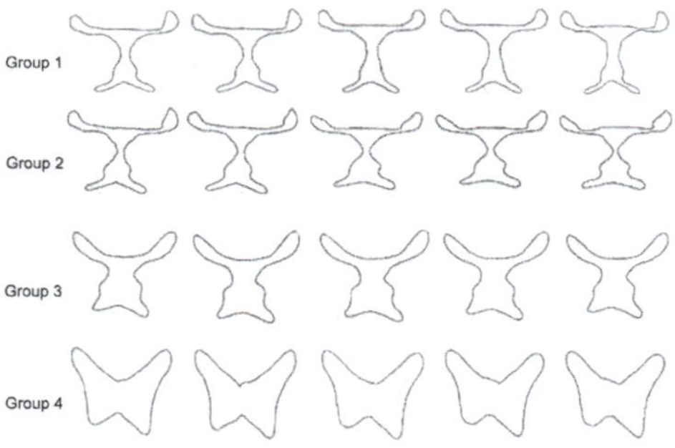

Fig. 4. The first mode ($m = 1$) of variation for the four groups of 5 contiguous slices taken from MR brain data. Range of variation $-3\sqrt{\lambda} \leq \beta_i \leq 3\sqrt{\lambda}$.

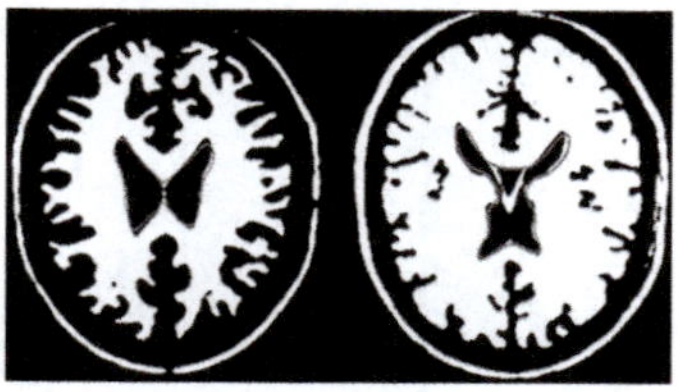

Fig. 5. Superimpose shape instances to the training set

Table 2. A quantitative comparison of various neurons adapted to the ventricle model with total variance per group

Groups	64 neurons	100 neurons	144 neurons	169 neurons
V_{T_1}	9.8340	1.9385	3.9668	3.9235
V_{T_2}	13.1873	1.7284	4.3672	3.1617
V_{T_3}	6.7822	2.0109	3.2260	4.0057
V_{T_4}	2.2567	1.6198	2.8398	3.5861

thick, we selected 4 groups of 5 contiguous slices to produce our point distribution model. In Figure 4 the modes of variation for all four groups are displayed by varying the first shape parameter $\beta_i\{\pm 3\sigma\}$ over the training set. The qualitatively results show that GNG leads to correct extraction of corners (sharp and smooth) of anatomical shapes and are compact when the topology preservation of the network is achieved.

In Figure 5 two shape variations from the automatically generated landmarks were superimposed to groups 4 and 3 from the training set. These modes effectively capture the variability of the training set and present only valid shape instances. Table 2 shows the total variance achieved by maps containing varying number of neurons used for the automatic annotation. The map of 100 neurons is the most compact since it achieves the least variance compared to 64, 144 and 169 neurons among the four groups. We have tested and compared our method with two other self-organising maps, the Kohonen and the NG map. The quantitative results show that GNG is significantly faster compared to Kohonen and NG, and the learning time is not so significant in GNG with the insertion of neurons compared to the other two where the adaptation process slows dramatically as the number of neurons increases. Figure 6 shows a comparative diagram of the learning time of various SOMs and at different number of neurons. The adaptation with 64 neurons is only 3 sec with GNG compared to the 57 sec and 52 sec with Kohonen and NG, but with 64 neurons the topology preservation in most of the shapes is lost independent of the selection of the SOM. A good adaptation with 100 and 144 neurons takes 6 and 11 seconds respectively at 1000 patterns to adapt to the contour of the ventricles.

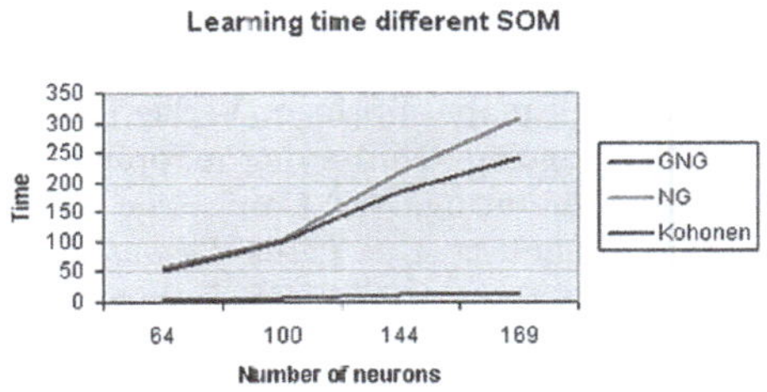

Fig. 6. Learning time for various SOMs and at various neurons

5 Conclusions

In this paper, we have used an incremental self-organising neural network to automatically annotate landmark points on a training set of hand and ventricle outlines. We have shown that the low dimensional incremental neural model (GNG) adapts successfully to the high dimensional manifold of the contour of the hands and the ventricles, allowing good eigenshape models to be generated completely automatically. The accuracy of our automated segmentation algorithm is comparable to other related SOMs and has better execution time. In future work, we could extend this technology so that it will generate 3*D* models directly. In addition, the generalisability of this model needs to be determined by applying it to various phantoms and other MRI standards. In addition, we will investigate what is the most suitable number of neurons for classifying ventricles. Lastly, we will investigate applying this technology to other brain tissue components in an effort to generate a complete MRI segmentation utility.

References

1. Baumberg, A., Hogg, D.: Learning flexible models from image sequences. 3rd European Conference on Computer Vision **1** (1994) 299–308
2. Davies, H.R., Twining, J.C., Cootes, F.T., Waterton, C.J., Taylor, J.C.: A minimum description length approach to statistical shape modeling. IEEE Transaction on Medical Imaging **21** (2002) 525–537

3. Thodberg, H.H., Olafsdottir, H.: Adding curvature to minimum description length shape models. In 14th British Machine Vision Conference **2** (2003) 251–260
4. Ericsson, A., Åstróm, K.: Minimizing the description length using steepest descent. In 14th British Machine Vision Conference **2** (2003)
5. Fatemizadeh, E., Lucas, C., Soltania-Zadeh, H.: Automatic landmark extraction from image data using modified growing neural gas network. IEEE Transactions on Information Technology in Biomedicine **7** (2003) 77–85
6. Angelopoulou, A., Psarrou, A., García, J., Kenneth, R.: Automatic landmarking of 2*d* medical shapes using the growing neural gas network. In Proc. IEEE ICCV Workshop on Computer Vision for Biomedical Image Applications, CVBIA 2005, LNCS 3765 (2005) 210–219
7. Cootes, T.F., Taylor, C.J., Cooper, D.H., J., G.: Training models of shape from sets of examples. 3rd British Machine Vision Conference (1992) 9–18
8. AL-Shaher, A., Hancock, R.E.: Learning mixtures of point distribution models with the EM algorithm. The Journal of Pattern Recognition **36** (2003) 2805–2818
9. Kohonen, T.: Self-organising maps. Springer Verlag (2001)
10. Ritter, H., Schulten, K.: Topology conserving mappings for learning motor tasks. In: Neural Networks for Computing, AIP Conf. Proc. (1986)
11. Martinez, T., Ritter, H., Schulten, K.: Three dimensional neural net for learning visuomotor-condination of a robot arm. IEEE Transactions on Neural Networks **1** (1990) 131–136
12. Nasrabati, M., Feng, Y.: Vector quantisation of images based upon kohonen self-organizing feature maps. In: IEEE Int. Conf. Neural Networks. (1988) 1101–1108
13. Fritzke, B.: A growing neural gas network learns topologies. In Advances in Neural Information Processing Systems 7 (1995) 625–632
14. Geoffrey, J., Goodhill, F., Terrence, J.: A unifying measure for neighbourhood preservation in topographic mappings. Proceedings of the 2nd Joint Symposium on Neural Computation **5** (1997) 191–202
15. Martinez, T.: Competitive hebbian learning rule forms perfectly topology preserving maps. In: ICANN. (1993)
16. Martinez, T., Schulten, K.: Topology representing networks. The Journal of Neural Networks **7** (1994) 507–522

Semi-metric Space: A New Approach to Treat Orthogonality and Parallelism

Jun-Sik Kim and In So Kweon

Dept. of EECS, KAIST
373-1 Kusong-dong, Yuseong-Gu, Daejeon, Korea
jskim@rcv.kaist.ac.kr, iskweon@kaist.ac.kr
http://rcv.kaist.ac.kr

Abstract. We propose a new method to recover 3D structures of artificial objects from scene pictures using orthogonality and parallelism. A new transformation group, "semi-metric space," is defined to describe the scenes of artificial objects consisting of orthogonal and parallel line features. A metric invariant called conic dual to the circular points has a simple diagonal form in the semi-metric space. Furthermore, under some assumptions, the metric reconstruction is possible using some affine properties. The algorithms are verified with real images captured with a camera in a commercial mobile phone.

1 Introduction

In the real world, there are many artificial objects. One of the most important properties of artificial objects is that they generally have many orthogonal and parallel structures. Orthogonality and parallelism are very useful cues to find structures of artificial objects, and there have been many approaches making use of them [1, 2, 3, 4, 5, 6, 7]. However, most methods have suggested using some independent information of the scenes or one of the cameras, in addition to orthogonality and parallelism [8].

Unfortunately there are few cases where the suggested independent information of the scene is obtained, if we want to work with *unknown* scenes. People can detect parallelism of line sets, and furthermore, orthogonality very easily. In fact, most of visual illusions are based on the properties of the human visual system. It means that human visual systems have been well-trained to detect parallelism and orthogonality. But it is quite difficult to find the suggested information, such as an exact aspect ratio of rectangles in three-dimensional space. As pointed out in [8, 5], this kind of information is critical to reveal the metric structures of the captured scenes.

In some instances, we cannot measure the scene physically and we do not have enough information about the cameras that are used to capture the scene. For example, there are many cases that we have some rectangles whose aspect ratios are unknown, if we are dealing with artificial objects. These cases occur when we want to use snapshot images captured in travel, or captured images from a

P.J. Narayanan et al. (Eds.): ACCV 2006, LNCS 3851, pp. 529–538, 2006.

television. What we are able to use is just information from the parallelism and the orthogonality.

In this paper, we study possibilities to use only parallelism and orthogonality with one or a few images in reconstructing artificial objects. First, we propose new transformation space called *semi-metric space* and study the properties of semi-metric space including *conic dual to the circular points*(CDCP) in the space, which plays an important role in reconstructing metric scene structures.

We extract the structures of the scenes from a single view and multiple ones using the proposed framework with images captured from a camera in a mobile phone.

2 Semi-metric Space

First, we define the new transformation space that deals with orthogonality and parallelism, called *semi-metric space.*

Semi-metric space is represented by a *semi-metric transformation.* A two-dimensional semi-metric transformation is expressed as

$$\mathbf{x}' = \mathsf{H}_{\mathsf{SM}}\mathbf{x} = \begin{bmatrix} s_1 & & \\ & s_2 & \\ & & 1 \end{bmatrix} \begin{bmatrix} \mathsf{R} & \mathbf{t} \\ \mathbf{0}^\top & 1 \end{bmatrix} \mathbf{x} \tag{1}$$

where R is a rotation matrix such that $\mathsf{R}^\top\mathsf{R} = \mathsf{R}\mathsf{R}^\top = \mathsf{I}$ and $\mathbf{t}$ is a translation vector. s_1 and s_2 are scale factors that are independent along the orthogonal axis.

Note that (1) is a kind of affine transformation and looks similar to the metric transformation with the exception of the diagonal scale matrix. In the semi-metric space, the metric properties along the parallel lines that are aligned to the X,Y axis in the warped plane are all preserved, but the ones not aligned to the axis are not preserved. Of course, affine properties are all preserved in the warped plane, because it is one of affine transformations.

Strictly speaking, the semi-metric transformation cannot be a general stratification of projective transformations because of these properties. However, semi-metric space provides a useful tool to analyze scenes that only contain information about the parallelism and orthogonality of certain planes.

2.1 Warping to the Semi-metric Space

For metric rectification of a projective distorted plane, there are several ways to find the rectifying homographies [7, 5]. Generally it is possible with five independent orthogonal line sets, or with a rectangle whose aspect ratio is known, or with a line at infinity and an orthogonal line pair. Essentially, these three conditions are all equivalent [5] to the case of a rectangle whose aspect ratio is known.

There are two ways to warp a projectively transformed image to semi-metric space. First one uses orthogonal vanishing points, and the other a standard rectangle.

Using Orthogonal Vanishing Points. We start from the general pinhole projection model as

$$\mathbf{x} \sim \mathsf{K} \begin{bmatrix} \mathbf{r}_1 \ \mathbf{r}_2 \ \mathbf{r}_3 \ \mathbf{t} \end{bmatrix} \begin{bmatrix} X \\ Y \\ Z \\ 1 \end{bmatrix} \tag{2}$$

where K denotes a camera matrix describing internal parameters of the camera, and $\mathbf{r}_1$, $\mathbf{r}_2$, $\mathbf{r}_3$, and $\mathbf{t}$ are column vectors of a rotation matrix and a translation vector. Without loss of generality, we set the reference plane as $Z = 0$. The vanishing points that correspond to the direction of $\mathbf{r}_1$, $\mathbf{r}_2$, and $\mathbf{r}_3$ are $\mathbf{v}_1$, $\mathbf{v}_2$, and $\mathbf{v}_3$. We assume that a circle is on the reference plane, and as derived in [9], the projected dual circle is expressed as

$$\begin{aligned} \mathsf{A}^{-1} &= s_1\mathbf{v}_1\mathbf{v}_1^\top + s_2\mathbf{v}_2\mathbf{v}_2^\top + s_3\mathbf{x}_c\mathbf{x}_c^\top \\ &= \begin{bmatrix} \mathbf{v}_1 \ \mathbf{v}_2 \ \mathbf{x}_c \end{bmatrix} \operatorname{diag}(s_1, s_2, s_3) \begin{bmatrix} \mathbf{v}_1 \ \mathbf{v}_2 \ \mathbf{x}_c \end{bmatrix}^\top \\ &\triangleq \mathsf{VDV}^\top \end{aligned}$$

where D is a diagonal scale matrix and V is a matrix that contains orthogonal vanishing points $\mathbf{v}_1$, $\mathbf{v}_2$ and an origin of the target plane $\mathbf{x}_c$. Assume that the plane homography is $\mathsf{P} \sim \mathsf{K} \begin{bmatrix} \mathbf{r}_1 \ \mathbf{r}_2 \ \mathbf{t} \end{bmatrix}$. As a consequence, the matrix V is expressed as

$$\mathsf{V} = \mathsf{P}\operatorname{diag}(a, b, c) \tag{3}$$

where a, b and c are proper scale factors that are needed to correct the scales. This means that warping with matrix V^{-1} makes planes independently scaled along to orthogonal axis, and this is a *semi-metric image.* The resulting warping matrix is V^{-1}.

Using a Standard Rectangle. On the other hand, a warping from the projected rectangle to a standard rectangle is sufficient to build semi-metric space. A standard rectangle is a predefined rectangle whose aspect ratio is known. Fig. 1 shows the concept of the warping method using a standard rectangle.

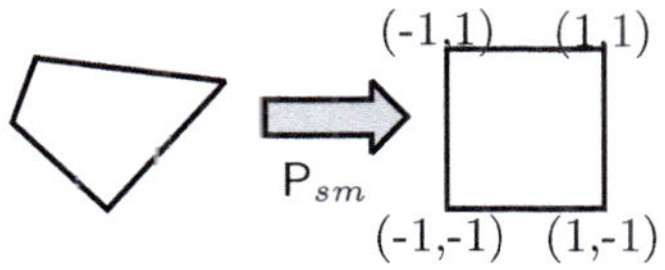

Fig. 1. Semi-metric warping using a standard rectangle

The warping matrix P_{sm} is computed by a conventional plane homography estimation algorithm using four points [7]. The matrix P_{sm} is equivalent to a warping matrix V^{-1} using vanishing points, because the resulting warped images using P_{sm} and one using V^{-1} can be transferred to each other by semi-metric transformations.

2.2 ICDCP in the Semi-metric Space

The conic dual to the circular points(CDCP) is the most important invariant feature to reconstruct the captured scene in metric space [7]. In semi-metric 2D space, the imaged CDCP(ICDCP) has a simple form. In this section, we derive the ICDCP in semi-metric space and the physical meanings of the parameters.

Theorem 1. *In semi-metric space, the ICDCP is given as* $\mathrm{diag}\left(R_m^2, R_{sm}^2, 0\right)$ *where* R_m *is an aspect ratio of the model rectangle, and* R_{sm} *is an aspect ratio of a semi-metric warped rectangle.*

Proof. Let's assume that a projection process of a plane is described as P. The inverse of semi-metric warping matrix V is represented as (3).

In model plane(Euclidean world), assume that there is a circle whose radius is r. Projection makes the circle into

$$\mathsf{A} = \mathsf{P}^{-\top}\mathrm{diag}(1, 1, -r^2)\mathsf{P}^{-1}.$$

The circle A' in semi-metric space is calculated as

$$\begin{aligned}\mathsf{A}' &= \mathsf{V}^{-\top}\mathsf{P}^{-\top}\mathrm{diag}(1, 1, -r^2)\mathsf{P}^{-1}\mathsf{V}^{-1} \\ &= \mathrm{diag}\left(1/a^2, 1/b^2, -r^2/c^2\right) \\ &\sim \mathrm{diag}\left(a'^2, b'^2, -1\right).\end{aligned} \tag{4}$$

Assume that there is a transformation T which maps a semi-metric space to a metric space. T is given as

$$\mathsf{T} = \mathrm{diag}\left(t_1, t_2, 1\right).$$

So, the circle A'' in a metric space is described as

$$\mathsf{A}'' = \mathrm{diag}\left(a'^2/t_1{}^2, b'^2/t_2{}^2, -1\right).$$

Because the circle in a metric space is also a circle, there has to be a relation as

$$\frac{a'^2}{t_1{}^2} = \frac{b'^2}{t_2{}^2}. \tag{5}$$

If there is a point on the circle whose coordinate is (X, Y) and its corresponding point in semi-metric space is (x_0, y_0), the point in metric space is expressed as (t_1x_0, t_2y_0). Also, the aspect ratio of metric space has to be equal to the Euclidean space, the relation

$$R_m \triangleq \frac{Y}{X} = \frac{t_2y_0}{t_1x_0} = \frac{t_2}{t_1}R_{sm} \tag{6}$$

is preserved.

From (5) and (6), we can find the relation

$$\frac{a'}{b'} = \frac{R_{sm}}{R_m}. \tag{7}$$

The CDCP is a dual circle whose radius is infinity, so ICDCP in semi-metric space is given as

$$\mathrm{diag}\left(1/a'^2, 1/b'^2, 0\right) \sim \mathrm{diag}\left(R_m^2, R_{sm}^2, 0\right)$$

from (4).

Corollary 1. *In projective space $\mathbb{P}^2$, the ICDCP is expressed as*

$$R_m^2 \mathbf{v}_1 \mathbf{v}_1^\top + R_{sm}^2 \mathbf{v}_2 \mathbf{v}_2^\top.$$

This is obvious from Theorem 1. Note that the aspect ratio R_{sm} in the semi-metric space can be measured without any metric knowledge of the world plane. R_{sm} is set to one if we choose a standard rectangle whose aspect ratio is one, like in Fig. 1.

2.3 About Off-the-Plane Features

When we warp a projectively distorted plane to a semi-metric space, there also are some interesting properties regarding the off-the-plane features. Since the original image is fully transformed projectively, there are a lot of feature points that are not on the reference plane. Although the semi-metric warping in two dimension is achieved, a projective distortion along the third orthogonal direction remains.

In this section, we investigate the position of the off-the-plane points after the semi-metric warping.

Points Off the Reference Plane in Semi-metric Space. Without loss of generality, we use a matrix V^{-1} as a semi-metric warping transformation. By warping $\mathbf{x}$ in (2) with V^{-1} in (3) to the semi-metric space, the warped point $\mathbf{x}'$ is

$$\mathbf{x}' \sim \mathsf{V}^{-1}\mathbf{x}. \tag{8}$$

(8) is rewritten as

$$\mathbf{x}' = \mathrm{diag}(c/a, c/b, 1)\left[X - Zm_1 \; Y + Zm_2 \; 1 + Zm_3\right]^\top, \tag{9}$$

where $\mathbf{m}$ is defined as

$$\mathbf{m} \triangleq \left[\mathbf{r}_1 \; \mathbf{r}_2 \; \mathbf{t}\right]^{-1} \mathbf{r}_3 = \left[m_1 \; m_2 \; m_3\right]^\top.$$

Using inhomogeneous coordinates, the position of points in the semi-metric space is expressed as

$$\left(\frac{c}{a}\frac{X + Zm_1}{1 + Zm_3}, \frac{c}{b}\frac{Y + Zm_2}{1 + Zm_3}\right). \tag{10}$$

Relative-Z Estimation. Based on (10), we can extract some useful information about the scene, which are distance ratios from the reference plane.

Assume that there are two points $(X_0, Y_0, 0)$ and $(-X_0, -Y_0, 0)$ on the reference plane. A length between the two points on the semi-metric space is calculated from (10) as

$$l_0 = \frac{c}{a} 2X_0. \tag{11}$$

In the same semi-metric image, a difference of X in the semi-metric space between two equal-Z points (X_1, Y_1, Z) and (X_2, Y_2, Z) is given by

$$l = \frac{c}{a} \frac{X_1 - X_2}{1 + Zm_3}. \tag{12}$$

From (11) and (12), the length ratio is given as

$$\frac{l}{l_0} = \frac{1}{1 + Zm_3} \frac{L}{L_0}$$

where $L \triangleq X_1 - X_2$ and $L_0 \triangleq 2X$.

So the relative Z, that is Zm_3, is calculated easily as

$$Zm_3 = \left(\frac{L}{L_0} \Big/ \frac{l}{l_0} \right) - 1. \tag{13}$$

It is not necessary to know m_3, because this equation gives us only *relative-Z* coordinates, if we know the ratio of differences between the X or Y coordinates of the two line segments in metric or Euclidean space. (13) shows that the value of m_3 determines the scales of the relative-Z.

3 Metric Upgrade from Semi-metric Space with a Static Camera

Under some assumptions, it is possible to upgrade semi-metric structures to metric space without any kind of metric knowledge. The metric upgrade is achieved by finding an aspect ratio R_m in the model plane.

ICDCP and Its Orthogonal Vanishing Point. Assume that we use a static camera. A static camera is a camera whose intrinsic parameters are constant. For static cameras, the following theorem is derived [10]. Due to the lack of space, the proof is omitted.

Theorem 2. *Let's assume that there are two ICDCPs $\boldsymbol{\Delta}_{2i}$ and $\boldsymbol{\Delta}_{2k}$ from planes i and k that are not parallel from images captured with a static camera. There is a non-zero and non-infinite scale ρ that satisfies*

$$Rank(\boldsymbol{\Delta}_{2i} - \rho \boldsymbol{\Delta}_{2k}) = 2.$$

To find ρ from two ICDCP matrices, we can see the problem as a generalized eigenvalue problem. The problem has two trivial solutions, zero and infinity, because the ranks of two ICDCPs are all two. We can mention the following corollary about the last nontrivial solution.

Corollary 2. *One of the generalized eigenvectors of the two ICDCP matrices appears as a line through the orthogonal vanishing points* $\mathbf{v}_{3i}$ *and* $\mathbf{v}_{3k}$ *with respect to the reference planes, physically.*

Physical Meaning of Rank($\boldsymbol{\Delta}_{2i} - \rho\boldsymbol{\Delta}_{2k}$) = 2. First, we investigate the physical meaning of Theorem 2. It can be formulated with the generalized eigenvalue problem, and the eigenvalue is ρ and its corresponding eigenvector is $\mathbf{l}_{ik}$. The problem is expressed as

$$\boldsymbol{\Delta}_{2i}\mathbf{l}_{ik} = \rho\boldsymbol{\Delta}_{2k}\mathbf{l}_{ik}.$$

As we studied in Sect. 3, $\mathbf{l}_{ik}$ is a line through two orthogonal vanishing points $\mathbf{v}_{3i}$ and $\mathbf{v}_{3k}$. Since $\boldsymbol{\Delta}_{2i}$ and $\boldsymbol{\Delta}_{2k}$ are dual conics, $\boldsymbol{\Delta}_{2i}\mathbf{l}_{ik}$ and $\boldsymbol{\Delta}_{2k}\mathbf{l}_{ik}$ are defined as a point in an image plane, by pole-polar relationships.

Regarding the theorem 2, we can prove the following lemma.

Lemma 1. $\boldsymbol{\Delta}_{2i}\mathbf{l}_{ik} = \rho\boldsymbol{\Delta}_{2k}\mathbf{l}_{ik} \sim \mathbf{p}_{ik}$ *is an intersection point of vanishing lines* $\mathbf{l}_{\infty i}$ *and* $\mathbf{l}_{\infty k}$ *which are defined by the reference planes, as shown in Fig. 2.*

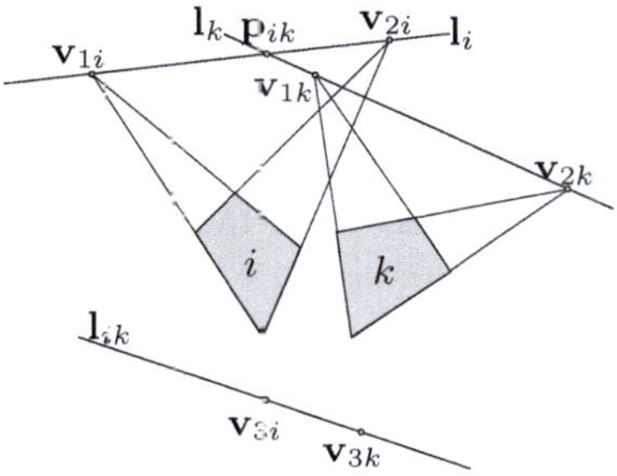

Fig. 2. Geometric meaning of rank($\boldsymbol{\Delta}_{2i} - \rho\boldsymbol{\Delta}_{2k}$) = 2

Proof. Let's assume that $\mathbf{l}_i$ and $\mathbf{l}_k$ are vanishing lines of the reference planes. So the relation with ICDCPs $\boldsymbol{\Delta}_{2i}$ and $\boldsymbol{\Delta}_{2k}$ are

$$\boldsymbol{\Delta}_{2i}\mathbf{l}_i = \boldsymbol{\Delta}_{2i}\mathbf{l}_k = 0.$$

In other words, $\mathbf{l}_i$ and $\mathbf{l}_k$ are null space of ICDCPs $\boldsymbol{\Delta}_{2i}$ and $\boldsymbol{\Delta}_{2k}$, algebraically. Therefore, the following relation is preserved.

$$(\boldsymbol{\Delta}_{2i}\mathbf{w})^\top \mathbf{l}_i = (\boldsymbol{\Delta}_{2k}\mathbf{w})^\top \mathbf{l}_k = 0$$

for all $\mathbf{w}$.

$\boldsymbol{\Delta}_{2i}\mathbf{l}_{ik}$, denoted as $\mathbf{x}_i$ have following relation.

$$\mathbf{x}_i^\top \mathbf{l}_i = 0.$$

Similarly $\mathbf{x}_k$ is also defined.

Since we deal with the features in homogeneous coordinate, physically $\mathbf{x}_i \sim \mathbf{x}_k$ from the Theorem 2. We denote the point as $\mathbf{p}_{ik}$. Then

$$\mathbf{p}_{ik}^\top \mathbf{l}_i = 0$$

and

$$\mathbf{p}_{ik}^\top \mathbf{l}_k = 0.$$

$$\therefore \mathbf{p}_{ik} = \mathbf{l}_i \times \mathbf{l}_k.$$

The plane vanishing lines $\mathbf{l}_i$ and $\mathbf{l}_k$ are obtained directly from semi-metric transformation matrices, because the semi-metric space is a kind of affine space. Practically, if the semi-metric transformation matrix P_{sm} is denoted as $\mathsf{P}_{sm} = \left[\mathbf{p}_1\ \mathbf{p}_2\ \mathbf{p}_3\right]$, the plane vanishing line is $\mathbf{l}_\infty = \mathbf{p}_1 \times \mathbf{p}_2$.

Linear Algorithm for Extracting the Model Aspect Ratio R_m with Two Views. Based on the previous study, we can determine the pole point $\mathbf{p}_{ik}$ with respect to the ICDCP and an orthogonal vanishing point of a plane, independent of the ICDCP, if we have sufficient information about the position of orthogonal vanishing points. In that case, we can extract the metric information from uncalibrated projective images. As we mentioned before, finding the model aspect ratio R_m is sufficient to obtain metric information of that plane using parameterization of semi-metric space.

Since the ICDCP of a plane can be expressed as like in Corollary 1, the equation presented in Lemma 1 can be formulated as

$$R_m^2 \mathbf{p}_1 \mathbf{p}_1 \mathbf{l}_{ik} + R_{sm}^2 \mathbf{p}_2 \mathbf{p}_2 \mathbf{l}_{ik} = \gamma \mathbf{p}_{ik}$$

where the plane homography $\mathsf{P}_{sm} = \left[\mathbf{p}_1\ \mathbf{p}_2\ \mathbf{p}_3\right]$ and γ is a scale factor. This equation has two unknowns R_m^2 and γ, and there are three equations. So we can linearly find the unknowns very easily.

Note that we do not assume that all views have the common aspect ratio R_m. That means we do not need to use the physically *same* plane for all images. Also we can find metric information from some affine properties like vanishing points and lines without any camera assumptions.

4 Experiments

In this section, we show an example of a reconstruction of semi-metric 3D with a real image. The left image of Fig. 3 shows an input image of a building scene. The image is captured using a camera module attached in a mobile phone, whose intrinsic parameters cannot be adjusted. There are several artificial planes, and

Fig. 3. Input images for verification of proposed algorithm

we can easily detect parallel line segments in the image. We selected three planes in the image to be reconstructed.

Fig. 4 shows a reconstructed 3D structure in semi-metric 3D space using the method in Sect. 2.3. Note that the lines along to the orthogonal axis are all orthogonal to each other, although we did not apply any kind of robust methods for estimating semi-metric 3D reconstruction. We used only easily obtainable information of the scene, for example, a rectangle, parallel lines to find the orthogonal vanishing points, and constraints for line segments whose length are all equal. Note that there were no extrinsic measurements in the process.

To reconstruct the structure in metric space, we need one more image of plane and its orthogonal vanishing points. The right image of Fig. 3 was used as the second image. In this image, we used the right plane of the building as the second reference plane to estimate the orthogonal vanishing points easily.

The resulting metric 3D is shown in the right image of Fig. 4. As shown in the right image of Fig. 4, the length ratios between the orthogonal axes are estimated well, although a semi-metric 3D structure does not have the sufficient information like in the left image of Fig. 4.

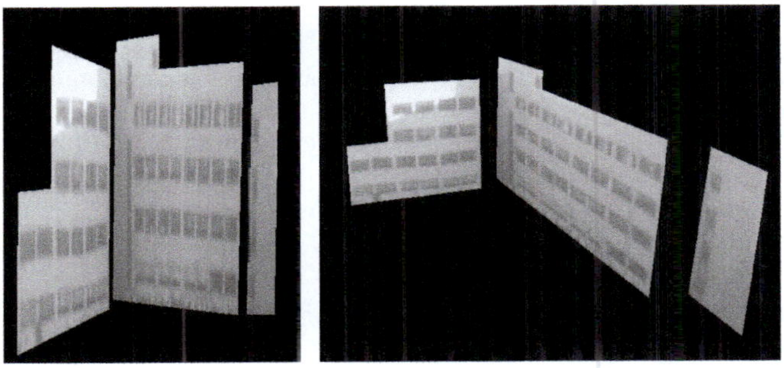

Fig. 4. Reconstructed semi-metric(left) and metric(right) 3D structure (VRML) model

5 Conclusion

In this paper, we propose a new method to reconstruct 3D structures of captured scenes using parallelism and orthogonality. First, we propose a new transformation group defined as *semi-metric space* and we reveal the properties of the space and its benefits. In semi-metric space, the metric properties aligned to each predefined orthogonal axis are preserved, but ones not aligned to predefined axis are not. From the semi-metric space, the partial structure of the scene can be retrieved from a single image and its easily obtainable scene features. The resulting 3D structure is called a semi-metric 3D structure, and we can find the scene structure up to semi-metric transformation even if we have only one image and no external measurements. Furthermore, we show that the metric invariants CDCPs in the semi-metric space have simple diagonal forms, and it can be used to make a much simpler algorithm to estimate the metric structure of the scene using two or more uncalibrated views. It gives a simple and useful parameterization of the CDCP. The CDCPs of the different planes have a rank constraint if we assume a static camera. The metric properties can be retrieved linearly from the two or more vanishing points and vanishing line sets.

Acknowledgments. This research has been partially supported by the Korean Ministry of Science and Technology for NRL Program(Grant number M1-0302-00-0064) and by Microsoft research Asia.

References

1. Caprile, B., Torre, V.: Using vanishing points for camera calibration. International Journal of Computer Vision **4** (1990) 127–140
2. Faugeras, O.: Three-Dimensional Computer Vision: A Geometric Viewpoint. MIT Press (1993)
3. Horry, Y., Anjyo, K., Arai, K.: Tour into the picture: using a spidery mesh interface to make animation from a single image. In Proceedings of the 24th annual conference on Computer graphics and interactive techniques, ACM Press/Addison-Wesley Publishing Co. (1997) 225–232
4. Criminisi, A., Reid, I., Zisserman, A.: Single view metrology. International Journal of Computer Vision **40** (2000) 123–148
5. Liebowitz, D.: Camera Calibration and Reconstruction of Geometry from Images. PhD thesis, University of Oxford (2001)
6. Wilczkowiak, M., Boyer, E., Sturm, P.: Camera calibration and 3D reconstruction from single images using parallelepipeds. In Proceedings of International Conference on Computer Vision. (2001) I: 142–148
7. Hartley, R., Zisserman, A.: Multiple View Geometry in Computer Vision. Cambridge (2000)
8. Liebowitz, D., Zisserman, A.: Combining scene and auto-calibration constraints. In Proceedings of International Conference on Computer Vision.(1999) 293–300
9. Kim, J.-S., Gurdjos, P., Kweon, I.S.: Geometric and algebraic constraints of projected concentric circles and their applications to camera calibration. IEEE Trans. Pattern Analysis and Machine Intelligence **27** (2005) 637–642
10. Gurdjos, P.: Pose from concentric circles (2004) Personal correspondence.

Boosting Multi-gabor Subspaces for Face Recognition

QingShan Liu[1,2], HongLiang Jin[1,2], XiaoOu Tang[2,3], HanQing Lu[2], and SongDe Ma[2]

[1] National Lab of Pattern Recognition, Institute of Automation, Chinese Academy of Sciences
{qsliu, hljin, luhq, masd}@nlpr.ia.ac.cn
[2] Department of Information Engineering, The Chinese University of Hong Kong
[3] Microsoft Research Asia, Beijing, P.R. China
xtang@ie.cuhk.edu.hk

Abstract. In this paper, we propose a new scheme of Gabor-based face recognition. Based on the fact that different Gabor filters have different properties, we first learn discriminating subspace for each kind of Gabor images respectively. Then the boosting learning is performed to fuse all the Gabor discriminating subspaces for recognition. Compared with previous work, the proposed method has three contributions: (1). We make sufficiently use of the respective properties of the Gabor filters, and learn different discriminant subspaces for different Gabor images respectively; (2). Boosting based fusing method adaptively determines the discriminating vectors and dimensionality of each subspace according to its discriminating capacity, so as to further improve the recognition performance; (3). The problem of computational complexity is well handled by subspace analysis and boosting based fusion. Extensive experiments show its encouraging performance.

1 Introduction

Appearance representation is a popular feature representation method for face recognition [1]. A basic characteristic of appearance representation is that it directly takes pixel intensity values as features. Because the dimensionality of the space constructed by pixel intensity values is very high, in most cases, subspace methods, such as, Principal Component Analysis (PCA) [2] and Linear Discriminant Analysis (LDA) [3], are performed to compress this high-dimensional image space into a compact low-dimensional intrinsic subspace of object. PCA tries to generate a set of orthonormal basis vectors aiming at maximizing variance over samples, but not at discriminating one class from others. LDA seeks to find a linear transformation that maximizes the between class scatter and minimizes the within class scatter, in order to generate discriminating features for recognition.

It is known that intensity value is sensitive to noises, especially illumination variation, so the performance of appearance-based recognition will collapse in some practical environments. Recently, Gabor representation has attracted much

P.J. Narayanan et al. (Eds.): ACCV 2006, LNCS 3851, pp. 539–548, 2006.

attention and is widely used in face recognition, because it can capture salient visual properties, such as spatial localization, spatial frequency characteristic, and orientation selectivity. In this paper, our work focuses on Gabor based face recognition.

The Gabor representation of an image is the convolution of the image with a family of Gabor filters with different scales and orientations. We denote the results of the convolution as Gabor images in the paper. Gabor features of an image are often composed of multiple Gabor images with different scales and orientations, so Gabor based face recognition demands higher computational power than appearance representation. In order to reduce the computational complexity, Liu, et al, down-sample the Gabor images to reduce the dimension of Gabor images [4]. In [5], the Gabor features are extracted around some fiducial points. Yang, et al, propose to select some Gabor features of discriminating points with Adaboost method [6]. Thus, these methods have two main problems. First, actually they are at the cost of losing information for computation reduction, for they do not use the Gabor features of all the pixels. Second, they all ignore the fact that different Gabor filters should have different properties. They put all the Gabor images with different scales and orientations together and treat them equally.

In this paper, we propose a new scheme of Gabor based face recognition. The flowchart of the training system is shown in Figure 1 . The input images are first filtered by 40 Gabor filters (5 scales and 8 orientations), and 40 kinds of Gabor images are produced. Then discriminant subspace analysis is performed

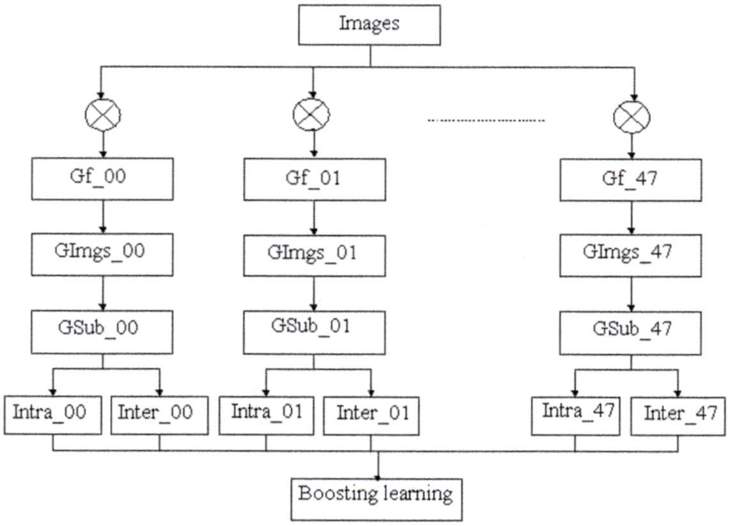

Fig. 1. The flowchart of the proposed method (Gf_00: Gabor filter with scale = 0 and orientation = 0, GImgs: Gabor images, GSub: Gabor subspace, Intra: Intra personal, and Inter: Interpersonal)

respectively on each kind of Gabor images. Finally the boosting learning is used to fuse all the Gabor subspaces, and a small set of optimal discriminating features is selected for recognition. Because the boosting learner often deals with two classes problem, we need to convert the multi-classes face recognition problem into a two-classes problem. We adopt the strategy in [5][7] to transfer the face classes into intra-personal (positive samples) and inter-personal (negative samples) classes.

Compared with previous work, the proposed method has three main contributions. (1) We first employ subspace analysis on each kind of Gabor images respectively, so the respective properties of different Gabor filters are considered and the Gabor features of all the pixels are used. (2) The boosting learning is performed to fuse all the Gabor subspaces for further improving the recognition performance. This fusion method can adaptively determines the discriminating vectors and dimensionality of each subspace based on its discriminating capacity. (3) The computational complexity is rapidly reduced by the subspace analysis and boosting based fusion. In our experiments, we test the proposed method on two benchmarks, i.e., the FERET database [8] and CAS-PEAL database [9], and we compare the proposed method with some related face methods [2][3][4][6], and two popular fusion strategies, i.e., PCA based fusion same as [10] and voting based decision.

2 Multi-gabor Subspaces

In this paper, we use Gabor representations for face recognition due to its advantages of capturing salient visual properties. Different from previous work, we first consider the fact that different Gabor filter has different properties, and learn a discriminating Gabor subspace for each kind of Gabor image respectively.

2.1 Gabor Images

Gabor filters attract much attention in face recognition [4][5][6], since they can capture salient visual properties, such as spatial localization, spatial frequency characteristic, and orientation selectivity. The Gabor filters can be defined as equation 1:

$$\psi_{\overrightarrow{k}}(\overrightarrow{z}) = \frac{\|\overrightarrow{k}\|^2}{\delta^2} exp(-\frac{\|\overrightarrow{k}\|^2 \cdot \|\overrightarrow{z}\|^2}{2\delta^2})[exp(i\overrightarrow{k} \cdot \overrightarrow{z}) - exp(-\delta^2/2)] \quad (1)$$

where $\overrightarrow{z} = (x, y)$ is the variable in spatial domain, $\|\cdot\|$ denotes the norm operator. $\overrightarrow{k}$ is the frequency vector, which determines the scale and the orientation of Gabor filters, and is defined as $\overrightarrow{k} = k_s e^{i\phi_d}$, where $k_s = \frac{k_{max}}{f^s}$ and $\phi_d = \frac{\pi d}{8}$. k_{max} is the maximum frequency, and f is the spacing factor between Gabor filters in the frequency domain. s and d define the scale and orientation of the Gabor filters.

The Gabor images of an image are the convolutions of the image with a family of Gabor filters with different scales and orientations. Same as most cases

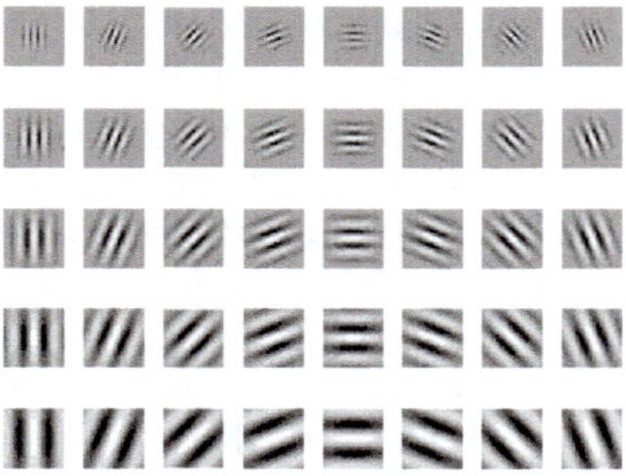

Fig. 2. The real part of 40 Gabor filters

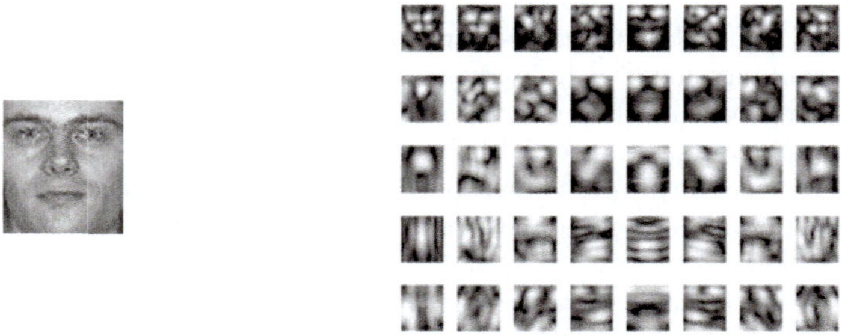

Fig. 3. Gabor images of an image

[4][6][11], we use Gabor filters of five different scales, $s \in 0, ...4$, and eight different directions, $d \in 0, ...7$ in this paper, and set $k_{max} = \pi/2, f = \sqrt{2}$. Then we get 40 different Gabor images of an image. Figure 2 gives an illustration of these 40 Gabor filters, and an example of their corresponding Gabor images is shown in Figure 3.

2.2 Gabor Subspaces

From Figure 2 and 3, we can see that different Gabor filters have different properties, so that each Gabor image has respective characteristic to enhance some different local features of face images. Thus, these different Gabor images should have different contribution for recognition. In previous work, few methods consider the different properties of Gabor filters. They put all the Gabor images together and treat them equally [4][5][6].

In this paper, we first learn 40 Gabor subspaces respectively according to 40 kinds of Gabor images. Comparing with previous work [4][5][6], we not only consider the properties of different Gabor filters, but also we use all the Gabor features. We deal with the problem of computation complexity with subspace analysis and the boosting based fusion. LDA based subspace learning is first performed on each kind of Gabor images, for LDA can extract the discriminating features of Gabor images. The idea of LDA is to maximize the between class scatter S_B and minimize the within class scatter S_W . Mathematically, it is equivalent to maximize the following Fisher rule: $J(w) = \frac{w^T S_B w}{w^T S_W w}$, and its solution is the leading eigenvectors of the matrix $S_W^{-1} S_B$. Often, there are not enough training samples to guarantee non-singularity of S_W , so some techniques are needed to deal with this numerical computation problem. Here, the strategy of unified subspace is used to overcome this problem because of its good performance [12]. The algorithm can be summarized as follows:

1. Perform PCA first, and adjust the PCA dimension to reduce noise.
2. Compute the between class scatter S_B and within class scatter S_W in the PCA subspace.
3. Compute the whiting transformation of S_W based on PCA, and reduce its dimension too.
4. Transfer with S_B the whiting transformation of S_W , and then apply PCA to compute the final discriminating features.

3 Boosting Based Fusion

Now we get 40 different Gabor subspaces. But there still exist two problems. (1) Though subspace analysis can lower computational complexity, the whole dimension size of all the 40 Gabor subspaces is still very high for classification. For example, if the dimension size of each subspace is only kept with 100, then the whole dimension size is up to $40*100 = 4000$. (2) It is obvious that different Gabor subspaces should have different discriminating abilities, so they should have different contributions to recognition. Thus, how to efficiently fuse them is still a key issue. A popular method is majority voting based decision. In [10], Tang and Li use PCA to fuse multi-subspaces for video based face recognition. However, these two fusion methods cannot well deal with above two problems.

In this paper, we present a boosting based fusion strategy to overcome the above two problems. Boosting is a method to combine a collection of weak learner to achieve a stronger classification function. AdaBoost is a popular boosting method, which can adaptively update the weights of samples according to the errors in previous learning [13]. Tieu and Viola [14] first employ the Adaboost for feature selection and enhancing classification in natural image retrieval. Here, we use the Adaboost to fuse multi-Gabor subspaces, i.e., selecting a small set of optimal discriminating vectors from all the Gabor subspaces. Because the Adaboost can only handle two classes problem, we need to convert the multi-classes face recognition problem into a two-classes problem. We adopt the strategy in [6][7] to transfer the face samples into intra-personal (positive samples) and inter -personal (negative samples) samples. Although we use LDA to discriminating features of Gabor images, the capacity of each discriminating vectors is still limited, especially for classifying inter-personal and intra- personal classes, so it is reasonable to use the Adaboost for discriminating vector selection here. The Adaboost algorithm can be summarized as follows:

- Input the training samples(x_1,y_1),...,(x_n,y_n) where the labels y_i=0,1 for negative and positive examples respectively.
- Initialize weights $D_{1,i} = \frac{1}{2m}, \frac{1}{2k}$ $y_i = 0, 1$ where m and k are the number of negatives and positives respectively.
- Do for $t = 1, ..., T$,
  - Normalize the weights to make $D_{1,i} = \frac{1}{2m}, \frac{1}{2k}$ $y_i = 0, 1$ respectively;
  - Train one hypothesis h_j for each feature with j with D_j, and calculate error $\epsilon_j = \sum_i D_i|h_j(x_i) - y_i|$;
  - Choose the classifier h_t with the lowest error;
  - Update the weights: $D_{t+1,i} = D_{t,i}\beta_t^{1-e_i}$ where $e_i = 0$ if x_i is classified correctly, $e_i = 1$ otherwise; and $\beta_t = \frac{\epsilon_t}{1-\epsilon_t}$, $\alpha_t = log(1/\beta_t)$;
- Output the final classifier:

$$h(x) = \begin{cases} 1, \text{ if } \sum_{t=1}^{T} \alpha_t h_t(x) \geq \frac{1}{2} \sum_{t=1}^{T} \alpha_t \\ 0, \text{ otherwise,} \end{cases}$$

Fig. 4. Adaboost

Here, we modify the weights normalization to keep the sum weights of both positive and negative samples with 0.5 during iterations for the imbalance between positive and negative samples in our experiments. Because the number of negative samples is grossly larger than that of the positive samples, in order to use almost all the negative samples, we adopt the re-sampling strategy same as [6]. In each training stage, we use all the positive samples and keep the ratio of positive samples to negative sample at 1:8 in the training set. The weak learner h_j is a threshold function as: $h_j(x) = 1$ if $|x - mean(P)| < \beta * std(P)$, otherwise, $h_j(x) = 0$, where $mean(P)$ and $std(P)$ are the mean and standard variation of positive samples. β is set to 1.625 in our experiments.

According to above description, we can see that the boosting based fusion has two advantages: (1) it can adaptively a small set of optimal discriminating vectors from all the Gabor subspaces to further improve the recognition performance. (2) The dimensionality of each subspace is adaptively determined according to its discriminating capacity, and the computational cost is reduced rapidly.

4 Experiments

We test the proposed method on two benchmarks, i.e., the FERET database [8] and CAS-PEAL database [9], and we compare the proposed method with three related face recognition methods, i.e., Gabor + ELDA [4], PCA [2], LDA [3]. In the experiments, we set the down-sampling factor $\rho = 4$ for Gabor + ELDA. In addition, in order to evaluate the performance of the boosting based fusion, two popular fusion methods are compared too, i.e., PCA based fusion same as [10] and majority voting based decision.

4.1 On the FERET Database

The FERET database has been widely used to evaluate face recognition methods. Our experimental data include FA and FB images of 1195 persons, and 1002 front view face images of 429 subjects in the training CD of the FERET database, which is independent of FA and FB images. There is only one image per person in FA and FB respectively. All the images are normalized to 48*54 by eye locations. Some samples are shown in Figure 5. No other pre-processing except histogram equalization is performed. We take all the 1002 images from training CD as training set. FA images are used for gallery images, and FB images are for probe images.

Fig. 5. Some samples on the FERET database

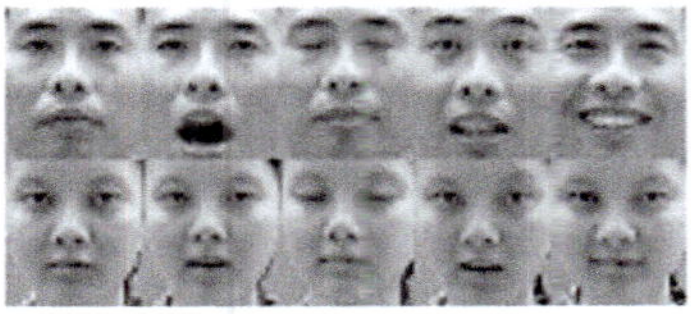

Fig. 6. Some Samples on the CAS-PEAL database

First, we compare the proposed method with some popular face recognition methods, i.e., Gabor + ELDA [4], PCA [2], LDA [3]. Figure 7 gives the comparison results, where the Gabor + ELDA and LDA at most can reach 428 features, because the number of training subjects are 429. We see that both Gabor based methods outperform two appearance based methods, i.e., PCA and LDA. The proposed method gives a higher recognition rate than Gabor + ELDA. The proposed method can achieve the recognition rate of 96.7% with 320 features, while the recognition rate of [4] is always below 93%. Because much information is lost during down-sampling in [4], and the properties of different Gabor filters

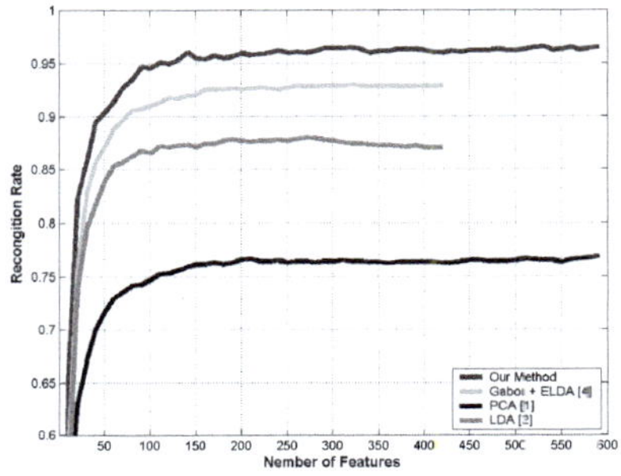

Fig. 7. Compare with Gabor + ELDA, LDA, and PCA

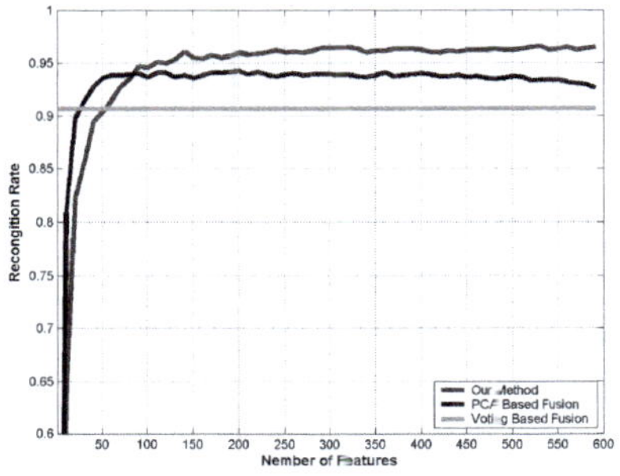

Fig. 8. Compare with PCA based fusion and Voting based fusion

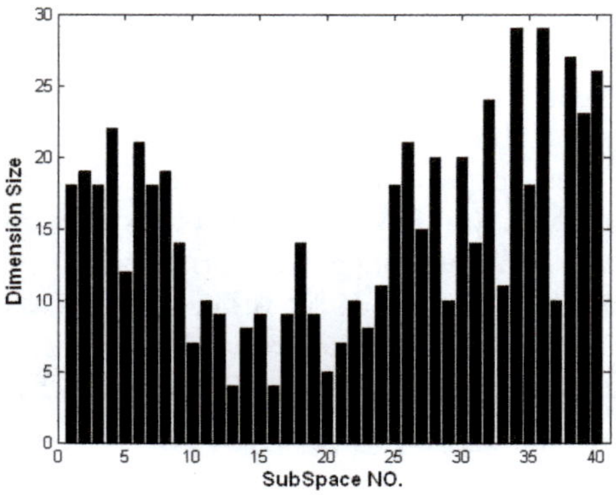

Fig. 9. The dimension size of each subspace

are not considered respectively. Since it is hard to repeat the experiments of [6], we do not implement it, but from the results report in [6], our results are also comparable with the best results on this set. They reported they got the best recognition rate of 95.2% with 700 features, because it directly constructs the weak learner with the original Gabor features, while we use the Adaboost to select the discriminating vectors from all the Gabor subspaces obtain by LDA.

In order to evaluate the performance of the boosting based fusion strategy, we compare it with PCA based fusion and voting based fusion. Figure 8 shows the comparison results of three fusion methods, and it is obvious to see the advantage of the proposed method. Because boosting can select a small set of optimal discriminating vectors for recognition, and treat each subspace according its importance, while actually PCA and voting rule treat 40 Gabor subspaces equally. Moreover, the proposed method not only gives a higher recognition rate, but also its computation complexity is low, because the dimension size of each subspace is adaptively determined according to its importance. Figure 9 reports the dimension size of each Gabor subspace, if 600 discriminating vectors are selected by boosting for recognition, where the x-axis is the subspace No. We denote No.1 for $s = 0, d = 0$, No.2 for $s = 0, d = 1$, and No.40 for $s = 4, d = 7$ by analogy. We can see that the dimension size of most subspaces is below 20.

4.2 On the CAS-PEAL Database

The CAS-PEAL database contains 99,594 images of 1,040 subjects, and unlike the above FERET database, all the people in this database are Asians. We take 376 subjects and each subject has 6 different front view images for the experiments, where each person has one image with normal expression. We crop the images to 48*54 by fixing eye locations too. Figure 6 shows some sample images. We randomly select 100 subjects for training. For the rest of the 276 subjects, we take the normal image of each person as gallery image, and the other 5 images as probe images. Histogram equalization is performed as pre-processing.

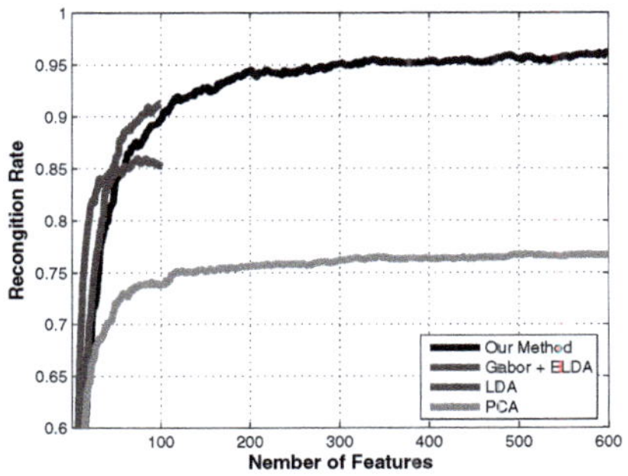

Fig. 10. Compare with Gabor + ELDA, LDA, and PCA

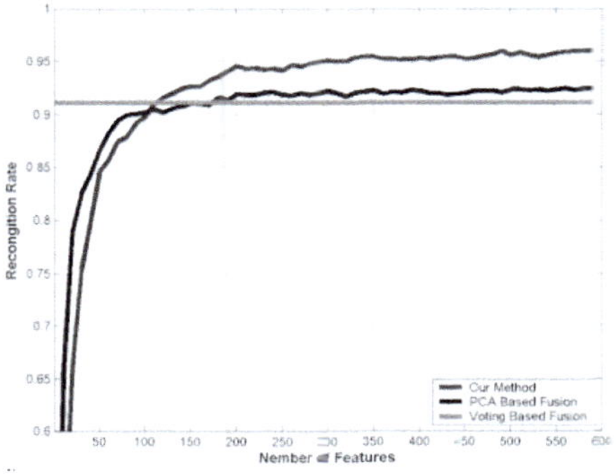

Fig. 11. Compare with PCA based fusion and Voting based fusion

Figure 10 reports the experimental results of the proposed method, Gabor + ELDA [4], PCA [2], LDA [3]. Because the number of training subjects are 100, the feature number of Gabor + ELDA and LDA can only reach 99. From Figure 6, it can be seen that the experimental results are similar to the results on the FERET database. The proposed method outperforms the other three methods, and the Gabor + ELDA is better than LDA and PCA. We also do an evaluation of the boosting based fusion method on this database. Figure 11 shows the comparison results of the boosting based fusion, PCA based fusion, and majority voting based fusion methods. Similarly, the proposed method achieves a better performance than PCA based fusion and majority based fusion methods.

5 Conclusions

In this paper, we propose a new scheme of Gabor based face recognition. Comparing with previous work, we make use of the respective properties of Gabor filters, and the problem of computational complexity is well handled without losing information by subspace dimension reduction and boosting based fusion. We first learn discriminating subspaces for each kind of Gabor images respectively, and then the boosting based fusion method is presented to fuse all the subspaces. This fusion strategy can adaptively determine the discriminating vectors and dimension size of each subspace. Moreover, it further improves the recognition performance. Experiments on the FERET and CAS -PEAL databases show its encouraging performance.

Acknowledgement

This work is supportted by Natural Sciences Foundation of China Under Grant No 60135020 and 60405005, the joint fund of NSFC-RGC under Grant No.60318003.

References

1. W.Zhao, R.Chellappa, A., P.J.Phillips.: Face recognition: A literature survey. CS-Tech Report-4167, University of Maryland (2000)
2. M.Turk, A.Pentland: Eigenfaces for recognition. Journal of Cognitive Neuroscience **3** (1991) 72–86
3. W.Zhao, R.Chellappa, P.: Subspace linear discriminant analysis for face recognition. Tech Report CAR-TR-914, Center for Automation Research, University of Maryland (1999)
4. C.J.Liu, H.Wechsler.: Gabor feature based classification using the enhanced fisher linear discriminant model for face recognition. IEEE Trans. On Image Processing **11** (2002)
5. M.Lades, J.C.Vorbrggen, J.J.C.R., W.Konen.: Distortion invariant object recognition in the dynamic link architecture. IEEE Trans on Computers **42** (1993) 300–311
6. P.Yang, S.G.Shan, W.S.L., D.Zhang.: Face recognition using ada-boosted gabor features. Proc.of Int'l Conf. on Automatic Face and Gesture Recognition (2004)
7. B. Moghaddam, T.J., Pentland., A.: Bayesian face recognition. Pattern Recognition **33** (2000) 1771–1782
8. P. J. Phillips, H. Wechsler, J.H., Rauss., P.: The feret database and evaluation procedure for face recognition algorithms. Image and Vision Computing **16** (1998)
9. W.Gao, B., S.G.Shan.: The cas-peal large-scale face database and evaluation protocols. Tech-Report JDL-TR-04-FR-001, JDL, CAS (2004)
10. X.Tang, Z.F.Li.: Frame synchronization and multi-level subspace analysis for video based face recognition. Proc. of Int'l Conf. Computer Vision and Pattern Recognition (2004)
11. D.Burr, M., D.Spinelli.: Evidence for edge and bar detectors in human vision. Vision Research **29** (1989)
12. X.Wang, X.Tang.: Unified subspace analysis for face recognition. Proc. of Int't Conf. Computer Vision (2003)
13. Y.Freund, R.E.Schapire.: A decision theoretic generalization of online learning and an application to boosting. J.Comp. ans Sys.Sci **55** (1997)
14. K.Tieu, P.Viola.: Boosting image retrieval. Proc. of Int'l Conf. Computer Vision and Pattern Recognition (2000)

A New Distance Criterion for Face Recognition Using Image Sets

Tat-Jun Chin* and David Suter

Institute of Vision Systems Engineering,
Monash University, Victoria, Australia
{tat.chin, d.suter}@eng.monash.edu.au

Abstract. A major face recognition paradigm involves recognizing a person from a set of images instead of from a single image. Often, the image sets are acquired from a video stream by a camera surveillance system, or a combination of images which can be non-contiguous and unordered. An effective algorithm that tackles this problem involves fitting low-dimensional linear subspaces across the image sets and using a linear subspace as an approximation for the particular face identity. Unavoidably, the individual frames in the image set will be corrupted by noise and there is a degree of uncertainty on how accurate the resultant subspace approximates the set. Furthermore, when we compare two linear subspaces, how much of the distance between them is due to inter-personal differences and how much is due to intra-personal variations contributed by noise? Here, we propose a new distance criterion, developed based on a matrix perturbation theorem, for comparing two image sets that takes into account the uncertainty of estimating a linear subspace from noise affected image sets.

1 Introduction

There are many merits to face recognition using image sets. It is conjectured that many still-image face recognition algorithms fail in practice because they were developed based in controlled environments which are hard to satisfy in the real world. Herein lies the strength of recognition using image sets– a set of images of a person under varying conditions contains more information than a single image, and possible variations and appearance of the person would have been encoded in the set. For algorithms that restrict the images in the set to be contiguous frames, temporal coherence between the images can be exploited to aid in recognizing a face [1]. For algorithms with no such restrictions, recognizing from image sets allows a convenient combination of long term observations captured at sequestered intervals [2].

Furthermore, many existing surveillance systems capture video sequences of their environment inconspicuously rather than a still image in a controlled setting which requires a high degree of cooperation from the subjects. Thus, a system based on matching image sets would be more natural and accommodating. The rapid advancement of face detection algorithms contributes immensely to face recognition using image sets.

* Tat-Jun Chin is a recipient of the Endeavour Australia-Asia Postgraduate Award 2004 conferred by the Department of Education, Science and Training of the Australian Government.

P.J. Narayanan et al. (Eds.): ACCV 2006, LNCS 3851, pp. 549–558, 2006.

In particular, algorithms such as [3] can perform multipose rotated face detection at high speed. Face recognition algorithms using image sets allow a seamless integration between face detection and face recognition, as the results from face detection can be used directly for recognition without much preprocessing.

In this paper, we focus on a class of face recognition algorithms that involves representing a face class by a single linear subspace [4, 5, 2, 6]. This model of a face is obtained via fitting low-dimensional linear subspaces across a set of images obtained under varying imaging conditions. Face recognition is performed on the premise that different faces generate different linear subspaces, and the distance or angles between the linear subspaces is used as a similarity measure. However, images will inevitably be corrupted by noise, and there is a certain degree of uncertainty in estimating linear subspaces from noisy samples. For a certain amount of noise, how far is our estimated subspace biased from the optimal one? Or equivalently, when we compare distance of subspaces, how much of the distance is contributed by inter-personal differences and how much is due to noise effects? We attempt to answer these questions by using a matrix perturbation theorem and propose a new distance criterion that takes into account the uncertainty of estimating linear subspaces.

Compared to more probabilistic approaches, linear subspace methods appear rather simplistic. For example, a recent method reported in [7] involves modeling the densities generated by image sets as Gaussian Mixture Models and evaluating the similarity between the sets via the Kullback-Leibler divergence. In [8], face appearances are modeled as a joint probability distribution of identity and motion using sequential importance sampling and the recognition decision is obtained via marginalization. Nonetheless, despite their straightforwardness, linear subspace methods are surprisingly rather effective, as reported in [7]. In particular, the CMSM method [6] accomplished an average accuracy of only 2% less than a more complex method proposed in [7]. Linear subspace methods are certainty very attractive and promising.

Linear methods do not provide theoretical justifications for using linear models to represent image sets of faces. Furthermore, it is conjectured that the manifold of faces within the image space is highly complex and non-linear [9], and hence linear methods will always suffer from model deficiencies. In other words, there is no such thing as an *unbiased* linear subspace for a particular image set. At most, we can estimate a linear subspace that best *approximates* an image set, and vestiges of the set not conforming to the linear model will introduce more within-class variations alongside other noise. Hence, it is desirable to have a qualified measurement of the uncertainty in subspace estimation over a noise affected image set and a distance criterion that isolates intra-personal variabilities from inter-personal differences.

2 Previous Work

One of the earliest algorithms for face recognition from image sets using linear subspaces was reported in [4]. The so-called *modified CLAFIC* method proposed is essentially about estimating low-dimensional linear subspaces across mean-adjusted image sets. This method is not entirely in the mould of the algorithms we consider here, since test samples used are single images rather than image sets. In this case, the projection distances of an image onto different subspaces are compared. A high accuracy of about 92% was reported. It should be noted that for this result, both training and test images were acquired under relatively well-controlled environments.

The Mutual Subspace Method (MSM) for face recognition was reported in [5]. Faces were first tracked using a face detection module and accumulated to form image sets. The distance measure was determined by comparing the smallest principal angles between subspaces generated by the image sets. A recent implementation [7] shows that the MSM yielded an accuracy of about 83%. A problem with the MSM is that the subspace estimation might be affected by noise or intra-class variabilities and these entities could contribute to the distance measure between subspaces, thus influencing the classification decision.

An extension of MSM is the Constrained Mutual Subspace Method (CMSM) [6], which is essentially an MSM performed on the projection of the original subspaces onto a *constrained* subspace. The constrained subspace contains the intra-class variabilities of the training images, and is constructed by the *difference vectors* within a face class. The similarity measures on this subspace should be robust against such variabilities present in the training images. A recent implementation [7] shows that the CMSM yielded an accuracy of about 92%, almost on par with a more sophisticated method proposed in [7]. A problem with CMSM is that if the constrained subspace does not contain all possible variations, the distance measure will still be influenced by some intra-class variabilities.

3 Angles Between Subspaces and Distance Metrics

The notion of angles between two subspaces, called *principal angles*, plays an integral part in quantifying the distance between two subspaces. The principal angles $\theta_1, \theta_2, \cdots, \theta_n \in [0, \pi/2]$ between two n-dimensional subspaces $\mathcal{P}$ and $\mathcal{Q}$, following the definition of [10], are defined by

$$\cos \theta_i = \max_{\mu \in \mathcal{P}} \max_{\nu \in \mathcal{Q}} \mu \cdot \nu = \mu_i \cdot \nu_i \ , \tag{1}$$

for $i = 1, ..., n$, subject to $\mu \cdot \mu = \nu \cdot \nu = 1$, $\mu \cdot \mu_j = 0$, $\nu \cdot \nu_j = 0 (1 \leq j \leq i-1)$. The vectors $\{\mu_i\}$ and $\{\nu_j\}$ are *principal vectors* corresponding to the pair $\mathcal{P}$ and $\mathcal{Q}$.

A type of distance metric between subspaces $\mathcal{P}$ and $\mathcal{Q}$ is the *gap distance*, defined by

$$d_s(\mathcal{P}, \mathcal{Q}) = \sin \theta_1 \ , \tag{2}$$

with $\theta_1, \theta_2, \cdots, \theta_n$ being the principal angles between $\mathcal{P}$ and $\mathcal{Q}$ and $\theta_1 \geq \theta_2 \geq \cdots \geq \theta_n$. Another widely used distance metric is the *chordal distance*, defined by

$$d_c(\mathcal{P}, \mathcal{Q}) = \sqrt{\sum_{i=1}^{n} \sin^2 \theta_i} \ , \tag{3}$$

with all the variables as defined previously. It can be seen that the chordal distance reduces to the gap distance for $n = 1$. Both distance measures have the necessary properties of metrics (e.g. non-negativity, symmetry, triangle inequality). Furthermore, they are essentially equivalent in the sense that they generate the same topology [11].

Let matrices P and Q be orthonormal bases for subspaces $\mathcal{P}$ and $\mathcal{Q}$ respectively. The *projection matrices* of $\mathcal{P}$ and $\mathcal{Q}$ are respectively

$$\mathsf{P} = PP^T \text{ and } \mathsf{Q} = QQ^T . \tag{4}$$

Unlike orthonormal bases, the projection matrices define their corresponding subspaces uniquely. The distance metrics defined above can be computed from projection matrices:

$$d_s(\mathcal{P}, \mathcal{Q}) = \|\mathsf{P} - \mathsf{Q}\|_2 , \tag{5}$$

$$d_c(\mathcal{P}, \mathcal{Q}) = \frac{1}{\sqrt{2}}\|\mathsf{P} - \mathsf{Q}\|_F , \tag{6}$$

with $\|\cdot\|_2$ and $\|\cdot\|_F$ representing the matrix 2-norm and the matrix Frobenius norm respectively. For a proof of the above, see [10, 11] for example.

4 The Effects of Noise on Subspace Distance Measure

All images are raster-scanned to form m-dimensional vectors. If no noise is present and n observations are recorded, we obtain a matrix $A \in \mathbb{R}^{m \times n}$. If noise is present, matrix A is perturbed by N and we observe matrix $\tilde{A}$, i.e.

$$\tilde{A} = A + N. \tag{7}$$

If the rank of A is r and $r < n$, we would like to find the r-dimensional linear subspace that spans the columns of A. An orthonormal basis of this subspace can be obtained by performing an SVD on A and retaining the first r left singular vectors. If our observations are affected by noise, A almost always becomes full rank. If we retain the first r left singular vectors of $\tilde{A}$ to form an orthonormal basis, how far potentially can this subspace differ from the uncorrupted subspace?

Let $A = U\Sigma V^T$ and $\tilde{A} = \tilde{U}\tilde{\Sigma}\tilde{V}^T$ with the singular values ordered decreasingly. Take note that if we subtract the mean from A before invoking an SVD, we would be performing a PCA– that is not the case here. Let the matrices U^r and $\tilde{U}^r$ contain the first r left singular vectors of A and $\tilde{A}$ respectively, i.e.

$$U^r = UE \text{ and } \tilde{U}^r = \tilde{U}E , \tag{8}$$

with $E = \begin{bmatrix} I_r \\ 0_{(m-r)\times r} \end{bmatrix}$, I_r being the identity matrix of dimension $r \times r$ and $0_{a\times b}$ being a zero matrix of dimension $a \times b$. By definition of the SVD, U and $\tilde{U}$ are orthogonal matrices, hence U^r and $\tilde{U}^r$ are sets of orthonormal vectors. The objective is to find an upper bound of the following:

$$\|U^r(U^r)^T - \tilde{U}^r(\tilde{U}^r)^T\|_a , \tag{9}$$

where a defines the type of norm. We will work exclusively with $a = F$, which effectively means that *"how far?"* in the question above is posed in terms of the chordal distance metric, and (9) is the difference in chordal distance between the column space of U^r and the column space of $\tilde{U}^r$.

Suppose the matrix $A \in \mathbb{R}^{m\times n}$ is perturbed by N and we observe $\tilde{A}$, i.e. $\tilde{A} = A + N$. Without loss of generality, we assume $m > n$. The matrix A can be decomposed via SVD into $A = U\Sigma V^T$, where $U \in \mathbb{R}^{m\times m}$ and $V \in \mathbb{R}^{n\times n}$ are orthogonal matrices and $\Sigma = \begin{bmatrix} S \\ 0_{(m-n)\times n} \end{bmatrix}$ with $S = \mathrm{diag}\{\kappa_1, \kappa_2, \cdots, \kappa_n\}$. Define $C = U^T NV$. **Theorem 1** [11]: Suppose κ_i is a simple non-zero singular value of A, then the first order perturbations of the singular values λ_i, the right singular vector x_i, and the left singular vector y_i of $\tilde{A}$ are respectively

$$\lambda_i = \kappa_i + C_{i,i} , \tag{10}$$

$$x_i = V_i + \sum_{j\neq i} \frac{\kappa_j C_{j,i} + \kappa_i C_{i,j}}{\kappa_i^2 - \kappa_j^2} V_j , \tag{11}$$

$$y_i = U_i + \sum_{j\neq i} \frac{\kappa_i C_{j,i} + \kappa_j C_{i,j}}{\kappa_i^2 - \kappa_j^2} U_j , \tag{12}$$

with $C_{j,i}$ representing the element of C at row j and column i, and U_i and V_i representing the i-th column of U and V respectively.

If A is of rank r, we can expect that only the first r singular values of A are non-zero. From Theorem 1, we can see that $\tilde{U}^r = UH$, with

$$H = \begin{bmatrix} 1 & P(1,2) & \cdots & P(1,r) \\ P(2,1) & 1 & \vdots & \vdots \\ \vdots & \cdots & \ddots & P(r\text{-}1,r) \\ P(r,1) & \cdots & P(r,r\text{-}1) & 1 \\ Q(r+1,1) & Q(r+1,2) & \cdots & Q(r+1,r) \\ \vdots & \vdots & \ddots & \vdots \\ Q(m,1) & Q(m,2) & \cdots & Q(m,r) \end{bmatrix} , \tag{13}$$

with $P(j,i) = \frac{\kappa_i C_{j,i} + \kappa_j C_{i,j}}{\kappa_i^2 - \kappa_j^2}$ and $Q(j,i) = \frac{C_{j,i}}{\kappa_i}$. H can be decomposed as such:

$$H = E + F + G, \text{ with } F = \begin{bmatrix} H_{1:r,1:r} - I_r \\ 0_{(m-r)\times r} \end{bmatrix} \text{ and } G = \begin{bmatrix} 0_{r\times r} \\ H_{(r+1):m,1:r} \end{bmatrix} \tag{14}$$

by borrowing a Matlab notation.

With the established results above, we can start to find the upper bound for (9). Trivially, by exploiting *unitary invariance* of the Frobenius norm, we can see the following:

$$\|\tilde{U}^r(\tilde{U}^r)^T - U^r(U^r)^T\|_F = \|HH^T - EE^T\|_F . \tag{15}$$

We make the assumption that $m \gg r$ such that the contribution of matrices with nearly $m\times m$ non-zero elements dominates over other sparse matrices. This assumption is valid for most computer vision applications where m is the number of pixels in an image with typical values anywhere from 400 to 10,000 and r range from 5 to 25 depending on specific methods. By using the decomposition of H above and dropping sparse matrices,

$$\|\tilde{U}^r(\tilde{U}^r)^T - U^r(U^r)^T\|_F = \|(E+F)\left(F^T+G^T\right)+GF^T + (F+G)E^T+GG^T\|_F \cong \|GG^T\|_F \,.$$

The matrix G can be decomposed further into $G = D \cdot S^{-r}$, with $D = \begin{bmatrix} 0_{r\times r} \\ C_{(r+1):m,\,1:r} \end{bmatrix}$ by using the Matlab notation again and $S^{-r} = \mathrm{diag}\{1/\kappa_1,\, 1/\kappa_2,\, \cdots,\, 1/\kappa_r\}$. Hence,

$$\|\tilde{U}^r(\tilde{U}^r)^T - U^r(U^r)^T\|_F \cong \|D\left(S^{-r}\right)^2 D^T\|_F \leq \|D\|_F^2 \cdot \|\left(S^{-r}\right)^2\|_F \qquad (16)$$

Suppose that each entry of A is corrupted with i.i.d. Gaussian noise with energy of σ_n^2, then each entry of C is drawn from the normal distribution $N\left(0, \sigma_n^2\right)$. We then make the following approximation:

$$\|D\|_F^2 = \sum_{j=r+1}^{m} \sum_{i=1}^{r} C_{j,i}^2 \cong (m-r)\, r\sigma_n^2 \,. \qquad (17)$$

Following [12], the maximal likelihood estimate of the noise level in an r-dimensional subspace estimated from a noise affected matrix $\tilde{A} \in \mathbb{R}^{m\times n}$ using SVD is

$$\sqrt{\frac{1}{(m-r)} \sum_{i=r+1}^{m} \tilde{\kappa}_i^2}\,, \qquad (18)$$

with $\{\tilde{\kappa}_i \,|\, i = 1, 2, \cdots, n\}$ being the singular values of $\tilde{A}$. By substituting the relevant equations, we arrive at the following upper bound:

$$\|\tilde{U}^r(\tilde{U}^r)^T - U^r(U^r)^T\|_F \leq r\left(\sum_{i=r+1}^{m} \tilde{\kappa}_i^2\right)\sqrt{\sum_{i=1}^{r} \frac{1}{\kappa_i^4}} \,. \qquad (19)$$

Of course, in realistic situations, A is never attainable, only $\tilde{A}$ is observed. We make the approximation of $\kappa_i \approx \tilde{\kappa}_i$ for $i = 1, 2, \cdots, r$. Secondly, usually only n samples are observed, so κ_i can be summed up to the n-th term only. This will not be invalid since κ_i for $i \gg r$ will be insignificant. Thirdly, our empirical results show that the upper bound given by (19) consistently overestimates the ground truth by a factor of at least r. Consequently, we drop the r term to arrive at the following result:

$$\|\tilde{U}^r(\tilde{U}^r)^T - U^r(U^r)^T\|_F \leq \left(\sum_{i=r+1}^{n} \tilde{\kappa}_i^2\right)\sqrt{\sum_{i=1}^{r} \frac{1}{\tilde{\kappa}_i^4}} \,. \qquad (20)$$

It should be noted that the value given by (20) is not equivalent to the optimal threshold for classification purposes. In essence, it is a mathematically qualified way of quantifying how far potentially our estimated subspace can be biased by noise, and is an indication of the quality of the estimation. Specifically, when the uncertainty of one subspace is larger than the distance from another subspace, these subspaces are practically indistinguishable despite their distance apart. A remedy would be to acquire cleaner samples for a re-estimation of the subspaces.

From (20), we can quantify the noise contribution to the distance between two subspaces learnt from noisy image sets. It can be considered intra-class variations that should be isolated from distance comparisons between subspaces of possibly distinct classes. For face recognition purposes, we propose the following distance criterion: suppose we have a test subspace $\mathcal{T}$ and a set of subspaces $\mathbb{L}$ learnt from noisy image sets, and all are r-dimensional. For nearest neighbour classification, the following distance criterion

$$\max\left(d_c(\mathcal{T}, \mathcal{P}) - N_{\mathcal{P}}, 0 \right) , \tag{21}$$

$$\text{with} \quad N_{\mathcal{P}} = \frac{1}{\sqrt{2}} \left(\sum_{i=r+1}^{n} \kappa_{P,i}^2 \right) \sqrt{\sum_{i=1}^{r} \frac{1}{\kappa_{P,i}^4}} , \tag{22}$$

should be used, where $\mathcal{P} \in \mathbb{L}$, P is the matrix from which we estimate $\mathcal{P}$ and $\kappa_{P,i}$ is the i-th singular value of P. Thresholds can then be applied onto the resultant distances as a closeness criterion.

As an afterthought, (20) is a manifestation of what we already know about the SVD: the quality of our basis in spanning the column space of a matrix is reflected by the singular values of the estimation. However, (20) not only provides a value of the estimation quality, but allows us to quantify by how far our subspace can potentially be biased by the uncertainty. Furthermore, it is mathematically justified.

5 Experimental Results

Experiments on synthetic data were performed to show the validity of (20). In the first experiment, a data matrix $A \in \mathbb{R}^{m \times n}$ of rank 15, with $100 \leq m \leq 3000$, $n = 65$ and $0 \leq A_{j,i} \leq 255$ was randomly created. A was perturbed to become $\tilde{A}$ with additive random Gaussian noise of zero mean and $\sigma = 5$. The uncertainty in the subspace estimation and the ground truth (9) were computed for each iteration of m (50 sub-iterations were performed for each m with the results averaged). Figure 1(a) shows that for a large range of m, our upper bound of the uncertainty consistently overestimates the ground truth by a factor of about 1.3. The design of experiment 2 remained the same, albeit with different parameters: m was fixed at 1000, $5 \leq r \leq 25$ and $n = r + 50$. Figure 1(b) shows that the overestimation over the ground truth increases to a factor of about 1.5 when $r = 25$. For experiment 3, the parameters are as follows: $m = 1000$, $n = 65$, $r = 15$ and $5 \leq \sigma \leq 10$. For this case, the overestimation over the ground truth increases to a factor of about 2.6 when $\sigma = 10$, as shown by Figure 1(c).

We implemented the MSM method to evaluate our results. A small face video database comprising 14 individuals from our department was constructed. The subjects were requested to sit on an office chair while looking straight at a webcam capturing at 10 fps with 320×240 pixel resolution. A face detector implementation of [13] was executed simultaneously at frame rate. To mimic real life scenarios, the recordings were done as candidly as possible, and the subjects were encouraged to perform some minor

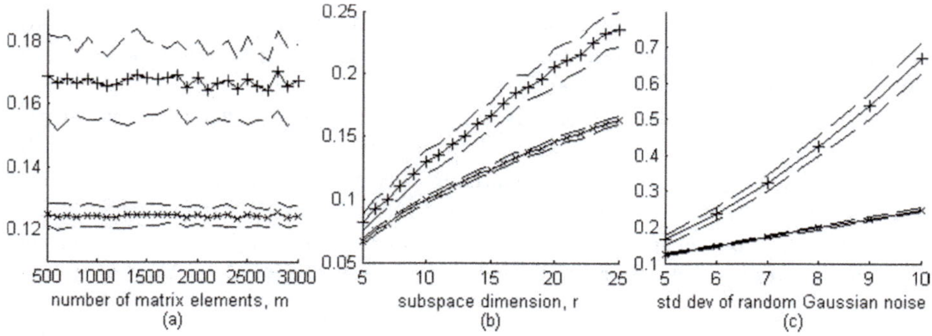

Fig. 1. (a)(b)(c) Experimental results with synthetic data. *y*-axis represents chordal distance. Lines with '+' depict chordal distance values estimated using (20), and lines with 'x' depict ground truth chordal distance values given by (9). Dashed lines encapsulating '+' and 'x' lines show standard deviation of chordal distance values for 50 iterations per changing parameter.

arbitrary movements like fidgeting, swiveling on the chair, translation, head rotation and talking. We do not consider illumination variations here, as the recordings were all done in an office environment with stable lighting conditions. Six recording sessions of 5s each were captured in this manner for each subject. The output of the face detector were resized to 32×32 pixels and used unaltered thereafter for face recognition. No background removal, false positive rejection or illumination normalization was performed.

To reduce computational requirements, only the first 10 face detector outputs of each sequence were used for training. Furthermore, we do not consciously filter out false positives and allow them to remain as noisy samples in the sequences. Examples of the actual images used are depicted in Figure 2(a). The optimal subspace dimension was empirically determined to be 5. Figure 3(a) depicts a comparison of the chordal distance of all subspaces against the subspace generated by Subject 1 Session 1. The estimation uncertainty of the reference subspace was computed using (20). It can be

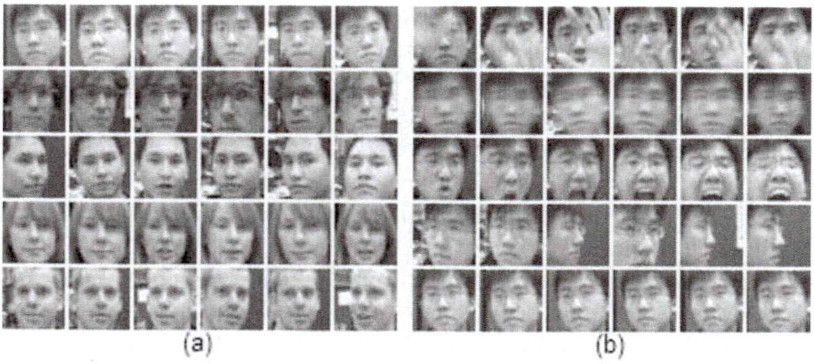

Fig. 2. (a) Examples of intra-class variations in the database. (b) Row 1–4: Examples of the extreme variations produced. Row 5: The control sequence.

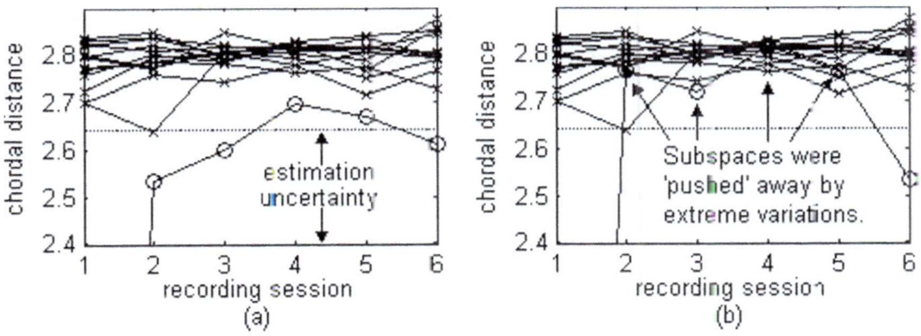

Fig. 3. Distance comparisons against Subject 1 Session 1, (a) using our face database. (b) with Sessions 2–6 of Subject 1 substituted with the sequences exemplified by Figure 2(b). 'x's denote chordal distances of Subjects 2–14, while 'o's denote chordal distances of Subject 1. Dotted lines show the estimation uncertainty.

seen that the subspaces of Subject 1 are noticeably closer to the reference subspace, some even dipping below the amount of uncertainty in the estimation, while subspaces of the other subjects are discernibly further away. Using the distance criterion (21) and a threshold level of zero, we were able to achieve an accuracy of 91% with our minimalist face recognition system.

To illustrate the ability of (20) in evaluating the quality of subspace estimation, Subject 1 was requested to intentionally produce several types of extreme variations while being recorded by our system above. Figure 2(b) depicts the types of variations produced: (according to the row order) deliberate occlusions, sudden/jerky movements, extreme facial variations and severe off-axis rotations. A control sequence captured under mild variations was included. Subspaces of dimension 5 were estimated for these sequences, and the amount of uncertainty computed using (20) are 3.6758, 2.8616, 2.9349, 3.2149 and 1.2970 respectively according to the order in Figure 2(b). We substituted these sequences into Sessions 2–6 of Subject 1 and reran our face recognition system. It is evident from Figure 3(b) that the extreme variations have biased the subspaces away from their true positions, while the control sequence remains close to Subject 1. Therefore, judging from the uncertainty values alone, we could have declined classification for these noisy test subspaces to prevent erroneous decisions and called for re-estimations using cleaner samples.

6 Conclusion

Face recognition using image sets has many merits compared to still image face recognition paradigms. An effective approach to tackle this problem involves fitting linear subspaces across the image sets and performing classification by comparing distances of subspaces. Based on a matrix perturbation theorem, we established the mathematical formulation of (20), which is the major contribution of this paper to quantify the uncertainty of estimating a linear subspace to approximate a noise affected image set. An immediate application is the evaluation of the quality of subspace estimation over noisy image sets, which we demonstrated with real life data. We performed experiments using artificial data to confirm the validity of our main result. Based on the established formulation, we proposed a more accurate distance criterion between subspaces, given by (21), that allows distance due to within-class variations be detached from distance comparisons between subspaces. A practical application of this was demonstrated through an MSM-based face recognition system using a small database of video sequences of faces which achieved comparable results with previous reported implementations.

References

1. Lee, K., Ho, J., Yang, M., Kriegman, D.: Video-based face recognition using probabilistic appearance manifolds. In: IEEE Conf. on Computer Vision and Pattern Recognition. (2003)
2. Shakhnarovich, G., Fisher, J.W., Darrell, T.: Face recognition from long-term observations. In: European Conference on Computer Vision. (2002)
3. Li, S., Zhang, Z.: Floatboost learning and statistical face detection. IEEE Transactions of Pattern Analysis and Machine Intelligence **26** (2004) 1–12
4. Ariki, Y., Ishikawa, N.: Integration of face and speaker recognition by subspace method. In: Int. Conf. on Pattern Recognition. Volume 3. (1996) 456–460
5. Yamaguchi, O., Fukui, K., Maeda, K.: Face recognition using temporal image sequence. In: Int. Conf. on Automatic Face and Gesture Recognition. (1998) 318–323
6. Fukui, K., Yamaguchi, O.: Face recognition using multi-viewpoint patterns for robot vision. In: 10th International Symposium of Robotics Research. (2003)
7. Arandjelovic, O., Shakhnarovich, G., Fisher, J., Cipolla, R., Darrell, T.: Face recognition with image sets using manifold density divergence. In: CVPR. (2005)
8. Zhou, S., Krueger, V., Chellappa, R.: Probabilistic recognition of human faces from video. Computer Vision Image Understanding **91** (2003) 214–245
9. Bichsel, M., Pentland, A.P.: Human face recognition and the face image set's topology. CVGIP: Image Understanding **59** (1994) 254–261
10. Golub, G.H., Loan, C.F.V.: Matrix Computations. 3rd edn. John Hopkins University Press (1996)
11. Stewart, G.W., Sun, J.G.: Matrix Perturbation Theory. Academic Press Inc. (1990)
12. Bishop, C.M.: Bayesian PCA. Advances in Neural Information Processing Systems **11** (1998) 382–388
13. Bradski, G., Kaehler, A., Pisarevsky, V.: Learning-based computer vision with Intel's open source computer vision library. Intel Technology Journal **9** (2005) 119–130

Face-Voice Authentication Based on 3D Face Models

Girija Chetty and Michael Wagner

HCC Laboratory, School of ISE, University of Canberra
Girija.Chetty@canberra.edu.au

Abstract. In this paper we propose fusion of shape and texture information from 3D face models of persons with the acoustic features extracted from spoken utterances, to improve the performance against imposter and replay attacks. Experiments conducted on two multimodal speaking face corpora, VidTIMIT and AVOZES, allowed less than 2 % EERs to be achieved for imposter attacks, and less than 1% for type-1 replay attacks for multimodal feature fusion of acoustic, shape and texture features. For type-2 replay attacks, more difficult type of spoof attacks, less than 7% EER was achieved.

1 Introduction

Person authentication systems based on video sequences of speaking faces, are less vulnerable to imposter and replay attacks because of their ability to process the information from both the face and voice of a person, [1]. The video containing temporal information, multiple instances of a speaking face, as well as a synchronous acoustic information makes imposter and spoof attacks less likely, as it is very difficult to spoof both the person's voice in synchronism with image of the person's speaking face. However, with recent advances in computer graphics(CG), and availability of inexpensive CG animation software tools , it is significantly easier to create photorealistic synthetic or fake 2D talking faces from a single image and pre-recorded audio, thus weakening anti-imposture and anti-spoof abilities of systems proposed in [2,3]. Moreover, since the systems proposed in [1,2,3] are based on two dimensional face models, they are more sensitive to pose, illumination and appearance variations in faces, imposing stringent pose and illumination normalization requirements on the biometric data presented to the system. Use of 3D face models will allow better handling of the pose and lighting variations, and can thwart most of the imposter/reply attacks at the same time,[4]. The 3D shape of a face does not change due to changes in head pose and illumination, and it possible to accurately model a normal talking face with rigid head movements, such as head turning right, left, back and forth while speaking using 3D models. There is an inherent synchrony between acoustic and visual signals for speaking faces. In addition, facial and head motion during speech is a direct consequence of vocal-tract motion which shapes the acoustics of the speech [5,6]. We propose feature fusion of 3D shape and texture features extracted from face images of the person, with acoustic features extracted from spoken utterances, for achieving invariance against pose and illumination variations, and enhance the performance against imposter and replay attacks. The feature fusion allows synchrony between audiovisual data to be preserved during the entire utterance, as opposed to

P.J. Narayanan et al. (Eds.): ACCV 2006, LNCS 3851, pp. 559 – 568, 2006.

independent processing of features in late fusion, [1]. Experiments with VidTIMIT and AVOZES, the two audiovisual speaking face corpora, allowed less than 2 % error rates (EERs) to be achieved for imposter attacks and less than 1% for type-1 replay attacks (pre-recorded audio with still photos) , and 4 – 6 % for type-I1 replay attacks(CG animated fake video from a still photo and pre-recorded audio).

Next section describes the speaking face data used for evaluating the potential of proposed 3D multimodal feature fusion, followed by face modeling technique in section 3. The details of the features extracted and the experiments carried out, is described in section 4 and 5, followed by conclusions in section 6.

2 Speaking Face Corpus

The speaking face data from two different databases, VidTIMIT and AVOZES were used for conducting imposter and spoof attack experiments. The VidTIMIT multimodal person authentication database [7] consists of video and corresponding audio recordings of 43 people (19 female and 24 male). The mean duration of each sentence is around 4 seconds, or approximately 100 video frames. A broadcast-quality digital video camera in a noisy office environment was used to record the data. The video of each person is stored as a sequence of JPEG images with a resolution of 512 384 pixels with corresponding audio provided as a 16-bit 32-kHz mono PCM file.

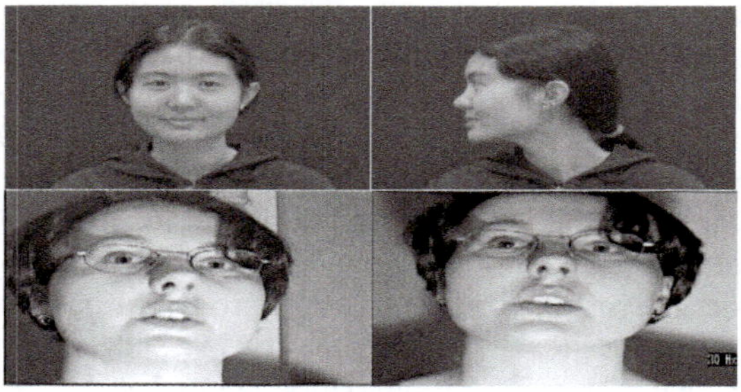

Fig. 1. Faces from (a) VidTIMIT above, (b) AVOZES

The second database used is the AVOZES database, an audiovisual corpus developed for automatic speech recognition research [8]. The corpus consists of 20 native speakers of Australian English (10 female and 10 male speakers), and the audiovisual data was recorded with a stereo camera system to achieve more accurate 3D measurements on the face. The recordings were made at 30 Hz video frame rate, and at 16bit, 48 kHz mono audio rate in a controlled acoustic environment with no external noise, and some background computer and air-conditioning noise. For each speaker there ware 3 continuous spoken utterances, 10 digit sequences, 18 phoneme sequences(CVC words in a carrier phrase) and 22 VCV phoneme sequences(VCV words in a carrier phrase. Figure 1a and Figure 1b show sample speaking-face data in different views available from VidTIMIT and AVOZES. The 3D face modeling technique used is described in next section, with VidTIMIT face data as an example.

3 3D Face Modeling

The VidTIMIT data base consists of frontal and profile view images of the faces, and AVOZES data comprises left(top) and right(bottom) images of the faces, as shown in Figure 1(a) and (b). We used a unified approach for 3D face modeling of faces from the databases, [4, 9]. The algorithm start by computing 3D coordinates of automatically extracted facial feature points. Correspondence between feature points in both images is established using epipolar constraints, and then depth information from front and profile views for VidTIMIT faces, and, left and right views for AVOZES faces, is computed using perspective projection. The 3D coordinates of the selected feature points are then used to deform a 3D generic face model to obtain a person specific 3D face model.

The generic model then undergoes global alignment and local refinement. The global alignment stage brings the generic model and facial measurements into same coordinate system. Then, local refinement is performed by generating 3D spline curves for each facial component and adjusting corresponding vertices of the 3D model accordingly.

The automatic facial feature extraction algorithm extracts 15 2D corresponding facial features from two views, based on skin color modeling, and morphogical segmentation in red-blue chrominance space, and then followed by pseudo-hue edge detection and matching with deformable templates corresponding to eyes, nose and mouth features, and [10]. The technique used allows automatic facial feature extraction with about 96% accuracy. These features are anchor points chosen because of their importance in representing a face. Figure 2 show some of the steps used in extracting the anchor points in front and profile views for VidTIMIT faces.

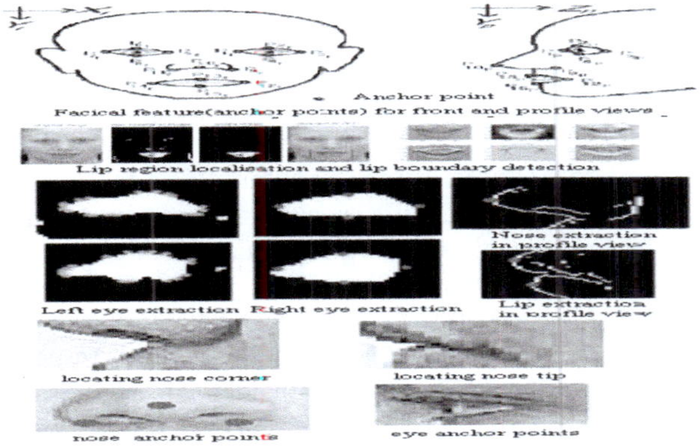

Fig. 2. Facial feature extraction from Front and Profile views for VidTIMIT faces

The global alignment of generic head model for each person's head shape involves deformation of 15 vertices (anchor points). The entire 3D generic model is brought as close as possible to the corresponding 3D coordinates of anchor points calculated from the images of the person's face. This is done by rotating, translating and scaling to match the calculated 3D points by minimizing the sum squared error criteria.

Given two sets of 3D points, namely 15 calculated anchor points, and 15 corresponding model points, global alignment algorithm finds the translation and rotation matrices that best match the corresponding data points. That is, it calculates the best fit of two similar sets of 3D data points; the global rigid alignment deforms successfully scales and aligns the generic model to the 3D feature points calculated from the face images.

Local refinement is then implemented by treating each of the facial features as separate non-rigid components, and the vertices of the generic model are brought closer to the calculated 3D anchor points of the person's face. Facial texture for all the vertices is computed by blending the R, G, B color components of two views of the face. Figure 3 shows the textured 3D face model for a male subject in VidTIMIT corpus by global and local alignment of generic face model.

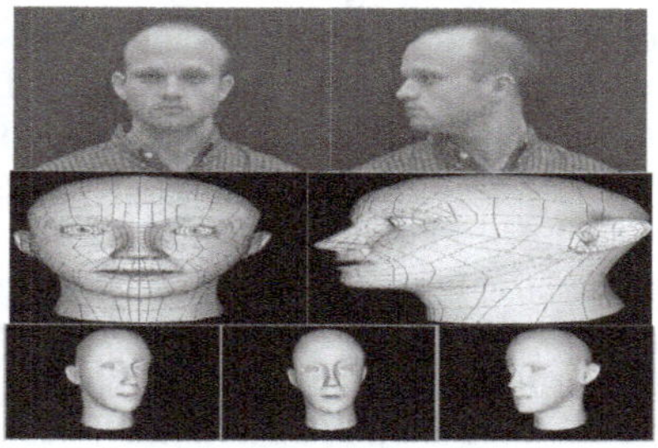

Fig. 3. 3D face model of VidTimit face by global and local alignment of generic face model shown in Figure 2

4 Shape and Texture Fusion

The techniques proposed till date for processing and integration of shape and texture features are in 3D face recognition domain, and have evolved based on the assumption that there is no correlation between shape and texture features of a 3D face. This might be true for static 3D faces, and most of research efforts so far have mainly addressed recognition of still 3D faces, [4, 9]. But a speaking face is a kinematic-acoustic system in motion, and the shape, texture and acoustic features during speech production must be correlated in some way or other. A number of studies carried out by Yehia et. al. [5,6] have established this correlation based on the anatomical facts, and shown that a single neuromotor source controlling the vocal tract behavior is responsible for both the acoustic and the visible attributes of speech production. Hence, for a speaking face not only the facial motion and speech acoustics is correlated, but the head motion and fundamental frequency (F0) produced during speech is also related.

Though there is no clear and distinct neuromotor coupling between head motion and speech acoustics, there is an indirect anatomical coupling created by the complex of strap muscles running between the floor of the mouth, through thyroid bone, and attaching to the outer edge of the cricothyroid cartilage. Due to this indirect coupling, speaker tends to raise the pitch when head goes up while talking. The head motion can modeled by tracking 3D face shapes with complementary and synchronous 2D facial feature variation, and 1D acoustic variation.

This unique and rich information is normally person-specific and cannot be easily spoofed either by a real imposter, or CG animated speaking faces. Hence a multimodal fusion of shape, texture and acoustic features at the feature-level as opposed to late fusion (where the features are independently processed) can enhance the performance of face-voice authentication systems against imposter and replay attacks.

The major deformations for speaking faces are in the lower part of the face compared to rest of the face. Hence the lower half of the face was used for extracting the shape and texture features and subsequent multimodal fusion. An alignment was done to account for variations in head orientation. The 3D model of lower part of the face consists of about 128 vertices and 200 surfaces. This means a fusion of acoustic vector with 128 dimensional shape (X, Y, Z) vector and similar size for texture feature vector values. This is too large a dimension for a reasonable performance to be achieved. However, after principal component analysis(PCA) of shape and texture vector separately, we learnt that about 6-8 principal components of shape vector and 3-4 components of texture vector explains more than 95% of variations in lip shapes and appearances during spoken utterances of most of the English language sentences.

The 8 eigen-values for shape vector correspond to jaw opening/closing, lip protrusion/retraction, lip opening/closing, and jaw protrusion/retraction as shown in Figure 4. Similarly, the 3-4 eigen values of texture vector describe most of the appearance variations mainly those corresponding to one rounded viseme with closed lips, (e.g. [‘u’]), one rounded viseme with open lips, and one spread viseme with spread lips, (e.g. [‘i’]).

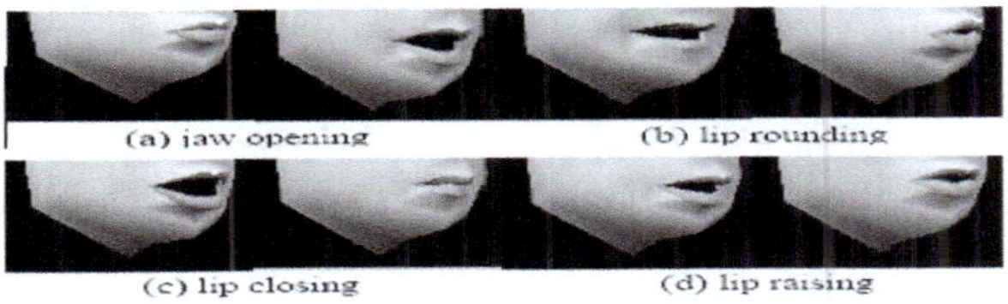

Fig. 4. Principal visemes during English speaking

For acoustic features, the Mel frequency cepstral coefficients (MFCC) as derived from the cepstrum information were used. The MFCC features were obtained by pre-emphasizing the audio signal first, and then processed with a 30ms Hamming window with one third overlap, yielding a frame rate of 50 Hz. An acoustic feature vector was determined for each frame by warping 512 spectral bands into 30 melspaced bands, and computing the 8 MFCCs. Cepstral mean normalization was performed on all MFCCs before they were used for training, testing and evaluation. In addition, fundamental frequency F0 computed by autocorrelation method was used.

5 Authentication Experiments

To investigate the potential of three dimensional face models against impostor attacks and spoof protection, different sets of experiments were conducted using 18 dimensional multimodal audio-visual feature vector(8 MFCCs + 1 F0 features, 6 Eigen-shape and 3 Eigen-texture features).

Table 1. Notation for different experimental modes

Notation	True Description
EER	Equal Error Rate
DB1	VidTIMIT corpus
DB2	AVOZES corpus
TDMO	Text dependent male only cohort
TDFO	Text dependent female only cohort
TIMO	Text independent male only cohort
TIFO	Text independent female only cohort

In the training phase, a 10-Gaussian mixture model of each client's feature vectors in the three dimensional space was built by constructing a gender-specific universal background model (UBM) and then adapting each UBM by MAP adaptation. Both text-dependent and text-independent experiments were conducted with VidTIMIT corpus and text-dependent experiments with AVOZES data. Table 1 shows the notation used for different experimental modes.

In the test phase, clients' live test recordings were evaluated against a client's model λ by determining the log likelihoods $log\ p(X|\lambda)$ of the time sequences X of audiovisual feature vectors.

For testing replay attacks, two types of replay-attack experiments were conducted. For *Type-1* replay attacks, a number of "fake" recordings were constructed by combining the sequence of audio feature vectors from each test utterance with ONE visual feature vector chosen from the sequence of visual feature vectors. Such a fake sequence represents an attack on the authentication system, which is carried out by replaying an audio recording of the client's utterance while presenting a still photograph to the camera. Four such fake audiovisual sequences were constructed from different still frames of each client test recording. Log-likelihoods $log\ p(X'|\lambda)$ were computed for the fake sequences X' of audiovisual feature vectors against the client model λ.

For *Type-2* replay attacks, a video clip was constructed from a still photo of each speaker. This represents a scenario of a replay attack with an impostor presenting a fake video clip constructed from pre-recorded audio and a still photo of the client animated with facial movements and voice-synchronous lip movements. The still photo of each client was voice-synched with the speech signal of each speaker, using a set of commercial software tools (Adobe Photoshop Elements, Discreet 3DSMax, and Adobe After Effects). We constructed several fake video clips by extracting ONE face (the first face) from the video sequence, which acts as a key frame, animated the lip region of the key frame by phoneme-to-viseme mapping, and then added random deformations and movements in the face and finally rendered lip and face movements with speech, all together as a new video clip. Such a fake clip emulates a normal talking head with certain facial and head movements in three dimensional space in synchronism with spoken utterance.

Different sets of experiments were conducted to evaluate the performance of the system in terms of DET curves and equal error rates. The results for only two types of

Table 2. Number of Client, Imposter and Replay attack (RA) trials

Corpus	**DB1TIMO**	**DB2TDFO**
Client Trials	144 (24 clients × 6 Utterances per client)	530 trials (10×53)
Impostor Trials	3312 trials (24×23 ×6)	4770 trials (10×9×53)
type-1 Replay-attack Trials	576 trials (24×6×4)	2120 trials (10×53×4)
type-2 attack Trials	144 trials	530 trials

data, that is DB1TIMO (VidTIMIT database text-independent male-only cohort) and DB2TDFO(AVOZES database text dependent female-only cohort) are reported here due to space limitations. For both types of data, both late-fusion and feature-level fusion of shape and texture features were examined. For late-fusion equal weights for shape and feature fusion was used.

For VidTimit corpus in text-independent mode there were 144 client trials (24×6) and 3312 impostor trials (24×23×6) for male subjects. For AVOZES there were 53 client trials and 4770(10×9×53) impostor trials. Next set of experiments were for testing the *Type-1* replay attacks. For the VidTimit database in text-independent mode, there were 144 client trials (24×6) and 576(24×6×4) replay attacks for male subjects. For AVOZES data, there were 53 client and 2120 (10×53×4) replay attack trials for both female subjects in text dependent mode. The third set of experiments is to test *Type-2* replay attacks, where the number of client and spoof attack trials were same as client trials. Table 2 shows the number of client, impostor and replay attack trials for each set.

Table 3. EERs for impostor and Replay attacks(RA)

% EER achieved	**VidTIMIT TIMO**	**VidTIMIT TIMO**	**AVOZES TDFO**	**AVOZES TDFO**
Fusion Type	*Late Fusion*	*Feature Fusion*	*Late Fusion*	*Feature Fusion*
Impostor Attacks	0.92	0.64	1.53	1.24
Type-1 RA	0.44	0.23	0.95	0.59
Type-2 RA	3.4	1.9	6.45	4.3

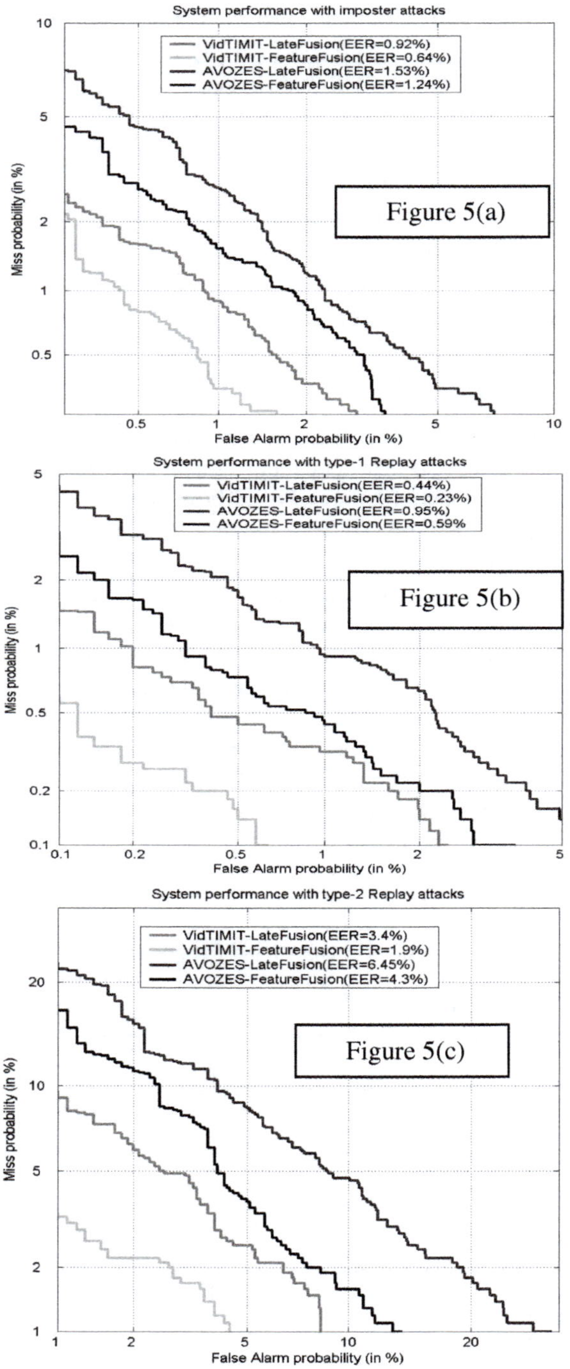

Fig. 5. DET curves for (a) impostor, (b) type-1 Replay, (c) type-2 Replay attacks

The DET curve and EER results in Table 3 and Figures 5 , show the potential of the proposed fusion of eigen-shape and eigen texture features with acoustic features (MFCC+f0) to thwart imposter and replay attacks for VidTIMIT data and AVOZES data. For VidTIMIT corpus, less than 1% EER achieved, with 0.92% for late fusion and 0.64% for feature fusion. Feature fusion performs better, a 30% improvement as compared to late fusion, due to synchronous processing of eigen-shape, eigen-texture and acoustic features. For AVOZES corpus, EER achieved is 1.24% with feature fusion as compared to 1.53 %, about 20% EER improvement. For type-1 replay attacks, less than 1 % EER is achieved for VidTIMIT and AVOZES, with feature-fusion performing better than late fusion (48% improvement for VidTIMIT data vs. 38% for AVOZES data). Less than 7% EER is achieved for type-2 replay attacks for both VidTIMIT and AVOZES data, with best EER equal to 1.9% for VidTIMIT TIMO data and worst EER of 6.45% for AVOZES TDFO data. The fusion of acoustic features with three dimensional shape and texture features allowed a significantly better performance, though type-2 replay attacks are more complex replay attacks to detect.

6 Conclusions

The potential of three-dimensional face models for thwarting imposter and still-photo/video-replay replay attacks for face-voice authentication has been shown in this study. The multimodal feature fusion of acoustic, shape and texture features allowed less than 2 % EERs to be achieved for imposter attacks, and less than 1% for *type-1* replay attacks. With less than 7% EER, significantly better performance has been achieved for more difficult *type-2* replay attacks. Currently, experiments to examine the improvements achieved when leaving out certain features, such as shape, texture or voice are in progress. Further work will involve investigations into more discriminative 3D features for improving *type-2* replay attacks.

References

1. Chetty, G. and Wagner, M., "'Liveness' Verification in Audio-Video Authentication", Proc. Int Conf on Spoken Language Processing ICSLP-04, Jeju, Korea, pp 2509-2512.
2. N. Poh and J. Korczak, 'Hybrid biometric person authentication using face and voice features," Proc. of Int. Conf. on Audio and Video-Based Biometric Person Authentification, Halmstad, Sweden, June 2001, pp. 348--353.
3. Conrad Sanderson and Kuldip K. Paliwal, "Identity verification using speech and face information", Digital Signal Processing, Volume 14, Issue 5, Pages 397-507 (September 2004)
4. R.L.Hsu and A.K.Jain, "Face Modeling for Recognition," Proceedings Int'l Conf. Image Processing, ICIP, Greece, Oct. 7-10, 2001.
5. Yehia, H., Rubin, P. and Vatikiotic-Bateson E. (1998), "Quantitative association of vocal track and facial behavior", Jorunal of Speech Communication 26(1-2), 23-43.
6. Hani Yehia, Takaaki Kuratate, Eric Vatikiotic-Bateson, "Linking Facial Animation, Head Motion and Speech Acoustics", Journal of Phonetics, Vol.30, Issue 3, 2002.

7. Sanderson, C. and K.K. Paliwal (2003), "Fast features for face authentication under illumination direction changes", Pattern Recognition Letters 24, 2409-2419.
8. R. Goecke and J.B. Millar, "The Audio-Video Australian English Speech Data Corpus AVOZES", Proceedings of the 8th International Conference on Spoken Language Processing INTERSPEECH 2004 - ICSLP, Volume III, pages 2525-2528, Jeju, Korea, 4 - 8 October 2004.
9. G.Gordon, "Face Recognition from Frontal and Profile Views," Proceedings Int'l Workshop on Face and Gesture Gesture Recognition, Zurich, 1995, pp.47-52.
10. Chetty, G. and Wagner, M., "Automated lip feature extraction for liveness verification in audio-video authentication", Proc. Image and Vision Computing 2004, New Zealand, pp 17-22.

Face Recognition Under Varying Illumination Based on MAP Estimation Incorporating Correlation Between Surface Points

Mihoko Shimano[1], Kenji Nagao[1],
Takahiro Okabe[2], Imari Sato[3], and Yoichi Sato[2]

[1] Panasonic Tokyo (Matsushita Electric Industrial Co., Ltd.,)
4–3–1 Tsunashima-higashi, Kohoku-ku, Yokohama City, Kanagawa 223–8639, Japan
shimano.mhk@jp.panasonic.com
[2] Institute of Industrial Science, The University of Tokyo,
4–6–1 Komaba, Meguro-ku Tokyo 153–8505, Japan
{takahiro, ysato}@iis.u-tokyo.ac.jp
[3] National Institute of Informatics,
2–1–2 Hitotsubashi, Chiyoda-ku Tokyo 101–8430, Japan
imarik@nii.ac.jp

Abstract. In this paper, we propose a new method for face recognition under varying illumination conditions using a single input image. Our method is based on a statistical shape-from-shading method which combines the strengths of the Lambertian model and statistical information obtained from a large number of images of different people under varying illumination. The main advantage of our method over the previous methods is that our method explicitly incorporates a correlation between surface points on a face in the MAP estimation of surface normals and albedos, so that a new image of the same face under novel illumination can be synthesized correctly even when the face is partially shadowed. Furthermore, our method introduces pixel grouping and reliability measure in the MAP estimation in order to reduce computational cost while maintaining accuracy. We demonstrate the effectiveness of our proposed method via experiments with real images.

1 Introduction

Face recognition has become one of the most actively studied areas in computer vision, and a number of methods have been proposed to recognize a person's face from input images [6, 21]. This is because face recognition technologies can be effectively used for a wide range of applications. One such application is the identification of a person with face recognition when only one image of the person is available beforehand, e.g., a picture on a driver's license or a passport. We believe this example is important because it is not always possible to provide a large number of training images for each person in real applications.

The appearance of a human face is highly dependent on many factors including the pose of a face, illumination conditions, and facial expression. In this

P.J. Narayanan et al. (Eds.): ACCV 2006, LNCS 3851, pp. 569–580, 2006.

work, we deal with the problem of recognizing a person's face under varying illumination conditions when only one training image is available for the person. Therefore, we do not consider appearance variations due to other factors such as poses or facial expression.

The task of face recognition becomes easier and robuster if a sufficient number of training images taken under different conditions are available for each person, so that we can model appearance variation for the person accurately. For instance, it is known that appearance variation of a human face due to illumination change is represented approximately with a low-dimensional linear subspace [4, 7, 2], and, as a result, existing methods for face recognition under varying illumination work fairly well as long as we have enough training images taken under different lighting conditions (for instance, [13, 11, 3, 7, 12, 17, 14, 15]).

On the other hand, face recognition under varying illumination becomes a challenging task when only one training image is available for each person. It is not trivial, and even may be impossible, to predict how the appearance of a person's face varies with different lighting conditions if we are given no information other than a single input image.

Several methods proposed recently [1, 18, 16, 5, 22, 10] can be used for solving this challenging problem. They are based on the idea of using a statistical model obtained from a set of images or laser-scanned images of different persons. With these methods, the shape and reflectance properties of a face are estimated from a single input image by using a statistical model of human faces. This is the key difference from conventional shape-from-shading techniques which estimate the shape of an object with more explicit assumptions such as the integrability constraint [8] and the assumption of face symmetry [20].

Although these methods have been used successfully to predict appearance variations in human faces for different lighting conditions, they share a common difficulty with the exception of Sim and Kanade's method [18]. That is, reflection components other than those represented by a simple reflection model such as the Lambertian model or the Phong model cannot be reproduced accurately with these methods. For instance, both Atick et al. [1] and Zhou et al.[22] assume that reflection on a human face can be represented with the Lambertian model. Blanz and Vetter [5] describe the shading observed on faces by using the Lambertian model and the Phong model. Matthews and Baker [10] represent appearance variations due to lighting as a linear combination of basis images. However, it is reported that reflections on human faces often deviate significantly from simple reflection models such as the Lambertian model and the Phong model [9].

Our method is most closely related to the method by Sim and Kanade [18], in that both methods estimate surface normals and albedos of surface points on a face from a given single input image via Maximum A Posteriori (MAP) estimation based on statistical information obtained from a set of images of different persons. Because reflection components other than those representable with the Lambertian model can also be estimated via MAP estimation, both methods have strengths in comparison with other statistical shape-from-shading methods in that subtle reflection components such as highlights and interreflections can be reproduced for novel lighting conditions.

The key difference between our method and Sim and Kanade's method is that our method explicitly incorporates the correlation between surface points on a face in MAP estimation of surface normals and albedos. This contributes to the distinct advantages of our method. For instance, a new image of the same face under novel illumination can be synthesized correctly with our method even when the face is partially shadowed, while Sim and Kanade's method fails to do so since each pixel is treated independently. In addition, we introduce the idea of pixel grouping and reliability measure in the MAP estimation in order to reduce computational cost while maintaining accuracy.

2 Our Proposed Method

Our method consists of three steps: i) *learning step* and ii) *modeling step* and iii) *rendering step*. In the *learning step*, our method computes statistics about human faces, i.e., the surface normal including albedo and an error term corresponding to reflection components other than the diffuse component, from a set of images of multiple people taken under varying illumination conditions. The set of images used for learning the statistics are referred to as bootstrap images. In the *modeling step*, a single image of a novel face, e.g., a picture on a driver's license or a passport, is used for predicting appearance variations for this person based on the statistics obtained in the learning step. We refer to this single image as a *training* image. Using this *training* image, our method first estimates the light source direction under which this *training* image was taken. Then, our method estimates the surface normal of the face via MAP estimation by using both the estimated light source direction and the learned statistics. Finally, in the *rendering step*, the error term for a novel illumination condition is computed by MAP estimation, and added to the diffuse reflection component to render the image of the face under the novel lighting. Images rendered this way are then used for face recognition under varying lightings. We will explain each of these steps in details.

2.1 Reflectance Equation

Our method assumes that a set of bootstrap images for the learning step and a single training image for the modeling step are taken under point light sources at infinity, that is, directional light sources. Then, the intensity i_p at the p-th pixel is represented as the sum of the diffuse component and the remaining component like in Sim and Kanade's method [18]

$$i_p = \boldsymbol{n}_p^T \boldsymbol{s} + e_p(\boldsymbol{s}), \tag{1}$$

where $\boldsymbol{n}_p = (n_{px}, n_{py}, n_{pz})^T$ is a product of the albedo and surface normal at the p-th pixel, and $\boldsymbol{s} = (s_x, s_y, s_z)^T$ is a product of the intensity and direction of a directional light source. The error term $e_p(\boldsymbol{s})$ describes reflection components other than diffuse reflection such as highlights, interreflections, and shadows.

To take into account the correlation between surface points explicitly, we represent the intensities of P pixels in each image as

$$\boldsymbol{i} = S^T\boldsymbol{b} + \boldsymbol{e}(\boldsymbol{s}), \tag{2}$$

$$\begin{pmatrix} i_1 \\ i_2 \\ \vdots \\ i_P \end{pmatrix} = \begin{pmatrix} \boldsymbol{s}^T & 0 & \dots & 0 \\ 0 & \boldsymbol{s}^T & & \vdots \\ \vdots & & \ddots & 0 \\ 0 & \dots & 0 & \boldsymbol{s}^T \end{pmatrix} \begin{pmatrix} \boldsymbol{n}_1 \\ \boldsymbol{n}_2 \\ \vdots \\ \boldsymbol{n}_P \end{pmatrix} + \begin{pmatrix} e_1(\boldsymbol{s}) \\ e_2(\boldsymbol{s}) \\ \vdots \\ e_P(\boldsymbol{s}) \end{pmatrix}.$$

Thus, $\boldsymbol{i}$, S, $\boldsymbol{b}$, and $\boldsymbol{e}$ are a P-dimensional vector, a $3P \times P$ matrix, a $3P$-dimensional vector, and a P-dimensional vector respectively.

2.2 Computing Statistics

Let us assume that a set of bootstrap images consists of images of L people taken under J known directional light sources $\boldsymbol{s}_j$ $(j = 1, 2, ..., J)$. For the l-th person, a set of images $I^{(l)}$ taken under J light sources are represented by

$$I^{(l)} = B^{(l)T}S' + E^{(l)}. \tag{3}$$

Here, $I^{(l)} = (\boldsymbol{i}_1^{(l)}, \boldsymbol{i}_2^{(l)}, \dots, \boldsymbol{i}_J^{(l)})$, $B^{(l)} = (\boldsymbol{n}_1^{(l)}, \boldsymbol{n}_2^{(l)}, \dots, \boldsymbol{n}_P^{(l)})$, $S' = (\boldsymbol{s}_1, \boldsymbol{s}_2, \dots, \boldsymbol{s}_J)$, and $E^{(l)} = (\boldsymbol{e}^{(l)}(\boldsymbol{s}_1), \boldsymbol{e}^{(l)}(\boldsymbol{s}_2), \dots, \boldsymbol{e}^{(l)}(\boldsymbol{s}_J))$ respectively. We assume that the illumination intensity $|\boldsymbol{s}_j|$ of the bootstrap images are same (We describe $|\boldsymbol{s}_j|$ as 1 in the rest of this paper.).

Then, we consider $E^{(l)}$ as Gaussian noise[1], and compute the least-squares solution of $B^{(l)}$ as

$$B^{(l)} = (S'S'^T)^{-1}S'I^{(l)}, \tag{4}$$

and the residuals, that is, the error $E^{(l)}$ as

$$E^{(l)} = I^{(l)} - B^{(l)T}S'. \tag{5}$$

Finally, we compute the statistics of the surface normal and the error term from the estimated surface normals and error terms for all people in the bootstrap images. With regard to the surface normals $\boldsymbol{b}$, all matrices $B^{(l)}$ for L people are converted into $3P$-dimensional vectors in a raster-scan manner, and then the mean vector $\mu_{\boldsymbol{b}}$ ($3P$-dimensional vector) and the covariance matrix $C_{\boldsymbol{b}}$ ($3P \times 3P$ matrix) are computed. For the statistics of the error term $\boldsymbol{e}(\boldsymbol{s})$, the mean vector $\mu_{\boldsymbol{e}}(\boldsymbol{s}_j)$ is computed from L error vectors $\boldsymbol{e}^{(l)}(\boldsymbol{s}_j)$ for each light source $\boldsymbol{s}_j$. The $PJ \times PJ$ covariance matrix $C_{\boldsymbol{e}}$ is computed from L error matrices $E^{(l)}$ in the same way as $C_{\boldsymbol{b}}$ is computed from $B^{(l)}$.Note that the difference between our

[1] In order to carefully recover $B^{(l)}$, we removed outliers such as highlights and shadows contained in bootstrap images.

proposed method and the previous method is that we incorporate the correlation between surface points rather than treating each point independently.

2.3 Modeling from a Single Image

The modelling step consists of two sub-steps; estimation of the light source direction under which a single training image of a subject was taken, and the estimation of the surface normals of the subject. We explain these sub-steps in detail.

Estimating Illumination

We estimate the illumination intensity and direction under which a single training image $\boldsymbol{i}$ was taken. Our method assumes that the subject has the average face shape and albedos which are represented by the Lambertian model, and computes the least-squares solution of the illumination[2]. We extended the illumination estimation method proposed by Sim and Kanade [18] so that we are able to take variations in intensity of illumination into consideration. Although it is assumed that the illumination intensities of the training image and the bootstrap images are same in Sim and Kanade's method [18], it is often the case that intensity of illumination changes between the bootstrap images and the training image.

The illumination intensity and direction of a single training image is estimated by using the average B_{avr} of the computed matrices $B^{(l)}$ for all people in the bootstrap images $\boldsymbol{i}_j^{(l)}$

$$\boldsymbol{s} = B_{avr}^{T+}\boldsymbol{i} = (B_{avr}B_{avr}^T)^{-1}B_{avr}\boldsymbol{i}. \tag{6}$$

Then the ratio α of the estimated illumination intensity to that of the bootstrap images is computed as $\alpha = |\boldsymbol{s}|$.

Estimating Surface Normals and Albedos

Taking into account the correlation between surface points, we recover surface normals and albedos by MAP estimate as $\boldsymbol{b}_{\mathrm{MAP}} = \arg\max_{\boldsymbol{b}} P(\boldsymbol{b}|\boldsymbol{i})$. According to the Bayes' rule,

$$\boldsymbol{b}_{\mathrm{MAP}} = \arg\max_{\boldsymbol{b}} P(\boldsymbol{i}|\boldsymbol{b})P(\boldsymbol{b}). \tag{7}$$

Because we assume that the probability density functions (PDFs) of $\boldsymbol{b}$ and $\boldsymbol{e}$ are Gaussian distributions, $P(\boldsymbol{b})$ is described by $\mu_{\boldsymbol{b}}$ and $C_{\boldsymbol{b}}$, and $P(\boldsymbol{i}|\boldsymbol{b})$ is described by the mean $S^T\boldsymbol{b} + \mu_{\boldsymbol{e}}(\boldsymbol{s})$ and the covariance $\Sigma_{\boldsymbol{e}}$. Here, we calculate the mean $\mu_{\boldsymbol{e}}(\boldsymbol{s})$ based on kernel regression method by using the known illumination $\boldsymbol{s}_j$, and the elements of $\Sigma_{\boldsymbol{e}}$ are also interpolated from the computed $C_{\boldsymbol{e}}$ as

$$\mu_{\boldsymbol{e}}(\boldsymbol{s}) = \alpha\beta\frac{\sum_{j=1}^{J} w_j \mu_{\boldsymbol{e}}(\boldsymbol{s}_j)}{\sum_{j=1}^{J} w_j}, \quad \sigma_{\boldsymbol{e}}(\boldsymbol{s})^2 = \alpha^2\beta^2\frac{\sum_{j=1}^{J} w_j \sigma_{\boldsymbol{e}}(\boldsymbol{s}_j)^2}{\sum_{j=1}^{J} w_j}, \tag{8}$$

[2] In order to carefully recover the illumination, we removed outliers such as highlights and shadows contained in a training image.

where $w_j = \exp(-(D(\boldsymbol{s}, \boldsymbol{s}_j)/\sigma_j)^2/2)$, $D(\boldsymbol{s}, \boldsymbol{s}_j) = |\boldsymbol{s}/\alpha - \boldsymbol{s}_j|$, and β is a coefficient which sets the norm of the estimated illumination vector to 1. The coefficient β is defined by $\boldsymbol{s}/\alpha = \beta(\sum_{j=1}^{J} w_j \boldsymbol{s}_j)/\sum_{j=1}^{J} w_j$. Substituting the above vectors and matrices into equation (7), $\boldsymbol{b}_{\mathrm{MAP}}$ is given by

$$\boldsymbol{b}_{\mathrm{MAP}} = (S\Sigma_{\boldsymbol{e}}^{-1}S^T + C_{\boldsymbol{b}}^{-1})^{-1}(S\Sigma_{\boldsymbol{e}}^{-1}(\boldsymbol{i} - \mu_{\boldsymbol{e}}) + C_{\boldsymbol{b}}^{-1}\mu_{\boldsymbol{b}}). \quad (9)$$

2.4 Rendering for Novel Lightings

In order to synthesize an image under a novel illumination condition, we estimate the error terms under the illumination condition, considering both the correlation between surface points and between illumination directions. Because we assume a jointly Gaussian distribution for the PDF of the error terms, by using the actual error $\boldsymbol{e} = \boldsymbol{i} - S^T\boldsymbol{b}_{\mathrm{MAP}}$, the MAP estimate of the error terms under a novel illumination condition S_{new} is given by

$$\boldsymbol{e}_{\mathrm{MAP}} = \mu_{\boldsymbol{e}_{\mathrm{new}}} + R^T\Sigma_{\boldsymbol{e}}^{-1}(\boldsymbol{e} - \mu_{\boldsymbol{e}}), \quad (10)$$

where $\mu_{\boldsymbol{e}_{\mathrm{new}}}$ and R is the mean error under the novel lighting and the covariance of the error terms between the lighting of the training image and the novel lighting respectively. These quantities are also interpolated from $\mu_{\boldsymbol{e}}$ and $\Sigma_{\boldsymbol{e}}$.

Thus, a new image under a novel lighting condition is synthesized as

$$\boldsymbol{i}_{\mathrm{new}} = S_{\mathrm{new}}^T\boldsymbol{b}_{\mathrm{MAP}} + \boldsymbol{e}_{\mathrm{MAP}} \quad (11)$$

by using the estimated surface normals and error terms.

3 Reduction of Computational Cost

In addition to the correlation between surface points, we introduce two important improvements for reducing computational cost of our method while maintaining accuracy.

3.1 Grouping Pixels

The computational cost of our method increases approximately at $O(P^3)$ for the number of pixels since our method incorporates correlation between pixels rather than treating them independently. Thus, in order to reduce the calculation cost and make our method more tractable, we divide an image into subareas and consider the correlation between pixels in each area.

It is worth noting that the grouping used for estimating surface normals and that used for estimating error terms are not necessarily the same. In our experiments, surface normals and albedos were estimated by incorporating the correlation between surface points as we described above. On the other hand, the error terms were treated independently with respect to surface points, and only the correlation between illumination conditions is taken into account, because the $PJ \times PJ$ covariance matrix requires a large amount of computational cost.

3.2 Considering Reliability

In order to correctly recover surface normals, we further introduce a reliability measure representing how reliable each pixel value. Based on the reliability measure, the surface normals at shadowed regions or at pixels with noise are estimated from reliable pixels rather than other unreliable pixels in the training image. In practice, the value of the error variance Σ_e are used as this reliable measure; if the variance of the error term at a pixel is high, the contribution of the pixel is decreased for calculation of the correlation C_b.

The threshold for this reliable pixel selection can be determined by preliminary experiments. In addition, this reliable pixel selection results in reducing the computational cost of our method.

4 Experiments

In order to evaluate the performance of our proposed method, we conducted experiments on face recognition. We used the same statistical model for all of our experiments, and the model was obtained by using the Yale database B [3] which contains 640 images of 10 individuals (each person has 64 different images) under various lighting conditions per pose. Among 640 images in a frontal pose, we omitted 24 images for each of 10 people which contain an excessive amount of shadows due to extreme lighting conditions and used the other 40 images for each person for computing statistics about human faces (400 images in total). Each image was manually cropped and resized to 40×30 pixels with aligned eye positions. We used two different segmentations for grouping pixels in our experiments on face recognition as shown in Figure 1.

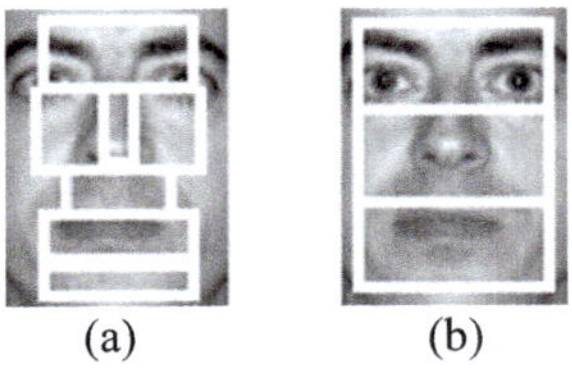

Fig. 1. Segmentations used for grouping pixels in our experiments: (a) 6 regions and (b) 3 regions. Note that left and right cheeks compose one region although they are not adjacent in (a).

4.1 Image Synthesis

Figure 2 shows one example of synthesized images by using our proposed method. The training image of a face illuminated from right (Figure 2 (a)) was used for synthesizing images under different lightings. As a ground truth, a real image of the same face taken under frontal illumination is shown in Figure 2 (d). Figure 2 (b) shows the image synthesized by our proposed method for frontal illumination with the grouping shown in Figure 1 (b). We can see both the diffuse reflection

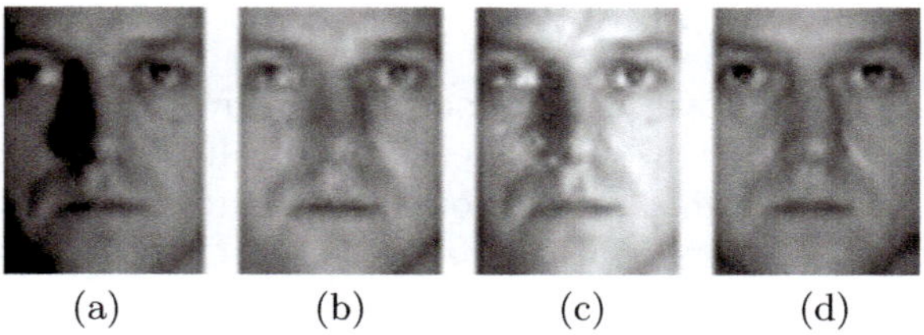

Fig. 2. Example of synthesized images with our method: (a) training image of a face illuminated from right, (b) synthesized image taken under frontal illumination with our method incorporating correlation between surface pixels, (c) synthesized image taken under frontal illumination without correlation , (d) real image taken under frontal illumination.

component and highlights are correctly synthesized even at surface points in shadows, e.g., the shadow cast by the nose and the attached shadow on the cheek. In contrast, it can be clearly seen that the image synthesized by using Sim and Kanade's method in Figure 2 (c) has problems for dealing with surface points in shadows.

4.2 Face Recognition

Two databases of face images taken under different illumination were used for our tests: our own database which contains frontal face images of 12 individuals illuminated from 11 different lighting directions and CMU-PIE database [19] which contains frontal images of 68 individuals illuminated from 21 different lighting directions.

All of the tests were conducted as follows. First, one image for each individual was used as a training image, and 40 images under different illumination (5 images only in the first experiment) were synthesized by using the training image and the statistical model learned from the Yale database B. Those 41 images were then used to generate the subspace for each individual. The rest of the images in the database were used as a test image and classified by searching for the subspace with the closest Euclidean distance to the test image.

In the first experiment, we compared the performance of our method with the most closely related method by Sim and Kanade [18] by using our own database. An image taken under frontal lighting was used as the single training image for each person for generating the person's subspace by Sim and Kanade's method and our proposed method. Table 1 shows recognition rates achieved by these two methods, and it shows significant improvement in recognition accuracy by incorporating correlations between surface points in MAP estimation as in our method.

In the second experiment, we used the CMU-PIE database, and the image of each person illuminated from the side was used as a training image. The result is shown in Table 2. As in the first experiment, recognition accuracy was significantly improved from 68% to 86% by incorporating correlations between surface points. Our method works well because both the diffuse reflection component

Table 1. Performance comparison of Sim and Kanade's method and our proposed method by using our face image database of 12 individuals

Methods	Recognition rate [%]
Sim and Kanade's method (without correlation)	88
Our method (with correlation in a group)	94

Table 2. Performance comparison of Sim and Kande's method and our proposed method by using CMU-PIE database

Methods	Recognition rate [%]
Sim and Kanade's method (without correlation)	68
Our method (with correlation in a group)	86

Table 3. Performance improvement by grouping pixels (3 areas) and the use of reliability measure in our method

Methods	Recognition rate [%]
Sim and Kanade's method (without correlation)	74
Our method (with correlation in a group without reliability)	81
Our method (with correlation in a group with reliability)	83

and highlights are correctly synthesized even at surface points in shadows as shown in Figure 2.

In the third experiment, we evaluated the effectiveness of pixel grouping and the reliability measure introduced in Section 3. The result is shown in Table 3. This experiment was done by using our database as in the first experiment except that face images illuminated from the side were used as a training image this time. First, we can see that the recognition rate was improved by almost 10% from 74% (*without correlation*) to 83% by incorporating correlations in MAP estimation. This also demonstrates that face recognition can be performed efficiently by using pixel grouping together with the reliability measure.

In the fourth experiment, we compared our method with Zhou et al.'s method [22] which is one of the most recently proposed methods for the same problem setting, i.e., face recognition under varying lightings by using a single training image. In order to compare the performance of our method with that of Zhou et al.'s method, we conducted experiments under the same condition as reported in [22]. The results of Zhou et al.'s method were taken from [22]. As we can see in Table 4, our method outperformed Zhou et al.'s method significantly. The recognition rate of our method (100%) is higher than that of Zhou et al's method (59%), when we used "f13" as a training set and "f16" as a test set, that is, both the training set and the test set contain face images illuminated from the same side. When we used "f08" under frontal illumination as a training set and "f15"

Table 4. Performance comparison of Zhou's method and our method by using CMU-PIE database

Methods	Recognition rate [%]	
	f13/f16(training/test)	f08/f15
Zhou et al.'s method	59	33
Our method	100	99

illuminated sideways as a test set, our method achieved high recognition rate (99%) in contrast with that of Zhou et al.'s method (33%).

The reason for our method's outperforming Zhou et al.'s method is attributed to the following two points. First, our method statistically models reflection components other than the diffuse component such as specular highlights and shadows, while Zhou et al.'s method assumes the Lambertian model. Second, our method takes into account correlations among surface points on a face so that a new image of the same face under novel illumination can be synthesized even when a single training image is partially shadowed.

5 Conclusions

In this work, we proposed a new method based on statistical shape from shading for face recognition under varying lighting conditions using a single training image for each person. Our method first learns a statistical model about human faces by using a set of training images of multiple people taken under varying illumination conditions. Then, the shape and albedo of a novel face are estimated via MAP estimation using the obtained statistical model and a single training image of the novel face. Finally, images of the face under novel lighting conditions are generated by using the obtained shape and albedo together with the error term estimated via MAP estimation.

The main advantage of our method over the previous methods is that our method explicitly incorporates a correlation between surface points on a face in the MAP estimation of surface normals and albedos, so that a new image of the same face under novel illumination can be synthesized correctly even when the face is partially shadowed. Furthermore, our method introduces pixel grouping and reliability measure in the MAP estimation in order to reduce computational cost while maintaining accuracy. The performance of our proposed method was demonstrated via experiments on face recognition by using real images.

We manually specified areas grouping pixels in this work, and automatic segmentation remains as a part of our future work. And we will further investigate the treatment of the error term. For instance, one possibility is to decompose the error term into different components such as specular highlights and shadows, and then treat them independently. We are also interested in extending our method for modeling the variations due to other factors such as poses.

References

1. J. J. Atick, P. A. Griffin, and A. N. Redlich, "Statistical approach to shape from shading: reconstruction of three-dimensional face surfaces from single two-dimensional images," *Neural Computation*, Vol.8, No.6, pp.1321–1340, 1996.
2. R. Basri, D. Roth, and D. Jacobs, "Clustering appearances of 3D objects," *Proc. IEEE Int. Conf. Computer Vision and Pattern Recognition*, pp.414–420, 1998.
3. P. N. Belhumeur, J. P. Hespanha, and D. J. Kriegman, "Eigenfaces vs. Fisherfaces: Recognition Using Class Specific Linear Projection," *IEEE Trans. Pattern Analysis and Machine Intelligence*, Vol.19, No.7, pp.711–720, 1997.
4. P. N. Belhumeur, and D. J. Kriegman, "What is the set of images of an object under all possible lighting conditions?," *Proc. IEEE Int. Conf. Computer Vision and Pattern Recognition*, pp.270–277, 1996.
5. V. Blanz and T. Vetter, "Face Recognition Based on Fitting a 3D Morphable Model," *IEEE Trans. Pattern Analysis and Machine Inteligence*, Vol.25, No.9, pp.1063–1074, 2003.
6. R. Chellappa, C. L. Wilson, and S. Sirohey, "Human and Machine Recognition of Faces, A Survey," *Proc. of the IEEE*, Vol.83, pp.705–740, 1995.
7. A. S. Georghiades, D. J. Kriegman, and P. N. Belhumeur, "Illumination cones for recognition under variable lighting: faces," *Proc. IEEE Int. Conf. Computer Vision and Pattern Recognition*, pp.52–58, 1998.
8. B. K. P. Horn, "Height and gradient from shading," *Int. J. Computer Vision*, Vol.5, pp.37–75, 1990.
9. S. R. Marschner, S. H. Westin, E. P. F. Lafortune, K. E. Torrance, and D. P. Greenberg, "Image-based BRDF Measurement Including Human Skin," *Proc. 10th Eurographics Workshop on Rendering*, pp.139–152, 1999.
10. I. Matthews and S. Baker, "Active appearance models revisited," *Int. J. Computer Vision*, Vol.60, No.2, pp.135–164, 2004.
11. H. Murase and S. K. Nayar, "Visual learning and Recognition of 3-D Objects from Appearance," *Int. J. Computer Vision*, Vol. 14, pp. 5–24, 1995.
12. K. Nagao, "Face recognition by distribution specific feature extraction," *Proc. IEEE Int. Conf. Computer Vision and Pattern Recognition*, pp.I-1278–1285, 2000.
13. E. Oja, "Subspace Methods for Pattern Recognition," *Research Studies Press Ltd.*, 1980.
14. T. Okabe and Y. Sato, "Object Recognition Based on Photometric Alignment Using RANSAC" *Proc. IEEE Int. Conf. Computer Vision and Pattern Recognition*, pp.I–221–228, 2003.
15. T. Okabe and Y. Sato, "Support Vector Machines for Object Recognition under Varying Illumination Conditions" *In Proc. Asian Conf. Computer Vision*, pp.724–729, 2004.
16. T. Shakunaga and K. Shigenari. "Decomposed Eigenface for Face Recognition under Various Lighting Conditions," *Proc. IEEE Int. Conf. Computer Vision and Pattern Recognition*, Vol.1, pp.864–871, 2001.
17. M. Shimano, K. Nagao, "Simultaneous Optimization of Class Configuration and Feature Space for Object Recognition," *Proc. Int. Conf. Pattern Recognition*, No.2, pp.7–10, 2004.
18. T. Sim and T. Kanade, "Combining Models and Exemplars for Face Recognition: An Illuminating Example," *Proc. IEEE Int. Conf. Computer Vision and Pattern Recognition Workshop on Models versus Exemplars in Computer Vision*, 2001.

19. T. Sim, S. Baker, and M. Bsat, "The CMU Pose, Illumination, and Expression (PIE) Database," *Proc. IEEE Int. Conf. Automatic Face and Gesture Recognition*, pp.53–58, 2002.
20. W. Zhao and R. Chellappa, "Illumination-insensive face recognition using symmetric shape-from-shading," *Proc. IEEE Int. Conf. Computer Vision and Pattern Recognition*, Vol.1, pp.286–293, 2000.
21. W. Zhao, R. Chellappa, J. Phillips and A. Rosenfeld, "Face Recognition in Still and Video Images: A Literature Surrey," *ACM Computing Surveys*, Vol. 35, pp. 399–458, Dec. 2003.
22. S. K. Zhou, R. Chellappa, and D. W. Jacobs, "Characterization of Human Faces under Illumination Variations Using Rank, Integrability, and Symmetry Constraints," *Proc. European Conf. Computer Vision (ECCV2004)*, Vol.1, pp.588–601, 2004.

Exploring Facial Expression Effects in 3D Face Recognition Using Partial ICP*

Yueming Wang[1], Gang Pan[1,**], Zhaohui Wu[1], and Yigang Wang[2]

[1] Dept. of Computer Science, Zhejiang University, Hangzhou, 310027, China
Tel:+86-571-87951647
[2] Virtual Reality Lab, Hangzhou Dianzi University, Hangzhou, 310037, China
{ymingwang, gpan}@zju.edu.cn

Abstract. This paper investigates facial expression effects in face recognition from 3D shape using partial ICP. The partial ICP method could implicitly and dynamically extract the rigid parts of facial surface by selecting a part of nearest points pairs to calculate dissimilarity measure during registration of facial surfaces. The method is expected to be able to get much better performance than other methods in 3D face recognition under expression variation for its dynamic extraction of rigid parts of facial surface at the same time of matching. We also present an effective method for coarse alignment of facial shape, which is fully automatic. Experiments on 3D face database of 360 models with 40 subjects, 9 scans with four different kinds of expression for each subject, show partial ICP is very promising, compared with PCA baseline.

1 Introduction

Automatic face recognition has been studied extensively over the past decade. Most efforts have been made for face recognition from 2D images[1] and a few approaches exploited 3D information [2, 3, 5, 6, 7, 8, 9, 10]. Although the 2D face recognition system has good performance under constrained conditions, since the 2D image essentially is a projection of the 3D human face, it is still challenged by changes in illumination, pose and expression [1, 17]. Utilizing 3D information can improve the system performance [17, 7] due to its explicit representation of facial surface. However, facial expression is still a big challenge even using 3D data in face recognition because in fact facial surface is a non-rigid object. Some efforts have been made to conquer the problem.

C.S.Chua et.al [5] extracted rigid parts of facial surface by a Gaussian model after registering the face range data with varying expression. These rigid parts were used to create a model library for indexing. After enrolling four scans for each subject, voting based on point signature was employed for recognition. It was reported that 100% recognition rate was obtained for total six persons. However, the model database is too small.. Furthermore, by Gaussian Distribution,

* The authors are grateful for the grants from the National Science Foundation of China (60503019, 60533040) and Program for New Century Excellent Talents in University (NCET-04-0545).

** Corresponding author.

P.J. Narayanan et al. (Eds.): ACCV 2006, LNCS 3851, pp. 581–590, 2006.

almost all extracted rigid parts of models only discarded mouth from full facial surface. Some expression may deform other areas of facial surface such as cheek.

K.Chang et.al [11] proposed a local region approach to coping with expression variation in 3D face recognition. The algorithm is based on traditional ICP after finding nose area of facial surface. On a database with about 355 subjects and 3205 3D models with seven different expressions, an average rank-1 rate 77.1% was obtained. The algorithm improved the recognition performance, compared with ICP-baseline method using complete facial shape. Their work treated nose area as the rigid region under varying expressions. But under certain expressions, parts of the nose still show some deformations.

A.M.Bronstein et.al [12] reported a 3D face recognition approach based on a representation of the facial surface that was invariant to isometric deformations resulting from expression variation. However, geodesic distance is definitely variant when facial surface with a "mouth open" expression.

There is a common assumption that though the face shape of the same person may change, sometimes greatly, due to various facial expressions, still there are regions which will keep their shape and position or be subjected to much less deformation among different expressions. If these regions can be identified, the 3D non-rigid face recognition problem can be reduced to the rigid case[5, 11].

However, there may be no large uniform subset of the face that is perfectly shape invariant across a broad range of normal expressions, and the deformation of facial surface of a certain person may be not as same as others with the similar expressions at all time. Figure 1(a) shows some deformation images of facial surface with three different expressions, smile, surprise and sad. The deformation image is obtained as follows. Registering neutral expression face with non-neutral face of same subject by nose area and subtracting the former from the latter along the depth value, we call the difference map deformation image, which indicates the deformation extent of surface region with certain expression relative to neutral facial surface. And the darker in the figure indicates more deformation and the lighter means less deformation. From the deformation images, it can be seen that:

(1) For a subject, almost no fixed large parts of facial surface are invariant along three expressions. Shown in left four columns in Fig.1(a), smile expression leads to shape deformation of mouth and cheek, surprise affects mouth and sad even changes the shape of nose and forehead area slightly.

(2) Comparing two subjects in Fig.1(a), the same expression of different subject affects different regions. Sad in left person changes shape of forehead, while affects mainly eyebrow in right person.

Thus, just extracting and matching the same relatively rigid parts for all facial surfaces is only a choice to solve the expression problem and may not be perfect. In this paper, after analysis of iterative closest point(ICP), we give the partial ICP for 3D facial shape recognition which can implicitly extract variant rigid regions of the face according to deformation extent under different expression during matching. The method does a proper selection of nearest points pairs

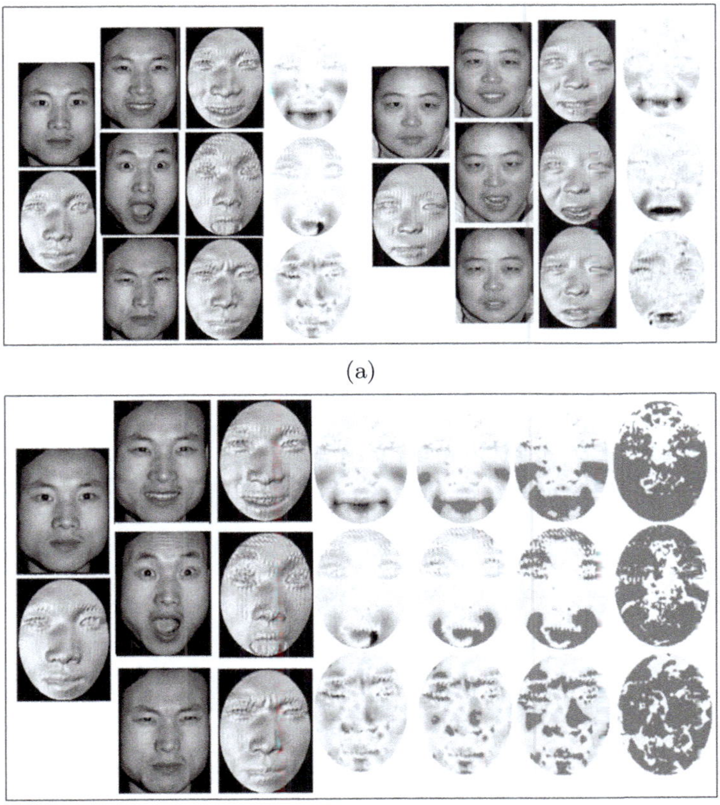

(a)

(b)

Fig. 1. (a) Deformation images for two subjects. The darker indicates the more deformation. (b) Discarded area in facial surface with different *p-rate*=0.9,0.7,0.2 (5th,6th,7th columns respectively). Regions in red indicate the removed parts. Removed areas are not fixed between facial surfaces under different expressions.

to calculate RMS when using ICP to match two surfaces. When applied the method to three expressions, smile, surprise and sad in our experiments, 96.88% rank-one matching rate is obtained. We also implement the PCA-based 3D face recognition as a baseline algorithm.

This paper is organized as follows: Sec. 2 analyzes the ICP algorithm and presents our method of implicitly extracting rigid parts of facial surface. Sec. 3 describes the data preparing. The experimental results and conclusions are in Sec. 4 and Sec. 5 respectively.

2 Analysis of Iterative Closest Point (ICP)

The ICP algorithm, developed by Besl and Mckay [16], is used to register the point sets by an iterative procedure which is widely used in field of 3D rigid object registration. Let point set $P_1 = \{p^1{}_1, \cdots, p^1{}_M\}$ and point set $P_2 = \{p^2{}_1, \cdots, p^2{}_N\}$. The ICP algorithm is summarized as:

$P_2(0) = P_2$, l=0
Do
    For each point $p^2{}_i$ in $P_2(l)$
        Find the closest point y_i in P_1
    End For
    The closest points y_i form a new point set $Y(l)$ where
     the pairs of points $\{(p^2{}_1, y_1), \cdots, (p^2{}_N, y_N)\}$
     describe the correspondences between P_1 and $P_2(l)$.
    If registration error E between P_1 and
      $P_2(l)$ is too large
        Compute transformation $T(l)$ between $(P_2(l), Y(l))$,
        including translation and rotation.
        Apply transformation $P_2(l+1) = T(l) \bullet P_2(1)$,$l$=$l$+1
    Else
        Stop
    End If
While $\|P_2(l+1) - P_2(l)\|$ >threshold

where point y_k in set $Y(l)$ denotes the closest point in P_1 to the point $p^2{}_k(l)$ in $P_2(l)$ and the registration error between P_1 and $P_2(l)$ is

$$E = \frac{1}{N} \sum_{k}^{N} \|y_k - p_k^2(l)\|^2 \tag{1}$$

For convergence of ICP, a coarse registration step usually is carried out before the iterative process. Generally, in ICP-based 3D face recognition, two facial surfaces are registered by the above method, then the value of E computed in the last time of iterative steps is treated as dissimilarity measure of two faces.

When matching two facial surfaces with different expressions, the difference between the pairs of nearest points may become large due to shape deformation which may have a large effect when performing least-squares minimization and E is no longer accurate as a dissimilarity metric. Thus, there is a significant performance drop by ICP-Based method in 3D face recognition when expression varies between gallery and probe, from average 93.6% to 61.1%, as reported by K.Chang [11]. If only those pairs of points with relatively less deformation can be selected as input of calculation of E, the registration error E may be still able to distinguish different subjects while remain small when matching models of same subjects with different expression.

While the traditional ICP-based method uses all point pairs in computing transformation $T(l)$ and E [11], we do it by selecting parts of the point pairs. After sorting the distances of pairs of points in increasing order, we reject the worst $n\%$ of pairs based on distance in each pair. That is, only first (1-$n\%$) part of distances and corresponding point pairs from sorted distances are chosen to compute transformation E and $T(l)$. Considering the last E that is used as dissimilarity measure of matching, discarding $n\%$ of pairs means removing those points in non-rigid region of facial surface. Thus, it is a implicit method to extract points in rigid parts of facial surface to register and match and the rigid parts extracted are varied according to deformation of facial surface among different matching models. We denote it *partial ICP* for 3D face recognition approach and call (1-$n\%$) *p-rate*.

Figue 1(b) shows some deformation images in which the areas in red indicate those removed by setting different *p-rate*. From the removed area, it could be seen that red regions completely come from darker area in deformation images. When *p-rate* equals 0.7, 70 percent of face area is kept to match and most non-rigid parts are discarded. Thus, the method is expected to be able to get much better performance in 3D face recognition with expressions than other rigid-parts-based methods for its dynamically extracting rigid areas of facial surface at the same time of matching.

3 Data Preparing

Considering the convergence problem of partial ICP, we firstly transform all models into a canonical coordinate system by finding the symmetric plane of facial surface and detecting two fiducial points, nose tip and nose base. Then, facial regions for all models are well extracted by trimming face mesh models with a elliptical cylinder which coarsely extracts same facial regions for all models, as shown in Fig.1. After trimming face models, following two strategies are applied:

(1) To compensate for the effect of resolution,we simplify trimmed models using mesh optimization [15]. Then, all facial surface meshes put into experiments have about 2000 vertices.

(2) When finding nearest point pairs between two point face meshes in partial ICP, the nearest distance from point to surface is computed instead of nearest distance between vertices of meshes.

The details of alignment and trimming are described as follows.

3.1 Transforming to the Canonical Coordinate System

Suppose central profile passes through nose tip, nose base and is in the symmetric plane of the facial surface. From profile, we identify following information: nose tip p_{nt}, nose base p_{nb} and direction of symmetric plane d_s. Obviously, six degrees of freedom of facial surface can be fixed by p_{nt}, p_{nb} and d_s. After detecting these information for each facial surface, all models can be coarsely registered in a canonical coordinate frame.

Finding Facial Central Profile. We apply our early work [13, 14] to detect the curve of the central profile of facial surface, as reviewed briefly as follows.

Let $S(p_i)$ denotes a point set of facial surface, where p_i is a point in the set and $S^m(p_i^m)$ denotes its mirror to some certain plane, where p_i^m is corresponding mirrored point of p_i. When $S^m(p_i^m)$ has been registered to S(p_i), $S^m(p_i^m)$ is transformed into $S^{m'}(p^{m'}_i)$. From $S^{m'}(p^{m'}_i)$ and S(p_i), we can fit symmetric plane of facial surface from point set A(x_i), where each point x_i obtained by:

$$x_i = (p_i + p^{m'}_i)/2 \tag{2}$$

We use the basic idea of the ICP to get a registration between facial surface and its mirror and find the symmetric plane by equation 2. Finally, we calculate the intersection of symmetric plane and the triangulated surface of S(p_i) to get the central profile, shown in Fig.2.

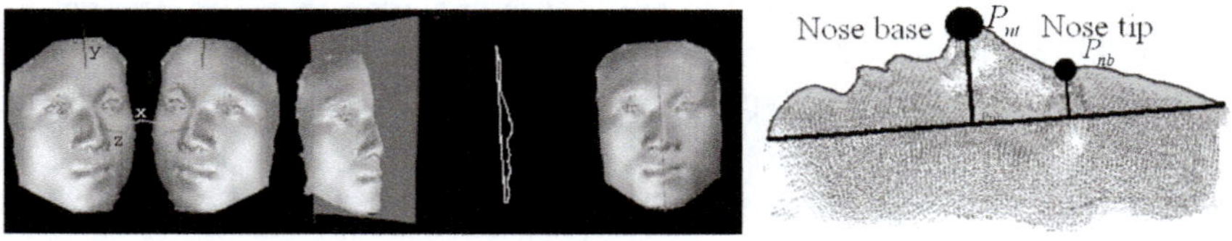

(a) (b) (c) (d) (e) (f)

Fig. 2. Symmetric plane detection and profile finding using ICP. (a) original model, (b) mirrored model, (c) detected symmetric plane, (e) profile and symmetric plane seen from another view, (f) determination of nose tip and nose base in profile.

Locating Nose Tip and Nose Base. Since central profile curve passes through nose tip and nose base , we locate their positions based on the curve. Let C denotes the central profile curve extracted, l_e denotes the line through both end points of the curve C , p_{nt} and p_{nb} denote nose tip point and nose base point respectively. Before location, we suppose following assumption hold up.

(1) The nose tip p_{nt} is a point on the curve C, with the maximum distance to the line l_e.
(2) The nose base p_{nb} is a point on the profile curve C, and is the first distance extremum point to the line l_e from p_{nt} to forehead, as shown in Fig. 2(f).

It can be formalized as:

$$p_{nt} = argmax_{p \in C} dist(p, l_e) \tag{3}$$

$$L = \{p|p \in C, y_p > y_{p_{nt}}, dist'(p, l_e) = 0\} \tag{4}$$

$$p_{nb} = argmin_{p \in L}(y_p) \tag{5}$$

where $dist(\cdot,\cdot)$ is the Euclidean distance function from a point to a line segment, y_p is y-axis coordinate of point p, $dist'(\cdot,\cdot)$ denotes first derivative of Euclidean distance to the point position at line l_e extend to forehead.

If facial surface is sampled only frontal view discarding hair and neck area, our assumption is appropriate so that p_{nb} and p_{nt} can be located accurately.

However, some certain samples of facial surface may be grotesque in shape which doesn't keep the assumption. To date we have never encountered a model on which failure happen in our experimental data set.

Aligning Model. Given nose tip p_{nt}, nose base p_{nb} and normal direction v_{sp} of symmetric plane for each model, a canonical coordinate system of all models can be determined. Subtracting p_{nb} from p_{nt}, we get unit vector v_y after normalized. Taking p_{nt} as the origin, v_{sp} as x-axis, v_y as y-axis, a new right-hand coordinate system is defined. Then all models are registered by transforming facial surface into the new coordinate system. Furthermore, we rotate the model 20 degree around x-axis counterclockwise in the new coordinate system for non-duplicate happened in projecting depth to x-y plane used in PCA-based face recognition. Some results are shown in Fig.3 (a). All our experiments are based on the aligned models.

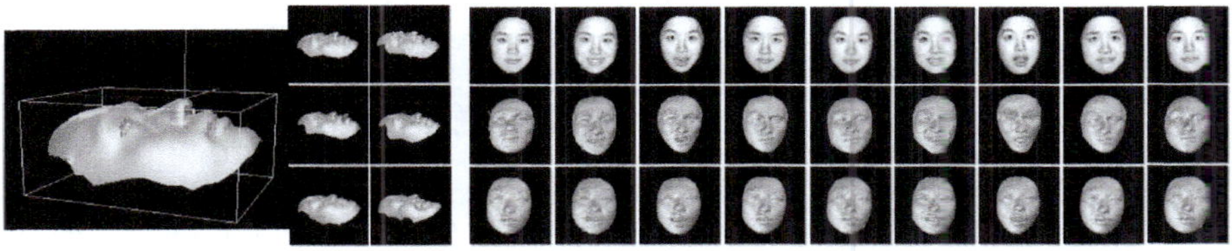

(a) (b)

Fig. 3. (a) The canonical coordinate system for aligned models. Axis in red is z-axis, blue is y-axis, green is x-axis. (b) Face models acquired by InSpeck 3D MEGA Capturor DF. Each row shows 9 scans of one subject. The models in first row are rendering with texture.

3.2 Trimming Models

Given aligned model mesh, facial regions can be extracted by removing those points and triangles of facial surfaces in the outer of following elliptical cylinder:

$$\frac{(x-x_1)^2}{a^2} - \frac{(y-y_1)^2}{b^2} = 1 \qquad (5)$$

Since all models are in a canonical coordinate, the facial regions of all models produced by above equation are not only full frontal area, but also roughly same between models which is an important condition for our partial ICP method. For consistency, we set parameters as x_1=0, y_1=20, a=60 and b=80 which works well for all 360 models in our experiments.

4 Experiments

4.1 Data Acquisition

Experiments use the 3D facial expression database **ZJU-3DFED**, collected by the authors. In ZJU-3DFED database, there are 40 different subjects, nine scans for each, and total 360 scans. Each subject has two scans with smile expression, two scans with surprise expression, 2 scans with sad expression and 3 scans with neutral expression. Facial surfaces of same subject with same expression are slightly different in extent. All face models are acquired by InSpeck 3D MEGA Capturor DF[18]. The facial models are in triangular mesh.

We manually cut out the parts out of the face regions from the original model data and this is the only manual work in our whole works. Each facial mesh then have about 25000 points and 50000 triangles and the resolution is 0.04 mm. After mesh simplification [15], each scan has about 2000 points and about 4000 triangles. Figure 3(b) shows 3 subjects and 27 scans of face models. The face models have both shape and texture information, we only use shape information in the experiments.

We put one neutral expression face model for each subject into gallery and the other 320 scans are classified into 4 probe sets. All 80 smile scans form smile-set, so do surprise scans, sad scans and neutral scans. A special probe set composed of the 320 scans is made for whole recognition results, called whole-set.

4.2 Results by Partial ICP with Different *p-Rate*

Twelve different values of *p-rate* { 0.05, 0.1, 0.2, 0.3, 0.4, 0.5,0.6, 0.7, 0.8, 0.9, 0.95, 1} are tested in our experiments. Additionally, we also consider a extreme instance that only a pair of nearest points is input into calculation of dissimilarity measure E after ICP process which use all points pair in iterative. The results are in Fig. 4.

Fig. 4. (a) Rank-1 recognition rate of different *p-rate* with partial ICP method on five probe sets. (b) zooming out part of (a).

From Fig.4, it can be seen that:

(1) For three non-neutral probe sets, none of them has a rank-1 rate larger than 90% when *p-rate* equals 1(that is same as the traditional ICP-based matching method). But when setting *p-rate* value between 0.1 and 0.95, none of them has a rank-1 rate smaller than 90%. The largest improvements of rank-1 rate of three non-neutral sets are 7.5% for smile-set, 11.25% for surprise-set, 10% for sad set.

(2) Both highest rank-1 rates of smile-set and sad-set are 96.25% and obtained at *p-rate* =0.8 while that of surprise-set are 97.5% and obtained at *p-rate*= 0.1 or *p-rate*= 0.2. It is partly due to facial surface with surprise expression has a larger deformation area than the other expressions.

(3) When setting *p-rate* as 0.1 which means 90% of facial surface is removed before matching using partial ICP method, an average rank-1 rate 94.17% is still reached on non-neutral probe sets. It is a cue indicating that small parts of facial surface still have enough information for recognition if nice extraction is performed.

(4) As a whole, our method get an average rank-1 rate 95% on three non-neutral probe sets when *p-rate*=0.2 and 96.88% on whole-set.

4.3 PCA v.s. Partial ICP

PCA-based method is implemented in our experiments for comparison. After models are trimmed, PCA-based method can easy be applied to 3D face recognition by projecting the trimmed models to x-y plane. We use the first 40 eigenvectors when test PCA-based method which hold 96.46% energy. We compare the performance between PCA-based method and partial ICP method on all five probe sets. The results are shown in Fig.5.

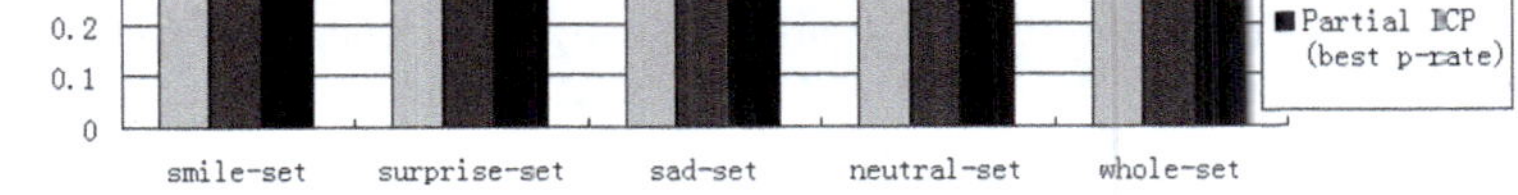

Fig. 5. Rank-1 rate: PCA v.s. partial ICP

The partial ICP method outperforms PCA-based-method on rank-1 performance among all probe sets. PCA-based-method is well known that is sensitive to noise. On all non-neutral expression probe set, PCA-based-method get average rank-1 rate 75.41% and the worst rank-1 rate 65% on surprise-set because shape deformation with different expressions act as a role of noise in a way. Between neutral and non-neutral expression probe sets, the rank-1 rate drop from 92.5% to an average 75.41% with PCA-Base method in recognition. The partial ICP with *p-rate*=1 gets a whole rank-1 recognition rate 89.69%. The partial ICP with best *p-rate* obtains an average rank-1 rate 96.88% on all probe sets. By well selecting the *p-rate*, partial ICP method is insensitive to expression variant in 3D face recognition.

5 Conclusion

We propose a method, partial ICP method, which is capable of dynamically extracting rigid parts of facial surface. The extraction is completely dependent on the deformation extent of facial surface and extracted areas are varied between different expressions. Based on partial ICP, we perform several experiments for 3D face recognition on a database with 360 models. A rank-1 rate 96.88% demonstrate the high performance of our method in 3D face recognition with different expressions. The experimental results also show that our method significantly outperforms PCA-based method.

References

1. W.Zhao, R.Chellappa, P.J.Phillips, A.Rosenfeld. Face recognition: a literature survey. *ACM Computing Surveys*, 35(4):399-458, 2003
2. J.C.Lee, E.Milios. Matching range images of human faces. *Proc. IEEE ICCV*, p.722-726, 1990.
3. G.G.Gordon. Face recognition from depth maps and surface curvature . *SPIE Conf. on Geometric Methods in Computer Vision*, 1570:234-247, 1991.
4. C.S.Chua, R.Jarvis. Point signatures: A new representation for 3D object recognition. *IJCV*, 25(1):63-85, 1997.
5. C.S.Chua, F.Han, Y.K.Ho. 3D Human Face Recognition Using Point Signature. *IEEE FG'00*, pp.233-238, 2000.
6. M.W.Lee, S.Ranganath. Pose-invariant face recognition using a 3D deformable model. *Pattern Recognition*, 36(8):1835-1846, 2003.
7. V.Blanz, S.Romdhani, T.Vetter. Face identification across different poses and illumination with a 3D morphable model. *Int'l Conf. on FG*, p.202-207, 2002.
8. C.Beumier, M.Acheroy. Automatic 3D face authentication. *Image Vision Computing*, 18(4):315-321, 2000
9. W. Zhao, R. Chellappa. Illumination-insensitive face recognition using symmetric shape-form-shading. *Proc. IEEE ICCV*, 1:286-293, 2000.
10. G. Pan, Z. Wu, and Y. Pan, Automatic 3D face verification from range data, in Proc. IEEE ICASSP, vol.3, pp.193-196, 2003.
11. K.Chang, K.Bowyer, P.Flynn. Effects on Facial Expression in 3D Face Recognition, *Proc. of the SPIE*, Volume 5779, pp. 132-143,2005.
12. A.M.Bronstein, M.M.Bronstein, R.Kimmel. Expression-invariant 3D face recognition. *Proc. AVBPA'03, LNCS,* vol.2688, 62-70, 2003.
13. Yijun Wu, Gang Pan, Zhaohui Wu. Face Authentication based on Multiple Profiles Extracted from Range Data. *Proc. AVBPA'03, LNCS*, vol.2688, pp.515-522, 2003.
14. Gang Pan, Zhaohui Wu, "3D Face Recognition from Range Data," Int'l Journal of Image and Graphics, 5(3):573-593, 2005.
15. H.Hoppe, T.DeRose, T.Duchamp, J.McDonald and W. Stuetzle, Mesh optimization, *Computer Graphics(SIGGRAPH'93 Proceedings)*, 27:19-26, Auguest, 1993.
16. P.J.Besl, N.D.McKay, A method for registration of 3-D shapes, IEEE Trans.Pattern Anal.Mach.Intell. 14:239-256, 1992.
17. Face Recognition Vendor Test 2002, http://www.frvt.org/.
18. InSpeck Inc., http://www.inspeck.com/.

Vision Based Speech Animation Transferring with Underlying Anatomical Structure

Yuru Pei and Hongbin Zha

National Laboratory on Machine Perception,
Peking University, Beijing, P.R. China
{peiyuru, zha}@cis.pku.edu.cn

Abstract. We present a novel method to transfer speech animation recorded in low resolution videos onto realistic 3D facial models. Unsupervised learning is utilized on a speech video corpus to find underlying manifold of facial configurations. K-means clustering is applied on the low dimensional space to find key speaking-related facial shapes. With a small set of laser scanner captured 3D models related to the clustering centroid, the facial animation in 2D videos is transferred onto 3D shapes. Especially by virtue of a weak perspective projection model, the underlying mandible rotation is recovered from videos and is utilized to drive 3D skull movements. The adaption of a generic skull onto facial models is guided by a 2D image, Tissue Map. With parsimonious data requirements, our system realizes the animation transferring and gains a realistic rendering effect with the underlying anatomical structure.

1 Introduction

Vision based speech animation transferring is to capture speaking motions recorded in low resolution video clips and retarget them onto a high resolution 3D model. The goal is to acquire moving vectors of dense point clouds on facial geometry at video-speed. Animation transferring is famed for the personal performance transmission at low cost in human-machine interaction, games, etc.

Drawing inspiration from Ezzat's speech animation system on multidimensional morphable model (MMM) [1], we employ the Isomap to reduce dimensionality of facial configurations to discover the intrinsic speech structure. K-means clustering is applied on the low dimensional manifold to find key viseme definitions corresponding to a training corpus, which is selected to cover all vowels and consonants in Mandarin. Obviously, all the possible occurrence of co-articulation could not be covered. Especially in Mandarin there is a large set of compound vowels, fixed composition of vowels and nasal consonants, which makes the Mandarin's phoneme framework more perplexing. Our vision-based method skips such an intricate phoneme frame, and instead uses an example based blending technique.

Compared with the vision-based animation system described in [2], we do not need the large database from motion capturing, and just utilize a small set of key shapes obtained with a laser scanner. The key shape is defined by the

P.J. Narayanan et al. (Eds.): ACCV 2006, LNCS 3851, pp. 591–600, 2006.

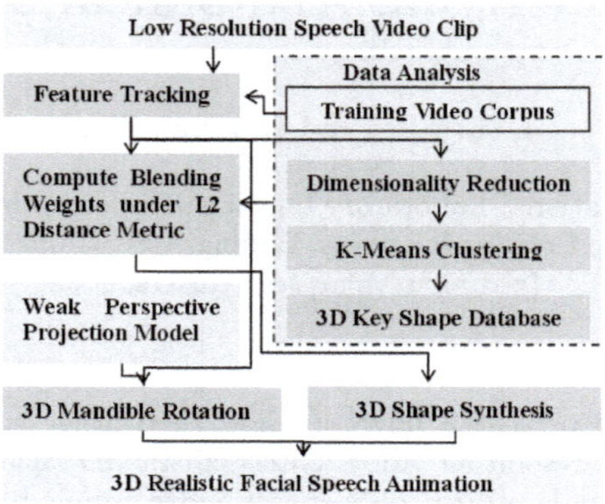

Fig. 1. Flow chart of transferring system

unsupervised learning of the video corpus. As to dense per vertex correspondence between different scans, a non-rigid registration algorithm similar to Allen's [3] is developed. Semantic constraints on human faces are imposed during the optimization process and deformation is restricted in a predefined speaking-related region. With a weak perspective projection model, underlying mandible rotation is recovered from videos. A generic textured skull model is driven to move along with facial deformations. It solves the teeth appearance during the speaking animation. A Tissue Map extracted from CT image is utilized to control the generic skull fitting.

Our main contribution is to propose a novel mechanism for extracting intrinsic geometry of speech video space with the Isomap and finding out key viseme definitions. Moreover, we recover the underlying skull movement from videos automatically and adapt the generic skull onto facial models based on a Tissue Map. With underlying anatomical structure, a realistic animation transferring is achieved.

2 Related Work

Vision based speech animation systems generally utilize a large video database [1, 4, 5, 6] and recently 3D motion capturing data [2] for training. The data analysis may be based on machine learning [1, 2, 4, 6, 7] or probabilistic framework [5]. Ezzat et al. [1] employ a variant of MMM to synthesize mouth configurations of a novel speech. Cao et al. [6] generate a data structure called Anime Graph to encapsulate motion captured facial motion database along with speech information. Voice Puppetry [5] utilizes a probabilistic framework to find an optimal trajectory for the whole utterance based on facial gestures learned from videos. Vlasic et al. [7] use a multilinear model to separate different attributes of facial models, e.g. expression and visemes, and connect multilinear model directly to videos for a time-series of poses and attribute parameters.

As to the generation of facial models with anatomical structure, multilayer generic template is used [8, 9, 10, 11]. Skin, muscle layer and skull are represented as polygonal meshes [8, 9] or as volumetric elements [10, 11]. The dynamical mechanism is simulated by the mass-spring system or finite elements analysis [10, 11]. In our system, the anatomical structure includes triangle meshes of face and skull, and the in-between space defined by the Tissue Map extracted from a CT image.

It is intuitive that the continuous movements can be embedded into a low dimensional manifold. A common method for dimensionality reduction is Principle Component Analysis (PCA) [12], which has been used in human figure and face shape representations [3, 13, 14]. Multi-Dimensional Scaling (MDS) [15] is another approach to finding an embedding that preserves the pairwise distances of original data. Cao et al. [16] use ICA [17] to extract meaningful parameters in speech motions without data annotation. Above methods are efficient to observations with linear intrinsic structure. Two main techniques, Isomap [18] and Locally Linear Embedding (LLE) [19] have been used in nonlinear dimensionality reduction. The global coordinates of Isomap provide a simple way to analyze and manipulate high dimensional observations. Juan et al. [20] use a variant of Isomap to discover a low dimensional structure of cartoon data. The LLE is an unsupervised learning algorithm with the assumption that each point and its neighbors lie on a locally linear patch of the manifold. LLE has been used in facial expression analysis [21, 22].

3 Data Analysis

The goal of analysis module is to extract key speaking-related facial shapes from video corpus and generate corresponding 3D viseme database. Firstly, feature tracking is applied on training video corpus. Consequently facial configurations are represented as a combination of feature curves. By virtue of the Isomap, the manifold of facial configurations, especially the variations in mouth region are embedded in a low dimensional space. The independent components related to facial variations are decoupled. K-means clustering is to find key facial shapes called pseudo visemes. With a laser scanner, the corresponding 3D viseme shapes are captured from a subject. In order to define the trajectory among different 3D visemes, the correspondence between scans is established by a non-rigid registration algorithm.

3.1 Feature Tracking

The image (320×240) can be considered as a point in a k dimensional space ($k = 230,400$). It is formidable to operate data in such a high dimensional space directly. To represent the facial configurations with the combination of several feature curves is intuitive. Active Appearance Model (AAM) proposed by Cootes et al. [23] is utilized for the feature tracking. Some 30 frames are annotated manually as training data. The feature template has 73 points and every frame is considered as a point in $146(2 \times 73)$ dimensional space.

The unavoidable subtle head movements have no apparent influence on the feature tracing, whereas they will cause accumulated offset errors in mouth configuration analysis. Linear conformal transformation is applied to frame alignments in preprocessing.

3.2 Dimensionality Reduction with Isomap

Given the inherent continuous motions, the video data are assumed to have some underlying surfaces in a low dimensional space. The Isomap [18] is employed for its capability in discovering nonlinear degrees of freedom and finding the globally optimal solution. Given high dimensional space X, the Isomap finds the embedding in a low dimensional manifold Y with dimension d, which preserves the manifold's estimated intrinsic geometry.

The true dimension of data can be found out by the decrease of residual value while increasing the dimension of embedded space. As shown in Fig. 2, when the dimension of embedded space is 6, it can cover more than 97% variance of whole facial features. In common sense the behavior of mouth motions represented by feature curves can be simply classified into opening and extruding. The resampling of mouth feature points along cubic Hermite curve is fed into the Isomap training. The embedding results verify such classification, as two dimensions can cover more than 95% variance of original data.

Isomap is suitable to the animation feature analysis because it can automatically extract a few components and decouple the key features in speech animations. Since the input of Isomap is graph distance, the distance metric is crucial to the Isomap based dimensionality reduction. L2 distance is selected. Given two frames F_i, F_j represented by 2D coordinate sequence as $F_i = (x_1^i, y_1^i, ..., x_n^i, y_n^i)(n = 73)$, the distance is:

$$D(F_i, F_j) = \sqrt{\|F_i - F_j\|^2} = \sqrt{\sum_{i=1}^{n}(x_k^i - x_k^j)^2 + \sum_{i=1}^{n}(y_k^i - y_k^j)^2} \,. \qquad (1)$$

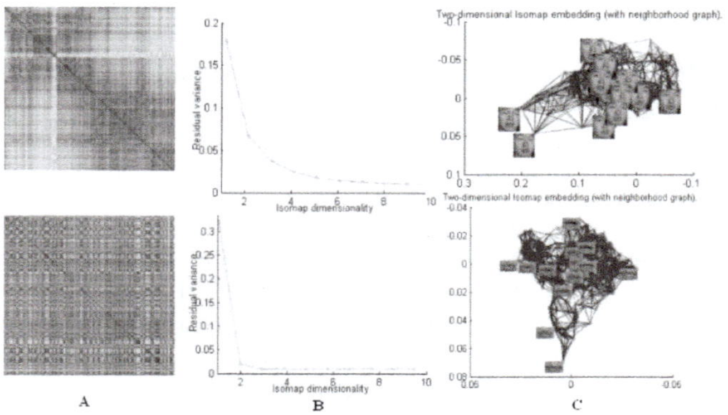

Fig. 2. Dimensionality reduction. (A) L2 distance matrix. (B) Variance plot. (C) 2D visualization on embedded space. The Upper row is on whole facial features; the bottom row is on resampling data of mouth contours.

3.3 K-Means Clustering and 3D Viseme Database

Once the low dimensional embedding of speech video corpus is obtained, K-means clustering is employed to extract key mouth configurations, which are called pseudo-visemes. They are just distinct mouth shapes and have no necessary relations with the ordinary phoneme system. The MATLAB function kmeans, a two phase iterative algorithm, is employed. Predefined cluster number and low dimensional data are fed into the procedure. The clustering returns centroids. Moreover, the distance of every point to each centroid can be obtained. The centroid is considered as pseudo viseme as shown in Fig. 3. The cluster number is defined empirically, which is comparably less than that used in MMM [1]. The reason is that in facial feature template, the teeth markers are excluded as their appearance could not be traced robustly due to the low quality of video clips. The concurrent teeth movement is realized by underlying skull structure described in Sect. 4.

With the clustering, every image in the training video is mapped as a 12 dimensional vector. Generally speaking, the more clusters, the more realistic synthesis result there will be. There should be reconciliation between the fidelity of facial animation and synthesis cost. With the observation of Mandarin phoneme system, our cluster number is comparably small. This situation sounds plausible in that the same lip shape can account for several phonemes and the pronouncements are not related to mouth configurations exclusively.

With the instruction of video cluster centroid, the 3D static shapes of pseudo visemes are captured with a laser scanner. With a non-rigid template fitting algorithm under an energy minimization frame, the correspondence between scans is established. The problem is formulated as morphing the base mesh B onto the target T with energy

$$E(p) = w_s E_s + w_d E_d + w_f E_f \ . \qquad (2)$$

The distance term E_d is to measure the gap between the base variation and target mesh. Feature term E_f is to evaluate the feature matching by virtue of some

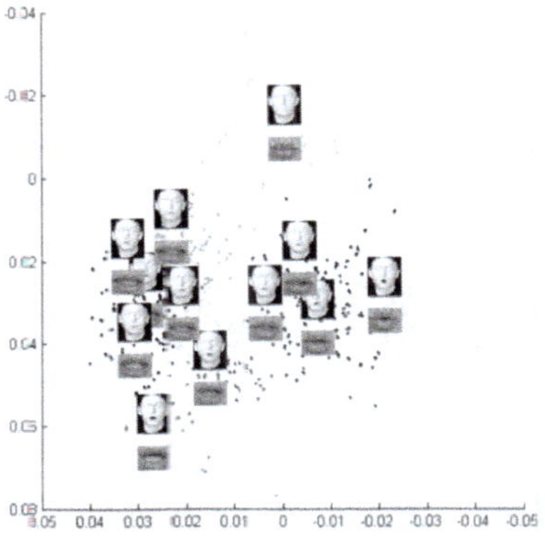

Fig. 3. K-means clustering in a low dimensional space

20 points pairs selected manually and feature curves. Smoothness of base mesh is preserved by virtue of 1-ring neighbors $Ring(v_i^B) = \{v_j^B | (i,j) \in Edges(B)\}$. The shape of 3D viseme can be represented as a vector of all vertices' Euclidean coordinate sequence. The base mesh is denoted as $S_0 = (x_1^0, y_1^0, z_1^0, ..., x_n^0, y_n^0, z_n^0)$. Once the optimization is applied onto the entire scans, a set of variations $S_{v_i} = (x_1^{v_i}, y_1^{v_i}, z_1^{v_i}, ..., x_n^{v_i}, y_n^{v_i}, z_n^{v_i})$ with close shapes to the captured visemes is obtained. The shape of viseme is extracted as:

$$\delta(S_{v_i}) = |S_{v_i} - S_0| \ . \tag{3}$$

4 Underlying Skull Movement

In this section the underlying skull movement is recovered from video clips by a weak perspective projection model. As the teeth are fixed on mandible and maxilla, the movement of teeth is consistent with skulls. Thus the teeth appearance during speaking is solved simultaneously. Compared with general approaches to teeth movement generation by defining mapping between phonemes and teeth poses, our automatic method is easier.

4.1 Skull Alignment

From the CT image of a live person, 3D skull and facial models are reconstructed. The in-between tissue layer is extracted and represented as a 2D image called Tissue Map. Every pixel has a pseudo color related to depth residual of corresponding sampling on face and skull models under cylindrical projection as shown in Fig. 4. The skull and its related Tissue Map are looked as the reference. The referent skull model has to adapt different faces. Firstly an affine transformation is used to achieve a coarse mapping, and then a small set of marker P_s is selected manually on skull with tissue thickness *Dep* extracted automatically from the Tissue Map. Their counterparts P_f on the facial surface are computed by a cylindrical projection. The target poses of skull marker

$$P_s' = P_f - Dep \ . \tag{4}$$

Some parts P_{si} on the skull with no correspondence on the facial model are hold still during the fitting. RBF is employed to realize the skull shape deformation.

Fig. 4. Tissue Map extraction

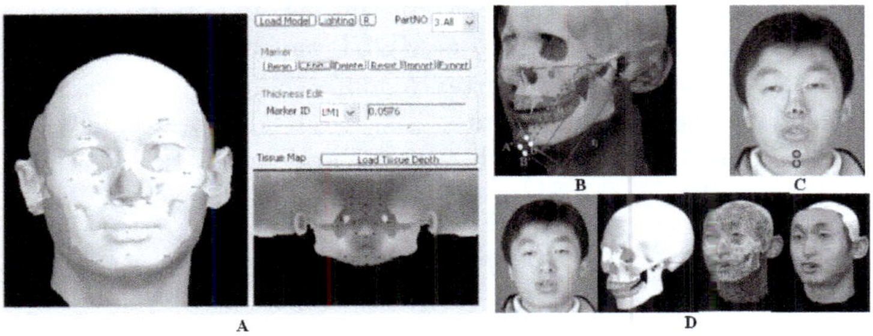

Fig. 5. Skull alignment and mandible rotation recovering from video. (A) Skull alignment by virtue of Tissue Map. (B) Mandible rotation angle on 3D model. (C) Jaw marker displacement vector on 2D image. (D) Recovering results.

$$\bar{y} = f(\bar{x}) = \sum_{i=1}^{N} w_i h(\|\bar{c}_i - \bar{x}\|) + \sum_{j=1}^{k} d_j p_j(\bar{x}) , \tag{5}$$

where $h(r) = \sqrt{r^2 + c^2}$; c_i is the fitting centers including p_s and p_{si}; $p_j(.)$ is the polynomial to accommodate for the affine transform. The training data is of the same size as the centers. Original and target poses of training data are $[p_s, p_{si}]$ and $[p'_s, p_{si}]$. To make the fitting process more editable, the thickness value can be modified for idiosyncrasies as shown in Fig. 5.

It is obvious that the skull should underlie the facial surface. Therefore, after every fitting cycle there should be a collision detection. If the collision occurs, more centers are added and continue next cycle of iteration.

4.2 Mandible Movement

For simplicity, we put only one freedom on skull, that is, mandible rotation. The angle θ is computed as $\theta = \widehat{AB}/r_s$, $\widehat{AB}$ is the arc length on jaw's trajectory. r_s is the radius. With an assumption that during speaking with a neutral expression there is no evident shape variation on jaw muscles, the facial jaw marker's movement is considered identical as that on the skull. Moreover, the rotation is subtle and the arc length approximates to the vertical displacement. Thus

$$\theta = \widehat{A'B'}/r_f \approx |y_{A'} - y_{B'}|/r_f . \tag{6}$$

The problem is formulated as determining the Y-direction offset from the video sequence. A bijection $\Delta y = \psi(v_a, v_b)$ has to be solved. With a weak perspective projection model, MDLT [24], the mapping of 3D coordinates and 2D pixels is established. The marker pairs on salient facial feature are selected manually for the MDLT parameter estimation.

$$d = A(P, L) , \tag{7}$$

where $d(u, v)$ is 2D vector of pixel position, and $p(x, y, z)$ is 3D coordinate of vertex on facial surface. $L = \{l_1, ..., l_{11}\}$ is MDLT parameters. Generally speaking, 3D position could not be obtained from a single image. However, the interested points are constrained on facial center line. The related x and u can be measured from 3D models and video clips as x_0 and u_0. Thus y is determined as $y = \zeta(v, L, x_0, u_0)$. The mandible rotation angle is recovered as

$$\theta = \Delta(y)/r_f = |\zeta(v_a, L, x_0, u_0) - \zeta(v_b, L, x_0, u_0)|/r_f \ . \tag{8}$$

5 3D Facial Shape Synthesis

During the synthesis, the distance of each frame to cluster centroid is computed to obtain clustering index. Then the frame sequence is colored according to the index assignment. The frames with the largest affiliation value and those adjacent to silence segments are selected as the keyframes automatically. The geometry of keyframes is generated by the convex linear interpolation of 3D key visemes with the weight

$$w_i^k = \frac{D(F_k, C_i)^{-1}}{\sum_j (D(F_k, C_j))^{-1}} \ , \tag{9}$$

where $D(F_k, C_i)$ is L2 distance of current frame F_k with clustering centroid C_i. The geometry of the keyframes is

$$S_k = S_0 + \alpha\delta(S_{v_d}) + \beta \sum_i w_i^k \delta(S_{v_i}) \ , \tag{10}$$

where α and β are used to balance the influence of dominant cluster and neighboring clusters. Poly-cosine function [25] is to simulate acceleration and deceleration during transition between keyframes. Then the geometry of in-between frames can be obtained by linear interpolation along the transition curve.

6 Experiments

We use several video clips to test the transferring ability of our system. The video used as the training data is collected with an ordinary digital camera. The detailed video setting is as follows: the frame size is 320 × 240; the sequence was digitalized under 25 fps D1/DV PAL frame rate; the audio rate is 32 kHz. The subject is instructed to read the predefined corpus with a neutral expression at an ordinary speed and avoid dramatic head movements. There are some 10000 frames (approx. 6 minutes) in the video. The analysis of training data and clustering is done in system initialization process just once. The underlying skull movement is recovered concurrent with facial animation synthesis. Then the audio track is resynchronized with 3D speech animation and played back. The environment is rendered with the billboard technique, where one flat polygon is mapped with a landscape image as shown in Fig. 6.

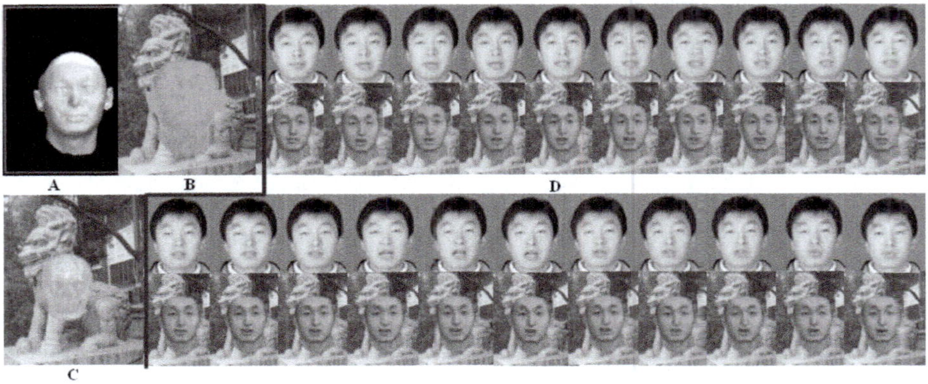

Fig. 6. Transferring result of [pei], [tçi η], [dà], [çyε]. (A) Overlapping of facial and skull model. (B) Facial model with billboard background. (C) Skull model. (D) Transferring result (upper row is original video sequence; lower row is transferring results on 3D model with underlying skull).

7 Conclusions

In this paper, we present a novel method to transfer speech animation in low quality videos onto realistic 3D facial models. We embed the video corpus into a low dimensional space with nonlinear dimensionality reduction, and obtain pseudo viseme definition by applying clustering. With 3D static visemes, the transferring is achieved based on shape blending along a poly-cosine curve. Underlying skull movement is recovered from videos at the same time and aligned onto the face with the help of a Tissue Map. With our system a realistic 3D speech animation is generated with parsimonious data requirement.

References

1. Ezzat, I., Geiger, G., Poggio, T.: Trainable videorealistic speech animation. ACM Transactions on Graphics **21** (2002) 388–398
2. Chai, J., Xiao, J., Hodgins, J.: Vision-based control of 3d facial animation. In: Proc. ACM SIGGRAPH/ Eurographics Symp. on Computer Animation, San Diego, CA, Eurographics Association Aire-la-Ville (2003) 193–206
3. Allen, B., Curless, B., Popovic, Z.: The space of all body shapes: Reconstruction and parameterization from range scans. In: Proc. ACM SIGGRAPH, San Diego, CA, Addison-Wesley (2003) 587–594
4. Bregler, C., Covell, M., Slaney, M.: Video rewrite: Driving visual speech with audio. In: Proc. ACM SIGGRAPH, Los Angeles, CA, ACM Press/Addison-Wesley Publishing Co. (1997) 353–360
5. Brand, M.: Voice puppetry. In: Proc. ACM SIGGRAPH, Los Angeles, CA, ACM Press/Addison-Wesley Publishing Co. (1999) 21–28
6. Cao, Y., Faloutsos, P., Kohler, E., Pighin, F.: Real-time speech motion synthesis from recorded motions. In: Proc. ACM SIGGRAPH/Eurographics Symp. on Computer Animation, Grenoble, France (2004) 347–355

7. Vlasic, D., Brand, M., Pfister, H., Popovic, J.: Face transfer with multilinear models. ACM Transactions on Graphics **24** (2005) 426 – 433
8. Albrecht, I., Haber, J., Kahler, K., Schroder, M., Seidel, H.P.: May i talk to you? facial animation from text. In: Proc. tenth Pacific Conference on Computer Graphics and Applications, Beijing, P.R.China, IEEE Computer Society (2002) 77–86
9. Lee, Y., Terzopoulos, D., Waters, K.: Realistic modeling for facial animations. In: Proc. ACM SIGGRAPH'95, Los Angeles, CA, ACM Press (1995) 55–62
10. Koch, R.M., Gross, M.H., Carls, F.R., Buren, D.F., Fankhauser, G., Parish, Y.I.H.: Simulating facial surgery using finite element methods. In: Proc. ACM SIGGRAPH'96, New Orleans, LA, ACM Press (1996) 421–428
11. Sifakis, E., Neverov, I., Fedkiw, R.: Automatic determination of facial muscle activations from sparse motion capture marker data. ACM Transactions on Graphics **24** (2005) 426–433
12. Jolliffe, I., ed.: Principal Component Analysis. Pringer Verlag, New York (1986)
13. Pyun, H., Kim, Y., Chae, W., Kang, H.Y., Shin, S.Y.: An example-based approach for facial expression cloning. In: Proc. ACM SIGGRAPH/ Eurographics Symp. on Computer Animation, San Diego, CA (2003) 167–176
14. Chuang, E.S., Deshpande, H., Bregler, C.: Facial expression space learning. In: Proc. 10th Pacific Conference on Computer Graphics and Applications, Beijing, P.R.China, IEEE Computer Society (2002) 68–76
15. Kruskal, J.B., Wish, M., eds.: Multidimensional Scaling. Sage Publications, Beverly Hills (1978)
16. Cao, Y., Faloutsos, P., Pighin, F.: Unsupervised learning for speech motion editing. In: Proc. ACM SIGGRAPH/ Eurographics Symp. on Computer Animation, San Diego, CA (2003) 225–231
17. Hyvarinen, A., Karhunen, J., Oja, E., eds.: Independent Component Analysis. John Wiley Sons, New York (2001)
18. Tenenbaum, J.B., Silva, V., Langford, J.C.: A global geometric framework for nonlinear dimensionality reduction. Science **290** (2000) 2319–2323
19. Roweis, S., Saul, L.: Nonlinear dimensionality reduction by locally linear embedding. Science **290** (2000) 2323–2326
20. Juan, C., Bodenheimer, B.: Cartoon textures. In: Proc. ACM SIGGRAPH/ Eurographics Symp. on Computer Animation, Grenoble, France (2004) 267–276
21. Hu, C., Chang, Y., Feris, R., Turk, M.: Manifold based analysis of facial expression. In: Proc. Computer Vision and Pattern Recognition Workshop, IEEE Computer Society (2004) 81– 81
22. Wang, Y., Huang, X., Lee, C.S., Zhang, S., Li, Z., Samaras, D., Metaxas, D., Elgammal, A., Huang, P.: High resolution acquisition, learning and transfer of dynamic 3-d facial expressions. In: Proc. Annual Conf. of the European Association for Computer Graphics, Grenoble, France (2004) 677–686
23. Cootes, T.F., Edwards, G.J., Taylor, C.J.: Active appearance models. In: Proc. 5th European Conference on Computer Vision, Freiburg, Germany, Springer (1998) 484–498
24. Hatze, H.: High-precision three-dimensional photo- grammetric calibration and object space reconstruction using a modified dlt-approach. J. Biomechanics **21** (1988) 533–538
25. Pei, Y., Zha, H.: Transferring speech video onto 3d realistic human faces. In: Proc. thirteenth Pacific Conference on Computer Graphics and Applications, Macao, P.R.China (2005) 13–15

A Level Set Approach for Shape Recovery of Open Contours*

Min Li[1], Chandra Kambhamettu[1], and Maureen Stone[2]

[1] Department of Computer & Information Sciences,
University of Delaware Newark, DE 19716, USA
[2] Dept of Biomedical Sciences and Orthodontics,
Vocal Tract Visualization Lab, University of Maryland Dental School
Baltimore, MD 21201, USA

Abstract. In this paper, a geometric deformable model for shape recovery of open contours in noisy images is presented. We use two level set functions to model the open contour and find the end points of the open contour as the intersection of the two level set functions. The evolutions of both level set functions do not depend on the gradient of the images, as in the classical geometric deformable models, but are decided by a region-based "*band velocity*". The "*band velocity*" is different from region information introduced by other deformable models which can only be used to find the closed contours in images, it is designed for evolutions of both closed and open contours and particularly unique for contours which are open and do not enclose any region. Prior shape information is also integrated into the contour evolution process, which prevents two level set functions from intersecting at other places than at the contour end points. With the described method open contours can be recovered from noisy images. Successful experiments on several data sets are presented in this paper.

1 Introduction

Image segmentation or shape recovery in 2D/3D images is an important problem in computer vision and medical imaging. The presence of noise, different artifacts, complex background and intensity inhomogeneities in images requires more sophisticated algorithms rather than some low-level image processing methods for recovering the objective shape from images. Deformable model based approach is such a popular technique. Deformable models are active curves or surfaces that deform within 2D or 3D images. In general, deformable models can be classified as either parametric deformable models or geometric deformable models.

Compared with the parametric deformable model, the geometric deformable model has some advantages such as the topology flexibility and the easy geometry properties (normal, curvature) calculation. Since it was introduced by Caselles

* This work is partially done under National Institutes of Health, Grant No. R01 DC01758.

P.J. Narayanan et al. (Eds.): ACCV 2006, LNCS 3851, pp. 601–611, 2006.

et al. [1] and by Malladi et al. [2], significant effort [3][4][5][6] has been devoted to geometric deformable models. However, all these existing geometric deformable models are aimed at closed curves/surfaces. As pointed out by Osher and Fedkiw [7], " *Level set methods are used to represent closed curves and surfaces that may begin and end at the boundaries of the computational domain. However, it is not clear how to devise methods for curves and surfaces that have ends or edges (respectively) within the computational domain.*"

A first step of using level set method for open curve evolution was carried out by Smereka [8] in spiral crystal growth research. In [8], the end points of an open curve (the step-line) are fixed during the curve evolution. Solem et al. [9] developed a level set method to reconstruct open surfaces from unorganized data points. This method allows the surface boundary to move during the surface evolution. The key technique of these methods is that two curves/surfaces are used to represent the open curve/surface and the boundary of the open curve/surface is defined as the intersection of these two curves/surfaces. Similar technique has also been used to track regions on surfaces [10]. But none of the above deals with open contour recovery from images.

Finding open contours in images is necessary in many situations of speech research [11], such as the ultrasound images of human tongue and MRI images of vocal tract, where only part of the object surface is captured thus the object shape is represented with a open contour. An example ultrasound image of human tongue is shown in Figure 1(a). In this image, the bright white band is the air reflection at the upper surface of the tongue. The lower edge of the band is the upper surface of the tongue, and the upper edge of the band is not related.

In this paper, we present a geometric deformable model to recover the shapes of open contours from noisy images. The objective open contour and end points of the open contour are modeled with two separate level set functions. To deal with the noise, different artifacts and intensity inhomogeneities presented in images, we introduce a region-based "*band velocity*" which controls the evolutions of both level set functions. Though region information has been extensively used in many deformable models such as [5][12], none of these models can deal with open contours since there is no region enclosed by a open contour. We also integrate

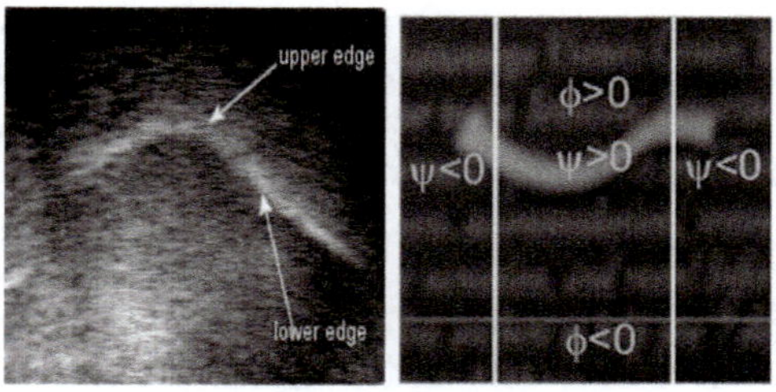

(a) (b)

Fig. 1. (a) An example of ultrasound images of the tongue. (b) The initial zero level sets.

prior shape information into the curve evolution process as Leventon et al. did in [6]. The prior shape information prevents two level set function from intersecting at other places than at the contour end points, which makes the shape recovery of open contours possible.

2 Level Set Representation of the Open Contour

In the level set method, a closed contour Γ is implicitly represented as the zero level set of a Lipschitz function ϕ as both Γ and ϕ being dependent on time t:

$$\Gamma(t) = \{\mathbf{x}; \phi(\mathbf{x}, t) = 0\} \tag{1}$$

where $\mathbf{x} \subset \Omega$ and Ω is the image domain.

ϕ is usually defined as a signed distance function such that:

$$\phi(\mathbf{x}, t) = \begin{cases} < 0 \text{ inside } \Gamma \\ = 0 \text{ on } \Gamma \\ > 0 \text{ outside } \Gamma \end{cases} \tag{2}$$

In case that Γ is open, the end points of Γ can be included into the definition by using another level set function ψ [8]. The open contour with end points inside the image domain is given by :

$$\Gamma(t) = \{\mathbf{x}; \phi(\mathbf{x}, t) = 0,\ \psi(\mathbf{x}, t) > 0\}. \tag{3}$$

Figure 1(b) shows an initial configuration of level set functions ϕ and ψ for detecting the lower (or upper) edge of a small elastic piece placed on complex background. In this figure, the zero level set of ϕ, where $\phi = 0$, is the horizontal line and the two vertical lines, where $\psi = 0$, are the zero level set of ψ. The set $\phi = 0$ contains two parts: the $\psi > 0$ part defines the open contour we are interested and the $\psi < 0$ part is the artificial contour. End points of the open contour are defined as the intersections of the horizontal line and the vertical lines, where $\phi = 0$ and $\psi = 0$.

3 The Band Velocity

Starting from the initialization, contour evolves until the objective shape is recovered. Let's first examine the evolution of ϕ, ψ evolves in the same fashion.

The evolution of the zero level contour of ϕ in the normal direction amounts to solve a partial differential equation [7]:

$$\phi_t = -v_\phi |\nabla \phi|,\ \phi(0) = \phi_0. \tag{4}$$

Where v_ϕ is the velocity in the normal direction and ϕ_0 is the initial configuration of ϕ.

In most geometric deformable models, v_ϕ is the combination of the mean curvature motion and a stop term coming from image gradient. For example, in [13]:

$$v_\phi = v_g(u_0)(\kappa + \nu). \tag{5}$$

Where u_0 is the given image, ν is a constant. $v_g(u_0)$ is a function of image gradient:

$$v_g(u_0) = \frac{1}{1 + |\nabla G_\sigma(\mathbf{x}) * u_0(\mathbf{x})|^p},\ p \geq 1. \tag{6}$$

Where $G_\sigma(\mathbf{x}) * u_0(\mathbf{x})$ is the convolution of the image u_0 with the Gaussian $G_\sigma(\mathbf{x}) = \sigma^{-1/2} e^{-|\mathbf{x}|^2/4\sigma}$.

With the velocity defined in Eq. 5, the zero level contour evolves in the normal direction and stops at the desired boundary, where g vanishes.

The above evolution velocity depends on the image gradient. In reality, images are generally noisy and there are always high-contrast unrelated edges which make the gradient information insufficient. By constraining the homogeneity of intensity (the image brightness) in a region, the edge of a region in a noisy image can be successfully extracted [5].

For open contours, the region homogeneity is not applicable since there is no inside and outside regions defined. To solve this problem, we compare the statistics of two regions $R(\Gamma)$ and $R'(\Gamma)$ which are locally around the evolving contour Γ but reside in different sides of Γ (see Figure 2), instead of considering the statistics of two regions which form the whole image domain. $R(\Gamma)$ and $R'(\Gamma)$ form a narrow band around the evolving contour Γ.

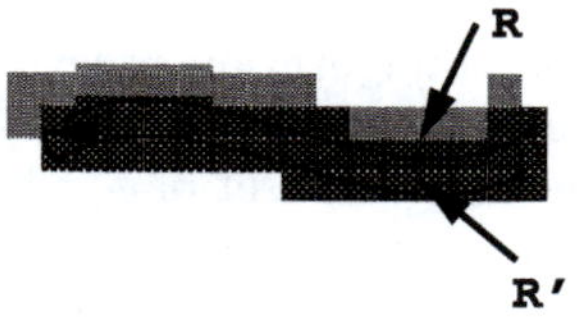

Fig. 2. R and R' around the contour

Recall that the lower edge of the bright band is the contour of interest (the real tongue surface) in the ultrasound tongue image (Figure 1(a)). If we define R as the local region on the side of normal direction (upward normal for the contour of tongue), R' as the local region on the opposite side, $S(R)$ as some statistics of R (e.g. the mean intensity of R), the observation is that $S(R) - S(R')$ is the maximum when Γ is located to the contour of interest. The only requirement of the above statement is that the depth of R and R', β, is small enough so that R is inside the white band in the ultrasound image.

The contour of interest can be located by minimizing a "*band energy*":

$$F(\Gamma) = 1 - (S(R) - S(R'))/N \tag{7}$$

where N is a normalization constant.

For the level set approach, we replace the unknown Γ by the unknown signed distance function ϕ:

$$F(\phi) = 1 - \left(\frac{1}{Nn}\int_{0<\phi\leq\beta} u_0(x,y)dxdy - \frac{1}{Nn'}\int_{-\beta\leq\phi<0} u_0(x,y)dxdy\right) \tag{8}$$

where u_0 is the given image, $(x,y) = \mathbf{x}, \mathbf{x} \subset \Omega$, n and n' are the numbers of pixels inside R and R', respectively. We then have:

$$S(R) = \frac{1}{n}\int_{0<\phi\leq\beta} u_0(x,y)dxdy \; S(R') = \frac{1}{n'}\int_{-\beta\leq\phi<0} u_0(x,y)dxdy \tag{9}$$

Having defined the "*band energy*" $F(\phi)$, we can define a corresponding "*band velocity*" for the evolving contour $\phi = 0$ as:

$$v_b(\phi = 0) = \begin{cases} 0 & F(\phi) < \rho \\ \tau F(\phi) & F(\phi) \geq \rho \end{cases} \tag{10}$$

where ρ is a constant threshold and $\tau > 0$ is a constant. In the ultrasound image, the speckle noises which have high gradient values can not stop the contour evolution since v_b is estimated over regions around $\Gamma(t)$. To give different evolution velocities to different parts on Γ, v_b of a specific part can also be calculated using informations from local regions around this part instead of the whole R and R'.

4 The Evolution Equations

Denote the normal velocities of ϕ and ψ with v_ϕ and v_ψ, respectively, we write the evolution equations of ϕ and ψ as:

$$\phi_t = -v_\phi|\nabla\phi| \quad \psi_t = -v_\psi|\nabla\psi| \tag{11}$$

v_ϕ now includes the "*band velocity*" introduced in the last section:

$$v_\phi = (\lambda_g v_g + \lambda_b v_b)(\kappa_\phi + \nu) \tag{12}$$

where λ_g and λ_b decide the relative importance of v_g and v_b.

v_ψ is defined as $v_\psi = v_\phi$ but is in the normal direction of ψ. Note the value of v_ψ is not decided by ψ, ψ stops evolution when v_ϕ vanishes See details in the next section.

5 Integrating Prior Shape Models

Prior shape information integrated into the deformable model can significantly help the shape recovery process. Leventon et al. [6] first combined the statistical shape model into the level set approach. In [6], the shape model is computed by principal component analysis over the signed distance function of the object shape to be recovered. An estimation of a novel shape (a signed distance function) ϕ^* can be represented by the parameters α of the projection of ϕ^* onto the

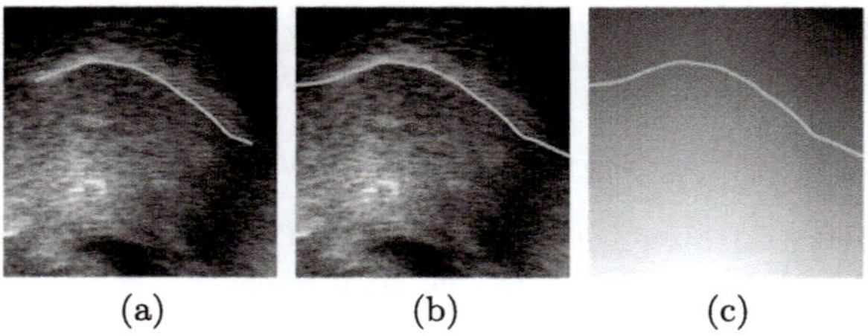

Fig. 3. An instance from a training set. (a) The training contour. (b) The kriged contour. (c) The distance map with the kriged contour overlapped.

relevant eigenvectors. The advantage of using signed distance function to represent shape is that slightly misaligned pixels in the distance map are generally highly correlated. Thus the correspondence problem during training process can be avoided.

Rousson and Paragios [14] have also proposed a level set approach using shape prior for 2D closed contour recovery. We follow the method of [6] but aim at open contour recovery using the statistical shape model. During the training process, a training open contour is first extended using a kriging[15] technique, then the signed distance map of the kriged contour is constructed. Prior shape model is acquired from constructed distance maps. In Figure 3, one instance from a training set for human tongue is shown.

At a given time t, a novel shape $\phi^*(t)$ is estimated using the maximum a posteriori (MAP) approach.

$$\phi^*_{MAP} = \text{argmax}_{\phi^*} P(\phi^*|\phi, u_0) \tag{13}$$

ϕ^* is represented by the parameters α of the projection of ϕ^* onto the relevant eigenvectors and its location in image is decided by its pose M. So the MAP of ϕ^* can be estimated by maximizing the following posterior probability:

$$P(\alpha, M|\phi, u_0) = \frac{P(\phi,u_0|\alpha,M)P(\alpha,M)}{P(\phi,u_0)} = \frac{P(\phi|\alpha,M)P(u_0|\alpha,M,\phi)P(\alpha)P(M)}{P(\phi,u_0)} \tag{14}$$

The first term in Eq. 14 computes the probability of a certain evolving contour, ϕ, given ϕ^* (or α, M). In our approach, we do not constrain the relative positions of ϕ and ϕ^*. $P(\phi, u_0|\alpha, M) = \mu(-\infty, \infty)$. The second term which comes from the image information is estimated by minimizing the "*band energy*" F defined in Eq. 7. $P(u_0|\phi*) = \exp(-F)$. The shape prior $P(\alpha)$ is a Gaussian model, as defined in [6]. $P(\alpha) = \frac{1}{((2\pi)^k|\Sigma_k|)^{1/2}}\exp(-\frac{1}{2}\alpha^T\Sigma_k^{-1}\alpha)$. where Σ_k contains the first k columns of the singular value matrix which is obtained after a Singular Value Decomposition of the covariance matrix of the training set. Similar to [6], the pose is not constrained in our approach. It could be any possible rotation and translation. $P(M) = \mu(-\infty, \infty)$.

The estimated $\phi^*(t)$ at each time step t guides a global evolution of $\phi(t)$ towards $\phi^*(t)$. At time $t+1$, $\phi(t+1)$ can be estimated as:

$$\phi(t+1) = \lambda_1\phi'(t+1) + \lambda_2(\phi^* - \phi(t)) \tag{15}$$

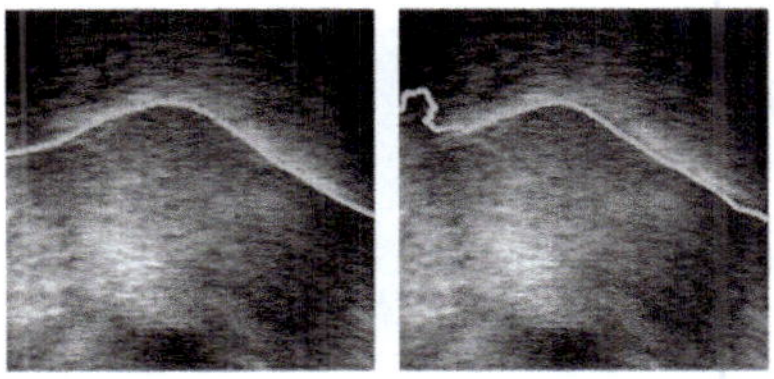

(a) (b)

Fig. 4. Shape model

where $\phi^{'}(t+1)$ is estimated from the local evolution defined in Eq. 11. λ_1 and λ_2 are the weighting parameters.

The integration of prior shape model is not only useful for the evolution of ϕ, it is also helpful for deciding the boundary of open contours. In the level set approaches for open curve/surface, it is important that the two level set functions, ϕ and ψ, never intersect at places other than the boundary of the open curve/surface since this would create some new boundaries. The approach in [8] moves the contour of interest (where $\phi = 0$, $\psi > 0$) in one direction but the artificial contour (where $\phi = 0$, $\psi < 0$) in the opposite direction. The problem with this approach is that the end points are fixed. [9] allows the surface boundary to move but requires good initializations of ϕ and ψ. In our approach, we do not distinguish the contour of interest and the artificial contour during the evolution of ϕ. The shape of ϕ is constrained by the prior shape information, which prevents the unnecessary intersections between ϕ and ψ. Figure 4(a) shows the final zero level set of ϕ, which is obtained by adding the global evolution from prior shape model to the local evolution. This contour is in the same class as contours in the training set and it is possible to evolve ψ to decide end points of this contour. But without the prior shape information, evolution of left part of this contour can not be stopped since the "*band energy*" at that part is high (no tongue surface there). Figure 4(b) shows the zero level set of ϕ which continues to evolve without the global evolution constraint from the prior shape model. It is impossible to decide the left end point of the tongue from this zero level set contour since there will be more than one intersection between ϕ and ψ sometimes when ψ is evolved over the left part of ϕ.

6 Experiments

Our method is quantitatively evaluated on both noisy synthetic and real images. The difference between the automatically detected contour, U, and the ground truth contour, V, is calculated using a Mean Sum of Distances(MSD) which measures the distances between the closest contour elements of each contour. Suppose the elements U and V are $U = [u_1, u_2, ..., u_n]$ and $V = [v_1, v_2, ..., v_n]$ for U and V respectively, The MSD between U and V is defined as: $MSD(U,V) = \frac{1}{2n}(\sum_{i=1}^{n} \min_j |v_i - u_j| + \sum_{i=1}^{n} \min_j |u_i - v_j|)$. The error of end point recovery is computed as the distance between the automatically detected end points and the ground truth end points along the recovered contour. For real images, ground truth is obtained by manually detecting the shape and end points.

6.1 Synthetic Images

The synthetic experiments are performed on images as shown in Figure 5(a) to recover the lower edge of a bright band as seen in each image. The target shape is created manually. It belongs to a training set of a tongue contour sequence, but is not among the training set. Shape model obtained from this training set is used as the prior shape information to guide the level set evolution during the contour recovery process.

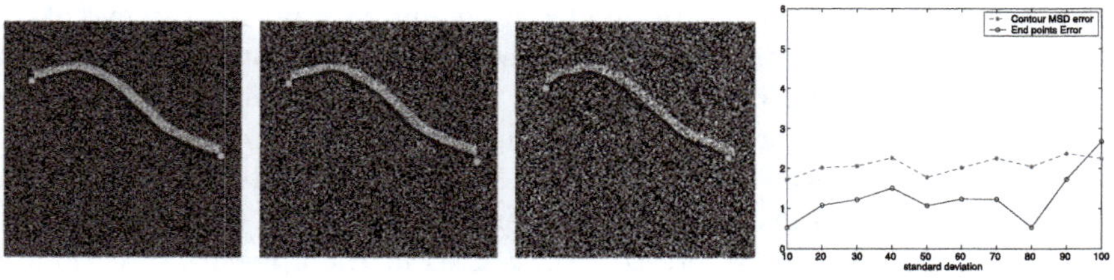

(a) (b)

Fig. 5. (a) Synthetic images with normally distributed noise added with the standard deviation of 40, 60, 100. Each shown with final contour and end points. (b) Errors of the synthetic image experiments (in pixels).

The synthetic experiment demonstrates the effect of noise on our method, by adding normally distributed noise with zero mean and different standard deviations, to the created synthetic image. The result is shown in Figure 5(b). The standard deviation of the added noise varies from 10 to 100. Note the errors in different noise levels do not change dramatically.

6.2 Real Images

The experiments on real images were first performed on five sequences of ultrasound images of the human tongue. The training set for the shape model in each experiment comes from few images at the beginning of the speech sequence to be analyzed. However, this can come from other sequences also and thus not restricted. In speech research, studies on comparing the same speech by different subjects and multiple repetitions of the same speech by the same subject are widely carried out. Principle tongue shape of the same speech can be captured in one sequence and applied to other sequences as the shape model.

Some tested ultrasound images are shown in the first row of Figure 6(a). The recovered tongue shapes and end points (cyan dots) for these images are shown in the second row of Figure 6(a). Note in the first experiment, though there is still part of bright band outside the detected left end point, it is the extension of the

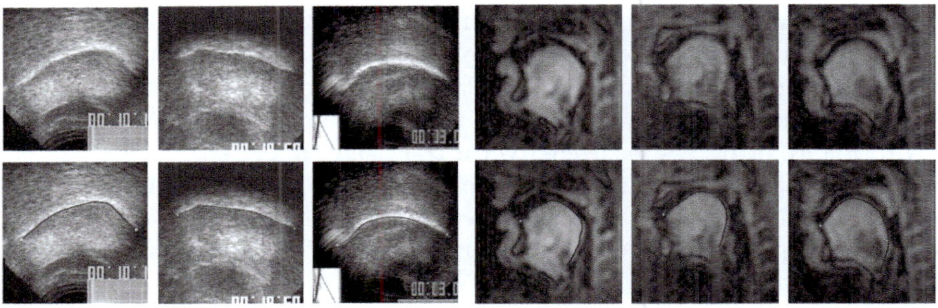

(a) (b)

Fig. 6. (a) Results of ultrasound tongue images. (b) MRI vocal tract images.

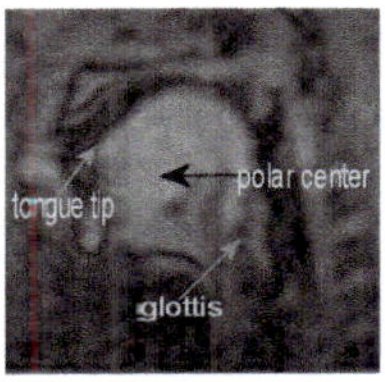

Fig. 7. An example of MRI vocal tract image

upper edge of the air reflection and proved to be noise produced by ultrasound imaging.

For each image sequence, five images are tested. The averaged errors of shape recovery and end point detection for each sequence are shown in Figure 8(a). All errors are less than the typical measurement error (5 pixels, or 1.5mm, in ultrasound images) [16].

We also tested our method on MRI images of the vocal tract. Sample MRI vocal tract image is shown in Figure 7. The vocal tract shape is extracted from the tongue tip to the glottis. Due to the MRI image quality that we currently

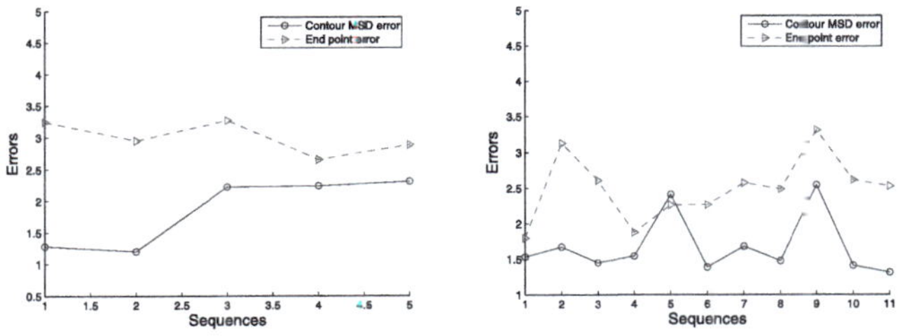

(a) (b)

Fig. 8. (a) Ultrasound Results. Errors are in pixels. (b) MRI Results. Errors are in pixels.

have, end points are only automatically recovered at the tongue tip. At the glottis, the end point is decided as the position which has the same angle as the mean glottis of the training set (A polar center is defined for MRI images to calculate angles of points). Some tested vocal tract images are shown in the first row of Figure 6(b). The recovered vocal tract shapes and end points for these images are shown in the second row of Figure 6(b). Quantitative evaluation on eleven MRI sequences was performed. For each sequence, five images were tested. Averaged errors of shape recovery and end point detection are shown in Figure 8(b).

7 Conclusion

Open contour recovery is an important problem in medical imaging such as the heart and speech research [11]. We present a level set approach to automatically recover the shape and detect the end points of open contours. We use two level set functions to model the open contour and find the end points of open contour as the intersection of the two level set functions. A novel "*band velocity*" is introduced to control the level set evolution, which makes our approach robust to noise. We also integrate the prior shape information into the contour evolution process, which prevents two level set functions from intersecting at other places than at the contour end points. Experiments on noisy images are shown and the results are verified by quantitative evaluations.

References

1. Caselles, V., Kimmel, R., Sapiro, G.: Geodesic active contours. IJCV **22** (1997) 61–79
2. Malladi, R., Sethian, J., Vemuri, B.: Shape modeling with front propagation: A level set approach. PAMI **17** (1995) 158–175
3. Han, X., Xu, C., Prince, J.: Topology preserving level set method for geometric deformable models. PAMI **25** (2003) 755–768
4. Niethammer, M., Tannenbaum, A.: Dynamic geodesic snakes for visual tracking. In: CVPR04. (2004) I: 660–667
5. Chan, T., Vese, L.: Active contours without edges. IP **10** (2001) 266–277
6. Leventon, M., Grimson, W., Faugeras, O.: Statistical shape influence in geodesic active contours. In: CVPR00. (2000) I: 316–323
7. Osher, S., Fedkiw, R.: Level Set Methods and Dynamic Implicit Surfaces. Springer (2003)
8. Smereka, P.: Spiral crystal growth. Physica D **138** (2000) 282–301
9. Solem, J., Heyden, A.: Reconstructing open surfaces from unorganized data points. In: CVPR04. (2004) II: 653–660
10. Bertalmio, M., Sapiro, G., Randall, G.: Region tracking on level-sets methods. MedImg **18** (1999) 448–451
11. Stone, M.: A guide to analyzing tongue motion from ultrasound images. International Journal of Clinical Linguistics and Phonetics **19** (2005) 455–502

12. Chalana, V., Costa, W.S., Kim Y.: Integrating region growing and edge detection using regularization. In: Proc. SPIE Vol. 2434, p. 262-271, Medical Imaging 1995: Image Processing, Murray H. Loew; Ed. (1995) 262–271
13. Caselles, V., Catte, F., Coll, T., Dibos, F.: A geometric model for active contours in image processing. Number. Math. **66** (1993) 1–31
14. Rousson, M., Paragios, N.: Shape priors for level set representations. In: ECCV02. (2002) II: 78.
15. Parthasarathy, V., Stone, M., Prince, J.: Spatiotemporal visualization of the tongue using ultrasound and kriging. In: Proc. Of SPIE-Medical Imaging. (2003)
16. Li, M., Kambhamettu, C., Stone, M.: Tongue motion averaging from contour sequences. International Journal of Clinical Linguistics and Phonetics **19** (2005) 515–528

Statistical Shape Models Using Elastic-String Representations

Anuj Srivastava[1], Aastha Jain[2], Shantanu Joshi[1], and David Kaziska[3]

[1] Florida State University, Tallahassee, FL, USA
[2] Indian Institute of Technology, N. Delhi, India
[3] Air Force Institute of Technology, Dayton, OH, USA

Abstract. To develop statistical models for shapes, we utilize an elastic string representation where curves (denoting shapes) can bend and locally stretch (or compress) to optimally match each other, resulting in geodesic paths on shape spaces. We develop statistical models for capturing variability under the elastic-string representation. The basic idea is to project observed shapes onto the tangent spaces at sample means, and use finite-dimensional approximations of these projections to impose probability models. We investigate the use of principal components for dimension reduction, termed tangent PCA or TPCA, and study (i) Gaussian, (ii) mixture of Gaussian, and (iii) non-parametric densities to model the observed shapes. We validate these models using hypothesis testing, statistics of likelihood functions, and random sampling. It is demonstrated that a mixture of Gaussian model on TPCA captures best the observed shapes.

1 Introduction

Analysis of shapes is emerging as an important tool in recognition of objects from their images. As an example, one uses the contours formed by boundaries of objects, as they appear in images, to characterize the objects themselves. Since the objects can occur at arbitrary locations, scales, and planar rotations, without changing their appearances, one is interested in the *shapes* of these contours, rather than the contours themselves. This motivates the development of tools for statistical analysis of shapes of simple, closed curves in $\mathbb{R}^2$. A statistical analysis is beneficial in many situations. For instance, in cases where the observed image is low quality due to clutter, low resolution, or obscuration, one can use the contextual knowledge to impose prior models on expected shapes, and use a Bayesian framework to improve shape extraction performance. Such applications require a broad array of tools for analyzing shapes: geometric representations of shapes, metrics for quantifying shape differences, algorithms for computing shape statistics such as means and covariances, and tools for testing competing hypotheses on given shapes.

Analysis of shapes of planar curves has been of a particular interest recently in the literature. Klassen [1] have described a geometric technique to parameterize curves by their arc lengths, and to use their angle functions to represent

P.J. Narayanan et al. (Eds.): ACCV 2006, LNCS 3851, pp. 612–621, 2006.

and analyze shapes. Similar constructions for analysis of closed curves were also studied in [2, 3]. Using the representations and metrics described in [1], [4] describe techniques for clustering, learning, and testing of planar shapes. One major limitation of this approach is that all curves are parameterized by arc length, and the resulting transformations from one shape into another are restricted to **bending only**. Local stretching or compression of shapes is not allowed. Mio [5] resolved this issue by introducing a representation that allows both bending and stretching of shapes to match each other. The geodesic paths resulting from this approach seem more natural as interesting features, such as corners, are better preserved while constructing geodesics, in this approach. This representation of planar shapes is called an *elastic string model*.

Our goal in this paper is to use elastic string model to study several probability models for capturing observed shape variability. Similar to approaches presented in [6, 4], we project observed shapes onto the tangent spaces at sample means, and further reduce their dimensions using PCA. Thus, we obtain a low-dimensional representations of shapes called *TPCA*. On tangent principal components (TPCs) of observed shapes we study: (i) Gaussian, (ii) nonparametric, and (iii) mixture of Gaussian models. The first two have been studied earlier for non-elastic shapes in [4]. To study model performances, we: (i) synthesize random shapes from these models, (ii) test amongst competing models using likelihood ratio, and (iii) compare statistics of likelihood on training and test data. This framework leads to stochastic shape models that can be used as priors in future Bayesian extraction of shapes from low-quality images. To illustrate these ideas we have used shapes from the ETH databases.

Rest of this paper is organized as follows. Section 2 summarizes elastic-string models for shape representations. Section 3 proposes three candidate probability models for capturing shape variability, while Sections 4 and 5 study these probability models via synthesis and hypothesis testing.

2 Elastic Strings Representation

Here we summarize the main ideas behind elastic-string representations of planar shapes, originally described in Mio et al [5].

2.1 Shape Representation

Let $\alpha\colon [0, 2\pi] \to \mathbb{R}^2$ be a smooth parametric curve such that $\alpha'(t) \neq 0$, $\forall t \in [0, 2\pi]$. The velocity vector is $\alpha'(t) = e^{\phi(t)} e^{j\theta(t)}$, where $\phi\colon [0, 2\pi] \to \mathbb{R}$ and $\theta\colon [0, 2\pi] \to \mathbb{R}$ are smooth, and $j = \sqrt{-1}$. The function ϕ is the log-speed of α and θ is the angle function. $\phi(t)$ measures the rate at which the interval $[0, 2\pi]$ is stretched or compressed at t to form the curve α; $\phi(t) > 0$ indicates local stretching near t, and $\phi(t) < 0$ local compression. Curves parameterized by arc length have $\phi \equiv 0$. We will represent α via the pair (ϕ, θ) and denote by $\mathcal{H}$ the collection of all such pairs.

Parametric curves that differ by rigid motions or uniform scalings of the plane, or by re-parameterizations are treated as representing the same shape. The pair

(ϕ, θ) is already invariant to translations of the curve. Rigid rotations and uniform scalings are removed by restricting to the space,

$$\mathcal{C} = \{(\phi,\theta) \in \mathcal{H} : \int_0^{2\pi} e^{\phi(t)}dt = 2\pi,\ \frac{1}{2\pi}\int_0^{2\pi} \theta(t)e^{\phi(t)}dt = \pi, \int_0^{2\pi} e^{\phi(t)}e^{j\theta(t)}dt = 0\},$$

$\mathcal{C}$ is called the *pre-shape spaces* of planar elastic strings. There are two possible ways of re-parameterizing a closed curve, without changing its shape: (i) One is to change the placement of origin $t = 0$ on the curve. This change can be represented as the action of a unit circle $\mathbb{S}^1$ on a shape (ϕ, θ), according to: $s \cdot (\phi(t), \theta(t)) = (\phi(t - s), \theta(t - s) + s)$. (ii) Re-parameterizations of α that preserve orientation and the property that $\alpha'(t) \neq 0,\ \forall t$, are those obtained by composing α with an orientation-preserving diffeomorphism $\gamma\colon [0, 2\pi] \to [0, 2\pi]$. Let $\mathcal{D}$ be the group of all such mappings. These mappings define a right action of $\mathcal{D}$ on $\mathcal{H}$ by

$$(\phi, \theta) \cdot \gamma = (\phi \circ \gamma + \log \gamma', \theta \circ \gamma). \tag{1}$$

$\circ$ denotes composition of functions. The space of all (shape-preserving) reparametrization of a shape in $\mathcal{C}$ is thus given by $\mathbb{S}^1 \times \mathcal{D}$. The resulting shape space is the space of all equivalence classes induced by these shape preserving transformations. It can be written as a quotient space $\mathcal{S} = (\mathcal{C}/\mathcal{D})/\mathbb{S}^1$.

What metric can used to compare shapes in this space? Mio [5] suggests that, given $(\phi, \theta) \in \mathcal{H}$, let h_i and f_i, $i = 1, 2$, represent infinitesimal deformations of ϕ and θ, resp., so that (h_1, f_1) and (h_2, f_2) are tangent vectors to $\mathcal{H}$ at (ϕ, θ). For $a, b > 0$, define $\langle(h_1, f_1), (h_2, f_2)\rangle_{(\phi,\theta)}$ as

$$a\int_0^1 h_1(t)h_2(t)\, e^{\phi(t)}\, dt + b\int_0^1 f_1(t)f_2(t)\, e^{\phi(t)}\, dt. \tag{2}$$

It can be shown that re-parameterizations preserve the inner product, i.e., $\mathbb{S}^1 \times \mathcal{D}$ acts on $\mathcal{H}$ by isometries. The elastic properties of the curves are built-in to the model via the parameters a and b, which can be interpreted as *tension* and *rigidity coefficients*, respectively. Large values of the ratio a/b indicate that strings offer higher resistance to stretching and compression than to bending; the opposite holds for a/b small. In this paper we fix a value of a/b that balances between bending and stretching.

2.2 Geodesic Paths in Shape Spaces

An important tool in this shape analysis is to construct geodesic paths, i.e. paths of smallest lengths, between arbitrary two shapes. Given the complicated geometry of $\mathcal{S}$, this task is not straightforward, at least not analytically. One solution is to use a computational approach, where the search for geodesics is treated as an optimization problem with iterative numerical updates. This approach is called the *shooting* method. Given a pair of shapes $\alpha_1 \equiv (\phi_1, \theta_1)$ and $\alpha_2 \equiv (\phi_2, \theta_2)$, one solves:

$$\min_{s\in\mathbb{S}^1, \gamma\in\mathcal{D}, g\in T_{\alpha_1}(\mathcal{C})} \|\Psi_1(\alpha_1; g) - (s \cdot (\alpha_2)) \cdot \gamma\|^2 \tag{3}$$

where $\Psi_t(\alpha; g)$ denotes a geodesic path starting at a shape α in the direction g, and parameterized by time t. Also, $\|\cdot\|$ is the $\mathbb{L}^2$ norm on $\mathcal{H}$. Basically, one solves for the shooting direction g^* such that the geodesic from α_1 in the direction g^* gets as close to the orbit of α_2 under shape preserving transformations [5]. Let $d(\alpha_1, \alpha_2) \equiv \|g^*\|$ denote the length of geodesics connecting the shapes α_1 and α_2. This construction helps define the exponential map: $\exp_\alpha(g) = \Psi_1(\alpha; g)$ and its inverse $\exp_\alpha^{-1}(\beta) = g$ such that $\Psi_1(\alpha; g) = \beta$.

2.3 Sample Mean of Shapes

Since the shape space $\mathcal{S}$ is nonlinear, the definitions of sample statistics, such as means and covariances, are not conventional. Earlier papers [7, 8] suggest the use of *Karcher mean* to define mean shapes as follows. For $\alpha_1, \ldots, \alpha_n$ in $\mathcal{S}$, and $d(\alpha_i, \alpha_j)$ the geodesic length between α_i and α_j, the Karcher mean is defined as the element $\mu \in \mathcal{S}$ that minimizes the quantity $\sum_{i=1}^{n} d(u, \alpha_i)^2$. A gradient-based, iterative algorithm for computing the Karcher mean is presented in [8, 1]. Shown in Figure 1 are some examples of three classes of shapes – dogs, pears, and mugs – used in the experiments here, and the Figure 2 shows Karcher means of shapes in these three classes. Let μ be the mean shape and for any shape α, let $g \in T_\mu(\mathcal{S})$ be such that $\Psi_1(\mu; g) = \alpha$. Then, α called the exponential of g, i.e. $\exp_\mu(g)$, and conversely, $g = \exp_\mu^{-1}(\alpha)$. As described next, statistics of α are studied through statistics of its map onto the tangent space at the mean.

Fig. 1. Examples of three classes of shapes – dogs, pears, and mugs – from the ETH database that are studied in this paper, with the numbers used in test and training

3 Statistical Shape Models

Our goal is to derive and analyze probability models for capturing observed shapes. The task of learning probability models on spaces like $\mathcal{S}$ is difficult for two main reasons. Firstly, they are nonlinear spaces and therefore classical statistical approaches, associated with the vector spaces, do not apply directly. Secondly, these are infinite-dimensional spaces and do not allow component-by-component modeling that is traditionally followed in finite-dimensional vector spaces. The solution involves making two approximations. First, we project elements of $\mathcal{S}$ onto the tangent space $T_\mu(\mathcal{S})$, which is a vector space, and therefore, better suited to statistical modeling. This is performed using the inverse exponential map $\exp_\mu^{-1}$. Second, we perform dimension reduction in $T_\mu(\mathcal{S})$ using PCA. Together,

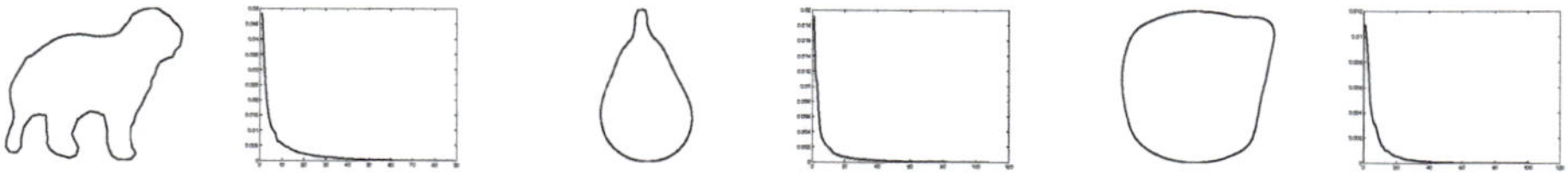

Fig. 2. In each case, left image shows the Karcher mean of shapes and right shows plots of the singular values of sample covariance matrix

these two approximations given rise to TPCA representation. These ideas were first proposed for landmark-based shape analysis in [6].

To start TPCA, we use the Gram-Schmidt algorithm to find an orthonormal basis of the given vectors: Set $i = 1$ and $r = 1$.

1. Set $Y_i = g_r - \sum_{j=1}^{i-1} \langle Y_j, g_r \rangle Y_j$.
2. If $\langle Y_i, Y_i \rangle \neq 0$,
   Set $Y_i = Y_i / \sqrt{\langle Y_i, Y_i \rangle}$, $i = i + 1$, $r = r + 1$, and go to Step 1.

   Else

   If $r < k$

   Set $r = r + 1$ and go to Step 1.

   Else Stop

Say the algorithm stops at some $i = n \leq k$. So now we have an n-dimensional subspace $\mathcal{Y}$ spanned by an orthonormal basis with elements $\{Y_1, Y_2, \ldots, Y_n\}$. The next step is to project each of the observed vector into $\mathcal{Y}$ as follows. Let $x_{ij} = \langle g_i, Y_j \rangle$ and define a vector $\mathbf{x}_i = [x_{i1}, x_{i2}, \ldots, x_{in}] \in \mathbb{R}^n$. Then, the projection of g_i into $\mathcal{Y}$ is given by $\sum_{j=1}^{n} x_{ij} Y_j$. Each $g_i \in T_\mu(\mathcal{S})$ is now represented by a smaller vector $\mathbf{x}_i \in \mathbb{R}^n$. Next, we perform PCA in $\mathbb{R}^n$ using the projected observations $\{\mathbf{x}_1, \mathbf{x}_2, \ldots, \mathbf{x}_k\}$. That is, from their sample covariance matrix $C \in \mathbb{R}^{n \times n}$, find its singular value decomposition $C = U \Sigma U^T$, and use the first d-columns of U to form a basis for the principal subspace of $\mathbb{R}^n$, with $d \leq n$. The vector $\mathbf{x} \in \mathbb{R}^n$ maps to a smaller vector $\mathbf{a} \in \mathbb{R}^d$ such that $x = \sum_{j=1}^{d} a_j U_j$. The choice of d is made using the singular values of C; shown in Figure 2 are the plots of singular values of C for the three classes: dogs, pears, and mugs.

3.1 Probability Models on TPCs

We impose a probability model on α implicitly by imposing a probability model on its tangent principal components (TPCs) $\mathbf{a}$. What probability models can be used in this situation? In this paper, we study the following three models: nonparametric, Gaussian and mixtures of Gaussian. The first two models were studied for non-elastic shapes in [4].

1. **Nonparametric Model:** Assuming that the TPCs, a_js, are statistically independent of each other, one can estimate their probability densities directly from the data using a kernel estimator. Let $f_j^{(1)}$, $j = 1, \ldots, d$ be the kernel estimate of the density function of a_j, the jth TPC of the shape α. In the experiments presented here we used a Gaussian Kernel. Then, assuming independence of

TPCs, we obtain: $f^{(1)}(\alpha) = \prod_{j=1}^{d} f_j(a_j)$. Shown in Figure 3 are some examples of estimated $f^{(1)}$ for several js. For each shape class, we display three examples of non-parametric density estimates for modeling TPCs.

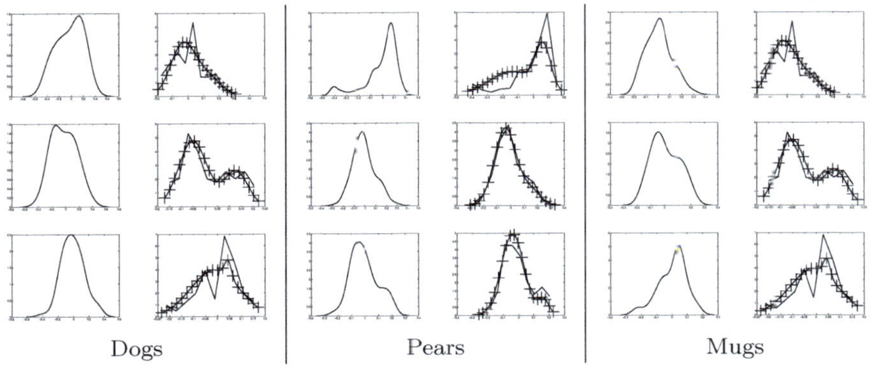

Fig. 3. We show three examples of modeling TPCs in each class. For each example, the left figure shows nonparametric estimate $f^{(1)}$ while the right figure shows the mixture of Gaussian $f^{(3)}$ (using cross-lines) drawn over observed densities (plain lines).

2. **Gaussian Model:** Let $\Sigma \in \mathbb{R}^{d\times d}$ be the diagonal matrix in SVD of C, the sample covariance of $\mathbf{x}_i$s. Then, we can model the component a_j as a Gaussian random variable with mean zero and variance $\sqrt{\Sigma_{jj}}$. Denoting the Gaussian density function as $h(y; z, \sigma^2) \equiv \frac{1}{\sqrt{2\pi\sigma^2}} \exp(-(y-z)^2/(2\sigma^2))$, we obtain the Gaussian shape model $f^{(2)}(\alpha) = \prod_{j=1}^{d} h(a_j; 0, \Sigma_{jj})$.

3. **Mixture of Gaussian:** Another candidate model is that a_j follows the density

$$f_j^{(3)}(\alpha) = \prod_{j=1}^{d} \left(\sum_{k=1}^{K} p_k h(a_j; z_k, \sigma_k^2) \right), \quad \sum_k p_k = 1,$$

a finite mixture of Gaussian. For a given K, EM algorithm can be used to estimate the means and variances of components. Based on empirical evidence, we have used $K = 2$ in this paper to estimate $f^{(3)}$ from observed data. Shown in Figure 3 are some examples of estimated $f^{(3)}$ for some TPCs. In each panel, the marked line shows the estimated mixture density and, for comparison, the plane line shows the observed histograms.

4 Empirical Evaluations

We have analyzed and validated the proposed shape models using: (i) random sampling, (ii) hypothesis testing, and (iii) statistics of log-likelihoods. We describe these results next.

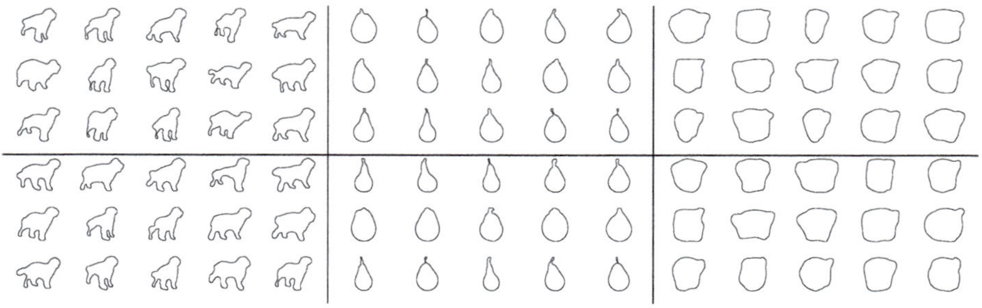

Fig. 4. Sample shapes synthesized from the nonparametric model (top) and the mixture model (bottom)

Shape Sampling: As a first step, we have synthesized random shapes from the three probability models $f^{(i)}$, $i = 1, 2, 3$. In each case the synthesis involves generating a random TPC according to its probability model- kernel density, Gaussian density or mixture of Gaussian- and then reconstructing the shape represented by that set of TPCs. For the generated values of TPCs, we form the vector $\mathbf{x} = \sum_{j=1}^{d} a_j U_j$, and the tangent direction $g = \sum_{i=1}^{n} x_i Y_i$, and eventually the shape $\alpha = \exp_\mu(g)$. Shown in Figure 4 are examples of random shapes generated from the models $f^{(1)}$ (top row) and $f^{(3)}$ (bottom row). We found that all three models seem to perform reasonably well in synthesis, with $f^{(1)}$ and $f^{(3)}$ being slightly better than $f^{(2)}$.

Testing Shape Models

In order to test proposed models for capturing observed shape variability, we use the likelihood ratio test to select among the candidate models. For a shape $\alpha \in \mathcal{S}$, the likelihood ratio under any two models is:

$$\frac{f^{(m)}(\alpha)}{f^{(n)}(\alpha)} = \prod_{j=1}^{d} \frac{f_j^{(m)}(a_j)}{f_j^{(n)}(a_j)}, \quad m, n = 1, 2, 3 \ ,$$

and the log-likelihood ratio is

$$l(\alpha; m, n) \equiv \sum_{j=1}^{d} \left(\log(f_j^{(m)}(a_j)) - \log(f_j^{(n)}(a_j)) \right) .$$

If $l(\alpha; m, n)$ is positive then the model m is selected, and vice-versa. Taking a large set of test shapes, we have evaluated $l(\alpha; m, n)$ for each shape and have counted the fraction for which $l(\alpha; m, n)$ is positive. We define:

$$P(m, n) = \frac{|\{i | l(\alpha_i; m, n) > 0\}|}{k} \ ,$$

where k is the total number of shapes used in this test. This fraction is plotted versus the component size d in Figure 5, for two pairs of shape models: $P(1, 3)$ in

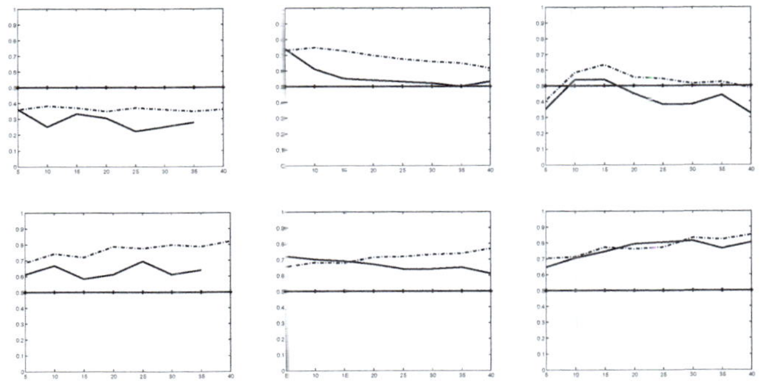

dogs pears mugs

Fig. 5. $P(m,n)$ plotted versus vs d, for each of the three classes. Top row: $m = 1$, $n = 3$, and bottom row: $m = 3$, $n = 2$.

the top row and $P(3,2)$ in the bottom row. $P(m,n) > 0.5$ implies that model m outperforms n. Two sets of results are presented in each of these plots. The solid line is for the test shapes that were not used in estimation of shape models, and the broken line is for the training shapes that were used in model estimation. Also, we draw a line at 0.5 to clarify which model is performing better. As these indicate, the mixture model seems to perform the best in most situations. On the training shapes, for pears and mugs, the nonparametric model is better than the mixture model. This result in expected since nonparametric model is derived from these training shapes themselves. However, on the test shapes, the mixture model is either comparable or better than the other two models. We conclude that for this data set, the mixture model is better for capturing variability in both training and test shapes. Furthermore, it is efficient due to its parametric nature.

Statistics of Model Likelihoods

Another technique for model validation is to study the variability of a model-based "sufficient statistic" when evaluated on both training and test shapes. In case the distributions of this statistic are similar on both training and test shapes, this validates the underlying model. In this paper, we have chosen the sufficient

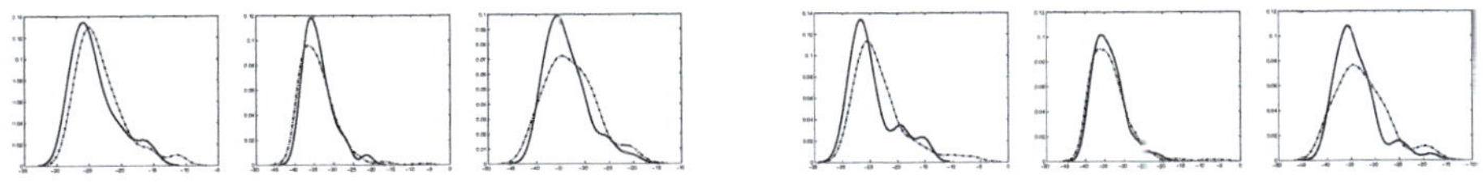

dogs pears mugs dogs pears mugs

Fig. 6. Histograms of $\nu^{(i)}(\alpha)$ for test (solid) and training shapes (broken). First three are for nonparametric model, and the last three are for mixture of Gaussians.

statistic to be proportional to *negative log-likelihood* of an observed shape. That is, we define $\nu^{(i)}(\alpha) \propto -\log(f^{(i)}(\alpha))$, where the proportionality implies that the constants have been ignored. Shown in Figure 6 are some examples of this study for the nonparametric (first three) and the mixture model (last three). These plots shows histograms of $\nu^{(i)}(\alpha)$ values for both test and training shapes, for each of the three shape classes. It is evident that the histograms for training and test sets are quite similar in all these examples, and hence, validate the proposed models.

Acceptance/Rejection Under Learned Models: In the final experiment, we performed acceptance/rejection for each test shape under the mixture model, $f^{(3)}$, for each shape class (dogs, pears, and mugs). Using threshold values estimated using training data of each class, we compute the value of $\nu^{(3)}(\alpha)$ for each test shape α; if it is below the threshold we accept it, otherwise we reject it. For example, we have

$$\nu^{(3)}(\alpha) \underset{\text{dog accept}}{\overset{\text{dog reject}}{\gtrless}} \kappa_{dog}.$$

This is done for each of the three classes – dogs, pears, and mugs, and the results are summarized in the next table. This table lists the percentage of times a shape from a given test class was accepted by each of the three shape classes. For example, test shapes in dog class were accepted 96.67% times by shape model for dog class, 1.67% by pear model, and 0.83% by cup model. Also, 1.67% of test shapes in dog class were rejected by all three models. Since a shape can be accepted by more than one model, the sum in each row can exceed 100%. Notice that the test shapes also include other objects such as horses, cows, apples, cars, and tomatoes. Some of the cows (35%) are accepted under dog model, but are easily rejected under pear and mug models; most of the cows (64%) are rejected under all three models. Tomatoes are mostly accepted by pear and mug models. Overall, the mixture model $f^{(3)}$ demonstrates a significant success in capturing shape variability and in discriminating between object classes. It also enjoys the efficiency of being a parametric model.

Test class	Dog Accepts (%)	Pear Accepts (%)	Cups Accepts (%)	No Accepts (%)
Dogs	96.67	1.67	0.83	1.67
Pears	10.45	99.00	41.79	0.99
Cups	9.95	28.35	98.01	1.49
Horses	43.97	0.00	0.52	56.02
Apples	0	78.71	96.53	0.99
Cows	35.83	0.00	0.00	64.17
Cars	16.91	0.99	46.76	38.30
Tomatoes	0.99	67.66	72.13	19.90

5 Conclusion

We have presented results from statistical analysis of planar shapes under elastic string models. Using TPCA representation of shapes, three candidate models were presented: nonparametric, Gaussian, and a mixture of Gaussian. We evaluated these models using (i) random sampling, (ii) likelihood ratio tests, (iii) similarity of (distributions of) sufficient statistics on training and test shapes, and (iv) acceptance/rejection of test shapes under the models estimated from the corresponding training shapes. All three models do reasonably well in random sampling and likelihood ratio test. However, the mixture model emerges as the best model for capturing shape variability and efficiency. We therefore conjecture that mixture of Gaussians are sufficient for modeling TPCs of observed shapes for use as prior shape models in future Bayesian inferences.

References

1. Klassen, E., Srivastava, A., Mio, W., Joshi, S.: Analysis of planar shapes using geodesic paths on shape spaces. IEEE Pattern Analysis and Machine Intelligence **26** (March, 2004) 372–383
2. Younes, L.: Optimal matching between shapes via elastic deformations. Journal of Image and Vision Computing **17** (1999) 381–389
3. Michor, P.W., Mumford, D.: Riemannian geometries on spaces of plane curves. Journal of the European Mathematical Society **to appear** (2005)
4. Srivastava, A., Joshi, S., Mio, W., Liu, X.: Statistical shape analysis: Clustering, learning and testing. IEEE Transactions on Pattern Analysis and Machine Intelligence **27** (2005) 590–602
5. Mio, W., Srivastava, A.: Elastic string models for representation and analysis of planar shapes. In: Proc. of IEEE Computer Vision and Pattern Recognition. (2004)
6. Dryden, I.L., Mardia, K.V.: Statistical Shape Analysis. John Wiley & Son (1998)
7. Le, H.L., Kendall, D.G.: The Riemannian structure of Euclidean shape spaces: a novel environment for statistics. Annals of Statistics **21** (1993) 1225–1271
8. Karcher, H.: Riemann center of mass and mollifier smoothing. Communications on Pure and Applied Mathematics **30** (1977) 509–541

Minimal Weighted Local Variance as Edge Detector for Active Contour Models

W.K. Law and Albert C.S. Chung

Lo Kwee-Seong Medical Image Analysis Laboratory,
Department of Computer Science,
The Hong Kong University of Science and Technology,
Clear Water Bay, Kowloon, Hong Kong
{maxlawwk, achung}@cs.ust.hk

Abstract. Performing segmentation of narrow, elongated structures with low contrast boundaries is a challenging problem. Boundaries of these structures are difficult to be located when noise exists or intensity of objects and background is varying. Using the active contour methods, this paper proposes a new vector field for detection of such structures. In this paper, unlike other work, object boundaries are not defined by intensity gradient but statistics obtained from a set of filters applied on an image. The direction and magnitude of edges are estimated such that the minimal weighted local variance condition is satisfied. This can effectively prevent contour leakage and discontinuity by linking disconnected boundaries with coherent orientation. It is experimentally shown that our method is robust to intensity variation in the image, and very suitable to deal with images with narrow structures and blurry edges, such as blood vessels.

1 Introduction

Active contour models are widely used in solving medical image segmentation problems. For instance, blood vessel segmentation is one of the applications in medical image segmentation. To separate vascular structures from the image background, researchers consider utilizing image gradient as a criterion to label blood vessel boundaries. In the Gradient Vector Flow (GVF) method [1], a moving parametric contour is driven by the minimization of energy $\mathcal{E}$,

$$\mathcal{E}(\mathcal{C}) = \int\int \mu(u_x^2 + u_y^2 + v_x^2 + v_y^2) + |\nabla f|^2|\mathbf{v} - \nabla f|^2 dxdy,$$

where $f = |\nabla I(x,y)|^2$ represents the edge map of an image I, $\mathbf{v}(x,y) = (u(x,y), v(x,y))^T$ denotes the flow vector, which is obtained using two diffusion based partial differential equations in the whole image domain, $\mu\nabla^2 u - (u - f_x)(f_x^2 + f_y^2) = 0$ and $\mu\nabla^2 v - (v - f_y)(f_x^2 + f_y^2) = 0$. As such, the diffusion process creates a competition of forces exerting from the image gradient at different locations. The GVF method outperforms the classical Snakes [2] because

P.J. Narayanan et al. (Eds.): ACCV 2006, LNCS 3851, pp. 622–632, 2006.

the above diffusion processes enable GVF to have long range interaction between boundaries and moving contours.

Apart from the parametric contours, Malladi *et at.* [3] have proposed to use the level set framework [4] for modeling of moving curves. The level set formulation can handle merging or splitting of contours naturally. One of the main ideas in [3] is that there is an advection term, which keeps the front of the level set function expanding (or contracting) with the speed controlled by a function, namely *edge detector*, $g(\nabla I(x,y)) = \frac{1}{1+|\nabla G_\sigma * I(x,y)|^p}, p \geq 1$. This formulation keeps the contours exploring the image and eventually halted on the object boundaries, where the edge detector gives small value.

However, these methods are not suitable for elongated or low contrast objects such as blood vessels in the brain. For example, for the GVF method, it favors the conceptual edges and usually discards the narrow regions rather than including them in the segmentation results. Also, the edge detector relies on high image gradient magnitude to halt the moving contours, and can fail to detect low contrast boundaries.

To deal with this problem, Vasilevskiy *et al.* proposed the use of flux maximizing geometric flows for image segmentation [5]. Different from the above methods, object boundaries are detected by incorporating image gradient direction and magnitude. The contour motion is governed by

$$\mathcal{C}_t = \nabla(\mathcal{V}(x,y))\mathcal{N}, \tag{1}$$

where $\mathcal{V}(x,y)$ is the gradient vector of an image and $\mathcal{N}$ is the normal direction on the curve $\mathcal{C}$. Contour evolution direction is guided by the direction perpendicular to the image gradient. It does not fail in the situation where gradient magnitude is small or object structures are elongated and thin.

Along the same line, Xiang *et al.* introduced an elastic model [6] for segmentation of thin concave and convex structures. This method also integrates the information of both the magnitude and direction of image gradient in the similar fashion. In [6], the image gradient magnitude is extended to whole image domain rather than locally defined, as in [5]. The dynamics of an active contour is defined by minimizing the energy,

$$\mathcal{E}(\mathcal{C}) = \frac{1}{2}\int \mathbf{w}\cdot\mathbf{w}dxdydz, \tag{2}$$

subject to the constraint,

$$\nabla \times \mathbf{w} = \delta_{\mathcal{C}}\mathbf{t}, \tag{3}$$

where $\mathbf{w}$ is a three dimensional vector field, $\delta_{\mathcal{C}}$ is Dirac delta-function which is zero everywhere except on the curve $\mathcal{C}$. $\delta_{\mathcal{C}}\mathbf{t}$ is approximated by $\delta(z)\cdot \left(\frac{\partial(G_\sigma * I)}{\partial y}, -\frac{\partial(G_\sigma * I)}{\partial x}, 0\right)^T$ such that $\mathcal{C}$ can be attracted towards the object boundaries by minimizing the energy above.

On the other hand, without considering image gradient, Chan and Vese suggested to perform image segmentation by solving the minimal partition problem in [7]. The segmentation result is the minimizer of an energy functional,

$$F(c_1, c_2, \mathcal{C}) = \mu \mathcal{C}_{Length} + \nu \mathcal{C}_{Area} + \lambda_1 \int_{\mathcal{C}_{in}} |I - c_1|^2 dxdy + \lambda_2 \int_{\mathcal{C}_{out}} |I - c_2|^2 dxdy,$$

where $\mu \geq 0, \nu \geq 0, \lambda_1 \geq 0, \lambda_2 \geq 0$ are fixed parameters, c_1 and c_2 are the average intensity values of pixels inside and outside contour $\mathcal{C}$ respectively. This approach is capable of dealing with low contrast objects, blurry edges or noisy image that cause failure in many gradient based segmentation methods. Furthermore, choosing a large value for μ in the above formulation encourages linking disconnected boundaries through conceptual edges. However, due to background noise and overlapping of different structures which commonly exist in medical images, the intensity values of vascular structures and the background are varying from regions to regions. Minimizing the energy functional can lead to a situation that the bright regions of background and dark portions of vessels belong to the same object.

Although approaches in [5] and [6] are robust to intensity variation of objects and background, they are confused by the fluctuating gradient of object boundaries in such case. The locally defined flux cannot recover the weak edges that are longer than the radius of the target object. Similarly, the elastic model is insensitive to small gradient of weak edges. This can lead to contour leakage. Besides, noise also generates intensity gradient across thin objects. It creates small gaps (discontinuities) on those narrow structures. The approaches above do not encode with the information about contour continuity. They tend to regard those single objects with small gaps as separated and disconnected structures.

In this paper, we propose a new vector field to incorporate with the active contour models for image segmentation. Calculation of the vector field is based on satisfying minimal weighted local variance calculated from the statistics after applying a set of filters on the image. Under this formulation, the magnitude and direction of an edge are not depending on its local gradient but the statistics estimated from a local region. The advantage of our method is that edges are extended along their direction so that the discontinued portion of the edges can be recovered without blurring or shifting effect. It is essential to recover those weak parts of edges in order to prevent contour leakage and discontinuity.

2 Methodology

2.1 The Proposed Model

Let $g(x, y)$ be a spatial filter which has its peak value at the center and decays gradually away from the center, for instance, Gaussian filter. We split the filter $g(x, y)$ into two filter sets according to a parameter $\theta, \theta \in [0, \pi)$. Each filter should be summed to one. Namely, $g_1(x, y, \theta)$ and $g_2(x, y, \theta)$ are defined as,

$$g_1(x, y, \theta) = \frac{g_1'(x, y, \theta)}{\int g_1'(x', y', \theta) dx'dy'},$$

$$g_2(x,y,\theta) = \frac{g_2'(x,y,\theta)}{\int g_2'(x',y',\theta)dx'dy'},$$
$$g_1'(x,y,\theta) = \begin{cases} g_\theta(x,y) & \text{if } (x,y)^T \cdot \hat{n_\theta} < 0, \\ 0 & \text{otherwise,} \end{cases}$$
$$g_2'(x,y,\theta) = \begin{cases} g_\theta(x,y) & \text{if } (x,y)^T \cdot \hat{n_\theta} > 0, \\ 0 & \text{otherwise,} \end{cases} \tag{4}$$

where $\hat{n_\theta} = (\cos\theta, \sin\theta)^T$, and $g_\theta(x,y) = g(x\cos(\theta+\frac{\pi}{2}) - y\sin(\theta+\frac{\pi}{2}), x\sin(\theta+\frac{\pi}{2}) + y\cos(\theta+\frac{\pi}{2}))$ is the rotated version of $g(x,y)$ (Fig.1a).

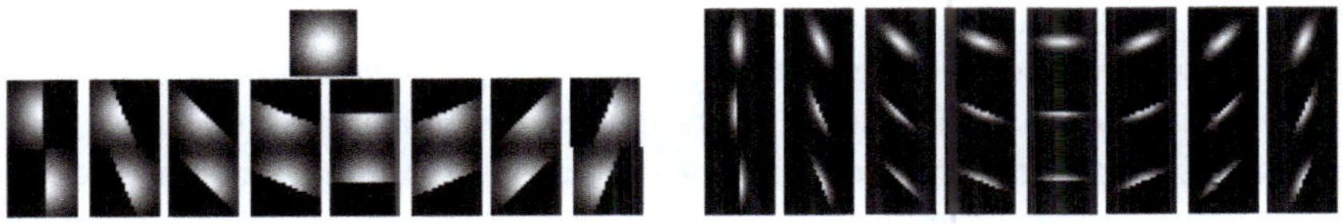

(a) (b)

Fig. 1. (a) Top: $G_{\sigma=4}$. Second row: Corresponding filter set g_1. Third row: Corresponding filter set g_2. From left to right, $\theta = 0, \frac{\pi}{8}, \frac{2\pi}{8}, \frac{3\pi}{8}, \frac{4\pi}{8}, \frac{5\pi}{8}, \frac{6\pi}{8}, \frac{7\pi}{8}$. (b) First row: $G_{\sigma_x=3,\sigma_y=1}$. Second row: Corresponding filter set g_1. Third row: Corresponding filter set g_2. From left to right, $\theta = 0, \frac{\pi}{8}, \frac{2\pi}{8}, \frac{3\pi}{8}, \frac{4\pi}{8}, \frac{5\pi}{8}, \frac{6\pi}{8}, \frac{7\pi}{8}$.

We obtain $\theta'(x,y)$ satisfying the following condition,

$$\theta'(x,y) = \arg\min_\theta \left\{ \int\int \{g_1(x'-x, y'-y, \theta)\cdot(I(x',y') - \mu_1(x,y,\theta))^2 + g_2(x'-x,y'-y,\theta)\cdot(I(x',y') - \mu_2(x,y,\theta))^2 \} dx'dy' \right\}. \tag{5}$$

Here $\mu_1 = \int g_1(x'-x, y'-y, \theta)I(x',y')dx'dy'$ and $\mu_2 = \int g_2(x'-x,y'-y,\theta)I(x',y')dx'dy'$. The terms $\mu_1(x,y)$ and $\mu_2(x,y)$ are the weighted averages of the neighboring pixels of (x,y) in different sides split by the line $\hat{n}_{\perp\theta(x,y)} = (\cos(\theta(x,y)+\frac{\pi}{2}), \sin(\theta(x,y)+\frac{\pi}{2}))^T$. Equation (5) is the weighted sum variance of the neighboring pixels from the both sides of the line $\hat{n}_{\perp\theta(x,y)}$. We call this condition, minimal weighted local variance.

Now we define the vector field, $\mathcal{V}$, using the $\theta'(x,y)$ obtained from minimal weighted local variance, $\mathcal{V}(x,y)$ is found as follows,

$$\mathcal{V}(x,y) = \{\mu_2(x,y,\theta'(x,y)) - \mu_1(x,y,\theta'(x,y))\}\cdot \hat{r}_{\theta'(x,y)} \tag{6}$$

By finding $\theta'(x,y)$ that satisfies the minimal weighted local variance condition, the direction of $\mathcal{V}(x,y)$ is pointing from one region to another region such that the weighted sum variance of these two regions is minimized. Its magnitude is determined by the difference of weighted averages of these two regions.

2.2 Properties

The main goal of defining $\theta'(x,y)$ is to find the direction pointed by the vector $\hat{n}_{\perp\theta'(x,y)}$, that is the best choice to partition the neighborhood of the pixel (x,y) into two regions. For an ideal sharp edge that separates two regions with distinct constant intensity, $\mathcal{V}(x,y)$ gives similar results to the smoothed intensity gradient vector of the edge.

The major difference of the above formulation and Chan's [7] minimal partition problem is that we localized the calculation of variance and the contour evolution is guided by the direction of $\hat{n}_{\perp\theta'(x,y)}$ at every point. For medical images, intensity of an object such as blood vessel is largely varying from regions to regions. Therefore, the sum variance of objects and background is not necessary to be minimal for correct segmentation result in those situations. Since the intensity variance of objects themselves is also large, minimizing the sum variance of inside and outside contours causes oversensitivity on those objects whose intensity is varying. In contrast, calculation of sum variance in a localized manner avoids this problem.

The localized sum variance of every pixel does not depend on the topology of contours. Instead, it depends only on the neighborhood of pixel. Obviously, the calculation of localized sum variance should be more sensitive to those pixels nearby and less sensitive to those pixels far away. The neighborhood is defined by the filter $g(x,y)$. A filter which has its peak value at the center and decays gradually away from the center is a good choice of $g(x,y)$, for example, Gaussian function.

In Equation (6), $|\mathcal{V}(x,y)|$ is given by $\mu_2(x,y,\theta'(x,y)) - \mu_1(x,y,\theta'(x,y))$, which is the difference of weighted intensity average of the regions separated by $\hat{n}_{\perp\theta'(x,y)}$. Such difference reflects how well the direction $\hat{n}_{\perp\theta'(x,y)}$ partitions the regions around (x,y).

Considering a vascular structure with fluctuating intensity value (Fig.2a,b), the intensity of some segments of blood vessel is very similar to the background. Distinguishing those regions from background is difficult without referring to the neighbors. That's the reason why leakage problem commonly exists in different active contour models.

Those confusing regions can be recovered by referring to the intensity of pixel neighbors. In our formulation, $|\mathcal{V}|$ depends on the weighted intensity average difference of pixel neighbors. The filters $g_1(\cdot,\theta'(x,y))$ and $g_2(\cdot,\theta'(x,y))$ in (4) are chosen to be split along direction of $\hat{n}_{\perp\theta'(x,y)}$, which is the tangent direction of boundaries extracted from minimal weighted local variance condition. Thus, $|\mathcal{V}(x,y)|$ are referring to two regions that are separated by a straight line along the direction of $\hat{n}_{\perp\theta'(x,y)}$. It plays an important role in extending edges along their direction and links the boundaries that have coherent orientation.

On the other hand, for those weak edges having no coherent orientation to their neighbors, their field magnitude is suppressed by smoothing effect of weighted average. Linking weak edges are only performed for those boundaries with coherent edge direction. Thus, noise is suppressed which has weak interaction with its neighbors.

In addition, our formulation only recovers those low contrast boundaries with high contrast edges along analogous direction in its neighborhood. Without considerable prior knowledge on the shape of target regions, the information extracted in minimal weighted local variance is not going to reconstruct those structures that are significantly confused with the background.

For vascular segmentation, target regions consist of elongated and thin structures. To make the field sensitive to these structures, we suggest to use a Gaussian kernel with different standard deviation in x and y directions, $G_{\sigma_x,\sigma_y}(x,y) = \frac{1}{2\pi\sigma_x\sigma_y}\exp\{-\frac{x^2}{2\sigma_x^2} - \frac{y^2}{2\sigma_y^2}\}$. The value of σ_x controls the strength to extend boundaries along their direction, and σ_y controls the width scale of the objects to be detected which should be set roughly smaller than the width of target structure. Large ratio of $\frac{\sigma_x}{\sigma_y}$ (Fig.1b) makes calculation of weighted average and weighted variance consider less pixels along the direction of $\hat{n}_{\theta'(x,y)}$ than direction of edges, $\hat{n}_{\perp\theta'(x,y)}$. As a result, the vector field $\mathcal{V}$ calculated by such filter favors elongated objects such as blood vessels.

2.3 Implementation

The crucial step to estimate $\mathcal{V}(x,y)$ is to find $\theta'(x,y)$. It can be achieved by defining a set of discrete values, θ_k, where $k \in \{0,\ldots,K-1\}$ and $\theta_k = \frac{k\pi}{K}$. The $\theta'(x,y)$ is obtained in discrete fashion,

$$\theta'(x,y) = \arg\min_{\theta_k}\left\{\sum_{x',y'}\{g_1(x'-x,y'-y,\theta_k)\cdot(I(x',y')-\mu_1(x,y,\theta_k))^2 \right. \\ \left. +g_2(x'-x,y'-y,\theta_k)\cdot(I(x',y')-\mu_2(x,y,\theta_k))^2\}\right\}. \quad (7)$$

In our experiments, we have used $K = 36$ for $\theta_k \in [0,\pi)$. Therefore, there are totally 36 filters for both $g_1(x,y,\theta_k)$ and $g_2(x,y,\theta_k)$ to detect 72 distinct edge orientations.

The vector field $\mathcal{V}(x,y)$ is then calculated by Equation (6). It is defined in the whole image domain and is not affected by the dynamics of moving contours. We utilize the elastic model proposed in [6] to model the interaction between boundaries detected by the minimal weighted local variance. This model is used because of its long range interaction ability and high sensitivity to both concave and convex regions. Resulting contour is the minimizer of energy associated with moving contours and a vector field, $\mathbf{w}$, as stated in Equation (2) subject to the constraint in Equation (3). Here we approximate $\delta_C\mathbf{t}$ with $\delta(z)\cdot(v_2,-v_1,0)^T$ where $\mathcal{V} = (v_1,v_2)^T$ and use zero level of level set surface to represent moving contours [4], which is evolving according to the following equation,

$$\phi_t = F|\nabla\phi|, \quad (8)$$

where F is the normal velocity that the curve evolves.

We can solve F in frequency domain similar to [6]. m, n, l denote the frequencies in x, y and z directions respectively and $\widetilde{F}(m, n, l)$ is the frequency component of $F(x, y) \cdot \delta(z)$,

$$\widetilde{F}(m, n, l) = i\frac{m \cdot a_1(m, n) + n \cdot a_2(m, n)}{m^2 + n^2 + l^2}, \tag{9}$$

where $a_1(m, n)$ and $a_2(m, n)$ are frequency components of $v_1(x, y)$ and $v_2(x, y)$, respectively. Assume that the 3D space is continuous and extending to infinity in z direction, discrete and periodic in both x and y directions,

$$\begin{aligned} F(x, y) &= \frac{1}{2\pi}\int_{l=-\infty}^{l=\infty}\left\{\sum_{m,n}\frac{i \cdot (ma_1(m, n) + na_2(m, n)) \cdot e^{imx+iny}}{m^2 + n^2 + l^2}\right\} dl, \\ &= \sum_{m,n}\frac{i(ma_1(m, n) + na_2(m, n))}{2\sqrt{m^2 + n^2}}e^{imx+iny}. \end{aligned} \tag{10}$$

Note that we have added a very small constant into the variable m and n in our implementation, which avoids singularity of the solution when m and n are both zero. The above formulation find $(v_{1x} + v_{2y})$ and diffuses it to whole image domain with inverse square decay rate. The opposite sign of $(v_{1x} + v_{2y})$ on two different sides over an edge creates zero-crossing boundary that halts the evolution of contour.

In [6], intensity gradient vector is used instead of $\mathcal{V}(x, y)$ in Equation (9). In this case, a_1 and a_2 are replaced with the frequency components of $-I_x$ and I_y respectively. Finding the corresponding $\widetilde{F}$ is equivalent to applying the Laplacian filter on the image and diffusing it with inverse square decay rate. As a result, [6] is similar to the work in [8] about edge integration by finding zero-crossing after applying Laplacian filter on an image. It also has a close relationship with [5] , where the Equation (1) is equivalent to $\mathcal{C}_t = (\nabla^2 \cdot I)\mathcal{N}$.

Neither the inverse square decay rate of [6] nor discrete summation of Equation (1) over circular disc proposed in [5] carries information about contour continuity. In contrast, the minimal weighted local variance added those information by extending edges along their direction which is useful for segmentation of narrow and low contrast structures in noisy images.

Finally, to speed up evolution process, we replace $F(x, y)$ in Equation (8) with a sigmoid function $\frac{2}{1-e^{-F(x,y)/\sigma_F}} - 1$ in our implementation, where σ_F is the standard deviation of $F(x, y)$. This function has similar effect of $sign(F)$ when magnitude of F is very large while keeping increasing linearly as magnitude of F is small.

3 Experimental Results

This section presents results obtained from real images (Fig.2) consisting of two digital subtraction angiography (DSA) obtained from the Department of Diagnostic Radiology and Organ Imaging, Prince of Wales Hospital, Hong Kong,

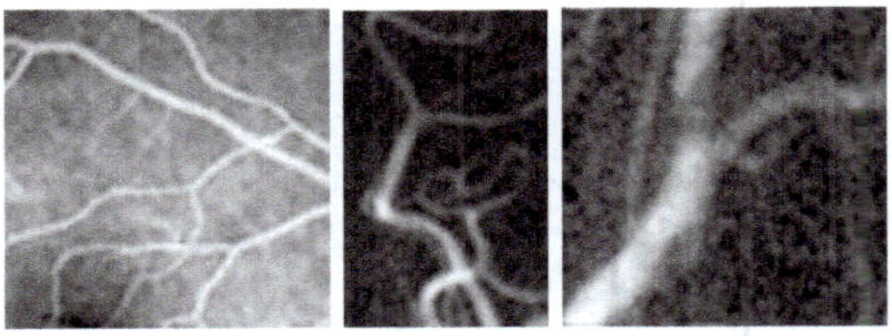

(a) (b) (c)

Fig. 2. (a) 128 × 128 retinal angiography. The intensity variation of vessel and background causes the gradient of vessel boundaries varying in different regions (top and bottom portion of the image). (b) 80 × 128 DSA. Intensity of the object is dropped at the Y-shape and circular structure at the middle of the image. (c) 128 × 128 DSA. A portion of the vessel has relatively lower intensity than the other parts.

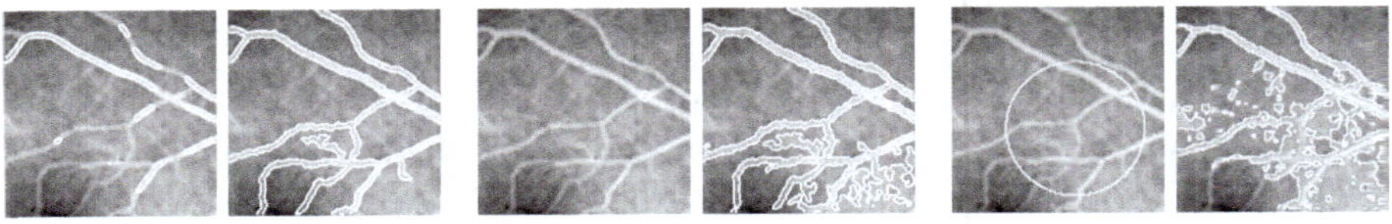

(a) (b) (c)

Fig. 3. Left: Initial contours. Right: Final results. (a): FM with $r = 1, 2, 3$, image is preprocessed with $G_{\sigma=0.8}$, initial contour obtained automatically from regions with the highest 5% inward flux which is further smoothed under curvature flows for 200 steps. (b): ACM-EI, the image is preprocessed with $G_{\sigma=0.8}$, manually selected initial contour. (c): ACWE with $\mu = 0.000\ 01 \cdot 255^2, \lambda_1 = \lambda_2 = 1, \nu = 0, h = 1$, manually selected initial contour.

and one retinal angiography [9]. Comparison is performed between the proposed method with three different approaches including "Flux Maximizing Geometric Flows" (FM) [5], "A New Active Contour Method based on Elastic Interaction" (ACM-EI) [6] and "Active Contours without Edges" (ACWE) [7].

The first example (Fig.2a) shows a retinal angiography. The background intensity is generally lower in left-bottom, left-top and right-top regions. Since the ACWE method partitions the image into high intensity group and low intensity

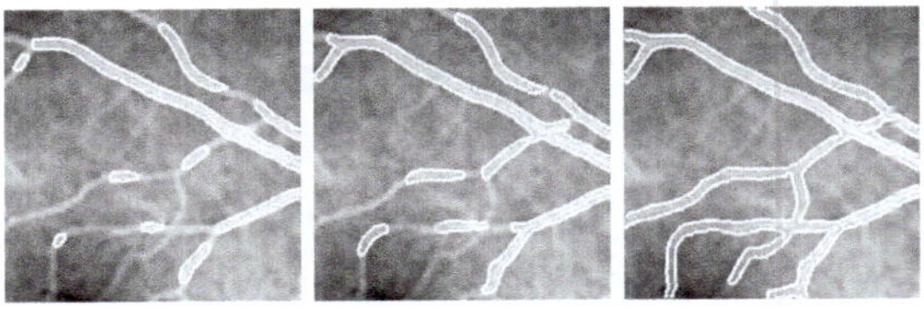

Fig. 4. Result of the proposed method using $\sigma_x = 1.6$ and $\sigma_y = 0.8$. Left: Initial contour obtained automatically from regions with the highest 5% field value which is further smoothed under curvature flows for 200 steps. Middle: Intermediate step. Right: Final result.

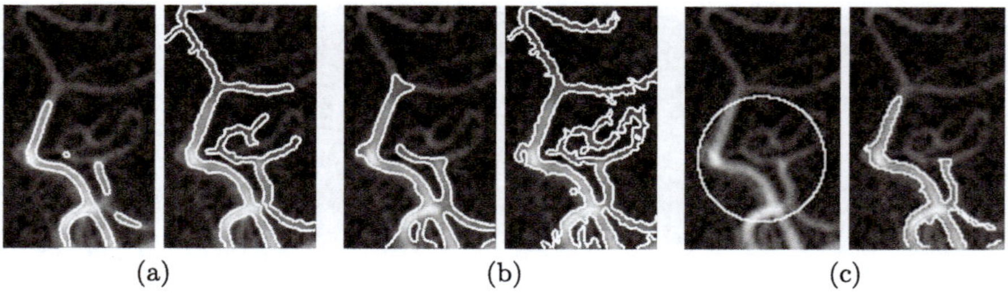

Fig. 5. Left: Initial contours. Right: Final results. (a): FM with $r = 1, 2, 3$, image preprocessed with $G_{0.8}$, initial contour obtained automatically from regions with the highest 10% inward flux which is further smoothed under curvature flows for 200 steps. (b): ACM-EI initial contour obtained automatically using the heuristic approach presented in [6] with $\sigma_1 = 0.8$ and $\sigma_2 = 10$. (c): ACWE with $\mu = 0.000\,01 \cdot 255^2, \lambda_1 = \lambda_2 = 1, \nu = 0, h = 1$, manually selected initial contour.

group, it cannot give a satisfactory result as the low intensity vessel is excluded from the contour while high intensity background is included (Fig.3c).

On the other hand, ACM-EI tends to ignore weak edges when strong edges are present. Therefore, the contour is guided by noise and leaks through blurred boundaries at the bottom of the image (Fig.3b). We have manually placed the initial contour of ACM-EI inside the blood vessel as the heuristic approach in [6] cannot locate the vessel position in this low contrast situation. FM selects initial contour correctly and indicates side vessel as well (Fig.3a). In contrast, our method favors smooth contour and keeps branches be connected without leakage. Fig.4 shows that our method locates the main vessel correctly, and can handle intensity variation in the object and background regions because of the calculation of minimal variance in a localized manner. It also avoids leakages in the low contrast regions since edges are extended along its direction.

In Fig.2b, we have shown a DSA where the intensity of the object is dropped significantly at two positions (the Y-shape structure and the circular structure at the middle of the image). As shown in Fig.5c, similar to the results previously shown, ACWE cannot capture objects in the dim regions. Besides, as shown

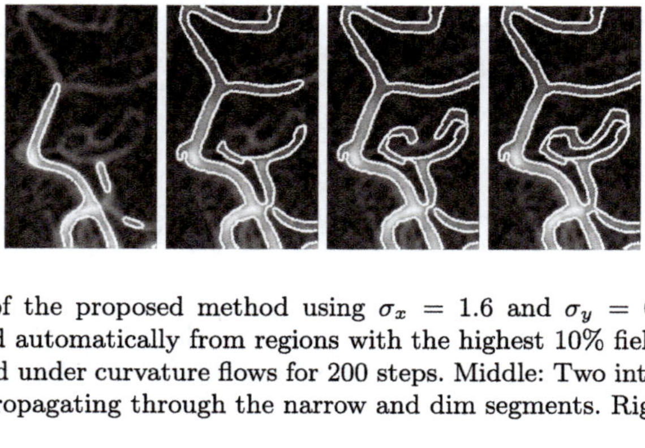

Fig. 6. Result of the proposed method using $\sigma_x = 1.6$ and $\sigma_y = 0.8$. Left: Initial contour obtained automatically from regions with the highest 10% field value which is further smoothed under curvature flows for 200 steps. Middle: Two intermediate steps, the contour is propagating through the narrow and dim segments. Right: Final result.

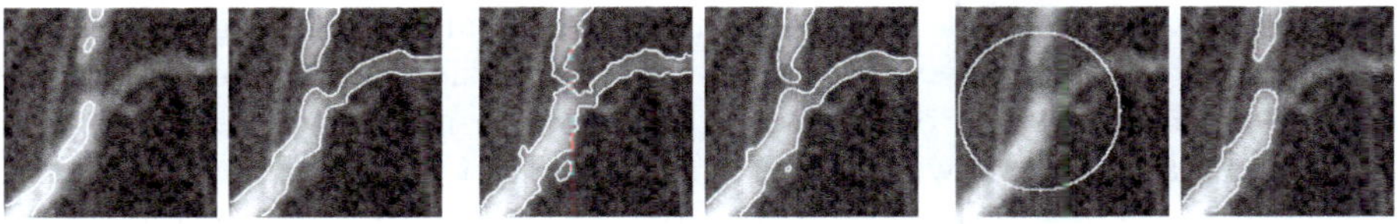

(a) (b) (c)

Fig. 7. Left: Initial contours. Right: Final results. (a): FM with $r = 4, 5, 6, 7$, image pre-processed with $G_{\sigma=3}$, initial contour obtained automatically from regions with the highest 5% inward flux which is further smoothed under curvature flows for 200 steps. (b): ACM-EI, initial contour obtained automatically using the heuristic approach presented in [6] with $\sigma_1 = 3, \sigma_2 = 10$. (c): ACWE with $\mu = 0.4 \cdot 255^2, \lambda_1 = \lambda_2 = 1, \nu = 0, h = 1$, manually selected initial contour.

in Fig.5a, the contour of FM is halted when the gradient along the vessel is comparable to the gradient of object boundaries.

ACM-EI can capture the vessel but the result is noisy (Fig.5b), although it is the best results obtained among different combinations of parameters. The contour follows the noisy regions attached to the vessels rather than the weak vessel boundaries. Increasing either the σ of the Gaussian filter or curvature term as authors suggested in [6] dose not help and results in contour halted at dim or narrow parts. In contrast, our method extends boundaries along their direction to recover the discontinued boundaries over dim and tiny segments. Thus, the contour can propagate through the dim and narrow regions (Fig.6).

The last example (Fig.2c) shows a vessel with a dim portion. It aims to examine the ability of different approaches to connect a gap, which has size comparable to the object width. FM, ACM-EI and ACWE cannot merge the contours across the portion with low intensity value (Figs.7a, b and c). The value of σ of the Gaussian filter being used in ACM-EI and FM cannot be too large. Otherwise, they cannot handle the narrow branch at the right portion

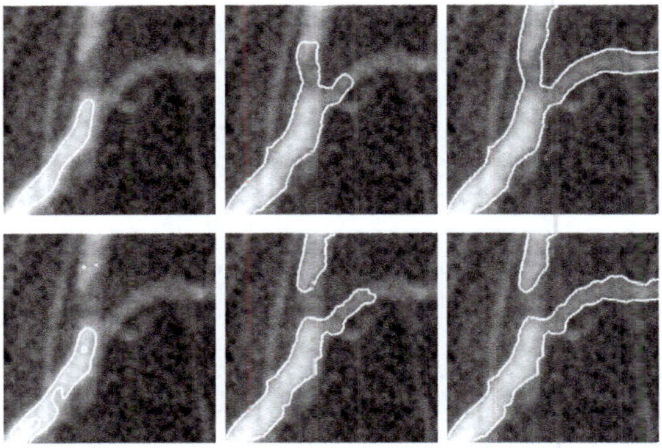

Fig. 8. Results of the proposed method using $\sigma_x = \sigma_y = 3$ in the top row and $\sigma_x = 1, \sigma_y = 3$ in the bottom row. Left: Initial contour obtained automatically from regions with the highest 5% field value which is further smoothed under curvature flows for 200 steps. Middle: Intermediate step. Right: Final result.

of the image. ACWE fails to detect the narrow branch using different values of μ because of the significant intensity variation. Therefore, we only show the result with a large value of μ, in which contour is not halted far away from vessel boundaries, as shown in Fig.7c. It shows that ACWE cannot recognize the vessel as a single object. Here the proposed method is able to connect the top and bottom portions of the vessel (Fig.8a). As mentioned in Section 2.2, a small value of σ_x can be used to reduce the strength of boundary extension. We have demonstrated to use a small value of σ_x for identifying the target region as separated objects in (Fig.8b).

4 Conclusion

This paper proposed a new vector field for the detection of objects with narrow and elongated structures. The field is incorporated in the active contour models. The direction of boundaries is estimated based on the minimal weighted local variance condition, which extrapolates edges along their direction so that disconnected boundaries can be linked. In the experiments, the proposed method has been validated and compared to three different approaches. It is shown that the proposed method can effectively prevent contour leakage or discontinuity, which may happen in the segmentation of narrow structures with low contrast boundaries. Finally, our method is robust to intensity variation inside objects and background regions.

Acknowledgment. The authors would like to thank Dr. Yu of the Department of Diagnostic Radiology and Organ Imaging, Prince of Wales Hospital, Hong Kong, for providing the DSA images.

References

1. C. Xu and J. Prince, "Snakes, shapes, and gradient vector flow," *IEEE T. Image Processing*, (7):359-369, 1998.
2. M. Kass, A. Witkin, and D. Terzopoulos, "Snakes: Active contour models," *Intern. J. Computer Vision*, (1):321-331, 1988.
3. R. Malladi, J. Sethian, B. Vemuri, "Shape modeling with front propgagtion: A level set approach," *IEEE T. PAMI.*, (17):158-175, 1995.
4. S. Osher, J. Sethian, "Fronts propagating with curvature dependent speed: algorithms based on hamilton-jacobi formulations," *J. Comp. Phys.*, (79):12-49, 1988
5. A. Vasilevskiy, K. Siddiqi, "Flux Maximizing Geometric Flows" *IEEE T. PAMI.*, (24):1565-1578, 2002.
6. Y. Xiang, A.C.S. Chung, J. Ye, "A New Active Contour Method based on Elastic Interaction," *IEEE Conf. CVPR.*, (1):452-457, 2005.
7. T.F. Chan, L.A. Vese, "Active Contours without Edges," *IEEE T. Image Processing*, (10):266-277, 2001.
8. D. Marr, E. Hildreth, "Theory of Edge Detection," *Proc. Royal Soc. of London*, (B207):187-217, 1980.
9. Bonnie M. Gauer, OD, MS, "Using Fluorescein Angiography To Assess Retinal Disease," *http://www.opt.pacificu.edu/ce/catalog/12059-PS/FA.html*

A New Active Contour Model: Curvature Gradient Vector Flow

Jifeng Ning[1,2], Chengke Wu[1], Shigang Liu[1], and Peizhi Wen[1]

[1] Xidian University, National Key Laboratory of ISN, 710071, Xi'an, China
jf_ning@sina.com, ckwu@xidian.edu.cn, xdlsg@hotmail.com
[2] Northwest A&F University, College of Information Engineering, 712100, Yangling, China

Abstract. The paper presents a new external force field for active contour model, which is called CGVF (Curvature Gradient Vector Flow). CGVF improves on classical GVF by simplifying the formulas and increasing the item of curvature, so that the edge information can be kept well and diffused more quickly. Several standard images are used to segmenting experiments, and the results show that CGVF has obvious advantages compared with GVF in the iteration number of force field, the evolvement number of curve and the accuracy of convergence. In particular, when the initial curve is far from the edge of object, the convergence will be more superior.

1 Introduction

The variational method has been a research focus of image processing in recent years [1,2,3,6,11,12,13,15]. Notably active contours, know as *snakes*, have been widely studied and applied, their applications mainly include edge detection [17], segmentation of objects [10,18], shape modeling [6] and motion tracking [14]. Active contours were first introduced in 1988 by Kass et al[1]. They are closed curves or surfaces expressed by parametric equation. An energy function is associated with these curves, which convert the problem of finding objects into the process of energy minimizing. Affected by both internal force and external force, the parametric curves move to the direction of minimum energy. The internal force is decided by the curves themselves, and the external force is decided by the image, so the external force is also called *imageforce*. The traditional force field has small capture range, and is sensitive to the initial snake curve. In order to enable the curves to converge the edge of objects rapidly, many improved models of image force field were put forwarded. Cohen [4] presented the balloon model in 1991, which enlarges the capture range of snakes, but could not enter into the concavities of the objects' edge. Additional, external forces defined as the negative gradient of a Euclidean distance map were widely used [5].

Xu et a.l [7, 8] proposed a new external force model, known as GVF, which uses a spatial diffusion of the gradient of an edge map of the image to create a dynamic force field. It solves perfectly the flaw of small capture range of traditional snakes' model, and can go into the concavities of the objects' edge in

P.J. Narayanan et al. (Eds.): ACCV 2006, LNCS 3851, pp. 633–642, 2006.

principle. And so far, GVF has been the most popular external force model. However, sometimes GVF enter into the concavities with low speed, or even could not do, which induced relatively poor efficiency of GVF.

This paper presents a new external force field for active contour model, which is called CGVF (Curvature Gradient Vector Flow). CGVF improves on classical GVF by simplifying the formulas and increasing the item of curvature, so that the edge information can be kept well and diffused more quickly, which made this force field could enter into the concavities of image edge with higher speed and accuracy than GVF did.

2 Active Contour Model

2.1 Snakes

In 2D, snake is a curve $c(s) = (x(s), y(s), s \in [0,1])$ that moves through the spatial domain of an image to minimize the energy functional:

$$E_{snakes} = \int_0^1 \frac{1}{2}(\alpha|c'(s)|^2 + \beta|c''(s)|^2) + E_{ext}(c(s))ds \tag{1}$$

where α and β are weighting parameters that control the snake's tension and rigidity, respectively, and $c'(s)$ and $c''(s)$ denote the first and second derivatives of $c(s)$ with respect to s. The external energy function E_{ext} is derived from the image, and it takes on its smaller values at the features of interest, such as boundaries. Given a gray-level image $f_0(x,y)$, viewed as a function of continuous position variables (x,y), typical external energies designed to lead an active contour toward step edges [1] are

$$E^1_{ext}(x,y) = -|\nabla f_0(x,y)|^2 \tag{2}$$

$$E^2_{ext}(x,y) = -|\nabla[G_\sigma(x,y) * f_0(x,y)]|^2 \tag{3}$$

where $G_\sigma(x,y)$ is a two-dimensional Gaussian function with standard σ and ∇ is the gradient operator.

In (3), large σ will increase snake's capture range, but it will blur the image edge at the same time, which causes inaccurate location of snakes. This is the defect of traditional external energy.

In (1), A snake that minimizes E must satisfy the Euler equation:

$$\alpha c''(s) - \beta c''''(s) - \nabla E_{ext} = 0 \tag{4}$$

This can be viewed as a force balance equation

$$F_{int} + F_{ext} = 0 \tag{5}$$

where $F_{int} = \alpha c'' - \beta c''''(s)$ and $F_{ext} = -\nabla E_{ext}$.

The traditional snakes are intrinsically weak in three main aspects:

(1) They are very sensitive to parameters.

(2) They have small capture range and the convergence of the algorithm is mostly dependent of the initial position.

(3) The have difficulties in going into boundary concavities.

2.2 GVF(Gradient Vector Flow)

Xu et al [7, 8] proposed famous external force field, known as GVF which has large capture range. GVF is the vector field $V(x,y) = [u(x,y), v(x,y)]$, which minimizes the energy functional:

$$Q = \int\int \mu(u_x^2 + u_y^2 + v_x^2 + v_y^2) + |\nabla f|^2 |V - \nabla f\ ^2 dxdy \tag{6}$$

where f is the result of the original image processed by edge detect operator and μ is weighting parameters.

Using the calculus of variations, it can be shown that the GVF field can be found by solving the following Euler equations:

$$\mu\nabla^2 u - (u - f_x)(f_x^2 + f_y^2) = 0, \mu\nabla^2 v - (v - f_y)(f_x^2 + f_y^2) = 0 \tag{7}$$

where ∇^2 is the Laplacian operator.

GVF is a dynamic force field, which diffuses along the directions of x and y of image gradient simultaneously, and could remain the image's edge information well after numerous iterations. GVF has favorable convergence and could enter into the concavities of the objects' edge in principle, so it has been one of the models which are used most wildly. However, the diffusion speed of the edge information of GVF is very low, consequently, only after a large number of iterations can the force field go into the concavities of the objects' edge, which will lose some edge information and deduce the accuracy of segmentations and performances of force field.

Xu et al[9] have improved the GVF and proposed GGVF in 1998. However, there is no essential difference between GGVF and GVF. The force field of GGVF still could be derived from two partial differential equations and enters into the concavity of edge after substantial iteration numbers.

3 Proposed Model

3.1 Curvature Gradient Vector Flow

Because the concavities of the objects' edge have large curvature, if taking into account of edge curvature when generating force field, the edge information will be remained and could diffuse with higher speed. Based on the above idea, CGVF is proposed:

$$\nabla^2 I + w_1 k - w_2 f^2 (I - f) = 0 \tag{8}$$

$$k = \nabla \cdot \frac{\nabla I}{|\nabla I|} = div(\frac{\nabla I}{|\nabla I|}) \tag{9}$$

where k is the curvature of image edge map, and w_1, w_2 are weighting parameters.

In GVF, the concavity edge's the same diffusion coefficient as other edge's. However, the additive curvature k in the CGVF force field equation (8) behaves as increasing the weight of concavity edge, which makes edge map of concavity diffuse faster than that of other edge map. Minimal energy functional corresponding to equation(8) is:

$$E_{CGVF} = \int\int |\nabla I|^2 + w_1|\nabla I| + w_2 f^2 (I - f)^2 dxdy \tag{10}$$

$$I_0 = f(x, y) \tag{11}$$

where I_0 is are initial value of I, and $f(x, y)$ is the edge information of original image.

Equation (8) can be solved, then calculate the gradient of I, and the corresponding CGVF field is obtained:

$$[CGVF_x, CGVF_y] = -\nabla I \tag{12}$$

Contrast with two force fields by equation (7) and (8), we can see that the classical GVF is generated by two partial differential equations, while there is only one equation to generate CGVF, and CGVF still has favorable properties.

3.2 Numerical Implementation

Equations (8) can be solved by treating u as functions of time and solving:

$$I_t(x, y, t) = \nabla^2 I(x, y, t) + w_1 \nabla \cdot \frac{\nabla I(x, y, t)}{|\nabla I(x, y, t)|} - w_2 f^2 (I(x, y, t) - f) \tag{13}$$

$$I(x, y, 0) = f(x, y) \tag{14}$$

The steady-state solution of this linear parabolic equation is the desired solution of the Euler equation (13).

The discrete process of (13) is:

$$I_t = \frac{I_{i,j}^{n+1} - I_{i,j}^n}{\triangle t} \tag{15}$$

$$\nabla^2 I = \frac{I_{i+1,j}^n + I_{i,j+1}^n + I_{i-1,j}^n + I_{i,j-1}^n - 4I_{i,j}^n}{\triangle x \triangle y} \tag{16}$$

$$|\nabla I| = \sqrt{I_x^2 + I_y^2} \tag{17}$$

$$k = \nabla \cdot \frac{\nabla I}{|\nabla I|} = \frac{I_{xx} I_y^2 - 2 I_x I_y I_{xy} + I_{yy} I_x^2}{(I_x^2 + I_y^2)^{\frac{3}{2}}} \tag{18}$$

$$I_{i,j}^{n+1} = I_{i,j}^n + \triangle t[\frac{I_{i+1,j}^n + I_{i,j+1}^n + I_{i-1,j}^n + I_{i,j-1}^n - 4I_{i,j}^n}{\triangle x \triangle y} + w_1 k - w_2 f_{i,j}^2 (I_{i,j}^n - f_{i,j})] \tag{19}$$

where indices i, j and n correspond to x, y and t, respectively, and let the spacing between pixels be $\triangle x$ and $\triangle y$, and time step for each iteration be $\triangle t$. In the image domain, $\triangle x = \triangle y = 1$. According to CFL condition, when $\triangle t < \frac{1}{4}$, equation(19) will converge.

I could be derived from equation (19), then calculate the gradient of I by central difference, and the gradient is the CGVF:

$$CGVF_x^{i,j} = -\frac{1}{2}(I_{i+1,j} - I_{i-1,j}), CGVF_y^{i,j} = -\frac{1}{2}(I_{i,j+1} - I_{i,j-1}) \tag{20}$$

Now the equation(5) can be rewrote as :

$$F_{int} + F_{CGVF} = 0 \tag{21}$$

4 Experimental Results

We compare the force filed properties and the segmentation effects of GVF with those of CGVF using Matlab6.5.

The parameters of the experiments as follows:

$\alpha = 0.05, \beta = 0, r = 1, k = 0.6, d_{min} = 0.5, d_{max} = 2, w_1 = 0.05, w_2 = 0.5$

4.1 The Comparison of Performance

In this paper, we test fig1.a with the size of 64×64-pixel. The force fields of GVF and CGVF after 30 iterations are showed respectively.

Fig.1b and Fig. 1c show that GVF and CGVF have similar properties. Both of them are global force fields and can maintain the image's edge map. However, Fig.1 (b) implies that GVF force field is close to horizontal in the rectangle on the image, which will not lead snake curve to convergence the concavity of image unless increase the iteration number of GVF force field Whereas Fig.1 (c) suggests that CGVF field in the rectangle on the image points to the concavity of edge, which induces snake curve can convergence more quickly to the concavity of image.

4.2 Image Segmentation

Five typical images are selected to contrast the segmentation accuracy between GVF and CGVF.

4.2.1 Image Without Noise

Fig.2 (a) is evolved by initial curve. The iteration numbers of two force fields are 40 respectively. As for GVF, the curve will converge after 165 evolvements, whereas, to CGVF, the curve only needs 100 evolvements. The processes of the curve's evolvements show that the convergence speeds of GVF and CGVF are nearly same when the initial curves are far from the object's edge, but as the curves enter into the concavities of images edge, the speed of convergence of CGVF is obviously faster than that of GVF, which also could be seen visually from the force fields of Fig.1.

Therefore, in the following experiments, we will focus on comparing the segmentation accuracy of CGVF with that of GVF.

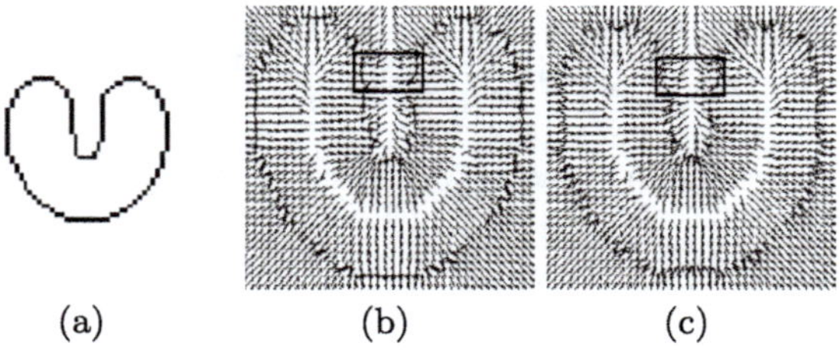

Fig. 1. GVF and CGVF force field; (a) Original image; (b) GVF field; (c) CGVF field

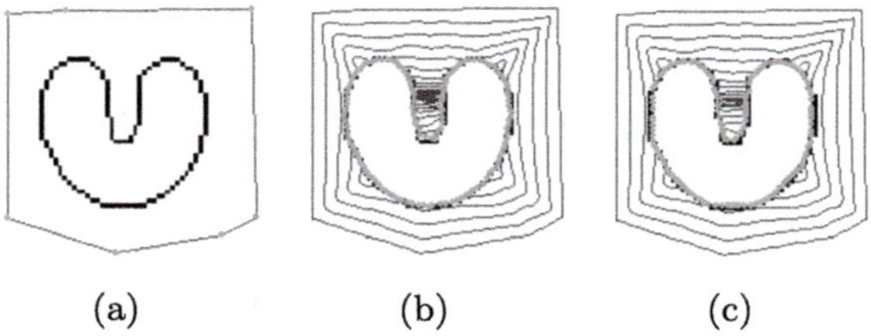

Fig. 2. (a) Initial curve; (b) Segmenting by GVF; (c) Segmenting by CGVF

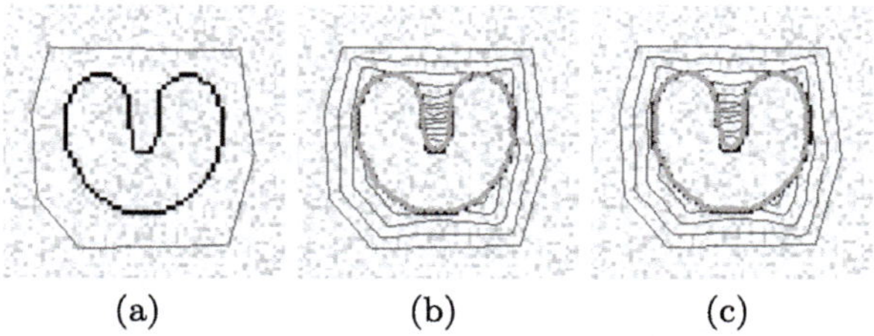

Fig. 3. Image with speckle noise(σ=0); (a) Initial curve; (b) Segmenting by GVF; (c) Segmenting by CGVF

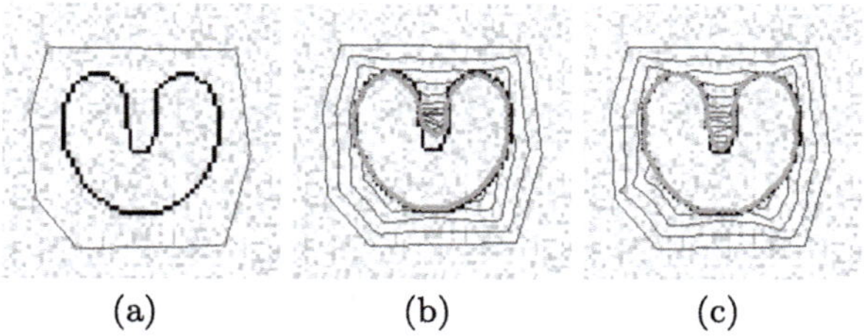

Fig. 4. Image with speckle noise(σ=1.5); (a) Initial curve; (b) Segmenting by GVF; (c) Segmenting by CGVF

4.2.2 Images with Noise

The paper contrasts the abilities of restraining different types of noise between GVF and CGVF from two aspects: one is segmenting images directly without preprocessing; the other is segmenting images after removing noise by Gaussian function.

The Gaussian function is:

$$f(x, y) = |G_\sigma(x, y) * f_0(x, y)| \tag{22}$$

where f_0 is orginal image.

In the following experiments, for compare, we let σ =1.5 Δt=0.2.

Fig.3a is not preprocessed. We can see from Fig.3(b)-(c) that for the image with speckle noise, both CGVF and GVF will have perfect segmentation results.

Fig.4a is filtered by Gaussian function. Although the noise is restrained in some extent, it causes some losses in the edge maps of the images. The segmentation results show that segmentation by CGVF is more accurate than segmentation by GVF.

Fig.5a is not preprocessed. The segmentation results tell us that the salt noise has different effects to GVF and CGVF. In the GVF force field, the curve will be attracted by some isolated noise spots, so it won't converge; while in the CGVF force field, the curve is still able to converge to the concavities of the image.

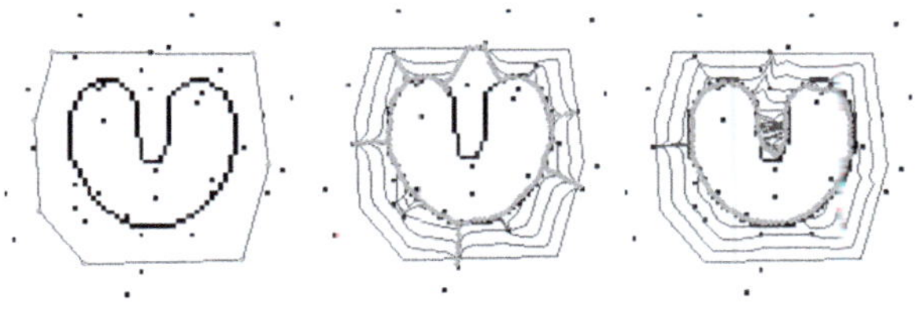

(a) (b) (c)

Fig. 5. Image with salt noise(σ=0); (a) Initial curve; (b) Segmenting by GVF; (c) Segmenting by CGVF

Fig. 6a suggests that after the image is filtered by Gaussian function, the salt noise has little effects on the segmentation results. When the curve is relatively far from the edge of the objects, both GVF and CGVF could converge, and the segmentation result of CGVF is obviously more accurate that that of GVF.

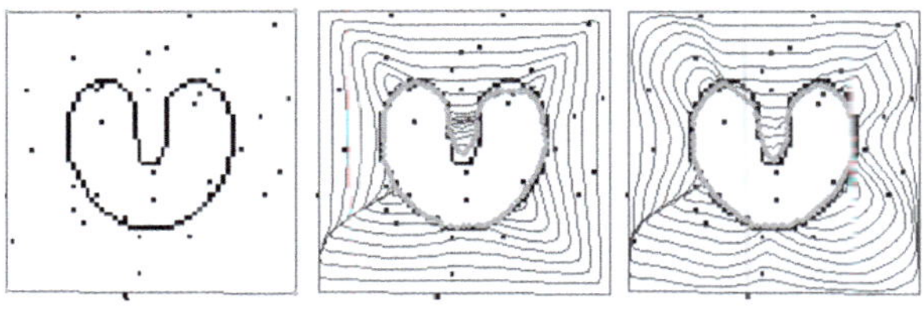

(a) (b) (c)

Fig. 6. Image with salt noise(σ=1.5); (a) Initial curve; (b) Segmenting by GVF; (c) Segmenting by CGVF

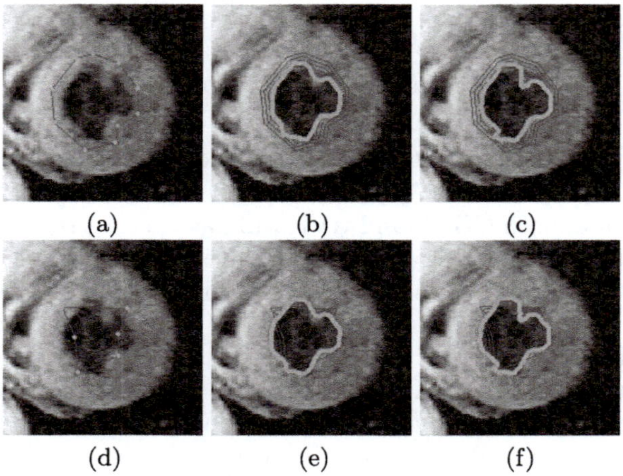

Fig. 7. Heart image; (a) initial curve1; (b) Segmenting by GVF; (c) Segmenting by CGVF; (d) Initial curve2; (e) Segmenting by GVF; (f) Segmentation by CGVF

Fig. 8. Dog image; (a)initial curve; (b) Segmenting by GVF; (c) Segmenting by CGVF

4.2.3 Real Images

Fig.7 and Fig.8 are medical image and natural image. We get the edge map of image by the (23) before segmenting:

$$f(x, y) = |\nabla[G_\sigma(x, y) * f_0(x, y)]| \tag{23}$$

where let $\sigma = 1.5$ In the following experiment,we let $\Delta t = 0.1$

Fig.7 shows that both GVF and CGVF are insensitive to the initial curves. However, as for the weak edge, CGVF could also converge well, whereas the convergence result of GVF is not very well. It suggests that CGVF can remain the edge map of the image perfectly.

As for the image with complex background, due to the disturbance by noise, it needs numerous iterations of force field when the initial curve is far from object, so the generated force field will lose some edge map. While Fig.8 shows that even after lots of force field iterations, CGVF could also remain the edge map of objects well, and the GVF could not do this.

5 Conclusions

CGVF, a new external force field for active contour model in our paper is presented. It deduces classical two GVF formulas to one and adds the item of curvature in the new model. Compared with GVF, CGVF keep the advantages of GVF and has more excellent properties. The edge map of image in the GVF force filed is remained, and at the same time it can diffuse with high speed, which makes the snake curve will converge to the concavities of image edge rapidly and accurately. In general, CGVF has great capture range and strong restrain ability to all kinds of noises, and is insensitive to the initial curve.

Acknowledgment

This paper was supported by NSFC(No.60473119). The authors would like to thank anonymous reviews for providing suggestions to improve the paper.

References

1. Kass M., Withkin A., Terzopoulos D., Snakes:Active contour models. Internat. J.Computer Vision. 1988, 321-331.
2. S.Osher, J.A.Sethian, Fronts propagating with curvature dependent speed: algorithms based on Hamilton-Jacobi formulations. J.Comput.Phys. 1988, 79, 12-49.
3. A.A. Amini,T.E. Weymouth, R.C. Jain, Using dynamic programming for solving variational problems in vision. IEEE Trans. Pattern Anal. Machine Intell. 1990, 12(9), 855-867.
4. T.F.Cohen, On active contour models and balloons. Comput.Vision Graph. Image Process(Image Understanding). 1991, 53(2), 211-218.
5. L.D.Cohen,I.Cohen, Finite-element methods for active contour models and balloons for 2-D and 3-D images. IEEE Trans.Pattern Anal. Machine Intell.. 1993, 15, 1131-1147.
6. R.Malladi,J.A. Sethian,B.C. Vermuri, Shape modeling with front propagation: a level set approach. Machine Intell, 1995, 17(2), 158-175.
7. C.Xu,J.L. Prince, Gradient vector flow: A new external force model for snakes. in IEEE Proc. Conf. on Computer Vision and Pattern Recognition. 66-71, 1997.
8. C.Xu,J.L. Prince, Snakes,shapes,and Gradient Vector flow. IEEE trans. Image Processing. 1998, 7, 359-369.
9. C.Xu,J.L. Prince, Generalized gradient vector flow external forces for active contours. Signal Processing. 1998, 71, 131-139.
10. Yuen P.C,Feng. G.C,Zhou,J.P., Contour detection method:Initialization and contour model. Pattern Recognition Letters. 1998, 20, 141-148.
11. A.Jain,Y.Zhong,M.Dubuisson-Jolly, Deformable template models: A review. Signal Processing. 1998, 71, 109-129.
12. Vicent Caselles,Jean-Michel Morel, Catalina Sbert, An axiomatic approach to image interpolation. IEEE trans. Image Processing. 1998, 7(3), 376-386.
13. J.A. Sethian, Level set methods and fast marching methods. Cambridge University Press. 1999, Cambridge.
14. Y.Zhong,A.K.Jain,M.Dubuisson-Jolly, Object tracking using deformable templates. IEEE Trans.Pattern Anal.Machiine Intell. 2000, 22, 544-549.

15. Park,j.,J.M. Keller, Snake on the watershed. IEEE Trans.Pattern Anal. Machine Intell. 2001, 23, 1201-1205.
16. Visen N.S.,N.S. Shashidhar,J.Paliwal,D.S.Jayas, Identification and segmentation of occluding groups of grain kernels in a grain sample image. J.Agric. Eng.Res. 2001, 79(2), 159-166.
17. T.F. Chan,L.A. Vese, Active contours without edges. IEEE Trans. Image Processing. 2001, 10(2), 266-277.
18. Y.-C. Wang, J.-J.Chou, Automatic segmentation of touching rice kernels with an active contour model. Transaction of ASAE. 2004, 47(5), 1803-1811.

Dynamic Open Contours Using Particle Swarm Optimization with Application to Fluid Interface Extraction

M. Thomas[1], S.K. Misra[2], C. Kambhamettu[1], and J.T. Kirby[2]

[1] Video/Image Modeling and Synthesis Lab, Dept. of Computer and Info. Sciences, University of Delaware, Newark, DE

[2] Center for Applied Coastal Research, Dept. of Civil and Env. Engineering, University of Delaware, Newark, DE

Abstract. This paper describes a method for the estimation of a dynamic open contour by incorporating a modified particle swarm optimization technique. This scheme has been applied to a "Particle Image Velocimetry" experiment for the analysis of fluid turbulence during a hydraulic jump. Due to inter reflections within the medium and refractions across different media interfaces, the imagery contains spurious regions, which have to be eliminated prior to the estimation of turbulence statistics at the fluid surface. The PIV image sequences provide a strict test bed for the performance analysis of this estimation mechanism due to the occurrence of intense specularity and extreme non-rigid motion dynamics.

1 Introduction

Edge detection and image segmentation is a crucial initial step in most computer vision applications prior to performing high-level tasks such as object recognition and scene interpretation. The presence of noise and other non-linearities imposes a strict restriction on this segmentation process. Since its formulation, the active contour model [1] tries to combine low level image information with high level structural information to provide a lucid description of the underlying structure in the presence of non-linearities. Usually this balance is brought about by two energy components, an internal energy component that characterizes the contour smoothness making it possible to estimate contour elements in places with incomplete image information and an external energy component that incorporates the low level image characteristics.

Among the variants of the active contour, notable ones include the greedy algorithm proposed by Williams and Shah [2], the balloon model by Cohen [3], the region based model by Ronfard [4] and the gradient vector flow based snake formulations by Xu and Prince [5]. Contour modeling via state space estimation was performed by Isard et al. [6] where the contour was represented as a state element and sequential importance sampling was used to track the contour state over time. Pérez et al. [7] described a contour extraction procedure,

P.J. Narayanan et al. (Eds.): ACCV 2006, LNCS 3851, pp. 643–652, 2006.

called Jetstream, that was also based on importance sampling with each contour location being used to compute the position of next contour location. Most active contour formulations depend on the availability of high image gradient for efficient processing. In image sequences with weak gradient information, these methods have difficulty in estimating the contour accurately. Statistical snakes as proposed by Ivins et al. [8] and the discriminant snakes proposed by Pardo et al. [9] tackle contour formulation by incorporating statistical information from the image and thus have been shown to be robust under noise and low gradient imagery.

In this paper, we attempt to extract a dynamic open contour that is built along the lines of the statistical snakes with multiple candidate hypotheses extracted from the image via a modified swarm optimization model. The swarm optimization scheme, "consume and move" has been developed to obtain multiple candidates, which could subsequently be used in computing the contour. The paper begins by giving a brief description of the interface extraction problem. This is followed by the description of the Particle Swarm Optimization model. The processing methodology that was developed for the minimization framework is described subsequently along with the results obtained from the algorithm. Finally, we present our conclusions and possible future directions.

2 Problem Description

In analyzing the salient structures in the velocity fields of incompressible turbulent fluid flows, such as water in confined channels [11], insertion of probes and measuring gauges into the fluid flow could create artificial turbulent deformations. In a regular Particle Image Velocimetry (PIV) experiment, the flow is seeded with suitable tracer particles, illuminated by a planar laser sheet and time-lapsed images are recorded. The displacement of the particles in the images is measured in the plane of the image, and is used to determine the flow (see [12] and the references therein). PIV has thus become an established non-

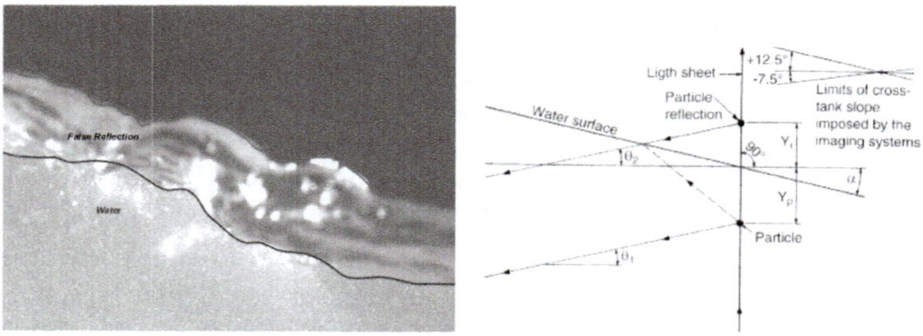

(a) (b)

Fig. 1. (a) Example of the interface extraction problem (b) Geometry of the problem - *Image taken from [10], Figure 4, page 432* intrusive measurement technique to measure the kinematics of turbulent fluid flow in controlled laboratory experiments.

It is often imperative to obtain detailed instantaneous flow velocities near the air-water (2-phase) interface, which necessitates an accurate estimation of the interface. This is inherently a difficult problem since most intensity based edge detection methods fail due to the presence of interface reflections in a PIV image [13]. Typically, the interface is concurrently visualized by a technique called Laser Induced Fluorescence (LIF) in which a fluorescent dye is added to one phase and excited to a particular wavelength by the laser thereby obtaining the interface as a sharp gradient at the specific wavelength[14]. A simultaneous PIV and LIF experiment therefore requires two separate imaging systems which add both complexity and cost to the entire estimation process.

Given the characteristics of fluid flow, the main problem that arises in estimating the interface from cross sectional images are the presence of badly defined boundaries that occurs due to the translucency of the fluid. The other problem that is often encountered is the presence of false regions of reflection (Fig. 1(a)). These regions occur due to the imaging device, which captures light undergoing total internal reflections from various sections in the fluid flow (Fig. 1(b)). Manual calculation of the interfaces remains a daunting task due to the large volume of data that is typically obtained in a regular PIV experiment. A robust, objective and automated method, which would be able to tackle these problems and calculate the interface solely based on the available image information, is thus very essential.

3 Processing Methodology

3.1 Particle Swarm Optimization

"Particle Swarm Optimization (PSO) is a population-based stochastic optimization technique for optimizing complex functions through the *interaction of individuals* in a population of particles." ([15], pp 2). The original formulation was proposed by Kennedy and Eberhart [16] and was based on the simulation of social behavior among flocks of birds. Each particle in the population (also called the swarm) adjusts its trajectory towards its own best position and towards the best position attained by the whole group [17]. The system dynamics are governed by the following equations.

$$\mathbf{v}_i^{(t)} = \omega \mathbf{v}_i^{(t-1)} + c_1\chi_1(\mathbf{p}_i^{(t-1)} - \mathbf{x}_i^{(t-1)}) + c_2\chi_2(\mathbf{g}^{(t-1)} - \mathbf{x}_i^{(t-1)}) \quad (1)$$

$$\mathbf{x}_i^{(t)} = \mathbf{x}_i^{(t-1)} + \mathbf{v}_i^{(t)} \quad (2)$$

where $\chi_1, \chi_2 \sim U[0,1]$ are two $N_s \times N_s$ diagonal matrices of uniform random numbers with N_s being the total number of particles in the swarm. ω is the "inertia weight" that regulates the trade-off between the global (wide-ranging) and the local (nearby) exploratory capabilities of the swarm [17]. $\mathbf{x}_i^{(t-1)}$ is the ith particle in the swarm at the $(t-1)^{th}$ iteration and $\mathbf{v}_i^{(t-1)}$ is its corresponding "velocity" component. $\mathbf{p}_i^{(t-1)}$ corresponds to the position of the best fitness value for the ith particle while $\mathbf{g}^{(t-1)}$ corresponds to the best fitness value for the entire swarm.

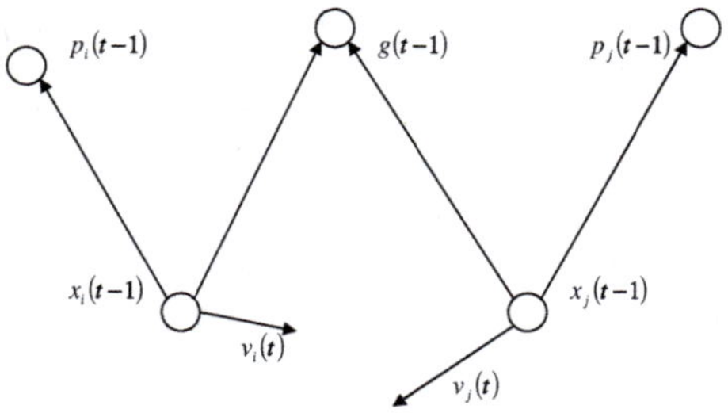

Fig. 2. Particle system in the Particle Swarm Optimization model for a two particle ($\mathbf{x}_i^{(t-1)}$ and $\mathbf{x}_j^{(t-1)}$) system

Among the three components of this dynamical equation, $\omega\mathbf{v}_i^{(t-1)}$ is the "inertial component", which constrains the velocity state estimate along the direction of $\mathbf{v}_i^{(t-1)}$. The second component, the "cognitive term" for each particle, $c_1\chi_1(\mathbf{p}_i^{(t-1)} - \mathbf{x}_i^{(t-1)})$ constrains the particle motion in the direction of its previous best value while the third component, the "social component", $c_2\chi_2(\mathbf{g}^{(t-1)} - \mathbf{x}_i^{(t-1)})$, directs the particles towards the best among all the elements in the swarm. The random variables χ_1 and χ_2 provide for the stochastic parameters for the search with c_1 and c_2 as two positive weights that control each of the components (Figure 2). An important aspect of PSO systems, for performing functional optimizations, is that the entire dynamical update is performed using additions and multiplications alone and is thus computationally very efficient.

"Explorers and Settlers" Paradigm. One of the variants to the particle swarm model was the "Explorers and Settlers" model as proposed by Kennedy and Eberhart [16]. In this paradigm, the swarm is composed of having two kinds of agents, the "explorers" and the "settlers". The "settlers" provided for micro-level function optimization of "known" regions of the problem domain while the "explorers" searched for regions outside for better "solutions". But as discussed by Kennedy and Eberhart [16] this scheme did not provide a significant improvement in the tests that they conducted.

In contrast, tackling the interface problem requires estimating multiple candidate hypothesis from a given search space so that the final open contour is drawn across the best possible candidates. To tackle this requirement we modified the "explorers and settlers" scheme to provide a mechanism for the swarm to continue in the exploratory phase after a goal is reached. This model, called the "consume and move", can be described in terms of migratory systems where the swarms continue moving in search for new pastures after the consumption of one specific region.

The essential principle of this model is to decrease the fitness metric of the search space after the swarm has converged at a specific goal $\mathbf{g}^{(t)}$. Depending on ω, c_1 and c_2, a subset of particles $x_i^{(t)}, i = \{1 \ldots N_1\}$ ($N_1 \leq N_s$), would converge to the best fitness value in the search space. For every particle $\mathbf{x}_i$ in the swarm, the fitness functional is cumulatively scaled down in proportion to the proximity of the particle to the goal. This scaling could be accomplished using the affinity function $\exp(-\|\mathbf{x}_i^{(t)} - \mathbf{g}^{(t)}\|^2/2\sigma^2)$ with the fitness at the position of the particles that coincide with the goal node being scaled more than the others. This scaling would thus "consume" the fitness functional to a greater extent at regions that are at a closer proximity to point of convergence of the swarm particles. Thus, iterating the search mechanism with this modified fitness space would constrain the swarm to "move" out and look for other possible candidate positions.

3.2 Contour Estimation

Kass [1] defined an active contour as a parametric contour $\mathbf{v}(s) = (x(s), y(s)), s \in [0, 1]$ that balances the internal energies E_{int} and the external energies E_{ext} (Eq. 3)

$$E^* = \int_0^1 [w_1 E_{int}(\mathbf{v}(s)) + w_2 E_{ext}(\mathbf{v}(s))] ds \quad (3)$$

where w_1 and w_2 are the weights that control the importance of one energy term over the other. Assuming a discrete approximation of Eq. 3, we have

$$E = \sum_{i=1}^{N} [\alpha E_{dist}(\mathbf{v}_i) + \beta E_{smo}(\mathbf{v}_i) + \gamma E_{ext}(\mathbf{v}_i)] \quad (4)$$

where α, β, γ are the weighting parameters, N is the number of discrete contour samples and

$$E_{dist}(\mathbf{v}_i) = \left| \frac{(\|\mathbf{v}_i - \mathbf{v}_{i-1}\| + \|\mathbf{v}_{i+1} - \mathbf{v}_i\|)}{\frac{2}{N-1} \Sigma_{j=2}^{N} \|\mathbf{v}_j - \mathbf{v}_{j-1}\|} - 1 \right|$$

$$E_{smo}(\mathbf{v}_i) = 1 - \cos(\theta_i) = 1 - \frac{(\mathbf{v}_{i+1} - \mathbf{v}_i) \cdot (\mathbf{v}_i - \mathbf{v}_{i-1})}{\|\mathbf{v}_{i+1} - \mathbf{v}_i\| \|\mathbf{v}_i - \mathbf{v}_{i-1}\|}$$

with θ_i being the smoothness term as defined in [18]. The external energy E_{ext} is derived from the image information and is usually the magnitude of the image gradient information.

Pixel Likelihood Estimation. The external energy term (E_{ext}) in a dynamic contour transfers the low level image information to the high level structural information. Most active contour methods are derived using the image gradient as the external energy constraint, but in images where the gradient is hard to estimate or the estimated gradient is inaccurate, the external energy functional has to be modeled using other image characteristics.

In a PIV image, the tracer particles have a distinct signature [19] which would enable a high-pass filter to approximately intensify the particle zones and

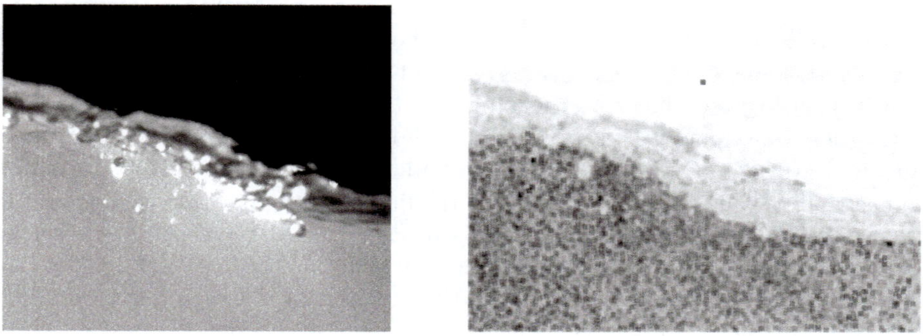

(a) (b)

Fig. 3. (a) Input PIV image (b) PIV image after PCA over the feature space

suppress the other regions. Local image statistics such as entropy, mean and standard deviation are extracted from the high-pass filtered image $I_{\mathcal{H}}$. Each of these features would provide information regarding the local data variation in $I_{\mathcal{H}}$. Principal Component Analysis (PCA) of this feature space is subsequently used to transform this space so as to maximize the data variation along individual eigen-directions. As shown in the figure 3(b), this PCA based transformation of the local image statistics provide a more succinct description of the underlying particle distribution.

In the PIV data, the likelihood that a pixel belongs to the surface was computed as the difference between the average intensity on the top and bottom of the pixel spatial position. Pixels very close to the actual surface, described a higher value of the likelihood as against the pixels elsewhere. This likelihood formed the fitness metric that was used in the "consume and move" swarm optimization strategy (section 3.1) to obtain multiple snaxel candidates.

Contour Optimization. Given the candidate hypotheses, finding the contour that minimizes the internal and external energy functional is performed using the dynamic programming (DP) approach as described by Amini et al. [20]. Depending on the pixel likelihood, different snaxels would have different hypotheses and thus energy minimization using DP is well-suited in tackling this contour optimization problem. The overall energy minimization would be achieved by minimizing the intermediate variables ξ_k such that

$$\mathbf{v}_k = \min \xi_k, \ k = 1 \dots N \tag{5}$$

under the constraint that

$$\xi_k = \xi_{k-1} + \min_{\mathbf{z}_k \in \mathcal{C}_k} \{E_{int}(\mathbf{z}_{k-1}, \mathbf{z}_k, \mathbf{z}_{k+1}) + E_{ext}(\mathbf{z}_k)\} \tag{6}$$

where $\mathbf{z}_k$ are the candidate snaxels positions and E_{int} and E_{ext} are the internal and external energies computed at each of the candidate positions $\in \mathcal{C}_k$. ξ_1 is initialized as the $\min_{\mathbf{z}_1 \in \mathcal{C}_1} E_{ext}(\mathbf{z}_1)$. The completion of the entire forward and reverse iterations of the DP presents the best possible positional estimates, $\mathbf{v}_k$.

4 Experimental Setup

The experiments were performed in a recirculating water tank that is sixteen feet long and one foot wide, with glass side walls and a solid bottom. The water was seeded with 14 μm silver coated hollow glass spheres and was pumped into the upstream end of the channel. A 120 mJ/pulse Nd-Yag New Wave solo laser source was mounted onto a custom-built submersible periscope which was lowered into the water so that the laser beam emerged as a planar light sheet parallel to the water tank wall. The flow was captured by a Kodak Megaplus 1.0 camera with a 1016 × 1008 pixel resolution (see [19] for details).

5 Results and Analysis

The algorithm that has been developed in the previous section has been tested on 1020 Particle Image Velocimetry image pairs. As can be easily seen these images are subject to extreme non rigid motion due to the fluid motion being captured and would thus be ideal in testing out the efficiency of the algorithm. The current implementation of the interface calculation is embedded in a hierarchical framework with coarse initial contours being used to guide subsequent finer contours. The entire process is iterated until the cumulative temporal variation of the contour elements, $\|\mathbf{v}_{1:N}(t-1) - \mathbf{v}_{1:N}(t)\|$ is $\leq 0.1N$, which is used as a metric to indicate the stabilization of the contour.

5.1 Quantitative Comparison

Due to the unavailability of ground truth, the result from the algorithm was assessed with respect to human perception. 10 randomly sampled PIV images were distributed among 4 participants with expertise in fluid dynamics. A short problem description was provided and the subjects were asked to find out the contour as they best perceived it. Since the inputs obtained from the subjects were sparse, a least square B-spline was used to compute the contour for the entire width of the image. In comparing the results of the algorithm with the output from the human participants, it is essential that the contours computed by the participants be considered as **NOT** significantly different from one another. It is also necessary to statistically show that the estimated contour does not significantly differ from those obtained from the participants. This analysis was accomplished using an independent sample one-way ANOVA. Figure 4(a) shows the box plots for the average contour variation across the 10 images for each of the participants (S1, S2, S3, S4). Figure 4(b) shows the average contour variation of the estimated contour in tandem with the output from the four participants. Also indicated are the corresponding p-values to provide a quantitative metric of similarity between the contours across the image pairs. The

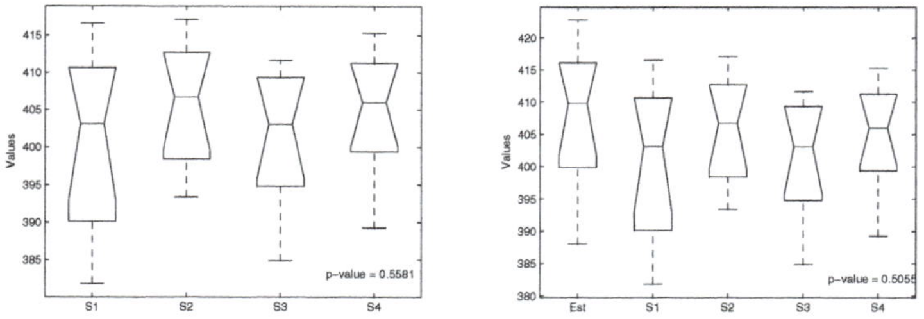

(a) (b)

Fig. 4. Results using the One-way ANOVA (a) Testing for inter subjects variability (p-value = 0.5581) (b) Testing if the estimated contour differed significantly from the "ground truth" contours (p-value = 0.5055)

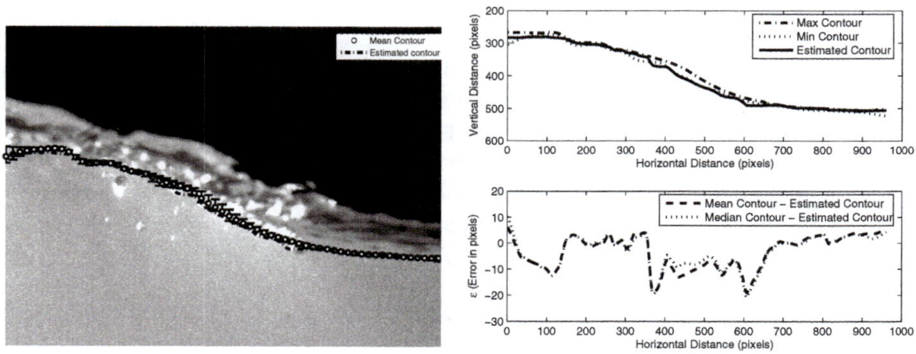

(a) (b)

Fig. 5. (a) Estimated contour points plotted in comparison with the mean variation of the "ground truth" contours (b) Mean and Median error deviation of the estimated contour

large p-values indicate that the individual sample means are not significantly different from one another or from the contour estimated by our algorithm.

Figure 5 is one of the test images (Contour 68) shown in conjunction with the error between the estimated contour and the mean of the contours from the 4 participants. The error bars show the maximum deviation from the mean and it is evident that the estimated contour falls within the upper and lower bounds of the contours obtained from the experts to a large extent. This method, thus provides a good initial estimate so as to apply free-surface kinematics to determine the exact position of the interface.

The algorithm was developed using MATLAB and has been tested with 1020 PIV images. Repeated trials indicate that the algorithm is stable and computationally efficient (The algorithm required $\sim$ 20 seconds to process a 128×960

Table 1. Error Analysis for 10 images, where the ground truth was extracted by the 4 subjects with expertise in fluid dynamics. The plot indicates the error variation ($\frac{1}{N}\sum_i^N \| \mathbf{x}_i - \mu_i \|$) between the contour estimated by the algorithm and the ground truth.

Contour	$Subject_1$	$Subject_2$	$Subject_3$	$Subject_4$
4	0.6527	0.6245	0.7504	0.7682
8	0.2791	0.2389	0.3310	0.3008
14	0.3493	0.3343	0.6700	0.6099
29	0.3550	0.5628	0.5312	0.5964
33	0.3687	0.2692	0.3573	0.4072
68	0.3998	0.2193	0.2364	0.2393
269	0.3503	0.4056	0.3093	0.3663
217	0.6549	0.3696	0.3262	0.3151
301	0.6733	0.2508	0.3732	0.4026
362	0.3813	0.3540	0.3454	0.3483

image, using $\sim$ 100 particles at each contour location). The average MSE, across the 10 images, are shown in Table 1 to further clarify the accuracy of the algorithm.

6 Conclusions

This paper describes a method to extract dynamic contours using particle swarm optimization and dynamic programming. The algorithm is robust and computationally efficient. The algorithm developed was applied to the free surface estimation in a 2-phase fluid flow using a PIV setup. Due to the lack of ground truth, the estimated contours have been compared with the results obtained from experts in the field of fluid dynamics. It has been observed that the estimated contour is not statistically different from the expert estimation. The method has now been tested over a sequence of 1020 PIV image pairs that have been further processed to compute instantaneous and ensemble average velocities at the interface.

References

1. Kass, M., Witkin, A., Terzopoulos, D.: Snakes: Active contour models. IJCV 1 (1988) 321–331
2. Williams, D.J., Shah, M.: A fast algorithm for active contours and curvature estimation. CVGIP: Image Underst. **55** (1992) 14–26
3. Cohen, L.D.: On active contour models and balloons. CVGIP **53** (1991) 211–218
4. Ronfard, R.: Region based strategies for active contour models. International Journal of Computer Vision **13** (1994) 229–251
5. Xu, C., Prince, J.L.: Snakes, shapes, and gradient vector flow. IEEE Transactions on Image Processing **3** (March 1998) 359–369

6. Isard, M., Blake, A.: Condensation – conditional density propagation for visual tracking. International Journal of Computer Vision **29(1)** (1998) 5–28
7. Pérez, P., Blake, A., Gangnet, M.: Jetstream: Probabilistic contour extraction with particles. In: ICCV. (2001) 524–531
8. Ivins, J., Porrill, J.: Statistical snakes: Active region models. In: Proc. British Machine Vision Conference. Volume 2. (1994) 377–386
9. Pardo, X.M., Radeva, P.: Discriminant snakes for 3d reconstruction in medical images. In: Proc. International Conference on Pattern Recognition (ICPR'00). Volume 4. (2000)
10. Peirson, W.L.: Measurement of surface velocities and shear at a wavy air-water interface using particle image velocimetry. Experiments in Fluids **23** (1997) 427–437
11. Zhong, J., Huang, T.S., Adrian, R.J.: Extracting 3d vortices in turbulent fluid flow. IEEE Transactions on Pattern Analysis and Machine Intelligence **20(2)** (1998) 193–199
12. Raffel, M., Willert, C., Kompenhas, J.: Particle Image Velocimetry, a Practical guide. Springer-Berlin (1998)
13. Lennon, J.M., Hill, D.F.: Particle image velocimetry measurements of undular and hydraulic jumps. Submitted to J. Hydraulic Engg. (2004)
14. Westerweel, J., Hofmann, T., Fukushima, C., Hunt, J.: Experimental investigation of the turbulent/non-turbulent interface at the outer boundary of a self-similar turbulent jet. Experiments in Fluids **33** (2002) 873–878
15. Battiti, R., Brunato, M., Pasupuleti, S.: Do not be afraid of local minima: Affine shaker and particle swarm. Technical report DIT-05-049, university of Trento, Italy (2005)
16. Kennedy, J., Eberhart, R.C.: Particle swarm optimization. In: Proceedings of IEEE International Conference on Neural Networks. (1995) 1942–1948
17. Parsopoulos, K.E., Vrahatis, M.N.: Particle swarm optimization method for constrained optimization problems. In: Proceedings of the Euro-International Symposium on Computational Intelligence. (2002)
18. Akgul, Y.S., Kambhamettu, C.: A coarse-to-fine deformable contour optimization framework. IEEE Transactions on Pattern Analysis and Machine Intelligence **25(2)** (2003) 174–186
19. Misra, S.K., Thomas, M., Kambhamettu, C., Kirby, J.T., Veron, F., Brocchini, M.: Estimation of complex air-water interfaces from PIV images. Experiments in Fluids (accepted for publication)
20. Amini, A., Weymouth, T., Jain, R.: Using dynamic programming for solving variational problems in vision. PAMI **12** (1990) 855–867

Attractor-Guided Particle Filtering for Lip Contour Tracking

Yong-Dian Jian[1], Wen-Yan Chang[1,2], and Chu-Song Chen[1,3]

[1] Institute of Information Science, Academia Sinica, Taipei, Taiwan
[2] Department of Computer Science and Information Engineering, National Taiwan University, Taipei, Taiwan
[3] Graduate Institute of Networking and Multimedia, National Taiwan University, Taipei, Taiwan
{ydjian, wychang, song}@iis.sinica.edu.tw

Abstract. We present a lip contour tracking algorithm using attractor-guided particle filtering. Usually it is difficult to robustly track the lip contour because the lip contour is highly deformable and the contrast between skin and lip colors is very low. It makes the traditional blind segmentation-based algorithms often fail to have robust and realistic results. But in fact, the lip contour is constrained by the facial muscles, the tracking configuration space can then be represented by a lower dimensional manifold. With this observation, we take some representative lip shapes as the attractors in the lower dimensional manifold. To resolve the low contrast problem, we adopt a color feature selection algorithm to maximize the separability between skin and lip colors. Then we integrate the shape priors and the discriminative feature into the attractor-guided particle filtering framework to track the lip contour. The experimental result shows that we can track the lip contour robustly and efficiently.

1 Introduction

Lip contour is useful information for human-machine interface application such as lipreading and facial expression analysis. However, there is a major problem with regard to robust lip contour extraction in practical situations: the boundary between the skin and the lip, particularly the lower lip, is often unclear. This problem makes the edge-based information unreliable.

To extract the lip contour, there are three techniques which can work independently or collaboratively. The first is blob-based approach which uses heuristic color threshold and morphological operations to find out the location and rough shape of the lip. However, the segmentation result is often very rough because there is no shape or smoothness constraint. Oliver et al. [1] used normalized red and green color to detect the blob of lip region. A sequence of the area and axis ratio of the blob area is classified by hidden Markov model (HMM) to perform facial expression recognition. Zhang et al. [2] used hue and edge information to achieve mouth localization and segmentation. The second approach is based on snake [3]. Although it takes smoothness and elasticity constraints into account,

P.J. Narayanan et al. (Eds.): ACCV 2006, LNCS 3851, pp. 653–663, 2006.

most of the time it is very difficult to tune the parameters of the snakes, and the snakes often converge to wrong results. Chan [4] converted RGB values to a single measurement with maximized discriminability between lip and skin color with Linear Discriminant Analysis (LDA). Wakasugi et al. [5] extended Chan's idea to region separability to direct the snake evolution. The control point of the snake searches the position with maximum region separability in the normal direction of the contour. Eveno et al. [6] used "jumping snakes" to detect several predefined control points at the first frame and uses optical flow to track the control points for the following frames. The third approach uses *a priori* shape knowledge to make the segmentation more robust and realistic. By designing a global shape model, the supplementary constraints ensure that the detected boundary belongs to possible lip shape space. For example, Cootes et al. [7] proposed the active shape models (ASMs) to model shapes with principal component analysis. In this method, a large training set is needed to cover the lip shape variability, and the images of this training set have to be cautiously calibrated. The tracking algorithm also uses edge-based information and iterative optimization procedures to make the control points converge to the right places. Matthews et al. [8] trained a 44-points ASM to track the visual features for lipreading.

However, most of the existing methods treat this problem as a detection framework without using temporal information. Instead of deterministic detection, a probabilistic propagation framework is introduced in this paper for lip contour extraction. In general, tracking the lip contour is difficult because lip is highly deformable and the edge and corner information are often unreliable. Isard et al. [9] introduced the concepts of particle filters for real-time tracking. But the required number of particles might grow exponentially due to the curse of dimensionality [10]. To overcome this problem, Wu et al. [11] collected some basis configurations to characterize the state subspace. The tracking configuration space can then be represented by a lower dimensional manifold. Chang et al. [12] introduced the concept of *attractor* to improve the tracking performance. For a visual tracking problem, attractors are some reference states and serve as prior knowledge to guide the tracking in a high-dimensional space.

In this paper, we introduce the concept of attractor-guided particle filtering for lip contour tracking. First, we manually segment some representative lip contours as the shape priors. We adopt the radial vector model [13] to represent the lip contours which can avoid the effort of manually labeling the control points as in the ASM method. Second, to boost the discriminability between lip and skin colors, we use the feature selection method proposed in [14]. It transforms the three dimensional RGB vector to an one dimensional feature value. Finally, we use a modified attractor-guided particle filtering framework to track lip contours. Kaucic et al. [15] shares the similar idea with this paper, but their state transition model is more similar to [11] where the state space is fully constrained by the training data.

The rest of the paper is organized as follows. Section 2 describes the lip contour model used in this paper. Section 3 introduces the attractor-guided particle filtering method and presents the details of our lip tracking algorithm. Experimental results are shown in Section 4 and we conclude this paper in Section 5.

2 Lip Contour Model

A snake is an open or closed elastic curve represented by a set of control points [3]. The evolution of the snake is guided by iteratively searching for a nearby local minimum of an energy function, which consists of the internal energy that imposes smoothness and continuity constraints on the snake curve and the external energy that indicates the degree of matching for the target features.

In practice, the snake may collapse or be trapped by spurious local minima because the edge information is often unreliable, that is, the boundary between lip and skin is not clear. To resolve this problem, we adopt the radial vector model [13] to generate some shape priors that serve as the prior knowledge to guide the tracking. The radial vectors are uniformly spread in 360°, and each of them originates from the centroid of the snake contour and links to a snake point. The shape of the contour is deformed by varying the lengths $(l_1, l_2, \ldots, l_n)$ of radial vectors and the centroid of the contour moves during the deformation. The angular interval θ controls the smoothness and the number of control points of the lip contour which equals to $n = \frac{360}{\theta}$. Figure 1 illustrates the radial vector model. There are two main advantages of using this representation. First, we can spare the labeling effort of control points as that in the ASM method which is often time consuming and prone to have inaccurate results. Second, we can easily control the dimension of state variables to compromise between tracking time and visual results.

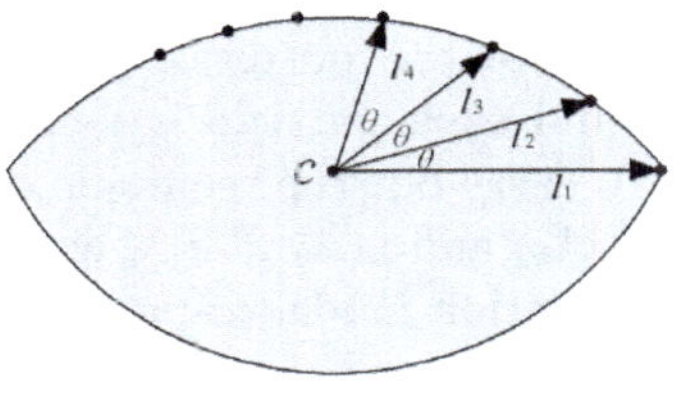

Fig. 1. Radial vector representation decomposes the lip contour into $(n = 360/\theta)$ control points. c is the centroid of the lip contour and l_i is the length of the i_{th} radial vector.

3 Attractor-Guided Particle Filtering Framework

In this paper, the radial vector and the centroid of the lip contour serve as the state variable for tracking. We also collect some lip contours in advance

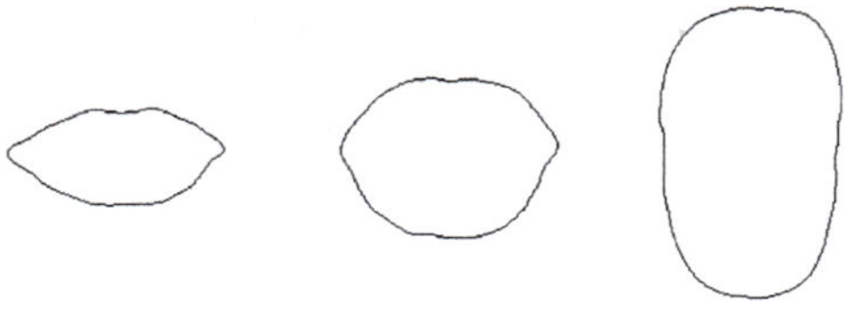

Fig. 2. Lip shape priors. From left to right, they are closed, half-open and full-open lip shapes respectively. Some of the shape priors will be dynamically selected as the attractors.

and represent them with the radial vector model. In our tracking algorithms, they will be regarded as the shape priors and we will dynamically select them as the attractors. Some of the manually segmented lip contours are shown in Figure 2.

3.1 Particle Filtering

Particle filtering is a successful technique in visual tracking. The idea of particle filtering [9] is to infer the marginal posterior distribution of the state $\mathcal{X}_t$ given the previous observation $\mathcal{Z}_{0:t}$. From the Bayes' formula and first-order Markov chain, a recursive form of the posterior probability can be derived as

$$p(\mathcal{X}_t|\mathcal{Z}_{0:t}) \propto p(\mathcal{Z}_t|\mathcal{X}_t) \int_{\mathcal{X}_{t-1}} p(\mathcal{X}_t|\mathcal{X}_{t-1})p(\mathcal{X}_{t-1}|\mathcal{Z}_{0:t-1}) \tag{1}$$

This recursive form allows us to use the posterior at time step $t-1$ as the prior for time step t. To compute the posterior probability, $p(\mathcal{X}_t|\mathcal{Z}_{0:t})$, a Bayesian optimal solution with an integral over all possible state values is formulated in [9]. However, it is computationally intractable. Particle filtering is the technique to efficiently approximate the posterior $p(\mathcal{X}_{t-1}|\mathcal{Z}_{0:t-1})$ by a finite set $\{X_{t-1}^k\}_{k=1}^K$ of K particles and each particle is associated with a weight π_{t-1}^k to form $\{X_{t-1}^k, \pi_{t-1}^k\}_{k=1}^K$. To carry out the recursion of particle filtering, we still need two probabilities, $p(\mathcal{Z}_t|\mathcal{X}_t)$ and $p(\mathcal{X}_t|\mathcal{X}_{t-1})$, which correspond to an observation model and a state transition model respectively.

3.2 Attractor-Guided Particle Filtering

The primary difficulty of the model-based tracking problem is because of the high degree of freedom (DoF). Searching in a high dimensional state space is highly inefficient due to the curse of dimensionality. Fortunately, the lip motion is constrained by the facial muscles, and then the tracking configuration space can be represented by a lower dimensional manifold. In the previous works of articulated hand tracking [11, 12], they integrate the hand motion constraints and appearance information to improve the tracking performance.

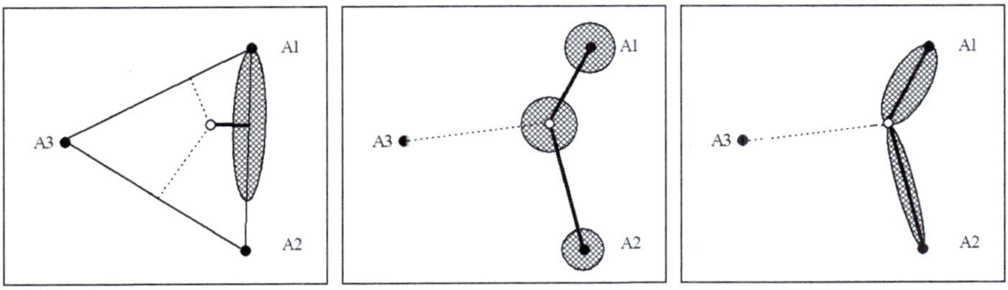

(a) Wu et al. [11] (b) Chang et al. [12] (c) The proposed method

Fig. 3. Difference of the three particle generation mechanisms. The white circle is the current state and the black circles are the predefined shape priors. The shaded area is where the corresponding algorithm generates its particles. The first approach finds out the linear manifold with minimum projection distance and generate particles around the projection point. In the second and third approaches, for example, two shape priors are selected as attractors. The second approach generates particles around the current state and the attractors. In the proposed method, we generate particles between the linear manifold spanned by the current state and the attractor.

In this paper, we apply this concept in lip contour tracking. Wu et al. [11] assumes that any intermediate state can be approximated by the linear manifold spanned by two nearest priors. The manifold with minimum Euclidean distance to the previous state is selected as the nearest one. The particles are then generated around the nearest manifold. Chang et al. [12] incorporated appearance information to find the possible attractors, and generate particles both around the previous state and the attractors. The attractors are some state variables whose appearance information are known in advance.

The algorithm presented in this paper combines the advantages of their methods. Let us note that, instead of using classical particle filtering (1) that allows no prior appearance information being incorporated into the probability propagation, we can formulate the attractor-guide particle filtering framework as in [12]

$$p(\mathcal{X}_t|\mathcal{Z}_{0:t},\mathcal{A}) \propto p(\mathcal{Z}_t|\mathcal{X}_t)\int_{\mathcal{X}_{t-1}} p(\mathcal{X}_t|\mathcal{X}_{t-1},\mathcal{A})p(\mathcal{X}_{t-1}|\mathcal{Z}_{0:t-1},\mathcal{A}) \qquad (2)$$

where $\mathcal{A}$ is the set of attractors. Note that the collected shape priors serve as the candidates for selecting the attractors in the state space. The proposed method generates particles around the manifold spanned by the previous state and the attractor. The first approach is constrained by the skeleton spanned by the shape priors, it forbids any state far away from the skeleton. The second approach retains the original formulation of particle filtering [9], but it independently emphasizes the importance of the previous state and the attractors. Figure 3 illustrates the difference between the three particle generation mechanisms.

3.3 Attractor-Guided Lip Contour Tracking Algorithm

The state variable is defined as $\mathcal{X}_t = (x_t, c_t)$, where $(x_t = \{l_1, l_2, \ldots, l_n\} \in \Re^n)$ represents the n radial vector defined in Section 2 and c_t is the centroid of the lip. The DoF of c_t depends on the behavior of head movement. The lip contour is piecewisely approximated by the cubic spline of any four consecutive control points. We define a $(m * m)$ window around the centroid of the contour as the interested area. Therefore, we can define the interior region for lip and exterior region for skin.

Since the colors of skin and lip are similar, we have to find out the most discriminative feature to separate the skin and lip region. Collins et al. [14] proposed a feature selection algorithm for tracking. We use their method to train a linear color projection function $w : I \rightarrow F$ such that the feature value $\mathcal{F} \equiv w(I) \equiv w(R, G, B) \equiv (w_1 R + w_2 G + w_3 B)$ has the most discriminability between skin and lip colors. Given a $(m * m)$ feature $\mathcal{F}$ image block, let $h_{lip}(i)$ be a histogram of the feature's value for pixels inside lip contour, and $h_{bg}(i)$ be a histogram for pixels from outside, where index i ranges from 1 to 2^b, the number of histogram bins. We form an empirical discrete probability density $A(\cdot)$ for the lip, and $B(\cdot)$ for the background, by normalizing each histogram by the number of elements in them. Collins et al. [14] defines a variance ratio (VR) to quantify the separability of $A(\cdot)$ and $B(\cdot)$ under feature $\mathcal{F}$. Our observation likelihood $p(\mathcal{Z}_t|\mathcal{X}_t)$ is defined as being proportional to the variance ratio between the interior and exterior histogram.

$$p(\mathcal{Z}_t|\mathcal{X}_t) \propto VR(A, B) \tag{3}$$

Figure 4 shows the comparison of gray level image and the proposed feature image.

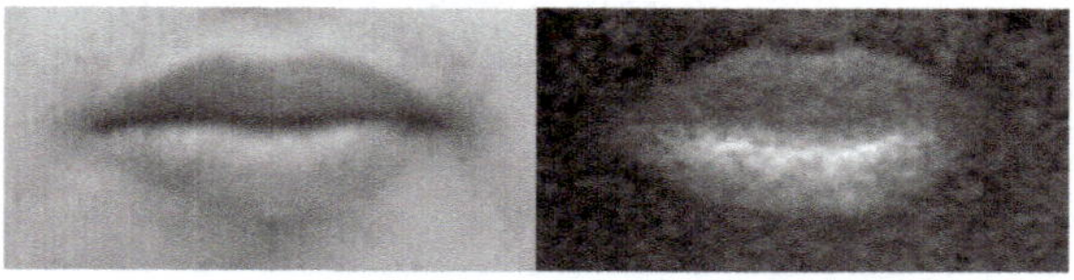

(a) gray level image **(b)** feature image

Fig. 4. Comparison of the gray level image and feature image

The state transition model is embedded in the manifold constructed by the current state and neighborhood attractors. Here we define

$$\mathcal{S} = \{\mathcal{S}_1, \mathcal{S}_2, \ldots, \mathcal{S}_M\}$$

as the collected shape prior set. At time t, first we have to select r most-likely attractors from $\mathcal{S}$ according the previous state x_{t-1} and current observation $\mathcal{Z}_t$.

To do this, we consider the probability $p(S_i|x_{t-1}, \mathcal{Z}_t), i = 1, \ldots, M$. Let β_t be a permutation sequence $(\beta_{t,1}, \beta_{t,2}, \ldots, \beta_{t,M})$ of $(1, 2, \ldots, M)$ such that

$$p(S_{\beta_{t,1}}|x_{t-1}, \mathcal{Z}_t) \geq \ldots \geq p(S_{\beta_{t,M}}|x_{t-1}, \mathcal{Z}_t)$$

The definition of probability $p(\mathcal{S}_{\beta_{t,i}}|x_{t-1}, \mathcal{Z}_t)$ depends on the tracking target, and it will reflect our knowledge of how to measure the similarity between shape prior and observation. Here we define this similarity by using the absolute area difference. Let $D_{t,i}$ be the absolute difference between the area of $\mathcal{S}_i$ and the segmented region by using the general lip color model [13]. The probability $p(\mathcal{S}_i|x_{t-1}, \mathcal{Z}_t)$ is defined as being proportional to

$$p(\mathcal{S}_i|x_{t-1}, \mathcal{Z}_t) \propto \left(\frac{D_{t,i}}{\sum_{i=1}^{r} D_{t,i}}\right)^{-1}$$

where r is the number of selected attractors from the shape prior set.

Then we can construct the attractor set $\mathcal{A}_t$ and its corresponding probability α_t as

$$\mathcal{A}_t = \{\mathcal{A}_{t,1}, \ldots, \mathcal{A}_{t,r}\} = \{S_{\beta_{t,1}}, \ldots, S_{\beta_{t,r}}\} \text{ and} \tag{4}$$

$$\alpha_t = \{\alpha_{t,1}, \ldots, \alpha_{t,r}\} = \frac{1}{\gamma_t}\{p(\mathcal{S}_{\beta_{t,1}}|x_{t-1}, \mathcal{Z}_t), \ldots, p(\mathcal{S}_{\beta_{t,r}}|x_{t-1}, \mathcal{Z}_t)\} \tag{5}$$

where $\gamma_t = \sum_{i=1}^{r} \alpha_{t,i}$.

After constructing $\mathcal{A}_t$ and α_t, the state transition model $p(\mathcal{X}_t|\mathcal{X}_{t-1}, \mathcal{A})$ in (2) is defined as

$$p(\mathcal{X}_t|\mathcal{X}_{t-1}, \mathcal{A}_t) = p(x_t, c_t|x_{t-1}, c_{t-1}, \mathcal{A}_t) = p(x_t|x_{t-1}, \mathcal{A}_t)p(c_t|c_{t-1}, \mathcal{A}_t) \tag{6}$$

and here we assume that the global and local movement of lip contour are independent. The local movement transition model is defined as a mixture of r component density functions, and each of them corresponds to one attractor as shown in the following:

$$p(x_t|x_{t-1}, \mathcal{A}_t) = \sum_{i=1}^{r} p(x_t|x_{t-1}, \mathcal{A}_{t,i}) \tag{7}$$

$$p(x_t|x_{t-1}, \mathcal{A}_{t,i}) = \alpha_{t,i} U(x_{t-1}, \mathcal{A}_{t,i})$$

where $U(\mathbf{a}, \mathbf{b})$ is a probability density function concentrated along the hyper line segment $\overline{\mathbf{ab}}$. The selection of $U(\mathbf{a}, \mathbf{b})$ implies our confidence level in the current state and the attractor. Here the state transition model $U(\mathbf{a}, \mathbf{b})$ is defined as a uniform distribution between the current state and the attractor. In addition, the global movement transition model is defined as a Gaussian distribution centered on the previous state

$$p(c_t|c_{t-1}, \mathcal{A}_t) = N(c_{t-1}, \Sigma_c) \tag{8}$$

where $N(\mu, \Sigma)$ is Gaussian distribution with mean μ and covariance matrix Σ.

Substituting (3) and (6) into (2) completes the proposed attractor-guided particle filtering framework. Algorithm 1 summaries the iterative steps for the attractor-guided lip contour tracking algorithm.

Algorithm 1. Lip Contour Tracking Algorithm

Input: Image frames $\{I_t\}_{t=0}^{T}$, initial configuration of the first frame, the angular interval θ, the number of tracking particles K, shape prior set $\mathcal{S} = \{\mathcal{S}_1 \cdots \mathcal{S}_M\}$, number of attractors r for local manifold, the color projection function w, the gaussian covariance matrix Σ_c of centroid, the length m of the local window surround lip

Initialization:

Generate the particle set $P_0 = \{X_0^k, \pi_0^k\}_{k=1}^K$;

Set $t \leftarrow 1$;

while $t < T$ **do**

  Acquire a new image frame I_t ;

  Construct feature image $F_t = w(I_t)$;

  for $k = 1$ **to** K **do**

    1. Sample a particle from P_{t-1} ;
    2. Construct attractor set $\mathcal{A}_t$ and probability α_t by (4) and (5) ;
    3. Estimate next particle state X_t^k by (6) ;
    4. Compute particle weight π_t^k by (3) ;

  Normalize $\sum_{k=1}^{K} \pi_t^k = 1$;

  $t \leftarrow t+1$;

4 Experimental Results

In our experiments, we manually segment the lip contour in the first frame. The images are of size 640*480 and stored as uncompressed format. The angular interval θ is 20°, therefore, we have ($\frac{360}{20} = 18$) control points. We use ($K = 50$) particles for tracking, ($M = 6$) shape priors and ($r = 2$) attractors. To generate the discriminative feature image, we train the color projection axis with some manually segmented images, and project every testing image on the axis. The color projection function used in our experiment is $F = (R - 2G + B)$, and the number of bins for lip and background histogram is 32. The surrounding window size is fixed to 251*251 in the experiment. The covariance matrix Σ_c of the centroid is set to identity matrix.

In the first experiment, we use the snake algorithm to track the lip contour. Because the contrast between the skin and the lip region is often reduced by transformation from the RGB to the gray level intensity, the snake algorithm either cross or stay away from the lip boundary. To track the lip contour by snake algorithm is possible, but the parameter tuning process is time consuming and often case by case. Figure 5a shows a common failure of the snake algorithm.

In the second experiment, we use the classical particle filtering to track the lip contour, and the tracking result is shown in Figure 5b. The contour drifts quickly and becomes ragged in the images because there are no shape priors to constrain the lip motion.

In the third and fourth experiments we use the proposed attractor-guided particle filtering algorithm to track the same image sequence. In order to exam

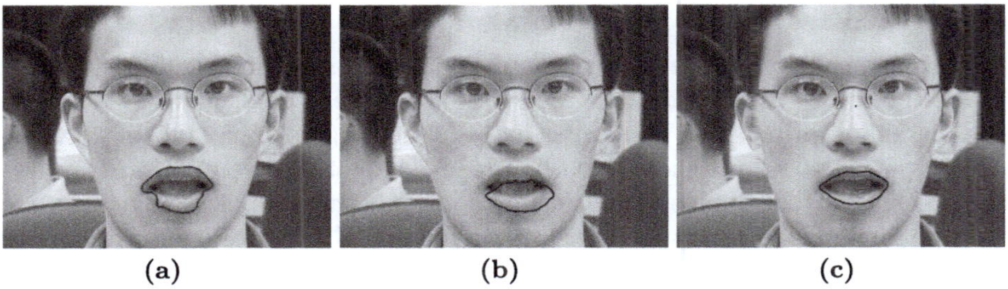

Fig. 5. Tracking results in the 25_{th} frame: (a) snake algorithm (b) unconstrained particle filter (c) the proposed algorithm but with gray level feature

the effectiveness of the selected feature, we use the gray level feature and the discriminative feature in the third and fourth experiments respectively. In the third experiment, although the tracking results are perfect in some frames, most of the time the tracked lip contours are unsatisfactory. It implies the gray level intensity is not discriminative enough to separate the skin and lip color regions; the tracking result is shown in Figure 5c.

In the fourth experiment, we use the proposed algorithm and the discriminative feature to track the same image sequence, and part of the tracking results are shown in Figure 6. With the guide of shape priors and the discriminative feature, our algorithm can recover rapid motions that are difficult to track by traditional particle filtering. In addition, unlike edge-based approaches, the proposed algorithm can handle the low contrast problem by taking advantage of the motion transition model defined on the linear manifold.

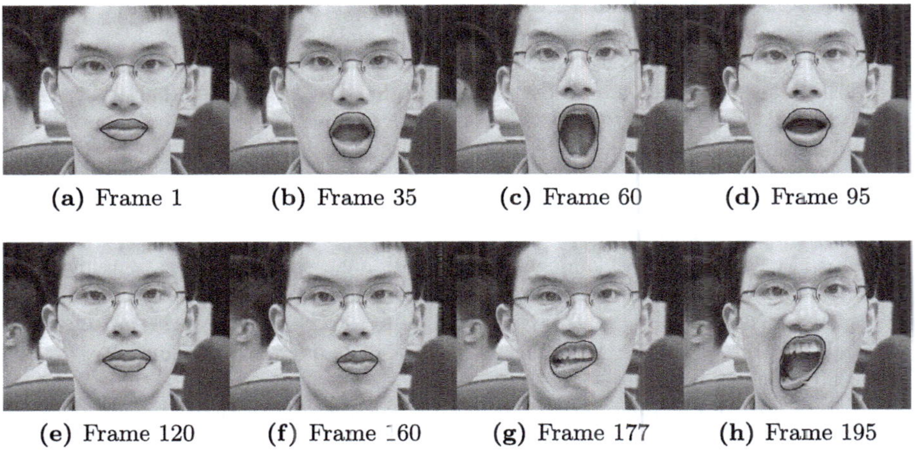

Fig. 6. Tracking results of the proposed algorithm

5 Conclusions

In this paper, we propose an attractor-guide particle filtering framework to track the lip contour. Although the lip shape is very deformable, we use the idea of shape priors with discriminative feature to guide the tracking process. The experiment results show that the proposed algorithm can perform successful tracking in the image sequence. In addition, the proposed algorithm can also be generalized to track other deformable facial features such as eyes and eyebrows.

Acknowledgements

This work was supported in part under grants NSC 94-2752-E-002-007-PAE, NSC 94-2213-E-001-002 and NSC 94-2213-E-002-026.

References

1. Oliver, N., Pentland, A., Berard, F.: Lafter: a real-time face and lips tracker with facial expression recognition. Pattern Recognition **33** (2000) 1369–1382
2. Zhang, X., Mersereau, R.M., Clements, M., Broun, C.C.: Visual speech feature extraction for improved speech recognition. In: Proc. of IEEE Internation Conference on Acoustic, Speech and Signal Processing. (2002)
3. Kass, M., Witkin, A., Terzopoulos, D.: Snakes: Active contour models. International Journal of Computer Vision (1988) 321–331
4. Chan, M.T.: Automatic lip model extraction for constrained contour-based tracking. In: Proc. of IEEE International Conference on Image Processing. (1999)
5. Wakasugi, T., Nishiura, M., Fukui, K.: Robust lip contour extraction using separability of multi-dimensional distribution. In: Proc. of IEEE International Conference on Automatic Face and Gesture Recognition. (2004)
6. Eveno, N., Caplier, A., Coulon, P.Y.: Accurate and quasi-autimatic lip tracking. IEEE Trans. on Circuits and Systems for Video Technology **14** (2004) 706–715
7. Cootes, T., Taylor, C., Cooper, D., Graham, J.: Active shape models: Their training and application. Computer Vision and Image Understanding **61** (1995) 38–59
8. Matthews, I., Cootes, T.F., Bangham, J.A., Cox, S., Harvey, R.: Extraction of visual features for lipreading. IEEE Trans. on Pattern Analysis and Machine Intelligence **24** (2002) 198–213
9. Isard, M., Blake, A.: Condensation–conditional density propagation for visual tracking. International Journal of Computer Vision **29** (1998) 5–28
10. MacCormick, J., Isard, M.: Partition sampling, articulated objects and interface-quality hand tracking. In: Proc. of European Conference of Computer Vision. (2000)
11. Wu, Y., Lin, J.Y., Huang, T.S.: Capturing natural hand articulation. In: Proc. of IEEE International Conference on Computer Vision. (2001)
12. Chang, W.Y., Chen, C.S., Hung, Y.P.: Appearance-guided particle filtering for articulated hand tracking. In: Proc. of IEEE International Conference on Computer Vision and Pattern Recognition. (2005)

13. Chiou, G.I., Hwang, J.N.: Lipreading from color video. IEEE Trans. on Image Processing **6** (1997) 1192–1195
14. Collins, R.T., Liu, Y.: On-line selection of discriminative tracking features. In: Proc. of IEEE International Conference on Computer Vision. (2003)
15. Kaucic, R., Blake, A.: Accurate, real-time, unadorned lip tracking. In: Proc. of International Conference on Computer Vision. (1998)
16. Jones, M., Rehg, J.: Statistical color models with application to skin detection. International Journal of Computer Vision **46** (2002) 81–96

Tracking with the Kinematics of Extremal Contours

David Knossow, Rémi Ronfard, Radu Horaud, and Frédéric Devernay

INRIA Rhone-Alpes, 655 Av. de l'Europe, 38330 Montbonnot, France

Abstract. This paper addresses the problem of articulated motion tracking from image sequences. We describe a method that relies on an explicit parameterization of the extremal contours in terms of the joint parameters of an associated kinematic model. The latter allows us to predict the extremal contours from the body-part primitives of an articulated model and to compare them with observed image contours. The error function that measures the discrepancy between observed contours and predicted contours is minimized using an analytical expression of the Jacobian that maps joint velocities onto contour velocities. In practice we model people both by their geometry (truncated elliptical cones) and with their articulated structure – a kinematic model with 40 rotational degrees of freedom. We observe image data gathered with several synchronized cameras. The tracker has been successfully applied to image sequences gathered at 30 frames/second.

1 Introduction and Background

In this paper we address the problem of tracking complex articulated motions, such as human motion, from visual data. More precisely, we describe humans by a set of kinematically-articulated body parts with smooth surfaces. These surfaces project onto images as extremal contours. We observe humans with several cameras, we extract image contours and we estimate the motion parameters by minimizing the discrepancy between predicted extremal contours and image contours.

The problem of human motion recovery has been thoroughly studied in the recent past using either one or several cameras and without artificial markers [1]. Previous work may be classified into two main approaches.

One approach extracts image features that can be used in the same way as markers, such as texture [2] or point features [3]. Those methods can be implemented in a straightforward manner since they have an explicit differential model of the kinematics, and the latter can be inverted using non-linear least squares methods. The difficulty is then to relate the positions of the features with a geometric model of the human body. In practice, this usually implies full knowledge of both the geometry and the appearance of the human actor [4], although recent advances in multi-body factorization may provide solutions for simultaneously recovering the motion *and* the structure [5].

P.J. Narayanan et al. (Eds.): ACCV 2006, LNCS 3851, pp. 664–673, 2006.

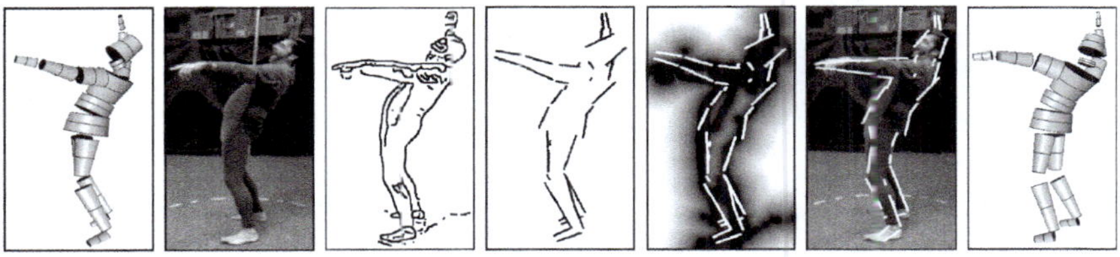

Fig. 1. From left to right : The current model is matched against a new image. The contours extracted from this image are compared with the extremal contours predicted from the model using the chamfer-distance image. Finally, the newly estimated model is consistent with this image.

Another approach relies on contours [6] or on silhouettes [7, 8, 9]. It is possible to relate the deformation of a 2-D (image) silhouette to the geometry and the motion of the articulated object which generated that silhouette. Methods based on deformable silhouettes [10] can cope only with limited changes in viewpoint and pose, and cannot deal with occlusions between primitives. Statistical methods in general and regressive models in particular are used to relate the shape of a silhouette with three-dimensional motion in a lower-dimensional motion space, learned from examples of a specific activity [11].

A slightly different approach was taken in [12], [13] for tracking mechanical parts with sharp edges. By parameterizing the allowable contour deformations with the actual degrees of freedom of the underlying rigid motions of the parts, they demonstrated increased robustness and efficiency over fully deformable active contours for tracking such objects. In the case of human motion tracking, the task is made harder by the fact that the human body has fewer sharp edges (if none), and its silhouette stems from the projection of smooth surfaces rather than surfaces with sharp edges.

Problem Formulation and Originality. We model articulated objects such as humans using *truncated elliptical cones* as basic primitives. These primitives are joined together to form an articulated structure. Each joint has one to three rotational degrees of freedom: let $\boldsymbol{\Phi}$ be an n-dimensional vector whose components are the motion parameters – the joint angles. The smooth surface of a primitive projects onto an image as an *extremal contour*. The apparent motion of this contour is a function of both the motion of the primitive and the motion of the *contour generator* lying onto the smooth surface. An important contribution of this work is to establish the relationship between the joint-angle velocities, $\dot{\boldsymbol{\Phi}} = \partial\boldsymbol{\Phi}/\partial t$, and the image velocity of a point lying onto an extremal contour, $\boldsymbol{v}$

$$\boldsymbol{v} = \mathbf{J}\dot{\boldsymbol{\Phi}} \tag{1}$$

Matrix $\mathbf{J}$ will be referred to as the *extremal contour Jacobian*. The analytic expression of this Jacobian allows us to cast the tracking problem into a non-linear optimization problem. Therefore, the problem of articulated-motion tracking will be formulated as the problem of minimizing a distance function between sets of image contours (gathered simultenously from several cameras) and sets of extremal contours. This can be written as:

$$\min_{\boldsymbol{\Phi}} E(\mathcal{Y}, \mathcal{X}(\boldsymbol{\Phi})) \tag{2}$$

where E is an error or a distance function, $\mathcal{Y}$ is the set of observed image contours and $\mathcal{X}(\boldsymbol{\Phi})$ is the set of predicted extremal contours. There are several ways of computing the distance between image and model contours, including the sum over point-to-point distances, the Hausdorff distance, and so forth. We use the chamfer distance and has several interesting features. It does not require model-contour-to-image contour matches and its computation is fast. Moreover, we treat the chamfer distance as a differentiable function. In practice, a chamfer-distance image is computed from the data. It combines image edges with a binary silhouette which acts both as a mask and as a way to suppress artifacts in the chamfer-distance image.

Paper Organization. The remainder of this paper is organized as follows. In section 2 we derive an analytical solution that relates the motion of an extremal contour to joint parameters of an articulated object. In section 3 we provide an explicit expression for measuring the distance between image contours and extremal contours; Moreover, we explain the advantages of using both edges and silhouettes. Finally, we present examples with complex and realistic motions that require several cameras (section 4).

2 Kinematics of Extremal Contours

As we already explained above, we use truncated elliptical cones as our basic primitives, i.e., Figure 2. These primitives are linked together with rotational joints (with one, two, or three degrees of freedom) to form a kinematic chain. Therefore, the motion of each such primitive is a constrained motion. Let $\mathbf{R}$ and $\boldsymbol{t}$ denote the rotation and translation of a primitive-centered frame with respect to a world-centered frame. Both $\mathbf{R}$ and $\boldsymbol{t}$ are therefore parameterized by the joint angles $\boldsymbol{\Phi} = (\phi_1, \dots, \phi_n)$, i.e., we have $\mathbf{R}(\boldsymbol{\Phi})$ and $\boldsymbol{t}(\boldsymbol{\Phi})$.

Moreover we consider the smooth surface of the elliptical cone. This surface is present in the image under the form of extremal contours. The image motion of a point belonging to such an extremal contour should, therefore, depend on the kinematic motion of the corresponding cone. One can further define a *contour generator* onto the cones's smooth surface – the locus of points where the surface is tangent to lines of sight. When the cone moves, the contour generator moves as well and is constrained both by the kinematic motion of the cone itself and by the relative position of the cone with respect to the camera. Therefore, the contour generator has two motion components and we must explicitly estimate these components. First, we will develop an analytical solution for computing the contour generator as a function of the motion parameters. The extremal contour is simply the projection of the contour generator. Second, we will develop an expression for the image Jacobian that maps joint-velocities onto image point-velocities.

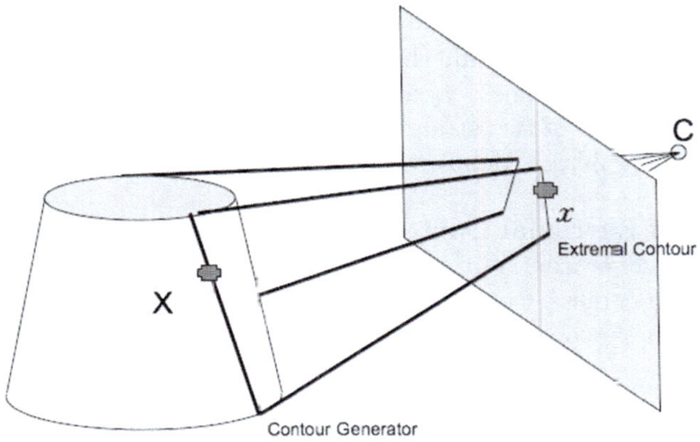

Fig. 2. A truncated elliptical cone projects onto an image as a pair of *extremal contours*. The 2-D motion of these extremal contours is a function of both the motion of the cone and the sliding of the *contour generator* along the smooth surface of the cone.

The Kinematics of the Contour Generator. Let X be a 3-D point that lies onto the smooth surface of a body part.

We derive now the constraint under which this surface point lies onto the contour generator associated to a camera. This constraint simply states that the line of sight associated with this point is tangent to the surface. Both the line of sight and the surface normal should be expressed in a common reference frame, and we choose to express these entities in the world reference frame: $(\mathbf{R}\boldsymbol{n})^\top (\mathbf{R}\boldsymbol{X} + \boldsymbol{t} - \boldsymbol{C}) = 0$, where vector $\boldsymbol{n} = \frac{\partial \boldsymbol{X}}{\partial z} \times \frac{\partial \boldsymbol{X}}{\partial \theta} = \boldsymbol{X}_z \times \boldsymbol{X}_\theta$ is normal to the surface at $\boldsymbol{X}$, and $\boldsymbol{C}$ is the camera optical center in world coordinates. The equation above becomes:

$$X^T \boldsymbol{n} + (\boldsymbol{t} - C)^T \mathbf{R}\boldsymbol{n} = 0 \tag{3}$$

For any rotation, translation, and camera position, equation (3) allows to estimate $\boldsymbol{X}$ as a function of the surface parameters.

The surface of a truncated elliptical cone is parametrized by an angle θ and a height z:

$$X(\theta, z) = \begin{pmatrix} a(1+kz)\cos(\theta) \\ b(1+kz)\sin(\theta) \\ z \end{pmatrix} \tag{4}$$

where a and b are the minor and major half-axes of the elliptical cross-section, k is the tapering parameter of the cone, and $z \in [z_1, z_2]$. With this parameterization, eq. (3) can be developed to obtain a trigonometric equation of the form $F\cos\theta + G\sin\theta + H = 0$ where F, G and H depend on $\boldsymbol{\Phi}$ and C but do not depend on z. With the standard substitution $t = \tan\frac{\theta}{2}$ we obtain a second-degree polynomial

$$(H - F)t^2 + 2Gt + (F + H) = 0 \tag{5}$$

This equation has two real solutions, t_1 and t_2, (or, equivalently, θ_1 and θ_2) whenever the camera lies outside the cone that defines the body part. Note that in the case of elliptical cones, θ_1 and θ_2 do not depend on z and the contour generator is composed of two straight lines, $X(\theta_1, z)$ and $X(\theta_2, z)$. From now on and without ambiguity, $\boldsymbol{X}$ denotes a point lying onto the contour generator.

The Motion of Extremal Contours. The extremal contour is the projection of the contour generator. Without loss of generality, let the world frame be aligned with the camera frame. A point $\boldsymbol{x}$ of the extremal contour is therefore defined by its image coordinates: $x_1 = X_1^w/X_3^w$ and $x_2 = X_2^w/X_3^w$, with

$$\boldsymbol{X}^w = \mathbf{R}\boldsymbol{X} + \boldsymbol{t} \tag{6}$$

The velocity of x, $\boldsymbol{v}$ is computed with:

$$\boldsymbol{v} = \mathbf{J}_I \left(\dot{\mathbf{R}}\boldsymbol{X} + \dot{\boldsymbol{t}} + \mathbf{R}\dot{\boldsymbol{X}} \right) = \mathbf{J}_I(\mathbf{A} + \mathbf{B}) \begin{pmatrix} \boldsymbol{\Omega} \\ \boldsymbol{V} \end{pmatrix} \tag{7}$$

where $\mathbf{A}$ and $\mathbf{B}$ are defined below and $\mathbf{J}_I$ is the classical 2×3 matrix:

$$\mathbf{J}_I = \begin{bmatrix} 1/X_3^w & 0 & -X_1^w/(X_3^w)^2 \\ 0 & 1/X_3^w & -X_2^w/(X_3^w)^2 \end{bmatrix}$$

Eq. (7) reveals that the motion of extremal contours has two components: a component due to the rigid motion of the smooth surface, and a component due to the sliding of the contour generator onto the smooth surface. The first component is:

$$\dot{\mathbf{R}}\boldsymbol{X} + \dot{\boldsymbol{t}} = \dot{\mathbf{R}}\mathbf{R}^\top(\boldsymbol{X}^w - \boldsymbol{t}) + \dot{\boldsymbol{t}} = \mathbf{A} \begin{pmatrix} \boldsymbol{\Omega} \\ \boldsymbol{V} \end{pmatrix} \tag{8}$$

where $\mathbf{A} = [-[X^w]_\times \ \ \mathbf{I}]$ and $(\boldsymbol{\Omega}, \boldsymbol{V})$ is the kinematic screw. The notation $[\boldsymbol{m}]_\times$ stands for the skew-symmetric matrix associated with a vector $\boldsymbol{m}$.

The second component can be made explicit by taking the time derivative of the contour generator constraint, i.e., eq. (3). After some algebraic manipulations, we obtain:

$$\mathbf{R}\dot{\boldsymbol{X}} = \mathbf{B} \begin{pmatrix} \boldsymbol{\Omega} \\ \boldsymbol{V} \end{pmatrix} \tag{9}$$

where $\mathbf{B} = b^{-1}\mathbf{R}\boldsymbol{X}_\theta \ (\mathbf{R}\boldsymbol{n})^\top \ [[\boldsymbol{C} - \boldsymbol{t}]_\times \ \ -\mathbf{I}]$ is a 3×6 matrix and $b = (X^g + \mathbf{R}^T(\boldsymbol{t} - C))^T \boldsymbol{n}_\theta$ is a scalar.

The sliding of the contour generator infers an image velocity that is tangent to the extremal contour. Approaches based on the estimation of the optical flow for tracking [14] cannot take into account this tangential component of the velocity field. Within our approach this term is important and it will be argued in the experimental section below that it speeds up the convergence of the tracker by a factor of 2.

Finally we notice that the kinematic screw of a body-part can be related to the joint velocities associated with a kinematic chain [15], where $\mathbf{J}_K$ is the chain's

Jacobian matrix: $(\boldsymbol{\Omega} \ \ \boldsymbol{V})^\top = \mathbf{J}_K\dot{\boldsymbol{\Phi}}$. By combining this formula with eq. (7) we obtain eq. (1):

$$\boldsymbol{v} = \mathbf{J}_I(\mathbf{A} + \mathbf{B})\mathbf{J}_K\dot{\boldsymbol{\Phi}} \tag{10}$$

3 Fitting Extremal Contours to Images

We now go back to the error function introduced in eq. (2). A well known difficulty is that one can only recover noisy and cluttered image contours and, therefore, the error function should be able to cope with this problem. One possible choice for the error funtion, that works well in practice, is the sum of the distances to the nearest image contour over all the predicted extremal contours points. Thus, the error function writes:

$$E(\mathcal{Y}, \mathcal{X}(\boldsymbol{\Phi})) = \sum_{i=1}^{N} D^2(\mathcal{Y}, \boldsymbol{x}_i(\boldsymbol{\Phi})), \tag{11}$$

where N is the number of predicted extremal contour points and D is a scalar function that returns the minimum distance to an observed contour in $\mathcal{Y}$, evaluated at image location $\boldsymbol{x}$.

The distance from a predicted extremal-contour point to the nearest image-contour point can be computed as a chamfer distance performed after edge detection. But in general one can only observe the silhouette of the actor, obtained through background subtraction, and the edges of a small number of body parts within that silhouette (figure 4). The distance we use in practice is the sum of the minimum distances to both the silhouette *and* the edges observed by all cameras. In the remainder of this section, we explain the advantages of using this particular combination of silhouettes and edges.

For clarity of the presentation, we consider the case of a single body part and we analyse the error function along an image row. Fig.3-(b) is a plot of the error function when only the silhouette is used. The chamfer distance is zero everywhere within the silhouette. Hence, the error function has a large and flat minimum – or infinitely many local minima – thus ill-suited for numerical optimization. Fig. 3-(c) is a plot of the error function when only the edges are considered. As it can be noticed, the error function is flat near the edges and the error function is also ill-suited. Eventually, Fig. 3-(d) is a plot of the error function when using the sum of the two previously proposed distances. The error function is never constant and there exists only one local minimum, where the model contour coincides exactly with the observed contour.

Thus, the simulteneous use of the chamfer distances of both the edges and the silhouette avoids such local minima. As explained above, minimizing the silhouette distance pushes model contours inside the image silhouettes while minimizing the edge distance attracts the model contours to high image gradients within that silhouette, without explicitly representing the contour orientations.

Now that we have chosen the error function to be minimized, we can track our model by iteratively minimizing the error in all views, using a non-linear

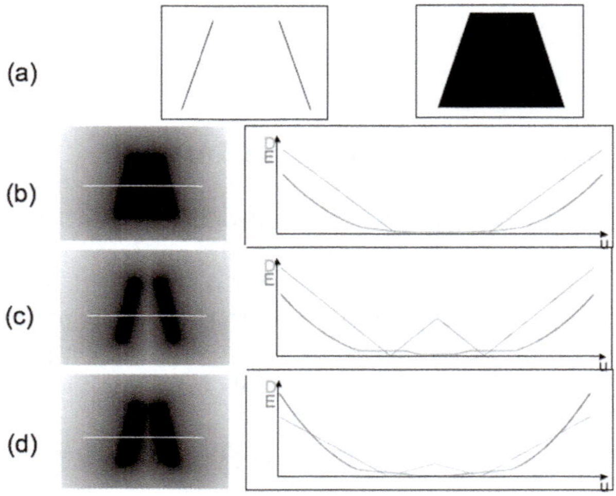

Fig. 3. (a) Observed edges (left) and silhouette (right). (b) Chamfer distance on the silhouette. (c) Chamfer distance on the edges. (d) Sum of both distances. The graphs illustrate the distance (blue or thin curve) and the error (red or bold curve) along a row (white lines).

least-squares optimization technique such as Levenberg-Marquardt. Using the results from section 2 together with a bilinear interpolation of the chamfer distance images, we compute the Jacobian analytically, which results in an efficient implementation, as described in the next section.

4 Experimental Results and Discussion

We performed experiments with realistic and complex human motions using a setup composed of 6 cameras that operate at 30 frames/second. The cameras are

Fig. 4. From left to right: A raw image, the silhouette, the edges inside the silhouette, and the chamfer-distance image associated with the silhouette

Fig. 5. A set of six calibrated cameras provides six image sequences whose frames are synchronized

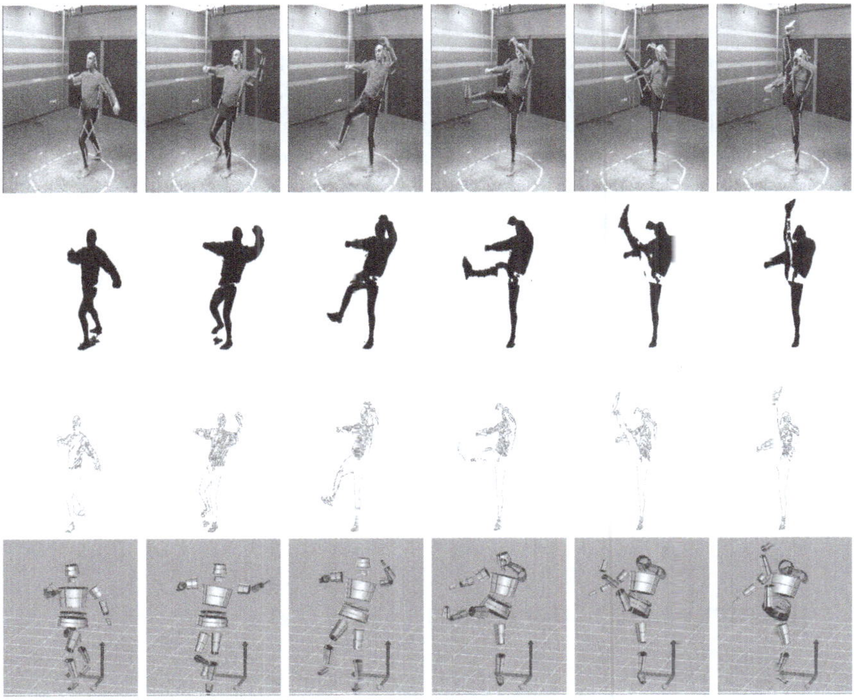

Fig. 6. Tracking a "taekwondo" sequence. From top to bottom: Extremal contours predicted from the previously estimated pose; Silhouettes extracted with a background subtraction algorithm; Edges inside the silhouettes, and the estimated pose of the articulated model.

both finely synchronized (within 10^{-6}s) and operate at the same shutter speed (10^{-3}s.) thus allowing us to cope with fast motions. The 3-D human model is composed of 18 body parts with a total of 40 degrees of freedom[1]. We validated

[1] 2 degrees of freedom for the head, 3 for the torso, 3 for the abdomen, 6 for the two clavicles, 6 for the two shoulders, 4 for the two elbows, 6 for the hips, and 4 at the knees, keeping the feet and the hands rigidly attached to the ankles and forearms.

our tracker using realistic data sets consisting of movements performed by professionals (Fig. 1 and 6). Silhouettes and edges were extracted using standard techniques (statistical background subtraction and edge detection). In the first sequence (Figure 1) we tracked the motion over 700 frames, starting from a reference pose. In the second sequence (Figure 6), we tracked a very fast motion over 100 frames. In both cases, the optimization always converged in less than 5 iterations per frame. The RMS error on both sequences is close to one pixel. Given the roughness of the parameters modelling the person's features (length of arms, feet, thighs, etc.), this error is quite satisfactory and could probably be improved further with better estimates of the anthropometric dimensions of the human model.

We evaluated the importance of the sliding motion term in the minimization process since it was asserted to be negligible in [14]. With both synthetic and real data, we found that we could ignore the correction terms and still obtain the same results, at the expense of doubling the number of iterations, on an average. This gives experimental evidence that the correction introduced by the sliding motion of the contour generators may be important, if not critical, for real-time/best-effort implementations.

With our current algorithms we did not restrict the joint angles to biomechanically feasible limits. As a result, most of our tracker failures occurred because of incorrect assignments during matching, which resulted in collisions between body parts. We believe we can solve this problem by implementing collision detection and collision prevention more carefully. Another important issue that should be addressed in future work, is the automatic calibration of the parameters of our human-body model. Obtaining optimal values for all the constant geometric and kinematic parameters in the anthropomorphic model will be important for evaluating and improving further the quality, robustness, and precision of our tracker.

5 Summary and Conclusion

We described a method for using image silhouettes and edges from several cameres in order to estimate the articulated motion of a person. Our approach works well with relatively difficult motions, using non-textured clothes with shadows and folds. We presented a derivation of the image Jacobian for that case, and demonstrated experimentally that the resulting tracker converges in fewer (typically less than five) iterations per frame, compared to the classical rigid-motion approximation.

Future work will be devoted to extend the method to other body part shapes such as the head, hands and feet, to combine information form the contours with point features and textures, when they are available, to fit the constant geometric and kinematic parameters of our models automatically, and to feed the results into a Kalman or particle-filter representation of human dynamics.

References

1. Gavrila, D.M.: The visual analysis of human movement: A survey. Computer Vision and Image Understanding **73** (1999) 82–98
2. Bregler, C., Malik, J., Pullen, K.: Twist based acquisition and tracking of animal and human kinematics. International Journal of Computer Vision **56** (2004) 179–194
3. Deutscher, J., Blake, A., Reid, I.: Articulated body motion capture by annealed particle filtering. In: Computer Vision and Pattern Recognition. (2000) 2126–2133
4. Hilton, A.: Towards model-based capture of a persons shape, appearance and motion. In: Proceedings of the IEEE International Workshop on Modelling People. (1999)
5. Yan, J., Pollefeys, M.: A factorization approach to articulated motion recovery. In: Conference on Computer Vision and Pattern Recognition. Volume 2. (2005) 815–821
6. Drummond, T., Cipolla, R.: Real-time tracking of highly articulated structures in the presence of noisy measurements. In: ICCV. (2001) 315–320
7. Sminchisescu, C., Telea, A.: Human pose estimation from silhouettes. a consistent approach using distance level sets. In: WSCG International Conference on Computer Graphics, Visualization and Computer Vision. (2002)
8. Delamarre, Q., Faugeras, O.: 3d articulated models and multi-view tracking with physical forces. Computer Vision and Image Understanding **81** (2001) 328–357
9. Niskanen, M., Boyer, E., Horaud, R.: Articulated motion capture from 3-d points and normals. In Clocksin, Fitzgibbon, T., ed.: British Machine Vision Conference. Volume 1., Oxford, UK, BMVA, British Machine Vision Association (2005) 439–448
10. Blake, A., Isard, M.: Active Contours. Springer-Verlag (1998)
11. Agarwal, A., Triggs, B.: Learning to track 3d human motion from silhouettes. In: International Conference on Machine Learning, Banff (2004) 9–16
12. Drummond, T., Cipolla, R.: Real-time visual tracking of complex structures. IEEE Trans. Pattern Analalysis Machine Intelligence **24** (2002) 932–946
13. Martin, F., Horaud, R.: Multiple camera tracking of rigid objects. International Journal of Robotics Research **21** (2002) 97–113
14. Rosten, E., Drummond, T.: Rapid rendering of apparent contours of implicit surfaces for real-time tracking. In: British Machine Vision Conference. Volume 2. (2003) 719–728
15. McCarthy, J.M.: Introduction to Theoretical Kinematics. MIT Press, Cambridge (1990)

Multiregion Level Set Tracking with Transformation Invariant Shape Priors

Michael Fussenegger[1], Rachid Deriche[2], and Axel Pinz[1]

[1] Institute of Electrical Measurement and Measurement Signal Processing,
Graz University of Technology,
Schießstattgasse 14b, 8010 Graz, Austria
{Fussenegger, Axel.Pinz}@tugraz.at
http://www.emt.tugraz.at

[2] INRIA, 2004 route des Lucioles, BP 93,
06902 Sophia Antipolis, France
Rachid.Deriche@sophia.inria.fr
http://www-sop.inria.fr/odyssee/

Abstract. Tracking of regions and object boundaries in an image sequence is a well studied problem in image processing and computer vision. So far, numerous approaches tracking different features of the objects (contours, regions or points of interest) have been presented. Most of these approaches have problems with robustness. Typical reasons are noisy images, objects with identical features or partial occlusions of the tracked features. In this paper we propose a novel level set based tracking approach, that allows robust tracking on noisy images. Our framework is able to track multiple regions in an image sequence, where a level set function is assigned to every region. For already known or learned objects, transformation invariant shape priors can be added to ensure a robust tracking even under partial occlusions. Furthermore, we introduce a simple decision function to maintain the desired topology for multiple regions. Experimental results demonstrate the method for arbitrary numbers of shape priors. The approach can even handle full occlusions and objects which are temporarily hidden in containers.

1 Introduction

Tracking of regions and object boundaries in image sequences is an important problem in computer vision (scene analysis and interpretation), video processing (video surveillance, object based video database search) and human-computer interaction.

Numerous tracking approaches have been developed, including early tracking algorithms to track feature points [1] and edge segments [2, 3], and several recent contributions to track parametric contours [4, 5]. Most of them had difficulties in handling topological changes such as the merging and splitting of overlapping object regions. For this, the level set method [6, 7, 8] is a more powerful technique. In the last few years various models have been proposed (see [9, 10, 11, 12, 13, 14, 15]). But there is always a problem with tracking multiple regions and none of these approaches uses the benefit of prior information to obtain a more robust tracking result. In this paper, we propose a novel approach that extends the well known level set model, such that it can simultaneously handle an arbitrary number of regions and competing shape priors.

P.J. Narayanan et al. (Eds.): ACCV 2006, LNCS 3851, pp. 674–683, 2006.

An early work on region based tracking proposed by Bertalmio et al. [9] is based on morphing images. Paragios and Deriche [10] use a geodesic model that combines motion and edge information. Using the difference between the current image and the reference background, a region based model was proposed by Besson et al [11]. In [12, 14] feature distributions of the object and the background were used for tracking. Freedman and Zhang [13] track a predefined distribution for the object region by minimizing a Kullback-Leibler or Bhattacharyya distance. All these approaches are restricted to one level set function and can only track one region. Shi and Karl [15] propose a new fast level set implementation that can handle multiple regions, but do not use prior information.

The integration of prior knowledge (in our case shape priors) into PDE based segmentation methods has delivered promising results (see [16–22]). Usually, the knowledge of one single shape prior is introduced into the contour evolution in a way that corrupted versions of a familiar object are reconstructed and all unfamiliar image structures are suppressed and often the localization of the shape must be known. Leventon et al. [18] use a Gaussian model to describe their shape priors. They assume a uniform distribution over pose parameters, that model translation and rotation. Rousson and Paragios [19] propose a transformation (scale, rotation and translation) for the shape prior that allows to segment familiar objects with an unknown position in the image scene. But like the approach of Leventon et al. they can handle only one shape prior and unfamiliar image structures are ignored. Cremers et al. ([23], [21]) presented an approach with dynamic labeling, that allows to use more than one shape prior and does not suppress unfamiliar image structures, but all shape priors are assigned to one level set function. Raviv et al. [22] present a novel approach that allows a projective transformation of the shape prior, but their approach is also limited to one region, furthermore the projective transformation needs too much calculation time for tracking applications. In [24] we present a segmentation level set framework that can handle an arbitrary number of regions with or without shape priors. Our segmentation algorithm in [24] is used in the initialization step of the multiple object tracking approach with shape priors, which we propose in this article.

The outline of the paper is as follows: Section 2 presents a level set formulation that can easily be extended with a single pose invariant shape prior (section 3). In section 4, we introduce our tracking algorithm. For the case of multiple object regions, we extend our tracking algorithm and introduce a logic function Ψ to incorporate topology in subsection 4.1. Results are presented in section 5. Finally conclusions are drawn in section 6.

2 A Level Set Framework

In this section, we define a level set framework, that aims to maximize the color value homogeneity of the different regions. We assume each image of a video sequence is composed of a background region Ω_0 and N independent objects of interest $\Omega_1, ..., \Omega_N$. Each of these $n = 1..N$ objects of interest is described with a level set function $\Phi_n : \Omega_n \rightarrow \mathbb{R}$, with $\Phi_n(\mathbf{x}) > 0$, if $\mathbf{x} \in \Omega_n$ and $\Phi_n(\mathbf{x}) < 0$, if $\mathbf{x} \in \Omega_0$.

There are different level set formulations, which could be possible choices [8, 25, 26, 27]. In this work, we use the level set formulation proposed by Paragios and Deriche [27, 28] to minimize the energy for each object region:

$$E_{D_n}(\Phi_n, p_n, p_0) = -\int_\Omega (H(\Phi_n)\log p_n + (1 - H(\Phi_n))\log p_0)d\mathbf{x} + \nu \int_\Omega |\nabla H(\Phi_n)|d\mathbf{x}. \quad (1)$$

H denotes the regularized Heaviside function and p_0 and p_n are the probability densities $p_i = p(\mathbf{x}|\Omega_i)$ of the background regions Ω_0 and the object region Ω_n, which cover the whole image domain Ω. For color images, we use the following multivariate Gaussian density:

$$p(\mathbf{x}|\Omega_i) = \frac{1}{(2\pi)^{d/2}|\Sigma_i|} e^{-\frac{1}{2}(\mathbf{x}-\mu_i)^T \Sigma_i^{-1}(\mathbf{x}-\mu_i)}, \quad (2)$$

with the mean μ_i and the covariance matrix Σ_i of the multivariate color distribution of the region Ω_i. The last term of equation 1 takes into account the length of the contour weighted by the parameter ν. The minimization of the energy term in equation 1 can now be estimated according to the gradient descent equation

$$\frac{\partial \Phi_n}{\partial t} = \delta(\Phi_n)\Big[\nu \mathrm{div}\Big(\frac{\nabla \Phi_n}{|\nabla \Phi_n|}\Big) - log\frac{p_n}{p_0}\Big], \quad (3)$$

where $\delta(\Phi_n)$ is the derivative of $H(\Phi_n)$ with respect to its argument.

3 Adding a Shape Prior

To add a shape prior to the energy equation 1, we define a straight forward extension

$$E_n(\Phi_n, \Phi_0, p_n, p_0) = E_{D_n}(\Phi_n, p_n, p_0) + \lambda E_{S_n}(\Phi_n, \Phi_0), \quad (4)$$

with

$$E_{S_n}(\Phi_n, \Phi_0) = \int_\Omega \delta(\Phi_n)(\Phi_n - \Phi_{0n})^2 d\mathbf{x}, \quad (5)$$

where Φ_{0n} is the level set of the given training shape or the mean of a set of training shapes. $\lambda \geq 0$ indicates the weight of the prior. This formulation is simplified and does not consider invariance of the shape prior with respect to similarity transformations of the level set function. Nevertheless, equation 5 can be extended in this direction (cf. [18, 19, 20]), see section 3.1.

The minimization of the energy term can again be estimated according to the gradient descent equation:

$$\frac{\partial \Phi_n}{\partial t} = \delta(\Phi_n)\Big[\nu \mathrm{div}\Big(\frac{\nabla \Phi_n}{|\nabla \Phi_n|}\Big) - log\frac{p_n}{p_0} - 2\lambda(\Phi_n - \Phi_{0n})\Big] \quad (6)$$

3.1 A Pose Invariant Formulation

During an image sequence the pose and the location of an object can change and the shape model has to be aligned. Possible solutions for simple or planar objects are presented in [19, 20], where a set of pose parameters are associated with the given prior

Φ_{0n}. Rousson and Paragios [19] assume a global deformation A_n between Φ_n and Φ_{0n} that involves the parameters $[\mathcal{A} = (s; \theta; \mathbf{T})]$ with a scale factor s, a rotation angle θ and a translation vector $\mathbf{T}$. The corresponding shape energy

$$E_{S_n}(\Phi_n, \Phi_0(\mathcal{A}_n)) = \int_\Omega \delta(\Phi_n)(s\Phi_n - \Phi_{0n}(\mathcal{A}_n))^2 d\mathbf{x} \tag{7}$$

is simultaneously optimized with respect to the segmentation level set function Φ_n and the pose parameters s, θ and $\mathbf{T}$. The function is expanded with $\delta(\Phi_n)$, so that the shape prior is only estimated within the vicinity of the zero-crossing of the level set representation, which has a better performance than considering the whole image domain. Minimizing equation 7 leads to the following gradient descent for the level set function Φ_n:

$$\frac{\partial \Phi_n}{\partial t} = \delta(\Phi_n)\Big[\nu div\Big(\frac{\nabla\Phi_n}{|\nabla\Phi_n|}\Big) - log\frac{p_n}{p_0} - 2\lambda(s_n\Phi_n - \Phi_{0n}(\mathcal{A}_n))\Big] \tag{8}$$

The transformation $\mathcal{A}_n$ is also dynamically updated to map Φ_n and Φ_{0n} in the best possible way. The calculus of variations for the parameter of $\mathcal{A}_n$ derives to the system:

$$\begin{aligned}
\frac{\partial s}{\partial t} &= 2\int_\Omega p(-\Phi_n + \nabla\Phi_{0n}(\mathcal{A}_n)\frac{\partial}{\partial s}\mathcal{A}_n)d\mathbf{x} \\
\frac{\partial \theta}{\partial t} &= 2\int_\Omega p(\nabla\Phi_{0n}(\mathcal{A}_n)\frac{\partial}{\partial \theta}\mathcal{A}_n)d\mathbf{x} \\
\frac{\partial \mathbf{T}}{\partial t} &= 2\int_\Omega p(\nabla\Phi_{0n}(\mathcal{A}_n)\frac{\partial}{\partial \mathbf{T}}\mathcal{A}_n)d\mathbf{x},
\end{aligned} \tag{9}$$

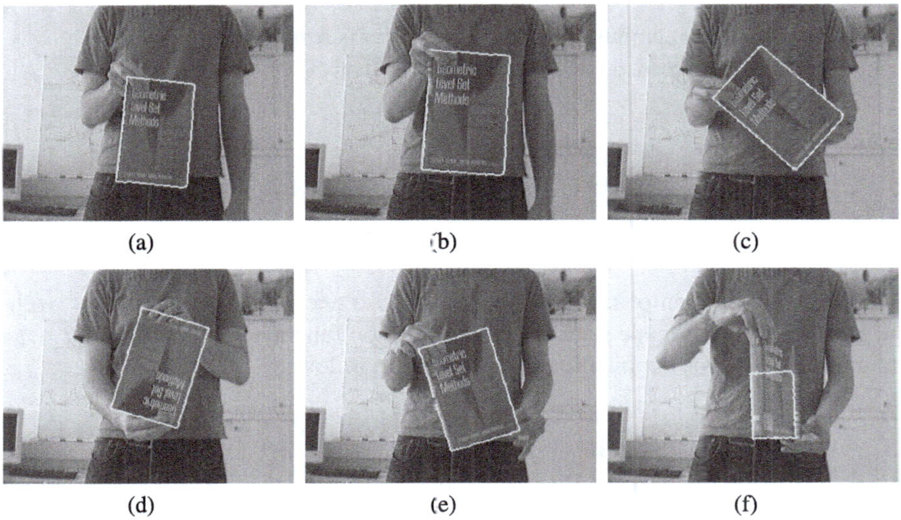

Fig. 1. Transformations of an object during a tracking sequence

with

$$p = \delta(\Phi_n)(s\Phi_n - \Phi_{0n}(\mathcal{A}_n)). \tag{10}$$

Figure 1 shows the possible transformations of the shape prior: translation, rotation and scale. In figure 1(f) the limitation of our transformation model is shown at perspective distortions. Raviv et al. [22] presented an approach that allows a projective transformation of the shape prior, but their approach needs too much calculation time for tracking applications.

4 Tracking Algorithm

In the initialization stage, we use the regions from the result of our multi region level set segmentation [24]. For every region of interest, we initialize a level set function Φ and calculate the means and covariance matrices for each region and the background. For important or already learned objects, we assign a shape prior Φ_0 to the corresponding level set function Φ.

For the re-distancing step of the level set function Φ, we use a mixed approach: the PDE is used for reinitialization [29] in a small neighborhood of the zero level while the Fast Marching [30, 31] permits to extend the distance function to a larger band.

To track the object boundary, we compute the speed at all pixels in the band of the level set function Φ with equation 8 and calculate the new contour in the re-distancing step. In our implementation, the curve evolution stops when any of the following stopping conditions is satisfied:

1. Either, the transformation change of a pixel $\mathbf{x}$ is smaller than ε_1:

$$||\mathbf{x}_i - \mathbf{x}_{i-1}|| < \varepsilon_1, \text{ or} \tag{11}$$

2. a pre-specified maximum number of iterations is reached, or
3. the sum of the speed at each pixel is smaller than ε_2:

$$\sum_{\Omega_n} |\frac{\partial \Phi}{\partial t}| < \varepsilon_2. \tag{12}$$

4.1 Tracking of Multiple Objects

For the representation of multiple objects, we use one level set function Φ_n with or without an assigned shape prior Φ_{0n} and a decision function Ψ_n for each of N objects of interest. The decision function Ψ_n is defined as follows:

$$\Psi_n(x) = \begin{cases} 1 & \Phi_n(x) < 0, \Phi_l(x) > 0 \ (n \neq l) \\ 0 & \Phi_n(x) < 0, \Phi_l(x) < 0 \mid \exists \Phi_{0n} \ (n \neq l) \\ -1 & \Phi_n(x) < 0, \Phi_l(x) < 0 \mid \nexists \Phi_{0n} \ (n \neq l) \end{cases}$$

In the case of overlapping regions the different values for objects with and without shape priors allow an arbitrary topology, where objects with shape prior survive even with occlusions and they are handled as more important than regions without a shape prior. Our tracking algorithm consists of the steps shown in table 1.

Adding Ψ_n to equation 8 leads to following gradient descent:

$$\frac{\partial \Phi}{\partial t} = \begin{cases} u(x) - v(x) & , \text{for } \Psi_n = 1 \\ v(x) & , \text{for } \Psi_n = 0 \\ |u(x)| & , \text{for } \Psi_n = -1 \end{cases}$$

Table 1. Tracking algorithm

- Step1:
  - Initialize all level set functions Φ_n.
  - Initialize all shape priors Φ_{0n} and assign them to the corresponding level set function Φ_n.
  - Calculate all means and covariance matrices for the regions and the background.
- Step2: (one cycle for region n)
  - Compute the parameters of transformation $\mathcal{A}_n$ for all shape priors Φ_{0n}.
  - Compute the gradient descent (equation 8) for all pixels in the band of Φ_n.
- Step3:
  - If the stopping condition is satisfied stop curve evolution for the actual region.
  - Else calculate the re-distancing for the actual region.
- Step4:
  - If the stopping condition for all regions is satisfied load new frame and start with step 2 with first region.
  - Else start with step 2 with next region.

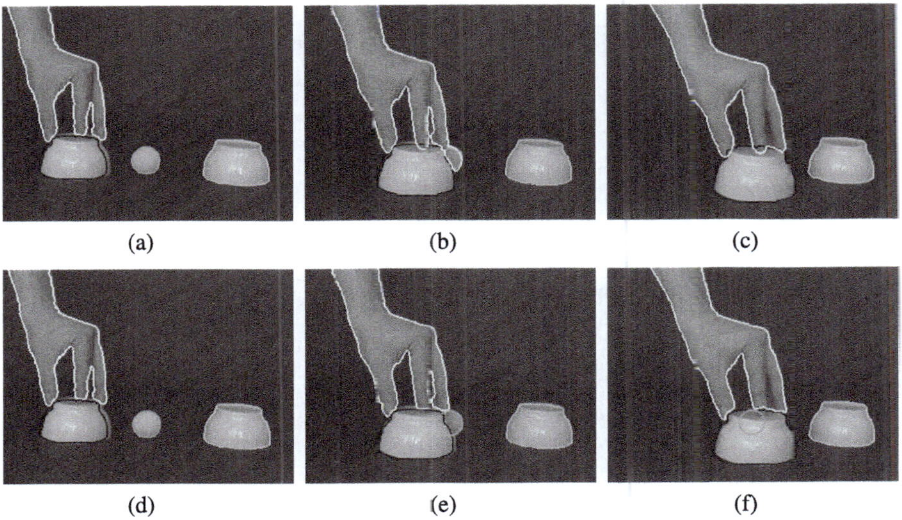

Fig. 2. Different tracking results of the *Game* sequence. First row without, second row with Ψ.

$u(x)$ and $v(x)$ are defined as follows:

$$u(x) = \delta(\Phi_n)\Big[\nu \mathrm{div}\Big(\frac{\nabla\Phi_n}{|\nabla\Phi_n|}\Big) - log\frac{p_n}{p_0}\Big], \tag{13}$$

and

$$v(x) = 2\alpha_n\delta(\Phi_n)(s_n\Phi_n - \Phi_{Sn}(\mathcal{A}_n)). \tag{14}$$

the weighting parameter $\lambda = 0$ when there is no shape prior Φ_{0n} assigned to the level set function Φ_n. The scale s_n of the transformation $\mathcal{A}_n$ does not change for $\Psi_n \neq 1$.

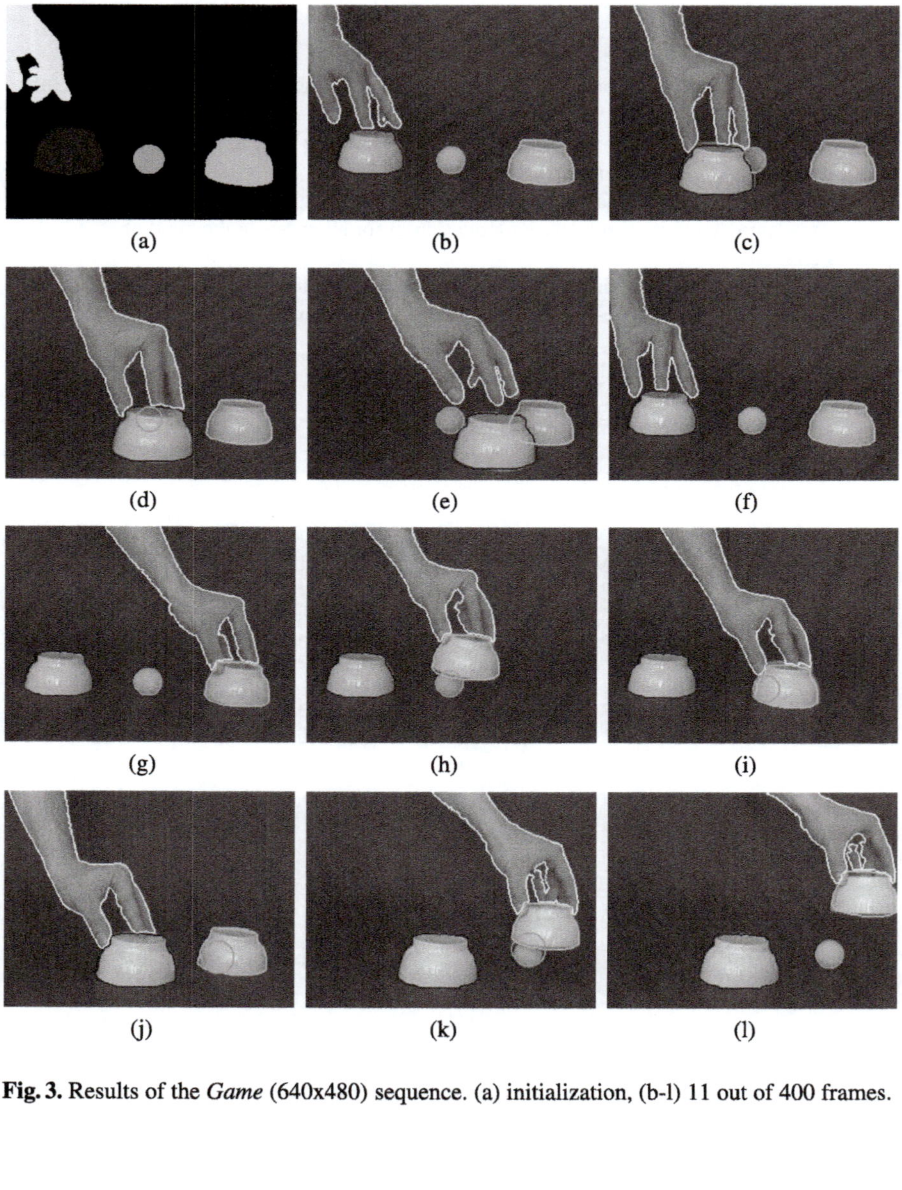

Fig. 3. Results of the *Game* (640x480) sequence. (a) initialization, (b-l) 11 out of 400 frames.

Figure 2 demonstrates the value of Ψ. The first row shows three tracking results without the use of the decision function Ψ. In figure 2(b) the hand region grows into the ball because the color information is similar and in figure 2(c) the ball has vanished because it is totally occluded by the cup. In the second row, these problems do not occur because of the use of the decision function Ψ.

5 Tracking Results

We present two results of our tracking implementation, which run on a 2.0GHz PC under Linux. In all experiments, the segmentation result of frame 0 calculated with [24] is used for the initialization. Region tracking from frame to frame is performed via the algorithm described in table 1. We use the same parameters: $\nu = 1$, $\lambda = 1$ when a shape prior is assigned to the region and $\lambda = 0$ when not, for all experiments. The maximum number of iteration steps is set to 30, which assures a robust tracking even at fast movements. The first tracking experiment (figure 3) is performed on the *Game* sequence over 400 frames. We successfully track all objects in the image (hand, two cups, ball). The first image (figure 3(a)) shows the segmentation result from [24], which is used for the initialization. The hand region is tracked without prior information, because the changes of the hand shape can not be modeled with our shape priors. Shape priors are assigned to all other regions. The tracking speed strongly depends on the number of regions to track and on the length of the contour. For example we need only 0.1s per frame when we track only the ball with shape prior but 0.8s for the hand without shape prior. In this experiment we need an average time of 1.4s per frame for all objects. The second experiment (figure 4) is performed on the *Book 1* sequence over 250 frames. In this sequence, we track the book with shape prior and the orange object only with color

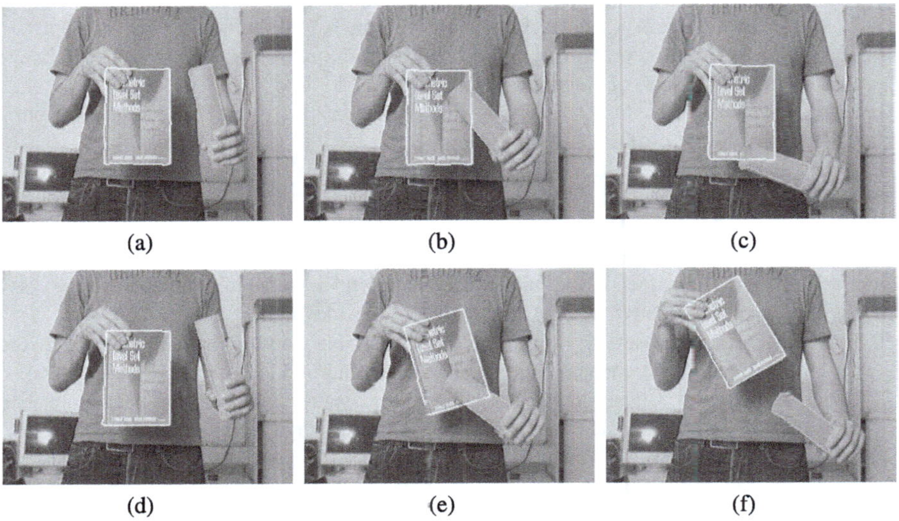

Fig. 4. Results of the *Book 1* (640x480) sequence. 6 frames of 250 are shown.

information. Both objects are successfully tracked with 0.5s per frame. Our videos can be downloaded from `http://www.emt.tugraz.at/~pinz/data`.

6 Conclusion

We have introduced a novel level set based tracking framework that allows to track multiple object regions. Furthermore, we can add an arbitrary number of planar shape priors for already known or learned objects to get a more robust tracking result. Each shape prior is given by a fixed template (a given training shape or the mean of a set of training shapes) and respective pose parameters. A simple decision function Ψ ensures the desired topology for multiple regions tracking. Our approach can combine data-driven and recognition-driven information in the tracking process, and can for example be used to improve a cognitive vision system. Our approach has been successfully tested on a large number of real images, and it can even handle full occlusions which are temporally hidden in containers.

Acknowledgement

This research has been partly funded by the Austrian Science Foundation (FWF, project S9103-N04), the European project IMAVIS HPMT-CT-2000-00040 within the framework of the Marie Curie Fellowships Training Sites Programme and by the European project LAVA (IST-2001-34405). This is gratefully acknowledged.

References

1. Sethi, I.K., Jain, R.: Finding trajectories of feature points in an monocular image sequence. In: IEEE Trans. Pattern Anal. Machine Intell. Volume 9. (1987) 56–73
2. Crowley, J.L., Stelmaszyk, P., Discours, C.: Measuring image flow by tracking edge line. In: Proc. Second Int. Conf. of Computer Vision. (1988) 658–664
3. Deriche, R., Faugeras, O.D.: Tracking line segments. In: Proc. First European Conf. of Computer Vision. (1992) 259–268
4. Chen, Y., Rui, Y., Huang, T.S.: JPDAF based HMM for real-time contour tracking. In: Proc. of CVPR. (2001) 543–550
5. Comaniciu, D., Ramesh, V., Meer, P.: Kernel-based object tracking. In: IEEE Trans. Pattern Anal. and Machine Intell. (2003) 564–577
6. Dervieux, A., Thomasset, F.: A finite element method for the simulation of Rayleigh-Taylor instability. In: Lecture Notes in Mathematics. (1979) 145–159
7. Dervieux, A., Thomasset, F.: Multifluid incompressible flows by a finite element method. In: International Conference on Numerical Methods in Fluid Dynamics. (1980) 158–163
8. Osher, S.J., Sethian, J.A.: Fronts propagation with curvature depend speed: Algorithms based on Hamilton-Jacobi formulations. In: Journal of Comp. Phys. Volume 79. (1988) 12–49
9. Bertalmio, M., Sapiro, G., Randall, G.: Morphing active contours: A geometric approach to topology-independent image segmentation and tracking. In: Proceedings of ICIP. (1998) 318–322
10. Paragios, N., Deriche, R.: Geodesic active contours and level sets for the detection and tracking of moving objects. In: IEEE Trans. Pattern Anal. Machine Intell. (2000) 266–280

11. Besson, S., Barlaud, M., Aubert, G.: Detection and tracking of moving objects using a new level set based method. In: Proceedings of ICPR. (2000) 1100–1105
12. Mansouri, A.: Region tracking via level set PDEs without motion computation. In: IEEE Trans. Pattern Anal. Machine Intell. (2002) 947–961
13. Freedman, D., Zhang, T.: Active contours for tracking distributions. In: IEEE Trans. Image Processing. (2004) 518–526
14. Yilmaz, A., Li, X., Shah, M.: Contour-based object tracking with occlusion handling in video acquired using mobile cameras. In: IEEE Trans. Pattern Anal. Machine Intell. (2004) 1531–1536
15. Shi, Y., Karl, W.C.: Real-time tracking using level sets. In: Proceedings of CVPR. (2005)
16. Yuille, A., Hallinan, P.: Deformable templates. In: A. Blake and A. Yuille, editors, Active Vison. (1992) 21–38
17. Cootes, T.F., A. Hill, C.J.T., Haslam, J.: Use of active shape models for locating structures in medical images. In: Image and Vison Computing. Volume 12:6. (1994) 355–365
18. Leventon, M.E., Grimson, W.E.L., Faugeras, O.: Statistical shape influence in geodesic active contour. In: Proceedings of Conference Computer Vision and Pattern Recognition. Volume 1. (2000) 316–323
19. Rousson, M., Paragios, N.: Shape priors for level set representations. In: Proceedings of European Conference of Computer Vision. Volume 2351 of LNCS. (2002) 78–92
20. Chen, Y., Tagare, H.D., Thiruvenkadam, S., Huang, F., Wilson, D., Gophinath, K.S., Briggs, R.W., Geiser, E.A.: Using prior shapes in geometric active contours in a variational framework. In: International Journal of Computer Vison. Volume 50(3). (2002) 315–328
21. Cremers, D., Sochen, N., Schnoerr, C.: Multiphase dynamic labeling for variational recognition-driven image segmentation. In: Proceedings of European Conference of Computer Vision. (2004) 74–86
22. Riklin-Raviv, T., Kiryati, N., Sochen, N.A.: Unlevel-sets: Geometry and prior-based segmentation. In: Proccedings of ECCV. (2004) 50–61
23. Cremers, D., Sochen, N., Schnoerr, C.: Towards recognition-based variational segmentation using shape priors and dynamic labeling. In: Proceedings of Scale-Space 2003. (2003) 388–400
24. Fussenegger, M., Deriche, R., Pinz, A.: Multiregion level set tracking with transformation invariant shape priors. In: Proceedings of ACCV. (2006)
25. Chan, T., Vese, L.: Active contours without edges. In: IEEE Transaction on Image Processing. Volume 10(2). (2001) 266–277
26. Tsai, A., Yezzi, A.J., Willsky, A.S.: Curve evolution implementation of the mumford-shah functional for image segmentation, denoising, interpolation and magnification. In: IEEE Transaction on Image Processing. Volume 10(8). (2001) 1169–1186
27. Paragios, N., Deriche, R.: Geodesic active regions : a new framework to deal with frame partition problems in computer vision. In: Journal of Visual Communication and Image Representation. Volume 13(1/2). (2002) 249–269
28. Paragios, N., Deriche, R.: Geodesic active regions and level set methods for motion estimation and tracking. In: Computer Vision and Image Understanding. Volume 97(3). (2005) 259–282
29. Sussman, M., Smereka, P., Osher, S.: A level set approach for computing solutions to incompressible two phase flow. In: Journal of Computational Physics. (1994) 146–159
30. Adalsteinsson, D., Sethian, J.: A fast marching level set method for propagating interfaces. In: Journal of Computational Physics. (1995) 269–277
31. Sethian, J.A.: A fast marching level set method for monotonically advancing fonts. In: Proceedings of the National Academy of Sciences of USA. (1996) 1591–1595

Multi-view Object Tracking Using Sequential Belief Propagation*

Wei Du and Justus Piater

University of Liege, Department of Electrical Engineering and Computer Science,
Institut Montefiore, B28, Sart Tilman Campus, B-4000 Liege, Belgium
weidu@montefiore.ulg.ac.be, justus.piater@ulg.ac.be

Abstract. Multiple cameras and collaboration between them make possible the integration of information available from multiple views and reduce the uncertainty due to occlusions. This paper presents a novel method for integrating and tracking multi-view observations using bidirectional belief propagation. The method is based on a fully connected graphical model where target states at different views are represented as different but correlated random variables, and image observations at a given view are only associated with the target states at the same view. The tracking processes at different views collaborate with each other by exchanging information using a message passing scheme, which largely avoids propagating wrong information. An efficient sequential belief propagation algorithm is adopted to perform the collaboration and to infer the multi-view target states. We demonstrate the effectiveness of our method on video-surveillance sequences.

1 Introduction

Visual tracking involves object detection and recursive inference of the target states in time. A popular approach is to generate target hypotheses and then to verify them by matching with a pre-learned reference model. However, a drawback of this approach is that if the target is occluded, a partial or – even worse – complete target observation is missing, making the comparison with the reference model impossible. The problem is particularly severe in the context of single-camera tracking in crowded scenes such as surveillance and team sports. However, the use of multiple cameras and collaboration between them make possible the integration of multi-view information and reduce the uncertainty due to occlusions.

A potential problem of conventional multi-view tracking is that wrong information may be integrated and propagated from one view to other views. To solve this problem, this paper presents a novel method for integrating and tracking multi-view observations using bidirectional belief propagation. The method is based on a dynamic graphical model where target states at different views are represented as different but correlated random variables, and image observations at one view are only associated with the target states at the same view. As all views are correlated with each other, the graphical model is fully connected. The tracking processes at different views exchange information using a message passing scheme, which largely avoids propagating

* This work has been sponsored by the Région Wallonne under DGTRE/WIST contract 031/5439.

P.J. Narayanan et al. (Eds.): ACCV 2006, LNCS 3851, pp. 684–693, 2006.

wrong information. Hua and Wu introduced an efficient Sequential Belief Propagation (SBP) algorithm to perform the multi-scale visual tracking [1]. In the present paper, we adapt the approach to our multi-view tracking task and our specific graphical model. In particular, we apply SBP to integrate individual trackers at different views so that the multi-view target states are inferred based on the multi-view observations.

Similar multi-camera tracking frameworks have been presented, e.g. in the context of video surveillance [2] or soccer player tracking [3]. Targets are tracked by individual trackers at different views, and the results are fused by a fusion module. To prevent wrong information integration, uncertainties of individual trackers are computed and used during fusion. However, with no interaction between individual trackers, the multi-view information is not fully exploited and the robustness of these systems is limited.

Particle filters are popular in multi-view tracking [4, 5]. Both cited approaches are based on the best-view-selection strategy: the target states are estimated using mainly those views that contain the most likely information. The problem is that the targets of interest may not be sufficiently distinctive from clutter and as a result, the wrong selection of the best view will cause the complete loss of tracks.

Different from previous work, our approach involves both recursive inference of target states using particle filters [6], making the system capable of coping with non-Gaussian clutter and non-linear dynamics, and exchanging information across views using belief propagation [7, 8], making the system robust to occlusions. Belief propagation provides a systematic solution for propagating uncertainties in a graphical model. The specific flavor of belief-propagation that we use, sequential belief propagation, enables us to reduce the risk of wrong information propagation. A fully connected graphical model for multi-view tracking is proposed based on a multi-view target state representation. We demonstrate the effectiveness of our method on video-surveillance sequences.

Section 2 describes the multi-view representation and the graphical models. Sequential Belief Propagation is introduced in Section 3. Section 4 introduces the SBP-based multi-view tracking algorithm. Results on sequences of video surveillance from PETS2001 datasets [9] are illustrated in Section 5.

2 A Graphical Model for Multi-view Tracking

The target state at each view is denoted by x_i, where $i = 1, \ldots, L$ is the view index. Putting all states at different views together results in a multi-view representation for the target, denoted by $X = \{x_1, \ldots, x_L\}$. The benefit of this representation is that the multi-view target model makes possible the integration of multi-view image observations, which helps overcome the occlusion problem if the target is not occluded in all views. The image observation associated with x_i in the same view is denoted by z_i, and $Z = \{z_1, \ldots, z_L\}$.

Given the above definitions, our approach performs bidirectional belief propagation in a graphical model shown in Figure 1, and recursively infers the multi-view target states in a dynamic graphical model shown in Figure 2.

In both figures, the undirected link between $x_{t,i}$ and $x_{t,j}$ describes the mutual influence of multiple views and is associated with a potential function $\psi^t_{i,j}(x_{t,i}, x_{t,j})$, and the directed link from $x_{t,j}$ to $z_{t,j}$ represents the image observation process and is associated with an image likelihood function $p_j(z_{t,j}|x_{t,j})$. In Figure 2, the directed

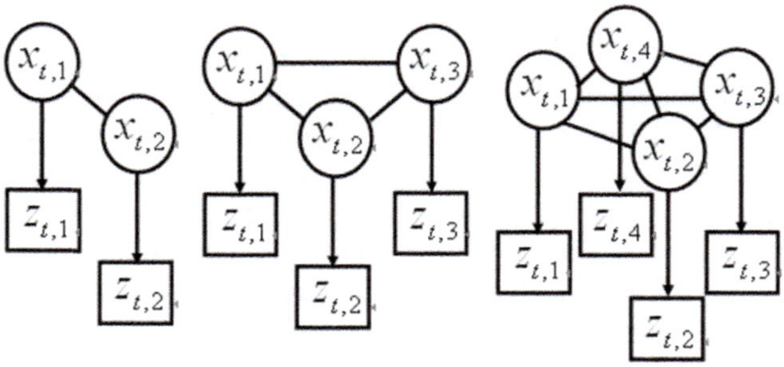

Fig. 1. Graphical models for the multi-view states at a time instant. From left to right, 2, 3 and 4 views are used respectively.

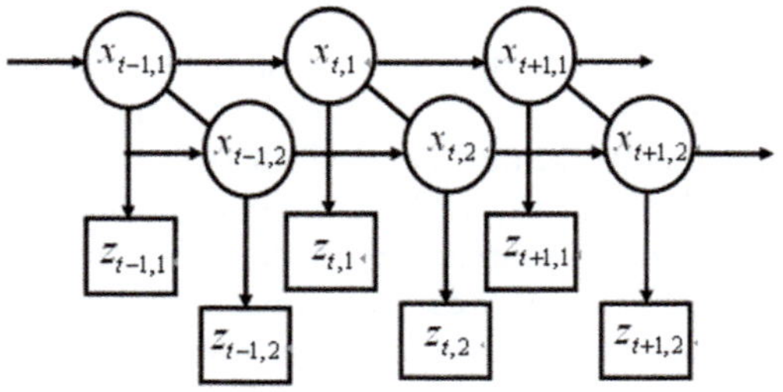

Fig. 2. Dynamic graphical model for the multi-view states. Only a two-view model is illustrated as an example.

link from $x_{t-1,i}$ to $x_{t,i}$ represents the prior dynamics and is associated with a dynamic model $p(x_{t,j}|x_{t-1,j})$.

According to Bayes' rule, the recursive inference of the posterior distribution of the multi-view state $p(X_t|Z^t)$ is formulated as

$$\begin{aligned} \textbf{predict:}\quad & P(X_t|Z^{t-1}) = \int P(X_t|X_{t-1})\, P(X_{t-1}|Z^{t-1})\, \mathrm{d}\, X_{t-1} \\ \textbf{update:}\quad & P(X_t|Z^t) \quad \propto P(Z_t|X_t)\, P(X_t|Z^{t-1}) \end{aligned}$$

X_t is the multi-view state at time t, and $Z^t = \{Z_1, \ldots, Z_t\}$ are the image observations up to time t.

The inference of the joint multi-view state is difficult due to the lack of a closed-form solution. In practice, we infer the posterior of the single-view states $P(x_{t,j}|Z^t)$, $j = 1, \ldots, L$. We show in the following sections how the inference is done using sequential belief propagation.

3 Sequential Belief Propagation

Sequential belief propagation, a non-parametric and sequential version of belief propagation, was first introduced by Hua and Wu [1]. We borrow the idea and apply it to our specific task.

The basic idea of the multi-view tracking algorithm is to calculate the inference of multi-view states through a message passing process. The local message passed from view i to view j in the graphical model in Figure 1 is

$$m_{ji}(x_{t,j}) \leftarrow \int \left(\prod_{k \in N(x_{t,i}) \setminus j} m_{ik}(x_{t,i}) \right) p_i(z_{t,i}|x_{t,i})\, \psi^t_{i,j}(x_{t,i}, x_{t,j})\, \mathrm{d}\, x_{t,i}, \quad (1)$$

where $N(x_{t,i})$ denotes the set of views connected to $x_{t,i}$ through an undirected link, and $N(x_{t,i})\setminus j$ means the neighboring views of $x_{t,i}$ except $x_{t,j}$. The first part of the right side of Equation 1 is the message that view i receives from its neighbors except j, the second part is the information of the image likelihood in view i, and the last part is the potential function mapping these information from view i to view j.

To infer $P(x_{t,j}|Z^t)$, $j = 1, \ldots, L$ based on the dynamic graphical model in Figure 2, we take into consideration the message from the previous time instants.

We assume independent dynamic models at each view,

$$P(X_t|X_{t-1}) = \prod_j p(x_{t,j}|x_{t-1,j}). \quad (2)$$

Given the posterior at the previous time instant $P(x_{t-1,j}|Z^{t-1})$, $j = 1, \ldots, L$, Equation 1 is updated as

$$\begin{aligned} m_{ji}(x_{t,j}) \leftarrow \int \Bigg[\int p(x_{t,i}|x_{t-1,i})\, P(x_{t-1,i}|Z^{t-1})\, \mathrm{d}\, x_{t-1,i} \\ \left(\prod_{k \in N(x_{t,i}) \setminus j} m_{ik}(x_{t,i}) \right) p_i(z_{t,i}|x_{t,i})\, \psi^t_{i,j}(x_{t,i}, x_{t,j}) \Bigg] \mathrm{d}\, x_{t,i}. \end{aligned} \quad (3)$$

Actually, only the information from the previous time instant is integrated into the new message passing process in the graphical model in Figure 2.

Thus, the marginal posterior $P(x_{t,j}|Z^t)$ is given by

$$\begin{aligned} P(x_{t,j}|Z^t) \propto \\ p_i(z_{t,j}|x_{t,j}) \left(\prod_{i \in N(x_{t,j})} m_{ji}(x_{t,j}) \right) \int p(x_{t,j}|x_{t-1,j})\, P(x_{t-1,j}|Z^{t-1})\, \mathrm{d}\, x_{t-1,j}. \end{aligned} \quad (4)$$

In fact, the new marginal posterior of Equation 4 is the traditional version plus a message passing process that integrates information from other views.

In practice, the SBP algorithm, implemented using sequential Monte Carlo methods, iterates the message passing process until convergence. Consult Hua and Wu [1] for the details of SBP and its Monte Carlo implementation.

4 Multi-view Tracking Using SBP

Our goal is to solve the occlusion problem in single-view tracking by exploiting multi-view information. The SBP algorithm introduced above is well suited for the task.

4.1 The Monte Carlo Implementation

The key of the approach is to propagate the marginal posterior $P(x_{t,j}|Z^t)$ in time using Equation 2, 3, 4. Both the posterior and the messages are represented by weighted particles,

$$m_{ji}(x_{t,j}) \sim \{s_{t,j}^{(n)}, \omega_{t,j}^{(i,n)}\}_{n=1}^{N}, \; i \in N(x_{t,j}),$$
$$P(x_{t,j}|Z^t) \sim \{s_{t,j}^{(n)}, \pi_{t,j}^{(n)}\}_{n=1}^{N}, \quad j = 1, \ldots, L,$$

where $s_{t,j}^{(n)}$ is the particles sampled at view j, $\omega_{t,j}^{(i,n)}$ is the weight of the message received from view i, and $\pi_{t,j}^{(n)}$ is the belief of the particle based on the observations at all the views. N is the number of particles. Note that the same particle set is used to represent the message and the posterior distribution. The Monte Carlo implementation of the algorithm is described in Algorithm 1.

It is easy to see that the occlusion problem can be effectively solved by the proposed algorithm unless the target is occluded in all the views. Our approach is superior to the best view selection strategy proposed in [4, 5] in that the full information at all the views is taken into consideration during tracking. Even a view in which the target is completely occluded "contributes" to the tracking results by propagating uniformly distributed belief to other views. Although the view isn't informative, it will not affect the inference of the target states at other views. As a result, wrong information propagation is avoided.

Algorithm 1 is similar to the one proposed by Hua and Wu [1]. We extend the original algorithm by adding a fusion module to infer the target states on the ground plane and by modifying the potential function to fit the mulit-view tracking task.

4.2 The Potential Function

An issue in Algorithm 1 is the potential function that describes the spatial relation between the states at two different views. To simplify the problem, we model the target in a view as a rectangle so that the view state x_j is a 4D vector (u_j, v_j, h_j, w_j), where (u_j, v_j) is the middle point of the bottom of the bounding box and (h_j, w_j) is the 2D size.

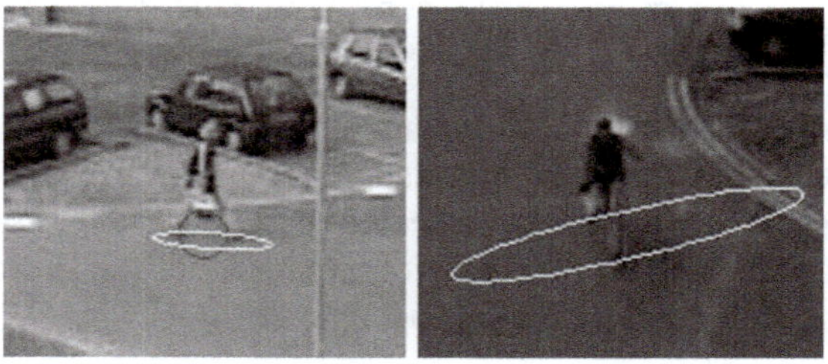

Fig. 3. Uncertainty propagation. The red circle in each view is the uncertainty of the target position in the current view (we assume constant and diagonal gaussian noise), and the white ellipse is the uncertainty propagated from the other view. It is clear that the transformation from the right view to the left is more certain.

Algorithm 1. SBP based Multi-view Tracking

Require: Given $\{s_{t-1,j}^{(n)}, \pi_{t-1,j}^{(n)}\}_{n=1}^{N}, j = 1, \dots, L$

Ensure: Generate $\{s_{t,j}^{(n)}, \pi_{t,j}^{(n)}\}_{n=1}^{N}, j = 1, \dots, L$

1. INITIALIZATION: $k \longleftarrow 1$, for $j = 1, \dots, L$

1.1 *Resampling*: resample $\{s_{t-1,j}^{(n)}, \pi_{t-1,j}^{(n)}\}_{n=1}^{N}$ to get $\{s_{t-1,j}^{(n)}, 1/N\}_{n=1}^{N}$

1.2 *Prediction*: generate $\{s_{t,j,k}^{(n)}\}_{n=1}^{N}$ from $p(x_{t,j}|x_{t-1,j})$

1.3 *Belief Initialization*: for $n = 1, \dots, N$

$$\pi_{t,j,k}^{(n)} = p_j(z_{t,j,k}^{(n)}|s_{t,j,k}^{(n)})$$

1.4 *Message Initialization*: for $n = 1, \dots, N, i \in N(j)$

$$\omega_{t,j,k}^{(i,n)} = \frac{1}{N} \quad \text{(uniformly distributed)}$$

2. ITERATION: SBP

2.1 *Importance Sampling*: Sample $\{s_{t,j,k+1}^{(n)}\}_{n=1}^{N}$ from $P(x_{t,j}|x_{t-1,j})$

2.2 *Message Reweighting*: for $n = 1, \dots, N, i \in N(j)$

$$\omega_{t,j,k+1}^{(i,n)} = G_{t,j}^{(i)}(s_{t,j,k+1}^{(n)}) \Big/ \left(\frac{1}{N}\sum_{r=1}^{N} p(s_{t,j,k+1}^{(n)}|s_{t-1,j}^{(r)})\right),$$

where

$$G_{t,j}^{(i)}(s_{t,j,k+1}^{(n)}) = \sum_{m=1}^{N}\left[\pi_{t,i,k}^{(m)} p_i(z_{t,i,k}^{(m)}|s_{t,i,k}^{(m)}) \left(\prod_{l\in N(i)\backslash j} \omega_{t,i,k}^{(l,m)}\right) \left(\frac{1}{N}\sum_{r=1}^{N} p(s_{t,i,k}^{(m)}|s_{t-1,i}^{(r)})\right) \psi_{i,j}(s_{t,i,k}^{(m)}, s_{t,j,k+1}^{(n)})\right].$$

Normalize so that $\sum_n \omega_{t,j,k+1}^{(i,n)} = 1$.

2.3 *Belief Reweighting*: for $n = 1, \dots, N$

$$\pi_{t,j,k+1}^{(n)} = p_j(z_{t,j,k+1}^{(n)}|s_{t,j,k+1}^{(n)}) \left(\prod_{l\in N(j)} \omega_{t,j,k+1}^{(l,n)}\right) \left(\frac{1}{N}\sum_{r=1}^{N} p(s_{t,j,k+1}^{(n)}|s_{t-1,j}^{(r)})\right)$$

Normalize so that $\sum_n \pi_{t,j,k+1}^{(n)} = 1$.

2.4 *Iteration*: $k \longleftarrow k + 1$, iterate until convergence.

3. INFERENCE ESTIMATION:

$$p(x_{t,j}|Z_t) \sim \{s_{t,j,k}^{(n)}, \pi_{t,j,k}^{(n)}\}_{n=1}^{N}, \quad j = 1, \dots, L$$

4. FUSION: The target states in 3D are estimated by fusing the individual view states.

We assume that the targets of interest always move on a calibrated ground plane, which is usual in video surveillance and team sports senarios, so that the positions

(u_j, v_j) at different views are related to each other by a homography between each pair of views [3]. The propagation of the target sizes between views is a little more difficult because we need the full camera calibration information, by which we can infer the real target sizes in 3D and then project to other views. Fortunately, this information is available in most video surveillance applications where still cameras are used.

Therefore, the potential function $\psi_{i,j}$ is defined as

$$\psi_{i,j}(x_i, x_j) \propto \lambda N(x_i; u_{x_i}, \Lambda_i) + (1-\lambda) N\left(x_i; \Pi_j(x_j), \Sigma_j(x_j)\right), \tag{5}$$

where the first term is the standard Gaussian outlier process, Π_j is a function that transforms the view state x_j to view i, and Σ_j is a function that propagates the uncertainty of x_j to view i using techniques from perturbation theory [10], see Fig. 3.

5 Results

Since 2-view data are most readily available, a SBP-based 2-view tracker was developed. The same principles apply when three or more views are used, although loops exist in the graphical model. For such situations, it was shown that loopy BP typically still yields good approximate results [8].

As described in Section 4.2, the target state $x_{t,j}$ is defined as a 4D vector with two coordinates for the position and the other two for the size to handle the scale changes. The motion model $p(x_{t,j}|x_{t-1,j})$ at each view is the standard constant-velocity model.

Following Perez et al. [11], a classical color observation model based on HSV color histograms is adopted which has the advantage of being insensitive to illumination effects. Thus, the observation process is to match the color histogram in a candidate region, a particle, with a pre-learned reference model, where the Bhattacharyya similarity coefficient is computed to measure the distance. The effectiveness of this model has been shown previously [11, 12, 4] and is confirmed by this work. In all the experiments, we manually initialize the regions of targets of interest at the first frame of each camera and learn the reference color models.

5.1 Video Surveillance

PETS2001 Dataset Two contains sequences taken from two calibrated cameras and is used to evaluate the above algorithm. Figure 4 shows the result of tracking a pedestrian in subsequences of Camera 1 and Camera 2 from Frame 600 to Frame 800. The pedestrian is completely occluded by a tree in Camera 1 but is visible all the time in Camera 2. Thus, the algorithm successfully tracks the target during the occlusion in Camera1 by receiving messages from Camera 2. Although the result is a little biased due to the uncertainty propagation, it is corrected when the target reappears after the occlusion.

Figure 5 shows the result of tracking the same pedestrian from Frame 775 to Frame 850 and the comparison with Condensation [13]. Since we learn a simple color model of the target from only one frame, sometimes it is not very distinctive from the background. As a result, Condensation fails at the 805th frame of Camera 1 and at the 819th frame of Camera 2. However, our multi-view tracking algorithm keeps tracking by exchanging information across views. We agree that the problem may be solved by learning a better

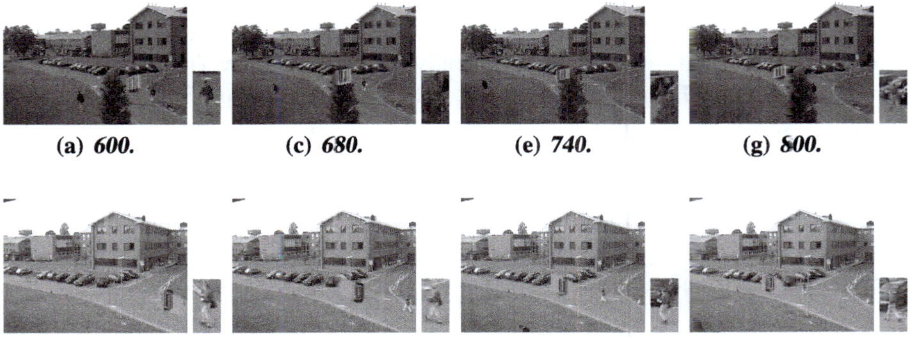

(a) *600.* (c) *680.* (e) *740.* (g) *800.*

(i) *600.* (k) *680.* (m) *740.* (o) *800.*

Fig. 4. Result of tracking a pedestrian. Blue rectangles are the particles sampled in the current view, while the green ones are the particles mapped from the other view using the homography between the two views. The white rectangles are the estimated target states of the view, whereas the red rectangles are the target states of the other view which are mapped to the view using the same homography.

(a) ***SBPMVT-805.*** (b) ***Condensation-805.*** (c) ***SBPMVT-819.*** (d) ***Condensation-819.***

Fig. 5. Comparison of the SBP-based multi-view tracker (SBPMVT) with Condensation

(a) ***Camera 1 (600-850).*** (b) ***Camera 2 (600-850).*** (c) ***Camera 1 (1300-1800).*** (d) ***Camera 2 (1300-1800).***

Fig. 6. Results of tracking several different targets

model or using another color space, but the problem still exists: if the target is not distinctive from clutter, it is difficult to maintain the target distribution with a small and fixed number of particles. By integrating multi-view observations, the algorithm is capable of dealing with unstable appearance in one view if stable appearance can be obtained in another view.

Other tracking results can be seen in Figure 6. Note that the two targets that are tracked from Frame 600 to Frame 850 in Figure 6 (a) and (b) are lost afterwards because they become too small to track using only color information. The tracking of a car from Frame 1300 to Frame 1800 is shown in Figure 6 (c) and (d). Since the car turns around in the subsequences of both cameras causing significant appearance changes, it is impossible to learn the reference color model from only one frame. To solve this problem, we sample particles in this experiment from both the motion prior and a proposal distribution obtained from a change detection process based on a background model [14].

Thus, the importance sampling function is

$$(1-\alpha)p(x_{t,j}|x_{t-1,j}) + \alpha p(x_{t,j}|B_{t,j}), \tag{6}$$

where $B_{t,j}$ is the observation of the foreground.

5.2 Discussion

We find that the potential function $\psi_{i,j}(x_i, x_j)$ is critical to the success of the multi-view tracking algorithm. As is described in Section 4.2, the target states at one view are transformed to another view by a homography under the assumption that the targets move on the ground plane. However, the transformation has large uncertainty if the camera view direction is highly oblique, for instance, when the camera position is close to the ground plane. In this case, more particles are needed to model the target distribution. This motivates the use of more views (> 2) which will reduce the uncertainty.

The extra fusion module that combines results at each view can be removed by adding a node representing the target states in 3D (2D ground) in the graphical model in Figure 2. The addition of this global node does not only change the current, fully-connected graphical model to a two-level, tree-structured graphical model, making the system more scalable and flexible to varying numbers of cameras, but also enables us to infer the 3D target states inside the SBP algorithm.

6 Conclusion and Future Work

This paper presents a novel multi-view tracking method that addresses the occlusion problem using bidirectional belief propagation. The strength of the method relies on the fact that information is integrated and exchanged across views so that a collaborative tracking scheme is formed. Technically, the tracking processes at different views perform the inference of the target states separately but based on the multi-view observations. A sequential and purely non-parametric belief propagation algorithm is adopted to allow individual trackers to collaborate in each view, which largely avoids the problem of propagating wrong information. As demonstrated, the method is robust and capable of dealing with occlusions as long as the targets of interest are visible in at least one view.

We are currently extending this work by adding one node in the graphical model representing the 3D target states. Another extension which is also ongoing is to track multiple targets simultaneously, which will broaden the applicability of the system.

References

1. Hua, G., Wu, Y.: Multi-scale visual tracking by sequential belief propagation. In: IEEE Conference on Computer Vision and Pattern Recognition. (2004)
2. Black, J., Ellis, T.: Multi camera image tracking. In: the Second IEEE International Workshop on Performance Evaluation of Tracking and Surveillance, Hawaii, USA (2001)
3. Hayet, J.B., Mathes, T., Czyk, J., Piater, J., Verly, J., Macq, B.: A modular multi-camera framework for team sports tracking. In: International Conference on Advanced Video and Signal based Surveillance, Como, Italy (2005)
4. Nummiaro, K., Koller-Meier, E., Svoboda, T., Roth, D., Van Gool, L.: Color-based object tracking in multi-cameras environment. In: 25th Pattern Recognition Symposium, DAGM. (2003)
5. Wang, Y., Wu, J., Kassim, A.: Multiple cameras tracking using particle filtering. In: IEEE International Workshop on Performance Evaluation of Tracking and Surveillance, Breckenridge, USA (2005)
6. Doucet, A., de Freitas, N., Gordon, N.: sequnetial Monte Carlo methods in practice. Springer-Verlag, New York (2001)
7. Sudderth, E., Ihler, A., Freeman, W., Willsky, A.: Nonparametric belief propagation. In: IEEE Conference on Computer Vision and Pattern Recognition, Madison, USA (2003) 605–612
8. Freeman, W., Pasztor, E.: Learning low-level vision. In: International Conference on Computer Vision, Greece (1999)
9. Ferryman, J.: (Pets websites: http://visualsurveillance.org/pets2001)
10. Criminisi, A., Reid, I., Zisserman, A.: A plane measuring device. In: British Machine Vision Conference. (1997)
11. Pérez, P., Hue, C., Vermaak, J., Gangnet, M.: Color-based probabilistic tracking. In: European Conference on Computer Vision. Volume 1. (2002) 661–675
12. Okuma, K., Taleghani, A., Freitas, N., Little, J., Lowe, D.: A boosted particle filter: multitarget detection and tracking. In: European Conference on Computer Vision. (2004) 28–39
13. Isard, M., Blake, A.: Condensation-conditional density propagation for visual tracking. International Journal of Computer Vision **29** (1998) 5–28
14. Stauffer, C., Grimson, W.: Adaptive background mixture models for real-time tracking. In: IEEE Conference on Computer Vision and Pattern Recognition. (1999)

Online Updating Appearance Generative Mixture Model for Meanshift Tracking

Jilin Tu[1], Hai Tao[2], and Thomas Huang[1]

[1] Elec. and Comp. Engr. Dept.
Univ. of Illinois at Urbana and Champaign,
Urbana, IL 61801
{jilintu, huang}@ifp.uiuc.edu
[2] Elec. Engr. Dept.
Univ. of Calif. at Santa Cruz,
Santa Cruz, CA 12345
tao@soe.ucsc.edu

Abstract. This paper proposes an appearance generative mixture model based on key frames for meanshift tracking. Meanshift tracking algorithm tracks object by maximizing the similarity between the histogram in tracking window and a static histogram acquired at the beginning of tracking. The tracking therefore may fail if the appearance of the object varies substantially. Assume the key appearances of the object can be acquired before tracking, the manifold of the object appearance can be approximated by some piece-wise linear combination of these key appearances in histogram space. The generative process can be described by a bayesian graphical model. Online EM algorithm is then derived to estimate the model parameters and to update the appearance histogram. The updating histogram would improve meanshift tracking accuracy and reliability, and the model parameters infer the state of the object with respect to the key appearances. We applied this approach to track human head motion and to infer the head pose simultaneously in videos. Experiments verify that, our online histogram generative updating algorithm constrained by key appearance histograms avoids the drifting problem often encountered in tracking with online updating, that the enhanced meanshift algorithm is capable of tracking object of varying appearances more robustly and accurately, and that our tracking algorithm can infer the state of the object(e.g. pose) simultaneously as a bonus.

1 Introduction

Visual tracking of object in complex environments is currently one of the most challenging and intensively studied tasks in machine vision field. Various visual cues have been employed in tracking, such as motion flow, edge, color, depth, etc. As low level visual cues usually tend to be noisy, *a prior* knowledge of the object being tracked is usually applied as global constraints during the tracking. In [1] the appearance statistics of the object is modeled by an appearance eigenspace and a so-called Eigentracking technique is introduced. The success

P.J. Narayanan et al. (Eds.): ACCV 2006, LNCS 3851, pp. 694–703, 2006.

of tracking is therefore largely dependent on the consistency between the actual object appearance and the *a prior* knowledge learnt off-line. This assumption however might be violated due to occlusion, or changing of illumination, etc.

In order to take the novelties into consideration during tracking, people proposed tracking algorithms with online model updating. [2] extended Eigentracking by online updating the object appearance PCA eigenspace using sequential *Karhunen-Loeve* algorithm. Noticing PCA eigenspace results from fitting subspace to data using L_2 norm, Ho[3] took a step further and suggested that fitting appearance subspace to data using L_∞ norm leads to subspace obtained by Gramm-Schmitt orthogonalization. The resulting algorithm incorporates observation novelties into subspace representation in a timely manner, and is able to track objects subject to pose changes, occlusions, and illumination variations, etc. Along the other direction, Jepson [4] proposed to model the appearance of an object as a mixture of stable image structure, outliers, and two frame information obtained from optical flow. An online EM algorithm is employed to infer the model parameters. The inferred stable image structure is adapted to model slow appearance variations of the object, such as variations caused by pose change, and illumination changes. Short time disturbances, such as occlusions, are modeled as outlier processes. While tracking with online learning has the advantage of handling occlusions and appearance variations, they all suffer from drifting problem more or less. The appearance model with online updating tends to drift away from the actual appearance of the object as the tracking error accumulates after tracking of very long period.

Comaniciu[5] proposed a meanshift tracking algorithm that tracks the object by comparing the similarity between histogram of the tracking window and a static histogram acquired before the tracking. Comparing to the other tracking techniques, this algorithm was well-known for real-time computation and robustness against partial occlusion. Afterwards people have proposed many extensions of this algorithm to accommodate different tracking scenarios based on different assumptions. Collins[6] first proposed to improve the ad-hoc kernel scale selection technique in mean-shift tracking algorithm by using scale space techniques. Zivkovic[7] reformulated the mean-shift process as a EM optimization process and the scale selection problem is solved as a variance estimation problem in a way similar to mean estimation. To avoid the distraction caused by background pixels in tracking window during mean-shift tracking, Porikli[8] proposed to weight the mean-shift kernel by foreground likelihood.

While all the extensions of mean-shift algorithms focuses on the adaption of kernel parameters, they all assume the histogram of the tracked object does not change much during the tracking. This assumption limited its application in scenario where the appearance of the object changes substantially. For example, the histogram of the frontal face of a person may be substantially different from that of the rear view of the person's head, therefore mean-shift tracker with histogram of the frontal face could become unstable when the person turns his face away from the camera. In [9], Birchfield attacked similar problem by using histogram intersection to blend both skin color and hair color when computing histogram similarity. This idea however can not be applied directly in mean-shift algorithm due to different tracking mechanism.

In this paper, we propose to adapt the static histogram in meanshift tracking algorithm by modeling it as random variable generated by piecewise linear combination of some histogram pairs in a generative framework. The model parameters can be estimated using on-line Expectation Maximizition(EM) techniques. With the histogram updated online, the meanshift tracker is able to track object of vast varying appearances. In the mean time, the constraints of the key appearance histograms prevent the tracking from drifting. We applied our algorithms to human head tracking. The experiments indicate that our algorithms can achieve more robust and accurate tracking performance comparing to ordinary meanshift algorithm. In the mean time, the head poses are successfully inferred based on the generative model parameters inferred during the tracking.

We first brief meanshift tracking algorithm in Section 2. In Section 3, the framework of meanshift tracking with online histogram updating is introduced. Section 4 introduces our histogram generative model and online EM algorithm. Section 5 presents the experimental evaluation on human head motion tracking and pose estimation using meanshift tracking with/without our histogram updating technique. We summarize the benefits of histogram updating and discuss some future works in Section 6.

2 Meanshift Tracking[5]

Suppose the appearance of the object is represented by normalized color histogram, denoted as $\mathbf{h}_1 = \{h_1(n)\}$, and the histogram of the tracking window centered at y be $\mathbf{h}_2(y) = \{h_2(y,n)\}$. The similarity between the two histograms can be represented by $\rho[\mathbf{h}_1, \mathbf{h}_2(y)] = \sum_n \sqrt{h_1(n)h_2(y,n)}$.

Denote a kernel centered at pixel p_i as $k(p_i)$, the Meanshift tracking algorithm can be summarized as follows:

1. Compute the histogram $\mathbf{h}_2(y_0)$ in the current frame, calculate $\rho_0 = \rho[\mathbf{h}_1, \mathbf{h}_2(y_0)] = \sum_n \sqrt{h_1(n)h_2(y_0,n)}$.
2. Compute likelihood ratio β_i between the current frame and the previous frame at each pixel in the tracking window : $\beta_i = \sum_n^N \delta[I(p_i) - n]\sqrt{\frac{h_1(n)}{h_2(y,n)}}$, i=1,..,R.
3. Compute the new location y_1 by meanshift $y_1 = \frac{\sum_i^R p_i \beta_i k(p_i)}{\sum_i^R \beta_i k(p_i)}$ and compute $\rho_1 = \rho[\mathbf{h}_1, \mathbf{h}_2(y_1)]$.
4. Quit with failure if $|\rho_1| < \epsilon_0$, quit with success if $|\rho_1 - \rho_0| < \epsilon_1$, else $y_0 = y_1$, goto 1.

3 Meanshift Tracking with Online Appearance Updating

As the template histogram $\mathbf{h}_1 = \{h_1(n)\}$ is kept static, the performance of meanshift tracking algorithm would become unpredictable in scenario where the appearance of the object has been undergoing huge variations.

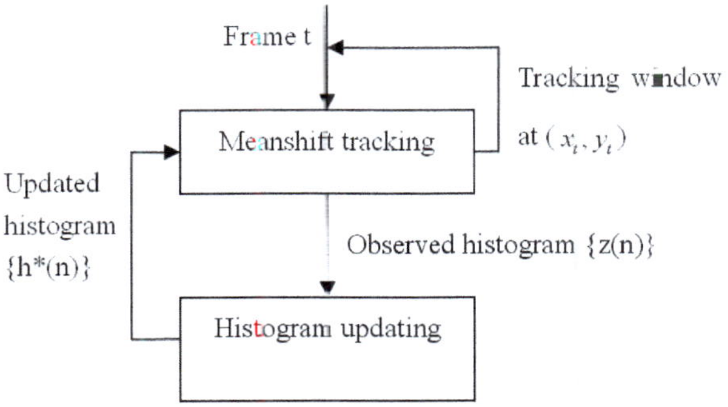

Fig. 1. The flowchart for meanshift tracking with histogram updating

A solution to this problem is to do online histogram updating. As we mentioned at the beginning of the paper, tracking with online model updating without constraints results in drifting problem. We therefore would rather constrain the online updating process by some key appearances acquired before the tracking. The key appearances can be acquired manually from some representative frames in the video. Or they can be acquired automatically. As tracking with online learning usually provides good performance for short clips without drifting problem, the tracked appearances in the tracking window can be clustered into key frames and be used by our algorithm for tracking video of very long period. Therefore our algorithm is an effective complement to the current available tracking tools.

The flowchart for meanshift tracking with histogram updating is illustrated in Figure 1. At frame t, meanshift tracking is carried out with an approximated histogram constrained on the manifold defined by key appearance histograms given the histogram observed in the tracking window of frame $t-1$. The approximated histogram is then updated based on the histogram observation in the updated tracking window of frame t. This procedure may iterate several times till the center of the tracking window converges. The question is now how to generate a histogram that approximates the observed histogram subject to the manifold constraints imposed by the key appearance histograms. We propose two bayesian inference approaches to attack this problem.

4 Generating Histogram from Piece-Wise Linear Combination of Key Appearance Histogram Pairs

Suppose K key appearances of the object can be acquired before the tracking. Denote their histograms as $\{h_1(n)\}$, $\{h_2(n)\}$,..., $\{h_K(n)\}$. And suppose the histogram of the object being tracked at current frame $\{z^*(n)\}$ can be piece-wise linearly approximated by some pairs of the key appearance histograms. The formulation is thus as follows:

$$z^*(n) = \sum_{t=1}^{M} \{w_t h_{L(t)}(n) + (1 - w_t) h_{R(t)}(n)\}[m = t] \quad (1)$$

where [.] is a boolean operator, e.g. $[m = t] = 1$ if $m = t$, otherwise $[m = t] = 0$, m is a discrete hidden variable, $w_t \in [0\,1], t = 1, ..., M$ is the model parameter. $L(t), R(t) \in [1, ..., K]$ specifies the pairs of key appearance samples and defines the configuration of the appearance manifold that is piece-wise linearly approximated. The $\{L(t), R(t) : t = 1, ..., M\}$ pairs are specified by user according to domain knowledge. In the simple case where every pair of key appearance samples are considered, we have $M = K(K-1)/2$.

The bayesian generative model is illustrated in Figure 2.

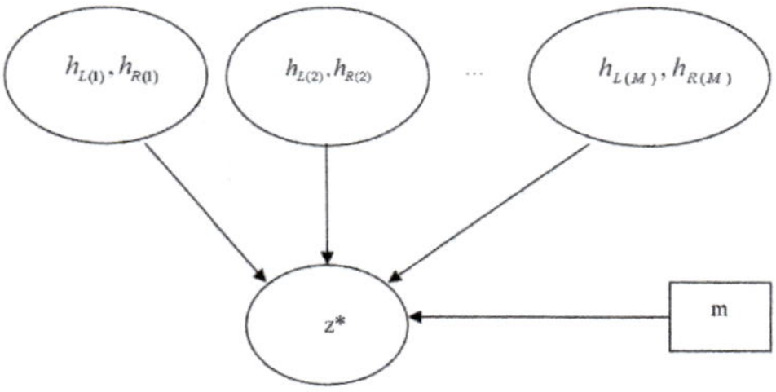

Fig. 2. The generative model for piece-wise linearly approximation of key appearances

Assuming gaussian distribution for simplicity, the joint distribution of the observation $z(n)$ at histogram bin n and the hidden variable m can be modeled as $P(z(n), m) = p(m)p(z(n)|m)$, where

$$p(m) = \frac{1}{M}, \; for \; m = 1, ..., M$$
$$p(z(n)|m) = \prod_{t=1}^{M} [G(z(n); w_t h_{L(t)}(n) + (1 - w_t) h_{R(t)}(n), \Psi)]^{[t=m]} \quad (2)$$

where $G(; \mu, \Psi)$ denotes Gaussian distribution with mean μ and covariance Ψ.

We can conveniently obtain the *a posterior* probability of m given observation z,

$$p(m|z) = \frac{p(z,m)}{p(z)} = \frac{p(z,m)}{\sum_{t=1}^{K} p(z,t)} = \frac{p(z|m)}{\sum_{t=1}^{K} p(z|t)} \quad (3)$$

The expectation of log likelihood of the observation of histogram $\{z(n)\}$ is

$$E[LL(\{z(n)\}|m, \mathbf{w})] = \sum_{n} \sum_{m=1}^{M} p(m|z(n)) \log p(z(n), m)$$
$$\sim \sum_{n} \sum_{m=1}^{M} p(m|z(n)) \log G(z(n); w_m h_{L(m)} + (1 - w_m) h_{R(m)}, \Psi).$$

Let $\frac{\partial E[LL]}{\partial w_m} = 0, m = 1, ..., M$, the following updating rule is obtained:

$$\hat{w}_m = \frac{\sum_n [z(n) - h_{R(m)}(n)][h_{L(m)}(n) - h_{R(m)}(n)]p(m|z(n))}{\sum_n [h_{L(m)}(n) - h_{R(m)}(n)]^2 p(m|z(n))}$$

Intuitively, we can tell this updating rule computes a probability weighted similarity measure between $\{z(n)\}$ and $h_{R(m)}(n)$, $h_{L(m)}(n)$.

If we further consider the past histogram observations under an exponential envelope located at the current time u, $C_u(k) = \alpha e^{-(u-k)/\tau}$, for $k \leq u$. $\alpha = 1 - e^{-\tau}$ so that $\sum_{k=-\infty}^{u} C_u(k) = 1$. The expectation of log likelihood of the observation of histogram $\{z_l(n) : l = -\infty, ..., u\}$ becomes

$$E[LL(\{z_l(n)\}|\{m_l, \mathbf{w}_l\}, l = -\infty...u)] = \sum_{l=u}^{-\infty} C_u(l) E[LL(\{z_l(n)\}|m_l, \mathbf{w}_l)]$$

With the assumption that the histogram of the object does not change very quickly, we have the approximation $p(m_u = t|z_l(n)) \sim p(m_l = t|z_l(n)), t = 1, ..., M$ if time l and u are close enough. Taking the derivative of expectation of log likelihood, we obtain the updating rules

$$D^1_{t,u} = \alpha \sum_n [z_u(n) - h_{R(t)}(n)][h_{L(t)}(n) - h_{R(t)}(n)]p(m_u = t|z_u(n)) + (1 - \alpha)D^1_{u-1}$$

$$D^2_{t,u} = \alpha \sum_n [h_{L(t)}(n) - h_{R(t)}(n)]^2 p(m_u = t|z_u(n)) + (1 - \alpha)D^2_{u-1}$$

$$\hat{w}_{t_u} = \frac{D^1_{t,u}}{D^2_{t,u}} \tag{4}$$

Therefore given histogram $\{z_u(n)\}$ as observation and $\{\hat{w}_{t_{u-1}}\}$ as initialization of the model parameters $\{\hat{w}_t\}$ at frame u, the model parameters can be inferred as follows:

E-Step. Compute $p(m|z_u(n))$ using Eq. 3 with $p(z(n)|m)$ defined in Eq. 2.
M-Step. Compute $\hat{w}_t, t = 1, ..., M$ using Eq. 4,

Finally, the approximated histogram given current histogram observation $\{z(n)\}$is

$$h^*(n) = E[z^*(n)|z(n)] = \sum_{t=1}^{M} \{\hat{w}_t h_{L(t)}(n) + (1 - \hat{w}_t)h_{R(t)}(n)\}p(m = t|z(n))$$

Loosely speaking, $\{h^*(n)\}$ can be understood as the point closest to the histogram observation on the manifold approximated by the key frame histograms in a probabilistic sense. We then use $\{h^*(n)\}$ as the color histogram template for meanshift tracking.

Suppose the histogram bin size is of $D \times D \times D$, and M pairs of key appearance histograms are specified, the computation complexity is asymptotically $O(MD^3)$ per iteration.

5 Experiments

One frequently encountered application scenario in human machine interaction is to track a person's head and to detect the person's head pose. The detection of the person's frontal face in particular can trigger some other face analyzing tools to reveal the person's identity, facial expression, eye gaze, lip movement, etc.

We find our algorithm a perfect application to this scenario as the head pose could be inferred directly according to the online updated histogram generative model parameters. For evaluation purpose, a video sequence is shot in which the subject moves his head around with different head poses starting with frontal view pose. The background contains a lot of shading, the color of which resembles the hair color, thus could be distraction of meanshift tracker. The frame size of the video is of 180 by 120. Because human head motion is relatively slow, the video is down-sampled to 4 frames/second.

For convenience of notation, the algorithms we are going to evaluate are indexed as follows:

MS_STATIC. Meanshift algorithm with static histogram
MS_UPDATE. Meanshift algorithm with histogram updating

We first applied algorithm **MS_STATIC** to the video. The histogram is computed in RGB color space with bin size $10 \times 10 \times 10$. The histogram bin size remains the same for the rest of the experiment. Similar to CAMShift in OpenCV[10], the window size is automatically adapted according to the 2-nd order moment of the object likelihood image. Some frames of the tracking result are shown in the first column of Figure 3. As template histogram is static and can not exactly characterize the appearance of the object in motion, the tracking window lags behind the head motion. The last 3 frames show that the shading in the background resembles the hair color and distracts the tracking window after the subject turns his head sideways.

To apply the meanshift algorithm with histogram updating, we acquired the human head appearances of frontal view, side view, and rear view before the tracking. Denote their histograms as $\{h_1(n)\}$, $\{h_2(n)\}$, and $\{h_3(n)\}$ respectively.

Fig. 3. Results for meanshift tracking with/without histogram updating. (a) **MS_STATIC**; (b)**MS_UPDATE**.

We assumed that the histogram of the human head appearance at arbitrary pose can be approximated by either the linear combination of frontal view and side view histograms, or that of side view and rear view. The piece-wise linearly approximation model is thus formulated as

$$z(n) = \{w_1 h_1(n) + (1 - w_1)h_2(n)\}[m = 1] \\ +\{w_2 h_3(n) + (1 - w_2)h_2(n)\}[m = 2] \quad (5)$$

We let $\alpha = 0.2$ so that the past 5-10 frames can be taken into consideration during on-line EM updating, and we empirically specified $\Psi = 0.1$. The key frames of the tracking result are shown in the second row of Figure 3. Comparing to the result of **MS_STATIC** in the first row, the new histogram updating mechanism enabled the meanshift tracker to track the head very closely when the head is turning away from the camera.

After histogram normalization, the approximation error between the observed histogram and the updated histogram is 0.164. Therefore the histogram updated with piece-wise linear combination constraint approximated the observed histogram in tracking windows pretty accurately.

As we collected appearance histogram for three key head poses(frontal, side, and rear views), we wish to infer these head poses through the estimated histogram generative model parameters. using the rule as follows taking Eq. 5 into consideration:

1. If majority vote of hidden variable m is frontal-side view combination, and $w_1 > T$, predict the head pose is frontal view.
2. If majority vote of hidden variable m is rear-side view combination, and $w_2 > T$, predict the head pose is rear view.
3. Otherwise, predict the head pose is side view.

The threshold T is set to 0.5 by default, but user may adjust it in practice. Figure 4 compares the pose estimation accuracy against ground truth during the video. The ground truth is labeled by visual inspection. We can tell our algorithm was able to make correct estimation despite background clutters and illumination variations, except the estimation result is in general lagging behind the ground truth.

We also notice abnormality at frame 140 where the estimation predicted the ground truth when the subject is turning from rear view to side view. This is

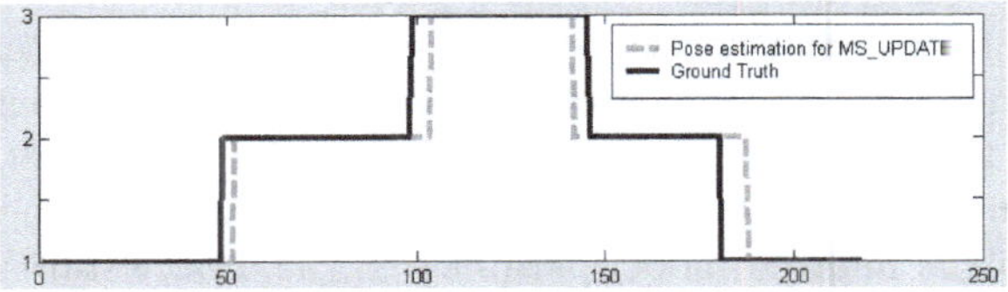

Fig. 4. Comparison of the pose estimation against ground truth for the whole video sequence. Frontal view–1; Side view–2; Rear view–3

actually caused by tracking inaccuracy. The tracking at this frame is somewhat distracted by background clusters, and give inaccurate pose estimation which happens to be the pose which the subject is about to turn to.

Finally, we applied our algorithm to some video sequences provided by Birchfield[11], some key frames for tracking one of the video are shown in Figure 5. The video contains a lot of head movements and pose changes. The background contains a lot of clutters, and some clutters has color components resembles skin color. As the head moves, the shading on the face also varies. In the middle of the video, the subject waves yellow folders and hands in front of his face. Therefore it is a very challenging video for tracking and pose estimation. Our algorithm is able to track the whole sequence, and reaches pose recognition accuracy 77% after comparing to ground truth. Comparing to Birchfield's tracking result provided by [11], our algorithm is less likely to be distracted by background clutters and motion dynamics, and can provide head pose estimation as a bonus.

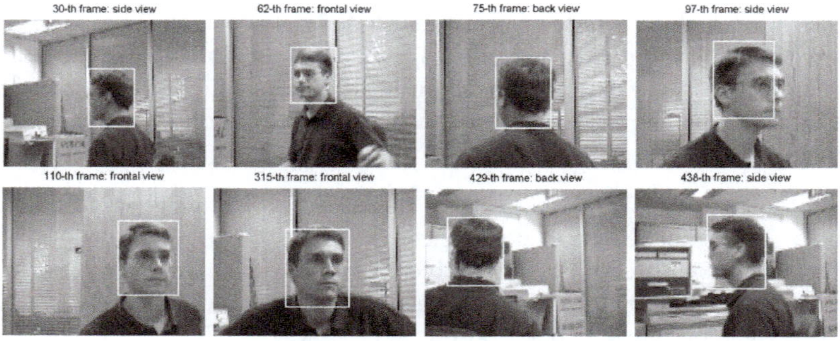

Fig. 5. More results for tracking and pose estimation with algorithm**MS_UPDATE**

6 Summary

In this paper, we proposed a generative mixture model and online EM updating algorithm for histogram updating. Experiment showed that, our model enabled meanshift tracking to achieve more robust tracking performance than that with static histogram. Based on the estimated model parameter, the object state(head poses) could be easily inferred.

Comparing to meanshift tracking with static histogram, meanshift tracking with histogram updating yields more robust and accurate tracking performance. Comparing to the past online learning techniques for visual tracking, our online EM algorithm with key appearance constraints avoids the notorious drifting problem. With the inferred model parameters, the object states(e.g. head pose) can be inferred as bonus.

Taking all these benefits into consideration, acquisition of more than one key appearances for the object, the only overhead added to the tracking algorithm, become worthwhile. Therefore our proposed online histogram updating technique for meanshift tracking is indeed an effective complement to the current tracking techniques. Besides, our proposed histogram generative model with its corresponding online EM updating algorithm is not confined by meanshift algorithm. It can be considered as an general object appearance model that can provide likelihood measure in other bayesian tracking frameworks.

References

1. Black, M., Jepson, A.: Eigentracking: Robust matching and tracking of articulated objects using a view-based representation. Intenational Journal of Computer Vision **26** (1998) 63–84
2. Ross, D., Lim, J., Yang, M.H.: Probabilistic visual tracking with incremental subspace update. In: ECCV. Volume 2. (2004) 470–482
3. Ho, J., Lee, K.C., Yang, M.H., Kriegman, D.: Visual tracking using learned linear subspace. In: IEEE CVPR. (2004)
4. Jepson, A.D., Fleet, D.J., El-Maraghi, T.F.: Robust on-line appearance models for visual tracking. IEEE Transactions on Pattern Analysis and Machine Intelligence **25** (2003) 1296–1311
5. Comaniciu, D., Ramesh, V., Meer, P. Real-time tracking of non-rigid objects using mean shift. In: IEEE Conf. Computer Vision and Pattern Recognition (CVPR'00). Volume 2., Hilton Head Island, South Carolina (2000) 142–149
6. Collins, R.: Mean-shift blob tracking through scale space. In: Computer Vision and Pattern Recognition (CVPR'03), IEEE (2003)
7. Zivkovic, Z., Krose, B.: An em-like algorithm for color-histogram-based object tracking. In: IEEE Computer Society Conference on Computer Vision and Pattern Recognition. Volume 1. (2004) 798–803
8. Porikli, F.: Human body tracking by adaptive background models and mean-shift analysis. In: IEEE International Workshop on Performance Evaluation of Tracking and Surveillance. (2003)
9. Birchfield, S.: Elliptical head tracking using intensity gradients and color histograms. In: Proceedings of the IEEE Conference on Computer Vision and Pattern Recognition. (1998) 232–237
10. G.R., B.: Computer vision face tracking as a component of a perceptual user interface. In: IEEE workshop on Application of Computer Vision, Princeton (1998) 214–219
11. Birchfield, S.: (http://www.ces.clemson.edu/ stb/research/headtracker/)

Theory and Calibration for Axial Cameras

Srikumar Ramalingam[1,2], Peter Sturm[1], and Suresh K. Lodha[2]

[1] INRIA Rhône-Alpes, Montbonnot St Martin, France
{Srikumar.Ramalingam, Peter.Sturm}@inrialpes.fr
[2] University of California, Santa Cruz, USA
lodha@soe.ucsc.edu

Abstract. Although most works in computer vision use perspective or other central cameras, the interest in non-central camera models has increased lately, especially with respect to omnidirectional vision. Calibration and structure-from-motion algorithms exist for both, central and non-central cameras. An intermediate class of cameras, although encountered rather frequently, has received less attention. So-called *axial cameras* are non-central but their projection rays are constrained by the existence of a line that cuts all of them. This is the case for stereo systems, many non-central catadioptric cameras and pushbroom cameras for example. In this paper, we study the geometry of axial cameras and propose a calibration approach for them. We also describe the various axial catadioptric configurations which are more common and less restrictive than central catadioptric ones. Finally we used simulations and real experiments to prove the validity of our theory.

1 Introduction

Many camera models have been considered in computer vision and related fields and even more taylor-made calibration methods have been developed. Most of those are designed for central cameras, but approaches and studies for non-central or general ones also exist [1, 2, 3, 4, 5, 6, 7, 8, 9]. An intermediate class of cameras, lying between central and fully non-central ones, is that of so-called *axial cameras*: their projection rays are constrained by the existence of a line that cuts all of them, the **camera axis**, but they may not go through a single optical center.

The axial model is a rather useful one (cf. figure 1(a) and (b)). Many misaligned catadioptric configurations fall under this model. Such configurations, which are slightly non-central, are usually classified as a non-central camera and calibrated using an iterative nonlinear algorithm [10, 11, 12]. For example, whenever the mirror is a surface of revolution and the central camera looking at the mirror lies anywhere on the revolution axis, the system is of axial type. Furthermore, two-camera stereo systems or systems consisting of three or more aligned cameras, are axial. Pushbroom cameras [13] are another example, although they are of a more restricted class (there exist two camera axes [14]).

In this paper, we propose a generic calibration approach for axial cameras, the first to our knowledge. It uses images of planar calibration grids, put in

P.J. Narayanan et al. (Eds.): ACCV 2006, LNCS 3851, pp. 704–713, 2006.

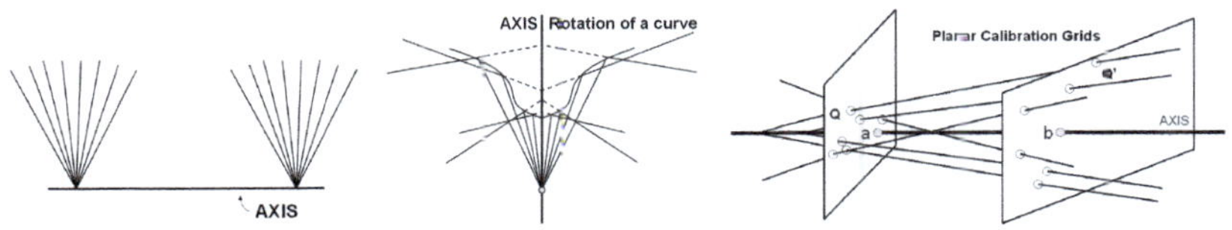

(a) (b) (c)

Fig. 1. Examples of axial imaging models (a) stereo camera (b) a mirror formed by rotating a planar curve about an axis containing the optical center of the perspective camera.(c) Calibration of axial cameras using calibration grids: The projection rays, camera axis and two grids are shown. The axis intersects at **a** and **b** on the first and the second calibration grids respectively.

unknown positions. We show the existence of multi-view tensors that can be estimated linearly and from which the pose of the calibration grids as well as the position of the camera axis, can be recovered. The actual calibration is then performed by computing projection rays for all individual pixels of a camera, constrained to cut the camera axis.

The paper is organized as follows. The problem is formalized in section 2. In section 3, we show what can be done with two images of calibration grids. Complete calibration using three images, is described in section 4, followed by a bundle adjustment algorithm in section 5. Various types of axial catadioptric cameras are listed in section 6. Experimental results and conclusions are given in sections 7 and 8.

2 Problem Formulation

In the following, we will call **camera axis** the line cutting all projection rays. It will be represented by a 6-vector $\mathbf{L}$ and the associated 4×4 skew-symmetric Plücker matrix $[\mathbf{L}]_\times$:

$$[\mathbf{L}]_\times = \begin{pmatrix} 0 & -L_4 & L_6 & -L_2 \\ L_4 & 0 & -L_5 & -L_3 \\ -L_6 & L_5 & 0 & -L_1 \\ L_2 & L_3 & L_1 & 0 \end{pmatrix}$$

The product $[\mathbf{L}]_\times \mathbf{Q}$ gives the plane spanned by the line $\mathbf{L}$ and the point $\mathbf{Q}$. Consider further the two 3-vectors:

$$\mathbf{A} = \begin{pmatrix} L_5 \\ L_6 \\ L_4 \end{pmatrix}, \quad \mathbf{B} = \begin{pmatrix} L_2 \\ L_3 \\ L_1 \end{pmatrix}$$

for which the Plücker constraint holds: $\mathbf{B}^\mathsf{T}\mathbf{A} = 0$. $\mathbf{A}$ represents the point at infinity of the line. The Plücker matrix can be written as:

$$[\mathbf{L}]_\times = \begin{pmatrix} 0 & -L_4 & L_6 & -L_2 \\ L_4 & 0 & -L_5 & -L_3 \\ -L_6 & L_5 & 0 & -L_1 \\ L_2 & L_3 & L_1 & 0 \end{pmatrix} = \begin{pmatrix} [\mathbf{A}]_\times & -\mathbf{B} \\ \mathbf{B}^\mathsf{T} & 0 \end{pmatrix}$$

The calibration problem considered in this paper is to compute projection rays for all pixels of a camera, from images of planar calibration grids in unknown positions. We assume that dense point correspondences are given, i.e. for (many) pixels, we are able to determine the points on the calibration grids that are seen in that pixel. Computed projection rays will be constrained to cut the camera axis. The coordinate system in which calibration will be expressed, is that of the first calibration grid. Calibration thus consists in computing the position of the camera axis and of the projection rays, in that coordinate system. The proposed approach proceeds by first estimating the camera axis and the pose of all grids but the first one.

3 What Can Be Done with Two Views of Calibration Grids?

Consider some pixel and let $\mathbf{Q}$ and $\mathbf{Q}'$ be the corresponding points on the two calibration grids, given as 3D points in the grids' local coordinate systems. Since we consider planar grids, we impose $Q_3 = Q'_3 = 0$.

We have the following constraint on the pose of the second grid $(\mathsf{R}', \mathbf{t}')$ as well as the unknown camera axis $\mathbf{L}$: the line spanned by $\mathbf{Q}$ and $\mathbf{Q}'$ cuts $\mathbf{L}$, hence is coplanar with it. Hence, for the correct pose and camera axis, we must have:

$$\mathbf{Q}^\mathsf{T}[\mathbf{L}]_\times \begin{pmatrix} \mathsf{R}' & \mathbf{t}' \\ \mathbf{0}^\mathsf{T} & 1 \end{pmatrix} \mathbf{Q}' = 0$$

Hence:

$$\begin{pmatrix} Q_1 \\ Q_2 \\ Q_4 \end{pmatrix}^\mathsf{T} \begin{pmatrix} 0 & -L_4 & L_6 & -L_2 \\ L_4 & 0 & -L_5 & -L_3 \\ L_2 & L_3 & L_1 & 0 \end{pmatrix} \begin{pmatrix} \bar{\mathsf{R}}' & \mathbf{t}' \\ \mathbf{0}^\mathsf{T} & 1 \end{pmatrix} \begin{pmatrix} Q'_1 \\ Q'_2 \\ Q'_4 \end{pmatrix} = 0$$

where $\bar{\mathsf{R}}'$ refers to the 3×2 submatrix of R' containing only the first and the second rows. We thus have the following 3×3 tensor that can be estimated linearly from point correspondences:

$$\mathsf{F} \sim \begin{pmatrix} 0 & -L_4 & L_6 & -L_2 \\ L_4 & 0 & -L_5 & -L_3 \\ L_2 & L_3 & L_1 & 0 \end{pmatrix} \begin{pmatrix} \bar{\mathsf{R}}' & \mathbf{t}' \\ \mathbf{0}^\mathsf{T} & 1 \end{pmatrix} \qquad (1)$$

It has only 7 degrees of freedom (9 - 1 for scale, -1 for rank-deficiency) so the 10 unknowns (4 for the camera axis, 3 for R' and 3 for $\mathbf{t}'$) can not be recovered from it.

We now look at what can actually be recovered from F. Let us first notice that its left null-vector is $(L_3, -L_2, L_4)^\mathsf{T}$ (it truly is the null-vector, as can be easily verified when taking into account the Plücker constraint). We thus can recover 2 of the 4 parameters of the camera axis. That null-vector contains actually the coordinates of the camera axis' intersection with the first grid (in plane coordinates). Its 3D coordinates are given by $(L_3, -L_2, 0, L_4)^\mathsf{T}$. Similarly, the right null-vector of F gives the plane coordinates of the axis' intersection with the second grid. Besides this F also gives constraints on R' and $\mathbf{t}'$. For example R' can be extracted up to 2 to 4 solutions. We will later observe that once we locally shift the intersection points, between the camera axis and calibration grids, to the origins of the respective grids the vector $\mathbf{t}'$ will lie on the camera axis. Inspite of all these additional constraints, arising from axial geometry, two views of calibration grids are not sufficient to uniquely extract R' and $\mathbf{t}'$. Thus we use three calibration grids as described below.

4 Full Calibration Using Three Views of Calibration Grids

Let $\mathbf{Q}$, $\mathbf{Q}'$, $\mathbf{Q}''$ refer to the grid points corresponding to a single pixel in the three grids. The poses of the grids are $(\mathsf{I}, \mathbf{0})$, $(\mathsf{R}', \mathbf{t}')$ and $(\mathsf{R}'', \mathbf{t}'')$ respectively. Since the three points $\mathbf{Q}$, $\mathbf{Q}'$ and $\mathbf{Q}''$ are collinear we use this constraint to extract the poses of the calibration grids [7]. Every 3×3 submatrix of the following 4×3 matrix has zero subdeterminant.

$$\begin{pmatrix} \mathbf{Q} & \begin{pmatrix} \mathsf{R}' & \mathbf{t}' \\ \mathbf{0}^\mathsf{T} & 1 \end{pmatrix} \mathbf{Q}' & \begin{pmatrix} \mathsf{R}'' & \mathbf{t}'' \\ \mathbf{0}^\mathsf{T} & 1 \end{pmatrix} \mathbf{Q}'' \end{pmatrix}$$

The submatrices constructed by removing the first and the second rows lead to the constraints $\sum C_i T1_i = 0$ and $\sum C_i T2_i = 0$ respectively (as described in Table 1). These are nothing but homogeneous linear systems of the form $AX = 0$. The unknown vector X is formed from the 14 variables (C_i). Each of these variables are coupled coefficients of the poses of the grids. The matrix A is constructed by stacking the trilinear tensors $T1$ and $T2$, which can be computed from the coordinates of $\mathbf{Q}$, $\mathbf{Q}'$ and $\mathbf{Q}''$. In future when we refer to the rank of a linear system $AX = 0$, we refer to the rank of the matrix A. The rank has to be one less than the number of variables to estimate them uniquely upto a scale. For example, each of the above linear systems must have a rank of 13 to estimate the coefficients (C_i) uniquely. These systems were used to calibrate completely non-central cameras [10]. However in the case of axial cameras, these systems were found to have a rank of 12. This implies that the solution can not be obtained uniquely. In order to resolve this ambiguity we will need more constraints.

4.1 Intersection of Axis and Calibration Grids

Using the technique described earlier we compute the intersection of the camera axis with the three grids at **a**,**b** and **c** respectively. We translate the local

Table 1. Trifocal tensor in the generic calibration of completely non-central cameras

i	Motion (C_i)	$T1_i$	$T2_i$	i	Motion (C_i)	$T1_i$	$T2_i$
1	R'_{31}	$Q_2Q'_1Q''_4$	$Q_1Q'_1Q''_4$	13	$R'_{22}R''_{32} - R'_{32}R''_{22}$	$Q_4Q'_2Q''_2$	0
2	R'_{32}	$Q_2Q'_2Q''_4$	$Q_1Q'_2Q''_4$	14	$R'_{11}t''_3 - R'_{31}t''_1$	0	$Q_4Q'_1Q''_4$
3	R''_{31}	$-Q_2Q'_4Q''_1$	$-Q_1Q'_4Q''_1$	15	$R'_{12}t''_3 - R'_{32}t''_1$	0	$Q_4Q'_2Q''_4$
4	R''_{32}	$-Q_2Q'_4Q''_2$	$-Q_1Q'_4Q''_2$	16	$R'_{21}t''_3 - R'_{31}t''_2$	$Q_4Q'_1Q''_4$	0
5	$t'_3 - t''_3$	$Q_2Q'_4Q''_4$	$Q_1Q'_4Q''_4$	17	$R'_{22}t''_3 - R'_{32}t''_2$	$Q_4Q'_2Q''_4$	0
6	$R'_{11}R''_{31} - R'_{31}R''_{11}$	0	$Q_4Q'_1Q''_1$	18	$R''_{11}t'_3 - R''_{31}t'_1$	0	$-Q_4Q'_4Q''_1$
7	$R'_{11}R''_{32} - R'_{31}R''_{12}$	0	$Q_4Q'_1Q''_2$	19	$R''_{12}t'_3 - R''_{32}t'_1$	0	$-Q_4Q'_4Q''_2$
8	$R'_{12}R''_{31} - R'_{32}R''_{11}$	0	$Q_4Q'_2Q''_1$	20	$R''_{21}t'_3 - R''_{31}t'_2$	$-Q_4Q'_4Q''_1$	0
9	$R'_{12}R''_{32} - R'_{32}R''_{12}$	0	$Q_4Q'_2Q''_2$	21	$R''_{22}t'_3 - R''_{32}t'_2$	$-Q_4Q'_4Q''_2$	0
10	$R'_{21}R''_{31} - R'_{31}R''_{21}$	$Q_4Q'_1Q''_1$	0	22	$t'_1t''_3 - t'_3t''_1$	0	$Q_4Q'_4Q''_4$
11	$R'_{21}R''_{32} - R'_{31}R''_{22}$	$Q_4Q'_1Q''_2$	0	23	$t'_2t''_3 - t'_3t''_2$	$Q_4Q'_4Q''_4$	0
12	$R'_{22}R''_{31} - R'_{32}R''_{21}$	$Q_4Q'_2Q''_1$	0				

grid coordinates such that these intersection points become their respective origins. Without loss of generality we continue to use the same notations after the transformations.

$$\mathbf{Q} \longleftarrow \mathbf{Q} - \mathbf{a}, \ \mathbf{Q}' \longleftarrow \mathbf{Q}' - \mathbf{b}, \ \mathbf{Q}'' \longleftarrow \mathbf{Q}'' - \mathbf{c},$$

We can obtain a collinearity constraint by putting these origins in the same coordinate system. Every 3×3 subdeterminant of the following 4×3 matrix vanishes.

$$\left(\begin{pmatrix} \mathbf{0} \\ 1 \end{pmatrix} \quad \begin{pmatrix} \mathsf{R}' & \mathbf{t}' \\ \mathbf{0}^\mathsf{T} & 1 \end{pmatrix} \begin{pmatrix} \mathbf{0} \\ 1 \end{pmatrix} \quad \begin{pmatrix} \mathsf{R}'' & \mathbf{t}'' \\ \mathbf{0}^\mathsf{T} & 0 \end{pmatrix} \begin{pmatrix} \mathbf{0} \\ 1 \end{pmatrix} \right) = \begin{pmatrix} 0 & t'_1 & t''_1 \\ 0 & t'_2 & t''_2 \\ 0 & t'_3 & t''_3 \\ 1 & 1 & 1 \end{pmatrix}$$

The camera axis passes through O, $\mathbf{t}'$ and $\mathbf{t}''$. This enables us to express $\mathbf{t}''$ as a multiple of $\mathbf{t}'$ using some scalar Δ: $\mathbf{t}'' = \Delta\mathbf{t}'$. As a result, the variables C_{22} and C_{23} from Table 1 disappear.

$$C_{22} = t'_1t''_3 - t'_3t''_1 = t'_1\Delta t'_3 - t'_3\Delta t'_1 = 0$$

$$C_{23} = t'_2t''_3 - t'_3t''_2 = t'_2\Delta t'_3 - t'_3\Delta t'_2 = 0$$

On disappearing, C_{22} and C_{23} reduce the size of the linear systems $\sum C_iT1_i = 0$ and $\sum C_iT2_i = 0$ each by one. Inspite of this reduction there still exists a rank deficiency of 2 in both these systems. The rank of each of these systems is 11 with 13 nonzero coefficients to be estimated. In the next section we provide the details of the usage of a coplanarity constraint, which exists in axial cameras, to remove the degeneracy problems.

4.2 Coplanarity Constraints in Axial Cameras

The camera axis cuts all the projection rays. As observed earlier both $\mathbf{O}$ and $\mathbf{t}'$ lie on the camera axis. Along with these two points, we consider two grid points $\mathbf{Q}'$ and $\mathbf{Q}''$ lying on a single projection ray. Since these four points are coplanar, the determinant of the following 4×4 matrix disappears.

Table 2. Bifocal tensor from the coplanarity constraint on $\mathbf{O}$, $\mathbf{t}'$, $\mathbf{Q}'$ and $\mathbf{Q}''$

i	j	α_{ij}
1	1	$t'_1(R'_{2,1}R''_{3,1} - R''_{2,1}R'_{3,1}) - t'_2(R'_{1,1}R''_{3,1} - R''_{1,1}R'_{3,1}) + t'_3(R'_{1,1}R''_{2,1} - R''_{1,1}R'_{2,1})$
1	2	$t'_1(R'_{2,1}R''_{3,2} - R''_{2,2}R'_{3,1}) - t'_2(R'_{1,1}R''_{3,2} - R''_{1,2}R'_{3,1}) + t'_3(R'_{1,1}R''_{2,2} - R''_{1,2}R'_{2,1})$
2	1	$t'_1(R'_{2,2}R''_{3,1} - R''_{2,1}R'_{3,2}) - t'_2(R'_{1,2}R''_{3,1} - R''_{1,1}R'_{3,2}) + t'_3(R'_{1,2}R''_{2,1} - R''_{1,1}R'_{2,2})$
2	2	$t'_1(R'_{2,2}R''_{3,2} - R''_{2,2}R'_{3,2}) - t'_2(R'_{1,2}R''_{3,2} - R''_{1,2}R'_{3,2}) + t'_3(R'_{1,2}R''_{2,2} - R''_{1,2}R'_{2,2})$

$$\left(\begin{pmatrix} 0 \\ 0 \\ 0 \\ 1 \end{pmatrix} \quad \begin{pmatrix} t'_1 \\ t'_2 \\ t'_3 \\ 1 \end{pmatrix} \quad \begin{pmatrix} \mathsf{R}' & \mathbf{t}' \\ \mathbf{0}^\mathsf{T} & 1 \end{pmatrix} \mathbf{Q}' \quad \begin{pmatrix} \mathsf{R}'' & \mathbf{\Delta} t' \\ \mathbf{0}^\mathsf{T} & 1 \end{pmatrix} \mathbf{Q}'' \right)$$

The corresponding constraint is a linear system $\sum \alpha_{ij} Q'_i Q''_j = 0$ (see table 2). Note that Q'_4 and Q''_4 are not present because of the three zeros in the first column. We can solve this linear system to computer the solutions for α_{ij}. We expand the above linear system and do some algebraic manipulation.

$$\alpha_{11}Q'_1Q''_1 + \alpha_{12}Q'_1Q''_2 + \alpha_{21}Q'_2Q''_1 + \alpha_{22}Q'_2Q''_2 = 0$$

$$Q_4(\alpha_{11}Q'_1Q''_1 + \alpha_{12}Q'_1Q''_2 + \alpha_{21}Q'_2Q''_1 + \alpha_{22}Q'_2Q''_2) = 0$$

$$Q_4Q'_2Q''_2 = -\frac{\alpha_{11}}{\alpha_{22}}Q_4Q'_1Q''_1 - \frac{\alpha_{12}}{\alpha_{22}}Q_4Q'_1Q''_2 - \frac{\alpha_{21}}{\alpha_{22}}Q_4Q'_2Q''_1$$

This will enable us to represent both $T2_9$ and $T1_{13}$, from the earlier systems, in terms of other variables in the tensors $T1$ and $T2$ respectively.

$$T2_9 = -\frac{\alpha_{11}}{\alpha_{22}}T2_6 - \frac{\alpha_{12}}{\alpha_{22}}T2_7 - \frac{\alpha_{21}}{\alpha_{22}}T2_8$$

$$T1_{13} = -\frac{\alpha_{11}}{\alpha_{22}}T1_{10} - \frac{\alpha_{12}}{\alpha_{22}}T1_{11} - \frac{\alpha_{21}}{\alpha_{22}}T1_{12}$$

Using the above relation we obtain two new constraints given by $\sum A_i A1_i = 0$ and $\sum A_i A2_i = 0$. Note that each of these constraints are linear systems with 12 nonzero coefficients each. Both of them have a rank of 11 and thereby producing unique solutions for their coefficients (A_i). The individual elements in the poses of the grids are extracted from these coupled coefficients using orthonormality constraints of the rotation matrix [7].

5 Bundle Adjustment Formulation

We give the details of a bundle adjustment which refines the estimated camera axis and poses of the calibration grids. This is similar to our earlier method [10], except that we have an additional constraint coming from the camera axis. The

Table 3. Trifocal tensor for the generic calibration of axial cameras

i	Motion (A_i)	$A1_i$	$A2_i$	i	Motion (A_i)	$A1_i$	$A2_i$
1	R'_{31}	$Q_2Q'_1Q''_4$	$Q_1Q'_1Q''_4$	11	$C_{12} - \frac{\alpha_{21}}{\alpha_{22}}C_{13}$	$Q_4Q'_2Q''_1$	0
2	R'_{32}	$Q_2Q'_2Q''_4$	$Q_1Q'_2Q''_4$	12	$\Delta(R'_{11}t'_3 - R'_{31}t'_1)$	0	$Q_4Q'_1Q''_4$
3	R''_{31}	$-Q_2Q'_4Q''_1$	$-Q_1Q'_4Q''_1$	13	$\Delta(R'_{12}t'_3 - R'_{32}t'_1)$	0	$Q_4Q'_2Q''_4$
4	R''_{32}	$-Q_2Q'_4Q''_2$	$-Q_1Q'_4Q''_2$	14	$\Delta(R'_{21}t'_3 - R'_{31}t'_2)$	$Q_4Q'_1Q''_4$	0
5	$t'_3 - t''_3$	$Q_2Q'_4Q''_4$	$Q_1Q'_4Q''_4$	15	$\Delta(R'_{22}t'_3 - R'_{32}t'_2)$	$Q_4Q'_2Q''_4$	0
6	$C_6 - \frac{\alpha_{11}}{\alpha_{22}}C_9$	0	$Q_4Q'_1Q''_1$	16	$R''_{11}t'_3 - R''_{31}t'_1$	0	$-Q_4Q'_4Q''_1$
7	$C_7 - \frac{\alpha_{12}}{\alpha_{22}}C_9$	0	$Q_4Q'_1Q''_2$	17	$R''_{12}t'_3 - R''_{32}t'_1$	0	$-Q_4Q'_4Q''_2$
8	$C_8 - \frac{\alpha_{21}}{\alpha_{22}}C_9$	0	$Q_4Q'_2Q''_1$	18	$R''_{21}t'_3 - R''_{31}t'_2$	$-Q_4Q'_4Q''_1$	0
9	$C_{10} - \frac{\alpha_{11}}{\alpha_{22}}C_{13}$	$Q_4Q'_1Q''_1$	0	19	$R''_{22}t'_3 - R''_{32}t'_2$	$-Q_4Q'_4Q''_2$	0
10	$C_{11} - \frac{\alpha_{12}}{\alpha_{22}}C_{13}$	$Q_4Q'_1Q''_2$	0				

bundle adjustment is done by minimizing the distance between the grid points and the corresponding projection rays. The cost function is given below.

$$Cost = \sum_{i=1}^{n} \sum_{j=1} (\mathbf{A} + \lambda_i \mathbf{D} + \mu_{ji} \mathbf{D}_i - [\mathsf{R}_j \mathbf{T}_j] \mathbf{Q}_{ji})$$

- $(\mathbf{A}, \mathbf{D})$ - represents the axis (point, direction)
- $\mathbf{D}_i$ - unit direction vector of the i_{th} projection ray
- λ_i - parameter selecting the intersection of the i_{th} ray and the axis
- $\mathbf{Q}_{ji}$ - grid point on the j_{th} grid lying the i_{th} ray
- μ_{ji} - parameter selecting the point on the i_{th} ray closest to Q_j
- $(\mathsf{R}_j, \mathbf{T}_j)$ - pose of the calibration grid

6 Axial Catadioptric Configurations

Our formulation can classify a given camera into either axial or not. For example on applying our method on axial data we obtain unique solutions. On the other hand, a completely non-central camera will lead to an inconsistent (no solution), whereas a central camera will produce a rank deficient system (ambiguous solutions). Thus our technique produces unique solutions only for axial configurations. This can be used as a simple test in simulations to study the nature of complex catadioptric arrangements (as shown in Figure 2(a)). Since axial cameras are less restrictive than central cameras, they can be easily constructed using various combinations of mirrors and lenses. For example there are very few central configurations [15] (also see Table 4). Furthermore these configurations are difficult to build and maintain. For example, in a central catadioptric camera with hyperbolic mirror and perspective camera, the optical center has to be placed precisely on one of the mirror's focal points. On the other hand, the optical center can be anywhere on the mirror axis to have an axial geometry.

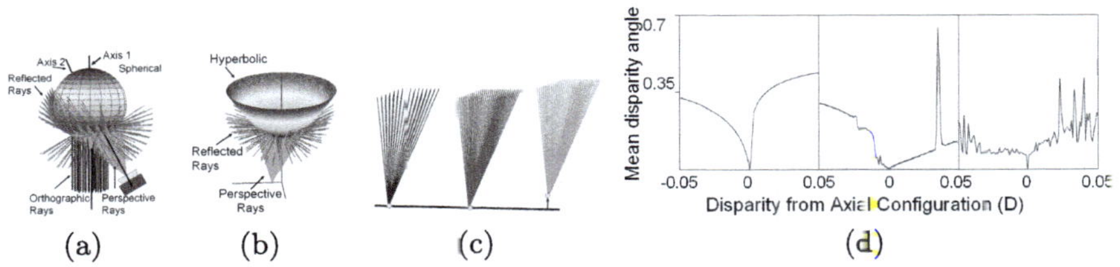

Fig. 2. Test for axial configuration. (a) Catadioptric (spherical mirror +pers.camera+ortho.camera): becomes non-central when the two optical centers and the sphere center are not collinear (as shown).(b) Catadioptric (Hyperbolic mirror+pers.camera): becomes non-central if the optical center is not on the axis of the hyperbolic mirror (as shown). (c) Tristereo when one of the cameras is axially misplaced (as shown). (d) shows the mean angular error between the original and reconstructed projection rays w.r.t disparity. The graphs shown in left, middle and right correspond to scenarios in (a), (b) and (c) respectively (see text for more details).

Table 4. Catadioptric configurations. Notations: ctrl (pers) - central configuration with perspective camera, nctrl (ortho) - non-central configuration with orthographic camera, mir-rot - mirror obtained by rotating a planar curve about the optical axis o - optical center of the perspective camera, f - focus of the mirror. MA - major axis of mirror, OA - optical axis of the camera, = refers to same location, ∈-lies on, ||-parallel, ∦-not parallel.

mirror	ctrl (pers)	axial (pers)	nctrl (pers)	ctral (ortho)	axial (ortho)	nctrl (ortho)
hyperbolic	o=f	$o \in MA$	$o \notin MA$	-	OA | MA	OA ∦ MA
spherical	-	always	-	-	always	-
parabolic	-	$o \in MA$	$o \notin MA$	OA || MA	-	OA ∦ MA
elliptic	o = f	$o \in MA$	$o \notin MA$	-	OA | MA	OA ∦ MA
cone	-	$o \in MA$	$o \notin MA$	-	OA | MA	OA ∦ MA
planar	always	-	planar	-	-	-
mir-rot	-	always	-	-	always	-

7 Experiments

7.1 Simulation

We started with perfect axial configurations for three scenarios (as shown in Figures 2(a), (b) and (c)) and gradually change the configurations to make them non-central. We quantify this change from the perfect axial configuration as disparity. For example, in Figure 2(a), the disparity represents the distance between the optical center of the perspective camera and the orthographic camera axis passing through the center of the sphere. This optical center is initially at a distance of 3 units from the center of the sphere (which is of radius 1 unit). In Figure 2(b), the disparity represents the distance between the optical center of the perspective camera and the major axis of the hyperboloid. Initially the optical center is at a distance of 5 units from the tip of the hyperboloid, whose two radii are 5 and 10 units. In Figure 2(c), the disparity represents the distance

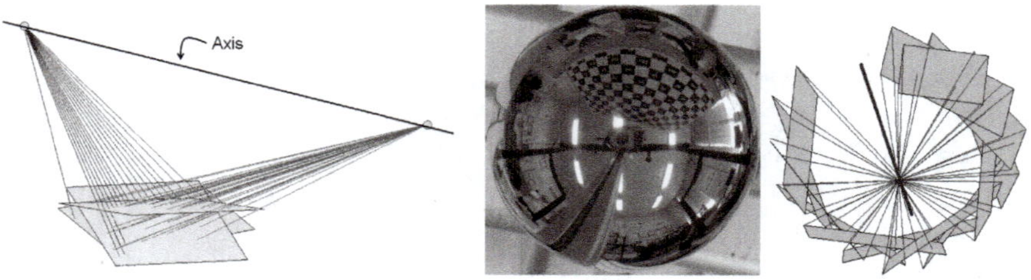

Fig. 3. Axial calibration: (a) Calibration of a stereo system (b) Image captured by a catadioptric system with a spherical mirror and a perspective camera. (b) Estimated poses of several grids along with the camera axis.

between the optical center of the third camera and the line joining the first two cameras. The distance between two consecutive centers of the cameras is 40 units. We calibrate these systems in the presence of disparities. We compute the mean angular error between the original and the reconstructed projection rays in Figure 2(d). Note that the the mean angular error (given in radians) reaches zero only at the precise axial configuration.

7.2 Stereo Camera

We captured three images of a calibration grid using two different cameras. The goal is to reconstruct the projection rays of both the cameras in the same generic framework using our axial calibration algorithm. Here the camera axis is the line joining the two optical centers (see Figure 3(a)). The image of the combined system is formed by concatenating the images from the two cameras. Figure 2(d) shows that our algorithm is very sensitive to noise. However using RANSAC, it is possible to obtain a good calibration. Once we compute the pose of the grids we can compute the rays corresponding to individual cameras in the stereo system. These rays can also be made to intersect separately and parameterized using a pinhole model. The RMS bundle adjustment error, based on the distance between the projection rays and grid points on the calibration grids, is of the order of 0.29% w.r.t overall size of the scene. The estimated camera parameters are close to the correct results. The reconstructed projection rays and grids are shown in Figure 3(a).

7.3 Spherical Catadioptric Cameras

We calibrated a real spherical catadioptric camera and extracted the camera axis. We start with an initial calibration using three grids using the above axial algorithm. This enables us to obtain an initial estimate for the axis and the projection rays. Using this partial calibration, we use pose estimation to incrementally compute the pose of newer grids. We followed our earlier method to obtain complete calibration [10]. The calibration grid captured by a spherical catadioptric camera is shown in Figure 3(b). We estimated the pose of several grids on a turntable sequence using the calibration. The grid positions and the axis are shown in Figure 3(c). For more details about results and other experimental issues please refer to [16].

8 Conclusions

We studied the theory and proposed a linear calibration algorithm for an intermediate class of cameras called axial cameras. Further line of investigation needs to be carried out to test the accuracy of this approach with respect to parametric and completely non-central approaches.

Acknowledgments. We thank Tomáš Pajdla, Branislav Mičušík and Diana Mateus for the data.

References

1. Grossberg, M., Nayar, S.: A general imaging model and a method for finding its parameters. In: ICCV. (2001)
2. J. Neumann, C.F., Aloimonos, Y.: Polydioptric camera design and 3d motion estimation. In: CVPR. (2003)
3. Pajdla, T.: Stereo with oblique cameras. IJCV (2002)
4. S. Peleg, M.B.E., Pritch, Y.: Omnistereo: Panoramic stereo imaging. PAMI (2001)
5. Pless, R.: Using many cameras as one. In: CVPR. (2003)
6. Seitz, S., Kim, J.: The space of all stereo images. In: IJCV. (2002)
7. Sturm, P., Ramalingam, S.: A generic concept for camera calibration. In: ECCV. (2004)
8. R. Swaminathan, M.G., Nayar, S.: A perspective on distortions. In: CVPR. (2003)
9. Bakstein, H., Pajdla, T.: An overview of non-central cameras. In: Computer Vision Winter Workshop. (2001)
10. S. Ramalingam, P.S., Lodha, S.: Towards complete generic camera calibration. In: CVPR. (2005)
11. Aliaga, D.: Accurate catadioptric calibration for real-size pose estimation of room-size environments. In: ICCV. (2001)
12. Micusik, B., Pajdla, T.: Autocalibration and 3d reconstruction with non-central catadioptric cameras. In: CVPR (2004)
13. Gupta, R., Hartley, R.: Linear pushbroom cameras. PAMI (1997)
14. Doron Feldman, T.P., Weinshall, D.: On the epipolar geometry of the crossed-slits projection. In: ICCV. (2003)
15. Baker, S., Nayar, S.: A theory of catadioptric image formation. In: ICCV. (1998)
16. S. Ramalingam, P.S., Lodha, S.: Generic calibration of axial cameras. INRIA Research Report (2005)

Error Characteristics of SFM with Erroneous Focal Length

Loong-Fah Cheong and Xu Xiang

Department of Electrical and Computer Engineering,
National University of Singapore,
4 Engineering Drive 3, Singapore 117576
{eleclf, engp0965}@nus.edu.sg

Abstract. This paper presents a theoretical analysis of the behavior of "Structure from Motion" (SFM) algorithms with respect to the errors in intrinsic parameters of the camera. We demonstrate both analytically and in simulation how uncertainty in the calibration parameters gets propagated to motion estimates. We studied the behavior of the estimation of the focus of expansion (FOE) in the case that the camera is well calibrated except that the focal length is estimated with error. The results suggest that the behavior of the bas-relief ambiguity is affected by the erroneous focal length. The amount of influence depends on the relative direction of the translation and rotation parameters of the camera, the field of view and scene depth. Simulation with synthetic data was conducted to support our findings.

1 Introduction

Structure from Motion has been the central problem of computer vision and constantly received attention from numerous researchers since 1980s. Much work about the SFM error analysis has been done in the last 15 years [1, 5, 10]. Various ambiguities such as bas-relief ambiguity and opposite minimum were reported in the literature and were mainly attributed to the presence of noise in the image measurements [1, 5, 4]. In [9], Xiang and Cheong argued that all the major ambiguities are actually inherent to the optimization criteria adopted and thus are algorithm-independent and will persist even with noiseless input. Although dealing with the statistical adequacy of the optimization criteria is important for understanding the effect of noise, it is equally important to understand the detailed nature of the inherent ambiguities caused by the geometry of the problem itself and thus cannot be removed by any statistical schemes. In this paper, we adopt such geometrical approach and further the analysis of SFM with erroneous intrinsic calibration and uncalibrated scenario.

In a recent critique of SFM research, Oliensis [7] argues that more comprehensive theoretical as well as phenomenological analyses of algorithm behavior should be carried out under all sorts of typical scenarios. Such analyses are important not only for understanding algorithms' properties, but also for conducting good experiments and for developing the best algorithms. Based on the

P.J. Narayanan et al. (Eds.): ACCV 2006, LNCS 3851, pp. 714–723, 2006.

work of [9], we propose in this paper an approach that lends itself towards understanding the behavior of SFM algorithms in uncalibrated scenario. In particular, we are concerned with the limitation of SFM algorithms in the face of errors in the estimation of the focal length. This is important for camera systems with zoom capability and online calibration cannot be always done with the requisite accuracy. Instead of dealing with specific algorithms each using different optimization techniques, we study one class of algorithms based on the weighted differential epipolar constraint. It is based on the difference between the original optical flow and the reprojected flow obtained via a back projection of the reconstructed depth, analogous to the distance between the observed feature and the reprojection of the recovered structure in the discrete case. This criterion permits a unifying view of these different algorithms. It also allows us to develop a simple and explicit expression for the residual error in terms of the errors in the 3-D motion estimates and the intrinsic parameters and enables us to predict the exact conditions likely to cause ambiguities. The error surfaces under a wide range of motion-scene configurations are plotted, from which several results are drawn.

1.1 SFM with Erroneous Estimation of Focal Length

Like the SFM algorithms, calibration algorithms are also sensitive to noise and lack robustness and reliability. Given the difficult of calibrating the camera precisely, projective approaches aim to perform SFM without calibration, that is, all the calibration information is neglected and the intrinsic camera parameters are assumed to vary freely from frame to frame. Although in some applications a full-fledged Euclidean reconstruction is not necessary, for instance in visual servoing or in image-based rendering, the projective approach may be too general to a fault. Although enormous amount of work on developing projective algorithms have been carried out by researchers, we still do not know when the projective approach is the right tool for its main task of dealing with calibration uncertainty. The projective approach assumes zero knowledge of the calibration. In practice, there is always something we may say about the intrinsic camera parameters. It is questionable whether such neglect of available information leads to an increased or decreased robustness. To answer this, one thing we need to know is whether the calibration uncertainty is large enough in practice to affect the goal of motion estimation and depth reconstruction. Oliensis [7] reported that even small errors in the estimation of focal length led to significant errors in the 3-D motion estimation. In this paper, we use the error surface to illustrate the behavior of egomotion estimation with erroneous calibration of the focal length.

If such an understanding can be achieved, we can better judge if there is a need of constant recalibration using robust but computationally intensive algorithms, or we can accept certain errors in the focal length estimate but at the same time are fully aware of the limit of the applicability of such algorithm. Due to space limitation, we assume in this paper no errors in other intrinsic parameters.

However the extension to those cases is not difficult and the results remain largely the same.

2 Background and Prerequisite

2.1 Models

A pinhole camera model with perspective projection is assumed as shown in Figure 1. In the figure, the camera is moving with a translational velocity $v = (U, V, W)^T$ and a rotation velocity $r = (\alpha, \beta, \gamma)^T$. The motion of the camera about a static environment results in a scene point P moving with a 3-D velocity (respective to the camera) as follows:

$$\dot{P} = -t - r \times p, \tag{1}$$

from which the well known 2-D motion field equations [6] can be derived: If we separate the motion in the horizontal and vertical directions, we can rewrite the above equation as follow:

$$u = \frac{W}{Z}x - f\frac{U}{Z} + \frac{xy}{f}\alpha - f\left(1 + \frac{x^2}{f^2}\right)\beta + \gamma y \tag{2}$$

$$v = \frac{W}{Z}y - f\frac{V}{Z} - \frac{xy}{f}\beta + f\left(1 + \frac{y^2}{f^2}\right)\alpha - \gamma x. \tag{3}$$

where (x, y) defines a feature point on the image plane. We define $\dot{p}_{tr} = (u_{tr}, v_{tr})^T$ and $\dot{p}_{rot} = (u_{rot}, v_{rot})^T$, where $\frac{\dot{p}_{tr}}{Z}$ and $\dot{p}_{rot}$ are the flows components due to translation and rotation respectively. Since only the translational direction can be recovered from the flow field, we can set $W = 1$ without loss of generality.

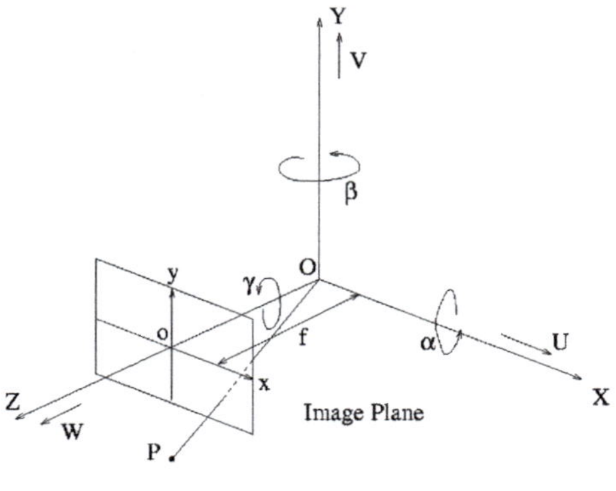

Fig. 1. The pinhole camera model

2.2 Optimization Criteria for SFM

The goal in motion estimation is to determine the translational and rotational parameters that are most consistent with the given set of point correspondences (discrete case) or flow fields (differential case). This goal is normally accomplished through the minimization of a cost function. Most of the existing cost functions for SFM are based on some weighted form of the epipolar constraint. The epipolar constraint relates the 3-D motion parameters with the image displacements, independent of depth. While the epipolar constraint was first formulated in the discrete case, it can also be developed in the differential case analogous to the discrete case:

$$p^T \hat{t} \dot{p} + p^T \hat{t} \hat{r} p = 0. \quad (4)$$

In [9] a cost function based on a weighted version of the above constraint is proposed:

$$J_R = \sum_{i=1}^{n} \left(\frac{([\dot{p}_i]_2 - \dot{p}_{rot_i}) \cdot \hat{p}_{tr_i}}{\hat{p}_{tr_i} \cdot \mathbf{n}_i} \right)^2 . \quad (5)$$

where $\mathbf{n}_i$ is a unit vector in the image plane representing a particular direction associated with the ith image point and $\dot{p}_i$ is the optical flow at the same point. In this paper, we denote any estimated parameter with the hat symbol ($\hat{}$) and error in the estimated parameter with the subscript e. Thus, error of any estimate s is defined as $s_e = s - \hat{s}$. It was shown in [9] that the various cost functions using in different algorithms correspond to different choices of $\mathbf{n}_i$ in the preceding expression.

3 Error Analysis of Motion Estimation Algorithms with Erroneous Estimation of Focal Length

In this section, we will investigate the behavior of motion estimation under the circumstance of inaccurate camera calibration with error in the estimate of the focal length.

First, we need to express the cost function J_R in terms of the various component errors in the 3-D motion estimates. This allows us to obtain a more obliging form for analyzing the ambiguity behavior over a wide range of conditions in more specific details. Substituting $\hat{p}_{tr_i} = (x_i - \hat{x}_0, y_i - \hat{y}_0)^T$ (where (x_0, y_0) is the focus of expansion FOE), $[\dot{p}_i]_2 = (u_i, v_i)^T = \left(\frac{x_i - x_0}{Z_i} + u_{rot_i}, \frac{y_i - \hat{y}_0}{Z_i} + v_{rot_i}\right)^T$ and $\dot{p}_{rot_i} = (\hat{u_{rot_i}}, \hat{v_{rot_i}})^T$ into Equation (5) we have:

$$J_R = \sum_{i=1}^{n} \left(\frac{(x - \hat{x}_0, y - \hat{y}_0) \cdot \left(v_{rot_e} - \frac{y_{0_e}}{Z}, \frac{x_{0_e}}{Z} - u_{rot_e}\right)}{(x - \hat{x}_0, y - \hat{y}_0) \cdot \mathbf{n}} \right)^2 , \quad (6)$$

where the various error terms are as follows:

$$
\begin{aligned}
(x_{0_e}, y_{0_e}) &= (x_0 - \hat{x}_0, y - \hat{y}_0) \\
u_{rot_e} &= -\left(\beta f - \hat{\beta}\hat{f}\right) + \left(\frac{\alpha}{f} - \frac{\hat{\alpha}}{\hat{f}}\right) xy \\
&\quad - \left(\frac{\beta}{f} - \frac{\hat{\beta}}{\hat{f}}\right) x^2 + \gamma_e y \\
v_{rot_e} &= \left(\alpha f - \hat{\alpha}\hat{f}\right) + \left(\frac{\alpha}{f} + \frac{\hat{\alpha}}{\hat{f}}\right) y^2 \\
&\quad - \left(\frac{\beta}{f} - \frac{\hat{\beta}}{\hat{f}}\right) xy - \gamma_e x.
\end{aligned}
$$

Besides the usual errors in the extrinsic motion parameters, we have introduced the inaccurate focal length estimate $\hat{f}$ in the above expression. For notational convenience, we omit the subscript i in the expression of J_R, although the summation runs over all feature points. Furthermore, we denote the terms in the numerator of Equation (6) $(x - \hat{x}_0, y - \hat{y}_0)^T$ and $\left(v_{rot_e} - \frac{y_{0_e}}{Z}, \frac{x_{0_e}}{Z} - u_{rot_e}\right)^T$ as t_1 and t_2 respectively, as in [9]. We also adopt the similar terminology that for the vectors t_1 and t_2, $t_{1,n}$ and $t_{2,n}$ denote the nth order component with respect to x and y; thus we have:

$$
\begin{aligned}
t_1 &= t_{1,0} + t_{1,1} \\
t_2 &= t_{2,0} + t_{2,1} + t_{2,2} + t_{2,z},
\end{aligned} \tag{7}
$$

where

$$
\begin{aligned}
t_{1,0} &= (-\hat{x}_0, -\hat{y}_0)^T \\
t_{1,1} &= (x, y)^T \\
t_{2,0} &= \left(\left(\alpha f - \hat{\alpha}\hat{f}\right), \left(\beta f - \hat{\beta}\hat{f}\right)\right)^T \\
t_{2,1} &= (-\gamma_e x, -\gamma_e y)^T \\
t_{2,2} &= \begin{pmatrix} \left(\frac{\alpha}{f} - \frac{\hat{\alpha}}{\hat{f}}\right) y^2 - \left(\frac{\beta}{f} - \frac{\hat{\beta}}{\hat{f}}\right) xy \\ - \left(\frac{\alpha}{f} - \frac{\hat{\alpha}}{\hat{f}}\right) xy + \left(\frac{\beta}{f} - \frac{\hat{\beta}}{\hat{f}}\right) x^2 \end{pmatrix} \\
t_{2,z} &= \left(-\frac{y_{0_e}}{Z}, \frac{x_{0_e}}{Z}\right)^T.
\end{aligned}
$$

The depth Z may depend on x and y in a complex manner, thus the notation $t_{2,z}$ is used and the order is unspecified.

Equation (5) shows that for any given data set (x, y, Z), the residual error is a function of the true FOE (x_0, y_0), the estimated FOE $(\hat{x}_0, \hat{y}_0)$, the error in the rotation estimates $(\alpha_e, \beta_e, \gamma_e)$ and the estimated focal length $\hat{f}$. We immediately note the estimation of γ is not affected by the inaccurate focal length, thus can be estimated with high accuracy.

The following two conditions should be satisfied to make the numerator of the cost function vanish: (1) making t_1 and t_2 perpendicular to each other and (2) making $||t_2||$ small. Condition (2) helps because condition (1) can never be completely satisfied at every image point under general situation. Making $||t_1||$ small does not help since it appears in both the numerator and the denominator (2). When both these conditions are approached, ambiguities arise.

From the expression of t_2 in Equation (7), we can see that $t_{2,0}$ and $t_{2,Z}$ are pointing towards constant directions for all the feature points. If we consider $t_{1,1}$ as a perturbation to the vector $t_{1,0}$ and $t_{2,1}+t_{2,2}$ as perturbation of $(t_{2,0}+t_{2,Z})$, then making $(t_{2,0}+t_{2,z})$ perpendicular to $t_{1,0}$ is a reasonable choice for the minimization of J_R.

$$\frac{y_{0e} - \alpha_e f Z - \hat{\alpha} f_e Z}{x_{0e} + \beta_e f Z + \hat{\beta} f_e Z} = \frac{y_0}{x_0}. \tag{8}$$

Note that in the calibrated case ($\hat{f} = f$), the preceding condition can be broken down into two independent constraints, one relating to translational parameters $\frac{x_0}{y_0} = \frac{\hat{x_0}}{\hat{y_0}} = \frac{x_{0e}}{y_{0e}}$ and the other relating to rotational parameters $\frac{\alpha_e}{\beta_e} = -\frac{\hat{y_0}}{\hat{x_0}}$. The first constraint characterizes the bas-relief valley. However, in the uncalibrated case, when the error in f is significant, α_e and β_e cannot be freely varied such that $\frac{\alpha_e}{\beta_e} = -\frac{\hat{y_0}}{\hat{x_0}}$ is satisfied. Thus constraint (8) cannot be broken down into two independent constraints. Rather, due to the significant error in f, the term $t_{2,2}$ can no longer be treated as second order effect and be ignored. Making $t_{2,2}$ small is just as important towards minimizing the cost function. Thus the rotational estimates are subject to the following constraint:

$$\frac{\alpha}{f} = \frac{\hat{\alpha}}{\hat{f}}, \frac{\beta}{f} = \frac{\hat{\beta}}{\hat{f}}. \tag{9}$$

In summary, satisfying both constraints (8) and (9) simultaneously is the best that can be done when there is error in the focal length estimate. Combining (8) and (9), we obtain

$$\frac{y_{0e} - \alpha f Z\left(1 - \frac{\hat{f}}{f}\right)}{x_{0e} + \beta f Z\left(1 - \frac{\hat{f}}{f}\right)} = \frac{y_0}{x_0}. \tag{10}$$

Equation (10) suggests that with error in the focal length, the bas-relief valley [9] whose direction in the error surface is originally defined by $\frac{x_{0e}}{y_{0e}} = \frac{x_0}{y_0}$ in the calibrated case, will now undergo a rotation due to the additional terms that appear in the LHS of Equation (10). The direction of the rotation depends on the sign of $\hat{\alpha}$, $\hat{\beta}$ and f_e in a complex manner. We illustrate the dependence using the particular situation $\alpha > 0$, $\beta > 0$, $x_0 > 0$, $y_0 > 0$. The results will be extended to general situations in the next section.

In the case when $\hat{\alpha} > 0$, $\hat{\beta} > 0$, the direction depends on the sign of f_e in the following way. If $f_e > 0$, i.e. the focal length is under-estimated, the signs of the terms of $\alpha f Z\left(1 - \frac{\hat{f}}{f}\right)$ and $\beta f Z\left(1 - \frac{\hat{f}}{f}\right)$ in Equation (10) are both positive. It is then clear from Equation (10) that the bas-relief valley will rotate in the

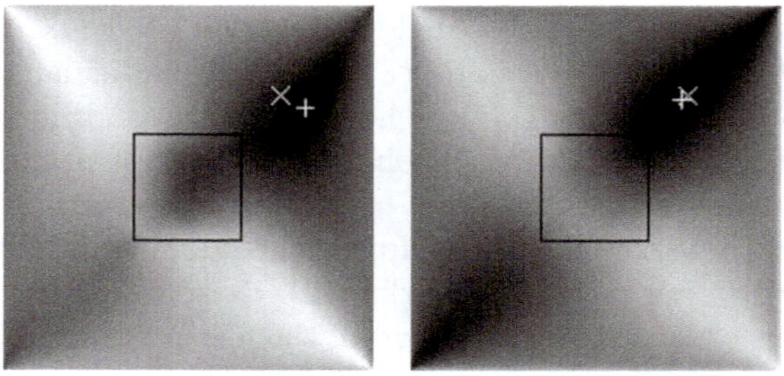

(a) (b)

Fig. 2. The phenomenon of the rotation of the bas-relief valley. $v = (1, 1, 1)$, $w = (0.001, 0.001, 0.001)$, $f = 512$ pixels for all figures. True FOEs and global minima are highlighted by "×" and "+" respectively. (a)focal length under-estimated $\hat{f} = 256$,with distinct rotation of the bas-relief valley, (b)focal length overestimated $\hat{f} = 1024$, rotation of the bas-relief valley not conspicuous.

clockwise direction. See Figure (2a) in the next section. Conversely, when $f_e < 0$, the rotation in the bas-relief valley is in the anti-clockwise direction. However the amount of rotation is not so conspicuous compared to the case of $f_e > 0$ (Figure 2b). The reason for this anisotropy with respect to the sign of f_e can be seen from Equation (8). There are two terms in the numerator involving α_e and $\hat{\alpha}$ and two terms in the denominator involving β_e and $\hat{\beta}$. When $f_e < 0$, Equation (9) dictates that the signs of α_e and β_e are both negative and the signs of $\hat{\alpha}$ and $\hat{\beta}$ are both positive. Plugging these signs into Equation (8), it is readily seen that the two aforementioned terms in the numerator are counteracting against each other, and similarly for the two terms in the denominator. This explains the less distinct shift in the bas-relief valley for $f_e < 0$.

4 Experiments and Discussion

In this section, we perform simulations on synthetic images to both visualize and verify the predictions obtained in the preceding section. These simulations were carried out based on the "epipolar reconstruction" scheme, that is, setting **n** to be along the estimated epipolar direction, but we emphasize that the results obtained in the preceding section are valid for all choices of **n**. All the combinations of different signs of translation and rotation parameters with over- and under-estimation of the f are simulated.

To visualize the residual error surface, it is easier to deal with a 3-D surface. We use the translation error surface for this purpose. Each point on this surface represents a FOE candidate, i.e., the FOE value is fixed. The rotation variables are then solved in terms of the fixed FOE so as to minimize J_R. The procedure is carried out under three cases: no error in $\hat{f}$, over-estimation in $\hat{f}$ and under-estimation in $\hat{f}$. To describe the entire residual surface completely, J_R is computed for each FOE candidate using the following:

$$J_R = \sum_{i=1}^{n} \left(\frac{c_{1_i} - \left(c_{1_i}\hat{\alpha} + c_{3_i}\hat{\beta} + c_{4_i}\hat{\gamma} \right)}{\eta_i} \right)^2 . \tag{11}$$

where

$$\begin{aligned}
c_{1_i} &= u(y - \hat{y_0}) - v(x - \hat{x_0}) \\
c_{2_i} &= \frac{xy}{f}(y - \hat{y_0}) - (\frac{y^2}{f} + f)(x - \hat{x_0}) \\
c_{3_i} &= \frac{xy}{f}(x - \hat{x_0}) - (\frac{x^2}{f} + f)(y - \hat{y_0}) \\
c_{4_i} &= x(x - \hat{x_0}) + y(y - \hat{y_0}) \\
\eta_i &= \sqrt{(x - \hat{x_0})^2 + (y - \hat{y_0})^2}.
\end{aligned}$$

We obtain the rotation variables by the SVD (singular value decomposition) method, a typical linear least squares fitting algorithm. We perform this fitting for each fixed FOE candidate over the whole 2-D search space and obtained the corresponding reprojected flow difference J_R. The residual values were then plotted in such a way that the image intensity encoded the relative value of the residual (bright pixel corresponded to high residual value and vice versa). The imaging surface was a plane with a dimension of 512×512 pixels; its boundary was delineated by a small rectangle in the center of the plots. The residuals were plotted over the whole FOE search space covering the entire hemisphere in front of the camera. We used visual angle in degree rather than pixel as the FOE search step thus the coordinates in the plots were not linear in the pixel unit. The synthetic experiments have the following parameters: the focal length was 512 pixels which meant a FOV of approximately 53°; there were 200 feature points distributed randomly over the image plane. The camera was undergoing a general translation with the translational parameters being $(1, 1, 1)$.

We conducted experiments under the following conditions:

1. under- and over- estimation of focal length;
2. different sign combination of α, β, x_0 and y_0;

The case when $\alpha > 0$ and $\beta > 0$ are explained and plotted in Figure 2. The numerical data of simulations showed that there were large errors in the estimate of α and β when the focal length was over- or under-estimated, compared to the case of focal length well calibrated. To facilitate further discussion, we define the direction of various vectors as follows. For instance, when $\alpha > 0$ and $\beta > 0$, we say that the direction of the rotation (more exactly the in-plane rotation) is in the first quadrant. Figure 3 list all the influence of the erroneous focal length on the bas-relief valley.

The property of bas-relief valley can be summarized as follow:

Under- versus over-estimation of focal length. Under-estimation of focal length always has a stronger rotational effect on the bas-relief valley than over-estimation. This may suggest that robust translation estimation under uncertain

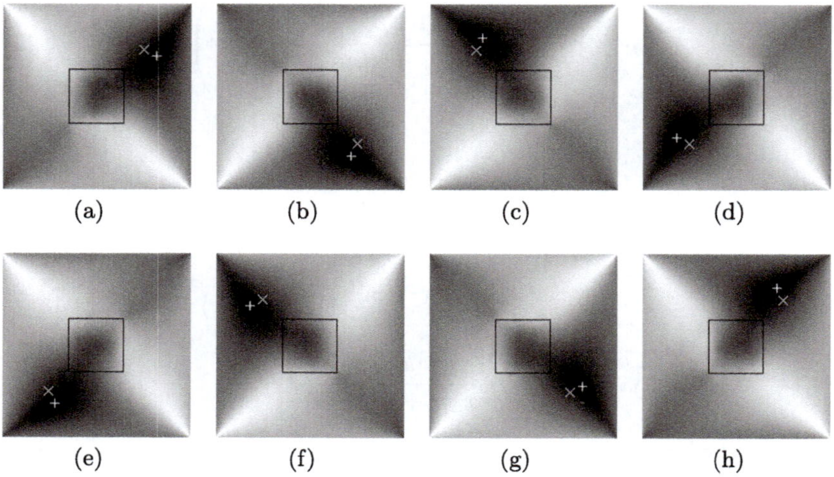

Fig. 3. Rotation of bas relief valley for different translation and rotation configurations with under-estimated focal length. In first row, where translation and rotation are at the same direction, bas-relief valley experienced a clockwise rotation; whereas in the second, translation and rotation are at the opposite direction, bas-relief valley rotate in an anti-clockwise direction.

calibration can be better accomplished by setting a larger-than-true focal length. Similar idea has been explored to design robust motion estimation algorithms using the depth-is-positive constraint [2].

Direction of rotation of bas-relief valley. For the case of under-estimation, if the "direction" of the rotation is the same as the direction of the translation, the bas-relief valley rotates in a clockwise direction (Figure (3), first row). If the two directions are opposite to each other, the bas-relief valley rotates in an anti-clockwise direction (Figure (3), second row). In Figure (3) $W = 1$, $\gamma = 0.001$ $f = 512$ and $\hat{f} = 256$ for all diagrams. The other translational and rotational parameters are (a) $(U, V) = (1, 1)$, $(\alpha, \beta) = (0.001, 0.001)$ (b) $(U, V) = (1, -1)$, $(\alpha, \beta) = (0.001, -0.001)$ (c) $(U, V) = (-1, 1)$, $(\alpha, \beta) = (-0.001, 0.001)$ (d) $(U, V) = (-1, -1)$, $(\alpha, \beta) = (-0.001, -0.001)$ (e) $(U, V) = (-1, -1)$, $(\alpha, \beta) = (0.001, 0.001)$ (f) $(U, V) = (-1, 1)$, $(\alpha, \beta) = (0.001, -0.001)$ (g) $(U, V) = (1, -1)$, $(\alpha, \beta) = (-0.001, 0.001)$ (g) $(U, V) = (1, 1)$, $(\alpha, \beta) = (-0.001, -0.001)$.

Extent of the erroneous focal length. If the "direction" of the rotation is "perpendicular" to the direction of the translation (i.e. they are in adjacent quadrants), the effect of erroneous focal length is smaller than the case where the "directions" of rotation and translation are the same or in the opposite direction. Due to space limitation, the plot results are not shown.

Large versus small scene depth. From Equation (8), we observe that big value of Z tends to have a stronger rotation effect on the bas-relief valley).

Thus the numerically less stable case of large depth points is more susceptible to the influence of error in $\hat{f}$.

5 Conclusions

In this paper we have developed expressions describing the error behavior of egomotion estimation when the focal length is calibrated with error. The key results in this paper are independent of both the egomotion estimation as well as the calibration algorithms. One important suggestion is that, provided that one knows the rough range of the true focal length, setting a larger-than-true focal length helps to estimate the direction of translation better. Similar idea has been explored to design robust motion estimation algorithms using the depth-is-positive constraint.

The results also show that the effect of erroneous focal length on the FOE estimate is not the same over different translation and rotation directions. The structure of the scene (depth) affects the shifting of the FOE estimate as well.

For the case of varying calibration parameters (f dynamically changing), additional analyses are in order. The results established in [3]—that zoom field crucially influence properties of depth reconstruction —raise the possibility that the results might be quite different.

References

1. G. Adiv. Inherent ambiguities in recovering 3-D motion and structure from a noisy flow field. *PAMI*, 11(5):477–489, May 1989.
2. L.F. Cheong and C.H. Peh. Depth distortion under calibration uncertainty. *CVIU*, 93(3):221–244, March 2004.
3. L.F. Cheong and T. Xiang. Characterizing depth distortion under different generic motions. *IJCV*, 44(3):199–217, September 2001.
4. A. Chiuso, R. Brockett, and S. Soatto. Optimal structure from motion: Local ambiguities and global estimates. *IJCV*, 39(3):195–228, September 2000.
5. K. Daniilidis and M.E. Spetsakis. Understanding noise sensitivity in structure from motion. In *Visual Navigation: From Biological Systems to Unmanned Ground Vehicles*, Y. Aloimonos (Ed.), Lawrence Erlbaum Assoc. Pub., 1993.
6. H.C. Longuet-Higgins. A computer algorithm for reconstructing a scene from two projections. *Nature*, 293:133–135, September 1981.
7. J. Oliensis. A critique of structure-from-motion algorithms. *CVIU*, 80(2):172–214, November 2000.
8. J. Oliensis. A New Structure-from-Motion Ambiguity. *PAMI*, 22(7):685–700, July 2000.
9. T. Xiang and L.F. Cheong. Understanding the behavior of SFM algorithms: A geometric approach. *IJCV*, 51(2):111–137, February 2003.
10. G.S. Young and R. Chellappa. Statistical analysis of inherent ambiguities in recovering 3-D motion from a noisy flow field. *PAMI*, 14(10):995–1013, October 1992.

Interpreting Sphere Images Using the Double-Contact Theorem

Xianghua Ying and Hongbin Zha

National Laboratory on Machine Perception, Peking University, Beijing, P.R. China
{xhying, zha}@cis.pku.edu.cn
http://www.cis.pku.edu.cn/vision/Visual&Robot/people/ying/

Abstract. An occluding contour of a sphere is projected to a conic in the perspective image, and such a conic is called a sphere image. Recently, it has been discovered that each sphere image is tangent to the image of the absolute conic at two double-contact image points. The double-contact theorem describes the properties of three conics which all have double contact with another conic. This theorem provides a linear algorithm to find the another conic if these three conics are given. In this paper, the double-contact theorem is employed to interpret the properties among three sphere images and the image of the absolute conic. The image of the absolute conic can be determined from three sphere images using the double-contact theorem. Therefore, a linear calibration method using three sphere images is obtained. Only three sphere images are required, and all five intrinsic parameters are recovered linearly without making assumptions, such as, zero-skew or unitary aspect ratio. Extensive experiments on simulated and real data were performed and shown that our calibration method is an order of magnitude faster than previous optimized methods and a little faster than former linear methods while maintaining comparable accuracy.

1 Introduction

Camera calibration is often required when recovering 3D information from 2D images. The parameters of a camera to be calibrated are divided into two classes: intrinsic and extrinsic. The intrinsic parameters describe the camera's imaging geometric characteristics, and the extrinsic parameters represent the camera's orientation and position with respect to the world coordinate system. Many approaches to camera calibration have been proposed and they can be classified into two categories: using calibration objects [6, 13, 16, 11, 1, 2, 8, 12, 14, 15], and self-calibration [7, 5, 9]. As we know, the occluding contour of a sphere is projected to a conic in the perspective image [1, 2, 5, 12, 14]. The image conic of a sphere is called a *sphere image* in this paper.

Here is a brief review of the existing methods for camera calibration using sphere images. Daucher et al. [2] found that the major axis of a sphere image passes through the principal point. Based on this observation, they further proposed to first determine the aspect ratio using three sphere images, then determine the principal point and finally determine the focal length. Note that this

P.J. Narayanan et al. (Eds.): ACCV 2006, LNCS 3851, pp. 724–733, 2006.

method can only recover four intrinsic parameters while assuming the skew factor equal to zero. Recently, a geometric invariant based method using sphere images proposed in [14](This method is originally proposed for catadioptric camera calibration) directly gave two constraint equations in the intrinsic parameters arising from one sphere image. Therefore, three sphere images may be used to recover all the five intrinsic parameters with nonlinear optimization techniques provided good initial guesses. The image of the absolute conic (IAC) plays a central role in camera calibration. Teramoto and Xu [12] first discovered the algebraic relation between the sphere image and the IAC, and then provided an efficient algorithm to solve for the camera parameters. However, in their approach the minimization is accomplished by means of a general-purpose nonlinear minimization and required a good initial estimation to start the minimization. Agrawal and Davis [1] utilized the dual representation instead, i.e., the algebraic relation between the dual form of a sphere image and the dual image of the absolute conic (DIAC), then employed semi-definite programming (SDP) to solve for the intrinsic parameters without requiring initial estimations. Base on the main principles derived in [12, 1], we further discovered that each sphere image is tangent to the IAC at two double-contact image points as described in [15].

In this paper, the double-contact theorem [3] is used to interpret the properties among three sphere images and the IAC. The IAC can be determined from three sphere images using the double-contact theorem. Therefore, a linear calibration method using three sphere images is obtained.

2 Preliminaries

2.1 Pinhole Camera Model

Let $\mathbf{M} = (X, Y, Z, 1)^T$ be a world point and $\mathbf{m} = (u, v, 1)^T$ be its image point, both in the homogeneous coordinates, they satisfy:

$$\mu \mathbf{m} = \mathbf{P}\mathbf{M}, \tag{1}$$

where $\mathbf{P}$ is a 3×4 projection matrix describing the perspective projection process. μ is an unknown scale factor. The projection matrix can be decomposed as:

$$\mathbf{P} = \mathbf{K}[\mathbf{R}|\mathbf{t}], \tag{2}$$

where

$$\mathbf{K} = \begin{bmatrix} f_x & s & u_0 \\ 0 & f_y & v_0 \\ 0 & 0 & 1 \end{bmatrix}. \tag{3}$$

Here the upper triangular matrix $\mathbf{K}$ is the matrix of the intrinsic parameters, and $(\mathbf{R}, \mathbf{t})$ denote a rigid transformation (i.e., $\mathbf{R}$ is a rotation matrix and $\mathbf{t}$ is a translation vector) which indicate the orientation and position of the camera with respect to the world coordinate system.

2.2 The Equation of a Sphere Image

Let the origin of the world coordinate system located in the vertex of a right circular cone **Q**, and the z-axis of the world coordinate system coinciding with the revolution axis of the right cone, then the right cone **Q** represented in the world coordinate system is:

$$\mathbf{Q} = \begin{bmatrix} 1 & 0 & 0 & 0 \\ 0 & 1 & 0 & 0 \\ 0 & 0 & -\alpha^2 & 0 \\ 0 & 0 & 0 & 0 \end{bmatrix}, \tag{4}$$

where $\alpha = \tan\frac{\theta}{2}$, and θ is the apex angle of the cone. A world point $\mathbf{M} = (X, Y, Z, 1)^T$ on the cone **Q** satisfies:

$$\mathbf{M}^T\mathbf{Q}\mathbf{M} = 0, \tag{5}$$

or

$$\overline{\mathbf{M}}^T\overline{\mathbf{Q}}\overline{\mathbf{M}} = 0, \tag{6}$$

where $\overline{\mathbf{M}} = (X, Y, Z)^T$ are the inhomogeneous coordinates of $\mathbf{M}$, and

$$\mathbf{Q} = \begin{bmatrix} 1 & 0 & 0 \\ 0 & 1 & 0 \\ 0 & 0 & -\alpha^2 \end{bmatrix}. \tag{7}$$

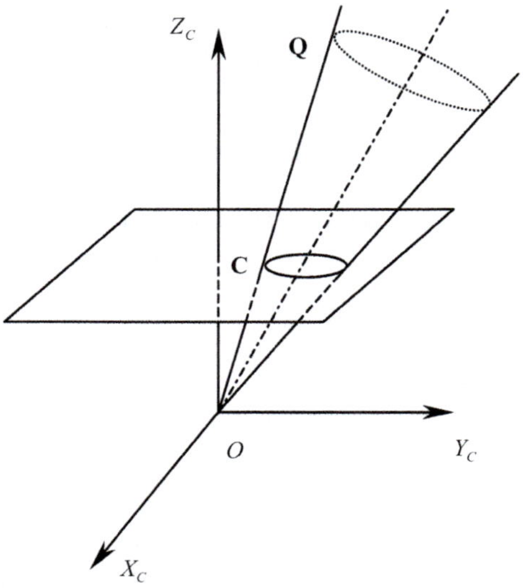

Fig. 1. A sphere image **C** obtained from a right cone **Q**

From Fig. 1 we know, the vertex of the cone $\mathbf{Q}$ is located in the camera's optical center. Therefore, only rotation exists between the world coordinate system and the camera coordinate system, i.e., $\mathbf{t} = (0,0,0)^T$. Then from (1) and (2), the image of a world point $\mathbf{M}$ on the cone $\mathbf{Q}$ satisfies:

$$\mu\mathbf{m} = \mathbf{PM} = \mathbf{K}[\mathbf{R}|\mathbf{0}]\mathbf{M} = \mathbf{KR}\overline{\mathbf{M}}. \tag{8}$$

Since $\mathbf{KR}$ is invertible, we have:

$$\overline{\mathbf{M}} = \mu\mathbf{R}^{-1}\mathbf{K}^{-1}\mathbf{m}. \tag{9}$$

Substituting (9) into (6), we obtain:

$$\mathbf{m}^T\mathbf{K}^{-T}\mathbf{R}^{-T}\overline{\mathbf{Q}}\mathbf{R}^{-1}\mathbf{K}^{-1}\mathbf{m} = 0, \tag{10}$$

or

$$\lambda\mathbf{C} = \mathbf{K}^{-T}\mathbf{R}^{-T}\overline{\mathbf{Q}}\mathbf{R}^{-1}\mathbf{K}^{-1}, \tag{11}$$

where λ is an unknown scale factor, and the image conic $\mathbf{C}$ is a sphere image obtained from $\mathbf{Q}$.

2.3 The IAC and the DIAC

The absolute conic Ω_∞ is a conic with purely imaginary points on the plane at infinity $\pi_\infty = (0,0,0,1)^T$, and its matrix form is:

$$\Omega_\infty = \begin{bmatrix} 1 & 0 & 0 \\ 0 & 1 & 0 \\ 0 & 0 & 1 \end{bmatrix}. \tag{12}$$

The mapping between π_∞ and its perspective image is given by the planar homography $\mathbf{H} = \mathbf{KR}$. Since the absolute conic Ω_∞ is on π_∞ one may compute the image of the absolute conic (IAC) under $\mathbf{H}$ as:

$$\omega = \mathbf{H}^{-T}\Omega_\infty\mathbf{H}^{-1} = (\mathbf{KR})^{-T}\mathbf{I}(\mathbf{KR})^{-1} = \mathbf{K}^{-T}\mathbf{K}^{-1}. \tag{13}$$

We may define the dual image of the absolute conic (DIAC) as:

$$\omega^* = \mathbf{KK}^{-T}. \tag{14}$$

2.4 The Algebraic Relation Between a Sphere Image and the IAC

Expand the right side of (11) using

$$\mathbf{Q} = \begin{bmatrix} 1 & 0 & 0 \\ 0 & 1 & 0 \\ 0 & 0 & 1 \end{bmatrix} + \begin{bmatrix} 0 & 0 & 0 \\ 0 & 0 & 0 \\ 0 & 0 & -(1+\alpha^2) \end{bmatrix}, \tag{15}$$

and after some manipulations we obtain:

$$\lambda\mathbf{C} = \omega - \mathbf{v}\mathbf{v}^T, \tag{16}$$

where ω is the IAC, and

$$\mathbf{v} = \sqrt{1+\alpha^2}\mathbf{K}^{-T}\mathbf{r}_3, \tag{17}$$

and $\mathbf{r}_3$ is the third column of $\mathbf{R}$.

2.5 The Algebraic Relation Between a Sphere Image and the DIAC

Inverse both side of (11), and after some manipulations as (15), we obtain:

$$\lambda'\mathbf{C}^* = \omega^* - \mathbf{v}'\mathbf{v}'^T, \tag{18}$$

where λ' is an unknown scale factor, and $\mathbf{C}^*$ is the inversion of the conic $\mathbf{C}$, i.e., the dual conic. ω^* is the DIAC, and

$$\mathbf{v}' = \sqrt{1 + \frac{1}{\alpha^2}}\mathbf{K}\mathbf{r}_3. \tag{19}$$

From (16) and (18), it is not difficult to find that the two equations have the same mathematical form, no matter whether the dual representation is adopted or not. In the rest of paper, we only discuss the interpretation for ω using the double-contact theorem and how to determine ω from this interpretation, because ω^* can be interpreted and determined in the same way.

2.6 Geometric Relations

Equation (16) can be rewritten as:

$$\lambda\mathbf{C} - \omega = -\mathbf{v}\mathbf{v}^T. \tag{20}$$

Since the rank of the matrix $-\mathbf{v}\mathbf{v}^T$ is one, the rank of the matrix $\lambda\mathbf{C} - \omega$ is one too. Consider the pencil of two conics $\mathbf{S}_1$ and $\mathbf{S}_2$, $\mathbf{S}_1 + \mu\mathbf{S}_2$ represents a conic which passes through all the common points of $\mathbf{S}_1$ and $\mathbf{S}_2$ [10]. Since two coincident lines (i.e., a repeated line) can be seen as a degenerate conic with rank 1, from the properties of a pencil of two conics described in [10], we know that $\mathbf{C}$ is tangent to ω at two image points, i.e., two double-contact points, and the chord of contact, $\mathbf{l}_d \propto \mathbf{v}$(derived from (20), where $\propto$ indicates equality up to a non-zero scale factor), passes through the two tangent points. Similar results can be obtained for $\mathbf{C}^*$ and ω^*.

3 Interpretation Using the Double-Contact Theorem

3.1 The Double-Contact Theorem

From the double-contact theorem [3] we know, if three conics $\mathbf{C}_1$, $\mathbf{C}_2$, $\mathbf{C}_3$ all have double contact with another conic ω, then each two of $\mathbf{C}_1$, $\mathbf{C}_2$ and $\mathbf{C}_3$ have a "distinguished" pair of opposite common chords (shown as solid lines in Fig. 2), and the three such pairs of common chords being the pairs of opposite sides of a complete quadrangle.

Let L_1 and M_1 be a pair of opposite common chords of $\mathbf{C}_2$ and $\mathbf{C}_3$, L_2 and M_2 be a pair of opposite common chords of $\mathbf{C}_1$ and $\mathbf{C}_3$, L_3 and M_3 be a pair of opposite common chords of $\mathbf{C}_1$ and $\mathbf{C}_2$. We assume that L_1, L_2 and L_3 are concurrent. Then from the double-contact theorem, we have,

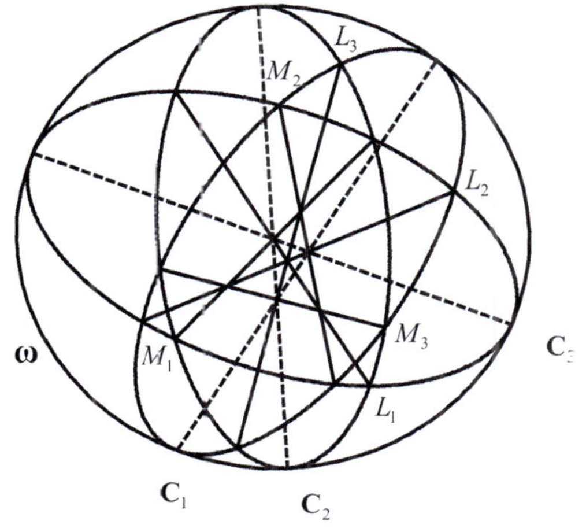

Fig. 2. Geometry for the double-contact theorem

$$\omega \propto 4k\mathbf{C}_1 + (M_2 + M_3 - M_1)^2 \equiv 4k\mathbf{C}_2 + (M_3 + M_1 - M_2)^2$$
$$\equiv 4k\mathbf{C}_3 + (M_1 + M_2 - M_3)^2 \quad (21)$$

where k is a scale factor which can be determined from L_1, L_2, L_3, M_1, M_2 and M_3 (see [3] for details). From (21), we obtain that the chords of contact satisfy:

$$\mathbf{l}_{d1} \propto M_2 + M_3 - M_1, \mathbf{l}_{d2} \propto M_3 + M_1 - M_2, \mathbf{l}_{d3} \propto M_1 + M_2 - M_3, \quad (22)$$

corresponding to $\mathbf{C}_1$, $\mathbf{C}_2$ and $\mathbf{C}_3$ respectively. We further find that each chord of contact (shown as dashed lines in Fig. 2) passes through two vertices of the triangle determined by the opposite sides of the complete quadrangle. This gives a geometric method to determine the chords of contact, i.e., $\mathbf{v}_i(i = 1, 2, 3)$, from the pairs of opposite common chords of $\mathbf{C}_1$ and $\mathbf{C}_2$, $\mathbf{C}_1$ and $\mathbf{C}_3$, $\mathbf{C}_2$ and $\mathbf{C}_3$. Note that Agrawal and Davis [1] only gave an algebraic method to solve for $\mathbf{v}_i$ and the solution for $\mathbf{v}_i$ is a very important part in the previous calibration algorithm, but no geometric interpretation for this is given in [1] and [15].

3.2 Interpretation for Sphere Images

From discussions in Sect. 2.6, we know that each sphere image is tangent to the IAC at two double-contact image points. The IAC has only purely imaginary points, but it shares the properties of any conic, such as the double-contact theorem. Therefore, three sphere images and the IAC can be interpreted by the double-contact theorem.

3.3 Determining the IAC

Given three sphere image $\mathbf{C}_i (i = 1, 2, 3)$, from (21), we can determine the IAC ω as follows:

$$\omega = \tfrac{1}{3}(4k\mathbf{C}_1 + (M_2 + M_3 - M_1)^2 + 4k\mathbf{C}_2 + (M_3 + M_1 - M_2)^2 + 4k\mathbf{C}_3 + (M_1 + M_2 - M_3)^2). \quad (23)$$

As we know, the IAC ω should be positive definite. The linear methods may fail in the case where the computed IAC ω is not positive definite. However, this did not occur in our experiments, except in the case where the noises are very large. After obtaining ω, it is not difficult to determine $\mathbf{v}_i$ from From (20).

4 Experiments

We perform a number of experiments, both simulated and real, to test our algorithms with respect to noise sensitivity, and make comparisons with the following algorithms:

- **DCT** and **DDCT**: Using the double-contact theorem related to the IAC and the DIAC, respectively.
- **GEO** and **DGEO**: Using the geometric interpretation related to the IAC and the DIAC, respectively [15].
- **SDP** and **DSDP**: Employing semi-definite programming with the representation of the IAC and the DIAC, respectively [1].

4.1 Calibration with Simulated Data

The simulated camera has the following parameters: $f_x = 1200$, $f_y = 1000$, $s = 20$, $u_0 = 400$, $v_0 = 300$. The resolution of the simulated image is 800×600. We generate an image containing three sphere images uniformly distributed within the image. On each sphere image we choose 100 points. Gaussian noise with zero-mean and σ standard deviation is added to these image points. We vary the noise level σ from 0 to 2 pixels. The conic fitting algorithm presented in [4] is used here. For each noise level, we perform 1,000 independent trials, and the mean values and standard deviations of these recovered parameters are computed over each run. The estimated results of these experiments are shown in Fig. 3. Since the performances of f_x and f_y, u_0 and v_0 are both very similar, the estimated results for f_y and v_0 are not shown here. From Fig. 3, it is not difficult to find that the estimated results from **SDP** and **DSDP** are almost identical to each other. In fact, there are only very small differences among the estimated results from these six different methods. We compare the runtimes of these methods using MATLAB implementations of all algorithms on a 1.7 GHz Pentium IV processor. Note that real-time performance is not expected for any of the algorithms under MATLAB, and our only goal is to provide comparison. All results are averaged over 1,000 trials and recorded in Table 1. Since **SDP** is a convex optimization

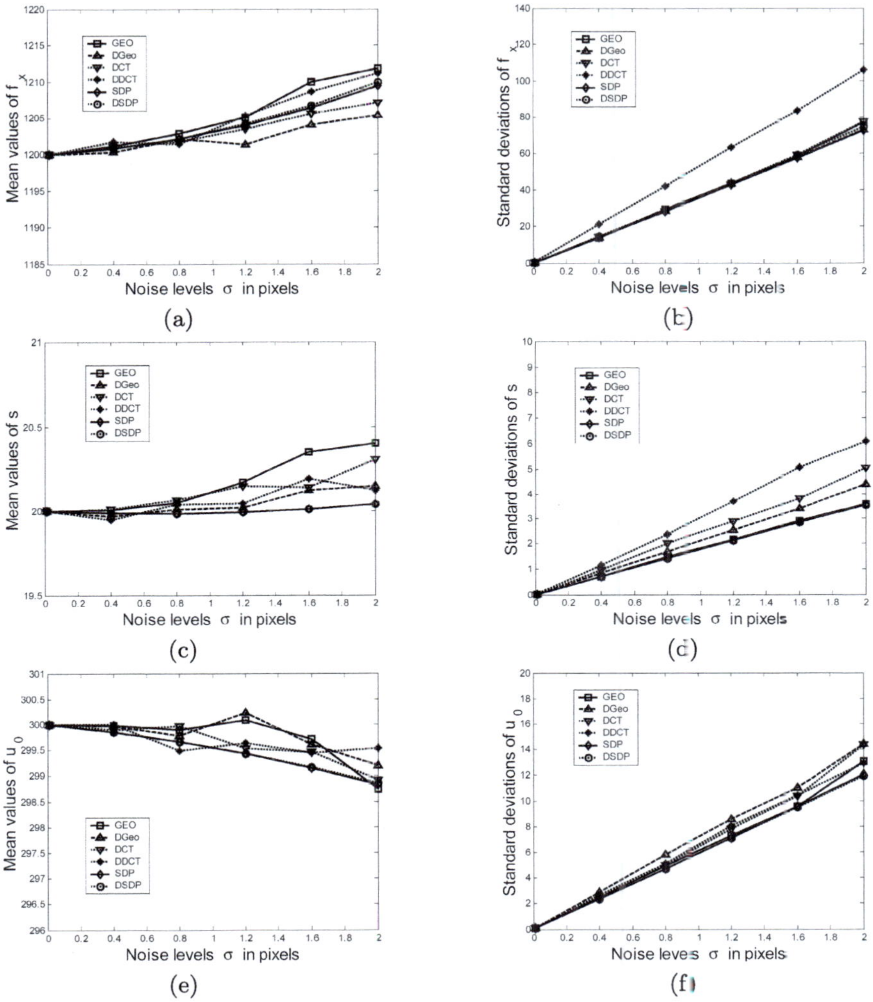

Fig. 3. The estimated results of simulated experiments. See text for details.

Table 1. Runtimes (in seconds) for the four algorithms

	DCT	DDCT	GEO	DGEO	SDP	DSDP
runtime	0.098	0.069	0.121	0.107	1.519	2.796

problem and has polynomial worst-case complexity, the runtimes of **SDP** and **DSDP** are about ten times slower than that using **DCT** and **DDCT**, whereas the runtimes of **GEO** and **DGEO** are a little slower than that using **DCT** and **DDCT**.

4.2 Calibration with Real Data

The test sphere for the real experiments is a billiard ball. The ball was placed in front of a white screen. We took images of the ball using a Sony DSC-F717 digital camera. Three sphere images are taken for the calibration purpose. The resolution of these images is 800 × 600. Edges were extracted using Canny's edge detector and the ellipses were obtained using a least squares ellipse fitting algorithm [4]. In order to obtain unbiased results, these sphere images should be uniformly distributed within the image. The ground truths for the camera parameters are unknown but the approach in [16] is applied before the experiments using a calibration pattern which serves as a reference. The calibration results with real data are listed in Table 2. From Table 2, one may find that the calibration results using these six methods are similar to one another.

Table 2. Calibration results with real data, where "Zhang" is the abbreviation for "the calibration method proposed by Z. Zhang [16]"

	f_x	f_y	s	u_0	v_0
Zhang	942.1	936.5	0.9	401.5	274.1
DCT	959.8	950.6	0.6	385.7	267.7
DDCT	974.6	959.1	0.5	403.1	263.6
GEO	958.5	952.0	2.3	388.3	258.8
DGEO	957.7	950.5	3.2	388.6	254.3
SDP	957.3	950.7	2.3	386.6	259.8
DSDP	963.2	956.5	2.3	390.2	259.1

5 Conclusions

In this paper, the double-contact theorem is used to interpret the relation between three sphere images and the IAC, and also the relation between the dual of sphere images and the DIAC. A novel geometric method is given to determine the chord of contact between each sphere image and the IAC from the pairs of opposite common chords of each two of these three sphere images, which is a very important part in the previous calibration algorithms. A linear calibration approach using sphere images is derived from this interpretation. As we know, the IAC should be positive definite. The linear methods may fail in the case where the computed IAC is not positive definite. However, this did not occur in our experiments, except in the case where the noises are very large. This novel algorithm has been tested in extensive experiments with respect to noise sensitivity.

Acknowledgements

This work was supported in part by the NSFC Grant (No. 60333010), and NKBRPC (No. 2004CB318000).

References

1. M. Agrawal and L. S. Davis, Camera Calibration using Spheres: A Semi-definite Programming Approach, Proc. Ninth Int'l Conf. Computer Vision, pp. 782-791, 2003.
2. N. Daucher, M. Dhome, and J. Lapreste. Camera Calibration from Spheres Images, Proc. European Conf. Computer Vision, pp. 449-454, 1994.
3. C. Evelyn, et al, The Seven Circles Theorem and Other New Theorems, London: Stacey International, 1974.
4. A. Fitzgibbon, M. Pilu, and R. Fisher, Direct Least Square Fitting of Ellipses, IEEE Trans. Pattern Analysis and Machine Intelligence, vol. 21, no. 5, pp. 476-480, 1999.
5. R. Hartley, An Algorithm for Self-calibration from Several Views, Proc. IEEE. Conf. Computer Vision and Pattern Recognition, pp. 908-912, 1994.
6. R. Hartley and A. Zisserman, Multiple View Geometry in Computer Vision. Cambridge University Press, 2000.
7. S. Maybank and O. Faugeras, A Theory of Self-calibration of a Moving Camera, Int'l J. Computer Vision, vol. 8, no.2, pp. 123-151, 1992.
8. M. Penna, Camera Calibration: A Quick and Easy Way to Determine the Scale Factor. IEEE Trans. Pattern Analysis and Machine Intelligence, vol. 13, no.12, pp. 1240-1245, 1991.
9. M. Pollefeys, R. Koch, and L. Van Gool, Selfcalibration and Metric Reconstruction in Spite of Varying and Unknown Internal Camera Parameters, Proc. Sixth Int'l Conf. Computer Vision, pp. 90-95, 1998.
10. J. Semple and G. Kneebone, Algebraic Projective Geometry, Oxford Science Publication, 1952.
11. P. Sturm and S. Maybank, On Plane-based Camera Calibration: A General Algorithm, Singularities and Applications, Proc. IEEE. Conf. Computer Vision and Pattern Recognition, pp. 432-437, 1999.
12. H. Teramoto and G. Xu, Camera Calibration by a Single Image of Balls: From Conics to the Absolute Conic, Proc. Asian Conf. Computer Vision, pp. 499-506, 2002.
13. R. Y. Tsai, A Versatile Camera Calibration Technique for High-accuracy 3D Machine Vision Metrology using Off-the-shelf TV Cameras and Lenses, IEEE J. Robotics and Automation, vol. 3, no.4, pp. 323-344, 1987.
14. X. Ying, Z. Hu, Catadioptric Camera Calibration Using Geometric Invariants, IEEE Trans. Pattern Analysis and Machine Intelligence, 26(10), pp. 1260-1271, 2004.
15. X. Ying, H. Zha, Linear Approaches to Camera Calibration from Sphere Images or Active Intrinsic Calibration using Vanishing Points, Proc. Tenth Int'l Conf. Computer Vision, pp. 596-603, 2005.
16. Z. Zhang, Flexible Camera Calibration by Viewing Planes from Unknown Orientations, Proc. Seventh Int'l Conf. Computer Vision, pp. 666-673, 1999.

New 3D Fourier Descriptors for Genus-Zero Mesh Objects

Hongdong Li and Richard Hartley

Research School of Information Sciences and Engineering,
The Australian National University,
Canberra Research Labs, National ICT Australia Ltd.

Abstract. The 2D Fourier Descriptor is an elegant and powerful technique for 2D shape analysis. This paper intends to extend such technique to 3D. Though conceptually natural, such an extension is not trivial in that two critical problems, the spherical parametrization and invariants construction, must be solved. By using a newly developed surface parametrization method–the *discrete conformal mapping (DCM)*—we propose a 3D Fourier Descriptor (3D-FD) for representing and recognizing arbitrarily-complex genus-zero mesh objects. A new DCM algorithm is suggested which solves the first problem efficiently. We also derive a method to construct a *truly complete* set of Spherical Harmonic invariants. The 3D-FD descriptors have been tested on different complex mesh objects. Experiment results for shape representation are satisfactory.

1 Introduction

3D object recognition is one central task of computer vision research. A good *shape representation* scheme is at the heart of a practical shape recognition system. This paper aims at developing a new 3D shape representation and recognition method for general mesh objects. Our method is based on Fourier Shape Analysis. Specifically, We intend to extend the well-known and powerful 2D Fourier descriptor technique to 3D Fourier Descriptors (3D-FD).

Although it is conceptually straightforward, in practice such an extension is non-trivial. The main challenges arise from two tasks: (1) spherical parametrization; and (2) invariant computation. In 2D-FD processing, the 2D shape (contour) is mapped onto a *unit circle*, by using an arc-length parametrization. This is followed by the Fourier analysis on this circle. Analogously, in 3D the object (surface) should be first mapped onto a *unit sphere*, then followed by a *Fourier analysis on the sphere.* Fourier analysis on a sphere is not a difficult task; Spherical Harmonic analysis (SH) is such a technique ([6]) and had been introduced to computer vision for 3D representation decades ago. The real difficulty comes from *surface parametrization.* Unlike in 2D where arc-length is a natural parametrization, there is no natural way of doing surface parametrization for a general 3D surface, even though it does have a spherical-topology. Some conventional spherical parameterizations techniques exist, but seldom do they provide satisfactory results (as will be explained later).

P.J. Narayanan et al. (Eds.): ACCV 2006, LNCS 3851, pp. 734–743, 2006.

To attack these difficulties, we propose a new method of discrete conformal mapping (DCM) in conjunction with the invariant Spherical Harmonics (SH). As will be shown in this paper, the method performs excellently in providing shape descriptors that can be used to represent 3D meshes in a set of coefficients. In principle, these descriptors are complete, therefore they can be used to reconstruct the original surface.

After the DCM mapping, we apply the spherical harmonics (SH) expansion to derive a *complete* and *invariant* shape representation. We recognize that both the **invariance** (w.r.t. irrelevant transformations) and the **completeness** are equally important issues for a good shape representation. By completeness we mean that the representation contains sufficient information for reconstructing the original shape (up to some non-essential transformations). Most existing SH-invariants methods, however, have overlooked the completeness issue. As a result, conventional SH invariants often leads to significant information loss. We propose a new method to construct truly *complete* SH invariants, basing on a recent paper of SH computation[10]. By this method the SH coefficients are made invariant to irrelevant transformations, as well as retaining the completeness strictly.

So far we have conducted experiments on a small set of meshes of complex geometries and different classes. But results already show that the obtained descriptors are invariant to rotation/translation/scale, and robust to different tessellation, triangulation and resolution, and noise. In addition, they preserve the geometric information of the original shape.

2 Previous Work

Spherical Parametrization. Because the Spherical Harmonics are defined on spherical domain, it is thereby important to find an appropriate *spherical parametrization* for a 3D surface.

Most conventional methods often choose a naive parametrization method (for example use center-emitted rays to intersect the object surface), they therefore can only handle convex objects or star-like objects [1]. Horn's EGI (and its many extensions) is a well-known and nice method for shape description[2][3]. It is based on the theory of Gauss map, hence has a solid theoretical ground. But, in general the Gauss map is not one-to-one for a concave object, therefore its many useful properties are enjoyed by convex objects only. Recent attempts at spherical parametrization of complex (e.g., concave, non-star-like, convolved, folded) 3D objects provide many other interesting approaches. A popular scheme is to gradually deform a surface until it maps onto the sphere (or conversely deform a sphere to the surface). Herbert et al's SAI [2], and Sijbers et al's 3D-Fourier [4] are examples of the kind. A shortcoming with them is the hardness to analyze the results, due to their heuristic nature. Brechbuhler et al proposed an interesting method based on solving a heat conduction equation inside the 3D object volume [9]. However, the computation burden is very heavy and the final result depends on some user specified landmark positions.

3 New Spherical Parametrization

Mathematical backgrounds. We base our method on Discrete Conformal mapping. Suppose M_1 and M_2 are two regular surfaces. A bijective differentiable mapping $f : M_1 \rightarrow M_2$ between the two surfaces is said to be *conformal* if it leaves the angle between curves on the surface invariant. A mapping between two surfaces is a conformal mapping if and only if it re-scales the *first fundamental forms* everywhere.

According to the celebrated `Riemann Mapping Theorem`, there always exists a conformal mapping between any two genus-zero surfaces. In particular, there exists a conformal mapping from any genus-0 surface to the unit sphere S^2—a spherical parametrization of the surface.

However, such a conformal mapping is not unique since two such maps may differ by a further conformal mapping of S^2 to itself. The set of such mappings form S^2 to S^2 forms a 6-dimensional Lie group, the Möbius group, as will be explained now.

We identify the 2-dimensional sphere S^2 with the one-point-compactified complex plane $\mathbb{C}\cup\{\infty\}$ via the stereographic mapping $\varphi(x,y,z) = (x/(1-z)+iy/(1-z))$ where (x,y,z) are the Euclidean coordinates of a point on the unit sphere. The conformal mappings S^2 to itself are then simply the group of Möbius transforms of the complex plane given by $m(z) = \frac{az+b}{cz+d}$, with $ad - bc \neq 0$, where z, a, b, c and $d \in\mathbb{C}$. This transform has 3 complex (6 real) parameters, since multiplication of a, b, c and d by a complex number does not change the transform. To be precise, the set of conformal mappings of S^2 are those mappings of the form $\varphi^{-1} \circ m \circ \varphi$. Another way of thinking of this is to identify $\mathbb{C} \cup \{\infty\}$ with the one-dimensional complex projective plane $\mathbb{PC}^1$. Points in $\mathbb{PC}^1$ are represented by complex 2-vectors. The space $\mathbb{PC}^1$ has the topology of a real 2-sphere S^2, and the stereographic mapping $\varphi : (x,y,z) \mapsto (x+iy, 1-z)$ provides the homeomorphism between these spaces. The Möbius transforms acting on $\mathbb{PC}^1$ are simply the group of projective transforms, represented by non-singular 2×2 complex matrices.

Harmonic mapping. In practice, the conformal mapping is often approximated by a harmonic mapping, denoted by f. Namely, it satisfies the following harmonic (Laplace) equation: $\triangle f = \textbf{div grad } f = 0$. For three-dimensional genus-0 surfaces, these two mappings are essentially the same. Therefore, the problem of finding a spherical conformal parametrization is reduced to a Laplace-on-Manifold problem, where the target manifold is the unit sphere S^2. Usually this is implemented by minimizing the following harmonic energy function ([23][21][14]):$E_H(f) = \frac{1}{2}\int_{M_1} \|\textbf{grad } f\|^2$. The overall procedure is thus: first find a spherical homeomorphic initialization for the given shape, then iteratively modify this initial mapping by minimizing the above energy function, till it converges to a conformal mapping. The later stage is known as *diffusion*.

Step-1: Initialization. We start from a triangulated closed mesh object homeomorphic to a sphere. The minimization of the harmonic energy is based on an iterative updating procedure. It thus requires a good initialization which serves as the starting point for the iteration. This initialization should be an approximation of the final conformal mapping.

Based on the fact that the connectivity (adjacency) graph of any genus-0 3D object is always a 2D *planar graph*, we propose a simple method for spherical initialization. Since our diffusion algorithm (described in the next subsection) has a relatively large convergence neighborhood, we do not require the initial mapping to be very close to the final result, as long as it is a homeomorphism. Our initialization procedure is: first choose an arbitrary surface triangle as the boundary, then apply a straight-line planar graph embedding to the graph, followed by an inverse stereographic mapping to get the initial spherical mapping.

Step-2: Diffusion. Having a homeomorphic spherical embedding as the initialization, the next step is to diffuse it to a conformal mapping. We accomplish this by solving a diffusion equation on the unit sphere, namely the Laplace-Beltrami equation: $\triangle_{S^2} f = \mathbf{div}_{S^2}\mathbf{grad}_{S^2} f = 0$. Note that the *Laplacian* is defined here in terms of the local geometry of the target manifold. We have found that creating a chart using the exponential map (or inversely, the logarithm map) gives significantly better results in terms of convergence, and independence of the initial function. The exp-map on a manifold intuitively corresponds to expanding geodesic curves to the tangent plane. Using the exponential map, all mesh vertices are mapped one-to-one onto a single chart. The actual computation of such exp-map on the sphere is also very simple, thanks to the Rodrigues' formula of matrix exponential [16].

Step-3: Möbius Normalization. After previous steps, a conformal mapping f from the surface M_1 to S^2 is obtained. However, this mapping is not unique, since it may be followed by another arbitrary conformal mapping of the sphere to itself. As seen in section 3 such a conformal mapping may be represented by a Möbius transform. Thus, there exists a 6-parameter family of such mappings. In the current section, we focus on *normalizing* the mapping from M_1 to S^2 so that the remaining ambiguity consists only of 3D rotations of the sphere, a 3-parameter family.

A nested-iteration algorithm is suggested for simultaneous diffusion and normalization [19]. However, this is computationally expensive, especially for large scale meshes. A simplified version by centering the mesh barycenter is thus further proposed, but it is still inefficient and sometimes produces degenerate solution as pointed out by Gotsman [21]. Gotsman suggests using anchor points to solve it, but this would depend on particular choice of the anchors.

We propose a new method here, which accomplishes the Möbius normalization task very efficiently, only at the expense of negligible computation. This is done by a process that balances the surface area (or "weight") distribution on the sphere by a Möbius factorization. Unlike [19][12], we carry out this normalization step after the diffusion process, rather than simultaneously. This leads to a significant improvement in efficiency.

Consider a surface element dA located at a point $\mathbf{x}$ on M_1. For the purpose of gaining an intuitive understanding of our method, we assume that this surface element has a "weight" proportional to area, and so the surface element may be thought of as having weight dA. Now, the mapping f maps this to an element of weight dA at point $f(\mathbf{x})$ on the sphere S^2. The centre of gravity of the surface mapped on to S^2 is given by $\int_{M_1} f(\mathbf{x})dA$. What we really want is to adjust the mapping f so that this centre-of-gravity is at the origin (centre-of-the-sphere).

If f_0 is an initial conformal mapping to S^2, then the most general conformal mapping $f : M_1 \rightarrow S^2$ is of the form $\varphi^{-1} \circ m \circ \varphi \circ f_0$, where m is a Möbius transform. We want to find a Möbius transform m such that

$$\int_{M_1} \varphi^{-1} \circ m \circ \varphi \circ f_0(\mathbf{x})dA = \mathbf{0} \ . \tag{1}$$

This could be done by searching over the 6-parameter family of all Möbius transforms. Note, however that applying a rotation to S^2 results in a rotation of the centre of gravity $\int_{M_1} f(\mathbf{x})dA$, and hence does not change the truth or falsehood of the condition (1). Rotations form a subgroup of the Möbius transforms of the sphere, and in seeking to enforce (1) we may factor out the rotations, thus reducing the search to a 3-parameter search.

Formally, it is verified that rotations of S^2 correspond precisely to those Möbius transforms represented by matrices of the form $\mathtt{Q} = \begin{bmatrix} q_1 & q_2 \\ -\bar{q}_2 & \bar{q}_1 \end{bmatrix}$. An arbitrary Möbius transform can be factored as

$$\mathtt{M} = \mathtt{Q} \cdot \mathtt{R} = \begin{bmatrix} q_1 & q_2 \\ -\bar{q}_2 & \bar{q}_1 \end{bmatrix} \cdot \begin{bmatrix} k & z_t \\ 0 & 1 \end{bmatrix} \ , \tag{2}$$

where $k \in \mathbb{R}$ and $z_t \in \mathbb{C}$. Thus, in enforcing (1), we may ignore the left-hand rotation matrix $\mathtt{Q}$, and constrain our search to Möbius transforms of the form given by the right-hand matrix above. Such a transformation is of the type $z \mapsto kz + z_t$, which represents a scaling, followed by a complex translation (by z_t) in the complex plane. Transformations of this type form a 3-parameter family.

The above discussion was derived in terms of continuous surfaces. In the case of a triangulated surface M_1, we may consider just the vertices $\mathbf{v}_i$ of the mesh, and to each one assign a weight equal to the area of the corresponding region in a dual tessellation. We then seek the solution to $\sum_i w_i \, \varphi^{-1} \circ m \circ \varphi \circ f_0(\mathbf{v}_i) = 0$ over all Möbius transforms of the form $m(z) = kz + z_t$. At first sight, this equation is nonlinear. By some very simple algebras, however, one can reduce it to an equivalent linear system, for which a least square technique suffices.

Once this is solved, applying the corresponding spherical affine transformation $\mathtt{R}$ to the diffused result will give us a unique solution up to rotation. As a matter of example, for the Stanford "bunny" mesh one of our experiments obtained the following affine factor:

$$\mathtt{R} = \begin{bmatrix} 0.21491 & -0.00932 + 0.00583i \\ 0.00000 & 1.00000 \end{bmatrix} \ ,$$

whose effect (as can be directly ascertained) is approximately re-scaling in the radial direction.

4 The Complete SH Invariants

Any bounded $\mathbf{L}^2$ continuous function (real or complex) $g(\theta, \varphi)$ defined on a sphere can always be decomposed into a finite set of SH coefficients C_ℓ^m, where $|m| \leq \ell$, $\ell = 0, 1, 2, 3, \ldots \ell_{max}$, ℓ is called the degree (or frequency) of the SH expansion. The SH expansion has been employed in many different areas. Its definition and fast computation can be found elsewhere. In this paper we mainly address the issue of how to construct *complete SH invariants* in the context of 3D shape representation.

As its 2D counterpart, 3D SH also has the nice property that the coefficients can be made invariant with respect to translation, rotation and scale change. We are most interested in the rotational invariance, because others can be easily eliminated by a trivial pre-alignment operation, whereas eliminating the rotation is not so easy. The PCA-pre-alignment technique [1], though was popularly adopted, proves to be neither accurate nor stable for noisy shapes or shapes with high-order symmetries.

Many authors suggest the use of the following Energy SH-Invariants (EIs) [6][7]:$EI(\ell) = \sum_{|m| \leq \ell} ||C_\ell^m||^2$, which is based on the fact that the squared magnitude of the SH coefficients at every frequency ℓ is independent of rotation. This method has drawbacks:

1. These invariants are not complete. This results in difficulty in discriminating shapes. For example, distinct shapes may have the same descriptors, and similar shapes may not be distinguishable. Moreover, it may not be possible to reconstruct the original shape from the invariants.
2. There is not only information loss but serious computation waste. For SH coefficients up to degree ℓ_{max}, there should be $((\ell_{max} + 1)^2)$ independent complex invariants. However, only $(\ell_{max} + 1)$ real energy invariants are obtained by the conventional method.

Our complete SH invariants. We provide a method of constructing a *complete* set of SH invariants. Completeness implies that the shape descriptors suffer no ambiguity in shape classification and recognition. We make use of a recent algorithm of estimating orientation from SHs [10]. The principle is the fact that SH coefficients at every frequency ℓ, $\ell \geq 1$, form an irreducible representation of the $SO(3)$ group. In other words, when a rotation is applied to the original function, the resulting SH coefficients will transform among themselves in exactly the same way. Specifically, if we apply a rotation denoted by the Euler angles (α, β, γ), we get new C_ℓ^m from the original $C_\ell^{m'}$ defined by:

$$C_\ell^m = e^{-im(\alpha+\pi/2)} \cdot \sum_{|m'|<\ell} e^{-im'(\gamma+\pi/2)} C_\ell^{m'} \cdot \sum_{|k|<\ell} \mathcal{P}_\ell^{m'k}(0) \mathcal{P}_\ell^{mk}(0) e^{-ik(\beta+\pi)} \quad , \tag{3}$$

where the two $\mathcal{P}_\ell(\cdot)$ are the *associated Legendre polynomials*. Specifying some of the SH coefficients with some *canonical* values, we can estimate a *canonical* rotation $\mathbf{R}(\alpha^\star, \beta^\star, \gamma^\star)$ by which the SH coefficients are transformed into complete rotation invariants. For instance, when $\ell = 2$, we can use the following *canonical* values [11]:

$$\begin{aligned} C_2^1(\alpha^\star, \beta^\star, \gamma^\star) &= 0 \ , \\ C_2^2(\alpha^\star, \beta^\star, \gamma^\star) & \quad \textit{real, positive and maximal,} \\ Re(C_1^1(\alpha^\star, \beta^\star, \gamma^\star)) &\geq 0 \ , \\ Im(C_1^1(\alpha^\star, \beta^\star, \gamma^\star)) &\geq 0 \ . \end{aligned}$$

We use $\ell = 2, 3, 4, 5$ in a least square fashion in our experiments for robust rotation-estimation. The subspace $\ell = 1$ is discarded as it is equivalent to the PCA-pre-alignment. An intuitive explanation for cases when $\ell \geq 2$ is to use the SH basis shapes to fit the original shape.

Theoretically, this method of invariants construction is not entirely satisfactory, because it relies on the identification of a canonical rotation and we suspect that this may lead to a 2-fold ambiguity. Nevertheless, it has given good results in experiments. We continue to look for better ways of defining rotationally invariants SH coefficients.

Shape functions in use. Now that we know how to compute a set of rotation-invariant SH coefficients of *shape functions*, we need to specify which function to use. One choice is the density, or *area ratio* function on S^2 induced by the conformal mapping $f : M_1 \rightarrow S^2$. Let T' be a facet in the dual mesh of M_1, corresponding to a vertex $\mathbf{v}$ of the triangulation, and let $f(T')$ be the corresponding facet on S^2. We define a function g on S^2 facet by facet on the mesh. The value assigned to each point of a facet $f(T')$ is equal to the area ratio $\text{Area}(T')/\text{Area}(f(T'))$. Note that this is essentially independent of the triangulation of the surface M_1. For computational purposes, a delta-function of weight $\text{Area}(T')$ placed at $f(\mathbf{v})$ may be used instead.

In the future we will pursue a more ambitious target as follows. It seems that specifying both the density-ratio and mean-curvature functions on the sphere provides redundant information for a global genus-0 closed surface. We are not aware, however, how to specify a *minimal* amount of information to determine the surface. We think it is an interesting *inverse problem*, where we argue that a *regularization* approach might help. Some preliminary reconstruction results can be found in [18].

5 Experiments and Results

We have tested our algorithm on 26 genus-0 meshes of different classes, and some have very complex geometries. The full program was implemented in C++, and ran on an Intel-P4 2.4Ghz PC with win-XP OS. All the 26 meshes converge quickly. The code was not meant to be runtime optimal. Both the planar graph drawing and the SH expansion have fast algorithms [15] [10], our main concern is thereby the time for the diffusion and normalization.For the wolf meshes of 308

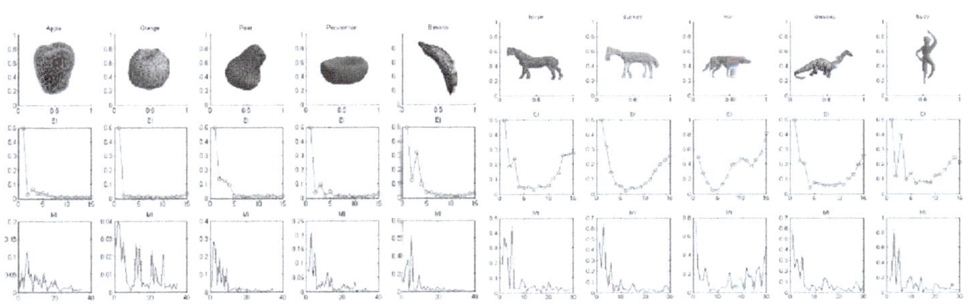

Fig. 1. This figure show some mesh objects, their corresponding energy-invariants (row-2) and our 3D-FD shape descriptors (row-3, magnitude part only). For better illustration, we only depict the first 36 coefficients. The actual number is about 200.

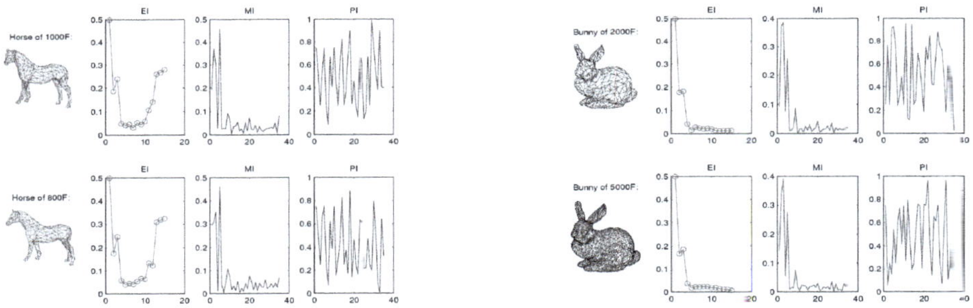

Fig. 2. Obtained 3D-FD shape descriptors of the same object but with different triangulations and resolutions. Here the two horses have 1000 facets and 800 facets respectively. The two rabbits have 2000 facets and 5000 facets and with different levels of noise added.

facets, the diffusion and normalization cost 18.2 seconds. While the computations of the horse-2k and rabbit-2k meshes, each has 2k facets, cost about 106s and 87s resp (average in 10 trials). We also implemented the nested-iteration method for simultaneous diffusion and normalization ([19]), but got no convergence after 20 minutes running. We have verified that the results of our spherical conformal mappings are indeed unique up to rotation, by applying the algorithm to other randomly rotated versions of the same object.

The current shape support function used in experiments is a complex-valued function with the real and imaginary parts given by the radius and area-ratios resp. Figure 1 gives some resultant SH invariants. The first row gives the original meshes. The second row shows the obtained EI invariants up to degree 15. The bottom row shows our complete invariant shape descriptors (magnitude part only). Pay attention to the similarity between alike shapes and the difference between unalike ones. Both descriptors capture the shape geometry, while ours retains more information due to its completeness nature.

Table 1. Euclidean distance matrix

	0.0000	0.0636	0.1469	0.5116	0.4682	0.5977
	0.0636	0.0000	0.1670	0.4227	0.3817	0.4078
	0.1469	0.1670	0.0000	0.3645	0.3391	0.4381
	0.5116	0.4227	0.3645	0.0000	0.2172	0.1839
	0.4682	0.3817	0.3391	0.2172	0.0000	0.1452
	0.5977	0.4078	0.4381	0.1839	0.1452	0.0000

We tested the robustness of our algorithm to different triangulations, resolution and noise. We did this through first perform both subdivision-based *refinement* and edge-collapse-based *simplification* to the original meshes, in order to alter the resolution and tessellation, then introduce isotropic Gaussian noise to the coordinates. Apply our algorithm to the obtained meshes, the newly obtained 3D-FD descriptors are shown very stable, which indicates that both the parametrization process and the invariant computation procedures are robust. Figure 2 gives results on the horse and "bunny" meshes. Note that even the phase parts of the new descriptors are rather consistence. Table-1 gives the Euclidean distance matrix for classifying several objects.

6 Conclusions and Future Work

The method of using Spherical Harmonics applied to a new conformal spherical parametrization, proposed in this paper seems to work well in discriminating mesh objects of different shape, while being invariant to rotation, robust to triangulation and noise in the model description.

We have not yet fully demonstrated the procedure of reconstructing from the SH invariants to the original shape. Nevertheless, the proposed new algorithm already provide practical improvements over existing methods, and already shows good results. All these have added to the confidence of applying the DCM to various vision problems. Of course, much more work is yet to be done for better demonstrating our method, and for many real-world applications (e.g, medical anatomic shape comparison, 3D model indexing/retrieval). Another fascinating and challenging problem is to represent shape using *minimal* amount of information. This can find many applications in geometric compression, and will be a priority in our future work in this area.

Acknowledgments. NICTA is funded through the Australian Governments Backing Australias Ability Initiative, in part through the Australian Research Council. Thank Fredrik Kahl for many insightful discussions. The mesh objects used in experiments were obtained from C. Grimm //www.cs.wustl.edu/cmg/.

References

1. Vranic, An improvement of rotation invariant 3D shape descriptor, *Proc.IEEE-ICIP-2003*, 2003.
2. H. Shum, M. Hebert, K. Ikeuchi, On 3D shape similarity, *Proc IEEE-CVPR-1996, pp.526-531*,1996.
3. S.B. Kang, K.Ikeuchi The Complex EGI: A New Representation for 3-D Pose Determination, *IEEE-T-PAMI, pp.707-721*,1993.
4. J.Sijbers, T. Ceulemans, D. V. Dyck, Algorithm for the Computation of 3D Fourier Descriptors, *Proc.ICPR-2002,vol-2, pp.11-15*, 2002.
5. X.Liu,R.Sun,S.Kang and H.Shum, Directional histogram model for 3D shape similarity, *Proc. IEEE-CVPR, pp.813-820*, 2003.
6. M.Kazhdan, T.Fukhouser, S.Rusinkiewicz, Rotation invariant Spherical Harmonic Representation of 3D descriptors, *Eurographcs'03 Symp. on Geometry Process*,2003.
7. M.Novotni,R.Klein, 3D Zenike descriptors for content based shape retrieval, *Proc. ACM solid model'03*, 2003.
8. J. Tangelder, R. Veltkamp, Survey of content based 3D shape retrieval methods, *Proc. Shape Modeling Int'04*, 2004.
9. M.Quicken, C. Brechbhler, J.Hug, H.Blattmann, and G.Szkely, Parameterization of Closed Surfaces for Parametric Surface Description, *Proc.IEEE-CVPR-2000*,2000.
10. A.Makadia, K.Daniilidis. Rotation estimation from spherical images, *Proc. IEEE-ICPR-2004*,2004.
11. G.Burel, H.Henocq, Determination of the orientation of 3D objects using spherical harmonics,*CVGIP:GMIP, Vol(57),no 5, pp.400-408*,1996.
12. M.Jin et al. Optimal global conformal surface parameterization, *Proc. IEEE-Vis'04, pp.267-274*,2004.
13. G.Kamberov, G. Kamberova, Conformal method for quantitative shape extraction: performance evaluation,*Proc.ICPR-2004*, 2004.
14. M.S. Floater and K. Hormann, Surface parameterization: a tutorial and survey, *Advances in Multiresolution for Geometric Modelling, pp 157-186*, Springer, 2005.
15. J.Boyer and W. Myrvold, Stop minding your p's and q's: a simplified $O(n)$ planar embedding algorithm, *Proc. ACM-SIAM Symposium on Discrete Algorithms,pp140-146*, 1999.
16. J.J.Koenderink,*Solid shape*, MIT Press,1990.
17. R. Hartley and A. Zisserman, *Multiple View Geometry in Computer Vision,2nd edition,* Cambridge University Press, 2004.
18. Hongdong Li,Richard Hartley, Hans Burkhardt, Discrete Conformal Shape Representation and Reconstruction of 3D Mesh Objects, in Proc. ICIAP-2005, 2005.
19. X.Gu,et al. Genus Zero Surface Conformal Mapping and Its Application to Brain Surface Mapping, *IEEE Trans on Medical Imaging, VOL.23, NO.8*,2004.
20. X. Gu, S. Yau. Surface Classification Using Conformal Structures, *Proc. ICCV-2003, pp.701-708*, Nice,France, 2003.
21. C.Gotsman, X.Gu, A.Sheffer. Fundamentals of spherical parameterization for 3D meshes, *ACM Trans on Graphics,vol-22,iss-3,pp.358-363*, 2003.
22. X.Gu, Y.Wang, et al., Geometric compression using Riemann surface structure,*Comm. in info. sys., Vol.3, No.3,pp.171-182*,2004.
23. S. Angenent, S.Haker, A.Tannenbaum,et al, On the Laplace-Beltrami Operator and Brain surface flattening, *IEEE-T-Medical Imaging, vol-18,no-8,pp.700-711*, 1999.

High Dynamic Range Global Mosaic

Dae-Woong Kim and Ki-Sang Hong

Division of Electrical and Computer Engineering, POSTECH, Pohang, Korea
{dwkim, hongks}@postech.ac.kr
http://cafe.postech.ac.kr

Abstract. This paper presents a global approach for constructing high dynamic range mosaic from multiple images with large exposure differences. By relating image intensities to scene radiances with a convenient distortion model, we robustly estimated registration parameters for the high dynamic range global mosaic (HDRGM), simultaneously estimating scene radiances and distortion parameters in a single framework. Also, a simple detail-preserving contrast reduction method is introduced.

1 Introduction

Mosaicing is a popular method of effectively increasing the field of view of a rotating and zooming camera by allowing several views of a scene to be combined into a single image. Most work focuses on the accurate estimation of geometric transformations between pairwise images. Although the pairwise registrations are accurate, the concatenation of these transformations often causes error accumulations when registering multi-frame images. To minimize the error accumulation problem, several global mosaic approaches [1–3] have been proposed.

Unintentional situations can occur in the construction of a mosaic using conventional methods, since vision systems use low dynamic range image detectors that typically provide 8 bits of brightness data at each pixel. When a camera moves to a different part of the scene with zooming and rotating about its optical center, the exposure can change automatically or manually, especially for scenes containing both areas of low and high illumination. The observed intensities of a scene point may not be the same in differently exposed images, which may deteriorate the registration accuracy.

To register images with large exposure differences, it is necessary to reconstruct original scene radiances of the observed image intensities. It has been obtained by calibrating the nonlinear radiometric response curve from multiply exposed images [4–7]. However, the obvious alignment issue has not been considered assuming that the image registration process is successful. Thus, registration and radiometric calibration should not be dealt separately, especially for differently exposed images taken from a hand-held camera. Combining the two problems in a single framework, the accurate image registration for image mosaic with high dynamic range is still an open issue and is the subject of this paper.

P.J. Narayanan et al. (Eds.): ACCV 2006, LNCS 3851, pp. 744–753, 2006.

To minimize registration errors caused by intensity mismatches in the image space, we propose to use the scene radiance space. The observable intensity space has many distortions including lens distortion, photometric distortion, and intentional non-linear radiometric distortion. By relating image intensities to scene radiances with a convenient distortion model, we robustly estimated registration parameters in the scene radiance space, simultaneously estimating scene radiances and distortion parameters in a single framework using a computationally optimized LM (Levenberg Marquardt) approach. By registering all images onto a high dynamic range scene radiance plane without distortion, error accumulations can be avoided, which is a major goal of the global mosaic.

We adapted a skipped mean estimator to estimate parameters robust to outliers such as moving objects and saturated pixels, and incorporated it into the optimization. Also, constraints of rotating and zooming cameras and radiometric curve are introduced, resulting in a MAP solution. We call our method *high dynamic range global mosaic* (HDRGM) because the final results are in the geometrically and photometrically undistorted high dynamic range scene radiance space, producing accurate and clean mosaic images without error accumulations. To reduce the contrast of the estimated scene radiance, we also introduced a new detail-preserving tone mapping method.

2 Related Work

In the realm of wide angle views with high dynamic range, Aggarwal and Ahuja [8] captured large fields of view at high resolutions by placing a graded transparency mask in front of the sensor. Similarly, Schechner and Nayar [9] mounted a fixed filter on the camera causing an intended vignetting. While they showed successful results for panoramic images based on specialized hardware, registration parameters were separately estimated.

Closer to our proposal are the works in [10] and [11]. Hasler and Süsstrunk [10] estimated parametric camera responses and camera motions separately using color mismatches in the overlapped region of a mosaic picture between two images. Mann [11] simultaneously extended the field of view and dynamic range by exploiting the automatic gain control feature of a camera with a gamma curve. However, they used only pairwise local relations while our method is a global approach in that it uses multiple images in a single framework. In the sense of global mosaic, the work of Sawhney and Kumar [3] is related to our work. However, it is quite different in that we related geometric and photometric distortion model to the scene radiance space, while they considered only geometric distortion in the intensity space.

Given registered images taken with an automatic gain control, Kim and Hong [12] estimated scene radiances with a photometric distortion model, and Litvinov and Schechner [13] dealt with a similar problem with non parametric models. In this paper, we extend our previous work in [12] by concentrating on the global registration issue with large exposure differences, also by considering geometric lens distortion.

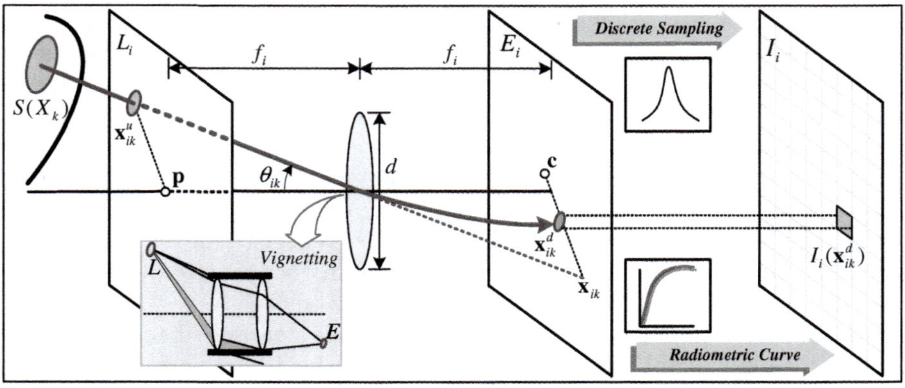

Fig. 1. Image distortion model for i-th image

3 Distortion Model

Most cameras have some effects causing distortions from scene radiances to image intensities. The distortions are closely related with intrinsic and extrinsic camera parameters. The goal of this section is to provide a convenient distortion model to calibrate camera parameters and scene radiances.

As depicted in Figure 1, the scene radiance $S(X_k)$ of a scene point X_k is linearly related to the image irradiance $E_i(\mathbf{x}_{ik})$ at the corresponding point $\mathbf{x}_{ik}$ in i-th image sensor array centered on $\mathbf{c}$, which is given by

$$E_i(\mathbf{x}_{ik}) = \mathcal{G}_i(\mathbf{x}_{ik})S(X_k), \tag{1}$$

where

$$\mathcal{G}_i(\mathbf{x}_{ik}) = t_i \underbrace{(1 - \alpha r_{ik})}_{Vignetting} \left[\frac{\pi}{4}\left(\frac{d}{f_i}\right)^2 \cos^4\theta_{ik}\right], \tag{2}$$

t_i is the exposure time, α is the constant representing the loss of light due to optical vignetting, r_{ik} is the distance from the principal point $\mathbf{p}(= [p_x, p_y]^T)$, d is the lens diameter, and f_i is the focal length.

Without translational motion of camera, the geometrical point relationship between X_k and $\mathbf{x}_{ik}$ can be represented by $\mathbf{x}_{ik} = K_i R_i X_k$, where R_i is the rotation matrix and K_i is the camera calibration matrix in the form of

$$K_i = K_c F_i = \begin{bmatrix} 1 & s & p_x \\ 0 & \gamma & p_y \\ 0 & 0 & 1 \end{bmatrix} \begin{bmatrix} f_i & 0 & 0 \\ 0 & f_i & 0 \\ 0 & 0 & 1 \end{bmatrix}, \tag{3}$$

where γ is the aspect ratio and s is the skew. The parameters in K_i represent the properties of the image formation system and they are closely related to $\cos\theta_{ik}$ $(=\sqrt{f_i^2/(f_i^2 + r_{ik}^2)})$. The distance from the principal point, r_{ik}, can be measured in the plane L_i with $\|\mathbf{x}_{ik}^u\|$, where $\mathbf{x}_{ik}^u$ is the projected point of X_k on L_i satisfying

$$\mathbf{x}_{ik}^u = F_i X_k = F_i F_i^{-1} K_c^{-1} \mathbf{x}_{ik} = K_c^{-1} \mathbf{x}_{ik}. \tag{4}$$

Ideally, the light rays coming from the scene should pass through the optical center linearly, but in practice, lens systems are composed of several optical elements introducing nonlinear distortion to the optical paths and the resulting images. With a simplified cubic term of radial lens distortion, $\mathbf{x}_{ik}$ is transformed nonlinearly with the lens distortion parameter κ, as given by

$$\mathbf{x}_{ik}^{d} = \mathbf{x}_{ik} + \kappa \mathbf{x}_{ik}^{u} \left[r_{ik}^{2} \; r_{ik}^{2} \; 0 \right]^{T} . \tag{5}$$

Images containing negative distortion, $\kappa < 0$, exhibit barreling effect and such images are corrected by applying positive distortion (and vice-versa for pin-cushion effect).

After the discrete sampling process of the CCD unit, the irradiance reaching the image sensor is nonlinearly mapped by the radiometric response curve g.

The final relation between scene radiance $L_i(\mathbf{x}_{ik}^u)$ and image intensity $I_i(\mathbf{x}_{ik}^d)$ can be expressed as

$$I_i(\mathbf{x}_{ik}^{d}) = g\big(\mathcal{G}_i(\mathbf{x}_{ik}) L_i(\mathbf{x}_{ik}^{u})\big). \tag{6}$$

We call L_i the scene radiance plane of I_i. It is noted that no distortion exists in L_i because $S(X_k) = L_i(\mathbf{x}_{ik}^u)$ ignoring losses in the lens. We will utilize this property in the registration.

4 High Dynamic Range Image Registration from a Rotating and Zooming Camera

Scene radiances have been obtained by calibrating the radiometric curve and exposure ratios [5–7]. But, they did not consider other photometric and geometric distortions which are closely related to intrinsic camera parameters as shown in Equation (2) and (5). These parameters can be estimated in a unified framework using the geometry of a rotating and zooming camera.

For simplicity, consider two images I_i and I_r obtained from a rotating and zooming camera as depicted in Fig 2. The point relationship can be represented by a 3×3 homography, H_i, given by

$$\mathbf{x}_{ik} = H_i \mathbf{x}_{rk} = K_i R_i K_r^{-1} \mathbf{x}_{rk}, \tag{7}$$

Because two matching points are on the same ray in 3D space passing through the camera center, $I_i(\mathbf{x}_{ik})$ and $I_r(\mathbf{x}_{rk})$ are originated from the same radiance $S(X_k)$ satisfying $L_i(\mathbf{x}_{ik}^u) = L_r(\mathbf{x}_{rk}^u)$. Therefore, the solution can be found in least square sense using the relation in Equation (6).

Notice that, given constant c, replacing $\mathcal{G}_i(\mathbf{x}_{ik}) L_i(\mathbf{x}_{ik}^u)$ with $\mathcal{G}_i(\mathbf{x}_{ik}) c c^{-1} L_i(\mathbf{x}_{ik}^u)$ results in the same solution in Equation (6). Thus, $c^{-1} L_i(\mathbf{x}_{ik}^u)$ can be another solution for scene radiances. A constraint for the scene radiance is needed to solve this ambiguity, and we assumed that $L_r(\mathbf{p}) = g^{-1}(I_r(\mathbf{p}))$. For this, we rewrite Equation (2) as

$$\tilde{\mathcal{G}}_i(\mathbf{x}_{ik}) = D_i(1 - \alpha_i r_{ik}) \Big(\frac{f_r f_i}{f_i^2 + r_{ik}^2} \Big)^2 , \tag{8}$$

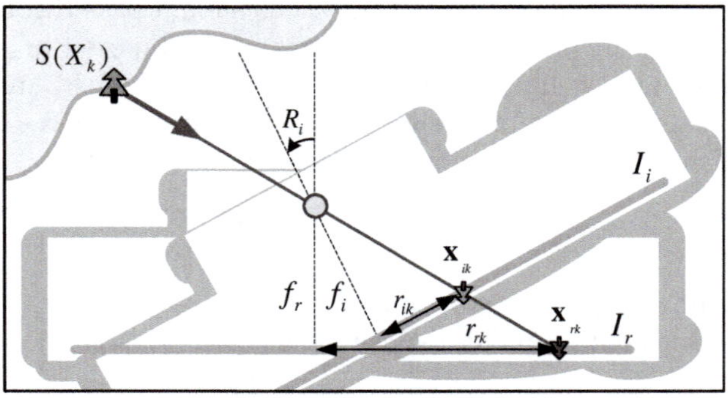

Fig. 2. Geometry of a rotating and zooming camera

where $D_i(= \pi t_i d^2/4f_r^2)$. Noting that $\tilde{\mathcal{G}}_r(\mathbf{p}) = D_r$, we can make $L_r(\mathbf{p})$ equal to $g^{-1}(I_r(\mathbf{p}))$ with $D_r = 1$. Then, the parameter $D_i(= t_i/t_r)$ should be a constant representing the ratio of exposure times between I_r and I_i. For some cases, it also contains the ratio of white balances and illumination change. In this sense, scene radiances can be reconstructed only up to scale and only the ratio of exposure times can be reconstructed.

As for the reference, we simply choose the frame with the smallest exposure time as I_r, and L_r is designated as the reference scene radiance plane. It is noted that L_r does not coincide with I_r because L_r has no distortion. By using L_r as the reference plane instead of I_r, we can avoid intensity mismatches causing error accumulation in the registration, which is a key idea of this paper.

Hence, assuming that all observed images $I(=\{I_i \mid i = 1 \sim N\})$ are corrupted by zero mean Gaussian noise and distorted by nonlinear mapping, all intrinsic camera parameters $\Theta(=\{f_i, D_i, g, \kappa, \alpha, p_x, p_y, \gamma, s \mid i = 1 \sim N\})$, homographies from the reference plane $H(=\{H_i \mid i = 1 \sim N\})$ and scene radiances $L(=\{L(\mathbf{x}_k) \mid \mathbf{x}_k \in \Omega, \Omega$: overlapping region in the reference plane$\})$ can be found with LM optimization minimizing

$$E_\rho = \langle \rho(e_{ik}, \sigma) \rangle, \tag{9}$$

where ρ is a error norm, $\langle \cdot \rangle$ is the average operator, σ is a constant, and e_{ik} is the residual error given by

$$e_{ik} = I_i(\mathbf{x}_{ik}^d) - g\big(\tilde{\mathcal{G}}_i(\mathbf{x}_{ik}) L_r(\mathbf{x}_{rk}^u)\big). \tag{10}$$

It should be noted that simultaneous estimation of Θ, H and L makes our algorithm use multiple images in a single framework avoiding error accumulations.

Among the bulk of noisy data in the overlapping region, there may be outliers such as moving objects and saturated intensities due to the small dynamic range of the sensor. A way of overcoming the outlier problem in estimation is by using robust statistics [14] which allows the estimator to be less affected by outliers in a statistical sense. The choice of the ρ-functions results in different robust estimators, and the robustness of a particular estimator refers to its insensitivity to outliers. In this paper, we used a Huber-type skipped means estimator [14] for ρ. It rejects everything which is more than $\sigma(=5.2 \text{ median})$ and takes the mean of the remainder. The second derivative is always positive, which is a very important property for incorporating the robust estimator into the LM optimization.

5 MAP Solution Using Priors

It is possible that the energy function contains local minima and the optimization procedure can get trapped by these. Therefore, we need some constraints on the parameter space. This can be achieved by defining the prior probabilities resulting in maximum a posterior (MAP) solution.

MAP estimate of Θ, H and L given multiple observed images I can be computed as

$$\hat{\Theta}, \hat{H}, \hat{L} = \arg \max_{\Theta, H, L} p(\Theta, H, L|I). \tag{11}$$

Noting that L is independent of Θ and H, Equation (11) can alternatively be represented as an energy minimization problem given by

$$\hat{\Theta}, \hat{H}, \hat{L} = \arg \min_{\Theta, H, L} \left[E_\rho + \lambda_c E_c + \lambda_p E_p\right], \tag{12}$$

where $E_\rho \sim -\log p(I|\Theta, L, H)$, $E_c \sim -\log p(H|\Theta)$, $E_p \sim -\log p(\Theta)p(L)$, λ_c and λ_p are Lagrange multiplier related with ratios of noise terms.

5.1 Infinite Homography Constraint (IHC) : E_c

Considering a rotating and zooming camera, we can use a constraint on H_i for $i = 1 \sim N$. Since $R_i(= K_i^{-1} H_i K_r)$ is a rotation matrix in Equation (7), it satisfies the property that $R_i = R_i^{-T}$. This can be equivalently represented by

$$\omega_i^* = K_i K_i^T = H_i K_r K_r^T H_i^T = H_i \omega_r^* H_i^T, \tag{13}$$

where ω^* is called the dual image of the absolute conic. This equation is known as the infinite homography constraint (IHC). It relates the camera calibration matrices to the infinite homographies and has been used as a measure for the self-calibration [15]. Using IHC, the conditional density function $p(H|\Theta)$ can be modeled using an energy function given by

$$E_c = \langle \| \omega_i^* - H_i \omega_r^* H_i^T \|_F^2 \rangle, \tag{14}$$

where F is Frobenius norm.

5.2 Priors and Penalties : E_p

We assumed that L has a uniform distribution and some intrinsic camera parameters are fixed and almost known via Gaussian prior: $\gamma \sim N(1, 0.1^2), s \sim N(0, 0.1^2)$, $(p_x, p_y) \sim N(0, 20^2)$.

As for the non-linear mapping function g, we adapt the polynomial model in [5] to give a broad flexibility to the shape. To guarantee the increasing shape of g, we used a new penalty type energy function using sigmoid function $Si(x)(=(1+e^{-ax})^{-1})$ given by

$$S_{b_1}^{b_2}(x) = (1 - Si(x - b_1))^2 + (1 - Si(b_2 - x))^2. \tag{15}$$

Because the sigmoid function is very close to the unit step function with a large value of $a(= 10^6)$, positive gradient of g, positive α, and negative (or positive for some case) κ can be guaranteed by minimizing

$$E_p = \int_0^1 S_0^{\infty}(g'(x))dx + S_0^{\infty}(\alpha) + S_{-\infty}^{0}(\kappa) + E_g, \tag{16}$$

where E_g is the energy term relating Gaussian priors.

The minimum of the final cost function in Equation (12) can be found using the LM (Levenberg-Marquardt) optimization. To handle a large motion of hand-held cameras and a wide dynamic range, we used a coarse-to-fine approach through a Gaussian pyramid. Because our algorithm finds too many parameters in L, direct implementation of LM optimization is not efficient. However, noting that scene radiance depends only on each pixel location, our formulation can be optimized by taking advantage of the diagonal block structure of the normal equation in the LM optimization.

6 Contrast Reduction

The final scene radiance can be obtained from the estimated $\hat{L}$ directly, or from a weighted average of all $L_i(\mathbf{x}_{ik}^u)$. The scene radiance need to be contrast reduced to be displayed on a common device with a limited dynamic range.

To reproduce I_c, we introduced a new tone mapping function given by

$$I_c(\mathbf{x}) = F(L(\mathbf{x}))L(\mathbf{x}), \tag{17}$$

where $F(L) = (e+1)/(e+L)$ with control parameter $e(> 0)$. It is noted that the behavior of F is very similar to the exposure time with the maximum value of $(e+1)/e$ for $L = 0$ and the minimum value of 1 for $L = 1$.

The global tone mapping curve and an example are shown in Figure 3. Although the global tone mapping method is very simple, image details can be lost in textured areas of images, as shown in (c). Instead of using F, we introduced spatially varying exposure $\tau(\mathbf{x})$ in each location $\mathbf{x}$ given by

$$\tau(\mathbf{x}) = \arg\min_{t(\mathbf{x})} \int_T \left[|\nabla t(\mathbf{x})| + \lambda_t \big(t(\mathbf{x}) - F(L(\mathbf{x}))\big)^2 \right] d\mathbf{x}, \tag{18}$$

$$\text{subject to } t(\mathbf{x})L(\mathbf{x}) \leq 1,$$

where T is the scene radiance domain and λ_t is Lagrange multiplier.

Using the total variation norm $|\nabla t(\mathbf{x})|$ as in [16], we obtain anisotropically diffused $F(L)$ as shown in (d). With $\tau(\mathbf{x})$, we can avoid halo effect in uniform regions, also preserving image details in textured regions as shown in (e).

(a) $F(x)\cdot x$ (b) L (c) $F(L)\cdot L$ (d) τ (e) $\tau\cdot L$

Fig. 3. Tone mapping example: $\lambda_t = 0.05$, $e = 0.1$

7 Experimental Results

In this section, we present experimental results of applying our global method to real digital still images with $\lambda_c = 0.01$, $\lambda_p = 1.0$, $\lambda_t = 0.05$, and $e = 0.3$.

In Figure 4, we show results from twelve digital images taken with a Sony DSC-P72 digital camera without zoom. Each image has a different exposure setting depending on the automatic gain control of the camera. Especially, one can observe that the brightness of the first frame is greater than that of the reference frame (the 12th frame), and the exposure times of the 4th, 8th, and 12th frame are very close to each other as depicted in the estimated parameters in (c). The lens distortion parameter κ was found -0.025553 which is the scaled value with the maximum distance from the image center. It can be noticed that straight lines of the stairs are

(a) Input image (b) Final mosaic result

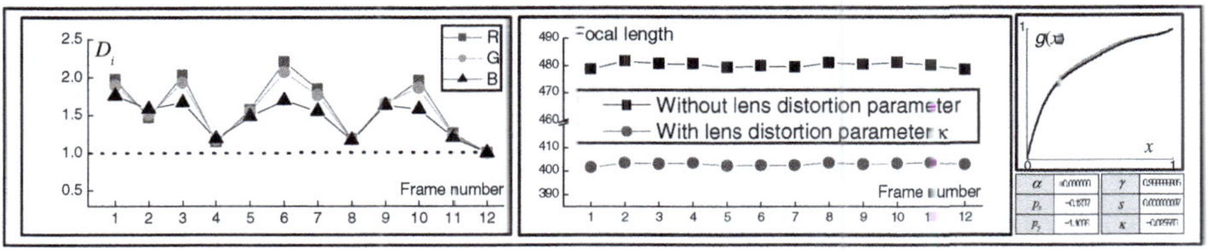

(c) Estimated camera parameters

Fig. 4. Result from Sony DSC-P72 with auto mode

(a) Original images

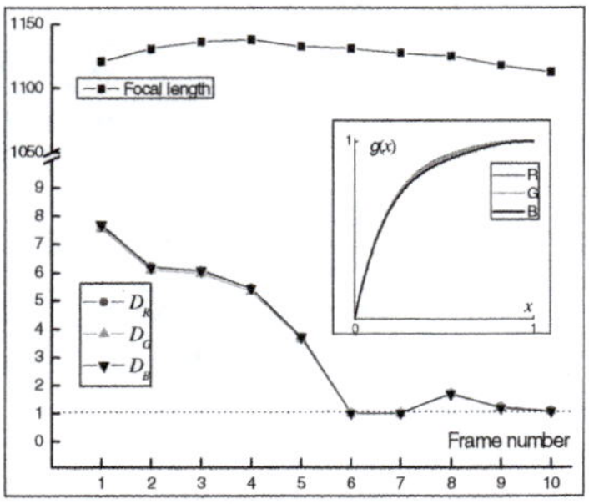

(b) Estimated camera parameters

(c) Final mosaic result

Fig. 5. Result from Sony DCR-TRV30 with manual mode

preserved, showing effective compensation for lens distortion. From [17], it is known that barreling lens distortion ($\kappa < 0$) can cause gross overestimates of focal length. This is depicted in (c) where the focal length is overestimated without lens distortion parameter κ compared with the result including κ. Note that the estimated focal lengths are almost constant because the images are taken without zoom. As expected, the radiometric curve shows an increasing shape, and p_x, p_y, γ, s are very close to the mean values of Gaussian prior. With the estimated scene radiance $L(\mathbf{x})$ and $\tau(\mathbf{x})$, the final global mosaic result is shown in (b).

In Figure 5, we show another calibration result with images (640x480) taken from Sony DCR-TRV30 in manual mode. This example shows a general situation using the manual mode of hand-held cameras, where we selectively adjust camera settings until a subjective satisfactory representation is obtained. It should also be noticed that some frames (1-5) contain many saturated intensities. With the estimated camera parameters in (b), an accurate and seamless mosaic result is obtained, also preserving image details as shown in (c).

8 Concluding Remarks

We presented a robust and global approach for constructing a high dynamic range mosaic from multiple images considering hand-held cameras with automatic or manual exposure control. By incorporating intrinsic camera parameters into the distortion model and using IHC as prior information, we could self-calibrate intrinsic and extrinsic camera parameters. In the experiment, we compared the effect of lens distortion on the estimated focal length. In future research, the photometric distortion model will be further exploited in conjunction with the self-calibration of rotating and zooming cameras considering the effect of translation, degenerated motion of camera, etc. Also, we expect the distortion models can be used as a constraint in many applications such as super-resolution, structure from motion, and optical flow where multiple images are obtained from an arbitrarily moving camera.

References

1. Shum, H., Szeliski, R.: Construction and refinement of panoramic mosaics with global and local alignment. ICCV (1998) 953–958
2. Brown, M., Lowe, D.G.: Recognising panoramas. ICCV **2** (2003) 1218–1225
3. Sawhney, H.S., Kumar, R.: True multi-image alignment and its application to mosaicing and lens distortion correction. IEEE Trans. on Pattern Analysis and Machine Intelligence **21** (1999) 235–243
4. Debevec, P.E., Malik, J.: Recovering high dynamic range radiance maps from photographs. SIGGRAPH97 (1997) 369–378
5. Mitsunaga, T., Nayar, S.: Radiometric self calibration. CVPR **1** (1999) 373–380
6. Grossberg, M.D., Nayar, S.K.: Modeling the space of camera response functions. IEEE Trans. on Pattern Analysis and Machine Intelligence **26** (2004) 1272–1282
7. Pal, C., Szeliski, R., Uyttendaele, M., Jojic, N.: Probability models for high dynamic range imaging. CVPR **2** (2004) 173–180
8. Aggarwal, M., Ahuja, N.: High dynamic range panoramic imaging. ICCV **1** (2001) 2–9
9. Schechner, Y.Y., Nayar, S.K.: Generalized mosaicing: High dynamic range in a wide field of view. Int'l Journal of Computer Vision **53** (2003) 245–267
10. Hasler, D., Süsstrunk, S.: Mapping colour in image stitching applications. Journal of Visual Communication and Image Representation **15** (2004) 65–90
11. Candocia, F.M.: A least squares approach for the joint domain and range registration of images. ICASSP **4** (2002) 3237–3240
12. Kim, D.W., Hong, K.S.: Enhanced mosaic blending using intrinsic camera parameters from a rotating and zooming camera. ICIP **5** (2004) 3303–3306
13. Litvinov, A., Schechner, Y.Y.: Addressing radiometric nonidealities: A unified framework. CVPR **2** (2005) 52–59
14. Rousseeuw, P.J., Hampel, F.R., Ronchetti, E.M., Stahel, W.A., eds.: Robust statistics: The approach based on influence function. New York: Wiley (1986)
15. Agapito, L.D., Hayman, E., Reid, I.: Self-calibration of rotating and zooming cameras. Int'l Journal of Computer Vision **42** (2001) 107–127
16. Chan, T.F., Osher, S., Shen., J.: The digital tv filter and nonlinear denoising. IEEE Trans. on Image Processing **10** (2001) 231–241
17. Tordoff, B., Murray, D.W.: Violating rotating camera geometry The effect of radial distortionon self-calibration. ICPR **1** (2000) 423–427

Image-Based Calibration of Spatial Domain Depth-from-Defocus and Application to Automatic Focus Tracking

Soon-Yong Park[1] and Jaekyoung Moon[2]

[1] Computer Engineering Department, Kyungpook National University, 1370 Sankyuk-dong, Buk-gu, Daegu 702-701, Korea
sypark@mail.knu.ac.kr

[2] Sensor Technology Research Center, Kyungpook National University, 1370 Sankyuk-dong, Buk-gu, Daegu 702-701, Korea
jkmoon@ee.knu.ac.kr

Abstract. Image-based defocus calibration (IBDC) and automatic focus tracking techniques are presented. The proposed technique is based on a Spatial-Domain Convolution/Deconvolution method (STM) developed by Subbarao and Surya [1]. STM uses two blur parameters, σ and β, of a camera lens system to determine a lens step of the best focus. However calibration of these parameters requires internal camera parameters such as focal length, image distance, etc. Without knowing accurate internal parameters, STM is subject to fail to obtain accurate defocus and depth information. We propose image-based *sigma* and *beta* calibration techniques for accurate depth measurement. We also show that *beta* calibration can be applied for automatic focus tracking of a moving object.

1 Introduction

Depth-from-Defocus (DFD) is useful in obtaining depth to an object or automatic focusing (AF) of a digital camera [2, 3, 4, 1]. DFD is very fast in comparison with Depth-from-Focus which searches for the best focus lens position [5, 6, 7]. Suppose a camera has a thin lens system as shown in Figure 1, where f, u and s are focal length, object distance, and image distance of the camera, respectively. Then, we can obtain

$$R = s\frac{D}{2}\left(\frac{1}{f} - \frac{1}{u} - \frac{1}{s}\right), \tag{1}$$

where D is the diameter of the lens, R is the radius of the blur circle when the object is not in focus. A blur circle is formed by the convolution of the point object and the point spread function (PSF) of the lens in the spatial domain. PSF is commonly modeled by a 2-D Gaussian function and a blur parameter σ which is the standard deviation of the function. In practice, it is found that σ is proportional to the blur circle R [8, 1]. DFD is to find the blur parameter σ or R using defocused images. Most techniques use two defocused images to estimate

P.J. Narayanan et al. (Eds.): ACCV 2006, LNCS 3851, pp. 754–763, 2006.

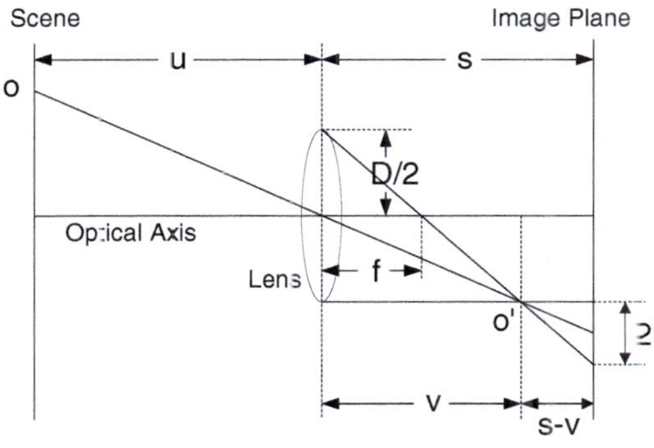

Fig. 1. Image formation in a convex lens

the parameter, while there are other approaches which use one or more than two defocused images [9, 3, 10].

Regardless of the number of defocused images, DFD needs precise calibration of internal camera parameters[8, 1]. For example, object distance depends on some internal camera parameters such as image distance, lens diameter, and focal length according to the lens equation. Most DFD techniques use either camera calibration techniques [10] or specially designed vision systems to precisely control and measure the settings of the lens [9, 5]. However, most camera calibration techniques assume a camera is the pin-hole lens system, while DFD employs the thin lens system. In addition, precise vision systems are expensive to implement.

Tsai and Lin [10] employ an artificial neural network for depth estimation using a single image. They train the neural network using the blur level of multiple defocused images and corresponding depth of a known object. They use 144 data points in three different distances to calibrate internal camera parameters. Rajagopalan and Chaudhuri [8] consider the camera as a shift variant system to enhance DFD performance. In their experiments with real objects, it is mentioned that a special object is used for camera calibration. Subbarao and Surya [1] introduce a spatial domain approach called Spatial-domain Convolution/Deconvolution Transform Method (STM). They determine camera parameters using the lens specification, however results of σ calibration does not exactly match with the blur level of acquired defocused images.

We propose a new image-based defocus calibration technique. By using two defocus images at a reference distance, we estimate an internal camera parameter called *beta* (β). With this parameter, we calibrate *sigma* at different object distances. The new sigma table yields not only accurate defocus information but also accurate depth to real objects. We also introduce a new defocus calibration table called *beta table* to facilitate focus tracking of a moving object. We calibrate the beta table by changing the focus lens step of one of the two defocus images. With respect to a reference defocus image, we show that the other defocus image gives different values of *beta*. By dynamically obtaining two defocus images of a moving object, we estimate *beta* of the images and track the object.

2 Spatial-Domain Transform Method

In this section, we briefly describe the STM technique and the calibration of blur parameters. Let g_f be a focus image of an object, g_1 and g_2 be two different defocused images of the object, σ_1 and σ_2 be the corresponding blur levels of the two images. σ_1 and σ_2 determine the amount of image defocus of g_1 and g_2 with respect to the focus image g_f. When g_f is modeled as a cubic polynomial, the relationship between the two defocused images and the focused image is expressed as

$$g_f = g_i - \frac{1}{4}\sigma_i^2 \nabla^2 g_i, i = 1, 2, \tag{2}$$

where ∇^2 is the Laplacian operator [1]. When a PSF of a lens is modeled by the 2-D Gaussian, $\sigma_i, i = 1, 2$ is the standard deviation of the PSF. For a rotationally symmetric function, σ_i is proportional to blur radius R (in practice $\sigma = R/\sqrt{2}$), then from Equation (1) we get

$$\sigma_i = m_i u_{-1} + c_i \tag{3}$$

where,

$$m_i = -\frac{D_i s_r}{2\sqrt{2}}, c_i = -m_i \left(\frac{1}{f} - \frac{1}{s_i}\right), \tag{4}$$

D_i is aperture diameter, and s_i is image distance in which two defocused images are obtained. s_r in the above equation is a reference image distance such that $s_r = s_2$ in this paper. We set the second defocused image as the reference image, because the scale of the first image is normalized to that of the second one. From Equation (3), we obtain

$$u^{-1} = \frac{\sigma_i - c_i}{m_i}. \tag{5}$$

If we express σ_1 in terms of σ_2 using the above equation, we obtain

$$\sigma_1 = \alpha\sigma_2 + \beta, \tag{6}$$

where α and β are determined by camera parameters as follows:

$$\alpha = \frac{m_1}{m_2}, \quad and \quad \beta = c_1 - c_2\frac{m_1}{m_2}. \tag{7}$$

Suppose we adjust image distance to obtain defocused images, then $D_1 = D_2$ and $s_1 \neq s_2$. Therefore, Equation (7) becomes

$$\beta = c_1 - c_2 = \sigma_1 - \sigma_2. \tag{8}$$

From Equation (2) we obtain

$$g_1 - g_2 = \frac{1}{4}(\sigma_1^2 - \sigma_2^2)\nabla^2 g, \tag{9}$$

$$where \ \nabla^2 g = \frac{\nabla^2 g_1 + \nabla^2 g_2}{2}.$$

By letting

$$(\sigma_1^2 - \sigma_2^2) = G, \tag{10}$$

we obtain

$$G = 4\frac{g_1 - g_2}{\nabla^2 g}. \tag{11}$$

which is a measure of blur difference between the two defocused images. By combining Equation (8) and Equation (10), we compute σ_2 from G as

$$\sigma_2 = \frac{G - \beta^2}{2\beta}. \tag{12}$$

Suppose we know the focal length and the aperture diameter of the camera, then c_1 and c_2 depend on s_1 and s_2, respectively. In addition, inverse distance u^{-1} also depends on two unknown parameters σ_2 and c_2. From Equation (12) and Equation (5), we know there are still two unknown parameters s_1 and s_2 to compute u^{-1}. In [1], Subbarao and Surya set $s_1 = \delta_s s_2$ to get a unique solution, where δ_s is an arbitrary scaling factor between the two image distances. However this method cannot solve the equations up to a known scale factor. In result, STM fails to compute accurate depth information.

In STM, a sigma (σ) table is calibrated at several different object distances. At each distance, they obtain two defocus images and record σ_2 of the reference image. Then they use the table as a look-up table for automatic focusing of a digital camera. To focus on an object of interest, they obtain two defocused images of the object, compute σ_2, and look for the lens step which is the inverse mapping of σ_2 in the table. See [1] for more information.

3 Image-Based Sigma (σ) Calibration

3.1 Sigma Calibration

Instead of obtaining β from inaccurate internal camera parameters, we investigate an image-based technique to estimate β and accurate internal parameters. From Equation (12), we can introduce a simple constraint to measure β as follows. When an object is at a certain distance in which the reference lens position s_2 focuses, $\sigma_2 = 0$ in an ideal case because there is no image blur for the object at the reference distance. Therefore, $G = \beta^2$ at the same reference distance.

Let u_r be the reference distance, p_1 and p_2 be lens step numbers to obtain two defocus images, and $p_r = p_2$ be the reference step number which focuses on the reference distance. Suppose there is an object at u_r. Then by obtaining two defocus images of the object and using Equation (11), we can obtain $\beta = \pm\sqrt{G_r}$ (We define β is positive if $p_1 < p_2$, negative if $p_1 > p_2$), where G_r is the value of G at the reference distance. Then, we can compute internal parameters by deriving equations as follows:

$$\beta = c_1 - c_2$$

$$= \frac{Ds_2}{2\sqrt{2}}\left(\frac{1}{f} - \frac{1}{s_1}\right) - \frac{Ds_2}{2\sqrt{2}}\left(\frac{1}{f} - \frac{1}{s_2}\right)$$

$$= \frac{Ds_2}{2\sqrt{2}}\left(\frac{1}{s_2} - \frac{1}{s_1}\right)$$

$$= \frac{D}{2\sqrt{2}}\left(1 - \frac{s_2}{s_1}\right)$$

$$= k\left(1 - \frac{s_2}{s_1}\right), \ where \ k = \frac{D}{2\sqrt{2}} \tag{13}$$

Then,

$$\frac{s_2}{s_1} = 1 - \frac{\beta}{k} = k' \tag{14}$$

Therefore,

$$s_2 = k' s_1 \tag{15}$$

If we know the reference object distance u_r, we can use the lens equation to compute s_2 as

$$\frac{1}{u_r} = \frac{1}{f} + \frac{1}{s_2}. \tag{16}$$

Using Equation (15) and (16), we can compute the image distances s_1 and s_2. In addition, by substituting s_2 into Equation (4), we can compute c_2 and inverse distance u^{-1}.

3.2 Comparison of Defocus Calibration Techniques

Let us show an example of defocus calibration of the original STM and the proposed image-based defocus calibration (IBDC). We use an Olympus C3030 zoom camera which lens step number ranges from 0 (closest) to 150 (infinity). Two defocus images are obtained at step number $p_1 = 30$ and $p_2 = 65$ to measure image defocus G. Step number 65 is set to the reference step $p_r = p_2$. To compute δ_s in STM, we use following techniques. Using the lens equation, we first compute image distances at step number 1 and 150, for example s_{p1} and s_{p150}. Then δ_s is computed as $(s_{p1} - s_{p150})/150$ and $s_2 = \delta_s(150 - 65) + s_{p150}$. However, in a real

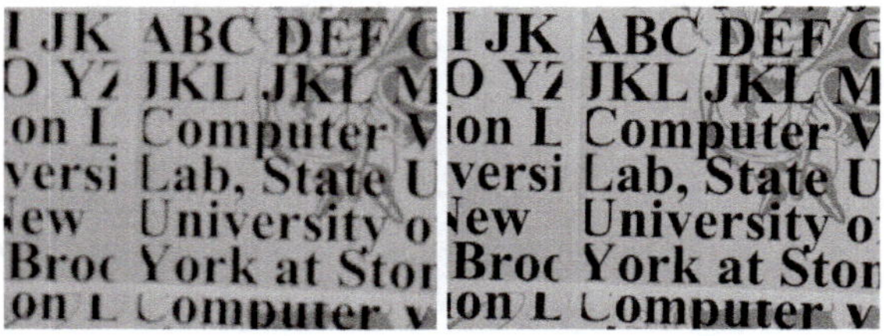

(a) (b)

Fig. 2. Two defocus images of an object at the reference distance (a) Step 32 (b) Step 65 (reference)

Table 1. Camera and blur parameters obtained by two defocus calibration techniques

Method	β	s_1	s_2
STM	2.3175	20.071	19.860
IBDC	2.2797	20.289	20.080

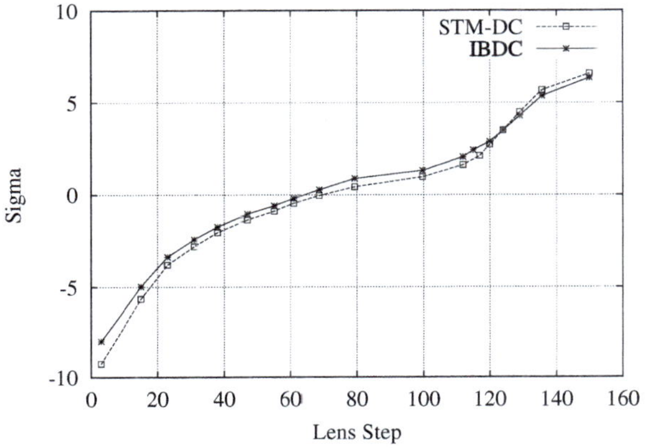

Fig. 3. Comparison of sigma tables from two different defocus calibration techniques. Compared to the curve from STM, the IBDC curve exactly passes zero at step 65.

situation, it is necessary to adjust δ_s in a trial-and-error manner so that STM yields zero sigma value at p_r. This job is very time-consuming because any small change of δ_s makes a large difference in sigma computation. Therefore there is no way to get an acceptable value of δ_s except a lot of trial-and-error.

In contrast, β estimation using the IBDC technique is very simple. We first place an object at the reference distance u_r and obtain two defocus images of the object. Then we use Equation (11) to obtain G and β. Figure 2 shows two defocus images at step 30 and 65. The image at step 65 is best focused since the object is at the reference distance. Table 1 shows β and two image distances s_1 and s_2 computed by two different defocus calibration techniques. Figure 3 shows graphs of two sigma tables calibrated from different techniques. We record σ_2 at about 18 different object distances. The dotted curve is obtained by STM and the solid curve is obtained by IBDC. Two graphs look very similar, however we actually need a lot of trial-and-error to get the graph of STM. Compared to the STM graph, the IBDC graph exactly passes zero at step 65, which is the reference step.

Using Equation (5), we compute inverse distance of several object distances as shown in Figure 4. To compare to a ground truth model we also measure the object distances using the Depth-from-Focus (DFF) technique. We assume that the results from DFF are more accurate than those from DFD. Compared to the DFF curve, the STM curve shows significant errors. However, distance computation using tBDC is very accurate as shown in the figure.

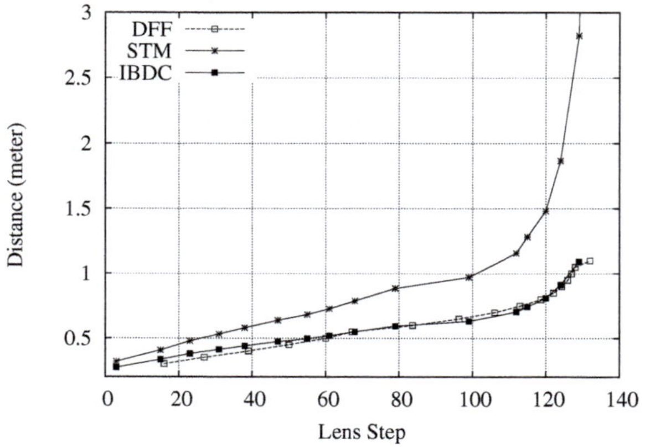

Fig. 4. Comparison of distance computation between STM and IBDC

4 Image-Based Beta (β) Calibration

Using IBDC, we introduce a new calibration table to facilitate automatic focus tracking (AFT) of a digital camera. We call this *Beta* (β) calibration, because we obtain β of two defocus images by changing the position of lens step p_1. Figure 5 shows a conventional plot of a sigma calibration table. p_1 and p_2 are two lens steps where two differently defocused images are obtained. To generate a sigma calibration table, we fix the lens positions of p_1 and p_2, obtain defocus images an object at different distances, and measure σ_2 to generate the sigma table.

Suppose there is an object at u_r, where the image obtained with the reference step p_r focuses on the object. Then we know σ_2 of the reference image g_2 is zero and $\sigma_1 = \beta$, where σ_1 is the defocus measure of the image obtained at step p_1.

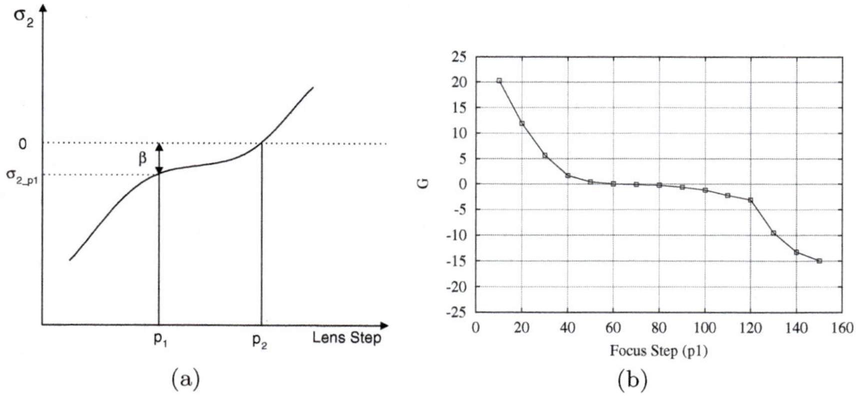

Fig. 5. (a) A conventional sigma plot with respect to lens step number (b) Beta table obtained by the proposed image-based calibration technique

Because $\sigma_1 - \sigma_2$ is a constant, we can expect that σ_2 at step p_1 (let us call this $\sigma_{2_p 1}$) is $-\beta$ as shown in Figure 5. This property of the sigma calibration yields a very useful technique for AFT. When we measure σ_2 using two defocus images, $\sigma_1 = \beta$ if an object is at u_r. Similarly, $\sigma_2 = -\beta$ if the object is at such distance that step p_1 focuses the object.

In the previous section, we fix the step number p_1 and p_2 at 50 and 65, respectively. Now consider to change p_1 from step number 0 to 150, but with fixed step number for $p_2 = 65$. If an object is fixed at u_r, we can compute β using two defocus images for different step number p_1. Figure 5(b) shows the plot of a beta table computed by Equation (11). This graph actually shows values of G, however β is computed by the square root of G. Depends on the position of p_1 with respect to p_2, the sign of G or β changes. We arrange of the sign of G so that it is positive if $p_1 < p_2$ and negative if $p_1 > p_2$.

5 Automatic Focus Tracking (AFT)

Let us consider tracking of a moving object along the camera's optical axis. When the object moves along the optical axis, focus to the object also changes. To obtain focused images continuously, we need to track the object by estimating the depth to the object. A simple way is to obtain defocus images very fast and move the lens to the estimated focus position. If the camera obtains the images fast enough so that there is little difference between two defocus images, we can implement an automatic focusing mechanism to a moving object. A block diagram of this mechanism is shown in Figure 6. To obtain a focus image, we need at least three images at each tracking step, two defocus images and one focus image. Strictly speaking this is a continuous automatic focusing because it estimates the focus position of the object at each step.

Using the beta table shown in Figure 5(b), we introduce an object tracking technique called Image-Based Focus Tracking (IBFT). Figure 5(b) shows that σ_2 changes with respect to different p_1. Suppose there is an object at a certain distance in which the camera lens focuses with a step number n. If we obtain two defocus images $g_1(t)$ and $g_2(t)$ at time t, $p_1 = n(t)$, and $p_2 = n_r$, where n_r is the reference step number (65 in our experiments), we can expect that $\sigma_2(t)$

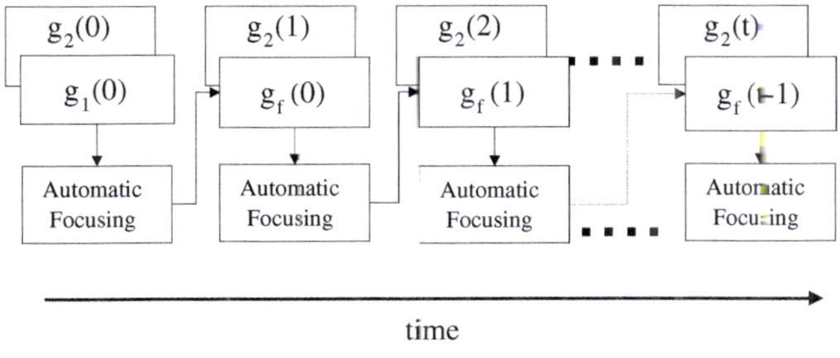

Fig. 6. Focus tracking using β calibration

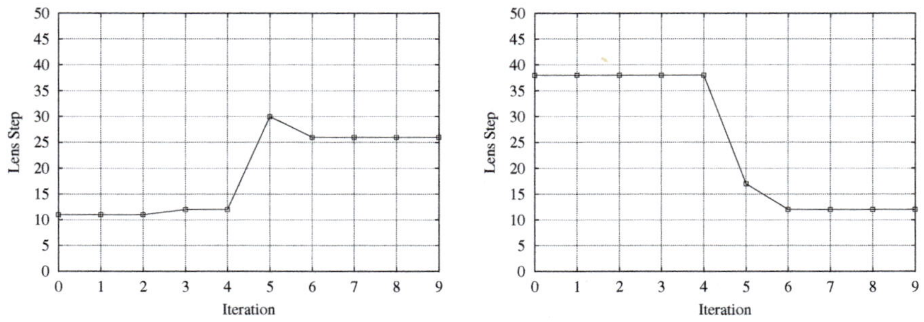

Fig. 7. Results of focus tracking

is the square root of $G(n(t))$ in the beta table. Suppose again that the object moves and two image $g_1(t+1)$ and $g_2(t+1)$ are obtained at the same steps, $p_1 = n(t)$ and $p_2 = n_r$, respectively. Then we know that $\sigma_2(t+1)$ will change. By assuming that σ_2 is locally linear, we can estimate the next focus position as $n(t+1) = G^{-1}(t+1)$.

A block diagram of IBFT is shown in Figure 6. We estimate an initial focus position using STM and obtain a focus image $g_f(t)$ at time t. Because we know that the step number of the focus image, we use the image as $g_1(t+1)$ image at the next step. With another image $g_2(t+1)$ obtained at the reference step number n_r, we can estimate the next focus step number $n(t+1)$ as described above. In this procedure, we need only two images at each tracking step. Compared to the continuous focus tracking technique, we can implement an efficient focus tracking system.

Experimental results of our IBFT technique is shown in Figure 7. We print black and white letters and pictures on a regular paper and put on a planar surface. The object is initially placed at the front of the camera facing the printed side to the camera. We use a 128×128 tracking window in defocus images and assume there is no focus difference in the window. In Figure 7 (a), we move the object away from the camera after the fourth iteration. Focus step number of the camera also tracks the object so that the camera obtains focus images continuously. In Figure 7 (b), another object moves in the opposite direction and the graph shows that IBFT tracks the object efficiently.

6 Conclusions

Image-based defocus calibration technique is presented for depth estimation and focus tracking of a digital camera. Using defocus information of images obtained from the camera, we calibrate a *sigma* table to do automatic focusing of the camera and accurate depth measurement. Compared to the conventional STM-based DFD approach, our technique yield a very accurate sigma table and depth computation results. By changing lens positions of obtaining defocus images, we calibrate another defocus table called a *beta* table. Using the *beta* table, we implement a focus tracking algorithm to continuously obtain focus images of a moving object.

References

1. Subbarao, M., Surya, G.: Depth from defocus: A spatial domain approach. Int. Journal of Computer Vision **13** (1994) 271–294
2. Favaro, P., Soatto, S.: Learning shape from defocus. In: Proc. of the European Conference on Computer Vision. (2000) 735–745
3. Pentland, A.: A new sense for depth of field. IEEE Transactions on Pattern Analysis and Machine Intelligence **9** (1987) 523–531
4. Schechner, Y.Y., Kiryati, N.: Depth from defocus vs. stereo: How different really are they? Int. Journal of Computer Vision **89** (2002) 141–162
5. S. Nayar, M.W., Noguchi, M.: Real-time focus range sensor. IEEE Transactions on Pattern Analysis and Machine Intelligence **18** (1996) 1186–1198
6. M. Subbarao, T.S.C., Nikzad, A.: Focusing techniques. Journal of Optical Engineering **32** (1993) 2824–2836
7. Xiong, Y., Shafer, S.: Depth from focusing and defocusing. In: Proc. of IEEE Conference on Computer Vision and Pattern Recognition. (1993) 68–73
8. Rajagopalan, A., Chaudhuri, S.: Space-variant approaches to recovery of depth from defocused images. Computer Vision and Image Understanding **68** (1996) 309–329
9. Hiura, S., Matsuyama, T.: Depth measurement by the multi-focus camera. In: Proc. of the IEEE Conference on Computer Vision and Pattern Recognition. (1998) 953–959
10. Tsai, D., Lin, C.: A moment-preserving approach for depth from defocus. Pattern Recognition **31** (1998) 551–560

Effects of Image Segmentation for Approximating Object Appearance Under Near Lighting

Takahiro Okabe and Yoichi Sato

Institute of Industrial Science, The University of Tokyo,
4-6-1 Komaba, Meguro-ku, Tokyo 153-8505, Japan
{takahiro, ysato}@iis.u-tokyo.ac.jp

Abstract. Shading analysis of an object under near lighting is not an easy task, because the direction and distance of the light source vary over the surface of the object. Observing a small area on the surface, however, techniques assuming far lighting are applicable, because variations of the direction and distance are small in the area. In this paper, we present two contributions to image segmentation for approximating object's appearance under near light sources. First, we experimentally evaluate the accuracy of approximations using rectangular segmentation for images of objects under near light sources, and confirm the effects of image segmentation itself. Second, we propose a novel segmentation method for approximating images under near light sources. Our proposed method plans appropriate segmentations in terms of approximation accuracy, considering properties of objects and variable illumination conditions.

1 Introduction

The effect of illumination on the appearance of objects is one of the most important research topics in computer vision. For the last decade, analysis of object's appearance under *far lighting* has made great progress.

For instance, Shashua [22] represented images of a Lambertian object under directional light sources by using three basis images of the object. Belhumeur and Kriegman [4] proved that a set of images of a convex Lambertian object under arbitrary directional light sources forms the illumination cone which is constructed from as few as three images of the object. Ramamoorthi-Hanrahan [17] and Basri-Jacobs [2] theoretically showed that the illumination cone can be approximately represented by linear combinations of 4 to 9 basis images. Based on these analyses assuming far lighting, a number of methods have been proposed for problems such as face recognition [10, 2, 5, 15], shape from motion [24, 7], forward rendering [19, 25, 21], and inverse rendering [18, 14].

To take one step further, we think that now is a good time for reconsidering the effects of *near lighting* on object's appearance. Let us consider an object with a size s illuminated by a point light source from a distance d. When the distance between the light source and the object is much larger than the size

P.J. Narayanan et al. (Eds.): ACCV 2006, LNCS 3851, pp. 764–775, 2006.

of the object ($s \ll d$), we can consider the light source as far lighting, that is, a directional light source. On the other hand, when the distance is less than or comparable to the size ($s > d$ or $s \sim d$), the light source should be treated as near lighting. It is well known that the analysis of object's appearance under near lighting is difficult because the direction and distance of the light source vary over the surface of the object.

The basic idea of our study is that, by segmenting an image of an object under near lighting, we can treat the image as if it were taken under far lighting. In other words, observing a small domain on the object surface, the domain size $\triangle s$ can become much smaller than the light source distance ($\triangle s \ll d$), even though the object size is larger than the distance. Therefore, techniques assuming far lighting are applicable to each domain on the object's surface.

Obviously, the assumption of directional lighting becomes more accurate as the number of domains increases. However, in practice, it is not appropriate to merely increase the number of domains for applying techniques assuming directional lighting. In the context of forward rendering [25], for example, more computing time is required as the number of domains increases. The performance of face recognition based on linear subspaces [10, 2] would get worse as the number of domains increases, because reconstruction errors due to false identity are also decreased. In addition, inverse rendering such as estimation of illumination [13] becomes ill-conditioned, as each domain gets close to an infinitesimal flat surface.

Accordingly, we discuss how to segment images of an object for applying techniques assuming directional lighting. More specifically, we propose a new segmentation method for approximating images under near light sources, in analogy with principal component analysis (PCA) that is optimal in the sense of approximation. Our proposed method finds the optimal segmentation in terms of approximation accuracy based on the difference between appearance under near lighting and that under far lighting, provided that the number of domains is given. In particular, our method enables us to plan appropriate segmentations considering properties of objects and variable illumination conditions

The main contributions of our study are summarized as follows. First, we experimentally evaluate the accuracy of approximations using rectangular segmentation, and confirm the effects of image segmentation itself. As far as we know, no study has been done even on the effects of simple rectangular segmentation for dealing with the appearance of objects under near light sources. Second, we propose a new segmentation method for approximating images under near lighting. To demonstrate the effectiveness of our proposed method, we conducted a number of experiments by using synthetic and real images.

2 Related Work

The effect of near lighting has been studied in the both fields of image analysis and image synthesis. In the field of computer graphics, the effect of near lighting on the appearance of objects is often represented by interpolation [25] or extrapolation [1]. For example, Sloan *et al.* [25] compute angular distributions of illumination at some points on an object's surface in terms of spherical harmonics coefficients, and interpolate them over the surface.

In the field of computer vision, two different approaches are possible for the analysis of object appearance under near lighting: a *direct approach* and an *indirect approach.*

Direct Approach

The brightness of a point on an object's surface under a near point light source is represented by a nonlinear function with respect to the depth of the point and the position of the light source. We call the approach that explicitly solves the nonlinear equation relating the brightness with the depth and the light source position the direct approach. This approach has been studied for a long time, focusing mainly on how to stably solve nonlinear equations.

Iwahori *et al.* [11] proposed a method for acquiring the surface normal and depth of a Lambertian object from images of the object taken under a controlled point light source. Then, Kim and Burger [12] investigated the relationship between arrangement of the light sources and uniqueness of the solution of the nonlinear equations. Furthermore, Clark [6] extended photometric stereo under near point light sources to that under a moving point light source.

Thus, the direct approach has achieved important progress in modeling objects. However, it is not trivial to extend these methods to deal with complex light sources, because they assume simple illumination conditions such as a single point light source.

Indirect Approach

In contrast to the direct approach, the indirect approach does not deal with the nonlinear function explicitly, but approximately represents object's appearance under near lighting. As described in Section 1, image segmentation is one of the feasible ways for approximating images under near lighting.

The idea of image segmentation is not necessarily new for object recognition. Zhao and Yang [26, 27] proposed the mosaic image method in the context of PCA with outliers such as occlusions, specular highlights, and shadows. The method segments an image into rectangular blocks and applies PCA to each block. They described that the assumption of directional lighting becomes more accurate by segmenting images. However, effects of image segmentation on object's appearance under near lighting were not examined.

Image segmentation is applied also to face recognition under varying illumination conditions. Batur and Hayes [3] divided an image into a set of small images with similar surface normals, and applied the linear subspace method [22] to each small image. Sakaue and Shakunaga [20] also combined rectangular segmentation with PCA-based face recognition. However, the main purpose of these studies was to achieve robust face recognition against shadows under directional light sources. Therefore, effects of near light sources were not examined.

Another way for approximating images under near light sources was recently proposed by Frolova *et al.* [9]. It is well known that images of a Lambertian object under directional light sources are approximately represented by using low-frequency terms of spherical harmonics [17, 2]. The point of the study is to represent effects of near lighting by using high-frequency terms of spherical harmonics. It is reported that the method using high-frequency terms works well for images of a sphere. However, the method is not applicable to objects such as a plane, because the basis images depend only on surface normals.

3 Proposed Method

3.1 Overview

We consider a set of images of a static object taken from a fixed viewpoint under variable illumination conditions. We assume that the shape and reflectance properties of the object and the statistical properties of the variable illumination are known. For simplicity, we assume that an illumination distribution is represented by a set of point light sources[1].

Let us segment the surface of an object into c domains and consider points on the object surface that belong to one of the domains. When a point p on the object surface belongs to the i-th domain D_i whose center is a point P_i, we denote the approximation error at the point p by $\mathrm{err}(p, P_i)$. Our proposed method minimizes the objective function J described by

$$J = \textstyle\sum_{i=1}^{c} \sum_{p \in D_i} \mathrm{err}(p, P_i), \tag{1}$$

in order to find the optimal segmentation in terms of approximation accuracy[2].

In Section 3.2, we define the error function $\mathrm{err}(p, P_i)$ of a scene where an object is illuminated by a single point light source. In Section 3.3, we extend the error function to the scene under complex and variable illumination distributions. Finally, in Section 3.4, we describe the detailed algorithm of our method based on k-means clustering [8].

3.2 Criterion I: Single Point Light Source

Let us consider an object illuminated by a single point light source with unit radiance, and denote the positions of the point p, the center P_i, and the light source by $\boldsymbol{x}$, $\boldsymbol{X}$, and $\boldsymbol{R}$ respectively (Fig. 1). Assuming the Lambertian model[3], the brightness I at the point p is represented by

$$I = \rho \boldsymbol{n} \cdot (\boldsymbol{R} - \boldsymbol{x}) S_{\boldsymbol{n}, \boldsymbol{R}-\boldsymbol{x}} / |\boldsymbol{R} - \boldsymbol{x}|^3, \tag{2}$$

where ρ and $\boldsymbol{n}$ are the albedo and surface normal at the point. The coefficient $S_{\boldsymbol{n}, \boldsymbol{R}-\boldsymbol{x}}$ represents both attached and cast shadows. Namely, $S_{\boldsymbol{n}, \boldsymbol{R}-\boldsymbol{x}} = 0$ if

---

1 Here, we assume isotropic lighting. Thus, we do not take account of anisotropic light sources such as a projector.

2 Because our objective is to approximate images, we sum up the approximation errors not over the surface of an object but over the image plane.

3 We can extend the following discussion to other reflectance models except for mirror-like reflectance.

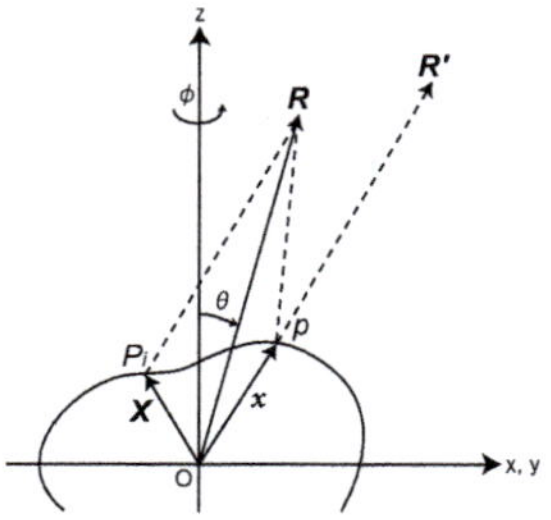

Fig. 1. Coordinate system

$\boldsymbol{n} \cdot (\boldsymbol{R} - \boldsymbol{x}) < 0$ or the direction of the light source $(\boldsymbol{R} - \boldsymbol{x})$ is occluded by the object, and $S_{\boldsymbol{n},\boldsymbol{R}-\boldsymbol{x}} = 1$ otherwise.

If the assumption of far lighting is accurate over the domain, the brightness of the point p is nearly constant when the position of the light source seen from the point p, that is, $(\boldsymbol{R} - \boldsymbol{x})$ is replaced by that seen from the center of the domain P_i, that is, $(\boldsymbol{R} - \boldsymbol{X})$. In other words, we can consider the point p as if it were illuminated by a point light source located at $\boldsymbol{R}' = \boldsymbol{x} + (\boldsymbol{R} - \boldsymbol{X})$. Thus, we consider I' defined by

$$I' = \rho \boldsymbol{n} \cdot (\boldsymbol{R} - \boldsymbol{X}) S_{\boldsymbol{n},\boldsymbol{R}-\boldsymbol{X}} / |\boldsymbol{R} - \boldsymbol{X}|^3 \quad (3)$$

as the brightness at the point p under the assumption of directional lighting, and define the error function as

$$\mathrm{err}(p, P_i) = (I - I')^2. \quad (4)$$

3.3 Criterion II: General Illumination Condition

Our objective is to minimize the approximation error of a set of images taken under variable illumination conditions. Let $L(\boldsymbol{r})$ denote the average illumination radiance at each 3D point $\boldsymbol{r}$ in a scene, which is the average with respect to the variable illumination conditions. Then, we can simply extend the error function in equation (4) to that under the variable illumination conditions, by summing up $(I - I')^2$ for each point light source with the weight corresponding to the average distribution $L(\boldsymbol{r})$ of the variable illumination. Replacing the summation by an integral, the error functions of an object illuminated by light sources at the distance $|\boldsymbol{R}| = R$, for example, are represented by integrals such as $\int_0^{2\pi} \int_0^{\pi} (I - I')^2 L(R, \theta, \phi) \sin\theta d\theta d\phi$. Here, $L(R, \theta, \phi)$ is the average distribution of illumination represented by the spherical coordinates. In the same way, we can take into account variations of distances from the object to light sources.

However, the above extension is not practical in terms of computational cost. In the segmentation algorithm described later, we have to calculate the above integrals for each iteration step, or compute them in advance. In the latter case, because the integrands depend both on the point p and on the domain center P_i, we have to precompute them for all combinations of pixels. Then, the number of integrations required becomes $O(N^2)$ for an image with N pixels. Therefore, this simple extension requires a large amount of computing time or storage.

Accordingly, taking the Taylor series expansion of $(I-I')$ under the conditions that $|\boldsymbol{R}| > |\boldsymbol{x}|$ and $|\boldsymbol{R}| > |\boldsymbol{X}|$, we focus on the first order effect represented by

$$I - I' \simeq (\rho/R^3)[(3\boldsymbol{R}\cdot\boldsymbol{n}/R^2)\boldsymbol{R} - \boldsymbol{n}]\cdot(\boldsymbol{x} - \boldsymbol{X})S_{\boldsymbol{n},\boldsymbol{R}}, \tag{5}$$

when the assumption of far lighting begins to break down. As a result, the error function is represented as

$$\mathrm{err}(p, P_i) = \textstyle\sum_{j=1}^{3}\sum_{k=1}^{3} g_{jk}(x_j - X_j)(x_k - X_k). \tag{6}$$

This means that we should calculate the error, that is, "distance" between the point p and the center P_i with the "metrics" g_{jk} defined by

$$g_{jk} \equiv \frac{\rho^2}{R^6}\int_0^{2\pi}\int_0^{\pi}\left(\frac{3\boldsymbol{R}\cdot\boldsymbol{n}}{R^2}R_j - n_j\right)\left(\frac{3\boldsymbol{R}\cdot\boldsymbol{n}}{R^2}R_k - n_k\right)S_{\boldsymbol{n},\boldsymbol{R}}L(R,\theta,\phi)\sin\theta d\theta d\phi, \tag{7}$$

based on properties of the object and illumination, instead of the Euclidean metrics ($g_{jk} = \delta_{jk}$). The approximation in equation (5) makes our method more tractable. We can numerically precompute $O(N)$ metrics[4], because the integrand in equation (7) is independent of the domain center P_i and depends only on the point p.

3.4 Segmentation Method

Our proposed method finds the image segmentation that minimizes the objective function J in equation (1). Basically, we give initial positions of domain centers. Then, we assign a point p to the domain that minimizes $\mathrm{err}(p, P_i)$ with respect to P_i, and update the center of domain $P_i'(\in D_i)$ so that $\sum_{p\in D_i}\mathrm{err}(p, P_i')$ is minimized. The last two steps are repeated until the segmentation converges.

In order to alleviate the problem of local minima, we take a coarse-to-fine approach. Actually, we repeat the above steps and update the temporary optimal positions of domain centers if the i-th value of the objective function J_i is minimal at the time. For the coarse search of the minimum, initial positions of centers are randomly sampled in the first N_{sample} iterations. On the other hand, in the last N_{resample} iterations, we resample these positions around the temporary optimal positions for the fine search[5].

---

[4] We computed the integrals by using Gaussian quadratures [16] assuming that the bandwidth of the integrands equals 50. Thus, we sampled the integrands at about 5000 directions.

[5] We set $N_{\mathrm{sample}} = 1000$ and N_{resample}=9000, based on preliminary experiments.

4 Experiments

4.1 Qualitative Properties

To begin with, we describe qualitative properties of the image segmentation obtained by using our proposed method.

We considered a part of a Lambertian sphere with uniform albedo as a target object (Fig. 2 (a)), and planned appropriate segmentations for three different average distributions of illumination. Let (r, θ, ϕ) be the spherical coordinates whose center $(r = 0)$ and north pole $(\theta = 0)$ are the center of the sphere and the direction of the z axis (the line of sight) respectively. The first condition corresponds to a point light source located at $(r, \theta, \phi) = (2r_s, \pi/4, 3\pi/4)$. Here, r_s is the radius of the sphere. The second one corresponds to a point light source that distributes at $\Omega = \{(\theta, \phi) | \pi/6 \leq \theta \leq \pi/2, 0 \leq \phi \leq \pi/2\}$ with uniform probability density. The third one is $L(R, \theta, \phi) = \text{const.}$ in equation (7), that is, a point light source that uniformly distributes around the sphere.

We show segmentation results as gray images in Fig. 2. The first, second, and third conditions correspond to (b), (c), and (d). The number of domains is 9 (16) in the upper (lower) row. The gray value of a pixel is proportional to the number of pixels belonging to the same domain as the pixel does. Therefore, the darker a pixel is, the smaller domain the pixel belongs to. Portions of images are saturated, because we set the gray value of the domain with average pixel number ($= N/c$) to 128.

This study shows three important properties as follows. (i) *Points in a domain are not necessarily close to each other in the sense of the Euclidean distance.* As mentioned in Section 3.3, the size of a domain changes according to the geometric and photometric properties of the scene. (ii) *The size of a domain becomes smaller as the domain comes close to light sources.* This property is consistent with our intuition. Variations of domain size are dominant when the average distribution of illumination is concentrated in a small solid angle as in results (b) and (c). (iii) *The size of a domain becomes smaller as variations of depth becomes larger in the domain.* As shown in results (d), this property is dominant when an average illumination distribution is isotropic. This shows that we should segment images of a scene based on the depth, even though we cannot obtain any prior knowledge about illumination as in the case of inverse lighting.

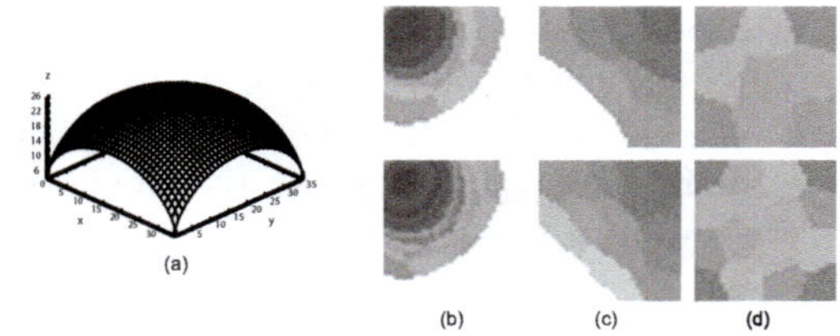

Fig. 2. (a) 3D shape of a target object and segmentation results of the object under (b) a point light source, (c) a set of point light sources with an area distribution, and (d) uniform illumination

4.2 Approximation Accuracy of Synthetic Images

Second, we conducted a number of experiments by using synthetic images so that we could rigorously evaluate the approximation accuracy. As described below, we reconstructed diffuse reflection components of the target object under point light sources by projecting input images to the basis images.

Let I_j be the brightness of a point p_j corresponding to the j-th pixel ($j = 1, 2, ..., N$), and $\boldsymbol{b}_j$ be the basis vector defined by

$$\boldsymbol{b}_j = \rho_j \boldsymbol{n}_j, \tag{8}$$

where ρ_j and $\boldsymbol{n}_j$ are the albedo and surface normal at the point. We calculated the coefficients $\boldsymbol{s}_i$ of the basis vectors in the i-th domain by minimizing $\sum_{p_j \in D_i} w_j (I_j - \boldsymbol{s}_i \cdot \boldsymbol{b}_j)^2$. Here, we set $w_j = 0$ if $I_j = 0$ and $w_j = 1$ otherwise so that shadows are removed. Then, we defined the reconstruction error as

$$\epsilon = \sum_{i=1}^{c} \sum_{p_j \in D_i} w_j (I_j - \boldsymbol{s}_i \cdot \boldsymbol{b}_j)^2 / \sum_{j=1}^{N} I_j^2. \tag{9}$$

We tested three average distributions of illumination. The first and second conditions correspond to point light sources located at $(2r_s, \pi/4, 3\pi/4)$ and $(3r_s, \pi/4, 3\pi/4)$ respectively. The third one is a point light source uniformly distributed at $\Omega = \{(\theta, \phi) | \pi/6 \leq \theta \leq \pi/2, 0 \leq \phi \leq \pi/2\}$.

Under the first illumination condition, we synthesized an input image of the object and reconstructed it. In Fig. 3, we show (a) the input image and reconstructed images (b) without image segmentation, (c) by using rectangular segmentation with 16 domains, and (d) by using our proposed method with the same number of domains. The reconstruction error against the number of domains is shown in Fig. 4 (a). The solid and dotted lines represent the errors of rectangular segmentation and our method respectively. One can find that image segmentation drastically improves the approximation accuracy. In the case of rectangular segmentation with 36 domains, for example, the error decreases about 2 orders of magnitude. Furthermore, the error of our method is several factors smaller than that of rectangular segmentation. In other words, our method achieves higher approximation accuracy by using smaller number of domains. For the second illumination condition, we obtained a similar result (Fig. 4 (b)).

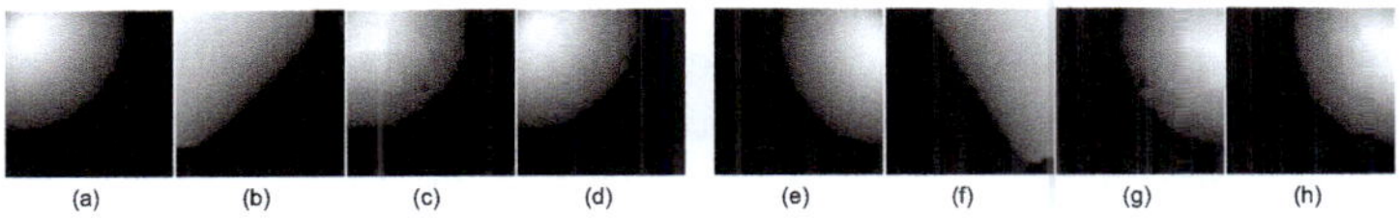

Fig. 3. Image reconstruction based on segmentation (sphere): (a) an input image under a point light source, reconstructed images (b) without segmentation, (c) with rectangular segmentation, and (d) with the segmentation obtained by using our method. Images (e) through (h) are those under another average distribution of illumination

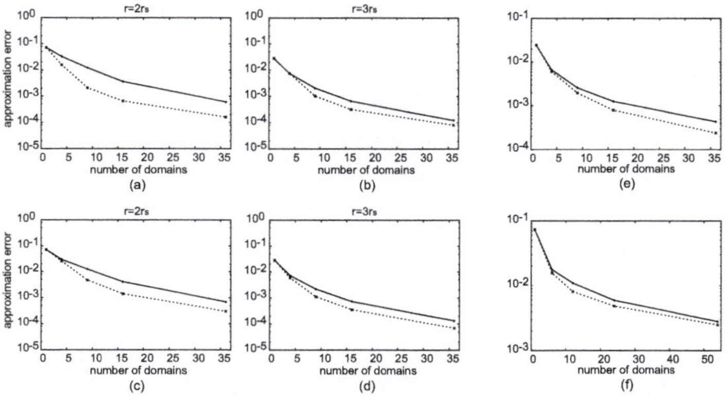

Fig. 4. Reconstruction errors of sphere images against the number of domains under a point light source located at (a) $2r_s$ or (b) $3r_s$, and under a set of point light sources located at (c) $2r_s$ or (d) $3r_s$. The solid and dotted lines represent the errors of rectangular segmentation and our method respectively. Reconstruction errors of images of a plaster sphere and those of a Napoleon figure are shown in (e) and (f).

For the third condition, we synthesized 100 images under point light sources located at a distance $2r_s$ or $3r_s$ and uniformly distributed within Ω, and reconstructed them (Fig. 3 (e), (f), (g), and (h)). The average reconstruction errors shown in Fig. 4 (c) and (d) behave in a similar manner to those under the first and second conditions.

4.3 Approximation Accuracy of Real Images

Third, we report the result of experiments using real images. In the experiments, various images of a plaster sphere were taken under far or near light sources by using SONY DXC-9000 camera and Matrox Meteor-II frame grabber. The distances between the center of the sphere and the far (near) light sources are more than 10 (about 2∼3) times the radius of the sphere.

We estimated three basis images of the sphere from 12 images taken under unknown far light sources by using singular value decomposition with missing data (SVDMD) [23]. We used 10 images taken under near light sources to confirm the effects of image segmentation for approximating the appearance. All images were cropped and down-sampled so that the geometry of the scene is the same as that in the experiments using synthetic images. The distribution of the near light sources roughly obeyed the third condition in the previous section.

In Fig. 4 (e), we show the average reconstruction error against the number of domains. One can find that the average reconstruction errors behave like those in Fig. 4 (a) through (d). Moreover, our method improves the approximation accuracy about 40% compared with rectangular segmentation. Hence, we can conclude that image segmentation, especially our proposed method, works well for approximating object's appearance under near light sources.

4.4 Discussion

Finally, we discuss the applicability of our proposed method to face recognition[6] under near light sources. More specifically, we conducted two experiments to confirm (i) whether segmentation results of different people resemble each other, and (ii) whether the image segmentation of the average face works well for other faces.

In the first experiment, we used the face database provided by the Max-Planck Institute for Biological Cybernetics [5]. This database contains laser-scanned face models of four persons and an average face model.

Fig. 5. Images and segmentation results of faces: (a) an average, and (b)∼(e) four persons

In Fig. 5, we show images under a typical point light source and segmentation results of (a) the average face and those of (b)∼(e) four persons. We assumed that the average distribution of illumination is uniform within $\Omega = \{(\theta, \phi) | \pi/6 \leq \theta \leq \pi/2, 0 \leq \phi \leq \pi/2\}$. One can see that these segmentation results resemble each other: pixels in the upper right and right regions belong to smaller domains than those in the lower left and left regions.

In the second experiment, we used images of a plaster Napoleon figure taken in a similar manner to that in Section 4.3. The average reconstruction error against the number of domains is shown in Fig. 4 (f). One can find that the average reconstruction errors behave in a similar manner to other results in Fig 4. In spite of different geometry and deviations from our assumptions such as interreflections, our method improves the approximation accuracy about 20% compared with rectangular segmentation.

These experimental results imply that, for approximating face images under near lighting, we can substitute the segmentation result of the average face for those of individuals. Therefore, a combination of image segmentation for the average face and PCA-based face recognition *etc.* would be one of the feasible methods for face recognition under near light sources, even when 3D models of individuals are unavailable.

5 Conclusions and Future Work

In this paper, we discussed image segmentation in terms of approximation accuracy, which is a necessary condition for applying techniques assuming directional

[6] Strictly speaking, we investigate not recognition but approximation. However, the notion of Eigenfaces shows image approximation or compression is important also for face recognition.

light sources. In summary, the main contributions of the present study consist of (i) the experimental evaluation of image segmentation for dealing with object's appearance under near lighting, (ii) a method for planning appropriate segmentations considering properties of objects and variable illumination conditions.

In the future, we will extend our framework for image segmentation by considering sufficient conditions for specific applications such as face recognition and inverse rendering. Along with the compatibility with techniques assuming directional light sources, we believe that image segmentation is one of the most promising approaches to a number of applications dealing with images under near light sources.

Acknowledgements

A part of this work was supported by Grants-in-Aid for Scientific Research from the Ministry of Education, Culture, Sports, Science and Technology of Japan (No. 13224051).

References

1. T. Annen, J. Kautz, F. Durand, and H.-P. Seidel, "Spherical harmonic gradients for mid-range illumination", In *Proc. Eurographics Sympo. Rendering 2004*, pp.331–336, 2004.
2. R. Basri and D. Jacobs, "Lambertian reflectance and linear subspaces", *IEEE Trans. PAMI*, 25(2), pp.218–233, 2003.
3. A. Batur and M. Hayes, "Linear subspaces for illumination robust face recognition", In *Proc. IEEE CVPR 2001*, pp.II-296–301, 2001.
4. P. Belhumeur and D. Kriegman, "What is the set of images of an object under all possible lighting conditions?", *Int'l. J. Computer Vision*, 28(3), pp.245–260, 1998.
5. V. Blanz and T. Vetter, "Face recognition based on fitting a 3D morphable model", *IEEE Trans. PAMI*, 25(9), pp.1063–1074, 2003.
6. J. Clark, "Active photometric stereo", In *Proc. IEEE CVPR '92*, pp.29–34, 1992.
7. F. Du, T. Okabe, Y. Sato, and A. Sugimoto, "Reflectance estimation from motion under complex illumination", In *Proc. IAPR ICPR 2004*, pp.218–222, 2004.
8. R. Duda, P. Hart, and D. Stork, *Pattern Classification*, John Wiley & Sons, 2001.
9. D. Frolova, D. Simakov, and R. Basri, "Accuracy of spherical harmonics approximations for images of Lambertian objects under far and near lighting", In *Proc. ECCV 2004*, LNCS 3021, pp.574–587, 2004.
10. A. Georghiades, P. Belhumeur, and D. Kriegman, "From few to many: illumination cone models for face recognition under variable lighting and pose", *IEEE Trans. PAMI*, 23(6), pp.643–660, 2001.
11. Y. Iwahori, H. Sugie, and N. Ishii, "Reconstructing shape from shading images under point light source illumination", In *Proc. IEEE ICPR '90*, pp.I-83–87, 1990.
12. B. Kim and P. Burger, "Depth and shape from shading using the photometric stereo method", *CVGIP: Image Understanding*, 54(3), pp.416–427, 1991.
13. A. Marschner and D. Greenberg, "Inverse lighting for photography", In *Fifth Color Imaging Conference*, pp.262–265, 1997.

14. T. Okabe, I. Sato, and Y. Sato, "Spherical harmonics vs. Haar wavelets: basis for recovering illumination from cast shadows", In *Proc. IEEE CVPR 2004*, pp.I-50–57, 2004.
15. T. Okabe and Y. Sato, "Object recognition based on photometric alignment using RANSAC", In *Proc. IEEE CVPR 2003*, pp.I-221–228, 2003.
16. W. Press, S. Teukolsky, W. Vetterling, and B. Flannery, *Numerical Recipes in C*, Cambridge University Press, 1992.
17. R. Ramamoorthi and P. Hanrahan, "On the relationship between radiance and irradiance: determining the illumination from images of a convex Lambertian object", *J. Opt. Soc. Am. A*, 18(10), pp.2448–2459, 2001.
18. R. Ramamoorthi and P. Hanrahan, "A signal-processing framework for inverse rendering", In *Proc. ACM SIGGRAPH 2001*, pp.117–128, 2001.
19. R. Ramamoorthi and P. Hanrahan, "An efficient representation for irradiance environment maps", In *Proc. ACM SIGGRAPH 2001*, pp.497–500, 2001.
20. F. Sakaue and T. Shakunaga, "Face recognition by parallel partial projections", In *Proc. ACCV 2004*, pp.144–150, 2004.
21. I. Sato, T. Okabe, Y. Sato, and K. Ikeuchi, "Appearance sampling for obtaining a set of basis images for variable illumination", In *Proc. IEEE ICCV 2003*, pp.800–807, 2003.
22. A. Shashua, "On photometric issues in 3D visual recognition from a single 2D image", *Int'l. J. Computer Vision*, 21(1/2), pp.99–122, 1997.
23. H.-Y. Shum, K. Ikeuchi, and R. Reddy, "Principal component analysis with missing data and its application to polyhedral object modeling", *IEEE Trans. PAMI*, 17(9), pp.854–867, 1995.
24. D. Simakov, D. Frolova, and R. Basri, "Dense shape reconstruction of a moving object under arbitrary, unknown lighting", In *Proc. IEEE ICCV 2003*, pp.1202–1209, 2003.
25. P. Sloan, J. Kautz, and J. Snyder, "Precomputed radiance transfer for real-time rendering in dynamic, low frequency lighting environments", In *Proc. ACM SIGGRAPH 2002*, pp.527–536, 2002.
26. L. Zhao and Y.-H. Yang, "Theoretical analysis of illumination in PCA-based vision systems", *Pattern Recognition*, 32(4), pp.547–564, 1999.
27. L. Zhao and Y.-H. Yang, "Mosaic image method: a local and global method", *Pattern Recognition*, 32(8), pp.1421–1433, 1999.

Fast Feature Extraction Using Approximations to Derivatives with Summed-Area Images

Paul Wyatt and Hiroaki Nakai

Multimedia Laboratory, Toshiba Corporate RDC, 1 Komukai-Toshiba-cho, Saiwai-ku, Kawasaki, 212-8582, Japan
wyatt@eel.rdc.toshiba.co.jp, hiroaki.nakai@toshiba.co.jp

Abstract. Accurate and stable identification of feature points is a requirement for such varied applications as wide-baseline stereo, object recognition and simultaneous localisation and mapping. Although a wide variety of feature extraction methods exist, certain aspects remain active areas of research.

In this paper, a feature model is proposed which makes use of the summed area images in achieving scale invariance at the loss of theoretical rotational invariance. By making use of approximations to first and second derivatives, as well as the Laplacian, a wide variety of features may be obtained. Additionally, the stability of this method is increased by an improved approach to ordering of features.

Evaluation is performed versus other common approaches using tests on precision, recall and information content of the extracted points.

1 Introduction

Identification of stable feature points is a core requirement of many applications; e.g. wide-baseline stereo matching or reconstruction as well as being useful in classification or recognition. Feature points are useful if a small subset of points contain the information required for a task as they then provide a means to reduce the computational burden.

In calculation of feature points, two dimensional points, in particular corners, are of interest [1]. More recently, region detectors have also become popular [2–4], partly as testing suggested they were more stable for image deformations [5]. Increasingly, there has been a desire for invariance to image deformations, in general scale [6, 3] and more recently affine invariance [2, 4, 7]. Whilst desirable for wide-baseline stereo, for applications such as 'simultaneous localisation and mapping' (SLAM) or object recognition affine invariance is not necessarily of great importance as the underlying assumptions are unlikely to hold for objects close to the camera. Additionally, affine invariant algorithms tend not to be fully affine invariant: they perform local searches from identified scale invariant points [2, 5, 7]. Instead, whilst scale invariance remains desirable, faster detection which is invariant to changes in contrast as the camera moves is probably more useful than affine invariance for SLAM or recognition. Consequently, in this paper we focus on fast, contrast independent, scale invariant detection of feature points.

P.J. Narayanan et al. (Eds.): ACCV 2006, LNCS 3851, pp. 776–786, 2006.

In particular, we wish to solve two problems: one relating to scale invariance, one to reducing dependence on illumination.

Scale invariant points are often found through convolving the image with a set of bandpass filters with gradually increasing spatial extent, then looking for maxima across scale and space [6, 7, 3]. As convolution is order N, for separable filters, to improve computation speed the image is normally down-sampled at each octave, e.g. [3]. Truncation of filters can, introduce small steps into the output, proportional to the local contrast which, lead to spurious maxima. Additionally, localisation of points can be poor at higher scales owing to the required interpolation step for down-sampled images [3]. The second problem which we solve results from the dependence of the derivatives and hence energy function on local intensity and contrast, a problem region methods suffer to less extent [2, 4]. As the set of scale space maxima is often reduced by tests on energy and curvature [3], features with poor contrast can be easily lost.

To solve these problems we propose the following. First, using the summed-area table, or integral image, transform [8, 9]. Bandpass filters at any scale can be calculated using 8 additions/subtractions on the integral image and are easily normalized for scale invariance. This avoids down-sampling the image and the associated problems with interpolation and truncation. Additionally, 'convolution' becomes significantly faster leading to a speed increase. Secondly, we propose selecting features as a subset of the identified maxima, except that instead of ordering these points by derivative energy (which is illumination dependent), they will be ordered by an illumination independent property. For this purpose, entropy, curvature and a measure based on normalised odd and even derivatives are considered. We therefore make two contributions. Firstly, a feature model to detect both points of high curvature and blobs using first and second order gradients. Secondly, a fast stable implementation of this model.

2 Feature Models

In this section, we consider the types of points we wish to detect and requirements to make functions scale invariant. We propose three types of points for detection and show how they relate to first and second order derivatives, and/or the Laplacian. We then briefly note how to make these points scale invariant and describe our procedure for obtaining maxima from the resulting scale-space.

Figure 1(a,b) shows a diagram of a corner like structure: a point with significant intensity change in one direction and with high curvature. Figure 1(c,d) shows a blob type structure: a point having significant change in its second order derivatives in all directions. Labels x and y denote the image co-ordinate system, with u and v denoting a second set of axes aligned at $\frac{\pi}{4}$ to this. θ is an axis estimated from image gradients, $\tan\theta = \left(\frac{\partial \mathcal{I}}{\partial y} / \frac{\partial \mathcal{I}}{\partial x}\right)$, where $\mathcal{I}$ is the intensity function. To detect corners, as described in figure 1 there are two conditions. Firstly, denoting noise η, it is required that

$$\left|\frac{\partial \mathcal{I}}{\partial \theta}\right| > \alpha\eta \text{ where } \alpha = \{0, 1, 2 \cdots\} \tag{1}$$

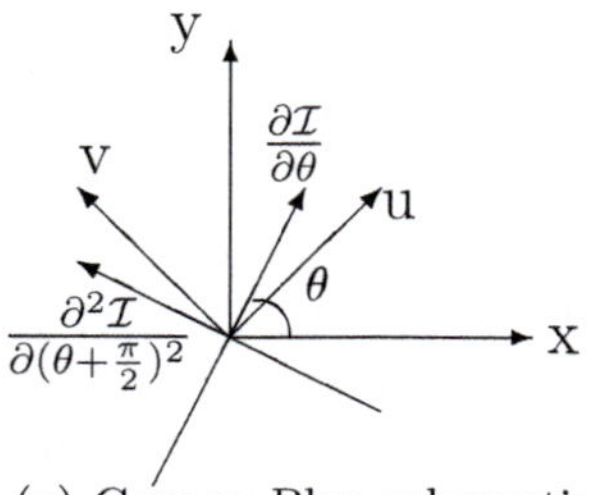

(a) Corner: Plan schematic

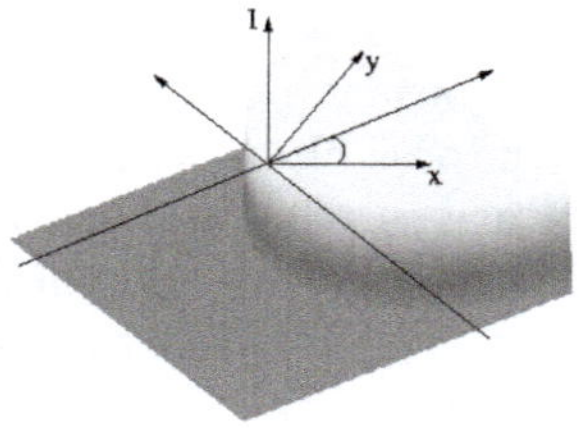

(b) Corner: Isometric view

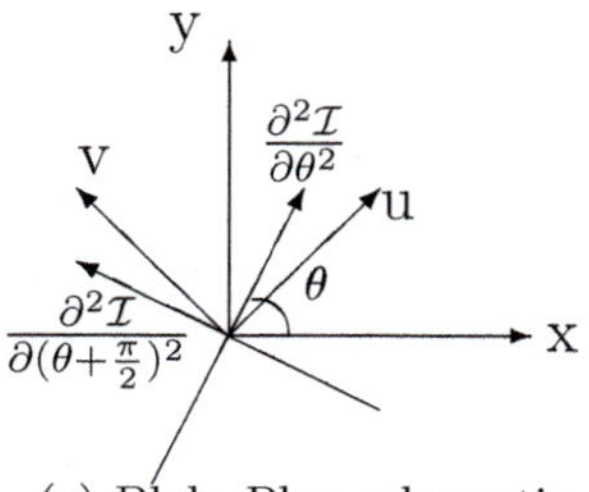

(c) Blob: Plan schematic

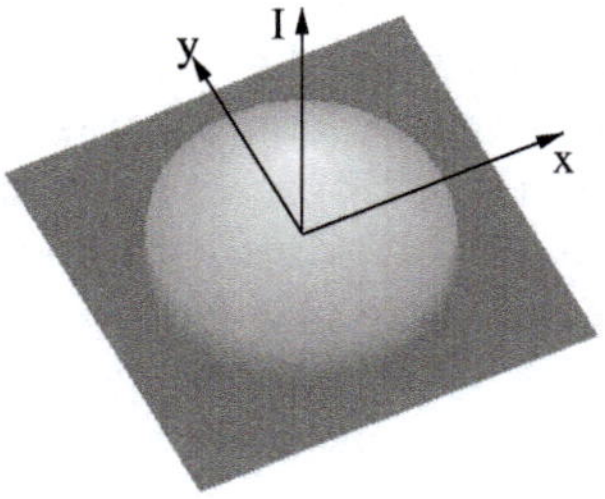

(d) Blob: Isometric view

Fig. 1. Schematic for general corner and blob-like points. A corner is defined as a point with high curvature and significant (relative to noise) change in intensity in direction θ. A blob has significant change in its second derivatives in all directions. Examples of corner-like points might be the corners of eyes or junctions between two lines. Examples of blob-like points might be centres of cheeks, or regions with little texture.

Secondly, to remove edge points, the point's curvature must be significant;

$$\kappa = \frac{\frac{\partial \mathcal{I}}{\partial \theta}\frac{\partial^2 \mathcal{I}}{\partial(\theta+\frac{\pi}{2})^2} - \frac{\partial \mathcal{I}}{\partial(\theta+\frac{\pi}{2})}\frac{\partial^2 \mathcal{I}}{\partial \theta^2}}{\left[\left(\frac{\partial \mathcal{I}}{\partial \theta}\right)^2 + \left(\frac{\partial \mathcal{I}}{\partial(\theta+\frac{\pi}{2})}\right)^2\right]^{\frac{3}{2}}} > \kappa_t \,, \tag{2}$$

where κ_t is a threshold set to remove curves which are insufficiently corner-like. Note that, if equation 1 is true then it is likely that $\frac{\partial^2 \mathcal{I}}{\partial \theta^2} \sim 0$. Consequently, instead of evaluating the whole of equation 2, the requirement simplifies to requiring $\|\frac{\partial^2 \mathcal{I}}{\partial(\theta+\frac{\pi}{2})^2}\|$ to be large. We can therefore search for feature points of this type by identifying locations where both 1 and $\|\frac{\partial^2 \mathcal{I}}{\partial(\theta+\frac{\pi}{2})^2}\|$ are maxima. According to the sign of $\frac{\partial \mathcal{I}}{\partial \theta}$ we can identify two types of feature.

Our third feature type results from identifying blob-like points such as shown in figure 1(c,d). As the structure is symmetrical, we must examine second rather than first derivatives. There is therefore a choice. Either we can use a single filter based on the Laplacian, or compute $\partial^2 \mathcal{I}$ in two orthogonal directions. Computing the two orthogonal directions brings the possibility of affine invariance, though as discussed earlier this is not necessarily an advantage. Using the Laplacian, or the difference of Gaussian approximation, yields the method of [3].

To make derivatives scale invariant, we must normalise them with respect to scale. Given the Gaussian $\mathcal{G}(x) = \frac{1}{\sqrt{2\pi}\sigma} \exp\left(\frac{-x^2}{2\sigma^2}\right)$, it is easy to show that

$$\int_{-\infty}^{\infty} \left|\frac{d\mathcal{G}}{dx}\right| dx = \sqrt{\frac{2}{\pi}}\frac{1}{\sigma} \text{ and } \int_{-\infty}^{\infty} \left|\frac{d^2\mathcal{G}}{dx^2}\right| dx = \sqrt{\frac{2}{\pi}}\frac{e^{-0.5}}{\sigma^2} . \tag{3}$$

This agrees with the standard definition that the scale normalised Gaussian derivative $\partial^n \mathcal{G}$ is $\sigma^n \partial \mathcal{G}$ [6]. Equations 3 highlight that for comparing odd and even (first and second) derivatives an additional factor of $\exp(-0.5)$ is required.

2.1 Maxima Detection and Feature Ordering

To summarise, the features illustrated in figure 1(a,b,c,d). will be obtained using first and second order scale normalised derivatives. From these derivatives, we obtain maxima and determine which are stable; proceeding in two stages. Firstly, following Lowe [3], we look for maxima in a 3x3x3 block consisting of a point's nearest neighbours in space and scale. Second, we order the points.

As discussed, intensity derivatives are dependent upon the illumination and hence unreliable for deciding between stable and unstable points. Retaining features based on the intensity derivatives tends to lead to points being clustered in bright regions with few points found in darker regions. To remove noise points, we estimate global noise using the median of the distribution of first order derivatives at the highest frequency level [10]. We suggest that *having identified points with repeatable 2D shape from maxima that are not noise, the actual feature energy is not directly related to the extent to which they are interesting.* Consequently, we wish to identify measures which are unrelated to intensity but not susceptible to noise. For this purpose we consider three alternatives. Firstly, the ratio of derivatives $\left|\frac{\partial \mathcal{I}}{\partial \theta} / \frac{\partial^2 \mathcal{I}}{\partial(\theta+\frac{\pi}{2})^2}\right|$. Second, the local entropy assessed from sampling the image at the feature scale into an 8 bin histogram where bins are set according to local minimum and maximum intensity. Thirdly, we use a method based on normalising the first and second order derivatives. Figure 2 shows odd and even scale normalised filter coefficients across scale for a 1D intensity profile. Note that where the odd response is large, the even response is near zero and vice-versa. For Gabor filters, the odd and even filters are exactly $\frac{\pi}{2}$ out of phase, making them orthogonal [10]. Although odd and even derivatives do not follow this property exactly, we make the approximation and use their absolute values to normalise their response. Then, for this normalised response we calculate the mean and variance over all scales, for both odd and even derivatives. We take the average of these variances as our interest measure. Points which have larger variance indicate more change and hence presumably are more interesting. Unchanging points indicate that the structure does not vary and is uninteresting. Defining normalised derivatives $\partial \mathcal{I}_o = \frac{\partial \mathcal{I}}{\sqrt{(\partial \mathcal{I})^2 + (\partial^2 \mathcal{I})^2}}$, σ_o^2 is estimated as:

$$\sigma_o^2 = \frac{1}{N}\sum_s (\partial \mathcal{I}_o)^2 - \mu_o^2, \text{ where } \mu_o = \frac{1}{N}\sum_s \partial \mathcal{I}_o \tag{4}$$

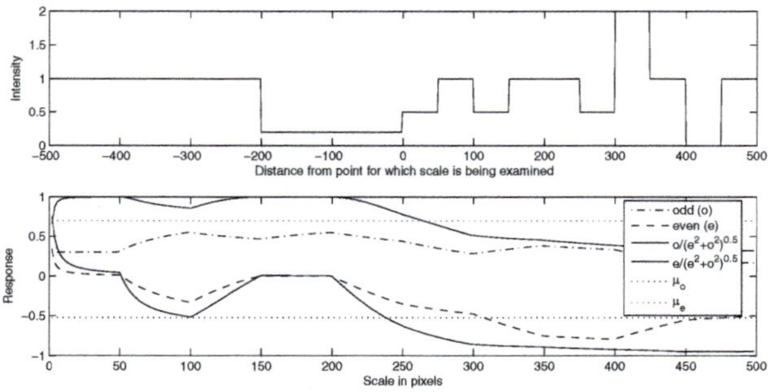

Fig. 2. Diagrams showing a 1D intensity profile (top) and the scale space response of the central point (bottom) for odd and even filters, their normalisations and means

Finally, points are added to our feature list via a method which attempts to spatially distribute them based on the extent to which they are a local maxima [11]. This reduces the tendency for points to bunch in one (textured) area.

3 Implementation

We have defined the types of points we wish to detect as maxima to bandpass filters of first and second order. However, as stated earlier, we do not implement these using the steerable Gaussian approach. Instead, to avoid down-sampling and potential errors in interpolation we will approximate these filters using the integral image representation [8, 9]. As these filters are not rotationally invariant, we implement them in four directions, along axes x,y,u and v as defined earlier in figure 1. As these filters require only 8 additions/subtractions, in addition to calculation of the integral image, they are highly efficient. We now describe this transform and define the scale invariant filters.

Denoting an image $\mathcal{I}$, summed-area image $\mathcal{I}_A$ at point (x, y) is defined as

$$\mathcal{I}_A(x, y) = \sum_{i=0}^{y} \sum_{j=0}^{x} \mathcal{I}(j, i) \; . \tag{5}$$

The image is calculated recursively: $\mathcal{I}_A(x, y) = \mathcal{I}(x, y) + \mathcal{I}_A(x-1, y) + \mathcal{I}_A(x, y-1) - \mathcal{I}_A(x-1, y-1)$, with boundary conditions $\mathcal{I}_A(-1, x) = \mathcal{I}_A(y, -1) = 0$. This allows the sum around a point (x,y), at scale s, $\mathcal{I}_S(x, y, s)$ to be calculated from addition/subtraction of four points:

$$\begin{aligned} \mathcal{I}_S(x, y, s) = & \; \mathcal{I}_A(x+s, y+s) - \mathcal{I}_A(x-s, y+s) - \\ & \; \mathcal{I}_A(x+s, y-s) + \mathcal{I}_A(x-s, y-s) \; . \end{aligned} \tag{6}$$

Now, consider figure 3. It shows a plan view of the three types of filter: second order (even), first order (odd) and an approximation to the Laplacian. White

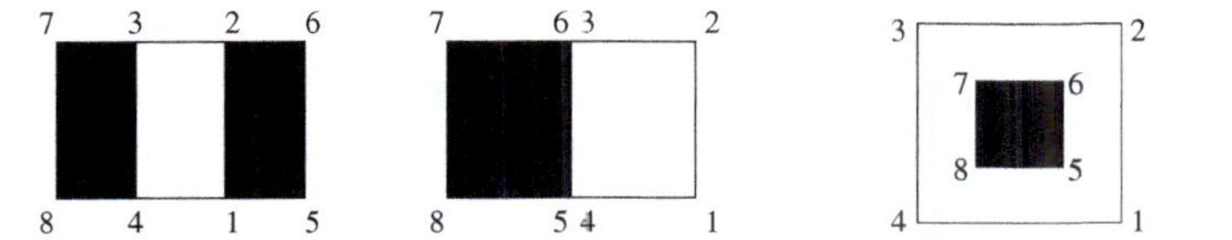

(a) Even Filter X Direction (b) Odd Filter X Direction (c) Approximation to Laplacian

Fig. 3. Box filters: approximations to derivatives with summed-area tables. White indicates a positive value, black negative. The filters are normalized such that the sum of coefficients of area 1234 is always equal to that of 5678.

indicates a positive response and black negative. Note that each filter can be formed from the subtraction of one block (1234) from the other (5678). However, such filters are not necessarily scale invariant, and unless scaled so that the coefficients of area (1234) equal those of area (5678) have a DC response. To obtain scale invariance, we must normalise the filters at all scales. Consider that the Laplacian, $\partial^2\mathcal{G}$, of a Gaussian $\mathcal{G}_\sigma$, is scale invariant after multiplication by a factor of σ^2: $\sigma^2\partial^2\mathcal{G}$, where σ is its standard deviation [6]. In [3], Lowe approximates this by the difference of two Gaussians, where their standard deviations are σ and $k\sigma$, k being a constant. The key difference between the sums of equation 6 and the Gaussian integral is that the point sums are not normalized. This is easily remedied by dividing equation 6 by factor $4s^2$. The difference of two such sums then yields a box filter approximation to the difference of Gaussians [3] and to the Laplacian $\mathcal{L}^2(x, y, s)$:

$$\mathcal{L}^2(x, y, s) \approx \frac{1}{4s^2}\mathcal{I}_S(x, y, s) - \frac{1}{4k^2s^2}\mathcal{I}_S(x, y, ks)\,. \tag{7}$$

This method of normalisation also works for the first and second order directional filters. At scale s, the first derivatives $\frac{\partial\mathcal{I}}{\partial x}$ are defined by

$$\frac{\partial\mathcal{I}(x, y, s)}{\partial x} = \frac{1}{s^2}\left[\mathcal{I}_S(x + \frac{s}{2}, y, \frac{s}{2}) - \mathcal{I}_S(x - \frac{s}{2}, y, \frac{s}{2})\right] \tag{8}$$

Derivative $\frac{\partial\mathcal{I}}{\partial y}$ is defined similarly, with a shift in y replacing that in x. Derivatives $\frac{\partial\mathcal{I}}{\partial u}, \frac{\partial\mathcal{I}}{\partial v}$ are defined using $\mathcal{I}_S(x \pm \frac{s}{2}, y \mp \frac{s}{2}, \frac{s}{2})$ etc.. The second order derivatives use the same idea. The only difference is that an extra parameter is required to express the ratio between the sum extent in the different directions, i.e. $\mathcal{I}_S(x, y, s_x, s_y)$ although the ratio between s_x and s_y is set to be constant and equal to $\frac{1}{2}$. In the x direction, $\frac{\partial^2\mathcal{I}}{\partial x^2}$ is defined as

$$\frac{\partial^2\mathcal{I}(x, y, s)}{\partial x^2} = \frac{2}{s^2}\mathcal{I}_S(x, y, \frac{s}{2}, \frac{s}{4}) - \frac{1}{s^2}\mathcal{I}_S(x, y, s, \frac{s}{4})\,. \tag{9}$$

Again, similar filters are defined for the other three directions. These filters use the same scales as the Laplacian approximation, although there is not any particular reason that this must be so. Practically, all first derivatives, and second derivatives $\mathcal{L}^2$, $\frac{\partial^2\mathcal{I}}{\partial x^2}$, $\frac{\partial^2\mathcal{I}}{\partial y^2}$, require 8 operations. However, $\frac{\partial^2\mathcal{I}}{\partial u^2}$ and $\frac{\partial^2\mathcal{I}}{\partial v^2}$ require 12.

There are two advantages and one disadvantage to this approach. Firstly, in [3], filters with standard deviations from $\sigma = 1.2$ to 3.2 are used. Assuming Gaussians are truncated at two standard deviations, filters span between 5 and 13 pixels. A separable filter implemented convolution requires between 10 and 26 operations, vs. 4 for the summed-area images. This significantly increases speed. The second advantage to the box filters is that, using the summed-areas, there is no need to downsample the image to improve convolution speed. This is useful as it should reduce delocalisation associated with this process. [3] uses interpolation to improve position estimates for maxima on downsampled images. Using a Taylor expansion, about a point, the estimate is altered using the approximation $\mathbf{x} = -\frac{\partial^2 \mathcal{L}}{\partial \mathbf{x}^2}^{-1} \frac{\partial \mathcal{L}}{\partial \mathbf{x}}$. Still, it might reasonably be assumed that estimates will deviate by $\sigma \sim 0.1$ pixels. This leads to an error of $\sigma \sim 0.8$ pixels for the third pyramid level which will decrease the number of matching features between consecutive images. The one weakness to implementation using integral images, is that the filter is a lower fidelity approximation to the first and second order derivatives than is achievable using Gaussian derivatives. In particular, it is not rotationally symmetric: implying lower performance for rotation about the axis through the camera lens and focal plane. Less importantly, the image grid limits the choice of k if we wish to the bandpass filters to have constant bandwidth. We specify our filter at scales $\lfloor 2k^n \rfloor, n = 0, 1, 2..$, where $\lfloor \bullet \rfloor$ means taking the floor value of the expression and k=1.5. This leads to scales 2,3,5,7,10,15,23,34,51,77,115 etc.. For 240x320 sized images we use the first 10 scales.

4 Experiments and Results

To measure performance, we adopt a similar test strategy to [5], aiming to compare accuracy and information content of points. Consequently, the number of points found on average is also given. Additionally, as a key aim of the paper was an efficient implementation for scale invariance, timings for frames/second processed are provided. Tests compare some or all of the following methods *of detecting feature points* (not describing them): (1) Corner detection using eigenvalues [1], (2) SIFT [3], (3) Laplacian of Harris corners (LHC) [5], (4) Gray-level Extremal Regions (GER) [4], (5) (proposed method) scale-invariant Laplacian box filters (SILBF) and (6) (proposed method) scale-invariant derivative box filters (SIDBF). All the images used in testing were obtained courtesy of http://www.inrialpes.fr/lear/people/Mikolajczyk/.

Table 1. Average mean entropy of points over 100 images. Entropy is calculated for all methods using the Local Jet [12]. The mean entropy of a random point was 2.10.

Method	KLT	SIFT	LHC	SILBF	SIDBF
Entropy	3.58	3.70	4.23	3.71	3.8
Pts. Detected	800	250	400	350	900

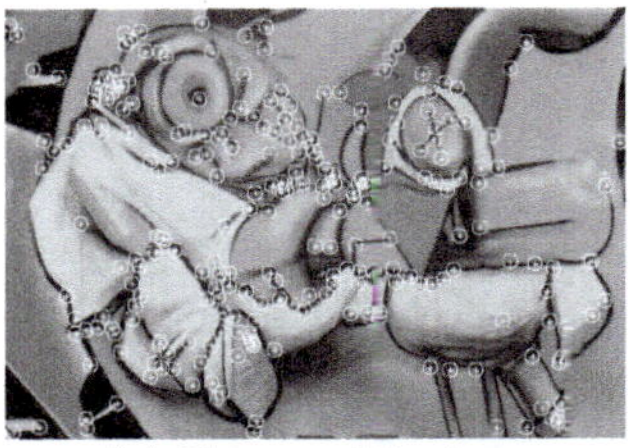

(a) Energy Maxima

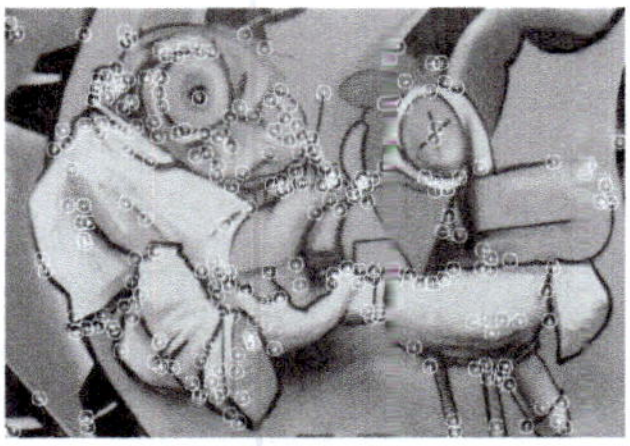

(b) Entropy Maxima

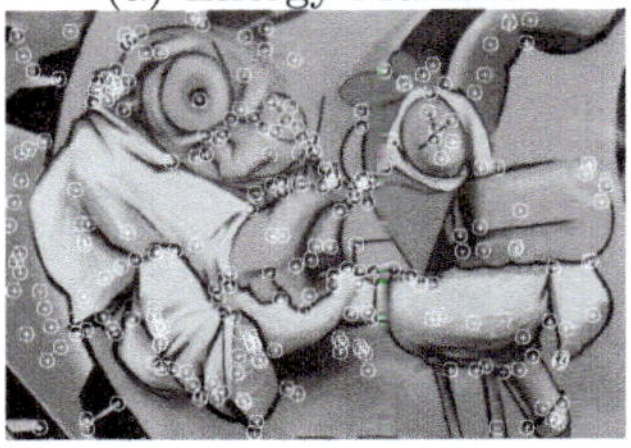

(c) Eigenvalues Ratio Maxima

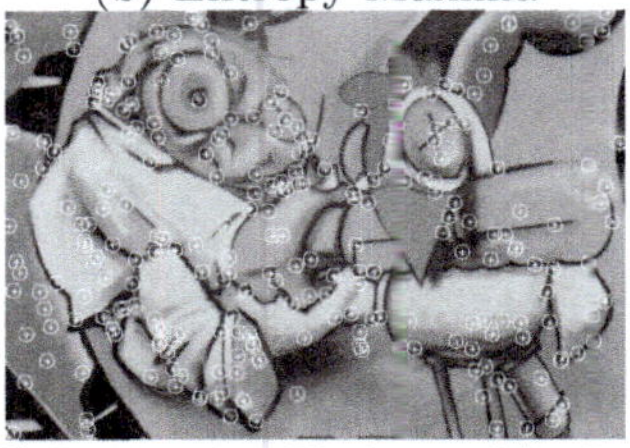

(d) Derivative Variance Maxima

Fig. 4. Comparison of obtaining maxima using various descriptors versus the standard maxima of energy of derivatives, for box filter method SILBF. Points are marked by white circles with a central cross.

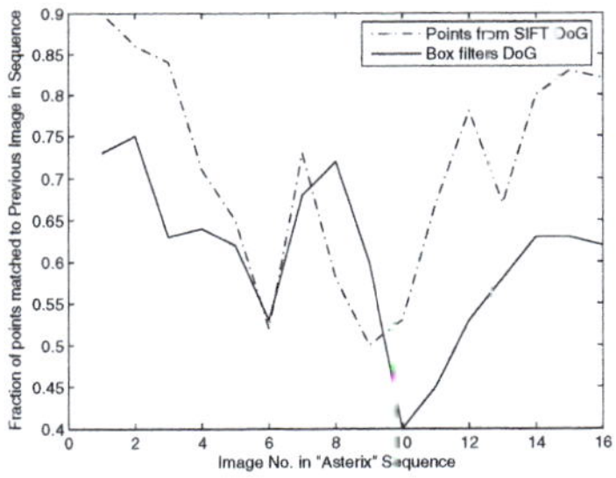

(a) Scale change

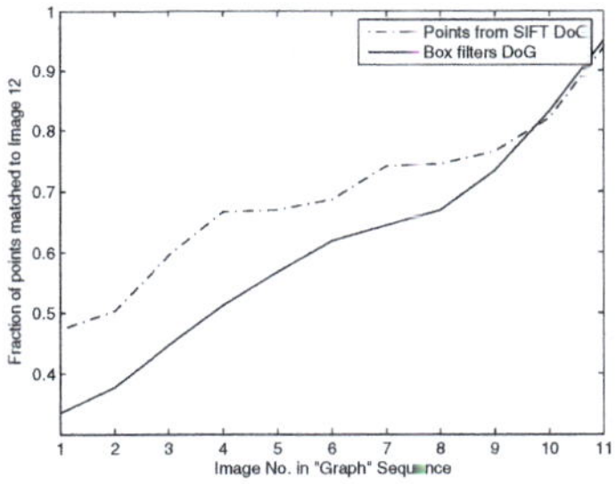

(b) Illumination change

Fig. 5. A comparison of points detected through data sequences with significant changes in a scale or illumination

Table 1 shows the entropy of the feature points found for various methods. Note that the entropy of SIFT and SILBP is similar, as expected, given they approximate the same function. All are significantly higher than the random entropy. Note that LHC points have higher entropy than SIFT or SILBF. This is as they find boundaries between regions rather than centres of them: change is inevitably greater. Table 2 shows comparison of the different methods for speed of processing. The speed was obtained by taking the shortest processing time from 200 trials. Note in particular that the proposed method SILBF is quickest, a factor of 2 faster than the second fastest and nearly a factor of 3 quicker than SIFT, its ideological equivalent. SIDBF is slower, as it calculates four times as many derivatives as SILBF, also requiring more comparisons to

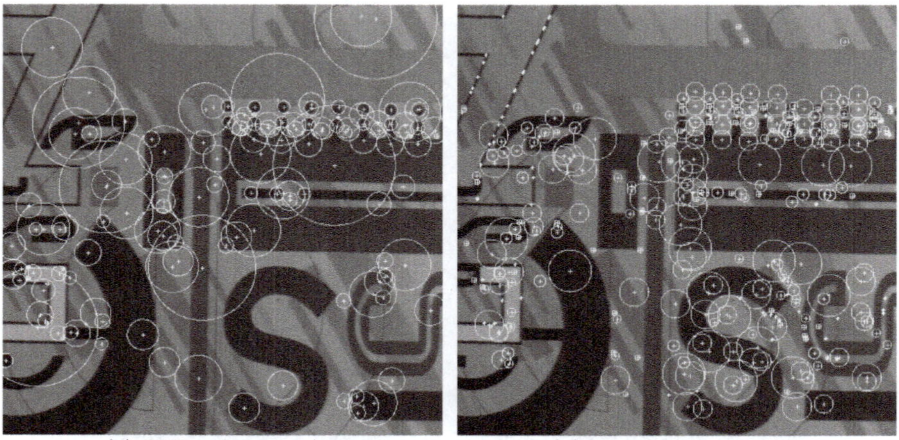

(a) SIFT, Graph 1/12 (b) SILBF, Graph 1/12

(c) SIFT, Graph 12/12 (d) SILBF, Graph 12/12

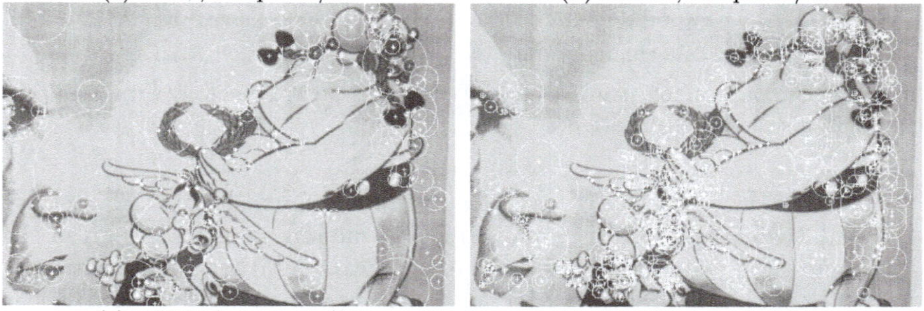

(e) SIFT, Asterix 10/16 (f) SILBF, Asterix 10/16

Fig. 6. Visual comparison of SIFT and SILBF for type of points produced. Note that although both the SIFT and SILBF obtain points which look like the centre of regions, they are in fact not identical. Noticeably, the Block filter approach seems to produce smaller regions and has difficulty with obtaining large scale feature points (compare (e) to (f)). This can affect performance for large scale changes.

Table 2. Comparison of algorithm speed for processing a single frame and for frames/sec. Comparisons were made on a P4, 2.5GHz with 512KB cache, 512MB RAM. The first number is total processing time, the second the time spent on detecting maxima. Time for computing the scalespace trees (or regions) is their difference.

	Milliseconds/Frame		Frames/sec	
Method	240x320	480x640	240x320	480x640
KLT	170(35)	280(35)	5.88	3.57
SIFT	155(14)	654(45)	6.45	1.53
LHC	531(14)	2437(42)	1.88	0.41
GER	100(7)	301(12)	10	3.32
SILBF	53(17)	185(38)	18.7	5.4
SIDBF	240(24)	1070(81)	4.17	0.93

identify maxima. Whilst [3] suggests upsampling the image as a preprocessing step, for timing comparisons this is not done.

Figure 4 shows a comparison of the different maxima ordering approaches on the "graffiti1" image. The strongest 250 points are shown. Although differences are small, the derivative variance maxima are slightly better distributed across the image. Figure 5 shows the results of testing for scale and illumination invariance on the Asterix and Graph sequences. Although the performance of SIBF is inferior to SIFT, it is not so much so. Where speed is of importance, it may be an acceptable tradeoff.

5 Conclusions

We have demonstrated a method for fast feature detection using box filters obtained from summed-area images. The approximated Laplacian improves in speed on SIFT by a factor of three and the approximated derivative filters on affine Harris by a similar factor. Performance for scale and illumination change remains similar. Future work will examine SILBF on non-intensity functions, e.g. colour or object models, and look to improve the stability of extracted maxima.

References

1. Shi, J., Tomasi, C.: Good features to track. In: Proceedings of CVPR. (1994)
2. Kadir, T., Zisserman, A., Brady, M.: An affine invariant salient region detector In: Proceedings of ECCV. (2004) 404–416
3. Lowe, D.: Distinctive image features from scale-invariant keypoints. IJCV **60(2)** (2004) 90–110
4. Matas, J., Chum, O., Urban, M., Pajdla, T.: Robust wide baseline stereo from maximally stable extremal regions. Image and Vision Computing **22(10)** (2004) 761–767
5. Mikolajczyk, K., Schmid, C.: A performance evaluation of local descriptors. In: Proceedings CVPR, Part 2. (2003) 257–263

6. Lindeberg, T.: Feature Detection with Automatic Scale Selection. IJCV **30(2)** (1998) 79–116
7. Mikolajczyk, K., Schmid, C.: Scale and affine invariant interest point detectors. IJCV **60(1)** (2004) 63–86
8. Crow, F.: Summed Area Tables for Texture Mapping. SIGGRAPH **18(3)** (1984) 207–212
9. Viola, P., Jones, M.: Robust real-time face detection. IJCV **57(2)** (2004) 137–154
10. Kovesi, P.: Image Features from Phase Congruency. Videre: Journal of Computer Vision Research **1(3)** (1999) 1–27
11. Brown, M., Szeliski, R., Winder, S.: Multi-image matching using multi-scale oriented patches. In: Proceedings CVPR, Part 1. (2005) 510–517
12. Florack, L., ter Haar Romeny, B., Koenderink, J., Viergever, M.: The gaussian scale-space paradigm and the multiscale local jet. IJCV **18** (1996) 61–75

Detecting Faces from Low-Resolution Images

Shinji Hayashi[1] and Osamu Hasegawa[1,2]

[1] Tokyo Institute of Technology, Nagatsuta, Yokohama, Japan
{hayashi, hasegawa}@isl.titech.ac.jp
[2] PRESTO Japan Science and Technology Agency (JST)

Abstract. Face detection is a hot research topic in Computer Vision; the field has greatly progressed over the past decade. However, to our knowledge, face detection in low-resolution images has not been studied. In this paper, we use a conventional AdaBoost-based face detector to show that the face detection rate falls to 39% from 88% as face resolution decreases from 24 × 24 pixels to 6 × 6 pixels.

We propose a new face detection method comprising four techniques. As a result, our method improved the face detection rate from 39% to 71% for 6 × 6 pixel faces of MIT+CMU frontal face test set. We also show our method can detect 6×6 faces in real scene other than MIT+CMU frontal face test set.

1 Introduction

In recent years, numerous methods for detecting faces in general scenes have been proposed [1]. Those methods work efficiently for frontal face detection [2]. However, faces in real images are not necessarily frontal; moreover, they are usually taken in various illumination conditions. Therefore, many studies have been undertaken for face detection, which is robust for variation of poses and illumination conditions [3][4].

On the other hand, considering the security use of discovering suspicious persons from surveillance images, it is better to detect a face immediately when a small face is captured in the distance. Nevertheless, conventional face detection technique usually detects face images larger than 20 × 20 pixel or 24 × 24 pixel. Face detection from low-resolution images has not been explicitly studied.

There are two studies related to this field. One is Torralba's psychological experiment[5]. That result indicates that a human can recognize a face in a low-resolution image better when using an upper-body image than using merely a face image. We use this knowledge to improve the face detection rate in section 3. The other is Kruppa and Schile's study[6]. They also used the knowledge of Torralba's experiment and applied "local context detector" for half resolution MIT+CMU ftontal face test set. However, the advantage of using "local context detector" is not clearly shown. In the graph of their paper, "object-centered detector (conventional method)" outperforms "local context detector" at the point of the same false positives.

In this paper, we investigate the relation between resolution and the face detection rate systematically in section 2. We made four kinds of evaluation images

P.J. Narayanan et al. (Eds.): ACCV 2006, LNCS 3851, pp. 787–796, 2006.

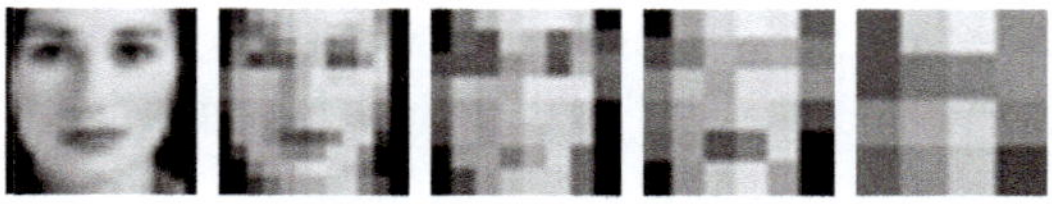

Fig. 1. Various face resolutions; face size is from left 24 × 24, 12 × 12, 8 × 8, 6 × 6, 4 × 4 pixel

from the MIT+CMU frontal face test set and trained four kinds of AdaBoost-based detectors. These four kinds indicate four levels of resolution. We evaluated face detection rates for these four kinds of detectors by plotting ROC curves as relations between false positives and the face detection rates. This evaluation shows that a detection rate decreases from 88% to 39% as the resolution of faces decreases from 24 × 24 pixel to 6 × 6 pixel. Section 3 presents our new method for detecting faces from low-resolution images. This method comprises four techniques, "Using the upper-body", "Expansion of input images", "Frequency-band limitation of features", and "Combination of two detectors". Our results showed that a 39% face detection rate for 6 × 6 pixel faces increases to 71% by our proposed method. In section 4, we applied our proposed method to real data. In section 5, we summarize our research.

In this paper, 'resolution' means the face size. We defined the face size as 2.4 times the interval between an individual's eyes.

2 Conventional Method

Recently, many methods for face detection have been proposed. Especially, the AdaBoost-based face detector by Viola [7] is used widely in face detection research because of its speed and accuracy [8][9]. The AdaBoost-based face detector is recognized as a standard method for face detection. For that reason, we use an AdaBoost-based face detector for our research and show the result of their application to low-resolution images.

2.1 Application to Low-Resolution Images

First, we determine the resolutions to investigate. Cropping faces in various sizes and observing, we judged that 6 × 6 pixel was near the boundary of resolution for an image to be recognizable as a face. Figure 1 shows cropped faces as 24 × 24, 12 × 12, 8 × 8, 6 × 6, and 4 × 4 pixels. The 4 × 4 pixel face has become unrecognizable as a face, but 6 × 6 pixel face is barely recognizable as a face. Therefore, we designate 6 × 6 pixel as the minimum resolution to investigate in this study. We selected 24 × 24 pixel as the maximum resolution. 12 × 12, 8 × 8 pixel were added. These are the four kinds of resolution investigated here.

Next, we describe application of an AdaBoost-based face detector to low-resolution images. Resolution of training data is the minimum size of face detection because, in the face detection process, an input image pyramid is produced

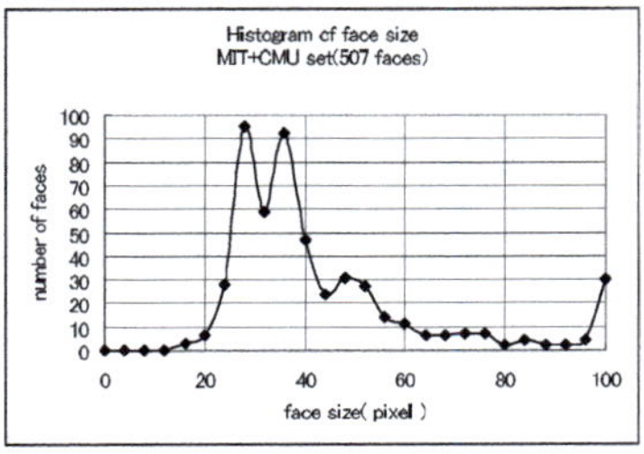

Fig. 2. Face size histogram of the MIT+CMU set

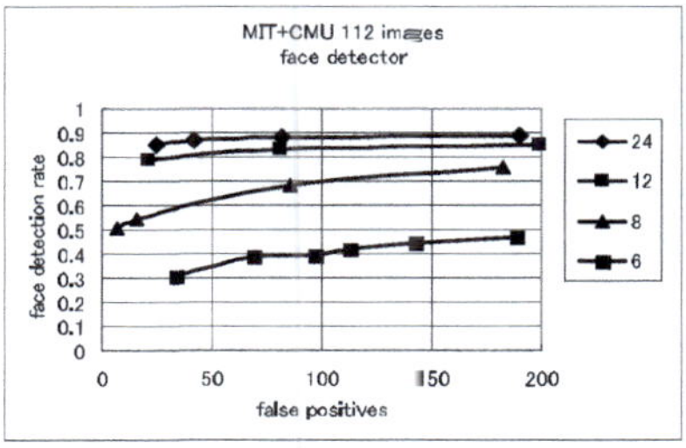

Fig. 3. Relation between resolutions and face detection rates

by scaling down. Consequently, it is necessary to lower the resolution of training data for detecting low-resolution faces. In this regard, not only the AdaBoost-based face detector but neural network-based face detectors and other devices are similar.

We use the MIT+CMU frontal face test set [10] for test data[1]. From the ground truth file, we calculated a histogram of face sizes of 507 faces in MIT+CMU frontal face test set. This is shown in Figure. 2. Because the minimum detectable face size is the size of the training data, most faces contained in the MIT+CMU set can be detected using a 24 × 24 pixel face detector. However, our research is intended to detect faces smaller than 24 × 24 pixels. Therefore, the MIT+CMU set, in which the small face is not contained, cannot be used as it is. Evaluation images for face detection from low-resolution images were created as follows.

- Eliminate 13 images that contain no faces and eliminate 5 images that contain line-drawn faces. Thereby, 130 images become 112 images.
- The "average face size" is calculated in the image, and the whole image is reduced using bicubic so that the "average face size" might reach a desired size. (24 × 24, 12 × 12, 8 × 8, or 6 × 6 pixels). Bicubic was chosen to perform the smoothest possible reduction.
- The above is repeated for 112 images and four kinds of sizes.

That process yielded four kinds of evaluation images. Respective averages of the face sizes contained in the four kinds of evaluation images are 24 × 24, 12 × 12, 8 × 8, or 6 × 6 pixels.

Four kinds of detectors were made using 5131 face images of 24 × 24, 12 × 12, 8 × 8, and 6 × 6 pixels and 5316 non-face images as training data. Evaluation results for the four detectors are shown in Figure. 3. This is the result obtained using conventional AdaBoost-based face detectors applied to low-resolution images. The horizontal axis of Figure. 3 expresses the number of false positives; the vertical axis expresses the face detection rate.

[1] This set comprises 130 images containing 507 ftonral faces.

Fig. 4. Examples of detection results: average face size is 24×24(upper left), 12×12(upper right), 8×8(lower left), and 6×6(lower left) pixels. Thresholds were set to obtain almost the same number of false positives for 112 images.

In Figure. 3, at the point of 100 false positives, the face detection rate declines from 88% to 39% as the face resolution is reduced from 24 × 24 pixel to 6 × 6 pixel. Therefore, it can be said that we can not obtain a sufficient face detection rate for 6 × 6 pixel faces merely using 6 × 6 pixel faces as training data. An example of detection results is shown in Figure. 4.

3 Proposed Method

When face size became 6 × 6 pixels, the detection rate fell extremely using conventional AdaBoost-based face detector. We chose 6 × 6 pixels as the minimum face size to detect; in this study, only 6 × 6 pixel evaluation images are used hereafter.

In this section, we show our proposed method "Using upper-body", "Expansion of input images", and "Combination of two detectors".

The final algorithm is shown below.

- An input image is expanded by a factor of six.
- Apply the face detector and the upper-body detector to the expanded image.
- The two detectors' results are inputted into a SVM. Final judgement is performed by the SVM.

3.1 Using Upper-Body Images

Torralba performed a psychological experiment for the face recognition from low-resolution images. This indicates that a man can recognize a face in a low-resolution image better when using an upper-body image than a simple face image.

Using this knowledge, we attempted to use upper-body images as training data. We choose 12 × 12 pixels as the size of upper-body images. This is double the resolution of face images. 4191 upper-body images of 12 × 12 pixels were prepared as training data; a detector was made using these images and 5316 non-face images. Figure 5 is a 12 × 12 upper-body image and a 6 × 6 face image. Each face size is the same.

Figure 6 portrays the result of 12 × 12 upper-body detector applied to 6 × 6 pixel evaluation images. For comparison, the result for a 6 × 6 face detector

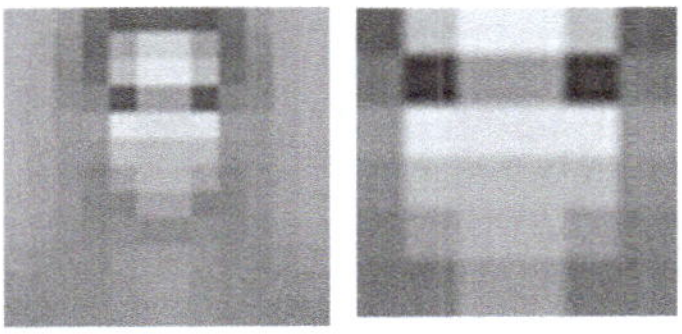

Fig. 5. Left:12 × 12 pixel upper-body image. Right:6 × 6 pixel face image.

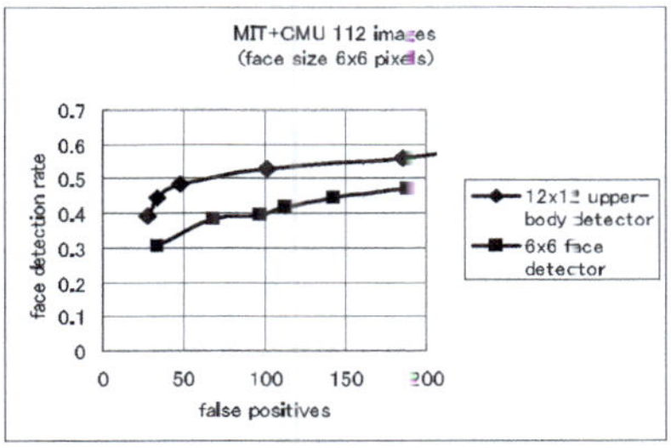

Fig. 6. Effect of using upper-body images

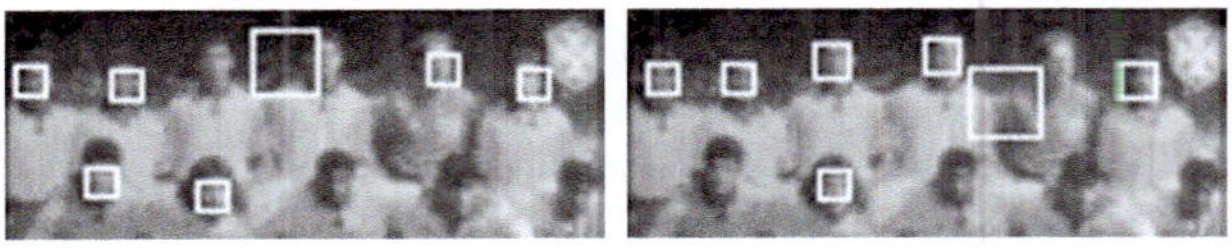

Fig. 7. Left:6 × 6 pixel face detector's result. Right:12 × 12 pixel upper-body detector's result (a detection window is drawn at the face region).

applied to 6 × 6 evaluation images is plotted. At the point of 100 false positives, the 6 × 6 face detector detects about 39% of faces, while the 12 × 12 upper-body detector detects 52% of faces.

We intended to use the upper-body detector only. However after seeing the detection results, we noticed that there are faces that only the upper-body detector can detect and that only the face detector can detect. An example is shown in Figure. 7. This indicates that these two detectors complement each other. Therefore, we use not only the upper-body detector, but also the face detector. Finally, we will try to combine these two detectors into one system.

3.2 Expansion of Input Images

In face detection, two or more "face coordinates candidates" usually occur around one face. This is because a detector judges the image as a face even if the position and size vary somewhat. Two or more detection coordinates generated around one face are merged; they finally are aggregated into one face detection coordinate for each face.

Figure 8 depicts detected results of 24 × 24 and 6 × 6 pixel faces. Face coordinate candidates in Figure. 8 are not merged. There are more face coordinate candidates in a 24 × 24 pixel face than in a 6 × 6 pixel face. We counted number of face coordinate candidates by respectively applying a face detector to 100 24 × 24 pixel face images and 6 × 6 face images. For the 24 × 24 pixel face images, the average number of face-coordinate candidates is 20. For 6 × 6 pixel face images, the average number of face coordinates candidates is two. This difference

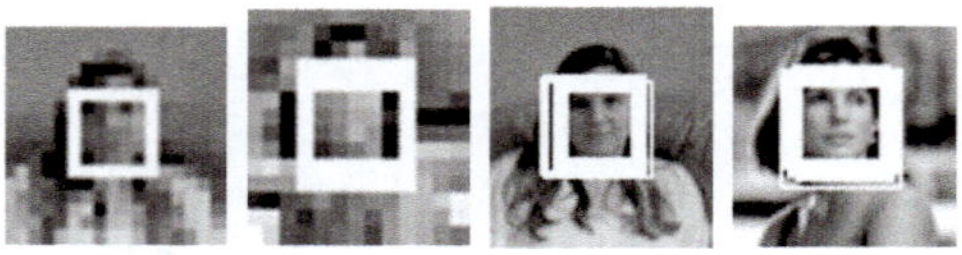

Fig. 8. Difference of the number of face-coordinate candidates. The two left images contain 6 × 6 pixel faces. The right two images contain 24 × 24 pixel faces.

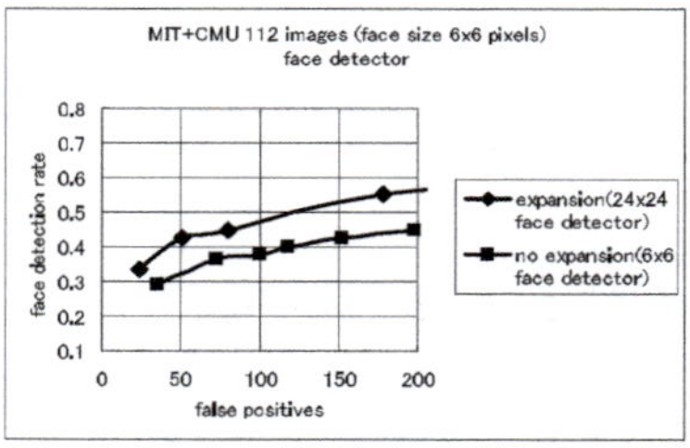

Fig. 9. Effect of expansion: face detector

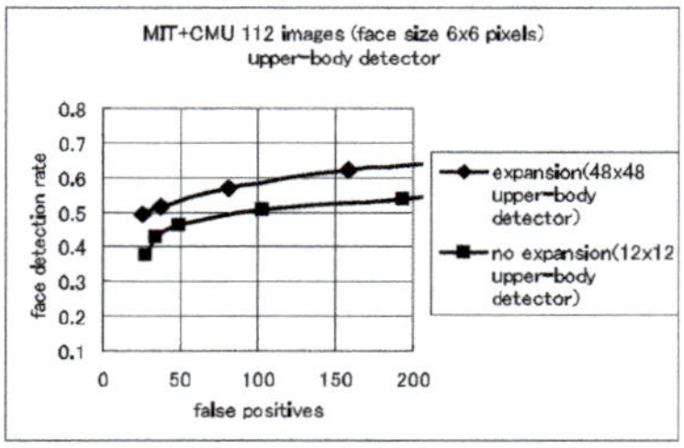

Fig. 10. Effect of expansion: upper-body detector

is the difference of robustness for position and size changes. We inferred that this is one reason why the face detection rate for 6 × 6 pixel evaluation images is so low.

Therefore, to detect 6 × 6 pixel faces, we propose to expand the whole input image by bicubic, and to detect faces using a 24 × 24 pixel face detector. The minimum scaling factor is four, meaning that 6 × 6 pixel faces are expanded to 24 × 24 pixel faces. However, considering the size variation in 6 × 6 pixel faces, it is better to select a larger scaling factor than four. On the other hand, a large scaling factor implies more numerous scanning patches, which leads to more false positives. Based on the above, we choose six as a scaling factor.

We expanded 6 × 6 pixel evaluation images by a factor of six, and applied the 24 × 24 face detector to these images. This result is depicted in Figure. 9. For comparison, the result of a 6 × 6 face detector applied to 6 × 6 pixel evaluation images is plotted. At the point of 100 false positives, the 39% face detection rate is improved to 48% using this expansion.

To evaluate the effect of expansion for an upper-body detector, we made a 48 × 48 pixel upper-body detector using 4191 upper-body images of 48 × 48 pixels and 5316 non-face images. We applied it to 6 × 6 pixel expanded evaluation images. The result is shown in Figure. 10. For comparison, the result of the 12 × 12 pixel upper-body detector applied to 6 × 6 pixel evaluation images is plotted. At the point of 100 false positives, the 52% face detection rate is improved to 58% using expansion.

The face detection rate is improved through the use of expansion of input images for both the face detector and the upper-body detector.

3.3 Frequency-Band Limitation of Features

A classifier that constitutes a detector uses four simple features. We use the same features as Viola used. These features can take all positions and lengths possible in a 24 × 24 pixel image. When 6 × 6 pixel face images are expanded by a factor of four, fewer than 4 pixel cycle data in 24 × 24 pixel face images are meaningless. However, when we made detectors before, AdaBoost selected features from all possible features. Features selected by AdaBoost included features whose frequency is less than four. We inferred that this is one reason for the low detection rate for expanded 6 × 6 pixel evaluation images. Therefore, we produced a new face detector and upper-body detector using conditions in eq. (1). H and W are shown in Figure. 11.

$$H \geq 4, W \geq 4 \tag{1}$$

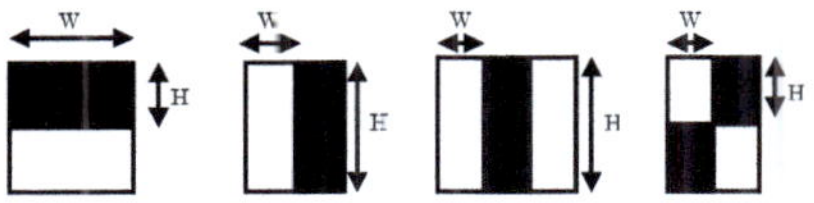

Fig. 11. W,H of features

These two detectors were applied to 6 × 6 pixel evaluation images. The results are shown as "frequency-band limitation" in Figure. 12 and Figure. 13. In each evaluation, 6 × 6 pixel evaluation images are expanded by a factor of six; then a 24 × 24 face detector or 48 × 48 upper-body detector is used. For comparison, results before using frequency-band limitation are plotted as "no frequency band limitation" in Figure. 12 and Figure. 13.

At the point of 100 false positives, the face detection rate of the face detector is improved from 48% to 58%. The face detection rate of an upper-body detector is improved from 58% to 67%.

3.4 Combination of Two Detectors

In this section, the face detection rate is improved through the combined use of the face detector and the upper-body detector.

Because two detectors are used, two face-likenesses for the image are detected. Making a final judgment based on this information requires determination of the domain of face and non-face in the 2D plane that takes face-likenesses as both axes. In our research, this is achieved using a SVM. The face-likeness is defined as eq. (2). $h_i(x)$ is a weak learner and α_i is the weight of the weak learner. k is the number of "face coordinates candidates" and i is the number of weak learners.

$$z_k = \sum_{weak\ learners} \alpha_i h_i(x) \tag{2}$$

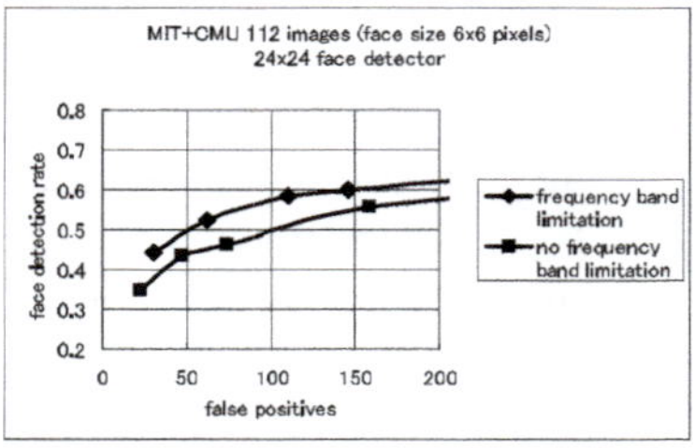

Fig. 12. Effect of frequency band limitation: face detector

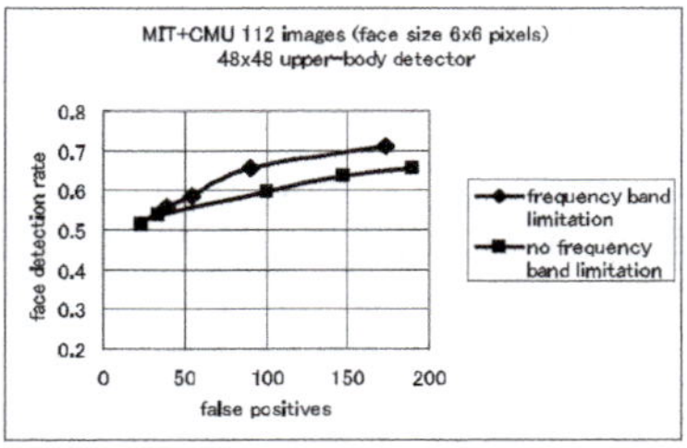

Fig. 13. Effect of frequency band limitation: upper-body detector

Two or more "face coordinate candidates" generated around one face are merged. Then one set of coordinates is finally made to correspond to one face in the detection process. When merging candidate locations,

$$Z = \sum_k z_k \tag{3}$$

is calculated, which corresponds to "face coordinates" that were made by merging "face coordinate candidates". This value is inferred as a "face-likeness".

Now, two detectors are applied independently to an input image and the 2D vector Z is obtained for an image that is finally detected by further merging the result. Final judgement is made by a SVM whose input is this 2D vector Z.

We applied the proposed method to 6 × 6 pixel evaluation images. The result is presented in Figure. 14. The results before combined use are shown as "48 × 48 upper-body detector" and "24 × 24 face detector" in Figure. 14. At the point of 100 false positives, the face detection rates are improved to 71% from 58% (24 × 24 face detector) and 67% (48 × 48 upper-body detector). The result of the 6 × 6 face detector is plotted for comparison. The face detection rate is improved to 71% from 39% by our proposed method. Figure 15 is the result of our proposed method applied to the lower left image in Figure. 4.

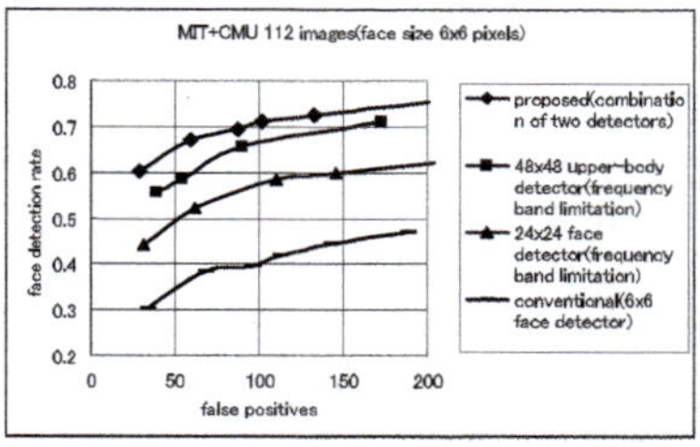

Fig. 14. Combination of two detectors in a SVM

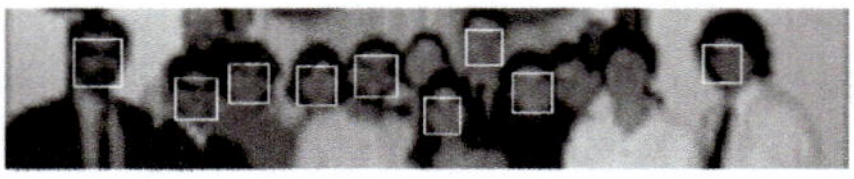

Fig. 15. Results of the proposed method as applied to 6 × 6 pixel evaluation images

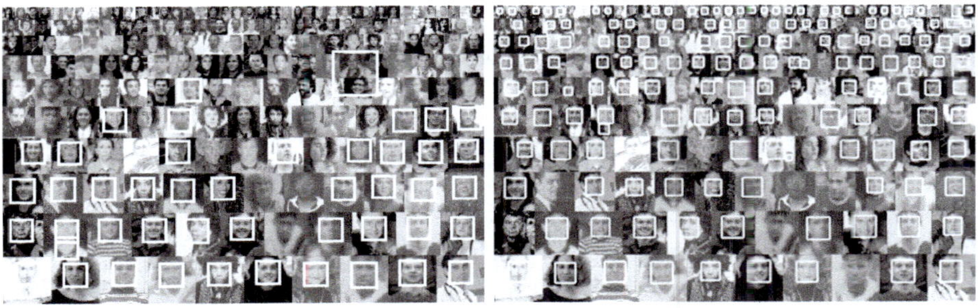

Fig. 16. Left: detected using a 24 × 24 face detector. Right: detected by the proposed method.

In addition, although 6 × 6 pixel faces have been studied so far, the proposed method can also detect a higher-resolution face image. Figure 16 shows this. An image in Figure. 16 consists of 10 layers. The top layer's resolution is 6 × 6 pixels; the bottom layer's resolution is 24 × 24 pixels. The left is the detected result of 24 × 24 face detector. Low-resolution faces are not detected at all. The right is the detection results of the proposed method. Faces of various sizes from 6 × 6 to 24 × 24 pixel are detected well.

4 Application to Real Data

We also applied our proposed method to real images other than MIT+CMU frontal face test set. Fig.17 is the detected result of our proposed method applied to a 720×480 pixel image (Face size is 6×6 pixel or 7×7 pixel). This image is a frame extracted from a movie. Fig.18 is an expanded image around pedestrians in Fig.17. Faces are correctly detected and some false positives are shown. We see false positives mostly appear in different places in each frames of the movie,

Fig. 17. Result of the proposed method applied to real data

Fig. 18. An expanded image around pedestrians in Fig. 17

so we think we can decrease the number of false positives by using information of two or more frames. Future studies will explore those areas.

5 Conclusions

We proposed a new method to detect faces from low-resolution images. A conventional AdaBoost-based face detector can detect only 39% of faces in 6×6 pixel evaluation images, but our proposed method can detect 71% of faces in those same evaluation images.

Although the AdaBoost-based detector was used for face detection in this paper, our proposed method is applicable also to other face detection methods. For example, as for Schneiderman's method, what is necessary for "Frequency band limitation" is to directly restrict the use of the high-frequency wavelet coefficient.

This study applied detectors to expanded low-resolution images, but the number of scanning patches was increased by expanding images. To resolve the increase in the number of false positives and processing time, it is better to scan without expanding an input image at first, then to detect by expanding only the region that offers the high possibility of being a face. This is a future work.

References

1. M.H. Yang, D.J. Kriegman and N. Ahuja. "Detecting Faces in images:A Survey," IEEE Trans. on PAMI, vol.24, no.1, pp.34-58, January, 2002.
2. H. Schneiderman. "Feature-Centric Evaluation for Efficient Cascaded Object Detection," in Proc. of CVPR, vol.2, pp.29-36, June, 2004.
3. M. Osadchy and D. Karen. "Image Detection Under Varying Illumination and Pose," in Proc. of ICCV, vol.II, pp.668-673, July, 2001
4. B. Wu, H. Ai, C. Huang, and S. Lao. "Fast Rotation Invariant Multi-view Face Detection Based on Real Adaboost," in Proc. of FGR, pp.79-84, May, 2004.
5. A. Torralba and P. Shina. "Detecting Faces in Impoverished Images," AI Memo 2001-028, CBCL Memo 208, 2001
6. Hannes Kruppa, Bernt Schiele. Using Local Context To Improve Face Detection. in BMVC,2003
7. P. Viola and M. Jones. "Rapid Object Detection Using a Boosted Cascade of Simple Features," in Proc. of CVPR, vol.1, pp.511-518, December, 2001
8. S.Z. Li, L. Zhu, Z.Q. Zhang, A. Blake, H.J. Zhang and H. Shum. "Statistical Learning of Multi-View Face Detection," in Proc. of ECCV, pp.67-81, May, 2002.
9. C. Liu and H.Y. Shum. "Kullback-Leibler Boosting," in Proc. of CVPR, vol.1, pp.587-594, June, 2003.
10. H.A. Rowley, S. Baluja, and T. Kanade. "Neural Network-Based Face Detection," IEEE Trans. on PAMI, vol.20, pp.23-38, January, 1998

Human Distribution Estimation Using Shape Projection Model Based on Multiple-Viewpoint Observations

Akira Utsumi[1], Hirotake Yamazoe[1], Ken-ichi Hosaka[1], and Seiji Igi[2]

[1] ATR Media Information Science Laboratories,
2-2-2 Hikaridai, Seikacho, Sorakugun, Kyoto, Kyoto 619-0288, Japan
{utsumi, yamazoe, hosaka}@atr.jp
[2] National Institute of Information and Communications Technology,
3-5 Hikaridai, Seikacho, Sorakugun, Kyoto, Kyoto 619-0289, Japan
igi@nict.go.jp

Abstract. This paper describes a method for estimating human distributions (quantities and locations) based on multiple-viewpoint image sequences. In the field of human image analysis, inter-human occlusion is a significant problem: when a scene includes a large number of occlusions, tracking of individual persons becomes difficult. Therefore updating a tracking-based model is not enough to estimate the distribution in complex scenes. In our method, the number of persons and their locations are directly estimated from a set of input images based on the fitting of a projected shape model. The model's complexity (number of persons) is determined based on the MDL (minimum description length) criterion. In addition, the image areas occluded by static objects are also detected and automatically excluded from the human distribution computations. We confirmed the feasibility of the proposed method through experiments using both synthesized and real images. Results show the effectiveness of our method.

1 Introduction

Vision-based human detection can be applied almost anywhere due to its lack of physical contact and its ability to detect unknown persons. Detecting and understanding human behavior is a challenging research domain in computer vision, and many vision researchers have already proposed methods for human motion detection/tracking [1, 2, 3, 4, 5, 6]. Most of these systems deal with the 3-D tracking of human movements. Dominant applications include human-machine interfaces using body movements, remote surveillance systems, and so on.

In vision-based human tracking, the most significant problem is occlusion. Since a human body is a three-dimensional articulated object, the appearance of human bodies can drastically change according to their distributions: when two or more persons are in a scene, one person can easily occlude others. In addition, a change of clothes and illumination conditions can also reduce the system's robustness.

P.J. Narayanan et al. (Eds.): ACCV 2006, LNCS 3851, pp. 797–806, 2006.

In an effort to solve this problem, we have investigated a multiple camera based human detection method [7]. Because of its strong ability to reduce the impact of occlusions, multiple-camera-based tracking has attracted the attention of many researchers [8, 9, 10, 11, 12].

Generally speaking, however, the number of required viewpoints in multiple-camera systems changes drastically depending on the size of the observation area and the human distributions (distances among persons). In addition, it becomes difficult to avoid occlusions by adding more cameras when people get too close to each other. In most conventional systems, each person in the scene is independently tracked in accordance with their motions. Therefore, failure of the tracking process can break down the system permanently. One way to tackle these problems is to improve the human-detection performance [7, 13]. By detecting observed humans accordingly, the system can restart the tracking process of them when the occlusion state finishes; however, it is difficult to process occluded humans by this approach. In this paper, instead, we model the mechanism of occlusions by also using a 3-D projection model, in which human distributions are directly estimated from observed images. By applying this method, our system can obtain estimations without breakdown even if the scene includes many occlusions.

In the next section, we briefly summarize related works and introduce our algorithm, which uses a model selection criterion. In Section 3, we outline our observation projection model, and in Section 4 we briefly introduce the minimum description length principle. Section 5 gives the detailed algorithm of distribution estimation and Section 6 describes the experiments conducted to clarify the effectiveness of our method. Finally, Section 7 concludes this paper.

2 Estimating Human Distribution Using Model Selection Criteria

In the analysis of human images, the number of persons existing in scene is generally unknown. However, if one could observe each person independently without occlusions, determination of the number becomes relatively easy; in fact, most human-tracking systems assume individual tracking to initialize their models [8, 9, 10, 12]. Such systems can work properly when the number of occlusions is small, though individual tracking becomes difficult in more complex scenes. In the proposed method, the number of persons in a scene and their locations that have the highest likelihood are directly estimated by model adaptation. According to the method, we can deal with input images that feature strong occlusions.

Generally, if a model is fitted to the observed data without limiting the number of model parameters, the model with a larger number of parameters has a smaller fitting error. Therefore, if a model is selected based only on the fitting errors, the model having more parameters is always selected. This problem is known as model selection, and several statistical criteria such as AIC and MDL have been proposed to obtain models of balanced size. This paper also applies the model selection method to determine the number of humans in a scene.

Regarding a statistical model for object tracking in vision research, a sophisticated model has already been proposed that approximates an object's motion as the motion of multiple particles [14]. In such a method, however, the model selection method is still required to determine the model's complexity. Furthermore, in the case of human tracking where the shape of the target object is approximately known, a method to directly model the relation between the target (a unit of a moving object) and its projection in images is more helpful.

In the next section, we describe our shape-projection model.

3 Shape Projection Model

In this section, we describe the shape-projection model used in the proposed method. By assuming the well known pin-hole camera model, the relation between a 3-D point (X, Y, Z) and its 2-D projection point in the image (x, y) follows the equation below.

$$k \begin{bmatrix} x \\ y \\ 1 \end{bmatrix} = \boldsymbol{S} \begin{bmatrix} \boldsymbol{R}\, \boldsymbol{t} \end{bmatrix} \begin{bmatrix} X \\ Y \\ Z \\ 1 \end{bmatrix} \tag{1}$$

Here, $\boldsymbol{S}$ is an intrinsic parameter for determining perspective projection, while $\boldsymbol{R}$ and $\boldsymbol{t}$ denote 3-D camera pose and position, respectively. An input image can be considered as the result of projecting a single or multiple human shapes according to the relation above.

Here, we divide the detection area (floor) into M blocks; x_j denotes the existence of people at block j $(1 \leq j \leq M)$.

$$x_j = \begin{cases} 0 \text{ (a person exists at block } j) \\ 1 \text{ (no person exists at block } j) \end{cases} \tag{2}$$

A human distribution can then be described as an M-dimensional vector $\boldsymbol{X}$ as follows:

$$\boldsymbol{X} = \begin{bmatrix} x_1\, x_2 \cdots x_M \end{bmatrix}'. \tag{3}$$

On the other hand, we denote an input image of the distribution $\boldsymbol{X}$ observed by camera k as $\boldsymbol{A}_k$.

$$\boldsymbol{A}^k = \begin{bmatrix} a_1^k\, a_2^k \cdots a_N^k \end{bmatrix}' \tag{4}$$

Here, a_i^k is a pixel value of i-th pixel at camera k (N is the size of an image).

$$a_i^k = \begin{cases} 0 \text{ (} a_i^k \text{ belongs to human region)} \\ 1 \text{ (} a_i^k \text{ does not belong to human region)} \end{cases} \tag{5}$$

Now, we consider the relation between them, focusing on the case where a person exists on a specific block l only and is represented as $\boldsymbol{X}_l$:

$$\begin{aligned} \boldsymbol{X}_l &= \begin{bmatrix} x_1\, x_2 \cdots x_M \end{bmatrix}' \\ x_j &= \begin{cases} 1\ (j = l) \\ 0\ (j \neq l) \end{cases} . \end{aligned} \tag{6}$$

$\boldsymbol{P}_0$ (0 degree) $\boldsymbol{P}_{45}$ (45 degree) $\boldsymbol{P}_{90}$ (90 degree)

Fig. 1. Average images

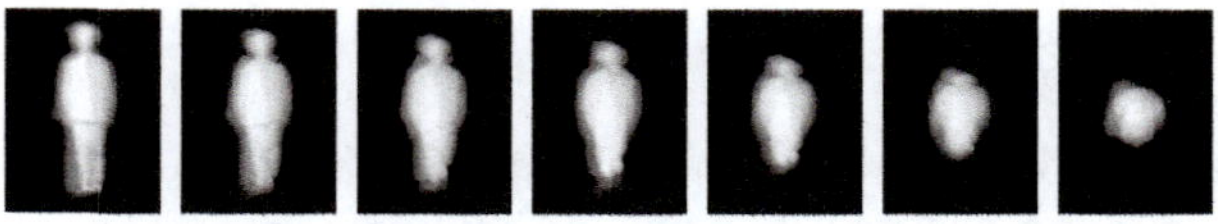
$\theta = 0$ $\theta = 15$ $\theta = 30$ $\theta = 45$ $\theta = 60$ $\theta = 75$ $\theta = 90$

Fig. 2. Examples of projected images

We denote the input image in this situation by camera k as $\boldsymbol{A}_l^k$.

In the case where multiple persons are present, the input images of projections of one or more persons overlap. For instance, in the case where L persons are located at $x_{l_1}, \cdots, x_{l_L}$, the observed image $\boldsymbol{A}^k$ can be expressed as follows:

$$\boldsymbol{A}^k = \boldsymbol{A}_{l_1}^k \cup \boldsymbol{A}_{l_2}^k \cup \cdots \cup \boldsymbol{A}_{l_L}^k . \tag{7}$$

When we have K cameras, a set of the model image is described as follows:

$$\boldsymbol{A} = \left[\boldsymbol{A}^{1'}\ \boldsymbol{A}^{2'} \cdots\ \boldsymbol{A}^{K'}\right]' . \tag{8}$$

In real situations, the projected image can vary according not only to the position, but also to the build and posture of each person. Consequently, we can create a 3-D shape model based on multiple subjects with multiple appearances. Here, we model the human shapes based on about 100 sample images for three observation directions (Fig. 1). Figure 2 shows an example of the generated model.

4 MDL Principle

The MDL (Minimum Description Length) principle is a method for determining a proper model to describe observed data [15]. Under the MDL principle, a model is selected based on both the complexity and fitting errors between the model and input data. In general, MDL can be defined as follows:

$$\text{MDL} = -(\text{Maximum Log Likelihood}) + \frac{F}{2} \log n, \tag{9}$$

where F represents the degrees of freedom for the model considered. The MDL principle has already seen used in many computer-vision and image-processing studies such as image segmentation [16], curve fitting [17], and so on.

In this paper, we apply that principle to human image analysis. In human images, the number of persons in a scene is generally unknown and has to be estimated somehow. As mentioned before, occlusions in images make accurate tracking difficult, thus raising the need for a method to directly estimate the number of humans and their locations. Our method divides the target area into several discrete blocks and estimates the existence of persons for each block based on the 3-D/2-D shape-projection model using the MDL principle.

We describe the estimation process in the following section.

5 Estimation of Human Distributions

In this section, we explain our method of estimating human distributions.

5.1 Observation Vector

Here, assuming color image inputs, an image $\boldsymbol{C}^K$ for camera K consisting of N pixels can be described as follows:

$$\boldsymbol{C}_t^k = \left[\boldsymbol{c}_1^k \; \boldsymbol{c}_2^k \cdots \boldsymbol{c}_N^k\,\right]', \tag{10}$$

$$\boldsymbol{c}_{i,t}^k = \left[r_{i,t}^k \; g_{i,t}^k \; b_{i,t}^k\right]'. \tag{11}$$

To simplify the calculation, here we select the pixels largely changed in a certain time period as human regions. We can then produce input vector $\boldsymbol{Z}^k$ for camera k, as follows:

$$\boldsymbol{Z}_t^k = \left[z_{1,t}^k \; z_{2,t}^k \cdots z_{N,t}^k\right], \tag{12}$$

$$z_i^k = \begin{cases} 0 \; ((\boldsymbol{c}_{i,t}^k - \bar{\boldsymbol{c}}_{i,t}^k)'(\boldsymbol{c}_{i,t}^k - \bar{\boldsymbol{c}}_{i,t}^k) < threshold) \\ 1 \text{ (otherwise)}, \end{cases} \tag{13}$$

$$\bar{\boldsymbol{c}}_{i,t}^k = \frac{1}{s}\sum_{j=t-s}^{t-1} \boldsymbol{c}_{i,t-j}, \tag{14}$$

For k cameras, a set of observation vectors $\boldsymbol{Z}_t$ can be defined as follows:

$$\boldsymbol{Z}_t = \left[\boldsymbol{Z}_t^{1'} \; \boldsymbol{Z}_t^{2'} \cdots \boldsymbol{Z}_t^{K'}\right]'. \tag{15}$$

5.2 Mask-Based Obstacle Representations

In a vision based tracking, the existence of occluding objects also cause serious problems to model reconstruction as well as inter-human occlusions. Fortunately, in our method, distribution estimation process can work correctly by just excluding the occlusion area from the evaluation process. Here, we represent the occluding area in camera k as the mask image $\boldsymbol{M}_k$.

$$\boldsymbol{M}^k = \left[m_1^k \; m_2^k \cdots m_N^k\right]', \tag{16}$$

$$m_i^k = \begin{cases} 0 \text{ (pixel } i \in \text{occluding area)} \\ 1 \text{ (otherwise).} \end{cases} \quad (17)$$

5.3 Model Description

In real situations, ideal observations are not allowed due to observation errors. Here, we model the observation errors as phenomena in which the observation values are inversed. At this point, we describe the probability of $z_j = 0$ for a human region as p and the probability of $z_j = 1$ for the background region as q.

Then, the observation probability of a set of images $\boldsymbol{Z}$ under the model distribution $\boldsymbol{A}$ becomes

$$P(\boldsymbol{Z}|\boldsymbol{A}) = p^{n_a}(1-p)^{n_b} q^{n_c}(1-q)^{n_d}. \quad (18)$$

Here, n_a, n_b, n_c and n_d are the total pixel numbers of $(a = 1, z = 1)$, $(a = 1, z = 0)$, $(a = 0, z = 1)$ and $(a = 0, z = 0)$, respectively, as follows:

$$\begin{aligned} n_a &= (\boldsymbol{A} \cap \boldsymbol{M} \cap \boldsymbol{Z})' \cdot (\boldsymbol{A} \cap \boldsymbol{M} \cap \boldsymbol{Z}), \\ n_b &= (\boldsymbol{A} \cap \boldsymbol{M} \cap \bar{\boldsymbol{Z}})' \cdot (\boldsymbol{A} \cap \boldsymbol{M} \cap \bar{\boldsymbol{Z}}), \\ n_c &= (\bar{\boldsymbol{A}} \cap \boldsymbol{M} \cap \boldsymbol{Z})' \cdot (\bar{\boldsymbol{A}} \cap \boldsymbol{M} \cap \boldsymbol{Z}), \\ n_d &= (\bar{\boldsymbol{A}} \cap \boldsymbol{M} \cap \bar{\boldsymbol{Z}})' \cdot (\bar{\boldsymbol{A}} \cap \boldsymbol{M} \cap \bar{\boldsymbol{Z}}). \end{aligned} \quad (19)$$

As a result a log likelihood of input vector $\boldsymbol{Z}_t$ to a model $\boldsymbol{A}$ can be drawn:

$$\begin{aligned} -\log P(\boldsymbol{Z}|\boldsymbol{A}) = &-n_a \log p - n_b \log(1-p) - n_c \log q \\ &-n_d \log(1-q). \end{aligned} \quad (20)$$

Then, the description length for this model can be calculated:

$$\begin{aligned} D_s(\boldsymbol{A}, \boldsymbol{Z}) = &-n_a \log p - n_b \log(1-p) - n_c \log q \\ &-n_d \log(1-q) - \frac{h}{2} \log M + \text{const.} \end{aligned} \quad (21)$$

In the next section, we attempt to determine whether the human distributions match the input images based on this criterion.

5.4 Search Process for Human Distribution Estimation

According to the criteria above, we search for human locations in the scene that match a set of input images. In the search process, we start with the 0-person case and gradually increase the number of model humans incrementally. For a every person added to the model, reallocations of all other persons are considered. Finally, when the addition of a new person does not decrease the score (description length L), then the search process is terminated.

This process is summarized as follows:

Algorithm: Search Process

$L := 0$
$D_{min} := D(\boldsymbol{O}, \boldsymbol{Z})$
do
  flag $= 0$
  for $i = L : 1$
    for $l_i = 1 : M$
      $\boldsymbol{A} = \boldsymbol{A}_{l_1} \cup \boldsymbol{A}_{l_2} \cup \cdots \cup \boldsymbol{A}_{l_L}$
      if $D(\boldsymbol{A}, \boldsymbol{Z}) + \frac{L}{2} \log M < L_{min}$ **then**
        $D_{min} := D(\boldsymbol{A}, \boldsymbol{Z}) + \frac{L}{2} \log M$
        ans $:= \left[l_1 \; l_2 \cdots l_L\right]'$
        flag $:= 1$
      end if
    end for
  end for
while flag=1

6 Experiments

To confirm the efficiency of the proposed method, we conducted several experiments.

First, by using images synthesized with a shape projection model, we performed human position estimations. In the experiment, the detection area was approximately 330 × 330 cm. We installed three cameras around that area, divided the area into 30 × 30 cm blocks (11 × 11 blocks in total), and constructed our shape projection models for the three cameras. Figure 3 shows the camera configurations.

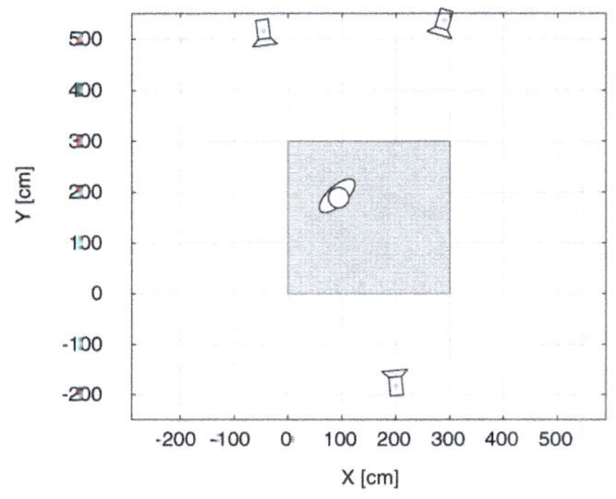

Fig. 3. Camera positions

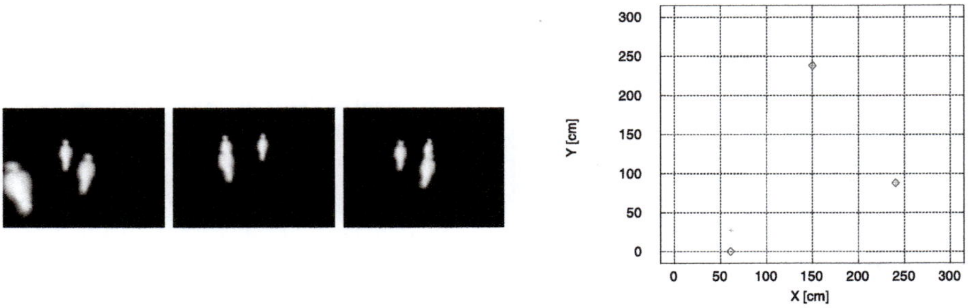

Fig. 4. Example of human distribution estimation (synthesized data)

As an example, we placed three 'virtual' human subjects at $(x, y) = (150, 240)$, $(x, y) = (60, 0)$ and $(x, y) = (240, 90)$ and synthesized images for the three cameras, which are shown in Fig. 4 left. Figure 4 right illustrates the result of position estimation. Here, $\diamond$ denotes the actual positions of subjects and $+$ denotes the estimation results. As the figure shows, our system could correctly estimate number of humans and their positions except for one person (his position is one block off.)

Fig. 5. Input images

Fig. 6. Results for an outdoor scene

Next, we applied our method to a set of real images. Using real cameras in the identical configuration with above, we captured sets of human images with one, two, three, four and five persons by locating the subjects at randomly selected locations. Figure 5 shows the part of input images. Figure 7 shows

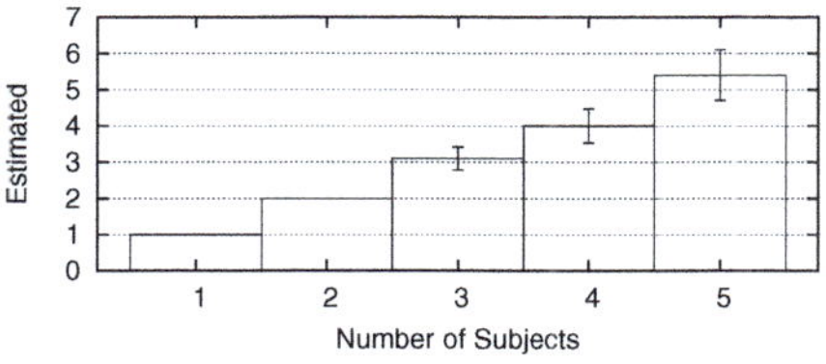

Fig. 7. Estimated number of humans

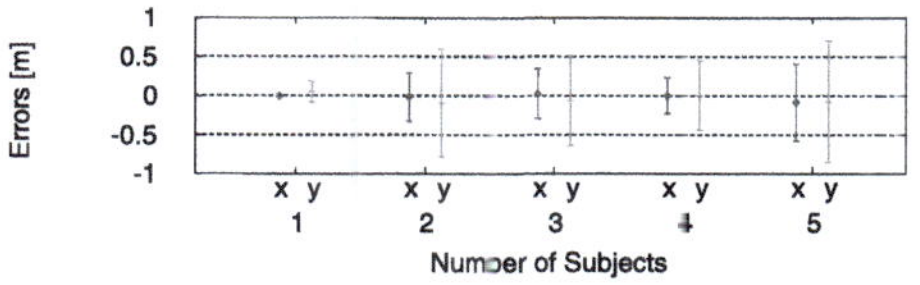

Fig. 8. Estimated Positions of Humans

averages and standard deviations of human number estimations, and Fig. 8 shows averages and standard deviations of distances between each estimated position and nearest correct location. As we can see, the proposed method can estimate human distributions with less than ±80-cm errors in position and ±1 error in number of humans. On the other hand, the error for the estimation of the number of persons becomes large when the number of humans increases. We consider this to be due to occlusions.

Finally, we applied our method to an outdoor scene. Figure 6 shows an example of the captured outdoor scene, The image sequence of which was captured from a camera set 10 m above the sidewalk. The right-hand side of Fig. 6 shows the result of the distribution estimation, indicating that our method also works well for sequences of real images.

7 Conclusion

In this paper, we presented a method to estimate the distribution of humans in a scene using MDL-based adaptation of a projection model founded on multiple camera observations. In our method, human distributions that have maximum likelihood for input images are estimated with a shape projection model, which models the relation between human position and input image. We confirmed the stability and efficiency of the proposed method through experiments using both synthesized and real data streams.

Future works include improving the calculation algorithm to obtain superior performance and to enhance the estimation accuracy.

This research was supported in part by the National Institute of Information and Communications Technology.

References

1. O'Rourke, J., Badler, N.J.: Model-based image analysis of human motion using constraint propagation. IEEE Pattern Analysis and Machine Intelligence **2** (1980) 522–536
2. Azarbayejani, A., Pentland, A.: Real-time self-calibrating stereo person tracking using 3-d shape estimation from blob features. In: Proceedings of 13th International Conference on Pattern Recognition. (1996) 627–632

3. Wren, C., Azarbayejani, A., Darrell, T., Pentland, A.: Pfinder: Real-time tracking of the human body. In: SPIE proceeding vol. 2615. (1996) 89–98
4. Waggg, D.K., Nixon, M.S.: On automated model-based extraction and analysis of gait. In: Proc. of the 6th IEEE International Conference on Automatic Face and Gesture Recognition. (2004) 11–16
5. Lim, J., Kriegman, D.: Tracking humans using prior and learned representations of shape and appearance. In: Proc. of the 6th IEEE International Conference on Automatic Face and Gesture Recognition. (2004) 869–874
6. Leibe, B., Seemann, E., Schiele, B.: Pedestrian detection in crowed scenes. In: Proc. of Computer Vision and Pattern Recognition. (2005) Volume1, 20–25
7. Utsumi, A., Tetsutani, N.: Human detection using geometrical pixel value structures. In: Proc. of the 5th IEEE International Conference on Automatic Face and Gesture Recognition. (2002) 372–377
8. Segen, J., Pingali, S.: A camera-based system for tracking people in real time. In: Proceedings of 13th International Conference on Pattern Recognition. (1996) 63–67
9. Cai, Q., Mitiche, A., Aggarwal, J.K.: Tracking human motion in an indoor environment. In: Proceedings of 2nd International Conference on Image Processing. (1995) 215–218
10. Cai, Q., Aggarwal, J.K.: Tracking human motion using multiple cameras. In: Proceedings of 13th International Conference on Pattern Recognition. (1996) 68–72
11. Kettnaker, V., Zabih, R.: Counting people from multiple cameras. In: Proc. of the IEEE International Conference on Multimedia Computing and Systems. (1999) Volume2, 7–11
12. Arita, D., ichiro Taniguchi, R., Yonemoto, S., Hamada, Y.: A real-time multi-view image processing system on pc cluster. In: Proceedings of Fourth Asian Conference on Computer Vision. (2000) 270–275
13. Papageorgiou, C., Evgeniou, T., Poggio, T.: A trainable pedestrian detection system. In: Proc. of Intelligent Vehicles. (1998) 241–246
14. Isard, M., Blake, A.: Condensation - conditional density propagation for visual tracking. International Journal of Computer Vision **29** (1998) 5–28
15. Rissanen, J.: A universal prior for integers and estimation by minimum description length. The Annals of Stat. **11** (1983) 416–431
16. Zhu, S.C., Yoille, A.: Region competition: Unifying snakes, region growing, and bayes/mdl for multiband image segmentation. IEEE Pattern Analysis and Machine Intelligence **18** (1996) 884–900
17. Cham, T., Cipolla, R.: Automated b-spline curve representation incorporating mdl and error-minimizing control point insertion strategies. IEEE Pattern Analysis and Machine Intelligence **21** (1999) 49–53

Modelling the Effect of View Angle Variation on Appearance-Based Gait Recognition

Shiqi Yu, Daoliang Tan, and Tieniu Tan

National Laboratory of Pattern Recognition,
Institute of Automation, Chinese Academy of Sciences,
P.O.Box 2728, Beijing, 100080, China
{sqyu, dltan, tnt}@nlpr.ia.ac.cn

Abstract. In recent years, many gait recognition algorithms have been developed, but most of them depend on a specific view angle. However, view angle variation is a significant factor among those that affect gait recognition performance. It is important to find the relationship between the performance and the view angle. In this paper, we discuss the effect of view angle variation on appearance-based gait recognition performance. A multi-view gait database (124 subjects and 11 view directions) is created for our research. We propose two models, a geometrical one and a mathematical one, to model the effect of view angle variation on appearance-based gait recognition. These models will be valuable for designing robust gait recognition systems.

1 Introduction

Gait, as an attractive biometric for human identification at a distance, has received an increasing interest from researchers in the computer vision community. The study by Murray et al. [1] is supportive of the uniqueness of gait for a person. More importantly, gait has the advantages of being non-contact, non-invasive and easily acquired at distance in contrast with other biometrics.

Among the factors which affect gait recognition performance such as view angle, clothing, shoe type, carrying condition and surface type [2], view angle variation is a significant one since for a given gait recognition system, it is impossible to expect all the subjects to walk in a particular direction. Furthermore, most appearance-based gait recognition algorithms depend upon a specific view angle. Some researchers in computer vision have been devoting their efforts to designing view-invariant and multi-view algorithms. Johnson et al. [3] propose a multi-view algorithm, which recovers static body parameters of subjects and uses these view-invariant parameters to recognize people. Kale et al. [4] use a sophisticated method to eliminate the effect from view angle change. They synthesize the side view from another arbitrary view using a single camera through the perspective projection model or the optical flow-based structure from motion equations.

Although many gait recognition algorithms for human identification have been proposed and developed over the past years, most of them are view-dependent, which will limit their practical applications. In addition, there are two remaining open problems.

P.J. Narayanan et al. (Eds.): ACCV 2006, LNCS 3851, pp. 807–816, 2006.

One is which view is the most suitable for gait recognition and why it is. Kale et al [4] declare that the side view is the best choice in practice, but no theoretical results, for the time being, have been given to prove that. Another open problem is how view angle variation affects the performance of gait recognition. Intuitively, the greater the angle between the gallery (training) set and the probe (test) set is, the worse the recognition performance. However, there are not been experimental or theoretical results on the relationship between gait recognition performance and view angles. It is obvious that the answers to the above questions are significant for designing robust gait recognition systems.

This paper proposes two models, a geometrical one and a mathematical one, in an attempt to address these two questions. The purpose of this paper is to investigate and analyze the effect of view angle on the performance of appearance-based gait recognition.

The remainder of this paper is organized as follows. Section 2 presents our definition of performance function. In Section 3, we discuss a multi-view gait database. Then, Section 4 introduces our experiments and gives experimental results. Two models are given in Section 5. Finally, this paper is concluded in Section 6.

2 Performance Evaluation Function

In our experiments, the correct classification rate (CCR) is used to evaluate the performance of gait recognition. Suppose, without the loss of generality, that the angle between the view direction of gallery set and the walking direction is θ_g, and the angle constituted by the view direction of probe set and the walking direction is θ_p. Obviously the CCR is a function of variables θ_g and θ_p.

$$CCR = f(\theta_g, \theta_p) \quad \theta_g \in [0^\circ, 360^\circ), \theta_p \in [0^\circ, 360^\circ) \tag{1}$$

If we can get the analytic expression of the function $f(\theta_g, \theta_p)$, then how θ_g and θ_p affect the recognition performance can be solved with ease. Discovering the expression of $f(\theta_g, \theta_p)$, however, can not be easily achieved. It is impossible to precisely obtain the value of $f(\theta_g, \theta_p)$ at any point in space $\mathbb{P} = [0^\circ, 360^\circ) \times [0^\circ, 360^\circ)$ by way of experimental methods as $\mathbb{P}$ is a continuous space. A sophisticated way to solve this problem is to compute the value of $f(\theta_g, \theta_p)$ through experiments at a discrete and limited subset of $\mathbb{P}$. The subset can be $P = \{\Delta\theta, 2\Delta\theta, \cdots, 360^\circ\} \times \{\Delta\theta, 2\Delta\theta, \cdots, 360^\circ\}$, and $\Delta\theta$ is a small angle.

As mentioned above, the video data ought to be collected from view angles ranging from $\Delta\theta$ to 360° at an increment $\Delta\theta$. When the camera is far from the subject, the silhouette taken from the left hand side of the subject is, from the perspective of geometry, basically similar to that from the right hand side. Therefore, the video data just need to be collected from only one side (the left side in this paper). The video data in our experiments is collected at view angles $\{0^\circ, \Delta\theta, 2\Delta\theta, \cdots, 180^\circ\}$, and $\Delta\theta = 18^\circ$. The CCR in the discrete subset $\{0, 1, 2, \cdots, \lfloor \frac{180}{\Delta\theta} \rfloor\} \times \{0, 1, 2, \cdots, \lfloor \frac{180}{\Delta\theta} \rfloor\}$ can be obtained by experiments and be formulated as Equation(2).

$$CCR = F(n,k) = f(n \cdot \Delta\theta, k \cdot \Delta\theta)$$
$$n = 0, 1, 2, \cdots, \left\lfloor \frac{180}{\Delta\theta} \right\rfloor \quad (2)$$
$$k = 0, 1, 2, \cdots, \left\lfloor \frac{180}{\Delta\theta} \right\rfloor$$

An algebraic formula $\tilde{f}(\theta_g, \theta_p)$, which is an approximation to $f(\theta_g, \theta_p)$ and satisfies $\tilde{f}(\theta_g, \theta_p) \approx f(\theta_g, \theta_p)$, can be acquired by data fitting and interpolation to $F(n,k)$. A simple yet useful and reasonable model $\tilde{f}(\theta_g, \theta_p)$ is presented in Section 6 on the basis of numerically analyzing the experimental results. The CCR at arbitrary θ_g and θ_p can be predicted or estimated with this model. It is easy to imagine that this work has a great practical meaning.

3 A Multi-view Gait Database

To analyze the impact of view angle changes on gait recognition performance, a multi-view gait database is needed. In addition to consisting of a great number of subjects, the database should be composed of the gait data collected from many view angles. The minimum angle interval ought to be relatively small.

For the purpose of developing gait recognition algorithms, a variety of gait databases have been created by many research units, such as USF [2], Soton [5], CASIA [6],

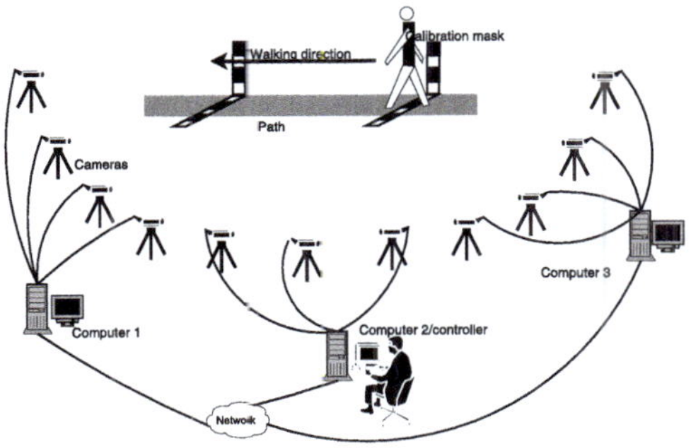

Fig. 1. The schematic diagram of gait data collection system

Fig. 2. Sample frames from 11 view angles

UMD, etc. The existing gait databases are either not large enough, or only captured from few view angles. These gait databases do not fulfill the requirements of view angle variation research. We develop a gait data collection system for creating a multi-view gait database which meets the requirements of view angle variation research. 11 cameras were used to capture gait videos as illustrated in Fig. 1.

All the subjects are asked to walk naturally on the concrete ground along a straight line in an indoor environment. The videos can be simultaneously captured by 11 cameras from different view directions. At last we successfully collect 124 subjects' gait data (94 males and 30 females). The view angle θ between the view direction and the walking direction takes on the values of $0°, 18°, 36°, \cdots$, and $180°$, as delineated in Fig. 1. Each subject walks along the straight line 10 times (6 for normal walking, 2 for walking in a coat and 2 for walking with a bag), and 11 video sequences are captured each time. Thus, there are 110 sequences for each subject, and a total of $110 \times 124 = 13640$ video sequences in our database. All the video sequences have the same resolution of 320×240 pixels. Some sample frames from 11 cameras are shown in Fig. 2.

Our database comprises those factors affecting gait recognition: view angles (11 views), clothing (with or without in a coat), and carrying condition (with or without a bag). Only view angles is studied here, though other factors are interesting to study too.

4 Gait Feature Extraction

There are many appearance-based gait features in the literature. Most of them are extracted from human silhouettes or outer contours. Here we choose one typical feature from each category. One is gait energy image (GEI), and it is extracted from human silhouettes. GEI is introduced in [7], which is the average of all silhouettes in a video sequence. The other is key Fourier descriptors (KFDs), and it is extracted from human outer contours. KFD method is proposed by Yu et al. [8], which is the key component of Fourier descriptors computed from human contours. Finally, we use the nearest neighbor classifier to perform classification.

4.1 Silhouette Segmentation

Given a fixed camera, the human silhouette can be extracted by background subtraction and thresholding. We take advantage of the method given in [9] to segment human silhouette from image sequences. The sizes of the silhouettes we extracted are not unique, and the silhouettes need to be normalized to the same size.

4.2 GEI Feature Extraction

The gait energy image is reported as a good feature which is robust to silhouette errors and image noise, and is defined by [7]

$$G(x, y) = \frac{1}{N} \sum_{t=1}^{N} I(x, y, t) \tag{3}$$

where N is the number of frames in the sequence $I(x, y, t)$, t is the frame number, x and y are the image coordinate [7].

4.3 KFD Feature Extraction

To extract KFD feature, the outer contour first needs to be obtained. The outer contour can be easily derived using a border-following algorithm based on connectivity. Then all the contours and the gait cycle are normalized to have the same number (N) of sample and the same number (T) of frame, respectively. All Fourier descriptors $g(i)$ can be obtained by discrete Fourier transform. The KFDs are defined as in [8]:

$$G = \left[\frac{|g(2T)|}{|g(T)|}, \frac{|g(3T)|}{|g(T)|}, \ldots, \frac{|g((N-1)T)|}{|g(T)|} \right] \tag{4}$$

where N is the number of sample points of each contour, and T is the number of frames in a gait cycle.

5 Experimental Results and Analysis

Each subject has 6 normal walking sequences at each view angle. Wet put the first 4 sequences into the gallery set, and the last 2 sequences into the probe set. A number of experiments are carried out to discover the relationship between gait recognition performance and view angles. Fig. 3 and Table 1 show the CCRs of the experiments which take GEI as a feature. It can be noticed from Fig. 3 that there exist two peaks on the CCR curves in each subfigure. and that CCR reaches the first peak at $\theta_p = \theta_g$ and the second peak at $\theta_p = 180° - \theta_g$. A geometrical model is proposed for explaining the existence of these two peaks. Fig. 4 and Table 2 display the CCRs of the experiments which take KFDs as a feature. As in Fig. 3 and Table 1, a similar phenomenon can be found in Fig. 4 and Table 2.

We can get that CCRs basically remains a constant C_M along the major diagonal line ($\theta_g = \theta_p$) of Tables 1 and 2, and a constant C_m along the major skew diagonal line ($\theta_g = 180° - \theta_p$) except $(\theta_g, \theta_p) \in \{(108°, 72°), (90°, 90°), (72°, 108°)\}$.

From Figures 3(f) and 4(f), it can be seen that the CCR basically remains high when θ_p varies around 90°. Thus, the CCR at the side view is robust to view angle change with respect to other views.

Table 1. CCR table (%) for GEI (rank=1)

Gallery angle θ_g	Probe angle θ_p										
	0°	**18°**	**36°**	**54°**	**72°**	**90°**	**108°**	**126°**	**144°**	**162°**	**180°**
0°	99.2	31.9	9.3	4.0	3.2	3.2	2.0	2.0	4.8	12.9	37.9
18°	23.8	99.6	39.9	8.9	4.4	3.6	3.6	5.2	13.7	33.5	10.9
36°	4.4	37.9	97.6	29.8	11.7	6.9	8.1	13.3	23.4	13.3	2.0
54°	2.4	3.6	29.0	97.2	23.0	16.5	21.4	29.0	21.4	4.8	1.2
72°	0.8	4.4	7.3	21.8	97.2	81.5	68.1	21.0	5.6	3.6	1.6
90°	0.4	2.4	4.8	17.7	82.3	97.6	82.3	15.3	5.2	3.6	1.2
108°	1.6	1.6	2.0	16.9	71.4	87.9	95.6	37.1	6.0	2.0	2.0
126°	1.2	2.8	6.0	37.5	33.5	22.2	48.0	96.8	26.6	4.4	2.0
144°	3.6	5.2	28.2	18.5	4.4	1.6	3.2	43.1	96.4	5.6	2.8
162°	12.1	39.1	15.7	2.4	1.6	0.8	0.8	2.4	5.2	98.4	28.6
180°	41.1	19.8	8.1	3.2	2.0	0.8	1.6	3.6	12.5	51.2	99.6

Table 2. CCR table (%) for KFD (rank=1)

Gallery angle θ_g	**Probe angle θ_p**										
	0°	**18°**	**36°**	**54°**	**72°**	**90°**	**108°**	**126°**	**144°**	**162°**	**180°**
0°	71.8	5.2	5.2	2.4	0.8	1.2	1.2	0.8	1.6	3.2	33.1
18°	3.6	49.2	14.5	4.4	2.8	3.2	4.0	3.6	4.0	8.9	4.0
36°	2.8	12.1	72.6	11.7	3.6	2.8	2.0	3.2	14.1	10.9	2.4
54°	2.0	3.2	10.5	69.4	7.7	2.4	4.4	14.9	10.9	3.2	0.8
72°	0.4	0.8	2.8	12.9	77.8	16.9	25.0	8.9	2.4	1.2	0.0
90°	0.4	0.8	3.6	4.4	23.0	75.0	20.6	4.0	2.0	0.8	1.2
108°	0.4	2.4	3.2	5.2	20.6	21.4	69.8	10.5	2.8	1.2	0.8
126°	0.8	3.6	4.8	14.9	11.7	5.6	14.1	71.4	10.5	3.6	1.6
144°	2.0	6.9	16.1	12.1	4.0	2.4	2.8	12.5	71.0	11.7	3.2
162°	2.8	10.9	10.9	1.6	2.0	2.4	2.8	6.0	11.3	72.2	3.6
180°	30.6	3.2	4.8	1.6	2.0	2.4	1.2	2.8	3.6	7.3	67.7

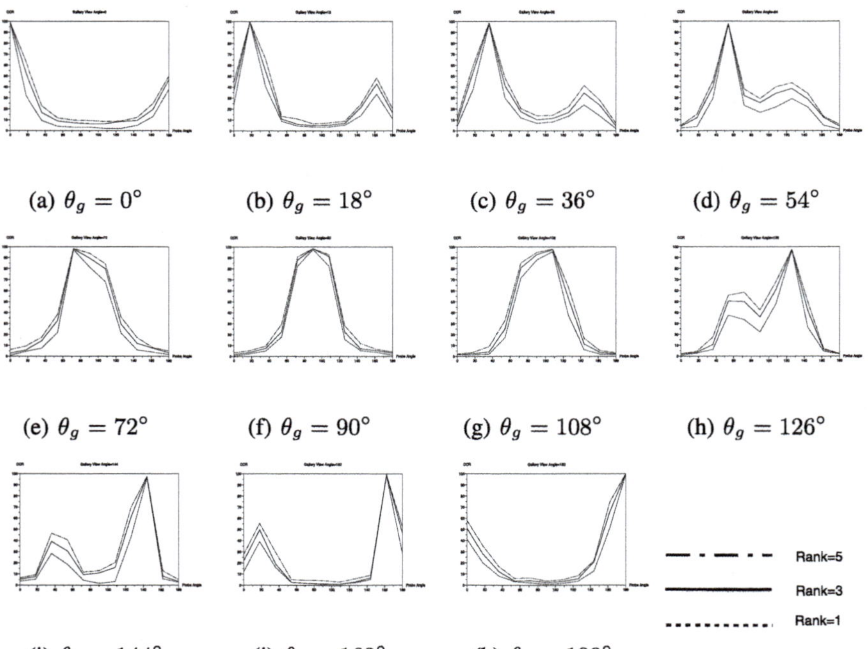

(a) $\theta_g = 0°$ (b) $\theta_g = 18°$ (c) $\theta_g = 36°$ (d) $\theta_g = 54°$

(e) $\theta_g = 72°$ (f) $\theta_g = 90°$ (g) $\theta_g = 108°$ (h) $\theta_g = 126°$

(i) $\theta_g = 144°$ (j) $\theta_g = 162°$ (k) $\theta_g = 180°$

Fig. 3. CCRs(%) for GEI(the abscissa is θ_p, and the ordinate is CCR)

5.1 A Geometrical Model

Why are there two symmetrical (though not strictly) peaks on the curves in Fig. 3 and 4? In our opinion, it is the human body symmetry that results in this phenomenon. Suppose that 3 images are, respectively, taken from 3 different view angles θ, $180° - \theta$, and $180° + \theta$, as illustrated in Fig. 5, and that the cameras are far away from the subject.

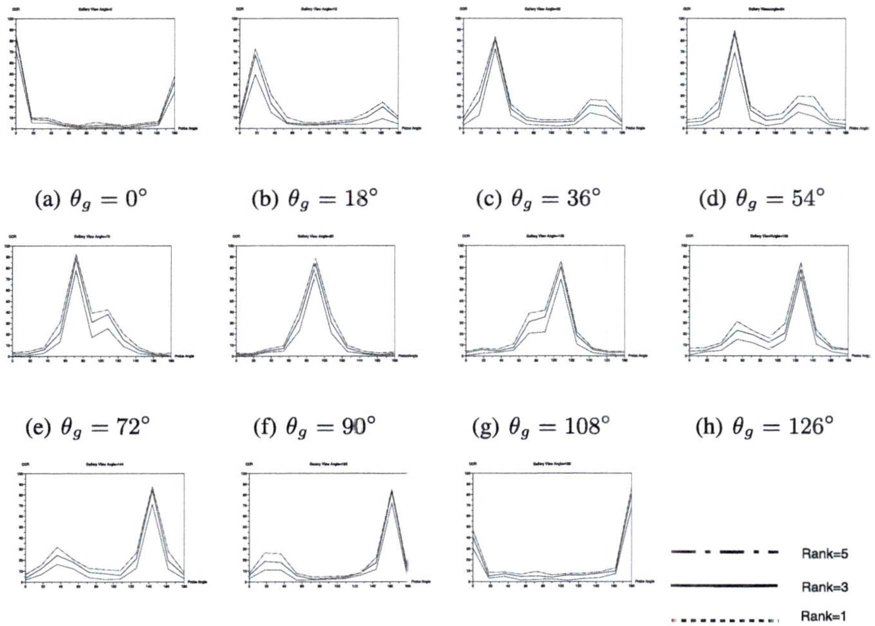

(a) $\theta_g = 0°$ (b) $\theta_g = 18°$ (c) $\theta_g = 36°$ (d) $\theta_g = 54°$

(e) $\theta_g = 72°$ (f) $\theta_g = 90°$ (g) $\theta_g = 108°$ (h) $\theta_g = 126°$

(i) $\theta_g = 144°$ (j) $\theta_g = 162°$ (k) $\theta_g = 180°$

Fig. 4. CCRs(%) for KFD(the abscissa is θ_p, and the ordinate is CCR)

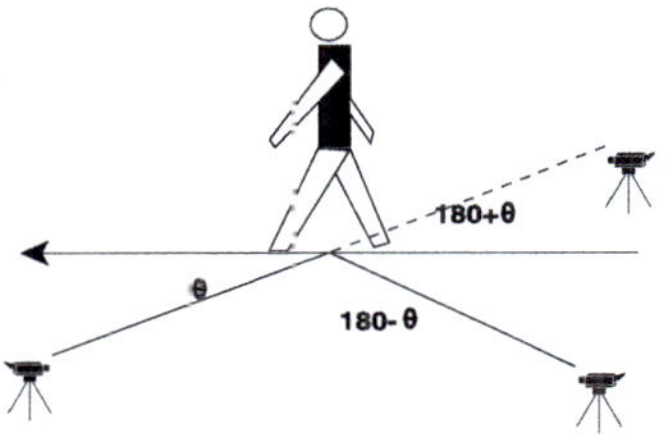

Fig. 5. Images at 3 view angles

$S(\theta)$, $S(180° - \theta)$ and $S(180° + \theta)$ represent the 3 human silhouettes extracted from the 3 corresponding images. For the distance between the cameras and the subject is large, we can reasonably consider:

$$S(\theta) \approx \overrightarrow{S}(180° + \theta) \tag{5}$$

where the symbol $\rightarrow$ means flip horizontally. On the other hand, human body has the symmetry, so we have

$$\overrightarrow{S}(180° + \theta) \approx S(180° - \theta) \tag{6}$$

Walking can partly break this symmetry with respect to a fixed view angle, which is the reason for using the symbol $\approx$ in Equation (6).

From Equations (5) and (6), it is straightforward to get Equation (7):

$$S(\theta) \approx S(180^\circ - \theta) \tag{7}$$

This implies that the silhouette from view angle θ is similar to that from view angle $180^\circ - \theta$. Thus, when the gallery angle is θ, using the data from $180^\circ - \theta$ as probe can produce relative higher CCR, from which a local peak positioned at $180^\circ - \theta$ naturally occurs, compared with the values of CCR at other view angles distant from θ.

5.2 A Mathematical Model

Based on the analysis in Section 6.1, there are two peaks on CCR curves in Figures 3 and 4. By observing the shapes of curves, we can reasonably use a mixed Gaussian function to model CCR curves.

The analytical expression of the mathematical model is defined as:

$$\tilde{f}(\theta_g, \theta_p) = C_M e^{-\frac{(\theta_g - \theta_p)^2}{2\sigma^2}} + C_m e^{-\frac{(180^\circ - \theta_g - \theta_p)^2}{2\sigma^2}} \left[1 - e^{-\frac{(\theta_g - \theta_p)^2}{2\sigma^2}}\right] \tag{8}$$

where C_M and C_m are the same as previous definitions. and σ is treated as a constant in our experiments, which indicates the level of performance deterioration when the probe view departs from the gallery view. The value of σ is optimized by the Curve Fitting Toolbox in Matlab, and it takes 15° here. $C_M e^{-\frac{(\theta_g - \theta_p)^2}{2\sigma^2}}$ and $C_m e^{-\frac{(180^\circ - \theta_g - \theta_p)^2}{2\sigma^2}}$ are two Gaussian functions which simulate the two ridges in Figures 6 and 8. $1 - e^{-\frac{(\theta_g - \theta_p)^2}{2\sigma^2}}$ is a weighting term which makes sure that $\tilde{f}(\theta_g, \theta_p)$ does not exceed unity.

The CCRs in Table 1 are shown in Fig. 6. Fig. 8 displays the CCRs in Table 2. Fig. 7 and Fig. 9 are the continuous versions of Fig. 6 and Fig. 8 obtained from our mathematical model (equation (8)), respectively. The theoretical results computed from Equation (8) generally conform to the experimental ones in Table 1 and Table 2.

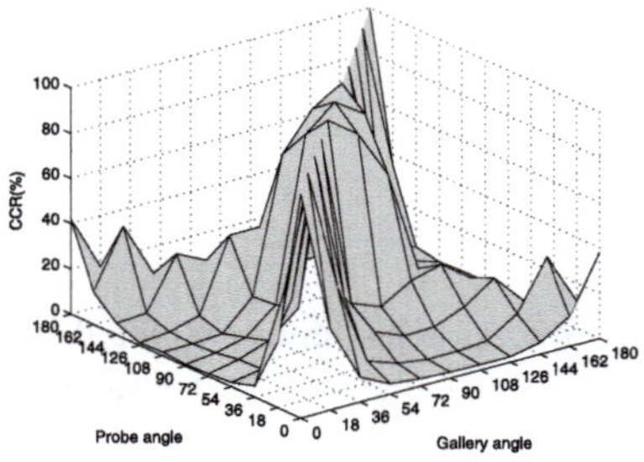

Fig. 6. CCRs for GEI

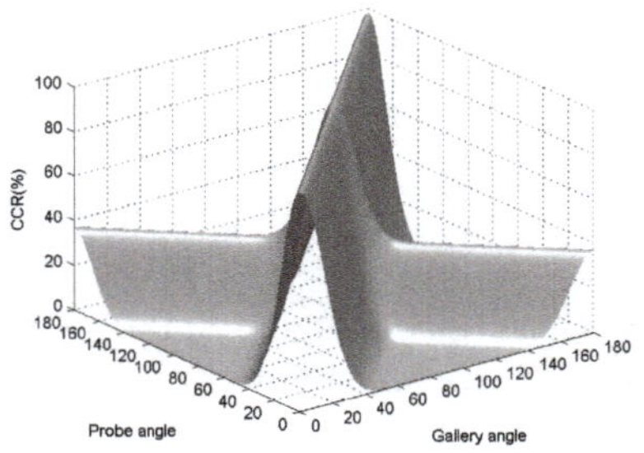

Fig. 7. The modelled CCRs for GEI

From Equation (8), Fig. 7 and Fig. 9, there are two perpendicular ridges which superpose each other. It is this superposition that makes the CCR around the site $(90^\circ, 90^\circ)$ much higher than in other regions. Thus, the CCR at the side view is robust to view angle variation.

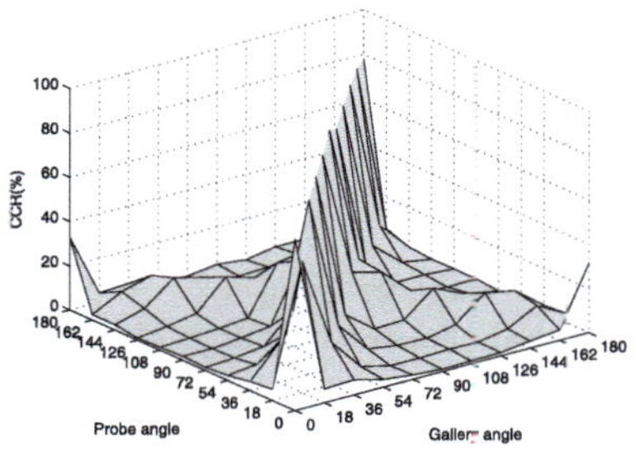

Fig. 8. CCRs for KFD

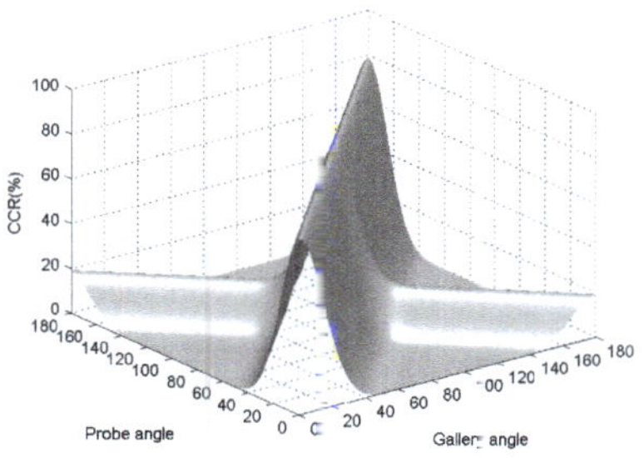

Fig. 9. The modelled CCRs for KFD

6 Conclusions and Future Work

In this paper, we have presented an analysis of the effect of view angle variation on the performance of appearance-based gait recognition methods the proposed and models. The novelty of our work is three-fold: first, it is a systematic study on multi-view gait recognition; secondly, it investigates how the performance is affected by view angle changes with a useful mathematical model depicting the relationship between view angle and performance(despite the current simplicity); last but obviously not least, it answers two open questions: why the side view is more suitable to recognize human gaits, and how view angle variation impacts the gait recognition performance. Our future work will be focused on view-invariant gait feature extraction, a better mathematical model taking into account the effect of θ_g, θ_p and features on σ, and the establishment of a multi-view gait database in an outdoor environment.

Acknowledgement

This work is partly supported by National Natural Science Foundation of China (Grant No. 60335010), National Basic Research Program of China (Grant No. 2004CB318100) and International Cooperation Program of Ministry of Science and Technology of China (Grant No. 2004DFA06900).

References

1. Murray, M.P.: Gait as a total pattern of movement. American Journal of Physical Medicine **46** (1967) 290–332
2. Sarkar, S., Phillips, P.J., Liu, Z., Vega, I.R., Grother, P., Bowyer, K.W.: The humanid gait challenge problem: Data sets, performance and analysis. IEEE Transactions on Pattern Analysis and Machine Intelligence **27** (2005) 162–177
3. Johnson, A.Y., Bobick, A.F.: A multi-view method for gait recognition using static body parameters. In: Proc. of 3rd International Conference on Audio and Video Based Biometric Person Authentication, Halmstad, Sweden (2001) 301–311

4. Kale, A., Chowdhury, A.K.R., Chellappa, R.: Towards a view invariant gait recognition algorithm. In: Proc. of IEEE Conference on Advanced Video and Signal Based Surveillance, FL, USA (2003) 143–150
5. Shutler, J.D., Grant, M.G., Nixon, M.S., Carter, J.N.: On a large sequence-based human gait database. In: Proc. of the 4th International Conference on Recent Advances in Soft Computing, Nottingham, UK (2002) 66–72
6. : (Center for biometrics and security research, casia. http://www.cbsr.ia.ac.cn)
7. Han, J., Bhanu, B.: Statistical feature fusion for gait-based human recognition. In: Proc. of the 2004 IEEE Computer Society Conference on Computer Vision and Pattern Recognition, Washington DC, USA (2004) II842–II847
8. Yu, S., Wang, L., Hu, W., Tan, T.: Gait analysis for human identification in frequency domain. In: Proc. of the 3rd International Conference on Image and Graphics, Hong Kong, China (2004) 282–285
9. Wang, L., Tan, T., Ning, H., Hu, W.: Silhouette analysis-based gait recognition for human identification. IEEE Transactions on Pattern Analysis and Machine Intelligence **25** (2003) 1505–1518

Gesture Recognition Using Quadratic Curves

Qiulei Dong, Yihong Wu, and Zhanyi Hu

National Laboratory of Pattern Recognition, Institute of Automation,
Chinese Academy of Sciences, P.O. Box 2728, Beijng 100080, P.R. China
{qldong, yhwu, huzy}@nlpr.ia.ac.cn

Abstract. This paper presents a novel method for human gesture recognition based on quadratic curves. Firstly, face and hands in the images are extracted by skin color and their central points are kept tracked by a modified Greedy Exchange algorithm. Then in each trajectory, the central points are fitted into a quadratic curve and 6 invariants from this quadratic curve are computed. Following these computations, a gesture feature vector composed of $6n$ such invariants is constructed, where n is the number of the trajectories in this gesture. Lastly, the gesture models are learnt from the feature vectors of gesture samples and an input gesture is recognized by comparing its feature vector with those of gesture models. In this gesture recognition method, the computational cost is low because the gesture duration does not need to be considered and only simple curvilinear integral and matrix computation are involved. Experiments on hip-hop dance show that our method can achieve a recognition rate as high as 97.65% on a database of 16 different gestures, each performed by 8 different people for 8 different times.

1 Introduction

Gesture recognition has many prospective applications in human-computer interfaces, visual surveillance and etc. It can be considered as a classification problem through matching the test data with the labeled spatial-temporal models representing typical gestures [1].

In recent years, gesture recognition has attracted much attention in computer vision field. One kind of major extant methods for gesture recognition is using Hidden Markov Models (HMMs). Gestures characterized by spatial-temporal structures are modeled using HMMs, and an unknown input gesture is recognized by maximizing the probability of its observed sequence. For example, Yamato et al. [2] used HMMs to recognize tennis actions from a set of time-sequential images. Starner and Pentland [3] presented an HMM-based system for recognizing American Sign Language. Brand and Kettnaker [4] showed that an HMM's internal state machine can be made to organize observed activity into meaningful states by minimizing the entropy of the joint distribution. By using HMMs, only a probabilistic value is produced for each possible model and a great number of gesture sequences are usually required in the training stage. Therefore, many other methods have been introduced. Dynamic Time Warping (DTW), a template-based dynamic programming matching technique, was

P.J. Narayanan et al. (Eds.): ACCV 2006, LNCS 3851, pp. 817–825, 2006.

used to match an unknown test sequence with a deterministic sequence of states [5], where a lot of templates had to be constructed to model a range of variations. Shin et al. [6] proposed a geometric method using Bezier curves for the trajectory analysis and classification of gestures from registered 3-D data. An approach based on assumption generation and verification was used by Wada and Matsuyama [7] to recognize multiple object behaviors from unsegmented image sequences. Campbell and Bobick [8] developed a system for recognizing ballet steps using a "phase space" representation of human movement. Bobick and Davis [9] presented a view-based method to represent and recognize human movements. In their method, temporal templates containing Motion-Energy Image (MEI) and Motion-History Image (MHI) were used as the representations of human movements. And then a matching algorithm using invariant moments for the temporal templates was proposed. The method is relatively fast because it does not involve explicit temporal analysis but may suffer from generating multiple random motion regions due to image differencing during creating MHI and MEI.

In this work, we propose a practical method for gesture recognition. It is fast, independent of the performing rhythm, and insensitive to noise as well as tracking errors.

We think the centers of the performer's hands and face from several orderly selected frames of a gesture sequence are sufficient for gesture recognition in despite of shape changes of these motion regions. So in this work, we use the centers of the performer's hands and face regions for gesture recognition. The main steps of our method are:

1. The centers of the performer's hands and face regions are located from the selected frames.
2. A modified version of Greedy Exchange algorithm [10] is used to establish the correspondences of the central points across the frames as different sets.
3. The coordinates of the central points in these sets are normalized using a practical and simple normalization approach.
4. Different quadratic curves are fitted to these different sets of corresponding central points by the least-squares method. The quadratic curves are shown capable of representing effectively the real trajectories. One quadratic curve represents one trajectory. And one gesture is represented by several quadratic curves since one gesture is generally composed of several trajectories. We set up 6 invariants for each quadratic curve and then each gesture is represented by a feature vector composed of $6n$ invariants, where n is the number of quadratic curves in this gesture.
5. Gesture models are learnt from the feature vectors of the gesture samples and then an unknown input is assigned to the gesture model whose feature vector has the shortest Mahalanobis distance to the feature vector of the input.

Our method is tested through the recognition of 16 predefined gestures of hip-hop dance. The results show that our method can yield a high recognition rate and does not need complex training. Fig. 1 shows two of the 16 predefined gestures.

Fig. 1. Two predefined gestures in our experiments. Each row corresponds to one predefined gesture.

The remainder of this paper is organized as follows: Section 2 reports the modified Greedy Exchange algorithm and the establishment of the central point correspondences. Section 3 describes the quadratic curve fitting, the gesture feature vector extraction, and the gesture recognition. Experiments are performed in Section 4, and followed by some concluding remarks in Section 5.

2 Image Preprocessing and Central Point Tracking

2.1 Foreground Detection

At first, the background model is constructed as in [11]. Then, several frames (7-11 frames) are selected orderly from the image sequence of each gesture automatically. In each selected frame, the foreground region is located by the method of [11]. The median point M of the foreground region is computed, followed by reconstructing the minimum bounding rectangle R , which is defined as the smallest rectangle containing the foreground region in the first frame of each gesture sequence. As shown in Fig. 2, L_A is the axis going through M and perpendicular to the bottom of R, and D is the distance of the median point M to the bottom of R .

(a) (b)

Fig. 2. (a) The foreground region. (b) The median point M, the minimum bounding rectangle R , the axis L_A and the distance D.

2.2 Hand and Face Location

Hand and face location is the important basis for gesture recognition and directly influences the later processes. Color is proved to be one of the most prominent and distinctive features for hand and face detection, so we use the skin detection method [12] to locate the hands and face in each selected frame of the image sequence. Then, using clustering, all the pixels with skin color are classified into three regions corresponding to hands and face in each frame in general (in case of occlusion, there may be less regions).

2.3 Central Point Tracking

After hand and face location, we are to match the central points of different regions obtained in Subsection 2.2 across frames by a modified Greedy Exchange algorithm.

Now, the Greedy Exchange algorithm [10] is recalled. It is based on the assumption of path coherence, i.e., the motion direction and speed change gradually. Let $X_{i,m}$ represent the location of the ith trajectory in the mth frame, the path coherence function is formulated as follows:

$$\begin{aligned} d_i^m &= \Psi(\overline{X_{i,m-1}X_{i,m}}, \overline{X_{i,m}X_{i,m+1}}) \\ &= 0.1(1 - \frac{\overline{X_{i,m-1}X_{i,m}} \bullet \overline{X_{i,m}X_{i,m+1}}}{\|\overline{X_{i,m-1}X_{i,m}}\|\|\overline{X_{i,m}X_{i,m+1}}\|}) \\ &\quad + 0.9(1 - 2\frac{\sqrt{\|\overline{X_{i,m-1}X_{i,m}}\|\|\overline{X_{i,m}X_{i,m+1}}\|}}{\|\overline{X_{i,m-1}X_{i,m}}\| + \|\overline{X_{i,m}X_{i,m+1}}\|}) \end{aligned} \tag{1}$$

where "•" is the inner product of two vectors. And the cost function is:

$$D = \sum_{i=1}^{n} \sum_{m=2}^{s-1} d_i^m \tag{2}$$

where n is the number of the trajectories, and s is the number of the frames.

Let d_i^{*m}, d_j^{*m} denote the new path coherence measures for the ith and jth trajectories after exchanging the points in the $(m+1)$th frame on the ith and jth trajectories. The exchange gain can be expressed as:

$$g_{i,j}^m = d_i^m + d_j^m - (d_i^{*m} + d_j^{*m}) \tag{3}$$

For all possible gains $g_{i,j}^m (i = 1, 2, \ldots, n-1,\ j = i+1, i+2, \ldots, n)$, if $\max\limits_{i,j}(g_{i,j}^m) = g_{p,q}^m > 0$, the points in the $(m+1)$th frame on the pth and qth trajectories will be exchanged and the corresponding path coherence measurement $d_p^{*m} + d_q^{*m}$ will replace $d_p^m + d_q^m$. Based on this criterion, the original algorithm iteratively exchanges the locations of points between trajectories to minimize the cost function (2), where the initialization is determined by the nearest neighbor criterion.

Since the original Greedy Exchange algorithm cannot deal with occlusion, in addition, since the number of the trajectories we need to deal with in our work is no more than three, we modify the original algorithm as :

1. If the candidate tracking location $X_{i,m+1}$ becomes invisible, the values of d_i^m, d_i^{m+1} and d_i^{m+2} are set to a fixed large constant.
2. Furthermore, in our case, the exchange gain function is modified as:

$$g^m = d_1^m + d_2^m + d_3^m - (d_1^{*m} + d_2^{*m} + d_3^{*m}) \tag{4}$$

By using this modified Greedy Exchange algorithm, three sets of corresponding points for the three trajectories are obtained. Then if the distance between any two points within a set is less than ζ, a small predefined threshold, this set is considered to represent a static hand or face. Otherwise, it represents a moving hand or face. In the next section, we only consider those sets from moving hands or face.

3 Feature Extraction and Gesture Recognition

3.1 Quadratic Curve Fitting and Feature Extraction

Because the lengths of different persons' arms are different in general, the coordinates of the located central points in Subsection 2.3 have to be normalized first. The normalization is carried out in our work by dividing the coordinates of the central points by the distance D(see Fig. 2 for D).

A lot of experiments have shown that the trajectories of basic human gestures can be represented approximately by quadratic curves. The special traits of quadratic curves make gesture recognition easy and fast. Therefore, we are to fit the normalized points in each set by different quadratic curves.

The equation of a quadratic curve is:

$$ax^2 + 2bxy + cy^2 + 2dx + 2ey + f = 0 \tag{5}$$

Substitute each normalized point (x, y) in the established set of Subsection 2.3 into (5), we obtain linear equations on a, b, c, d, e, f , then solve out them by the least-squares method under the constraint $a^2 + b^2 + c^2 + d^2 + e^2 + f^2 = 1$. The estimated (a, b, c, d, e, f) is used as the representation of this quadratic curve.

From each of the representations of quadratic curves, three entities are computed as:

$$A = a + c \tag{6}$$

$$J = \begin{vmatrix} a & b \\ b & c \end{vmatrix} \tag{7}$$

$$\Delta = \begin{vmatrix} a & b & d \\ b & c & e \\ d & e & f \end{vmatrix} \tag{8}$$

These three entities are invariants under translation and rotation on the points of this quadratic curve [13].

In order to distinguish two different quadratic curves having the same three invariants, we introduce other three invariants: the central moment with order (1+1) [14] and two angles as follows:

The central moment of order $(p+q)$ of a line l is defined as:

$$\mu_{p,q} = \int_l (x-\overline{x})^p (y-\overline{y})^q f(x,y) dl \tag{9}$$

where

$$f(x,y) = \begin{cases} 1 & (x,y) \in l \\ 0 & (x,y) \notin l \end{cases}, \ \overline{x} = \frac{1}{L}\int_l x f(x,y) dl, \ \overline{y} = \frac{1}{L}\int_l y f(x,y) dl, \ L = \int_l dl.$$

For each quadratic curve, we only use its central moment of order (1+1), i.e. $\mu_{1,1}$ in our work.

The two angles α, β are defined as: for each quadratic curve, let L_S be the line going through M (see Fig. 2 for M) and the starting point of this quadratic curve, and L_E the line going through M and the end point of this quadratic curve. Then, $\alpha(\beta)$is the included angle between $L_S(L_E)$ and the axis L_A (see Fig. 2 for L_A).

The three invariants (6), (7), (8) and the central moment (9) are global features, and the two angels α, β are local features. Combining all these 6 features, we get different feature vectors for different quadratic curves. Thus the feature vector of a gesture consisting of n trajectories or n quadratic curves is expressed as:

$$\begin{aligned} H = (&\mu_{1,1}^1, \alpha_1, \beta_1, A_1, J_1, \Delta_1, \cdots, \mu_{1,1}^i, \alpha_i, \beta_i, A_i, \\ &J_i, \Delta_i, \cdots, \mu_{1,1}^n, \alpha_n, \beta_n, A_n, J_n, \Delta_n)^T \end{aligned} \tag{10}$$

The order of different feature vectors of different quadratic curves in H is decided based on the location. $(\mu_{1,1}^1, \alpha_1, \beta_1, A_1, J_1, \Delta_1)^T$ is for the most down left trajectory and $(\mu_{1,1}^n, \alpha_n, \beta_n, A_n, J_n, \Delta_n)^T$ is for the most upper right trajectory.

Remark. The primary reason that we here use the invariants for gesture recognition rather than by direct curve matching is from our experimental observation that usually direct curve matching is prone to local curve distortion and is of high computational load. However, our invariants based method seems much robust to local distortion and random noise, and is computationally efficient.

3.2 Gesture Recognition

The steps of recognizing an unknown input gesture are:

First, the unknown input gesture is classified by its feature vector's dimensionality.

Second, for those gesture models whose feature vectors have the same dimensionality as that of the input gesture, a Mahalanobis distance is calculated between the input feature vector and those of the models. The model that has the shortest Mahalanobis distance is selected as the final recognition.

4 Experiments

We test our method on hip-hop dance, a popular youth dance. 16 basic hip-hop gestures, each of which is performed by eight people for eight different times, are obtained. Fig. 1 shows two of the gestures. The gesture sequences are captured by a digital camcorder and each of them contains 20-50 frames. Then all the sequences are converted to 300×240 BMP files and we have $1024 (=16 \times 8 \times 8)$ gesture sequences.

We arbitrarily select 640 gesture sequences, 40 from each gesture, for training. The rest gestures are used for testing.

In the training stage, several frames (7-11 frames) are selected orderly from the image sequence of each gesture for foreground detection. Then the central points are extracted from the selected frames and their correspondences between frames are established using the modified version of Greedy Exchange algorithm in Subsection 2.3. Fig. 3 shows a tracking example with temporal occlusion of a

Fig. 3. A tracking example with temporal occlusion of a hand

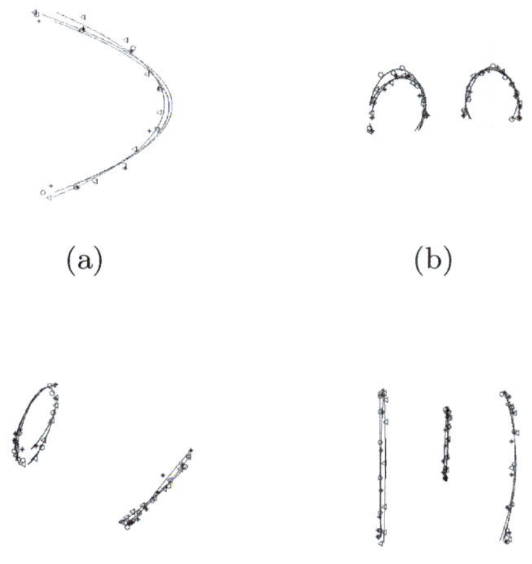

(a) (b)

(c) (d)

Fig. 4. Examples: (a) several fitted curves in Gesture 1, (b) several fitted curves in Gesture 4, (c) several fitted curves in Gesture 10, (d) several fitted curves in Gesture 16

Table 1. Experimental results

Gesture No.	1	2	3	4	5	6	7	8	9	10	11	12	13	14	15	16	Total
#Training	40	40	40	40	40	40	40	40	40	40	40	40	40	40	40	40	640
#Testing	24	24	24	24	24	24	24	24	24	24	24	24	24	24	24	24	384
#Correct	24	24	24	23	24	22	24	24	22	24	24	24	22	22	24	24	375

hand, where the points being "$*$" represent the central points of one moving hand and the points being "$\circ$" represent the centroids of another moving hand from eleven selected frames. It can be seen that although there is temporal occlusion for one hand, the exact correspondences are obtained. We fit the corresponding points across frames by a quadratic curve, and construct the feature vector for each gesture using the method of Section 3. Four examples of fitted quadratic curves are shown in Fig. 4. The final recognition results are shown in Table 1. The recognition rate on the testing data is 97.65%.

We also compare the proposed method with direct curve matching. It is noticed that direct curve matching is sensitive to noise and prone to local curve distortion extremely.

Besides, we apply LIBSVM [15] to classify these gestures. Guassian function is selected as the RBF kernel. The recognition rate is also high.

5 Conclusions

A novel quadratic curve based method for gesture recognition is proposed and validated by hip-hop gesture recognition on a database of 16 different gestures, each performed by 8 different people for 8 different times. The recognition rate is as high as 97.65%.

The main characteristics of our method are: (i) The computational cost is low because only simple curvilinear integral and matrix computation are involved. (ii) Since the used features do not depend on the gesture duration, the recognition is greatly simplified. (iii) The feature vector includes not only global features but also local features to make this method more flexible.

In future, gesture recognition from multiple views will be studied to further increase the recognition rate.

Acknowledgment. This work was supported by the National Natural Science Foundation of China under grant Nos (60303021, 60375006).

References

1. Hu, W.M., Tan, T.N., Wang, L.: A survey on visual surveillance of object motion and behaviors. IEEE Transaction on Systems, Man, and Cybernetics-Part C: Applications and Reviews **34** (2004) 334–352
2. Yamato, J., Ohya, J., Ishii, K.: Recognizing human action in time-sequential images using hidden markov model. In: Proc. IEEE Conf. Computer Vision and Pattern Recognition, champaign, IL (1992) 379–385

3. Starner, T., Pentland, A.: Visual recognition of american sign language using hidden markov models. In: Proc. International Workshop on Automatic Face and Gesture Recognition, Zurich, Switzerland (1995) 189–194
4. Brand, M., Kettnaker, V.: Discovery and segmentation of activities in video. IEEE Trans. Pattern Analysis and Machine Intelligence **22** (2000) 844–851
5. Bobick, A.F., Wilson, A.D.: A state-based approach to the representation and recognition of gesture. IEEE Trans. Pattern Analysis and Machine Intelligence **19** (1997) 1325–1337
6. Shin, M.C., Tsap, L.V., Goldgof, D.B.: Gesture recognition using bezier curves for visualization navigation from registered 3-d data. Pattern Recognition **37** (2004) 1011–1024
7. Wada, T., Matsuyama, T.: Multiobject behavior recognition by event driven selective attention method. IEEE Trans. Pattern Analysis and Machine Intelligence **22** (2000) 873–887
8. Campbell, L., Bobick, A.: Recognition of human body motion using phase space constraints. In: Proc. IEEE International Conference on Computer Vision, Cambridge, MA (1995) 624–630
9. Bobick, A., Davis, J.: The recognition of human movement using temporal templates. IEEE Trans. Pattern Analysis and Machine Intelligence **23** (2001) 257–267
10. Sethi, I., Jain, R.: Finding trajectories of feature points in a monocular image sequence. IEEE Trans. Pattern Analysis and Machine Intelligence **9** (1987) 56–73
11. Haritaoglu, I., Harwood, D., Davis, L.: W4: Real-time surveillance of people and their activities. IEEE Trans. Pattern Analysis and Machine Intelligence **22** (2000) 809–830
12. Kjeldsen, R., Kender, J.: Finding skin in color images. In: Proc. IEEE Workshop on Automatic Face and Gesture recognition, Killington, Vermont, USA (1996) 312–317
13. Sun, J.X., Wang, X.H., Zhong, S., Zhang, F., Shi, H.M.: Feature extraction in pattern recognition and computer vision invariants. National Defence Industry Press, Beijing, China (2001)
14. Wen, W., Lozzi, A.: Recognition and inspection of manufactured parts using line moments of their boundaries. Pattern Recognition **26** (1993) 1461–1471
15. Ma, J., Zhao, Y., Ahalt, S.: Osu svm classifier matlab toolbox. (Software available at http://www.ece.osu.edu/~maj/osu_svm/)

From Motion Patterns to Visual Concepts for Event Analysis in Dynamic Scenes

Lun Xin and Tieniu Tan

National Laboratory of Pattern Recognition,
Institute of Automation, Chinese Academy of Sciences, 100080 Beijing, P.R. China
{lxin, tnt}@nlpr.ia.ac.cn

Abstract. The analysis of events in dynamic scenes has become an important and challenging problem increasingly in recent years. Events can be considered as obvious changes of important features with semantic meanings. From this viewpoint, the fundamental task of events analysis is to extract semantically meaningful changes and associate all of these basic motion patterns and changes with relevant visual concepts of moving objects in dynamic scenes. In this paper, we propose a method to extract lower level motion patterns and associate them with visual concepts respectively in a well-defined structure. Furthermore we also analyze latent spatial-temporal relationships among these basic visual concepts for event modeling and analysis. Finally, we present experimental results which prove the effectiveness of our approach on some real-world videos of dynamic scenes.

1 Introduction

As a challenging problem, semantic analysis of dynamic scenes has been paid more attention by researchers in recent years. Furthermore many methods have been presented for dealing with it. Some of these methods define and analyze semantic meanings based on the global statistical properties of the movement. From the global viewpoint, this kind of methods usually ignores semantics of features exhibited in a lesser temporal scale. On the other hand, considering basic semantic meaningful features in small temporal interval is useful for the semantic understanding of the entire event. The basic flowchart of a video surveillance system will include elementary procedures such as environment modeling, object detection, tracking and recognition. However, each of these is not the termination of semantic analysis in a dynamic scene; there should be some further missions for achieving semantic understanding and interpretation of what behaviors or events performed by those moving objects in this dynamic scene. Compared with the lower level processing, the higher level phase involves spatio-temporal relationship mining, reasoning under uncertainty, semantic representation, and so on [1].

The basic requirement of the event analysis is to extract semantically meaningful motion patterns in the scene [2]. In different research areas, semantics has quite different meanings. There is a restrictive definition in semiotics that semantics implies the relationship between signs and objects. But for language science, semantics means the meaning and relationship of words. In our research work, we adopt the definition that semantics is the mapping and integration between related concepts [3].

P.J. Narayanan et al. (Eds.): ACCV 2006, LNCS 3851, pp. 826 – 835, 2006.

But there is a gap between measurable features and semantic meanings. According to the ability and the procedure of human in perception and understanding for the world, event can be considered as the semantically meaningful changes in the scenes. The basic elements for event analysis and understanding are various concepts. Each concept denotes a special semantic meaning. And all these concepts are grouped into different clusters according to their semantic functions. For the purpose of semantic analysis and understanding of events in dynamic scenes, all related concepts should be obtained firstly, and all these concepts should be organized in a well-defined structure.

As declared by some genres in philosophy, the world can be considered as the integration of different kinds of entities. From this viewpoint, all existing things in a special dynamic scene, such as different regions, moving or static objects can be treated as different entities with their own relative properties. Further more, given concepts can be used to denote these entities and their properties. The semantic analysis in the special domain can be achieved from these concepts and their relationships.

The three fundamental components of a concept are an entity, a term or a word and corresponding attributes [4]. Each concept is described as a sign by a term or a word to distinguish each other. And the difference or the similarity of different concepts can be defined on all these measurable attributes.

The difficulty for a certain definition of event is due to various demands from different domains. Thibadeau [5] defines first-order change descriptions as motion and the second-order ones as action, and Newtson [6] treats activity as the maintenance of first-order primitive properties. In this paper we consider events as obvious changes of important features as mentioned in [7].

High-level analysis and understanding of dynamic scenes is the final goal of computer vision. Compared with the traditional vision tasks such as tracking and recognizing moving objects, high-level vision is to achieve deeper analysis of spatial-temporal relationships exhibited by all visible and measurable data in dynamic scenes [8]. Contextual spatial-temporal information acts as an important clue for semantic understanding.

This paper proposes a method to associate semantic meaningful motion patterns with corresponding visual concepts for semantic analysis of events in dynamic scenes. Sections in this paper are organized as follows. Section 2 outlines previous work of event modeling and analysis. Methods for motion pattern extraction and concept modeling are described in Section 3 and Section 4 respectively. Then experimental results are showed and analyzed in Section 5. Finally, we draw conclusions and discuss future work in Section 6.

2 Previous Work

Existing work on event analysis is usually based on trajectory analysis of moving objects. Methods for trajectory extraction and simple object classification are based on some traditional methods proposed in [10, 11, 12, and 13]. Since more expressive semantically meaningful features can be extracted from trajectories, they are not organized in a proper structure for farther semantic analysis. That means each semantically meaningful feature should be associated with a concept, and the relationship of these concepts should also be considered seriously.

In [14], events are modeled and recognized by exhibited periodically variational patterns. Similar work proposed in [15] treats human activities as descriptions of their basic spatial-temporal characteristics. Ivanov and Bobick [16] extract primitive features by using HMM and recognize activities with a context-free parsing mechanism. Event or activity can also be divided into elementary components, and can be detected, represented and identified at different levels in a uniform framework [17, 18, 19, 20, and 21]. Kojima et al. [21] employ a case frame with syntactic components to model events in office scene. All syntactic components are associated with related semantic features, and the model can provide natural language descriptions of those official events. Chaudron et al. [22] represent the interpretation of event in dynamic scene as a symbolic layered prototype by Petri nets.

In recent years, more and more researchers tend to use probabilistic frameworks to express and analyze events, such as Bayesian networks, hidden Markov models, etc. All these models have a common peculiarity that stochastic parameters can be acquired automatically without any assumptions of prior knowledge under uncertainty. Considering idiographic demands under different circumstances, some variations have emerged. Galata et al. [23] mention a method to present human behavior by variable length Markov models (VLMM). The algorithm of coupled hidden Markov models (CHMM) to model two-handed interactions is presented in [24]. At the same time, the superiority of these methods mentioned above brings obvious shortages. The computation of parameters for the given structure of a model is time-costly. To fit another problem, the structure of the model must be changed, and the learning for variable structures is more difficult.

From Birnbaum et al., who use ontology to define causal changes in their attention controller in [25] , ontology related methods [26, 27, and 28] are increasingly applied in various areas, such as semantic web, data mining, knowledge management, information fusion, linguistics and etc.

3 Motion Patterns Extraction

In a visual surveillance system, scenes of the environment captured by fixed cameras can be looked as combinations of all kinds of visual entities exhibited in the video data. These entities are regions with different spatial positions and appearances, moving objects and their different motion and interaction patterns, and so on. The semantic analysis of the scene can be looked as mining and analysis for all kinds of relationship of related visual concepts. So at the beginning of this kind of work, all visual concepts must be defined and constructed in a unified form.

3.1 Location States Extraction

To determine locations of moving objects in a dynamic scene, we can look the scene as different adjacent regions which are labeled with their attributes, such as grassplot, road, sideway, intersection, crosswalk, etc. There is a pre-hypothesis that the semantic attribute of each region blob in the scene is homogeneous. So each region has its unique semantic label. Examples of semantic attributes of different labeled regions are showed in Table 1. At the same time, different spatial regions have invariable topological adjacent relationship under a fixed camera. Figure 1 shows an example of topological adjacent relationship for different regions in a special scene.

Table 1. Semantic Attributes of Labeled Regions

Labeled Regions	Semantic Attributes
Road	Vehicles and other moving objects can move in it.
Sideway	Only allow foot passengers moving in it.
Grassplot	Any motion of moving objects occurs in it is not allowed.
Crossway	Any stop of moving objects in it is not allowed.
Parking Lot	Only allow vehicle parking in it.

As illustrated in Figure 1, nine nodes denote nine different regions, and edges refer the adjacent spatial relationship of these regions. Different color of these nodes means different semantic attributes of these regions and highlighted edges indicate that moving objects can transit between two connected nodes. All related constraints can be defined in this topological graph.

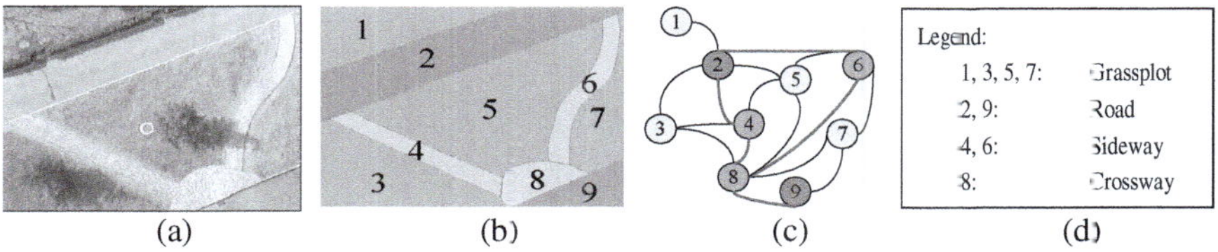

Fig. 1. Topological Relationship of Regions in the Scene

We use central points of moving regions as the approximate locations of moving objects. Mapping coordinates of central points to the semantically labeled image, we can obtain regions objects occupied. When objects move through different regions, label sequences of region transitions can also be obtained.

3.2 Motion States Extraction

All moving objects are leading actors in dynamic scenes. Event modeling and semantic analysis are focused on them. We can extract and express motion states of moving objects separately. Under a fixed camera, a trajectory of a moving object is represented as temporally sequential pairs of coordinates in frames. These pairs of coordinates can be presented like this format:

$$L = \{(x_1, y_1), (x_2, y_2), \cdots, (x_t, y_t), \cdots\} \quad (1)$$

where (x_t, y_t) is the coordinates of a moving object at time t or is at the t th sequence number of the current frame.

The basic motion states of a single moving object are "*Move*" and "*Stay*", and the basic direction states are "*Go Straight*", "*Turn Left*" and "*Turn Right*". The small trajectory segments of moving objects with the temporal scale about two seconds (50~60 frames) can be divided into these basic elements.

Figure 2 shows an example of two moving objects separately labeled by m and n . When each moving object has appeared in the scene, a sub-coordinate is set up for

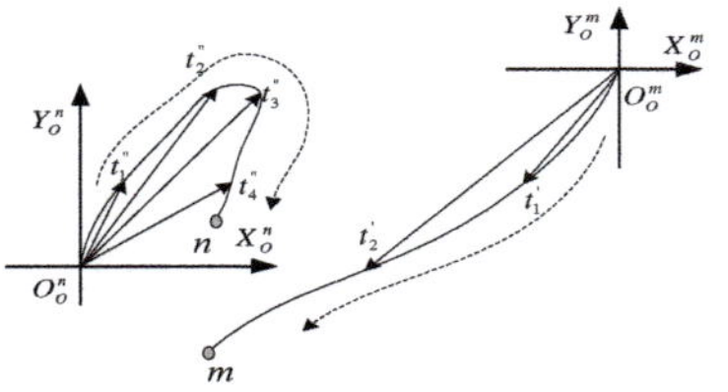

Fig. 2. Motions in Different Coordinates

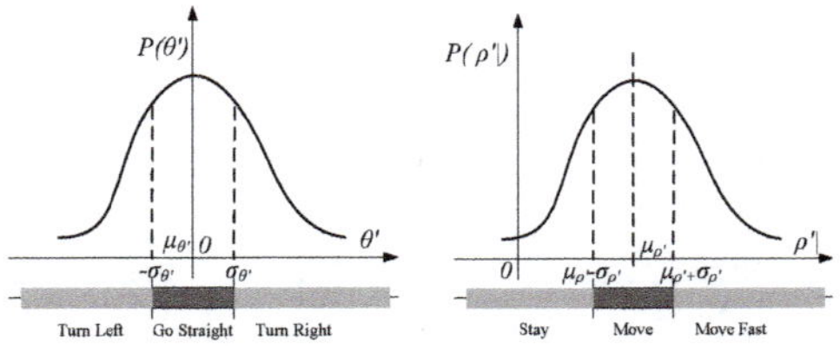

Fig. 3. Motion States Mapping

this object, and all related motion status can be extracted and calculated in this sub-coordinate. The origin of each sub-coordinate is the initial position of each moving object. For easy calculation, we present a trajectory in Polar Coordinate,

$$L_{\rho-\theta} = \{(\rho_1,\theta_1),(\rho_2,\theta_2),\cdots,(\rho_t,\theta_t),\cdots\} \tag{2}$$

and define the interval change ρ' and θ' as

$$\begin{aligned} \rho' &= \{(\rho_{i+l} - \rho_i)\},\ \rho' \sim N(\mu_{\rho'},\sigma_{\rho'}^{\ 2}) \\ \theta' &= \{(\theta_{i+l} - \theta_i)\},\ \theta' \sim N(\mu_{\theta'},\sigma_{\theta'}^{\ 2}) \end{aligned} \tag{3}$$

where l is an interval.

Based on statistical analysis of training data, we make an assumption that $|\rho'|$ and θ' obey the Gaussian distribution under the existing noise. The motion patterns about movement M_{Status} and direction Dir_{Status} can be mapped into different status as shows in Figure 3. All these parameters are all learned from videos of special scenes under special viewpoints. As a result, when zoom ratio or viewpoint changed, all these parameters should also be recalculated.

3.3 Interaction States Extraction

When we analyze the interaction between moving objects, we should consider opposite distances of these objects in a unique coordinate of the whole image (see object *i*, *j* and their opposite distance in Figure 4. (a)). The basic varieties of opposite distances can be increase, reduce and without obvious changes. By using learned thresholds, we can distinguish opposite distance *d(i,j)* between object *i* and *j* as one of those three basic varieties. And all these thresholds are also view or scale based. When several moving objects are very close to each other, it is hard for our tracking algorithm, even for human, to determine whether they should belong to a whole moving object or regard as separate objects. In the same way, when objects are so far from each other, it is unnecessary for considering their interactions. To deal with this problem, we can define different region scales (Figure 4. (b)) for each moving object. The size of each region scale is related to the size of each moving object. By using these region scales, we can determine interaction states of moving objects easily.

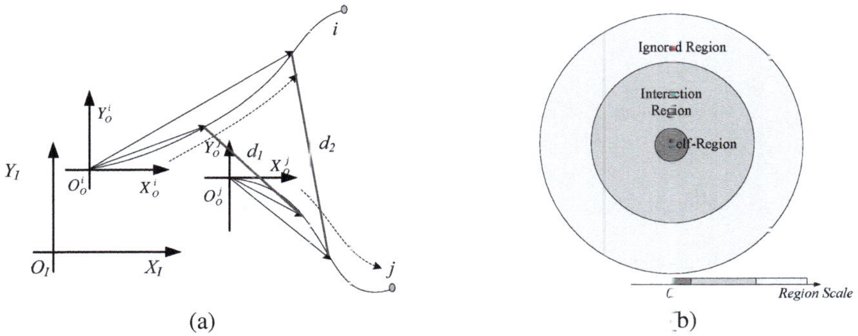

Fig. 4. (a) Opposite Distances between Objects. (b) Region Scale for Interactions.

4 States Transition-Based Concept Modeling

The definition of concept in Webster's dictionary is "an abstract or generic idea generalized from particular instances", it is the basic element of human thought. As a symbolic abstraction of the essence of reality, a concept contains some related measurable attributes. It is exhilarative that location states, motion states and different interaction categories of moving objects mentioned above are all based on measurable attributes. For further semantic analysis of events performed by moving objects in dynamic scenes, we should associate all these states, patterns and categories with corresponding concepts in certain temporal sequences. Some of concepts and verbs used in our model are chosen from the classification of motion verbs in traffic scene given by Badler [9] formerly.

All related visual concepts can be defined on transitions among those states. Figure 5. illustrates transitions on the basic states, such as "*Move*", "*Stay*", "*Go Straight*", "*Turn Left*" and "*Turn Right*". These transitions can present all semantically meaningful features of moving objects. In each temporal scale, motion patterns can be classified into basic semantic states, and we can obtain temporal sequences of those states showed below, and some related visual concepts can be associated with different segments of states transition sequences.

$MM \cdots MM$	*Move*
$SS \cdots SS$	*Stay*
$\cdots MMSS \cdots$	*Stop*
$\cdots SSMM \cdots$	*Startup*
$\cdots MMS \cdots SMM \cdots$	*Halt*
$G_SG_S \cdots G_SG_S$	*Go Straight*
$\cdots (G_SG_S)T_LT_L \cdots$	*Turn Left*
$\cdots (G_SG_S)T_RT_R \cdots$	*Turn Right*
$\cdots$	$\cdots$

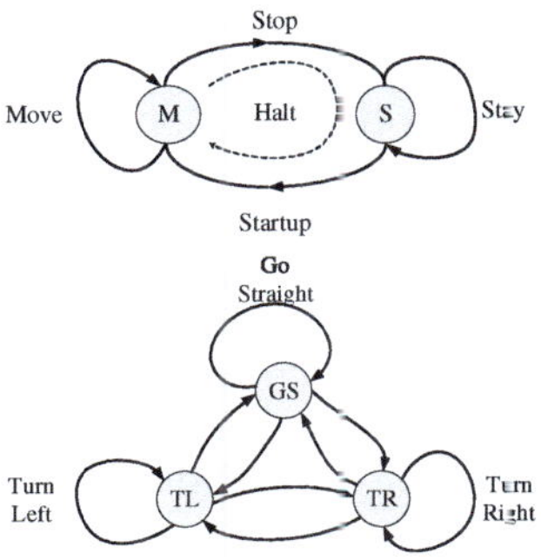

Fig. 5. Transitions Model of Basic States

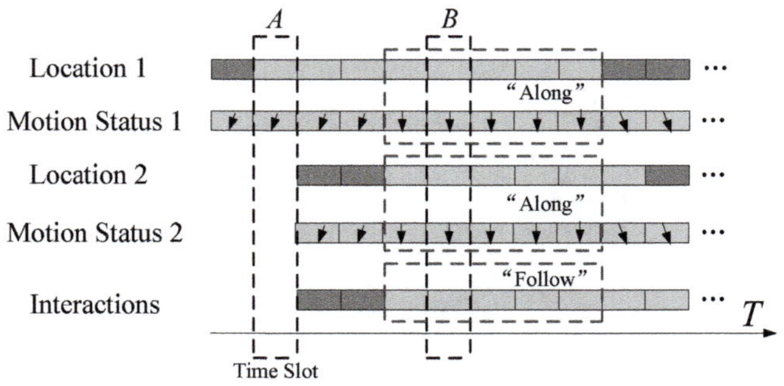

Fig. 6. Conceptual Vectors and Semantic Representations

By using this method, we can obtain all kinds of related visual concepts. For the aspect of motion, we can describe it as "*Go Straight*", "*Turn Right*", "*Turn Left*", "*Retrace*", etc. And there are different interactions in the scene. Interactions between moving objects and special regions can be represented as spatial relationships, such as "*Occupy*", "*Enter*", "*Transfer*", "*Appear*", etc. Interactions of two moving objects can be "*Close To*", "*Away From*", "*Encounter*", "*Follow*", "*Retrace*", etc. And we should choose different concept for vehicles and passengers.

In a certain time slot, we can integrate all these obtained visual concepts into a conceptual vector (see Figure 6.). In this figure, each block denotes a corresponding visual concept with different color, and each arrow expresses different motion direction of this moving object in a certain time slot. By using each conceptual vector, simple semantic representation of event performed by moving objects can be obtained.

All concepts in visual surveillance are obtained at different scales. That means some basic concepts are components of other concepts, such as "*Move*" and "*Halt*", "*Go Straight*" and "*Retrace*". So concepts with similar meanings can be presented in dendriform structure as different clusters.

5 Experimental Results

From our multi-camera visual surveillance system, we choose two fixed cameras which can capture wide visual fields from taller points of views. Under this condition, the influence of 3D to 2D perspective can be reduced, and then we can use the coordinates of moving objects in the image plane as the probable positions of them in the real scene.

According to the method mentioned above, we calculate all parameters from training video, and then analyze all related motion patterns of moving objects in the certain temporal scale. After associating these motion patterns with corresponding visual concepts in conceptual vectors, simple semantic representations will be obtained by using these related concepts in a time slot.

Figure 7 explains complex events performed by moving objects in two selected scenes and shows simple semantic representations of these events. As showed in Figure 6., we will select "Along" to express the motion of an object if it moves unremittingly in the same region without obvious direction change in several adjacent time slots. In the same way, "Follow" will be adopted if two objects are moving in the similar direction and their opposite distance keeps reducing.

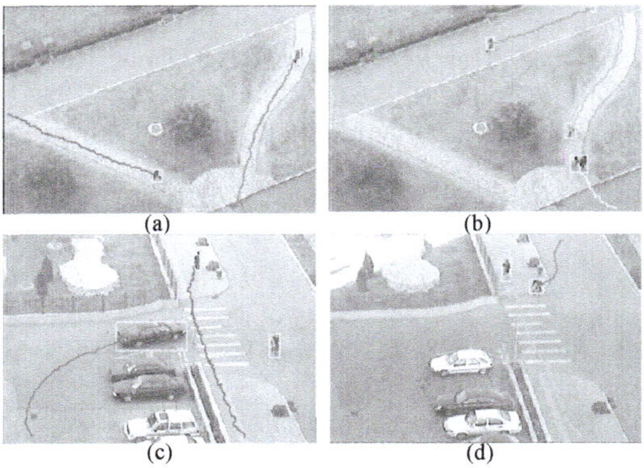

(a) {Person 1 Walk Along Sideway}
{Person 2 Walk Along Sideway}
(b) {Person 1 Walk Along Sideway}
{Person 2 Walk Along Road}
{Person 3 Walk Sideway}
{Person 2 Person 3 Meet Sideway}
(c) {Car 1 Enter Crossway}
{Person 1 Walk Along Sideway}
{Person 2 Walk Fast Along Road}
(d) {Person 1 Walk Sideway}
{Person 2 TurnRight Enter Crossway}

(e)

Fig. 7. Complex Events and Simple Semantic Representations

6 Conclusion and Future Work

In this paper, we have presented a method to associate motion patterns with corresponding visual concepts for event analysis seen in dynamic scenes. The key points of our method are extraction of motion patterns, concept generation and modeling. Simple semantic representations of events in the dynamic scenes are obtained in some real world videos, and the result also validates the effectiveness of this method.

Manually labeling of different regions in the dynamic scene and negligence the uncertainty of observed data are main limitations of our methods. In the future, we will adopt some learning methods to achieve semantic labels by using texture and motion information. To handle the uncertainty problem of our method, probabilistic mechanism should be a good choice. Extended experiments and embedded polishing are also needed for our method.

Acknowledgement

The work reported in this paper was funded by research grants from the National Basic Research Program of China (No. 2004CB318100), the National Natural Science Foundation of China (No. 60335010) and the International Cooperation Program of Ministry of Science and Technology of China (No. 2004DFA06900).

References

[1] Mubarak Shah: Guest Introduction: The Changing Shape of Computer Vision in the Twenty-First Century. International Journal of Computer Vision. Vol. 50. No. 2. (2002) 103-110

[2] A. Ekinci, A. M. Tekalp Generic Event Detection in Sports Video using Cinematic Features. In Second IEEE Workshop on Event Mining (EVENT'03). (June 2003) 17-24

[3] Fauconnier, G.: Mapping in Thought and Language. Cambridge University Press. (1997)

[4] Dahlberg, I.: Conceptual Definitions for Interconcept. International Classification. Vol. 8. No. 1. (1981) 16-22

[5] R. Thibadeau: Artificial Perception of Actions. Cognitive Science. 10(2). (1986) 117-149
[6] D. Newtson: Foundations of Attribution: the Perception of Ongoing Behaviour. New Directions in Attribution Research. Laurence Erlbaum. Hillsdala. NJ. (1976) 147-223
[7] R.J. Howarth, H. Buxton: Conceptual Descriptions from Monitoring and Watching Image Sequences. Image and Vision Computing. Vol. 18. (2000) 105-135
[8] Bernd Neumann: A Conceptual Framework for High-level Vision. Bericht. FB Informatik. FBI-HH-B245/02. (Juli 2002)
[9] Badler, N.I.: Temporal Scene Analysis: Conceptual Descriptions of Object Movements. Technical Report No. 80. Dept. of Computer Science. University of Toronto. (1975)
[10] S.S. Intille, J.W. Davis, A.F. Bobick: Real Time Closed World Tracking. IEEE Proc. Computer Vision and Pattern Recognition. (1997) 697-703
[11] A. J. Lipton, H. Fujiyoshi, R.S. Patil: Moving Target Classification and Tracking from Real Time Video. Proc. Fourth IEEE Workshop Application of Computer Vision. (1998) 8-14
[12] I.Haritaoglu, D.Harwood, L.S.Davis: W4: real-time surveillance of people and their activities. IEEE Transactions on Pattern Analysis and Machine Intelligence. Vol. 22. Issue: 8, (Aug. 2000) 809-830
[13] C.R. Wren, A. Azarbayejani, et al.: Pfinder: Real Time Tracking of the Human Body. IEEE Trans. Pattern Analysis and Machine Intelligence. Vol. 19. No. 7. (July 1997)
[14] L. Davis, R. Chelappa, A. Rosenfeld, D. Harwood, I. Haritaoglu, R. Cutler: Visual Surveillance and Monitoring. In DARPA Image Understanding Workshop. (1998) 73-76
[15] A. Galton: Towards an Integrated Logic of Space, Time and Motion. Proc. International Joint Conf. Artificial Intelligence (IJCAI). (Aug. 1993)
[16] Yuri A. Ivanov, Aaron F. Bobick: Recognition of Visual Activities and Interactions by Stochastic Parsing. IEEE Trans. on Pattern Analysis and Machine Intelligence. Vol. 22. No. 8. (Aug. 2000) 852-872
[17] Dance, S., Caelli, T.: A Symbolic Object-oriented Picture Interpretation Network: SOOPIN. In Advances in Structural and Syntactic Pattern Recognition. Proceedings of the International Workshop. H. Bunke, Ed. World Scientific Publishing Co. (1993) 530-541
[18] M. Haag, H.-H. Nagel: Incremental Recognition of Traffic Situations from Video Image Sequences. Image and Vision Computing. Vol. 18. (2000) 137-153
[19] R. J. Howarth, H. Buxton: Conceptual descriptions from Monitoring and Watching Image Sequences. Image and Vision Computing. Vol. 18. (2000) 105-135
[20] Nuria Oliver, Ashutosh Garg, Eric Horvitz: Layered Representations for Learning and Inferring Office Activity from Multiple Sensory Channels. Computer Vision and Image Understanding. Special Issue on Event Detection in Video. Vol. 96. Issue 2. (Nov. 2004) 163-180
[21] Atsuhiro Kojima, Takeshi Tamura, Kunio Fukunaga: Natural Language Description of Human Activities from Video Images Based on Concept Hierarchy of Actions. International Journal of Computer Vision. Vol. 50. No. 2. (Nov. 2002) 171-184
[22] Laurent Chaudron, Corine Cossart, Nicolas Maille, Catherine Tessier: A Purely Symbolic Model for Dynamic Scene Interpretation. International Journal on Artificial Intelligence Tools. Vol. 6. No. 4. (Dec. 1997) 635-664
[23] Aphrodite Galata, Neil Johnson, David Hogg: Learning Structured Behaviour Models Using Variable Length Markov Models. Computer Vision and Image Understanding (CVIU) Journal. Vol. 81. No. 3. (March 2001) 398-413
[24] M. Brand, N. Oliver, A. Pentland: Coupled Hidden Markov Models for Complex Action Recognition. Proc. of the Conference on Computer Vision and Pattern Recognition (CVPR '97). (1997) 994-998

[25] L. Birnbaum, M. Brand, P. Cooper: Looking for Trouble: Using Causal Semantics. Proceedings of the Fourth International Conference on Computer Vision. Berlin. Germany. IEEE Computer Society Press. Silver Spring. MD. (1993) 49-56

[26] Christopher Town: Ontology-driven Bayesian Networks for Dynamic Scene Understanding. Proceedings of the 2004 IEEE Computer Society Conference on Computer Vision and Pattern Recognition Workshops (CVPRW'04). (27-02 June 2004) 116-123

[27] P. Varga, T. Mészáros, Cs. Dezsényi, T.P. Dobrowiecki: An Ontology-based Information Retrieval System. The 16th International Conference on Industrial & Engineering Applications of Artificial Intelligence and Expert Systems. Loughborough. U.K. (23-26 June 2003)

[28] Yanmei Wang, Zhonghua Yang, Pe Hin Hinny Kong, Robert Kheng Leng Gay: Ontology-based Web knowledge management. Proceedings of the 2003 Joint Conference of the Fourth International Conference on Information, Communications and Signal Processing. Vol. 3. (15-18 Dec. 2003) 1859 -1863

Probabilistic Modeling for Structural Change Inference

Wei Liu and Véronique Prinet

National Laboratory of Pattern Recognition (NLPR),
Sino-French research Laboratory in Information,
Automation and Applied Mathematics (LIAMA),
Institute of Automation, Chinese Academy of Sciences (CASIA)
prinet@nlpr.ia.ac.cn

Abstract. We view the task of change detection as a problem of object recognition from learning. The object is defined in a 3D space where the time is the 3rd dimension. We propose two competitive probabilistic models. The first one has a traditional regard on change, characterized as a 'presence-absence' within two scenes. The model is based on a logistic function, embedded in a framework called 'cut-and-merge'. The second approach is inspired from the Discriminative Random Fields (DRF) approach proposed by Ma and Hebert [KUMA2003]. The energy function is defined as the sum of an association potential and an interaction potential. We formulate the latter as a 3D anisotropic term. A simplified implementation enables to achieve fast computation in the 2D image space. In conclusion, the main contributions of this paper rely on : 1) the extension of the DRF to a 3D manifold ; 2) the *cut-and-merge* algorithm. The application proposed in the paper is on remote sensing images, for building change detection. Results on synthetic and real scenes and comparative analysis demonstrate the effectiveness of the proposed approach.

1 Introduction

This paper focuses on probabilistic modeling for object structural change inference.

Probabilistic modeling emerged as an increasingly efficient framework for segmentation and object recognition tasks. From Markov Random Fields [13] to recently introduced part-based modeling for recognition [4], the goal is to find a 'best' global configuration of a random variable associated to a label. Set as an energy minimisation problem, the basic challenges are : i) to define appropriately the functional to be optimised ; it is in general characterised by a data features term and a constraint or regularisation term; the latter is mainly derived from prior knowledge and enable to introduce smoothness or to sharpen edges. ii) to set efficient computational solution to reduce the combinatorial calculation burden [22].

The Remote Sensing (RS) image processing field has so far be little influenced by Pattern Recognition (PR) and Computer Vision (CV) works. However, the

P.J. Narayanan et al. (Eds.): ACCV 2006, LNCS 3851, pp. 836–846, 2006.

two communities deal with very similar key problems –restoration, segmentation and classification, flow vector field, reconstruction,... Far to be easy cases to handle, the complexity of the scenes and the high level of noise existing in RS images challenge the models developed from PR and CV, which often are not robust nor generic enough. RS images are characterised in particular by illumination changes, shadowing, projective distortion, occlusion, stochastic noise –thermal effect during the acquisition– and geometric noise. Geometric noise refers to all small size objects that appear in the scene and disturb the segmentation or detection process, such as cars, trees, etc. A contrary to man-made object detection in natural scenes, an RS image scene covering an urban area is mainly composed of objects which have similar structured and polygonal shapes: roads and buildings. To takle this problem, previous works on buildings detection in dense urban areas are mainly based on models which include high and restrictive constraints, therefore lacking of genericity and uncapable to work on a large set of images [6,11].

The present work was inspired from a recent publication from Kumar [8], in which he introduced a Discriminative Random Field (DRF) model, for man-made objects detection in natural scenes. This model formulates the constraint term of the Gibbs energy as a function of the global image.

We show in this paper how to generalise the concept of DRF modeling to a multi-dimensional space without increasing computational cost. Application is on building change retrieval from high resolution optical remote sensing images covering dense urban areas. The rest of this article is organized as follows: the next section introduces structural object change inference from a Kernel approach based on a so-called *cut-and-merge* algorithm and maximum likelihood. Section 3 presents the 3D anisotropic model derived from DRF and its practical implementation. Results are illustrated in section 4; the 5th section concludes the paper.

2 Structural Change Recognition

2.1 Overview

The main idea of structural change recognition is to first perform object segmentation in each of the two images, then to analyse the probability of change, for each individual object. We do not perform a 'hard' segmentation, in the sense that an object can be detected even if its likelihood of being a building is low. It enables us to estimate the change as a cross product of probability functions, which appears to be much more powerful than computing a simple difference. The rest of this section gives the main cues of the approach.

2.2 Cut-and-Merge Algorithm

The cut-and-merge algorithm performs binary segmentation without explicit thresholding. The *cut* task will blindly binarize the input image and create a set of black-and-white images, without knowledge of the object's type we are seeking for. The *merge* task will make use of prior knowledge and fuse this segmented set of data such as to retrieve the regions which maximise a given 'criteria'.

Cut : A band-pass filter is convolved several times with the original image [18]. The filter is characterised by the min and max values of the band. All pixels x with intensity level $I(x)$ satisfying $min < I(x) < max$ are retained. From one convolution to an other, min and max values are progressively incremented, thus generating a set of binary images. In each of these images, aggregated pixels define regions which closed contours are extracted.

Merge : The likelihood of a each region and its closed contour R_i to be a object-building is given by $p_i = p(R_i)$ (see section 2.3). For two overlapping regions R_i and R_j resulting from two different pass-band filters, we calculate $p_{ij} = p(R_i \bigcap R_j)$. We then merge the overlapping regions by retaining the one R_k that verifies :

$$k = arg \max_{k \in \{1,j,ij\}} (p_i, p_j, p_{ij})$$

In an iterative procedure, we can therefore eliminate all regions unlikely to correspond to our searched object.

2.3 Functional and Features

The problem is to determine whether a segmented area R_i –called "element"– is likely to be a object-building or not. The label assigned to R_i is represented by a random value x_i. Assuming that events are independent, finding the configuration X that maximizes the probability P over the image is equivalent to maximizing the probability density function at each site R_i : $P(X|y) = \Pi_i p(x_i|y_i)$ where y_i is the features vector computed at element R_i. We define $p(x|y)$ by a logistic function :

$$p(x_i|y_i) = \sigma(x_i w^T f(y_i))$$

w is the unknown parameters vector and f is an application that transforms the data features to a higher dimensional space: $f : y_i \rightarrow [1, y_i, y_i y_i^T, \tilde{y}]$, where $\tilde{y}$ is defined as the product of each feature with an other. A total of eight individual feature are computed —it includes : region entropy, edges points, intensity mean, standard deviation, gradient direction moment and their difference, shadow parameter–, leading to a parameter vector size of 45 degrees of freedom. Parameters are retrieved by maximizing the log-likelihood of P via a ICM module.

2.4 Object Change Detection

We consider two images I^1 and I^2 acquired at t^1 and t^2 respectively. We estimate the probability density function p.d.f. at each of the elements i of R^1 and j of R^2: $p_i^1 = p(y_i^1)$ and $p_j^2 = p(y_j^2)$ respectively.

The probability function that an object appears in the two images simultaneously is given by $p_{nc} = p_i^1 p_j^2$, while the probability function for an object to appear in one of the image only is : $p_c = p_i^2(1-p_i^1) + p_i^1(1-p_j^2)$. Selecting candidate contours that verify $p_c > 0.5$ provides us with the changed structured objects.

3 Change Inference from 3D DRF

3.1 The Model

We first recall some basic notations and define the main concept of 3D DRF modeling. A image is represented as a graph $G = (V, E)$, where E are the nodes of the graph and V are the vertices. In order to create G, the image is divided into regular patches. Each patch is a node and two mutually connected nodes within a n-neighborhood determine a clique. Each node $e \in E$ is characterised by the data it encompasses – it can also be features computed from the data– : y_e. The label associated to each node is a random variable $X_{e \in E} = \{-1, 1\}$, where value 1 stands for 'true' (i.e. "there is a building-like object in this patch") and -1 for 'false' ("no building-like object here").

Considering the set of multi-temporal images as a 3D data, G is defined in the 3D space (2 spatial dimensions + 1 temporal dimension). G is the sum of k 2D spatio-subgraphs $G^{s,i \in \{1,..,k\}}$, linked by temporal vertices V^t, where s and t denote the spatial and temporal indices respectively, and $V = \{\bigcup_i V^{s,i}, \bigcup_j V^{t,j}\}$. $G = \{\bigcup_i G^i, \bigcup_i V^{t,j}\}$, $i \in \{1,..,k\}, j \in \{1,..,k-1\}$. Then, in the specific case of two images: $G^{s,i=\{1,2\}} = (E^{s,i}, V^{s,i})$ with $i = \{1,2\}$. Pair-wise cliques associated to each node e cover a 5-neighborhood characterised by its four vertices in $x-y$ space, V^s, augmented with a unique vertex in t space, V^t.

In the Gibbs formalism, the probability distribution to retrieve the configuration X given the features $y = \{y_{e \in G}\}$ is expressed by :

$$P(X|y) = \frac{1}{Z}e^{-U}$$

where $U = U(X, y)$ is the potential energy and Z is known as the partition constant. In [8], Kumar defines U as the sum of an association potential A and an interaction potential I, such that :

$$-U(X,y) = \sum_{e \in G} \gamma_e A(x_e, y_e) + \sum_{e \in G} \sum_{e' \in N_e} \beta_{e,e'} I(x_e, y_e, x_{e'})$$

N_e is the five-neighboring. $A(x_e, y_e)$ is the association potential; the interaction term $I(x_e, y_e, x_{e' \in N_e})$ is a smoothness factor. It determines how much a site is similar or not to its associated neighboring sites. A and I are defined as parametric logistic functions which exact formulation can be found in [8].

Knowing that object changes are characterised by continuity in spatial neighborhood and discontinuity in temporal neighborhood, we consider an anisotropic formulation of U given by:

$$\beta_{e,e'} = \beta_{e,e''} \quad iif \quad (e,e',e'') \in G^{s,i}$$

$$\beta_{e,e'} \neq \beta_{e,e''} \quad otherwise$$

The anisotropic constraint will enable to detect any 3D object having a structured –building-like– shape in the space dimension s, but which is lost over the time. We call $C = \{C_e\}_{e \in G^1}$ the hidden variable defined such as : $C_e = X_e^1 X_{e'}^2$, for which e is connected to e' by $V(e,e') \subset V^t$. Then, in a straightforward manner:

$$P(C|y) \equiv P(X|y)$$

$P(C|y)$ is the probability of structural changes, defined at each node of each of the 2D images taken individually. Note that C is defined over the *projection* of G_1 and G_2 in the spatial dimension and has 'lost' the 3rd temporal dimension.

3.2 Computational Issues

In order to fasten the computation, it is possible to implement the model in its 2D formulation, while modifying the choice of the features, such that new features by them selves are charactistics of a structural change. The simplest way is to define new features' vector as the difference of features computed from bi-dimensional images.

Parameters are estimated by maximizing the pseudo-likelihood of $P(y|C)$ using a large training image set and manually detected objects. On the testing images set, the optimal configuration C is obtained via ICM computation.

4 Results Analysis

The two proposed methods have been implemented and validated on composite and real remote sensing images. Com-posite images were artificially created by mapping locally some small textured patches onto real images: it will validate the method without illumination change. Remote sensing images are from Quickbird satellite (resol. 0.6m/pixel, panchromatic, acquired in 2002 and 2003 ; covering the area of Beijing city). Ground truth is given by manual segmentation. Note that Beijing area is particularly interesting to study because of the rapid undergoing changes in preparation of the 2008 Olympic games.

We used, for the two models, a training set of nearly 2000 object sites manually detected from 10 sub-images. The Kernel computation (section 2) takes about 4mn on Pentium4. Cost comes from contour feature calculation while the optimization per see only takes less than 10 seconds.

Figure 1 illustrates the principle of the *cut-and-merge* algorithm and building candidates selection. Results from the object change detection Kernel approach are shown in figures 2 and 4. Tables 1 and 2 give statistical analysis of the results. We recall that the ultimous purpose is not to delineate precisely the new/old buildings, but to locate the changed objects, as indicated by the crosses. The kernel approach gives a precise counting of the changed objects.

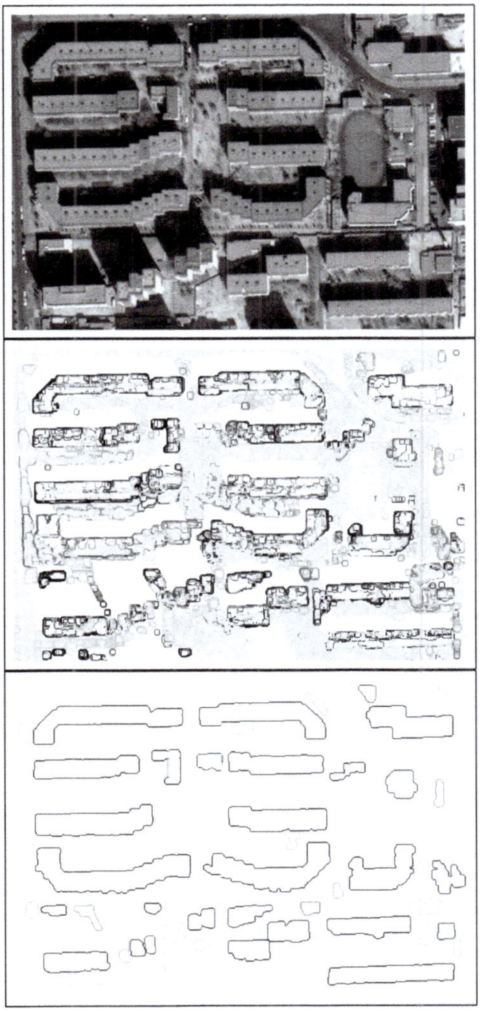

Fig. 1. Illustration of the *cut-and-merge* algorithm. Top: original image. Middle: superimposition of the contours extracted during the *cut* step; Bottom: building candidates resulting from the *merge* step. The grey level of the contours is inversely proportional to the probability to delineate a building-like object.

Good performance obtained from 3D DRF (section 3) on a toy picture without noise validate the model definition and features choice (fig.5). Note that only the changes of structured objects are detected. Figures 3 and 4 illustrate the approach and compare it to the kernel method. The DRF model acts as a region-of-interest detector, by giving rough location of areas where structural changes have appeared.

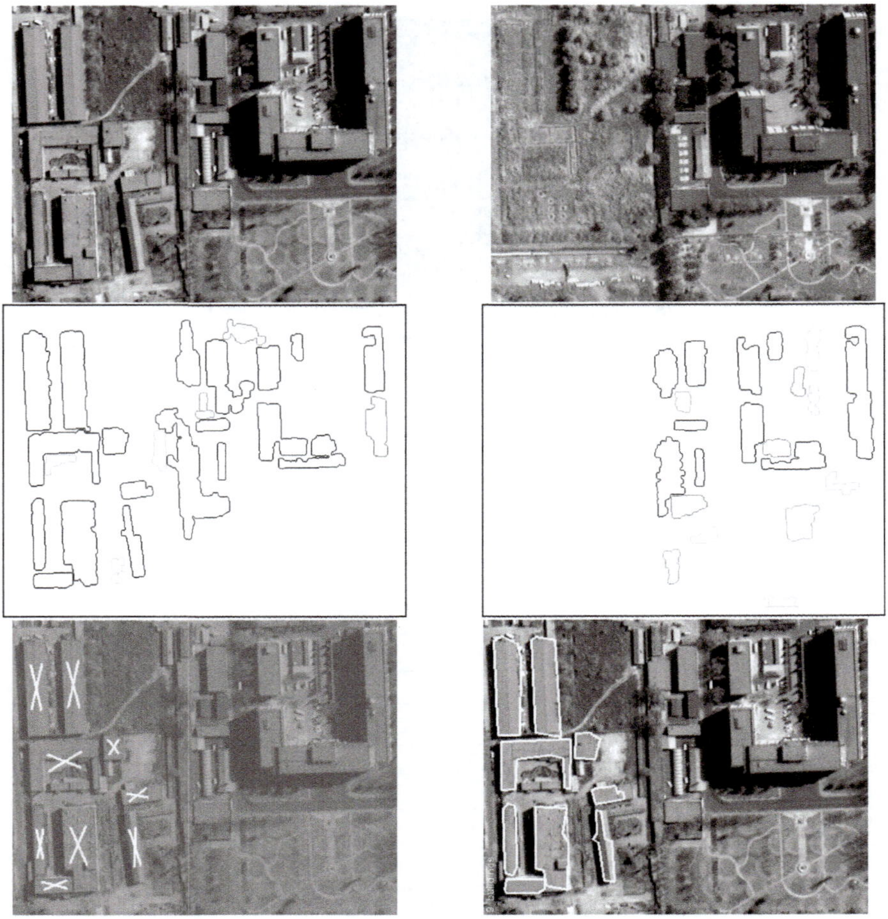

Fig. 2. Top: Original images. Center: candidate buildings' contours retrieved from *cut-and-merge*; Bottom: building-object changes represented by polygonal approximation of the contours (right) or marked with a cross (left) –black for new building, white for disappeared.

5 Conclusion

We proposed in this paper two probabilistic framework for structural change inference in complex scenes. The first one, closely related to classical differential methods, computes the changes based on a likelihood function, which makes the approach very robust and enable to decrease erroneous detections rate. The second model is derived from 3D DRF modeling, where the third dimension is the temporal component. Its fast implementation in 2D space makes it extremely efficient. One may notice however that the proposed model formulation is not invariant by symetry with respect to temporal axis. From a practical point of

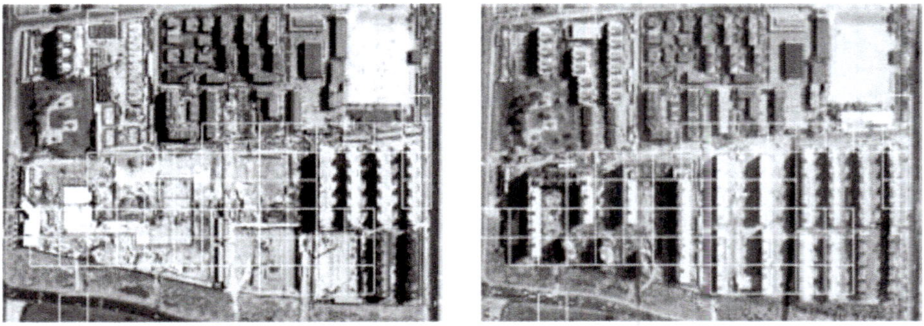

Fig. 3. Illustration of the 3D DRF on real Quickbird images acquired in 2002 (right) and 2003 (left). Patches indicate areas detected as changes (patch size=64x64pixels). New buildings are properly recovered but false detections also appear.

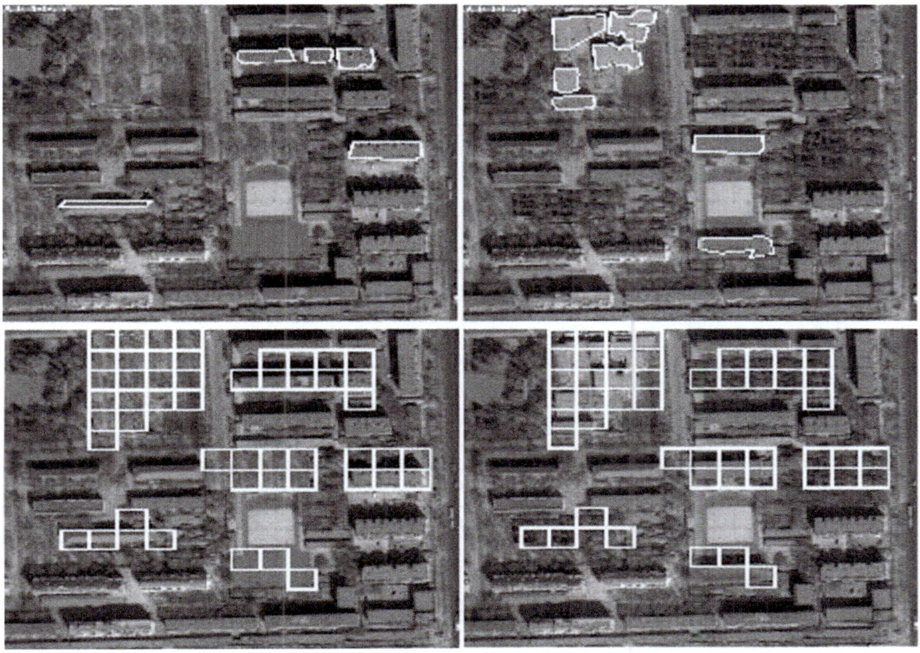

Fig. 4. Results comparison from 3D DRF (bottom) and kernel based approaches (top), on a composite image. Top: white lines indicate the changed objects retrieved as destroyed and new buildings ; Bottom: White squares indicate the location of structural changes, as detected by the DRF model.

view, the two approaches differ by the output they provide: 3D DRF gives a rough location of structural changes ; the minimal area is set by the size of the patches used for the computation ; a contrario, in the *cut-and-merge* algorithm,

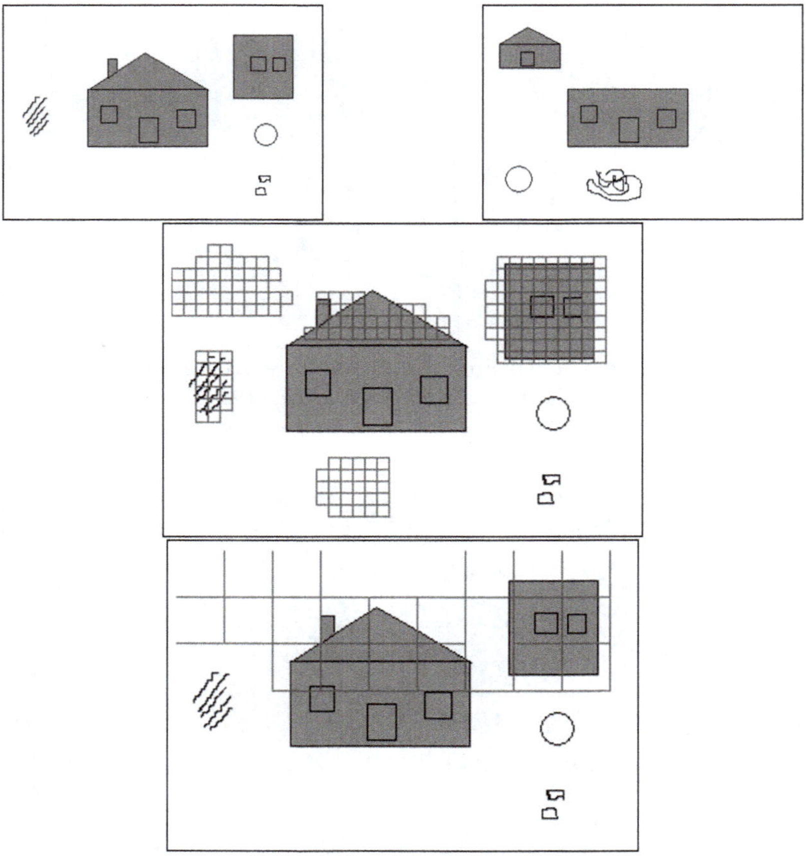

Fig. 5. Structural changes from 3D DRF - Application to a toy picture. Top: original images. Middle and bottom: patches –computing size = 8x8 (middle) and 32x32pixels (bottom) indicating the detected changes are superimpose to one of the input image. Note that only the structured object changes are retrieved.

Table 1. Statistical figures on change detection (section 2). GT=Nber of changed-objects given by the ground truth; TP=True positive; FP=False positive; DR=Detection rate=TP/GT ; CR= Correctness rate=FP/(FP+TP).

GT	TP	FP	DR	CR
62	45	22	0.72	0.67

the segmentation step delineates the buildings' shape and makes possible the counting of changed objects. Extension of this work could be on object tracking from video sequence.

Table 2. Statistical figures on building detection from cut-and-merge. FN=False negative; AreaTrueRate: rate of the surface size of the object that have been correctly recovered; AreaErrorRate: rate of the surface area which is out side true building AreaLostRate: rate of the surface area which has not been detected.

TP	FP	FN	AreaTrueR
0.834	0.058	0.166	0.861
AreaErrorR	AreaLosetR	Peri Rate	AreaRate
0.060	0.139	0.244	0.189

Acknowledgement. This work was partially supported by the LIAMA and by the Chinese Ministry of Science and Technology 863 program under the project "Multi-source geospatial data fusion for digital map updating and urban development decision support".

References

1. J. Besag. "On the statistical analysis of dirty pictures". Journal of Royal Statistical Soc., B-48:259-302, 1986
2. L. Garcin, X. Descombes, J. Zerubia, and H. Le Men. "Building extraction using a Markov point process". In Proc. ICIP, Greece, 2001.
3. L.M.T. Carvalho, L.M.G.Fonseca. "Digital change detection with the aid of multiresolution wavelet analysis". Int. J. Remote. Sens., 2001, vol.22, no.18, pp.3871-3876.
4. D. Crandall and P. Felzenszenzwald. "Spatial priors for part-based reco-gnition using statistical methods". In Proc.CVPR, SanDiego, June 2005
5. S. Geman and D. Geman. "Stochastic relaxation, Gibbs Distribution and Bayesian Restoration of Images", IEEE PAMI vol.6, no.6, Nov. 1984.
6. R.B. Irvin and D.M. McKeown. "Method for exploiting the relationship between buildings and their shadows in aerial imagery". IEEE Trans. Syst. Man Cybern., vol. 19, pp.1564-1575, 1989.
7. K. Kulschewski. "Building recognition with Bayesian Networks". Workshop on Semantic Modelling for the Acquisition of Topographic Images and Maps, Bonn, Germany, 1997.
8. S. Kumar and M. Hebert. "Discriminative Random Fields: A Discriminative Framework for Contextual Interaction in Classification". In Proc. ICCV, 2003.
9. S. Kumar and M. Hebert. "Man-Made Structure Detection in Natural Images using a Causal Multiscale Random Field". In Proc. CVPR, 2003.
10. S. Krishnamrchari and Ag. "Delineating Buildings by Grouping Lines with MRFs". IEEE Trans. on Image Processing, vol. 5, NO. 1., 1996.
11. C.G. Lin and R. Nevatia. "Building Detection and Description from a Single Intensity Image". CVIU, vol 72, no2, Nov.1998, pp101-121.
12. J. Lafferty, A. McCallum, and F. Pereira. "Conditional random fields: Probabilistic models for segmenting and labeling sequence data". In Proc ICML, 2001.
13. S. Z. Li. Markov Random Field Modeling in Computer Vision. Springer-Verlag, Tokyo, 2001.
14. D. Marr. Vision. Ed. Freeman and Company, NY, 1982.

15. Hans-Gerd Maas. "Closed solutions for the determination of parametric building models from invariant moments of airborne laserscanner data". IAPRS, vol. XXXII (B3), 1999.
16. Helmut Mayer."Automatic Object Extraction from Aerial Imagery: A Survey Focusing on Buildings". CVIU, vol. 74 no.2, pp. 138-149, 1999.
17. T. P. Minka. "Algorithms for Maximum-Likelihood logistic Regression". Statistics Tech Report 758, Carnegie Mellon University.
18. Open CVcourses, CVPR01 course "(http://sourceforge.net/projects/opencvlibrary)".
19. N. Paparoditis, M. Cord, M. Jordan, and J.-P. Cocquerez. "Building Detection and Reconstruction from Mid- and High-Resolution Aerial Imagery". CVIU, vol 72 no2, Nov.1998.
20. V. Venkateswar and R. Chellappa. "A hierachical approach to detection of buildings in aerial images". Tech. Rep. CAR-TR 567, Univ. of Maryland, 1991.
21. Special section on Syntactic and structural pattern recognition, IEEE pattern analysis and machine intelligence, vol.27 no.7, July 2005
22. Y. Boykov. "Discrete Optimization Methods in Computer Vision", SanDiego, In Proc. CVPR 2005.

Robust Occluded Shape Recognition*

Ronak Shah, Anima Mishra, and Subrata Rakshit

Centre for Artificial Intelligence and Robotics,
Defence Research and Development Organisation,
High Grounds, Raj Bhavan Circle,
Bangalore-560001
{ronak, anima, subrata }@cair.res.in

Abstract. The primary reason for shape characterization and matching is to use it for characterization and recognition of the associated objects. However, the shapes obtained from segmentation and/or edge detection of real world images are, at best, approximations of the actual shapes of objects. Unsupervised segmentations often deviate from object boundaries to include parts of other objects or background. Similarly, objects of interest may be partially occluded by other objects in natural scenes. We address the problem of adapting known shape characterization and retrieval methods to make them robust to errors in the basic input - the binarised shape image corresponding to an object. An effort is made to retain the ability to deal with scale, rotation and translation.

The presented method is based on the centroid distance shape signature, but which does not sample the perimeter points evenly along the perimeter length. Instead, the sampling is done evenly using an angular measure. This property of our signature localizes the changes due to occlusion. For similar reasons, we do not derive a shape descriptor where each feature potentially depends on the entire shape signature. The onus of achieving various invariances is shifted to the definition of our similarity metric. Again, to take care of the changes in the perimeter, the similarity measure has been designed to produce small changes for small segmentation errors. The approach presented here can be applied to many applications such as Content Based Image Retrieval (CBIR), Target Detection, Medical Imaging etc. The limitations of the method are its inability to deal with complex shapes that have perforations, tendrils etc.

Index terms: Shape, Shape signature, Similarity measure, Occlusion.

1 Introduction

Shape, color (intensity) and texture are important features used to describe and identify objects in images. Of these, shape cannot be directly sensed or measured. It is necessary to first delineate an object, either by segmenting it

* This work was funded by DRDO through Proj CAR-008. Authors wish to thank Director CAIR, ISYS-DO and colleagues in CVG for their support.

P.J. Narayanan et al. (Eds.): ACCV 2006, LNCS 3851, pp. 847–857, 2006.

on the basis of color and/or texture or by detecting its edge. The basic input for shape charcterization is noisy as niether of the above said processes are guaranteed to work perfectly and sometimes also due to projection of a 3D object on a 2D plane. So for applications such as CBIR [1] and target detection ability to deal with the imperfect segmentation results is critical as manual segmentation makes a little sense. Last, but not least, distance and view angle can lead to translation, scaling and rotation of objects across scenes making the task of object recognition using shapes a very difficult task.

The challenges addressed for reliable classification and retrieval of well segmented shapes have been oriented towards achieving invariance to translation, scale, rotation and affine transforms and in forming compact descriptors and computationally efficient match algorithms. Traditionally, shape representation is divided into two types - contour based and region based depending on what they describe. Each is further subdivided into two categories - structural and global based on how they describe shape [2].

Contour-based structural methods use different criteria to break up the shape boundary into segments (or representations) and so the similarity measure is generally based on graph or string matching. Such similarity measure allows for partial match based on substring matching methods. One of the important methods in Contour-based structural methods is Curvature Scale Space, which is based on tracking the inflection points, obtained by successive filtering of the shape boundary from variable width low-pass filters [3]. The problem of this method lies in defining events, which essentially are features from the shape, which can give a stable and a compact representation of the interval tree (Result of the smoothing process).

Contour-based global methods have two steps: the extraction of a shape signature and the computation of a shape descriptor based on the signature. The shape signature is a 1D function defined along the perimeter which can encode various quantities like centroid distance, curvature, area swept etc [4]. The switch from shape signature to a global descriptor is necessary in order to obtain the scale, rotation and translation invariances. Shape signatures pick up minor perturbations at the fringes of the segmented objects.

Region-based global techniques such as moments, medial axis etc. take into account all the pixels within a shape region to obtain the representation. In this way they are robust to minor shape distortions at the periphery. They are computationally very expensive as lower order moments are not able to represent the shape successfully.

The global methods are better able to deal with invariances, besides being more computationally efficient. However, when two shapes do not match, the global descriptors do not have the ability to localize the cause of difference. Without the ability to localize the mismatch or identify a partial match, it is hard to deal with occlusion. The problem with the structural methods is that they do not allow for good similarity metrics and are not invariant to scale and rotation and require very large length descriptors.

In this paper, a new approach to shape recognition is described. The shape descriptor chosen here is based on the centroid distance signature. However, the exact method of computing is altered to give more robustness to occlusion. The similarity measure defined here provides scale and rotation invariance for the described shape signature. This enables us to eliminate the requirement for a shape descriptor based on a global transform. The final strategy for robustness lies in searching for the best choice of origin within the shape rather than relying strictly on the centroid.

The approach described here also tries to satisfy the requirements set by MPEG-7 [5][6]. However, the emphasis is on dealing with the type of object segmentation errors expected for real images. Our method will perform poorly for very complicated shapes, but we do not expect to accurately segment such complicated shapes from natural scenes anyway.

The rest of the paper is organized as follows. In section 2, we describe the approach for shape recognition, which includes Shape Descriptor, Similarity Measure and Center Point Search Algorithm. The Results, Summary and Future Work are described in section 3, which is followed by the references.

2 Approach

In order to deal with occlusions and segmentation errors, we modify the centroid distance based Fourier descriptor for shapes, which has been reported in [4] as being the most suitable for shape representation and retrieval. This section describes the formulation of a modified centroid based shape descriptor and its associated similarity metric. By themselves they only ensure shape representation and scale - rotation - translation invariant recognition. The utilisation of this modified descriptor for occlusion is dealt with in the next section. However, the requirements for robustness to occlusion are mentioned here in order to motivate the formulation of the descriptor.

2.1 Shape Descriptor

In this section, a contour based shape descriptor is presented which is a modification of the centroid distance signature. The computation of the usual centroid distance signature and its associated Fourier descriptor (FD) involves [4]

1. Computation of the centroid (x_c, y_c).
2. Computation of the distance of each perimeter point to the centroid

$$r(t) = ([x(t) - x_c]^2 + [y(t) - y_c]^2)^{\frac{1}{2}} \tag{1}$$

   where the perimeter is represented parametrically as the set of $(x(t), y(t))$ with $t = 0, \cdots, T-1$.
3. Computation of the DFT $R(n)$, $n = 0, \cdots, T-1$
4. Normalization of the magnitudes of the DFT coefficients by the dc $(R(0))$ and selection of the first N components to define the N dimensional FD.

By using a parametric representation for perimeter $(x(t), y(t))$, it is possible to generate shape signatures for contours of any simply connected shape. The FD is typically truncated to a fixed length and a Euclidean metric used to determine the similarity. The FD is invariant to translation, scale and rotation transformations.

When the perimeter length is changed due to occlusion or segmentation errors, the shape changes by a process of addition or subtraction. The FD as computed above turns out to be sensitive to such changes due to three factors.

1. Change in the position of the centroid, (x_c, y_c).
2. Change in the perimeter length, T, which in effect changes the associated harmonic bases (in case of occlusion) used in the DFT computation.
3. The global computation of the DFT coefficients means that a local change in the perimeter affects all the DFT coefficients to varying degrees.

Large changes in the descriptor for local perimeter changes indicate the limitation of such descriptors in handling occluded shapes. Figure 1 shows the true shape (a) and an erroneously segmented version (b) of that shape. While distinctive features are preserved, an extra rectanguler region has been added. Figure 2

(a) original shape (b) occluded shape

Fig. 1. Selected Shape

indicates the change in the descriptor. Here the obtained descriptor for shape (b) at a new and old center point (centroid for shape (a)) differ drastically from the original one. The peak obtained for shape (a) is shifted from 6 to 7 for shape (b). This makes the comparision virtually impossible. The extra peak obtained in the new descriptor is due to a low frequency change in the original shape. Ideally, the signature and descriptor must be designed such that there are small changes for small changes in the perimeter. Additionally, so as to handle occluded shapes, the perturbations must be localised. The properties of scale, rotation and translation invariance while applying similarity measure continues to be important. In order to satisfy all these contraints, the present work modifies the centroid signature/descriptor, the similarity metric introduces an additional search process. Any descriptor that depends on a computed geometrical entity like the centroid will necessarily be changed due to addition or subrtaction of regions from the shape. The solution proposed here is to initiate a directed search that finds the best *centre* point ($\boldsymbol{c}$) for defining the descriptor such as to match some given reference descriptor. The Fourier descriptors make such a search computationally

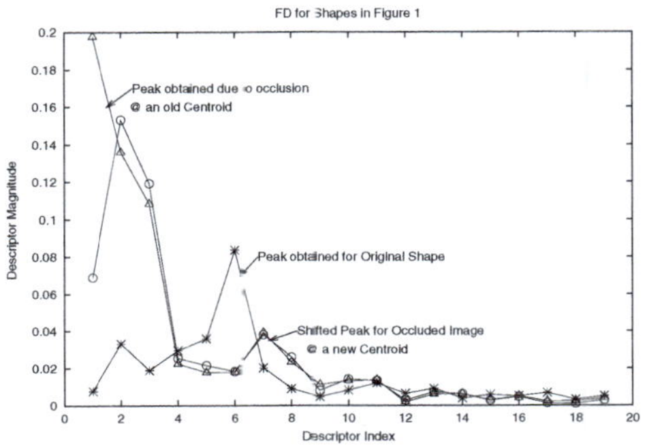

Fig. 2. FD obtained for shapes indicated above

expensive. We formulate a simpler descriptor that allows for an efficient search for $\boldsymbol{c}$ and a localization of occlusion induced error.

In order to isolate the changes due to occlusions, the shape descriptor is generated from the shape signature by a process of sampling rather than a global process like series summation. Outward rays from the chosen centre point (default being centroid) are extended till the perimeter at fixed angular intervals and the distance to the perimeter is measured. When a perimeter is changed due to addition or subtraction, the descriptor elements corresponding to the unchanged portion remain unchanged. The drawback of this formulation is that the descriptor loses its ability to appropriately characterize highly nonconvex shapes. The descriptor itself is no longer invariant to size and orientation, but that is dealt with by modifying the similarity metric.

The computation of this modified centroid distance based descriptor involves

1. Selection of the descriptor length, N.
2. Computation of the center point $\boldsymbol{c} = (x_c, y_c)$. By default this is the centroid but other choices will be introduced later.
3. Computation of the distance from $\boldsymbol{c}$ to perimeter along N directions $\theta_n = 2n\pi/N$, for $n = 0, \cdots, N-1$. If (x_n, y_n) denotes the point on the perimeter that is closest to (x_c, y_c) along θ_n, then the N signature points are

$$\delta_n = [(x_n - x_c)^2 + (y_n - y_c)^2]^{\frac{1}{2}} \tag{2}$$

4. The δ_ns define the elements of the feature descriptor $\boldsymbol{\lambda}$, which may be denoted as

$$\boldsymbol{\lambda}(\boldsymbol{c}) = [\delta_0 \delta_1 \delta_2 \cdots \delta_{(N-1)}] \tag{3}$$

where the arguement $\boldsymbol{c}$ makes explicit the dependency of $\boldsymbol{\lambda}$ on the chosen center point $\boldsymbol{c}$.

Figure 3 [7] illustrates the signature. This signature is translation invariant and computationally inexpensive. This descriptor helps in obtaining only the local changes in the description when small changes in the perimeter occurs. In

(a) Shape Descriptor Process (b) Shape Descriptor

Fig. 3. Shape Descriptor Process Using Regular Angular Sampling of Centroid Distance

this way, it removes the problem related to the global change in the description for occluded shapes. Figure 4 indicates the fact. It can be seen that at the *center* point the descriptor for occluded shape matches to the descriptor of the original one closely (except for the occluded portion). Here the descriptors represent the shapes shown in figure 1. A change in the perimeter will affect only

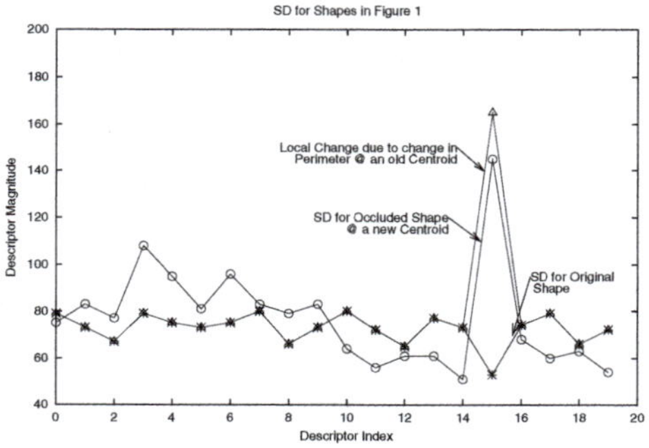

Fig. 4. Descriptor obtained for shapes indicated in figure 1

selected descriptor elements, *provided the center point remains unchanged.* That can happen only if, after starting with the new centroid as the center point, we can devise a method for determining the earlier centroid when comparing the occluded shape to a shape similar to its original shape. Such a method requires an iterative maximization of similarity between a fixed $\boldsymbol{\lambda_{ref}}$ and our new $\boldsymbol{\lambda}(\boldsymbol{c})$. Before describing such a scheme, the similarity metric is defined for $\boldsymbol{\lambda}$.

2.2 Similarity Measure

This feature descriptor obtained is translation invariant as $\boldsymbol{c}$ is computed based on the shape itself (centroid being default). For a scaled shape the feature vector obtained will be related to the original by

$$\boldsymbol{\lambda_s} = \alpha\boldsymbol{\lambda} \tag{4}$$

i.e., the magnitude of the vector will scale but the orientation will remain unchanged. For a rotated shape, the new feature descriptor is approximated by a shifted version of the original. For a rotation by a multiple of $2\pi/N$, say by $\theta_n = 2n\pi/N$, the new descriptor can be represented as

$$\boldsymbol{\lambda_r} = [\delta_n \delta_{n+1} \delta_{n+2} \cdots \delta_{((N-1+n))_N}] \tag{5}$$

where the components of the original descriptor have been indicated as per the earlier notation. Clearly, the descriptor is itself not invariant to scale and rotation. A constraint while defining the similarity measure is to ensure that the above properties are utilized to ensure that the similarity metric is invariant to translation, scale and rotation. In addition, it is desirable that the metric is not dominated by a few large mismatches among the N descriptor components.

The function used here for defining the similarity between two shapes is the maximum of the normalized circular convolution of the shape descriptors. The normalization ensures scale invariance and the maximum of the circular convolution ensures rotation invariance. The product form used in the convolution ensures that the metric measures overall similarity while ignoring a few large mismatches in the descriptor components, as opposed to the squared difference based Eucledian norm. Formally, let

$$\boldsymbol{\lambda_1} = [\delta_{10} \delta_{11} \delta_{12} \cdots \delta_{1(N-1)}] \tag{6}$$

and

$$\boldsymbol{\lambda_2} = [\delta_{20} \delta_{21} \delta_{22} \cdots \delta_{2(N-1)}] \tag{7}$$

be two shape descriptors, where the dependence on center points has been suppressed for notational simplicity. The normalized circular convolution between these may be denoted as:

$$\psi(\boldsymbol{\lambda_1}, \boldsymbol{\lambda_2}, n) = \sum_k \frac{\lambda_1(k)\lambda_2(k-n)}{\Lambda_1 \Lambda_2} \tag{8}$$

where $\Lambda_i = ||\boldsymbol{\lambda_i}||$. The similarity measure between two shape descriptors can now be defined as

$$\tilde{S}(\boldsymbol{\lambda_1}, \boldsymbol{\lambda_2}) \triangleq \max_n \psi(\boldsymbol{\lambda_1}, \boldsymbol{\lambda_2}, n) \tag{9}$$

This similarity measure, $\tilde{S}$, indicates the best fit of the shapes for the chosen center points used for $\boldsymbol{\lambda_1}$, $\boldsymbol{\lambda_2}$. Without loss of generality, assume that $\boldsymbol{\lambda_1}$ is computed with the centroid as the center point. The similarity measure S can now be written explicitly as a function of the second center point as:

$$\tilde{S}(\boldsymbol{\lambda_1}, \boldsymbol{\lambda_2}(\boldsymbol{x})) = \tilde{S_{12}}(\boldsymbol{x}) \triangleq \max_n \psi(\boldsymbol{\lambda_1}, \boldsymbol{\lambda_2}(\boldsymbol{x}), n) \tag{10}$$

In order to remove the dependency on centroid variation and capitalize on the ability of the shape signature to localise changes due to occlusion, the occlusion-resistant version of the similarity measure is defined as

$$S_{12} = \max_{\boldsymbol{x}} \tilde{S_{12}}(\boldsymbol{x}) \tag{11}$$

Compared to the usual centroid distance based Fourier descriptor, S_{12} is far more computationally costly as it involves two searches for maxima: a 1D search for orientation (n) and a 2D search for center point ($\boldsymbol{x}$). While a search based invariance is costlier, it has the benefit of not being blind. The knowledge of the n and $\boldsymbol{x}$ that maximise the measures allows us to recover the relative orientation and probable occlusion regions. The rotation invariance of the FD, on the other hand, means that no measure based on it can be used to recover orientation. The search for n is the price one pays for localizing shape descriptor changes for occlusions. Of the two searches, the search for optimum $\boldsymbol{x}$ is by far more computationally expensive. While the search for best n can be exhaustive (1D, with $\sim$ 30-100 elements), an exhaustive search for the best center point is impractical. A directed search algorithm is required which can incrementally give the direction of a better center point, with good convergence and stability properties. This search technique is explained next.

2.3 Center Point Search Algorithm

The search for the solution of Equation(11) is handicapped by the fact that there is no analytic definition of the perimeter. As a result one cannot formulate a general expression for $S_{12}(\boldsymbol{x})$ in terms of $\boldsymbol{x}$ and directly solve for $\boldsymbol{x}$. The direct solution being ruled out, the second best alternative would be a gradient based search: start at some $\boldsymbol{x}$, say the centroid, and determine the direction one should go in order to maximise the similarity measure $\tilde{S}$. The lack of an analytic definition of the perimeter precludes an analytic estimate of the gradient of $\tilde{S}(\boldsymbol{x})$ as well. This forces us to numerically estimate the local gradients of $\tilde{S}(\boldsymbol{x})$ by evaluating it for neighboring values of $\boldsymbol{x}$. In effect, we would have to find by actual evaluation

$$\underset{\boldsymbol{\epsilon}}{argmax}[S(\boldsymbol{x}+\boldsymbol{\epsilon})] \tag{12}$$

and then update $\boldsymbol{x} = \boldsymbol{x} + \boldsymbol{\epsilon}^*$. The $\boldsymbol{\epsilon}$ are displacements in various directions with a fixed small magnitude ϵ. If the number of directions is set equal to N, the number of directions sampled in defining the feature descriptor, it becomes computationally expensive to find N shape signatures and evaluate N similarity measures $\tilde{S}$. Two approximations can be used to accelerate the computation without compromising the final result.

1. $\boldsymbol{\lambda}(\boldsymbol{x}+\boldsymbol{\epsilon})$ can be estimated based on $\boldsymbol{\lambda}(\boldsymbol{x})$ for small ϵ. If $\epsilon << \delta_i$, the descriptor components, then the new descriptor components can be approximated by $\delta_i^\epsilon = \delta_i - \cos(\gamma) \cdot \epsilon$ where γ is the angle between $\boldsymbol{\epsilon}$ and the direction θ_n of the descriptor component.
2. The computation of $\tilde{S}$ involves a search over orientations and is an $O(N^2)$ computation. However, for finding $argmax(\boldsymbol{\epsilon})$, the two shapes are not being rotated with respect to each other. For small ϵ, the shape of $\boldsymbol{\lambda}(\boldsymbol{x})$ will be very close to $\boldsymbol{\lambda}(\boldsymbol{x}+\boldsymbol{\epsilon})$. Hence the value of n that maximises $\tilde{S}(\boldsymbol{\lambda_1}, \boldsymbol{\lambda_2}(\boldsymbol{x}))$ can be assumed to maximise $\tilde{S}(\boldsymbol{\lambda_1}, \boldsymbol{\lambda_2}(\boldsymbol{x}+\boldsymbol{\epsilon}))$

The magnitude of $\boldsymbol{\epsilon}$ is critical for the dynamics of the search. If it is too small, the search will take a long time to settle to a solution. If it is too big, then the

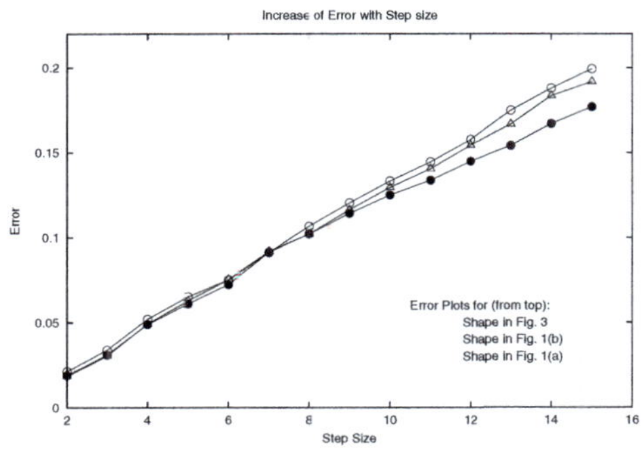

Fig. 5. Error v/s Stepsize Graph

errors made in approximating the shape descriptors will misdirect the search. This error varies for different shapes and for different step sizes for the same shape. This may be calculated as following

$$Error = \frac{\|\boldsymbol{\lambda}(x+\boldsymbol{\epsilon}) - \boldsymbol{\lambda}_{anal}(x+\boldsymbol{\epsilon})\|}{\Lambda} \tag{13}$$

where $\Lambda = \|\boldsymbol{\lambda}(x+\boldsymbol{\epsilon})\|$ and $\boldsymbol{\lambda}_{anal}$ is the descriptor obtained from the method used for accelerating the computation. The approximation error as a function of ϵ is shown in Figure 5. As expected error is a monotonically increasing function of ϵ. Here the step size may be selected by setting the upper threshold for error (which was 0.1 for our case). In order to prevent accumulation of error, the shape descriptor and similarity measure were explicitly recomputed for each new center point before continuing the search.

The center point search algorithm for matching two shapes can be summarized as follows:

1. Compute the centroid and the shape descriptor for Shape1, $\boldsymbol{\lambda_1}$.
2. Set the center point for Shape2, $\boldsymbol{x}$, to be its centroid. Compute the shape descriptor for Shape2 at the chosen center point, $\boldsymbol{\lambda_2}(\boldsymbol{x})$.
3. Compute the similarity $\tilde{S_{12}}(\boldsymbol{x})$, noting the value of n, n^*, that maximizes the circular convolution.
4. Approximate $\boldsymbol{\lambda_2}(\boldsymbol{x}+\boldsymbol{\epsilon})$ from $\boldsymbol{\lambda_2}(\boldsymbol{x})$ for N directions of $\boldsymbol{\epsilon}$.
5. For each $\boldsymbol{\lambda_2}$ above, evaluate $\tilde{S_{12}}$ by computing the circular convolution for only $n = n^*$
6. If none of the new descriptors score higher, EXIT
7. Select the $\boldsymbol{\epsilon}$ that maximises $\tilde{S_{12}}$ and set the new center point to $\boldsymbol{x} = \boldsymbol{x} + \boldsymbol{\epsilon}$. Goto Step 2.

3 Results

The proposed method is tested using the shapes shown in Figure 6. The top row shows four reference shapes while the bottom row shows four query shapes. The

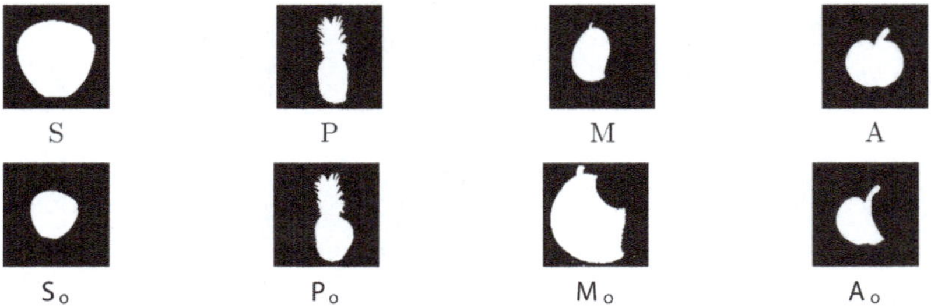

Fig. 6. Selected Original and Occluded Shapes

Table 1. Similarity Metric at a new centroid

SHAPES	S	P	M	A
S_o	**1.0000**	0.9017	0.9862	0.9954
P_o	0.9242	**0.9885**	0.9653	0.9296
M_o	0.9851	0.9507	**0.9939**	0.9842
A_o	0.9810	0.9263	**0.9836**	0.9807

Table 2. Similarity Metric at a center point

SHAPES	S	P	M	A
S_o	**1.0000**	0.9072	0.9863	0.9956
P_o	0.9249	**0.9919**	0.9688	0.9334
M_o	0.9857	0.9515	**0.9944**	0.9861
A_o	0.9832	0.9370	0.9854	**0.9857**

shape S has been subjected to scaling and rotation, P has an added portion, M has been scaled and then truncated and A has a portion removed. The similarity metric computed between each query shape and the four reference shapes are given below. Table1 shows the results of using the proposed descriptor and metric using the true centroids in each case. Table 2 shows the metric based on finding the best centre point. In each case, S_o scores a perfect match with S showing the scale-orientation invariance of the proposed method. The shapes P_o and M_o also find their correct best matches. However, A_o is misclassified as M in Table 1. With the centre point search, A_o is correctly classified as shown in Table 2.

3.1 Summary and Future Work

Ability to handle occluded shapes plays an important role in selection of the shape descriptor and in turn in shape recognition. The Fourier based descriptors are not optimised to handle occlusions, as the change in the descriptor is global for a local changes in the perimeter. The approach described here for shape recognition can handle occlusions. The aim here is to ensure that there are only local changes in the descriptor for local perimeter changes. The descriptor and metric formulated here is shown to retain the scale-orientation invariance while ensuring this localisation.

There are two extensions of this work which are being explored. After finding the best centre point, scale and orientation for a fit, one can suitably recompute the descriptor taking the scale, centre point and orientation into account. The difference between the descriptors of the reference shape and query shape can then be analysed to decide if, and where, an occlusion has taken place. Secondly, the definition of the descriptor may be extended to include an additional N elements based on a (possible) second intersection of the oriented rays with the perimeter. This will improve the ability to deal with more complex shapes.

References

[1] Remco C. Veltkamp, Mirela Tanase: Content-Based Image Retrieval Systems: A Survey. Technical Report UU-CS-2000-34 (October, 2000).

[2] Sven Loncavic: A Survey of Shape Analysis Techniques. Pattern Recognition **31(8)** (1998) 983–1001.

[3] Dengsheng Zhang, Guojun Lu: Review of Shape Representation and Description Techniques. Pattern Recognition **37** (2004) 1–19.

[4] Dengsheng Zhang, Guojun Lu: A Comparative Study of Fourier Descriptors for Shape Representation and Retrieval. Asian Conference on Computer Vision (January, 2002).

[5] Dengsheng Zhang, Guojun Lu: A Comparative Study of Three Region based Shape Descriptors. Digital Image Computing Techniques and Applications (January, 2002).

[6] H.Kim, J.Kim: Region-based Shape Descriptor invarient to rotation, scale and translation. Image Communication **16** (2000) 87-93.

[7] Christopher M. Cyr, Ahmed F. Kamal, Thomas B. Sebastian, Benjamin B. Kimia: 2D-3D Registration based on Shape Matching. Proceedings on Mathematical Methods in Bio-Medical Image Analysis (June, 2000) 198-203.

Interactive Contour Extraction Using NURBS-HMM

Debin Lei[1], Chunhong Pan[2], Qing Yang[2], and Minyong Shi[1]

[1] Communication University of China, Beijing, China
{007, myshi}@cuc.edu.cn
[2] National Laboratory of Pattern Recognition (NLPR),
Institute of Automation, Chinese Academy of Sciences, China
{chpan, qyang}@nlpr.ia.ac.cn

Abstract. In the paper, we attempt to develop a novel method to offer the possibility even for a non-expert to extract easily the contour of an object. A NURBS-HMM framework aiming at the interactive image contour extraction is proposed. We fit the initial points input by users with Non-Uniform Rational B-Spline(NURBS). Due to the local controllability of NURBS, the control points are considered as the states of Hidden Markov Model(HMM) framework, and the boundary features and uniformity along the boundary are integrated as the observations. The experimental results show the robustness of our method. As an interactive method, the method interacts with users in an efficient and comfortable way.

1 Introduction

Image segmentation and contour extraction techniques are of practical use for various applications including image analysis, image composition, key extraction, etc. Approaches in this area are numerous, ranging from fully automatic methods to fully manual methods. The first ones are an unsolved problem due to a wide variety of image sources, contents, and complexity, even if they are well adapted to specific cases. Their success cannot be guaranteed in more general cases. The second ones are time-consuming, hardly reproducible and inaccurate. To overcome these problems, a lot of work has been done in interactive methods. The typical methods include Active Contour[1, 2, 3], Intelligent Paint[4], Intelligent Scissors[5, 6, 7], Bayesian Matting[8], Graph Cut[9], Lazy snapping[10], GrabCut[11] and so on.

Interactive segmentation exploits user's knowledge on the target object for tracing its boundary. The key points are high performance and simple interactive process. High performance in this task emphasizes accurate segmentation of object from background. The simple interaction means that a non-expert can finish the interaction, and obtain the accurate contour by an efficient and comfortable way. The less interaction may lead to wrong segmentation, while high performance usually needs too much interaction. Our objective in the paper is to achieve high performance at the cost of the modest interactive effort on the part of the user.

P.J. Narayanan et al. (Eds.): ACCV 2006, LNCS 3851, pp. 858–867, 2006.

In this paper, A new NURBS-HMM framework targeted at interactive image contour extraction is proposed. The user firstly inputs a few initial points around the object boundary. The input points are then fitted with Non-Uniform Rational B-Spline(NURBS)[12]. Due to local controllability of NURBS, control points of NURBS are considered as states of HMM, while observations of HMM are the boundary features of the image and the uniformity of an object area. Then, a state transition model based on the contour smoothness constraint is calculated. Finally, we find the optimal contour efficiently with Viterbi algorithm.

The rest of the paper is organized as follows. Hidden states of HMM are discussed in Section 2. Section 3 gives the detailed description on the observations of HMM. Section 4 introduces how to extract the contour with Viterbi algorithm. Section 5 gives the experimental results on different types of images and videos. Comparisons with three typical methods: Active Contour, Intelligent Scissors, and GrabCut are also included in this section. Concluding remarks are given in Section 6.

2 Contour Extraction Using HMM

Hidden Markov Model (HMM)[13] is a stochastic model which offers a high level of flexibility for modeling the structure of observations. It also provides a powerful and efficient way to incorporate multiple features by expanding the observations. This subsection below will describe the structure and basic theory of hidden Markov model used in our work.

2.1 Hidden States of HMM

A HMM[14] is specified by a number of states, say s_ϕ, the observation model $P(O_\phi|s_\phi)$, and the transition probability $P(s_\phi|s_{\phi-1})$. The graphic model of HMM is shown in Fig.1. Here, our aim is to accurately extract contour by some initial points given by users. First, these input points are fitted with the NURBS. The

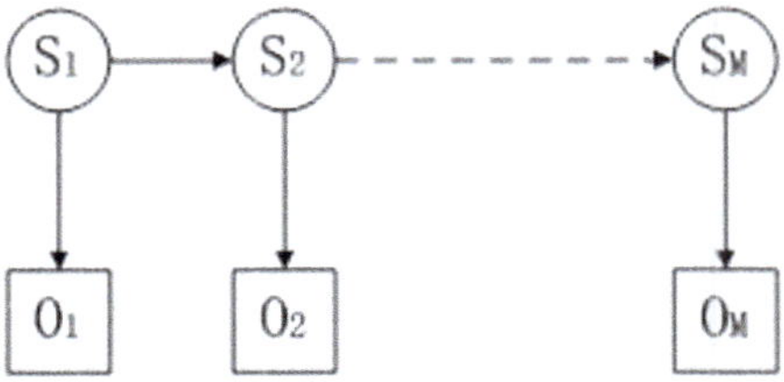

Fig. 1. Graphic model of contour extraction

control points are defined as HMM hidden states. If s_i is the control point of NURBS[15], the states can be denoted as $s = \{s_1, \ldots, s_\phi, \ldots, s_M\}$. Because NURBS allows us to interpolate curve and compute tangents at any locations along the curves. A set of normal lines of the contour can be obtained due to the parametrical representation of the contour. Let $\phi = 1, \ldots, M$, be the index of the normal lines and $\lambda = -N, \ldots, N$, be the index of pixels along a normal line. Each normal line has $2N+1$ pixels, which are indexed from $-N$ to N. The center point of each normal line, index as 0 is placed on the NURBS curve. If the fitted curve is accurate enough, the detected contour points on all normal lines should be exactly at the center, i.e., $c(\phi) = 0, \forall \phi \in [1, M]$. The observations of the HMM, denoted as $O=\{O_1, \ldots, O_\phi, \ldots, O_M\}$, are collected along each normal line ϕ. For detecting the contour accurately, different features such as: region smoothness, edge features, and the prior constraints such as: contour smoothness constraint are integrated into the HMM framework.

Given the current state s_ϕ, the observation O_ϕ is assumed to be independent of previous state $s_{\phi-1}$ and previous observation $O_{\phi-1}$. The assumption can be guaranteed due to the local controllability property of NURBS , e.g. the location change of control point s_i can only affect the curve segment $\mathbf{C_g}(u)$, where $u \in [u_i, u_{i+d+1})$, instead of the whole curve. Therefore, it is reasonable to define the control points of NURBS as the states of HMM. In HMM, transition probabilities are defined as $p(s_\phi|s_1, s_2, \ldots, s_{\phi-1})$. Here the first order HMM is used in our work. It means that the next state is dependent only upon the current state. Therefore, we have $p(s_\phi|s_1, s_2, \ldots, s_{\phi-1}) = p(s_\phi|s_{\phi-1})$.

3 Observations of HMM

Given a hidden state s_i, the segment controlled by this hidden state can be uniquely determined due to the local controllability property of NURBS. Let $\phi = 1, 2, \ldots, M$ be the index of the normal lines. If there are $2N+1$ pixels along each normal line, for each normal line, we will have $2N+1$ possible edges ($z_\phi= z_1, z_2, \ldots, z_{2N+1}$)(see Fig.2). The boundary features and region feature along the possible edges are defined as the observations of our HMM.

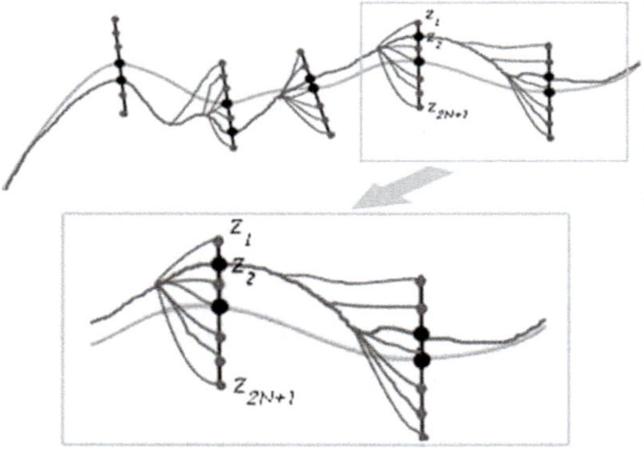

Fig. 2. Boundary detection

3.1 Boundary Features

If p, q are two pixels at two neighboring normal lines, then $P(p, q)$ represent the properties of the contour connecting pixels p, q and of its environment (gray levels of the contour, of the background, etc.). These features are then mapped through the use of a so-called cost assignment function (CAF) into cost functions which are similar to the "potential" instances of active contour models. Once these individual cost functions are defined, they are combined into a total cost function as follows.

$$P(p, q) = \omega_g C_g(q) + \omega_l C_l(q) + \omega_d C_d(p, q) + \omega_i C_i(q) + \omega_o C_o(q) + \omega_e C_e(q)$$

where each ω_x is the weight of the corresponding cost function, and the cost functions C_x associated to some features are respectively defined as: C_g, gradient magnitude; C_d, direction of the gradient magnitude; C_l, Laplacian feature; C_i, intensity on the positive (inside) side of the boundary; C_o, intensity on the negative (outside) side of the boundary; C_e, intensity on the contour (boundary).

The cost assignment depends on how one wants to emphasize one or another value of the features. For the gradient magnitude the inverse can for example be taken as a CAF in order to favor high contrasts, but a Gaussian function, centered on the gradient value that one wants to highlight, could also be applied. For the Laplacian feature, the CAF is usually a zero-crossing detector. Some other types of CAF can be used too.

The energy of a path to minimize with Dijkstra[16] is defined by

$$Epath = \sum_{(p,q)\in path} P(p, q) \tag{1}$$

$Epath_\phi = (e_1, e_2, \ldots, e_{2N+1})$ is the value of z_ϕ(see Fig.2). Let $Epath_\phi$ be the cost function related to any segment controlled by any control points , and $Epath_{min}$ be the minimum cost function of all possible edges between the beginning and ending normal lines of this segment, e.g. $Epath_{min} = min\{e_1, \ldots, e_{2N+1}\}$. The observation likelihood model of boundary can be defined as:

$$p(O_\phi | s_\phi) = \frac{1}{\sqrt{2\pi}\sigma} e^{-(e_\phi - Epath_{min})^2/2\sigma^2} \tag{2}$$

where σ is a predefined constant.

3.2 Uniformity Along the Boundary

In addition to the features of boundary likelihood model, the feature about the region uniformity of the foreground and background is considered here. The boundary separates the region along the boundary into two parts, foreground (R_f) and background (R_b). If the detected contour is exactly the boundary region, then foreground region should follow a similar gray distribution.

$$E(FG) = \sum_{k=1}^{N_f} x_k \quad E(BG) = \sum_{k=1}^{N_b} x_k \tag{3}$$

$$Var(FG) = \sum_{k=1}^{N_f} [x_k - E(FG)]^2 p_k \quad Var(BG) = \sum_{k=1}^{N_b} [x_k - E(BG)]^2 p_k \tag{4}$$

Where N_f and N_b are the number of the pixels of region R_f and R_b . The x_k is the value of kth pixel. The $Var(FG)$, $Var(BG)$ are the variance of the area R_f, R_b.

$$I(FG) = -\sum_{k=1}^{N_f} p_k \log p_k \quad I(BG) = -\sum_{k=1}^{N_b} p_k \log p_k \tag{5}$$

Where the probabilities of x_k is p_k, and the $I(FG)$, $I(BG)$ are the entropy of the area R_f, R_b. When the shortest path $Epath_\phi$ is the true contour, the foreground (R_f) and background (R_b) should have the similar distributions. It means that the $Var(FG)_\phi$, $Var(BG)_\phi$ should be minimal. On the other hand, for a homogeneous region, for example, if the occurrence probability of the intensity levels is uniformly distributed, then $p_k = const$, for $k \in \Omega$, and I is high. Therefore, the $I(FG)_\phi + I(BG)_\phi$ should be maximal. This is shown in Fig.3.

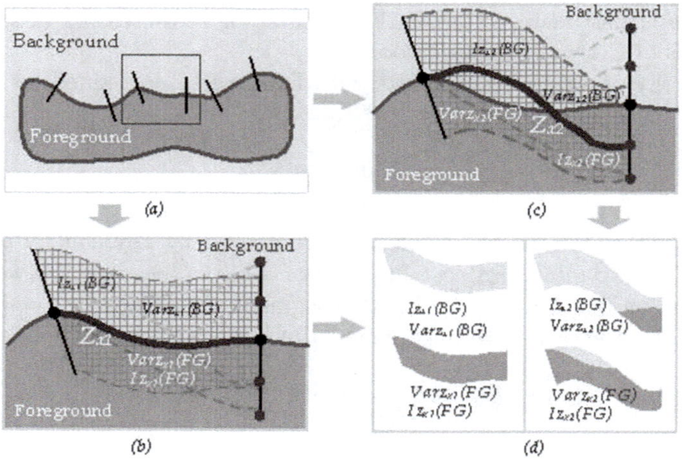

Fig. 3. The region uniformity of the foreground and background

Combining the features of boundary likelihood model and the uniformity of the region probabilities, we have the following multi-features observations likelihood function:

$$P(O_\phi|s_\phi) = c \cdot p(z_\phi|s_\phi) \cdot Var_N(FG)_\phi \cdot Var_N(BG)_\phi \cdot Id_{N\phi} \tag{6}$$

where $Var_N(FG)_\phi$, $Var_N(BG)_\phi$, $Id_{N\phi}$ are the normalization of $Var(FG)_\phi$, $Var(BG)_\phi$, Id_ϕ, and c is a predefined constant.

4 Contour Extraction by Viterbi Algorithm

An important component in HMM is the transition probability. It determines how a state transits to another state. In this section, we will use the standard contour smoothness constraint to derive the transition probability. Here we follow the philosophy in traditional snake model and use an internal energy term to penalize the roughness of the contour. But we encode this constraint in transition probabilities instead of using an internal energy in an optimization framework. The smoothness constraint has to be represented in a causal form to achieve this. One can see that when the normal lines are dense, the true contour points on adjacent normal lines tend to have the similar displacement from the predicted contour position (indexed as 0 on each normal line). This correlation is causal and can be captured by transition probabilities $p(s_\phi|s_{\phi-1})$:

$$p(s_\phi|s_{\phi-1}) = c * e^{-(s_\phi - s_{\phi-1})^2/\sigma_s^2} \tag{7}$$

where c is a normalization constant and σ_s is a predefined constant that regulates the smoothness of the contour. This transition probability will penalize sudden changes of the contour points between adjacent segments, hence resulting in a smooth contour. The best contour can be obtained by the Viterbi algorithm [14] described in the following.

Given the observation sequence $O = \{O_\phi, \phi \in [1, M]\}$ and the transition probabilities $a_{i,j} = p(s_{\phi+1}|s_\phi = i)$, the best contour can be found by finding the most likely state sequence s^*. This can be efficiently accomplished by the Viterbi algorithms:

$$s^* = arg \max_s P(s|O) = arg \max_s P(s, O) \tag{8}$$

Let's define

$$V(\phi, \lambda) = max_{s_{\phi-1}} P(O_\phi, s_{\phi-1}, s_\phi = \lambda) \tag{9}$$

Using the Markov conditional independence assumptions, it can be recursively computed as follows:

$$V(\phi, \lambda) = P(O_\phi|s_\phi = \lambda) \cdot \max_j P(s\phi = \lambda|s_{\phi-1} = j)V(j, \phi - 1) \tag{10}$$

$$j^*(\phi, \lambda) = P(O_\phi|s_\phi = \lambda) \cdot \arg\max_j P(s\phi = \lambda|s_{\phi-1} = j)V(j, \phi - 1) \tag{11}$$

with the initialization $V(1, \lambda) = max_{s_1} P(O_1|s_1)P(s_1)$, where the initial state probabilities $P(s_1) = \frac{1}{2N+1}, s_1 \in [-N, N]$. The term $j^*(\phi, \lambda)$ records the "best previous state" from state λ at line ϕ. We therefore obtain at the end of the sequence $max_s P(O, s) = max_\lambda V(M, \lambda)$. The s^* can be obtained by back tracking j^*, starting from $s^*_M = argmax_\lambda V(M, \lambda)$, with $S^*_{\phi-1} = j^*(s^*_\phi, \phi)$. The computation cost of the Viterbi algorithm is $O(M \cdot (2N + 1))$. Unlike traditional active contour model, this method can give us the optimal contour without recursively searching the 2D image plane. Given the best state sequence $s^* = \{s^*_1, \ldots, s^*_M\}$, we denote the corresponding image coordinate of the best contour point s^*_ϕ on line ϕ by $[x_\phi, y_\phi]$.

5 Experiments

To validate the efficiency and robustness of the proposed method, we use the different types of images and videos to test our algorithm. Our method offers an easy and comfortable interactive way for the user. First, the user inputs a series of initial points around the contour that one hope to extract, then the algorithm is able to find the contour automatically. Fig.4 is the SAR (Synthetic Aperture Radar)[17] image, and the red points is the initial points input by user. It is well known that SAR is obtained with coherent illumination and presents a noisy appearance due to the speckle noise phenomenon. Therefore, it is very challenging to extract robustly the contour in SAR image. The yellow line in Fig.4 **(a)** (right) is the resultant contour by using the proposed method. If the resultant contour is not satisfied, then the user can repeat the above procedure until the real contour is achieved. **(b)** (left) is the result of the first iteration, and it is unsatisfied. Then we repeat the above procedure by using the result of the first iteration as the initial contour of the next iteration. **(b)** (right) shows the contour after the third iteration. Some results on the ordinary images are shown in Fig.5. From the experimental results, one can see that our method can extract robustly the contour from the different types of images with a modest interaction.

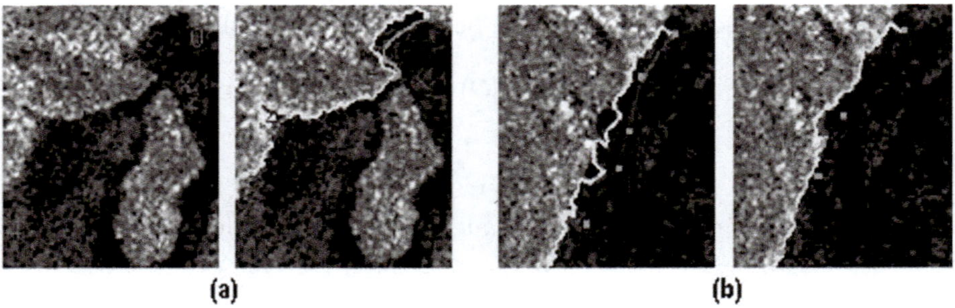

Fig. 4. The red points are set by the user. The green line is fitted using NURBS through the red points. The yellow line is found by our algorithm. The yellow line in (b)(left) is the result of the first iteration, and the contour in the right image is the result of the third iteration. The green points of (b)(right) is the control points of the yellow contour.

Furthermore, we apply our method to video segmentation. First, we input the initial points along the boundary at the first frame of the video, and obtain the contour at this frame, then the extracted contour is propagated to the next frame, and regarded as the initial contour of this frame, repeat the procedure until the final frame is processed. Fig.6 (upper) gives some sampled frames of the video that one man is moving, and the segmentation results of head are shown in Fig.6(lower). Another example is shown in Fig.7. The upper array of the figures

Fig. 5. Some experimental results on ordinary images. The user inputs a series of points around an object, and the object is then extracted automatically.

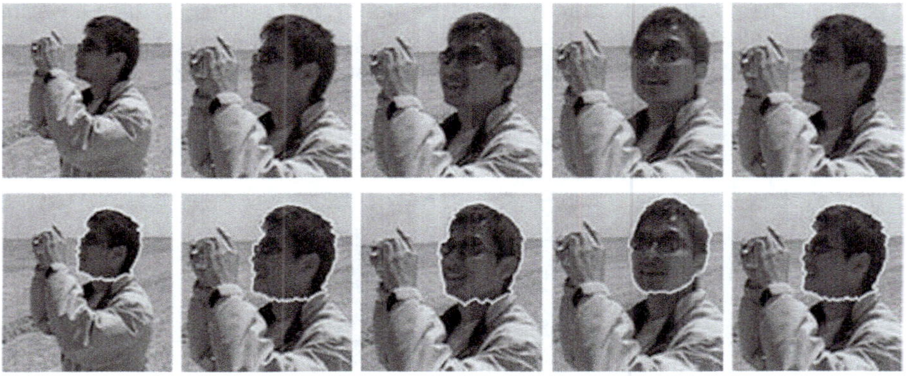

Fig. 6. Segmentation of a video sequence

are the sampled images of a medical image video, and the lower array are the segmentation results.

In order to demonstrate the performance of the proposed method, we compare our method with another three typical methods, Active Contour, Intelligent Scissors, and GraphCut. It is well known that active contour method is greatly dependent on the selection of initial points. It is initialized manually with a rough approximation to a boundary of interest, then allowed to iterate over the contour to determine the boundary that minimizes energy functional. If the resulting contour is not satisfactory due to converging to the local minimum, this may in turn be followed by one or more iterations of user input and reapplication of the algorithm. Fig.8(left) shows that segmentation result from Active Con-

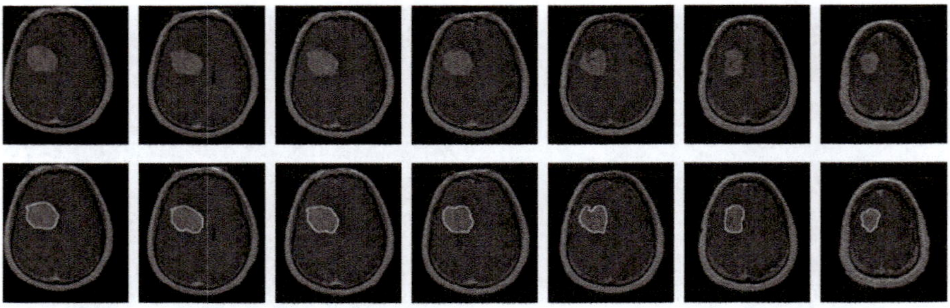

Fig. 7. Segmentation of a medical images sequence

tour method. The Intelligent Scissors is able to achieve a satisfied segmentation result when given the enough interaction, but it needs more interaction than our method. Fig.8 (middle left) shows the segmentation result by using Intelligent Scissors. One can see that although the method can obtain a similar result as our one, it needs to input more initial points accurately along the boundary that one hope to extract. Finally, Fig.8 (middle right) shows the segmentation result of the GrabCut. Fig.8 (right) is the result of our method. Obviously, our method can result in the more satisfied segmentation than the GrabCut when their interactions are similar.

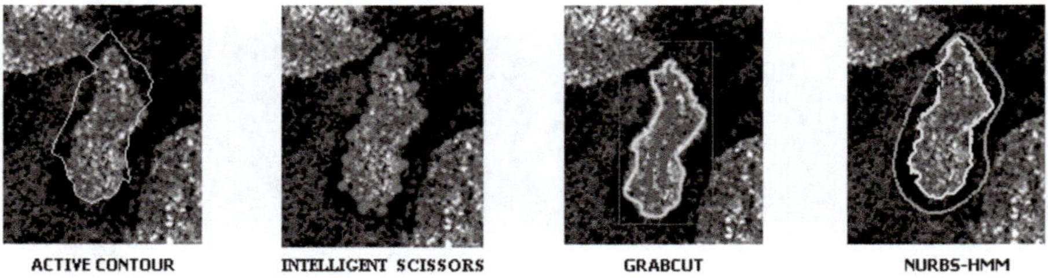

Fig. 8. Comparison with other methods

6 Summary and Conclusions

In this paper, a new algorithm aiming at the interactive contour extraction is proposed. It allows user to have a full of control of the drawing process, and even a non-specialist user is able to extract the contour with an efficient and comfortable way. We fit the initial points input by user with NURBS, and iteratively search the best contour using Viterbi algorithm. Our proposed framework can also integrate all kinds of observations such as boundary features and region features in a similar way. The experimental results demonstrate that our method is efficient and robust.

References

1. Kass, M., Witkin, A., Terzopoulos, D.: Snakes: Active contour models. IJCV **1** (1988) 321–331
2. Cohen, L., Kimmel, R.: Global minimum for active contour models: A minimal path approach. IJCV **24** (1997) 57–78
3. Blake, A., Isard, M.: the Active Contours book. Springer-Verlag, Berlin Heidelberg New York (1998)
4. Reese, L.: Intelligent Paint:Region-Based Interactive Image Segmentation. Masters Thesis, Department of Computer Science, Brigham Young University (1999)
5. Falcao, A., Udupa, J.: User-steered image segmentation paradigms: Live-wire and live-lane. GMIP **60** (1998) 233–260
6. Mortensen, E., Morse, B., Barrett, W., Udupa, J.: Adaptive boundary detection using live-wire two-dimensional dynamic programming. IEEE Proc. of Computers in Cardiology (1992)
7. Mortensen, E., Barrett, W.: Intelligent scissors for image composition. Proc. of Computer Graphics, SIGGRAPH (1995)
8. CHUANG, Y.-Y., CURLESS, B., SALESIN, D., SZELISKI, R.: A bayesian approach to digital matting. Proc. IEEE Conf. Computer Vision and Pattern Recog (2001)
9. Boykov, Y., Jolly, M.P.: Interactive graph cuts for optimal boundary and region segmentation of objects in nd images. ICCV (2001)
10. Li, Y., Sun, J., Tang, C.K., Shum, H.Y.: Lazy snapping. ACM Transactions on Graphics (2004)
11. Rother, C., Kolmogorov, V., Blake, A.: Interactive foreground extraction using iterated graph cuts. ACM Transactions on Graphics (2004)
12. Piegl, L., Shah, M.: The NURBS Book. 2rd edn. Springer-Verlag (1997)
13. Rabiner, L., Juang, B.: An introduction to hidden markov models. IEEE ASSP Mag (1986)
14. Chen, Y., Rui, Y., Huang, T.: Jpdaf based hmm for real-time contour tracking. Proc. of the IEEE CVPR (2001)
15. Liang, K., Rajeswari, M., Khoo, B.: Free form shape representation using nurbs modeling. Proc. of the Int. CGVCV (2002)
16. Dijkstra, E.: A note on two problems in connection with graphs. Numerische Mathematic **1** (1959) 269–271
17. Derrode, S., Pieczynski, W.: Sar image segmentation using generalized pairwise markov chains. SPIE's International Symposium on Remote Sensing (2002)

Learning Parameter Tuning for Object Extraction

Xiongcai Cai[1], Arcot Sowmya[1], and John Trinder[2]

[1] School of Computer Science and Engineering, University of New South Wales and National ICT Australia, Sydney, NSW 2052, Australia
{xcai, sowmya}@cse.unsw.edu.au
[2] School of Surveying and Spatial Information Systems, University of New South Wales, Sydney, NSW 2052, Australia
j.trinder@unsw.edu.au

Abstract. This paper presents a learning-based method for parameter tuning of object recognition systems and its application to automatic road extraction from high resolution remotely sensed (HRRS) images. Our approach is based on region growing using fast marching level set method (FMLSM), and machine learning for automatically tuning its parameters. FMLSM is used to extract the shape of objects in images. Parameters are introduced into the speed function of the FMLSM to improve flexibility and reflect the variety of images. The parameters are tuned using machine learning and utilizing background knowledge. The primary contribution of our approach is the ability to learn the parameters for a FMLSM model for object extraction. Experimental results on 11 HRRS image datasets, 1024*1024 pixels each with ground resolution of 1.3 meters, demonstrate the validity of the proposed algorithm. We are able to extract the roads without the use of heuristic parameters and other manual intervention.

1 Introduction

Automatic shape extraction of objects and its application to road extraction from remotely sensed images is an active area of research. The general approaches adopted include image processing techniques [1, 2], edge detection and linking[3], tracking and region growing [4, 5, 6, 7, 8], grouping and clustering [9, 10] and machine learning techniques [11]. Recently, advances have led to the inclusion of prior knowledge as well as multi-scale and multi-resolution methods [12], and multi-temporal, multi-spectral and hyper-spectral analysis [13].

Region growing methods attempt to group pixels into homogeneous regions starting from seeds, and agglomerate points around the seeds that satisfy certain homogeneity criteria. A recently developed algorithm in this approach is the level set method, which has the ability of smart handling of propagating contours [14]. To apply this method to automatic object extraction, two well known problems must be solved: automatically deciding the stopping criterion and initialization of seeds. Although attempts at automatic seed selection exist [15], the stopping criterion determination remains heuristic in the literature [14][16].

P.J. Narayanan et al. (Eds.): ACCV 2006, LNCS 3851, pp. 868–877, 2006.

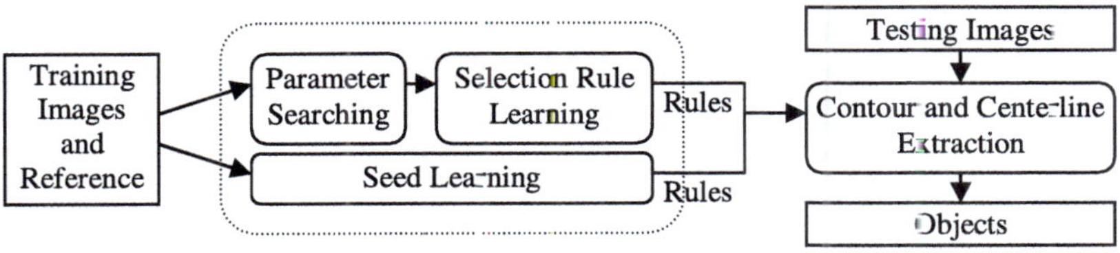

Fig. 1. Overview of the proposed algorithm

In this paper, we propose an automatic parameter tuning method for the speed function of FMLSMs for object shape and centerline extraction and its application to roads extraction from HRRS images. By parameter tuning of the speed function, we automatically determine the stopping criterion for FMLSMs. Our approach makes use of searching strategies and machine learning techniques and consists of two stages, namely learning and extraction. In the first stage, rules for selecting parameters are learned from training images. The second stage consists of object extraction from new images using the speed function with learned parameters. Given the training images with their ground truth, we utilized genetic search to discover the optimal parameters of the FMLSM speed function for every training image. These parameters, with their image characteristics, were then input to a support vector machine (SVM) regression machine learning procedure to generalize rules of relationship between image characteristics and parameters, which were then used to derive parameter values for new images. Finally, a FMLSM model using these values was deployed to discover the shape of objects. An overview of the proposed algorithm is shown in Fig. 1.

Cooperating with a seed selection procedure and a centerline extraction procedure, we applied this approach to automatically extract roads to evaluate our algorithm and show its strengths. Our major contribution is automatic parameter tuning of region growing methods for object extraction.

The paper is organized as follows. In section 2, we discuss related work. FMLSM is introduced in section 3. Automatic parameter tuning for speed function is described in section 4. Experiments on road extraction from HRRS images are presented in section 5. Conclusions are presented in section 6.

2 Related Work

Deformable contour models or snakes were first presented [7] for detection and localisation of boundaries for the image segmentation problem. Cohen [4] uses the balloon model to reduce the requirement of initialisation of snake model. This has been improved [8] using a geodesic formulation in a Riemannian space for active contours derived from the image content. Level set method has been utilised for shape modelling [14]. In [16], level set method is used to extract road network from multi-spectral images, where multi-spectral features are extracted using pixel classification masks and then level set method employed to extract road contours. Geman and Jedynak [17] present an active testing model to reduce uncertainty in tracking roads in satellite images using entropy and statistical inference. Cohen and Kimmel [18] describe a shape modeling method by interpretation of the snake as a path of minimal cost which is solved using numerical methods. Bhanu et al. [19] develop a general adaptive framework for image segmentation and illustrate it using genetic algorithm and nearest neighbour learning. Chen et al. [9] proposed an adaptive and trainable multi-level road extraction system using inductive meta-learning and clustering to tune parameters and choose the algorithm. Recently, we proposed a method for road recognition based on learning and fusion of road segment and junction information [11].

In this paper, we present a machine learning based dynamic FMLSM model for automatic shape extraction of objects by automated tuning of parameters of the speed function. We also determine the stopping criterion of the level set and select its starting seeds automatically. The proposed approach differs from our earlier work [11] in that we introduce and tune two parameters rather than one for the speed function of FMLSM, and perform sophisticated genetic algorithm based random search instead of sequential search to discover their optimal values. We also experimentally compare the proposed approach with standard level set method. Compared to Bhanu et al. [19], we tackle both the parameter tuning and seed selection problem that are specific to level set methods and use SVM regression for learning parameter selection rules rather than simply use nearest neighbor technique.

3 Fast Marching Level Set Method

For the purpose of completeness, level set method and fast marching method are briefly described here. In [14], the classical level set boundary is defined as the zero level set of an implicit function $z = \phi(x, y, t)$ defined on the entire image domain. The contour at time t must satisfy the function $\phi(x, y, t) = 0$. If each pixel in the image is visited once and the time step is fixed to 1, this will lead to a simple boundary value formulation $F\,|\nabla\mu(x, y)| = 1$, where μ is the arrival time of the contour and F is the speed function. Combined with an optimal sorting technique, this leads to a very fast solution, namely the fast marching algorithm.

4 Automatic Parameter Tuning

In this section, we define the speed function of the FMLSM and describe the parameter tuning approach. Seed selection is highly specific to the application and will be discussed in the next section.

4.1 Speed Function Design

A key aspect of successfully designing the FMLSM based shape detector is to design its speed function since it will finally determine the precision of the method. The speed function must model the desired requirement of maintaining positive evolution speed whenever the evolving contour remains inside the object area, and zero speed as the boundary approaches the border. In related research [4, 7, 8, 14], the speed function consists of constant speed, curvature constrained speed and underlying velocity. We use a combination of intensity distribution, texture statistics and gradient information together, defined as following:

$$F(x,y) = [e^{-\frac{1}{2}(\hat{c}(x,y)-\bar{\mu_0})\Sigma^{-1}(\hat{c}(x,y)-\bar{\mu_0})^T} + e^{-|T(x,y)-T_0|}] \times \frac{1}{1+|\nabla I(x,y)|^P} \ . \quad (1)$$

where $\hat{c}(x,y)$ is the intensity value at image location (x,y), $\bar{\mu_0}$ denotes the mean of intensity of seeds. T(x,y) is the texture feature of the image at point (x,y), T_0 is the mean of those from seeds, and $\nabla I(x,y)$ is the gradient of the image at location (x,y). P and Σ are parameters that will be automatically tuned.

A similar speed function has been used by Keaton and Brokish [16] in a semi-automatic road detection system. Our speed function differs from Keaton and Brokish's in that we utilise the pixel intensity and texture from multiple seeds instead of a single seed. Thus, $\bar{\mu_0}$ and T_0 are defined as following:

$$\bar{\mu_0} = \frac{1}{n}\sum_{i=1}^{n} I_i, T_0 = \frac{1}{n}\sum_{i=1}^{n} T_i \ . \quad (2)$$

where I_i and T_i are the intensity and texture feature vector of the i_{th} seed. Our approach reduces the uncertainty of a single seed by averaging the features of all seeds.

4.2 Parameter Tuning for Stopping Criterion

A common problem with region growing algorithms including the fast marching method is the determination of the stopping criterion. For object extraction, the contrast, noise and other spatial and spectral properties present in different images can change. Since the speed function is essential to the success and precision of the FMLSM, it must be properly adjusted to reflect these changes. There are two parameters embedded in the speed function of our approach, namely the gradient power P and Σ intensity covariance matrix S, which together work as a global constraint and enable adjustment of the stopping criterion. Given a set of training images and objects appearing in them, the parameter tuning problem is defined as finding optimal parameters θ for a FMLSM to properly extract the objects in the training images with respect to an evaluation metric, and creating a set of rules to derive parameters for new images. We utilize search strategies and machine learning to automatically tune the parameters.

Given merely the training image and ground truth, there is no direct relationship between training images and parameters that can be used to discover good parameters. Thus, training data must be first processed to search for parameters with good performance of shape extraction for every training image. There exist two approaches to parameter value search [20]. One is the filter approach, which has the disadvantage of being heuristic and does not directly take into account the effect of the underlying shape extractor. Another is the wrapper

```
initialize θ, P_co, P_mut, L n-bit chromosomes
do determine fitness of each chromosome
  rank the chromosomes
  do random select two chromosomes
    if Rand[0, 1) < P_co then
      crossover the pair at a randomly chosen bit
    else
      change each bit with probability P_mut
      remove the parent chromosomes
  until L offspring have been created
until reach the maximum iteration limitation θ
return highest fitness chromosome
```

Fig. 2. Genetic Algorithm (GA)

```
Training:
  initialize training images and references
  for each training image
    find optimal parameters by GA
    create features
  build parameter selection rules by learning
  return parameter selection rules
Testing:
  initialize parameter selection rules, new images
  for each new image
    calculate features
    find parameters using selection rules
  return parameters
```

Fig. 3. Parameter Tuning Algorithm

approach, where parameters are selected through a search using the extractor itself as part of the evaluation function. We use the wrapper approach. For each search iteration, we make an attempt at guessing parameter values, and call the FMLSM extractor, whose results are compared to the ground truth to discover good parameter values. Furthermore, in order to apply the wrapper approach to shape extraction, we must overcome the efficiency problem, since each search in this approach must call the shape extraction procedure once, which is time intensive and requires an efficient search algorithm. We utilise the genetic algorithm based random search method rather than analytical methods or exhaustive search, to avoid constructing a complicated model using a priori and to reduce the computation burden, [19] as shown in Fig. 2.

The fitness for genetic algorithm is an evaluation metric of the performance of FMLSM, which is defined in Sect. 5 . To get the fitness, the algorithm uses FMLSM to extract objects using the gene values in the current generation. The evaluation metrics used as the fitness are then calculated over the extraction results. We use chromosomes of 2 genes and 5 bits per gene, to represent two parameters of the speed function. This constructs a search space of size of 32*32.

After the optimal parameters for every single training image has been estimated, machine learning is deployed to generalize the relationship between image characteristics and parameters. This is because different images usually have different characteristics such as contrast and noise, which can significantly affect the performance of the shape extractor. For a reusable and robust shape extraction algorithm, tuning a variety of parameter values to be applied on images with different characteristics is a nontrivial problem. We use SVM regression to discover the mapping from image characteristics to optimal speed function parameters of the FMLSM. Various texture features of seed candidates including energy, correlation, contrast, dissimilarity, homogeneity, entropy, maximum and sum based on co-occurrence matrix and mean, variance, skewness, kurtosis, energy and entropy based on histogram are extracted [21, 22]. The image intensities are re-sampled into 64 bins with a bin size of 4 and the texture features are derived. We construct a set of training instances from the training images, each containing the texture features and the parameters found by the genetic algorithm. SVM regression [23] is trained over these instances to derive the parameter selection rules as a regression function over the texture feature values, which are then used to find optimal parameters for new images.

Once the selection rules are created, the parameter selection for a new image is done simply by calculating the texture features of the new image and applying the rules on these texture features to find the parameters.

The algorithm for tuning the parameters is described in Fig. 3. Although the training of this algorithm may take time, testing very fast after the parameter selection rules are created.

5 Application to Road Extraction

5.1 Problem Formulation

We apply our approach to road extraction from HRRS images. The problem of road extraction is to infer a road object centerline from an input HRRS image. Let x be the representation of the HRRS image and y the road centerline. Our goal is to learn the relation between x and y from a training set of 99 image patches created from 11 HRRS images, and their centerline ground truths. Since we use FMLSM, this is basically a problem of identifying seeds and speed function parameters for this method. We first learn the seeds and then use the seeds to learn parameters.

5.2 Experimental Setup

A dataset consisting of 11 grey-scale HRRS images from a rural area were used. The size of each image is 1024*1024 pixels and they are cropped from a larger image of ground resolution 1.3 meters per pixel. Each image is further split into 9 patches to construct a 99 image patch training set. Leave-one-out cross validation is used in order to learn from the largest available dataset and obtain effective test sets. Our approach makes use of the centerline vector reference model based on Wiedemann et al. [24]. References are provided as line vectors and the evaluation is performed by comparing the recognized road centerline vectors with the reference vector, which are delineated manually. The evaluation measures are given by:

$$completeness = \frac{length_{TP}}{length_{reference}}, correctness = \frac{length_{TP}}{length_{classified}} . \quad (3)$$

where $length_{TP} = length(reference \cap classified)$. The two measures above are combined into a general measure of quality, called CXC which is defined as:

$$CXC = completeness \times correctness^2 . \quad (4)$$

The CXC is also used as the fitness for the genetic algorithm.

5.3 Experimental Results

Our approach makes use of partial candidates of road segments and junctions provided by other independent methods. Briefly, a road segment is represented as a set of twin-linked edge pairs each containing four single line vectors. A junction contains three edge pairs. For each image, we first import the road junctions and segments and then find seed candidates by extracting centre points from the convex polygon of junction edge pairs [9]. We construct a texture feature set of seeds as described in the previous section. We then train a SVM [25] based on the texture feature set and the images to learn good seeds from seed candidates. This produces rules that are used in the classification phase to determine the good seeds. After training is completed, seed selection is performed by calculating the texture features of a new image and its junction centre points and applying the acquired rules on them. The Weka implementation of SVMs and their default parameters [26] are used. Our seed detector routinely achieved 89% correctness by leave-one-out cross validation. Although there were about 11% of seeds misclassified, only 4% of them were false positive and introduced false positive road contours and centerlines. The effect of false negative seeds on FMLSM is slight and may be ignored.

Firstly, we find optimal parameters for every training image by genetic algorithm based search of parameter space. We use crossover and mutation as genetic operators and the probabilities for crossover and mutation are both set to 0.6. We perform 10 generations of evolution, where each generation has a population of 10, with respect to the fitness measured by evaluating the performance of the FMLSM using the gene values. We then take the best fitness gene values within the populations of 10 generations as the optimal parameters for that image.

Then a set of texture features as described in Sect. 4 are calculated from the training images with the optimal parameters, to construct the training set for further machine learning. SVM regression is run over this new training data set with a polynomial kernel function whose exponent is 3. We use the Weka implementation of SVM Regression algorithm [26]. This creates a regression function over all texture features, which will be used to calculate the parameters for new images.

We then apply the seeds and the parameters found to our extended FMLSM to extract the road contours [16]. After the contour is extracted, we apply the FMLSM again to extract the road centerline, based on [27]. Finally, the centerline points are thinned into a one pixel-width line, which is subsequently converted into vectors and linked to create the centerlines.

We compared the output of our algorithm with those obtained using the standard level set method described in [28], where the speed function is:

$$F(x,y) = \frac{1}{1 + |\nabla G_\sigma * I(x,y)|} . \tag{5}$$

We also ran the road extractor with the speed function described in section 4.2, but fixed the intensity covariance matrix Σ to be identity and the gradient power P to be 1, and compared it with our algorithm.

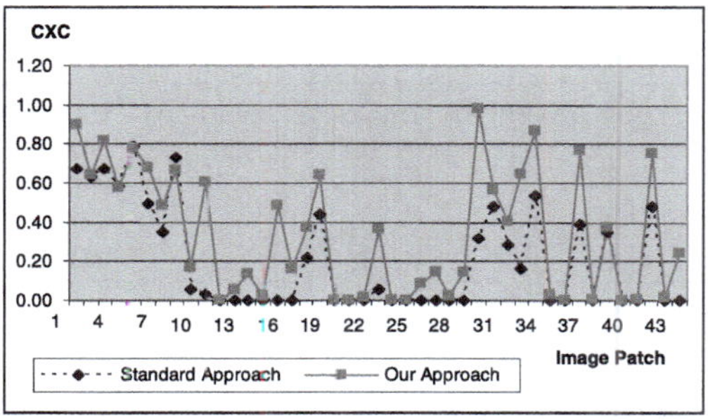

Fig. 4. Comparative Results

Fig. 5. Image A (1024*1024 pixels) - Learning approach (CXC 0.64 in average)

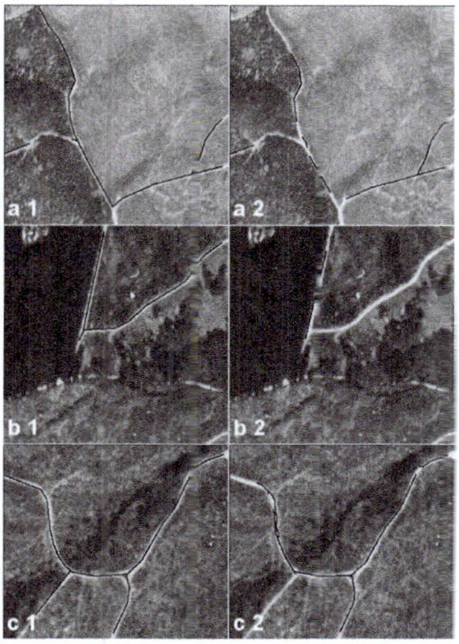

Fig. 6. Patches results: a1, b1 and c1 by learning approach; a2, b2 and c2 by standard approach. The patches are extracted from large images (not shown here except for A, from which a1 and a2 is extracted).

We ran our algorithm in 3 passes over the 99 image patches to produce 3 sets of parameters and then calculated the CXC evaluation measures for every parameter set. Due to some patches containing no seeds, and thus not contributing to the performance of the algorithm, we only show comparative results for 44 patches. We average the 3 CXCs for every image and then compare the averaged CXCs of our learning approach with those obtained by the other two. We found that the standard approach works as well as the fixed parameter approach since they produce similar CXC values, therefore only one of them is shown here.

Table 1. Comparative results for shown images (CXC values) - High CXC is better

	All (average)	Image A (average)	Patch a	Patch b	Patch c
Learning Approach	0.34	0.64	0.90	0.98	0.87
Standard Approach	0.20	0.55	0.67	0.31	0.53
Improvement	0.14	0.09	0.23	0.67	0.34

However, our learning approach outperforms the other two approaches by an average of 0.14 in CXC, as shown in Fig. 4. Results mapped back to images are illustrated in Fig. 5 and Fig. 6, whose CXC values are compared in Table 1. Space constraints preclude inclusion of all patches.

6 Conclusion

This paper proposes a method for automated tuning and learning for object shape extraction and its application to road extraction. A region growing approach based on FMLSM is used to extract the shape of objects. We extend the FMLSM and apply machine learning techniques to the problem of automated seed selection and parameter tuning, which results in a fully automatic approach for object shape extraction. Experimental results have demonstrated the feasibility of the proposed method.

Acknowledgement

National ICT Australia is funded through the Australian Government's *Backing Australia's Ability* initiative, in part through the Australian Research Council.

References

1. Zhang, C., Murai, S., Baltsavias, E.: Road network detection by mathematical morphology. In: ISPRS Workshop on 3D Geospatial Data Production: Meeting Applicat, Requirements, Paris (1999) 185–200
2. Amini, J., Sarahjian, M.: Image map simplification by using mathematical morphology. ISPRS Journal of Photogrammetry and Remote Sensing **33** (2000)
3. Sowmya, A., Singh, S.: Rail: Extracting road segments from aerial images using machine learning. In: Proc. ICML 99 Workshop on Learning in Vision. (1999) 8–19
4. Cohen, L.: On active contour models and balloons. CVGIP Image Understanding **53** (1991)
5. Baumgartner, A., Hinz, S., Wiedemann, C.: Efficient methods, and interfaces for road tracking. In: Proc. ISPRS-Commision III Symp. Photogrammet. Compu. Vision (PCV'02), Graz (2002) 28–31
6. Laptev, I., Mayer, H., Lindeberg, T., Eckstein, W., Steger, C., Baumgartner, A.: Automatic extraction of roads from aerial images based on scale space and snakes. Machne Vision Applicat. **12** (2000) 23–31

7. Kass, M., Witkin, A., Terzopoulos, D.: Snakes: Active contour models. International Journal of Computer Vision (1988) 321–331
8. Caselles, V., Kimmel, R., Sapiro, G.: Geodesic active contours. In: ICCV'95. Cambridge, USA (1995) 694–699
9. Chen, A., Donovan, G., Sowmya, A., Trinder, J.: Inductive clustering: automatic low level segmentation in high resolution images. In: ISPRS Photogrammet. Comput. Vision. Volume A., Graz, Austria (2002) 73
10. Agouris, P., Doucette, P., Stefanidis, A.: Spatiospectral cluster analysis of elongated regions in aerial imagery. IEEE International Conference on Image Processing(ICIP) **2** (2001) 789–792
11. Xiongcai, C., Sowmya, A., Trinder, J.: Learning to recognise roads from high resolution remotely sensed images. In: The 2nd International Conference on Intelligent Sensors, Sensor Networks and Information Processing, Melbourne (2005)
12. Baumgartner, A., Steger, A., Mayer, C., Eckstein, W., Ebner, H.: Automatic road extraction based on multi-scale, grouping and context. Photogrammet. Eng. Remotely Sensing **65** (1999) 777–786
13. McKeown, D., Cochran, S., Ford, S., Mcglone, J., Shufelt, J., Yocum, D.: Fusion of hydice hyperspectral data with panchromatic imagery for cartographic feature extraction. IEEE Trans. Geosci. Remote Sensing **27** (1999) 1261–1277
14. Malladi, R., Sethian, J.A., Vemuri, B.C.: Shape modeling with front propagation: a level set approach. IEEE Transactions on Pattern Analysis and Machine Intelligence **17** (1995)
15. Zlotnick, A., Carnine, P.: Finding roads seeds in aerial images. In: CVGIP, Image Understanding. Volume 57. (1993) 243–260
16. Keaton, T., Brokish, J.: Evolving roads in ikonos multispectral imagery. In: Proceedings of International Conference on Image Processing. (2003)
17. Geman, D., Jedynak, B.: An active testing model for tracking roads in satellite images. IEEE Trans. Pattern Anal. Machine Intell. **18** (1996)
18. Cohen, L.D., Kimmel, R.: Global minimum for active contour models: A minimal path approach. In: IEEE Computer Society Conference on Computer Vision and Pattern Recognition. (1996) 666–673
19. Bhanu, B., Sungkee, L., Ming, J.: Adaptive image segmentation using a genetic algorithm. Systems, Man and Cybernetics, IEEE Transactions on **25** (1995) 1543
20. Kohavi, R., John, G.: Wrapper for feature subset selection. Journal of Artificial Intelligence **97** (1997) 273–324
21. Pratt, W.: Digital Image Processing. Wiley (1991)
22. Haralick, R.: Statistical and structural approaches to texture. Proc. IEEE **67** (1979) 786–804
23. Smola, A.J., Sch, B.: A tutorial on support vector regression. NeuroCOLT2 Technical Report Series (1998)
24. Wiedemann, C., Heipke, C., Mayer, H., Hamet, O.: Empirical evaluation of automatically extracted road axes. CVPR Workshop on Empirical EvaluationMethods in Computer Vision (1998) 172–187
25. Burges, C.: A tutorial on support vector machines for pattern recognition. Data Mining and Knowledge Discovery **2** (1998) 121–167
26. Witten, I.H., Frank, E.: Data Mining: Practical Machine Learning Tools and Techniques with Java Implementations. Morgan Kaufmann Publishers (2000)
27. Telea, A., Vilanova, A.: A robust level-set algorithm for centerline extraction. Joint EUROGRAPHICS - IEEE TCVG Symposium on Visualization (2003)
28. Malladi, R., Sethian, J.: A unified approach to noise removal, image enhancement, and shape recovery. IEEE Trans. on Image Processing **5** (1996) 1554–1568

Region-Level Motion-Based Foreground Detection with Shadow Removal Using MRFs

Shih-Shinh Huang[1], Li-Chen Fu[1], and Pei-Yung Hsiao[2]

[1] Department of Computer Science and Information Engineering,
National Taiwan University, Taipei, Taiwan, R.O.C.
powwhuang@gmail.com
[2] Department of Electronics Engineering,
Chang Gung University, Tao-Yuan, Taiwan, R.O.C.
pyhsiao@mail.cgu.edu.tw

Abstract. This paper presents a new approach to automatic segmentation of foreground objects with shadow removal from an image sequence by integrating techniques of background subtraction and motion-based foreground segmentation. First, a region-based motion segmentation algorithm is proposed to obtain a set of motion-coherence regions and the correspondence among regions at different time instants. Next, we formulate the foreground detection problem as a graph labeling over a region adjacency graph (RAG) based on Markov random fields (MRFs) statistical framework. A background model representing the background scene is built and then is used to model a *likelihood* energy. Besides the background model, the temporal and spatial coherence are also maintained by modeling it as *a prior* energy. Finally, a labeling is obtained by maximizing *a posterior* energy of the MRFs. Experimental results for several video sequences are provided to demonstrate the effectiveness of the proposed approach.

1 Introduction

In many applications, success of detecting foreground regions from a static background scene is an important step before high-level processing, such as object identification and event understanding. However, in real-world situations, there exist several kinds of environment variations that will make the foreground detection more difficult. In order to cope with that, the approach here should be able to immune to these variaitions, i.e., being invariant to them or adapting to them.

1.1 Related Works

Techniques for foreground detection can be grouped into two categories, background subtraction and motion-based foreground segmentation. We will give a brief review of these two kinds of techniques. In order to adapt to changes, the background is usually represented by the background model and updated over

P.J. Narayanan et al. (Eds.): ACCV 2006, LNCS 3851, pp. 878–887, 2006.

time. This kind of technique is based on an assumption that the background scene is available and the camera is only subject to minimal vibration without loss of generality. A simply method is to represent the gray level or color intensity of each pixel in the image as an independent and uni-modal distribution [1, 2]. However, in the real world, the appearance of a pixel in most video sequences is in multi-modal distribution. The usage of a mixture of Gaussian distributions is common in modeling multi-model distribution. To overcome this problem, [3] modeled the pixel intensity as a weighted mixture of three Gaussian distributions respectively corresponding to road, vehicle, and shadow. The works in [4] model each pixel as a K mixture of Gaussian distributions where K depends on memory.

However, not all distributions are in Gaussian form[5]. In [5], a non-parametric background model based on non-parametric density estimation was proposed to handle the situations where the background scene is non-static but contains minimal motion. The currently proposed approaches are used to represent the background scene by a set of independent models without taking any semantic information into consideration. This makes false detection likely when changes or noise occur. It is here where some sophisticated modeling or updating strategies are applied.

The technique of motion-based foreground segmentation is based on the idea that appearance of foreground objects are always accompanied by motion. In general, such technique consists of two steps, i.e., motion segmentation and region classification. The aim of motion segmentation is to divide an image into a set of regions with motion coherence, whereas that of region classification is to assign a label, foreground or background, to each segmented region. For providing a meaningfully semantic description of video, Wang and Adelson [6] employed a k-means clustering algorithm in the affine parameter space to find a small number of motion classes. Finally, each flow vector is assigned to one of the resulting motion classes. Borshukov [7] later improved Wang and Adelson's algorithm through a merging and multi-stage approach to perform motion segmentation in a more robust way. The aforementioned approaches incur inaccurate segmentation due to inexact motion estimation near the object boundary. In order to overcome this problem, color information is introduced to obtain more accurate segmentation. In [8, 9], an initial segmentation proceeds with color segmentation. Then, regions are merged on the basis of temporal or spatial similarity.

1.2 System Overview

In this paper, we integrate these two kinds of approaches to perform the foreground detection in a more effective manner. Figure 1 shows the block diagram of the proposed algorithm. The main idea is to regard the background model as a portion of knowledge for classification. And, motion-based segmentation is to generate a set of regions for classification in the semantic level. After segmentation, the statistical framework, MRFs, is introduced to formulate the foreground detection problem as a labeling problem. The optimization over the MRFs model is then performed, or specifically *a posterior* probability is maximized to obtain a classification result. Finally, regions which have the same classification label and similar colors are merged to derive a more meaningful segmentation. Finally, the background model and the resulting region map are updated accordingly.

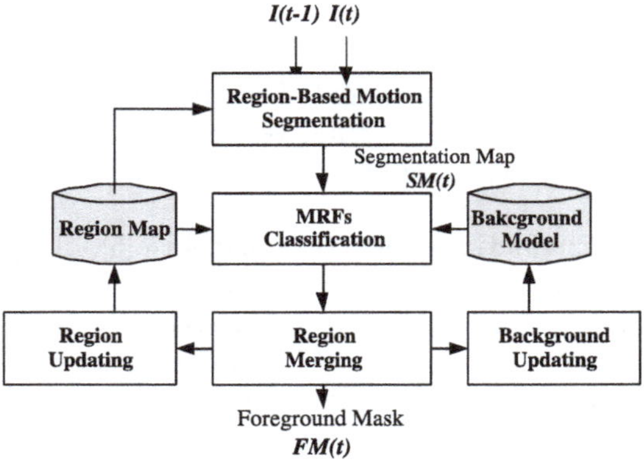

Fig. 1. The block diagram of the proposed algorithm

The remainder of this paper is organized as follows. In section 2, we introduce the region-based motion segmentation algorithm to obtain a set of motion-coherence regions. Section 3 addresses problems of background modeling and updating. The classification process based on the MRFs statistical framework is described in section 4. In section 5, we demonstrate the effectiveness of the developed approach by providing some appealing experimental results. Finally, we conclude the paper in section 6 with some relevant discussion.

2 Region-Based Motion Segmentation

First of all, Horn and Schunck's method [10] is used to estimate dense optical flow for describing motion vector, $(u(x,y), v(x,y))$, of every pixel (x,y) between two consecutive image frames $I(t-1)$ and $I(t)$. Segmented regions of the previous image frame, $I(t-1)$, will then be projected to the current image frame, $I(t)$. Regions with coherent motion are extracted as initial motion markers. Pixels not ascribed to any region are labeled uncertain ones. Finally, a watershed algorithm [11] based on motion and color is utilized to join uncertain pixels to the nearest similar marker.

2.1 Region Projection

Because of inaccuracy in estimating motion of region's boundary using Horn and Schunck's method, a parametric affine motion model is adopted to represent the motion of a region. Let the affine motion model A_i represent the motion of a region R_i, then it is a six-parameter model denoted as the parametric motion vector, i.e. $A_i(x, y; R_i)$, of any relevant pixel $(x, y) \in R_i$. Specially, A_i can be expressed as $A_i(x, y; R_i) = [U_i(x, y), V_i(x, y)]$

Given the affine motion model,any pixel $(x, y) \in R_i$ in the previous frame, $I(t-1)$, should be projected to the location (x', y'), where $(x', y') = (x + U_i(x, y), y + V_i(x, y))$. Due to quantization error, we define the projection error $e_p(x, y)$ of the pixel (x, y) as

$$e_p(x, y) = \min_{(i,j)\in N_4(x\prime,y\prime)\cup(x,y)} |I(x, y; t-1) - I(i, j; t)|, \tag{1}$$

where $N_4(x', y')$ is the set of four connected pixels surrounding (x', y'). $|I(x, y; t-1) - I(i, j; t)|$ is the Euclidean distance of RGB color vectors between two pixels (x, y) and (i, j) at different time instant. If $e_p(x, y)$ is less than a given threshold Th_p, then the region label of (x', y') is assigned to the same one of (x, y). Otherwise, the pixel which has large projection error is labeled as uncertain ones to indicate that the projecting from the previous frame to the current one is failed.

2.2 Motion Marker Extraction

The output of this step is a set of motion-coherent regions, that is, all pixels within a region comply with a motion model. Here, each such region is referred to as a motion maker. By starting to grow from these markers, we can eventually obtain a segmentation. Motion markers here are derived in two ways. First, the regions projected from the previous time frame are one kind of motion markers because each of them arises from an affine motion model. In addition to those, the regions resulting from the newly introduced object(s) may be another kind of motion markers, To handle this situation, a method similar to [12] is used to extract this kind of motion marker.

Next, an affine motion model A_i is evaluated to describe the motion of each region, R_i, according to the least square method in [13]. We then exclude the pixel (x, y) from R_i if the motion error, $e_m(x, y)$, of the pixel (x, y) associated with A_i is larger than a predefined threshold Th_m, where the motion error is defined as

$$e_m(x, y) = |(u(x, y), v(x, y)) - A_i(x, y; R_i)| \tag{2}$$

After exclusion, the region is the motion marker if the area of it is above a threshold. The set of these motion markers is denoted as $\mathcal{M} = \{\mathcal{M}_i | i = 1, 2, ...m\}$, where m is the number of motion markers. Each motion marker, $\mathcal{M}_i$ stands for a segmented region.

2.3 Boundary Determination

After motion marker extraction, the number of the regions to be segmented is known. However, a large number of pixels are not yet assigned to any region. These uncertain pixels are mainly around the contours of the regions. Through the use of the watershed algorithm [11], uncertain pixels will be merged to one of the markers. Finally, we obtain a set of segmented regions with coherent motion.

3 Background Modeling

In this paper, we use the method proposed by [4] to model and update the background scene. A brief description of Stauffer and Grimson's work is first given and then we introduce the Bhattacharyya distance as the difference measure between the region from the region-based motion segmentation and the one represented by the background model to successfully remove the shadow effect.

3.1 Adaptive Gaussian Mixture Models

The probability of a specific pixel which has an observation $o(t)$ at time instant t can be expressed as

$$P(o(t)) = \sum_{i=1}^{K} w_i(t)\eta(o(t); \mu_i(t), \Sigma_i(t)), \tag{3}$$

where $w_i(t)$ is the weight of the ith Gaussian distribution at time t, $\mu_i(t)$ and $\Sigma_i(t)$ are the mean vector and covariance matrix of the ith Gaussian distribution at time t, and $\eta(o; \mu, \Sigma)$ is the Normal Gaussian distribution.

3.2 Bhattacharyya Distance

Now, we want to introduce how to measure the similarity between the segmented region and the one represented by the background model. Let the region R_s is the one obtained from the region-based motion segmentation process, and let the color observation of the pixel $p(x, y)$ belongs to R_s be denoted as $o(x, y)$. Then, the color of $p(x, y)$ representing by the background model is then defined as the mean vector of the Gaussian distribution that has the minimum Mahalanobis distance [14] from $o(x, y)$. Now, suppose the notation R_b is used to denote the region represented by the background model, then the colors of the regions, R_s and R_b, are both assumed to be of Gaussian distributions.

Suppose that μ_s and Σ_s are the mean vector and covariance matrix of R_s, respectively, and similarly for μ_b and Σ_b are of R_b. The distance measure between R_s and R_b can be related to the probability of classification error in statistical hypothesis testing, which naturally leads to the Bhattacharyya distance [14, 15]. The Bhattacharyy distance, $d_{bhat}(.,.)$, is formally defined as follows:

$$\begin{aligned} d_{bhat}(R_s, R_b) &= \tfrac{1}{8}(\mu_s - \mu_b)^T |\tfrac{\Sigma_s + \Sigma_b}{2}|^{-1}(\mu_s - \mu_b) \\ &+ \tfrac{1}{2} \ln \frac{|\frac{\Sigma_s+\Sigma_b}{2}|}{\sqrt{|\Sigma_s||\Sigma_b|}} \end{aligned} \tag{4}$$

However, the region similarity defined in this way will lead to mis-classification of the background region where direct light is blocked by the foreground object. The region of this kind is referred to as shadow. According to [16], the intensity of the pixel in shadow will be scaled down by a factor λ with $\lambda_f \leq \lambda \leq 1$, where λ_f is a constant.

If the actual color vector of a pixel is $v = (r, g, b)$, it will become $v' = (r', g', b')$ after being covered by shadow. In an ideal case, $v' = \lambda v$. Due to light fluctuation and noise effect, the ideal situation hardly takes place. Thus, the scaling factor is defined to be λ^*, which minimizes $f(\lambda) = (r' - \lambda r)^2 + (g' - \lambda g)^2 + (b' - \lambda b)^2$. By differentiating $f(\lambda)$ with respect to λ, we can obtain λ^* according to the following equations.

$$
\begin{aligned}
&\tfrac{df(\lambda^*)}{d\lambda} = 0 \\
&\Rightarrow \lambda^*(r^2 + g^2 + b^2) = rr' + gg' + bb' \\
&\Rightarrow \lambda^* = \tfrac{rr'+gg'+bb'}{r^2+g^2+b^2}
\end{aligned}
\tag{5}
$$

In order to obtain the measure for region similarity invariant to shadow effect, the pixel in the current image should be scaled down at the first place. But, this is impractical due to expensive computation. Instead of doing this, we just use the mean vectors of R_s and R_b to evaluate λ^* and scale down the distribution (μ_s, Σ_s) of R_s to $(\lambda^* \mu_s, (\lambda^*)^2 \Sigma_s)$.

4 MRFs-Based Classification

Next, we describe how to incorporate the background model to classify every region into either a foreground object or a background one by Markov Randome Fields (MRFs). The formally statistical framework of MRFs can be found in [17]. Before that, a graph called region adjacency graph (RAG) is used to represent the set of segmented regions. Let $G = (S, E)$ be an RAG, where $S = \{s_1, s_2, ..., s_n\}$ is the set of nodes in graph and each node S_i corresponds to a region R_i, and E is the set of edges with $(s_i, s_j) \in E$ if R_i and R_j being neighboring regions.

Here, we describe how to define $U(O|\omega)$ and $U(\omega)$ so as to incorporate the background model as well as temporal and spatial coherence under MRFs framework. The terms, $U(O|\omega)$ and $U(\omega)$ are the *likelihood* and *prior* energy over all sites, respectively. $L = \{\omega_1, \omega_2, ..., \omega_m\}$ is a set of labels. In the foreground detection problem denoted as $L = \{F, B\}$, F and B stand for foreground and background, respectively. $O = \{o_1, o_2, ..., o_n\}$: a set of observations associated with each site.

The term $U(o_i|s_i = \omega_i)$ represents the likelihood energy of the site s_i to be classified as the label ω_i. Two functions, $f^F_{likelihood}(.)$ and $f^B_{likelihood}(.)$ are defined as depicted in Figure 2(a) to evaluate $U(o_i|\omega_i = F)$ and $U(o_i|\omega_i = B)$, whereas $U_{likelihood}$ and $Th_{likelihood}$ in Figure 2(a) are two constants. Based on the background model, the distance we use to measure the likelihood energy is $d_{bhat}(R_i, R_{b(i)})$, where $R_{b(i)}$ is the region represented by the background model as mentioned in section 3.

The *prior* energy is composed of singleton, $U_1(.)$, and pairwise, $U_2(.,.)$ energies. The term $U_1(.)$ is related to the temporal coherence and is defined as:

$$
U_1(\omega_i) = \begin{cases} -r_B d_{bhat}(R_i(t), R_i(t-1)) \text{ if } \omega_i = B \\ -r_F d_{bhat}(R_i(t), R_i(t-1)) \text{ if } \omega_i = F \end{cases}, \tag{6}
$$

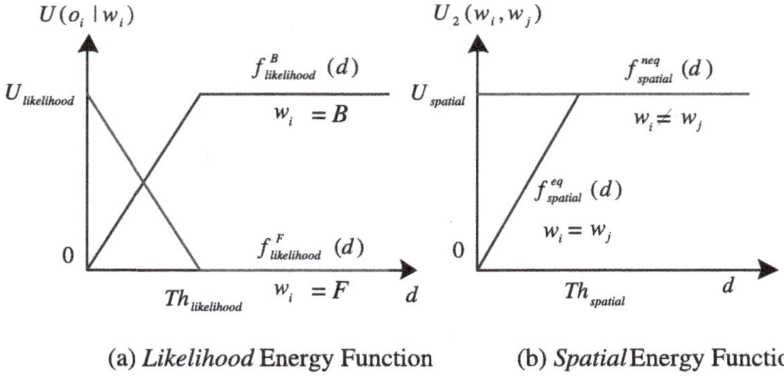

Fig. 2. Energy Functions: (a) shows two functions, $f^B_{likelihood}(.)$ and $f^F_{likelihood}(.)$ to evaluate the *likelihood* function, $U(o_i|w_i)$. (b) shows two functions, $f^{neq}_{spatail}(.,.)$ and $f^{eq}_{spatial}(.,.)$, that are for evaluating spatial function $U_2(.,.)$.

where $R_i(t-1)$ is the corresponding region of $R_i(t)$ at frame $I(t-1)$ which can be obtained by using affine motion model, r_B is the ratio of pixels in $R_i(t-1)$ that have been classified as background at time instant $t-1$, and, $r_F = 1 - r_B$. The purpose of introducing this term is to impose the temporal coherence, that is, the region obtained at current time instant tends to be classified as the same label as the corresponding region at the previous time instant.

As for the term $U_2(.,.)$, we relate it to spatial coherence which means that two neighboring regions with similar color should be assigned to the same label. Therefore, $U_2(w_i, w_j)$ for two neighboring sites s_i and s_j can be evaluated by using two functions, $f^{neq}_{spatial}(.)$ and $f^{eq}_{spatial}(.)$, as depicted in Fig. 2(b), which are used under the cases $\omega_i \neq \omega_j$ and $\omega_i = \omega_j$, respectively.

The optimization is carried out by using iterative conditional mode (ICM) algorithm to find the most proper label assignment of every region. After classification, the regions neighboring to one another will be merged and used to update the background model and region map.

5 Experiment

In this section, one standard MPEG-4 test sequence as well as two image sequences captured from intelligent home (e-home) demon room belonging to the Intelligent Robotics Laboratory at National Taiwan University are considered to validate our proposed method. Additionally, we compare our algorithm with the one proposed in [18] which is used to extract foreground objects for further human identification.

Figure 3(a) illustrates the original frames 15, 25, 50, and 75 of the *Hall Monitoring* image sequence. Images in Fig. 3(b) and Fig. 3(c) show the detection results of Wang's approach and ours, respectively. Frame 15 here is to exhibit that our algorithm can automatically detect newly introduced objects.

The second case is the image sequence exhibiting the gradual illumination variation and local motion. When a person enters, the background will gradually

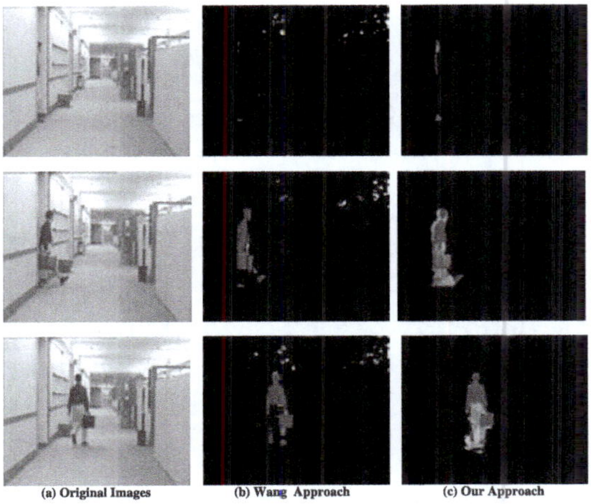

Fig. 3. *Hall Monitoring* Sequence. (a) are the frames, 15, 25, and 50 of the *hall monitoring* sequence. (b) and (c) are the detection result of Wang's approach and our proposed approach, respectively.

brighten. This is due to radiance from the fluorescent lamp that is reflected back into the background scene. After leaving the scene, he will wave the curtains to make it flutter. Some possible false positives due to Wang's algorithm under the condition with gradual illumination variation and local motion are shown in Fig. 4(b). As shown in Fig. 4(c), the detection results of our approach are more robust in such situations.

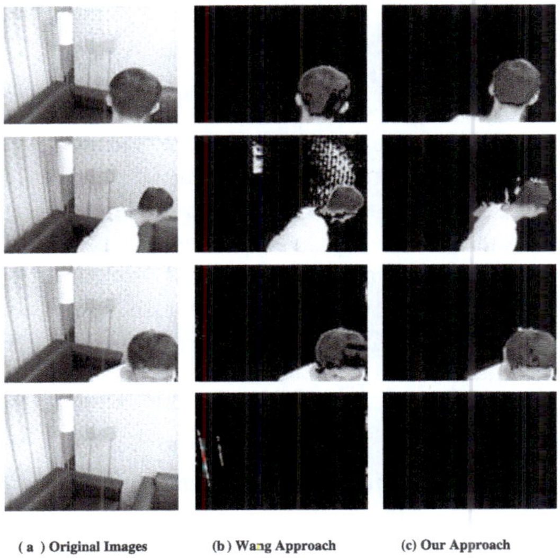

Fig. 4. Gradual illumination variation in e-home demo room. (a) Original images. (b) Detection result of Wang's approach. (c) Detection results of our approach.

(a) Original Images

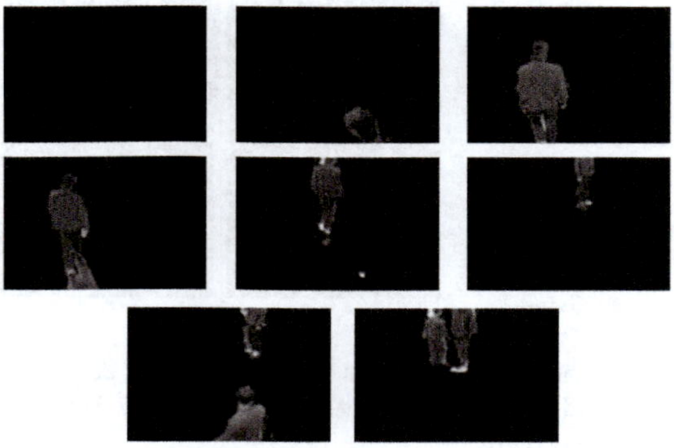
(a) Foreground Detection of Our Appraoch

Fig. 5. Shadow Effect Elimination. (a) Original images. (b) Detection results of our approach.

The final case features two persons entering the scene in order and crossing each other at the top of the image. Our proposed method will eliminate most of the shadow effect by applying the aforementioned scaling factor λ^* before evaluating Bhattacharyya distance. Empirically, λ_f is set to 0.7 in this paper.

6 Conclusion

In this paper, we performed the foreground detection at the region level which means that contextual information is taken into consideration. A statistical framework, MRFs, fuses the cues from background model and *prior* knowledge including temporal and spatial coherence to detect the foreground objects in a more accurate and elegant way. Experimental results demonstrate that our proposed method can successfully extract the foreground objects even under situations with illumination variation, shadow, and local motion.

References

1. Gupte, S., Masoud, O., Martin, R.F.K., Papanikolopoulos, N.P.: "Detection and Classification of Vehicles". IEEE Transactions on Intelligent Transportation Systems **3** (2002) 37–47
2. Haritaoglu, I., Harwood, D., Davis, L.S.: "W4: Real-Time Surveillance of People and Their Activities". IEEE Transactions on Pattern Analysis and Machine Intelligence **22** (2000) 809–830

3. Friedman, N., Russell, S.: "Image Segmentation in Video Sequence: A Probabilistic Approach". International Conference on Uncertainty in Artificial Intelligence (1997)
4. Stauffer, C., Grimson, W.: "Adaptive Background Mixture Models for Real-Time Tracking". IEEE Computer Society Conference on Computer Vision and Pattern Recognition **2** (1999)
5. Elgammal, A., Duraiswami, R., Harwood, D., Davis, L.S.: "Background and Foreground Modeling Using Nonparametric Kernel Density Estimation for Visual Surveillance". Proceedings of the IEEE **90** (2002) 1151–1162
6. Wang, J.Y.A., Adelson, E.H.: "Spatio-Temporal Segmentation of Video Data. Proceedings of the SPIE: Image and Video Processing (1994)
7. Borshukov, G.D., Bozdagi, G.: "Motion Segmentation by Multistage Affine Classification. IEEE Transactions on Image Process **6** (1997) 1591–1594
8. Tsaig, Y., Averbuch, A.: "Automatic Segmentation of Moving Objects in Video Sequences: A Region Labeling Approach". IEEE Transactions on Circuits and Systems for Video Technology **12** (2002) 597–612
9. Altunbasak, Y., Eren, P.E., Tekalp, A.M.: "Region-Based Parametric Motion Segmentation Using Color Information". Graphical Models and Image Processing: GMIP **60** (1998) 013–023
10. Horn, B.K.P., Schunck, B.G.: "Determining Optical Flow". AI Memo 572, Massachusetts Institue of Technology (1980)
11. Salembier, P., Pardas, M.: "Hierarchical Morphological Segmentation for Image Sequence Coding". IEEE Transaction on Image Processing **3** (1994) 639–651
12. Choi, J.G., Lee, S.W., Kim, S.D.: "Spatio-Temporal Video Segmentation Using a Joint Similarity Measure. IEEE Transactions on Circuits and Systems for Video Technology **7** (1997) 279–286
13. Wang, J.Y.A., Adelson, E.H.: "Representation Moving Images with Layers. IEEE Transactions on Image Processing **3** (1994) 625–638
14. Duda, R.O., Hart, P.E., Stork, D.G.: "Pattern Classification". Wiley Interscience (2000)
15. Mak, B., Barnard, E.: "Phone Clustering Using the Bhattacharyya Distance". Fouth International Conference on Spoken Language Processing (ICSLP) **4** (1996) 2005–2008
16. Elgammal, A., Harwood, D., Davis, L.S.: "Non-parametric Model for Background Subtraction". IEEE International Conference on Computer Vision Frame-Rate Workshop (1999)
17. Li, S.Z.: "Markov Random Field Modeling in Computer Vision". Proceedings of European Conference in Computer Vision (1994)
18. Wang, L., Tan, T., Ning, H., Hu, W.: "Silhouette Analysis-Based Gait Recognition for Human Identification". IEEE Transaction on Pattern Analysis and Machine Intelligence **25** (2003) 1505–1518

Waterfall Segmentation of Complex Scenes*

Allan Hanbury[1] and Beatriz Marcotegui[2]

[1] Pattern Recognition and Image Processing Group (PRIP), Institute of Computer-Aided Automation, Vienna University of Technology, Favoritenstraße 9/1832, A-1040 Vienna, Austria
hanbury@prip.tuwien.ac.at
http://www.prip.tuwien.ac.at

[2] Centre de Morphologie Mathématique, Ecole des Mines de Paris, 35, rue Saint-Honoré, 77305 Fontainebleau cedex, France
marcoteg@cmm.ensmp.fr
http://cmm.ensmp.fr

Abstract. We present an image segmentation technique using the morphological Waterfall algorithm. Improvements in the segmentation are brought about by using improved gradients. These are based on the detection of object boundaries learnt from human segmentations introduced by Martin et al. (2004). We avoid the usual pitfall found when applying Watershed algorithms to these boundaries, namely that the boundary lines usually contain gaps, by making use of distance functions on the boundary image. Two types of distance function are used: the classic distance function and a distance function for numerical images recently introduced by Beucher (2005). Resulting segmentations are compared to human segmentations using the Berkeley segmentation benchmark. The benchmark results show that the proposed segmentation algorithm produces segmentations comparable to those produced by the Normalised Cuts algorithm.

1 Introduction

Image segmentation is often used as a first step in general object recognition in complex, natural scenes, for example in [1, 2]. The object recognition is simplified if the regions produced by the segmentation algorithm already correspond to "meaningful" objects. Nevertheless, even humans often cannot agree on the best segmentation of such a scene [3].

Many algorithms for image segmentation are available, two of the most popular being the Normalised Cuts (NCuts) [4] and the Watershed [5]. Both of these algorithms require a way of measuring the similarity (or difference) between pixels in an image. The Watershed, for example, is usually applied to some sort of gradient of an image. A particularly promising algorithm for detecting the

* This work was supported by the European Union Network of Excellence MUSCLE (FP6-507752), and the Austrian Science Foundation (FWF) under grant SESAME (P17189-N04).

P.J. Narayanan et al. (Eds.): ACCV 2006, LNCS 3851, pp. 888–897, 2006.

boundaries in an image based on brightness, colour and texture cues learnt from human segmentations of an image was presented in [6], and is briefly described in Section 2. Unfortunately, these boundaries are not suitable to be used as a gradient for a Watershed algorithm due to gaps in the boundary lines. In this paper, we present a solution to this problem, which is to fill the small gaps by applying a distance transform to the boundary image, as described in Section 3. An enhanced version of the Watershed algorithm, the Waterfall algorithm (Section 4), is used to segment the images. The complete algorithm is summarised in Section 5. The comparison of the Waterfall algorithm with the NCuts algorithm using the Berkeley Segmentation Benchmark is presented in Section 6.

2 Boundaries Based on Learning

We briefly review the boundaries based on learning introduced by Martin et al. [6]. They make use of brightness, colour and texture gradients to compute the boundaries. To calculate the gradients, a circular area is moved over the image. At each pixel, for a number of orientations of a line dividing the circle into two halves, the χ^2 histogram difference is evaluated for histograms of the features in the two halves. For brightness and colour, the features are the values of L^*, a^* and b^* in the CIELAB space (taken separately) and for texture, the features are 64 textons used in [6]. For each feature, the gradient is taken to be the maximum value obtained over all the orientations of the line dividing the circle. The result of this algorithm is therefore a vector of four gradient values at every pixel (3 colour and 1 texture).

These gradients are combined to form a boundary probability by using a logistic model, where the weights for each gradient are obtained by supervised training of the model on the human segmentations. We made use of the weights provided by the authors of [6] in their software[1]. The resultant boundary probabilities are in the range $[0, 1]$. As an example, the boundaries detected in Figure 1(a) are shown in Figure 1(b).

3 Distance Functions

A common problem when attempting to segment a boundary image produced by the algorithm outlined in the previous section is the gaps in the boundary lines. These can be clearly seen in Figure 1(c), which is an enlargement of part of Figure 1(b). This results in very few local minima in the image (often only one), which makes applying Watershed based segmentation algorithms dificult. Our solution to the problem is to attempt to close the gaps by calculating a *distance function* of the boundary image.

The classic distance function takes as input a binary image. It associates with each foreground pixel the distance to the closest background pixel. See Figure 2

[1] Downloadable on the Berkeley Segmentation Benchmark page: `http://www.cs.berkeley.edu/projects/vision/grouping/segbench/`

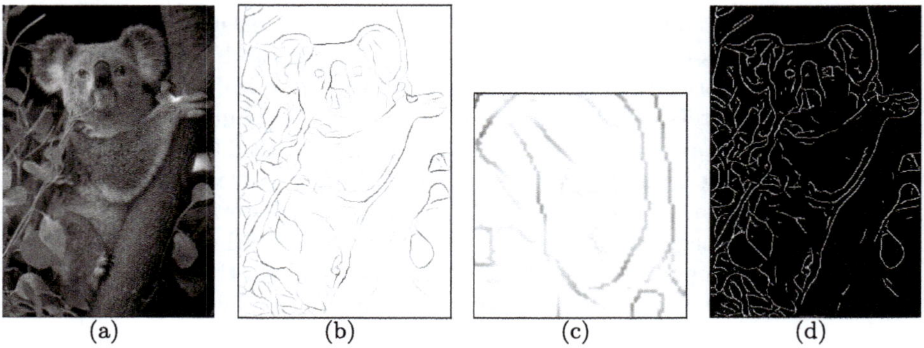

Fig. 1. (a) An image and its (b) boundary probabilities (darker pixels indicate higher probability). (c) Detail of (b) showing the gaps in the contour. (d) Threshold of (b).

for an example. The maxima of the distance function (pixels represented with a hatched pattern in Figure 2(b)) mark the different particles contained in the connected component. The Watershed applied to the inverse of the distance function is a well known approach for segmenting overlapping binary objects [7, 8]. In Figure 2(b), the Watershed line is represented by the grey pixels. We can see that this line correctly separates the two particles of the connected component.

If we take the boundaries detected by the Martin et al. algorithm as the background, the distance function encodes the shortest distance to each of the detected boundary lines. The value of the distance function within small gaps in the detected boundaries will therefore be lower. In the inverse of this distance function, the detected boundaries will have the maximum possible value. The lower values of the distance function in small gaps lead to higher values in the inverse, effectively closing the gaps in the topographical representation of the image used by the Watershed. Two distance functions were used: the classic distance function and the quasi-distance function.

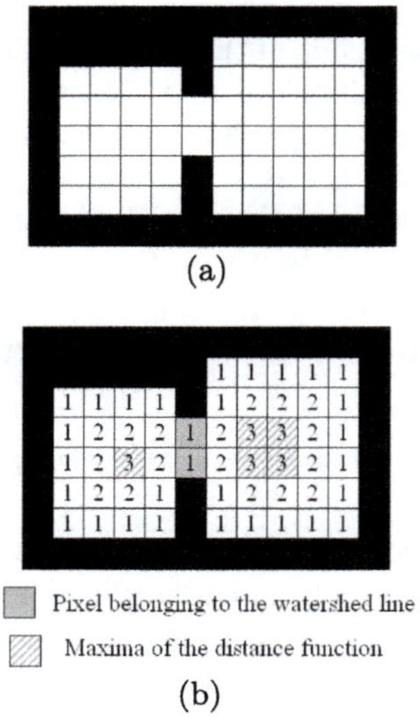

Fig. 2. (a) Binary image. (b) Associated distance function.

As the classic distance function requires a binary image as input, a threshold at level t is applied to the boundary image. We used a relatively low value of $t = 0.07$ for all experiments. This was found by experiment on a number of images to be the value below which the boundaries are mostly due to noise. The threshold of Figure 1(b) is shown in Figure 1(d). The classic distance function applied to this thresholded image is shown in Figure 3(a), with a zoomed in area shown in Figure 3(b).

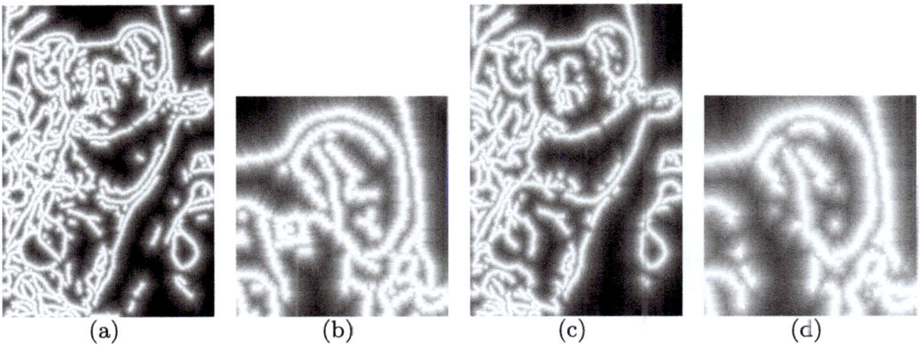

Fig. 3. (a) Distance on the thresholded boundary image. (b) Detail of (a). (c) Quasi-distance on the boundary image (without threshold). (d) Detail of (c).

To avoid the necessity of choosing this threshold we also made use of the quasi-distances introduced by Beucher [9]. The quasi-distance qd of an image I is defined as:

$$qd(x, y) = \arg\max_{i}(\epsilon_{i-1}(x, y) - \epsilon_i(x, y)) \quad (1)$$

where ϵ_i is the morphological erosion of size i, and (x, y) a given pixel of the image I. In other words, the quasi-distance associates with each pixel (x, y) the size i of the erosion that produces the biggest change in greylevel, among all possible sizes of erosions. Thus the quasi-distance is able to characterize the size of objects in a greylevel image without applying a threshold first. The quasi-distance function applied to the boundary image in Figure 1(b) is shown in Figure 3(c), with a zoomed in area shown in Figure 3(d).

4 Waterfall Algorithm

The Watershed algorithm usually leads to a strong over-segmentation of an image. The Waterfall [10] is a hierarchical approach that selects among all the contours of the Watershed those that are completely surrounded by more contrasted contours. By removing these contours, a simplified partition is obtained. The process may be iterated. At the end, a single region covering the whole image is obtained. An efficient graph-based Waterfall algorithm is presented in [11].

Examples of the Waterfall algorithm applied to the classic distance function and quasi-distance function of the detected boundary image are shown in Figures 4 and 5 respectively. In these figures, image (a) shows the result of applying the Watershed algorithm to the distance function, image (b) is the result of applying the Waterfall algorithm once (referred to as level 1 of the hierarchy) and image (c) is the result of two iterations of the Waterfall (level 2). Segmentation results on the 100 images of the Berkeley segmentation test dataset are available on the author's home page[2].

[2] `http://www.prip.tuwien.ac.at/~hanbury/ACCV06`

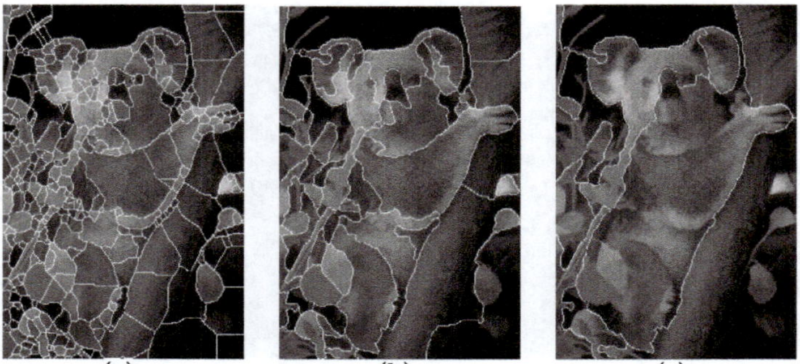

(a) (b) (c)

Fig. 4. (a) Watershed of distance function on the thresholded boundary probability image (level 0). (b) Waterfall level 1. (c) Waterfall level 2.

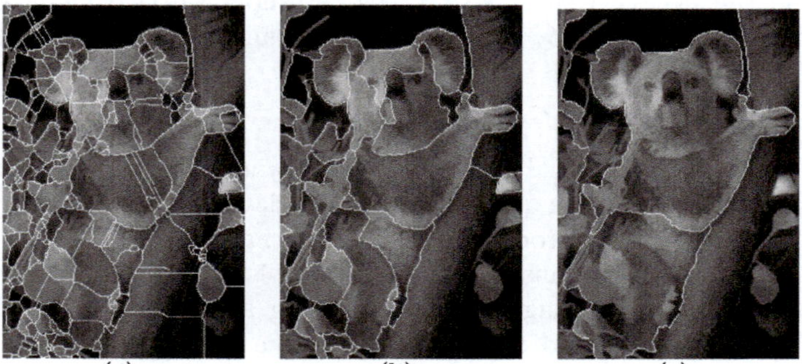

(a) (b) (c)

Fig. 5. (a) Watershed of quasi-distance on the boundary probability image (level 0). (b) Waterfall level 1. (c) Waterfall level 2.

5 Complete Segmentation Algorithm

We summarise here the algorithm used to perform the segmentation:

1. Calculate the learning-based boundaries (we used the combined colour and texture gradients [6]).
2. Calculate one of the two distance functions described in Section 3: the classic distance function on the threshold of the boundary image (abbreviated TD) or the quasi-distance function directly on the boundary image (QD).
3. Calculate the Waterfall hierarchy on the inverse of the distance function. The results of this Waterfall are referred to as "WF xD level y", where x is 'T' or 'Q', referring to the type of distance function used, and y gives the level of the Waterfall hierarchy, where level 0 is the result of the Watershed algorithm, level 1 is the first Waterfall level, etc.

6 Results and Evaluation

The results of the proposed segmentation approach are compared to those produced by the NCuts algorithm using the error measures proposed in [3].

6.1 Error Measure Definitions

To benchmark the results of the algorithms, we made use of the Berkeley segmentation benchmark [3]. Two measures of the difference between two segmentations S_1 and S_2 are introduced in [3]: the Global and Local Consistency Errors (GCE and LCE). As the GCE is a tougher measure, we make use of only this measure.

Let S_1 and S_2 be two segmentations of an image. The region $R(S, p_i)$ is the set of pixels corresponding to the region in segmentation S that contains pixel p_i. A segmentation S_1 is a *simple refinement* of S_2 if at every pixel p_i, $R(S_1, p_i) \subseteq R(S_2, p_i)$. The GCE is defined in terms of the local refinement error:

$$E(S_1, S_2, p_i) = \frac{|R(S_1, p_i) \setminus R(S_2, p_i)|}{|R(S_1, p_i)|} \quad (2)$$

where $\setminus$ denotes the set difference and $|x|$ is the cardinality of set x. As can be seen, this error measure is not symmetric. If, at pixel p_i, $R(S_1, p_i) \subseteq R(S_2, p_i)$, then $E(S_1, S_2, p_i) = 0$, but $E(S_2, S_1, p_i) > 0$. The GCE of segmentations S_1 and S_2 is defined as

$$\mathrm{GCE}(S_1, S_2) = \frac{1}{n} \min\left\{\sum_i E(S_1, S_2, p_i), \sum_i E(S_2, S_1, p_i)\right\} \quad (3)$$

where n is the number of pixels and the sums are over all pixels. If S_1 (resp. S_2) is a simple refinement of S_2 (resp. S_1), then $\mathrm{GCE}(S_1, S_2) = 0$. As the local refinement error is not symmetrical, the minimum of the local refinement error sums calculated in both directions is taken.

We used the 100 colour test images from the Berkeley Segmentation Dataset and Benchmark as well as the corresponding human segmentations. For each of the images, at least 5 segmentations produced by different people are available. To evaluate a segmentation algorithm, it was first applied to each of the 100 images. Then, for each image, the GCE of the segmentation produced by the algorithm with respect to each of the available human segmentations for that image was calculated. The mean of these values gives the mean GCE per image, which was plotted in a histogram. The global GCE was calculated as the mean of these 100 mean GCE values.

As the human segmentations often differ considerably, we first calculated a "best possible" GCE by comparing each human segmentation of an image to the remaining segmentations for that image. The "best possible" global GCE is 0.08 and the histogram of its distribution is shown in Figure 6(c).

For each algorithm, the mean of the number of regions produced by the segmentation algorithm for each of the 100 images was also calculated (for the

Table 1. The Global GCE, average number of regions and region number agreement with the human segmentations for various segmentation algorithms. These are: the Waterfall algorithm (WF) operating on different types of distance function (TD and QD) for two different levels of the hierarchy, and the NCuts algorithm. The results of the human-human segmentation comparison are also shown.

Method	GCE	Ave. #Reg.	#Reg. Agree.
WF TD level 1	0.16	51.4	24
level 2	0.23	7.8	39
WF QD level 1	0.21	28.6	46
level 2	0.22	5.6	35
N. Cuts (5 reg)	0.34	5.0	31
N. Cuts (16 reg)	0.24	16.0	63
N. Cuts (28 reg)	0.18	28.0	45
Human	0.08	16.8	-

human segmented images, this is 16.8). Finally, for each image, the mean $\bar{m}$ and standard deviation σ_m of the number of regions in the human segmentations is calculated. This allows the number of images for which the segmentation algorithm produces a region count lying within this range ($\bar{m} \pm \sigma_m$) to be determined (this is referred to as the *region number agreement*, shown in the rightmost column of Table 1).

6.2 Comparison of Segmentation Algorithms

We calculated the global GCE values for levels 1 and 2 of the WF TD and the WF QD, as well as for a segmentation by the NCuts algorithm[3]. These GCE values are shown in Table 1. Histograms showing the distributions of the mean GCE values of each of the 100 images are shown in Figure 6. Note that some of the segmentations at level 2 of the Waterfall hierarchy consist of only one region. As the GCE for such a segmentation is zero, we chose to use level 1 of the hierarchy if the number of regions in level 2 was smaller than 3.

The NCuts algorithm was applied directly to the boundary images. The implementation of the NCuts used requires that the number of regions required be passed as a parameter. We used values of 5, 16 and 28, corresponding to the average number of regions obtained by respectively the WF QD level 2, humans and WF QD level 1. The average number of regions produced by each algorithm as well as the region number agreement are also shown in Table 1.

6.3 Discussion

The lowest GCE value in Table 1 (excepting humans) was obtained by the WF TD level 1. However, as the average number of regions for this method

[3] We used an implementation by J. Shi available here: `http://www.cis.upenn.edu/~jshi/software/`

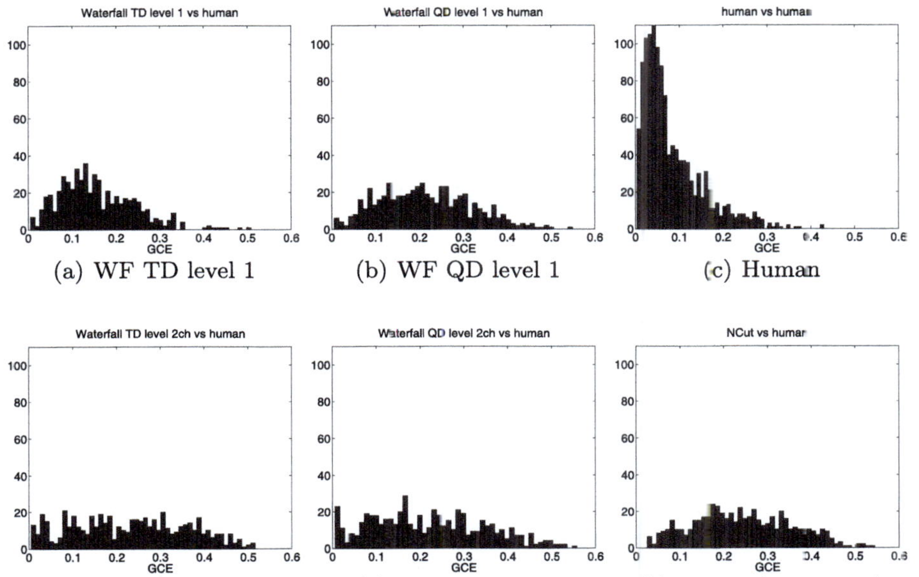

(a) WF TD level 1 (b) WF QD level 1 (c) Human

(d) WF TD level 2 (e) WF QD level 2 (f) NCuts (16 regions)

Fig. 6. Histograms of the distribution of the mean GCE for each of the 100 test images for: (a, b, d, e) the four different applications of the Waterfall algorithm, (f) the NCuts algorithm with 16 regions, and (c) the human-human comparison (note that this has more than 100 values as the human segmentations for each image are compared using a leave-one-out approach)

is 51.4, it appears that the images are over-segmented. It is mentioned in [3] that as the GCE measure is tolerant of refinement (splitting of regions), an over-segmentation can result in a smaller GCE value. This method also has the smallest region number agreement.

The other three Waterfall-based methods produce GCE values between 0.21 and 0.23, even though the average number of segments is much higher for the WF QD level 1 than for the two level 2 results. The WF QD level 1 has the smallest GCE of three along with the highest region number agreement. The GCE distributions for these three methods shown in Figure 6(b), (d) and (e) are similar. Figure 7(a) shows the mean and standard deviations of the GCE obtained for each of the 100 images when comparing the segmentation obtained by the WF QD level 1 to the corresponding human segmentations. The large differences in the mean GCE as a function of the image, as well as the large standard deviations due to significant differences in the human segmentations are clearly visible.

Concerning the number of segments produced, level 1 of the Waterfall-based methods tends to be an over-segmentation of the image, whereas level 2 tends to be an under-segmentation. This can be seen when comparing the average number of regions obtained (given in Table 1) with the average number of 16.8

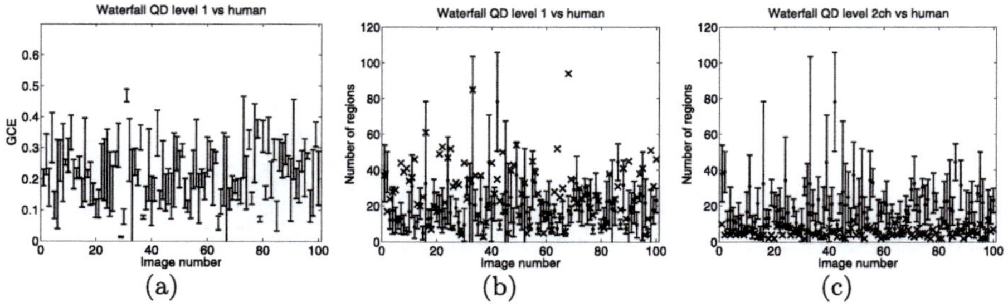

Fig. 7. (a) Mean and standard deviation of the GCE calculated for the WF QD level 1 with respect to the corresponding human segmentations for each test image. (b, c) Mean and standard deviation of the number of regions in the human segmentations for each of the test images (bars) and the number of regions in the (b) WF QD level 1 and (c) WF QD level 2 (crosses).

obtained for the human segmentations. Figure 7(b) and (c) give a more detailed view of the number of regions obtained per image. The bars show the mean and standard deviations of the number of regions in the human segmentations for each image, while the crosses show the number of regions obtained respectively by the WF QD level 1 and level 2. The large variation in the number of regions in the human segmentations of some of the images are visible. Furthermore, one can see that the majority of crosses are above the error bars for level 1 and below for level 2. This suggests the introduction of an alternative (less strict) merging rule in the Waterfall algorithm.

The Waterfall-based approaches produce smaller global GCE values than the NCuts with 5 and 16 regions. The GCE for level 2 of the Waterfall methods, even with the small number of regions, is significantly lower than the GCE of the NCuts for 5 regions. This suggests that the regions found by the Waterfall method are a better match to the human segmentations. The NCuts with 16 regions has a GCE value similar to those of the majority of Waterfall methods. The distribution of these GCE values are shown in Figure 6(f). This method also has the highest region number agreement. The second smallest GCE value in Table 1 corresponds to the NCuts with 28 regions, nevertheless it is possible that this is again due to over-segmentation. The Waterfall-based approaches have the advantage that the number of regions do not need to be specified in advance. There is a version of the NCuts which determines the number of regions automatically [12], but we currently have no implementation of it.

7 Conclusion

We have compared a morphological Waterfall-based segmentation algorithm to the Normalised Cuts algorithm using the Berkeley Segmentation Benchmark. Both segmentation algorithms are applied to boundary images obtained from a learning-based algorithm. These boundary images are not suitable for use with Watershed-based algorithms due to gaps in the boundary lines, a problem we have solved by calculating a distance function of the boundary images. Two types of distance function were tested, with one of them requiring no parameters as it operates directly on the greyscale images.

Based on the results of the benchmark, it is difficult to make a final pronunciation on which of the tested algorithms are better. For a small number of regions, the Waterfall algorithm has a lower GCE than the NCuts, but the GCE values are similar for segmentations with a higher number of regions The Waterfall algorithm tends to produce too many regions at the first level of its hierarchy and too few at the second level. It should be possible to change the region merging criteria to improve this. It would also be interesting to test the version of the NCuts which does not require the number of regions to be specified in advance.

References

1. Barnard, K., Duygulu, P., de Freitas, N., Forsyth, D., Blei, D., Jordan, M.I.: Matching words and pictures. Journal of Machine Learning Research **3** (2003) 1107–1135
2. Chen, Y., Wang, J.Z.: Image categorization by learning and reasoning with regions. Journal of Machine Learning Research **5** (2004) 913–939
3. Martin, D., Fowlkes, C., Tal, D., Malik, J.: A database of human segmented natural images and its application to evaluating segmentation algorithms and measuring ecological statistics. In: Proc. 8th Int'l Conf. Computer Vision. Volume 2. (2001) 416–423
4. Shi, J., Malik, J.: Normalized cuts and image segmentation. IEEE Trans. on Pattern Analysis and Machine Intelligence **22** (2000) 888–905
5. Beucher, S., Meyer, F.: The morphological approach to segmentation: the watershed transformation. In Dougherty, E., ed.: Mathematical Morphology in Image Processing. Marcel Dekker (1993) 433–481
6. Martin, D., Fowlkes, C., Malik, J.: Learning to detect natural image boundaries using local brightness, color, and texture cues. IEEE Transactions on Pattern Analysis and Machine Intelligence **26** (2004) 530–549
7. Lantuejoul, C., Beucher, S.: On the use of geodesic metric in image analysis. Journal of Microscopy **121** (1981) 39–49
8. Soille, P.: Morphological Image Analysis. second edn. Springer (2002)
9. Beucher, S.: Numerical residues. In: Mathematical Morphology and its Applications to Image Processing, Proc. ISMM'05. (2005) 23–32
10. Beucher, S.: Watershed, hierarchical segmentation and waterfall algorithm. In: Mathematical Morphology and its Applications to Image Processing, Proc. ISMM'94. (1994) 69–76
11. Marcotegui, B., Beucher, S.: Fast implementation of waterfall based on graphs. In: Mathematical Morphology and its Applications to Image Processing, Proc. ISMM'05. (2005) 177–186
12. Malik, J., Belongie, S., Leung, T., Shi, J.: Contour and texture analysis for image segmentation. International Journal of Computer Vision **43** (2001) 7–27

Markovian Framework for Foreground-Background-Shadow Separation of Real World Video Scenes

Csaba Benedek[1] and Tamás Szirányi[2]

[1] Pázmány Péter Catholic University, Department of Information Technology, H-1083 Budapest, Práter utca 50/A, Hungary
benedek@digitus.itk.ppke.hu
[2] Analogical Computing Laboratory, Computer and Automation Institute, Hungarian Academy of Sciences, H-1111 Budapest, Kende u. 13-17, Hungary
sziranyi@sztaki.hu

Abstract. In this paper we give a new model for foreground-background-shadow separation. Our method extracts the faithful silhouettes of foreground objects even if they have partly background like colors and shadows are observable on the image. It does not need any a priori information about the shapes of the objects, it assumes only they are not point-wise. The method exploits temporal statistics to characterize the background and shadow, and spatial statistics for the foreground. A Markov Random Field model is used to enhance the accuracy of the separation. We validated our method on outdoor and indoor video sequences captured by the surveillance system of the university campus, and we also tested it on well-known benchmark videos.

1 Introduction

Detection of foreground objects is a crucial task in visual surveillance systems. If we can retrieve the accurate shapes of the objects, their high-level description becomes much easier, so it is favorable e.g. in detection of people or activity analysis.

In the present paper, we exploit information from pixel-level estimation and neighborhood connection, while motion and structure are not considered. Based on the present results, more sophisticated segmentation methods can be developed by using tracking [12], object model matching [13], or edge information [4] [14]. However, all these developments can be preceded by an exact model on generating still background and reasonable shadow/foreground classes.

For foreground separation based on pixel intensity, Stauffer and Grimson [10] proposed an adaptive, real time algorithm, but it cannot handle some important problems. Shadows become part of moving objects, and since some parts of the objects may have similar color to the background, holes appear often in the silhouettes. The above mentioned problems can be observed on the silhouette images of Figure 1.

P.J. Narayanan et al. (Eds.): ACCV 2006, LNCS 3851, pp. 898–907, 2006.

Fig. 1. Results of foreground detection with Stauffer-Grimson algorithm. Left: School Entrance in the afternoon ('SE pm') video, right: 'Highway' test sequence.

Usually shadows have to be handled separately, because they do not belong to moving objects but their color properties are different from the background. [8] gives an overview on the state-of-the-art methods.

Classification of background, shadow and foreground areas is basically a Bayesian approach [1]. For this reason we must have statistical information about the a priori and conditional probabilities of the different clusters and the observable pixel values. The spatial interaction constraint of the neighbouring pixels can be modelled by Markov Random Fields (MRF) [5].

Previously published Bayesian models are lack of some information. They skipped shadow modelling [7][15], or the conditional probabilities of the shadow and foreground processes were oversimplified functions [9][14]. Therefore these methods are less effective on complex lighting conditions. Our goal was to develop a model with correct estimation of shadow in different lightning and coloring effects, and to detect foreground pixels of different colored and textured objects. Namely, the present paper is based on the former results, introducing more adequate models for conditional probabilities.

For validation we used real surveillance videos and also the benchmark sequences from [8]. Our model was successful in experiments with non-ideal conditions, like motley background and low contrast.

2 Markov Model

Since the work of Geman and Geman [5] there are several examples where MRFs are used for solving image-labeling problems. We used a similar model to that in [2] to classify the pixels of the video images into the following three classes: foreground (fg), background (bg) and shadow (sh). The *definitions* are the following:

S - set of pixels (or sites)

$X = \{x_s \mid s \in S\}$, - set of image data (x_s is the value of pixel s)

L={bg,sh,fg} - labels or classes.

$\Omega = \{\omega_s \mid s \in S\}$ - global labeling ($\omega_s \in L$ is the label of pixel s).

$p_k(s) = P(x_s|\omega_s = k), k \in L$ - conditional probability density function. E.g. $p_{\mathrm{bg}}(s)$ is the probability of that the background process generates the color value x_s at pixel s.

According to the model the optimal labeling is the following:

$$\widehat{\Omega} = \operatorname{argmin}_{\Omega} \sum_{s \in S} -\log p_k(s) + \sum_{r,s \in S} V(\omega_r, \omega_s) \tag{1}$$

where $V(\omega_r, \omega_s) = 0$ if s and r are not neighboring pixels, otherwise:

$$V(\omega_r, \omega_s) = \begin{cases} -\beta \text{ if } \omega_r = \omega_s \\ +\beta \text{ if } \omega_r \neq \omega_s \end{cases}$$

Our task is to define the $p_k(s)$ density functions, set the constant $\beta > 0$, and choose the energy optimization technique which finds the best or at least a good suboptimal labeling according to 1. We describe exactly how to get the $p_k(s)$ probability terms in Sections 3.1, 3.2 and 3.3. In Section 6, we show the applied MRF-optimization methods. In the following color images are considered, so the pixel value is a three dimensional vector: $x_s = [x_r(s), x_g(s), x_b(s)]$.

3 Probability Model Elements

3.1 Background Probabilities

The distribution of the color values for a given background pixel is modeled by Gaussian density function with mean value $\mu_{\text{bg}}(s)$ and covariance matrix $\Sigma_{\text{bg}}(s)$. [10] proposed an effective algorithm to determine the model parameters from the color video-flow. In [14] a similar method has already been successfully used in the MRF model. The covariance matrix is in the form of $\Sigma_{\text{bg}} = \sigma^2_{\text{bg}} \cdot I$, where I is the 3×3 identity matrix. With this simplification we avoid matrix inversion and determinant recovering during the calculation of the probabilities:

$$p_{\text{bg}}(s) = \frac{1}{\sqrt{(2\pi)^3} \cdot \sigma^3_{\text{bg}}(s)} \exp\left(-\frac{\|x_s - \mu_{\text{bg}}(s)\|^2}{2\sigma^2_{\text{bg}}(s)} \right) \qquad (2)$$

3.2 Shadow Probabilities

[6] appointed since a shadowed pixel represents the background surface under different illumination, the effect of illumination on pixel appearance is typical for a situation. The effect was approximated by a diagonal A matrix as a multiplicative term in the RGB color space, and the shadow probabilities were directly derived from the background model:

$$p_{\text{sh}}(s) = \eta\left(x_s, A \cdot \mu_{\text{bg}}(s), A^2 \cdot \Sigma_{\text{bg}}(s)\right)$$

where $\eta(.,.,.)$ marks Gaussian density function.

In case of motley background each surface may have different reflection properties, therefore the approximation of the darkening factor with a global constant causes considerable model error. In [14] a heuristic additional shadow noise parameter was used to correct the deviation term, but in practical surveillance videos, a more sophisticated method is needed.

Instead of modelling the probability density functions of the shadowed values independently at each pixel location s, we modelled the density of the darkening ratios globally in the image. We considered one global transformation, however

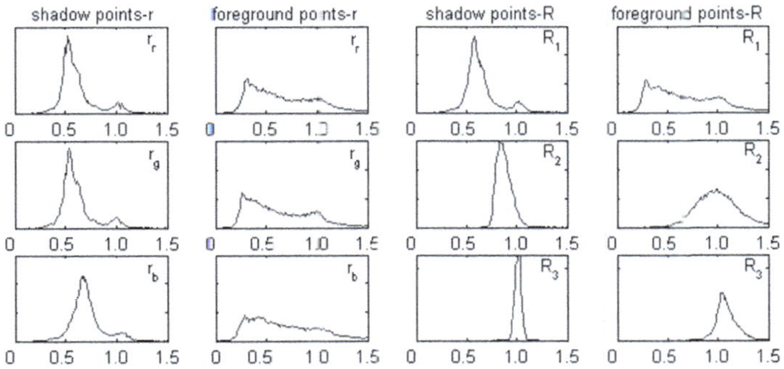

Fig. 2. Histograms for r_r, r_g, r_b, R_1, R_2 and R_3 values of shadowed and foreground points from 'SE pm' sequence

in case of images with multiple lighting and separated scene areas, the transformation parameters should be estimated in each subregion separately. With notation $\mu_{bg}(s) = [b_r(s), b_g(s), b_b(s)]$ we introduce vector containing ratios of the color values in the background and in the shadow for each pixel and for each color channel: $r(s) = [r_r(s), r_g(s), r_b(s)]$, where

$$r_r = \frac{x_r}{b_r}, \quad r_g = \frac{x_g}{b_g}, \quad r_b = \frac{x_b}{b_b}.$$

In Figure 2 the first and second columns show the histogram of the occurring r_r,r_g, and r_b values for manually marked shadowed and foreground points of the School entrance in the afternoon (SE pm) sequence. We also executed this experiment on other videos with similar results. We can observe, if we neglect the small second peaks, the 1 dimensional ratio values in shadow have approximately Gaussian distribution. However, Table 1 shows that the correlation between the elements of vector r is high, so if we model the shadowed r ratios with Gaussian distribution, the covariance matrix cannot be considered diagonal. Therefore we have searched for further quantities, and found the following ones: $R = [R_1, R_2, R_3]$

$$R_1 = \frac{r_r + r_g + r_b}{3}, \quad R_2 = \frac{r_r}{r_b}, \quad R_3 = \frac{r_g}{r_b}.$$

In Figure 2 and Table 1 we can observe R_1, R_2, and R_3 values are generated also approximately by Gaussian distribution, but their correlation is definitely smaller. Therefore we characterize shadow via R values. The resulting shadow

Table 1. Average of the absolute values of nondiagonal elements in the autocorrelation matrix for r and R values of shadowed points

	Corr(r)	Corr(R)
SE pm:	0.967	0.374
Highw:	0.987	0.360

probability term for pixel s, and parameters of our shadow model are the following:

$$p_{\mathrm{sh}}(s) = \eta\left(R(s), \mu_{\mathrm{sh}}, \Sigma_{\mathrm{sh}}\right) \tag{3}$$

$$\mu_{\mathrm{sh}} = [\mu_{\mathrm{sh},1}, \mu_{\mathrm{sh},2}, \mu_{\mathrm{sh},3}], \quad \Sigma_{\mathrm{sh}} = diag\{\sigma^2_{\mathrm{sh},1}, \sigma^2_{\mathrm{sh},2}, \sigma^2_{\mathrm{sh},3}\}. \tag{4}$$

3.3 Foreground Probabilities

The description of background and shadow characterizes the scene and lighting properties so it is possible to collect statistical information about them in time. Unfortunately, the color distribution of foreground areas is unpredictable in the same way. However it is often inappropriate to model the foreground by uniform distribution, like in [9][14]. Figure 3 shows some resulting segmented images after applying MRF optimization for our background and shadow model but using uniform foreground distribution. Since the objects may have large background or shadow-like connected parts, big holes appear in the silhouettes, and the suggested Markovian model cannot remove these errors.

Instead of temporal statistics we used spatial color information to overcome this problem. First we assume that a pre-processing step is able to locate most of the foreground pixels. That process, which we introduce in Section 4, gives a preliminary foreground mask to the algorithm. Denote F the set of pixels marked as foreground elements in that mask. We have two assumptions for a given foreground pixel:

- In the neighborhood there are some foreground pixels
- The color of the pixel matches to the color distribution of set of the neighbouring foreground pixels.

In the following V_s denotes the set of the neighbouring pixels around s, considering rectangular neighborhood with window size v. F_s is the set of neighbouring pixels determined as 'foreground' by the preprocessing step: $F_s = F \cap V_s$. To deal with textured or multi level foreground components, the estimated probability density function of the color channels for F_s is in the following form:

$$f_{F_s, x_s}(x) = w_s \cdot \eta(x, \mu_{\mathrm{fg}}(s), \Sigma_{\mathrm{fg}}(s))) + (1 - w_s) \cdot f(x)$$

Namely, we divide the neighborhood pixels in two clusters: the ones, whose color-distance from x_s is smaller than a threshold, are characterized by one Gaussian term, while $f(x)$ is the residual density function with constraint: $f(x) = 0$, if

Fig. 3. Results of using MRF model with uniform foreground distribution

$\|x_s - x\| < \tau$, $0 < w_s < 1$. Accordingly, the color values of the site s are statistically characterized by the distribution of its neighborhood in the color domain:

$$p_{\text{fg}}(s) = f_{F_s,x_s}(x_s) = w_s \cdot \eta(x_s, \mu_{\text{fg}}(s), \Sigma_{\text{fg}}(s)). \quad (5)$$

To approximate the foreground model parameters we compose a subset of F_s by

$$F_s^D = \{r \mid r \in F_s, \ \|x_s - x_r\| < \tau\}.$$

Empirical mean value and deviation of the pixel values in F_s^D estimate the parameters $[\mu_{\text{fg}}(s), \Sigma_{\text{fg}}(s)]$. Weight w_s is calculated as a ratio of the cardinality of sets F_s^D and F_s. We also used an extra term to keep the probability low, if there are any or only a few pre-classified foreground pixels in the neighborhood.

4 Preliminary Foreground-Shadow-Background Classifier

The foreground model introduced in Section 3.3 needs a pre-processing step, which is able to find most of the foreground pixels. To achieve this task we used a deterministic classifier which uses the existing background and shadow model parameters from Section 3. The background matching step is the same as it was used in [10]. Pixel s is classified as background, if:

$$\|x_s - \mu_{\text{bg}}(s)\|^2 < 2c \cdot \sigma_{\text{bg}}^2(s)$$

Non-background the pixels are matched to the shadow constraints and labeled as shadow, if

$$(R_i(s) - \mu_{\text{sh},i})^2 < 2c/3 \cdot \sigma_{\text{sh},i}^2, \quad i \in \{1, 2, 3\}$$

Other way the pixel gets foreground label.

5 Parameter Settings

Our method has scene dependent and condition dependent parameters. *Scene dependent* parameters can be considered constant in a specific field, and are influenced by e.g. camera settings, expected size and shape of the objects or reflection properties. We give strategies how to set these parameters given a territory of a surveillance camera. *Condition dependent* parameters vary in time in a scene, we used adaptive algorithms to follow them.

The background parameter estimation and update procedure is automated, based on the work of [10]. It has a parameter (α in [10]), which controls the speed of model update. In our experiences it was set uniformly to 0.02.

5.1 Foreground Model Parameters

The foreground parameters are scene dependent constants. Window size s depends on the expected size of the objects in the scene. If T_B is the approximate average territory of the objects bounding boxes, we used $v = 1/3\sqrt{T_B}$.

The threshold parameter τ defines the maximum distance in the RGB color space between pixels generated by one Gaussian process. We used outdoors $\tau = 50$, indoors $\tau = 20$.

5.2 Shadow Parameters

The parameters are defined by Eq. 4. Except of window-less rooms with constant lightning, $\mu_{sh,1}$, the average background luminance darkening factor in shadow is strongly condition dependent. Outdoors, it can vary from 0.4 in sunburst to 0.9 in overcast weather. We observed the other shadow parameters (5 scalar values more) being approximately constant in time, letting us to estimate them once in a scene.

We built an adaptive algorithm to follow the changes of $\mu_{sh,1}$. For a given image we collected histogram from the R_1 values of those pixels, which are marked as non background point by the Stauffer-Grimson algorithm. If the image contains considerable shadowed parts, a peak appears in the histogram near the desired $\mu_{sh,1}$ value. Figure 4 shows 3 typical situations from the video 'SE pm', where the optimal $\mu_{sh,1}$ was definitely 0.68. On the first image, a large shadow is observable, and the peak in the histogram is very significant. On the second one, the peak is still in the right place, however it is smaller. On the third image there is small shadow and the histogram is flat. Denote $h[k]$ the location of the peak in the histogram of the k-th image, $v[k]$ is the maximum value, $\overline{v}[k]$ is the average value. $h[k]$ can be a good estimation for $\mu_{sh,1}$, if peak-value $v[k]$ is high and significant: $\frac{v[k]}{\overline{v}[k]}$ is high. We define the update process by the following:

$$\mu_{sh,1}[k+1] = \rho \cdot h[k] + (1-\rho) \cdot \mu_{sh,1}[k], \qquad \rho = \alpha \cdot v[k] \cdot \frac{v[k]}{\overline{v}[k]}$$

where $\alpha = 0.001$ is a constant factor, and we perform the parameter update only, if there are enough non-background points in the image.

We tested this method on videos recorded by the 'School entrance' camera in case of ten different lightning conditions, and appointed it can follow the lightning changes caused by clouds well, or in case of randomly chosen $\mu_{sh,1}$ it finds the correct value quite fast. However the performance of the adaption was lower round noon, when the shadows are smaller, and the corresponding darkening ratio is not so dominant in the statistics.

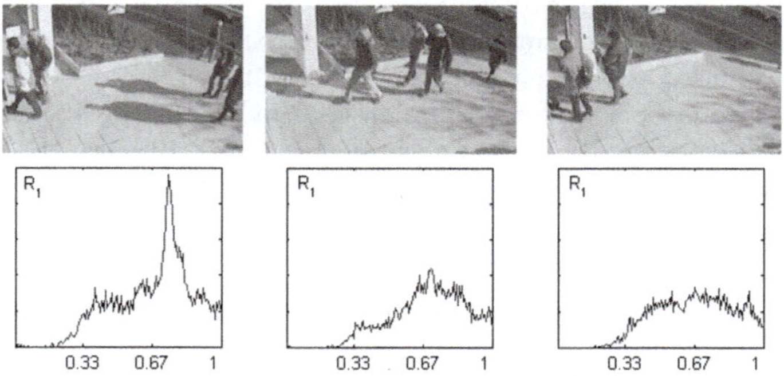

Fig. 4. Three images from sequence 'SE pm' and the corresponding histograms for the R_1 values of the non-background pixels

6 MRF Optimization and Speed of the Algorithm

The presented algorithm segments the video images via MRF optimization. First, the probability terms $p_{bg}(s)$, $p_{sh}(s)$, $p_{fg}(s)$ are calculated for each pixel s, according to (2)(3)(5). The second level is to find a good labeling considering the energy term of (1). The results showed on Figure 5 were made using the Modified Metropolis method [2], which is not real time on a sequential architecture, however [11] have already suggested a fast parallel implementation for a special array processor.

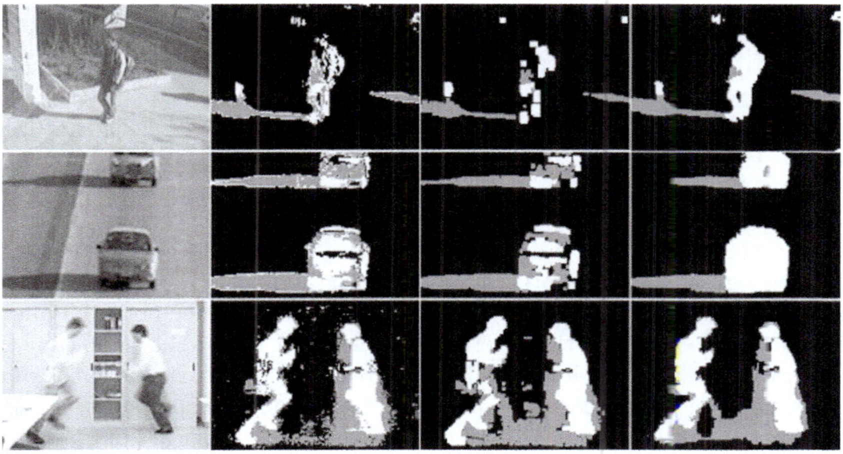

Fig. 5. *Segmentation results.* 1st column: video image, 2nd: result of the preliminary classifier, 3rd: pre. classifier result enhanced by morphology, 4th: MRF result. *Images* are from the following videos: a) Sequence 'SE pm', b) 'Highway', c) 'Laboratory'.

A well-known quick deterministic optimization method for MRF is the ICM algorithm, which gives a good sub-optimal solution in a few (2-5) iteration of steps with linear complexity. Although the quality of the segmentation produced by ICM is significantly worse than the we got by MMD, it is still enough for connected component based object detection.

We have tested out method on color videos with the resolution 320×240. The running speed was 2 fps using Intel Pentium 4 2400 MHz Processor.

7 Results

Model verification was made through manually generated ground truth sequences. Since the goal is foreground detection, the crossover between shadow and background does not count for errors.

Denote with TP (*true positive*) the number of correctly identified foreground pixels of the evaluation sequence. Similarly we introduce TN for well classified

Table 2. *Evaluation result.* SG: Stauffer-Grimson algorithm (without shadow filtering), Pre: preliminary classifier, Mor: the output of pre. enhanced by morphology, MMD: the result got by our MRF model, with MMD optimization. 'SE am' sequence was recorded in the morning by the campus' camera and contains large shadows.

	Fg. detection rate (D) %				Fg. accuracy rate (A) %			
Sequence	SG	Pre.	Mor.	MMD	SG	Pre.	Mor.	MMD
SE am	83.7	78.6	72.7	93.1	38.3	76.8	88.0	86.9
SE pm	82.9	67.6	66.7	80.7	62.5	79.3	88.4	90.1
Highw	87.4	56.5	43.9	83.1	55.9	78.2	88.8	88.5
Lab.	95.3	88.7	94.7	93.2	54.3	89.8	92.4	93.8

non-foreground points, FP for misclassified non-foreground points, and FN for misclassified foreground points.

Evaluation metrics: D is the foreground detection rate, A is the accuracy of the detection.

$$D = \frac{TP}{TP + FN} \qquad A = \frac{TP}{TP + FP}$$

The results in Table 2 are valid without postprocessing. The applied MRF model increased significantly the foreground detection and accuracy rate, compared to the deterministic step. We tried to reach homogenous regions by applying morphology on the output of the deterministic classifier but at the same time the D and A ratios became much worse. The improvement is remarkable in the difficult scenes, while on the 'Laboratory' benchmark sequence the simpler methods gave also very good results. Some examples for segmented images are in Figure 5.

8 Conclusion and Future Work

We introduced a realistic model of shadow effects and a new foreground probability calculus for segmenting videos by MRF model optimization. We measured significant improvements versus previous methods in real world videos, where the background and foreground is textured, and the color ranges of the different clusters are strongly overlapping. Our future work is to improve the automated parameter estimation process, and to speed up energy calculation of the foreground model. We want to complete our method with texture analysis, and exploit the advantages using more adequate color spaces (CIE-L*a*b* or CIE-L*u*v*). We will try to deal with difficult situations like shadow in the shadow and reflection from glass doors.

References

1. Cs. Benedek, T. Szirányi: A Markov Random Field Model for Foreground-Background Separation, Joint Hungarian-Austrian Conference on Image Processing and Pattern Recognition (HACIPPR), Veszprém, Hungary, May 11-13, (2005)
2. M. Berthod, Z. Kato, S. Yu, J. Zerubia: Bayesian image classification using Markov Random Fields. Image and Vision Computing 14 (1996) 285-295

3. R. Cucchiara, C. Grana, G. Neri, M. Piccardi, and A. Prati: The Sakbot System for Moving Object Detection and Tracking. Video-Based Surveillance Systems-Computer Vision and Distributed Processing (2001) 145-157
4. L. Czúni, T. Szirányi: Motion Segmentation and Tracking with Edge Relaxation and Optimization using Fully Parallel Methods in the Cellular Nonlinear Network Architecture. Real-Time Imaging Vol.7, No.1, (2001) 77–95
5. S. Geman and D. Geman: Stochastic relaxation, Gibbs distributions and the Bayesian restoration of images. IEEE Transactions on Pattern Analysis and Machine Intelligence (1984) 721-741
6. I. Mikic, P. Cosman, G. Kogut and M. M. Trivedi: Moving Shadow and Object Detection in Traffic Scenes, Proc. ICPR, (2000) 321-324
7. N. Paragios, V. Ramesh. A MRF-based Real-Time Approach for Subway Monitoring. In IEEE Conference in Computer Vision and Pattern Recognition (CVPR) (2001) 1034-1040
8. A. Prati, I. Mikic, M. M. Trivedi, R. Cucchiara: Detecting moving shadows: algorithms and evaluation. PAMI(25), (2003) 7, pp. 918–923
9. J. Rittscher, J. Kato, S. Joga and A. Blake: A Probabilistic Background Model for Tracking Proc. European Conf. Computer (2000)
10. C. Stauffer and W. E. L. Grimson: Learning Patterns of Activity Using Real-Time Tracking, IEEE Trans. Pattern Anal. Mach. Intell. (2000) 22(8): 747-757
11. T. Szirányi, J. Zerubia: Markov Random Field Image Segmentation using Cellular Neural Network , IEEE Tr. Circuits and Systems (1997) I., V.44, pp.86-89,
12. A. Yilmaz, X. Li, M. Shah Object Contour Tracking Using Level Sets. Asian Conference on Computer Vision, ACCV 2004, Jaju Islands, Korea, (2004)
13. P. Viola, M. Jones: Rapid Object Detection Using a Boosted Cascade of Simple Features, Proc. IEEE Conf. Computer Vision and Pattern Recognition, (2001)
14. Y. Wang, T. Tan, and K.-F. Loe:A Dynamic Hidden Markov Random Field Model for Foreground and Shadow Segmentation Seventh IEEE Workshops on Application of Computer Vision, Breckenridge, Colorado, (2005)
15. Yue Zhou, Yihong Gong, and Hai Tao: Background segmentation using spatial-temporal multi-resolution MRF, IEEE Motion05, (January 2005)

Separation of Reflection and Transparency Using Epipolar Plane Image Analysis

Thanda Oo[1], Hiroshi Kawasaki[1], Yutaka Ohsawa[1], and Katsushi Ikeuchi[2]

[1] Saitama University, Department of Information and Computer Science, 255, Shimo-okubo, Sakura-ku, Saitama 338-8570, Japan
{thanda, kawasaki, ohsawa}@mm.ics.saitama-u.ac.jp
[2] The University of Tokyo, Institute of Industrial Science, 6-4-1 Komaba, Meguro-ku, Tokyo 153-8505, Japan
ki@cvl.iis.u-tokyo.ac.jp

Abstract. The effect of reflection and transparency is superimposed in many real world scenes, which is caused by glass-like shiny and transparent materials. The presence of such incidental effect in a captured image has made it difficult to apply computer vision algorithms and has lead to erroneous results. Moreover, it disturbs the texture acquisition of the real-world scene. This paper presents an optimal method for the separation of reflection and transparency components. The method is based on the Epipolar Plane Image (EPI) analysis. The method is not like the ordinary edge-based EPI analysis, but instead it is an edge and color-based EPI analysis. To demonstrate the effectiveness of our method, we present the results of experiments using synthesized and real images which include indoor and outdoor scenes, from which we successfully extracted the reflection and transparency components from the input image sequences. ...

1 Introduction

Texture acquisition of a real-world scene is one of the critical research areas in computer vision and can be used in other application areas such as computer graphics (CG) including 3D city modeling projects. Moreover, to acquire texture without noise (e.g., a shadow, a specularity, a reflected image) is vital for such work. Generally, many of the buildings are covered with glass windows and glass usually produces reflection and transparency effects. Therefore, the observed color of such a scene is a combination of the light transmitted from an actual object behind the glass and a reflected object (virtual object) in front of the glass. This situation strongly disturbs the texture acquisition of the real-world scenes. One possible solution to this problem is to separate the component images. Many researchers have tried to separate the reflection and transparency components and many valuable methods have already been proposed. Some proposed methods are based on layer motion [1] [2]. Szeliski [2] proposed layer extraction technique even in the presence of reflection and transparency based on constrained least square method. Likewise, some other

P.J. Narayanan et al. (Eds.): ACCV 2006, LNCS 3851, pp. 908–917, 2006.

techniques [1] [3] based on motion for image enhancement and transparency separation are proposed. Schechner worked out to separate transparent layers using focus [4][5]. Moreover, there have been some proposed methods to separate real and virtual objects using an optical property called polarization [6] [7] [8]. On the other hand, a number of research works using independent component analysis [9] [10] [11] and layer information exchange[12] have been proposed. Some of above mentioned methods need a polarization filter to be operated with camera and need to capture more than one image by rotating the polarization filter or focusing either layer separately for every scene.

According to our knowledge, all of the previously proposed methods are considered only for static camera and/or single depth. Moreover, for the purpose of the texture acquisition of real-world scene, a huge amount of outdoor scene images are originally required and the captured images usually contain 3D objects. As a result, these methods can not be applied for the texture acquisition of outdoor scene. In this paper, we propose a new method to separate the reflection component form image sequence which has been taken by a motion camera. This method is based on the epipolar plane image (EPI) analysis. Unlike previous EPI analysis, which usually analyze the edges, we propose a color-based EPI analysis, which can robustly separate two component layer images.

The remainder of this paper is organized as follows. A detailed explanation of EPI analysis is described in Section 2. In Section 3, we discuss on the separation method of reflection and transparency components. Experimental results can be seen in Section 4 and we provide conclusion in Section 5.

2 EPI Analysis

2.1 EPI Construction and Conventional EPI Analysis

EPI can be produced by accumulating epipolar line in each frame of image sequence along the time axis. The first step is to make spatio-temporal image volume and slice it horizontally to acquire EPI. The camera motion is assumed to constant speed and straight path. Certainly, the restriction is not strictly required in actual experiment, because we can use GPS, gyro sensor and other vehicle speed sensors. The camera is set to arbitrary direction, therefore the rectification of captured image sequence is required before accumulation to make spatio-temporal image volume. Ideally, the frontal surface of any object appears as an area bounded by two distinct parallel boundaries on the EPI (we call this area the EPI-strip, or strip). Since we restrict the camera movement along a straight line and the depth of all the objects are not the same in the real world, all the strips do not lie in a parallel direction. This depth difference gives a special character to the EPI, as shown in Fig.1(bottom). We can clearly see that the inclination angles of the EPI strips are directly proportional to the depth d of the object. Furthermore, strip 2 is totally covered by the other opaque strips at the overlap areas. Therefore, the boundary edges of strip 2 cannot be detected at the overlap areas and strip 2 is divided into separate areas. Since the areas are separated, we can still understand that these areas produce an EPI strip by analyzing the edges parallelism and color similarity.

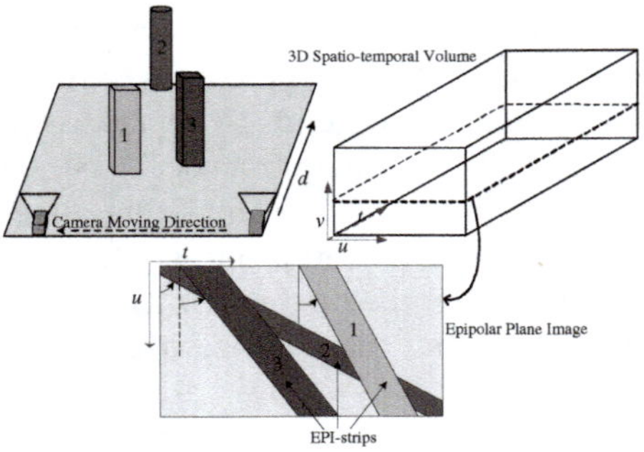

Fig. 1. Appearance and nature of actual objects in the EPI

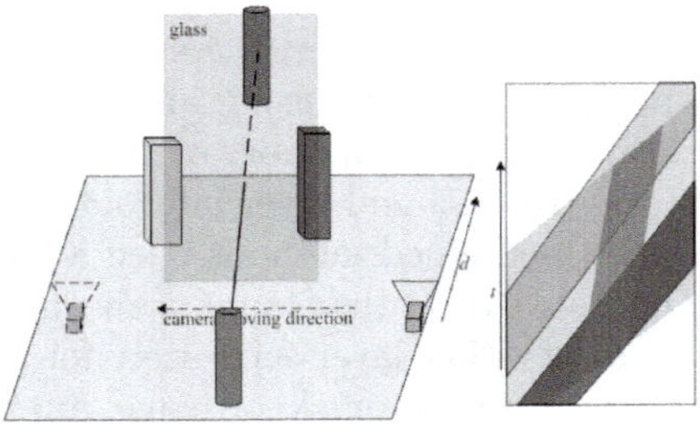

Fig. 2. Appearance and nature of transparent and reflected objects in an EPI

With such an edge-based analysis, we can retrieve the 3D information from the EPI and the scene. Such kind of EPI analysis assumes the object appearance does not depend on the view direction.

2.2 Color-Based EPI Analysis

In a real-world scene, the color sometimes drastically changes depending on the view direction because of the superimposed reflection and transparency, specularity and other effects. To conduct a further analysis with an EPI in a real-world scene, we have to understand how color is produced on an EPI and we must include view dependent effect. We have considered only for superimposed reflection and transparency effect in this work. A color change on an EPI can be basically explained by two reasons: one is the changes of material or color of the target objects and the other is reflection and transparency effect caused by the glass-like shiny objects in the target scene. It should be noted that we do not consider complicated bi-directional reflectance distribution function (BRDF) in this paper.

2.3 Reflection and Transparency on an EPI

As shown in Fig.2, a reflected object is observed as if it exists on the opposite side of glass; therefore, the object simply describes an EPI-strip on an EPI. However, since glass is transparent, the observed color is a mixture of transparent and reflected objects. Therefore, since the reflected object makes a single band, its color changes abruptly when it intersects the EPI-strips of the transparent objects and vice versa. Note that, under such conditions, we can still distinguish each EPI-strip robustly; such distinction is usually difficult to achieve by simple image processing techniques such as tracking applied on the original image sequence.

3 Separation of Reflection and Transparency

We now describe a technique to separate the two component layers of the EPI and estimate the underlying original colors of the overlap regions. The technique first detects the inclination lines of the EPI-strips. EPI is then rectified by inclination angle of EPI-strip, so that trails within strip are vertical. Original color estimation can be done by applying the proposed method along the vertical scan line as describe in Sec 3.2. Once separation is achieved, the corresponding region is labeled and excluded from further computations.

3.1 Defining Strips on an EPI

Since the camera is assumed to move linearly, each object in the scene is bounded by two parallel lines on the EPI. As a result, parallel line detection by using Hough transform is sufficient to detect the boundary lines of the EPI-strips. We used only high energy peaks of the Hough space to detect the distinct edges such as boundaries of the building. Fig3(a) represents the selection result of 16 maximum energy peaks of the Hough transformation result of Fig.3(b) and Fig.3(c) shows the detection result. Generally the reflected object (virtual object) is assumed farther than the target objects (wall of the building and other actual objects close to the wall). Therefore, the inclination angles of reflected EPI-strips usually greater than that of the EPI-strips of the actual objects. Then, we detect the boundaries of all EPI-strips and the separation method is applied to each EPI-strip within the detected boundary lines in the increasing order of inclination angles until the whole image area is applied. For Fig.3(b) we could recover all overlap areas by applying the proposed separation method to EPI-strips those inclination angles are lass than 50.

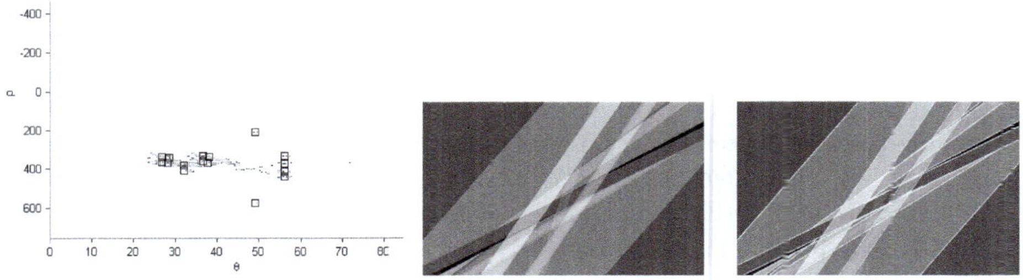

(a) (b) (c)

Fig. 3. (a) Hough transform result of (b), (b) Input EPI, (c) The detected boundary lines

3.2 Separation of the EPI

Considering the presence of both the reflection and transparency components at the same image point, if we suppose the color of the overlap area is the linear combination of two color components, the observed color of that image point can be described as

$$M_c(x, y) = f_t \sigma_c^{act}(x, y) + f_r \sigma_c^{virt}(x, y) \tag{1}$$

where c represents the type of sensor (r, g and b), (x, y) is the two-dimensional image coordinate, $\sigma_c^{act}(x, y)$ and $\sigma_c^{virt}(x, y)$ represent for the color of the actual and virtual objects, respectively. f_t and f_r are the factors of transparency and reflection, respectively. For simplicity, equation (1) can be rewritten as

$$M_c(x,y) = A_c(x,y) + V_c(x,y) \tag{2}$$

The system first rectified the EPI-strip by it's inclination angle, so that trails within the strip are vertical. The separation is performed to each vertical line of the rectified strip. Since each point in a vertical line of EPI-strip represents for the same image point of the object of each image frame, equation (3) should be true for every pixels within one scan line.

$$A_c(x,y_i) = A_c(x,y_j) \qquad \ldots \qquad (i \neq j) \tag{3}$$

from equation (2) and (3) we can obtain

$$M_c(x,y_i) - M_c(x,y_j) = V_c(x,y_i) - V_c(x,y_j) \tag{4}$$

From this equation, V_c values for all pixels can be calculated if we assume one V_c value as an initiator. Therefore we can obtain infinite sets of V_c values for that line due to initiators. Since all pixels in the scan line are collected from same image point of each image frame, the minimum color value along the entire line should be an original color of that line due to the linear color combination property of reflection and transparency. Therefore, $V_c(x,y_i)$ is assumed to 0 where $M_c(x,y_i)$ is the minimum of entire scan line. In our actual implementation we estimate the minimum color along entire scan line and substitute it for all pixels along entire line. However, it is not suitable to apply real-world EPI because of noise and artifact. Therefore, the histogram thresholding method is used for real-EPI separation. The basic task of this method takes the pixel value of the first peak nearest to zero intensity, which is larger than threshold, and substitute for all pixels which are brighter than that along the entire scan line. After applying the separation algorithm the EPI-strip is rectified back to the original one. Another component image can be obtained by subtracting the result image from the original EPI. Since there remains base color ambiguity with this method, this technique cannot produce the correct color value. However, the result can be effectively used for texture acquisition of the real-world scene and human interaction can produce a reasonable result.

3.3 Separation of the Original Image

By using the decomposition results of the EPIs as described above, we can separate the original image into two component images by two ways. The first is a straightforward method which creates EPIs for all horizontal lines and applies the separation algorithm to each EPI (we call the iterative method), and the second is based on color clustering.

The detailed procedure of second approach is as follows.

- create sparse EPIs from the captured image sequence and decompose the EPIs by the separation algorithm.
- get the (x,y) coordinate and the color information (r, g, b) from the EPI for the desired input frame as an initial point.

- perform color clustering of the original image by the region-growing method, which starts from an initial point and merges neighboring pixels by using their color information in 3D space.
- after clustering, the component image can be extracted by substituting the expected original color for the clustered pixels, which can be obtained from the resulting EPI.

4 Experiments

We performed several experiments to test the effectiveness of our method. In the following two experiments, we used a synthesized image sequences and a real images captured in our laboratory and outdoor scenes.

4.1 Synthesized Images

The image sequences used to test our method have been created by using CG software. As a target object, we constructed a model room which has a front wall covered by glass to create a reflected image of the objects placed in front

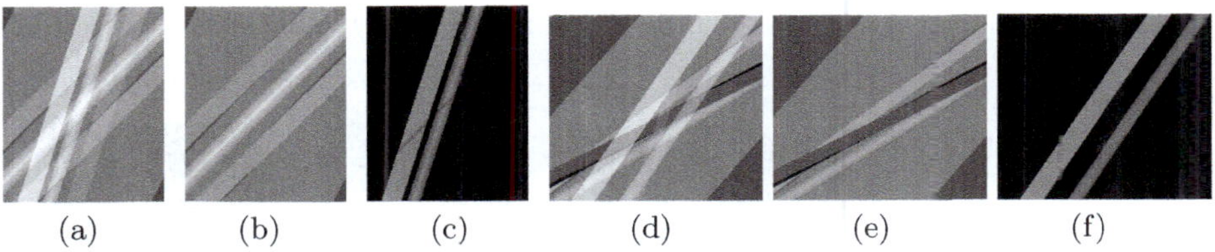

Fig. 4. Result of the EPI analysis. (a),(d) Input synthesized EPIs. (b),(c),(e),(f) Separation results.

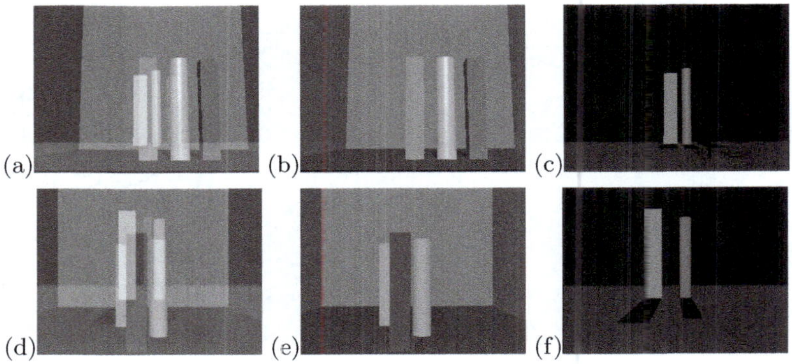

Fig. 5. The separation results of synthesized images. First row: the input synthesized image with specularity and its separation results. Second row: the input synthesized image including different depth objects and separation results.

of the glass wall, as well as transparent images of the objects placed inside the room. We assumed that the factors of reflection and transparency for all captured frames are constant, and the camera motion along a straight path that produces regularly sampled images for creating the EPI volume. The EPI was successfully separated into component images can be seen in Fig.4. However, in Fig.4(c), we can observe small artifacts on EPI strips which are caused by color saturation on the synthesized images. To avoid such artifacts, using a high dynamic range image is a practical solution.

The left column of Fig.5 shows an arbitrary frame of two input image sequences, and the recovered transparent and reflected component images are shown in the middle and right columns.

4.2 Real Images

We have conducted several tests on real images captured using Sony three-CCD(640×480) digital camera. The motorized stage has been used to control the linear movement of the camera in the indoor image capturing process as shown in Fig.6(a). Fig.6 (first and second rows) show the input EPIs and separation results of indoor image sequences. The original images and their separation results are presented in the Fig.7. In Fig.6(d) and Fig.7(c), we can observe some artifacts because of the non-linearity of camera sensor since we can successfully separate synthesized images. Therefore, the linearization of camera sensor is required be-

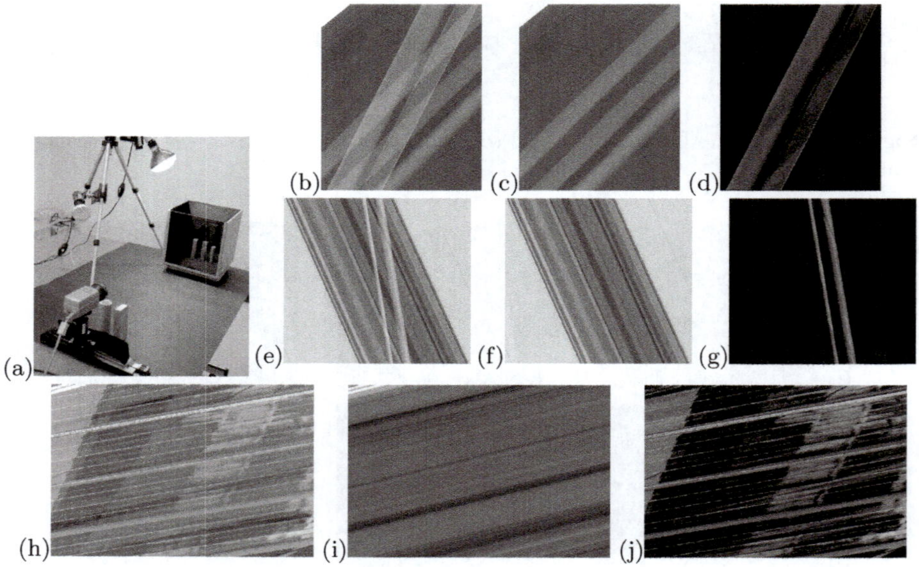

Fig. 6. The scene of the indoor image capturing process (a) and EPI Separation results of real images. (b),(e) input indoor EPIs. (c),(d),(f),(g) separation results of indoor EPIs. (h) input outdoor EPI. (i),(j) separation results.

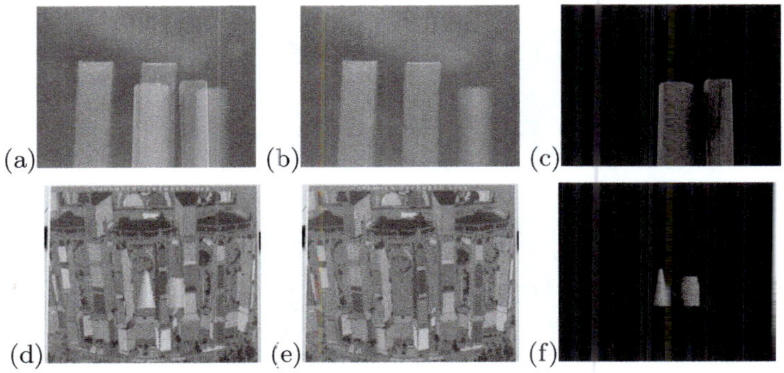

Fig. 7. Separation of indoor images.(a),(d) input images. (b),(c),(e),(f) separation results.

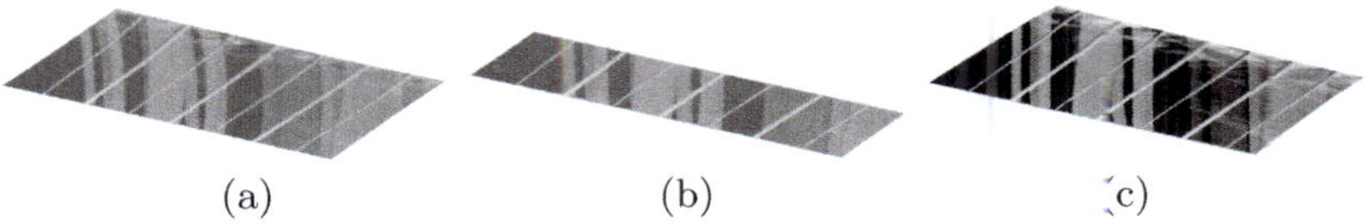

Fig. 8. Rectified EPIs of outdoor image sequence (a) using all EPI range (b) using reduced EPI range (c) fitted with tracking result

fore the proposed method is applied. For the separation of original indoor image as described in Fig.7(a), we used second approach (color clustering), because the image texture is simple. The another image sequence is decomposed by iterative method as shown in Fig.7 second row.

Car mounted video camera has been used to capture outdoor image sequences by controlling constant car speed and driving along straight path Since we restrict the constant car speed, a tiny un-constancy of car speed has occurred between each successive image frames. Therefore, the trials within the rectified EPI-strips are not strictly vertical as shown in Fig.8 (a) and the separation results of original image is almost noisy as describe in Fig 9(second row). To solve this problem, we first apply simple and straightforward method, which is to reduce the number of image frames in EPI until the rectified strip appears as vertical as shown in Fig.8 (b). Since this method could produce a reasonable result as described in Fig.9 third row, the method will fail when the number of image frames in reduced EPI are too few. The estimation of car speed and adjusting it to every successive image frame is required to produce more modest results. For this purpose, we implement the algorithm, which sampled features from non-transparent image area and tracking for all image frames to detect the motion speed in pixel. The detected pixel difference values have been used to fit the rectified EPI-strip to vertical as described in Fig.8 (c). The separation results of original outdoor image can be seen in Fig.9 bottom row. As a result, the proposed method can extract two component layers even the image texture is complicated as we can observe specular effect on the reflected buildings.

Fig. 9. Input outdoor image and separation results: first row shows the input outdoor image, second row shows the separation results using all EPI range, the results describe in third row are created by using reduce EPI range. Bottom row shows the results by using motion tracking data in EPI rectification process. The right column of the result images are enhanced to make them easier to see.

5 Conclusion

In this paper, we proposed a new EPI analysis based on a color analysis, since the conventional EPI analysis does not consider the view-dependent effects of reflection and transparency, which usually exist in real-world scenes. Our proposed method completely assumes these complicated effects and successfully analyzes them. By using our EPI analysis, a scene consisting of glass-like objects which produce both a transparent and reflective effect could be robustly separated into component images. Furthermore, most of our separation method could be performed automatically. Since, many computer vision algorithms usually fail to handle the complicated scene images, our technique can provide a practical solution by separating the image into component images. For city modeling purposes, since many buildings are typically covered with glass windows and it is difficult to retrieve textures of good quality, our technique can provide a practical solution.

References

1. Toro, J., Owens, J., Medina, R.: Using known motion fields for image separation in transparency. Pattern Recognition Letters **24** (2003) 594–605
2. Szeliski, R., Avidan, S., Anandan, P.: Layer extraction from multiple images containing reflections and transparency. In: CVPR. (2000) 1246–1253

3. Irani, M., Peleg, S.: Motion analysis for image enhancement: resolution, occlusion, and transparency. Journal of Visual Communication and Image Representation (**4(4)**) 324–335
4. Schechner, Y.Y., Kiryati, N., Basri, R.: Separation of transparent layers using focus. International Journal of Computer Vision **39** (2000) 25–39
5. Schechner, Y.Y., Kiryati, N., Shamir, J.: Blind recovery of transparent and semi-reflected scenes. In: Computer Vision and Pattern Recognition. Volume 1. (2000) 38–43
6. Schechner, Y.Y., Kiryati, N., Shamir, J.: Separation of transparent layers by polarization analysis. In: Scandinavian Conference on Image Analysis. Volume 1. (1999) 235–242
7. Schechner, Y.Y., Shamir, J., Kiryati, N.: Polarization-based decorrelation of transparent layers: The inclination angle of an invisible surface. In: ICCV. Volume 2. (1999) 814–819
8. Schechner, Y.Y., Shamir, J.: Vision through semireflecting media: polarization analysis. Optics Letters **24** (1999) 1088–1090
9. Hermanto, Barros, A.K., Yamamura, T., Ohnishi, N.: Separating virtual and real objects using independent component analysis. IEICE TRANS **E84-D** (2001)
10. Bronstein, A.M., Bronstein, M.M., Zibulevsky, M., Zeevi, Y.Y.: Blind separation on reflections using sparse ICA. In: 4th International Symposium of Independent Component Analysis and Blind Signal Separation. (2003) 227–232
11. Farid, H., Adelson, E.H.: Separating reflections from images using independent components analysis. Journal of the Optical Society of America **16** (1999) 2136–2145
12. Sarel, B., Irani, M.: Separating transparent layers through layer information exchange. In: ECCV. Volume 4. (2004) 328–341

Fast Approximated SIFT*

Michael Grabner, Helmut Grabner, and Horst Bischof

Institute for Computer Graphics and Vision,
Graz University of Technology, Austria
{mgrabner, hgrabner, bischof}@icg.tu-graz.ac.at

Abstract. We propose a considerably faster approximation of the well known SIFT method. The main idea is to use efficient data structures for both, the detector and the descriptor. The detection of interest regions is considerably speed-up by using an integral image for scale space computation. The descriptor which is based on orientation histograms, is accelerated by the use of an integral orientation histogram. We present an analysis of the computational costs comparing both parts of our approach to the conventional method. Extensive experiments show a speed-up by a factor of eight while the matching and repeatability performance is decreased only slightly.

1 Introduction

In the last few years we have witnessed an explosion of object recognition methods based on the detection of local key-points and construction of local photometric descriptors around these key-points (e.g. [1, 2, 3, 4]). The basic idea of these approaches is to first detect salient structures in images (e.g., corners, high entropy regions, scale space maxima, etc.) and to construct from the region or its surrounding a discriminative description which is used for matching. The requirement is that the structures can be re-detected with high reliability and that the descriptor is robust (e.g. to illumination changes) and possesses certain invariance properties (e.g. affinely invariant). The big advantage of these approaches is that they do not require a segmentation of the image and due to the local nature they are robust to occlusions.

Local approaches have demonstrated considerable success in a variety of applications, like recognition of objects [1], wide-base line stereo [4], robot navigation [5], image retrieval [6, 7], building of panoramas [8], etc. Probably the most popular and widely used local approach is the DoG detector with the SIFT descriptor as proposed by Lowe [1]. SIFT has been used with success in all of the above mentioned application areas. Evaluations and comparison

* The project results have been developed in the MISTRAL Project which is financed by the Austrian Research Promotion Agency (www.ffg.at). This work has been sponsored in part by the Austrian Federal Ministry of Transport, Innovation and Technology under P-Nr. I2-2-26p VITUS2 and by the Austrian Joint Research Project Cognitive Vision under projects S9103-N04 and S9104-N04, the EC funded NOE MUSCLE IST 507572.

P.J. Narayanan et al. (Eds.): ACCV 2006, LNCS 3851, pp. 918–927, 2006.

(e.g. [9]) demonstrate the excellent performance of the method compared to other approaches. The DoG detector detects blobs in the Laplacian scale space. The SIFT descriptor is basically a histogram (in fact 16 concatenated ones) of gradient orientations of the normalized (with respect to scale and orientation) DoG region. One key issue for its success is that DoG points and SIFT are normalized with each other and can be computed fast.

Due to the high popularity of SIFT, it is no surprise that several variants and extensions of SIFT have been proposed. For example Ke and Sukthankar proposed the so called PCA-SIFT [10] that applies Principal Components Analysis (PCA) to the normalized gradient patch. The Gradient location and orientation histogram (GLOH) [9] changes SIFTs location grid and uses PCA to reduce the size of SIFT. The primary focus of these extensions is to gain improved performance.

In this paper we propose a modified SIFT method for recognition purpose. Our primary motivation is to significantly speed up the SIFT computation while at the same time keep the excellent matching performance. We demonstrate that by using approximations (mainly employing integral images) both the DoG detector (see section 2) and the SIFT-descriptor (see section 3) we can speed-up the SIFT computation by at least a factor of eight compared to the binaries provided by Lowe. Extensive experimental evaluations (see section 4) show that the loss in matching performance is negligible.

2 DoG Detector

In order to detect scale invariant key-points Lowe suggests to repeatedly smooth the input image and identify key locations in scale space. In order to detect even very small scales Lowe extends this approach and proposes to double the input image before building the scale space. The different scale levels are produced by recursive filtering with a variable-scale Gaussian kernel. A local maxima search is finally applied to the Difference-of-Gaussian images which can be computed of adjacent scale images, in order to detect key-points in scale space.

To accelerate this approach we propose several approximations and changes, see Table 1. The key idea of our method is to considerably reduce the costs for computing the scale space by using Difference-of-Mean (DoM) images instead of Difference-of-Gaussians (DoG). This DoM images can be computed very efficiently by using a box filter in combination with an *integral image* as introduced

Table 1. Major differences between Lowe's detector [1] and our proposed approach

SIFT	Fast approximated SIFT
image doubling	-
-	calculate integral image
DoG scale space	DoM scale space
post-processing	-

by Viola and Jones [11] (capturing the main idea of [12]). Once the integral image is computed, it allows to compute the mean within a rectangular region in constant time independent of the size of the region. This property allows fast box filtering and can be used for linear sampling of the scale axis which is realized by successively increasing the size of the filter kernel. Adjacent scale space images are subtracted and a local maxima search is applied to the Difference-of-Mean images in order to detect key-points. For a reliable detection of key-points at all scales it is important to normalize the DoM response with

$$sensitivity \cdot \left(1 - \frac{s_1^2}{s_2^2}\right) \tag{1}$$

where s_1, s_2 corresponds to the size of the small and larger box filter, respectively. The parameter *sensitivity* captures the minimal contrast of the mean gray values of the inner region (s_1) and the outer region ($s_2 - s_1$) and can be used to adjust the sensitivity of the detector. Since experiments with DoG indicate that small scales cannot be reliably matched we skip the doubling of the image size, which again provides a significant speed-up. Once the key-points have been detected we do not make any further post-processing like an accurate key-point localization because due to the use of integral images we have already pixel accuracy at each scale. But note that the accuracy of the obtained points is not as precise as with the DoG, nevertheless the detected points are good for recognition tasks but less suitable for geometric tasks like estimation of the fundamental matrix.

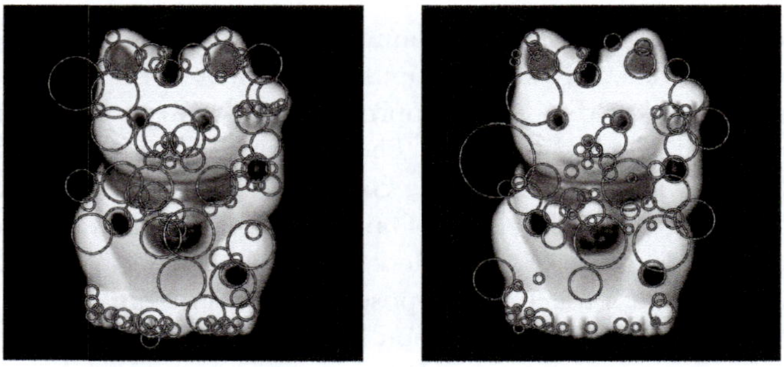

Fig. 1. Comparison of the DoM key-points (left) detected by our approach to DoG key-points (right) detected by the approach of Lowe

2.1 Computational Costs

The box filtering approach using integral images is depicted in Algorithm 1. Once the integral image is pre-computed which takes 2 additions for each image pixel, a single box filter response can be computed, independent of its size, with 4 memory accesses, 3 additions and a single multiplication which is needed for normalizing the box region. In Table 2 which has been adapted from [13], we compare the box filtering approach to other commonly used Gaussian filtering

Algorithm 1. Integral image computation

```
// pre-computation
for each image point do
    Propagate integral image {1 addition}
    Increase value {1 addition}
end for
// apply box filter with a given kernel size
for each image point do
    Compute intersection {3 addition}
    Normalize {1 multiplication}
end for
```

Table 2. Comparison of various filtering techniques (calculations per pixel)

Filter technique	Additions	Multiplications
2D-Gauss	N^2	$N^2 - 1$
Separated Gauss	$2 \cdot N - 2$	$N + 2$
Recursive Gauss	6	14
FFT	$2 \cdot log(W \cdot H)$	$2 \cdot log(W \cdot H) + 1$
Box filter	$2 + 3$	1

techniques. Simple 2-D convolution is the slowest one since the complexity for each pixel is $O(N^2)$, where N corresponds to the filter size. Much more efficient is to make use of the separability of the Gaussian function which allows convolution by applying two passes of the 1-D function in the horizontal and vertical directions. This leads to linear costs in the kernel size N. Other methods like FFT are independent with respect to the filter kernel size but depend on the size of the input image $W \times H$. However, as can be seen in Figure 2(a), the computational costs are higher than for the separable Gaussian for a kernel size of 7×7 (as proposed by Lowe in [14]). A similar result holds for recursive Gaussian filters which allow convolution in constant time but are still computationally more demanding for small filter kernels.

3 SIFT Descriptor

Reliable matching of key-points is performed by feature vectors generated from their local neighborhoods. Lowe suggests to use the gradient information around a key-point. Initially a consistent orientation is assigned to the key-point such that the descriptor can be represented relative to this orientation, thereby achieving rotation invariance. Gradients within a circular region are used to compute an orientation histogram, and local maxima in the histogram are used as characteristic orientations.

To obtain a descriptor Lowe proposes to divide the surrounding region into 4×4 sub-patches. From each sub-patch an orientation histogram with 8 bins is computed and concatenated to form a single feature vector. Since orientation histograms form the basic computation for the descriptor this leads to the idea to use integral histograms [15]. Integral histograms are an extension of integral images using for each histogram bin (e.g. orientation) a separate integral image. Once the integral orientation histogram is computed, histograms can be accessed in constant time independent of the size of the region. Similar to integral images integral histograms can only provide histograms of rectangular regions.

For orientation histogram computation we use un-weighted squared regions. Furthermore, for the descriptor we rotate the midpoints of each sub-patch relative to the orientation and compute the histograms of overlapping sub-patches without aligning the squared region but shifting the sub-patch histogram relative to the main orientation. The main advantage of our method is that we make use of the full resolution of the input image without additional computational costs.

3.1 Computational Costs

The major question is how many descriptors have to be calculated in order to obtain a speed up for the integral version compared to the conventional approach. We define the costs for single histogram computation for both approaches which has been done by adapting the analysis from [15]. We assume that the gradient image has already been computed. In addition we assume computing histograms only over squared regions.

Algorithm 2. Conventional histogram computation

```
//histogram computation
for each histogram do
  for each gradient within window do
    Find bin { 1 multiplication}
    Increase bin value { 1 addition}
  end for
end for
```

The conventional method for histogram computation is given in Algorithm 2. Once the gradient image is available, for each gradient in the observed region an assignment to the correct bin value must be done. Consequently the conventional method strongly depends on the number of gradients contributing to the histogram which leads to the complexity $O(N^2)$ for a squared region where N corresponds to the window size. In addition the computational costs for a squared region is

$$k \cdot N^2 \cdot (c_{add} + c_{mult}) \tag{2}$$

where k corresponds to the number of histograms, c_{add} represent costs for an addition and c_{mult} are the costs for a multiplication.

Considering the integral histogram computation illustrated in Algorithm 3, we see that equivalent to integral images some pre-computations have to be

---

Algorithm 3. Integral histogram computation

//pre-computation
for each gradient **do**
  for each bin **do**
    Propagate integral histogram { *1 addition*}
  end for
  Find bin { *1 multiplication*}
  Increase bin value { *1 addition*}
end for
//histogram computation
for each histogram **do**
  for each bin **do**
    Compute intersection { *3 additions*}
  end for
end for

---

done. Once the integral orientation histogram has been computed, orientation histograms can accessed in $k \cdot b \cdot 3 \cdot c_{add}$, where b corresponds to the number of bins (in our case 16 bins are used). Similar to integral images rectangular regions can be accessed. The costs for histogram computation does not depend on the number of gradients within a region.

Consequently the total costs including the computation of the integral orientation histogram can be written as

$$W \cdot H \cdot (b \cdot c_{add} + c_{add} + c_{mult}) + k \cdot b \cdot 3 \cdot c_{add} \tag{5}$$

where $W \times H$ represents the input image size.

Figure 2(b) compares standard histogram and integral histogram computation, where we have used relative costs for additions and multiplications from [15]

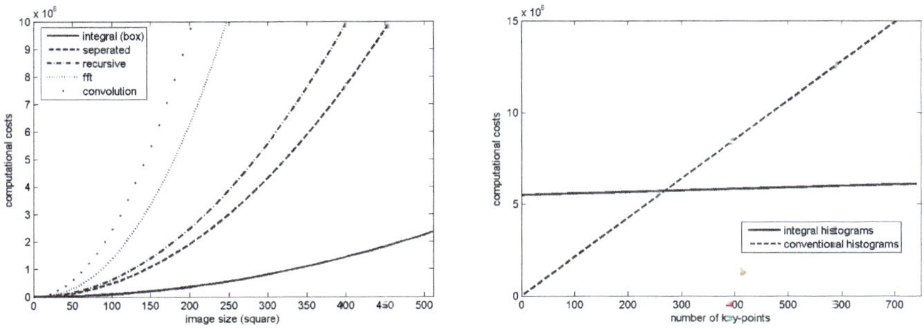

(a) Different filtering techniques for a 7 × 7 filter kernel

(b) Conventional and integral technique for orientation histogram computation

Fig. 2. Comparison of computational costs for detector (left) and the descriptor (right)

(addition:1 - multiplication:4). Other parameters of the cost functions, such as the histogram patch size, have been experimentally determined. As we can see in Figure 2(b), initially the costs for the integral histogram are much higher however once the integral image is computed the costs increase very slowly. In contrast the costs of the conventional method increase linearly with the number of computed descriptors.

Integral orientation histograms are profitable especially when calculated over large regions. This is especially suited for our approach because we always compute the descriptors on the original resolution. Consequently, we take advantage of using the whole information of the input image.

4 Experimental Results

We compare our novel approach to Lowe's method with respect to performance and speed. For matching performance we run two types of experiments to explore the effects of the approximations made in our approach. First, both methods are examined with respect to rotation, scale and perspective invariance on a data-set of 15 commonly used images. Second, an evaluation comparing both, detectors and descriptors, on 2 images of the popular Graffiti data-set has been done using the framework of Mikolajczyk [9]. Finally we compare the runtime of our approach to Lowe's publicly available binaries [1].

4.1 Artificial Transformations

For all artificial transformations we used the same criterions for determining repeatability of the detector and the matching score of the descriptor. The repeatability is obtained through a simple location criterion while for the matching score a key-point match and the corresponding nearest descriptor match is required.

Due to the box filter approximation the rotation is the worst case scenario for the detector. Even for the descriptor the worst case because no rotational sampling is done. Therefore we artificially rotate each image from 0°to 90°of our data-set with steps of 15°. In Figure 3 we see that both, the detector and the descriptor of the approximated SIFT implementation behave worst at a rotation of 45°. However, at the same time the performance is not much worse to SIFT. The strong performance decrease of SIFT can be explained by the fact that the small scale key-points are lost because of the smoothing effect after the bilinear transformation.

Second, scale invariance is tested. As a reference image we used a down scaled image (0.8) in order to have scale changes in both directions. Figure 4(a) shows that our approach which passes on detecting key-points with small scales performs slightly better than SIFT.

Finally, we examined the repeatability of the detector and the matching of the descriptor by generating different projective transformations of the image.

[1] Available at http://www.cs.ubc.ca/ lowe/keypoints/

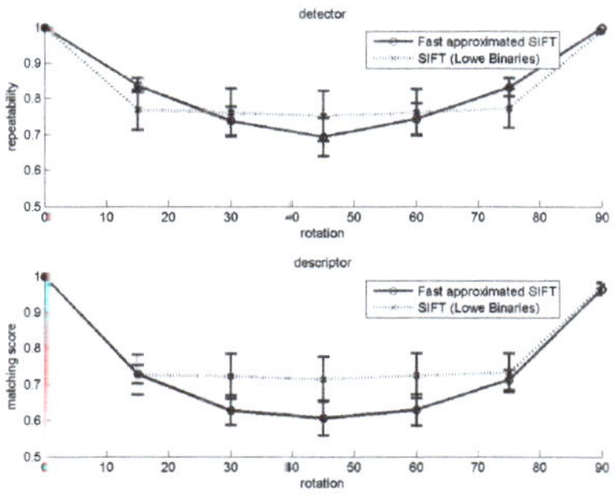

Fig. 3. Even in the worst case of a rotation of 45 °, approximated SIFT shows only a slight decrease in performance of the detector (above) and the descriptor (lower)

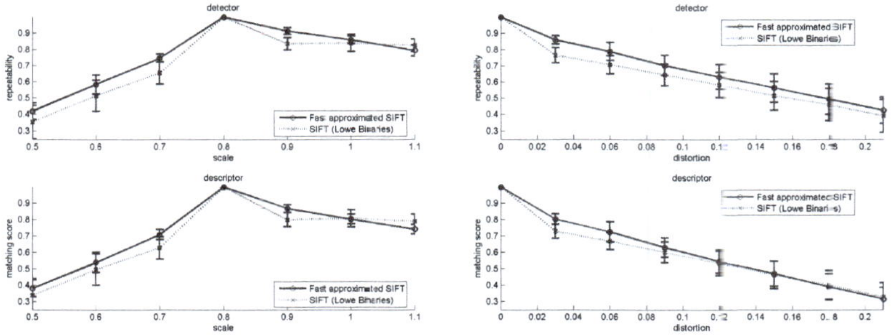

(a) Scale transformations (b) Projective transformations

Fig. 4. The proposed approximations of our method do not have any effects on scale or projective invariance

Again the results in Figure 4(b) show good performance for the approximated SIFT implementation.

4.2 Mikolajzyk Framework

We compared our method to Lowe's approach using the recently proposed framework from Mikolajzyk [9]. Two images of the Graffiti data-set have been used. The repeatability of both detectors are shown in Figure 5. When the overlap error tolerance is large enough the approximated SIFT implementation performs even better than the original version. However, allowing only a small overlap error, the approximation effects can be seen which lead to a slightly decreased performance. In Figure 5(b) we see a similar result for the descriptor.

4.3 Speed

We have a non optimized C++ implementation of the approximated SIFT which has been compared to the SIFT binaries provided by Lowe. In Table 3 the

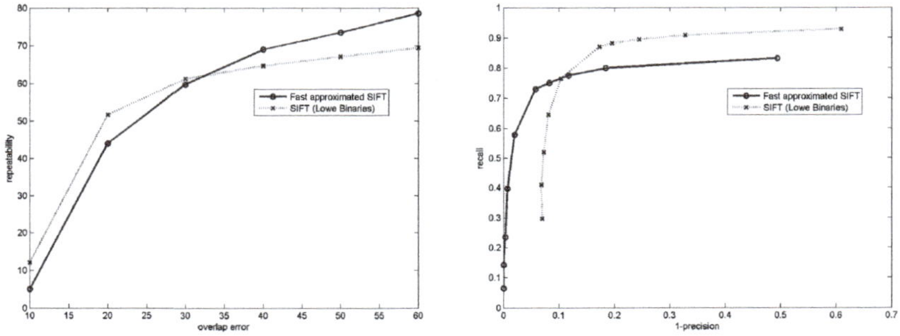

(a) Repeatability of the detector

(b) Descriptor evaluation using the ratio-nearest-neighbor matching criterion

Fig. 5. Evaluation results with the framework from Mikolajzyk

Table 3. Comparison of speed with respect to the image size

image size	SIFT (Binaries)	Approx. SIFT
800x640	4.24 s	0.625 s
400x320	1.34 s	0.180 s
200x160	0.44 s	0.075 s

processing times for feature detection of different image sizes are listed. This experiment was done on a Pentium 4 with 3.2 GHz. Results show that approximated SIFT provides a speed-up of a factor 8 with this non optimized implementation where the major benefit is obtained in the detection process. Optimizing the implementation we expect to achieve at least a factor 12 to 16.

5 Conclusion

In this paper we have presented a novel approximation of the SIFT method that achieves a considerable speed-up of the original method (at least a factor of eight using our non optimized C++ implementation) while at the same time achieving comparable matching performance. We have carefully analyzed the speed-up gain theoretically and have performed extensive experimental evaluations.

This new fast SIFT variant opens several venues of further research which we are currently investigating. Once we have calculated the integral images the costs for the descriptor calculation is negligible. Therefore, we can perform a local neighbor search around a key-point for more discriminative/reliable descriptors. This should further increase the matching performance. Having such a fast method, tracking using SIFT becomes feasible. This should result in highly robust trackers. Another idea that is currently investigated is to use SIFT in an Adaboost framework. This has already been proposed by Zhang et al. [16], but having a fast SIFT will considerably speed-up the training process.

References

1. Lowe, D.G.: Distinctive image features from scale-invariant keypoints. IJCV **60** (2004) 91–110
2. Mikolajczyk, K., Schmid, C.: Indexing based on scale invariant interest points. In: Proc. ICCV, Vancouver, Canada (2001) 525–531
3. Mikolajczyk, K., Schmid, C.: Scale & affine invariant interest point detectors. In: Proc. CVPR. Number 1 (2004) 63–86
4. Matas, J., Chum, O., Urban, M., Pajdla, T.: Robust wide baseline stereo from maximally stable extremal regions. In: Proc. BMVC. (2002)
5. Se, S., Lowe, D., Little, J.: Local and global localization for mobile robots using visual landmarks. In: Proc. IROS. Volume 2. (2001) 414–420
6. Ke, Y., Sukthankar, R., Huston L.: An efficient parts-based near-duplicate and sub-image retrieval system. In: Proc. Int. Conf. on Multimedia. (2004) 869–876
7. Tuytelaars, T., Gool, L.V.: Content-based image retrieval based on local affinely invariant regions. In: Proc. Int. Conf. on Visual Information and Information Systems. (1999) 493–500
8. Brown, M., Lowe, D.: Recognising panoramas. In: Proc. ICCV. (2003) 1218–1225
9. Mikolajczyk, K., Schmid, C.: A performance evaluation of local descriptors. IEEE Trans. PAMI **27** (2005) 1615–1630
10. Ke, Y., Sukthankar, R.: PCA-SIFT: A more distinctive representation for local image descriptors. In: Proc. CVPR. Volume 2. (2004) 506–513
11. Viola, P., Jones, M.: Rapid object detection using a boosted cascade of simple features. In: Proc. CVPR. Volume I. (2001) 511–518
12. Simard, P., Bottou, L., Haffner, P., LeCun, Y.: Boxlets: A fast convolution algorithm for signal processing and neural networks. In: Proc. NIPS. (1998) 571–577
13. Geusebroek, J., Smeulders, A., van de Weijer, J.: Fast anisotropic Gauss filtering. In: Proc. ECCV. (2002) 99–112
14. Lowe, D.: Object recognition from local scale-invariant features. In: Proc. ICCV. Volume 2. (1999) 1150–1157
15. Porikli, F.: Integral histogram: A fast way to extract histograms in cartesian spaces. In: Proc. CVPR. Volume 1. (2005) 829–836
16. Zhang, W., Yu, B., Zelinsky, G., Samaras, D.: Object class recognition using multiple layer boosting with heterogeneous features. In: Proc. CVPR. Volume 2. (2005) 323–330

Image Matching by Multiscale Oriented Corner Correlation

Feng Zhao[1,2], Qingming Huang[2], and Wen Gao[1,2]

[1] Institute of Computing Technology, Chinese Academy of Sciences,
Beijing 100080, China
[2] Graduate School of the Chinese Academy of Sciences,
Beijing 100039, China
{fzhao, qmhuang, wgao}@jdl.ac.cn

Abstract. In this paper we present a simple but effective method for matching two uncalibrated images. Feature points are firstly extracted in each image using a fast multiscale corner detector. Each feature point is assigned with one dominant orientation. The correspondence of feature points is then established by utilizing a multilevel matching strategy. We employ the normalized cross-correlation defined as the similarity measure between two feature points in the matching procedure. The orientation of the correlation window is determined by the dominant orientation of the feature point to achieve rotation invariance. Experimental results on real images demonstrate that our method is effective for matching two images with large rotation and significant scale changes.

1 Introduction

Matching two images of the same scene is one of the fundamental problems in computer vision. Image matching plays an important role in many applications such as stereo vision, motion analysis, image registration and mosaicing. It has been an extensively studied topic in the last several decades and a large number of matching algorithms have been proposed [1] [2] [3].

The methods for image matching can be broadly divided into two classes: area-based matching and feature-based matching. Area-based matching directly compares the gray value distribution in image patches and the similarity is measured by cross-correlation or least-squares techniques. Feature-based matching extracts salient features such as corners in the two images and then establishes reliable feature correspondences. There also have been some matching methods that can be regarded as the combination of the two classes [4] [5].

Normalized cross-correlation is widely used as an effective similarity measure for matching tasks. Normalized cross-correlation is invariant to linear brightness and contrast variations and its easy hardware implementation makes it useful for real-time applications.However, traditional correlation-based image matching methods will fail when there are large rotation or significant scale changes between the two images. This is because the normalized cross-correlation is sensitive to rotation and scale changes. There are also generalized versions of cross

P.J. Narayanan et al. (Eds.): ACCV 2006, LNCS 3851, pp. 928–937, 2006.

correlation that calculate the cross correlation for each assumed geometric transformation of the correlation windows [6] [7]. Although they are able to handle more complicated cases, the computational load grows very fast in the mean time.

In this paper, we propose a new method for matching two uncalibrated images based on normalized cross-correlation. Our work addresses the problem of matching image pairs with large rotation and significant scale changes, which cannot be efficiently solved by traditional correlation-based methods. We first build a multiscale pyramid for each image and extract corner points as feature points in each level of the pyramid. Compared with other multiscale feature point detectors, our implementation is simple and fast. Only one Gaussian smoothing operation is required for building a multiscale pyramid and there is no scale-space extrema detection included. Each feature point is assigned with one dominant orientation. Then a multilevel matching strategy is used to establish the correspondence of feature points. The multilevel matching strategy makes our method more efficient by removing the redundant computation in the matching procedure.

For similarity measure between two feature points, we adopt the rotation invariant normalized cross-correlation. The orientation of the correlation window is determined by the dominant orientation of the feature point to achieve rotation invariance. Moreover, both the shape and the size of the correlation window is fixed, which contributes to the simplicity of our method. The epipolar geometry constraint is imposed to reject the false matches. We also provide a simple method to further improve the quality of matching results. Experimental results on real images of various content demonstrate that our method is effective for matching two images with large rotation and significant scale changes.

The rest of this paper is organized as follows. Section 2 describes the multiscale feature point detection and the assignment of dominant orientation. Section 3 presents in detail the multilevel matching strategy and the calculation of similarity measure between feature points based on rotation invariant normalized cross-correlation. Section 4 describes rejecting the false matches by imposing epipolar geometry constraint and also provides a further method to improve the quality of matching results. Section 5 shows some experimental results on real image pairs and conclusions are presented in Section 6.

2 Multiscale Feature Point Detection

Corners are highly informative image locations and they are considered as good candidates for feature points in many computer vision applications. Many algorithms for detecting corners have been reported up to now. Among the most popular corner detectors, the Harris corner detector [8] is known to be robust against camera noise, image rotation and illumination changes [9]. Using Harris corners as feature points has been proved to be effective for image matching applications [5] [10] [11].

However, the Harris corner detector is sensitive to changes in image scale. Its repeatability rate significantly decreases when the scale change between two images is large [12]. In the recent literature some scale adapted feature point detectors have been proposed to deal with the problem of scale change [13] [14] [15].

2.1 Fast Multiscale Corner Detection

A fast multiscale corner detector is used to extract feature points in our method. We first build a multiscale pyramid representation for the image. The pyramid consists of four levels. The first level of the pyramid is the image itself. Other levels of the pyramid are created by sampling the image with a set of scale factors $k_n(n = 1, 2, 3)$. The original image is smoothed by a Gaussian function with $\sigma_{init} = 1$ before downsampling. The scale factor k_n should be chosen carefully since it greatly affects the matching result. The standard Harris detector cannot provide a satisfying repeatability rate when the scale change between two images is beyond 1.5 [12]. Considering this and after experimentation with different sets of scale factors, we choose the set of scale factors $\{2/3, 1/3, 0.23\}$ in our method as it gives the most stable results. Compared with the traditional Gaussian pyramid representation, only one Gaussian smoothing operation is required for building the multiscale pyramid and the scale factor between consecutive levels is not a constant.

Feature points are then extracted using a standard Harris corner detector in each level of the multiscale pyramid. The Harris corner detector is based on the auto-correlation matrix, which is built as follows:

$$M = g(\sigma_h) * \begin{bmatrix} I_x^2 & I_x I_y \\ I_x I_y & I_y^2 \end{bmatrix} , \tag{1}$$

where I_x and I_y indicate the x and y directional derivatives respectively. The auto-correlation matrix performs a smoothing operation on the products of the first derivatives by convolving with a Gaussian window function. The Harris corner strength measure is then calculated from the determinant and the trace of this matrix as follows:

$$C_H = \det(M) - \alpha \text{trace}^2(M) , \tag{2}$$

where α is a constant. A threshold t_h is used to select corner points. A point is identified as a corner if $C_H > t_h$ and C_H is the local maximum in its 8-neighborhood. In our implementation, I_x and I_y are computed by convolution with the mask $[-1\ 0\ 1]$. The parameter σ_h and α are set to 1.0 and 0.04 respectively. In order to select corners with high significance, threshold t_h is set to 15000.

We also employ a strategy that will help to restrict the total number of the feature points. If the number of corners detected in one scale level is larger than N_l, we reorder all the corners decreasingly according to C_H and choose the first N_l corners. We use $N_l = 2000$ in our implementation. Experimental results show that using this strategy can effectively speed up the matching procedure while almost not affecting the quality of matching result. For typical images with medium resolution such as 850×680 pixels, the average number of feature points extracted using our multiscale corner detector is about 4000, with the above parameter setting.

2.2 Dominant Orientation Assignment

Each feature point is assigned one dominant direction to achieve invariance to rotation. We adopt the histogram-based approach for dominant orientation assignment [15]. Some modifications are made for better results. An orientation histogram with 36 bins covering the range of 360 degrees is used to accumulate the local gradient orientations within a square region centered on a feature point. The size of the region equals to the size of the correlation window used in the matching procedure, which is set to be 11×11 pixels in our implementation. The pixel differences for computing the gradient magnitude and orientation are calculated on the pyramid level at which the feature point is detected. The pixel value is obtained by smoothing with a Gaussian window function with $\sigma_p = 1$. The gradient orientation of each sample in the region is weighted by its gradient magnitude and by a Gaussian window function with $\sigma_r = 1.7$.

After building the orientation histogram, we perform a smoothing operation on the histogram by iterative local averaging of every 3 consecutive bins in a cyclical fashion. The orientation corresponding to the largest bin in the smoothed histogram is selected to be the dominant orientation of the feature point.

3 Multilevel Matching Based on Correlation

3.1 Multilevel Matching Strategy

A multilevel matching strategy is used to establish the correspondence of feature points. Feature points are divided into 4 groups according to the pyramid level at which they are detected. The traditional matching strategy performs full group-to-group matching, which requires 16 group-to-group matching operations. We can speed up the matching procedure by removing the redundant computation. Only 7 group-to-group matching operations are required in our matching strategy, as shown in Fig. 1.

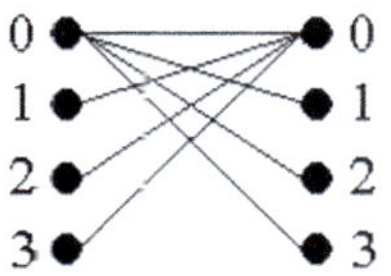

Fig. 1. Matching between feature point groups

The black dots labeled with number represent the feature point groups of different pyramid level in the two images. Each line segment connecting two feature point groups denotes one group-to-group matching operation. The multi-level matching strategy reduces the computation cost in the matching procedure and makes our method more efficient.

3.2 Similarity Measure Based on Rotation Invariant Correlation

Traditional similarity measure based on correlation is not invariant to image rotation. In our method, rotation invariant normalized cross-correlation is used to estimate the difference between feature points. The orientation of the correlation window is determined by the dominant orientation of the feature point. Therefore the similarity measure between feature points is invariant to rotation. The calculation of similarity measure is presented in detail as follows:

Let $p = L_m(x, y)$ be a feature point at the m-th pyramid level in the first image with dominant orientation θ_1 and $q = L'_n(x', y')$ be a feature point at the n-th pyramid level in the second image with dominant orientation θ_2. W_1 and W_2 are two correlation windows of size $(2w+1) \times (2w+1)$ centered on each feature point. W'_1 is the correlation window generated by rotating W_1 clockwise by θ_1 around p and W'_2 is the correlation window generated by rotating W_2 clockwise by θ_2 around q. Then W'_1 and W'_2 can be represented as two $(2w+1) \times (2w+1)$ arrays of pixel intensities A and B:

$$\begin{aligned} A_{uv} &= L_m(x + u\cos\theta_1 - v\sin\theta_1, y + v\cos\theta_1 + u\sin\theta_1) , \\ B_{uv} &= L'_n(x' + u\cos\theta_2 - v\sin\theta_2, y' + v\cos\theta_2 + u\sin\theta_2) , \end{aligned} \tag{3}$$

where $u, v \in [-w,\ w]$. A_{uv} and B_{uv} are calculated using bilinear interpolation. The similarity measure between p and q is defined as:

$$C_{pq} = \frac{\sum_{u=-w}^{w} \sum_{v=-w}^{w} [A_{uv} - \overline{A}] \cdot [B_{uv} - \overline{B}]}{(2w+1)(2w+1)\sigma(A)\sigma(B)} , \tag{4}$$

where $\overline{A}$ ($\overline{B}$) is the average and $\sigma(A)$ ($\sigma(B)$) is the standard deviation of all the elements in A (B). As mentioned in Section 2, w is set to be 5 in our experiments. Since the similarity measure is computed with respect to a canonical orientation, the matching procedure is invariant to image rotation. The similarity measure decreases monotonically from 1 to -1 with the increase of difference between two feature points.

Suppose there are m feature points in the first group and n feature points in the second group. Consider a matrix $G \in M_{m,n}$ whose element G_{ij} stands for the similarity measure between the i-th feature point in the first group and the j-th feature point in the second group. If G_{ij} is the greatest element both in its row and in its column, the i-th feature point in the first group and the j-th feature point in the second group will be identified as a candidate match. A threshold t_c is used to reject the unstable candidate matches with a low correlation score, which is set to be 0.7 in our experiments. The initial set of feature point matches between two groups can be established by selecting all such elements in G.

4 Rejection of False Matches

For each group-to-group matching operation, we obtain an initial set of feature point matches. The initial set of feature point matches usually contains some false matches due to the inaccurate characterization of feature point or the improper matches established in the matching procedure. In the case of matching two uncalibrated images, the epipolar constraint can be used to reject the false matches [16]. In our experiments, the epipolar constraint is imposed based on the widely used robust estimator RANSAC [17]. The feature point matches that are not consistent with the estimated epipolar geometry are identified as false matches and rejected.

Suppose F is the fundamental matrix. Point $p(x, y)$ can be represented as: $\widetilde{p} = [x\ y\ 1]^T$. For a feature point match (p, q), the epipolar line of point p is defined as: $l_p = F\widetilde{p}$. If the match is perfect, point q should lie on the epipolar line l_p exactly. The distance d_q of point q to the epipolar line l_p is calculated by

$$d_q = \frac{|\ \widetilde{q}^T F\widetilde{p}\ |}{\sqrt{(F\widetilde{p})_1^2 + (F\widetilde{p})_2^2}}\ , \tag{5}$$

where $(F\widetilde{p})_i$ is the i-th component of vector $F\widetilde{p}$. The distance d_p of point p to the epipolar line l_q is calculated similarly. Then a threshold t_e can be used to find the bad matches. A feature point match will be identified as a false match if $\max(d_p, d_q) > t_e$. False matches are removed from the initial set of feature point matches.

After rejecting the false matches by using epipolar constraint, we obtain the refined matching result for each group-to-group matching. The matching result that has the largest number of feature point matches will be selected as the matching result between the two images.

We find that there still exist a few false matches in the selected matching result. The feature points of these false matches happen to locate around the epipolar lines. Therefore, they cannot be identified only using epipolar constraint. A simple constraint is employed to further improve the quality of the selected matching result. For all good matches, the difference between the dominant orientations of the two feature points should be almost equal. Considering the fact that the number of the false matches is usually very small, we use the following process to identify these false matches.

The average of the differences between the dominant orientations in all feature point matches is calculated. Suppose the average is $\overline{\theta}$ and the difference between the dominant orientations of the i-th feature point match is θ_i. t_θ is a threshold. If $|\theta_i - \overline{\theta}| > t_\theta$, the i-th feature point match will be identified as a false match. The threshold t_e and t_θ are set to be 0.8 and 40 (in degrees) respectively.

5 Experimental Results

In this section, we will demonstrate some experimental results on real images of various content. The images used in our experiments are from the public

Table 1. Final matching results for Fig. 2-Fig. 5

	Correct Matches	Average Distance
Residence	76	0.577
Boat	53	0.458
East_south	45	0.552
Bark	44	0.571

Fig. 2. Matching result for image pair **Residence** (frame 0 and 9 of "**Resid**" sequence). The scale factor is 4.7 and the rotation angle is 5 degrees.

Fig. 3. Matching result for image pair **Boat** (frame 0 and 9 of "**Boat**" sequence). The scale factor is 4.3 and the rotation angle is 45 degrees.

image database in INRIA [1]. Fig. 2-Fig. 5 show the final matching results for four different image pairs with significant camera motions (translation, rotation

[1] http://lear.inrialpes.fr/people/Mikolajczyk/Database/index.html

Fig. 4. Matching result for image pair **East_south** (frame 0 and 9 of "**East_south**" sequence). The scale factor is 5.2 and the rotation angle is 59 degrees.

and scaling). The numbers of correct matches and the average distances from epipolar lines are illustrated in Table 1.

Fig. 2 shows the matching result for image pair **Residence** with significant scale changes and translation. There also exist self-similarity structures in the two images. Fig. 3 and Fig. 4 show the matching results for image pair **Boat** and **East_south** with large rotation and scale changes. We also test our method on the images of the textured scene. Fig. 5 shows the matching result for the image pair **Bark** of a textured scene with large rotation and scale changes.

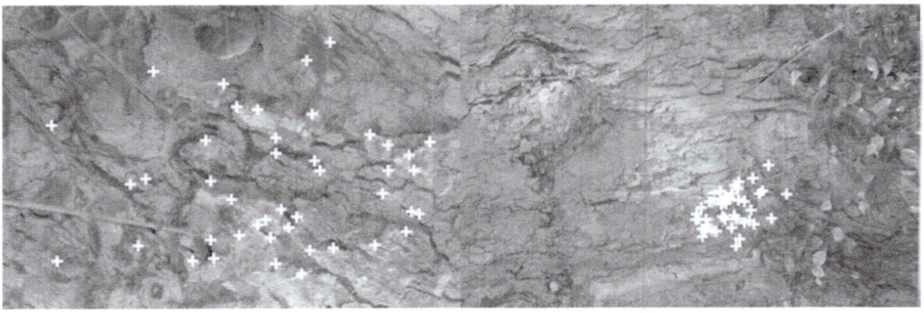

Fig. 5. Matching result for image pair **Bark** (frame 1 and 6 of "**Bark**" sequence). The scale factor is 4.0 and the rotation angle is 154 degrees.

6 Conclusions

This paper presents a simple but effective method for matching two uncalibrated images. The method is based on matching multiscale feature points using rotation invariant normalized cross-correlation. Feature points with dominant orientation are firstly extracted in each image using a fast multiscale corner detector.

Then a multilevel matching strategy is used to establish the correspondence of feature points. We employ the rotation invariant normalized cross-correlation defined as the similarity measure between two feature points in the matching procedure. The final matching result is obtained after the false matches rejection process. Experimental results on real images of various content demonstrate that our method is effective for matching two uncalibrated images with large rotation and significant scale changes.

Acknowledgements

This work is supported by National Hi-Tech Development Programs of China under grant No. 2003AA142140.

References

1. Brown, L.G.: A survey of image registration techniques. ACM Comput. Surv. **24** (1992) 325–376
2. Heipke, C.: Overview of image matching techniques. OEEPE Official Publications **33** (1996) 173–189
3. Zitová, B., Flusser, J.: Image registration methods: a survey. Image Vision Comput. **21** (2003) 977–1000
4. Förstner, W.: A feature-based correspondence algorithm for image matching. Intern. Arch. of Photogrammetry and Remote Sensing **26** (1986) 150–166
5. Zhang, Z., Deriche, R., Faugeras, O.D., Luong, Q.T.: A robust technique for matching two uncalibrated images through the recovery of the unknown epipolar geometry. Artif. Intell. **78** (1995) 87–119
6. Hanaizumi, H., Fujimura, S.: An automated method for registration of satellite remote sensing images. In: Proceedings of the International Geoscience and Remote Sensing Symposium IGARSS'93. (1993) 1348–1350
7. Berthilsson, R.: Affine correlation. In: Proceedings of the 14th International Conference on Pattern Recognition. (1998) 1458–1461
8. Harris, C., Stephens, M.: A combined corner and edge detector. In: Proceedings of the 4th Alvey Vision Conference. (1988) 147–151
9. Schmid, C., Mohr, R., Bauckhage, C.: Comparing and evaluating interest points. In: Proceedings of the 6th International Conference on Computer Vision. (1998) 230–235
10. Harris, C.: Geometry from visual motion. In Blake, A., Yuille, A., eds.: Active Vision. MIT Press (1992) 263–284
11. Schmid, C., Mohr, R.: Local grayvalue invariants for image retrieval. IEEE Trans. Pattern Anal. Mach. Intell. **19** (1997) 530–534
12. Schmid, C., Mohr, R., Bauckhage, C.: Evaluation of interest point detectors. International Journal of Computer Vision **37** (2000) 151–172
13. Dufournaud, Y., Schmid, C., Horaud, R.: Matching images with different resolutions. In: Proceedings of the IEEE Conference on Computer Vision and Pattern Recognition. (2000) 612–618
14. Mikolajczyk, K., Schmid, C.: Indexing based on scale invariant interest points. In: Proceedings of the 8th International Conference on Computer Vision. (2001) 525–531

15. Lowe, D.G.: Distinctive image features from scale-invariant keypoints. International Journal of Computer Vision **60** (2004) 91–110
16. Hartley, R., Zisserman, A.: Multiple View Geometry in Computer Vision. Cambridge University Press (2000)
17. Fischler, M.A., Bolles, R.C.: Random sample consensus: A paradigm for model fitting with applications to image analysis and automated cartography. Commun. ACM **24** (1981) 381–395

Surface Registration Using Extended Polar Maps

Elsayed E. Hemayed

Computer Engineering Department, Cairo University, Giza, Egypt
hemayed@ieee.org

Abstract. In this paper, we are presenting a new surface signature-based representation that is orientation-independent and can be used to match and align surfaces under rigid transformation including uniform scaling. The proposed scheme represents the surface signatures as extended polar maps. Correlation of the maps is used to establish point correspondences between two views; from these correspondences a rigid transformation, including uniform scaling, that aligns the views is calculated. The effectiveness of the proposed scheme is demonstrated through several registration experiments.

1 Introduction

Many applications require the construction of precise 3D object models of physical objects, preserving as much information as possible [1, 2]. It is usually necessary to scan the scene from different viewpoints in order to build a complete 3-D model of a complex scene. The registration of the acquired data sets into a common coordinate system has been a subject of much research during the last 15 years.

Several of the proposed methods [3, 4, 5, 6, 7, 8, 9] can be seen as extensions or improvements of the Iterative Closest Point (ICP) algorithm [10]. ICP is an iterative procedure minimizing the mean squared error (or the sum of the squared distances) between points in one view and the respective closest points in the other view. At each ICP iteration, the geometric transformation that best aligns the two images with respect to this criterion is calculated.

Another approach [11, 12, 13] to registering two images is to find the geometric transformation through a pose-space search, rather than the correspondence-based search of ICP. The search space of geometric transformations contains solutions that can be used to align two views. In this case, the objective is to find, in a huge search space, a solution acceptably close to the global optimum, in a reasonable time.

Recently, researchers have developed and discussed different surface representations that are effective in finding point corresponding between the two sets to be registered. In this case, the registration problem is addressed in two steps, where the first step is to establish the point corresponding between the surface sets then to use these points to compute the transformation that aligns the two surfaces. These surface representations are known as surface signature-based representation. They include the splash representation [14], the point signatures

P.J. Narayanan et al. (Eds.): ACCV 2006, LNCS 3851, pp. 938–947, 2006.

[15], the spin image representation [16], the spherical spin image representation [17], the surface point signatures [18], the harmonic shape images [19], the local surface descriptors [20] and the point fingerprints [21]. In this paper, we are proposing an extension for these representations to solve the registration problem.

Our approach to surface registration is based on establishing point correspondences using a new surface signature-based representation for matching points on the surfaces of objects. Next, sets of geometrically consistent point correspondences are used to compute the transformation that aligns the views [22]. While many registration algorithms do not address scaled surfaces, our approach solves for the general registration problem including rigid rotation, translation and uniform scaling. Furthermore, we speeded up the registration time by applying a selection process to select feature points on the surface to be used in the matching process.

The proposed representation technique, Surface Extended Polar Map -will be known as SEPMap-, transforms the surface from the Cartesian coordinate system where surface descriptions vary with transformation and scaling to an extended polar coordinate system where surface descriptions are invariant to rigid transformation and the scale factor can be estimated. In this artificial domain, every surface patch, its center of gravity, is represented by one SEPMap. As a surface signature-based representation, SEPMap places few restrictions on object shape and topology and can be used to match surfaces in the presence of clutter and occlusion.

This paper is organized as follows: The SEPMap scheme is described in Section 2. The alignment process using SEPMap scheme is described in Section 3. Experimental results are presented and discussed in Section 4. Finally, conclusion and future work are presented in Section 5.

2 SEPMap Scheme

In this paper, surfaces are defined by a dense collection of 3D points and surface normals [23]. In SEPMap, we are extending the surface signature representation to handle uniform scaling. Our approach is to use three parameters (θ, ϕ, r) to represent the positions and the curvature of each point with respect to the basis of other points on the surface. In this representation, (θ, ϕ) capture the relative curvature and they are independent of the object scaling while 'r' captures the relative displacement between the surface points and can be used to compute the scaling factor between the object and the model.

SEPMaps generated for two corresponding points on different surfaces would be similar, so oriented points can be matched based on a comparison of their SEPMaps. SEPMaps are descriptive enough that correspondences between points can be established based on a comparison of SEPMaps alone. Since SEPMaps can be generated for any point on the surface of an object, the proposed algorithm will generate a representation that is robust to clutter and occlusion, so segmentation of scene data is not necessary for surface matching in cluttered scenes.

In order to speed up the registration process, a selection process is applied to select only those points that can serve as landmarks of the surface. The SEPMaps are generated only for the selected points and hence the registration process is applied to these points only; saving long processing time. The process of generating the SEPMaps are presented in this section along with the object model representation and the feature selection process.

2.1 Object Model Representation

The object model is defined by a set of triangles. Each triangle composed of three-vertices defined by their Cartesian coordinates in the object coordinate systems. In the SEPMap generation process, each surface patch (triangle) in the model is represented by a map that is independent of the object coordinate system. The map is generated at each surface patch by recording the relative curvature and displacement of that surface patch and all other surface patches in the model. In order to simplify the generation process, the triangle's center-of-gravity and its normal are used instead of the actual triangle. So the object model can be seen as a set of oriented points (represent the triangle's center-of-gravity) and the surface normal at these points.

In mathematical form, the object model is defined by Eq. 1.

$$G = \{g_i = (p, n_p)_i,\ i = 1..N\} \tag{1}$$

Where $p = (x, y, z)$ is the Cartesian coordinates of the triangle's center of gravity and $n_p = (n_x, n_y, n_z)$ is the triangle's surface normal. g is known as an oriented point. The SEPMap of an oriented point $g = (p, n_p)$ is defined by Eq. 2,

$$M = \{m_j = (\theta, \phi, r)_j,\ j = 1..N-1\} \tag{2}$$

2.2 Feature Points Selection

In many objects, the majority of points forming the surface are of low curvature value and do not serve as landmarks of the object. These points can be eliminated to speed up the process. In a mathematical form, an oriented point $g = (p, n)$ is considered a feature point if its relative curvature, S_g, is higher than a certain positive value, ε. For a triangle patch, represented by its oriented point $g = (p, n)$, and having three neighbors' triangle patches, represented by their oriented points $g_1 = (p_1, n_1), g_2 = (p_2, n_2)$, and $g_3 = (p_3, n_3)$, the relative curvature of g, S_g, is defined as follows:

$$S_g = 1 - \frac{S_1 + S_2 + S_3}{3} \tag{3}$$

Where $S_i = n \bullet n_i,\ i = 1, 2, 3$ and '$\bullet$' denotes dot-product. Based on the feature points' selection, the object model, defined before in Eq. 1, is re-defined by Eq. 4.

$$G = \{g_i = (p, n_p)_i,\ i = 1..N,\ S_{g_i} > \varepsilon > 0\} \tag{4}$$

Where N is the number of triangle patches (oriented points) in the original object model G. The selection process will keep only N' oriented points where $N' << N$.

Since the selection of ε can vary from an object to another, in our experiments we auto-select ε based on the number of oriented points in the object. Basically, we define N' in terms of N, e.g., $N' \geq 0.1N$, we obtained the histogram of $N'()$ and select ε such that $N'() \geq 0.1N$.

2.3 SEPMap Generation

For an object model G defined by Eq. 4, the SEPMap M of an oriented point $g \in G$, $g = (p, n_p)$ is defined by Eq. 2 (where N is the number of featured points), and is generated as follows:

For each oriented point $g_j \in G$, $g_j = (q, n_q)_j$ where $g_j \neq g$,

1. Define $v =$ the vector $\overrightarrow{pq}$,
2. Calculate (θ, ϕ, r) as follows, see Fig. 1.
   (a) $\theta =$ the angle between n_p and v
   (b) $\phi =$ the angle between n_q and v
   (c) $r =$ the length of v (the distance between p and q)
3. Record $m_j = (\theta, \phi, r)$ in M

The SEPMap generation process is repeated for all $g_i \in G$, each will produce a SEPMap, M_i, $i = 1..N$. The set of SEPMaps are used to represent the object model G. So the new representation of G (SEPMap) is defined as

$$G = \{M_i, \ i = 1..N\},$$
$$M_i = \{m_j = (\theta, \phi, r)_j, \ j = 1..N-1\} \qquad (5)$$

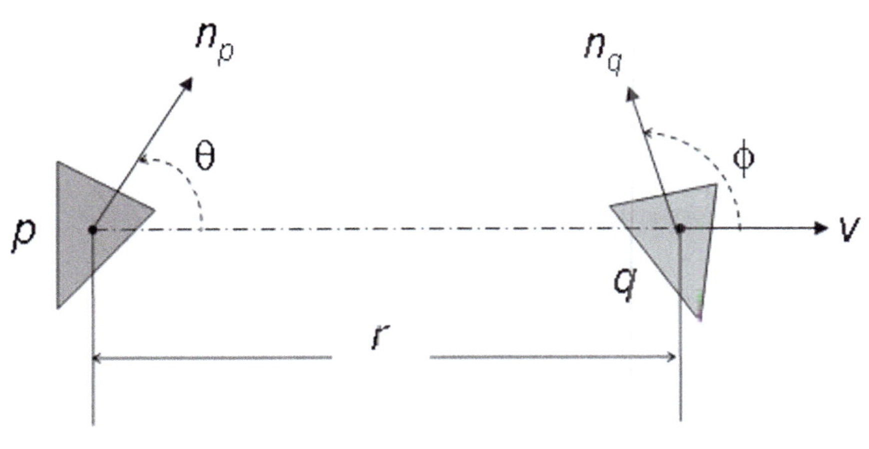

Fig. 1. The calculation of a SEPMap tuple $m = (\theta, \phi, r)$ of two oriented points (p, n_p) and (q, n_q)

3 Registration Process Using SEPMaps

The problem of registering two different surfaces defined by their SEPMaps is solved in a two-step process, SEPMap matching and the transformation matrix estimation. In the first step, the SEPMaps of the two surfaces's points are matched establishing points corresponding between the two surfaces as well as estimating the scaling factor. The matched points are then fed into the second step where a modified ICP algorithm [22] is used to estimate the rotation and translation matrices to align the two surfaces. The SEPMap matching and the transformation estimation are presented in this section.

3.1 SEPMap Matching and Scale Estimation

The idea of the SEPMap matching is to establish point corresponding between the two surfaces that maximize the similarity between them. In our case, the two objects are represented by their SEPMaps. Mathematically, the SEPMap matching problem is defined as follows:

Given the SEPMap representation of two objects

$$\begin{aligned} G &= \{M'_i,\ i = 1...N'\}, \\ H &= \{M''_i,\ i = 1...N''\} \end{aligned} \tag{6}$$

where N' and N'' are the number of oriented points in G and H, respectively. Find the point correspondence between the two objects that maximizes the similarity between them.

In order to measure the similarity between two objects G and H, we first measure the similarity, P, between their pair-wise SEPMaps defined in Eq. 6. The similarity, P, between two SEPMaps, M' and M'', defined in Eq. 7, is measured by the percentage of matching records between the two SEPMaps recorded for specific scaling factor.

Given two SEPMaps

$$\begin{aligned} M' &= \{m'_i = (\theta, \phi, r)'_i,\ i = 1..N'\}, \\ M'' &= \{m''_j = (\theta, \phi, r)''_j,\ j = 1..N''\} \end{aligned} \tag{7}$$

we measure the scaling factor, $s = r'/r''$, for all pair-wise records, m' and m''. The matching process can be summarized in the following steps:

1. $\forall M'_i \in G$ and $M''_j \in H$, calculate the similarity measure, P_{ij}, and the corresponding scaling factor, S_{ij}, as follows:
   (a) $\forall m'_k \in M'_i$ and $m''_l \in M''_j$ and $\left|(\theta,\phi)'_k, (\theta,\phi)''_l\right| \leq \delta$, calculate $s_{kl} = r'_k/r''_l$. δ is used to account for sampling errors. In our experiments, we used $\delta = 5$ degrees. That is the variations of the surface normal due to sampling noise.
   (b) The similarity measure between M'_i and M''_j, P_{ij}, is the maximum number of similar s_{kl}. The scaling factor, S_{ij}, is the s_{kl} that yields the maximum P_{ij}.

(c) If $P_{ij} > \Delta$ then M_i' and M_j'' are said to be a matched pair and the corresponding scaling factor S_{ij} is accepted as a possible scaling factor between the two objects G and H. Δ is used to account for occlusions and missing points. In our experiments, we used $\Delta = 20\%$. That is the percentage of occlusions between the two objects.

2. The overall similarity measure, P, and the scaling factor, S, between G and H, is determined by a simple counting approach for the possible scaling factors reported in step 1-c above. Basically, we calculate P as the maximum number of similar scaling factor S_{ij}. The overall scaling factor, S, is the S_{ij} that yield the maximum P.

The overall scaling factor and the overall similarity measure are compared against the pair-wise scaling factor and similarity measure recorded in step 1b above. Only the points that yield similar overall scaling factor with high similarity measure are considered as trusted match and added to the pair-wise correspondences list that will be used in estimating the transformation matrix.

3.2 Transformation Matrix Estimation

The aim of the registration process is to compute the transformations, which, when applied to the points in that view, it brings the two surfaces into alignment. The desired transformations are expressed by the 3x3 rotation matrix R and 3x1 translation vectors t. The registration procedure can be posed as the minimization of a cost function which measures the sum of squared distances between the transformed corresponding points.

$$\mathrm{E} = \sum_{i=1}^{N_1}\sum_{j=1}^{N_2} u_{ij} \left\| p_i' - (Rp_j'' + t) \right\|^2, \tag{8}$$

$$u_{ij} = \begin{cases} 1 \;\; if\ (p_i', p_j'')\ forms\ pairwise\ correspondence \\ 0 \;\; otherwise \end{cases}$$

where N_1 and N_2 are the numbers of points in the two surfaces. The Iterative Closest Point (ICP) algorithm proposed by Besl and McKay [10] is a commonly used framework for solving this surface registration problem. In our work, we used an enhanced ICP algorithm, developed by Williams and Bennamoun [22] to solve the registration problem.

4 Experimental Results

The registration process using SEPMap scheme has been applied to several object models. In this paper, we present the results of registering full and partial objects of three chess pieces (from 3D CAFE website); a chess king, a rook, and a queen models. In the first experiment, we applied rigid transformation (rotation, translation and scaling) to the three objects. The feature selection process is applied to the transformed objects, their SEPMaps are generated and the matching process is applied against the models library. In another experiment, we simulate a form of occlusion where the object does not have a complete 3D-model. In this experiment, we cut a piece of the objects and applied to them rigid transformation. Tables 1 and 2 show the transformation parameters of the experimental objects, full and partial respectively. The transformation parameters shown are the scaling factor, rotation axis, rotation angle and the translation vector. Figures 2 and 3 illustrate the two experiments before and after registration. Models are shown in light grey-level (gold color) while objects are shown in dark grey-level (purple color).

To verify the accuracy of the registration process, we define two forms of registration errors using the Euclidean distances between the model and the registered objects points. The first registration error (sum) is the squared sum of the Euclidean distance between the model and the registered object. The second registration error (average) is the average of the sum error. Table 3 shows the sum and the average registration errors of the chess pieces registration experiments. The results demonstrate the effectiveness of the proposed technique visually and analytically. and the ability of the technique in handling the general registration problem of full and partial objects.

Table 1. Transformation parameters for the chess pieces full size objects

	King	Rook	Queen
Scaling factor	0.5	0.3	2.0
Rotation Axis	z-axis	x-axis	x-axis
Rotation Angle	30	15	45
Translation vector	[0, -5, 0]	[-20, 0, -20]	[30, 30, 33]

Table 2. Transformation parameters for the chess pieces partial size objects

	King	Rook	Queen
Scaling factor	2.0	3.0	0.5
Rotation Axis	x-axis	y-axis	x-axis
Rotation Angle	-30	45	-45
Translation vector	[4, 0, 0]	[30, 30, 20]	[30, -20, 30]

Table 3. The registration errors (sum and average of distances between the registered surfaces) for the chess pieces experiments

Model	**Full Object**		**Partial Object**	
	Sum	**Average**	**Sum**	**Average**
King	0.117	0.0003	0.067	0.00017
Rook	0.305	0.0008	2.917	0.0077
Queen	1.296	0.0033	1.209	0.0031

Fig. 2. Chess pieces model experiment for full size objects. (top) before registration, (bottom) after registration.

Fig. 3. Chess pieces model experiment for partial size objects. (top) before registration, (bottom) after registration.

All experiments was conducted in a laptop computer with Pentium-M processor 1.8 GHz and 512 MB RAM and assuming the rule of keeping 10% of the original patches as landmarks of the object during the feature selection process. The average feature selection and SEPMap generation total time (user + I/O + CPU) is less than 2 seconds in a model of 1000 original triangles. The matching total time (registration time is negligible) between a model and object with 100 landmarks triangle patches is less than 10 seconds. The computational and memory requirements are proportional to the number of original triangle patches in the feature selection process however it is proportional to the number of landmarks patches in the SEPMap generation and matching. Usually the number of the landmarks is much less than the original number of patches.

5 Conclusion and Future Work

SEPMap is a surface signature-based representation scheme that is orientation-independent and can be used to align surfaces under rigid transformation including uniform scaling. In order to speed up the registration process, a feature point selection process is applied to the surfaces' points. The experimental results demonstrate the effectiveness of the proposed technique and the ability to handle general registration problem of full and partial objects. Several items will be considered in the future work. Among those items are , studying the impact of noise on the discrimination effectiveness of the SEPMap, experimenting with clutter scenes and different triangulation sampling, applying the SEPMap scheme to the 3D segmentation problem.

References

1. Bernardini, F., Martin, I., Mittleman, J., Rushmeier, H., Taubin, G.: Building a digital model of michelangelo's florentine pieta. IEEE Computer Graphics & Applications **22(1)** (2002) 59–67
2. Ikeuchi, K., Sato, Y., eds.: Modeling From Reality. Kluwer Academic Publishers (2001)
3. Rusinliewicz, S., Levoy, M.: Efficient variants of the icp algorithm. In: Proc. of the 3th Int. Conf. on 3-D Digital Imaging and Modeling. Volume 1. (2001) 145–152
4. Zhang, H., Hall-Holt, O., Kaufman, A.: Range image registration via probability field. In: Proc. of the Computer Graphics International (CGI'04), Crete, Greece (June 2004) 546–552
5. Blais, G., Levine, M.D.: Registering multiview range data to create 3d computer objects. IEEE Trans. on Pattern Analysis and Machine Intelligence **17(8)** (1995) 820–824
6. Eggert, D.W., Lorusso, A., Fisher, R.B.: Estimating 3d rigid body transformations: a comparison of four major algorithms. Machine Vision and Applications **9** (1997) 272–290
7. Zhang, Z.: Iterative point matching for registration of freeform curves and surfaces. IEEE Trans. on Pattern Analysis and Machine Intelligence **13(2)** (1994) 119–152
8. Okatani, I., Sugimoto, A.: Registration of range images that preserves local surface structures and color. In: Proc. of the 2nd International Symposium on 3D Data Processing, Visualization, and Transmission (3DPVT'04). (2004) 789–796
9. Sharp, G.C., Lee, S.W., Wehe, D.K.: Icp registration using invariant features. IEEE Trans. on Pattern Analysis and Machine Intelligence **24(1)** (2002) 90–102
10. Besl, P., McKay, N.: A method for registration of 3-d shapes. IEEE Trans. on Pattern Analysis and Machine Intelligence **14(2)** (1992) 239–256

11. Fan, Y., Jiang, T., Evans, D.: Medical image registration using parallel genetic algorithms. LNCS (Applications of Evolutionary Computing) **2279** (2002) 304–314
12. Robertson, C., Fisher, R.: Parallel evolutionary registration of range data. Computer Vision and Image Understanding **87(1)** (2002) 39–50
13. Silva, L., Bellon, O.R.P., Boyer, K.L.: Precision range image registration using a robust surface interpenetration measure and enhanced genetic algorithms. IEEE Trans. on Pattern Analysis and Machine Intelligence **27(5)** (2005) 762–776
14. Stein, F., Medioni, G.: Structural indexing: efficient 3-d object recognition. IEEE Trans. on Pattern Analysis and Machine Intelligence **14(2)** (1992) 125–145
15. Chua, C.S., Jarvis, R.: Point signatures: A new representation for 3-d object recognition. International Journal of Computer Vision **25(1)** (1997) 63–85
16. Johnson, J., Hebert, M.: Using spin images for efficient object recognition in cluttered 3d scenes. IEEE Trans. on Pattern Analysis and Machine Intelligence **21(5)** (1999) 433–449
17. Correa, S., Shapiro, L.: A new signature-based method for efficient 3-d object recognition. In: Proc. IEEE Conf. Computer Vision and Pattern Recognition. Volume 1. (2001) 769–776
18. Yamany, S.M., Farag, A.A.: Surface signatures: An orientation independent free-form surface representation scheme for the purpose of objects registration and matching. IEEE Trans. on Pattern Analysis and Machine Intelligence **24(8)** (2002) 1105–1120
19. Zhang, D., Herbert, M.: Harmonic maps and their applications in surface matching. In: Proc. IEEE Conf. Computer Vision and Pattern Recognition. Volume 2. (1999) 524–530
20. Chen, H., Bhanu, B.: 3d free-form object recognition in range images using local surface patches. In: Proc. of the 17th International Conference on Pattern Recognition, Cambridge, UK (August 2004) 524–530
21. Sun, Y., Paik, J., Koschan, A., Page, D.L., Abidi, M.A.: Point fingerprint: A new 3-d object representation scheme. IEEE Trans. On Systems, Man and Cybernetics - Part B: Cybernetics **33(4)** (2003) 712–717
22. Williams, j., Bennamoun, M.: Simultaneous registration of multiple corresponding point sets. Computer Vision and Image Understanding **81(1)** (2001) 117–142
23. Hemayed, E.: A scalable approach for 3d mesh generation. In: Proc. of the 7th World Multi-Conference on Systemics, Cybernetics and Informatics (SCI 03), Oralndo, FL (July 2003)

Multiple Range Image Registration by Matching Local Log-Polar Range Images

Takeshi Masuda

National Institute of Advanced Industrial Science and Technology (AIST),
Tsukuba, Ibaraki 305-8568, Japan
t.masuda@aist.go.jp

Abstract. We propose a method for coarse registration of multiple range images. A local log-polar range image is computed at every surface point of all input range images, and an invariant feature vector is generated from it. The correspondence of point pairs is determined by finding the closest feature vector pairs derived from different range images. The correspondence is validated, and the RANSAC is applied for extracting inlier point pairs to determine pairwise transformations between input range images. Finally, the global registration is determined by construcing the view tree of the input range images. The result of coarse registration is used as the initial state for the fine registration which is followed by the object shape modelling.

1 Introduction

A range image is an image that contains a 3-D coordinate information of depth or range at each image pixel. Many optical range sensors have been developed based on various principles like stereoscopy, (de-)focus, structured light, and time-of-flight of the light. They have been important sources of shape information for object tracking, object recognition, computer simulation and shape modeling in many engineering research fields including CV, CG, CAD, VR, mechanics and robotics. Range sensors can measure only a part of the object surface due to occlusion. For measuring the complete object surface, measurements from multiple viewpoints are necessary. Registration is the process for estimating the geometric alignment of the viewpoints from the measured range images.

Registration of range images can be segmented in two stages: coarse and fine stages. In the coarse stage, the input range images measured from very different viewpoints are registered. Many object recognition methods share their techniques with the coarse registration methods. Once the coarse registration is established, the result can be used as the initial value for the fine registration stage. In this stage, we can assume that the input range images are roughly registered within some accuracy. Correspondence can be established mostly by finding geometrically closest point pairs. The ICP algorithm [1, 2], direct meth-

P.J. Narayanan et al. (Eds.): ACCV 2006, LNCS 3851, pp. 948–957, 2006.

ods [3, 4], and simultaneous registration for modelling [5] are classified in the fine stage. The method to be presented belongs to the coarse registration.

In practical cases, coarse registration can be determined by special hardwares like attached markers, robot arms, rotation table, or positioning devices like GPS. These hardwares are not always available due to the object's size, materials and surrounding environment. Coarse registration can also be achieved by manual operation with GUI, but the operator's load is not feasible when the number of input range images increases.

The invariant features for shape recognition and coarse registration should satisfy the following conditions: 1) translation invariant, 2) rotation invariant, 3) general, 4) local, and 5) robust [6]. If a feature contains much information, correspondence can be established easily. A feature with larger support contains much information, but can be fragile to occlusion. Also, a feature with small support has a problem of stability. An invariant local feature should balance a trade-off between locality and robustness.

Surface curvatures are mathematically defined differential geometric features invariant to the Euclidean transformation. Feldmar and Ayache [7] used curvatures and principal directions for coarse registration between range images. Because curvatures are differential properties determined on the infinitely small support, computing them from a real data is not stable. Also, they have only two components (maximum/minimum, Gaussian/mean etc.), and are not descriptive enough for establishing point correspondence.

Many features extracting much more information from a local support have been proposed. The support is extended in curves such as zero-mean-curvature curves [8] and bitangent curves [9]. Features can also be determined from a ring region surrounding the center point such as the point signatures proposed by Chua and Davis [10] and 'splash' features proposed by Stein and Medioni [6]. Johnson and Hebert [11] proposed the spin image which is a local 2-D histogram generated by accumulating surface points by rotating the image plane around the surface normal. Huber and Hebert [12] used the spin images for pairwise range image registration, and they applied various validations for automatic registration of multiple range images. Frome *et al.*[13] proposed the harmonic shape contexts which is computed from a local 3-D histogram of the surface point around the center point.

In this paper, we propose a coarse registration algorithm of multiple range images based on an invariant feature generated from the local log-polar range images. All feature vectors are mapped in a common feature space, and the pairs are established by searching the nearest feature pairs. Various validations are applied to filter out false correspondence, and the RANSAC algorithm is employed for estimating pairwise registrations along with extracting inliers. The view tree of all range images are constructed for determining the global registration, and the result is used as the initial value of the fine registration and integration of range images. In the following part, we explain the feature vector generation in Sec. 2, correspondence establishment and validation in Sec. 3, experimental results in Sec. 4, and the conclusion in Sec. 5.

2 Feature Vector Generation

2.1 Local Log-Polar Range Image

We assume that we have multiple input range images of an object: $S^{\alpha}(1 \leq \alpha \leq N_S)$. The proposed method is organized without assuming any specific sensor or projection type. We specify the allowance of registration: δ.

A local log-polar range image (LR) is a local range image orthogonally projected on the tangent plane on which the 2-D location is represented by the log-polar coordinate system[14, 15]. The location on the image plane (u, v) in the Cartesian coordinate system is represented by $(\xi, \theta) = (\log r, \arctan(v/u))$ in the log-polar coordinate system, where $r = \sqrt{u^2 + v^2}$ and we use δ as the unit length of the local coordinate system.

We generate local log-polar range images on every surface point of all input range images. For fast generation, we reduce the resolution of the input range images by the signed distance field (SDF) as proposed by Masuda [5]. The 3-D space is sampled at each lattice point whose interval is δ, and a SDF sample at the sampling point $\boldsymbol{p}$ is composed by the properties of the signed distance to the surface s, surface normal $\boldsymbol{n}$ and closest point on the surface $\boldsymbol{c}$ (Fig. 1). The surface normal $\boldsymbol{n}$ is determined by normalizing the vector $\boldsymbol{p} - \boldsymbol{c}$, which is more robust than using the differentials. We use the closest points $\boldsymbol{c}$ as the center of a LR and the surface normal $\boldsymbol{n}$ as its image plane. In the current implementation, we store SDF samples only near the object surface satisfying $|s| < 2\delta$.

For each surface point $\boldsymbol{c}_i$, other surface points within the neighborhood $\boldsymbol{c}_j$ are projected on the image plane. The depth is determined by $\boldsymbol{n}_i \cdot (\boldsymbol{c}_j - \boldsymbol{c}_i)$, and it is stored in the orthogonally projected pixel whose log-polar coordinates are (ξ, θ) (Fig. 2). We set the neighborhood a cylindrical shape whose radius is R and depth limit is $\pm R$, and we use the samples whose surface normal is in the same direction as the center ($\boldsymbol{n}_i \cdot \boldsymbol{n}_j > 0$). When multiple depths are mapped on a pixel, their maximum value is used as the pixel value. The pixels with no value due to occlusion are filled by 0. We generate LRs when the SDF sample of the center point is close to the surface, $|s| < \delta$, and approximately at least one center point exists within an area of δ^2 on the surface. The LR generated

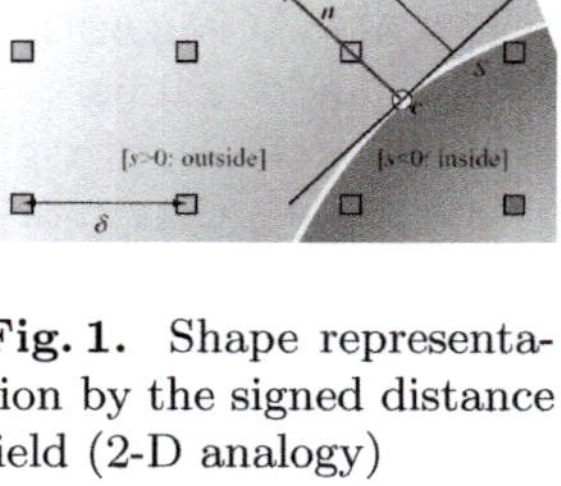

Fig. 1. Shape representation by the signed distance field (2-D analogy)

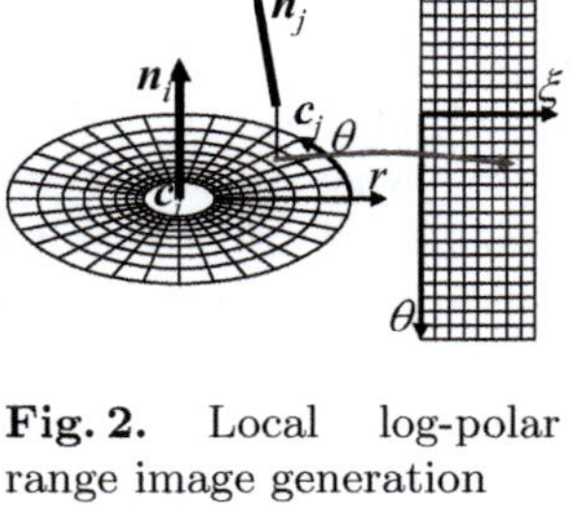

Fig. 2. Local log-polar range image generation

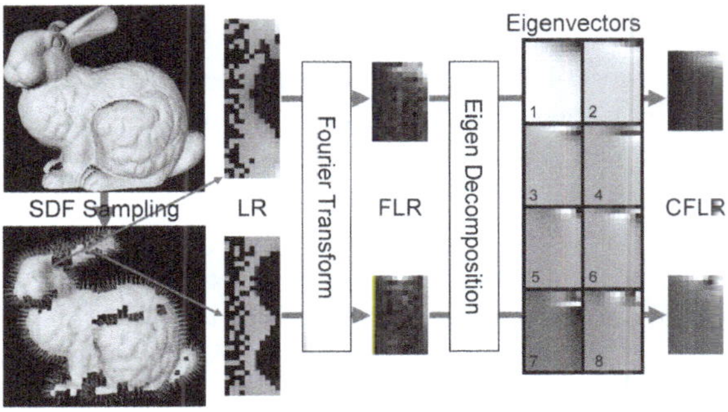

Fig. 3. The input range image is first downsampled by the SDF. The local log-polar range image (LR) is generated at each SDF sample. The Fourier transform is applied for computing the power spectrum in the θ-axis to generate FLR. They are compressed by the eigen decomposition, and the FLRs are approximated by the coefficients of eigenvectors (CFLR). The reconstructed FLRs from the CFLRs are similar to the original FLRs.

from the α-th input range image S^α at the surface point $\boldsymbol{c}_i^\alpha$ is represented by $\mathsf{LR}[\boldsymbol{c}_i^\alpha](\xi, \theta)$.

The 2-D coordinates (ξ, θ) are uniformly quantized for determining integer pixel coordinates. When θ is quantized in $2N_\theta$ directions, the i-th ξ coordinate satisfies $\xi_i = \log r_i = (\pi/N_\theta)i$. The index range in ξ direction is $[0, N_\xi - 1]$, where $N_\xi = \lceil (N_\theta/\pi) \log R \rceil$. For example, when $N_\theta = 16$ and $R = 8$, the required LR dimension is $[0, 10] \times [-16, 15]$. Examples of generated LRs are shown in Fig. 3.

2.2 Invariant Feature Vector Generation

The generated LRs are not invariant to rotation about the surface normal. In generation of LRs, the local Cartesian frame are determined by the surface normal and principal directions [16]. It has an ambiguity of rotation of π, and its choice is instable at navel points. To normalize these ambiguities, we extract invariant features from the LRs.

The LR is cyclic in the θ-axis: $\mathsf{LR}(\xi, \theta) = \mathsf{LR}(\xi, \theta + 2\pi)$, and it can be expanded by the Fourier series. We use the Fourier power spectrum of an LR in the θ-axis as a phase invariant feature named FLR, which is determined by

$$\mathsf{FLR}(\xi, k) = \left| \frac{1}{\pi} \int_{-\pi}^{\pi} \mathsf{LR}(\xi, \theta) e^{-ik\theta} d\theta \right|,$$

where k signifies the frequency. This can be fast computed by the FFT. Because an LR is real valued, the transformed FLR is symmetric: $\mathsf{FLR}(\xi, k) = \mathsf{FLR}(\xi, -k)$, and a FLR requires a storage half of an LR. For example, the size of the FLR corresponding to the example beforehand is $[0, 10] \times [0, 15]$. We represent the number of pixels in FLR by $D_{\mathsf{FLR}} = N_\theta \times N_\xi$. We use this FLR as the invariant feature vector for establishing point correspondence.

2.3 Feature Vector Compression

As shown in Fig. 3, the components of FLRs are localized, and they can be compressed by applying the eigen decomposition on the set of FLRs. Assume that there are N_{FLR} FLRs generated at all surface points of all input range images. The FLRs are piled up to form a matrix of $N_{\mathsf{FLR}} \times D_{\mathsf{FLR}}$. This matrix is decomposed by the SVD, and we select the D_{CFLR} eigenvectors $\mathsf{EFLR}[\boldsymbol{c}_i^\alpha, l]$ $(1 \leq l \leq D_{\mathsf{CFLR}})$ corresponding to the largest D_{CFLR} singular values. The l-th coefficient of CFLR is determined by taking the inner products of the FLR with the l-th eigenvector, $\mathsf{CFLR}[\boldsymbol{c}_i^\alpha](l) = \mathsf{EFLR}[\boldsymbol{c}_i^\alpha, l] \cdot \mathsf{FLR}[\boldsymbol{c}_i^\alpha]$, and the compressed feature vector $\mathsf{CFLR}[\boldsymbol{c}_i^\alpha]$ is D_{CFLR}-dimensional. Due to the property of the eigen decomposition, the FLRs are well approximated by the CFLRs (Fig. 3).

3 Establishment of Correspondence

3.1 Point Pair Search

A CFLR can be considered as a point in the D_{CFLR}-dimensional feature space, and the correspondence can be established by searching the nearest CFLR pairs. We can employ any general nearest neighbor search algorithm, and we used the k-d tree algorithm [17]. For a CFLR of input S^α at $\boldsymbol{c}_i^\alpha$, if the nearest CFLR of other input range images $S^\beta (\beta \neq \alpha)$ is $\boldsymbol{c}_j^\beta$, we store the point pair $[\boldsymbol{c}_i^\alpha, \boldsymbol{c}_j^\beta]$ in the list of the point pairs. After the closest point is found for each feature vector, we select the mutual pairs, which are point pairs bidirectionally closest to each other.

3.2 Crosscorrelation Validation

Shift invariance in the θ-axis is desirable, which signifies that the pair of corresponding LRs satisfy $\mathsf{LR}[\boldsymbol{c}_i^\alpha](\xi, \theta) = \mathsf{LR}[\boldsymbol{c}_j^\beta](\xi, \theta + \theta_0)$. However, a FLR bear also the sign and orientation invariances which are not desirable. In these cases, a pair of corresponding LRs may satisfy some other equations such as $\mathsf{LR}[\boldsymbol{c}_i^\alpha](\xi, \theta) = -\mathsf{LR}[\boldsymbol{c}_j^\beta](\xi, \theta)$ and $\mathsf{LR}[\boldsymbol{c}_i^\alpha](\xi, \theta) = \mathsf{LR}[\boldsymbol{c}_j^\beta](\xi, \theta_0 - \theta)$. Asynchronous combination of these deformation also causes undesirable ambiguities.

These mismatches are eliminated by checking crosscorrelation between the paired LRs. For each sign $\pm$ and shift $\Delta\theta$, we generate the flipped and shifted LR by $\mathsf{LR}[\boldsymbol{c}_j^\beta](\xi, \pm\theta + \Delta\theta)$. This operation can be simply implemented by shift and swap operations of vector elements due to the log-polar coordinate system. Then, we compute the crosscorrelation by the inner product with the flipped and shifted LR. If the maximum of these crosscorrelations is less than a threshold $(= \cos(\pi/4)$ in the implementation) or the maximum is given with the flipped LR (the sign argument is '$-$'), the pair is considered to be falsely matched.

3.3 Euclidean Transformation Validation

The class of the transformation for registering rigid input range images is the Euclidean transformation of the group SE(3). For each pair of the input range

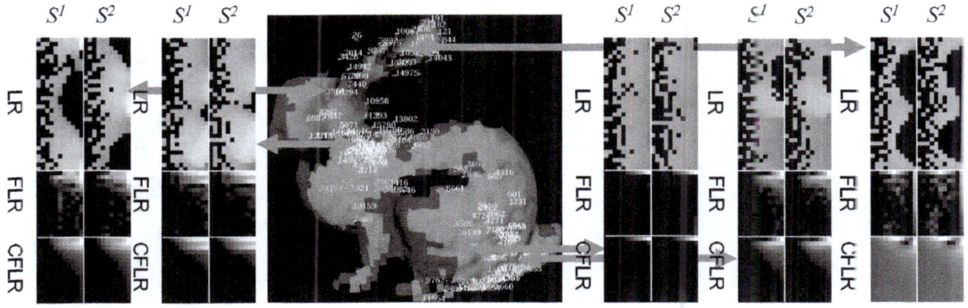

Fig. 4. The inlier point pairs and corresponded LRs between two input range images extracted by the Euclidean transformation validation

images, there should exists a Euclidean transformation which we need to estimate for registering them. For determining the transformation and extracting inliers, we apply the RANSAC algorithm between each pair of input range images. First, corresponded point pairs are classified according to the pair of input range images, for example, a point pair $[\boldsymbol{c}_i^\alpha, \boldsymbol{c}_j^\beta]$ is classified as a member of the input pair $[S^\alpha, S^\beta]$. For each input pair, we apply the RANSAC algorithm. For hypothesis generation, we use only mutual point pairs that is accepted by the crosscorrelation validation in Sec. 3.2. We make a hypothesis of Euclidean transformation from the following point pairs: a point pair along with the information of the correlation peak determined in Sec. 3.2, and a set of three point pairs. We use all combination of three point pairs when the number of point pairs is less than 22, otherwise point pairs are randomly selected for 10000 times.

We test the hypothesis of transformation by applying it to all point pairs including non-mutual point pairs between the input range images $[S^\alpha, S^\beta]$, and count the number of inlier point pairs that satisfy the following conditions: $||\boldsymbol{T}\boldsymbol{c}_i^\alpha - \boldsymbol{c}_j^\beta|| < \delta$, $\boldsymbol{R}\boldsymbol{n}_i^\alpha \cdot \boldsymbol{n}_j^\beta > \tau_{\boldsymbol{n}}(= \cos(\pi/8)$ in the implementation). The transformation of the maximum number of inliers $\boldsymbol{T}_\alpha^\beta$ is the result of registration between the input pair $[S^\alpha, S^\beta]$.

Examples of the extracted inlier point pairs are shown in Fig. 4. The paired inlier LRs are similar to each other regardless of rotation ambiguity in the θ-axis.

3.4 View Tree Construction

For determining registration of all input range images, we construct the view tree, which is a spanning tree of the input range images that maximize the sum of the number of inlier point pairs. For example, if the input pairs $[S_1, S_2]$, $[S_2, S_3]$ and $[S_1, S_3]$ have 588, 103 and 27 inlier point pairs respectively (Fig. 5), we use input pairs $[S_1, S_2]$ and $[S_2, S_3]$ minimally enough to connect these 3 views. The view tree is constructed by repeatedly adding a branch of the input pair with the maximum number of inliers among the unconnected input pairs. This iteration terminates when the maximum number of inliers of unconnected pairs becomes less than $\tau_{\mathsf{connection}}$ (=5 in the implementation).

	S^2	S^3	S^4	S^5	S^6	S^7	S^8	S^9	S^{10}
S^1	**588**	27	14	3	**322**	10	12	12	40
S^2		**103**	4	7	65	5	22	16	**68**
S^3			6	4	2	4	**49**	24	61
S^4				3	2	6	**153**	**120**	8
S^5					**98**	15	14	8	11
S^6						**54**	3	5	3
S^7							5	3	2
S^8								47	9
S^9									39

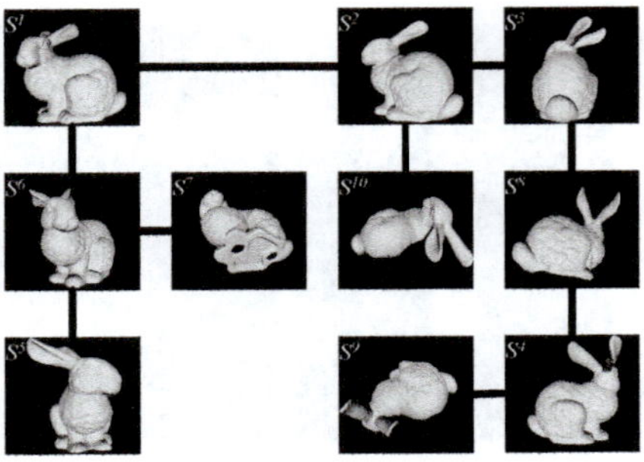

Fig. 5. For each input pair, the RANSAC algorithm is applied to estimate the transformations and the inlier point pairs. Numbers of inliers are stored in a table, and the spanning view tree maximizing the total number of inliers is generated.

With the view tree, we determine the registration of the all input range image. Starting from the base range image S_{base} ($= S_1$ in Fig. 5), we can determine the transformation $\boldsymbol{T}_\alpha$ of the α-th range image S^α relative to the base range image S_{base} by sequentially accumulating the $\boldsymbol{T}_\alpha^\beta$ on the branches of the view tree.

3.5 Refinement and Modeling

Once the transformations $\boldsymbol{T}_\alpha$ of input range images S^α are determined, the input range images are overlapped by the estimated transformations within the specified accuracy of δ, but the registration error is still accumulated.

We apply a synchronous fine registration algorithm proposed by Masuda [5] for refining the registration result (Fig. 6) by setting the initial state with the result of the proposed coarse registration method. By synchronously registering and integrating multiple range images, we obtain a continuous seamless surface model of the object. The model can be successively refined by applying the fine

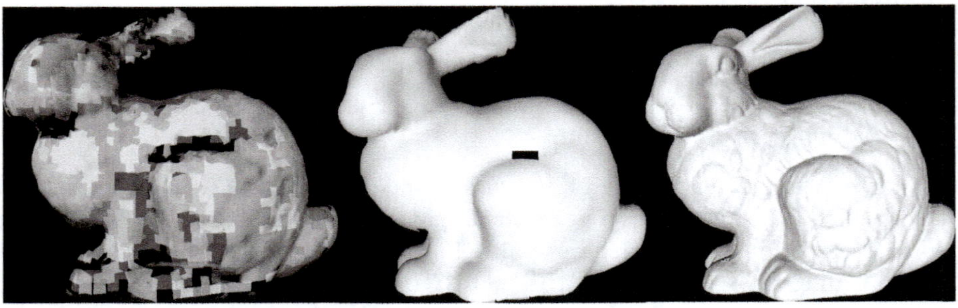

Fig. 6. The coarse registration result is shown by overlapping the transformed SDF representation of the input range images (left), and the result is refined by the synchronously fine registration and integration (middle). By refining the resolution to $\delta = 0.5$mm, a detailed shape model can be generated (right).

registration algorithm with reduced sampling interval δ. This modelling method generate the integrated surface model from the volumetric representation by the SDF, which we can use also as an input for the proposed method. It makes possible to decompose the problem of registration of large dataset into multiple processes of reduced size.

4 Experiments

4.1 Bunny

The figures shown in the preceding sections are the experimental results on the range image dataset named 'Bunny' obtained from the Stanford 3D Scanning Repository [18] (Fig. 5). The object is approximately 25cm in size, and the 10 range images were represented by the SDF with $\delta = 4$mm. The local log-polar range images were generated by $N_\theta = 16, R = 8, D_{\mathsf{FLR}} = 11 \times 16 = 176$, and their number was $N_{\mathsf{FLR}} = 19156$ in total. These images were compressed by the $D_{\mathsf{CFLR}} = 8$ eigenvectors with the cumulative proportion of 92.9%. By the nearest neighbor search, 19156 point pairs were extracted, and 3788 were the mutual point pairs. By applying crosscorrelation validation, 1125 point pairs were used by the RANSAC sampling. Finally, 1565 inlier point pairs in the spanning tree were used for the registration result as shown in Fig.5. It took about 1 min for loading 10 input range images and generating their SDF representation, 45 secs for generating local log-polar range images, about 2 mins for feature vector generation, 3 secs for nearest neighbor search, 30 secs for validation, and about 4 mins in total by a 2.8GHz processor.

The registration results of the same dataset with various settings are shown in Tab. 1. When R, D_{FLR} and N_θ are too small, registration failed due to poor information, and when R is too large, it failed because the radius of the support R exceeds the width of overlaps. The optimal setting is around the lower bound like $R = 4$, $D_{\mathsf{FLR}} = 8$ and $N_\theta = 4$, because more computational cost is required when these parameters are larger.

Table 1. Registration results with various parameters, where CP%: cummulative proportion at D_{CFLR} in %, #inliers: total number of inlier point pairs in the final view tree

N_θ	R	N_ξ	D_{FLR}	D_{CFLR}	CP%	#inliers	registered S^α
16	2	4	64	8	90.6	0	none
16	4	8	128	8	93.8	1028	all
16	8	11	176	8	92.9	1565	all
16	16	15	240	8	89.3	1310	/1,2,6/4,8,9/
16	8	11	176	2	73.5	132	/1,2,3/
16	8	11	176	4	86.9	540	/1,2,3,6,10/
16	8	11	176	16	96.1	2299	all
3	8	2	6	6	99.8	903	all
4	8	3	12	8	99.0	1800	all
8	8	6	48	8	94.4	1772	all

4.2 Dragon

The proposed method was applied on the 'Dragon' dataset obtained also from the Stanford 3D Scanning Repository [18] (Fig. 7). The object size is about 25cm in size, and the dataset is composed of 71 range images. We applied the proposed method with the settings of $\delta = 4$mm, $N_\theta = 4$, $R = 8$ and $D_{\mathsf{FLR}} = 8$. 100198 local log-polar range images were generated, and 8547 inlier point pairs forms a view tree of input range images. It took about 6.5 mins for loading input range images and generating their SDF representation, 3 mins for generating local log-polar range images, 3 mins for feature vector generation, 36 secs for nearest neighbor search, 2 mins for validation, and 12.5 mins in total. The coarse and fine registration and integration results are shown in Fig. 7.

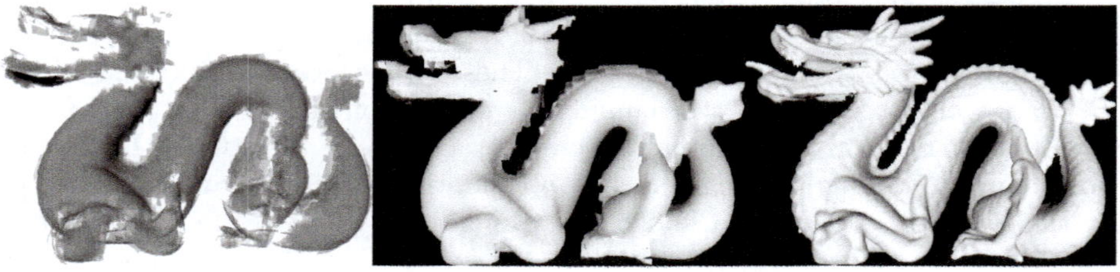

Fig. 7. The coarse registration result of 71 input range images (left) were used as the initial value for fine synchronous registration and integration (middle), and by refining the resolution up to $\delta = 1$mm, a fine shape model was generated (right)

5 Conclusion

We proposed a method for coarsely registering multiple range images by matching local log-polar range images. The invariant feature vector is generated by the power spectrum of the local log-polar range images, and it is compressed by the eigen decomposition for fast retrieval of correspondence, and various validations were applied to remove false matches. By constructing the view tree, the global registration is determined, which can be used as the initial value for the fine registration.

The approach has similarity with the spin images [11, 12]. Compared to the spin images, the proposed method does not depend on the homogeneity of the point density. The local log-polar range image is made invariant by the power spectrum, which is richer in information compared to the spin images that uses only accumulated number of point in a ring region. The advantage of using the log-polar coordinate system is the sparse sampling in the outskirts, which is usually corrupted by occlusion.

We currently determine the sampling interval δ about 1/64 of the object size for processing in a reasonable computational time. With $R = 8$, the input range images should be overlapped around 1/4 of the object size. The proposed method works well if the object is complex and the overlap of the input range images is large. We are examining the performance and limitations of the proposed method for its improvement. We think that the proposed method can be applied also to the shape recognition and shape retrieval.

References

1. Besl, P.J., McKay, N.D.: A method for registration of 3-D shapes. IEEE Trans. PAMI **14** (1992) 239–256
2. Rusinkiewicz, S., Levoy, M.: Efficient variants of the ICP algorithm. In: Proc. 3DIM2001. (2001) 145–152
3. Horn, B.K.P., Harris, J.G.: Rigid body motion from range image sequences. CVGIP: Image Understanding **53** (1991) 1–13
4. Yamamoto, M., Boulanger, P., Beraldin, J.A., Rioux, M.: Direct estimation of range flow on deformable shape from a video rate range camera. IEEE Trans. PAMI **15** (1993) 82–89
5. Masuda, T.: Registration and integration of multiple range images by matching signed distance fields for object shape modeling. Comput. Vis. Image Underst. **87** (2002) 51–65
6. Stein, F., Medioni, G.: Structural indexing: efficient 3-d object recognition. IEEE Trans. PAMI **14** (1992) 125–145
7. Feldmar, J., Ayache, N.: Rigid, affine and locally affine rewgistration of free-form surfaces. Int. J. Comput. Vision **18** (1996) 99–119
8. Krsek, P., Pajdla, T., Hlavac, V.: Differential invariants as the base of triangulated surface registration. Comput. Vis. Image Underst. **87** (2002) 27–38
9. Wyngaerd, J.V., van Gool, L.: Automatic crude patch registration: Toward automatic 3D model building. Comput. Vis. Image Underst. **87** (2002) 8–26
10. Chua, C.S., Jarvis, R.: Point signatures: A new representation for 3D object recognition. Int. J. Comput. Vision **25** (1997) 63–85
11. Johnson, A.E., Hebert, M.: Using spin images for efficient object recognition in cluttered 3d scenes. IEEE Trans. PAMI **21** (1999) 433–449
12. Huber, D., Hebert, M.: Fully automatic registration of multiple 3d data sets. In: Image and Vision Computing. Volume 21. (2003) 637–650
13. Frome, A., Huber, D., Kolluri, R., Bülow, T., Malik, J.: Recognizing objects in range data using regional point descriptors. In: Proc. ECCV04. (2004)
14. Wolberg, G., Zokai, S.: Robust image registration using log-polar transform. In: Proc. ICIP2000. (2000)
15. Hotta, K., Mishima, T., Kurita, T.: Scale invariant face detection and classification method using shift invariant features extracted from log-polar image. Trans. IEICE **E84-D** (2001) 867–878
16. Masuda, T.: Surface curvature estimation from the signed distance field. In: Proc. 3DIM2003. (2003) 361–368
17. Bentley, J.L.: Multidimensional binary search trees used for associative searching. Communications of the ACM **18** (1975)
18. : The stanford 3d scanning repository. `http://graphics.stanford.edu/data/3Dscanrep/`

Incremental Mesh-Based Integration of Registered Range Images: Robust to Registration Error and Scanning Noise

Hong Zhou[1], Yonghuai Liu[1], and Longzhuang Li[2]

[1] Department of Computer Science,
University of Wales, Aberystwyth, Ceredigion SY23 3DB, UK
[2] Department of Computer Science,
Texas A and M University, Corpus Christi, TX-78412, USA

Abstract. Existing integration algorithms often assume that the registration error of neighbouring views is an order of magnitude less than the measurement error [3]. This assumption is very restrictive that automatic registration algorithms can hardly meet. In this paper, we develop a novel integration algorithm, robust to both large registration errors and heavy scanning noise. Firstly, a pre-processing procedure is developed to automatically triangulate a single range image and remove noisy triangles. Secondly, we shift points along their orientations by the projection of their resulting correspondence vectors so that new correspondences can approach together, leading large registration errors to be compensated. Thirdly, overlapping areas between neighbouring views are detected and integrated, considering the confidence of triangles, which is a function of the including angle between the centroid point vector of a triangle and its normal vector. The outcome of integration is a set of disconnected triangles where gaps are caused by the removal of overlapping triangles with low confidence. Fourthly, the disconnected triangles are connected based on the principle of maximizing interior angles. Since the created triangular mesh is not necessarily smooth, finally, we minimize the weighted orientation variation. The experimental results based on real images show that the proposed algorithm significantly outperforms an existing algorithm and is robust to both registration error and scanning noise.

1 Introduction

Automatic 3D object model reconstruction from multiple registered range images is popular today in applications ranging from object modelling to computer graphics [1, 2, 9]. 3D object modelling usually involves the following four stages: (1) Scan object surface from various viewpoints; (2) Register the views; (3) Integrate the views; and finally (4) Render the integrated data.

Data acquisition involves scanning the surface of 3D objects from multiple viewpoints using laser range scanners like Minolta Vivid 700. The data used in this paper were downloaded from the range image database currently hosted by

P.J. Narayanan et al. (Eds.): ACCV 2006, LNCS 3851, pp. 958–968, 2006.

the Signal Analysis and Machine Perception Laboratory at Ohio State University. Each range image has a resolution of 200 by 200 and is depicted in local laser range scanner centred coordinate system. So these range images have to be first aligned into a global coordinate system. For this purpose, the registration algorithm [5] was employed. Through alignment, transformations between all pairs of views have been obtained. Integration then merges registered data from multiple views so that a single surface representation is created in the global coordinate system. Finally rendering stage will build a watertight and smooth surface based on the integrated data.

Existing integration algorithms can be classified into the following three main categories:

1. Mesh integration [8, 9]: Original data from each view is firstly built into mesh (normally triangulation). Doing so is justified by the fact that they can make full use of topological and geometrical information associated with each mesh (e.g., point neighbourhood, curvature, and surface orientation). The overlapped meshes are detected and discarded. The remaining meshes are connected to build the whole surface. Mesh based integration is powerful in discarding noisy mesh and is stable in detecting overlapping area by considering topological and geometrical information in mesh and can retain details of surface. However, the existing methods in this class often cannot handle the data with large registration error very well;
2. Volume based integration [2, 3]: It combines the integration of overlapping area detection and surface reconstruction together by using implicit volumetric reconstruction methods. It is applicable to objects with arbitrary topology. But it introduces a lot of noisy mesh when sampling noise is heavy. On the other hand, it cannot provide an exact surface topology due to interpolation that approximates the intersection between implicit surface and voxel edges; and finally,
3. Points based integration [7]: the Cartesian 3D space is first decomposed into multiple equally sized voxels and all points which fall into the same voxel are then integrated as a consensus point without considering much about topology between points. The main difference between volume and points based integration lies in that while the former applies the traditional marching cubes algorithm to extract triangular mesh, the latter considers the intersection between voxel edges and a plane perpendicular to the orientation at the consensus point. This method may fail due to a large registration error and when the density of points in 3D space changes significantly. In addition, the voxel size is difficult to decide.

All these methods succeed to varying degrees in different situations. Due to sampling noise and unpredicted registration error, the final reconstructed surface is often deformed and includes some artefacts such as holes and wrongly connected edges. Hence, the algorithm that is tolerable to both large registration and scanning errors is still desired to be developed.

So far, there is no universally stable registration algorithm that can always register any range data accurately. Moreover, the registration error is likely to accumulate continuously with new images added [1]. In this case, integration algorithms are desired to possess a mechanism to compensate these registration errors. For this purpose, we shift the points along their orientations. The magnitude of shifting is determined by the projection of their correspondence vectors along their orientations. The consequence of shift operation is to let point correspondences approach together and thus, leads large registration errors to be compensated. To deal with noise, three subroutines are developed: discontinuity preservation based triangulation, removing triangles with single neighbours, and smoothing the generated triangular mesh using a newly developed Gaussian filter. Within these three subroutines, the first two are used for pre-processing and the last is used for post-processing. A comparative study based on real images has shown that the proposed algorithm is promising for automatic 3D model reconstruction.

The rest of this paper is structured as follows: Section 2 describes how to triangulate a single image, Section 3 describes how to integrate the registered range images, while Section 4 describes how to smooth the generated mesh. Finally, the experimental results are presented and some conclusions are drawn in Section 5.

2 Single Range Image Triangulation

Most laser range scanners employ a polar coordinate system and the viewing volume is restricted by the horizontal and vertical maximal angles. The range measurements are stored as a 2D grid, from which the 3D coordinates of sampled object surface points can be recovered when the calibration parameters are known. For more accurate estimation of orientation of points, the scanned points data are first triangulated. For four neighbouring points, there are six possible configurations for triangulation (Figure 1).

Fig. 1. Six possible configurations for the creation of triangles from four neighbouring points

When two neighbouring range data measurements differ by more than a threshold, there is a step discontinuity. In this case, it is meaningless to join these two points directly with regard to the representation of surface geometry. The threshold is determined by the surface geometry and sampling resolution. However, the threshold is often difficult to determine. Here we develop a method to automatically determine the threshold based on a given raster range image:

1. Find all the non-boundary points $p(x, y, z)$. (Definition of non-boundary: If eight neighbours of a point p are all non-background, the point p is considered to be a non-boundary point). For each non-boundary point and its

three neighbouring non-boundary points, two triangles are then created with shorter diagonal length. As a consequence of this operation, a set of triangles have been generated without considering step discontinuity;

2. Calculate the dot product of the normal of the triangles and the normalized line of sight toward the centroids of these triangles. Find the triangles where the including angles between their normal and the line of sight toward their centroids are in the range of $[160°, 180°]$. Calculate the mean M of lengths of the longest edges of those triangles. This idea of determining threshold follows the range scanner's working mechanism: the measurement accuracy depends on the incident angle;
3. Multiply the mean M by a constant C: $D = C * M$ (C=1.4 in this paper). The constant increases the distance threshold and thus guarantees that some accurate points on boundary can be included in the resulting mesh.

After the distance threshold D has been calculated, we re-triangulate the points from the raster image file. For each non-boundary point and its three neighbouring points, if two of the three neighbouring points are invalid, then no triangle will be created. If one of the three neighbouring points is invalid, then we compute the interpoint distance. If all three interpoint distances are smaller than D, then a triangle will be created. If none of the three neighbouring points is invalid, then we compute just the distance between diagonal points, since the distance dn between two neighbouring points is in general smaller than that dd between two diagonal points. If dd is smaller than a threshold, then dn must be smaller than that threshold. Thus, doing so does not lose any triangles for the representation of surface details but gains computational efficiency. If only one of these two diagonal distances is smaller than D, then a single triangle will be created in one of the last four configurations in Figure 1. If both of these two distances are smaller than D, then two triangles will be created with the common edge being the one with a shorter length, as shown in the first two configurations in Figure 1. Otherwise, no triangle will be created. Consequently, more accurate triangular mesh that reflects surface geometry has been constructed.

In the triangular mesh built from a single range image, there are some points in isolated or boundary triangles that usually have only one neighbouring triangle. These points bring two troubles for the integration process: one is that they tend to be noisy and thus distort the shape of object. The other is that the orientation of points is difficult to estimate. As a result, we assume that a triangle with more than one neighbour is more accurate and stable than the triangles with one neighbour only. So an iterative procedure is proposed to remove the triangles with one neighbour only. Then the orientation N at all points on mesh can be calculated based on their area and neighbouring relation [7].

3 Integration of Multiple Registered Range Images

Integration of multiple registered range images consists of three main steps: overlapping area detection, shift along normal, and overlapping triangle detection and removal and surface reconstruction that are detailed as follows.

3.1 Front Face Checking and Overlapping Area Detection

When one range image R is transformed into the coordinate system in which the other range image R_{old} was described and becomes R_{new}, they can then be merged to obtain a single surface. Firstly, we check whether or not the triangular meshes in R_{new} are facing the viewpoint at which the range image R_{old} was captured. If the dot product of the normals of triangles and the rays from the viewpoint to the centroids of the triangles is negative, we say the triangles in R_{new} are "front facing". The triangles in R_{new} that overlap with those in R_{old} *must* be those front facing ones. Secondly, because every new range image can supply somewhat new information of surface geometry for the exiting range images, non-overlapping and overlapping areas with regard to "front facing" triangles found need to be further detected. If the distance between the centroid of a triangle in one range image and its closest centroid of a triangle in the other is smaller than a threshold, it is added into overlapping triangle sets $S_{old-overlapping}$ and $S_{new-overlapping}$. Otherwise, it is put into non-overlapping triangle set $S_{old-non-overlapping}$ or $S_{new-non-overlapping}$. Those triangles in non-overlapping sets $S_{old-non-overlapping}$ and $S_{new-non-overlapping}$ are left and directly added to form a new surface as new geometrical information supplied by the two range images. In this paper, the threshold was set as D/2 where D was estimated in Section 2. An example for the detection of overlapping area between two registered range images is illustrated in Figure 2.

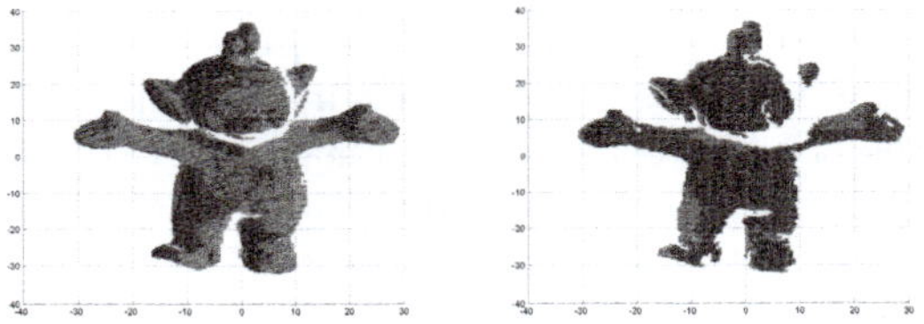

Fig. 2. Left: The registration result of $teletubby_{deg0}$ (no color) and $teletubby_{deg20}$ (green). Right: Their overlapping area.

3.2 Shift Along Normal

Because the fusion algorithm described here only utilizes the original points from all the range images, the points from two range images may be connected and triangulated together. In this case, the accuracy of registration imposes a remarkable effect on the final fusion result. Inaccurate registration leads the real overlapping area between two registered range images to stay apart. On the contrary, some non-overlapping areas are close to each other. As a result, false connections and gaps are often created, as demonstrated by Figure 8(left).

To deal with large registration errors, we propose a novel algorithm that is detailed as follows. Since the triangles in $S_{old-overlapping}$ are of higher quality and the number of triangles in $S_{new-overlapping}$ is smaller, thus the triangles in

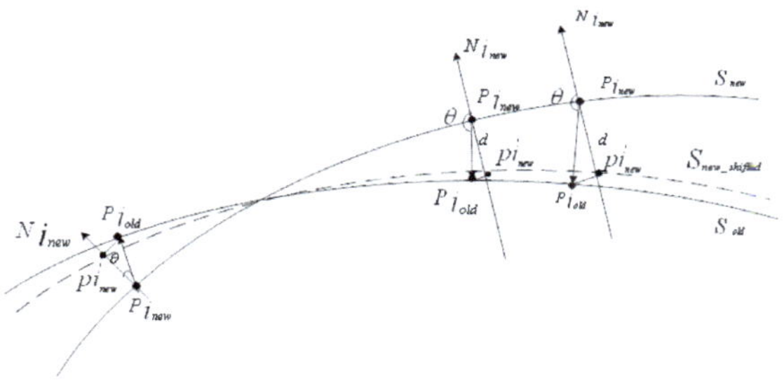

Fig. 3. Point integration along normal vector

$S_{old-overlapping}$ are used as reference. For each point pi_{new} in $S_{new-overlapping}$, the closest point pi_{old} in $S_{old-overlapping}$ is identified. Then the dot product d between vector $\vec{pi} = pi_{old} - pi_{new}$ and normal vector Ni_{new} at point pi_{new} is computed. Finally, we shift pi_{new} along Ni_{new} toward pi_{old} using the following formula (Figure 3):

$$pi'_{new} = pi_{new} + dNi_{new} \tag{1}$$

so that shifted point pi'_{new} is closer to pi_{old}. If vector $\vec{pi}$ is in the same direction as normal Ni_{new} at point pi_{new}, then d is positive. Otherwise, it is negative.

Note what we change is the point position, but the triangulation relationship among points in $S_{new-overlapping}$ are kept intact. Due to point position shift, self-intersection triangular meshes may emerge. In this case, we let the point position shift a minimum distance so that the original topology in $S_{new-overlapping}$ has not been changed. The finally obtained triangular mesh is called $S_{shifted-new-overlapping}$. An example of integrating registered range images with large registration error is shown in Figure 8.

3.3 Overlapping Triangles' Detection and Removal and Surface Reconstruction

To detect the overlapping triangles between $S_{old-overlapping}$ and $S_{shifted-new-overlapping}$, we only consider the x and y coordinates of points. Due to "front facing" detection in Section 3.1, no two triangles from $S_{old-overlapping}$ will occupy the same space on the xy plane. For each triangle T_{old} in $S_{old-overlapping}$, we first project it onto the xy plane and then compute its circum-circle CC_{old}. For any triangle in $S_{shifted-new-overlapping}$, if one of its three vertices or its centroid lies in CC_{old}, then that triangle is considered as overlapping with T_{old} and is called as $Tset_{new}$. This approach can find most intersection triangles. In some cases, the intersection triangles are left, but they do not affect the final result since either the number of such triangles or their intersection area is small. The purpose of overlapping triangle detection is to find the relative relationship between different triangles in $S_{shifted-new-overlapping}$ and $S_{old-overlapping}$ respectively, but the actual intersection information between these triangles is not needed by our integration

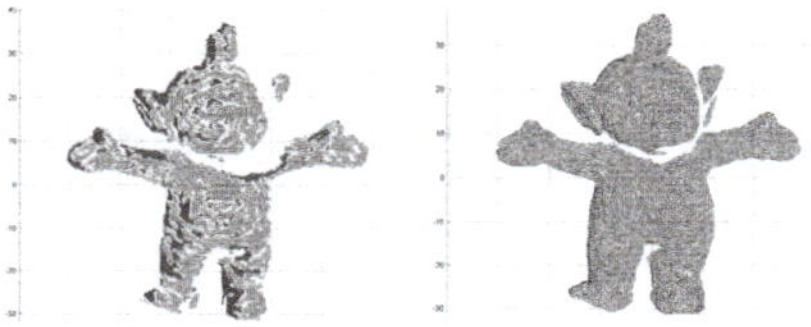

Fig. 4. Non-overlapping mesh between $teletubby_{deg0}$ and transformed $teletubby_{deg20}$ (left) and final mesh (right)

method and thus, is not computed. Consequently, computational load can be cut down.

When all overlapping triangles $Tset_{new}$ and T_{old} are found, for the sake of removing redundancy, we have to delete either the triangle T_{old} or all the triangles in $Tset_{new}$. To keep the best measurement, we define a confidence for the accuracy of each triangle as follows. The including angle θ between the normal of the triangle and the line of sight toward the centroid of the triangle is first computed. The length l of the vector from the original to the centroid of the triangle is then computed. Finally, the confidence of a triangle is computed as: $w = 1/(\theta l)$. The larger the angle θ and the smaller the length l, the more confidence in the triangle.

The following rule is developed to decide whether the triangles in $Tset_{new}$ or T_{old} are kept. To this end, the average confidence of all the overlapping triangles in $Tset_{new}$ is first computed. If the average is larger than that of the triangle T_{old}, then the partial surface described by triangles in $Tset_{new}$ is more accurate and stable than that described by the triangle T_{old}. In this case, the triangle T_{old} is deleted from $S_{old-overlapping}$ and the triangles in $Tset_{new}$ are retained in $S_{shifted-new-overlapping}$ and vice versa. As a consequence of this operation, a set of non-overlapping triangles is left in $S_{old-overlapping}$ and $S_{shifted-new-overlapping}$, as illustrated in Figure 4(left).

The connection method in [8] is employed here to fill the gaps among triangles in $S_{old-overlapping}$, $S_{shifted-new-overlapping}$, $S_{old-non-overlapping}$ and $S_{new-non-overlapping}$. After filling all the gaps, the finally reconstructed triangular mesh has been created for the representation of surface. One example of 2D triangular mesh from teletubby is presented in Figure 4(right).

4 Surface Smoothing Algorithm

The finally reconstructed surface in the last section is usually non-smoothing in the smooth area of real surface mainly due to a rapid change of orientation of reconstructed surface and the estimation of surface orientation is often sensitive to noise introduced by scanning, registration and integration. Therefore how to effectively combat noise on the surface mesh, while preserving desired features, is thus an active area of research. To this end, two main approaches have been proposed: One is to adjust vertex positions so that the overall surface becomes smoother [10], the other is to smooth the surface normals [11,12]. Surface normals play a critical role in most of the proposed surface smoothing algorithms since normals impose a greater impact on the model's perceived quality. Therefore, features of a surface can be determined more easily using surface normals than using vertex positions.

For this purpose, we develop here a simple method to accurately estimate the surface orientation as follows. The normal of each vertex in the mesh is firstly calculated by averaging the normals of all the triangles weighted by their areas [7] that share the vertex. This step of normal computation is different from that in Section 2. While the former may apply points from two images, the latter apply points only from a single image. The neighbouring vertices of a vertex are all other vertices of the triangles sharing the vertex.

If a surface is smooth, then the orientation of each vertex should be consistent with those of its neighbours. So the weighted orientation variation $\sum_{i=1}^{M}\sum_{j=1}^{N} W_{ij}\Delta\theta_{ij}$ should be minimum where M is the number of vertices in the mesh and N is the number of neighbouring vertices of a vertex. For each vertex V_i and its neighbouring vertices V_{i1}, V_{i2}, $\cdots$, V_{iN}, the including angles between normal vectors N_{imean} at V_i and N_{ij} at V_{ij} are $\Delta\theta_{ij}$: $N_{imean} = \frac{1}{N}\sum_{j=1}^{N} N_{ij}$, W_{ij} are the weights of $\Delta\theta_{ij}$.

To optimize W_{ij}, we apply the entropy maximization (EntMax) principle from statistical mechanics [4]. Thus, the following objective function is built to smooth noisy mesh: $J = \sum_{i=1}^{M}\sum_{j=1}^{N} W_{ij}\Delta\theta_{ij} - (-\frac{1}{\beta}\sum_{i=1}^{M}\sum_{j=1}^{N} W_{ij}\ln W_{ij})$. Differentiating this objective function about W_{ij} leads to: $\frac{\partial J}{\partial W_{ij}} = \Delta\theta_{ij} + \frac{1}{\beta}\ln W_{ij} + \frac{1}{\beta}W_{ij}\frac{1}{W_{ij}} = 0$. Thus, $W_{ij} = exp(-\beta\Delta\theta_{ij} - 1)$. Since in W_{ij}, exp(-1) is a constant, after normalization, W_{ij} can be expressed as: $W_{ij} = exp(-\beta\Delta\theta_{ij})$ Finally, the new orientation N_i at vertex V_i is updated as a weighted sum of N_{ij}: $N_{inew} = N_i + \sum_{j=1}^{N} W_{ij}N_{ij}$ where the parameter β controls how smooth the final surface is. The smaller the parameter β, the smoother the final surface (β= 0.005 and iteration number = 5).

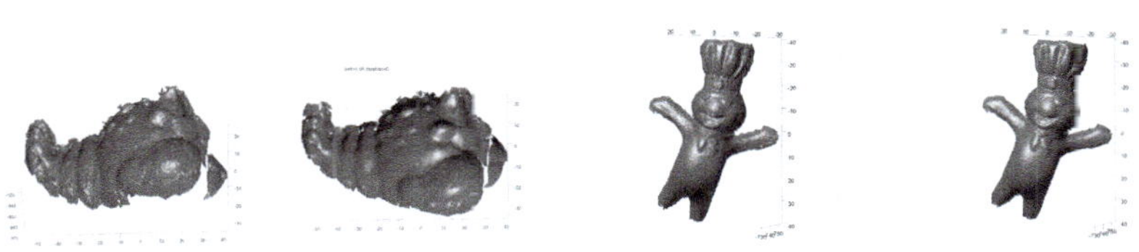

Fig. 5. Integration results of 3 views of lobster and 7 views of doughboy before (odd column) and after (even column) using our smoothing algorithm

Due to more accurate estimation of surface orientation, the finally reconstructed surface becomes smoother, as demonstrated in Figure 5 where after smoothing, fewer artefacts appear in the abdomen of the lobster and in the chest, mouth and hat of the doughboy. Meanwhile the geometric features such as corners and cease edges are desirably kept.

5 Experiment Results and Conclusions

To measure the accuracy of the original and improved integration algorithms, we defined the integration error as the average distance between vertices of remaining triangles in $S_{new-overlapping}$ and their closest vertices of those in $S_{old-overlapping}$. If the registration of two range images is quite accurate, then the remaining triangles in $S_{new-overlapping}$ should be close to those in $S_{old-overlapping}$, leading the integration error to be small. The experimental results about 6 objects with total 44 images are presented in Figures 6, 7, and 8 and Table 1.

Fig. 6. Integration results using our method. Left: bird(13 views). Second: bunny(6 views). Third: doughboy(7 views). Right: frog(7 views).

Fig. 7. Integration results with small(left two) and large (right two) registration errors for different algorithms. Odd column: the integration method [8]. Even column: our method.

From Figures 6, 7, and 8 and Table 1, it can be seen that our algorithm consistently outperforms the algorithm proposed in [8] in the sense that in all cases, the integration error has been reduced and more accurate, smooth and water-tight surfaces have been reconstructed. When the registration error is small, our method produces similar results to the method [8], as demonstrated by Figure 7.

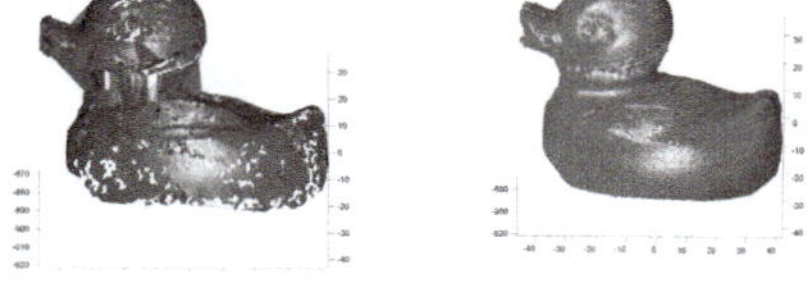

Fig. 8. Integration results with large registration error for different algorithms. Left: the integration algorithm [8]. Right: our method.

Table 1. Integration results using different algorithms and images. RE: Registration Error (RE)[5]. IE: Integration Error(IE1) [8]. IE: Integration Error(IE2) (our method).

Image	Views	Points	Face	Vertex	RE(mm)	IE1(mm)	IE2(mm)
Bird	13	102133	53531	27132	0.40	1.08	0.74
Bunny	6	30816	24890	12530	0.30	0.87	0.64
Doughboy	7	53460	25704	12956	0.45	1.10	0.75
Frog	7	46075	30767	15532	0.45	1.16	0.68
Tubby	6	30608	31464	15982	0.32	0.88	0.65
Duck	5	57194	39740	20031	0.65	1.58	0.97

But when the registration error is relatively large, our method considerably outperforms the method [8], as demonstrated by Figures 7 and 8. In this case, the registration algorithm [5] calibrated the rotation angle of the camera motion from the tubby and duck images to be 15.96° and 18.76° with an expectation of 20° respectively, yielding a relative calibration error in rotation angle of as large as 20.2%. For the duck images, the average registration error is 0.65mm. While the method [8] produced an integration error of 1.58mm, our integration algorithm produced the corresponding error of 0.97mm, leading the integration error to be reduced remarkably by 38%. While the method [8] created a lot of false connections and gaps, our method almost perfectly recovered all details of the duck about wing, eye, and neck as shown in Figure 8 and all details of the doughboy about hand, mouth and hat as shown in Figure 7. For the integration of various views of any object, it took less than 30 minutes on a Pentium 4 computer. The larger the number and sizes of images, the more time the integration requires.

The main reason for our algorithm to outperform the method [8] is that we explicitly took into account both registration errors and scanning noise. Our integration method has the following characteristics: (1) it is able to deal with noisy mesh and compensate the registration error; (2) it smoothes the surface efficiently due to the use of a Gaussian filter; and finally, (3) it is an automatic process with range images registered under typical conditions without any restrictive assumption [3]. The output is a watertight surface. In the future, we are planning to register and integrate all the views simultaneously using a star network [6] to avoid the registration error accumulation.

References

1. M. Andreetto, N. Brusco, G.M. Cortelazzo. Automatic 3D modelling of textured cultural heritage objects. *IEEE Trans. Image Processing* 13(2004) 354-369.
2. B. Curless and M. Levoy. A volumetric method for building complex models from range images. *Proc. SIGGRAPH*, 1996, pp. 303-312.
3. A. Hilton, J. Illingworth. Geometric fusion for a hand-held 3D sensor. *Machine Vision and Applications* 12(2000) 44-51.
4. E.T. Jaynes. Information theory and statistical mechanics. *The Physical Review*, 106(1957) 620-630.
5. Y. Liu, L. Li, and B. Wei. 3D shape matching using collinearity constraint. *Proc. ICRA*, 2004, pp. 2285-2290.

6. C. Oblonsek and N. Guid. A fast surface-based procedure for object reconstruction from 3-D scattered points. *CVIU* 69(1998) 185-195.
7. S. Rusinkiewicz, Olaf Hall-Holt and M. Levoy. Real-time 3D model acquisition. *Proc. SIGGRAPH*, 2002, pp. 438-446.
8. Y. Sun, C. Dumont. Mesh-based integration of range and color images. *Proc. of SPIE*, Vol. 4051, 2000, pp. 110-117.
9. G. Turk and M. Levoy. Zippered polygon meshes from range images. *Proc. SIGGRAPH*, 1994, pp. 311-318.
10. G. Taubin. A signal processing approach for fair surface design. *Proc. SIGGRAPH*, 1995, pp. 351-358.
11. J. Vollmer, R. Mencl, and H. Muller. Improved Laplacian smoothing of noisy surface meshes. *Proc. Eurographics*, 1999, pp. 131-138.
12. S.S. Wong, K.L. Chan. Multi-view 3D model reconstruction: exploitation of color homogeneity in voxel mask. *Proc. ICIG*, 2004, 146-149.

Author Index

Lecture Notes in Computer Science

For information about Vols. 1–3757

please contact your bookseller or Springer

Vol. 3860: D. Pointcheval (Ed.), Topics in Cryptology – CT-RSA 2006. XI, 365 pages. 2006.

Vol. 3855: E. A. Emerson, K.S. Namjoshi (Eds.), Verification, Model Checking, and Abstract Interpretation. XI, 443 pages. 2006.

Vol. 3852: P.J. Narayanan, S.K. Nayar, H.-Y. Shum (Eds.), Computer Vision - ACCV 2006, Part II. XXXI, 977 pages. 2006.

Vol. 3851: P.J. Narayanan, S.K. Nayar, H.-Y. Shum (Eds.), Computer Vision - ACCV 2006, Part I. XXXI, 973 pages. 2006.

Vol. 3850: R. Freund, G. Păun, G. Rozenberg, A. Salomaa (Eds.), Membrane Computing. IX, 371 pages. 2006.

Vol. 3842: H.T. Shen, J. Li, M. Li, J. Ni, W. Wang (Eds.), Advanced Web and Network Technologies, and Applications. XXVII, 1057 pages. 2005.

Vol. 3841: X. Zhou, J. Li, H.T. Shen, M. Kitsuregawa, Y. Zhang (Eds.), Frontiers of WWW Research and Development - APWeb 2006. XXIV, 1223 pages. 2005.

Vol. 3840: M. Li, B. Boehm, L.J. Osterweil (Eds.), Unifying the Software Process Spectrum. XVI, 522 pages. 2006.

Vol. 3838: A. Middeldorp, V. van Oostrom, F. van Raamsdonk, R. de Vrijer (Eds.), Processes, Terms and Cycles: Steps on the Road to Infinity. XVIII, 639 pages. 2005.

Vol. 3837: K. Cho, P. Jacquet (Eds.), Technologies for Advanced Heterogeneous Networks. IX, 307 pages. 2005.

Vol. 3836: J.-M. Pierson (Ed.), Data Management in Grids. X, 143 pages. 2005.

Vol. 3835: G. Sutcliffe, A. Voronkov (Eds.), Logic for Programming, Artificial Intelligence, and Reasoning. XIV, 744 pages. 2005. (Sublibrary LNAI).

Vol. 3834: D. Feitelson, E. Frachtenberg, L. Rudolph, U. Schwiegelshohn (Eds.), Job Scheduling Strategies for Parallel Processing. VIII, 283 pages. 2005.

Vol. 3833: K.-J. Li, C. Vangenot (Eds.), Web and Wireless Geographical Information Systems. XI, 309 pages. 2005.

Vol. 3832: D. Zhang, A.K. Jain (Eds.), Advances in Biometrics. XX, 796 pages. 2005.

Vol. 3831: J. Wiedermann, G. Tel, J. Pokorný, M. Bieliková, J. Štuller (Eds.), SOFSEM 2006: Theory and Practice of Computer Science. XV, 576 pages. 2006.

Vol. 3829: P. Pettersson, W. Yi (Eds.), Formal Modeling and Analysis of Timed Systems. IX, 305 pages. 2005.

Vol. 3828: X. Deng, Y. Ye (Eds.), Internet and Network Economics. XVII, 1106 pages. 2005.

Vol. 3827: X. Deng, D. Du (Eds.), Algorithms and Computation. XX, 1190 pages. 2005.

Vol. 3824: L.T. Yang, M. Amamiya, Z. Liu, M. Guo, F.J. Rammig (Eds.), Embedded and Ubiquitous Computing – EUC 2005. XXIII, 1204 pages. 2005.

Vol. 3823: T. Enokido, L. Yan, B. Xiao, D. Kim, Y. Dai, L.T. Yang (Eds.), Embedded and Ubiquitous Computing – EUC 2005 Workshops. XXXII, 1317 pages. 2005.

Vol. 3822: D. Feng, D. Lin, M. Yung (Eds.), Information Security and Cryptology. XII, 420 pages. 2005.

Vol. 3821: R. Ramanujam, S. Sen (Eds.), FSTTCS 2005: Foundations of Software Technology and Theoretical Computer Science. XIV, 566 pages. 2005.

Vol. 3820: L.T. Yang, X. Zhou, W. Zhao, Z. Wu, Y. Zhu, M. Lin (Eds.), Embedded Software and Systems. XXVIII, 779 pages. 2005.

Vol. 3819: P. Van Hentenryck (Ed.), Practical Aspects of Declarative Languages. X, 231 pages. 2005.

Vol. 3818: S. Grumbach, L. Sui, V. Vianu (Eds.), Advances in Computer Science – ASIAN 2005. XIII, 294 pages. 2005.

Vol. 3816: G. Chakraborty (Ed.), Distributed Computing and Internet Technology. XXI, 606 pages. 2005.

Vol. 3815: E.A. Fox, E.J. Neuhold, P. Premsmit, V. Wuwongse (Eds.), Digital Libraries: Implementing Strategies and Sharing Experiences. XVII, 529 pages. 2005.

Vol. 3814: M. Maybury, O. Stock, W. Wahlster (Eds.), Intelligent Technologies for Interactive Entertainment. XV, 342 pages. 2005. (Sublibrary LNAI).

Vol. 3813: R. Molva, G. Tsudik, D. Westhoff (Eds.), Security and Privacy in Ad-hoc and Sensor Networks. VIII, 219 pages. 2005.

Vol. 3810: Y.G. Desmedt, H. Wang, Y. Mu, Y. Li (Eds.), Cryptology and Network Security. XI, 349 pages. 2005.

Vol. 3809: S. Zhang, R. Jarvis (Eds.), AI 2005: Advances in Artificial Intelligence. XXVII, 1344 pages. 2005. (Sublibrary LNAI).

Vol. 3808: C. Bento, A. Cardoso, G. Dias (Eds.), Progress in Artificial Intelligence. XVIII, 704 pages. 2005. (Sublibrary LNAI).

Vol. 3807: M. Dean, Y. Guo, W. Jun, R. Kaschek, S. Krishnaswamy, Z. Pan, Q.Z. Sheng (Eds.), Web Information Systems Engineering – WISE 2005 Workshops. XV, 275 pages. 2005.

Vol. 3806: A.H. H. Ngu, M. Kitsuregawa, E.J. Neuhold, J.-Y. Chung, Q.Z. Sheng (Eds.), Web Information Systems Engineering – WISE 2005. XXI, 771 pages. 2005.

Vol. 3805: G. Subsol (Ed.), Virtual Storytelling. XII, 289 pages. 2005.

Vol. 3804: G. Bebis, R. Boyle, D. Koracin, B. Parvin (Eds.), Advances in Visual Computing. XX, 755 pages. 2005.

Vol. 3803: S. Jajodia, C. Mazumdar (Eds.), Information Systems Security. XI, 342 pages. 2005.

Vol. 3802: Y. Hao, J. Liu, Y.-P. Wang, Y.-m. Cheung, H. Yin, L. Jiao, J. Ma, Y.-C. Jiao (Eds.), Computational Intelligence and Security, Part II. XLII, 1166 pages. 2005. (Sublibrary LNAI).

Vol. 3801: Y. Hao, J. Liu, Y.-P. Wang, Y.-m. Cheung, H. Yin, L. Jiao, J. Ma, Y.-C. Jiao (Eds.), Computational Intelligence and Security, Part I. XLI, 1122 pages. 2005. (Sublibrary LNAI).

Vol. 3799: M. A. Rodríguez, I.F. Cruz, S. Levashkin, M.J. Egenhofer (Eds.), GeoSpatial Semantics. X, 259 pages. 2005.

Vol. 3798: A. Dearle, S. Eisenbach (Eds.), Component Deployment. X, 197 pages. 2005.

Vol. 3797: S. Maitra, C. E. V. Madhavan, R. Venkatesan (Eds.), Progress in Cryptology - INDOCRYPT 2005. XIV, 417 pages. 2005.

Vol. 3796: N.P. Smart (Ed.), Cryptography and Coding. XI, 461 pages. 2005.

Vol. 3795: H. Zhuge, G.C. Fox (Eds.), Grid and Cooperative Computing - GCC 2005. XXI, 1203 pages. 2005.

Vol. 3794: X. Jia, J. Wu, Y. He (Eds.), Mobile Ad-hoc and Sensor Networks. XX, 1136 pages. 2005.

Vol. 3793: T. Conte, N. Navarro, W.-m.W. Hwu, M. Valero, T. Ungerer (Eds.), High Performance Embedded Architectures and Compilers. XIII, 317 pages. 2005.

Vol. 3792: I. Richardson, P. Abrahamsson, R. Messnarz (Eds.), Software Process Improvement. VIII, 215 pages. 2005.

Vol. 3791: A. Adi, S. Stoutenburg, S. Tabet (Eds.), Rules and Rule Markup Languages for the Semantic Web. X, 225 pages. 2005.

Vol. 3790: G. Alonso (Ed.), Middleware 2005. XIII, 443 pages. 2005.

Vol. 3789: A. Gelbukh, Á. de Albornoz, H. Terashima-Marín (Eds.), MICAI 2005: Advances in Artificial Intelligence. XXVI, 1198 pages. 2005. (Sublibrary LNAI).

Vol. 3788: B. Roy (Ed.), Advances in Cryptology - ASIACRYPT 2005. XIV, 703 pages. 2005.

Vol. 3787: D. Kratsch (Ed.), Graph-Theoretic Concepts in Computer Science. XIV, 470 pages. 2005.

Vol. 3785: K.-K. Lau, R. Banach (Eds.), Formal Methods and Software Engineering. XIV, 496 pages. 2005.

Vol. 3784: J. Tao, T. Tan, R.W. Picard (Eds.), Affective Computing and Intelligent Interaction. XIX, 1008 pages. 2005.

Vol. 3783: S. Qing, W. Mao, J. Lopez, G. Wang (Eds.), Information and Communications Security. XIV, 492 pages. 2005.

Vol. 3782: K.-D. Althoff, A. Dengel, R. Bergmann, M. Nick, T. Roth-Berghofer (Eds.), Professional Knowledge Management. XXIII, 739 pages. 2005. (Sublibrary LNAI).

Vol. 3781: S.Z. Li, Z. Sun, T. Tan, S. Pankanti, G. Chollet, D. Zhang (Eds.), Advances in Biometric Person Authentication. XI, 250 pages. 2005.

Vol. 3780: K. Yi (Ed.), Programming Languages and Systems. XI, 435 pages. 2005.

Vol. 3779: H. Jin, D. Reed, W. Jiang (Eds.), Network and Parallel Computing. XV, 513 pages. 2005.

Vol. 3778: C. Atkinson, C. Bunse, H.-G. Gross, C. Peper (Eds.), Component-Based Software Development for Embedded Systems. VIII, 345 pages. 2005.

Vol. 3777: O.B. Lupanov, O.M. Kasim-Zade, A.V. Chaskin, K. Steinhöfel (Eds.), Stochastic Algorithms: Foundations and Applications. VIII, 239 pages. 2005.

Vol. 3776: S.K. Pal, S. Bandyopadhyay, S. Biswas (Eds.), Pattern Recognition and Machine Intelligence. XXIV, 808 pages. 2005.

Vol. 3775: J. Schönwälder, J. Serrat (Eds.), Ambient Networks. XIII, 281 pages. 2005.

Vol. 3774: G. Bierman, C. Koch (Eds.), Database Programming Languages. X, 295 pages. 2005.

Vol. 3773: A. Sanfeliu, M.L. Cortés (Eds.), Progress in Pattern Recognition, Image Analysis and Applications. XX, 1094 pages. 2005.

Vol. 3772: M.P. Consens, G. Navarro (Eds.), String Processing and Information Retrieval. XIV, 406 pages. 2005.

Vol. 3771: J.M.T. Romijn, G.P. Smith, J. van de Pol (Eds.), Integrated Formal Methods. XI, 407 pages. 2005.

Vol. 3770: J. Akoka, S.W. Liddle, I.-Y. Song, M. Bertolotto, I. Comyn-Wattiau, W.-J. van den Heuvel, M. Kolp, J. Trujillo, C. Kop, H.C. Mayr (Eds.), Perspectives in Conceptual Modeling. XXII, 476 pages. 2005.

Vol. 3769: D.A. Bader, M. Parashar, V. Sridhar, V.K. Prasanna (Eds.), High Performance Computing – HiPC 2005. XXVIII, 550 pages. 2005.

Vol. 3768: Y.-S. Ho, H.J. Kim (Eds.), Advances in Multimedia Information Processing - PCM 2005, Part II. XXVIII, 1088 pages. 2005.

Vol. 3767: Y.-S. Ho, H.J. Kim (Eds.), Advances in Multimedia Information Processing - PCM 2005, Part I. XXVIII, 1022 pages. 2005.

Vol. 3766: N. Sebe, M.S. Lew, T.S. Huang (Eds.), Computer Vision in Human-Computer Interaction. X, 231 pages. 2005.

Vol. 3765: Y. Liu, T. Jiang, C. Zhang (Eds.), Computer Vision for Biomedical Image Applications. X, 563 pages. 2005.

Vol. 3764: S. Tixeuil, T. Herman (Eds.), Self-Stabilizing Systems. VIII, 229 pages. 2005.

Vol. 3762: R. Meersman, Z. Tari, P. Herrero (Eds.), On the Move to Meaningful Internet Systems 2005: OTM 2005 Workshops. XXXI, 1228 pages. 2005.

Vol. 3761: R. Meersman, Z. Tari (Eds.), On the Move to Meaningful Internet Systems 2005: CoopIS, DOA, and ODBASE, Part II. XXVII, 653 pages. 2005.

Vol. 3760: R. Meersman, Z. Tari (Eds.), On the Move to Meaningful Internet Systems 2005: CoopIS, DOA, and ODBASE, Part I. XXVII, 921 pages. 2005.

Vol. 3759: G. Chen, Y. Pan, M. Guo, J. Lu (Eds.), Parallel and Distributed Processing and Applications - ISPA 2005 Workshops. XIII, 669 pages. 2005.

Vol. 3758: Y. Pan, D.-x. Chen, M. Guo, J. Cao, J.J. Dongarra (Eds.), Parallel and Distributed Processing and Applications. XXIII, 1162 pages. 2005.

GPSR Compliance

The European Union's (EU) General Product Safety Regulation (GPSR) is a set of rules that requires consumer products to be safe and our obligations to ensure this.

If you have any concerns about our products, you can contact us on ProductSafety@springernature.com

In case Publisher is established outside the EU, the EU authorized representative is:

Springer Nature Customer Service Center GmbH
Europaplatz 3
69115 Heidelberg, Germany

Batch number: 10682269

Printed by Printforce, the Netherlands